Fodor's

PACIFIC
NORTHWEST

18th Edition

Fodor's Travel Publications · New York, Toronto, London, Sydney, Auckland

www.fodors.com

Be a Fodor's Correspondent

Your opinion matters. It matters to us. It matters to your fellow Fodor's travelers, too. And we'd like to hear it. In fact, we need to hear it.

When you share your experiences and opinions, you become an active member of the Fodor's community. That means we'll not only use your feedback to make our books better, but we'll publish your names and comments whenever possible. Throughout our guides, look for "Word of Mouth," excerpts of your unvarnished feedback.

Here's how you can help improve Fodor's for all of us.

Tell us when we're right. We rely on local writers to give you an insider's perspective. But our writers and staff editors—who are the best in the business—depend on you. Your positive feedback is a vote to renew our recommendations for the next edition.

Tell us when we're wrong. We're proud that we update most of our guides every year. But we're not perfect. Things change. Hotels cut services. Museums change hours. Charming cafés lose charm. If our writer didn't quite capture the essence of a place, tell us how you'd do it differently. If any of our descriptions are inaccurate or inadequate, we'll incorporate your changes in the next edition and will correct factual errors at fodors.com immediately.

Tell us what to include. You probably have had fantastic travel experiences that aren't yet in Fodor's. Why not share them with a community of like-minded travelers? Maybe you chanced upon a beach or bistro or B&B that you don't want to keep to yourself. Tell us why we should include it. And share your discoveries and experiences with everyone directly at fodors.com. Your input may lead us to add a new listing or highlight a place we cover with a "Highly Recommended" star or with our highest rating, "Fodor's Choice."

Give us your opinion instantly at our feedback center at www.fodors.com/feedback. You may also e-mail editors@fodors.com with the subject line "Pacific Northwest Editor." Or send your nominations, comments, and complaints by mail to Pacific Northwest Editor, Fodor's, 1745 Broadway, New York, NY 10019.

You and travelers like you are the heart of the Fodor's community. Make our community richer by sharing your experiences. Be a Fodor's correspondent.

Happy Traveling!

Tim Jarrell, Publisher

FODOR'S PACIFIC NORTHWEST

Editors: Eric B. Wechter, Molly Moker

Writers: Shelley Arenas, Carissa Bluestone, Crai S. Bower, Cedar Burnett, Andrew Collins, Sarah Cypher, John Doerper, Mike Francis, Matt Graham, Carolyn B. Heller, Nick Horton, Heidi Leigh Johansen, Sue Kernaghan, Brian Kevin, Chris McBeath, Janna Mock-Lopez, Kerry Newberry, Deston S. Nokes, Rob Phillips, Dave Sandage, Jenie Skoy, Allecia Vermillion, Christine Vovakes, Crystal Wood

Production Editor: Carolyn Roth
Maps & Illustrations: David Lindroth, *cartographer;* Bob Blake, Rebecca Baer, *map editors;* William Wu, *information graphics*
Design: Fabrizio La Rocca, *creative director;* Guido Caroti, Siobhan O'Hare, *art directors;* Tina Malaney, Nora Rosansky, Chie Ushio, Jessica Walsh, Ann McBride, *designers;* Melanie Marin, *senior picture editor*
Cover Photo: (Looking Glass Lake, Oregon): Janis Miglavs/age fotostock
Production Manager: Steve Slawsky

18th Edition

ISBN 978-1-4000-0512-3

ISSN 1098–6774

SPECIAL SALES

This book is available at special discounts for bulk purchases for sales promotions or premiums. Special editions, including personalized covers, excerpts of existing books, and corporate imprints, can be created in large quantities for special needs. For more information, write to Special Markets/Premium Sales, 1745 Broadway, MD 6-2, New York, New York 10019, or e-mail specialmarkets@randomhouse.com.

AN IMPORTANT TIP & AN INVITATION

Although all prices, opening times, and other details in this book are based on information supplied to us at press time, changes occur all the time in the travel world, and Fodor's cannot accept responsibility for facts that become outdated or for inadvertent errors or omissions. So **always confirm information when it matters,** especially if you're making a detour to visit a specific place. Your experiences—positive and negative—matter to us. If we have missed or misstated something, **please write to us.** We follow up on all suggestions. Contact the Pacific Northwest editor at editors@fodors.com or c/o Fodor's at 1745 Broadway, New York, NY 10019.

PRINTED IN COLOMBIA

10 9 8 7 6 5 4 3

CONTENTS

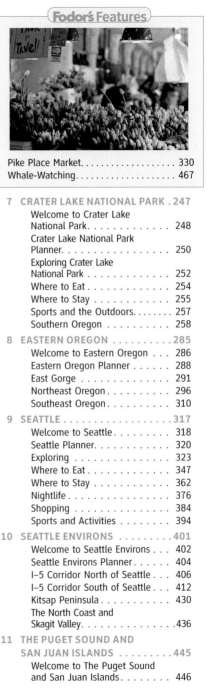

MAPS

ABOUT THIS BOOK

Our Ratings

Sometimes you find terrific travel experiences, and sometimes they just find you. But usually the burden is on you to select the right combination of experiences. That's where our ratings come in.

Sometimes a place is so unique that superlatives don't do it justice: you just have to be there to know. These sights, properties, and experiences get our highest rating, **Fodor's Choice** indicated by orange stars throughout this book.

Black stars highlight sights and properties we deem **Highly Recommended** places that our writers, editors, and readers praise again and again for consistency and excellence.

By default, there's another category: any place we include in this book is by definition worth your time, unless we say otherwise. And we will.

Disagree with any of our choices? Care to nominate a place or suggest that we rate one more highly? Visit our feedback center at www.fodors.com/feedback.

Budget Well

Hotel and restaurant price categories from ¢ to $$$$ are defined in the opening pages of each chapter. For attractions, we always give standard adult admission fees; reductions are usually available for children, students, and senior citizens. Want to pay with plastic? **AE, D, DC, MC, V** following restaurant and hotel listings indicate whether American Express, Discover, Diners Club, MasterCard, and Visa are accepted.

Restaurants

Unless we state otherwise, restaurants are open for lunch and dinner daily. We mention dress only when there's a specific requirement and reservations only when they're essential or not accepted—it's always best to book ahead.

Hotels

Hotels have private bath, phone, TV, and air-conditioning and operate on the European Plan (aka EP, meaning without meals), unless we specify that they use the Continental Plan (CP, with a continental breakfast), Breakfast Plan (BP, with a full breakfast), or Modified American Plan (MAP, with breakfast and dinner), or are all-inclusive (AI, including all meals and most activities). We always list facilities but not whether you'll be charged an extra fee to use them, so when pricing accommodations, find out what's included.

Listings	
★	Fodor's Choice
★	Highly recommended
⊠	Physical address
⊕	Directions or Map coordinates
⌂	Mailing address
☎	Telephone
🖷	Fax
⊕	On the Web
✎	E-mail
💳	Admission fee
⊙	Open/closed times
Ⓜ	Metro stations
▭	Credit cards
Hotels & Restaurants	
🏨	Hotel
⇄	Number of rooms
⚲	Facilities
⑩	Meal plans
✕	Restaurant
⌕	Reservations
🏛	Dress code
⬦	Smoking
⑨	BYOB
Outdoors	
⚑	Golf
⚠	Camping
Other	
♻	Family-friendly
⇨	See also
⊠	Branch address
☞	Take note

Experience the
Pacific Northwest

WHAT'S WHERE OREGON

Numbers refer to chapters.

2 Portland. With its pedestrian-friendly downtown and super public transit, Portland is easy to explore. The city has become a magnet for fans of artisanal food, beer, and wine, and its leafy parks and miles of bike lanes make it a mecca for outdoors enthusiasts.

3 The Oregon Coast. Oregon's roughly 300 miles of rugged coast is every bit as scenic as the more crowded and famous California coast. Oregon Dunes National Recreation Area, Bandon Dunes Golf Resort, the Oregon Coast Aquarium, and the Columbia River Maritime Museum are key highlights.

4 The Willamette Valley and Wine Country. Just beyond the Portland city limits and extending south for 120 miles to Eugene, the Willamette Valley is synonymous with exceptional winemaking. Salem, historic Oregon City, and the amazing cataracts of Silver Falls State Park offer a variety of activities.

5 The Columbia River Gorge and Mt. Hood. Less than an hour east of Portland, the Columbia Gorge extends for about 160 mi along the Oregon-Washington border. Wind sports and white-water rafting abound. Just 35 miles south of Hood River is massive Mt. Hood, a favorite destination for hiking and skiing.

6 Central Oregon. The semi-arid and generally sunny swatch of Oregon immediately east of the Cascade Range takes in a varied landscape, with the outdoorsy city of Bend as the regional hub. Make time for the funky mountain town of Sisters and the world-famous rock climbing of Smith Rock State Park near Redmond.

7 Crater Lake National Park. The 21-square-mi sapphire-blue expanse is the nation's deepest lake and a scenic wonder. The Klamath Falls region provides some of Oregon's best, under-visited scenery, while artsy Ashland and Old West–looking Jacksonville abound with sophisticated restaurants, shops, and wineries. Nearby, Oregon Caves National Monument is a fascinating natural attraction.

8 Eastern Oregon. The vast eastern reaches of the state promise plenty of memorable sights. The Wild West town of Pendleton and historic Baker City are just off Interstate 84. Farther afield are Burns and Frenchglen—excellent bases for exploring Steens Mountain and John Day Fossil Beds. Far northeast, Hells Canyon contains a stunning stretch of the Snake River.

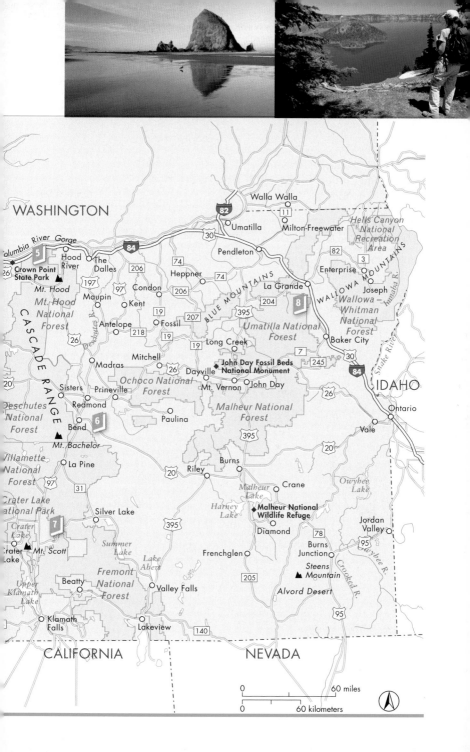

WASHINGTON

Walla Walla

Umatilla

Milton-Freewater

Hells Canyon
National
Recreation
Area

Columbia River Gorge

Hood
River

The
Dalles

Pendleton

Enterprise

Joseph

Crown Point
State Park

Mt. Hood

Mt. Hood
National
Forest

La Grande

WALLOWA MOUNTAINS

Wallowa–
Whitman
National
Forest

Maupin

Kent

Condon

BLUE MOUNTAINS

Baker City

CASCADE RANGE

Antelope

Fossil

Umatilla National
Forest

Snake River

Madras

Mitchell

Dayville

Long Creek

Mt. Vernon

John Day

John Day Fossil Beds
National Monument

Sisters

Ochoco National
Forest

IDAHO

Deschutes
National
Forest

Redmond

Prineville

Paulina

Malheur National
Forest

Ontario

Bend

Mt. Bachelor

Vale

Willamette
National
Forest

La Pine

Burns

Riley

Crane

Owyhee
Lake

Malheur
Lake

Crater Lake
National Park

Silver Lake

Harney
Lake

Malheur National
Wildlife Refuge

Jordan
Valley

Crater
Lake

Crater
Lake

Mt. Scott

Summer
Lake

Diamond

Burns
Junction

Owyhee R.

Upper
Klamath
Lake

Beatty

Fremont
National
Forest

Lake
Abert

Frenchglen

Steens
Mountain

Crooked R.

Klamath
Falls

Valley Falls

Alvord Desert

Lakeview

CALIFORNIA

NEVADA

0   60 miles

0   60 kilometers

WHAT'S WHERE WASHINGTON AND VANCOUVER

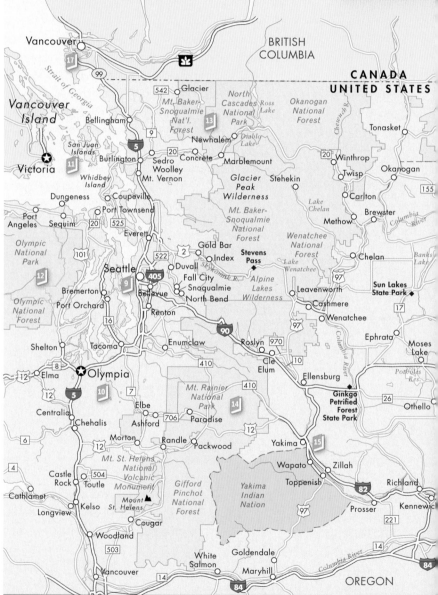

0   40 miles
0   40 kilometers

Okanogan National Forest

Colville National Forest

Colville National Forest

Republic

21   25   195

Colville

Colville Indian Reservation

Franklin D. Roosevelt Lake

Chewelah

231

Coulee Dam

Spokane Indian Reservation

Grand Coulee

2   Wilbur

247

Davenport

Spokane

16

28

Sprague

Ritzville

90

Washtucna

26

395

Snake R.

Pomeroy

Dayton

Umatilla National Forest

Walla Walla

12

Pendleton

9 Seattle. Seattle is a sprawling city shaped by many beautiful bodies of water. On the west is Puget Sound; on the east is massive Lake Washington. The Emerald City sits in the middle, bisected by highway I-5 and further divvied up by more lakes and canals.

10 Seattle Environs. Right outside Seattle there are many quintessential Washington experiences: touring the cities of Olympia and Tacoma, marveling at navy warships and vintage Boeing airplanes, or biking past tulip fields in the Skagit Valley.

11 The Puget Sound and San Juan Islands. You haven't experienced a Washington summer without a trip to the islands. The beauty of the San Juans—prime whale-watching territory—is unmatched, but Puget Sound also has plenty of beach walks and lazy country lanes.

12 Olympic National Park. Centered on Mount Olympus and framed on three sides by water, this 922,651-acre park covers much of Washington's forest-clad Olympic Peninsula. The region is still mostly undeveloped, except for a handful of small towns along Highway 101.

13 North Cascades National Park. This 505,000-acre expanse of mountain wilderness about 75 mi north of Seattle is part of an area with more than half of the glaciers in America.

14 Mount Rainier National Park. The fifth-highest mountain in the Lower 48, Mt. Rainier is massive and unforgettable. It's roughly 80 mi south of Seattle and 60 mi southeast of Olympia. Equally awe-inspiring is Mt. St. Helens to the south of the park.

15 Yakima River Valley. This fertile valley east of the Cascades has long been known for apple and cherry orchards, and in recent years as a highly prized winemaking area.

16 Eastern Washington. Characterized by rolling, dry, treeless hills and anchored by the state's second-largest city, Spokane, the state's eastern reaches take in the vast Columbia River valley and an eclectic mix of cities and towns. Walla Walla ranks among the top wine centers in the Northwest, with vineyards also proliferating in the Tri-Cities area to the west.

17 Vancouver and Victoria. Cosmopolitan Vancouver is a glorious city. Tall fir trees and rock spires tower close by, the ocean is at your doorstep, and international residents create a vibrant atmosphere. Victoria,, is a stunner, and is easily reached by a spectacular ferry ride from Seattle.

THE PACIFIC NORTHWEST PLANNER

Fast Facts	Border Crossing

Currency and Exchange. The units of currency in Canada are the Canadian dollar (C$) and the cent, in almost the same denominations as U.S. currency. A good way to be sure you're getting the best exchange rate is by using your credit card or ATM/debit card. The issuing bank will convert your bill at the current rate.

Packing. It's all about layers here. The weather can morph from cold and overcast to warm and sunny and back again in the course of a few hours, especially in spring and early fall. *See also Hiking 101 below.*

Taxes. Oregon has no sales tax, although many cities and counties levy a tax on lodging and services. Room taxes, for example, vary from 6% to 9½%. The state retail sales tax in Washington is 6.5%, but there are also local taxes that can raise the total tax to 11.5%, depending on the goods or service and the municipality; Seattle's retail sales tax is 8.9%. A Goods and Services Tax (GST) of 5% applies on virtually every transaction in Canada except for the purchase of basic groceries.

By Air and Ferry. You are required to present a passport to enter or reenter the United States. To enter Canada (or more precisely, to reenter the U.S. from Canada) by air you must present a valid passport or an Air NEXUS card; by land or sea you need to present one of the following: 1) passport, 2) a trusted-traveler program card (i.e., NEXUS, SENTRI, or FAST card, 3) a U.S. Passport Card, or 4) an Enhanced Driver's License (issued only in the states of Michigan, New York, Vermont, and Washington).

By Car. You will need one of the aforementioned documents (see above) to cross the border. In addition, drivers must carry owner registration and proof of insurance coverage, which is compulsory in Canada. The Canadian Non-Resident Inter-Provincial Motor Vehicle Liability Insurance Card, available from any U.S. insurance company, is accepted as evidence of financial responsibility in Canada. If you are driving a car that is not registered in your name, carry a letter from the owner that authorizes your use of the vehicle.

The main entry point into British Columbia from the United States by car is on I–5 at Blaine, Washington, 48 km (30 mi) south of Vancouver. Three highways enter British Columbia from the east: Highway 1, or the Trans-Canada Highway; Highway 3, or the Crowsnest Highway, which crosses southern British Columbia; and Highway 16, the Yellowhead Highway, which runs through northern British Columbia from the Rocky Mountains to Prince Rupert.

Border-crossing procedures are usually quick and simple, although the wait can be trying on weekends and during busy holiday periods. Every British Columbia border crossing is open 24 hours (except the one at Aldergrove, which is open from 8 AM to midnight). The I–5 border crossing at Blaine, Washington (also known as the Douglas, or Peace Arch, border crossing), is one of the busiest border crossings between the United States and Canada. Listen to local radio traffic reports for information about wait times.

U.S. Passport Information **U.S. Department of State** (☎ *877/487-2778* ⊕ *www.travel.state.gov/passport*).

1

Getting Around

You'll need a car to get around all but the major cities of the Pacific Northwest. Although a car will also grant you more freedom to explore the outer areas of Portland, Seattle, Vancouver, and Victoria, these four cities have adequate public transportation and taxi fleets. This is not the case in most other towns in the region, so even if bus or train service exists between two points, you may need a car to get around once you arrive.

I–5 is the major north-south conduit of the U.S. part of the region, offering a straight shot at high speeds—when there aren't traffic snarls, of course—from Oregon's southern border all the way up to the Canadian border. Seattle and Portland are both along I–5, and Vancouver is about 30 mi across the border from where it ends. This makes driving between the major hubs an easy option, though it's also possible to travel between them by train or bus, which may be preferable—except for the lower half of Oregon, below Eugene, I–5 isn't especially scenic, so it doesn't make for a very inspiring road trip.

U.S. 101, on the other hand, is one of the main attractions of the region. It starts in Washington west of Olympia, makes a very wide loop around Olympic National Park and then heads south through Oregon, hugging the coast almost the whole way down. Most of the road is incredibly scenic—the loveliest stretches are in northern and central Oregon—but this is not a very quick way to traverse either state. Make sure you want to commit to the coastal drive, which may be slow going in some parts, before getting on the 101—it takes some time to work your way over from I–5, so jumping back and forth between the two isn't a very practical option.

The Cascade Range cuts through the middle of Washington and Oregon, which means that east–west journeys often meander over mountain passes and can be either simply beautiful (summer) or beautiful and treacherous (winter). I–90 is the main east–west artery in Washington, connecting Seattle with Spokane, but Highway 20, which passes through the North Cascades National Park, is more scenic. I–84 is Oregon's major east–west artery; not far east of Portland it enters the stunningly picturesque Columbia River Gorge.

See also Car Travel in Travel Smart for driving times to various regions from Seattle and Portland.

When to Go

Hotels in the major tourist destinations often book up early in July and August, so it's important to make reservations well in advance. Spring and fall are also excellent times to visit, although rain is more prevalent then, especially in spring. Prices for accommodations, transportation, and tours can be lower (and the crowds much smaller!) in the most popular destinations. In winter, snow is uncommon in the lowland areas but abundant in the nearby mountains, where ski resorts abound but chains and snow tires are often required for driving.

CLIMATE

Average daytime summer highs are in the 70s; winter temperatures are generally in the 40s, but this depends heavily on elevation—in the mountains temperatures can drop much lower. Rainfall varies greatly from one locale to another. In the coastal mountains, for example, 160 inches of rain falls annually, creating temperate rain forests. In the eastern two-thirds of Oregon, Washington, and British Columbia, near-desert conditions prevail, with rainfall as low as 6 inches per year. Seattle has an average of only 36 inches of rainfall a year—less than New York, Chicago, or Miami—however, from October through March a light rain is almost always present. Portland is equally gray and drizzly in winter.

PACIFIC NORTHWEST TOP ATTRACTIONS

Crater Lake National Park

(A) The deepest lake in the United States is also the clearest, a fact readily grasped as soon as you behold this searing-blue body of water. It formed from rain and snowmelt that filled an ancient volcanic caldera. It's closed much of the year due to snow, but in summer this 21-square-mi lake is southern Oregon's foremost attraction—the nearly century-old Crater Lake Lodge, perched on the southern shore, makes a memorable overnight and dinner venue.

Oregon Sand Dunes

(B) The 41-mi of rolling bluffs that make up Oregon Dunes National Recreation Area bring out the kid in visitors of all ages—there's something inherently happy about frolicking amid these massive mountains of sand, some of them climbing nearly 500 feet higher than the surf. Here you can hike, ride horseback, and race on a dune buggy, and there's great boating and fishing (plus several excellent seafood restaurants) in the nearby town of Florence.

Hurricane Ridge, Olympic National Park

(C) Of the dozens of stunning panoramas within Olympic National Park, this 5,200-foot-high bluff offers the most memorable views—it takes in the vast Olympic mountain range as well as the Strait of Juan de Fuca and, beyond that, Vancouver Island. In summer, rangers lead tours through the wildflower- and wildlife-rich terrain.

Johnston Observatory, Mt. St. Helens

(D) Named for a brave volcanologist who perished in the terrifying 1980 eruption of Mount St. Helens, this visitor center and observatory affords mind-blowing views of the hulking—often steaming—lava dome that lies deep within the mountain's crater. You reach this spot by driving the scenic Spirit Lake Highway.

Powell's Bookstore

(E) The downtown Portland legend is the world's largest bookstore carrying both new and used titles, and with its coffee-house, late hours, and endless aisles of reading, it's also a prime spot for literary-minded people-watching.

Cannon Beach

(F) The nearest town on the dramatically rocky, windswept Oregon coast from Portland also happens to be one of the most idyllic communities in the coastal Northwest. This town anchored by 235-foot-tall Haystack Rock is rife with beach-side hiking trails, fine art galleries, and cafés specializing in organic coffee, Oregon wines, and fresh-caught seafood.

Stanley Park, Vancouver, BC

(G) Remarkably, this verdant 1,000-acre oasis of evergreen-shaded biking and hiking trails and pristine beaches lies just a few blocks from Vancouver's bustling business district. Stanley Park has plenty of notable attractions, too, including a miniature railway with rides that delight kids, eight intricately carved First Nation totem poles, and the Vancouver Aquarium Marine Science Centre.

Butchart Gardens, Victoria, BC

(H) Stroll through this 55-acre wonderland of gloriously arranged gardens and you may never believe this site once held a stone quarry. This beloved attraction lies just outside of Victoria, and comprises a magnificent variety of gardens, from Japanese to rose to formal Italian. Concerts are held on the grounds throughout the warmer months.

Pike Place Market

(I) The Pacific Northwest abounds with stellar farmers' markets, but downtown Seattle's creaky and colorful Pike Place is the mother of them all, established in 1907 and still thriving (despite a near brush with the wrecking ball during the 1960s).

TOP EXPERIENCES

The Laser-Light Show at Grand Coulee Dam, WA

You truly get a sense of the awesome magnitude of the Columbia River when you view some of the enormous hydroelectric facilities set along this meandering Northwest river. The Grand Coulee Dam, built in 1932, ranks among the world's biggest concrete structures, and towers over the landscape. On summer evenings, grab a seat and watch the nightly laser-light show projected across the dam. This is a favorite family activity in this otherwise relatively remote part of northeastern Washington.

Wine-tasting in Walla Walla, WA

Although you'll find super wine-making in several parts of the region, including Oregon's Willamette Valley and Washington's nearby Yakima and Columbia valleys, the dapper college town of Walla Walla has evolved into the Northwest's best overall wine-country hub. The handsomely revived historic downtown abounds with smart boutiques, lively cafés and restaurants, and several prominent tasting rooms. And throughout the surrounding vineyard-studded hills you'll find elegant inns and some of the most critically acclaimed, if still somewhat underrated, wineries in the country.

Skiing Mt. Hood, OR

Just 60 mi east of Portland, the state's highest mountain is the only place in the lower 48 where you can ski year-round. There are actually three different facilities on this mammoth, snowcapped mountain. Timberline Lodge Ski Area is the one that remains open year-round, and its runs pass beside the venerable Timberline Lodge, a restaurant and hotel dating to the 1930s. Nearby Mt. Hood Ski Bowl has less interesting terrain but the most night-skiing acreage in the country. Around the north side of the mountain, you'll find the most challenging, extensive, and interesting terrain at Mt. Hood Meadows Ski Resort, which offers some 2,000 acres of winter snowboarding and ski fun.

Picnicking at Silver Falls State Park, OR

The lush Silver Falls State Park, about 25 mi east of Salem, is so impressive that serious campaigns to admit it to the national park system have taken place recently. In the meantime, it's something of a secret treasure. The 8,700-acre swatch of sky-scraping old-growth Douglas firs climbs into the foothills of the Cascade Range, where rain and melting snow supply the torrent that roars through 14 different waterfalls, several of them more than 100 feet tall.

Driving Through the Columbia Gorge, OR/WA

The roughly 75-mi section of the mighty Columbia River that extends from just east of Portland to The Dalles provides some of the most stunning scenery in the Pacific Northwest. Towering cliffs on both the Washington and Oregon sides of the river form a dramatic backdrop, and meandering highways line both banks (on the Washington side, Hwy. 14 is slower but offers better views). There's much to see and do in the Gorge: visit the 620-foot-high Multnomah Falls, stroll among the restaurants and shops in quaint Hood River, or try your luck at sailboarding, a sport well suited to the river's high winds.

Attending the Oregon Shakespeare Festival in Ashland, OR

Sunny, hilly, and attractive Ashland is a charming, small city in its own right, with a bustling downtown popping with notable restaurants specializing in farm-to-table cuisine and wines from nearby vineyards. But the Oregon Shakespeare Festival, which presents world-class plays (from Shakespeare to classics to contemporary) on three different stages from mid-February to early November, really put this town on the map. Try to see a play in the largest venue, the Elizabethan, which replicates London's famed Fortune Theatre.

Coffeehouse-Crawling in Seattle, WA

Sure, for kicks, it's worth stopping by the original branch of Starbucks, which is across the street from Pike Place Market. But as arguably the nation's coffeehouse capital, Seattle has far more interesting java joints to consider. Especially fertile (coffee) grounds for coffeehouse-hopping include the Capitol Hill, Queen Anne, Ballard, and Fremont neighborhoods—try Vivace, Caffe Vita, Fremont Coffee Company, or Caffe Fiore for stellar espresso.

Shopping at the Portland Saturday Market, Portland, OR

Despite its name, this expansive outdoor market—the largest weekly arts-and-crafts gathering in the country—is actually open on both Saturdays and Sundays (from March through Christmas). The recently expanded market grounds are just below downtown's Burnside Bridge, and here you'll find every imaginable creation: offbeat patio sculptures, jewelry made from recycled wares, stylish yet practical housewares. Artists here are required to appear in person to sell their art, providing customers with a chance to chat and ask questions about potential purchases.

Biking around Lopez Island, WA

Whether you're an ardent cyclist or an occasional weekender, Lopez Island offers some of the best biking terrain in the West. This laid-back, gently undulating island that's part of Washington's fabled San Juan archipelago is ringed by a beatiful main road and dedicated bike paths. As you cycle past lavender fields, blackberry bushes, horse farms, and occasional patches of woodland, you'll encounter little automobile traffic. There are several bike-rental shops, and the Lopez Island Soda Fountain is a fine spot for a refreshment.

Riding the Ferry to Victoria, BC

This is a perfectly simple way to admire the region's coastal scenery, from the mountains in Olympic National Park to the meandering shorelines of the San Juan Islands (if you're coming from Washington) and Gulf islands (if you're coming from mainland British Columbia). Numerous ferries of many sizes ply the waters around Victoria and Vancouver Island, and the trip is best enjoyed on an open deck, while devouring a cup of clam chowder.

White-water Rafting on the Rogue River, Grants Pass, OR

Of the many excellent places for white-water rafting in Oregon, the Rogue River offers some of the most thrilling rides. Several outfitters offer trips along this frothy, 215-mi river in the southwestern part of the state, from half-day adventures well suited to beginners to multiday trips that include camping or overnights in local lodges.

IF YOU LIKE

Must-See Museums

Although you'll discover a plethora of art and history museums, the Pacific Northwest continues to fascinate visitors with its diverse selection of museums, all of which complement the region's equally diverse culture.

Columbia River Maritime Museum, Astoria, OR. A fully operational U.S. Coast Guard lightship and the personal belongings of the passengers of area shipwrecks are among the exhibits here.

Evergreen Aviation Museum, McMinnville, OR. Engrossing facts about aviation complement an awesome assortment of flying machines at this expansive repository best known as the address of Howard Hughes's "flying boat," the *Spruce Goose,* which has a wingspan longer than a football field and its end zones.

High Desert Museum, Bend, OR. Evocative and intricate walk-through dioramas and an indoor-outdoor zoo with creatures great and tiny convey the High Desert's past and present in a delightfully airy and family-friendly space.

Poulsbo Marine Science Center, Poulsbo, WA. The creatures of Puget Sound squirm, swim, and squirt. You can have a first-hand experience (excuse the pun) with some of them thanks to the center's touch tanks.

Seattle Asian Art Museum. Pick an Asian country—any Asian country—and you're likely to find its art or artifacts inside this stately art deco museum in leafy Volunteer Park.

Wing Luke Museum, Seattle, WA. Costumes, crafts, and photographs of immigrants from Asia and the Pacific islands all under one roof.

Distinctive Lodging

Accommodations in the Northwest include urban boutique hotels, simple chain hotels in the suburbs, luxury mountain retreats, ski chalets, national park cabins, and local motels. Bed-and-breakfasts are especially popular with rooms in historic homes, sprawling log cabins amid the rain forest, and weathered cedar mansions beside a lake or bay.

Allison Inn & Spa, Newberg, OR. Elegant yet refreshingly contemporary, this 80-room boutique resort and spa has finally given Oregon's scenic Willamette Valley an accommodation worthy of the region's ethereal pinot noirs.

Cave B Inn at Sagecliffe, Quincy, WA. A stay here puts you on the edge of the Columbia Gorge in the middle of wine country. Opt for one of the secluded cliff houses, and be sure to dine at the superb regional Northwest restaurant, Tendrils.

Heceta House, Heceta Head, OR. Occupying the same dramatic promontory as a working lighthouse, this Queen Anne–style B&B has views of the Pacific that inspire many a marriage proposal.

Hotel 1000, Seattle, WA. The pride of the city's recent hotel boom, this chic beauty offers plenty of high-tech sensors and gadgets to fiddle with, along with the city's only state-of-the-art virtual driving range.

Shangri-la Hotel, Vancouver, BC. The tallest building in Vancouver houses the very first North American outpost of the luxe Asian hotel brand. The sybaritic Chi Spa and sleekly understated Pan-Asian decor add up to a supremely relaxing stay.

CRUISES

Seattle's cruise industry welcomes some of the world's largest ships to its docks on Elliott Bay. Vancouver is the major embarkation point for Alaska cruises, and virtually all Alaska-bound cruise ships call there; some also call at Victoria and Prince Rupert. Cruise Lines International Association (⊕ www.cruising.org) is a good starting point if you don't have a specific carrier in mind.

Major Cruise Lines

Carnival Cruises. They call themselves "fun ships" for good reason, with lots of entertainment and youthful things to do aboard. Singles, couples, children, and even older folks will enjoy these cruises. The kids' programs earn rave reviews. ☎ 888/227–6482 ⊕ www.carnival.com.

Celebrity Cruises. Celebrity's focus is on service. From their waitstaff to their activity directors, every aspect of your trip is well thought out. They cater to adults more than children, so this may not be the best line for families. ☎ 800/647–2251 ⊕ www.celebrity.com.

Holland America. The grande dame of cruise lines, Holland America has a reputation for service and elegance. ☎ 877/932–4259 ⊕ www.hollandamerica.com.

Norwegian Cruise Line. Billing its relatively relaxed, family-friendly cruises as "freestyle," NCL was one of the earliest companies to specialize in the Caribbean. It boasts the youngest fleet on the planet. ☎ 866/234–7350 ⊕ www.ncl.com.

Princess Cruises. Princess's prices start out a little higher, but you get more (affordable balcony rooms, nice decor, more restaurants to choose from, personalized service). It aims to offer affordable luxury and draws a slightly older crowd. ☎ 800/774–6237 ⊕ www.princess.com.

Regent Seven Seas. Aiming for the high-end market with deluxe staterooms, noteworthy speakers, and performance troupes, this company's ships are among the most sophisticated afloat. ☎ 877/505–5370 ⊕ www.rssc.com.

Royal Caribbean. Royal Caribbean is known for its spacious and stylish mega-liners. In keeping with its reputation for being all things for all people, Royal Caribbean offers a huge variety of activities and services on board and more excursions on land than any other cruise line. ☎ 866/562–7625 ⊕ www.royalcaribbean.com.

Seabourn. With the most luxurious vessels afloat, Seabourn has smaller ships that specialize in intimate service and a tranquil cruise experience for the moneyed crowd. ☎ 800/929–9391 ⊕ www.seabourn.com.

Silversea. Silversea serves deluxe cruisers with small vessels renowned for exquisite decor and attentive service. Expect classical performers among the entertainers. ☎ 877/760–9052 ⊕ www.silversea.com.

Smaller Cruise Lines

Smaller ships explore narrower inlets, from the Columbia River to BC's Gulf Islands, and offer more personalized service. America Safari Cruises and Cruise West offer trips in British Columbia (some venturing all the way up to Alaska) and along the Columbia and Snake rivers in Washington and Oregon. Bluewater Adventures provides a number of tours along the coast of British Columbia. **American Safari Cruises** (☎ 888/862–8881 ⊕ www.amsafari.com). **Bluewater Adventures** (☎ 888/877–1770 ⊕ www.bluewateradventures.ca). **Cruise West** (☎ 888/851–8133 ⊕ www.cruisewest.com).

PORTLAND WITH KIDS

Many of Oregon's best kids-oriented attractions and activities are in greater Portland. Just getting around the Rose City—via streetcars and light-rail trains on city streets and kayaks, excursion cruises, and jet boats on the Willamette River—is fun. For listings of family-oriented concerts, performances by the Oregon Children's Theatre, and the like, check the free *Willamette Weekly* newspaper.

Museums and Attractions
On the east bank of the Willamette River, the **Oregon Museum of Science and Industry** (OMSI) is a leading interactive museum, with touch-friendly exhibits, an Omnimax theater, the state's biggest planetarium, and a 240-foot submarine moored just outside in the river. Along Portland's leafy Park Blocks, both the **Oregon Historical Society** and the **Portland Art Museum** have exhibits and programming geared toward kids.

In Old Town, kids enjoy walking amid the ornate pagodas and dramatic foliage of the **Lan Su Chinese Garden**. This is a good spot for a weekend morning, followed by a visit to the **Portland Saturday Market**, where food stalls and musicians keep younger kids entertained, and the cool jewelry, toys, and gifts handcrafted by local artisans appeal to teens. Steps from the market is the **Oregon Maritime Museum**, set within a vintage stern-wheeler docked on the river. And just up Burnside Street from the market, **Powell's City of Books** contains enormous sections of kids' and young adults' literature.

Parks
Portland is dotted with densely wooded parks—many of the larger ones have ball fields, playgrounds, and picnic areas. The most famous urban oasis in the city, **Forest Park** (along with adjoining **Washington Park**) offers a wealth of engaging activities. You can ride the MAX light rail right to the park's main hub of culture, a complex comprising the **Oregon Zoo, Portland Children's Museum,** and **World Forestry Discovery Center Museum**. Ride the narrow-gauge railroad from the zoo for 2 mi to reach the **International Rose Test Garden** and **Japanese Garden**. From here it's an easy downhill stroll to **Northwest 23rd and 21st avenues'** pizza parlors, ice-cream shops, and bakeries.

Outdoor Adventures
Tour boats ply the **Willamette River**, and a couple of marinas near OMSI rent **kayaks** and conduct **drag-boat races** out on the water. There are also several shops in town that rent **bikes** for use on the city's many miles of dedicated bike lanes and trails. There's outstanding **white-water rafting** just southeast of Portland, along the Clackamas River. On your way toward the Clackamas, check out **North Clackamas Aquatic Park** and **Oaks Amusement Park**, which have rides and wave pools galore.

Nearby **Mt. Hood** has camping, hiking, and biking all summer, and three of the most family-friendly ski resorts in the Northwest—**Timberline** is especially popular for younger and less experienced boarders and skiers. From summer through fall, the pick-your-own berry farms and pumpkin patches on **Sauvie Island** make for an engaging afternoon getaway—for an all day outing, continue up U.S. 30 all the way to **Astoria**, at the mouth of the Columbia River, to visit the **Columbia River Maritime Museum** and **Fort Stevens State Park**, where kids love to scamper about the remains of an early-20th-century shipwreck.

SEATTLE WITH KIDS

A city where floatplanes take off a few feet from houseboats, and harbor seals might be spotted on a routine ferry ride, doesn't have to try too hard to feel like a wonderland. And if (when) the rains fall, there are plenty of great museums to keep the kiddos occupied. A lot of child-centric sights are easily reached via public transportation, and the piers and the Aquarium can be explored on foot from most Downtown hotels. A few spots (Woodland Park Zoo, and Discovery and Gas Works parks) are easier to visit by car, especially if you're schlepping a lot of supplies.

Museums

Several museums cater specifically to kids, and many are conveniently clustered at the Seattle Center. The Center's winning trio includes the **Pacific Science Center,** which has interactive exhibits and IMAX theaters; the **Children's Museum,** which has exhibits on Washington State and foreign cultures plus plenty of interactive art spaces; and, of course, the **Space Needle.** For older, hipper siblings there's a skate park; the Vera Project, a teen music and art space; and the Experience Music Project/Science Fiction Museum.

Downtown there are miles of waterfront to explore along the piers. The **Seattle Aquarium** is here and has touch pools and otters—what more could you want?

Parks and Outdoor Attractions

Discovery Park has an interpretive center, a Native American cultural center, easy forest trails, and accessible beaches. **Alki Beach** in West Seattle is lively and fun; a wide paved path is the perfect surface for wheels of all kinds—you can rent bikes and scooters, or take to the water on rented paddleboats and kayaks. **Gas Works Park** has great views of the skyline and floatplanes over Lake Union, along with the rusty remnants of the old machinery. **Volunteer Park** has a shallow pool made for splashing toddlers and wide lawns.

The **Woodland Park Zoo** is easy to explore and has 300 different species of animals, from jaguars to mountain goats; cheap paid parking and stroller rentals are available. Watching an astonishing variety of boats navigate the ship canal at the **Ballard Locks** will entertain visitors of any age. The **Northwest Puppet Center** has a museum and weekend marionette plays.

Hotels

Downtown, the **Hotel Monaco** offers a happy medium between sophisticated and family-friendly. The colorful, eccentric decor will appeal to kids but remind adults that they're in a boutique property. Fun amenities abound, like optional goldfish in the rooms, and lobby events featuring tarot card readers and Guitar Hero showdowns. Surprisingly, one of the city's most high-end historic properties, the **Fairmont Olympic,** is also kid-friendly. The hotel's decor is a little fussy, but the grand staircases in the lobby will awe most little ones, and there's a great indoor pool area. In addition, it offers babysitting, a kids' room-service menu, as well as toys and board games.

Several properties offer kitchenette suites that help families save some money on food costs. The Silver Cloud Inn Lake Union has suites with kitchens. It's north of Downtown on Lake Union, which is slightly out of Downtown, but the South Lake Union streetcar is across the street and gets you into Downtown and to bus connections quickly.

HIKING 101

The Pacific Northwest is home to some true wilderness; below are some basic tips to help make your hiking trips safer and more comfortable.

What to Bring

The "10 Essentials" According to the Washington State Trails Association:

1. map of the area and trail

2. compass

3. flashlight

4. at least a day's worth of food (energy bars, gorp, and hardy fruits like apples and bananas are good)

5. warm clothing and/or rain gear (a hat and a light jacket may be needed even on hot summer days)

6. sunglasses, especially when walking across snow patches on sunny days

7. basic first-aid kit in a waterproof container or baggie

8. pocket knife or multipurpose tool

9. waterproof matches

10. fire starter like a candle or compressed wood chips (the Pacific Northwest is a damp place, and you may have trouble finding dry kindling).

Water, water, and more water. A good rule of thumb is two liters per person for the average day hike. Take regular water breaks—don't wait until you're very thirsty to stop.

Waterproof footwear or a change of shoes. Even if the sun is shining in Seattle, the weather may be very different at your destination. If there's even a hint of a coming rainstorm, make sure you have proper rain gear. Hiking in the rain can be exhilarating. Walking 3 or 4 mi in sopping wet shoes? Not so much.

Anything but cotton. Veteran hikers can't say enough bad things about cotton clothing. It gets soggy (and then heavy) easily and is a terrible insulator, especially when it's wet. Your cotton T will probably be fine for an easy nature walk, but if you plan to do an all-day hike, you'll fare better with wool or synthetic fabrics.

Sunblock. Even if it's cool enough to require a jacket and hat, you can still get sunburned—the sun is particularly intense above the tree line. And if there's even a remote possibility that you'll be encountering snowfields, sunblock is an absolute necessity.

Toilet paper. Though major parks usually have well-equipped public restrooms, the port-a-johns at less-traveled trailheads may not have any paper products.

Insect repellent. Rocky areas can get quite buggy with anything from gnats to horseflies. Mosquitoes start biting in late afternoon. Bugs aren't always a nuisance, but carrying a small supply of repellent is advised.

Northwest Forest Pass, if necessary. Some trails require the purchase of a $5 pass (one per vehicle), which allows you to park at the trailhead. Check out ⊕ *www.fs.fed.us/r6/passespermits* to see if your trail requires a pass; you can purchase them at any Forest Service station.

Safety

Don't overdo it. Injuries occur more often when you are tired and/or lack experience navigating a certain type of terrain. Know your ability and conditioning levels. The good thing about the Northwest is that great views can be found even on relatively easy trails—not everything requires a marathon slog up a mountainside.

Don't rely on cell phones to get you out of a jam. Service is spotty at best on trails, so don't let a cell phone in your pocket give you a false sense of security.

Hike in pairs. Although you'll see plenty of solo hikers, especially on the more heavily visited trails of the major parks, it's always wise to hike in pairs or groups, especially if you're a novice.

Exercise caution on Forest Service roads. Some Forest Service roads are mere steps from major highways; others consist of miles of twisting, often-unpaved stretches. Double-check road conditions, especially in late fall or early spring or after heavy winds or rainstorms, and make sure you have a full tank of gas before turning off main roads. If at any time you are unsure of your whereabouts, turn around and retrace your steps back to the main road.

Keep track of the time. Be sure to clock the first leg of a hike, calculate how long the return trip will take, and plan accordingly. Know what time the sun sets and remember that dense, old-growth forest trails can get dark even if the sun's still shining up top.

Share your plans with someone. Let someone know of your hiking plans, including the trail name, the approximate time you're starting the hike, and the approximate time you expect to be back.

Be bear aware. Bear sightings are rare, but black bears do make their homes in Northwest forests. Bone up on bear etiquette at ⊕ *www.nps.gov/noca/naturescience/bear-safety.htm.*

Lock up your car. Break-ins do happen at trailhead parking areas, so always lock your car and don't leave valuables in plain view.

Trail Etiquette

Don't litter. Even the region's busiest trails are widely free of garbage. Your mantra should be: Leave no trace.

Clam up. Avoid chatter and nonemergency cell-phone use. A big part of hiking's allure is the silence.

Stay on the trail. The delicate ecosystems of the state's busiest natural areas are under tremendous strain from all the foot traffic; wildlife habitats can also be disturbed by overzealous adventurers. Don't go off the trail, especially in spots where signs implore you to stay put.

Let horseback riders pass. Few hiking trails allow horseback riding, but if you encounter riders, step to the side and let them pass.

Let your fellow hikers pass. Step off to the side when you need a break or if you're moving slowly and sense you're causing a bottleneck on a narrow trail. In most cases, hikers going uphill have the right of way; hikers heading downhill should step aside until they pass. However, sometimes the hiker with the less difficult or roomier path will go first to give the other hiker more time to contend with the terrain.

Smile. It's common for hikers to greet each other as they pass by. Expect to get a nod, smile, or a "hello"—or all three.

FLAVORS OF THE PACIFIC NORTHWEST

Pacific Northwest cuisine highlights regional seafood, locally grown produce, and locally raised meats, often prepared in styles that borrow Pan-Asian, French, and Italian influences. All the region's major and even many smaller cities have top-rated, nationally renowned dining spots, as well as funky, inexpensive little eateries that also pride themselves on serving seasonal and often organic ingredients.

Seafood

The Northwest's dining scene is forever eclectic because of the combined abundance of fresh seafood and the imaginative ways it's cooked. Many restaurants, such as the Portland-based chain McCormick & Schmick's, print menus daily and feature a "fresh list" with more than 30 types of seafood represented, most of which are caught from local waters. And since Dungeness crab, salmon, tuna, sole, oysters, spotted prawns, scallops, and swordfish are all within pole's reach, chefs take serious and artful pleasure in discovering ways to fry, grill, bake, stir-fry, sear, poach, barbecue, and sauté the latest catch in new, inventive ways.

Elliott's Oyster House, Seattle, WA. Brave the touristy waterfront to belly up to the shellfish bar—you won't find better oysters or Dungeness crab in Seattle

Matt's in the Market, Seattle, WA. Right next to Seattle's prime source of fresh fish, Pike Place Market, Matt's serves a must-try oyster po'boy and Penn Cove mussels with chorizo or Dungeness crab bisque, and pan-roasted fillets of wild salmon and lingcod served with light vinaigrettes.

Jake's Famous Crawfish, Portland, OR. For more than 100 years Portlander's have come to Jake's. You should, too, especially during crawfish season (May–September).

Blue Water Café, Vancouver, BC. Ask the staff to recommend wine-pairings from the BC-focused list, and enjoy exquisitely prepared seafood, which may include overlooked varieties such as mackerel, sardines, and herring.

Foraged Foods

Pacific Northwest chefs are fanatical, in a delicious way, about sustainability, presenting dishes with ingredients raised, grown, or foraged within about 100 mi. Northwest chefs are so determined to maintain an unwavering connection to the land that many hire professional foragers, or on occasion can be found tromping off into the woods themselves. Bounties of morels, chanterelles, and bolete mushrooms (fall), stinging nettles and fiddlehead ferns (spring), and huckleberries and blackberries (summer) now dictate the menus of many restaurants. From both Portland and Seattle, farmland immediately surrounds urban boundaries; therefore, daily deliveries of asparagus, eggplant, pears, cherries, and other fruits and vegetables is achievable.

Sitka & Spruce, Seattle, WA. Wild greens and edible flowers always show up in salads or as garnishes alongside fresh seafood or free-range chicken from Vashon Island farms at Chef Matt Dillon's tiny temple to the Northwest.

Lark, Seattle, WA. Naturally raised veal sweetbreads come with a sunchoke puree, and spring nettles are stuffed into spinach ravioli at Lark, where the small menu names every local farm that contributes to its dishes.

The Herbfarm, Woodinville, WA. Every year the Herbfarm honors mushroom season with the Mycologist's Dream menu, which sees the fungi go into everything from ravioli to flan. The rest of the

year, blackberries may mingle with rose geranium in ice cream, or caviar may be accompanied by a jelly flavored with wild ginger and local rhizomes.

clarklewis, Portland, OR. Greens from Sauvie Island, seafood from the Oregon Coast, and pork belly and lamb loin cultivated from area suppliers appear on a daily changing menu of pastas, grills, and sides.

Paley's Place, Portland, OR. Talented chef Vitaly Paley produces incomparably fresh and complex fare utilizing strictly seasonal and regional ingredients, from local rabbit and squab to razor clams and wild mushrooms.

Wineries

Thanks to a mild climate with soil, air, water, and temperature conditions comparable to regions of France, the Northwest is recognized for producing prime varieties of wine. In charming, rural settings, some just outside the cities, petite to larger vineyards offer behind-the-scenes tours where sampling the merchandise is encouraged. The Northwest is also a notable region for its production of organic and biodynamic wines. In keeping with the sustainable food and farm movement, vineyards are developing fertilization, production, harvesting, and fermentation techniques that produce flavorful, ecofriendly varieties that set the standard in the wine world. A few of our favorites include:

Abacela Vineyards, Umpqua Valley, OR

Amity Vineyards, Willamette Valley, OR

Hedges Cellars, Yakima Valley, WA

L'Ecole No. 41, Walla Walla, WA

Sokol Blosser, Willamette Valley, OR

Artisanal Cocktails

The artisan drinks of the region are thoughtful and high-quality, often using local and seasonal ingredients, including fresh juices and herbs garnered from farmers' markets. Bourbon and gin lovers never had it so good, as these drinks seem to be at the base of most creations; for the rest, there are plenty of obscure lavender-infused liqueurs to choose from. If the idea of fresh honey, rhubarb, or ginger beer corrupting a fine liquor makes you queasy, rest assured that classic drinks are much appreciated in these parts. In Seattle, several bartenders are single-handedly restoring the dignity of the martini, the Manhattan, and the French 75. Note that Portland has recently become a hotbed of small-batch distilleries—standouts include Clear Creek (eau de vie), Aviation (gin), and New Deal (vodka).

Mint/820, Portland, OR. Bartender and owner Lucy Brennan wrote the book on creative cocktails—literally; she's the author of *Hip Sips*, which features more than 60 recipes.

Zig Zag, Seattle, WA. Zig Zag pours the best martinis in Seattle, along with more exotic fare like the Trident (cynar, aquavit, dry sherry, and peach bitters) and inventive, improvised cocktails.

Beaker & Flask, Portland, OR. This East Side newcomer has sophisticated elixirs utilizing everything from house-made bitter-orange liqueur to coconut-water ice cubes.

Licorous, Seattle, WA. Licorous customizes its nibbles to complement the drink list. Parmigiano-and-chorizo palmiers may be suggested to temper the sweet-and-sour Playa Rosa, made with tequila infused with hibiscus, and fresh lime and pineapple juices.

PACIFIC NORTHWEST DRIVING TOUR

North Cascades National Park

Day 1 Start in ❶**Sedro-Woolley,** where you can pick up information about ❷**North Cascades National Park** at the park head-quarters. From Sedro-Woolley it's a 45-minute drive on Route 20 to the park entrance. Take your first stroll through an old-growth forest from the visitor center in Newhalem, then devote the rest of the day to driving through the **Cascades** on Route 20, stopping at various overlooks. Exit the park and continue through the **Methow Valley.** Head south on Route 20, then Route 153, then U.S. 97, then I–82 (just over 300 mi total) to ❸**Yakima** to stay the night.

Mount Rainier National Park

Days 2 and 3 On the morning of Day 2, take U.S. 12 west from Yakima 102 mi to Ohanapecosh, the southern entrance to ❹**Mount Rainier National Park.** When you arrive, take the 31-mi two-hour drive on Sunrise Road, which reveals the "back" (northeast) side of Rainier. A room at the **Paradise Inn** is your base for the next two nights. On Day 3, energetic hikers will want to tackle one of the four- to six-hour trails that lead up among the park's many peaks. Or try one of the ranger-led walks through wildflower meadows. Another option is to hike to Panorama Point near the foot of the **Muir Snowfield** for breathtaking views of the glaciers and high ridges of Rainier overhead. After dinner at the inn, watch the sunset's alpenglow on the peak from the back porch.

Mount St. Helens and the Olympic Foothills

Day 4 Today, follow Routes 706 and 7 to U.S. 12 from Paradise, heading west to I–5. When you reach the interstate, drive south to Route 504 to spend the day visiting the ❺**Mount St. Helens National Volcanic**

THE PLAN

DISTANCE: 1,450 mi

TIME: 10 days

BREAKS: Overnight in Yakima, Mount Rainier National Park, Port Angeles, and Olympic National Park, WA; and Florence, Crater Lake National Park, and Ashland, OR.

Monument, where you can see the destruction caused from the 1980 volcanic eruption. Return to I–5 the way you came in and head north to Olympia, where you should pick up U.S. 101 North. The highway winds through scenic Puget Sound countryside, skirting the Olympic foothills and periodically dipping down to the waterfront. Stop at ❻**Port Angeles,** 136 mi (three hours) from the junction of Route 504 and I–5, to have dinner and spend the night.

Olympic National Park

Days 5 and 6 The next morning, launch into a full day at ❼**Olympic National Park.** Explore the **Hoh Rain Forest** and **Hurricane Ridge** before heading back to Port Angeles for the evening. Start Day 6 with a drive west on U.S. 101 to Forks and on to ❽**La Push** via Route 110, a total of about 45 mi. Here, an hour-long lunchtime stroll to **Second or Third Beach** will offer a taste of the wild Pacific coastline. Back on U.S. 101, head south to **Lake Quinault,** which is about 98 mi from Lake Crescent. Check into the Lake Quinault Lodge, then drive up the river 6 mi to one of the rain-forest trails through the lush Quinault Valley.

The Pacific Coast

Day 7 Leave Lake Quinault early on Day 7 for the long but scenic drive south on U.S. 101. Here the road winds through coastal spruce forests, periodically rising

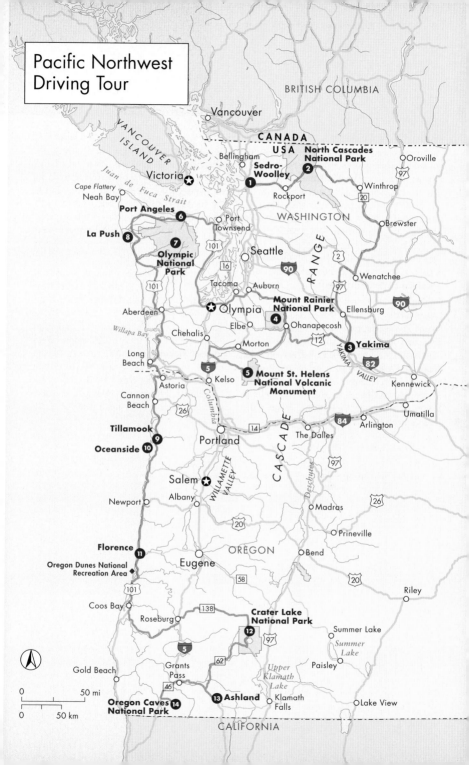

on headlands to offer Pacific Ocean panoramas. Once you're in Oregon, small seaside resort towns beckon with cafés, shops, and inns. In ❾**Tillamook** (famous for its cheese), take a detour onto the Three Capes Loop, a stunning 35-mile byway off U.S. 101. Stop in ❿**Oceanside** (on the loop) for lunch. Once you're back on U.S. 101, continue south. Your final stop is the charming village of ⓫**Florence,** 290 mi (six to eight hours) from Lake Quinault; spend the night.

Crater Lake National Park

Days 8 and 9 From Florence, take U.S. 101 south to Reedsport, Routes 38 and 138 east to Sutherlin, I–5 south to Roseburg, and Route 138 east again to ⓬**Crater Lake National Park,** 180 mi total. Once inside the park, you can continue along Rim Drive for another half hour for excellent views of the lake. Overnight in the park or in Fort Klamath.

The following morning, take the lake boat tour and a hike through the surrounding forest. In the afternoon, head south on Route 62 to I–5, and on to ⓭**Ashland,** 83 mi (about two hours) from Crater Lake. Plan to stay the night in one of Ashland's many superb B&Bs. Have dinner and attend one of the **Oregon Shakespeare Festival** productions (mid-February through early November).

Oregon Caves National Monument

Day 10 On Day 10, head back north on I–5 from Ashland to Grants Pass, then turn south on U.S. 199. At Cave Junction, 67 mi from Ashland, you can take a three-hour side trip to ⓮**Oregon Caves National Monument.** Guided tours of the unique marble caves last 90 minutes; in the summer the day's final tour is by candlelight, which will give you a sense of what it might have been like for early explorers.

—by John Blodgett

Portland

WORD OF MOUTH

I like to walk the bridges. There is a great walking path along the waterfront, so you can walk up one side of the river, cross the bridge and do the other side, and cross back on another bridge. You can also rent bikes and do this.

—sunbum1944

WELCOME TO PORTLAND

TOP REASONS TO GO

★ **Unleash your inner foodie.** Don't miss an amazingly textured range of global delights, created with fresh, locally harvested ingredients.

★ **Beer "hop."** (Pun intended.) Thirty-five local microbrews and offbeat varieties with such names as Hallucinator, Doggie Claws, and Sock Knocker await.

★ **Experience McMenamins.** Visit one of the local chain's beautifully restored properties, such as a renovated 1915 elementary school turned hotel.

★ **Take a stroll through Washington Park.** The International Rose Test Garden, Japanese Garden, Oregon Zoo, World Forestry Center, and Children's Museum are all here.

★ **Peruse pages at Powell's City of Books.** The aisles of this city block–sized shop are filled with more than a million new and used books. Top off hours of literary wanderlust with a mocha or ginseng tea downstairs at World Cup Coffee and Tea House.

1 Downtown. At the center of it all, Portland's downtown has museums, clubs, restaurants, parks, and unique shops. To get around downtown quickly, take the TriMet MAX light rail for free.

2 Pearl District and Old Town/Chinatown. The Pearl District, Portland's trendy and posh neighborhood, is teaming with upscale restaurants, bars, and shopping, along with pricey condos and artists' lofts. A visit here is

3 Nob Hill and Vicinity.
From funky to fabulous, this neighborhood is also referred to as "Northwest 23rd" or "Northwest District." The exciting shopping, restaurants, and bars draw a younger but still sophisticated crowd.

4 Washington Park. Keep busy at the Oregon Zoo, Children's Museum, World Forestry Center, Hoyt Arboretum, Japanese Garden, International Rose Test Garden, Vietnam Veterans Memorial, and Oregon Holocaust Memorial. Nearby Forest Park is the largest forested area within city limits in the nation.

5 East of Willamette River. Ten bridges span the Willamette over to Portland's east side. It offers much of what downtown does but with fewer tourists. If you visit, you'll be rewarded with under-the-radar neighborhoods such as Belmont, Eastmoreland, Hawthorne, Laurelhurst, and Sellwood in the southeast and Alameda, Alberta Arts, Irvington, and the Lloyd District in the northeast.

6 West of Downtown. The lush hills at the west end of downtown hold stately homes and excellent parks, and mark the starting point for much of the greater Portland metro area.

rewarded with tantalizing bakeries and chocolatiers. Old Town/Chinatown offers variety, from cutting-edge to old-fashioned. This is the area for Asian-inspired public art, the LanSu Chinese Garden, and tours of the city's Shanghai Tunnels.

GETTING ORIENTED

Geographically speaking, Portland is relatively easy to navigate. The city's 200-foot-long blocks are highly walkable, and mapped out into quadrants. The Willamette River divides east and west and Burnside Street separates north from south. "Northwest" refers to the area north of Burnside and west of the river; "Southwest" refers to the area south of Burnside and west of the river; "Northeast" refers to the area north of Burnside and east of the river; "Southeast" refers to the area south of Burnside and east of the river. As you travel around the Portland metropolitan area, keep in mind that named east and west streets intersect numbered avenues, run north–south, and begin at each side of the river. For instance, Southwest 12th Avenue is 12 blocks west of the Willamette. Most of downtown's streets are one-way.

PORTLAND PLANNER

Getting Here

Air Travel. It takes about 5 hours to fly nonstop to Portland from New York, 4 hours from Chicago, and 2½ hours from Los Angeles. Flying from Seattle to Portland takes just under an hour; flying from Portland to Vancouver takes an hour and 15 minutes. **Portland International Airport** (PDX) (☎ 877/739–4636 ⊕ www.flypdx.com) is a sleek, modern airport with service to many national and international destinations. **TriMet's Red Line MAX light rail** (☎ 503/238–7433 ⊕ www.trimet.org) leaves the airport for downtown about every 15 minutes. Trains arrive at and depart from just outside the passenger terminal near the south baggage claim. The trip takes about 35 minutes, and the fare is $2.30. By taxi, the trip downtown takes about 30 minutes and costs about $35.

Train Travel. Amtrak (☎ 800/872–7245) has daily service to Union Station from the Midwest and California. The *Cascades* runs between Seattle and Vancouver and between Seattle, Portland, and Eugene. The trip from Seattle to Portland takes 3½ hours and costs $28–$44. The *Empire Builder* travels between Portland and Spokane (7 hours, $75). From Portland to Eugene it's a 3-hour trip; the cost is $21–$35.

Getting Around

Bike Travel. It's tough to find a more bike-friendly city in America. Visitors are impressed by the facilities available for bicyclists—more than 300 miles of bike lanes, paths, and boulevards. ⇨ *See Bicycling in Sports and Outdoors.*

Car Travel. I–5 enters Portland from the north and south. I–84, the city's major eastern approach, terminates in Portland. U.S. 26 and U.S. 30 are primary east–west thoroughfares. Bypass routes are I–205, which links I–5 and I–84 before crossing the Columbia River into Washington, and I–405, which arcs around western downtown.

From the airport to downtown, take I–205 south to westbound I–84. Drive west over the Willamette River and take the City Center exit. If going to the airport, take I–84 east to I–205 north; follow I–205 to the airport exit.

Traffic on I–5 north and south of downtown and on I–84 and I–205 east of downtown is heavy between 6 AM and 9 AM and between 4 and 8 PM. Four-lane U.S. 26 west of downtown can be bumper-to-bumper any time of day going to or from downtown.

Most city-center streets are one-way only, and Southwest 5th and 6th avenues between Burnside and Southwest Madison are limited to bus traffic.

Though there are several options, parking in downtown Portland can be tricky and expensive. If you require more than several hours, your most affordable and accessible option is to park in one of seven city-owned "Smart Park" lots.

Rates range from $1.50 per hour (short-term parking, four hours or less) to $3–$5 per hour (long-term parking, weekdays 5 AM–6 PM), with a $15 daily maximum; rates are lower weekends and evenings. Participating merchants will validate tickets and cover the first two hours of parking when you spend at least $25 in their stores. There are numerous privately owned lots around the city as well; fees for those vary.

Street parking is metered only, and requires you to visibly display a sticker on the inside of your curbside window. The meters that dispense the stickers take coins or credit cards. Metered spaces are mostly available for 90 minutes to three hours; parking tickets for exceeding the limit are regularly issued. Once you get out of downtown and into residential areas, there's plenty of nonmetered street parking available.

Car-rental rates in Portland begin at $30 a day and $138 a week, not including the 17% Multnomah County tax if you rent in this county, which includes the airport. All major agencies are represented.

Taxi Travel. Taxi fare is $2.50 at flag drop plus $2.30 per mi for one person. Each additional passenger pays $1. Cabs cruise the city streets, or you can phone for one.

Contacts **Broadway Cab** (🖀 503/227–1234). **New Rose City Cab** (🖀 503/282–7707). **Portland Taxi Company** (🖀 503/256–5400). **Radio Cab** (🖀 503/227–1212).

TriMet/MAX Travel. TriMet operates an extensive system of buses, streetcars, and light rail trains. The Central City streetcar line runs between Legacy Good Samaritan Hospital in Nob Hill, the Pearl District, downtown, and Portland State University. To Nob Hill it travels along 10th Avenue and then on Northwest Northrup; from Nob Hill it runs along Northwest Lovejoy and then on 11th Avenue. Trains stop every few blocks. Buses can operate as frequently as every five minutes or only once an hour.

Metropolitan Area Express, or MAX light rail, links the eastern and western Portland suburbs with downtown, Washington Park and the Oregon Zoo, the Lloyd Center district, the Convention Center, and the Rose Quarter. From downtown, trains operate daily 5:30 AM–1 AM and run about every 10 minutes Monday–Saturday and every 15 minutes on Sunday and holidays.

Bus, MAX, and streetcar fare is $2 for one or two zones, which covers most places you'll go, and $2.30 for three zones, which includes all of the city's outlying areas. A "Fareless Square" extends through downtown from I–405 to the Willamette River, and from Northwest Irving to the South Waterfront area, and includes the Lloyd Center stop across the river. The free area applies to MAX light rail and Portland Streetcar only. To qualify, your entire trip must stop and start in the fareless area. Maps are posted at all downtown train and streetcar stops.

Day passes for unlimited system-wide travel cost $4.75. Three-day, weekly, and monthly passes are available. As you board the bus, the driver will hand you a transfer ticket good for one to two hours on all buses and MAX trains. Be sure to hold on to it whether you're transferring or not; it also serves as proof that you have paid for your ride.

Contacts **TriMet/MAX** (🖀 503/238–7433 ⊕ www.trimet.org).

Tour Options

Boat Tours. Portland Spirit (🖀 503/224–3900 or 800/224–3901 ⊕ www.portlandspirit.com) has a variety of tours on multiple types of marine craft. **Willamette Jetboat Excursions** (🖀 888/538–2628 or 503/231–1532 ⊕ www.willamettejet.com) offers whirling, swirling one- and two-hour tours along the Willamette River that include an up-close visit to the falls at Oregon City.

Trolley Tours. The **Willamette Shore Trolley** (🖀 503/697–7436 ⊕ www.oregonelectricrailway.org) provides scenic round-trips between suburban Lake Oswego and downtown, along the west shore of the Willamette River. The 6-mi route, which the trolley makes in 45 minutes, passes over trestles and through Elk Rock Tunnel along one of the most scenic stretches of the river.

Walking Tours. For a guided tour packed with information, the variety of options from **Portland Walking Tours** (🖀 503/774–4522 ⊕ www.portlandwalkingtours.com) ensures something for all touring tastes.

VISITOR INFORMATION

Contacts **Travel Portland Information Center** (✉ 701 S.W. 6th Ave., Pioneer Courthouse Sq. 🖀 503/275–8355 or 877/678–5263 ⊕ www.travelportland.com).

PORTLAND PLANNER

When to Go

Portland's mild climate is best from June through September. Hotels are often filled in July and August, so it's important to book reservations in advance. Spring and fall are also excellent times to visit. The weather usually remains quite good, and the prices for accommodations, transportation, and tours can be lower (and the crowds much smaller) in the most popular destinations. In winter, snow is uncommon in the city but abundant in the nearby mountains, making the region a skier's dream.

Average daytime summer highs are in the 70s; winter temperatures are generally in the 40s. Rainfall varies greatly from one locale to another. In the coastal mountains, for example, 160 inches of rain fall annually, creating temperate rain forests. Portland has an average of only 36 inches of rainfall a year—less than New York, Chicago, or Miami. In winter, however, the rain may never seem to end. More than 75% of Portland's annual precipitation occurs from October through March.

Forecasts National Weather Service (⊕ www.wrh.noaa. gov). **Weather Channel** (⊕ www.weather.com).

About the Restaurants

Lovers of ethnic foods have their pick of Chinese, French, Indian, Peruvian, Italian, Japanese, Polish, Middle Eastern, Tex-Mex, Thai, and Vietnamese specialties. Most of the city's trendier restaurants and reliable classics are concentrated in Nob Hill, the Pearl District, and downtown. A smattering of cuisines can also be found on the east side of town as well, near Fremont, Hawthorne Boulevard, Sandy Boulevard, and Alberta Street.

Compared to other major cities, Portland restaurants aren't open quite as late, and it's unusual to see many diners after 11 PM even on weekends, though there are a handful of restaurants and popular bars that do serve late. Many diners dress casually for even higher-end establishments; jeans are acceptable almost everywhere.

About the Hotels

The hotels near the city center and on the riverfront are appealing for their proximity to Portland's attractions. MAX light rail is within easy walking distance of most properties. Additional accommodations clustered near the Convention Center and the airport are almost all chain hotels that tend to be less expensive than those found downtown. Several beautiful B&Bs are the northwest and northeast residential neighborhoods.

Most of Portland's luxurious hotels can be booked for under $250 per night. If you are willing to stay outside of the downtown area, you can easily find a room in a suburban chain hotel for well under $100 per night. Before booking your stay, visit ⊕ www.travelportland.com to check out "Portland Perks" packages.

WHAT IT COSTS IN U.S. DOLLARS					
	¢	$	$$	$$$	$$$$
Restaurants	under $10	$10–$16	$17–$23	$24–$30	over $30
Hotels		under $100	$100–$150	$151–$200	$201–$250	over $250

Restaurant prices are per person, for a main course at dinner. Hotel prices are for two people in a standard double room in high season, excluding tax.

2

Updated by
Janna Mock-
Lopez and
Crystal Wood

What distinguishes Portland from the rest of America's cityscapes? Or from the rest of the world's urban destinations for that matter? In a Northwest nutshell: everything. For some, it's the wealth of cultural offerings and never-ending culinary choices; for others, it's Portland's proximity to the ocean and mountains, or simply the beauty of having all these attributes in one place.

Strolling through downtown or in one of Portland's numerous neighborhoods, you discover an unmistakable vibrancy to this city—one that is created by the clean air, the wealth of trees, and a blend of historic and modern architecture. Portland's various nicknames—Rose City, Bridgetown, Beervana, Brewtopia—tell its story in a nutshell as well.

Portland has a thriving cultural community, with ballet, opera, symphonies, theater, and art exhibitions both minor and major in scope. Portland also has long been considered a hub for indie music. Hundreds of bands flock to become part of the creative flow of alternative, jazz, blues, and rock that dominate the nightclub scene seven nights a week. Factor in an outrageous number of independent brewpubs and coffee shops—with snowboarding, windsurfing, or camping within an hour's drive—and it's easy to see why so many young people take advantage of Portland's eclectic indoor and outdoor offerings.

For people on a slower pace, there are strolls through never-ending parks, dimmed dining rooms for savoring innovative regional cuisine, and gorgeous cruises along the Willamette River aboard the *Portland Spirit*. Families can explore first-rate museums and parks, including the Children's Museum, the Oregon Museum of Science and Industry, and Oaks Park. At most libraries, parks, and recreational facilities, expect to find hands-on activities, music, story times, plays, and special performances for children. Many restaurants in and around Portland are family-friendly, and with immediate access to the MAX light rail and streetcars, toting kids around is easy.

PORTLAND IN A DAY

Spend the morning exploring downtown. Visit the Portland Art Museum or the Oregon History Center, stop by the historic First Congregational Church and Pioneer Courthouse Square, and take a stroll along the Park Blocks or Waterfront Park. Eat lunch and do a little shopping along Northwest 23rd Avenue or at Powell's Books in the early afternoon, and be sure to get a look at the beautiful historic homes in Nob Hill. From there, drive up into the northwest hills by the Pittock Mansion, and finish off the afternoon at the Japanese Garden and the International Test Rose Garden in Washington Park. If you still have energy, head across the river for dinner on Hawthorne Boulevard; then drive up to Mt. Tabor Park for Portland's best sunset.

EXPLORING PORTLAND

One of the greatest things about Portland is that there's so much to explore. This city rightfully boasts that there's something for everyone. What makes discovering Portland's treasures even more enticing is that its attractions, transportation options, and events are all relatively accessible and affordable.

DOWNTOWN

Portland has one of the most attractive, inviting downtown centers in the United States. It's clean, compact, and filled with parks, plazas, and fountains. Architecture fans find plenty to admire in its mix of old and new. Hotels, shops, museums, restaurants, and entertainment can all be found here, and much of the downtown area is part of the TriMet transit system's Fareless Square, within which you can ride the light rail or the Portland Streetcar for free.

Numbers in the margin correspond to numbers on the Downtown map.

TOP ATTRACTIONS

② **Central Library.** The elegant, etched-graphite central staircase and elaborate ceiling ornamentation make this no ordinary library. With a gallery space on the second floor and famous literary names engraved on the walls, this building is well worth a walk around. ⊠ *801 S.W. 10th Ave., Downtown* ☎ *503/988–5123* ◷ *Mon. and Thurs.–Sat. 10–6, Tues. and Wed. 10–8, Sun. noon–5.*

⑨ **Justice Center.** This modern building houses the jail, county courts, and police support offices. Visitors are welcome to browse the **Police Museum** (☎ *503/823–0019* ◰ *Free* ◷ *Tues.–Fri. 10–3*) on the 16th floor, which has uniforms, guns, and badges worn by the Portland Police Bureau. Motorcycles and a jail cell can also be explored. Photo ID is required to enter the main building. ⊠ *1111 S.W. 2nd Ave., Downtown* ⊕ *www.portlandpolicemuseum.com.*

⑦ **Keller Auditorium.** Home base for the Portland Opera, the former Civic Auditorium also hosts traveling musicals and other theatrical

WHAT'S FREE (OR CHEAPER) WHEN

Children's Museum: Free from 4–8 PM the first Friday of each month.

Crystal Springs Rhododendron Garden: Free the day after Labor Day through February.

Oregon Historical Society: Two free children for each adult the third Sunday of each month.

Oregon Museum of Science and Industry: $2 admission the first Sunday of each month.

Oregon Zoo: $4 admission the second Tuesday of each month.

Portland Art Museum: Free from 5–8 PM the fourth Friday of each month.

World Forestry Discovery Center Museum: $2 admission the first Wednesday of each month.

extravaganzas. The building itself, part of the Portland Center for the Performing Arts, is not particularly distinctive, but the **Ira Keller Fountain,** a series of 18-foot-high stone waterfalls across from the front entrance, is worth a look. ⊠ *S.W. 3rd Ave. and Clay St., Downtown* ☎ *503/274–6560* ⊕ *www.pcpa.com.*

5 **Old Church.** This building erected in 1882 is a prime example of Carpenter Gothic architecture. Tall spires and original stained-glass windows enhance its exterior of rough-cut lumber. The acoustically resonant church hosts free classical concerts at noon each Wednesday. If you're lucky, you'll get to hear one of the few operating Hook and Hastings tracker pipe organs. ⊠ *1422 S.W. 11th Ave., Downtown* ☎ *503/222–2031* ⊕ *www.oldchurch.org* ⊗ *Weekdays 11–3.*

3 **Oregon Historical Society.** Impressive eight-story-high trompe-l'oeil murals of Lewis and Clark and the Oregon Trail cover two sides of this downtown museum, which follows the state's story from prehistoric times to the present. A pair of 9,000-year-old sagebrush sandals, a covered wagon, and an early chainsaw are displayed inside "Oregon My Oregon," a permanent exhibit that provides a comprehensive overview of the state's past. Other spaces host large traveling exhibits and changing regional shows. The center's research library is open to the public Thursday through Saturday; its bookstore is a good source for maps and publications on Pacific Northwest history. Every month the Oregon Historical Society has a day on which kids are admitted for free. Check the Web site for dates. ⊠ *1200 S.W. Park Ave., Downtown* ☎ *503/222–1741* ⊕ *www.ohs.org* ▨ *$11* ⊗ *Tues.–Sat. 10–5, Sun. noon–5.*

1 **Pioneer Courthouse Square.** In many ways the living room, public heart, and commercial soul of downtown, Pioneer Square is not entirely square, rather an amphitheater-like brick piazza. Special seasonal, charitable, and festival-oriented events often take place in this premier people-watching venue. On Sunday **vintage trolley cars** (☎ *503/323–7363*) run from the MAX station here to Lloyd Center, with free service every half hour between noon and 6 PM. Call to check on the current schedule. You can pick up maps and literature about the city and the state here

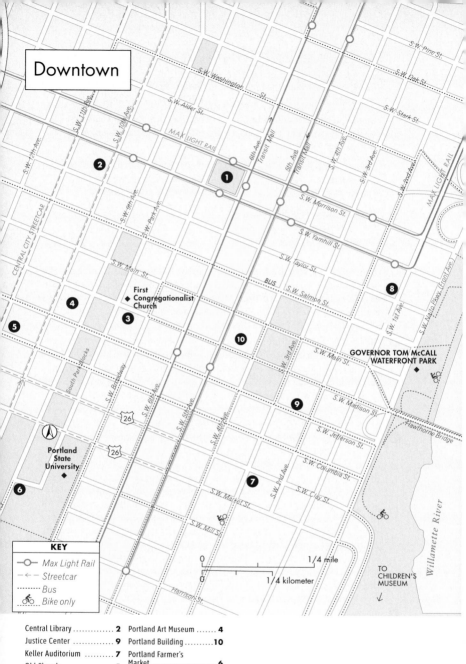

Downtown

KEY
- ⊶ Max Light Rail
- ←← Streetcar
- ····· Bus
- ☺○ Bike only

First Congregationalist Church

GOVERNOR TOM McCALL WATERFRONT PARK

Portland State University

Willamette River

TO CHILDREN'S MUSEUM

Pioneer Square, Downtown

at the **Portland/Oregon Information Center** (☎ *503/275–8355* ⊕ *www. travelportland.com* ☼ *Weekdays 8:30–5:30, Sat. 10–4*). Directly across the street is one of downtown Portland's most familiar landmarks, the classically sedate **Pioneer Courthouse**. Built in 1869, it's the oldest public building in the Pacific Northwest. ⊠ *701 S.W. 6th Ave., Downtown.*

❹ Portland Art Museum. The treasures at the Pacific Northwest's oldest arts facility span 35 centuries of Asian, European, and American art. A high point is the Center for Native American Art, with regional and contemporary art from more than 200 tribes. The **Jubitz Center for Modern and Contemporary Art** contains six floors devoted entirely to modern art, with the changing selection chosen from more than 400 pieces in the Museum's permanent collection. The film center presents the annual Portland International Film Festival in February and the Northwest Film Festival in early November. Also, take a moment to linger in the peaceful outdoor sculpture garden. Kids under 18 are admitted free. ⊠ *1219 S.W. Park Ave., Downtown* ☎ *503/226–2811, 503/221–1156 film schedule* ⊕ *www.portlandartmuseum.org* ☀ *$12* ☼ *Tues., Wed., and Sat. 10–5, Thurs. and Fri. 10–8, Sun. noon–5.*

Fodor's Choice
★

❻ Portland Farmers' Market. On Saturday from March through mid-December, local farmers, bakers, chefs, and entertainers converge at the South Park Blocks near the PSU campus for Oregon's largest open-air farmers' market. It's a great place to sample the regional bounty and to witness the local-food obsession that's revolutionized Portland's culinary scene. There's also a Wednesday market between Southwest Salmon and Southwest Main. ⊠ *South Park Blocks at S.W. Park Ave. and Montgom-*

ery St., Downtown ☎ *503/241–0032* ⊕ *www.portlandfarmersmarket. org* ⊙ *Mar.–mid-Dec., Sat. 8:30–2; May–Oct., Wed. 10–2.*

⑩ Portland Building. *Portlandia,* the second-largest hammered-copper statue in the world, surpassed only by the Statue of Liberty, kneels on the second-story balcony of one of the first postmodern buildings in the United States. Built in 1982, and architect Michael Graves's first major design commission, this 15-story office building is buff-color, with brown-and-blue trim and exterior decorative touches. A huge fiberglass mold of *Portlandia*'s face is exhibited in the second-floor Public Art Gallery, which provides a good overview of Portland's 1% for Art Program, and the hundreds of works on display throughout the city. ⊠ *1120 S.W. 5th Ave., Downtown* ⊙ *Weekdays 8–6.*

❽ Yamhill National Historic District. Trains glide by many examples of 19th-century cast-iron architecture on the MAX line between the Skidmore and Yamhill stations, where the streets are closed to cars. Take a moment at the Yamhill station to glance around at these old buildings, which have intricate rooflines and facades. Nearby, on Southwest Naito Parkway at Taylor Street, is **Mill Ends Park,** which sits in the middle of a traffic island. This patch of whimsy, at 24 inches in diameter, has been recognized by *Guinness World Records* as the world's smallest official city park. ⊠ *Between S.W. Naito Pkwy. and S.W. 3rd Ave. and S.W. Morrison and S.W. Taylor Sts., Downtown.*

PEARL DISTRICT AND OLD TOWN/CHINATOWN

The Old Town National Historic District, commonly called Old Town/ Chinatown, is where Portland was born. The 20-square-block section, bounded by Oak Street to the south and Everett Street to the north, includes buildings of varying ages and architectural styles. Before it was renovated, this was skid row. Vestiges of it remain in parts of Chinatown; older buildings are slowly being remodeled, and over the last several years the immediate area has experienced a surge in development. MAX serves the area with a stop at the Old Town/Chinatown station.

Bordering Old Town to the northwest is the Pearl District. Formerly a warehouse area along the railroad yards, the Pearl District is the fastest-growing part of Portland. Mid-rise residential lofts have sprouted on almost every block, and boutiques, outdoor retailers, galleries, and trendy restaurants border the streets. The Portland Streetcar passes through here on its way from Nob Hill to downtown and Portland State University, with stops at two new, ecologically themed city parks.

Numbers in the margin correspond to numbers on the Pearl District and Old Town/Chinatown map.

❸ Japanese-American Historical Plaza. Take a moment to study the evocative figures cast into the bronze columns at the plaza's entrance; they show Japanese and Japanese-Americans before, during, and after World War II—living daily life, fighting in battle for the United States, and marching off to internment camps. Simple blocks of granite carved with haiku poems describing the war experience powerfully evoke this dark episode in American history. ⊠ *N.W. Naito Pkwy. and Davis St., in Waterfront Park, Old Town/Chinatown.*

Pearl District and Old Town/Chinatown

Irving St.

Hoyt St.

N.W. Flanders St.

N.W. Everett St.

N.W. Davis St.

N.W. Couch St.

CHINATOWN

OLD TOWN

PEARL DISTRICT

W. Burnside St.

Burnside Bridge

Ankeny St.

S.W. Oak St.

S.W. Ash St.

S.W. Stark St.

S.W. Pine St.

S.W. Washington St.

S.W. Alder St.

CENTRAL CITY STREETCAR

MAX LIGHT RAIL

MAX LIGHT RAIL

S.W. Naito Pkwy. (Front Ave.)

S.W. Morrison St.

Morrison Bridge

S.W. Yamhill St.

S.W. Taylor St.

GOVERNOR TOM McCALL WATERFRONT PARK

S.W. Salmon St.

KEY
- —O— Max Light Rail
- — ← — Streetcar
- ········ Bus
- 🚲 Bike only

S.W. Main St.

0 _____ 1/4 mile

0 _____ 1/4 kilometer

Lan Su Chinese Garden, Old Town/Chinatown

❹ Lan Su Chinese Garden. In a twist on the Joni Mitchell song, the city of
Fodor's Choice Portland and private donors took down a parking lot and unpaved
★ paradise when they created this wonderland near the Pearl District
and Old Town/Chinatown. It's the largest Suzhou-style garden outside
China, with a large lake, bridged and covered walkways, koi- and water
lily–filled ponds, rocks, bamboo, statues, waterfalls, and courtyards.
A team of 60 artisans and designers from China literally left no stone
unturned—500 tons of stone were brought here from Suzhou—in their
efforts to give the windows, roof tiles, gateways, including a "moon-
gate," and other architectural aspects of the garden some specific meaning or purpose. Also on the premises are a gift shop and a two-story
teahouse overlooking the lake and garden. ⊠ *239 N.W. Everett, Old
Town/Chinatown* ☎ *503/228–8131* ⊕ *www.lansugarden.org* ✉ *$8.50*
⊙ *Nov.–Mar., daily 10–5; Apr.–Oct., daily 10–6.*

❷ Oregon Maritime Museum. Local model makers created most of this
☾ museum's models of ships that once plied the Columbia River. Contained within the stern-wheeler steamship *Portland*, this small museum
provides an excellent overview of Oregon's maritime history with
artifacts and memorabilia. The Portland was the last steam-powered
stern-wheeler built in the U.S. ⊠ *On steamship at end of S.W. Pine St.,
in Waterfront Park, Old Town/Chinatown* ☎ *503/224–7724* ⊕ *www.
oregonmaritimemuseum.org* ✉ *$5* ⊙ *Wed.–Sat. 11–4, Sun. 12:30–4:30.*

❶ Portland Saturday Market. On weekends from March to Christmas, the
☾ west side of the Burnside Bridge and the Skidmore Fountain area has
Fodor's Choice North America's largest open-air handicraft market. If you're looking
★ for jewelry, yard art, housewares, and decorative goods made from

every material under the sun, then there's an amazing collection of talented works on display here. Entertainers and food and produce booths add to the festive feel. If taking the MAX train to the market, get off at the Skidmore Fountain stop. ⊠ *Waterfront Park and Ankeny Park, both at S.W. Naito Pkwy and S.W. Ankeny, Old Town/Chinatown* ☎ *503/222–6072* ⊕ *www.saturdaymarket.org* ☉ *Mar.–Dec., Sat. 10–5, Sun. 11–4:30.*

❺ **Powell's City of Books.** The largest independent bookstore in the world, with more than 1.5 million new and used books, this Portland landmark can easily consume several hours. It's so big it has its own map available at the info kiosks, and rooms are color-coded according to the types of books, so you can find your way out again. Be sure to look for the pillar bearing signatures of prominent sci-fi authors who have passed through the store—the scrawls are protected by a jagged length of Plexiglas. At the very least, stop into Powell's for a peek or grab a cup of coffee at the adjoining branch of World Cup Coffee. ⊠ *1005 W. Burnside St., Pearl District* ☎ *503/228–4651* ⊕ *www.powells.com* ☉ *Daily 9* AM*–11* PM.

Fodor's Choice
★

NOB HILL AND VICINITY

The showiest example of Portland's urban chic is Northwest 23rd Avenue—sometimes referred to with varying degrees of affection as "trendythird"—a 20-block thoroughfare that cuts north–south through the neighborhood known as Nob Hill. Fashionable since the 1880s and still filled with Victorian houses, the neighborhood is a mixed-use cornucopia of Old Portland charm and New Portland hip. With its cafés, restaurants, galleries, and boutiques, it's a great place to stroll, shop, and people-watch. More restaurants, shops, and nightspots can be found on Northwest 21st Avenue, a few blocks away. The Portland Streetcar runs from Legacy Good Samaritan Hospital in Nob Hill, through the Pearl District on 10th and 11th avenues, connects with MAX light rail near Pioneer Courthouse Square downtown, and then continues on to Portland State University and RiverPlace on the Willamette River.

Numbers in the margin correspond to numbers on the Nob Hill and Vicinity map.

❷ **Clear Creek Distillery.** The distillery keeps such a low profile that it's practically invisible. But ring the bell and someone will unlock the wrought-iron gate and let you into a dim, quiet tasting room where you can sample Clear Creek's world-famous Oregon apple and pear brandies and grappas. ⊠ *2389 N.W. Wilson, Nob Hill* ☎ *503/248–9470* ⊕ *www.clearcreekdistillery.com* ☉ *Mon.–Sat. 9–5.*

❶ **The 3D Center of Art and Photography.** Half gallery and half museum, this center devoted to three-dimensional imagery exhibits photographs best viewed through red-and-blue glasses, in addition to artifacts on the history of stereoscopic art. A collection of rare Nazi-era stereocards is displayed next to View-Masters and 3-D snapshot cameras. A three-dimensional rendering of famous classical paintings is one of the many changing 3-D slide shows you might see in the backroom Stereo Theatre. ⊠ *1928 N.W. Lovejoy St., Nob Hill* ☎ *503/227–6667*

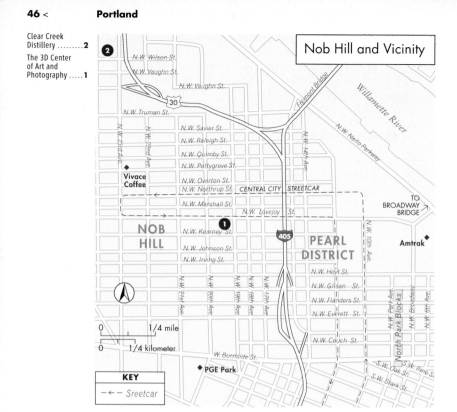

⊕ *www.3dcenter.us* ▣ *$5* ☽ *Thurs.–Sat. 11–5, Sun. 1–5; also 1st Thurs. of month 6 PM–9 PM.*

NEED A BREAK?   **Vivace Coffee** (✉ *1400 N.W. 23rd Ave.* ☎ *503/228–3667*) is inside Pettygrove House, a restored Victorian gingerbread house built in 1892 that was once the home of Francis Pettygrove, the man who named Portland after winning a coin-toss. Today it's a creperie and coffeehouse with colorful walls and comfortable chairs.

WASHINGTON PARK

The best way to get to Washington Park is via MAX light rail, which travels through a tunnel deep beneath the city's West Hills. Be sure to check out the Washington Park station, the deepest (260 feet) transit station in North America. Graphics on the walls depict life in the Portland area during the past 16.5 million years. There's also a core sample of the bedrock taken from the mountain displayed along the walls. Elevators to the surface put visitors in the parking lot for the Oregon Zoo, the World Forestry Center Discovery Museum, and the Children's Museum.

Portland Rose Festival parade

Numbers in the margin correspond to numbers on the Washington Park map.

❷ Children's Museum. Colorful sights and sounds offer a feast of sensations for kids of all ages where hands-on play is the order of the day. Visit nationally touring exhibits, catch a story time, a sing-along, or a puppet show in the Play It Again theater, create sculptures in the clay studio, splash hands in the water works display, or make a creation from junk in the Garage. To reach the museum's complex, take the "Zoo" exit off U.S. 26, or take MAX light rail to Washington Park station. ⊠ *4015 S.W. Canyon Rd., Washington Park* ☎ *503/223–6500* ⊕ *www.portlandcm. org* ⊡ *$8* ⊗ *Mar.–Aug., daily 9–5; Sept.-Feb., Tues.–Sun. 9–5.*

❸ Hoyt Arboretum. Ten miles of trails wind through the arboretum, which has more than 1,000 species of plants and one of the nation's largest collections of coniferous trees; pick up trail maps at the visitor center. Also here are the Winter Garden and a memorial to veterans of the Vietnam War. ⊠ *4000 S.W. Fairview Blvd., Washington Park* ☎ *503/865–8733* ⊕ *www.hoytarboretum.org* ⊡ *Free* ⊗ *Arboretum daily dawn–dusk, visitor center Mon.–Fri. 9–4, Sat. 9–3.*

❹ International Rose Test Garden. Despite the name, these grounds are not an experimental greenhouse laboratory, but rather three terraced gardens, set on 4 acres, where 10,000 bushes and 400 varieties of roses grow. The flowers, many of them new varieties, are at their peak in June, July, September, and October. From the gardens you can see highly photogenic views of the downtown skyline and, on fine days, the Fuji-shaped slopes of Mt. Hood, 50 mi to the east. Summer concerts take place in the garden's amphitheater. Take MAX light rail to Washington

Fodor's Choice
★

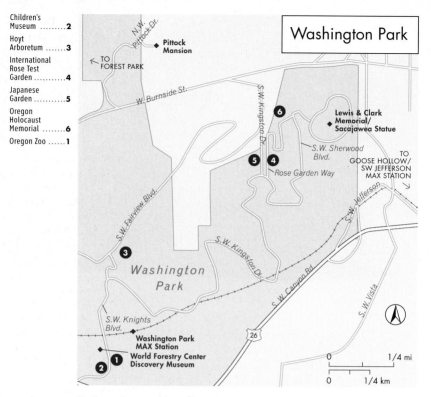

Park station, and transfer to Bus No. 63 or Washington Park Shuttle. ✉ *400 S.W. Kingston Ave., Washington Park* ☎ *503/823–3636* ⊕ *www. rosegardenstore.org* ✑ *Free* ☉ *Daily dawn–dusk.*

 Japanese Garden. The most authentic Japanese garden outside Japan
Fodor's Choice   takes up 5½ acres of Washington Park above the International Rose
★   Test Garden. This serene spot, designed by a Japanese landscape master, represents five separate garden styles: Strolling Pond Garden, Tea Garden, Natural Garden, Sand and Stone Garden, and Flat Garden. The Tea House was built in Japan and reconstructed here. The west side of the Pavilion has a majestic view of Portland and Mt. Hood. Take MAX light rail to Washington Park station, and transfer to Bus No. 63 or the Washington Park Shuttle. ✉ *611 S.W. Kingston Ave., Washington Park* ☎ *503/223–1321* ⊕ *www.japanesegarden.com* ✑ *$9.50* ☉ *Oct.–Mar., Mon. noon–4, Tues.–Sun. 10–4; Apr.–Sept., Mon. noon–7, Tues.–Sun. 10–7.*

❻ **Oregon Holocaust Memorial.** This memorial to those who perished during the Holocaust bears the names of surviving families who live in Oregon and Southwest Washington. A bronzed baby shoe, a doll, broken spectacles, and other strewn possessions await notice on the cobbled courtyard. Soil and ash from six Nazi concentration camps is interred beneath the black granite wall. Take MAX light rail to Washington

Park station, and transfer to Bus No. 63 or Washington Park Shuttle. ⊠ *S.W. Wright Ave. and Park Pl., Washington Park* ☎ *503/245–2733* ⊕ *www.ohrconline.org* 🖃 *Free* ⊘ *Daily dawn–dusk.*

1 **Oregon Zoo.** This beautiful animal park in the West Hills is famous for its Asian elephants. Major exhibits include an African section with rhinos, hippos, zebras, and giraffes. Steller Cove, a state-of-the-art aquatic exhibit, has two Steller sea lions and a family of sea otters. Other exhibits include polar bears, chimpanzees, an Alaska Tundra exhibit with wolves and grizzly bears, a penguin house, and habitats for beavers, otters, and reptiles native to the west side of the Cascade Range. In summer a 4-mi round-trip narrow-gauge train operates from the zoo, chugging through the woods to a station near the International Rose Test Garden and the Japanese Garden. Take the MAX light rail to the Washington Park station. ⊠ *4001 S.W. Canyon Rd., Washington Park* ☎ *503/226–1561* ⊕ *www.oregonzoo.org* 🖃 *$10.50, $4 2nd Tues. of month* ⊘ *Mid-Apr.–mid-Sept., daily 8–6; mid-Sept.–mid Apr., daily 9–4.*

EAST OF THE WILLAMETTE RIVER

Portland is known as the City of Roses, but the 10 distinctive bridges spanning the Willamette River have also earned it the name Bridgetown. The older drawbridges, near downtown, open several times a day to allow passage of large cargo ships and freighters. You can easily spend a couple of days exploring the attractions and areas on the east side of the river.

Numbers in the margin correspond to numbers on the East of the Willamette River map.

5 **The Grotto.** Owned by the Catholic Church, the National Sanctuary of Our Sorrowful Mother, as it's officially known, displays more than 100 statues and shrines in 62 acres of woods. The grotto was carved into the base of a 110-foot cliff, and has a replica of Michelangelo's *Pietà.* The real treat is found after ascending the cliff face via elevator, as you enter a wonderland of gardens, sculptures, and shrines, and a glass-walled cathedral with an awe-inspiring view of the Columbia River and the Cascades. There's a dazzling Festival of Lights at Christmastime (late November and December), with 250,000 lights and holiday concerts in the 600-seat chapel. Sunday masses are held here, too. ⊠ *8840 N.E. Skidmore St., main entrance at Sandy Blvd. at N.E. 85th Ave., near airport* ☎ *503/254–7371* ⊕ *www.thegrotto.org* 🖃 *Plaza level free; elevator to upper level $4* ⊘ *Mid-May–Labor Day, daily 9–8:30; Labor Day–late Nov. and Feb.–mid-May, daily 9–5:30; late Nov.–Jan., daily 9–4.*

3 **Hawthorne District.** This neighborhood stretching from the foot of Mt.

Fodor's Choice ★ Tabor to 30th Avenue attracts a more college-age, bohemian crowd than downtown or Nob Hill. With many bookstores, coffeehouses, taverns, restaurants, antiques stores, and boutiques filling the streets, it's easy to spend a few hours wandering here. ⊠ *S.E. Hawthorne Blvd. between 30th and 42nd Aves., Hawthorne District.*

North Mississippi Avenue. Four blocks of old storefronts reinvented as cafés, collectives, shops, and music venues along this north Portland

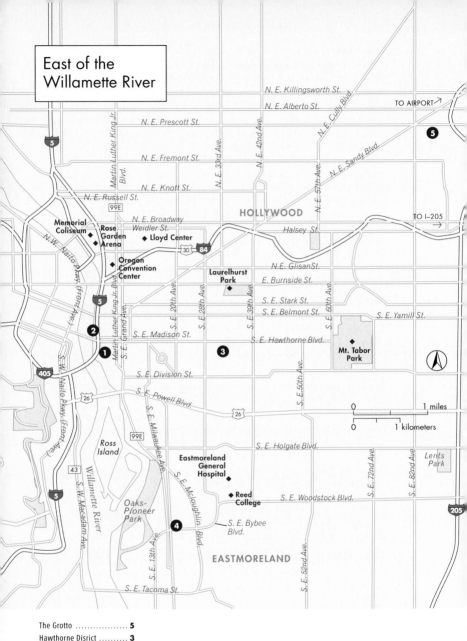

East of the Willamette River

N. E. Killingsworth St.

N. E. Alberto St.

N. E. Prescott St.

TO AIRPORT

Martin Luther King Jr. Blvd.

N. E. 42nd Ave.

N. E. Cully Blvd.

N. E. Sandy Blvd.

5

N. E. Fremont St.

N. E. 33rd Ave.

N. E. Knott St.

N. E. Russell St.

99E

HOLLYWOOD

N. E. 57th Ave.

TO I-205

Memorial Coliseum

Rose Garden Arena

N. E. Broadway
Weidler St.

Halsey St.

Lloyd Center

N.W. Naito Pkwy. (Front Ave.)

30   84

Oregon Convention Center

Laurelhurst Park

N.E. Glisan St.

E. Burnside St.

Martin Luther King Jr. Blvd.

S. E. Grand Ave.

S. E. 20th Ave.

S. E. 28th Ave.

S. E. 39th Ave.

S. E. Stark St.

S. E. Belmont St.

S. E. 60th Ave.

S. E. Yamill St.

2

S. E. Madison St.

S. E. Hawthorne Blvd.

Mt. Tabor Park

3

1

405

S. E. Division St.

S. E. 50th Ave.

0   1 miles

26

S. E. Powell Blvd.

26

0   1 kilometers

43

99E

S. E. Holgate Blvd.

Lents Park

Ross Island

Eastmoreland General Hospital

S. E. 72nd Ave.

S. E. 82nd Ave.

Willamette River

S. E. Milwaukee Ave.

Oaks-Pioneer Park

Reed College

S. E. Woodstock Blvd.

205

S. W. Macadam Ave.

4

S. E. McLoughlin Blvd.

S. E. Bybee Blvd.

S. E. 52nd Ave.

S. E. 13th Ave.

EASTMORELAND

S. E. Tacoma St.

street showcase the indie spirit of the city's do-it-yourselfers and creative types. Bioswale planter boxes, found-object fences, and café tables built from old doors are some of the innovations you'll see around this hip new district. At the hub of it all is the ReBuilding Center, an outlet for recycled building supplies that has cob (clay-and-straw) trees and benches built into the facade. Take MAX light rail to the Albina/Mississippi station. ⊠ *Between N. Fremont and Shaver Sts., off N. Interstate Ave.*

Northeast Alberta Street. Quirky handicrafts by local artists are for sale inside the galleries, studios, coffeehouses, restaurants, and boutiques lining this street in the northeast Portland neighborhood. It's a fascinating place to witness the intersection of cultures and lifestyles in a growing city. Shops unveil new exhibits during an evening event called the Last Thursday Art Walk. The Alberta Street Fair in September showcases the area with arts-and-crafts displays and street performances. ⊠ *Between Martin Luther King Jr. Blvd. and 30th Ave., Alberta Arts District.*

❶ Oregon Museum of Science and Industry (OMSI). Hundreds of hands-on exhibits draw families to this interactive science museum, which also has an Omnimax theater and the Northwest's largest planetarium. The many permanent and touring exhibits are loaded with enough hands-on play for kids to fill a whole day exploring robotics, ecology, rockets, computers, animation, and outer space. Moored in the Willamette as part of the museum is a 240-foot submarine, the USS *Blueback,* which can be toured for an extra charge. ⊠ *1945 S.E. Water Ave., south of Hawthorne Bridge, on Willamette River* ☎ *503/797–4000 or 800/955–6674* ⊕ *www.omsi.edu* ☕ *Full package $21, museum $12, planetarium $5.75, Omnimax $8.50, submarine $5.75* ☉ *Mid-June–Labor Day, daily 9:30–7; Labor Day–mid-June, daily 9:30–5:30.*

❹ Sellwood District. The pleasant neighborhood that begins east of the Sellwood Bridge was once a separate town. Annexed by Portland in the 1890s, it retains a modest charm. On weekends the antiques stores along 13th Avenue do a brisk business. Each store is identified by a plaque that tells the date of construction and the original purpose of the building. More antiques stores, specialty shops, and restaurants are near the intersection of Milwaukie and Bybee. ⊠ *S.E. 13th Ave. between Malden and Clatsop Sts., Sellwood.*

❷ Vera Katz Eastbank Esplanade. A stroll along this 1½-mi pedestrian and
Fodor'sChoice cycling path across from downtown is one of the best ways to experience the Willamette River and Portland's bridges close-up. Built in ★ 2001, the esplanade runs along the east bank of the Willamette River between the Hawthorne and Steel bridges, and features a 1,200-foot walkway that floats atop the river, a boat dock, and public art. Pedestrian crossings on both bridges link the esplanade to Waterfront Park, making a 3-mi loop. Take MAX light rail to the Rose Quarter station. ⊠ *Parking at east end of Hawthorne Bridge, between Madison and Salmon Sts.*

NEED A BREAK? At the Bagdad Theatre and Pub (⊠ *3702 S.E. Hawthorne Blvd., Hawthorne District* ☎ *503/236–9234*) you can buy a pint of beer, a slice of pizza, and watch a movie in a large classic theater complete with dining tables.

WHERE TO EAT

Despite most restaurant menus' lack of foams or flash, Portland has quietly become a formidable food presence. The city fields a respectable number of chefs and restaurants that garner national attention and win major industry awards.

While temples of fine dining are few and far between, Portland offers a lively mix of memorable food in casual digs, like popular Thai spot **Pok Pok**, and the famed street carts clustered around town. Portland also has plenty of restaurants, like the venerable **Jake's Famous Crawfish**, that celebrate its proximity to the sea by offering oysters, tuna, and other fare that was swimming off the Pacific coast the previous day.

Popular destinations like **Bluehour** and **Andina**, have cemented the reputation of Northwest Portland's Pearl District as a restaurant hot spot. Otherwise, new restaurants tend to open on the east side of the Willamette River, where rents are cheaper.

DOWNTOWN

Finding a fabulous place to dine downtown is almost as easy as closing your eyes and pointing on the map. One thing visitors appreciate about lunch downtown is the plethora of food carts lining the streets. Smells of Greek, Russian, Japanese, Lebanese, and Mexican food permeate the air as the noon hour approaches. Lines of workers hover around the makeshift kitchen trailers, waiting to get their fill of the inexpensive and authentic selection of food.

¢ ✕ **Bijou Cafe.** This spacious, sunny restaurant with high ceilings has some
AMERICAN of the best breakfasts in town, and they're served all day: French-style crepes and oyster hash are both popular, as are fabulous pancakes and French toast. At lunch the breakfast dishes are joined by burgers, sandwiches, and soups. ⊠ *132 S.W. 3rd Ave., Downtown* ☎ *503/222–3187* ▭ *MC, V* ⊗ *No dinner* ✛ *E4.*

$ ✕ **Bo's Asian Bistro.** Combining the trend toward tapas and chic cocktails,
ASIAN this hotel bar brings both to delicious heights. The stylish dark walls accented by colorful modern art create a sleek setting in which to sip a specialty martini made with some esoteric liqueur. ⊠ *Hotel Lucia, 400 S.W. Broadway, Downtown* ☎ *503/222–2688* ⊕ *www.bobistro.com* ▭ *AE, DC, MC, V* ⊗ *Closed Sun.* ✛ *D4.*

$ ✕ **Dan & Louis's Oyster Bar.** Oysters at this Portland landmark near the
SEAFOOD river come fried, stewed, or on the half shell. The clam chowder is tasty, but the crab stew is a rare treat. Combination dinners let you mix your fried favorites. The collection of steins, plates, and marine art has grown since the restaurant opened in 1907 to fill beams, nooks, crannies, and nearly every inch of wall. ⊠ *208 S.W. Ankeny St., Downtown* ☎ *503/227–5906* ⊕ *www.danandlouis.com* ▭ *AE, D, DC, MC, V* ✛ *E4.*

El Gaucho, Downtown

$

JAPANESE

✕ **Departure.** If you want to sink into a swanky restaurant that could just as easily be in a much bigger city, then Departure is for you. The interior is over-the-top lush, and a scenic highlight for locals and visitors alike is the outdoor rooftop lounge, with gorgeous views of the city. The food is artfully prepared; most dishes, such as the Hamachi sashimi and calamari tempura come in smallish but flavorful portions. The fried ginger ice cream, for instance, is served with panko breadcrumbs, sesame seeds, and powdered sugar. ⊠ *525 S.W. Morrison St., Downtown* ☎ *503/802–5370* ⊕ *www.departureportland.com* ▭ *AE, MC, V* ☉ *Closed Sun. and Mon. No lunch* ✛ *D4.*

$$$$

STEAK

Fodor'sChoice

★

✕ **El Gaucho.** Three dimly lit dining rooms with blue walls and striped upholstery are an inviting place for those with healthy wallets. The specialty here is 28-day, dry-aged, certified Angus beef, but chops, ribs, and chicken entrées are also cooked in the open kitchen. The chateaubriand for two is carved tableside. Seafood lovers might want to try the tomato fennel bouillabaisse. Service is impeccable at this Seattle transplant in the elegant Benson Hotel. Each night live Latin guitar music serenades the dinner guests. ⊠ *319 S.W. Broadway, Downtown* ☎ *503/227–8794* ⊕ *www.elgaucho.com* ▭ *AE, DC, MC, V* ☉ *No lunch* ✛ *D4.*

$$$

AMERICAN

Fodor'sChoice

★

✕ **Gracie's.** Stepping into this dining room is like stepping into a prestigious 1940s supper club. Dazzling chandeliers, beautifully rich floor-to-ceiling draperies, velvet couches, and marble-topped tables exude class. Dishes like grilled swordfish and stuffed pork loin are perfectly seasoned and served with seasonal vegetables. On weekends there's a brunch menu that includes fresh fruit, waffles, and omelets. ⊠ *Hotel DeLuxe, 729 S.W. 15th Ave., Downtown* ☎ *503/222–2171* ⊕ *www. graciesdining.com* ▭ *AE, D, MC, V* ✛ *C4.*

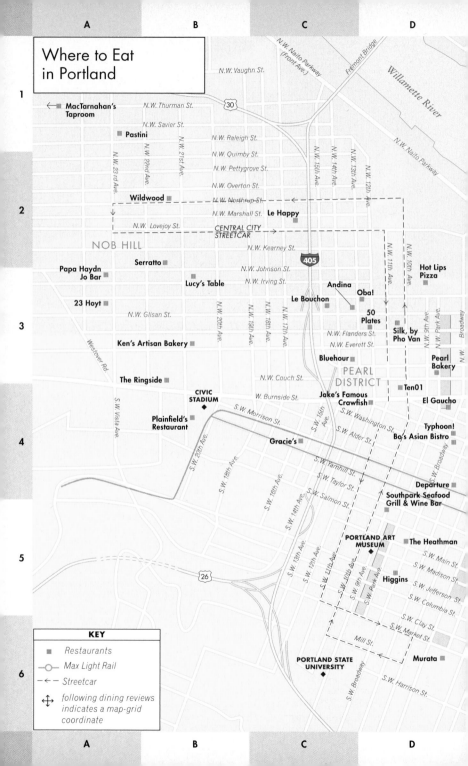

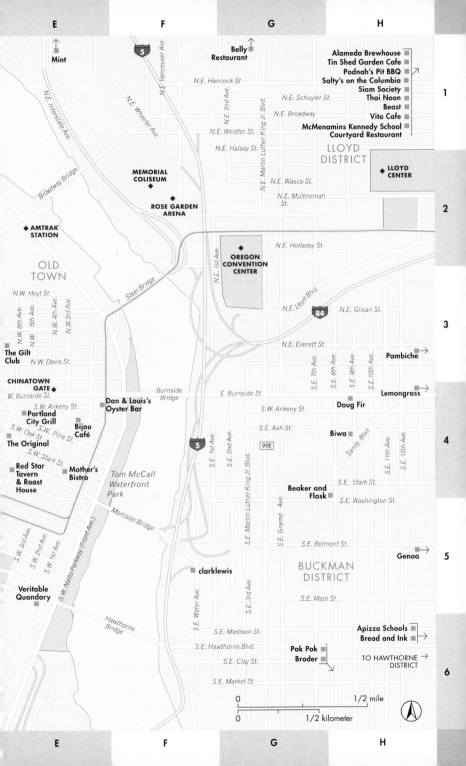

$$ ✕**The Heathman.** Chef Philippe Boulot revels in fresh ingredients of the
CONTINENTAL   Pacific Northwest. His menu changes with the season, and includes
entrées made with grilled and braised fish, fowl, veal, lamb, and beef.
Among the chef's Northwest specialties are a delightful Dungeness crab,
mango, and avocado salad and a paella made with mussels, clams,
shrimp, scallops, and chorizo. Equally creative choices are available for
breakfast and lunch. The dining room, scented with wood smoke and
adorned with Andy Warhol prints, is a favorite for special occasions.
⊠ *Heathman Hotel, 1001 S.W. Broadway, Downtown* ☎ *503/790–
7752* ⊟ *AE, D, DC, MC, V* ⊹ *D5.*

$$ ✕**Higgins.** Chef Greg Higgins, former executive chef at the Heathman
FRENCH   Hotel, focuses on ingredients from the Pacific Northwest and on organi-
Fodor'sChoice   cally grown herbs and produce while incorporating traditional French
★   cooking styles and other international influences into his menu. Start
with a salad of warm beets, asparagus, and artichokes, or the country-
style terrine of venison, chicken, and pork with dried sour cherries
and a roasted-garlic mustard. Main courses, which change seasonally,
might include dishes made with Alaskan spot prawns, halibut, duck,
or pork loin. Vegetarian options are available. A bistro menu is available in the adjoining bar, where comfortable leather booths and tables
provide an alternative to the main dining room. ⊠ *1239 S.W. Broadway, Downtown* ☎ *503/222–9070* ⊟ *AE, D, DC, MC, V* ⊗ *No lunch
weekends* ⊹ *D5.*

$$ ✕**Jake's Famous Crawfish.** Diners have been enjoying fresh Pacific
SEAFOOD   Northwest seafood in Jake's warren of wood-paneled dining rooms
for more than a century. The back bar came around Cape Horn dur-
ing the 1880s, and the chandeliers hanging from the high ceilings
date from 1881. The restaurant gained a national reputation in 1920,
when crawfish was added to the menu. White-coat waiters take your
order from an almost endless sheet of daily seafood specials year-
round, but try to come during crawfish season (May–September),
when you can sample the tasty crustacean in pie, cooked Creole style,
or in a Cajun-style stew over rice. ⊠ *401 S.W. 12th Ave., Downtown*
☎ *503/226–1419* ⊕ *www.mccormickandschmicks.com* ⊟ *AE, D, DC,
MC, V* ⊗ *No lunch Sun* ⊹ *D4.*

$ ✕**Mother's Bistro.** The menu is loaded with home-style favorites—maca-
AMERICAN   roni and cheese with extra ingredients of the day, soups, pierogi, matzo-
Fodor'sChoice   ball soup, pot roast, and meat loaf. For vegetarians there's a couscous
★   stew. The high ceilings in the well-lit dining room lend an air of spa-
ciousness, but the tables are a bit close together. The bar is open late
Friday and Saturday. ⊠ *212 S.W. Stark St., Downtown* ☎ *503/464–
1122* ⊕ *www.mothersbistro.com* ⊟ *AE, D, MC, V* ⊗ *Closed Mon. No
dinner Sun.* ⊹ *E4.*

$$ ✕**Murata.** Slip off your shoes and step inside one of the tatami rooms
JAPANESE   at Murata, Portland's best Japanese restaurant. You can also pull up a
chair at the corner sushi bar. So ordinary looking it barely stands out
among the office towers near Keller Auditorium, the restaurant draws a
crowd of locals, celebrities, and Japanese businesspeople who savor the
sushi, sashimi, tempura, hamachi, and teriyaki. Grilled salmon cheeks
stand out among many seafood specialties. ⊠ *200 S.W. Market St.,*

Mother's Bistro, Downtown

Downtown ☎ *503/227–0080* 🖃 *AE, MC, V* ☻ *Closed Sun. No lunch Sat.* ✛ *D6.*

$ ✕ **The Original.** At this upscale diner-ish restaurant, one of the oddest
AMERICAN foods in Portland can be ordered: a donut cheeseburger. It's made with
a Voodoo glazed donut, and only available on the late night menu.
Other specialties are more traditional—stroganoff, meatloaf, brisket,
and burgers—but have an upscale twist, many with a Pacific Northwestern flair. The food, service, and vibe makes this a restaurant that appeals
to almost everyone. 🖃 *300 S.W. 6th Ave., Downtown* ☎ *503/546–2666*
⊕ *www.originaldinerant.com* 🖃 *AE, D, MC, V* ✛ *E4.*

$$$ ✕ **Portland City Grill.** On the 30th floor of the US Bank Tower, Portland
AMERICAN City Grill has one of the best views in town. You can sit at a window
table and enjoy the Portland skyline while eating fine steak and seafood
with an Asian flair; it's no wonder that this restaurant is a favorite hot
spot. The adjoining bar and lounge has comfortable armchairs all along
its windowed walls, which are the first to get snatched up during the
extremely popular happy hour each day. 🖃 *111 S.W. 5th Ave., Down-
town* ☎ *503/450–0030* ⊕ *www.portlandcitygrill.com* 🖃 *AE, D, MC, V*
☻ *No lunch weekends* ✛ *E4.*

$$ ✕ **Red Star Tavern & Roast House.** Cooked in a wood-burning oven,
AMERICAN smoker, rotisserie, or grill, the cuisine at Red Star can best be described
as American comfort food inspired by the bounty of the Pacific Northwest. Spit-roasted chicken, maple-fired baby back ribs with a brown-
ale glaze, charred salmon, and crayfish étouffée (seasonal) are some
of the better entrées. The wine list includes regional and international
vintages, and 10 microbrews are on tap. The spacious restaurant, adjacent to Hotel Monaco, has tufted leather booths, murals, and copper

accents. ⊠ *503 S.W. Alder St., Downtown* ☏ *503/222–0005* ⊕ *www. redstartavern.com* ⊟ *AE, D, DC, MC, V* ✢ *E4.*

$$ ✕ **Southpark Seafood Grill & Wine Bar.** Wood-fired seafood is served in
SEAFOOD this comfortable, art deco–tinged room with two bars. Chef Broc Willis's Northwest-influenced menu includes wild king salmon with baked gnocchi, as well as Oregon-raised Carlton Farms rib eye. There's a wide selection of fresh Pacific Northwest oysters, and fine regional wines are available by the glass. Some of the desserts are baked to order. ⊠ *901 S.W. Salmon St., Downtown* ☏ *503/326–1300* ⊕ *www. southparkseafood.com* ⊟ *AE, D, MC, V* ✢ *D5.*

$$ ✕ **Typhoon!** A Buddha statue with burning incense watches over diners
THAI at this popular restaurant in the Lucia Hotel. Come enjoy the excellent food in a large, modern dining room filled with colorful art and sleek red booths. The spicy chicken or shrimp with crispy basil, the curry and noodle dishes, and the vegetarian spring and salad rolls are standouts. As for tea, 25 varieties are available, from $4 a pot to $10 for some of the world's rarest. ⊠ *410 S.W. Broadway, Downtown* ☏ *503/224–8285* ⊕ *www.typhoonrestaurants.com* ⊟ *AE, D, DC, MC, V* ✢ *D4.*

$$$ ✕ **Veritable Quandary.** There are so many delicious options at this long-
AMERICAN standing local favorite: the tantalizing French toast and revered chocolate soufflé pair well with the beautiful outdoor patio, where you're surrounded by roses, fuchsias, and hanging begonia baskets. The menu emphasizes fresh, flavorful produce and seafood; prices are reasonable for the quality, and the wine list is one of the best in town. ⊠ *1220 S.W. 1st Ave., Downtown* ☏ *503/227–7342* ⊕ *www.veritablequandary.com* ⊟ *AE, D, DC, MC, V* ✢ *E5.*

PEARL DISTRICT AND OLD TOWN/CHINATOWN

The Pearl District, once full of worn, empty warehouses and little more than a reminder of Portland's industrial past, is now the city's most bustling destination for arts and dining. Many of the warehouses have been refurbished into hot spots in which to gather for drinks and food. On any given day or night visitors can comb the scene for a perfectly selected glass of wine or a lush designer cocktail. Within this small area are global selections of Greek, French, Italian, Peruvian, Japanese, and more. Restaurants here tend to be slightly more upscale, though there are plenty of casual bakeries, coffee shops, and places to grab sandwiches. Keep in mind that the city's gallery walk event, held the first Thursday of every month, keeps restaurants jammed on that night.

$$$ ✕ **Andina.** Portland's sleekest, trendiest, and most brightly colored res-
PERUVIAN taurant gives an artful presentation to designer and traditional Peruvian
Fodor's Choice cuisine. Asian and Spanish flavors are the main influences here, and
★ they're evident in an extensive seafood menu that includes five kinds of ceviche, grilled octopus, and pan-seared scallops with white and black quinoa. There are also entrées with poultry, beef, and lamb. A late-night bar offers sangria, small plates, and cocktails; downstairs, a shrinelike wine shop hosts private multicourse meals. Live music Sunday through Saturday. ⊠ *1314 N.W. Glisan St., Pearl District* ☏ *503/228–9535* ⊕ *www.andinarestaurant.com* ⊟ *AE, D, MC, V* ✢ *C3.*

$$$ ╳ **Bluehour.** At this vast, towering restaurant the waitstaff is as sophis-
MEDITERRANEAN ticated as the white tablecloths and floor-to-ceiling curtains. The menu
changes daily, based on available ingredients and the chef's whims.
Four-course prix-fixe menus are available for lunch and dinner. Ongoing
appetizers to try are the "20 greens" salad and sea scallops wrapped in
applewood-smoked bacon with celery-root puree. Top the meal off with
a bittersweet chocolate chestnut torte with honey cream. ⊠ *250 N.W.
13th Ave., Pearl District* ☎ *503/226–3394* ⊕ *www.bluehouronline.com*
⊟ *AE, D, MC, V* ✛ *C3.*

$$ ╳ **50 Plates.** You wish you had more room to try everything here, where
AMERICAN everything seems designed to put mom's tried-and-true favorites to the
Fodor's Choice test. Evoking regional cuisine from all 50 states, the restaurant creates
★ fresh culinary interpretations. The delightful "silver dollar sammies"
include sweet and spicy Carolina pulled pork on a sweet-potato roll and
a smoked portobello rendition with butter lettuce, fried green tomatoes,
and herbed goat cheese. There's also a crowd-pleasing succotash whose
components vary depending upon the availability of locally harvested
ingredients. The rich desserts include dark-chocolate fudge cake served
with homemade brown-sugar ice cream, and bananas Foster. ⊠ *333
N.W. 13th Ave., Pearl District* ☎ *503/228–5050* ⊕ *www.50plates.com*
⊟ *AE, MC, V* ✛ *D3.*

$$ ╳ **The Gilt Club.** Cascading gold curtains, ornate showpiece chandeliers,
CONTINENTAL and high-back booths complement a swanky rich-red dining room.
The food is equally lush, with buttercup pumpkin gnocchi topped with
an Oregon venison ragù, and a truffle, red quinoa, and goat cheese
custard with roasted autumn baby vegetables. The drink menu is
loaded with flavor-embellished drinks such as "Tracy's First Love,"
with vodka, cucumber, basil, and lime. ⊠ *306 N.W. Broadway, Pearl
District* ☎ *503/222–4458* ⊕ *www.giltclub.com* ⊟ *AE, MC, V* ⊘ *Closed
Sun.* ✛ *E3.*

¢ ╳ **Hot Lips Pizza.** A favorite of Portland's pizza lovers, Hot Lips bakes
PIZZA organic and regional ingredients into creative pizzas, available whole
or by the slice. Seasonal variations might feature apples, squash, wild
mushrooms, and blue cheese. It also has soups, salads, and sandwiches.
Beverages include house-made berry sodas, a large rack of wines, and
microbrew six-packs. Dine inside the Ecotrust building, outside on the
"eco-roof," or take it all across the street for an impromptu picnic in
Jamison Square. This is one of five different citywide locations. ⊠ *721
N.W. 9th Ave., Pearl District* ☎ *503/595–2342* ⊕ *www.hotlipspizza.
com* ⊟ *AE, D, MC, V* ✛ *D3.*

$$ ╳ **Le Bouchon.** A warm, jovial waitstaff makes Francophiles feel right at
FRENCH home at this bistro in the Pearl District, which serves classic examples
Fodor's Choice of the cuisine for lunch and dinner. Duck confit, truffle chicken, bouil-
★ labaisse, and escargots are all cooked with aplomb by chef Claude
Musquin. And for dessert, chocolate mousse is a must-try. ⊠ *517 N.W.
14th Ave., Pearl District* ☎ *503/248–2193* ⊕ *www.bouchon-portland.
com* ⊟ *AE, MC, V* ⊘ *Closed Sun. and Mon.* ✛ *C3.*

$ ╳ **Le Happy.** This tiny crepe-maker outside of the hubbub of the Pearl
FRENCH District can serve as a romantic dinner-date spot or just a cozy place to
enjoy a drink and a snack. You can get sweet crepes with fruit, cheese,

and cream or savory ones with meats and cheeses; in addition, the dinner menu is rounded out with steaks and salads. It's a classy joint, but not without a sense of humor: Le Trash Blanc is a bacon-and-cheddar crepe served with a can of Pabst. ⊠ *1011 N.W. 16th Ave., Pearl District* 🕾 *503/226–1258* ⊕ *www.lehappy.com* ⊟ *MC, V* ⊗ *Closed Sun. No lunch* ✛ *C2.*

$$$ ✕ **Oba!** Many come to Oba! for the upscale bar scene, but this Pearl District salsa hangout also serves excellent Latin American cuisine, including coconut prawns, roasted vegetable enchiladas and tamales, and other seafood, chicken, pork, and duck dishes. The bar is open late Friday and Saturday. ⊠ *555 N.W. 12th Ave., Pearl District* 🕾 *503/228–6161* ⊕ *www.obarestaurant.com* ⊟ *AE, D, DC, MC, V* ⊗ *No lunch* ✛ *D3.*

LATIN AMERICAN

¢ ✕ **Pearl Bakery.** A light breakfast or lunch can be had at this popular spot, which is known for its excellent fresh breads and sandwiches. The cakes, cookies, croissants, and Danish are some of the best in the city. ⊠ *102 N.W. 9th Ave., Pearl District* 🕾 *503/827–0910* ⊕ *www. pearlbakery.com* ⊟ *MC, V* ⊗ *No dinner* ✛ *D3.*

CAFÉ

$ ✕ **Silk, by Pho Van.** This spacious, minimalist restaurant is the newer and trendier of the two Pho Van locations in Portland—the less expensive twin is on the far east side, on 82nd Avenue. A big bowl of pho (noodle soup) is delicious, enough to fill you up, and costs only $8 or $9. The friendly waitstaff will help you work your way through the menu, and can make suggestions to give you the best sampling of Vietnamese cuisine. ⊠ *1012 N.W. Glisan St., Pearl District* 🕾 *503/248–2172* ⊕ *www. phovanrestaurant.com* ⊟ *AE, D, MC, V* ⊗ *Closed Sun.* ⊠ *1919 S.E. 82nd Ave.* 🕾 *503/788–5244* ✛ *D3.*

VIETNAMESE

$$$ ✕ **Ten01.** Soft light, endless ceilings, and clean architectural lines make for a very chic dining room at Ten01. Indulge in practically plucked-off-the-farm entrées upstairs or dozens of available small plates downstairs. Save room for the signature chocolate-peanut-butter bread pudding served with malted-milk ice cream and peanut-butter caramel. The wine list is among the city's best. ⊠ *1001 N.W. Couch St., Pearl District* 🕾 *503/226–3463* ⊕ *www.ten-01.com* ⊟ *AE, DC, MC, V* ✛ *D4.*

AMERICAN

NOB HILL AND VICINITY

Head northwest to sample the broadest scope of this city's food scene. From the finest of the fine (Paley's Place, Wildwood, Papa Haydn, and Hoyt 23) to the come-as-you-are casual (McMenamins Blue Moon, Pizza Schmizza, and Rose's Deli), there's something for everyone within a handful of blocks. Most restaurants in the Nob Hill area are open for lunch and dinner and on weekends; reservations are recommended for the higher-end establishments. This neighborhood draws an eclectic crowd: progressives and conservatives, lifetime residents and recent transplants, wealthy as well as struggling students. There are numerous retail shops and galleries in the neighborhood to help you work up an appetite before or after your meal.

$$$ ✕ **23 Hoyt.** From the prominent antler chandelier to the owner's private collection of contemporary art on walls and in glass cases, an eclectic mix of fun in a chic, contemporary setting is what this place is about.

CONTINENTAL

2

The restaurant has received national accolades for its interpretation of Northwest cuisine. Choices, which change seasonally, may include a mixed-grill dish with juniper-rubbed quail, rabbit sausage, and smoky bacon; or a Moroccan couscous with Alaskan halibut, manila clams, squid, and sea scallops. If it's available, don't miss the strudel made with crispy phyllo layered with poached pears and caramel custard. In a savory twist, it's served with black-pepper ice cream. ⊠ *529 N.W. 23rd Ave., Nob Hill* ☏ *503/445–7400* ⊕ *www.23hoyt.com* ⊟ *AE, MC, V* ⊘ *Closed Sun. and Mon. No lunch* ✛ *A3.*

¢ ✕ **Ken's Artisan Bakery.** Golden crusts are the trademark of Ken's rustic
CAFÉ breads, croissants, tarts, and puff pastries, good for breakfast, lunch, and light evening meals. Sandwiches, barbecue pulled pork, and croque monsieur are served on thick slabs of freshly baked bread, and local berries fill the flaky pastries. And if the dozen tables inside the vibrant blue bakery are crammed (they usually are), you can sit outside at one of the sidewalk tables. On Monday nights they serve pizza, and the bakery stays open to 9 PM. ⊠ *338 N.W. 21st Ave. Nob Hill* ☏ *503/248–2202* ⊕ *www.kensartisan.com* ⊟ *MC, V* ⊘ *No dinner Tues.–Sun.* ✛ *B3.*

$$ ✕ **Lucy's Table.** In this regal purple and gold corner bistro chef Michael
CONTINTENTAL Conklin creates Northwest cuisine with a mix of Italian and French accents. The seasonal menu includes lamb, steak, pork, and seafood dishes. For dessert, try the *boca negra*, chocolate cake with Frangelico whipped cream and cherries poached with port and walnut Florentine. Valet parking is available Wednesday–Saturday. ⊠ *706 N.W. 21st Ave., Nob Hill* ☏ *503/226–6126* ⊕ *www.lucystable.com* ⊟ *AE, DC, MC, V* ⊘ *Closed Sun. No lunch* ✛ *B3.*

$ ✕ **MacTarnahan's Taproom.** The copper beer-making equipment at the
AMERICAN door tips you off to the specialty of the house: beer. This restaurant in the Northwest industrial district is part of a 27,000-sq-ft brewery complex. Start with a tasting platter of seven different beers. The hay-stack baby back ribs with garlic-rosemary fries are popular, and the fish-and-chips use a batter made with Mac's signature ale. Asparagus-artichoke lasagna is a good vegetarian option. You can enjoy it all on the patio overlooking the landscaped grounds. ⊠ *2730 N.W. 31st Ave., off N.W. Yeon St., Nob Hill* ☏ *503/228–5269* ⊕ *www.macsbeer.com* ⊟ *AE, DC, MC, V* ✛ *A1.*

$$ ✕ **Papa Haydn/Jo Bar.** Many patrons come to this bistro just for the lus-
AMERICAN cious desserts or for the popular Sunday brunch (reservations essential). Favorite dinner choices include pan-seared scallops, dinner salads, and grilled flatiron steak. Wood-fired, rotisserie-cooked meat, fish, and poul-try dishes plus pastas and pizza are available next door at the jazzy **Jo Bar.** ⊠ *701 N.W. 23rd Ave., Nob Hill* ☏ *503/228–7317 Papa Haydn, 503/222–0048 Jo Bar* ⊕ *www.papahaydn.com* ⊟ *AE, MC, V* ✛ *A3.*

¢ ✕ **Pastini.** It's hard to go wrong with anything at this classy Italian bistro,
ITALIAN which has more than two dozen pasta dishes under $10. Rigatoni *zuccati* comes in a light cream sauce with butternut squash, wild mushrooms, and spinach; *linguini misto mare* is a seafood linguine in white wine. It also has panini, antipasti, and dinner salads. Open for lunch and dinner, Pastini is part of a local chain. There's often a crowd, but from this loca-tion you can browse the shops while waiting for a table. ⊠ *1506 N.W.*

23rd Ave., Nob Hill ☎ *503/595–1205* ⊕ *www.pastini.com* ⟁ *Reservations not accepted* ▭ *AE, DC, MC, V* ◷ *No lunch Sun.* ✛ *A1.*

$$$$ ✕**Plainfield's Restaurant.** Portland's finest Indian food is served in an
INDIAN   elegant Victorian house. The tomato-coconut soup with fried curry
leaves and the vegetarian and vegan dishes are highlights. Appetizers
include the authentic Bombay *bhel* salad with tamarind dressing and
the *dahi wadi* (crispy fried lentil savory donuts in a spicy yogurt sauce).
Meat and seafood specialties include lobster in brown onion sauce and
tandoori lamb. ✉ *852 S.W. 21st Ave., one block south of Burnside,
close to Nob Hill* ☎ *503/223–2995* ⊕ *www.plainfields.com* ▭ *AE, D,
DC, MC, V* ◷ *No lunch* ✛ *B4.*

$$$ ✕**The Ringside.** This Portland institution has been famous for its beef
AMERICAN for more than 50 years. Dine in cozy booths on rib eye, prime rib, and
New York strip, which come in regular- or king-size cuts. Seafood lov-
ers will find plenty of choices: a chilled seafood platter with an 8-ounce
lobster tail, Dungeness crab, oysters, jumbo prawns, and Oregon bay
shrimp. The onion rings, made with the local Walla Walla sweets vari-
ety, are equally renowned. ✉ *2165 N.W. Burnside St., close to Nob
Hill* ☎ *503/223–1513* ⊕ *www.ringsidesteakhouse.com* ▭ *AE, D, MC,
V* ◷ *No lunch* ✛ *B3.*

$$$ ✕**Wildwood.** The busy center bar, stainless-steel open kitchen, and
CONTINENTAL blond-wood chairs set the tone at this restaurant serving fresh Pacific
Northwest cuisine. Chef Dustin Clark's entrées include dishes made
with lamb, pork loin, chicken, steak, and seafood. An obsession with
sustainable, fresh ingredients means that that menu changes often, and
that there's always a broad vegetarian selection. Wildwood also has
a family-style Sunday supper menu with selections for two or more
people. ✉ *1221 N.W. 21st Ave., Nob Hill* ☎ *503/248–9663* ⊕ *www.
wildwoodrestaurant.com* ▭ *AE, MC, V* ◷ *No lunch Sun.* ✛ *B2.*

EAST OF THE WILLAMETTE

A whole new food movement is sprouting up east of the river, just
outside downtown Portland. As restaurants become more daring and
inventive, they are also finding less-predictable locations. One benefit
of dining outside of downtown is that parking is less expensive and
easier to find. Getting from place to place, though, takes more time, as
these establishments are not necessarily concentrated in any one area.
But with some of Portland's most sought-after dining spots—such as
Genoa, Pok Pok, clarklewis—on the east side, a little research will go
a long way toward uncovering amazing new flavors.

$ ✕**Alameda Brewhouse.** The spacious room—with light wood, high ceil-
AMERICAN ings, and lots of stainless steel—feels chic while still managing to remain
friendly and casual. Many people come for the excellent microbrews
made here, but the food's worth a look too; this is no boring pub
grub. With creative pasta dishes such as mushroom-artichoke linguine,
salmon gyros, tuna tacos, and delicious burgers, it's clear that this restaurant has as much thought going into its menu and ingredients as it
does into its brewing. ✉ *4675 N.E. Fremont St., Alameda* ☎ *503/460–
9025* ⊕ *www.alamedabrewhouse.com* ▭ *AE, DC, MC, V* ✛ *H1.*

\$\$ ✕**Apizza Scholls.** You will pay more for this pizza, but the crispy yet
ITALIAN   chewy crust—the end result of 24-hour fermentation—is worth it. Slow
fermentation with a minimum of yeast produces acidity, which gives it
a creamy, textured flavor. Dough is made daily then topped by whole
fresh cheeses and a small amount of meats to spotlight the richness of
the crust and sauce flavorings. ⊠ *4741 S.E. Hawthorne Blvd., Hawthorne District* ☎ *503/233–1286* ⊕ *www.apizzascholls.com* ▭ *MC, V*
⊘ *No lunch* ✛ *H6.*

\$ ✕**Beaker and Flask.** Inspired by *The Gentleman's Companion*, an influ-
CONTINENTAL   ential cocktail manual published in 1946, the sassily named cocktails
here are modern twists on classics. For instance, there's the rum-based
Sal's Minion, served over coconut-water ice cubes, or the Chimney
Sweep, a concoction of ouzo, blended scotch, and Ramazzotti (an Italian bitters). Drink choices frequently change based on seasons and
available ingredients. The food, equally chic and selectively prepared,
often unites ingredients in unconventional ways, as in the macaroni
and cheese with blood sausage and a herb-thyme crust or the maple-
braised pork belly accompanied by creamed kale, squash, and apple
relish. ⊠ *720 S.E. Sandy Blvd., Buckman* ☎ *503/235–8180* ⊕ *www.
beakerandflask.com* ▭ *MC, V* ⊘ *Closed Sun.* ✛ *H4.*

\$\$\$\$ ✕**Beast.** This quintessential example of Portland's creative cuisine is in
CONTINENTAL   a nondescript red building with no signage. Inside, the seating is communal, at two large tables that seat 8 and 16. The frequently changing
menus are prix-fixe, and you have the option of either three or five
courses. The dishes that come from the open kitchen live up to the
restaurant's name: there might be chicken and duck-liver mousse, wine
and truffle-braised beef, or steak tartare with quail-egg toast. (Vegetarians may struggle to eat here.) There are two seatings per night; call
ahead for times and the day's menus. ⊠ *5425 N.E. 30th Ave., Concordia*
☎ *503/841–6968* ⊕ *www.beastpdx.com* ▭ *MC, V* ⊘ *Closed Mon. and
Tues. No dinner Sun.* ✛ *H1.*

\$ ✕**Belly Restaurant.** In this neighborhood restaurant people feel wel-
AMERICAN   comed, and can dine on an incredible meal made from sustainable
ingredients. The name "Belly" is about showing up with an appetite
big enough for the vast selection of small dishes—including potato
and kale soup or pork meatballs—or the hearty three-course meals.
Sunday brunches are also a hit: there's banana-bread French toast and
a chance to build your own biscuit sandwich stuffed with eggs, bacon,
sausage, and gravy. ⊠ *3500 N.E. Martin Luther King Jr. Blvd., Alameda* ☎ *503/249–9764* ⊕ *www.bellyrestaurant.com* ▭ *AE, D, DC, MC,
V* ⊘ *Sun. brunch only. Closed Mon.* ✛ *G1.*

\$ ✕**Biwa.** Taking ramen to whole new heights is what this bustling, indus-
JAPANESE   trial restaurant with an open kitchen does best. Homemade noodles
are the focal point of aromatic, flavorful soups enriched by accompaniments such as sliced pork and grilled chicken. Also try the thicker
udon noodles served in a soup made from dried fish and seaweed. A
fitting sendoff for the filling, authentic meals here would be one of the
many sakes. ⊠ *215 S.E. 9th Ave., Buckman* ☎ *503/239–8830* ⊕ *www.
biwarestaurant.com* ▭ *MC, DC, V* ⊘ *No lunch* ✛ *H4.*

$
AMERICAN

✕ **Bread and Ink.** The old-fashioned elegance will strike you as soon as you walk in; the dining room, done in cream and forest green and with high ceilings, is not trendy in any way. The look's impressive, but it's mainly the earnest dedication to quality food that's made Bread and Ink a neighborhood landmark. Breakfast, a specialty, might include brioche French toast, smoked fish, and blintzes (they're legendary). Lunch and dinner yield good choices, including burgers, poached salmon, and crab cakes. ⊠ *3610 S.E. Hawthorne Blvd., Hawthorne District* ☎ *503/239–4756* ⊕ *www.breadandinkcafe.com* ⊟ *AE, D, MC, V* ✛ *H6.*

¢
SWEDISH

✕ **Broder.** Smells of freshly brewed coffee and wonderful breads greet you as you walk into this friendly Swedish restaurant. Broder is known for its excellent takes on breakfast: if you can't decide between the many tasty, home-cooked options on the menu, go with the Swedish Breakfast Bord. For only 10 bucks, you get the best of what's offered: depending on the day, that could include walnut toasts, smoked trout, ham, seasonal fruit, yogurt and honey, a soft-boiled egg, and some sort of brilliant cheese. The coffee cakes, pastries, and breads are delectable. Lunch and dinner include a variety of sandwiches and salads—and yes, they serve meatballs. ⊠ *2508 S.E. Clinton St., Clinton* ☎ *503/736–3333* ⊕ *www.broderpdx.com* ⊟ *MC, V* ✛ *G6.*

$$
CONTINENTAL

✕ **clarklewis.** This cutting-edge restaurant, aka "darklewis" for its murky lighting, is making big waves for inventive farm-fresh meals served inside a former warehouse loading dock. Regional vegetables, seafood, and meat from local suppliers appear on a daily changing menu of pastas, entrées, and sides. Diners can order small, large, and family-style sizes, or let the chef decide with the fixed-price meal. Although the food is great, the lack of signage or a reception area can make your first visit feel a little like arriving at a party uninvited. ⊠ *1001 S.E. Water Ave., Buckman* ☎ *503/235–2294* ⊕ *www.clarklewispdx.com* ⊟ *AE, MC, V* ☾ *Closed Sun. No lunch weekends* ✛ *F5.*

¢
AMERICAN

✕ **Doug Fir.** In what resembles a futuristic lumberjack hangout, the surroundings make use of brick and glass, and the walls and ceilings are made from wood logs. Add a menu of hearty, homey dishes, and you've got a fun, eclectic restaurant. The morning shift can go for the banana-hazelnut pancakes or egg scrambles, and lunch crowds will appreciate big hearty sandwiches that include a signature hamburger. For dinner, grandma's meatloaf with gravy or Diego's marionberry chicken are both good. Downstairs is a concert venue open seven nights a week that attracts lots of wannabe rockers who come to hang out, drink, and socialize. ⊠ *830 E. Burnside St., Buckman* ☎ *503/231–9663* ⊕ *www.dougfirlounge.com* ⊟ *AE, MC, V* ✛ *H4.*

$$$$
ITALIAN
Fodor's Choice
★

✕ **Genoa.** Widely regarded as the finest restaurant in Portland, Genoa serves a five-course prix-fixe Italian menu that changes with the availability of ingredients and the season. Diners can chose from several entrées; the portions are hearty, thoughtfully crafted, and paired with some vibrant accompaniments such as sautéed brussels-sprout leaves or roasted root vegetables. As for the dining room, its dark antique furnishings, long curtains, and dangling light fixtures all help make it feel sophisticated. Seating is limited to a few dozen diners, so service is excellent. ⊠ *2822 S.E. Belmont St., near Hawthorne District*

☎ *503/238–1464* ⌕ *Reservations essential* ⊕ *www.genoarestaurant. com* ⊟ *AE, D, DC, MC, V* ☽ *No lunch* ✛ *H5.*

$ ✕ **Lemongrass.** Set in an old house, this lovely, intimate establishment
THAI consistently serves tantalizing pad Thai and a garlic basil chicken with
Fodor's Choice sauce so delicious you wish you had a straw. Fresh flowers adorn the
★ white-linen tables. Dishes are cooked to order, and just about everything
is delectable, including the chicken chili paste and peanut curry. ⊠ *1705
N.E. Couch St., Kerns* ☎ *503/231–5780* ⌕ *Reservations not accepted*
⊟ *No credit cards* ✛ *H4.*

$ ✕ **McMenamins Kennedy School Courtyard Restaurant.** Whether you are
AMERICAN coming to the Kennedy School to stay at the hotel, to watch a movie,
or just to enjoy dinner and drinks, the Courtyard Restaurant can add
to your evening. The food, with old reliables like burgers, salads, and
pizzas, fish-and-chips, pasta, prime rib, and beef stew, can satisfy most
any appetite. Several standard McMenamins microbrews are always
available, in addition to seasonal specialty brews. ⊠ *5736 N.E. 33rd
Ave., near Alberta District* ☎ *503/288–2192* ⊕ *www.kennedyschool.
com* ⊟ *AE, D, MC, V* ✛ *H1.*

$$ ✕ **Mint.** The owner of this cool, romantic restaurant also happens to
CONTINENTAL be a top-notch bartender. Drinks made with maple syrup, nutmeg, and
avocados are commonplace—and just as the beverages here are hard
to categorize, so too are the menu items. Global flavors influence an
evolving choice of interesting dishes like opah (a kind of fish) poached
in coconut lemongrass sake, and sautéed rabbit loin with garlic mashed
potatoes and wild-boar bacon. When you're done, slip next door to
820, the sister lounge to this suave establishment. ⊠ *816 N. Russell
St., Eliot* ☎ *503/284–5518* ⊕ *www.mintrestaurant.com* ⊟ *AE, MC, V*
☽ *Closed Sun–Tues. No lunch* ✛ *E1.*

$ ✕ **Pambiche.** Locals know that you can drive by Pambiche any night of
CARIBBEAN the week and find it packed. With traditional Cuban fare (plantains,
roast pork, mojitos, and Cuban espresso), it is no surprise why. If you
have some time to wait for a table, you should stop by and make an
evening of it at this hopping neighborhood hot spot. Don't miss out on
the incredible desserts here; they are the sole reason why some people
make the trip. Try the Selva Negra, a coconut chocolate cake filled
with mango and other tropical fruit. ⊠ *2811 N.E. Glisan St., near
Laurelhurst* ☎ *503/233–0511* ⊕ *www.pambiche.com* ⌕ *Reservations
not accepted* ⊟ *D, MC, V* ✛ *H3.*

$ ✕ **Podnah's Pit BBQ.** This nondescript little storefront diner hardly even
SOUTHERN declares itself with outdoor signage—but don't be fooled—the Texas-
and Carolina-style dishes at Podnah's are the stuff big boy barbecues are
made of. Melt-in-your-mouth pulled pork, ribs, chicken, and lamb are
all slow-smoked on hardwood and served up in a sassy vinegar-based
sauce. ⊠ *1469 N.E. Prescott St., Alberta District* ☎ *503/281–3700*
⊟ *MC, V* ☽ *Closed Mon.* ✛ *H1.*

¢ ✕ **Pok Pok.** There's no shortage of culinary adventure here. The food
ASIAN resembles what street vendors in Thailand would make: charcoal-grilled
game hen stuffed with lemongrass or shredded chicken and coconut
milk (made in-house). Diners have options of sitting outside by heated
lamps under tents, or down below in the dark, funky cave. Foods are

unique blends of flavors and spices, such as the coconut and jackfruit ice cream served on a sweet bun with sticky rice, condensed milk, chocolate syrup, and peanuts. ✉ *3226 SE Division St., Richmond* ☎ *503/232–1387* ⊕ *www.pokpokpdx.com* ▤ *MC, V* ⊹ *G6.*

$$$ ✕ **Salty's on the Columbia.** Pacific Northwest salmon (choose blackened or
SEAFOOD   grilled, a half or full pound) is what this comfortable restaurant overlooking the Columbia River is known for. Blackberry-barbecue-glazed salmon highlights local ingredients. Loaded with prawns, oysters, crab, mussels, and clams, the seafood platter offers plenty of variety. The menu also includes chicken and steak. There are both a heated, covered deck and an uncovered deck for open-air dining. ✉ *3839 N.E. Marine Dr., East Columbia* ☎ *503/288–4444* ⊕ *www.saltys.com* ▤ *AE, D, DC, MC, V* ⊹ *H1.*

$ ✕ **Siam Society.** Oversize red shutter doors, a beautiful outdoor patio
ASIAN   surrounded by full plants and flowers, and a lush upstairs lounge create an inviting atmosphere. Expect large portions of dishes such as chargrilled steak with a red-wine reduction and sweet-potato fries lightly sprinkled with white-truffle oil. The banana-roasted pork is made by slow-cooking pork shoulder for five days while wrapped in banana leaves; it's served with grilled pineapple. Drinks not to be missed include a ginger-lime cosmo and jalapeño-pear kamikaze. ✉ *2703 N.E. Alberta St., Alberta District* ☎ *503/922–3675* ⊕ *www.siamsociety.com* ▤ *MC, V* ⊹ *H1.*

¢   ✕ **Thai Noon.** The excellent traditional dishes here, including red, green,
THAI   and yellow curry; stir-fries; and noodle dishes, are served in a vibrant orange dining room with only about 12 tables. You can choose the spiciness of your meal, but beware that although "medium" may be milder than "hot," it's still spicy. Thai iced tea is also transformed into a boozy cocktail in the adjoining bar and lounge. Try the fried banana split or the mango ice cream for dessert. ✉ *2635 N.E. Alberta St., Alberta District* ☎ *503/282–2021* ⊕ *www.thainoon.com* ▤ *MC, V* ⊹ *H1.*

¢   ✕ **Tin Shed Garden Cafe.** This small restaurant is a popular breakfast
CAFÉ   spot known for its shredded potato cakes, biscuits and gravy, sweet-potato cinnamon French toast, creative egg and tofu scrambles, and breakfast burritos. The lunch and dinner menu has creative choices like a creamy artichoke sandwich, and a chicken sandwich with bacon, Gorgonzola, and apple, in addition to burgers, salads, and soups. A comfortable outdoor patio doubles as a beer garden on warm spring and summer evenings, and the adjacent community garden rounds off the property with a peaceful sitting area. ✉ *1438 N.E. Alberta St., Alberta District* ☎ *503/288–6966* ⌦ *Reservations not accepted* ⊕ *www.tinshedgardencafe.com* ▤ *MC, V* ⊹ *H1.*

¢   ✕ **Vita Cafe.** Vegan mac and cheese and vegetarian biscuits and gravy
VEGETARIAN   are just a few of the old favorites with a new, meatless spin. This hip restaurant along Alberta Street has a large menu with American, Mexican, Asian, and Middle Eastern–inspired entrées, and both herbivores and carnivores are sure to find something. There is also plenty of free-range, organic meat to go around. Finish off your meal with a piece of German chocolate cake or a peanut-butter fudge bar. ✉ *3023 N.E. Alberta St., Alberta District* ☎ *503/335–8233* ⊕ *www.vita-cafe.com* ▤ *MC, V* ⊹ *H1.*

WHERE TO STAY

DOWNTOWN

Staying downtown ensures that you'll have immediate access to just about everything Portland offers, including events, restaurants, cultural venues, shops, movie theaters, and more. Transportation options are abundant thanks to the MAX, bus lines, and taxis; in addition, many hotels offer shuttle service. Portland has clean streets and, overall, is considered relatively safe.

$$$ ⚏ **Avalon Hotel & Spa.** On the edge of Portland's progressive South Waterfront District and just a few minutes from downtown, this tranquil boutique property is sheltered among trees along the meandering Willamette River. Rooms range widely in size (from about 340 up to 1,030 sq ft), and they are all tastefully decorated with simple yet warm furnishings; most have a balcony. There are a full service spa and extensive fitness facility on-site. Aquariva, an Italian restaurant and wine bar on the premises, serves wonderful tapas and drinks. **Pros:** great river views; trails nearby for walking and jogging; breakfast served on each hotel floor. **Cons:** not in the center of downtown, spa tubs in the fitness facility are not coed; steep overnight parking fee. ⊠ *455 S.W. Hamilton Ct., Downtown* ☎ *503/802–5800 or 888/556–4402* ⊕ *www. avalonhotelandspa.com* ↝ *99 rooms* ⌂ *In-room: refrigerator (some), Wi-Fi. In-hotel: restaurant, room service, bar, gym, concierge, laundry service, Wi-Fi hotspot, parking (fee)* ▭ *AE, MC, V* ⦿| *CP* ✛ *D6.*

$$ ⚏ **Benson Hotel.** Portland's grandest hotel was built in 1912. The hand-carved Circassian walnut paneling from Russia and the Italian white-marble staircase are among the noteworthy design touches in the public areas. In the guest rooms expect to find small crystal chandeliers and inlaid mahogany doors. Some even have the original ceilings. Extra touches include fully stocked private bars and bathrobes in every room. **Pros:** beautiful lobby; excellent location. **Cons:** hallways could use updating. ⊠ *309 S.W. Broadway, Downtown* ☎ *503/228–2000 or 888/523–6766* ⊕ *www.bensonhotel.com* ↝ *287 rooms* ⌂ *In-room: refrigerator (some), dial-up, Wi-Fi. In-hotel: 2 restaurants, room service, bar, gym, concierge, laundry service, Wi-Fi hotspot, parking (fee)* ▭ *AE, D, DC, MC, V* ✛ *C4.*

$$ ⚏ **Courtyard by Marriott—Portland City Center.** Certified Gold LEED (Leadership in Energy and Design) for its energy efficiency, this 2009 hotel is one of just over a dozen U.S. hotels with this designation. The lobby, as welcoming as a living room, has individual kiosks rather than one big reception desk. The spacious rooms showcase local art and photography, and the bathrooms offer bins for recycling and water-saving toilets. The Original restaurant serves upscale twists on traditional diner-style fare. **Pros:** everything's new and environmentally conscious, great on-site restaurant. **Cons:** small gift shop; tubs available only in some rooms (on request). ⊠ *550 S.W. Oak St., Downtown* ☎ *503/505–5000* ⊕ *www.marriott.com* ↝ *256 rooms* ⌂ *In-room: refrigerator, Wi-Fi. In-hotel: restaurant, room service, bar, gym, laundry service, Wi-Fi hotspot, parking (fee)* ▭ *AE, D, DC, MC, V* ✛ *D4.*

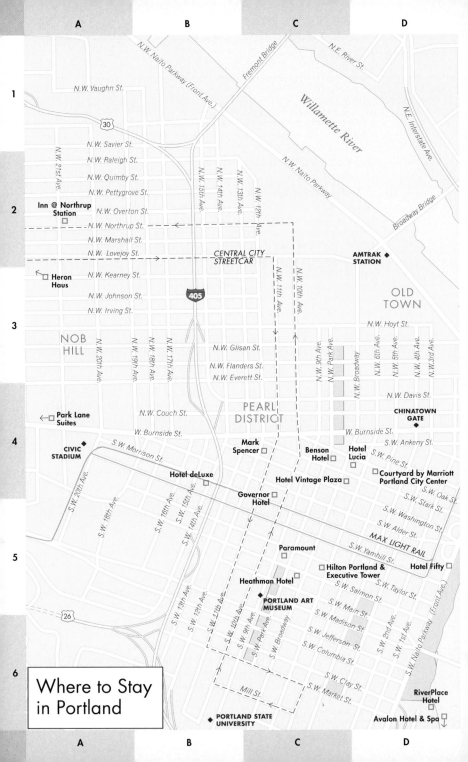

Where to Stay in Portland

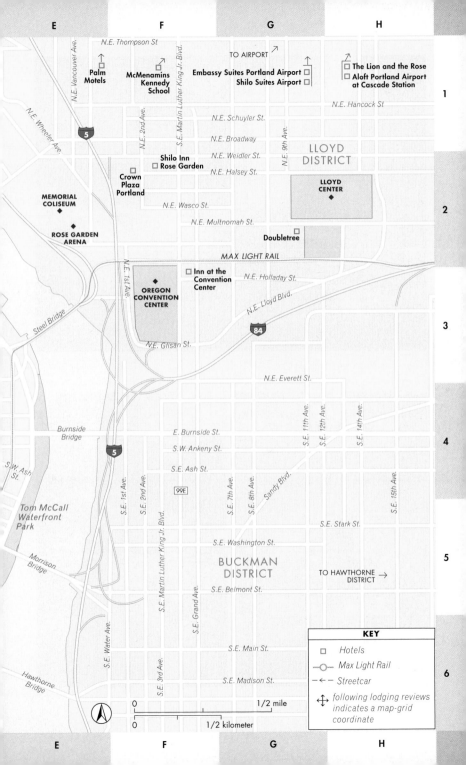

McMenamins Kennedy School

Hotel deLuxe

Heathman Hotel

2

$$ 📺 **Governor Hotel.** With mahogany walls and a mural of Pacific Northwest Indians fishing at Celilo Falls, the clubby lobby of the distinctive Governor helps set the 1920s Arts and Crafts style that's followed throughout the hotel. Painted in soothing earth tones, the tasteful guest rooms have large windows, honor bars, and bathrobes. Some have whirlpool tubs, fireplaces, and balconies. Jake's Grill is on the property, the streetcar runs right out front, and the hotel is one block from MAX. **Pros:** large rooms; beautiful 1920s property; excellent restaurant. **Cons:** some rooms in need of updates; limited late-night room-service menu. ⊠ *614 S.W. 10th Ave., Downtown* ☎ *503/224–3400 or 800/554–3456* ⊕ *www.govenorhotel.com* 🔊 *68 rooms, 32 suites* ⚒ *In-room: refrigerator, dial-up, Wi-Fi. In-hotel: restaurant, room service, bar, concierge, laundry service, Wi-Fi hotspot, parking (fee)* ▤ *AE, D, DC, MC, V* ✛ *C4.*

$$$ 📺 **Heathman Hotel.** The Heathman more than deserves its reputation
Fodor'sChoice for quality. From the teak-paneled lobby to the rosewood elevators
★ (with Warhol prints hung at each landing) and marble fireplaces, this hotel exudes refinement. The guest rooms provide the latest in customized comfort: a bed menu allows you to choose from Tempurpedic, European pillowtop, or European featherbed mattresses, and the bathrooms have plenty of marble and mirrors. The second-floor mezzanine—showcasing local art (works change every few weeks) and a small library (primarily filled with the signed editions of notable Heathman guests)—overlooks the high-ceiling Tea Court, a popular gathering spot in the evening. **Pros:** superior service; central location adjoining the Performing Arts Center; renowned on-site restaurant. **Cons:** small rooms; expensive parking. ⊠ *1001 S.W. Broadway, Downtown* ☎ *503/241–4100 or 800/551–0011* ⊕ *www.heathmanportland.com* 🔊 *117 rooms, 33 suites* ⚒ *In-room: refrigerator, Internet, Wi-Fi. In-hotel: restaurant, 24 hour room service, bar, fitness suite, concierge, laundry service, Wi-Fi hotspot, parking (fee), pets allowed* ▤ *AE, D, DC, MC, V* ✛ *C5.*

$$ 📺 **Hilton Portland & Executive Tower.** Together, two buildings comprise a gargantuan complex of luxuriously contemporary bedrooms, meeting rooms, two restaurants, and athletic center and gym, including two indoor swimming pools. The property is within walking distance of the Performing Arts Center, Pioneer Courthouse Square, the Portland Art Museum, and MAX light rail. **Pros:** nice workout facilities and indoor pools; prime downtown location near attractions and restaurants. **Cons:** sporadic downtown construction could mean noise and traffic; not for visitors looking for homier lodging. ⊠ *921 S.W. 6th Ave., Downtown* ☎ *503/226–1611 or 800/445–8667* ⊕ *www.hilton.com* 🔊 *773 rooms, 9 suites* ⚒ *In-room: Internet. In-hotel: 2 restaurants, bars, pools, gym, Wi-Fi hotspot, parking (fee)* ▤ *AE, D, DC, MC, V* ✛ *C5.*

$$ 📺 **Hotel deLuxe.** If you long to be transported back to the Hollywood
Fodor'sChoice glamour of the 1940s, this place is perfect. The more than 400 black-
★ and-white photographs on the corridor walls are arranged by cinematic themes (Music Masters, Rebels, Exiles, and Immigrants). If the standard King James Bible in the drawer doesn't ignite your spiritual flame, than choose from a selection of other texts found at the front desk, including Buddhist, Taoist, Catholic, and even Scientologist

offerings. **Pros:** "pillow menu" and other extra touches lend an air of luxury; artistic vibe. **Cons:** older windows in building can be drafty at night; cold bathroom floors. ⊠ *729 S.W. 15th Ave., Downtown* ☎ *503/219–2094 or 866/895–2094* ⊕ *www.hoteldeluxeportland.com* ⤳ *130 rooms* ⧖ *In-room: refrigerator, Wi-Fi. In-hotel: restaurant, room service, bar, Wi-Fi hotspot, parking (fee), some pets allowed* ⊟ *AE, D, DC, MC, V* ⦿| *CP* ⊹ *B4.*

$$ ⚏ **Hotel Fifty.** This reasonable boutique property recently underwent a major renovation, and the final results are pleasing. The decor is modern and clean, with glass, stone, and marble floor accents in the lobby. In the guest rooms, decorated with chocolate browns, deep purples, and oak highlights, there are 42-inch wall-mounted plasma HDTVs, ample work space, top-of-the-line memory-foam beds, and oversized walk-in showers. Another star attraction is the riverfront location. **Pros:** comfortable beds; river location. **Cons:** no gift shop; no on-site fitness facility. ⊠ *50 S.W. Morrison St., Downtown* ☎ *503/221–0711 or 877/237–6775* ⧉ *503/484–1417* ⊕ *www.hotelfifty.com* ⤳ *140 rooms 1 suite* ⧖ *In-room: refrigerator, Wi-Fi. In-hotel: restaurant, room service, bar, laundry service, Wi-Fi hotspot, parking (paid), some dogs allowed* ⊟ *AE, D, DC, MC, V* ⊹ *D5.*

$$$ ⚏ **Hotel Lucia.** Modern track lighting, black-and-white David Hume Kennerly celebrity photos, and comfy leather chairs adorn this nine-story boutique hotel in the heart of downtown—within walking distance of Nordstrom, Powell's, and the MAX line. The hotel's goal of "delivering calm" is accomplished in part through seven choices in pillows, stored customer profiles (so you automatically receive that same pillow next time), and Aveda soaps and lotions. The Pet Package comes with a special bed, set of dishes, treats, and bottled water. **Pros:** prime location; luxurious amenities; consistently good service. **Cons:** small rooms; limited shelf and storage space in the bathrooms; those with allergies should request a pet-free room. ⊠ *400 S.W. Broadway St., Downtown* ☎ *503/225–1717 or 877/225–1717* ⊕ *www.hotellucia. com* ⤳ *127 rooms, 16 suites* ⧖ *In-room: Wi-Fi. In-hotel: restaurant, room service, gym, laundry service, parking (fee), some pets allowed* ⊟ *AE, D, DC, MC, V* ⊹ *D4.*

$$ ⚏ **Hotel Vintage Plaza.** This historic landmark takes its theme from the area's vineyards. Guests can fall asleep counting stars in top-floor rooms, where skylights and wall-to-wall conservatory-style windows are some of the special details. Hospitality suites have extra-large rooms with a full living area, and the deluxe rooms have a bar. All are appointed in warm colors and have cherrywood furnishings; some rooms have hot tubs. Complimentary wine is served in the evening, and an extensive collection of Oregon vintages is displayed in the tasting room. Two-story town-house suites are named after local wineries. **Pros:** beautiful decor; nice complimentary wine selections; pet-friendly. **Cons:** those with allergies should ask for pet-free rooms; some street noise on the lower levels on the Washington Street side of the hotel. ⊠ *422 S.W. Broadway, Downtown* ☎ *503/228–1212 or 800/263–2305* ⊕ *www.vintageplaza. com* ⤳ *117 rooms, 21 suites* ⧖ *In-room: refrigerator, Wi-Fi. In-hotel:*

restaurant, room service, bar, gym, concierge, Wi-Fi hotspot, parking (fee), some pets allowed ═ AE, D, DC, MC, V ✛ C4.

$$ ⊡ **Mark Spencer.** The Mark Spencer, near Portland's gay-bar district and Powell's City of Books, is one of the best values in town. The rooms are clean and comfortable, and all have full kitchens. The hotel, a major supporter of local arts, offers special packages that include tickets to the Artists Repertory Theatre, Portland Opera, Oregon Symphony, Portland Art Museum, and Center Stage. **Pros:** complimentary breakfast; afternoon tea and cookies, and a weekly local wine tasting for all guests. **Cons:** some rooms could use updating; those with allergies should request a pet-free room. ⊠ 409 S.W. 11th Ave., Downtown ☎ 503/224–3293 or 800/548–3934 ⊕ www.markspencer.com ⟿ 102 rooms ♿ In-room: kitchen, Wi-Fi. In-hotel: laundry facilities, laundry service, Wi-Fi hotspot, pets allowed ═ AE, D, DC, MC, V ⍥◎ CP ✛ C4.

$ ⊡ **Paramount.** This pale-stone, 15-story hotel is two blocks from Pioneer Square, MAX, and the Portland Art Museum. The cozy rooms are adorned with earth tones, plush dark-wood furnishings, and dried flowers, and some have outdoor balconies and whirlpool tubs. The grand suites also have wet bars and gas fireplaces. Dragonfish, an excellent Pan-Asian restaurant, is on the premises. **Pros:** beautiful granite bathrooms; in-room honor bars. **Cons:** small fitness facilities. ⊠ 808 S.W. Taylor St., Downtown ☎ 503/223–9900 ⊕ www.portlandparamount. com ⟿ 154 rooms ♿ In-room: refrigerator, Wi-Fi. In-hotel: restaurant, room service, gym, concierge, laundry service, parking (fee) ═ AE, D, DC, MC, V ✛ C5.

$ ⊡ **Park Lane Suites and Inn.** A few blocks from Washington Park, Nob Hill, and downtown, this property is in a prime location, and consists of two buildings. Suites come with spacious, work-friendly living areas, and the kitchens come stocked with decent dishware, lots of cabinet space, and a full-size refrigerator, stovetop, microwave, and dishwasher. The standard rooms include flats-screen TVs. **Pros:** proximity to several of Portland's most prominent neighborhoods; expanded kitchen capacity. **Cons:** parking is free but limited; not enough soundproofing. ⊠ 809 S.W. King Ave., Downtown ☎ 503/226–6288 ⊕ www.parklanesuites. com ⟿ 44 rooms ♿ In-room: kitchen, refrigerator, Internet, Wi-Fi. In-hotel: laundry facilities, laundry service, some pets allowed ═ AE, D, DC, MC, V ✛ A4.

$$$$ ⊡ **RiverPlace Hotel.** All the guest rooms here have muted color schemes, Fodor's Choice Craftsman-style desks, and ergonomic chairs, and over a quarter of ★ them have amazing views of the river, marina, and skyline, as well as a landscaped courtyard. Extras include bathrobes, locally roasted coffee, Tazo tea in the room, and afternoon tea and cookies in the lobby. **Pros:** great location; wide selection of room options; great beds. **Cons:** no pool. ⊠ 1510 S.W. Harbor Way, Downtown ☎ 503/228–3233 or 800/227–1333 ⊕ www.riverplacehotel.com ⟿ 39 rooms, 45 suites ♿ In-room: DVD, Wi-Fi. In-hotel: restaurant, room service, concierge, parking (fee) ═ AE, D, DC, MC, V ✛ D6.

NOB HILL AND VICINITY

$$ **Heron Haus.** This lovely, bright B&B is inside a stately, 100-year-old three-floor Tudor-style mansion near Forest Park. Special features include a tulip-shaped bathtub in one room and a tiled, seven-head antique shower in another. You can enjoy a relaxing afternoon in the secluded sitting garden. All rooms have phones, work desks, and fireplaces. **Pros:** modern amenities; fancy continental breakfast included; plenty of room to roam on huge property. **Cons:** in a residential neighborhood; not immediately near public transportation. ⊠ *2545 N.W. Westover Rd., Nob Hill* ☎ *503/274–1846* ⊕ *www.heronhaus.com* ↗ *6 rooms* ⟐ *In-room: Wi-Fi. In-hotel: no elevator, Wi-Fi hotspot, parking (no fee)* ⊟ *MC, V* ¶⊙¶ *CP* ✢ *A3.*

$ **Inn @ Northrup Station.** Bright colors, original artwork, retro designs, and extremely luxurious suites fill this hotel in Nob Hill—it looks like a stylish apartment building from the outside, with patios or balconies adjoining most of the suites, and a garden terrace for all guests to use. The striking colors and bold patterns found on bedspreads, armchairs, pillows, and throughout the halls and lobby manage to be charming, elegant, and fun, never falling into the kitsch that plagues many places that strive for "retro" decor. All rooms have full kitchens or kitchenettes, two TVs, three phones, and large sitting areas. **Pros:** roomy suites feel like home; great location that's close to the shopping and dining on Northwest 21st Avenue. **Cons:** past guests have commented on the lack of noise insulation. ⊠ *2025 N.W. Northrup St., Nob Hill* ☎ *503/224–0543 or 800/224–1180* ⊕ *www.northrupstation.com* ↗ *70 suites* ⟐ *In-room: kitchen. In-hotel: Wi-Fi hotspot, parking (no fee)* ⊟ *AE, D, DC, MC, V* ¶⊙¶ *CP* ✢ *A2.*

EAST OF THE WILLAMETTE

The area east of the Willamette is not nearly as condensed as downtown Portland, which means fewer interesting buildings. It's also a little harder to get around, though thanks to MAX and excellent bus service it's still doable. Properties tend to be older, with lower prices than downtown, and with more rooms free. The majority of chain hotels are clustered around the Convention Center; nearby is Lloyd Center Mall, which has an ice-skating rink, movie theaters, and several levels of shops and restaurants. There are also a number of B&Bs on this side of town, tucked away in historical neighborhoods like Irvington.

$$ **Crowne Plaza Portland.** This sleek, modern hotel is close to the Rose Quarter, the Coliseum, and the Convention Center, and is within easy walking distance of Lloyd Center, the MAX line, and the Broadway Bridge leading to downtown. Given its attractive rooms and ample facilities, it's a reliable and convenient option for both business travelers and tourists. **Pros:** indoor pool; good selection of accommodations and room sizes. **Cons:** location near the Rose Quarter means traffic congestion during basketball games and concerts. ⊠ *1441 N.E. 2nd Ave., Lloyd District/Convention Center* ☎ *503/233–2401 or 877/777–2704* ⊕ *www.cpportland.com* ↗ *241 rooms* ⟐ *In-room: refrigerator, Wi-Fi. In-hotel: restaurant, bar, pool, gym* ⊟ *AE, D, DC, MC, V* ✢ *F2.*

2

$$ 🏨 **Doubletree Hotel.** This bustling business hotel maintains a huge traffic in meetings and special events. The public areas are a tasteful mix of marble, rose-and-green carpet, and antique-style furnishings. The large rooms, many with balconies, have views of the mountains or the city center. The Lloyd Center and the MAX light-rail line are across the street; the Oregon Convention Center is a five-minute walk away. **Pros:** convenient location; nice views, access to shops. **Cons:** pool is outdoors; can be crowded. ⊠ *1000 N.E. Multnomah St., Lloyd District* ☎ *503/281–6111 or 800/222–8733* ⊕ *www.doubletree.com* ⤶ *476 rooms* ♿ *In-room: Wi-Fi. In-hotel: 2 restaurants, room service, bar, pool, gym, concierge, laundry service, Wi-Fi hotspot, parking (fee)* ▭ *AE, D, DC, MC, V* ⊕ *G2.*

¢ 🏨 **Inn at the Convention Center.** Convenience is the big plus of this no-frills, independently run six-story hotel: it's directly across the street from the Convention Center, four blocks from Lloyd Center, and right along the MAX line. Rooms are simple and comfortable. **Pros:** right next to Convention Center; walking distance to Lloyd Center Mall. **Cons:** not wheelchair-friendly; could use updates. ⊠ *420 N.E. Holladay St., Lloyd District/Convention Center* ☎ *503/233–6331* ⊕ *www.innatcc. com* ⤶ *97 rooms* ♿ *In-room: refrigerator (some), Wi-Fi. In-hotel: laundry facilities, laundry service, Wi-Fi hotspot, parking (no fee)* ▭ *AE, D, DC, MC, V* ⊕ *F3.*

$$ 🏨 **Lion and the Rose.** Oak and mahogany floors, original light fixtures, antique silver, and a coffered dining-room ceiling set a tone of formal elegance here, while the wonderfully friendly, accommodating, and knowledgeable innkeepers make sure that you feel perfectly at home. May through October a full breakfast is included; November through April breakfast is continental. In a beautiful residential neighborhood, you're a block from the shops and restaurants that fill Northeast Broadway and within an easy walk of a free MAX ride downtown. Good last-minute rates are sometimes available; check the Web site. **Pros:** gorgeous house; top-notch service; afternoon tea available upon request. **Cons:** no elevator; fills up quickly (particularly in summer). ⊠ *1810 N.E. 15th Ave., Irvington* ☎ *503/287–9245 or 800/955–1647* ⊕ *www. lionrose.com* ⤶ *8 rooms* ♿ *In-room: Wi-Fi. In-hotel: no kids under 10* ▭ *AE, D, DC, MC, V* ⊕ *H1.*

Fodor's Choice
★

$ 🏨 **McMenamins Kennedy School.** In a renovated elementary school in northeast Portland, the Kennedy School may well be one of the most unusual hotels you'll ever encounter. With all of the guest rooms occupying former classrooms, complete with the original chalkboards and cloakrooms, the McMenamin brothers have created a multi-use facility that is both luxurious and fantastical. Go to the Detention Bar for cigars and one of the only two TVs on-site; visit the Honors Bar for classical music and cocktails. **Pros:** funky and authentic Portland experience; room rates include movie admission and use of the year-round outdoor soaking pool. **Cons:** no bathtubs (shower stalls only) in bathrooms; no TVs in rooms; no elevator. ⊠ *5736 N.E. 33rd Ave., near Alberta District* ☎ *503/249–3983* ⊕ *www.kennedyschool.com* ⤶ *35 rooms* ♿ *In-room: no TV, Wi-Fi. In-hotel: restaurant, bars, Wi-Fi hotspot, parking (no fee)* ▭ *AE, D, DC, MC, V* ⏐⊙⏐ *BP* ⊕ *F1.*

Fodor's Choice
★

¢ 📺 **Palms Motel.** Clean, simple, and accessible to downtown, this property offers an affordable alternative to some of the larger chains. It's close to freeway access, the MAX line, and buses. The rooms, renovated in 2008–09, are equipped with free Wi-Fi, microwaves, and refrigerators. **Pros:** affordable; friendly and eager staff. **Cons:** no frills; not immediately near shops and restaurants. ⊠ *3801 N. Interstate Ave., North Interstate* ☎ *503/287–5788 or 800/620–9652* ⊕ *www.palmsmotel.com* ➳ *55 rooms* ⬥ *In-room: refrigerator, Wi-Fi. In-hotel: Wi-Fi hotspot, parking (fee)* ⊹ *E1.*

$$ 📺 **Portland's White House.** Hardwood floors with oriental rugs, chandeliers, antiques, and fountains create a warm and romantic mood at this elegant B&B in the historic Irvington District. The Greek Revival mansion was built in 1910, and is on the National Register of Historic Landmarks. Rooms have private baths, flat-screen TVs, and mahogany canopy or four-poster queen- and king-size beds. A full breakfast is included in the room rate, and the owners offer vegetarian or vegan options. Smoking and pets are not allowed, and there's no elevator. **Pros:** romantic; authentic historic Portland experience; excellent service. **Cons:** located in residential neighborhood; shops and restaurants several blocks away. ⊠ *1914 N.E. 22nd Ave., Irvington* ☎ *503/287–7131 or 800/272–7131* ⊕ *www.portlandswhitehouse.com* ➳ *8 suites* ⬥ *In-room: dial-up, Wi-Fi. In-hotel: parking (free)* ⊟ *AE, D, MC, V* ⦿ *BP* ⊹ *G1.*

$ 📺 **Shilo Inn Rose Garden.** This family-friendly hotel provides respectable
☸   accommodations and great service. Some rooms have sofas, and all the furnishings and amenities are up-to-date. It's a five-minute walk to the MAX transit center, which has direct service to the airport. **Pros:** recently remodeled property; spa and sauna on-site. **Cons:** no shuttle service; off the beaten path from shops and restaurants. ⊠ *1506 N.E. 2nd Ave., Lloyd District* ☎ *503/736–6300 or 800/222–2244* ⊕ *www.shiloinns.com* ➳ *44 rooms* ⬥ *In-room: refrigerator, Wi-Fi. In-hotel: spa, no elevator, laundry service, Wi-Fi hotspot, parking (paid), some pets allowed* ⊟ *AE, D, DC, MC, V* ⦿ *CP* ⊹ *F2.*

PORTLAND INTERNATIONAL AIRPORT AREA

If you're flying in and out for a quick business trip, then staying by the airport may be a good idea. The lodging options here are only the larger chains. The airport is about a 20- to 25-minute drive away from downtown Portland.

Generally speaking, there's not much here in terms of noteworthy beauty, culture, restaurants, shops, or attractions—with the possible exception of Cascade Station, a newer mixed-use development for retail, lodging, and commercial office space. Cascade Station offers the convenience of several restaurants and larger chain stores, including IKEA and Best Buy. For all other attractions and nightlife, you'll have to travel into the city or to a neighboring town.

$$ 📺 **Aloft Portland Airport At Cascade Station.** High-end vibrant design, sophisticated amenities, and fresh new concepts in a hotel experience

make the first Aloft in Oregon a standout amid airport travel mediocrity. The ceilings are nine feet high, windows are oversized, and even the bathroom offers natural light with full-length frosted-glass panels surrounding walk-in showers. Other features include touchscreen kiosks for choosing your room, getting your key, and printing your departing flight's boarding pass. Dogs are not only welcomed, they're treated like royalty by receiving their own bed, toys, treats, and food bowl. Make time to relax in the re:mix lounge, which flows into the WXYZ bar, where there's a pool table and four-panel LCD TV "screenwall" for watching sports. **Pros:** lots of high-tech amenities; welcoming social areas; unique, spacious rooms; near IKEA. **Cons:** airport location; no sit-down restaurant. ⊠ *9920 N.E. Cascades Pkwy., Airport* ☎ *503/200–5678* ⊕ *www.starwoodhotels.com/alofthotels* ⇨ *136 rooms* ⌂ *In-room: refrigerator, Wi-Fi. In-hotel: bar, pool, gym, laundry facilities, laundry service, Wi-Fi hotspot, parking (free), some pets allowed* ⊟ *AE, D, DC, MC, V* ⊕ *H1.*

$ 🏨 **Embassy Suites Portland Airport.** Suites in this eight-story atrium hotel have beige walls and blond-wood furnishings. The lobby has a waterfall and koi pond. All suites come with separate bedrooms and living areas with sleeper sofas. It's on the MAX airport light-rail line. **Pros:** spacious suites; full breakfast included; free cocktails at happy hour. **Cons:** airport location. ⊠ *7900 N.E. 82nd Ave., Airport* ☎ *503/460–3000* ⊕ *www.portlandairport.embassysuites.com* ⇨ *251 suites* ⌂ *In-room: refrigerator. In-hotel: restaurant, room service, pool, gym, concierge, laundry service, airport shuttle, Wi-Fi hotspot, parking (no fee)* ⊟ *AE, D, DC, MC, V* ⦿*BP* ⊕ *G1.*

$ 🏨 **Red Lion Hotel on the River.** The rooms in this four-story hotel, on the Columbia River, have balconies and good views of the river and Vancouver, Washington. Public areas glitter with brass and bright lights that accentuate the greenery and the burgundy, green, and rose color scheme. **Pros:** river location; views from room balconies; close to the Jantzen Beach shopping center. **Cons:** pool is outdoors. ⊠ *909 N. Hayden Island Dr., east of I–5's Jantzen Beach exit, Jantzen Beach* ☎ *503/283–4466 or 800/733–5466* ⊕ *www.redlion.com* ⇨ *320 rooms, 24 suites* ⌂ *In-room: Wi-Fi. In-hotel: 2 restaurants, room service, bar, tennis court, pool, gym, laundry facilities, laundry service, Wi-Fi hotspot, parking (no fee)* ⊟ *AE, D, DC, MC, V* ⊕ *D1.*

$ 🏨 **Shilo Suites Airport.** Each room in this large, four-level all-suites inn is bright, with floral-print bedspreads and drapes, and has a microwave, wet bar, and two oversize beds. The indoor pool and hot tub are open 24 hours. **Pros:** large indoor pool; spacious rooms; free local calls. **Cons:** airport location. ⊠ *11707 N.E. Airport Way, Airport* ☎ *503/252–7500 or 800/222–2244* ⊕ *www.shiloinns.com* ⇨ *200 rooms* ⌂ *In-room: refrigerator. In-hotel: restaurant, room service, bar, pool, gym, laundry facilities, laundry service, airport shuttle, Wi-Fi hotspot, parking (no fee)* ⊟ *AE, D, DC, MC, V* ⦿*CP* ⊕ *G1.*

NIGHTLIFE AND THE ARTS

Portland is quite the creative town. Every night performances from top-ranked dance, theater, and musical talent take the stage somewhere in the city. Expect to find never-ending choices for things to do, from taking in true independent films, performance art, and plays to checking out some of the Northwest's (and the country's) hottest musical groups at one of the city's many nightclubs.

As for the fine art scene, galleries abound in all four corners of Portland, and if you take the time and do a little research, you'll discover extraordinarily creative blends of artistic techniques. Painted, recycled, photographed, fired, fused, welded, or collaged—the scope and selection of art is one of the most notable attributes of what makes this city so metropolitan and alive.

NIGHTLIFE

Portland has become something of a base for young rock bands, which perform in dance clubs scattered throughout the metropolitan area. Good jazz groups perform nightly in clubs and bars. Top-name musicians and performers in every genre regularly appear at the city's larger venues.

BARS AND LOUNGES

From chic to cheap, cool to cultish, Portland's diverse bars and lounges blanket the town. The best way to experience some of the city's hottest spots is to check out the happy-hour menus found at almost all of Portland's bars; they offer excellent deals on both food and drinks.

DOWNTOWN

Many of the best bars and lounges in Portland are found in its restaurants.

At the elegant **Heathman Hotel** (✉ *1001 S.W. Broadway* ☎ *503/241–4100*) you can sit in the marble bar or the wood-paneled Tea Court.

Huber's Cafe (✉ *411 S.W. 3rd Ave.* ☎ *503/228–5686*), the city's oldest restaurant, is notable for its Spanish coffee and old-fashioned feel.

The young and eclectic crowd at the **Lotus Cardroom and Cafe** (✉ *932 S.W. 3rd Ave.* ☎ *503/227–6185*) comes to drink and play pool or foosball.

The **Rialto** (✉ *529 S.W. 4th Ave.* ☎ *503/228–7605*) is a large, dark bar with several pool tables and enthusiastic players as well as some of the best Bloody Marys in town.

Saucebox (✉ *214 S.W. Broadway* ☎ *503/241–3393*) attracts a sophisticated crowd that enjoys colorful cocktails and trendy DJ music Wednesday–Saturday evenings.

With more than 120 choices, **Southpark** (✉ *901 S.W. Salmon St.* ☎ *503/326–1300*) is a perfect spot for a post-symphony glass of wine.

At **Veritable Quandary** (✉ *1220 S.W. 1st Ave.* ☎ *503/227–7342*), next to the river, you can sit on the cozy, tree-filled outdoor patio or in the glass atrium.

CLOSE UP

Classic Cocktails

2

Classic cocktails are back with a vengeance chic enough to make James Bond proud, and they have a new twist: being infused with anything flavorful that grows under the sun. Throughout the Northwest, emphasis on freshness and sustainability has spilled over into the mixers, shakers, and blenders of creative mixologists. Avocados, cucumbers, chilies, green peppers, cilantro, nutmeg, rhubarb, and beets are some of the luminaries infusing tangy hints and boldness into rums, vodkas, and whiskeys. Regionally, drink swankiness and sophistication have reached soaring heights. The book *Hip Sips,* by Portland Mint/820 bartender and restaurateur Lucy Brennan is dedicated to this intoxicating topic, with more than 60 imaginative recipes to choose from.

PEARL DISTRICT AND OLD TOWN/CHINATOWN

The modern bar at **Bluehour** (⊠ *250 N.W. 13th Ave., Pearl District* ☎ *503/226–3394*) draws a chic crowd for specialty cocktails such as the Bluehour Breeze (house-infused grapefruit vodka with a splash of cranberry).

Henry's 12th Street Tavern (⊠ *10 N.W. 12th Ave., Pearl District* ☎ *503/227–5320*) has more than 100 beers on draft, plasma-screen TVs, and a billiards room in a building that was once Henry Weinhard's brewery.

At **Oba!** (⊠ *555 N.W. 12th Ave., Pearl District* ☎ *503/228–6161*), plush tans and reds with lime-green backlit walls create a backdrop for South American salsa.

NOB HILL AND VICINITY

Boisterous **Gypsy** (⊠ *625 N.W. 21st Ave., Nob Hill* ☎ *503/796–1859*) has 1950s-era furnishings.

Young hipsters pack **Muu-Muu's** (⊠ *612 N.W. 21st Ave., Nob Hill* ☎ *503/223–8169*) on weekend nights.

21st Avenue Bar & Grill (⊠ *721 N.W. 21st Ave., Nob Hill* ☎ *503/222–4121*) open until 2:30 AM, has a patio and outdoor bar.

An upscale martini-loving crowd chills at **Wildwood** (⊠ *1221 N.W. 21st Ave., Nob Hill* ☎ *503/248–9663*).

EAST OF WILLAMETTE RIVER

Artsy, hip east-siders, not to be mistaken for the jet-setters downtown, hang and drink martinis and wine at the minimalist **Aalto Lounge** (⊠ *3356 S.E. Belmont St.* ☎ *503/235–6041*).

One of the few bars on Northeast Alberta Street, **Bink's** (⊠ *2715 N.E. Alberta St.* ☎ *503/493–4430*) is a small, friendly neighborhood spot with cozy seats around a fireplace, a pool table, and a good jukebox. It serves only beer and wine.

Green lanterns glow on the curvy bar as hip patrons sip mojitos or other mixed drinks at the no-smoking hot spot **820** (✉ *820 N. Russell St.* ☎ *503/284–5518*).

A laid-back beer-drinking crowd fills the **Horse Brass Pub** (✉ *4534 S.E. Belmont St.* ☎ *503/232–2202*), as good an English-style pub as you will find this side of the Atlantic, with more than 50 beers on tap.

The open, airy **Imbibe** (✉ *2229 S.E. Hawthorne Blvd.* ☎ *503/239–4002*) serves up creative cocktails, such as its namesake, the Imbibe Infusion—a thyme-and-ginger-infused vodka and strawberry martini with a touch of lemon.

Noble Rot (✉ *1111 E. Burnside St., 4th fl.* ☎ *503/233–1999*) is a chic east-side wine bar with excellent food and red-leather booths.

Swift Lounge (✉ *1932 N.E. Broadway* ☎ *503/288–3333*), a popular tapas bar, draws a cocktail-sipping crowd of hipsters at night.

BREWPUBS, MICROBREWERIES, AND PUB THEATERS

Portland is the proclaimed beer capital of the world, affectionately deemed "Beervana" and "Munich on the Willamette," boasting 35 craft breweriesoperating within the city limits. Some have attached pub operations, where you can sample a foaming pint of house ale. "Pub theaters," former neighborhood movie houses where patrons enjoy food, suds, and recent theatrical releases, are part of the microbrewery phenomenon. Many are branches of McMenamins, a locally owned chain of bars, restaurants, nightclubs, and hotels, and some of these pubs can be found in restored historic buildings.

The **Bagdad Theatre and Pub** (✉ *3702 S.E. Hawthorne Blvd., Hawthorne District* ☎ *503/236–9234*) screens second-run Hollywood films and serves McMenamins ales and Pizzacato Pizza.

The first McMenamins brewpub, the **Barley Mill Pub** (✉ *1629 S.E. Hawthorne Blvd., Hawthorne District* ☎ *503/231–1492*), is filled with Grateful Dead memorabilia and concert posters. It's a fun place for families.

BridgePort Brewpub + Bakery (✉ *1313 N.W. Marshall St.* ☎ *503/241–3612* ⊕ *www.bridgeportbrew.com*). Visit the oldest microbrewery in Portland, a beautiful brick-and-ivy building that is listed on the National Register of Historic Places. Their heritage beer, Blue Heron, was first brewed in 1987, and honors Portland's official city bird. Brewery tours are free and take place on Saturday at, 1, 3, and 5 PM.

Hopworks Urban Brewery "HUB" (✉ *2944 S.E. Powell Blvd.* ☎ *503/232–4677* ⊕ *www.hopworksbeer.com*). In addition to brewing only organic beer, the brewery is powered with 100% renewable energy. Pint picks include the Organic Survival "Seven-Grain" Stout, finished with the iconic Stumptown Hairbender espresso and their namesake Organic

Last Thursday Art Walk on Alberta Street

Hopworks IPA, a Northwest classic. Brewery tours, which cost $5, take place on Saturday at 11 AM and 3 PM.

Inside an old warehouse with high ceilings and rustic wood tables, the **Lucky Labrador Brew Pub** (✉ *915 S.E. Hawthorne Blvd.* ☎ *503/236–3555*) serves handcrafted ales and pub food both in the brewery and on the patio, where your four-legged friends are welcome to join you.

First opened in 1987, the **Mission Theatre** (✉ *1624 N.W. Glisan St., Nob Hill* ☎ *503/223–4527*) was the first McMenamins brew theater. It shows recent Hollywood offerings.

Ringlers (✉ *1332 W. Burnside St., Downtown* ☎ *503/225–0627*) occupies the first floor of the building that houses the famous Crystal Ballroom (⇨ *Dancing*).

Ringlers Annex (✉ *1223 S.W. Stark St., Downtown* ☎ *503/525–0520*), one block east of Ringlers, is a pie-shaped corner pub where you can puff a cigar while drinking beer, port, or a single-malt scotch.

In a former church, the **St. John's Pub** (✉ *8203 N. Ivanhoe, East of Willamette River* ☎ *503/283–8520*) includes a beer garden and a movie theater.

Tugboat Brewery (✉ *711 S.W. Ankeny St., Downtown* ☎ *503/226–2508*) is a small, cozy brewpub with books and games, picnic tables, and experimental jazz several nights a week.

Widmer Brothers Brewing Company (✉ *929 N. Russell St.* ☎ *503/281–2437* ⊕ *www.widmer.com*). Founded in 1984, this is Oregon's largest brewery, and their Hefeweizen is still the top-selling craft beer in the state.

Brewery tours take place on Friday at 3 PM, and Saturday at 11 AM and noon.

COFFEEHOUSES AND TEAHOUSES

Coffee is to Portland as tea is to England. For Portlanders, sipping a cup of coffee is a right, a ritual, and a pastime that occurs no matter the time of day or night. There's no shortage of cafés in which to park and read, reflect, or rejuvenate for the long day or night of exploration ahead.

DOWNTOWN

Fodor's Choice ★ Serving quite possibly the best coffee around, **Stumptown Coffee Roasters** (⊠ *128 S.W. 3rd Ave., Downtown* ☎ *503/295–6144*) has three local cafés, where its beans are roasted daily on vintage cast-iron equipment for a consistent, fresh flavor.

NOB HILL AND VICINITY

Anna Bannanas (⊠ *1214 N.W. 21st Ave., Nob Hill* ☎ *503/274–2559*) serves great espresso and coffee, veggie sandwiches, soup, and smoothies. There's outdoor seating out front.

One of the more highly trafficked locales in the Portland coffee scene, **World Cup Coffee and Tea** (⊠ *1740 N.W. Glisan St., Nob Hill* ☎ *503/228–4152*) sells excellent organic coffee and espresso in Nob Hill, as well as at its store in the Pearl District at the Ecotrust building and at Powell's City of Books on Burnside.

EAST OF WILLAMETTE RIVER

Common Grounds (⊠ *4321 S.E. Hawthorne Blvd., East of Willamette River* ☎ *503/236–4835*) has plush couches and serves desserts plus sandwiches and soup.

Palio Coffee and Dessert House (⊠ *1996 S.E. Ladd St., East of Willamette River* ☎ *503/232–9412*), in the middle of peaceful residential Ladd's Addition, has delicious desserts and espresso, and is open later than many coffee shops in the area.

Post-collegiate sippers lounge on sofas and overstuffed chairs at **Pied Cow** (⊠ *3244 S.E. Belmont St., East of Willamette River* ☎ *503/230–4866*), a laid-back alternative to the more yuppified establishments.

Rimsky Korsakoffee House (⊠ *707 S.E. 12th Ave., East of Willamette River* ☎ *503/232–2640*), one of the city's first coffeehouses, is still one of the best, especially when it comes to desserts.

Stumptown Coffee Roasters (⊠ *4525 S.E. Division St.* ☎ *503/230–7702* ⊠ *3356 S.E. Belmont St.* ☎ *503/232–8889*) has two cafés on the east side. At the original site (S.E. Division), organic beans are still roasted daily. At the Stumptown Annex, the newer branch next door, patrons can participate in "cuppings" (tastings) daily at 3 PM.

With soft music and the sound of running water in the background, the **Tao of Tea** (⊠ *3430 S.E. Belmont St., East of Willamette River* ☎ *503/736–0119*) serves vegetarian snacks and sweets as well as more than 80 loose-leaf teas.

DANCING

A couple of cocktails and some good music are all that's needed to shake your groove thing at Portland's hot spots for dancing. Clubs feature both live bands and DJs spinning the latest in dance-floor favorites.

Part 1950s diner, part log cabin, the **Doug Fir** (⊠ *830 E. Burnside St., East of Willamette River* ☎ *503/231–9663*) hosts DJs and live rock shows from up-and-coming bands seven nights a week.

Tuesday through Saturday, the funky, Moroccan-style **Fez Ballroom** (⊠ *316 S.W. 11th St., Downtown* ☎ *503/221–7262*) draws a dancing crowd.

McMenamins Crystal Ballroom (⊠ *1332 W. Burnside St., Downtown* ☎ *503/225–0047*) is a famous Portland dance hall that dates from 1914. Rudolph Valentino danced the tango here in 1923, and you may feel like doing the same once you step out onto the 7,500-sq-ft "elastic" floor (it's built on ball bearings) and feel it bouncing beneath your feet. Bands perform everything from swing to hillbilly rock nightly except Monday.

GAY AND LESBIAN CLUBS

Portland's gay community has a decent selection of places to mingle, dance, and drink; several of these nightspots are open into the wee hours, until 4 AM or so.

Part of the same disco-bar-restaurant complex as the Fez Ballroom, **Boxxes** (⊠ *1035 S.W. Stark St., Downtown* ☎ *503/226–4171*) has multiple video screens that display everything from music to messages from would-be dates.

A bar attracting mostly gay men, **C.C. Slaughters** (⊠ *219 N.W. Davis Ave., Old Town* ☎ *503/248–9135*) has a restaurant and a dance floor that's crowded on weekend nights; weeknights bring karaoke and country dancing.

Egyptian Room (⊠ *3701 S.E. Division St., East of Willamette River* ☎ *503/236–8689*), Portland's lesbian bar-disco, has pool tables, video poker, and a medium-size dance floor.

Open till 4 AM, **Embers** (⊠ *11 N.W. Broadway Ave., Old Town* ☎ *503/ 222–3082*) is a popular after-hours place to dance; the club hosts occasional drag shows and theme nights.

Fox and Hounds (⊠ *217 N.W. 2nd Ave., Old Town* ☎ *503/243–5530*) is popular with both gay men and lesbians. A full menu is served in the evening, and the place is packed for Sunday brunch.

Scandals (⊠ *1125 S.W. Stark St., Downtown* ☎ *503/227–5887*) has plate-glass windows with a view of Stark Street and the city's streetcars. At this low-key place there's a small dance floor, video poker, and a pool table, and the bar serves light food noon to closing.

LIVE MUSIC

The city features a wealth of homegrown talent, thanks in part to the array of fresh-faced twenty-somethings moving into town every day with guitars slung over their shoulders and creative ideas circling in their minds. Well, they don't all have guitars; there are also saxophones, cellos, djembe drums, Moog synthesizers, and laptops.

It's not simply the number of outstanding musicians that makes Portland unique, but their eclecticism. It's a city where stray-far-from-the crowd individualism and a highly cooperative sense of community are prized in equal measure, and the local scene reflects that: talented, idiosyncratic musicians making all genres of music together.

Whether you're interested in listening to a singer-songwriter tell it like it is as you sip Stumptown Coffee, getting down and dirty in a rocking dive bar, or simply dancing the night away to electronic trance beats, Portland's got you covered.

BLUES, FOLK, AND ROCK

The **Aladdin Theater** (✉ *3017 S.E. Milwaukie Ave., East of Willamette River* ☎ *503/234–9694*), in an old movie theater, is one of the best music venues in town. It serves microbrews and pizza.

Berbati's Pan (✉ *10 S.W. 3rd Ave., Old Town* ☎ *503/226–2122*), on the edge of Old Town, has dancing and live music, everything from big band and swing to acid jazz, rock, and R&B.

The **Candlelight Room** (✉ *2032 S.W. 5th Ave., Downtown* ☎ *503/222–3378*) presents blues nightly.

Crystal Ballroom. Restored by the McMenamin brothers, this ballroom transformed into one of Portland's most interesting music venues. Home to shows by nationally touring acts as well as locals, the spring-loaded ballroom floor makes dancing extra fun. ✉ *1332 W. Burnside St., Downtown* ☎ *503/225–0047.*

Doug Fir. This intimate music venue with a Northwest log-cabin theme and crystal-clear acoustics also doubles as a bar and restaurant. Acts performing at the Doug Fir tend to be of acoustic guitar, folk, and Americana variety. ✉ *830 E. Burnside St., East of Willamette River* ☎ *503/231–9663.*

Dublin Pub (✉ *6821 S.W. Beaverton–Hillsdale Hwy., West of Downtown* ☎ *503/297–2889*), on the West Side, pours more than 50 beers on tap and hosts Irish bands and rock groups.

Hawthorne Theatre. Bang your head! While Portland is becoming recognized for indie-folk, this city was one of the original hotbeds of grunge music. The Hawthorne Theatre keeps that tradition alive as one of the best local rock venues. Their amps go to 11. ✉ *3862 S.E. Hawthorne Blvd., East of Willamette River* ☎ *503/233–7100.*

Kells Irish Restaurant & Pub (✉ *112 S.W. 2nd Ave., Old Town* ☎ *503/227–4057*) serves terrific Irish food and presents Celtic music nightly.

Locals crowd the **Laurelthirst Public House** (✉ *2958 N.E. Glisan St., East of Willamette River* ☎ *503/232–1504*) to eat tasty food, sit in cozy red booths, and listen to folk, jazz, country, or bluegrass music on its tiny stage. There are pool tables in an adjoining room.

The down-to-earth **Produce Row Cafe** (✉ *204 S.E. Oak St., East of Willamette River* ☎ *503/232–8355*) has a huge beer list, a great beer garden, and live bluegrass, folk, and acoustic music most nights of the week.

COUNTRY AND WESTERN

Duke's (✉ *14601 S.E. Division St., East of Willamette River* ☎ *503/760–1400*) books occasional country and country-rock performers and hosts nightly DJ dancing to country music.

Not your ordinary truck stop, the Ponderosa Lounge at **Jubitz Truck Stop** (⊠ *10350 N. Vancouver Way, East of Willamette River* ☎ *503/345–0300*) presents live country music and dancing Thursday through Saturday.

JAZZ Upstairs at the **Blue Monk** (⊠ *3341 S.E. Belmont St., East of Willamette River* ☎ *503/595–0575*) local artists' works are on display and patrons nosh on large plates of pasta and salads; the live-jazz venue downstairs displays jazz memorabilia and photos.

Dubbed one of the world's "top 100 places to hear jazz" by *DownBeat*, **Jimmy Mak's** (⊠ *300 S.W. 10th, Pearl District* ☎ *503/295–6542*) also serves Greek and Middle Eastern dishes and has a basement lounge outfitted with two pool tables and an Internet jukebox.

THE ARTS

For a city of this size, there is truly an impressive—and accessible— scope of talent from visual artists, performance artists, and musicians. The arts are alive, with outdoor sculptural works strewn around the city, ongoing festivals, and premieres of traveling Broadway shows. Top-name international acts, such as Bruce Springsteen, the Rolling Stones, Paul McCartney, and Billy Joel, regularly include Portland in their worldwide stops.

TICKETS Most Portland-based performing-arts groups have their own box-office numbers; *see individual listings.*

For tickets to most events, call **Ticketmaster** (☎ *800/745–3000* ⊕ *www. ticketmaster.com*). Tickets are also available from **TicketsWest** (☎ *503/ 224–8499* ⊕ *www.ticketswest.com*).

During the summer half-price tickets for almost any event are available the day of the show at Ticket Central in the **Visitor Information and Services Center** (⊠ *Pioneer Courthouse Sq., Downtown* ☎ *503/275–8358 after 10* AM), open Monday–Saturday 9–4:30. This is an outlet for tickets from Ticketmaster and TicketsWest. Credit cards are accepted, but you must buy tickets in person.

CLASSICAL MUSIC

OPERA **Portland Opera** (⊠ *222 S.W. Clay St.* ☎ *503/241–1802 or 866/739–6737* ⊕ *www.portlandopera.org*) and its orchestra and chorus stage five productions annually at the Keller Auditorium.

ORCHESTRAS The **Oregon Symphony** (⊠ *923 S.W. Washington* ☎ *503/228–1353 or 800/228–7343* ⊕ *www.orsymphony.org*), established in 1896, is Portland's largest classical group—and one of the largest orchestras in the country. Its season officially starts in September and ends in May, but throughout the summer the orchestra and its smaller ensembles can be seen at Waterfront Park and Washington Park for special outdoor summer performances. It also presents more than 40 classical, pop, children's, and family concerts each year at the Arlene Schnitzer Concert Hall.

The **Metropolitan Youth Symphony** (⊠ *4800 S.W. Macadam St., Suite 105* ☎ *503/239–4566* ⊕ *www.playmys.org*) performs family-friendly concerts throughout the year at various Portland venues, including the Arlene Schnitzer Concert Hall.

DANCE

Body Vox (☎ 503/229–0627 ⊕ www.bodyvox.com) performs energetic contemporary dance–theater works at several locations in Portland.

Do Jump! Extremely Physical Theatre (✉ 1515 S.E. 37th Ave. ☎ 503/231–1232 ⊕ www.dojump.org) showcases its creative acrobatic work at the Echo Theatre near Hawthorne.

Oregon Ballet Theatre (✉ 818 S.E. 6th Ave. ☎ 503/222–5538 or 888/922–5538 ⊕ www.obt.org) produces five classical and contemporary works a year, including a much-loved holiday *Nutcracker*. Most performances are at Keller Auditorium.

Since its founding in 1997, **White Bird Dance** (✉ 5620 S.W. Edgemont Pl. ☎ 503/245–1600 ⊕ www.whitebird.org) has been dedicated to bringing exciting dance performances to Portland from around the world.

FILM

Cinema 21 (✉ 616 N.W. 21st Ave., Nob Hill ☎ 503/223–4515) an art-movie house in Nob Hill, hosts the annual gay and lesbian film festival.

An over-80-year-old landmark, and another host of the annual gay and lesbian film festival, the **Hollywood Theatre** (✉ 4122 N.E. Sandy Blvd., East of Willamette River ☎ 503/281–4215) shows everything from obscure foreign art films to old American classics and second-run Hollywood hits, and hosts an annual Academy Awards viewing party.

The **Laurelhurst Theatre** (✉ 2735 E. Burnside, East of Willamette River ☎ 503/232–5511) is a beautiful theater and pub showing excellent second-run features and cult classics for only $3.

Not-to-be-missed Portland landmarks when it comes to movie-viewing, the **McMenamins theaters and brewpubs** offer beer, pizza, and inexpensive tickets to second-run blockbusters in uniquely renovated buildings that avoid any hint of corporate streamlining. The **Bagdad Theatre** (✉ 3702 S.E. Hawthorne Blvd., East of Willamette River ☎ 503/236–9234) is a local favorite. The **Kennedy School** (✉ 5736 N.E. 33rd St., East of Willamette River ☎ 503/249–3983) theater is in a renovated elementary school that also contains a bed-and-breakfast and a restaurant. The **Mission Theatre** (✉ 1624 N.W. Glisan, Nob Hill ☎ 503/223–4527) has a popular "Burger, Beer and a Movie" night.

The **Northwest Film Center** (✉ 1219 S.W. Park Ave., Downtown ☎ 503/221–1156 ⊕ www.nwfilm.org), a branch of the Portland Art Museum, screens art films, documentaries, and independent features and presents the three-week Portland International Film Festival in February and March. Films are shown at the Whitsell Auditorium, next to the museum.

THEATER

Artists Repertory Theatre (✉ 1516 S.W. Alder St., Downtown ☎ 503/241–1278 ⊕ www.artistsrep.org) stages seven productions a year—regional premieres, occasional commissioned works, and classics.

Imago Theatre (✉ *17 S.E. 8th Ave., East of Willamette River* ☎ *503/231–9581* ⊕ *www.imagotheatre.com*), considered by some to be Portland's most outstanding innovative theater company, specializes in movement-based work for both young and old.

Ⓒ **Oregon Children's Theatre** (☎ *503/228–9571* ⊕ *www.octc.org*) puts on three or four shows a year at major venues throughout the city for school groups and families.

Ⓒ **Tears of Joy Puppet Theater** (☎ *503/248–0557* ⊕ *www.tojt.org*) stages five children's productions a year at different locations in town.

SHOPPING

One of Portland's greatest attributes is its neighborhoods' dynamic spectrum of retail and specialty shops. The Pearl District is known for chic interior design and high-end clothing boutiques. Trek over to the Hawthorne area and you'll discover wonderful stores for handmade jewelry, clothing, and books. The Northwest has some funky shops for housewares, clothing, and jewelry, while in the Northeast there are fabulous galleries and crafts. Downtown has a blend of it all, as well as bigger options, including the Pioneer Place Mall and department stores such as Nordstrom and Macy's.

No Portland shopping experience would be complete without a visit to the nation's largest open-air market, Saturday Market, where an array of talented artists converge to peddle handcrafted wares beyond your wildest do-it-yourself dreams. It's also open Sunday.

Portland merchants are generally open Monday–Saturday between 9 or 10 AM and 6 PM, and on Sunday noon–6. Most shops in downtown's Pioneer Place, the east side's Lloyd Center, and the outlying malls are open until 9 PM Monday–Saturday and until 6 PM on Sunday.

SHOPPING AREAS

Portland's main shopping area is **downtown,** between Southwest 2nd and 10th avenues and between Southwest Stark and Morrison streets. The major department stores are scattered over several blocks near Pioneer Courthouse Square. Northeast **Broadway** between 10th and 21st avenues is lined with boutiques and specialty shops. **Nob Hill,** north of downtown along Northwest 21st and 23rd avenues, has eclectic clothing, gift, book, and food shops. Most of the city's fine-art galleries are concentrated in the booming **Pearl District,** north from Burnside Street to Marshall Street between Northwest 8th and 15th avenues, along with furniture and design stores. **Sellwood,** 5 mi from the city center, south on Naito Parkway and east across the Sellwood Bridge, has more than 50 antiques and collectibles shops along southeast 13th Avenue, plus specialty shops and outlet stores for sporting goods. You can find the larger antiques stores near the intersection of Milwaukie Avenue and Bybee. **Hawthorne Boulevard** between 30th and 42nd avenues has a selection of alternative bookstores, coffeehouses, antiques stores, and boutiques.

PORTLAND TOP 5 SHOPPING TIPS

■ Munch on a fresh-out-of-the-fryer elephant-ear pastry while perusing aisles of handmade wares at Portland's Saturday Market.

■ Scout for something totally fun and funky at one of Northwest 23rd Avenue's boutique gift shops.

■ Leisurely rifle through racks of clothes at some of Portland's more notable secondhand stores, such as

Buffalo Exchange downtown and Red Light in Hawthorne.

■ Visit Columbia Sportswear downtown to see just how surprisingly fashionable clothing options for every type of outdoor condition can be.

■ Saunter through Powell's City of Books and see what treasures are in its rare-books section.

MALLS AND DEPARTMENT STORES

DOWNTOWN

Shopping downtown is not only fun, it's also easy, thanks to easy transportation access and proximity to many of Portland's hotels. Locally based favorites Nike and Columbia Sportswear both have major stores downtown; REI has one in the Pearl District (⇨ *Outdoor Supplies, below*).

Macy's at Meier & Frank Square (✉ *621 S.W. 5th Ave., Downtown* ☎ *503/223–0512*), until 2005 the main location of the local Meier & Frank chain, has five floors of general merchandise.

Seattle-based **Nordstrom** (✉ *701 S.W. Broadway, Downtown* ☎ *503/224–6666*) sells fine-quality apparel and accessories and has a large footwear department. Bargain lovers should head for the **Nordstrom Rack** (✉ *245 S.W. Morrison St., Downtown* ☎ *503/299–1815*) outlet across from Pioneer Place Mall.

Pioneer Place (✉ *700 S.W. 5th Ave., Downtown* ☎ *503/228–5800*) has more than 80 upscale specialty shops (including April Cornell, Coach, J. Crew, Godiva, and Fossil) in a three-story, glass-roof atrium setting. You can find good, inexpensive ethnic foods from more than a dozen vendors in the Cascades Food Court in the basement. Paradise Bakery is known for fresh home-baked breads and delicious chocolate-chip cookies; Suki Hana has some yummy soups and noodle dishes.

Saks Fifth Avenue (✉ *850 S.W. 5th Ave., Downtown* ☎ *503/226–3200*) has two floors of men's and women's clothing, jewelry, and other merchandise.

BEYOND DOWNTOWN

Once you venture outside of downtown, you can find several major malls and outlets in which to shop 'til you drop. Both Woodburn (30 mi south of Portland) and Troutdale (20 mi east) have outlet malls with dozens of discount name-brand clothing stores.

Portland Saturday Market

EAST OF THE WILLAMETTE RIVER

Clackamas Town Center (✉ *Sunnyside Rd. at I–205 Exit 14, East of Willamette River* ☎ *503/653–6913*) has four major department stores, including Nordstrom and Macy's, as well as more than 180 shops. Discount stores are nearby.

Lloyd Center (✉ *N.E. Multnomah St. at N.E. 9th Ave., East of Willamette River* ☎ *503/282–2511*), on the MAX light-rail line, has more than 170 shops (including Nordstrom, Sears, and Macy's), an international food court, a multiscreen cinema, and an ice-skating pavilion. The mall is within walking distance of Northeast Broadway, which has many specialty shops, boutiques, and restaurants.

SPECIALTY STORES

Portland's specialty stores are as varied and authentic as the city itself. Residents applaud and encourage locally made quirky goods, so stores offering these creative wares are abundant. Discover all the innovative approaches to household items, art, jewelry, and clothing for a fun afternoon.

ANTIQUES

Moreland House (✉ *826 N.W. 23rd Ave., Nob Hill* ☎ *503/222–0197*) has eclectic antiques and gifts, with a notable selection of dog collectibles, old printing-press type, and fresco tiles.

Shogun's Gallery (✉ *1111 N.W. 23rd Ave., Nob Hill* ☎ *503/224–0328*) specializes in Japanese and Chinese furniture, especially the lightweight wooden Japanese cabinets known as *tansu*. Also here are chairs, tea tables, altar tables, armoires, ikebana baskets (originally for flower arrangements), and Chinese wooden picnic boxes, most at least 100 years old and at reasonable prices.

Stars Antique Mall (✉ *7027 S.E. Milwaukie Ave., East of Willamette River* ☎ *503/235–5990* ⊕ *starsantique.com*), Portland's largest antiques mall, has two stores across the street from each other in the Sellwood-Moreland neighborhood. Since it rents its space to about 300 antiques dealers; you might find anything from low-end 1950s kitsch to high-end treasures.

ART DEALERS AND GALLERIES

EVENTS **First Thursday** (☎ *503/295–4979* ⊕ *www.firstthursdayportland.com*) gives art appreciators a chance to check out new exhibits while enjoying music and wine. Typically, the galleries are open in the evening, but hours vary depending on the gallery. Find out what galleries are participating on the Web site.

The Alberta Arts District hosts a **Last Thursday Arts Walk** (☎ *503/972–2206* ⊕ *www.artonalberta.org*) each month.

Many galleries in the **Pearl District** (⊕ *www.firstthursday.org*) host First Thursday events.

GALLERIES **Butters Gallery, Ltd.** (✉ *520 N.W. Davis, Pearl District* ☎ *503/248–9378*) has monthly exhibits of the works of nationally known and local artists in its Pearl District space.

Exit 21 Gallery (✉ *1502 S.E. 21st, East of Willamette River* ☎ *503/867–8495*) has wall-mounted and floor-standing sculptures made from reclaimed materials as well as hand-knitted apparel. They are recognized for supporting local artists and showcasing an eclectic blend of works, with a wide range of prices.

The **Laura Russo Gallery** (✉ *805 N.W. 21st Ave., Nob Hill* ☎ *503/226–2754*) displays contemporary Northwest work of all styles, including landscapes and abstract expressionism.

Emphasizing sustainable and fair trade practices, the **Onda Gallery** (✉ *2215 N.E. Alberta St., East of Willamette River* ☎ *503/493–1909*) is a collective of Northwestern and Latin American artists. Gift items are also for sale.

Pulliam/Deffenbaugh Gallery (✉ *929 N.W. Flanders St., Pearl District* ☎ *503/228–6665*) generally shows contemporary abstract and expressionistic works by Pacific Northwest artists.

Quintana's Galleries of Native American Art (✉ *120 N.W. 9th Ave., Pearl District* ☎ *503/223–1729 or 800/321–1729*) focuses on Pacific North-

2

west Coast, Navajo, and Hopi art and jewelry, along with photogravures by Edward Curtis.

Talisman Gallery (⊠ 1476 N.E. Alberta St., East of Willamette River ☎ 503/284–8800 ⊕ talismangallery.com) showcases two artists each month—they may include local painters and sculptors.

Twist (⊠ 30 N.W. 23rd Pl., Nob Hill ☎ 503/224–0334 ⊠ Pioneer Pl., Downtown ☎ 503/222–3137) has a huge space in Nob Hill and a smaller shop downtown. In Nob Hill are contemporary American ceramics, glass, furniture, sculpture, and handcrafted jewelry; downtown carries an assortment of objects, often with a pop, whimsical touch.

BOOKS

Broadway Books (⊠ 1714 N.E. Broadway, East of Willamette River ☎ 503/284–1726 ⊕ www.broadwaybooks.net) is a fabulous independent bookstore with books on all subjects, including the Pacific Northwest and Judaica.

New Renaissance Bookshop (⊠ 1338 N.W. 23rd Ave., Nob Hill ☎ 503/224–4929), between Overton and Pettygrove, is dedicated to New Age and metaphysical books and tapes.

Fodor's Choice ★ **Powell's City of Books** (⊠ 1005 W. Burnside St., Downtown ☎ 503/228–4651 ⊕ www.powells.com), the largest retail store of used and new books in the world (with more than 1.5 million volumes), covers an entire city block on the edge of the Pearl District. It also carries rare and collectible books. There are also three branches in the Portland International Airport.

Powell's for Cooks and Gardeners (⊠ 3747 Hawthorne Blvd., East of Willamette River ☎ 503/235–3802), on the east side, has a small adjoining grocery.

CLOTHING

Eight Women (⊠ 3614 S.E. Hawthorne Blvd., East of Willamette River ☎ 503/236–8878) is a tiny boutique "for mother and child," with baby clothes, women's nightgowns, jewelry, and handbags.

Hanna Andersson sells high-quality, comfortable clothing for children and families from their **retail store** (⊠ 327 N.W. 10th Ave., Nob Hill ☎ 503/321–5275), next to the company's corporate office, as well as through their **outlet store** (⊠ 7 Monroe Pkwy., Lake Oswego ☎ 503/697–1953) in Oswego Towne Square, south of Portland.

Imelda's Designer Shoes (⊠ 3426 S.E. Hawthorne Blvd., East of Willamette River ☎ 503/233–7476) is an upscale boutique with funky, fun shoes for women with flair.

Magpie (⊠ 520 S.W. 9th St., Downtown ☎ 503/220–0920) sells funky retro garb that dates from the '50s through the '80s. Lots of jewelry, shoes, dresses, coats, and even rhinestone tiaras can be found here.

Portland's best store for fine men's and women's clothing, **Mario's** (⊠ 833 S.W. Morrison St., Downtown ☎ 503/227–3477) carries designer lines by Prada, Dolce & Gabbana, Etro, and Loro Piana—among others.

Niketown (⊠ 930 S.W. 6th Ave., Downtown ☎ 503/221–6453), Nike's flagship retail store, has the latest and greatest in "swoosh"-adorned products. The high-tech setting has athlete profiles, photos, and interactive displays.

Portland Nike Factory Store (⊠ *2650 N.E. Martin Luther King Jr. Blvd., East of Willamette River* ☎ *503/281–5901*) sells products that have been on the market six months or more.

Portland Outdoor Store (⊠ *304 S.W. 3rd Ave., Downtown* ☎ *503/222–1051*) stubbornly resists all that is trendy, both in clothes and decor, but if you want authentic Western gear—saddles, Stetsons, boots, or cowboy shirts—head here.

Portland Pendleton Shop (⊠ *S.W. 4th Ave. and Salmon St., Downtown* ☎ *503/242–0037*) stocks clothing by the famous local apparel maker.

Zelda's Shoe Bar (⊠ *633 N.W. 23rd Ave., Nob Hill* ☎ *503/226–0363*), two connected boutiques in Nob Hill, carries a sophisticated, highly eclectic line of women's clothes, accessories, and shoes.

GIFTS

Babik's (⊠ *738 N.W. 23rd Ave., Nob Hill* ☎ *503/248–1771*) carries an enormous selection of handwoven rugs from Turkey, all made from handspun wool and all-natural dyes.

The **Backyard Bird Shop** (⊠ *8960 S.E. Sunnyside Rd., Clackamas* ☎ *503/496–0908*) has everything for the bird lover: bird feeders, birdhouses, a huge supply of bird seed, and quality bird-theme gifts ranging from wind chimes to stuffed animals.

In addition to offering the best eat-in or take-out soups, salads, and desserts, **Elephants Delicatessen** (⊠ *111 N.W. 22nd Ave., Nob Hill* ☎ *503/299–6304*) has a vast gourmet food, cooking utensils, and household section.

Made in Oregon (☎ *866/257–0938*), which sells books, smoked salmon, local wines, Pendleton woolen goods, carvings made of myrtle wood, and other products made in the state, has shops at Portland International Airport, the Lloyd Center, Washington Square, and Clackamas Town Center.

Even without getting a nod from Oprah in her magazine, **Moonstruck** (⊠ *526 N.W. 23rd Ave., Nob Hill* ☎ *503/542–3400*) would still be known as a chocolatier extraordinaire. Just a couple of the rich confections might sustain you if you're nibbling—water is available for palate cleansing in between treats—but whether you're just grazing or boxing some up for the road, try the Ocumarian Truffle, chocolate laced with chili pepper; the unusual kick of sweetness and warmth is worth experiencing.

At **Stella's on 21st** (⊠ *1108 N.W. 21st Ave., Nob Hill* ☎ *503/295–5930*) there are eccentric, colorful, and artsy items for the home, including lamps, candles, and decorations, as well as jewelry.

OUTDOOR SUPPLIES

Andy and Bax (⊠ *324 S.E. Grand Ave., East of Willamette River* ☎ *503/234–7538*) is an Army-Navy/outdoors store that has good prices on camo gear, rafting supplies, and just about everything else.

Columbia Sportswear (✉ *911 S.W. Broadway, Downtown* ☎ *503/226–6800* ⊕ *www.columbia.com*), a local legend and global force in recreational outdoor wear, is especially strong in fashionable jackets, pants, and durable shoes.

Next Adventure Sports (✉ *426 S.E. Grand Ave., East of Willamette River* ☎ *503/233–0706*) carries new and used sporting goods, including camping gear, snowboards, kayaks, and mountaineering supplies.

REI (✉ *1405 N.W. Johnson St., Pearl District* ☎ *503/221–1938* ⊕ *www. rei.com*) carries clothes and accessories for hiking, biking, camping, fishing, bicycling, or just about any other outdoor activity you can possibly imagine.

PERFUME

Aveda Lifestyle Store and Spa (✉ *500 S.W. 5th Ave., Downtown* ☎ *503/248–0615*) sells the flower- and herb-based Aveda line of scents and skin-care products.

Perfume House (✉ *3328 S.E. Hawthorne Blvd., East of Willamette River* ☎ *503/234–5375*) carries hundreds of brand-name fragrances for women and men.

TOYS

Finnegan's Toys and Gifts (✉ *922 S.W. Yamhill St., Downtown* ☎ *503/221–0306*), downtown Portland's largest toy store, stocks artistic, creative, educational, and other types of toys.

Kids at Heart (✉ *3445 S.E. Hawthorne Blvd., East of Willamette River* ☎ *503/231–2954*) is a small, colorful toy store on Hawthorne with toys, models, and stuffed animals for kids of all ages.

Thinker Toys (✉ *7784 S.W. Capitol Hwy., West of Downtown* ☎ *503/245–3936*), which bills itself as Portland's "most hands-on store," offers puppets, games, educational toys, and a large wooden play house that kids can hang out in.

SPORTS AND THE OUTDOORS

Portlanders definitely gravitate to the outdoors, and they're well acclimated to the elements year-round—including winter's wind, rain, and cold. Once the sun starts to shine in spring and into summer, the city fills with hikers, joggers, and mountain bikers, who flock to Portland's hundreds of miles of parks, paths, and trails. The Willamette and Columbia rivers are used for boating and water sports—though it's not easy to rent any kind of boat for casual use. Locals also have access to a playground for fishing, camping, skiing, and snowboarding all the way through June, thanks to the proximity of Mt. Hood.

BICYCLING

Fodor's Choice
★   Bicycling is a cultural phenomenon in Portland—possibly the most beloved mode of transportation in the city. Besides the sheer numbers of cyclists you see on roads and pathways, you'll find well-marked bike lanes and signs reminding motorists to yield to cyclists.

BIKE RENTALS

Bikes can be rented at several places in the city. Rentals typically run from $20 to $50 per day with cheaper weekly rates from $75 to $150. Bike helmets are generally included in the cost of rental.

CityBikes Workers Cooperative (⊠ *734 S.E. Ankeny St., East of Willamette River* ☎ *503/239–6951*) rents hybrid bikes good for casual city riding.

Fat Tire Farm (⊠ *2714 N.W. Thurman St., West of Downtown* ☎ *503/222–3276*) rents mountain bikes, great for treks in Forest Park.

Waterfront Bicycle Rentals (⊠ *315 S.W. Montgomery St., Suite 3, Downtown* ☎ *503/227–1719*) is convenient for jaunts along the Willamette.

BIKING ROUTES

There are more than 300 mi of bicycle boulevards, lanes, and off-street paths in Portland. Accessible maps, specialized tours, parking capacity (including lockers and sheltered racks downtown), and bicycle-only traffic signals at confusing intersections make biking in the city easy. Cyclists can find the best routes by following green direction-and-distance signs that point the way around town, and the corresponding white dots on the street surface.

For more information on bike routes and resources in and around Portland, visit the **Department of Transportation** (⊕ *www.portlandonline. com/transportation*). You can download maps, or order "Bike There," a glossy detailed bicycle map of the metropolitan area.

If you're a social rider, group rides set out from several local shops. Check the events pages of **Bike Gallery** (⊕ *www.bikegallery.com*), **River City Bicycles** (⊕ *www.rivercitybicycles.com*), and **Fat Tire Farm** (⊕ *www. fattirefarm.com*).

The **Columbia Historic Highway** begins 17 mi east of Portland on U.S. 84 and rolls almost 90 mi along the Columbia River Gorge. This National Scenic Area will take you past a series of thundering waterfalls toward sporty Hood River, Oregon. You can shorten the route by turning around after the awe-inspiring river view at Mile 12, or after a breathtaking descent to Multnomah Falls at Mile 18. Many riders begin and end at McMenamins Edgefield, a comfortable resort where anyone (not just guests) can get a warm shower, cold beer, and good meal. Reach the Edgefield by bike, or shuttle there via TriMet's Bus 77

Leif Erikson Drive is an 11-mi off-road ride through Northwest Portland's Forest Park, accessible from the serene west end of Northwest Thurman Street. Leif's wide, doubletrack trail is popular with runners and mountain bikers, winding through a 5,000-acre city park far from the noise and distraction of neighborhood traffic. Its dense canopy occasionally gives way to river views. To reach the trailhead, bike up steep Thurman Street or shuttle there via TriMet Bus 15.

Bicycling **Sauvie Island**'s 12-mi loop is a rare treat. Situated near the mouth of the Willamette River and Columbia Slough, the island is entirely rural farmland. Besides the main loop, it also offers out-and-back jaunts to beaches and pristine wetlands. To get to Sauvie Island from Portland, you can brave the 10-mi ride in the wide bike lane of U.S. 30, or shuttle your bike there via TriMet Bus 17.

Runners crossing the Hawthorne Bridge

Bike paths on both sides of the **Willamette River** continue south of downtown, so you can easily make a mild, several-mile loop through Waterfront Park by crossing the Steel, Hawthorne, or Sellwood bridges to get from one side to the other.

FISHING

The Columbia and Willamette rivers are major sportfishing streams, with opportunities for angling virtually year-round. Though salmon can still be caught here, runs have been greatly reduced in both rivers in recent years, and the Willamette River is still plagued by pollution. Nevertheless, the Willamette still offers prime fishing for bass, channel catfish, sturgeon, crappies, perch, panfish, and crayfish. It's also a good stream for winter steelhead. June is the top shad month, with some of the best fishing occurring below Willamette Falls at Oregon City. The Columbia River is known for its salmon, sturgeon, walleye, and smelt. The Sandy and Clackamas rivers, near Mt. Hood, are smaller waterways popular with local anglers.

OUTFITTERS Outfitters throughout Portland operate guide services. Few outfitters rent equipment, though, so bring your own or be prepared to buy. **Northwest Flyfishing Outfitters** (✉ *10910 N.E. Halsey St., East of Willamette River* ☎ *503/252–1529 or 888/292–1137*) specializes in all things flyfishing, including tackle, rentals, and guided outings.

You can find a broad selection of fishing gear, including rods, reels, and fishing licenses, at **Stewart Fly Shop** (✉ *23830 N.E. Halsey St., East of Willamette River* ☎ *503/666–2471*).

Local sport shops are the best sources of information on current fishing hot spots, which change from year to year. Detailed fishing regulations are available from the **Oregon Department of Fish and Wildlife** (✉ *17330 S.E. Evelyn St., Clackamas* ☎ *503/947–6000* ⊕ *www.dfw.state.or.us*).

GOLF

There are several public and top-class golf courses within Portland and just outside the city where you can practice your putt or test your swing. Even in the wet months, Portlanders still golf—and you can bet the first clear day after a wet spell will mean courses fill up with those who have so faithfully waited for the sun. Depending upon the time of year, it's not a bad idea to call ahead and verify wait times.

At the 18-hole, par-72 **Colwood National Golf Club** (✉ *7313 N.E. Columbia Blvd., East of Willamette River* ☎ *503/254–5515*), the greens fees are $29–$33, plus $26 for an optional cart.

Heron Lakes Golf Course (✉ *3500 N. Victory Blvd., west of airport, off N. Marine Dr.* ☎ *503/289–1818*) consists of two 18-hole, par-72 courses: the Great Blue, generally acknowledged to be the most difficult links in the greater Portland area; and the Greenback. The greens fees at the Green, as it's locally known, are $26–$37, while the fees at the Blue run $30–$42. An optional cart at either course costs $26.

Pumpkin Ridge Golf Club (✉ *12930 N.W. Old Pumpkin Ridge Rd., North Plains* ☎ *503/647–4747 or 888/594–4653* ⊕ *www.pumpkinridge.com*) has 36 holes, with the 18-hole Ghost Creek par-71 course open to the public. According to *Golf Digest*, Ghost Creek is one of the best public courses in the nation. Pumpkin Ridge hosted the U.S. Women's Open in 1997 and in 2003. The greens fees are $150; the cart fee is $16.

Rose City Golf Course (✉ *2200 N.E. 71st Ave., East of Willamette River* ☎ *503/253–4744*) has one 18-hole, par-72 course. Greens fees are $28–$35; carts are $26 for 18 holes.

PARKS

Portland aspired to be a city of parks starting in 1852. Those first parks (now known as the Plaza Blocks and South Park Blocks) were designed to help residents enjoy the simple things in life, and to steer them away from those darker ones that tempted good Portlanders (ahem, beer). These days, more than 12,000 acres of parks and open spaces in more than 250 locations house six public gardens, 204 parks, five golf courses, and thousands of acres of urban forest.

True to the city's nicknames, Rose City or City of Roses, the fragrant favorite is found at many of the area's parks. There is no one official reason for the city's moniker, but many suggested ones. The first known reference was in 1888 at an Episcopal Church convention. And though the first Rose Festival was held in 1907, the city did not officially take the nickname until 2003.

The following parks are our top picks. After each listing, the ⛄ specifies who will especially enjoy the park. Washington Park and its gardens are not listed here; please see Washington Park for those listings.

Cathedral Park. Whether it's the view of the imposing and stunning Gothic St. John's Bridge or the historic significance of Lewis and Clark's having camped here in 1806, this park is divine. Though there's no church, the park gets its name from the picturesque arches supporting the bridge. It's rumored that the ghost of a young girl haunts the bridge, and that may be true, but if you're told that it was designed by the same man who envisioned the Golden Gate Bridge, that's just a popular misconception. Dog lovers, or those who aren't, should take note of the off-leash area. ⊠ *N. Edison St. and Pittsburg Ave., East of Willamette* ⏱ 5 AM—*midnight*⛄ *Good for: bridge buffs, dog lovers, ghost hunters, history lovers.*

Council Crest Park. The second-highest point in Portland, at 1,073 feet, is a superb spot to watch sunsets and sunrises. If you visit on a weekday, there are far fewer folks than on the busy weekends. Along with great views of the Portland metro area, a clear day also affords views of the surrounding peaks—Mt. Hood, Mt. St. Helens, Mt. Adams, Mt. Jefferson, and Mt. Rainier. A bronze fountain depicting a mother and child has been erected in the park twice; first in the 1950s and the second in the 1990s. The peaceful piece was stolen in the 1980s, uncovered in a narcotics bust ten years later, and then returned to the park. ⊠ *3400 Council Crest Dr., West of Downtown* ⏱ 5 AM–*midnight, closed to cars after 9* PM⛄ *Good for: picnickers, view seekers.*

Forest Park. One of the nation's largest urban wildernesses (5,000 acres), this city-owned, car-free park has more than 50 species of birds and mammals and more than 70 mi of trails. Running the length of the park is the 24½-mi Wildwood Trail, which extends into Washington Park. The 11-mi Leif Erikson Drive, which picks up from the end of Northwest Thurman Street, is a popular place to jog or ride a mountain bike. The **Portland Audubon Society** (⊠ *5151 N.W. Cornell Rd.* ☎ *503/292–6855* ⊕ *www.audubonportland.org*) supplies free maps and sponsors a flock of bird-related activities, including guided bird-watching events. There's a hospital for injured and orphaned birds as well as a gift shop stocked with books and feeders. ⊠ *Past Nob Hill in Northwest District* ☎ *503/823–7529* ⊕ *www.forestparkconservancy. org* ⏱ *Daily dawn–dusk* ⛄ *Good for: hikers, nature lovers, photographers, bird-watchers, mountain bikers.*

Fodor's Choice
★
Governor Tom McCall Waterfront Park. Named for a former governor revered for his statewide land-use planning initiatives, this park stretches north along the Willamette River for about a mile to Burnside Street. Broad and grassy, Waterfront Park's got a fine ground-level view of downtown Portland's bridges and skyline. Once an expressway, it's now the site for many events, among them the Rose Festival, classical and blues concerts, Cinco de Mayo, and the Oregon Brewers Festival. The arching jets of water at the **Salmon Street Fountain** change configuration every few hours, and are a favorite cooling-off spot during the dog days of summer. ⊠ *S.W. Naito Pkwy. (Front Ave.), from south*

of Hawthorne Bridge to Burnside Bridge, Downtown ⌂ Good For: families, bikers, walkers, runners.

Fodor's Choice
★

Laurelhurst Park. Completed in 1914, resplendent Laurelhurst Park is evocative of another time, and gives you the urge to don a parasol. It's no wonder that it was the first park to be put on the National Register of Historic Places. Take a stroll around the large spring-fed pond (granted a bit murky with algae) and keep an eye out for blue heron, the city's official bird. On the south side of this 26-acre park is one of the busiest basketball courts in town. Though the park is always beautiful, it is especially so in fall. ⊠ *SE 39th Ave. and Stark St., East of Willamette River ☉ 5 AM–10:30 PM ⌂ Good for: basketballers, dog lovers, anglers, picnickers, runners, nappers, lovers, volleyballers, horseshoes players.*

Marquam Nature Park. Itching to get a hike in but no time to get out of Portland? Just minutes from downtown are 176 acres of greenery and five miles of trails to explore. No playgrounds or dog parks here, just peace and quiet. Maps of trails that range from 1 to 3.5 miles are available at the shelter at the base of the trails or on the Friends of Marquam Park website. ⊠ *S.W. Marquam St. and Sam Jackson Park Rd., West of Downtown ⊕ www.fmp.org ☉ 5 AM–midnight ⌂ Good for: nature lovers, hikers, solitude seekers.*

Mt. Tabor Park. A playground on top of a volcano cinder cone? Yup, that's here. The cinders, or glassy rock fragments, unearthed in the park's construction, were used to surface the respite's roads; the ones leading to the top are closed to cars, but popular with cyclists. They're also popular with cruisers—each August there's an old-fashioned soapbox derby. Picnic tables and tennis, basketball, and volleyball courts make Mt. Tabor Park perfection. ⊠ *S.E. 60th and Salmon Sts., East of Willamette River ☉ 5 AM–midnight ⌂ Good for: families, picnickers, dog lovers, geologists, walkers, cyclists, sunset seekers.*

Fodor's Choice
★

Oaks Bottom Wild Refuge. Bring your binoculars, because birds are plentiful here; more than 400 species have been spotted, including hawks, quail, pintails, mallards, coots, woodpeckers, kestrels, widgeons, hummingbirds, and the sedately beautiful blue heron. The 140-acre refuge is a flood-plain wetland—rare because it is in the heart of the city. The hiking isn't too strenuous, but wear sturdy shoes, as it can get muddy; part of the park is on top of a landfill layered with soil. ⊠ *S.E. 7th and Sellwood Ave., East of the Willamette ☉ 5 AM–midnight ⌂ Good for: bird-watchers, hikers, cyclists.*

Fodor's Choice
★

Peninsula Park & Rose Garden. The "City of Roses" moniker started here, at this park that harks back to another time. The city's oldest (1909) public rose garden (and the only sunken one), houses almost nine thousand plantings and 65 varieties of roses. The daunting task of deadheading all these flowers is covered in classes taught to volunteers twice a season. The bandstand is a historic landmark, and the last of its kind in the city. There's also a 100-year-old fountain, playground, wading pool, tennis and volleyball courts, and picnic tables. ⊠ *700 N. Rosa Parks Way, East of the Willamette ☉ 5 AM–midnight ⌂ Good for: botanists, gardeners, runners, picnickers, romantics.*

DID YOU KNOW?

With a river running through the center of the city, Portland has one of the most interesting urban landscapes in the country, due in no small part to the several unique bridges that span the width of the Willamette River. Five of the city's 10 bridges are drawbridges that must be frequently raised to let barges go through, and there's something awe-inspiring and anachronistic in watching a portion of a city's traffic and hubbub stand still for several minutes as a slow-moving vessel floats through still water. Each bridge is beautiful and different: the St. John's Bridge has elegant 400-foot towers, the Broadway Bridge is a rich red hue, the arches of the huge two-level Fremont Bridge span the river gracefully, and the Steel Bridge has a pedestrian walkway just 30 feet above the water, allowing walkers and bikers to get a fabulous view of the river.

Tryon Creek State Natural Area. Portland is chock-full of parks, but this is the only state park within city limits. And at 670 acres, there's plenty of room for all its admirers. The area was logged starting in the 1880s, and the natural regrowth has produced red alder, Douglas fir, big leaf maple, and western red cedar, giving home to more than 50 bird species. The eastern edge has a paved trail, in addition to 14 miles of trails for bikes, hikers, and horses. Before heading to the trails, stop by the nature center to check out the exhibits and topographical relief map. ⊠ *S.W. Boones Ferry Rd. and Terwilliger Blvd., West of Downtown* ☎ *503/636–4398* ⊕ *www.tryonfriends.org* ☉ *Daily 7 AM–8 PM, Nature Center 9–4.* ⤓ *Good for: cyclists, bird-watchers, walkers, hikers.*

SPECTATOR SPORTS

Since Portland isn't home to a large national football or baseball team, fans tend to show a lot of support for their city's only true professional team, the NBA's Portland Trail Blazers. Fans are also loyal in cheering on their minor-league teams: hockey, auto racing, baseball, and soccer events are well-attended by excited crowds.

AUTO RACING

Portland International Raceway (⊠ *West Delta Park, 1940 N. Victory Blvd., west of I–5, along Columbia Slough* ☎ *503/823–7223*) presents bicycle and drag racing and motocross on weeknights and sports-car, motorcycle, and go-kart racing on weekends April–September.

BASKETBALL

The **Portland Trail Blazers** (⊠ *Rose Garden, 1 Center Ct., East of Willamette River* ☎ *503/797–9617*) of the National Basketball Association play in the Rose Garden.

ICE HOCKEY

The **Portland Winter Hawks** (✉ *Memorial Coliseum, 300 N. Winning Way, East of Willamette River* ☎ *503/236–4295*) of the Western Hockey League play home games September–March at Memorial Colisium and sometimes at the Rose Garden.

SOCCER

The **Portland Timbers** (✉ *PGE Park, 1844 S.W. Morrison St., Downtown* ☎ *503/553–5550 for Portland Timbers office, 503/553–5400 for PGE Park*), Portland's major-league Soccer team, play at the downtown PGE Park from April through September.

SKIING

With fairly easy access to decent skiing nearly eight months out of the year, it's no wonder that skiers love Portland. There are several ski resorts on Mt. Hood, less than an hour's drive away, including Ski Bowl, Mt. Hood Meadows, and Timberline Lodge.

Mountain Shop (✉ *628 N.E. Broadway, East of Willamette River* ☎ *503/288–6768*) rents skis and equipment. **REI** (✉ *1405 N.W. Johnson St., Pearl District* ☎ *503/221–1938*) can fill all your ski-equipment rental needs.

The Oregon Coast

WORD OF MOUTH

"I think the south coast, between Port Orford and Brookings, is the most dramatic. Might have something to do with the fact that it's also the most isolated."

—passerbye

WELCOME TO THE OREGON COAST

TOP REASONS TO GO

★ **A beach for everyone.** The Oregon Coast has breathtaking beaches, from romantic, bluffy stretches perfect for linking fingers with loved ones to creature-teeming tide pools great for exploring with kids.

★ **Blow a glass float.** Glass artisan shops dot the coast-line, where you can craft your own colorful creations.

★ **Ride the dunes.** Whether you're a screaming dune-buggy passenger or an ATV daredevil, southern Oregon's mountainous sand dunes are thrilling.

★ **Par a hole.** Oregon's golf Shangri-La, Bandon Dunes, has four beach courses of pure bliss.

★ **Wine and dine.** You don't have to spend a lot to enjoy fresh seafood, rich microbrews, and local wines. There are delicious coastal eateries for every budget.

1 North Coast. The north coast is the primary getaway for Portland and Vancouver residents. Its lighthouse-dotted shoreline stretches from the mouth of the Columbia River at Oregon's far northwestern corner south to Pacific City. The 90-mile region includes the revitalized working community of Astoria, the vacation town of Seaside, the art-fueled and refined Cannon Beach, the well-photographed Manzanita Beach, the dairy paradise of Tillamook, and Pacific City, where a colorful fleet of dories dots the wide, deep beach.

2 Central Coast. The 75-mile stretch from Lincoln City to Florence offers whale-watching, incomparable seafood, shell-covered beaches, candy confections, and close-up views of undersea life. At the north end, in Lincoln City, visitors can indulge in gaming, shopping, golfing, and beachcombing. The harbor town of Depoe Bay is a center for whale-watching, and nearby Newport offers a stellar aquarium and science center. It's also home to one of Oregon's largest fishing fleets. Yachats is a true vacation community, where the only demands are to relax and enjoy. Visitors will want to check in at the Sea Lion Caves in Florence, and enjoy crabbing, shopping, or riding the Oregon dunes.

3 South Coast. From the heart of Oregon dunes country in Reedsport to the southernmost Oregon town of Brookings, riding, hiking, and even surfing along the 134-mile south coast is a rollicking thrill. North Bend and Coos Bay are centers for timber, commercial fishing, and commerce. There's also clamming, gaming, sport fishing, and plenty of shopping. Bandon offers a wealth of golfing, camping, lighthouse gazing, and cranberries. Port Orford has gorgeous beach landscapes and windsailing, while Gold Beach, farther south, bathes in sunshine, and gives its visitors a chance to rip up the Rogue River on a jet boat. At Oregon's farthest southwestern corner is Brookings—the "Banana Belt" of the Oregon Coast.

3

GETTING ORIENTED

Oregon's coastline begins in the north in the town of Astoria, which lies at the mouth of the Columbia River on the Washington state line. It is a 363-mile drive south along U.S. Highway 101 to reach the small town of Brookings at Oregon's southwestern corner, just six miles from the California border. The Oregon Coast is bordered by the Pacific Ocean on the left and by the Coast Range on the right. Farther east across the Coast Range is the Willamette Valley, which includes the larger Oregon communities of Portland, Salem, Corvallis, and Eugene.

WASHINGTON

Columbia River

Astoria
Seaside
Cannon Beach **1**
Manzanita
Tillamook Bay
Tillamook
Pacific City
Lincoln City
Gleneden Beach
Depoe Bay
Yaquina Head Toledo
Newport
Waldport
Yachats
Florence
Reedsport
Oregon Dunes National Recreation Area
North Bend
Coos Bay
Bandon
Port Orford
Agness
Gold Beach
Brookings

Portland
McMinnville
Salem
Corvallis
Eugene

Tillamook State Forest
Mt. Hood National Forest
Willamette National Forest
Siuslaw National Forest **2**
COAST RANGE
WILLAMETTE VALLEY
Roseburg
UMPQUA VALLEY
Umpqua National Forest
Crater Lake National Park
Rogue River National Forest
Siskiyou National Forest
Grants Pass
Medford
Cave Junction
Ashland

PACIFIC OCEAN

3

CALIFORNIA

0   30 miles
0   30 kilometers

THE OREGON COAST PLANNER

When to Go

December through June are generally rainy months, but once the fair weather comes coastal Oregon is one of the most gorgeous, greenest places on earth. July through September offer wonderful, dry days for beachgoers.

Even with the rain, coastal winter and spring do have quite a following. Many hotels are perfectly situated for storm-watching, and provide a romantic proposition. Think of a toasty fire, sweet music, a smooth Oregon pinot, and your loved one, settled in to watch the waves dance upon a jagged rocky stage.

If you're looking for one time of year to experience what friendly frivolity can be found on the coast, check out the **Cannon Beach Sandcastle Contest** in May—if you can find a room or a parking spot. The **Newport Seafood and Wine Festival** occurs the last full weekend in February, and calls itself the premier seafood and wine event of the West Coast. Dozens of wineries are represented at this expansive celebration, which also features myriad crafts and eateries. In Bandon each October the **Cranberry Festival** comprises a fair and parade.

Getting Here and Around

Air Travel. The north coast is accessible from **Astoria Regional Airport** (AST) (☎ 800/860–4093 or 503/325–4521), which has daily flights from Portland on SeaPort Airlines. The central coast has daily flights into **Newport Municipal Airport** (ONP) (☎ 800/424–3655 or 541/867–3655) on SeaPort Airlines. The southern coast has flights from its new **Southwest Oregon Regional Airport** (OTH) (☎ 541/756–8531) in North Bend to Portland and San Francisco on United Express. Taxis are available at all airports; Hertz car rental is at the Astoria and Southwest airports.

Portland's airport is roughly 100 miles away from both Astoria and Lincoln City, and the drive takes about two hours; Newport is 150 miles and a 3-hour drive away. **PDX Shuttle Portland** (☎ 503/740–9485 ⊕ pdxshuttleportland. com) provides service from Portland's airport to the coast for around $200. **OmniShuttle** (☎ 800/741–5097) provides shuttle service from Eugene airport to the coast. The fare to Yachats is $135. It is more economical to rent a car.

Bus Travel. Greyhound (☎ 800/231–2222 ⊕ www. greyhound.com) serves Coos Bay, Newport, Toledo, and Waldport, connecting them with Corvallis, Salem, and Portland. **Sunset Empire Transportation** (☎ 503/861–7433 ⊕ www.ridethebus.org) travels between Portland and Astoria Monday, Wednesday, and Friday, and serves the north coast cities of Astoria, Warrenton, Hammond, Gearhart, Seaside, and Cannon Beach. **Porter Stage Lines** (☎ 541/269–7183) connects the Florence and Coos Bay area with Eugene.

Car Travel. Driving the coast is one of the singular pleasures of visiting Oregon. Car-rental agencies are available in the coast's larger towns; a branch of Enterprise is in Newport, Hertz is at the airports. U.S. 101 runs the length of the coast, sometimes turning inland for a few miles. The highway enters coastal Oregon from Washington State at Astoria and from California near Brookings. U.S. 30 heads west from Portland to Astoria. U.S. 20 travels west from Corvallis to Newport. Highway 126 winds west to the coast from Eugene. Highway 42 leads west from Roseburg toward Coos Bay.

About the Restaurants

Deciding which restaurant has the best clam chowder is just one of the culinary fact-finding expeditions you can embark upon along the Oregon Coast. Chefs here take full advantage of the wealth of sturgeon, chinook, steelhead, and trout found in coastal rivers. Fresh mussels, shrimp, and oyster shooters are also standard fare in many establishments. Newport's bounty is its Dungeness crab. When razor clams are in season, they appear as a succulent addition to restaurant menus throughout the state. Also popular are desserts made from Oregon's wealth of blueberries, marionberries, and huckleberries.

Away from the upscale resorts, most restaurants tend to be low-key and affordable. There are many hearty pizza establishments, and tasty fish-and-chips are easy to come by. In addition, Oregon Coast restaurants proudly serve reds and whites from Willamette Valley wineries and rich ales from local or on-site breweries.

About the Hotels

The Oregon Coast offers a pleasant variety of properties for visitors who either wish to wallow in luxury, stay at a beachside golf course, watch storms through picture windows, or take river-running fishing trips. There are plenty of chains in the area, as well as an eclectic assortment of properties: fascinating bed-and-breakfasts hosted by friendly folks with stories to tell, properties perched on cliffs, and hotels set in the midst of wilderness and hiking trails.

Properties in Seaside and Lincoln City fill up fast in the summer, so book in advance. Between June and October hotel rates nudge up for many properties, but with some research you'll find plenty that keep their rates fairly steady throughout the year. Many will require a minimum two-night stay on a summer weekend.

WHAT IT COSTS IN U.S. DOLLARS

	¢	$	$$	$$$	$$$$
Restaurants	under $10	$10–$16	$17–$23	$24–$30	over $30
Hotels	under $100	$101–$150	$151–$200	$201–$250	over $250

Restaurant prices are per person, for a main course at dinner. Hotel prices are for two people in a standard double room in high season, excluding tax.

Tour Options

Marine Discovery Tours (✉ Newport ☎ 800/903–2628) conducts a sealife cruise. The 65-foot excursion boat *Discovery*, with inside seating for 49 people and two viewing levels, departs throughout the day. Its public cruise season is March–October, while reserved group tours are welcome throughout the year.

NorthWest EcoExcursions (✉ Depoe Bay ☎ 541/765–2598 ⊕ www.nwecoexcursions.com) has kayaking, hiking, and whale-watching tours at various levels of difficulty. Its guides are experienced naturalists, with backgrounds in park-ranger service and education.

VISITOR INFORMATION

Central Oregon Coast Association (✉ 137 N.E. 1st St., Newport, ☎ 503/265–2064 or 800/767–2064 ⊕ www.coastvisitor.com). **Eugene, Cascades & Coast Adventure Center** (✉ 3312 Gateway St., Springfield ☎ 541/484–5307 ⊕ www.travellanecounty.org). **Oregon Coast Visitors Association** (✉ 137 N.E. 1st St., Newport ☎ 541/574–2679 or 888/628–2101 ⊕ www.visittheoregoncoast.com).

3

EXPLORING OREGON'S BEST BEACHES

Oregon's 300 miles of public coastline is the backdrop for thrills, serenity, rejuvenation, and romance. From yawning expanses of sand dotted with beach chairs to tiny patches bounded by surf-shaped cliffs, they're yours to explore.

(above) Surfing the Oregon Coast. (opposite page, top) Oregon Dunes National Recreation Area. (opposite page, bottom) Cannon Beach Sandcastle Contest

Most awe-inspiring are the massive rock formations just offshore in the northern and southern sections of the coast, breaking up the Pacific horizon. Beaches along the north coast, from Astoria to Pacific City, are perfect for romantic strolls on the sands. The central-coast beaches, from Lincoln City to Florence, are long and wide, providing perfect conditions for sunbathers, children, clam-diggers, horseback riders, and surfers. The southern-coast beaches from Reedsport to Brookings are less populated, ideal for getting away from it all.

In late July and August the climate is kind to sun worshipers. During the shoulder months, keep layers of clothing handy for the unpredictable temperature swings. Winter can be downright blustery, but plenty of beachfront hotels cater to visitors who enjoy bundling up to walk along the wet, wind-whipped surf.

—by Deston S. Nokes

GLASS FLOATS: FINDERS KEEPERS

Since 1997, between mid October and Memorial Day, more than 2,000 handcrafted glass floats made by local artists have been hidden along Lincoln City's 7.5 mi public beach. If you happen to come upon one, call *800/452-2151* to register it, and find out which artist made it. While antique glass floats are extremely rare, these new versions make great souvenirs.

FODOR'S CHOICE BEACHES

Cannon Beach. In the shadow of glorious **Haystack Rock**, this beach is wide, flat, and perfect for bird-watching, exploring tide pools, building sandcastles, and romantic walks in the sea mist. Each June the city holds a **sandcastle contest**, drawing artists and thousands of visitors. The rest of the year the beach is far less populated. The beachfront town is a cultural destination featuring much of Oregon's finest dining, lodging, and boutique shopping.

Pacific City. This beach is postcard perfect, with its colorful fleet of dories sitting on the sand. Dozens of them lie tilted in between early-morning fishing excursions to catch lingcod, surf perch, and rockfish. Like Cannon Beach, this town also has a huge (less famous) Haystack Rock that provides the perfect scenic backdrop for horseback riders, beachcombers, and people with shovels chasing sand-covered clams. With safe beach breaks that are ideal for beginners and larger peaks a bit to the south, this is a great spot for surfers. Storm-watchers love Pacific City, where winds exceeding 75 miles per hour twist Sitka spruce, and tides deposit driftwood and logs on the beach. Most stay inside to watch, but there are plenty of bold (or crazy) folks who enjoy the blast in their faces.

Samuel H. Boardman State Scenic Corridor. It doesn't get any wilder than this—or

more spectacular. The 12-mile strip of forested, rugged coastline is dotted with smaller sand beaches, some more accessible than others. Here visitors will find the amazing **Arch Rock** and **Natural Bridges** and can hike 27 miles of the **Oregon Coast Trail**. Beach highlights include **Whaleshead Beach, Secret Beach**, and **Thunder Rock Cove**, where you might spot migrating gray whales. From the 345-foot-high **Thomas Creek Bridge** you can take a moderately difficult hike down to admire the gorgeous, jagged rocks off **China Beach**.

Winchester Bay. One reason the Pacific Northwest isn't known for its amusement parks is because nature hurls more thrills than any rattling contraption could ever provide. This certainly is true at **Oregon Dunes National Recreation Area.** Here riders of all-terrain vehicles (ATVs) will encounter some of the most radical slips, dips, hills, and chills in the nation. It is the largest expanse of coastal sand dunes in North America, extending for 40 miles, from Florence to Coos Bay. More than 1.5 million people visit the dunes each year. For those who just want to swim, relax, and marvel at the amazing expanse of dunes against the ocean, there are spaces off-limits to motorized vehicles. Overlooking the beach is the gorgeous **Umpqua River Lighthouse**.

Updated by
Deston S.
Nokes

The Oregon Coast truly epitomizes the finest in Pacific Northwest living. Thanks to its friendly seaside towns, outstanding fresh seafood, and cozy wine bars sprinkled among small hotels and resorts, visitors have the region's finest choices for sightseeing, dining, and lodging. But the true draw here is the beaches, where nature lovers will delight at their first site of a migrating whale or a baby harbor seal sitting on a rock.

Oregon's coastline is open to all; not a grain of its 300 mi of white-sand beaches is privately owned. The coast's large and small communities are linked by U.S. Highway 101, which runs the length of the state. It winds past sea-tortured rocks, brooding headlands, hidden beaches, historic lighthouses, and tiny ports. This is one of the most picturesque driving routes in the country, and should not be missed. Embracing it is the vast, gunmetal-gray Pacific Ocean, which presents a range of moods with the seasons. On summer evenings it might be glassy and reflective of a romantic sunset. In winter the ocean might throw a thrilling tantrum for storm-watchers sitting snug and safe in a beachfront cabin.

Active visitors can indulge in thrills from racing up a sand dune in a buggy to making par at Bandon Dunes, one of the nation's finest golf experiences. Bicyclists can pedal along misty coastline vistas, cruising past historic lighthouses. Boaters can explore southern-coast rivers on jet boats, or shoot a rapid on a raft. If the weather turns, indoor venues such as the Oregon Coast Aquarium capture the imagination.

Shoppers will be equally engaged perusing fine-art galleries in Toledo or Cannon Beach; for more quirky shopping fun, giggle in the souvenir shops of Seaside or Lincoln City while eating fistfuls of caramel corn or chewing saltwater taffy.

NORTH COAST

Every winter Astoria celebrates fisherman poets: hardworking men and women who bare their souls as to what makes their relationship to Oregon's north-coast waters so magical. It's easy to understand their inspiration, whether in the incredibly tempestuous ocean or the romantic beaches. Throw in Victorian homes, tony art galleries, and memorable wine bars and restaurants, and you have yourself one heck of a vacation.

This is the primary beach playground for residents of Portland. What distinguishes the region historically from other areas of the Oregon Coast are its forts, its graveyard of shipwrecks, Lewis and Clark's early visit, and a town—Astoria—that is closer in design and misty temperament to San Francisco than any other in the West. It has more amazing cheese, quality ales, and fine-dining venues than any other coastal town.

ASTORIA

96 mi northwest of Portland on U.S. 30.

The mighty Columbia River meets the Pacific at Astoria, the oldest city west of the Rockies. It is named for John Jacob Astor, owner of the Pacific Fur Company, whose members arrived in 1811 and established Fort Astoria. In its early days Astoria was a placid amalgamation of small town and hard-working port city. With rivers rich with salmon, the city relied on its fishing and canning industries. Settlers built sprawling Victorian houses on the flanks of Coxcomb Hill; many of the homes have since been restored and are no less splendid as bed-and-breakfast inns. In recent years the city itself has awakened with a greater variety of trendy dining and lodging options, staking its claim as a destination resort town. But it retains the soul of a fisherman's town, celebrated each February during its Fisher Poets Gathering.

GETTING HERE

Astoria is about a two-hour drive from Portland on U.S. Highway 30. It's also accessible from Washington on U.S. Highway 101. Sea-Port Airlines offers an air shuttle between Portland and Seattle and Astoria's airport. The airport is 7 miles from downtown Astoria, with taxi service and car rental available. **Sunset Empire** (☎ *503/861-7433* ⊕ *www.ridethebus.org*) buses connect Portland with the northern coastal cities of Astoria, Warrenton, Hammond, Gearhart, Seaside, and Cannon Beach.

VISITOR INFORMATION

Astoria–Warrenton Area Chamber of Commerce (✉ *111 W. Marine Dr., Astoria* ☎ *503/325–6311 or 800/875–6807* ⊕ *www.oldoregon.com*).

EXPLORING

Astoria Column. For the best view of the city, the Coast Range, volcanic Mt. St. Helens, and the Pacific Ocean, scamper up the 164 spiral stairs to the top of the Astoria Column. When you get to the top, you can throw a small wooden plane and watch it glide to earth; each year some 35,000 gliders are tossed. The 125-foot-high structure sits atop

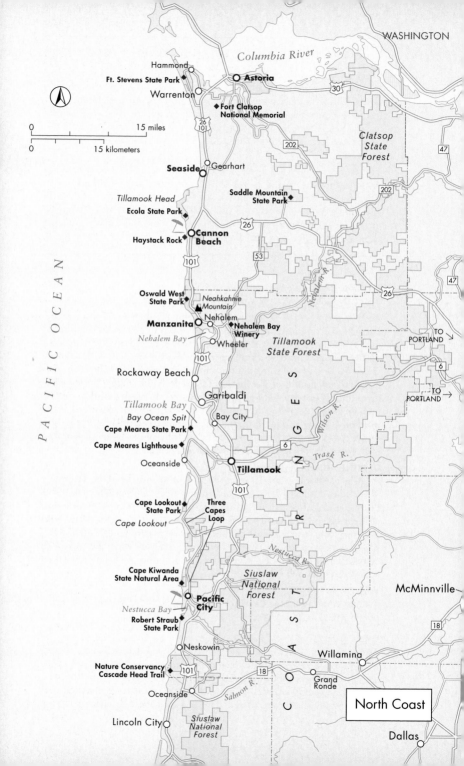

North Coast

Coxcomb Hill, and was patterned after Trajan's Column in Rome. There are little platforms to rest on if you get winded, or, if you don't want to climb, the column's 500 feet of artwork, depicting important Pacific Northwest historical milestones, are well worth study. ⊠ *From U.S. 30 downtown take 16th St. south 1 mi to top of Coxcomb Hill, Astoria* ☎ *503/325–2963* ⊕ *www.astoriacolumn.org* ☞ *$1 per car donation* ☉ *Daily 9–dusk.*

Fodor's Choice **Columbia River Maritime Museum.** One of Oregon's best coastal attractions
★ illuminates the maritime history of the Pacific Northwest and provides
☾ visitors with a sense of the perils of guiding ships into the mouth of the Columbia River. Guests can experience what it was to pilot a tugboat and participate in a Coast Guard rescue on the Columbia River Bar. There's the actual bridge of a WWII-era U.S. Navy destroyer, the U.S. Coast Guard lightship *Columbia,* and a 44-foot Coast Guard motor lifeboat. A captivating exhibit displays the personal belongings of some of the ill-fated passengers of the 2,000 ships that have foundered here since 1811. ⊠ *1792 Marine Dr., Astoria* ☎ *503/325–2323* ⊕ *www.crmm.org* ☞ *$10* ☉ *Daily 9:30–5.*

Fodor's Choice **Fort Clatsop National Memorial.** See where the 30-member Lewis and
★ Clark Expedition endured a rain-soaked winter in 1905-06, hunting,
☾ gathering food, making salt, and trading with Clatsop, Chinook, and Tillamook Indians. This memorial is a faithful replica of the log fort depicted in Clark's journal. The park has evolved into a 3,000-acre, forested wonderland, including an exhibit hall, gift shop, film, and trails. Park rangers dress in period garb during the summer and perform such early-19th-century tasks as making fire with flint and steel. Hikers will enjoy the 1.5-mile Netul Landing trail, or the 6.5-mile Fort to Sea trail. ⊠ *Fort Clatsop Loop Rd. 5 mi south of Astoria* ☎ *503/861–2471* ⊕ *www.nps.gov/focl* ☞ *$3* ☉ *Daily 9–5 (Summer 9–6).*

☾ **Fort Stevens State Park.** This earthen fort at Oregon's northwestern tip was built during the Civil War to guard the Columbia River against attack. None came until World War II, when a Japanese submarine fired upon it. The fort still has cannons and an underground gun battery. The park has year-round camping, with full hook-up sites and 15 yurts. There are also bike paths, boating, swimming, hiking trails, and a short walk to a gorgeous, wide beach where the corroded skeleton of the *Peter Iredale* pokes up through the sand. This century-old English four-master shipwreck is a reminder of the nearly 2,000 vessels claimed by these treacherous waters. ⊠ *Fort Stevens Hwy.* ☎ *503/861–2000 or 800/551–6949* ⊕ *www.visitfortstevens.com* ☞ *$5 per vehicle* ☉ *Mid-May–Sept., daily 10–6; Oct.–mid-May, daily 10–4.*

WHERE TO EAT

¢ ✕ **Blue Scorcher Bakery Café.** "Joyful work, delicious food and strong
CAFÉ community," is this tasty café's rallying cry. It serves up everything from huevos scorcheros and organic, handcrafted breads to a variety of foods using local and organic ingredients. The offerings change with the seasons, but there's always a vegan or gluten-free option. This workers' collective also has a Pie-of-the-Month Club. ⊠ *1493 Duane St., Astoria* ☎ *503/338–7473* ⊕ *www.bluescorcher.com* ▭ *D, MC, V* ☉ *No dinner.*

$$ ✕**Clemente's.** Serving possibly the best seafood on the Oregon Coast,
SEAFOOD chefs Gordon and Lisa Clement are making a significant critical and
Fodor'sChoice popular splash in Astoria. Grounded in Mediterranean cuisine from
★ Italy and the Adriatic Coast, Clemente's inventive specials feature the
freshest catches of that day. From succulent sea-bass salad to a hearty
sturgeon sandwich—meals are dished up for reasonable prices. Dunge-
ness crab cakes stuffed with crab rather than breading, and wild scallop
fish-and-chips liven up a varied menu. Not interested in fish? Try the
spaghetti with authentic meatballs. ⊠ *1198 Commercial St., Astoria*
☎ *503/325–1067* ⊕ *www.clementesrestaurant.com* ⊟ *AE, D, MC, V*
⊘ *No lunch Mon.*

$$ ✕**Columbian Cafe.** Locals love this unpretentious diner that defies cat-
ECLECTIC egorization by offering inventive, fresh seafood and spicy vegetarian
dishes, while it also cures and smokes its meat selections. Open for
breakfast, lunch, and dinner, it serves simple food, such as crepes with
broccoli, cheese, and homemade salsa for lunch; grilled salmon and
pasta with a lemon-cream sauce for dinner. The restaurant isn't shy
about its culinary prowess, claiming that the experience "will change
your life." Dishes are served by a staff that usually includes owner/chef
Uriah Hulsey. Come early; this place always draws a crowd. ⊠ *1114
Marine Dr., Astoria* ☎ *503/325–2233* ⊕ *www.columbianvoodoo.com/
cafe* ⊟ *No credit cards* ⊘ *Closed Mon.–Tues.*

WHERE TO STAY

$$$ ⬚**Cannery Pier Hotel.** Every room has a gorgeous view of where the
Fodor'sChoice mighty Columbia River meets the Pacific Ocean, and it's almost hyp-
★ notic to relax by a fire and watch the tugboats shepherding barges to
and fro. Built upon century-old pilings, this captivating property is in
the restored Union Fisherman's Cooperative Packing Company build-
ing, an integral part of the town's history. The interior, however, is mod-
ern and bright, with a liberal use of glass and polished wood, including
hardwood floors in the rooms. The property sits on the Astoria River-
walk and on the trolley line, with gourmet dining within walking dis-
tance. But don't leave until you enjoy the complimentary wine and lox,
served daily between 5 and 6 PM. Replica 1950s bicycles are available
for use, and the hotel offers complimentary chauffeur service in a 1939
Buick, 1938 Packard, or 1945 Cadillac. **Pros:** amazing river views, great
in-room amenities, nearby outstanding restaurants. **Cons:** no on-site
restaurant or room service. ⊠ *10 Basin St., Astoria* ☎ *503/325–4996
or 888/325–4996* ⊕ *www.cannerypierhotel.com* ↵ *46 rooms, 8 suites*
⅋ *In-room: refrigerator, DVD, Internet. In-hotel: gym, spa, some pets
allowed, parking.* ⊟ *AE, D, MC, V* ⎥⊙⎢ *CP.*

$$ ⬚**Hotel Elliott.** This upscale, five-story downtown hotel stands in the
heart of Astoria's historic district. The property retains the elegance
of yesteryear updated with modern comforts. On the rooftop you can
relax in the garden and enjoy views of the Columbia River and the
Victorian homes dotting the hillside. In your room you can warm your
feet on the heated stone floors in the bathroom. Downstairs, you can
sample fine wines in the Cabernet Room or enjoy a guilt-free cigar in
the tucked-away Havana Room. **Pros:** captures the city's historic ambience beautifully; every effort made to infuse the rooms with upscale

amenities; popular wine bar. **Cons:** some areas smell like cigar smoke; no on-site dining. ✉ *357 12th St., Astoria* ☎ *877/378–1924* ⊕ *www. hotelelliott.com* ⤴ *32 rooms* ⚭ *In-room: Internet, DVD. In-hotel: bar* ▭ *AE, D, MC, V.*

CANNON BEACH

25 mi south of Astoria on U.S. 101.

Cannon Beach is a mellow, trendy place to enjoy art, wine, and fine dining, and to take in the sea air. Shops and galleries selling surfing gear, upscale clothing, local art, wine, coffee, and food line Hemlock Street, Cannon Beach's main thoroughfare. One of the most charming hamlets on the coast, the town has beachfront homes and hotels. On the downside, the Carmel of the Oregon coast can be more expensive and crowded than other towns along Highway 101.

Every May the town hosts the Cannon Beach Sandcastle Contest, for which thousands throng the beach to view imaginative and often startling works in this most transient of art forms.

GETTING HERE

Cannon Beach is about an hour and a half's drive from Portland on U.S. Highway 26, and 25 miles south of Astoria on U.S. Highway 101. **Sunset Empire** (☎ *503/861-7433* ⊕ *www.ridethebus.org*) buses connect Portland with the northern coastal cities of Astoria, Warrenton, Hammond, Gearhart, Seaside, and Cannon Beach.

VISITOR INFORMATION

Cannon Beach Chamber of Commerce (✉ *207 N. Spruce St., Cannon Beach* ☎ *503/436–2623* ⊕ *www.cannonbeach.org*).

EXPLORING

Haystack Rock. Towering over the broad, sandy beach is a gorgeous, 235-foot-high dome that is one of the most-photographed natural wonders on the Oregon Coast. ■ TIP→ Please stay off the rock and enjoy the view from the beach. The rock is temptingly accessible during low tide, but the Coast Guard regularly airlifts stranded climbers from its precipitous sides, and falls have claimed numerous lives over the years.

EN ROUTE

A portion of the Oregon Trail crosses the summit of **Neahkahnie Mountain**, just south of Cannon Beach. Cryptic carvings on the beach rocks below and old Native American legends of shipwrecked Europeans have sustained the belief that survivors of a sunken Spanish galleon buried a fortune in doubloons somewhere on the side of the 1,661-foot-high mountain. U.S. 101 climbs 700 feet above the Pacific, providing dramatic views and often hair-raising curves as it winds along the flank of the mountain. There's a moderate but steep 3-mile climb to the summit, gaining 900 feet of elevation.

WHERE TO EAT

¢ × **Sleepy Monk.** In a region famous for its gourmet coffee, one small
CAFÉ roaster brews a cup more memorable than any chain. Sleepy Monk attracts java aficionados on caffeine pilgrimages from near and far to sample its specially roasted, certified organic, and fair trade beans.

Puffin Kite Festival, Cannon Beach

They are roasted without water, which adds unnecessary weight. Local, fresh pastries are stacked high and deep. If you're a coffee fan, this is your Shangri-la. It also opened a new restaurant on the premises, Irish Table. ⊠ *1235 S. Hemlock St., Cannon Beach* ☎ *503/436–2796* ⊕ *www. sleepymonkcoffee.com* ⊟ *MC, V* ☺ *Closed Mon.–Thurs.*

$$
IRISH
✕ **Irish Table.** This new restaurant has made a favorable splash into Cannon Beach's dining scene. Built adjacent to the Sleepy Monk café, it serves seasonal food with an Irish twist, such as potato kale soup and its heralded Irish stew. Other offerings include a perfect steak or delicate fresh halibut. Start with chicken-bacon chowder or the curried mussels. Soak up the sauce with slices of piping-hot soda bread. Naturally, there are plenty of libations, including Irish whiskey. It's a terrific stop for people seeking a little something different at the coast. ⊠ *1235 S. Hemlock St., Cannon Beach* ☎ *503/436–2796* ⊕ *www.sleepymonkcoffee. com* ⊟ *MC, V C Wed.*

$$$$
CONTINENTAL
Fodor'sChoice
★
✕ **Stephanie Inn.** As diners enjoy a romantic view of Haystack Rock, this upscale hotel's four-star dining room prepares a new menu nightly, crafting exquisite, four-course, prix-fixe dinners using fresh, local ingredients. Diners can expect dishes such as butternut squash risotto, cedar plank–roasted salmon, savory duck confit, and a lemon-curd tart with wild berry sauce. Naturally, it has an extensive regional and international wine list. The view, cuisine, and attentive service combine to make it one of the finest dining experiences in the Pacific Northwest. ⊠ *2740 S. Pacific St., Cannon Beach* ☎ *503/436–2221 or 800/633–3466* ⊕ *www.stephanie-inn.com* ⌂ *Reservations essential* ⊟ *AE, D, DC, MC, V.*

WHERE TO STAY

$$$ ⌂ **Arch Cape Inn and Retreat.** Between the artsy beach communities of Manzanita and Cannon Beach, this property lies along some of the most gorgeous stretch of coast in the region. It's perfect for those who want a little more of a getaway, putting some distance between themselves and the summer hordes. A three-course breakfast and nightly wine social are included in the room rate. No kids under 16 are permitted. **Pros:** elegant, distinctive rooms; fireplaces great in winter; most rooms have terrific ocean views. **Cons:** 200 yards from the beach. ✉ *31970 E. Ocean La., Cannon Beach* ☎ *503/436–2800* ⊕ *www.archcapeinn.com* ➷ *10 rooms* ⚭ *In-room: refrigerators, DVD In-hotel: Wi-Fi, parking, some pets allowed* ⊟ *AE, D, MC, V* ◯◐ *BP.*

$$$$
Fodor'sChoice
★
⌂ **Stephanie Inn.** One of the most beautiful views on the coast deserves one of the most splendid hotels. With a stunning view of Haystack Rock, the Stephanie Inn keeps its focus on romance, superior service, and luxurious rooms. Impeccably maintained, with country-style furnishings, fireplaces, large bathrooms with whirlpool tubs, and balconies, the rooms are so comfortable you may never want to leave. Generous country breakfasts are included in the room price, as are evening wine and hors d'oeuvres. The fresh-baked cookies in the lobby are a warm touch. No kids under 12 are permitted. Two-night minimum stays required during August, or during weekends throughout the year. **Pros:** one of the finest romantic getaways in Oregon. **Cons:** expensive. ✉ *2740 S. Pacific St., Cannon Beach* ☎ *503/436–2221 or 800/633–3466* ⊕ *www.stephanie-inn.com* ➷ *27 rooms, 14 suites* ⚭ *In-room: A/C, safe, refrigerator, Internet, DVD. In-hotel: parking, spa,* ⊟ *AE, D, DC, MC, V* ◯◐ *BP.*

SHOPPING

Cannon Beach Art Galleries. The numerous art galleries that line Cannon Beach's Hemlock Street are an essential part of the town's spirit and beauty. A group of 10 galleries featuring beautifully innovative works in ceramic, bronze, photography, painting, and other mediums have collaborated to form the Cannon Beach Gallery Group. Through its Web site, it helps to promote exhibitions and special events for all 10 venues. *S. Hemlock St., Cannon Beach* ⊕ *www.cbgallerygroup.com).*

MANZANITA

20 mi south of Cannon Beach on U.S. 101.

Manzanita is a secluded seaside community with only a few more than 500 full-time residents. It's on a sandy peninsula peppered with tufts of grass on the northwestern side of Nehalem Bay, a popular windsurfing destination. It is a tranquil small town, but its restaurants, galleries, and 18-hole golf course have increased its appeal to tourists.

GETTING HERE

Manzanita is in Tillamook County, a little under two hours from Portland on U.S. Highway 26. The town sits on Highway 101, about 40 mi south of Astoria and 27 mi north of Tillamook. The nearest airport is in Astoria. Tillamook County's bus, **The Wave** (☎ *503-815-8283*

⊕ *www.tillamookbus.com*), leaves from Portland's Union Station. The bus connects Manzanita, Tillamook, and Pacific City.

VISITOR INFORMATION

Oregon Coast Visitors Association (✉ *137 N.E. 1st St., Newport* ☎ *541/574–2679 or 888/628–2101* ⊕ *www.visittheoregoncoast.com*).

EXPLORING

Nehalem Bay Winery. Established in 1974, this winery is known for its pinot noir, chardonnay, blackberry, and plum fruit wines. The winery also has a busy schedule of events, with concerts, barbecues, an occasional pig roast, children's activities, and a bluegrass festival the third week of August. ✉ *34965 Hwy. 53, Nehalem* ☎ *503/368–9463 or 888/368–9463* ⊕ *www.nehalembaywinery.com* ⊙ *Daily 9–6.*

WHERE TO EAT AND STAY

¢   ✕ **San Dune Pub.** What was once just a tavern is now a local magnet for

AMERICAN   bodacious burgers, sweet-potato fries, and, on Tuesdays, baby back ribs. With 17 beers on tap, live music, and a 50-inch screen for sports, it's a one-stop shop. Patio seating on nicer days is a bonus. ✉ *127 Laneda Ave., Manzanita* ☎ *503/368–5080* ⊕ *www.sandunepub.com* ⊟ *MC, V* ⊙ *Closed Sun.*

$$ ⌂ **Inn at Manzanita.** This 1987 Scandinavian structure, filled with light-color woods, beams, and glass, is half a block from the beach. Shore pines on the property give upper-floor patios a treehouse feel; all rooms have decks, and two have skylights. There are also three child-friendly rooms and a new penthouse suite. A nearby café serves breakfast, and area restaurants are nearby. In winter the inn is a great place for storm-watching. There's a two-day minimum stay on weekends. **Pros:** wonderful ambience with a Japanese garden atmosphere, very light and clean. **Cons:** 20-day cancellation notice required. ✉ *67 Laneda Ave., Manzanita* ☎ *503/368–6754* ⊕ *www.innatmanzanita.com* ⇗ *13 rooms, penthouse* ⚙ *In-room: no phone (some), kitchen (some), refrigerator* ⊟ *AE, D, MC, V.*

SPORTS AND THE OUTDOORS

RECREATIONAL   **Oswald West State Park.** Adventurous travelers will enjoy a sojourn at

AREAS   one of the best-kept secrets on the Pacific coast, at the base of Neahkahnie Mountain. Park in one of the two lots on U.S. 101 and hike a ½-mi trail. There are several trails to the beach that lead to the Cape Falcon overlook or to the Oregon Coast Trail. The spectacular beach has caves and tidal pools. The trail to the summit (about 2 mi south of the parking lots marked only by a HIKERS sign) provides rewarding views of the surf, sand, forest, and mountain. Come in December or March and you might spot pods of gray whales. ✉ *Ecola Park Rd., Manzanita* ☎ *503/368–5943 or 800/551–6949* ⊕ *www.oregonstateparks.org* ▭ *Free* ⊙ *Day use only, daily dawn–dusk.*

GOLFING   **Manzanita Golf Course.** This short, 9-hole course is a fun, coastal option for a quick, pleasant round. Designed by Ted Erickson, it offers tree-lined fairways, easy walking, and a 5th hole with a 60-foot drop to the fairway below. With only 280 yards from the back tees, it provides players with a great chance for an eagle. The course is open year-round, and has a full-service pro shop. The driving range is open May–September. Call for reservations, since many other vacationers have the same idea. ✉ *Lakeview Dr., Manzanita* ☎ *503/368–5744* ⊕ *www.doormat.com/ mgc/mgc-1.htm* ⊡ *$10-$20.*

TILLAMOOK

27 mi south of Manzanita on U.S. 101.

More than 100 inches of annual rainfall and the confluence of three rivers contribute to the lush green pastures around Tillamook, probably best known for its thriving dairy industry and cheese factory. The Tillamook County Cheese Factory ships about 40 million pounds of cheese around the world every year. Just south of town is the largest wooden structure in the world, one of two gigantic buildings constructed in 1942 by the U.S. Navy to shelter blimps that patrolled the Pacific Coast during World War II. Hangar A was destroyed by fire in 1992, and Hangar B was subsequently converted to the Tillamook Naval Air Station Museum.

The **Three Capes Loop** over Cape Meares, Cape Lookout, and Cape Kiwanda offers spectacular views of the ocean and coastline.

GETTING HERE

Tillamook is a 90-minute drive from Portland on U.S. Highway 26 to Route 6. It sits on Highway 101 about 65 miles south of Astoria and 44 mi north of Lincoln City. Astoria's airport is the closest for air travel. Tillamook County's bus, **The Wave** (☎ *503-815-8283* ⊕ *www. tillamookbus.com*), leaves from Portland's Union Station. The bus connects Manzanita, Tillamook, and Pacific City.

VISITOR INFORMATION

Tillamook Chamber of Commerce (✉ *3705 U.S. 101 N, Tillamook* ☎ *503/842– 7525* ⊕ *www.GoTillamook.com*).

EXPLORING

Tillamook County Cheese Factory. More than 750,000 visitors annually journey to the largest cheese-making plant on the West Coast. Here the rich milk from the area's thousands of Holstein and brown Swiss cows becomes ice cream, butter, and cheddar and Monterey Jack cheeses. The product is heavenly—one of the true benefits of living in Oregon. Unfortunately the creamery's self-guided cheese-making tour is a letdown—fairly restrictive and lacking in personal interaction. Best cut to the chase and get to the cheese in the expansive store. There's also a selection of smoked meats and wonderful ice cream. Try the marionberry in a waffle cone. ✉ *4175 U.S. 101 N, Tillamook* ☎ *503/815–1300* ⊕ *www.tillamookcheese.com* ⊡ *Free* ⊙ *Sept.–mid-June, daily 8–6; mid-June–Sept., daily 8–8.*

Tillamook Naval Air Station Museum. In the world's largest wooden structure, a former blimp hangar south of town displays one of the finest private collections of vintage aircraft from World War II. It includes a P-38 Lightning, F4U-Corsair, P51-Mustang, PBY Catalina, SBD Dauntless dive bomber, and an ME-109 Messerschmidt. The 20-story building is big enough to hold half a dozen football fields. ✉ *6030 Hangar Rd.,*

3

Tillamook ☎ *503/842–1130* ⊕ *www.tillamookair.com* 🎫 *$9* ⊙ *Daily 9–5.*

WHERE TO EAT AND STAY

$$

SEAFOOD

✕ **Roseanna's.** Nine miles west of Tillamook in Oceanside, Roseanna's is in a rustic 1915 building on the beach opposite Three Arch Rock, a favorite resting spot for sea lions and puffins. The calm of the beach is complemented in the evening by candlelight and fresh flowers. Have halibut or salmon half a dozen ways, or the baked oysters or Gorgonzola seafood pasta. The evening's not complete without marionberry cobbler. ⊠ *1490 Pacific Ave., Oceanside* ☎ *503/842–7351* ⊛ *Reservations not accepted* ⊟ *MC, V.*

¢

▦ **Hudson House.** The son of the original owner of this 1906 farmhouse was a photographer who captured the area's rough beauty on postcards. The larger suite is downstairs, with a parlor and private porch overlooking the Nestucca Valley. The more popular upstairs suite has a bedroom in the house's turret. The two guest rooms are under the high-gabled roof. The house has a wraparound porch from which you can enjoy a view of the surrounding woods. ⊠ *37700 U.S. 101 S, Cloverdale* ☎ *503/392–3533 or 888/835–3533* ⊕ *www.hudsonhouse.com* ⤳ *2 rooms, 2 suites* ⅋ *In-room: no phone, no TV, Internet* ⊟ *MC, V* ⅃⊙⅃ *BP.*

SHOPPING

℃

Blue Heron French Cheese Company. This special shop specializes in Brie— traditional, herb & garlic, pepper, and its flavorful smoked variety. You'll want to snag a wheel and some crackers for your trip along the coast. There's a free petting zoo for kids, a sit-down deli with fresh-baked bread, wine and cheese tastings, and a gift shop that carries wines and jams, mustards, and other products from Oregon. ⊠ *2001 Blue Heron Dr., Tillamook* ☎ *503/842–8281* ⊕ *www.blueheronoregon.com* 🎫 *Free* ⊙ *Memorial Day–Labor Day, daily 8–8; Labor Day–Memorial Day, daily 8–6.*

PACIFIC CITY

24 mi south of Tillamook.

There's a lot to like about Pacific City, mostly that it's located three miles off of Oregon's busy coastal Highway 101. That means fewer sputtering recreation vehicles or squeaking truck brakes breaking up the serenity of the sea. Also, there's no backup at the town's only traffic light—a blinking-red, four-way stop in the center of town. There's just the quiet, happy ambience of a town living the good life in the midst of extraordinary beauty. The dining venues and brewery are outstanding, and the lodging is stellar. Plus, the opportunities for recreation and tourism epitomize the best of the Oregon Coast. The beach at Pacific City is one of the few places in the state where fishing dories (flat-bottom boats with high, flaring sides) are launched directly into the surf instead of from harbors or docks.

Three Capes Loop

Coastal views from the Three Capes Loop

The **Three Capes Loop**, a gorgeous 35-mi byway off U.S. 101, winds along the coast between Tillamook and Pacific City, passing three distinctive headlands—Cape Meares, Cape Lookout, and Cape Kiwanda. Bayocean Road heading west from Tillamook passes what was the thriving resort town of Bay Ocean, whichwashed into the seaby a raging Pacific storm more than 30 years ago.

WHAT YOU'LL SEE

Cape Meares State Park is on the northern tip of the Three Capes Loop. The restored **Cape Meares Lighthouse,** built in 1890 and open to the public May–September, provides a sweeping view over the cliff to the caves and sea-lion rookery on the rocks below. A many-trunked Sitka spruce known as the Octopus Tree grows near the lighthouse parking lot. ⊠ *Three Capes Loop, 10 mi west of Tillamook* ☎ *800/551–6949* ⊕ *www. oregonstateparks.org* 🏷 *Free* ⊙ *Park daily dawn–dusk. Lighthouse Apr.– Oct., daily 11–4.*

Cape Lookout State Park lies south of the beach towns of Oceanside and Netarts. A fairly easy 2-mi trail— marked on the highway as WILDLIFE VIEWING AREA—leads through giant spruces, western red cedars, and hemlocks, and ends with views of Cascade Head to the south and Cape Meares to the north. Wildflowers, more than 150 species of birds, and migrating whales passing by in early April make this trail a favorite with nature lovers. The park has a picnic area overlooking the sea and a year-round campground. ⊠ *Three Capes Loop, 8 mi south of Cape Meares, Oceanside* ☎ *800/551–6949* ⊕ *www. oregonstateparks.org* 🏷 *Day use $5* ⊙ *Daily dawn–dusk.*

Huge waves pound the jagged sandstone cliffs and caves at **Cape Kiwanda State Natural Area**. The much-photographed, 235-foot-high **Haystack Rock** juts out of Nestucca Bay to the south. Surfers ride some of the longest waves on the coast, hang gliders soar above the shore, and beachcombers explore tidal pools and take in unparalleled ocean views. ⊠ *Three Capes Loop, 15 mi south of Cape Lookout, Pacific City* ☎ *800/551–6949* ⊕ *www. oregonstateparks.org* 🏷 *Free* ⊙ *Daily sunrise–sunset.*

GETTING HERE

Located between Tillamook and Lincoln City, the unincorporated village of Pacific City is off U.S. Highway 101 on the south end of the beautiful Three Capes Loop. It is a two-hour drive from Portland on U.S. Highway 26 to Route 6. From Salem, Pacific City is a 90-minute drive on Route 22. Tillamook County's bus, **The Wave** (☎ *503-815-8283* ⊕ *www.tillamookbus.com*), leaves from Portland's Union Station. The bus connects Manzanita, Tillamook, and Pacific City. The nearest airport is in Newport, 47 mi south.

VISITOR INFORMATION

Pacific City-Nestucca Valley Chamber of Commerce (☎ *503/392–4340 or 888/549–2632* ⊕ *www.PacificCity.com*).

WHERE TO EAT AND STAY

¢   ✕ **Grateful Bread.** Open since 1991, this café uses the cod caught by
AMERICAN the local dories for its fish-and-chips. Everything it makes is fresh and from scratch. Its breads, pastries, breakfasts, and pizzas are simply perfect. ✉ *34805 Brooten Rd., Pacific City* ☎ *503/965–7337* ▭ *MC, V* ⊙ *Closed Tues. and Wed. No dinner.*

$$ ✕ **Pelican Pub and Brewery.** This beer-lover's jewel stands on the ocean-
AMERICAN front by Haystack Rock. While its microbrewery has garnered national and international acclaim for its beers, the Pelican Pub has elevated the art of beer cuisine by listing beer pairings on its menu. Many of its fine entrées are infused with its beers, such as the linguine with fresh clams flavored with Kiwanda Cream Ale, and the Tsunami Stout brownie sundae. The pub periodically hosts Brewers Dinners—splendid affairs that have explored beer pairings with Scottish, Greek, Italian, and Belgian cooking. Kids love the gourmet pizzas and children's menu. ✉ *33180 Cape Kiwanda Dr., Pacific City* ☎ *503/965–7007* ⊕ *www. pelicanbrewery.com* ▭ *AE, D, MC, V.*

$$$ ✕ **Riverhouse.** On the Nestucca River, this is the area's best place for
SEAFOOD fresh crab, oysters, and filet mignon. It also has more casual fare, such as sandwiches and salads. The interior has handmade redwood tables and art pieces displayed by local artists. Best of all, it's famous throughout the Pacific Northwest for its unmatched salad dressings, which are available at popular grocery stores throughout the region. Its bleu cheese flavor is so fine you'll make primitive sounds slurping it off your lettuce. ✉ *34450 Brooten Rd., Pacific City* ☎ *503/965–6722* ▭ *MC, V.*

$$$$ ▥ **Cottages at Cape Kiwanda.** For a five-star resort experience with a glorious beach view, the Cottages at Cape Kiwanda has 18 units for rent that can sleep four or six people. It's perfect for families or that beach get-together with friends. Each dwelling has fine decor, the latest electronics, and kitchen gadgets for proper entertaining or preparing your own feast. The concierge will help guests find the right trails or where to buy a kite or rent a surfboard. There's a two-night minimum. **Pros:** upscale, comfortable, and next to Pacific City eateries. **Cons:** there are ownership opportunities, so there might be a sales pitch. ✉ *33000 Cape Kiwanda Dr., Pacific City* ☎ *888/965–7001* ⊕ *www.kiwandacottages. com* ☎ *18 rooms* ⚹ *In-room: kitchen, refrigerator, DVD, Internet, some pets allowed* ▭ *AE, D, MC, V.*

3

¢ ⚈ **Inn at Cape Kiwanda.** You won't find a weather-beaten beach cottage here. Each of the 35 deluxe, fireplace-warmed rooms has a gorgeous view of Haystack Rock. Along with top amenities in every room, a workout facility, the Stimulus Espresso Café Coffee Shop, and pet-friendly rooms are available. It's within walking distance of Pacific City dining. **Pros:** Great views, some pets are welcome, terrific restaurants nearby. **Cons:** Guests might get hit up with a sales pitch. ⊠ *33105 Cape Kiwanda Dr., Pacific City* ☎ *888/965–7001* ⊕ *www.innatcapekiwanda. com* ↴ *35 rooms* ⚘ *In-room: refrigerator, DVD. In-hotel: Wi-Fi, gym, restaurant, some pets allowed.* ⊟ *AE, D, MC, V.*

SPORTS AND THE OUTDOORS

OFF THE
BEATEN
PATH
Nature Conservancy Cascade Head Trail. This dense, green trail winds through a rain forest where 100-inch annual rainfalls nourish 250-year-old Sitka spruces, mosses, and ferns. Emerging from the forest, hikers come upon grassy and treeless Cascade Head, a rare maritime prairie. There are magnificent views down to the Salmon River and east to the Coast Range. Continuing along the headland, black-tailed deer often graze and turkey vultures soar in the strong winds. You need to be in fairly good shape for the first and steepest part of the hike, which can be done in about an hour. The 270-acre area has been named a United Nations Biosphere Reserve. Coastal bluffs also make this a popular hang-gliding and kite-flying area. ⊠ *Savage Rd., 6 mi south of Neskowin off U.S. 101, Pacific City* ☎ *503/230–1221* ⊕ *www.nature.org* ⚐ *Free* ⊙ *Upper trail closed from Jan. to mid July.*

FISHING **Eagle Charters.** Within 3 minutes of launching from the beach, customers can be fishing in a dory and catching rockfish right in front of Haystack Rock. Groups of up to 5 people can be accommodated, and families with children are welcome. Fishing and eco-tourism trips last 6 hours except for halibut and tuna fishing, which are 10 to 12 hrs. ☎ *877/892–3679* ⊕ *www.eaglecharters.us* ⊟ *MC, V.*

Haystack Fishing, Inc. Offering ocean fishing for salmon, bottom fish, halibut, and crab, Haystack Fishing targets lingcod larger than 10 lbs. After a day of fishing, they'll fillet your catch. These guided dory trips last between 4 and 6 hours and accommodate up to 6 people. Fishing tours are held between June and Sept. ☎ *503/965–7555 or 866/965–7555* ⊕ *www.haystackfishing.com* ⊟ *MC, V.*

HORSEBACK **Oregon Beach Rides.** Saddle up for horseback rides that journey along
RIDING the beach, up coastal trails, to Robert Straub State Park and Nestucca River. Reserved rides can last from one hour up to a full day. There's even a romantic sunset trot along the beach. ☎ *971/237–6653* ⊕ *www. oregonbeachrides.com* ⚘ *Reservations required* ⊟ *AE, D, MC, V.*

CENTRAL COAST

This is Oregon's coastal playland, drawing shoppers, kite flyers, deep-sea fishing enthusiasts, surfers, and dune-shredding daredevils. Lincoln City offers a wealth of shops devoted to antiques and knickknacks, and visitors can even blow their own glass float. Depoe Bay has the world's smallest harbor, and Newport is designated the Dungeness crab capitol of the world. The best barbecue is in Toledo, and Oregon Dunes National Recreation Area provides the best thrills. Even if you're not intent on making tracks in the sand, the dunes provide vast, unforgettable scenery.

LINCOLN CITY

16 mi south of Pacific City on U.S. 101; 78 mi west of Portland on Hwy. 99 W and Hwy. 18.

Lincoln City is a captivating destination for families and lovers who want to share some time laughing on the beach, poking their fingers in tide pools, and trying to harness wind-bucking kites. Once a series of small villages, Lincoln City is a sprawling town without a center. But the endless tourist amenities make up for a lack of a small coastal-town ambience. Clustered like barnacles on the offshore reefs are fast-food restaurants, gift shops, supermarkets, candy stores, antiques markets, dozens of motels and hotels, a factory-outlet mall, and a busy casino. Lincoln City is the most popular destination city on the Oregon Coast, but its only real geographic claim to fame is the 445-foot-long D River, stretching from its source in Devil's Lake to the Pacific; *Guinness World Records* lists the D as the world's shortest river.

GETTING HERE

Lincoln City is a two hour drive from Portland. From Astoria, it's a 2-hour and 30 minute drive along U.S. 101. **Lincoln Transit** buses connect riders with Newport, Siletz, Lincoln City, and Yachats. Newport has the nearest airport, 31 miles away.

VISITOR INFORMATION

Lincoln City Visitors Center (✉ *801 S.W. U.S. 101, 4th Floor, Lincoln City* ☎ *541/996–1274 or 800/452–2151* ⊕ *www.oregoncoast.org*).

WHERE TO EAT

¢   ✕ **Beach Dog Café.** Dang, these are good dogs, dressed in 16 different
AMERICAN   ways. You'll find everything from Coney, Philly, and Kosher to Hot Dig-
Fodor'sChoice   gity. This family-owned joint has a galaxy of dog photos adorning its
★   walls. But its breakfasts have the morning crowds gathering. Roger and Sonja Seals offer a menu full of hearty potato dishes, scrambles, stuffed French toast, and incredible breakfast sandwiches. The apple-potato pancake with sour cream and a Polish sausage is the keystone to any nutritious breakfast. ✉ *1266 S.W. 50th St., Lincoln City* ☎ *541/996– 3647* ▭ *No credit cards* ☉ *Closed Mon. No dinner.*

$$ ✕ **Blackfish Café.** Owner and chef Rob Pounding serves simple-but-suc-
SEAFOOD   culent dishes that blend fresh ingredients from local fisherman and
Fodor'sChoice   gardeners. Before starting his own restaurant in 1999, Pounding was
★   the executive chef of acclaimed Salishan Lodge for 14 years, winning top national culinary awards. His skillet-roasted, "ocean trolled" chinook salmon, basted with fennel lime butter and Oregon blue-cheese potatoes, is flavorful and perfect. The Blackfish Ding Dong dessert, with mixed-berry sauce and whipped cream, is the best way to finish a meal. ✉ *2733 N.W. Hwy. 101, Lincoln City* ☎ *541/996–1007*

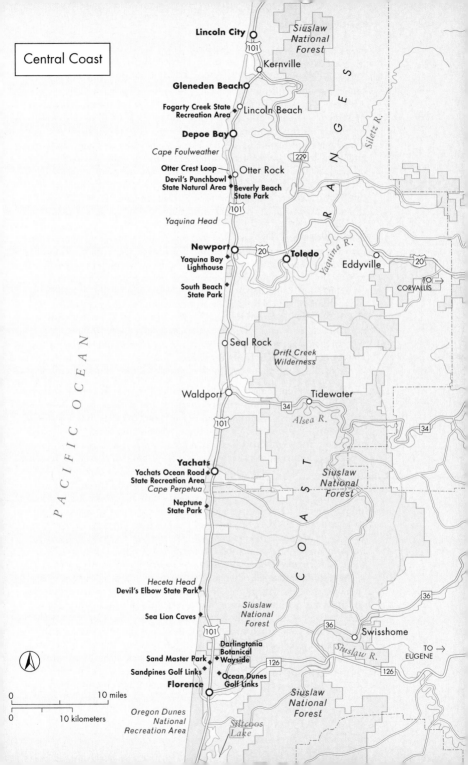

Central Coast

Lincoln City
101
Kernville
Gleneden Beach
Fogarty Creek State
Recreation Area
Lincoln Beach
Depoe Bay
Cape Foulweather
229
Otter Crest Loop
Otter Rock
Devil's Punchbowl
State Natural Area
Beverly Beach
State Park
101
Yaquina Head

Newport
20
Toledo
Yaquina Bay
Lighthouse
Eddyville
20
TO
CORVALLIS
South Beach
State Park

Seal Rock
Drift Creek
Wilderness

Waldport
34
Tidewater
Alsea R.
34

Yachats
Yachats Ocean Road
State Recreation Area
Cape Perpetua
Siuslaw
National
Forest
Neptune
State Park

Siuslaw
National
Forest
36
Heceta Head
Devil's Elbow State Park
Sea Lion Caves
Siuslaw
National
Forest
36
Swisshome
101
Darlingtonia
Botanical
Wayside
TO
EUGENE
Sand Master Park
126
Sandpines Golf Links
Ocean Dunes
Golf Links
Florence
Siuslaw
National
Forest

SIUSLAW RANGES

COAST RANGES

Siletz R.

Yaquina R.

Siuslaw R.

PACIFIC OCEAN

0   10 miles
0   10 kilometers

Oregon Dunes
National
Recreation Area
Siltcoos
Lake

⊕ *www.blackfishcafe.com* 🍴 *Reservations recommended* 🖃 *AE, D, MC, V* 🕾 *Closed Tues.*

$$$ ✕ **Culinary Center.** Whether she's conducting a small, hands-on class or
NEW AMERICAN orchestrating a full-blown cooking demonstration for dozens, executive chef Sharon Wiest loves sharing her passion for Pacific Northwest ingredients. Directly above the Visitor's Bureau, the Culinary Center is a wonderful stop for newcomers to the area. Guests can sign up to get their hands onto some food and learn, or they can sit back, sip wine, and enjoy learning what makes Oregon such a special place to dine. The center's schedule includes classes in oysters, pizza, sushi, tapas, Mexican, seafood, and even bacon. Chocolate-chip bacon-pecan cookie, anyone? ✉ *801 S.W. Hwy 101, Suite 401, Lincoln City* 🕾 *541/557–1125* ⊕ *www.oregoncoast.org/culinary/index.php* 🖃 *MC, V* 🕾 *Closed Mon. No dinner.*

¢ ✕ **Rockfish Bakery.** The seed for this phenomenal bakery began when
CAFÉ Rob Pounding, owner and chef for Blackfish Café, couldn't find any hamburger buns that met his standards. Now his bakery publishes a weekly bread schedule so customers will know when to buy the freshest sourdough, olive ciabatta, rye, or brioche with raisins. It makes the coast's best cinnamon rolls, cookies, excellent pizza, hearty sandwiches, and a soup du jour from the nearby. Blackfish Café. The Rockfish is a must for anyone who loves an upper-crust bakery. ✉ *3026 N.E Hwy. 101, Lincoln City* 🕾 *541/996–1006* ⊕ *www.rockfishbakery.com* 🖃 *MC, V* 🕾 *Closed Mon. and Tues. No dinner.*

WHERE TO STAY

$$$ 🛏 **Coho Oceanfront Lodge.** Set on a romantic cliff, the renovated Coho is
Fodor'sChoice a perfect hybrid of family-friendly lodging and a quiet, intimate hide-
★ away for couples. The expanded oceanfront property has 65 suites and rooms—14 of them in a brand-new south wing, which is relegated to adults. The Coho also has a concierge service, and is particularly adept at recommending nearby trails, restaurants, and evening fun. If you want to stay in, its lobby has plenty of games, an expansive DVD collection, and a complimentary continental breakfast daily. It even offers sand pails and kites to borrow for sandy fun. **Pros:** great value, family-friendly, concierge service, and shuttle to nearby casino. **Cons:** no restaurant. ✉ *1635 N.W. Harbor Ave., Lincoln City* 🕾 *541/994–3684* ⊕ *www.thecoholodge.com* 🛏 *33 studios, 32 suites* 🛁 *In-room: a/c, safe (some), kitchen (some), refrigerator (some), DVD, Wi-Fi. In-hotel: beachfront, parking, pool, fitness room* 🖃 *AE, D, MC, V* 🍴 *CP.*

¢ 🛏 **The Historic Anchor Inn.** This quirky bungalow might not be for everyone. But for those who appreciate a warm, spirited inn with a decidedly inventive and whimsical touch, this is a remarkable find. Started in the mid-1940s, it is the oldest hotel in Lincoln City. It's loaded with funky, fun treasures. The rooms are themed; check out the Web site for oodles of photos. Homemade breakfast is served between 9 and 10 AM, and dinner for groups and small parties can be arranged. **Pros:** a memorable, truly unique property with everything you need to explore Lincoln City. **Cons:** not on the beach, very quirky and rustic, which could be a pro too. ✉ *4417 S.W. U.S. 101, Lincoln City* 🕾 *541/996–3810* ⊕ *www.*

historicanchorinn.com ↩ *19 rooms* ⚴ *In-hotel: Wi-Fi, restaurant, some pets allowed* ═ *MC, V* ⍑⎜◯⎜ *BP*

NIGHTLIFE AND THE ARTS

Chinook Winds Casino Resort. Oregon's only beachfront casino has a great variety of slot machines, blackjack, poker, keno, and off-track betting. The Rogue River Steakhouse serves a great fillet and terrific appetizers. There's also the Siletz Bay Buffet, the Chinook Seafood Grill, a snack bar, and a lounge. An arcade will keep the kids busy while you are on the gambling floor. Big-name entertainers perform in the showroom. Players can take a break from the tables and enjoy a round of golf at the Chinook Winds Golf Resort next door. ⊠ *1777 N.W. 44th St., Lincoln City* ☎ *541/996–5825 or 888/244–6665* ⊗ *Daily, 24 hours* ═ *AE, D, MC, V.*

SHOPPING

Alder House II. The imaginative crafts folk at this studio turn molten glass into vases and bowls, which are available for sale. It is the oldest glass-blowing studio in the state. ⊠ *611 Immonen Rd., Lincoln City* ☎ *541/996–2483* ⊕ *www.alderhouse.com* ⊡ *Free* ⊗ *Mid-Mar.–Nov., daily 10–5.*

Jennifer L. Sears Glass Art Studio. Blow a glass float or make a glorious glass starfish, heart, or fluted bowl of your own design. The studio's expert artisans will guide you every step of the way. It's a fun, memorable keepsake of the coast. ⊠ *4821 S.E. Hwy. 101, Lincoln City* ☎ *541/996–2569* ⌦ *Call for an appointment* ⊕ *www.jennifersearsglassart.com* ⊡ *$65 for a glass float* ⊗ *Wed.–Sun. 10–6.*

SPORTS AND THE OUTDOORS

BOATING **Devil's Lake State Park.** Canoeing and kayaking are popular on this small lake, which is in turn popular with coots, loons, ducks, cormorants, bald eagles, and grebes. Visitors can sign up in advance for popular kayaking tours in the summer. It's the only Oregon Coast campground within the environs of a city. Hook-ups, tent sites, and yurts are available. ⊠ *1452 N.E. 6th St., Lincoln City* ☎ *541/994–2002 or 800/551–6949* ⊕ *www.oregonstateparks.org* ⊗ *Daily* ═ *MC, V.*

GLENEDEN BEACH

7 mi south of Lincoln City on U.S. 101.

Gleneden Beach is primarily a resort town with Salishan, its most famous property, perching high above placid Siletz Bay. This expensive collection of guest rooms, vacation homes, condominiums, restaurants, golf fairways, tennis courts, and covered walkways blends into a forest preserve; if not for the signs, you'd scarcely be able to find it.

GETTING HERE

The closest airport to Gleneden Beach is in Newport, 23 miles south. Bus service to Newport is provided by **Lincoln County Transit Bus/Dial-A-Ride** (☎ *541/265–4900*). **Caravan Airport Transportation** (☎ *541/994–9645*) provides shuttle service to Portland International Airport for Lincoln City, Depoe Bay, and Newport.

VISITOR INFORMATION

Central Oregon Coast Association (⊠ *137 N.E. 1st St., Newport* ☎ *503/265–2064 or 800/767–2064* ⊕ *www.coastvisitor.com*).

EXPLORING

Lawrence Gallery at Salishan. The well-respected gallery has a well-informed staff that will guide you through the collections of work by Northwest artists, including paintings (pastels, oils, and watercolors), glassworks, bronze and metal, furniture, and ceramics and porcelain. ⊠ *7755 N. U.S. 101, Gleneden Beach* ☎ *541/764–2318 or 800/764–2318* ⊕ *www.lawrencegallery.net* ☽ *Daily 10–5.*

WHERE TO EAT AND STAY

$$$$
STEAKHOUSE

✕ **Prime Steakhouse at Salishan.** If you're not on a budget, pull up a chair and slurp a bowl of Dungeness crab bisque, relish some oysters Rockefeller, and slice into a 28-day-aged steak or a mouth-watering seared scallop. It also serves game, lamb, and elegant desserts. The white-linen dining room has a gorgeous view of Siletz Bay and the private Salishan Spit, and there's a private dining room for those very special occasions. You could spend all evening perusing the wine list, as the resort's cellar has more than 17,000 bottles. ⊠ *7760 N. U.S. 101, Gleneden Beach* ☎ *541/764–2371 or 800/452–2300* ⚑ *Reservations essential* ▭ *AE, D, DC, MC, V* ☽ *No lunch.*

$$
CONTINENTAL

✕ **Sidedoor Café.** This dining room, with a high ceiling, exposed beams, a fireplace, and many windows just under the eaves shares a former tile factory with the Eden Hall performance space. The menu changes constantly—fresh preparations have included mushroom-crusted rack of lamb and broiled swordfish with citrus-raspberry vinaigrette over coconut-ginger basmati rice. ⊠ *6675 Gleneden Beach Loop Rd., Gleneden Beach* ☎ *541/764–3825* ▭ *AE, D, MC, V.*

$$

⌑ **BeachCombers Vacation Rentals.** This cluster of properties is right off the beach, and features spacious 1-, 2-, or 3-bedroom accommodations, some with a hot tub or in-room Jacuzzi. The property is near a golf course, art galleries, shopping, and outstanding restaurants. **Pros:** very friendly, comfortable, near the beach. **Cons:** expect a rustic beach property, not a resort. ⊠ *7045 N.W. Glen, Gleneden Beach* ☎ *541/764–2252 or 800/428–5533* ⊕ *www.beachcombershaven.com* ⤳ *14 homes* ⌂ *In-room: kitchen, DVD. In-hotel: Wi-Fi, beachfront, laundry service* ▭ *D, MC, V.*

$$$

⌑ **Salishan Lodge and Golf Resort.** Secluded and refined, this upscale property is located in a hillside forest preserve. Long revered as a luxury weekend away as well as a destination for tony corporate retreats, Salishan provides plenty of reasons to stay on the property. Its spa is outstanding, and there are different dining venues perfect for brunch, a casual bite after golf, or a polished, white-linen dining experience. The rooms are spacious, comfortable, and toasty with wood-burning fireplaces. Each has a balcony and original artwork by Northwest artists. Its par-71 golf course, redesigned by Peter Jacobsen, is one of the coast's finest. **Pros:** very elegant, secluded resort with a terrific golf course and plenty of activities on the property. **Cons:** ocean views are few, some reviewers mentioned that service can be a bit lax. ⊠ *7760 N. U.S. 101, Gleneden Beach* ☎ *541/764–3600 or 800/452–2300* ⊕ *www.*

Salishan Golf Resort, Gleneden Beach

salishan.com ⤵ 205 rooms ⚐ In-room: refrigerator, Wi-Fi. In-hotel: 3 restaurants, room service, bar, golf course, tennis courts, pool, gym, beachfront, laundry service ▭ AE, D, DC, MC, V.

SPORTS AND THE OUTDOORS

GOLF **Salishan Golf Resort.** Redesigned by Peter Jacobsen, this par-71 course is a year-round treat for hackers and aficionados alike. The front nine holes are surrounded by a forest of old-growth timber, while the back nine holes provide old-school, links-style play. It has an expansive pro shop with fine men's and women's sportswear, and a great bar and grill for relaxing after a "rough" day out on the links. It has rental clubs available, as well as lessons on its driving range and practice green. ✉ *7760 N. U.S. 101, Gleneden Beach* ☎ *541/764–3600 or 800/452–2300* ⊕ *www.salishan.com* ✉ *$119 weekends, cart included*

DEPOE BAY

5 mi south of Gleneden Beach on U.S. 101.

Depoe Bay calls itself the whale-watching capital of the world. The small town was founded in the 1920s and named in honor of Charles DePoe of the Siletz tribe, who was named for his employment at a U.S. Army depot in the late 1800s. With a narrow channel and deep water, its tiny harbor is also one of the most protected on the coast. It supports a thriving fleet of commercial- and charter-fishing boats. The Spouting Horn, a natural cleft in the basalt cliffs on the waterfront, blasts seawater skyward during heavy weather.

GETTING HERE

Depoe Bay is a short 12-mile drive north of Newport and its airport on Highway 101. **Lincoln Transit** provides bus service to Newport, Depoe Bay, Siletz, Lincoln City, and Yachats. Bus connections to Portland are accessible in Newport and are provided by **Greyhound** Newport and the **Valley Retriever** (☎ 541/265–2253 ⊕ www.kokkola-bus.com/ ValleyRetrieverBuslines.html). **Caravan Airport Transportation** (☎ 541/994–9645) provides shuttle service to Portland International Airport.

VISITOR INFORMATION

Depoe Bay Chamber of Commerce ⊠ 223 S.W. Hwy 101, Ste B, Depoe Bay ☎ 541/765–2889 ⊕ www.depoebaychamber.org.

EXPLORING

EN ROUTE Five miles south of Depoe Bay off U.S. 101 (watch for signs), the **Otter Crest Loop,** another scenic byway, winds along the cliff tops. Only parts of the loop are open to motor vehicles, but you can drive to points midway from either end and turn around. The full loop is open to bikes and hiking. British explorer Captain James Cook named the 500-foot-high **Cape Foulweather,** at the south end of the loop, on a blustery March day in 1778. Backward-leaning shore pines lend mute witness to the 100-mph winds that still strafe this exposed spot. At the viewing point at the **Devil's Punchbowl,** 1 mi south of Cape Foulweather, you can peer down into a collapsed sandstone sea cave carved out by the powerful waters of the Pacific. About 100 feet to the north in the rocky tidal pools of the beach known as **Marine Gardens,** purple sea urchins and orange starfish can be seen at low tide. The Otter Crest Loop rejoins U.S. 101 about 4 mi south of Cape Foulweather near **Yaquina Head,** which has been designated an Outstanding Natural Area. Harbor seals, sea lions, cormorants, murres, puffins, and guillemots frolic in the water and on the rocks below the gleaming, white tower of the **Yaquina Bay Lighthouse.**

WHERE TO EAT AND STAY

$$

BISTRO

✕ **Café Bella Mar.** This charming, colorful bistro provides a fine selection of wines, local brews, tasty panini sandwiches, and flatbread pizzas. Owner Lauren Stenzel will be there to greet you, adorned with one of her famous hats. Try the hot artichoke dip. ⊠ 8 Bella Beach Dr., Depoe Bay ☎ 541/764–4466w www.cafebellamar.com ⊟ MC, V.

$

SEAFOOD

✕ **Gracie's Sea Hag.** In 1963 Gracie Strom founded Gracie's Sea Hag Restaurant & Lounge, which specializes in fresh seafood, with an extensive buffet on Friday nights. Saturday the focus is prime rib with Yorkshire pudding. Several booths at the front of the restaurant have views of the "spouting horns" across the highway. The restaurant is kid-friendly, and there's an adjoining grown-up–friendly bar that gets hopping with live entertainment at night. ⊠ 58 U.S. 101, Depoe Bay ☎ 541/765–2734 ⊟ AE, D, DC, MC, V.

$$

The Harbor Lights Inn. This harborfront bed-and-breakfast provides a dreamy setting for watching boats and relaxing in a quaint, quiet atmosphere. Nine rooms have fireplaces as well as balconies or patios. Breakfast is served between 8:30 and 10 AM. **Pros:** small, quiet, and pretty; great breakfasts. **Cons:** not on the beach. ⊠ 235 S.E. Bay View Ave., Depoe Bay ☎ 541/765–2322 or 800/228–0448 ⊕ www.

theharborlightsinn.com ⤳ *13 rooms* ♿ *In-room: Wi-Fi,* DVD. *In-hotel: restaurant.* ▭ *AE, MC, V* ⑩| *BP.*

SPORTS AND THE OUTDOORS

RECREATIONAL AREAS

Fogarty Creek State Park. Bird-watching and viewing the tidal pools are the key draws here, but hiking and picnicking are also popular at this park 4 mi north of Depoe Bay on U.S. 101. Wooden footbridges arch through the forest. The beach is rimmed with cliffs. ⊠ *U.S. 101, Depoe Bay*☎ *541/265–9278 or 800/551–6949* ⊕ *www.oregonstateparks.org* ⊠ *Free* ☉ *Daily.*

OUTFITTERS

Coastal Outfitters provides kayak tours, rentals, and lessons for exploring area waters in Depoe Bay, Newport, and the Siletz River. Depending on the group and its ability, tours include whale-watching and cave exploring, Pacific Ocean tours, spotting blue heron and bald eagles up Beaver Creek, and a Yaquina Bay tour. Kayaks also can be rented by the day. ⊠ *104 N.E. Hwy. 101, Depoe Bay* ☎ *541/765–2776* ⊕ *coastaloutfitter.us* ⊠ *$35 per day for one-person kayak, $50 per day for two-person kayak; tours are $70 per hour* ▭ *AE, MC, V*

NEWPORT

12 mi south of Depoe Bay on U.S. 101.

Called the Dungeness crab capital of the world, Newport offers accessible beaches, a nationally renowned aquarium, a lively performing-arts center, and a local laid-back attitude. Newport exists on two levels: the highway above, threading its way through the community's main business district, and the old Bayfront along Yaquina Bay below (watch for signs on U.S. 101). With its high-masted fishing fleet, well-worn buildings, seafood markets, and art galleries and shops, Newport's Bayfront is an ideal place for an afternoon stroll. So many male sea lions in Yaquina Bay loiter near crab pots and bark from the waterfront piers that locals call the area the Bachelor Club. Visit the docks to buy fresh seafood or rent a kayak to explore the bay. In 2010 Newport was designated the National Oceanic and Atmospheric Administration's (NOAA) Pacific Marine Operations Center. That means that a new, $38 million, 5-acre facility (and a port for four ships), will open in May 2011.

GETTING HERE

Daily flights on SeaPort Airlines land at Newport Municipal Airport (ONP), just five miles from town. The city is served by **Greyhound, Valley Retriever** (☎ *541/265–2253* ⊕ *www.kokkola-bus.com/ValleyRetrieverBuslines.html*), and **Lincoln Transit** buses, connecting to Siletz, Lincoln City, Yachats, and Portland.

VISITOR INFORMATION

Greater Newport Chamber of Commerce (⊠ *555 S.W. Coast Hwy., Newport* ☎ *503/265–8801 or 800/262–7844* ⊕ *www.newportchamber.org*).

EXPLORING

The Flying Dutchman Winery. Perched on a cliff, this small, family-owned winery enjoys one of the most spectacular locations on the Oregon Coast. It buys grapes from five Oregon vineyards, and brings them over

Oregon Coast Aquarium, Newport

the Coast Range to its salt-air environment for fermenting. Guests can enjoy its award-winning vintages in the cozy tasting room, or take a quick tour of the oak barrels next door with owner Dick Cutler. ✉ *915 First St., Otter Rock* 🕾 *541/765-2553* ⊕ *www.dutchmanwinery.com* ☉ *June–Sept., daily 11–6; Oct.–May, daily 11–5.*

Fodor'sChoice
★
🕲

Oregon Coast Aquarium. One of the true jewels of the Oregon Coast, this 4½-acre complex brings visitors face to face with the creatures living in offshore and near-shore Pacific marine habitats: Flirting, frolicking sea otters, colorful puffins, pulsating jellyfish, and even a 60-pound octopus. There's a hands-on interactive area for children, including tide pools perfect for "petting" sea anemones and urchins. The aquarium houses one of North America's largest seabird aviaries, including glowering turkey vultures. Permanent exhibits include Passages of the Deep, where visitors walk through a 200-foot underwater tunnel with 360-degree views of sharks, wolf eels, halibut, and a truly captivating array of sealife. Large coho salmon and sturgeon can be viewed in a naturalistic setting through a window wall 9-feet high and 20-feet wide. The sherbet-colored nettles are hypnotizing. ✉ *2820 S.E. Ferry Slip Rd., Newport* 🕾 *541/867–3474* ⊕ *www.aquarium.org* 🎟 *$15.45* ☉ *Summer, daily 9–6; winter, daily 10–5.*

Yaquina Bay Lighthouse. The state's oldest wooden lighthouse was only in commission for three years (1871–1874), because it was determined that it was built in the wrong location. Today the well-restored lighthouse with a candy-apple top shines a steady white light from dusk to dawn. Open to the public, it is thought to be the oldest structure in Newport, and the only Oregon lighthouse with living quarters attached. ✉ *U.S.*

101 S, Newport ☎ 541/867–7451 ⊕ www.yaquinalights.org 🖃 Free
⊙ *Memorial Day–Oct., daily 11–5; Oct.–Memorial Day, daily 12–4.*

♻ **Yaquina Head Lighthouse.** The tallest lighthouse on the Oregon Coast
has been blinking its beacon since its head keeper first walked up its
114 steps to light the wicks on the evening of August 20, 1873. Next
to the 93-foot tower is an interpretive center. Bring your camera and
call ahead for tour times. ⊠ *4 mi north of bridge in Newport, Newport*
☎ *541/574–3100* ⊕ *www.yaquinalights.org* 🖃 *$7 per car, 9 passengers*
or fewer ⊙ *June–Labor Day, daily 9–4; Oct.–May, daily 12–4; closed*
Thanksgiving and Christmas.

WHERE TO EAT

$ ✕ **Mo's.** Started by Mohava Marie Niemi, Newport's crusty, big-hearted
SEAFOOD chain-smoking mother, Mo's has been delighting diners with its thick,
creamy chowder since about 1950. Mo passed away in 1992 at the age
of 79, but not before expanding beyond its original Newport location to
Mo's Annex in Newport, Mo's West in Otter Rock, and Mo's in Lincoln
City, Cannon Beach, and Florence. This coastal institution has consistently served great oysters, fish tacos, and other deep-water delicacies,
along with down-home service. There's a kids' menu too, and burgers
for the fish phobic. Mo's terrific fresh chowder and chowder base can
be purchased online. ⊠ *622 S.W. Bay Blvd., Newport* ☎ *541/265–2979*
w*www.moschowder.com* ▭ *AE, D, MC, V.*

¢   ✕ **Panini Bakery.** The owner, who operates this local favorite bakery
CAFÉ and espresso bar, prides himself on hearty and home-roasted meats,
hand-cut breads, and friendly service. The coffee's organic, the eggs
free-range, the orange juice fresh-squeezed, and just about everything
is made from scratch. Take a seat inside, or, in good weather, streetside
tables are a great place to view the Nye Beach scene. ⊠ *232 N.W. Coast*
Hwy., Newport ☎ *541/265–5033* ▭ *No credit cards* ⊙ *No dinner Wed.*

$ ✕ **Quimby's.** This unpretentious little place hosts a busy, happy crowd
SEAFOOD on almost any given night. With lots of oak on the inside and gorgeous
ocean views looking out, this restaurant proves that you don't have
to spend much to get great food on the coast. Start with the coast's
best clam chowder, loaded with deep-water clams, Yukon gold potatoes, onion, celery, and smoky bacon. The full bar has microbrews and
regional fine wines. ⊠ *740 W. Olive St., Newport* ☎ *541/265–9919 or*
866/784–6297 ⊕ *www.quimbysrestaurant.com* ▭ *AE, D, DC, MC, V.*

$$$ ✕ **Tables of Content.** The well-plotted prix-fixe menu at the restaurant
SEAFOOD of the outstanding Sylvia Beach Hotel changes nightly. Chances are
that the main dish will be fresh local seafood, perhaps a moist grilled
salmon fillet in a sauce Dijonnaise, served with sautéed vegetables,
fresh-baked breads, and rice pilaf; a decadent dessert is also included.
The interior is functional and unadorned, with family-size tables, but
be forewarned, dinners can be long, so young children may get restless.
⊠ *267 N.W. Cliff St., from U.S. 101 head west on 3rd St., Newport*
☎ *541/265–5428* ⊕ *www.sylviabeachhotel.com* ⊲ *Reservations essen-*
tial ▭ *AE, D, MC, V.*

WHERE TO STAY

$ ⛵ **Sylvia Beach Hotel.** Make reservations far in advance for this 1913-vintage beachfront hotel, where reading, writing, and old conversation eclipse technological hotel-room isolation. Its antiques-filled rooms are named for famous writers. A pendulum swings over the bed in the Poe room. The Christie, Twain, Tolkien, Woolf, and Colette rooms are all notable; all have fireplaces, decks, and great ocean views. A well-stocked split-level upstairs library has decks, a fireplace, slumbering cats, and too-comfortable chairs. Complimentary mulled wine is served nightly at 10. **Pros:** unique; great place to disconnect. **Cons:** no Internet access. ✉ *267 N.W. Cliff St., Newport* ☎ *541/265–5428 or 888/795–8422* ⊕ *www.sylviabeachhotel.com* ⟋ *20 rooms* △ *In-room: no phone. In-hotel: restaurant* ☰ *AE, MC, V* ⅋ *BP.*

$ ⛵ **The Whaler.** Located across the roadway from the coast, visitors enjoy wide views of the Pacific Ocean. Magnificent gray whales are often spotted offshore, and it's pleasant to watch the fishing boats leaving or returning to port. The Whaler is near the Newport Performing Arts Center and a short distance from Yaquina Bay, the Oregon Coast Aquarium, and the Newport Bayfront. **Pros:** great location, ocean views, roomy and clean. **Cons:** bland breakfast and rooms. ✉ *155 S.W. Elizabeth., Newport* ☎ *541/265–9261 or 800/433–9444* ⊕ *www.whalernewport.com* ⟋ *73 rooms* △ *In-room: Internet, refrigerator. In-hotel: pool, spa, gym, laundry facilities* ☰ *AE, D, MC, V* ⅋ *CP.*

NIGHTLIFE AND THE ARTS

Newport Symphony Orchestra. The only year-round, professional symphony orchestra on the Oregon Coast plays at the 400-seat Newport Performing Arts Center, just a few steps away from the seashore in Nye Beach. Adam Flatt is the music director and conductor, and actor and narrator David Ogden Stiers serves as associate conductor. The orchestra performs a popular series of concerts in the Newport Performing Arts Center September through May, and special events in the summer, including its popular free community concert every July 4. *777 W. Olive St., Newport* ☎ *541/574–0614* ⊕ *newportsymphony.org.*

SPORTS AND THE OUTDOORS

RECREATIONAL AREAS **Beverly Beach State Park.** Seven miles north of Newport, this beachfront park extends from Yaquina Head, where you can see the lighthouse, to the headlands of Otter Rock. It's a great place to fly a kite, surf the waves, or hunt for fossils. The campground is well equipped, with a wind-protected picnic area and a yurt meeting hall. It has a campground with 53 full hookups ($26), 75 electrical ($26), 128 tent sites ($21), a hiker/biker camp ($6), and 21 yurts ($40). ✉ *U.S. 101, Newport* ☎ *541/265–9278 or 800/551–6949* ⊕ *www.oregonstateparks.org/* ▭ *Free* ⊙ *Daily.*

Devil's Punch Bowl State Natural Area. A rocky shoreline separates the day-use from the surf. It's a popular whale-watching site just 9 mi north of Newport, and has excellent tidal pools. ✉ *9 mi north of Newport on U.S. 101, Newport* ☎ *541/265–9278* ▭ *Free* ⊙ *Daily.*

South Beach State Park. Fishing, crabbing, boating, windsurfing, hiking, and beachcombing are popular activities at this park. Kayaking tours are available for a fee. Pets welcome through September. A campground with Wi-Fi access has 228 electrical hookups ($27), 27 yurts ($40), group tent sites ($77), and a hiker/biker camp ($6). ⊠ *U.S. 101 S, Newport* ☎ *541/867–4715 or 541/867–7451* ⊙ *Daily.*

Yaquina Head Outstanding Natural Area. Thousands of birds—cormorants, gulls, common murres, pigeon guillemots—make their home just beyond shore on Pinnacle and Colony rocks, and nature trails wind through fields of sea grass and wildflowers, leading to spectacular views. There is also an interpretive center. ⊠ *750 N.W. Lighthouse Dr., Newport* ☎ *541/574–3100* ⊕ *www.yaquinalights.org* ⊠ *$7 per vehicle, 9 passengers or fewer* ⊙ *Interpretive center open June–Labor Day, daily 9–4; Oct.–May, daily 10–4.*

TOLEDO

7 mi east of Newport on U.S. 101.

Once a rustic mill town, Toledo has reinvented itself as an enclave for painters, artisans, antiques, and the most amazing barbecue this side of Missouri. Landscape artists Ivan Kelly and Michael Gibbons reside here, as well as metal sculptor Sam Briseno, potter Jean Inglis, and contemporary artist Jon Zander. Just seven miles inland from the coast on the Yaquina River, it is the only inland coastal community with a deep-water channel. The Yaquina is fished for sturgeon, fall-run chinook, and steelhead.

GETTING HERE

Toledo is served by **Greyhound** to Corvallis and Newport. The Newport Municipal Airport is the closest airport, located 12 miles away.

VISITOR INFORMATION

Toledo Chamber of Commerce (⊠ *311 N.E. 1st St., Toledo* ☎ *541/336–3183* ⊕ *www.visittoledooregon.com*).

WHERE TO EAT

$ ✕ **Pig Feathers.** "Everyone loves a great rack" is the rallying cry of the
SOUTHERN best barbecue restaurant in the Pacific Northwest. Owner and chef Stu
Fodor'sChoice Miller's sauces and rubs transform mere wings, pulled pork, and baby
★ back ribs into tastes so rich and rare that they've brought grown men to tears. The "OUCH," "Slather," and "Smokey Sweet" sauces are available to purchase. ⊠ *300 S. Main St., Toledo* ☎ *541/336–1833* ⊕ *www. pigfeathers.com* ⊟ *D, MC, V.*

YACHATS

31 mi south of Toledo on U.S. 101.

The small town of Yachats (pronounced "yah-*hots*") is at the mouth of the Yachats River, and from its rocky shoreline, which includes the highest point on the Oregon coast, trails lead to beaches and dozens of tidal pools. A relaxed alternative to the more touristy communities to the north, Yachats has all the coastal pleasures: B&Bs, good restaurants, deserted beaches, tidal pools, surf-pounded crags, fishing, and crabbing.

GETTING HERE

Yachats is 24 miles from Newport Municipal Airport, 84 miles from Eugene Airport, and 166 miles from Portland International Airport. **Lincoln Transit** provides bus service to Newport, Siletz, and Lincoln City. **Valley Retriever** (☎ *541/265–2553* ⊕ *www.kokkola-bus.com/ ValleyRetrieverBuslines.html*) and **Greyhound** bus connections to Corvallis are in Newport. The **Omni Shuttle** runs to the Eugene airport, and **Caravan Airport Transportation** runs shuttles to the Portland airport.

VISITOR INFORMATION

Yachats Visitors Center (✉ *241 Hwy. 101* ☎ *541/547–3530 or 800/929–0477* ⊕ *www.yachats.org*).

WHERE TO EAT AND STAY

$$ ✕ **Adobe Restaurant.** The extraordinary ocean views sometimes upstage SEAFOOD   the meal, but if you stick to the seafood, you'll be satisfied. The Baked Crab Pot is a rich, bubbling casserole filled with Dungeness crab and cheese in a shallot cream sauce. Its best dish is the Captain's Seafood Platter, heaped with prawns, scallops, grilled oysters, and razor clams. ✉ *1555 U.S. 101, Yachats* ☎ *541/547–3141* ⊟ *AE, D, DC, MC, V.*

$ ✕ **The Drift Inn.** This restaurant is a terrific find, with the best fresh razor SEAFOOD   clams on the coast. Each night a musician plays to the crowd that sits Fodor'sChoice   below a ceiling full of umbrellas, with views of the Yachats River where ★   it meets the ocean. Friday is open mike night, and Saturday there's a dance rock band. Family-friendly and lively, the Drift Inn features fresh seafood, all-natural steaks, and other local meats and produce. The bar stools are usually crowded, and it has a great selection of Oregon craft brews and wines. ✉ *124 Hwy. 101 N, Yachats* ☎ *541/547–4477* ⊕ *www.the-drift-inn.com* ⊟ *MC, V.*

$$$ ⚟ **Overleaf Lodge.** On a rocky shoreline at the north end of Yachats, Fodor'sChoice   the Overleaf Lodge is a romantic place to enjoy a spectacular sunset ★   in splendid comfort. Its well-kept, spacious rooms have a variety of options, including fireplaces, corner nooks, and whirlpool tubs with ocean views. The adjacent coastal walk is populated with seals. Continental breakfast is provided. **Pros:** best hotel in one of the coast's best communities. **Cons:** no dining, small exercise room. ✉ *280 Overleaf Lodge La., Yachats* ☎ *541/547–4880* ⊕ *www.overleaflodge.com* ⟱ *54 rooms and 4 suites* ⚏ *In-hotel: Wi-Fi, spa, gym, beachfront* ⊟ *AE, D, MC, V* ⏏⏐⏗ *CP.*

SPORTS AND THE OUTDOORS

RECREATIONAL   **Cape Perpetua.** The highest lookout point on the Oregon Coast, Cape AREAS   Perpetua towers 800 feet above the rocky shoreline. Named by Captain Cook on St. Perpetua's Day in 1778, the cape is part of a 2,700-acre scenic area popular with hikers, campers, beachcombers, and naturalists. General information and a map of 10 trails are available at the **Cape Perpetua Visitors Center,** on the east side of the highway, 2 mi south of Devil's Churn. The easy 1-mi **Giant Spruce Trail** passes through a fern-filled rain forest to an enormous 500-year-old Sitka spruce. Easier still is the marked Auto Tour; it begins about 2 mi north of the visitor center and winds through Siuslaw National Forest to the ¼-mi **Whispering Spruce Trail.** Views from the rustic rock shelter here extend 150 mi north and south, and 37 mi out to sea. The **Cape Perpetua Interpretive Center,** in the visitor center, has educational movies and exhibits about the natural forces that shaped Cape Perpetua. ⊠ *U.S. 101, 9 mi south of Yachats* ☎ *541/547–3289* 🚗 *Parking fee $5* ☉ *Daily 10–4.*

Yachats Ocean Road State Recreation Area. Drive this one-mile loop south of Yachats, and discover one of the most scenic viewpoints on the Oregon Coast. Park along the loop to see where the Yachats River meets the Pacific Ocean. There's fun to be had playing on the beach, poking around tidepools, and watching blowholes, summer sunsets, and whales spouting. ⊠ *U.S. 101 to Yachats Ocean Rd., Yachats* ☎ *541/997–3851 or 800/551–6949* ⊕ *www.oregonstateparks.org.*

FLORENCE

25 mi south of Yachats on U.S. 101, 64 mi west of Eugene on Hwy. 126.

Tourists and retirees have been flocking to Florence in ever-greater numbers in recent years. Its restored waterfront Old Town has restaurants, antiques stores, fish markets, and other diversions. But what really makes the town so appealing is its proximity to remarkable stretches of coastline. Seventy-five creeks and rivers empty into the Pacific Ocean in and around Florence, and the Siuslaw River flows right through town. When the numerous nearby lakes are added to the mix, it makes for one of the richest fishing areas in Oregon. Salmon, rainbow trout, bass, perch, crabs, and clams are among the water's treasures. Fishing boats and pleasure craft moor in Florence's harbor, forming a pleasant backdrop for the town's restored buildings. South of town, miles of white-sand dunes lend themselves to everything from solitary hikes to rides aboard all-terrain vehicles.

GETTING HERE

The closest airport is in Newport. **Eugene Porter Stage Lines** provides bus transportation from Florence to Eugene and Coos Bay.

VISITOR INFORMATION

Florence Area Chamber of Commerce (⊠ *290 U.S. 101* ☎ *541/997–3128* ⊕ *www.florencechamber.com*).

EXPLORING

♻ **Sea Lion Caves.** In 1880 a sea captain named Cox rowed a small skiff into a fissure in a 300-foot-high sea cliff. Inside, he was startled to discover a vaulted chamber in the rock, 125 feet high and 2 acres in size. Hundreds of massive sea lions—the largest bulls weighing 2,000 pounds or more—covered every available surface. Cox's discovery would become one of the Oregon Coast's premier tourist attractions. An elevator near the cliff-top ticket office descends to the floor of the cavern, near sea level, where vast numbers of Steller's and California sea lions relax on rocks and swim about (their cute, fuzzy pups can be viewed from behind a wire fence). This is the only known hauling-out area and rookery for wild sea lions on the mainland in the Lower 48, and it's an awesome sight and sound. In spring and summer the mammals usually stay on the rocky ledges outside the cave; in fall and winter they move inside. You'll also see several species of seabirds here, including migratory pigeon guillemots, cormorants, and three varieties of gulls. Gray whales are visible during their northern and southern migrations, October–December and March–May. The gift shop has amazing fudge—try the jalapeño. ✉ *91560 U.S. 101, 10 mi north of downtown Florence* ☎ *541/547–3111* 💲 *$12* 🕙 *Daily 9–5 w sealioncaves.com* ▭ *MC, V.*

NEED A BREAK?

Siuslaw River Coffee Roasters. This small, homey business serves cups of drip-on-demand coffee—you select the roast and they grind and brew it on the spot. Beans are roasted on-site, muffins and breads are freshly baked, and a view of the namesake river can be savored from the deck out back. ✉ *1240 Bay St., Florence* ☎ *541/997–3443 wwww.coffeeoregon.com* ▭ *D, MC, V.*

WHERE TO EAT AND STAY

$$
SEAFOOD
✕ **Bridgewater Seafood Restaurant.** Freshly caught seafood—20 to 25 choices nightly—is the mainstay of this creaky-floored, Victorian-era restaurant in Florence's Old Town. Whether you opt for patio dining during summer or lounge seating in winter, the varied menu of pastas, burgers, and soups offers something for everyone. A live jazz band provides some foot-tapping fun. ✉ *1297 Bay St., Florence* ☎ *541/997–1133* ▭ *AE, D, MC, V.*

$
SEAFOOD
✕ **Waterfront Depot Restaurant and Bar.** The detailed chalkboard menu says it all: from the fresh, crab-encrusted halibut to Bill's Flaming Spanish Coffee, this is a place serious about fresh food and fine flavors. Located in the old Mapleton train station, it has a great view of the Siuslaw River and the Siuslaw River Bridge. In the summer diners can enjoy patio seating right at the water's edge and chomp on the nice variety of tapas plates. ✉ *1252 Bay St., Florence* ☎ *541/902–9100* ⊕ *www.thewaterfrontdepot.com* ▭ *D, MC, V.*

$$$
Fodor's Choice
★
🏨 **Heceta House.** On a windswept promontory, this unusual late-Victorian B&B surrounded by a white-picket fence is one of Oregon's most remarkable bed-and-breakfasts. Now owned by the U.S. Forest Service, it is managed by Steve and Michelle Bursey, certified executive chefs who prepare a seven-course breakfast (included in the room rate) each morning. The menu changes according to the season. Meals include herbs and produce out of the Lightstation garden and highlight the best of Oregon: artisan cheeses, sausages, produce, and Carol Korgan's pastries. The nicest of the simply furnished rooms is the Mariner's, with a private bath and an awe-inspiring view. Filled with period detailing and antiques, the common areas are warm and inviting. If you're lucky, you may hear Rue, the resident ghost, in the middle of the night. **Pros:** you won't find any property quite like this— as though you were living in a novel. **Cons:** not within walking distance of the town or other activities. ✉ *92072 U.S. 101, Florence* ☎ *541/547–3696* ⊕ *www.hecetalighthouse.com* 🛏 *6 rooms, 4 with bath* ▭ *D, MC, V* 🍴 *BP.*

$$
🏨 **River House Inn.** Located on the beautiful Siuslaw River, this property has terrific accommodations and is near quaint shops and restaurants in Florence's Old Town. Golfing, horseback riding. and sand dune activities are nearby. Most rooms have a stunning river view of boats and wildlife. **Pros:** Spacious, well decorated. **Cons:** Not located

Umpqua Sand Dunes in Oregon Dunes National Recreation Area

on the beach. ✉ *1202 Bay St., Florence* ☎ *541/997–3933 or 888/824–2750* ⊕ *www.riverhouseflorence.com* ↪ *40 rooms* ⌂ *In-room: Wi-Fi, refrigerator* ⊟ *AE, D, MC, V* ⋈ *CP.*

NIGHTLIFE AND THE ARTS

Three Rivers Casino and Hotel. This casino has 700 of the newest slots and video games. It also has table games, including roulette, craps, blackjack, no-limit Texas hold 'em, as well as keno and bingo. Five dining venues—from the refined to the casual—suit every taste. Nearby are beaches, shopping, fishing, and two popular golf courses. ✉ *5647 Highway 126, Florence* ☎ *541/997–7529 or 877/374–8378* ⊕ *www. threeriverscasino.com.*

SPORTS AND THE OUTDOORS

RECREATIONAL
AREAS

Devil's Elbow State Park. A ½-mi trail from the beachside parking lot leads to **Heceta Head Lighthouse,** whose beacon, visible for more than 21 mi, is the most powerful on the Oregon Coast. ✉ *U.S. 101* ☎ *541/547–3416* ✉ *Day use $5, lighthouse tours free* ☉ *Lighthouse May–Oct., weekdays 11–1; Nov.–Feb. Park daily dawn–dusk.*

ⓒ
Fodor'sChoice
★

Oregon Dunes National Recreation Area. Open year-round, the Oregon Dunes National Recreation Area is the largest expanse of coastal sand dunes in North America, extending for 40 miles, from Florence to Coos Bay. The area contains some of the best ATV riding in the United States, with 5,930 acres of open sand and 6,140 acres with designated trails. More than 1.5 million people visit the dunes each year, and about 350,000 are ATV users, nearly half of them from outside Oregon. **Honeyman Memorial State Park,** 522 acres within the recreation area, is a base camp for dune-buggy enthusiasts, mountain bikers, hikers, boaters, horseback riders, and dogsledders (the sandy hills are an excellent training ground). It has 41 full sites $26; 121 electrical $26; 187 tent sites $21; hiker/biker sites $5; and yurts $39. The dunes are a vast playground for children, particularly the slopes surrounding cool **Cleawox Lake.** ⊠ *Oregon Dunes National Recreation Area office, 855 U.S. 101, Reedsport* ☎ *541/271–6000* ⊡ *Day use $5* ☉ *Daily dawn–dusk.*

ⓒ **Sandland Adventures.** This has everything you need to get the whole
Fodor'sChoice family together for the ride of their lives. Start off with a heart-racing
★ dune-buggy ride with a professional that will take you careening up, over, down, and around some of the steepest sand in the Oregon Dunes National Recreation Area. After you're done screaming and smiling, Sandland's park has bumper boats, a go-kart track, a miniature golf course, and a small railroad. ⊠ *85366 Hwy. 101 S* ☎ *541/997-8087* ⊕ *www.sandland.com.*

GOLF **Oregon Dunes Golf Links.** A favorite of locals year-round, Oregon Dunes
Fodor'sChoice Golf Links is a straightforward 18 holes that reward great shots and
★ penalize the poor ones. You won't find many sand bunkers, because the narrow course is surrounded by sand dunes. Instead, you'll encounter fairways winding about dunes lined with ball-swallowing gorse, heather, shore pines, and native sea grasses. Pot bunkers guard small greens, and play can get pretty frisky if the frequent wind picks up. However, the course is well drained and playable—even under the wettest conditions. ⊠ *3345 Munsel Lake Rd., Florence* ☎ *541/991–2744* ⊕ *www.oceandunesgolf.com* ⊡ *Summer rates: 18 holes $42, 9 holes $25.*

Sandpines Golf Links. This Scottish Links-style course is playable year-round. Designed by Rees Jones, the outward nine is cut out of pine forest and near blue lakes; and the inward nine provides some undulating fun, with the rolling dunes at the forefront from tee to green. While challenging, the course is generous enough to provide a great day on the links for beginners and more polished players. Sandpines has a fully equipped practice area with a driving range, bunkers, and putting greens. When it opened in 1993, *Golf Digest* named it the Best New Public Course in America. ⊠ *1201 35th St., Florence* ☎ *800/971–4653* ⊕ *www.sandpines.com* ⊡ *Summer rates: 18 holes $79.*

HIKING **Carl G. Washburne Memorial.** A trail from this park connects you to the Heceta Head Trail, which you can use to reach the Heceta Head Lighthouse. Its campground has 56 full hookups $26, 7 tent sites $21, hiker/biker sites $5, and 2 yurts $39. ⊠ *93111 U.S. 101 N, Florence* ☎ *541/547–3416* ⊕ *www.oregonstateparks.org.*

HORSEBACK **C & M Stables.** Ride year-round along the Oregon Dunes National Rec-
RIDING reation Area. The area is rich with marine life, including sea lions, whales, and coastal birds. Sharp-eyed riders also might spot bald eagles, red-tailed fox, and deer. Rides range from hour-long trots to half-day adventures. Children must be at least eight years old for the beach ride or six years old for the dune trail rides. There are also six overnight RV spaces. ⊠ *90241 U.S. 101 N, Florence* ☎ *541/997–7540* w*www. oregonhorsebackriding.com* ⊡ *$40–$150* ⊟ *AE, D, MC, V* ☉ *Daily 10–5.*

SANDBOARD-
ING

Sand Master Park. Everything you need to sandboard the park's private dunes is right here: Board rental, wax, eyewear, clothing, and instruction. The staff is exceptionally helpful, and will get beginners off on their sandboarding adventure with enthusiasm. However, what must be surfed, must first be hiked up, and so on. ⊠ *87542 Hwy 101 N, Florence* ☏ *541/997–6006* ⊕ *www.sandmasterpark.com* ⊙ *June–Sept. 10, daily 9–6:30; off-season, Mon.–Sat. 10–5, Sun. 11–5.*

SOUTHERN COAST

3

Outdoors enthusiasts will find a natural amusement park along this gorgeous stretch of coast from Reedsport to Brookings. Its northern portion has a continuation of the Oregon Dunes National Recreation Area, and is the location for its visitors center. The Umpqua Discovery Center is a perfect trip with the kids, or just yourself, to learn about the region's history and animals. In Bandon golfers will find one of the most celebrated cluster of courses in the nation at Bandon Dunes—plus it just opened a new, fourth course, Old Macdonald. Lovers of lighthouses, sailing, fishing, crabbing, elk-viewing, camping, and water sports will wonder why they didn't venture south sooner.

REEDSPORT

20 mi south of Florence on U.S. 101, 90 mi southwest of Eugene via I–5 and Hwy. 38.

The small town of Reedsport owes its existence to the Umpqua River, one of the state's great steelhead-fishing streams. Hikers will enjoy the picturesque, quiet hiking trails that wander through the forest, onto the dunes, and through the beach grass to the beaches. As in Florence to the north, there are plenty of ATV and dune-buggy riders on the dunes. The area is also a favorite of campers and nature lovers who watch herds of majestic elk in the Deer Creek Preserve.

GETTING HERE

From Reedsport, **Greyhound** bus lines provides limited service to Eugene. The nearest airport is 25 miles to the south in North Bend. Reedsport is 196 miles from Portland.

VISITOR INFORMATION

Reedsport/Winchester Bay Chamber of Commerce (⊠ *855 Highway Ave., Reedsport* ☏ *541/271–3495 or 800/247–2155* ⊕ *www.reedsportcc.org*).

EXPLORING

Oregon Dunes National Recreation Area Visitors Center. The natural forces that created the towering sand dunes along this section of the Oregon Coast (*see the listing in Florence, above*) are explained in interpretive exhibits. The center, which also sells maps, books, and gifts, is a good place to pick up free literature on the area. ⊠ *855 Highway Ave., south side of Umpqua River Bridge, Reedsport* ☏ *541/271–3611* ⊠ *Free* ⊙ *June–Aug., daily 8–4:30; Sept.–May, weekdays 8–4:30.*

Ⓒ **Umpqua Discovery Center.** Exhibits at this waterfront location provide a good introduction to the Lower Umpqua estuary and surrounding region. One of two state-of-the-art wings focuses on cultural history; the other, on natural history, has an indoor simulated walking trail, which whisks you through four seasons. ✉ *409 Riverfront Way, Reedsport* ☎ *541/271–4816* ⊕ *www.umpquadiscoverycenter.com* ▦ *Museum $8 adults, $6 ages 6–15, under 6 free* ⊙ *June–Sept., daily 9–5; Oct.–May, daily 10–4.*

Umpqua Lighthouse Park. Some of the highest sand dunes in the country are found in this 50-acre park 6 mi south of Reedsport. The first **Umpqua River Lighthouse,** built on the dunes at the mouth of the Umpqua River in 1857, lasted only four years before it toppled over in a storm. It took local residents 33 years to build another one. The "new" lighthouse, built on a bluff overlooking the south side of Winchester Bay and operated by the U.S. Coast Guard, is still going strong, flashing a warning beacon out to sea every five seconds. The **Douglas County Coastal Visitors Center** adjacent to the lighthouse has a museum and can arrange lighthouse tours. ✉ *Umpqua Hwy., west side of U.S. 101, Reedsport* ☎ *541/271–4631* ▦ *Donations suggested* ⊙ *Lighthouse May–Sept., Wed.–Sat. 10–4, Sun. 1–4.*

EN ROUTE

A public pier at **Winchester Bay's Salmon Harbor,** 3¼ mi south of Reedsport, juts out over the bay and yields excellent results for crabbers and fishermen (especially those after rockfish). There's also a full-service marina with a fish market, **the Sportsmen's Cannery,** which serves a fresh seafood barbecue on weekends (from Memorial Day to Labor Day).

WHERE TO EAT AND STAY

$ ✕ **Bedrocks on the Bay.** Outstanding pizza, sandwiches, and fresh fish-and-chips highlight this casual local restaurant on Winchester Bay's PIZZA Salmon Harbor. Be sure and try the halibut fish-and-chips. It also serves breakfast. ✉ *105 Coho Point Loop, Winchester Bay* ☎ *541/271–2431* ⊕ *bedrocksrestaurants.com* ▭ *MC, V.*

¢   🏨 **Anchor Bay Inn.** In the center of Reedsport, this clean, inexpensive motel has hospitable service and easy access to the dunes. **Pros:** frugal choice. **Cons:** road noise. ✉ *1821 Winchester Ave.* ☎ *541/271–2149 or 800/767–1821* ⊕ *www.u-s-history.com/or/a/anchobin.htm* ⟿ *21 rooms* ⌂ *In-hotel: pool, laundry facilities, some pets allowed* ▭ *AE, D, MC, V* ⦿ *CP.*

SPORTS AND THE OUTDOORS

RECREATIONAL AREAS

Ⓒ **Dean Creek Elk Viewing Area.** A herd of wild Roosevelt elk, Oregon's largest land mammal, roams within sight. Abundant forage and a mild winter climate enable the elk to remain at Dean Creek year-round. The best viewing times are early morning and just before dusk. ✉ *Hwy. 38, 3 mi east of Reedsport* ▦ *Free* ⊙ *Daily dawn–dusk.*

William M. Tugman State Park. On Eel Lake near the town of Lakeside, a dense forest of spruce, cedar, fir, and alder surrounds the little-known park. Recreational activities include fishing, swimming, canoeing, and sailing. ✉ *U.S. 101 S, North Bend* ☎ *541/888–4902 or 800/551–6949* ⊕ *www.oregonstateparks.org* ▦ *$5 per vehicle day-use fee.*

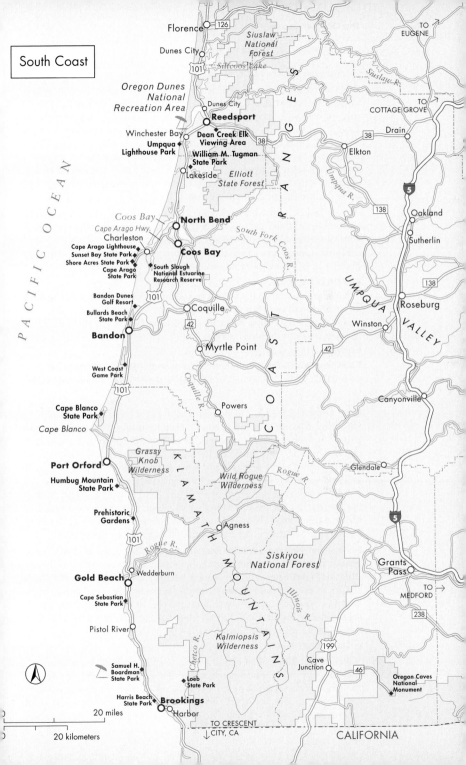

South Coast

BAY AREA: COOS BAY & NORTH BEND

27 mi south of Reedsport on U.S. 101.

The Coos Bay–Charleston–North Bend metropolitan area, collectively known as the Bay Area (population 25,000), is the gateway to rewarding recreational experiences. The town of Coos Bay lies next to the largest natural harbor between San Francisco Bay and Seattle's Puget Sound. A century ago, vast quantities of lumber cut from the Coast Range were milled in Coos Bay and shipped around the world. Coos Bay still has a reputation as a rough-and-ready port city, but with mill closures and dwindling lumber reserves it is looking to tourism and other industries for economic growth.

To see the best of the Bay Area, head west from Coos Bay on Newmark Avenue for about 7 mi to **Charleston**. Though it's a Bay Area community, this quiet fishing village at the mouth of Coos Bay is a world unto itself. As it loops into town, the road becomes the Cape Arago Highway and leads to several oceanfront parks.

GETTING HERE

Private and commercial jets use the Southwest Oregon Regional Airport in North Bend. Bus service to the airport and to south-coast communities is provided by **Curry Public Transit's Coastal Express** (☎ *800/921–2871* ⊕ *www.currypublictransit.org*).

VISITOR INFORMATION

Coos Bay - North Bend Visitors & Convention Bureau (✉ *50 Central Ave., Coos Bay* ☎ *541/269–0215 or 800/824–8486* ⊕ *www.oregonsadventurecoast.com*).

EXPLORING

Cape Arago Lighthouse. On a rock island just 12 mi offshore south of Coos Bay, this lighthouse has had several iterations; the first lighthouse was built here in 1866, but it was destroyed by storms and erosion. A second, built in 1908, suffered the same fate. The current white tower, built in 1934, is 44 feet tall and towers 100 feet above the ocean. If you're on a foggy day, listen for its unique foghorn. The lighthouse is connected to the mainland by a bridge. Neither is open to the public, but there's an excellent spot to view this lonely guardian and much of the coastline. From U.S. 101, take Cape Arago Highway to Gregory Point, where it ends at a turnaround, and follow the short trail.

South Slough National Estuarine Research Reserve. The reserve's fragile ecosystem supports everything from algae to bald eagles and black bears. More than 300 species of birds have been sighted at the reserve, which has an interpretive center, guided walks (summer only), and nature trails that give you a chance to see things up close. ✉ *Seven Devils Rd., 4 mi south of Charleston, Coos Bay* ☎ *541/888–5558* 🎫 *Free* ⊗ *Trails daily dawn–dusk, interpretive center daily 10–4:30.*

WHERE TO EAT AND STAY

$$

NEW AMERICAN

⨯ **Blue Heron Bistro**. You'll find subtle preparations of local seafood, chicken, and homemade pasta at this busy bistro. There are no flat spots on the far-ranging menu; even the innovative soups and desserts are excellent. The skylit, tile-floor dining room seats about 70 amid natural wood and blue linen. The seating area outside has blue awnings and colorful Bavarian window boxes that add a festive touch. Eighteen microbrews are available. ⊠ *100 W. Commercial St., Coos Bay* ☎ *541/267–3933* ▭ *D, MC, V* ⊗ *Closed Sun. Oct.–May.*

$$ ✕ **Portside Restaurant.** The fish served at this restaurant overlooking the
SEAFOOD   Charleston boat basin comes straight to the kitchen from the dock outside. Try the steamed Dungeness crab with drawn butter. The nautical furnishings—vintage bayside photos, boat lamps, navigational aids, coiled rope—reinforce the view of the harbor through the restaurant's picture windows. ⊠ *8001 Kingfisher Rd.,Charleston* ☎ *541/888–5544* ▭ *AE, MC, V.*

$$ ▦ **Coos Bay Manor.** Built in 1912 on a quiet residential street in Coos Bay, this 15-room Colonial Revival manor is listed on the National Register of Historic Places. Hardwood floors, detailed woodwork, high ceilings, and antiques and period reproductions offset the red-and-gold-flecked wallpaper. An unusual open balcony on the second floor leads to the large rooms. Innkeepers Jon & Felicia Noack serve a full breakfast (included in the rates), and are happy to fulfill dietary requests. Just let them know in advance. Kids and pets are welcome. **Pros:** very nicely kept and decorated. **Cons:** located in town, but only condos are on the beach. ⊠ *955 S. 5th St., Coos Bay* ☎ *541/269–1224 or 800/269–1224* ⊕ *www.coosbaymanor.com* ◄ᵤ *5 rooms* ♿ *In-hotel: Wi-Fi* ▭ *AE, MC, V* ⏐⊙⏐ *BP.*

NIGHTLIFE AND THE ARTS

The Mill Casino. This casino offers lively gaming, top-name touring entertainers, and a spacious hotel. The complex has a casino with more than 700 slots, craps, blackjack, poker, roulette, and bingo. Included in the property's five dining venues are a waterfront restaurant and a bakery. ⊠ *3201 Tremont Ave., North Bend* ☎ *541/756–8800 or 800/953–4800* ⊕ *www.themillcasino.com* ▭ *AE, D, MC, V.*

SPORTS AND THE OUTDOORS

RECREATIONAL   **Cape Arago State Park.** The distant barking of sea lions echoes in the air
AREAS   at a trio of coves connected by short but steep trails. The park overlooks the **Oregon Islands National Wildlife Refuge,** where offshore rocks, beaches, islands, and reefs provide breeding grounds for seabirds and marine mammals. ⊠ *End of Cape Arago Hwy., 1 mi south of Shore Acres State Park* ☎ *866/888–6100* ▱ *Free* ⊗ *Daily dawn–dusk. Trail closed Mar.–June* ⊕ *www.oregonstateparks.org.*

Shore Acres State Park. An observation building on a grassy bluff overlooking the Pacific marks the site that held the mansion of lumber baron Louis J. Simpson. The view over the rugged wave-smashed cliffs is splendid, but the real glory of Shore Acres lies a few hundred yards to the south, where an entrance gate leads into what was Simpson's private garden. Beautifully landscaped and meticulously maintained, the gardens incorporate formal English and Japanese designs. From March to mid-October the grounds are ablaze with blossoming daffodils, rhododendrons, azaleas, roses, and dahlias. In December the garden is decked out with a dazzling display of holiday lights. ⊠ *10965 Cape Arago Hwy., 1 mi south of Sunset Bay State Park, Coos Bay* ☎ *866/888–6100* ▱ *$5 per vehicle day-use fee* ⊗ *Daily 8–dusk.*

BANDON

25 mi south of Coos Bay on U.S. 101.

Referred to by some who cherish its romantic lure as Bandon-by-the-Sea, Bandon is both a harbor town and a popular vacation spot. Bandon is famous for its cranberry products, its cheese factory, as well as its artists' colony, complete with galleries and shops. Two national wildlife refuges, Oregon Islands and Bandon Marsh, are within the city limits. The Bandon Dunes links-style course is a worldwide attraction, often ranked in the top three golf courses in the U.S.

It may seem odd that tiny Bandon bills itself as Oregon's cranberry capital. But 10 mi north of town lie acres of bogs and irrigated fields where tons of the tart berries are harvested every year. Each October there's the Cranberry Festival, complete with a parade and a fair.

GETTING HERE

Bandon is 29 miles from the North Bend airport. Bus service is provided by **Curry Public Transit's Coastal Express** (☎ *800/921–2871* ⊕ *www.currypublictransit.org*), which travels the US Hwy 101 corridor from Smith River, Calif., northward through Brookings, Gold Beach, Port Orford, Bandon, Coos Bay, and North Bend.

VISITOR INFORMATION

Bandon Chamber of Commerce (*300 Second St., Bandon* ✉*541/347–9616 www.bandon.com*).

EXPLORING

Bandon Historical Society Museum. In the old City Hall building, this museum depicts the area's early history, including Native American artifacts, logging, fishing, cranberry farming, and the disastrous 1936 fire that destroyed the city. Its gift shop has books, knickknacks, jewelry, myrtlewood, and other little treasures. ✉ *270 Fillmore St., Bandon* ☎ *541/347–2164* ⊕ *bandonhistoricalmuseum.org* ✍ *$2* ☉ *Mon.–Sat. 10–4.*

West Coast Game Park. The "walk-through safari" on 21 acres has free-roaming wildlife: 450 animals and 75 species, including lions, tigers, snow leopards, bears, chimps, cougars, and camels, make it one of the largest wild-animal petting parks in the United States. The big attractions here are the young animals: bear cubs, tiger cubs, whatever is suitable for actual handling. It is 7 mi south of Bandon on U.S. 101. ✉ *U.S. 101, Bandon* ☎ *541/347–3106* ⊕ *www.gameparksafari.com* ✍ *$16* ☉ *Mid-June–Labor Day, daily 9–5 (last admittance 4:30).*

WHERE TO EAT AND STAY

$$$

STEAK

Fodor's Choice

★

✕ **Lord Bennett's.** His lordship has a lot going for him: a cliff-top setting, a comfortable and spacious dining area, sunsets visible through picture windows overlooking Face Rock Beach, and occasional musical performers on weekends. The rich dishes include prawns sautéed with sherry and garlic and steaks topped with shiitake mushrooms. A Sunday brunch is served. ✉ *1695 Beach Loop Rd., Bandon* ☎ *541/347–3663* ⊕ *www.lordbennett.com* ▭ *AE, D, MC, V* ☉ *No lunch Mon.–Thurs.*

3

$$$ 🏨 **Bandon Dunes Golf Resort.** This golfing lodge provides a luxurious
Fodor's Choice place to relax after a day on the links, with single rooms and four-bed-
★ room suites, many with beautiful views of the famous Bandon Dunes
Golf Course. There are cottages available that are designed for a quartet
of golfers. Each unit includes a gathering room with fireplace, outdoor
patio area, and four separate bedrooms with a king bed and private
bath. There are also other lodging options available throughout the
vast resort property, and five different restaurant and lounge choices.
Pros: if you're a golfer, this adds to an incredible overall experience;
if not, you'll have a wonderful stay anyway. **Cons:** the weather can
be coarse in the shoulder-season months. ⊠ *57744 Round Lake Dr.,
Bandon* ☎ *541/347–4380 or 800/345–6008* ⊕ *www.bandondunesgolf.
com* ⤴ *186 rooms* ⚹ *In-hotel: Wi-Fi, gym, parking, room service* ⊟ *AE,
D, DC, MC, V.*

SPORTS AND THE OUTDOORS

RECRE- **Bullards Beach State Park.** The octagonal **Coquille Lighthouse,** built in
ATIONAL AREA 1896 and no longer in use, stands lonely sentinel at the mouth of the
Coquille River. From the highway the 2-mi drive to reach it passes
through the Bandon Marsh, a prime bird-watching and picnicking area.
The beach beside the lighthouse is a good place to search for jasper,
agate, and driftwood. Note: 104 full hookups, 81 electrical $24; 13
yurts $36; horse camp 8 sites (3 single corrals, 3 double corrals, 2 four-
space corrals) $19; hiker/biker camp $5. ⊠ *U.S. 101, 2 mi north of
Bandon, Bandon* ☎ *800/551–6949; 541/347–3501 lighthouse* ⊠ *Free*
⊙ *Daily 9–5.*

GOLF **Bandon Dunes Golf Resort.** This playland for the nation's golfing elite is
Fodor's Choice no stranger to well-heeled athletes flying in to North Bend on private
★ jets to play on the resort's four distinct courses, including the new Old
Macdonald course, which opened in Spring 2010. The expectations at
Bandon Dunes are that you will walk the course with a caddy—adding
another refined, traditional touch. Greens fees range, according to sea-
son and other factors, $220–$275 a round from May to October, $75–
$265 other months. Caddy fees are $55 for single bag, $110 double.
⊠ *57744 Round Lake Dr., Bandon* ☎ *541/347–4380 or 800/345–6008*
⊕ *www.bandondunesgolf.com* ⊟ *AE, D, DC, MC, V.*

PORT ORFORD

30 mi south of Bandon.

The westernmost incorporated city in the contiguous United States, Port
Orford is surrounded by forests, rivers, lakes, and beaches. The jetty
at Port Orford offers little protection from storms, so every night the
fishing boats are lifted out and stored on the docks. Commercial fishing
boats search for crab, tuna, snapper, and salmon in the waters out of
Port Orford, and diving boats gather sea urchins for Japanese markets.
Visitors can fish off the Port Orford Dock or the jetty for smelt, sardine,
herring, lingcod, halibut, and perch. Dock Beach provides beach fishing.
The area is a favorite spot for sport divers because of the near-shore,
protected reef, and for whale-watchers in fall and early spring.

GETTING HERE

Port Orford is 56 miles from the North Bend airport. Bus service is provided by **Curry Public Transit's Coastal Express** (☎ *800/921–2871* ⊕ *www.currypublictransit.org*), which travels the US Hwy 101 corridor from Smith River, Calif., northward through Brookings, Gold Beach, Port Orford, Bandon, Coos Bay, and North Bend.

VISITOR INFORMATION

Port Orford Visitor's Center Information (⊠ *Battle Rock Wayside, Port Orford* ☎ *541/332–4106* ⊕ *www. discoverportorford.com*).

THE FAB 50

U.S. 101 between Port Orford and Brookings, often referred to as the "fabulous 50 miles," soars up green headlands, some of them hundreds of feet high, and past a seascape of cliffs and sea stacks. The ocean is bluer and clearer—though not appreciably warmer—than it is farther north, and the coastal countryside is dotted with farms, grazing cattle, and small rural communities.

EXPLORING

OFF THE BEATEN PATH

Prehistoric Gardens. As you round a bend between Port Orford and Gold Beach, you'll see one of those sights that make grown-ups groan and kids squeal with delight: a huge, open-jawed Tyrannosaurus rex, with a green brontosaurus peering out from the forest beside it. Twenty-three life-size dinosaur replicas are on display. ⊠ *36848 U.S. 101, Port Orford* ☎ *541/332–4463* 🏷 *$9* ⊗ *Summer, daily 9–6; winter, daily 9–5.*

WHERE TO STAY

$$ 🏨 **Floras Lake House by the Sea.** This cedar home rests beside freshwater Floras Lake, spring-fed and separated from the ocean by only a sand spit. It's a bit tricky to find. The owners run a windsurfing school on the lake. The interior of the house is light, airy, and comfortable, with picture windows, exposed beams, contemporary couches, and a wood-stove. There are four rooms, two with fireplaces, and all have private deck entrances. Outside, there's a garden, with a sauna beside the lake. ⊠ *92870 Boice Cope Rd., Langlois* ☎ *541/348–2573* ⊕ *www.floraslake. com* 🛏 *4 rooms* 🗘 *In-room: no phone, no TV, Wi-Fi* ▭ *MC, V* ⊗ *Closed Nov.–mid-Feb.* ⦁⊙⦁ *BP.*

$ 🏨 **Home by the Sea.** One of the oldest B&Bs in Oregon, this three-story shingle house is on a headland jutting into the Pacific. A nearby path leads down to the beach. Both guest rooms have views of the ocean, as does the lower-level solarium and breakfast room, a great spot for watching whales (October–May is the best time) and winter storms. ⊠ *444 Jackson St., Port Orford* ☎ *541/332–2855* ⊕ *www. homebythesea.com* 🛏 *2 rooms* 🗘 *In-room: Wi-Fi. In-hotel: laundry facilities* ▭ *MC, V* ⦁⊙⦁ *BP.*

SPORTS AND THE OUTDOORS

RECREATIONAL AREAS

Cape Blanco State Park. The westernmost point in Oregon and perhaps the windiest—gusts clocked at speeds as high as 184 mph have twisted and battered the Sitka spruces along the 6-mi road from U.S. 101 to the **Cape Blanco Lighthouse.** The lighthouse, atop a 245-foot headland, has been in continuous use since 1870, longer than any other in Oregon. No one knows why the Spaniards sailing past these reddish bluffs in

1603 called them *blanco* (white). One theory is that the name refers to the fossilized shells that glint in the cliff face. Campsites at the 1,880-acre park are available on a first-come, first-served basis. Saturday-evening tours are available in summer, with a donation suggested. ⊠ *Cape Blanco Rd., follow signs from U.S. 101, Sixes* ☎ *541/332–6774* ⊕ *www. oregonstateparks.org* 🗺 *Lighthouse tour $2. Park day use free* ☼ *Park daily dawn–dawn; lighthouse Apr.–Oct. 31, Tues.–Sun. 10–3:30.*

Humbug Mountain State Park. Six miles south of Port Orford, this park, especially popular with campers, usually has warm weather, thanks to the nearby mountains, which block the ocean breezes. Windsurfing and scuba diving are popular here. Hiking trails lead to the top of Humbug Mountain. The campground has 32 electrical ($20) and 62 tent sites ($17), and a hiker/biker camp ($5). 3 electrical and 4 tent sites are accessible to the disabled. ⊠ *U.S. 101, Port Orford* ☎ *541/332–6774 or 800/551–6949* ⊕ *www.oregonstateparks.org.*

GOLD BEACH

28 mi south of Port Orford on U.S. 101.

The fabled Rogue River is one of the few U.S. rivers to merit Wild and Scenic status from the federal government. From spring to late fall an estimated 50,000 visitors descend on the town to take one of the daily jet-boat excursions that roar upstream from Wedderburn, Gold Beach's sister city across the bay, into the Rogue River Wilderness Area. Black bears, otters, beavers, ospreys, egrets, and bald eagles are seen regularly on these trips.

Gold Beach is very much a seasonal town, thriving in summer and nearly deserted the rest of the year because of its remote location. It marks the entrance to Oregon's banana belt, where mild, California-like temperatures take the sting out of winter and encourage a blossoming trade in lilies and daffodils.

GETTING HERE

Gold Beach is 84 mi south of the North Bend airport. Bus service is provided by **Curry Public Transit's Coastal Express** (☎ *800/921–2871* ⊕ *www. currypublictransit.org*), which travels the US Hwy 101 corridor from Smith River, Calif., northward through Brookings, Gold Beach, Port Orford, Bandon, Coos Bay, and North Bend.

VISITOR INFORMATION

Gold Beach Visitors Center (⊠ *94080 Shirley La., Gold Beach* ☎ *541/247–7526 or 800/525–2334* ⊕ *www.goldbeach.org*).

WHERE TO EAT AND STAY

$ | NEW AMERICAN | Fodor's Choice ★ ✕ **Rollin 'n Dough Bakery & Bistro.** Patti Joyce greets people like family in her kitchen. Not only does she create exquisite pastries, cheesecakes, and breads, but her Rollin 'n Dough Deli also carries imported cheeses, ethnic meats, and gourmet lunches. The Bistro has table service for soups, salads, pasta dishes, specialty sandwiches, and desserts. It's a little tough to find, but worth seeking out: it's on the north bank of the Rogue River, across the street from Lex's Landing. ⊠ *94257 N. Bank*

Rogue, Gold Beach ☎ *541/247–4438* ▭ *D, MC, V* ☾ *Closed Mon. No dinner. Sporadic hours in winter.*

$$$$

Fodor's Choice

★

📺 **Tu Tu' Tun Lodge.** Pronounced "too-*too*-tin," this well-known fishing resort is a slice of heaven on the Rogue River, 7 mi upriver from Gold Beach. Owner Kyle Ringer is intent on providing his guests with a singular Northwest experience. All the units in this small establishment present rustic elegance. Some have hot tubs, others have fireplaces, and a few have both; private decks overlook the river. Two deluxe rooms feature outdoor soaking tubs with river views. Guided fishing trips and river activities here are popular, and nearby jet-boat excursions and world-class golf at Bandon Dunes are also draws. The restaurant (closed November–April) serves breakfast, lunch, and dinner; the last, open to outside guests (though reservations are hard to come by), consists of a five-course prix-fixe meal that changes nightly. **Pros:** warm, personable, beautiful and luxurious; delicious gourmet dining and wine tasting; activities to suit every taste. **Cons:** no TV, not well suited for young kids. ☒ *96550 N. Bank Rogue, Gold Beach* ☎ *541/247–6664* ⊕ *www.tututun.com* ⤶ *16 rooms, 2 suites* ♿ *In-room: no TV, Wi-Fi. In-hotel: restaurant, bar, golf course* ▭ *D, MC, V.*

SPORTS AND THE OUTDOORS

RECREATIONAL AREAS

Cape Sebastian State Park. The parking lots at this park are more than 200 feet above sea level. At the south parking vista you can see up to 43 mi north to Humbug Mountain. Looking south, you can see nearly 50 mi toward Crescent City, California, and the Point Saint George Lighthouse. A deep forest of Sitka spruce covers most of the park. There's a 1½-mi walking trail. Be warned: there's no drinking water. ☒ *U.S. 101, Gold Beach* ☎ *541/469–2021 or 800/551–6949* ⊕ *www. oregonstateparks.org.*

▮
EN
ROUTE

Between Gold Beach and Brookings you'll cross Thomas Creek Bridge, the highest span in Oregon. Take advantage of the off-road coastal viewing points along the 10-mi-long **Samuel H. Boardman State Park**— especially in summer, when highway traffic becomes heavy and rubbernecking can be dangerous.

BOATING

Jerry's Rogue Jets. These Rogue River jet boats operate in the most rugged section of the Wild and Scenic Rogue River, offering 64-, 80-, and 104-mi tours. Whether visitors choose a shorter, 6-hour lower Rogue scenic trip or an 8-hour white-water trip, folks will have a rollicking good time. Its largest vessels are 40-feet long and can hold 75 passengers. The smaller, white-water boats are 32-feet long and can hold 42 passengers. ☒ *29985 Harbor Way, Gold Beach* ☎ *541/247–4571 or 800/451–3645* ⊕ *www.roguejets.com.*

FISHING

Five Star Charters. Fishing charter trips range from a 4-hour bottom-fish outing to a full-day salmon, steelhead, or halibut charter. It offers all the tackle needed, and customers don't even need experience—they'll take beginners and experts. The outfit has 4 river boats, including 2 drift boats and 2 power boats, as well as 2 ocean boats. They operate year-round. ☒ *Port of Gold Beach, Gold Beach* ☎ *541/247–0217 or 888/301–6480* ⊕ *www.goldbeachadventures.com.*

Willamette Valley and Wine Country

WORD OF MOUTH

"Thanksgiving weekend is a big deal here in the Willamette Valley. Many wineries open their doors for tastings and it is an excellent way to see what there is. Many of the wineries are normally by appt only, so this is a great chance to check them out."

—mms

WELCOME TO WILLAMETTE VALLEY AND WINE COUNTRY

TOP REASONS TO GO

★ **Swirl and sip.** Each region in the Willamette Valley offers some of the finest vintages and dining experiences found anywhere.

★ **Soar through the air.** Newberg's hot-air balloons will give you a bird's eye view of Yamhill's wine country.

★ **Run rapids.** Feel the bouncing exhilaration and the cold spray of white-water rafting on the wild, winding McKenzie River outside Eugene.

★ **Walk on the wild side.** The Jackson Bottom Nature Preserve gives walkers a chance to view otters, beavers, herons, and eagles.

★ **Back the Beavers or Ducks.** Nothing gets the blood pumping like an Oregon State Beaver or University of Oregon Ducks football game.

1 **North Willamette Valley.** Most visitors begin their journey into wine country here, an area rich with upscale dining, shopping, the arts, and wineries. Close to Portland, North Willamette's communities provide all the amenities of urban life with a whole lot less concrete. Wine enthusiasts will relish the excellent vineyards in Beaverton, Hillsboro, and Forest Grove.

2 **Yamhill County.** This part of the state has undergone a renaissance in the last 20 years, as the world has beaten a path to its door, seeking the perfect pinot. Many of the Willamette's highest-rated wineries are here. There are gorgeous inns, wine bars, and unforgettable restaurants providing a complete vacation experience.

3 **Mid-Willamette Valley.** Agriculture is the mainstay of this region; its roadsides are dotted with fruit and veggie stands, and towns boast farmers' markets. Its flat terrain is ideal for bicycle trips and hikes. The state capitol is Salem, and Oregon State University is in Corvallis.

4 **South Willamette Valley.** Here visitors soak in natural hot springs, hike in dense forest, run the rapids, or cheer on the Oregon Ducks. Eugene has a friendly, youthful vibe, which is enhanced by the natural splendor of the region.

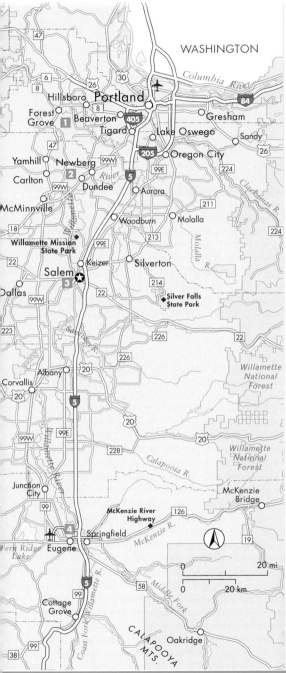

WASHINGTON

GETTING ORIENTED

The Willamette Valley is a fertile mix of urban, rural, and wild stretching from Portland at the north to Cottage Grove at the south. It is bordered by the Cascade Range to the east and the Coast Range to the west. The Calapooya Mountains border it to the south and the mighty Columbia River runs along the north. Running north and south, Interstate 5 connects communities throughout the valley. In the mid-1800s the Willamette Valley was the destination of emigrants on the Oregon Trail, and today is home to about two-thirds of the state's population. The Willamette Valley is 150 miles long and up to 60 miles wide, which makes it Oregon's largest wine-growing region.

4

WILLAMETTE VALLEY AND WINE COUNTRY PLANNER

When to Go

July to October are the best times to wander the country roads in the Willamette Valley, exploring the grounds of its many wineries. Fall itself is spectacular, with leaves at their colorful peak in late October. Winters are usually mild, but they can be relentlessly overcast and downright rainy. Visitors not disturbed by dampness or chill will find excellent deals on lodging. In the spring rains continue, but the wildflowers begin to bloom, which pays off at the many gardens and nature parks throughout the valley.

Look high in the sky for evidence of the colorful **Tigard Festival of Balloons** in June—hot-air balloons soar above the town throughout the weekend. Wine lovers flock to McMinnville to sample fine regional vintages in late July and early August during the **International Pinot Noir Celebration**. Eugene hosts the world-class **Oregon Bach Festival**, 19 summer days of classical music performances. In late August and early September the **Oregon State Fair** (📞 503/947–3247 ⊕ www.oregonstateparks.org) in Salem has 8,000 things to do, see, and taste, ranging from carnival rides, top-name concert performances, animals, carnival-style games, and bodacious rides.

Getting Here and Around

Air Travel. Portland's airport is an hour's drive east of the northern Willamette Valley; The **Aloha Express Airport Shuttle** (📞 503/356–8848 ⊕ www.alohaexpressshuttle.com) and the **Beaverton Airporter** (📞 503/760–6565 ⊕ www.beavertonairporter.com) provide shuttle service. **Eugene's Mahlon Sweet Airport** (📞 541/682–5544 ⊕ www.flyeug.com) is more convenient if you're exploring the region's southern end. It's served by Delta, Horizon, and United/United Express. The flight from Portland to Eugene is 40 minutes. There are smaller airports scattered throughout the valley for private aircraft.

Rental cars are available at the Eugene airport from Budget, Enterprise, and Hertz. Taxis and airport shuttles will transport you to downtown Eugene for about $22. **Omni Shuttle** (📞 541/461–7959 ⊕ www.omnishuttle.us) will provide shuttle service to and from the Eugene airport from anywhere in Oregon.

Bus Travel. In Forest Grove, Hillsboro, Beaverton, Tigard, Lake Oswego, and Oregon City, **TriMet** (📞 503/238–7433 ⊕ www.trimet.org) bus service provides frequent transportation into Portland and between these communities. **Greyhound** (📞 800/231–2222 ⊕ www.greyhound.com) provides bus service from Portland to Newberg, McMinnville, Salem, Corvallis, Albany, and Eugene. Many of the **Lane Transit District** (LTD) (📞 541/687–5555 ⊕ www.ltd.org) buses will make a few stops to the outskirts of Lane County, such as McKenzie Bridge. All buses have bike racks.

Car Travel. I–5 runs north–south the length of the Willamette Valley. Many Willamette Valley attractions lie not too far east or west of I–5. Highway 22 travels west from the Willamette National Forest from Salem to the coast. Highway 99 travels parallel to I–5 through much of the Willamette Valley. Highway 34 leaves I–5 just south of Albany and heads west, past Corvallis and into the Coast Range, where it follows the Alsea River. Highway 126 heads east from Eugene toward the Willamette National Forest; it travels west from town to the coast. U.S. 20 travels west from Corvallis. Rental cars are available from Budget (Beaverton), Enterprise, and Hertz (both Beaverton, Salem).

About the Restaurants

The buzzwords associated with fine dining in this region are "sustainable," "farm-to-table," and "local." Fresh salmon, Dungeness crab, mussels, shrimp, and oysters are harvested just a couple of hours away on the Oregon Coast. Lamb, pork, and beef are local and plentiful, and seasonal game appears on many menus. Desserts made with local blueberries, huckleberries, raspberries, and marionberries should not be missed. But what really sets the offerings apart are the splendid, local wines that receive worldwide acclaim.

Restaurants in the Willamette Valley are low-key and unpretentious. Expensive doesn't necessarily mean better, and locals have a pretty good nose for good value. Reasonably priced Mexican, Indian, Japanese, and Italian do very well. Food carts in the cities are a growing phenomenon. But there's still nothing like a great, sit-down meal at a cozy bistro for some fresh fish or lamb, washed down with a stellar pinot noir.

About the Hotels

One of the great pleasures of touring the Willamette Valley is the incredible selection of small, ornate bed-and-breakfast hotels sprinkled throughout Oregon's wine country. In the summer and fall they can fill up quickly, as visitors come from around the world to enjoy wine tastings at the hundreds of large and small wineries. Many of these have exquisite restaurants right on the premises, with home-baked goods available day and night. There are plenty of larger properties located closer to urban areas and shopping centers, including upscale resorts with expansive spas, as well as national chains that are perfect for folks who just need a place to lay their heads.

WHAT IT COSTS IN U.S. DOLLARS

	¢	$	$$	$$$	$$$$
Restaurants	under $10	$10–$16	$17–$23	$24–$30	over $30
Hotels	under $100	$100–$150	$151–$200	$201–$250	over $250

Restaurant prices are per person, for a main course at dinner. Hotel prices are for two people in a standard double room in high season, excluding tax.

Tour Options

Oregon Wine Tours and **EcoTours of Oregon** provide informative, guided outings across the Willamette Valley wine country.

Contacts **EcoTours of Oregon** (☎ 503/245–1428 or 888/868–7733 ⊕ www.ecotours-of-oregon.com). **Oregon Wine Tours** (☎ 503/681–9463 ⊕ www.orwinetours.com).

VISITOR INFORMATION

Contacts **Chehalem Valley Chamber of Commerce** (Newberg, Dundee, and St. Paul) (✉ 415 E. Sheridan, Newberg ☎ 503/538–2014 ⊕ www.chehalemvalley.org) **Oregon Wine Country/ Willamette Valley Visitors Association** (✉ 553 N.W. Harrison Blvd., Corvallis ☎ 866/548–5018 ⊕ www.oregonwinecountry.org). **Travel Lane County** (Eugene, Cascades, and Coast) (✉ 754 Olive St., Eugene ☎ 541/343–6335 or 800/547–5445 ⊕ www.travellanecounty.org). **Washington County Visitors Association** (Beaverton, Forest Grove, Hillsboro, Tigard, and Tualatin) (✉ 11000 SW Stratus St., Suite 170, Beaverton ☎ 503/644–5555 ⊕ www.visitwashingtoncountyoregon.com). **Yamhill Valley Visitors Association** (☎ 503/883–7770 ⊕ www.yamhillvalley.org).

4

Updated by
Deston S.
Nokes

The Willamette (pronounced "wil-*lam*-it") Valley has become a wine-lovers Shangri-La, particularly in the northern Yamhill and Washington counties. An entire tourism industry has sprung up between Interstate 5 and the Oregon Coast, encompassing small hotels and inns, cozy restaurants, and casual wine bars.

The valley divides two mountain ranges (the Cascade and Coast), and contains more than 200 wineries. The huge wine region is made up of six sub-appellations: Chehalem Mountains, Ribbon Ridge, Dundee Hills, Yamhill-Carlton, Eola-Amity Hills, and McMinnville. With its incredibly rich soil perfect for growing pinot noir, pinot gris, chardonnay, and Riesling, the valley has received worldwide acclaim for its vintages. The region's farms are famous for producing quality fruits, vegetables, and cheeses that are savored in area restaurants. During spring and summer there are many roadside stands dotting the country lanes, and farmers' markets appear in most of the valley's towns. Also delicious are the locally raised lamb, pork, and beef. The valley also is a huge exporter of plants and flowers for nurseries, with a large number of farms growing ornamental trees, bulbs, and plants.

The valley definitely has an artsy, expressive, and fun side, with its wine and beer festivals, theater, music, crafts, and even ballooning. Many folks are serious runners and bicyclists, particularly in Corvallis and Eugene, so pay attention while driving.

The entire state is riveted by the collegiate rivalry between the Willamette Valley–based Oregon State Beavers in Corvallis and University of Oregon Ducks in Eugene. In these towns businesses think nothing of closing for the home football games, and getting a ticket to the "Civil War" game between the two is a feat in itself.

NORTH WILLAMETTE VALLEY

Just outside Portland the suburban areas of Tigard, Hillsboro, and Forest Grove have gorgeous wineries, wetlands, rivers, and nature preserves. In the shadow of Nike headquarters, the area has a wealth of golfing, bicycling, and trails for running and hiking. From its wetlands to the residential neighborhoods, it's not unusual to spot red-tail hawks, beavers, and ducks on your route. Shopping, fine dining, and proximity to Portland make this a great area in which to begin your exploration of the Willamette Valley and the wine country.

EN ROUTE

Vineyard and Valley Scenic Tour. Oregon's newest driving route, the Vineyard & Valley Scenic Tour Route, is a 50-mile drive through the lush Tualatin Valley, which runs between the city of Sherwood to the southern part of the valley and the Swiss-settled Helvetia at the northern end. The rural driving route showcases much of Washington County's agricultural bounty, including 17 of the county's 21 wineries and several farms (some with stands offering seasonal fresh produce and/or u-pick), along with pioneer and historic sites, wildlife refuges, and scenic viewpoints of the Cascade Mountains. For more information, contact the **Washington County Visitors Association** (☎ *503/644–5555* ⊕ *www. visitwashingtoncountyoregon.com*).

HILLSBORO

20 mi southwest of Portland.

Hillsboro offers a wealth of eclectic shops, preserves, restaurants, and proximity to the valley's fine wineries. In the past 20 years Hillsboro has experienced rapid growth associated with the Silicon Forest, where high-tech business found ample sprawling room. Several of Intel's industrial campuses are in Hillsboro, as are the facilities of other leading electronics manufacturers. Businesses related to the town's original agricultural roots remain a significant part of Hillsboro's culture and economy. Alpaca ranches, nurseries, berry farms, nut and fruit orchards, and numerous wineries are among the area's most active agricultural businesses.

GETTING HERE

Hillsboro is about a 45-minute drive west from Portland International Airport. The **Aloha Express Airport Shuttle** (☎ *503/356–8848* ⊕ *www. alohaexpressshuttle.com*) and the **Beaverton Airporter** (☎ *503/760–6565* ⊕ *www.beavertonairporter.com*) provide shuttle service.

From downtown Portland it's a short, 20-minute car ride, or visitors can ride the MAX light rail. The TriMet Bus Service connects to the MAX light rail in Hillsboro, with connections to Beaverton, Aloha, and other commercial areas.

VISITOR INFORMATION

Washington County Visitors Association (✉ *11000 S.W. Stratus St., Suite 170, Beaverton* ☎ *503/644–5555* ⊕ *www.visitwashingtoncountyoregon.com*).

WINERY

Oak Knoll. This is one of the closest wineries to Portland, but once you're on the property, you're a world away, with views of the surrounding Chehalem mountain ridge. Its tastings offer a selection of Oak Knoll wines, some of which are only available at the winery. Oak Knoll is lauded for its pinot noir, chardonnay, Riesling, and pinot gris. It also produces an unoaked chardonnay, a slightly sweet, spätlese-styled Riesling, and a Native American varietal, Niagara. The vineyard's large manicured lawn is ideal for picnics or a wine-tour lunch stop. ⊠ *29700 S.W. Burkhalter Rd., Hillsboro* ☎ *503/648–8198 or 800/625–5665* ⊕ *www.oakknollwinery.com* ☉ *Weekdays 11–6, weekends 11–5.*

EXPLORING

Hillsboro Saturday Market. Fresh local produce—some from booths, some from the backs of trucks—as well as local arts and crafts are all here. Live music is played throughout the day, and it's just a block from the light-rail line. ⊠ *Main St. between 1st and 2nd Aves., and along 2nd Ave. between Main and Lincoln Sts., Hillsboro* ☎ *503/844–6685* ⊕ *www.hillsboromarkets.org* ☉ *May–Oct., Sat. 8–1:30.*

⟲ **Rice Northwest Museum of Rocks and Minerals.** In 1938 Richard and Helen Rice began collecting beach agates. Over the years they developed one of the largest private mineral collections in the United States. The most popular item here is the Alma Rose Rhodochrosite, a 4-inch red crystal. The museum (in a ranch-style home) also has petrified wood from all over the world and a gallery of Northwest minerals—including specimens of rare crystallized gold. ⊠ *26385 N.W. Groveland Dr., Hillsboro* ☎ *503/647–2418* ⊕ *www.ricenorthwestmuseum.org* ⬛ *$7* ☉ *Wed.–Sun. 1–5.*

⟲ **Washington County Museum and Historical Society.** Catch a glimpse of history through exhibits on early pioneers and the Tualatin Indians. Exhibits rotate, usually with a hands-on display geared toward children. ⊠ *17677 N.W. Springville Rd., Hillsboro* ☎ *503/645–5353* ⊕ *www.washingtoncountymuseum.org* ⬛ *$3; free on Mon.* ☉ *Mon.–Sat. 10–4.*

WHERE TO EAT

$
MEXICAN
✕ **Mazatlan Mexican Restaurant.** Though it's hidden away in a small shopping mall, this spot feels like a small village inside, with stunning murals and ceramic wall furnishings. Try the Mazatlan Dinner, a house specialty with sirloin, a chile relleno, and an enchilada, or *arroz con camarones*, prawns sautéed with vegetables. Save room for the flan or the *sopapillas* (fried dough). The kids' menu is a good value. ⊠ *20413 S.W. TV Hwy., Aloha* ⊕ *www.mazatlanmexicanrestaurant. com* ☎ *503/591–9536* ⬛ *AE, D, MC, V.*

$
JAPANESE
✕ **Syun Izakaya.** This Japanese restaurant has a large assortment of sushi and sashimi, soups, and salads. It also has wonderful grilled and fried meats and vegetables, and a vast sake selection. The tempura is a must. During happy hour (between 5 and 6 PM) there are lots of small plates for $5–$7. The chicken nuggets are a hit with the kids. ⊠ *209 N.E. Lincoln St., Hillsboro* ☎ *503/640–3131* ⬛ *MC, V* ☉ *No lunch Sun.*

SPORTS AND THE OUTDOORS

RECREATIONAL **Jackson Bottom Wetlands Preserve.** Several miles of trails lace this 710-acre
AREAS floodplain and woods that are home to thousands of ducks and geese,
deer, otters, beavers, herons, and eagles. Walking trails allow birders
and other animal watchers to explore the wetlands for a chance to catch
a glimpse of indigenous and migrating creatures in their own habitats.
The **Educational Center** has several hands-on exhibits, as well as a
real bald eagle's nest that was rescued from the wild, and completely
preserved (and sanitized) for public display. There's also an exhibit
hall with hands-on activities and a gift shop. No dogs or bicycles are
allowed. ✉ *2600 S.W. Hillsboro Hwy., Hillsboro* ☎ *503/681–6206*
⊕ *www.jacksonbottom.org* ✉ *$2 suggested donation* ☉ *Mon.–Sun.*
10–4.

4

♻ **L.L. "Stub" Stewart State Park.** This 1,654-acre, full-service park has hiking, biking, and horseback-riding trails for day use or overnight campers. There are full hookup sites, tent sites, small cabins, and even a
horse camp. Lush rolling hills, forests, and deep canyons are terrific for
bird-watching, wildflower walks, and other relaxing pursuits. ✉ *30380*
N.W. Hwy. 47, Buxton ☎ *503/324–0606* ⊕ *www.oregonstateparks.org*

FOREST GROVE

24 mi west of Portland on Hwy. 8

This small town is surrounded by stands of Douglas firs and giant
sequoia, including the largest giant sequoia in the state. There are
nearby wetlands, birding, the Hagg Lake Recreation Area, a new outdoor adventure park, and numerous wineries and tasting rooms. To
get to the wineries, head south from Forest Grove on Highway 47
and watch for the blue road signs between Forest Grove, Gaston, and
Yamhill.

GETTING HERE

Forest Grove is about an hour's drive west from Portland International
Airport. The **Aloha Express Airport Shuttle** (☎ *503/356–8848* ⊕ *www.*
alohaexpressshuttle.com) and the **Beaverton Airporter** (☎ *503/760–6565*
⊕ *www.beavertonairporter.com*) provide shuttle service.

From downtown Portland it's a short 35-minute car ride with only
one traffic light during the entire trip. TriMet Bus Service provides bus
service to and from Forest Grove every 15 minutes, connecting to the
MAX light rail 6 miles east in Hillsboro, which continues into Portland.
Buses travel to Cornelius, Hillsboro, Aloha, and Beaverton.

VISITOR INFORMATION

Forest Grove Chamber of Commerce (✉ *2417 Pacific Ave., Forest Grove*
☎ *503/357–3006* ⊕ *www.fgchamber.org*)

WINERIES

David Hill Vineyards and Winery. The David Hill Winery has splendid
views of the Tualatin Valley from one of Oregon's oldest winery sites. It
produces pinot noir, chardonnay, gewürztraminer, merlot, tempranillo,
pinot gris, Riesling, sauvignon blanc, and several Rhône blends. They're
well made and pleasant, especially the eclectic blends called Farmhouse

David Hill Vineyards and Winery, Forest Grove

Red and Farmhouse White and the estate pinot gris. Private tastings are only for groups of 8–20 people. ⊠ *46350 N.W. David Hill Rd., Forest Grove* ☎ *503/992–8545* ⊕ *www.davidhillwinery.com* ☉ *Daily 5:30–7.*

Elk Cove Vineyard. Founded in 1974 by Pat and Joe Campbell, Elk Cove Vineyards is another older, well-established Oregon winery, with 600 acres on four separate vineyard sites. The winery's focus is on Willamette Valley pinot noir, pinot gris, and pinot blanc. ⊠ *27751 N.W. Olson Rd., Gaston* ☎ *503/985–7760 or 877/355–2683* ⊕ *www.elkcove. com* ☏ *$5* ☉ *Daily 10–5.*

Montinore Estate. Locals chuckle at visitors who try to show off their French savvy when they pronounce "Montinore." The estate, originally a ranch, was established by a tycoon who'd made his money in the Montana mines before he retired to Oregon; he decided to call his estate "Montana in Oregon." Montinore has 232 acres of vineyards, and its wines reflect their high-quality soil and fruit. Highlights include a crisp gewürztraminer, a light Müller-Thurgau, an off-dry Riesling, a lush pinot noir, and a refreshing pinot gris that's a perfect partner for Northwest seafood. It also has a pinot noir port. The tasting-room staff is among the friendliest and most knowledgeable in Oregon wine country. ⊠ *3663 S.W. Dilley Rd., Forest Grove* ☎ *503/359–5012* ⊕ *www. montinore.com* ☉ *Daily 11–5.*

SakéOne. The world's only American-owned and -operated sakéry resides in Oregon. After SakéOne's founders realized that the country's best water supply for saké was the Pacific Northwest, they built their brewery in Forest Grove in 1997. Its free tours are a great way to develop an appreciation of fine saké and learn the importance of each ingredient. ⊠ *820 Elm St., Forest Grove* ☎ *503/357–7056 or 800/550–7253* ⊕ *www.sakeone.com* ⬚ *Flights $3–$10* ⊙ *Daily 11–5.*

EXPLORING

Pacific University. With 1,800 students, this shady campus provides a respite from wine tasting and other outdoor recreation. It was founded in 1849, making it one of the oldest educational institutions in the western United States. Concerts and special events are held in McCready Hall in the Taylor-Meade Performing Arts Center. ⊠ *2043 College Way, Forest Grove* ☎ *503/357–6151* ⊕ *www.pacificu.edu.*

WHERE TO STAY

🏨 **McMenamins Grand Lodge.** On 13 acres of pastoral countryside, this converted Masonic rest home has accommodations that run from bunk-bed rooms to a three-room fireplace suite. Its sturdy 1922 brick buildings also include pubs that serve several McMenamins draft beers. Rooms are furnished with period antiques such as oak nightstands and porcelain sinks. In the Compass Room Theater feature films are screened nightly; kids accompanied by a guardian are permitted at the early show. Often there's live music, too. **Pros:** relaxed, friendly brewpub atmosphere. **Cons:** not as refined as some tourists would like. ⊠ *3505 Pacific Ave., Forest Grove* ☎ *503/992–9533 or 877/992–9533* ⊕ *www.thegrandlodge.com* ⬚ *77 rooms* △ *In-hotel: 2 restaurants, bars, spa, golf* ⬚ *AE, D, DC, MC, V.*

SPORTS AND THE OUTDOORS

RECREATIONAL
AREAS
Scoggin Valley Park and Henry Hagg Lake. This beautiful area in the Coast Range foothills has a 15-mi-long hiking trail that surrounds the lake. Bird-watching is best in spring. Recreational activities include fishing, boating, waterskiing, picnicking, and hiking, and a 10½-mi, well-marked bicycle lane parallels the park's perimeter road. There's even a disc golf course. ⊠ *Scoggin Valley Rd., Gaston* ☎ *503/359–5732* ⊕ *www.co.washington.or.us* ⬚ *$5* ⊙ *Mar.–Nov., daily sunrise–sunset.*

Tree to Tree Adventure Park. This is the first public aerial adventure park in the Pacific Northwest—and only the second of its kind in the U.S. The park, which opened in June 2010, welcomes explorers of all ages to test their agility on 40 courses, featuring zip lines, ropes, and tunnels. The courses range from beginner to extreme, with certified and trained instructors providing guidance to adventurers. The park has a course for children and shorter adults less than 5-feet tall. Harnesses and helmets are provided, and no open-toed shoes are allowed. ⊠ *2975 S.W. Nelson Rd., Gaston* ☎ *503/357–0109* ⊕ *www.treetotreeadventurepark.com* ⬚ *$30 half course, $39 full course* ⊙ *Weekdays 10–4, weekends 10–4:30.*

TIGARD

10 mi southwest of Portland, 5 mi south of Beaverton.

This Portland suburb has made great strides in attracting visitors with its festivals and shopping options. Its old downtown Main Street is enjoying a rebirth with antiques shops, espresso bars, and fashionable

Tigard Festival of Balloons 2010

eateries. Its shopping center, Bridgeport Village, is a magnet for excellent dining, boutique shopping, and movies.

GETTING HERE

Tigard is about 20 miles southwest of Portland International Airport driving on I–84 and I–5. The **Aloha Express Airport Shuttle** (☎ *503/356–8848* ⊕ *www.alohaexpressshuttle.com*) and the **Beaverton Airporter** (☎ *503/760–6565* ⊕ *www.beavertonairporter.com*) provide shuttle service.

Sitting on 99W, Tigard also is the gateway to the Oregon wine country, just 17 miles from the small town of Dundee. Tigard has frequent TriMet bus service into Portland and the neighboring communities of Beaverton, Lake Oswego, and Tualatin. It also is 40 miles north of Salem on I–5.

VISITOR INFORMATION

Tigard Area Chamber of Commerce (✉ *12345 S.W. Main St., Tigard* ☎ *503/639–1656* ⊕ *www.tigardchamber.org*)

EXPLORING

Tualatin River Wildlife Refuge. The Tualatin River National Wildlife Refuge is located in Sherwood (about 12 miles south of downtown Portland). It is a sanctuary for indigenous and migrating birds, waterfowl, and mammals. As one of only a handful of national urban refuges in the U.S., it has restored much of the natural landscape common to western Oregon prior to human settlement. The refuge is home to nearly 200 species of birds, 50 species of mammals, 25 species of reptiles and amphibians, and a variety of insects, fish, and plants. It features an interpretive center, a gift shop, photography blinds, and restrooms. This restoration has attracted animals back to the area in great numbers, and with a keen eye, birders and animal watchers can catch a glimpse of these creatures year-round. In May the refuge holds its Migratory Songbird Festival. ✉ *19255 S.W. Pacific Hwy., Sherwood* ☎ *503/625–5945* ⊕ *wwwxfws. gov/tualatinriver.com.*

WHERE TO EAT AND STAY

$ ✕ **Café Allegro.** In the heart of Old Town Tigard, Café Allegro serves
ITALIAN authentic Italian cuisine in a cozy bistro setting. The rustic decor provides a funky backdrop to tasty fresh salads, hearty pasta dishes and pizzas, and a variety of desserts. The Greek fettuccine is a tantalizing choice, and the small football–size meat calzone is a mighty plunge into decadence. ✉ *12386 S.W. Main St., Tigard* ☎ *503/684–0130* ⊕ *www. cafeallegrotigard.com* ▭ *AE, D, MC, V* ⊗ *No lunch Sun.*

¢ ✕ **Sanchez Taqueria.** It may not look like much from the outside, but
MEXICAN the Mexican food at this simple family restaurant has no peer. From its
Fodor'sChoice mole and crispy sopes to its carnita enchiladas, the food is fresh and
★ sumptuously authentic. Wash it all down with a cup of orchata, a drink made of rice, milk, and cinnamon. ✉ *13050 S.W. Pacific Hwy., Tigard* ☎ *503/684–2838* ▭ *MC, V.*

$ ⛉ **The Grand Hotel at Bridgeport.** This independent hotel, opened in 2009, offers luxurious business-class accommodations and amenities, including a free, chef-prepared breakfast. Extremely attractive and comfortable, this property is steps away from tax-free shopping at Bridgeport Village, one of Oregon's premier shopping, dining, and entertainment centers. Built as a "green" hotel from the ground up, 124 rooms are dedicated to earth-friendly, sustainable practices, which include energy-efficient appliances and light bulbs, as well as recycling bins in all guest rooms and public areas. Each oversized room and suite comes with leather furniture in the living-room area and a desk. **Pros:** next to great shopping and dining. **Cons:** in a shopping center. ✉ *7265 S.W. Hazel Fern Rd., Tigard* ☎ *503/968–5757 or 866/968–5757* ⊕ *grandhotel-bridgeport.com* ⇥ *124 rooms* ⬧ *In-room: Wi-Fi, refrigerator. In-hotel: Pool, spa, gym, parking* ▭ *AE, MC, V* ⊙⛉ *BP.*

NIGHTLIFE AND THE ARTS

Broadway Rose Theatre Company. This professional musical theatre company has earned rave reviews for its productions, ranging from new to well-known musicals. Performances have included *A Chorus Line*, *The King and I*, and *Honky Tonk Angels*, and kids' productions, such as *Aladdin*. Its summer, performances are held in the Deb Fennell Auditorium. Other performances are held at the Broadway Rose New Stage Theatre. ✉ *Box office: 12850 S.W. Grant Ave., Tigard* ☎ *503/620–5262* ⊕ *www.broadwayrose.com* ⊙ *Mon–Fri., 10–6.*

SHOPPING

Bridgeport Village. This complex diverts more cars off Interstate 5 than any other site in the Willamette Valley. With 500,000 square feet of upscale shops, boutiques, eateries, and a luxury spa, the outdoor mall is a magnet for residents and visitors. It also has the largest multiscreen cinema in the state, including an IMAX theater. ✉ *7455 S.W. Bridgeport Rd.,*

Tigard ☎ *503/968–8940* ⊕ *www. bridgeport-village.com.*

Stash Tea & Catalog Retail Store. Daily tea tastings are a welcome change of pace at this nationally recognized tea producer. An exclusive retail store showcases a large selection of its bagged and loose-leaf teas. It also sells seasonal and rare varieties, as well as artful gifts and teapots for tea lovers. ✉ *7250 S.W. Durham Rd., Tigard* ☎ *503/603– 9905* ⊕ *www.bridgeport-village. com* ⊙ *Tues.–Fri. 10–6, Sat. and Sun. 10–4.*

SPORTS AND THE OUTDOORS

RECREATIONAL AREAS **Cook Park.** On the banks of the Tualatin River, this 79-acre park is where suburbanites gather to enjoy a variety of team sports. The park has horseshoe pits, a fishing dock, small boat ramp, picnic shelters, and several walking trails and bike paths. Wildlife includes great blue herons and river otters. Cook Park is located south of Durham Road at the end of 92nd Avenue near Tigard High School. ✉ *17005 S.W. 92nd Ave., Tigard* ☎ *503/718–2641.*

BOATING **Tualatin River.** The Tualatin River is a slow, meandering river, with fantastic opportunities for paddlers who are new to the sport, as well those who are experienced. With several launch points along the river, paddlers can plan to set out on the river independently, or as part as a planned expedition with the **Tualatin Riverkeepers** (☎ *503/620–7507* ⊕ *www.tualatinriverkeepers.org*).

YAMHILL COUNTY

Yamhill County, at the northern end of the Willamette Valley, has a fortunate confluence of perfect soils, a benign climate, and talented winemakers who craft world-class vintages. In recent years several new wineries have been built in Yamhill County's hills, as well as its flatlands. While vineyards flourished in the northern Willamette Valley in the 19th century, viticulture didn't arrive in Yamhill County until the 1960s and 1970s, with such pioneers as Dick Erath (Erath Vineyards Winery), David and Ginny Adelsheim (Adelsheim Vineyard), and David and Diana Lett (The Eyrie Vineyards). The focus of much of the county's enthusiasm lies in the Red Hills of Dundee, where the farming towns of Newberg, Dundee, Yamhill, and Carlton have made room for upscale bed-and-breakfasts, spas, wine bars, and tourists seeking that perfect swirl and sip.

The Yamhill County wineries are only a short drive from Portland, and the roads, especially Route 99W and Route 18, definitely can be crowded on weekends—that's because these roads link suburban Portland communities to the popular Oregon Coast.

NEWBERG

15 mi west of Tigard, 24 mi south of Portland on Hwy. 99W

Newberg sits in the Chehalem Valley, known as one of Oregon's most fertile wine-growing locations, and is called the Gateway to Oregon Wine Country. Many of Newberg's early settlers were Quakers from the Midwest, who founded the school that has become George Fox University, an accredited four-year institution. Newberg's most famous resident, likewise a Quaker, was Herbert Hoover, the 31st president of the United States. For about five years during his adolescence, he lived with an aunt and uncle at the Hoover-Minthorn House, now a museum listed on the National Register of Historic Places. Now the town is on the map for the nearby wineries, fine-dining establishments, and a spacious, spectacular resort, the Allison. St. Paul, a historic town with a population of about 325, is about 8 mi south of Newberg, and every July holds a professional rodeo.

4

GETTING HERE

Newberg is just under an hour's drive from Portland International Airport; **Caravan Airport Transportation** (☎ *541/994–9645* ⊕ *www. caravanairporttransportation.com*) provides shuttle service. The best way to visit Newberg and the Yamhill County vineyards is by car. Sitting on Highway 99W, Newberg is 15 miles outside of Tigard and 90 minutes from Lincoln City, on the Oregon Coast.

Yamhill County Transit Area (YCTA) (☎ *503/472–0457 ext. 122* ⊕ *www. yctransitarea.org*) provides bus service for Yamhill County, with links to Hillsboro/MAX, Sherwood/TriMet, and Salem/SAMT. Greyhound provides bus service to McMinnville.

VISITOR INFORMATION

Chehalem Valley Chamber of Commerce (Newberg, Dundee, and St. Paul) (✉ *415 E. Sheridan, Newberg* ☎ *503/538–2014* ⊕ *www.chehalemvalley.org*).

WINERIES

Adelsheim Vineyard. David Adelsheim is the knight in shining armor of the Oregon wine industry—tirelessly promoting Oregon wines abroad, and always willing to share the knowledge he has gained from his long viticultural experience. He and Ginny Adelsheim founded their pioneer winery in 1971. They make their wines from grapes picked on their 170 acres of estate vineyard, as well as from grapes they've purchased. Their pinot noir, pinot gris, pinot blanc, and chardonnay all conform to the Adelsheim house style of rich, balanced fruit and long, clean finishes. ✉ *16800 N.E. Calkins Ln., Newberg* ☎ *503/538–3652* ⊕ *www.adelsheim.com* 🍷 *$15* ⊗ *Open July–Oct. daily 11–4; winter hours Wed.–Sun. 11–4, by appointment Mon.-Tues.*

Rex Hill Vineyards. A few hundred feet off the busy highway, surrounded by conifers and overlooked by vineyards, Rex Hill seems to exist in a world of its own. The winery opened in 1982, after owners Paul Hart and Jan Jacobsen converted a former nut-drying facility. It produces first-class pinot noir, pinot gris, chardonnay, sauvignon blanc, and Riesling from both estate-grown and purchased grapes. The tasting room has a massive fireplace, elegant antiques, and an absorbing collection

Bountiful vineyards stretch along many of Willamette Valley's south-facing slopes.

of modern art. Another highlight is the beautifully landscaped garden, perfect for picnicking. ⊠ *30835 N. Hwy. 99W, Newberg* ☎ *503/538–0666 or 800/739–4455* ⊕ *www.rexhill.com* ✉ *$10* ☉ *Daily 10–5; closed major holidays.*

Vercingetorix. This small winery south of Newberg, which produces only pinot gris and pinot noir, is part of Willamette Farms, a grower of hazelnuts, trees, and wine grapes. The crisp, fruity pinot gris is especially worth seeking out. The winery has half a mile of Willamette River frontage, so you can claim a picnic table and keep your eyes peeled for wildlife (beavers, deer, ducks, geese, or raptors). Picnic baskets are for sale in the tasting room. ⊠ *800 N.E. Parrish Rd., Newberg* ☎ *503/538–9895* ⊕ *www.vxvineyard.com* ✉ *Prices vary* ☉ *Open weekends Memorial Day–Labor Day.*

EXPLORING

Champoeg State Park. Pronounced "sham-*poo*-ee," this 615-acre state park on the south bank of the Willamette River is on the site of a Hudson's Bay Company trading post, granary, and warehouse that was built in 1813. This was the seat of the first provisional government in the Northwest. The settlement was abandoned after a catastrophic flood in 1861, then rebuilt and abandoned again after the flood of 1890. The park's wide-open spaces, groves of oak and fir, modern visitor center, museum, and historic buildings provide vivid insight into pioneer life. Tepees and wagons are displayed here, and there are 10 mi of hiking and cycle trails.

Robert Newell was among the inaugural American settlers in the Willamette Valley and helped establish the town of Champoeg; a replica of his 1844 home, now the **Newell House Museum** (✉ *8089 Champoeg Rd. NE, St. Paul* ☎ *503/678–5537* ⊕ *www.newellhouse.com* ☞ *$4 adults, $3 seniors, $2 children* ☉ *Mar.–Oct., Fri.–Sun. 1–5*), was built inside the park grounds in 1959 and paid for by the Oregon State Society Daughters of the American Revolution. The first floor is furnished with 1860s antiques. Pioneer quilts and a collection of gowns worn by the wives of Oregon governors at inaugurations are displayed on the second floor. There's also a pioneer jail and schoolhouse.

Also on park grounds is the historic **Pioneer Mother's Memorial Log Cabin** (✉ *8035 Champoeg Rd. NE, St. Paul* ☎ *503/633–2237* ☞ *$4 adults, $3 seniors, $2 children* ☉ *Mar.–Oct., Fri.–Sun. 1–5*), with pioneer artifacts from the Oregon Trail era. ✉ *8239 Champoeg Rd. NE, St. Paul* ☎ *800/551–6949* ⊕ *www.oregonstateparks.org* ☞ *$5 per vehicle.*

Hoover-Minthorn House Museum. The boyhood home of President Herbert Hoover is the oldest and most significant of Newberg's original structures. Built in 1881, the preserved frame house still has many of its original furnishings. Outside is the woodshed that no doubt played an important role in shaping young "Bertie" Hoover's character. ✉ *115 S. River St., Newberg* ☎ *503/538–6629* ⊕ *www.nscda.org/museums/ oregon.htm* ☞ *$3* ☉ *Mar.–Nov., Wed.–Sun. 1–4; Dec. and Feb., weekends 1–4, closed Jan.*

WHERE TO EAT AND STAY

$$$
NEW AMERICAN

✕ **Jory.** This exquisite restaurant is named after one of the soils in the Oregon wine country. Here you can order grilled Muscovy duck over roasted grapes and watch it cook over a wood grill. Start off with butternut squash soup with shreds of fresh apple. Fish lovers will relish the saffron fettuccine in a tomato-fennel broth with bay scallops, prawns, and mussels. The dessert menu has orange-cardamom doughnuts accompanying a vanilla crème brûlée, and a brown-butter cake with hazelnut praline ice cream. Naturally, the restaurant has an expansive wine list. ✉ *2525 Allison La., Newberg* ☎ *503/554–2525* ⊕ *www. theallison.com* ⊟ *AE, D, DC MC, V* ☉ *No lunch Sun.*

$$$$
Fodor's Choice
★

▥ **The Allison Inn & Spa.** The new Allison (opened in Sept. 2009) provides a luxurious, relaxing base for exploring the region's 200 wineries. The attention to detail in its materials, art, grounds, and amenities is impressive. It's a great retreat for both locals and travelers. Each bright, comfortable room includes a gas fireplace, which is perfect for a misty day; original works of art, a soaking tub, impressive furnishings, bay-window seats, and views of the wine country from the terrace or balcony. The massive copper-coil curtain at the entrance to Allison's 15,000-square-foot spa conveys its opulence as a place to enjoy wines, a pinot pedicure, or mimosa massage in one of its 12 treatment rooms. The property lives up it its nickname, "the living room of the Willamette Valley." **Pros:** outstanding on-site restaurant, excellent gym and spa facilities, located in the middle of wine country. **Cons:** not many nearby off-property activities other than wine tasting. ✉ *2525 Allison La., Newberg* ☎ *503/554–2525* ⊕ *www.theallison.com* ⤳ *65 rooms, 20 suites* ☍ *In-room: bar, refrigerator, Wi-Fi. In-hotel: restaurant, pool, gym* ⊟ *AE, D, DC, MC, V.*

NIGHTLIFE AND THE ARTS

99W Drive-in. Ted Francis built this drive-in in 1953, and operated it until his death at 98; the business is now run by his grandson. The first film begins at dusk. ⊠ *Hwy. 99 W (Portland Rd.), just west of Spring-brook Rd. intersection, Newberg* ☎ *503/538–2738* ⊕ *www.99w.com* ✉ *$7 per person, $11 minimum vehicle charge* ⊙ *Fri.–Sun.*

SPORTS AND THE OUTDOORS

BALLOONING Hot-air balloon rides are nothing less than a spectacular, breath-taking thrill—particularly over Oregon's beautiful Yamhill County. **Vista Balloon Adventures** (☎ *503/625–7385 or 800/622–2309* ⊕ *www.vistaballoon.com*) launches several balloons daily from Sportsman Air-park. Flown by FAA-licensed pilots, they rise about 1,500 feet, and its pilots often can steer the craft down to skim the water, and up to view hawk's nests. A brunch is included afterwards.

DUNDEE

3 mi southwest of Newberg on Hwy. 99 W.

Dundee used to be known for growing the lion's share (more than 90%) of the U.S. hazelnut crop. Today it's better known for the numerous quaint and elegant wine bars, bed-and-breakfast inns, and restaurants that are products of its wine tourism. Exploring the area's wineries is an experience you won't want to miss.

GETTING HERE

Dundee is just under an hour's drive from Portland International Airport; **Caravan Airport Transportation** (☎ *541/994–9645* ⊕ *www.caravanairporttransportation.com*) provides shuttle service.

What used to be a pleasant drive through quaint Dundee on Highway 99W now can be a traffic hassle, as it serves as the main artery from Lincoln City to suburban Portland. Others will enjoy wandering along the 25 miles of Highway 18 between Dundee and Grande Ronde, in the Coast Range, which goes through the heart of the Yamhill Valley wine country.

Yamhill County Transit Area (YCTA) (☎ *503/472–0457 ext. 122* ⊕ *www.yctransitarea.org*) provides bus service for Yamhill County, with links to Hillsboro/MAX, Sherwood/TriMet, and Salem/SAMT.

VISITOR INFORMATION

Chehalem Valley Chamber of Commerce (Newberg, Dundee, and St. Paul) (⊠ *415 E. Sheridan, Newberg* ☎ *503/538–2014* ⊕ *www.chehalemvalley.org*)

WINERIES

Archery Summit Winery. Gary and Nancy Andrus, the owners of Pine Ridge winery in Napa Valley, started Archery Summit in the early 1990s; the first crush was in 1995. Because they believed that great wines are made in the vineyard, they adopted such innovative techniques as narrow spacing and vertical trellis systems, which give the fruit a great concentration of flavors. In addition, they did extensive clone research to develop the best possible vines for their more than 100 acres of estate vineyards. The Andruses focus on pinot noir, making their wines in a gravity-flow winery for the gentlest handling, and aging them in traditional caves—a rarity in Oregon—in French oak barrels. ✉ *18599 N.E. Archery Summit Rd., Dundee* ☎ *503/864–4300* ⊕ *www. archerysummit.com* 🎫 *$15* ☉ *Open daily.*

Argyle Winery. A beautiful establishment, Argyle has its tasting room in a Victorian farmhouse set amid gorgeous gardens. The winery is tucked into a former hazelnut processing plant—which explains the Nuthouse label on its reserve wines. Since Argyle opened in 1987, it has consistently produced sparkling wines that are crisp on the palate, with an aromatic, lingering finish and bubbles that seem to last forever. And these sparklers cost about a third of their counterparts from California. The winery also produces chardonnay, dry Riesling, pinot gris, and pinot noir. ✉ *691 Hwy. 99W, Dundee* ☎ *503/538–8520 or 888/427– 4953* ⊕ *www.argylewinery.com* 🎫 *Prices vary* ☉ *Open daily 11–5.*

Domaine Drouhin Oregon. When the French winery magnate Robert Drouhin ("the Sebastiani of France") planted a vineyard and built a winery in the Red Hills of Dundee back in 1987, he set local oenophiles abuzz. Be forewarned, though: this is one winery where you're expected to buy some wine if you tour, and the wines are not cheap. Ninety acres of the 225-acre estate had been planted. The hillside setting was selected to take advantage of the natural coolness of the earth and to establish a gravity-flow winery. A visit is well worth planning for, however, because the tasting includes Drouhin wines from both Oregon and France, allowing you to compare the two. ✉ *6750 N.E. Breyman Orchards Rd., Dundee* ☎ *503/864–2700* ⊕ *www.domainedrouhin.com* 🎫 *$10* ☉ *Open Wed.–Sun. Tours by appointment only.*

Duck Pond Cellars. Fronted by gardens north of Route 99W, Duck Pond is one of the region's jewels. Doug and Jo Ann Fries planted the vineyards in 1986 and opened the winery in 1993. They concentrate on estate-grown Willamette Valley pinot gris, pinot noir, and chardonnay, but also make cabernet sauvignon and merlot from grapes grown in Washington's Columbia Valley, where they have pioneered vineyard plantings on the Wahluke Slope above the Columbia River. The Duck Pond tasting room has a market that sells food and gifts, and the picnic area is a floral delight. ✉ *23145 Hwy. 99 W, Dundee* ☎ *503/538–3199 or 800/437–3213* ⊕ *www.duckpondcellars.com* 🎫 *Some tasting complimentary, others $2 taste, $5 flight* ☉ *Oct.–April, daily 11–5; May– Sept., daily 10–5.*

Erath Vineyards Winery. One of Oregon's pioneer wineries, Erath Vineyards opened more than a quarter of a century ago. Its owner and winemaker, Dick Erath, focused on producing distinctive pinot noir from grapes he'd been growing in the Red Hills since 1972—as well as full-flavored pinot gris, pinot blanc, chardonnay, cabernet sauvignon, Riesling, and late-harvest gewürztraminer. The wines were both excellent and reasonably priced. In 2006 the winery was sold to Washington State's giant conglomerate Ste. Michelle Wine Estate. The tasting room is in the middle of the vineyards, high in the hills, with views in nearly every direction: the hazelnut trees that covered the slopes not so long ago have been replaced with vines. The tasting-room terrace, which overlooks the winery and the hills, is a choice spot for picnicking. Crabtree Park, next to the winery, is a good place to stretch your legs after a tasting. ⊠ *9009 N.E. Worden Hill Rd., Dundee* ☎ *503/538–3318* ⊕ *www.erath.com* ✉ *$10* ⊘ *Open daily 11–5.*

Maresh Red Barn. When Jim and Loie Maresh planted two acres of vines in 1970, theirs became the fifth vineyard in Oregon and the first on Worden Hill Road. The quality of their grapes was so high that some of the Dundee Hills' best and most famous wineries soon sought them out. When the wine industry boomed in the 1980s, the Mareshes decided they might as well enjoy some wine from their renowned grapes. They transformed their old barn into a tasting room, where you can taste and purchase exceptional chardonnay, pinot noir, pinot gris, and sauvignon blanc. ⊠ *9325 N.W. Worden Hill Rd., Dundee* ☎ *503/537–1098* ⊕ *www.vineyardretreat.com* ✉ *$5* ⊘ *Open Wed.–Sun. 11–5 and by appointment. Closed Jan.–Feb.*

Sokol Blosser. Sokol Blosser is one of Yamhill County's oldest wineries (it was established in 1977), and it makes consistently excellent wines and sells them at reasonable prices. Set on a gently sloping south-facing hillside and surrounded by vineyards, lush lawns, and shade trees, it's a splendid place to learn about wine. A demonstration vineyard with several rows of vines contains the main grape varieties and shows what happens to them as the seasons unfold. ⊠ *5000 Sokol Blosser La., 3 mi west of Dundee off Hwy. 99W, Dundee* ☎ *503/864–2282 or 800/582–6668* ✉ *Tasting room $5–$15* ⊕ *www.sokolblosser.com* ⊘ *Open daily 10–4.*

Torii Mor Winery. Torii Mor, established in 1993, makes small quantities of handcrafted pinot noir, pinot gris, and chardonnay. The tasting room is in Torii Mor's Olson Vineyard, one of Yamhill County's oldest vineyards, with an amazing setting amid Japanese gardens with breathtaking views of the Willamette Valley. The owners, who love things Japanese, named their winery after the distinctive Japanese gate of Shinto religious significance; they added a Scandinavian mor, signifying "earth," to create an east-west combo: "earth gate." Jacques Tardy, a native of Nuits Saint Georges, in Burgundy, France, is the current winemaker. Under his guidance Torii Mor wines have become more Burgundian in style. ⊠ *18325 N.E. Fairview Dr., Dundee* ☎ *800/839–5004* ⊕ *www.toriimorwinery.com* ✉ *$10* ⊘ *Open daily 11–5.*

WHERE TO EAT AND STAY

$ ✗ **Dundee Bistro.** This highly regarded 80-seat restaurant run by the
CONTEMPORARY Ponzi wine family uses Northwest organic foods such as Draper Valley chicken and local foods such as locally produced wines, fruits, vegetables, nuts, mushrooms, fish, and meats. Vaulted ceilings provide an open feeling inside, warmed by abundant fresh flowers and the works of local Oregon artists. ⊠ *100-A S.W. 7th St., Dundee* ☎ *503/554–1650* ⊕ *www.dundeebistro.com* ▭ *AE, DC, MC, V.*

$$ ✗ **Farm to Fork.** The restaurant serves breakfast, lunch, dinner, and a
NEW AMERICAN Sunday brunch. Its deli offers a wide selection of Oregon and international cheeses, charcuterie, and fresh salads from the kitchen. Its farm,

located in the Chehalem Mountain AVA at de Lancellotti Family Vineyard, grows fruits, vegetables, herbs, and lavender for the restaurant. Request a custom picnic basket for a day of wine tasting, bike riding, hiking, or trail riding. Tastings in the Press Wine Bar are offered on the property, many from smaller, hard-to-find wineries. ⊠ *1410 N. Hwy. 99W, Dundee* ☎ *503/538–7970; wine bar 503/538–7989* ⊕ *www.www. innatredhills.com/farm_to_fork.html* ⊟ *AE, D, DC, MC, V.*

$$$ ✕ **Tina's.** Chef–proprietors Tina and David Bergen bring a powerful one-
FRENCH two punch to this Dundee favorite that often lures Portlanders away
Fodor's Choice from their own restaurant scene. The couple shares cooking duties—
★ Tina does the baking and is often on hand to greet you—and David brings his experience as a former caterer and employee of nearby Sokol Blosser Winery to the table, ensuring that you have the right glass of wine to match your course. Fish and game vie for attention on the country French menu—entrées might include grilled Oregon salmon or Alaskan halibut, or a braised rabbit, local lamb, or tenderloin. Avail yourself of any special soups, particularly if there's corn chowder in the house. A lunch menu includes soup, sandwiches, and Tina's grilled hamburger, made with free-range beef. Service is as intimate and laid-back as the interior. A double fireplace divides the dining room, with heavy glass brick shrouded by bushes on the highway side, so you're not bothered by the traffic on Highway 99. ⊠ *760 Hwy. 99W, Dundee* ☎ *503/538–8880* ⊕ *www.tinasdundee.com* ⊟ *AE, D, MC, V* ☉ *No lunch Sat.–Mon.*

$$$ ⬚ **Dundee Manor Bed and Breakfast.** This 1908-built traditional bed-
Fodor's Choice and-breakfast features expansive grounds, a perfect location, and trea-
★ sures and collectibles that add intrigue to each themed room: African, Asian, European, and North American. Visitors are greeted with pinot noir, chocolate, and afternoon appetizers. Its garden has gazebos with views of Mt. Hood, Mt. Jefferson, and Mt. Bachelor. Breakfasts are fresh, plentiful, and delicious, using local ingredients. There are fire pits, croquet, horseshoes, golf chipping, bocce ball, and 38 different places to sit and ponder your good fortune. Its concierge service will book tee times, fine-dining reservations, massages, and private vineyard tours. **Pros:** terrific amenities, lots of activities, attentive staff. **Cons:** few rooms. ⊠ *8380 N.E. Worden Hill Rd., Dundee* ☎ *503/554–1945 or 888/262–1133* ⊕ *www.dundeemanor.com* ⬎ *4 rooms* ☖ *In-room: Wi-Fi* ⊟ *AE, MC, V* ⏽ *BP.*

$$ ⬚ **The Inn at Red Hills.** This is about as local as it gets. From the materials in the building, the wines it serves, and the ingredients in the kitchen, the Inn at Red Hills works to be sustainable and to use Oregon's bounty. Located in downtown Dundee, the inn has 20 spacious, comfortable rooms, each with its own layout and impressive wine-country views. Wide-screen televisions and huge bathrooms add to the amenities. **Pros:** modern and upscale. **Cons:** located in the town rather than the country. ⊠ *1410 N. Hwy. 99W, Dundee* ☎ *503/538–7666* ⊕ *www.innatredhills. com* ⬎ *20 rooms* ☖ *In-room: a/c, Wi-Fi* ⊟ *AE, D, DC, MC, V.*

YAMHILL-CARLTON

14 mi west of Dundee

The small towns of Carlton and Yamhill are neatly combed benchlands and hillsides, an AVA established in 2004, and home to some of the finest pinot noir vineyards in the world. The area is a gorgeous quilt of nurseries, grain fields, and orchards. Come here for the wine tasting, and not much else.

GETTING HERE

Having your own car is the best way to explore this rural region of Yamhill County, located a little more than an hour's drive from Portland International Airport. The towns of Yamhill and Carlton are about an hour's drive from downtown Portland, traveling through Tigard, to Newberg and west on Highway 240.

Yamhill County Transit Area (YCTA) (☎ *503/472–0457 ext. 122* ⊕ *www. yctransitarea.org*) provides bus service for Yamhill County, with links to Hillsboro/MAX, Sherwood/TriMet, and Salem/SAMT.

VISITOR INFORMATION

Yamhill Valley Visitors Association (☎ *503/883–7770* ⊕ *www.yamhillvalley.org*).

WINERIES

Anne Amie Vineyards. Early wine country adopters Fred and Mary Benoit established this namesake hilltop winery in 1979. Since the winery changed hands in 1999, it has been concentrating on pinot blanc, pinot gris, and pinot noir, but still makes a dry Riesling. Both the winery and the picnic area have spectacular views across the hills and valleys of Yamhill County. ⊠ *6580 N.E. Mineral Springs Rd., McMinnville* ☎ *503/864–2991* ⊕ *www.anneamie.com* ⊟ *$5–$10* ⊙ *Open Mar.– Dec., daily 10–5; Jan.–Feb., Fri.–Sun. or by appointment.*

Carlton Winemakers Studio. Oregon's first cooperative winery was specifically designed to house multiple small premium wine producers. This gravity-flow winery has up-to-date winemaking equipment as well as multiple cellars for storing the different makers' wines. You can taste and purchase bottles from the different member wineries: Andrew Rich, Hamacher Wines, Ayoub Wines, Brittan Vineyards, Carlton Wine, Lazy River Vinex, and Wahle Vineyards and Cellars. The emphasis is on pinot noir, but more than a dozen other types of wines are poured, from cabernet franc to gewürztraminer to mourvèdre. From spring to autumn the studio holds winemakers' dinners on Wednesdays. Reservations are essential. ⊠ *801 N. Scott St., Carlton* ☎ *503/852–6100* ⊕ *www. winemakersstudio.com* ⊟ *$3 and up* ⊱ *Wed. winemaker dinner reservations essential* ⊙ *Open Feb.–Dec., daily 11–5.*

Raptor Ridge Winery. High up in the Chehalem Mountains, the raptors who fly over these vineyards (red-tail hawks, sharp-shinned hawks, and kestrels) give this small winery its name. Because the ridge intercepts the sea breeze, it's often foggy here. The fog cools the vineyards and imparts subtle, highly desirable flavors to the grapes, making for first-rate pinot noir, pinot gris, and chardonnay wines. This remained true even after the winery moved from the ridge to a new facility in downtown Carlton in autumn 2007, because the grapes still come from the

Carlton Winemakers Studio

old vineyards. The winery produces small lots of handcrafted wines, aging them in French oak barrels. An unusual touch is the synchronizing of racking with the full moon, to "help bring out natural flavors and delicate aromas of Willamette Valley grapes" (though whether this timing accomplishes that end is dubious). In addition to employing its own crops, Raptor Ridge buys grapes from five different vineyards in the northern Willamette Valley. ✉ *103 Monroe St., Carlton* ☎ *503/887–5595, tasting room appointments 503/367–4263* ⊕ *www.raptoridge. com* ☯ *Fri.–Sat. 11–4.*

Scott Paul Tasting Room and Winery. Pinot noir fans, listen up: this small spot in the center of Carlton is an outstanding pinot noir resource. It not only makes pinot noir from local grapes, but it also imports and sells pinot noirs from Burgundy. The three pinot noirs made from local grapes are Audrey, the finest wine of the vintage, La Paulée, a selection of the best lots of each vintage, and Cuvée Martha Pirrie, a fruit-forward, silky wine meant to be drunk young. All are splendid examples of the wines that can be made from this great, challenging grape. The tasting room, a quaint redbrick building, is across the street from the winery. Winery tours are by appointment only. Wine seminars are offered in the evening. ✉ *128 S. Pine St., Carlton* ☎ *503/852–7300* ⊕ *www.scottpaul.com* ✑ *$10* ☯ *Open Wed.–Sun. 11–4.*

Tyrus Evan Tasting Room. Carlton's former train depot is now the tasting room for Ken Wright's warm-climate label, Tyrus Evan. These wines are quite different from the Ken Wright pinots: they are warm-climate varieties like cabernet franc, malbec, syrah, and red Bordeaux blends, from grapes Wright buys from vineyards in eastern Washington and southern Oregon. The tasting room pours some Ken Wright wines alongside, as well as wines of other warm-climate producers. You can also pick up cheeses and other picnic supplies. ⊠ *120 N. Pine St., Carlton* ☎ *503/852–7010* ⊙ *Open Fri.–Sat. 11–6, Sun.–Thurs. 11–5.*

MCMINNVILLE

11 mi south of Yamhill on Hwy. 99 W.

The Yamhill County seat, McMinnville lies in the center of Oregon's thriving wine industry. There is a larger concentration of wineries in Yamhill County than in any other area of the state, and the vineyards in the McMinnville area produce the most award-winning wines. Among the varieties are chardonnay, pinot noir, and pinot gris. Most of the wineries in the area offer tours and tastings. McMinnville's downtown area, with a pleasantly disproportionate number of bookstores and art galleries for its size, is well worth exploring; many of the historic district buildings, erected 1890–1915, are still standing, and are remarkably well maintained.

GETTING HERE

McMinnville is a little more than an hour's drive from downtown Portland; **Caravan Airport Transportation** (☎ *541/994–9645* ⊕ *www.caravanairporttransportation.com*) provides shuttle service to Portland International Airport. McMinnville is just 70 minutes from Lincoln City on the Oregon Coast, and 27 mi west of Salem.

Yamhill County Transit Area (YCTA) (☎ *503/472–0457 ext. 122* ⊕ *www.yctransitarea.org*) provides bus service for Yamhill County, with links to Hillsboro/MAX, Sherwood/TriMet, and Salem/SAMT.

VISITOR INFORMATION

McMinnville Chamber of Commerce (⊠ *417 N.W. Adams St., McMinnville* ☎ *503/472–6196* ⊕ *www.mcminnville.org*)

WINERIES

Amity Vineyards. Its original tasting area was the back of a 1952 Ford pickup. Its Gamay noir label notes that the wine gives "more enjoyment to hamburgers [and] fried chicken." And the winery's current architecture still includes a trailer affectionately referred to as the "mobile chateau," already on the property when winemaker Myron Redford purchased the winery in 1974. These modest and whimsical touches underscore what seems to be Redford's philosophy: take your wine-making a lot more seriously than you take yourself. Taste the pinot blanc for Redford's take on the grape, and also linger in the tasting room to sample the pinot noir and the gewürztraminer, among other varieties. Chocolates made with Amity's pinot noir and other products are available for sale. ⊠ *18150 Amity Vineyards Rd. SE, Amity* ☎ *503/835–2362* ⊕ *www.amityvineyards.com* ⊙ *Oct.–May, daily noon–5; June–Sept., daily 11–5.*

Domaine Serene. In Dundee's Red Hills, this is a world-class five-level winery and a well-regarded producer of Oregon pinot noir, as well as chardonnay and syrah. ⊠ *6555 N.E. Hilltop La., Dayton* ☎ *503/864–4600* ⊕ *www.domaineserene.com* ⊙ *Wed.–Sun. 11–4.*

EXPLORING

Evergreen Aviation Museum. The claim to fame here is Howard Hughes' *Spruce Goose*, on permanent display. If you can take your eyes off the *Spruce Goose* there are also more than 45 other historic planes and replicas here from the early years of flight and World War II, as well as the postwar and modern eras. IMAX shows are on Friday and Saturday nights. There's a museum store and café—the Spruce Goose Café, of course—and there are ongoing educational programs and special events. ⊠ *500 N.E. Michael King Smith Way, McMinnville* ☎ *503/434–4180* ⊕ *www.sprucegoose.org* ☜ *$20* ☉ *Daily 9–5, closed holidays.*

Fodor's Choice ★

NEED A BREAK?

Serendipity Ice Cream provides a true, old-fashioned ice-cream parlor experience. Try a sundae, and take home some cookies made from scratch. The parlor is located in the historic Cook's Hotel, built in 1886. (⊠ *502 N.E. 3rd St., McMinnville* ☎ *503/474–9189* ⊕ *serendipityicecream.com*)

4

WHERE TO EAT AND STAY

$$$
CONTEMPORARY

✕ **Joel Palmer House.** Joel Palmer was an Oregon pioneer, and his 1857 home in Dayton is now on the National Register of Historic Places. There are three small dining rooms, each seating about 15 people. The chef specializes in wild-mushroom dishes; a popular starter is Heidi's three-mushroom tart. Entrées include rib eye au poivre, rack of lamb, breast of duckling, and coq au vin; desserts include apricot-walnut bread pudding and crème brûlée. Or, if you really, really like mushrooms, have your entire table order Jack's Mushroom Madness Menu, a five-course extravaganza for $75.00 per person. ⊠ *600 Ferry St., Dayton* ☎ *503/864–2995* ⊕ *www.joelpalmerhouse.com* ▭ *AE, D, DC, MC, V* ☉ *Closed Sun. and Mon. No Lunch.*

$$$
ITALIAN

✕ **Nick's Italian Cafe.** Famed for serving Oregon's wine country enthusiasts, this fine-dining venue is a destination for a special evening or lunch. Modestly furnished but with a voluminous wine cellar, Nick's serves spirited and simple food, reflecting the owner's northern Italian heritage. A five-course prix-fixe menu changes nightly for $65. À la carte options are also available. ⊠ *521 N.E. 3rd St., McMinnville* ☎ *503/434–4471* ☜ *Reservations essential* ▭ *AE, MC, V* ⊕ *www. nicksitaliancafe.com.*

¢

✂ **Hotel Oregon.** Built in 1905, this historic facility—the former Elberton Hotel—was rescued from decay by the McMenamins chain, renovated in 1998, and reopened the following year. It is a four-story brick structure, and its rooms have tall ceilings and high windows. The hotel is outfitted in late Victorian furnishings, but its defining design element is its art. The hotel is whimsically decorated by McMenamins' artists: around every corner, even in the elevator, you'll find art—sometimes serene, often bizarre—as well as photos and sayings scribbled on the walls. The Oregon has a first-floor pub serving three meals a day, a rooftop bar with an impressive view of Yamhill County, and a cellar wine bar, resembling a dark speakeasy, that serves only area vintages. **Pros:** inexpensive, casual yet lively. **Cons:** those seeking upscale ambience should look elsewhere. ⊠ *310 N.E. Evans St., McMinnville* ☎ *503/472–8427 or 888/472–8427* ⊕ *www.mcmenamins.com* ⇘ *42 rooms* ☝ *In-hotel: Wi-Fi, restaurant, 2 bars* ▭ *AE, D, DC, MC, V.*

$ Fodor's Choice ★ **Mattey House Bed & Breakfast.** Built in 1982 by English immigrant Joseph Mattey, a local butcher, this Queen Anne Victorian mansion—on the National Register of Historic Places—has several cheerful areas that define it. Downstairs are a cozy living room jammed with antiques, dual dining areas—a parlor with white wicker and a dining room with elegant furniture—and a porch with a swing. The four upstairs rooms are whimsically named after locally grown grape varieties—Riesling, chardonnay, pinot noir, and blanc de blanc—and are decorated in keeping with the character of those wines: the Chardonnay Room, for instance, has tall windows and crisp white furnishings, and the Pinot Noir has dark-wood pieces and reddish wine accents. A small balcony off the upstairs landing is perfect for sipping a glass of wine on a cool Yamhill Valley evening. A fine full breakfast might include poached pears with raspberry sauce, frittatas, and Dutch-apple pancakes. Or your hosts will have pastry and hot coffee available before you set off. **Pros:** refined B&B atmosphere. **Cons:** not many modern amenities in the rooms. ✉ *10221 N.E. Mattey La., off Hwy. 99 W, ¼ mi south of Lafayette, McMinnville* ☎ *503/434–5058* 🌐 *www.matteyhouse.com* *4 rooms* *In-room: no phone* *AE, MC, V* *BP.*

NIGHTLIFE AND THE ARTS

Spirit Mountain Casino and Lodge. Located 24 mi southwest of McMinnville on Highway 18, this is a popular casino owned and operated by the Confederated Tribes of the Grande Ronde Community of Oregon. The 90,000-square-foot casino has more than a thousand slots, as well as poker and blackjack tables, roulette, craps, Pai Gow poker, keno, bingo, and off-track betting. Big-name comedians and rock and country musicians perform in the 1,700-seat concert hall, and there's an arcade for the kids. There's complimentary shuttle service from Portland and Salem. Dining options include an all-you-can-eat buffet, a deli, and a café. ✉ *27100 S.W. Hwy. 18, Grande Ronde* ☎ *503/879–3764 or 888/668–7366* 🌐 *www.spirit-mountain.com.*

MID-WILLAMETTE VALLEY

While most of the wineries are concentrated in Washington and Yamhill counties, there are several finds in the Mid-Willamette Valley that are worth extending a wine enthusiast's journey. There are also flower, hops, berries, and seed gardens scattered throughout Salem, Albany, and Corvallis. The huge number of company stores concentrated on Interstate 5 will have you thinking about some new Nikes, and Oregon State University will have you wearing orange and black long after Halloween is over. Be aware that many communities in this region are little more than wide spots in the road. In these tiny towns you might find only a gas station, a grocery store, a church or two, and a school. Watch out for any "School Crossing" signs: Oregon strictly enforces its speed-limit laws.

SALEM

24 mi from McMinnville, south on Hwy. 99 W and east on Hwy. 22. 45 mi south of Portland on I–5.

Salem has a rich pioneer history, but before that it was the home of the Calapooia Indians, who called it Chemeketa, which means "place of rest." Salem is said to have been renamed by missionaries. Although trappers and farmers preceded them in the Willamette Valley, the Methodist missionaries had come in 1834 to minister to Native Americans, and they are credited with the founding of Salem. In 1842 they established the first academic institution west of the Rockies, which is now known as Willamette University. Salem became the capital when Oregon achieved statehood in 1859 (Oregon City was the capital of the Oregon Territory). Salem serves as the seat to Marion County as well as the home of the state fairgrounds. Government ranks as a major industry here, while the city's setting in the heart of the fertile Willamette Valley stimulates rich agricultural and food-processing industries. More than a dozen wineries are in or near Salem. The main attractions in Salem are west of I–5 in and around the Capitol Mall.

GETTING HERE

Salem is located on I–5 with easy access to Portland, Albany, and Eugene. **Hut Portland Airport Shuttle** (☎ *503/364–4444* ⊕ *www. portlandairportshuttle.com*) provides transportation to Portland International Airport, which is 1 hour and 15 minutes away. Salem's McNary Field no longer has commercial airline service, but serves general aviation aircraft.

Bus transportation throughout Salem is provided by **Cherriot's** (⊕ *www. cherriots.org*). Amtrak operates regularly, and its train station is located at 500 13th Street SE.

VISITOR INFORMATION

Salem Convention & Visitors Center (✉ *1313 Mill St. SE* ☎ *503/581–4325 or 800/874–7012* ⊕ *www.travelsalem.com*)

WINERIES

Bethel Heights Vineyard. The tasting room has one of the most glorious panoramic views of any winery in the state; its terrace and picnic area overlook the surrounding vineyards, the valley below, and Mount Jefferson in the distance. Founded in 1977, Bethel Heights was one of the first vineyards planted in the Eola Hills region of the Willamette Valley. It produces pinot noir, chardonnay, pinot blanc, and pinot gris. ✉ *6060 Bethel Heights Rd. NW* ☎ *503/581–2262* ⊕ *www.bethelheights.com* 🗫 *$5, refundable with purchase* ☉ *Varies by season.*

Witness Tree Vineyard. Named for the ancient oak that towers over the vineyard (it was originally used as a surveyor's landmark in 1854), this winery produces premium pinot noir made entirely from grapes grown on its 100-acre estate nestled in the Eola Hills northwest of Salem. Witness Tree Vineyard also produces limited quantities of estate chardonnay, viognier, pinot blanc, dolcetto, and a sweet dessert wine called Sweet Signé. Tours are conducted frequently. ✉ *7111 Spring Valley Rd.*

NW ☎ *503/585–7874* ⊕ *www.witnesstreevineyard.com* ☉ *Summer: Tues.–Sun. 11–5; weekends year-round.*

EXPLORING

Numbers in the margin correspond to the Salem map.

❺ Bush's Pasture Park. These 105 acres of rolling lawn and formal English gardens include the remarkably well preserved Bush House, an 1878 Italianate mansion at the park's far western boundary. It has 10 marble fireplaces and virtually all of its original furnishings. The house and gardens are on the National Register of Historic Places. Bush Barn Art Center, behind the house, exhibits the work of Northwest artists and has a sales gallery. ⊠ *600 Mission St. SE* ☎ *503/363–4714* ⊕ *www.salemart. org* ⌨ *$4* ☉ *Mar. and Apr., Tues.–Sun. 1–4; May–Sept., Tues.–Sun. 12–5; Oct.–Dec., Tues.–Sun. 1–4; Jan., Feb. call for times.*

❶ Elsinore Theatre. This flamboyant Tudor Gothic vaudeville house opened on May 28, 1926, with Edgar Bergen in attendance. Clark Gable (who lived in Silverton) and Gregory Peck performed on stage. The theater was designed to look like a castle, with a false stone front, chandeliers, ironwork, and stained-glass windows. It's now a lively performing arts center with a busy schedule of bookings, and there are concerts on its Wurlitzer pipe organ. Group Tours for $3.00 per person can be arranged. ⊠ *170 High St. SE* ☎ *503/375–3574* ⊕ *www.elsinoretheatre.com.*

❹ Mission Mill Village. The **Thomas Kay Woolen Mill Museum** complex (circa 1889), complete with working water wheels and millstream, looks as if the workers have just stepped away for a lunch break. Teasel gigging, napper flock bins, and the patented Furber double-acting napper are but a few of the machines and processes on display. The **Jason Lee House,** the **John D. Boon Home,** and the **Methodist Parsonage** are also part of the village. There is nothing grandiose about these early pioneer homes, the oldest frame structures in the Northwest, but they reveal a great deal about domestic life in the wilds of Oregon in the 1840s. The adjacent **Marion County Historical Society Museum** (☎ *503/364–2128*) displays pioneer and Calapooia Indian artifacts. ⊠ *Museum complex, 1313 Mill St. SE* ☎ *503/585–7012* ⊕ *www.missionmill.org* ⌨ *$6, includes tour* ☉ *Daily 10–5* ☞ *Guided tours of houses and woolen mill museum are given when possible.*

❻ Mount Angel Abbey. On a 300-foot-high butte, this Benedictine monastery was founded in 1882. It's the site of one of two American buildings designed by Finnish architect Alvar Aalto. A masterpiece of serene and thoughtful design, Aalto's library opened its doors in 1970, and has become a place of pilgrimage for students and aficionados of modern architecture. ⊠ *18 mi from Salem, east on Hwy. 213, and north on Hwy. 214* ☎ *503/845–3030* ⊕ *www.mountangelabbey.org* ⌨ *Free.*

❷ Oregon Capitol. A brightly gilded bronze statue of the *Oregon Pioneer* stands atop the 140-foot-high Capitol dome, looking north across the Capitol Mall. Built in 1939 with blocks of gray Vermont marble, Oregon's Capitol has an elegant yet austere neoclassical feel. East and west wings were added in 1978. Relief sculptures and deft historical murals soften the interior. Tours of the rotunda, the House and Senate

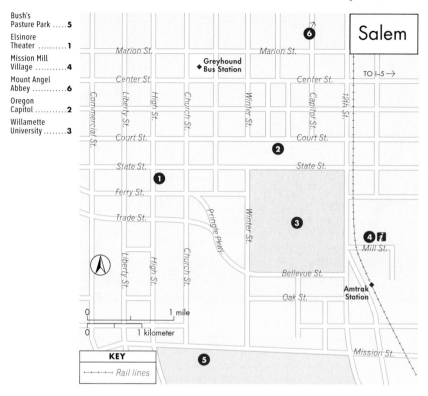

chambers, and the governor's office leave from the information center under the dome. ⊠ *900 Court St.* ☎ *503/986–1388* ⊕ *www.leg.state. or.us* ⊠ *Free* ☉ *Weekdays 8–5.*

❸ Willamette University. Behind the Capitol, across State Street but half a world away, are the brick buildings and grounds of Willamette University, the oldest college in the West. Founded in 1842, Willamette has long been a breeding ground for aspiring politicians. **Hatfield Library,** built in 1986 on the banks of Mill Stream, is a handsome brick-and-glass building with a striking campanile; tall, prim **Waller Hall,** built in 1867, is one of the oldest buildings in the Pacific Northwest. ⊠ *Information desk, Putnam University Center, Mill St.* ☎ *503/370–6300* ⊕ *www.willamette.edu* ☉ *Weekdays 8–5.*

WHERE TO EAT AND STAY

$$ ╳ **Bentley's Grill.** Located in the Grand Hotel in Salem, this steak and
AMERICAN seafood eatery strives to serve ingredients from the Northwest, whether it's Oregon bay shrimp, Rogue Valley bleu cheese, Oregon hazelnuts, or local beef. Its menu also has occasional wild game entrées. Rounding out its menu are selections from its pizza oven. ⊠ *201 Liberty St. SE* ☎ *503/779–1660* ⊕ *bentleysgrill.com* ⊟ *AE, DC, MC, V.*

Oregon Capitol building in Salem

\$\$ ✕ **DaVinci**. Salem politicos flock to this two-story downtown restaurant
ITALIAN for Italian-inspired dishes cooked in a wood-burning oven. No shortcuts
Fodor's Choice are taken in the preparation, so don't come if you're in a rush. But if
★ you're in the mood to linger over seafood and fresh pasta that's made
on the premises, this may be your place. The wine list is one of the most
extensive in the Northwest; the staff is courteous and extremely professional. There's wine tasting and live jazz Thursdays at 6 PM. ⊠ *180 High
St.* ☎ *503/399–1413* ⊕ *www.davincisofsalem.com*☐ *AE, DC, MC, V*
☾ *No lunch*.

\$ ⊞ **Grand Hotel in Salem**. Formerly known as the Phoenix Grand Hotel,
this property serves as the headquarters hotel for the new Salem Conference Center in downtown Salem. Its centrally located, a convenient
base for trips to nearby parks, shopping, and wineries. The rooms are
large, with comfortable, luxurious furnishings. It's restaurant, Bentley's
Grill, is a local favorite. **Pros:** spacious rooms, centrally located. **Cons:**
located on the street. ⊠ *201 Liberty St. SE, Salem* ☎ *503/540–7800
or 877/540–7800* ⊕ *www.GrandHotelSalem.com* ⟿ *143 rooms, 50
suites* ⚷ *In-Room: refrigerator, Internet. In-hotel: restaurant, Wi-Fi,
pool, gym* ☐ *AE, D, DC, MC, V*.

\$ ⊞ **Oregon Garden Resort**. Located 13 mi northeast of Salem, this luxu-
rious property neighbors the Oregon Garden. The rooms are bright,
roomy, and tastefully decorated. Rates include a full breakfast and
admission to the Oregon Garden. The hotel is great for weddings, meet-
ings and romantic getaways. Each room has a fireplace and a private,
landscaped patio or balcony. The resort has a full-service spa, an outdoor pool, and free parking. Some pet-friendly rooms are available.
Pros: gorgeous grounds, luxurious rooms, plenty of amenities. **Cons:**

outside of town, away from other activities. ⊠ *895 W. Main St., Silverton* ☎ *503/874–2500 or 800/966–6490* ⊕ *www.oregongardenresort.com* ⇆ *143 rooms, 50 suites* ⌂ *In-Room: a/c, refrigerator, Internet. In-hotel: restaurant, spa, pool, parking* ▭ *AE, D, DC, MC, V* ⏐⦿⏐ *BP.*

SHOPPING

Reed Opera House. Located in downtown Salem, this 1869 opera house now contains a compelling collection of locally owned stores, shops, restaurants, bars, and bakeries. Its Trinity Ballroom hosts special events and celebrations. ⊠ *189 Liberty St. NE* ☎ *503/391–4481* ⊕ *www.reedoperahouse.com.*

Woodburn Company Stores. Located 18 mi north of Salem on I–5 are more than 100 brand-name outlet stores, including Nike, Calvin Klein, Bose, Gymboree, OshKosh B'Gosh, Ann Taylor, Levi's, Chico's, Fossil, Liz Claiborne, Polo, and Columbia Sportswear, and plenty of places to eat. Chances are that someone in your traveling party would enjoy burning an hour or three browsing famous outlet stores. ⊠ *1001 Arney Rd., Woodburn* ☎ *503/981–1900 or 888/664–7467* ⊕ *www.shopwoodburn.com* ⊗ *Mon.–Sat. 10–8, Sun. 10–7.*

SPORTS AND THE OUTDOORS

Fodor's Choice ★ **Silver Falls State Park.** Hidden amid old-growth Douglas firs in the foothills of the Cascades, Silver Falls is the largest state park in Oregon (8,700 acres). South Falls, roaring over the lip of a mossy basalt bowl into a deep pool 177 feet below, is the main attraction here, but 13 other waterfalls—half of them more than 100 feet high—are accessible to hikers. The best time to visit is in the fall, when vine maples blaze with brilliant color, or early spring, when the forest floor is carpeted with trilliums and yellow violets. There are picnic facilities and a day lodge; in winter you can cross-country ski. Camping facilities include 52 year-round electrical $24; 45 tent (tent sites closed Oct. 31–Apr. 1) $19; group tent (3 areas) $71; horse camp $19–$58; 14 cabins $39. ⊠ *20024 Silver Falls Hwy. SE, Sublimity* ☎ *503/873–8681 or 800/551–6949* ⊕ *www.oregonstateparks.org* ⊡ *$5 per vehicle* ⊗ *Daily dawn–dusk.*

Willamette Mission State Park. Along pastoral lowlands by the Willamette River, this serene park holds the largest black cottonwood tree in the United States. A thick-barked behemoth by a small pond, the 265-year-old tree has upraised arms that bring to mind J. R. R. Tolkien's fictional Ents. Site of Reverend Jason Lee's 1834 pioneer mission, the park also offers quiet strolling and picnicking in an old orchard and along the river. The Wheatland Ferry, at the north end of the park, began carrying covered wagons across the Willamette in 1844, using pulleys. ⊠ *Wheatland Rd., 8 mi north of Salem, I–5 Exit 263* ☎ *503/393–1172 or 800/551–6949* ⊕ *www.oregonstateparks.org* ⊡ *Day use $5* ⊗ *Daily 8–dusk.*

ALBANY

20 mi from Salem, south on I–5 and west on U.S. 20.

Known as the grass-seed capital of the world, Albany has some of the most historic buildings in Oregon. Some 700 buildings, scattered over a 100-block area in three districts, include every major architectural style in the United States since 1850. The area is listed on the National Register of Historic Places. Eight covered bridges can also be seen on a half-hour drive from Albany.

GETTING HERE

Albany is located on I–5 with easy access to Portland, Salem, and Eugene. Portland International Airport is 1 hour, 40 min. away, and the Eugene airport is 1 hour away to the south. Several shuttle services are available from both airports.

Albany Transit System provides two routes for intercity travel. The Linn-Benton loop system provides for transportation between Albany and Corvallis. Albany is a destination stop for Amtrak.

VISITOR INFORMATION

Albany Visitors Association (✉ *250 Broadalbin SW, #110* ☎ *541/928–0911 or 800/526–2256* ⊕ *www.albanyvisitors.com*).

EXPLORING

Benton County Historical Society and Museum. The artifact collection of 66,000 items features local themes ranging from logging and technology to the arts. The museum also has artifacts of Camp Adair, which was a World War II military cantonment, and Philomath College, a United Brethren College that now houses the museum. ✉ *1101 Main St., Philomath* ☎ *541/929–6230* ⊕ *www.bentoncountymuseum.org* ⊗ *Tues.–Sat. 10–4:30.*

Monteith House Museum. The first frame house in Albany was Monteith House, built in 1849. Now a museum, restored and filled with period furnishings and historic photos, it is widely thought to be the most authentic restoration of a Pacific Northwest pioneer-era home. ✉ *518 2nd Ave. SW* ☎ *800/526–2256* ⊕ *www.albanyvisitors.com* ⊠ *Donation* ⊗ *Mid-June–mid-Sept., Wed.–Sat. noon–4; mid-Sept.–mid-June, by appointment.*

WHERE TO EAT

$$
ECLECTIC
Fodor's Choice
★
✕ **Sybaris.** This fine bistro in Albany's historic downtown strives to ensure that most of the menu's ingredients, including the lamb, eggs, and vegetables, are raised within 10 mi. Even the huckleberries in the ice cream are gathered in secret locations by their mushroom picker. With a monthly rotating menu—which can be viewed online—it serves upscale, flavorful cuisine at reasonable prices. ✉ *442 1st Ave. W* ☎ *541/928–8157* ⊕ *www.sybarisbistro.com* ⊗ *Closed Sun. and Mon. No lunch* ⊟ *AE, D, DC, MC, V.*

$
HUNGARIAN
✕ **Novak's Hungarian.** Since 1984, the Novak family has been a delightful fixture in Albany's dining scene. From Hungarian hash and eggs in the morning to chicken paprika served over homemade Hungarian pearl noodles, you can't go wrong in this establishment. There's a huge assortment of desserts as well. On Sunday they serve brunch. ✉ *2306 Heritage Way SE* ☎ *541/967–9488* ⊕ *www.novakshungarian. com* ⊟ *AE, D, MC, V.*

CORVALLIS

10 mi southwest of Albany on U.S. 20

To some, Corvallis is a brief stopping place along the way to Salem or Portland. To others, it's a small town that gives you a chance to escape the bigger cities. Driving the area's economy are a growing engineering and high-tech industry, a burgeoning wine industry, and more traditional local agricultural crops, such as grass and legume seeds. Corvallis is home to Oregon State University and its Beavers. It offers plenty of outdoor activities as well as scenic attractions, from covered bridges to wineries and gardens.

GETTING HERE

Corvallis Transit System (CTS) operates 8 bus routes throughout the city. **Hut Shuttle** (☎ *503/364–4444* ⊕ *www.portlandairportshuttle. com*) provides transportation between Corvallis and the Portland airport, located 1 hour, 53 minutes away. **OmniShuttle** (☎ *541/461–7959* ⊕ *www.omnishuttle.us*) provides transportation between Corvallis and the Eugene airport, 50 minutes away. Corvallis Municipal Airport is a public airport four miles south of the city.

VISITOR INFORMATION

Corvallis Tourism (⊠ *553 N.W. Harrison* ☎ *541/757–1544 or 800/334–8118* ⊕ *www.visitcorvallis.com*)

EXPLORING

Oregon State University. It's a thrill to be on campus on game day, as students are a sea of orange and black cheering on their beloved Beavers. This 400-acre campus, west of the city center, was established as a land-grant institution in 1868. OSU has more than 22,000 students, many of them studying the university's nationally recognized programs in conservation biology, agricultural sciences, nuclear engineering, forestry, fisheries and wildlife management, community health, pharmacy, and zoology. ⊠ *15th and Jefferson Sts.* ☎ *541/737–1000* ⊕ *oregonstate.edu.*

WHERE TO EAT AND STAY

$ ✕ **Gathering Together Farm.** When spring arrives, it means that the organic
NEW AMERICAN farmers outside of Philomath are serving their bounty. Fresh vegetables,
Fodor'sChoice pizzas, local lamb, pork, and halibut are frequent menu highlights.
★ Local wines and tempting desserts make the evening perfect. It also serves lunch four days a week and breakfast on Saturday. ⊠ *25159 Grange Hall Rd., Philomath* ☎ *541/929–4270* ⚑ *reservations essential* ⊟ *MC, V* ⊗ *Closed Mon. and Oct.–Mar. No dinner Sat.–Wed. No lunch Sun.*

$ ⊡ **Salbasgeon Suites & Conference Center.** Rooms here are spacious, clean, and equipped with new furnishings, although it doesn't shake the chain hotel feel. What's nice is its proximity to Oregon State University, Hewlett-Packard, movie theatres, and fine dining. **Pros:** close to Corvallis sights, in-hotel activities. **Cons:** suites seem a little cramped; bland and corporate. ⊠ *1730 N.W. 9th St., Corvallis* ☎ *541/753–4320 or 800/965–8808* ⊕ *www.salbasgeon.com* ⊲ *95 rooms* ⚐ *In-room: refrigerator, a/c. In-hotel: restaurant, bar, pool, gym, laundry facilities, Wi-Fi* ⎮⊙⎮ *BP* ⊟ *AE, D, MC, V.*

4

SPORTS AND THE OUTDOORS

RECREATIONAL AREAS

Fodor's Choice ★

Siuslaw National Forest. The highest point in the Coast Range (4,097 feet), Mary's Peak offers panoramic views of the Cascades, the Willamette Valley, and the rest of the Coast Range. On a clear day you can see as far as the Pacific Ocean. There are several picnicking areas, more than 10 mi of hiking trails, and a small campground. There are stands of noble fir and alpine meadows. The forest, just 2 mi from Corvallis, includes the Oregon Dunes National Recreation Area and the Cape Perpetua Interpretive Center. People usually access the Forest using one of several major highways: Highways 26, 6, and 18 all access the north central coast; Highways 20 and 34 access Newport and the central coast; Highway 126 accesses Florence and the north part of the Oregon Dunes; and Highway 38 accesses Reedsport and the southern section of the Oregon Dunes. ⊠ *4077 S.W. Research Way, Corvallis* ☎ *541/750–7000* ⊕ *www.fs.fed.us/r6/siuslaw* ⊠ *Free* ☉ *Daily dawn–dusk.*

SWIMMING

Osborn Aquatic Center. This is not the site of your ordinary lap pool. There are water slides, a water channel, water cannons, and floor geysers. The indoor lap pool is open all year. ⊠ *1940 N.W. Highland Dr.* ☎ *541/766–7946* ⊕ *www.ci.corvallis.or.us* ⊠ *$4* ☉ *June–Sept.*

SOUTH WILLAMETTE VALLEY

Lane County rests at the southern end of the Willamette Valley. It encompasses Eugene, Springfield, Drain, McKenzie Bridge, and Cottage Grove to the south. There are plenty of wineries to enjoy, but visitors can also sprinkle their sipping fun with some white-water rafting, deep-woods hiking, and cheering on the Oregon Ducks. To the west lies the Oregon Dunes Recreation Area, and to the east are the beautiful central Oregon communities of Sisters, Bend, and Redmond.

EUGENE

63 mi south of Corvallis on I–5.

Eugene was founded in 1846, when Eugene Skinner staked the first federal land-grant claim for pioneers. Eugene is consistently given high marks for its "livability." As the home of the University of Oregon, a large student and former-student population lends Eugene a youthful vitality and countercultural edge. Full of parks and oriented to the outdoors, Eugene is a place where bike paths are used, pedestrians *always* have the right-of-way, and joggers are so plentiful that the city is known as the Running Capital of the World. Shopping and commercial streets surround the Eugene Hilton and the Hult Center for the Performing Arts, the two most prominent downtown buildings. During football season you can count on the U of O Ducks being the primary topic of most conversations.

GETTING HERE

Eugene's airport has rental cars, cabs, and shuttles that make the 15-minute trip to Eugene's city center. By train, Amtrak stops in the heart of downtown. Getting around Lane County's communities is easy with **Lane Transit District** (LTD) (☎ *541/687–5555* ⊕ *www.ltd.org)*

public transportation. Eugene is very bicycle-friendly.

VISITOR INFORMATION

Eugene, Cascades & Coast Adventure Center (✉ *3312 Gateway St, Springfield* ☎ *541/484–5307* ⊕ *www.travellanecounty.org*).

WINERIES

King Estate Winery. This certified organic estate is committed to producing world-class pinot gris and pinot noir. The visitors center offers complimentary wine tasting, extensive flight selections, and production tours. ✉ *80854 Territorial Rd., Eugene* ☎ *541/942–9874 or 800/884–4441* ⊕ *www.kingestate.com* ✆ *$7* ⊙ *Daily 11–9, tours on the hour noon–5.*

Sweet Cheeks Winery. This estate vineyard lies on a prime sloping hillside in the heart of the Willamette Valley appellation. It also supplies grapes to several award-winning wineries. It has free Friday-night tastings with cheese pairings. Check the Web site for special dinners and events. ✉ *27007 Briggs Hill Rd., Eugene* ☎ *541/349–9463 or 877/309–9463* ⊕ *www.sweetcheekswinery.com* ⊙ *Daily noon–6; Fri.-night twilight tastings with cheese pairings 6–9.*

EXPLORING

Alton Baker Park. Named after the *Eugene Register-Guard* newspaper's publisher, Alton Baker Park is the site of many community events. Live music is performed in summer. There's fine hiking and biking at Alton Baker on the banks of the Willamette River. A footpath along the river runs the length of the park. Also worth seeing is the Whilamut Natural Area, an open space with 13 "talking stones," each with an inscription. Also, there is a very nice dog section. ✉ *Centennial Blvd. east of Ferry St. Bridge, Eugene* ☎ *541/484–5307 or 541/682–2000* ⊕ *www.eugene-or.gov* ⊙ *Daily 6* AM*–11* PM.

☾ **Cascades Raptor Center.** This birds of prey nature center and hospital has over 30 species of birds. This is a great outing for kids, where they can learn what owls eat, why and where birds migrate. Some of its full-time residents include turkey vultures, bald eagles, owls, hawks, falcons, and kites. ✉ *32275 Fox Hollow Rd., Eugene* ☎ *541/485–1320* ⊕ *www.eRaptors.org* ✆ *$7* ⊙ *Apr.–Oct., 10–6; closed Mon.*

5th Street Public Market. A former chicken-processing plant is the site of this popular shopping mall, filled with small crafts, art, and gifts stores. Dining includes sit-down restaurants, decadent bakeries, and the international diversity of the second-floor food esplanade. ✉ *5th Ave. and High St., Eugene* ☎ *541/484–0383* ⊕ *www.5stmarket.com* ⊙ *Shops Mon.–Sat. 10–7, Sun. 11–5.*

☾ **Mount Pisgah Arboretum.** This beautiful nature preserve near southeast Eugene includes extensive all-weather trails, educational programs

Fresh produce from Hey Bayles! Farm at the Eugene Saturday Market

for all ages, and facilities for special events. Its Visitor Center holds workshops, and features native amphibian and reptile terraria; microscopes for exploring tiny seeds, bugs, feathers, and snakeskins; "touch me" exhibits; reference books; and a working viewable bee hive. ⊠ *34901 Frank Parrish Rd., Eugene* ☎ *541/747–3817* ⊕ *www.mountpisgaharboretum.org* 🗺 *Donation suggested, $2 parking* ⊙ *Daily, dawn to dusk.*

Science Factory. Formerly the Willamette Science and Technology Center (WISTEC), and still known to locals by its former name, Eugene's imaginative, hands-on museum assembles rotating exhibits designed for curious young minds. The adjacent **planetarium,** one of the largest in the Pacific Northwest, presents star shows and entertainment events. ⊠ *2300 Leo Harris Pkwy., Eugene* ☎ *541/682–7888 museum, 541/461–8227 planetarium* ⊕ *www.sciencefactory.org* 🗺 *$7 for both Science Hall and Planetarium, $4 each* ⊙ *Wed.–Sun. 10–4. Closed Oregon Duck home football games and major holidays.*

University of Oregon. The true heart of Eugene lies southeast of the city center at its university. Several fine old buildings can be seen on the 250-acre campus; **Deady Hall,** built in 1876, is the oldest. More than 400 varieties of trees grace the bucolic grounds, along with outdoor sculptures that include *The Pioneer* and *The Pioneer Mother.* The two bronze figures by Alexander Phimster Proctor were dedicated to the men and women who settled the Oregon Territory and less than a generation later founded the university.

Eugene's two best museums are affiliated with the university. The **Jordan Schnitzer Museum of Art** (⊠ *1430 Johnson La.* ☎ *541/346–3027*

⊕ *www.uoma.uoregon.edu* ▣ *$5* ☉ *Tues.–Sun. 11–5*), next to the library, underwent a major renovation and expansion, nearly doubling its size. It includes galleries featuring American, European, Korean, Chinese, and Japanese art. Relics of a more local nature are on display at the **University of Oregon Museum of Natural History** (✉ *1680 E. 15th Ave.* ☎ *541/346–3024* ⊕ *www.natural-history.uoregon.edu* ▣ *$3* ☉ *Wed.–Sun. 11–5*), devoted to Pacific Northwest anthropology and the natural sciences. Its highlights include the fossil collection of Thomas Condon, Oregon's first geologist, and a pair of 9,000-year-old sagebrush sandals. *Agate St. and Franklin Blvd.* ⊕ *www.uoregon.edu.*

WHERE TO EAT

$$$
PACIFIC
NORTHWEST

✕ **Adam's Sustainable Table.** Serving delicious seasonal Northwest cuisine with an organic menu of local produce, meats, and sustainable seafood, Adam's works to obtain food from farms, ranches, and mills within a 75-mile radius, most within 25 miles to keep its ingredients as local as possible. Its most requested dish is the pasture-raised chicken picatta, and its produce is so fresh it will bring tears to your eyes. Adam's is a recipient of 10 *Wine Spectator* awards. ✉ *30 E Broadway, Eugene* ☎ *541/344–6948* ⊕ *www.adamsplacerestaurant.com* ▭ *AE, MC, V* ☉ *No lunch. Closed Sun. and Mon.*

$$
ITALIAN

✕ **Excelsior Café.** The expert cuisine enhances the appealing European elegance of this restaurant, bar, and bistro-style café across from the University of Oregon. The chef uses only fresh local produce, but Excelsior is best known for its authentic Italian cuisine, such as a delectable osso bucco Milanese and house-made artisan pasta. The menu changes according to the season, but staples include delicious salads and soups, gnocchi, grilled chicken, broiled salmon, and sandwiches. The dining room, shaded by blossoming cherry trees in the spring, has a quiet, understated feel. There's outdoor seating on the patio. Serves breakfast and Sunday brunch. ✉ *754 E. 13th Ave., Eugene* ☎ *541/342–6963 or 800/321–6963* ⊕ *www.excelsiorinn.com* ▭ *AE, D, DC, MC, V.*

$$$
FRENCH

✕ **Marché.** The name translates into "market," meaning that this renowned Eugene restaurant works with a dozen local farmers to bring the freshest, most organic local food to the table. Specialties include salmon, halibut, sturgeon, and beef tenderloin, braised pork shoulders, and outstanding local oysters. It has an extensive wine list with an emphasis on Oregon and France. There's also a Sunday brunch. ✉ *296 E. 5th Ave., Eugene* ☎ *541/342–3612* ⊕ *www.marcheprovisions.com* ▭ *AE, D, MC, V.*

$$
SOUTHWESTERN
Fodor's Choice
★

✕ **Red Agave.** Two local women managed to establish this cozy, romantic restaurant in an old building that at one point was a refuse dump, and the result is a hard-to-categorize winner that has Mexican and Latino influences. Menu items might include sesame-crusted salmon with chipotle barbecue glaze, which you can consider washing down with a tamarind margarita. Flans, like much of the menu, are seasonal; try the Kahlua flan or the orange flan with chocolate in the middle. ✉ *454 Willamette St., Eugene* ☎ *541/683–2206* ⊕ *redagave.net* ▭ *AE, D, DC, MC, V* ☉ *Closed Sun. No lunch.*

$$
AMERICAN

✕ **Sweetwaters.** The dining room at the Valley River Inn, which overlooks the Willamette at water level, specializes in Pacific Northwest cuisine. Try the salmon with Szechuan peppercorn crust and cranberry vinaigrette or the grilled beef fillet with Oregon blue-cheese crust. There is a bar area outside, as well as a deck for open-air dining. Sunday brunch and a kids' menu are available, too. ⊠ *1000 Valley River Way, Eugene* ☎ *541/687–0123* ⊕ *www.valleyriverinn/sweetwaters.com* ▭ *AE, D, DC, MC, V.*

WHERE TO STAY

$ ⊡ **Campbell House.** Built in 1892 on the east side of Skinner Butte, Campbell House is one of the oldest structures in Eugene. Restored with fastidious care, the luxurious B&B is surrounded by an acre of landscaped grounds. The parlor, library, and dining rooms have their original hardwood floors and curved-glass windows. Differing architectural details, building angles, and furnishings (a mixture of century-old antiques and reproductions) lend each of the rooms a distinctive personality. Suites have Jacuzzis. The room rates include a full breakfast including freshbaked pastries. The house now serves dinner seven nights a week, with a prix-fixe offering or à la carte. **Pros:** classic architecture, comfortable rooms, well-kept grounds. **Cons:** rooms lack the amenities of nearby hotels. ⊠ *252 Pearl St., Eugene* ☎ *541/343–1119 or 800/264–2519* ⊕ *www.campbellhouse.com* ↪ *12 rooms, 7 suites, 1 cottage* ⌂ *In-room: DVD (some), Wi-Fi* ▭ *AE, D, MC, V.*

$ ⊡ **C'est la Vie Inn.** Listed on the National Register of Historic Places,
Fodor'sChoice   the restored 1891 Queen Anne Victorian bed-and-breakfast has been
★   updated to provide Old World comfort with modern-day amenities. The inn serves as an excellent hub for enjoying Eugene, as it is close to downtown shops, restaurants, galleries, and bicycle paths. The Hult Center for the Performing Arts and the University of Oregon campus are also within walking distance. Each guest room is luxurious and romantic, with private bath and individual cooling/heating controls. The parlor and dining rooms are ornately decorated in period furnishings, and the inn offers concierge services for dry cleaning, theater tickets, and restaurant reservations. **Pros:** outstanding service and value. **Cons:** few rooms. ⊠ *1006 Taylor St., Eugene* ☎ *866/302–3014 or 541/302–3014* ⊕ *www.cestlavieinn.com* ↪ *3 rooms, 1 suite* ⌂ *In-room: DVD, Wi-Fi* ▭ *AE, MC, V.*

$$ ⊡ **Excelsior Inn.** This small hotel manifests a quiet sophistication com-
Fodor'sChoice   mensurate with lodgings found in quaint European villages. Crisply
★   detailed, with cherrywood doors and moldings, it has rooms furnished in a refreshingly understated manner, each with a marble-and-tile bath and some with fireplaces. The rates include a delicious breakfast. The ground-level Excelsior Café is one of Eugene's best restaurants. **Pros:** romantic accommodations, excellent service and restaurant. **Cons:** formal in a casual town. ⊠ *754 E. 13th Ave., Eugene* ☎ *541/342–6963 or 800/321–6963* ⊕ *www.excelsiorinn.com* ↪ *14 rooms* ⌂ *In-room: a/c, Wi-Fi. In-hotel: restaurant, parking* ▭ *AE, D, DC, MC, V* �🍽 *BP.*

$ ⊡ **Valley River Inn.** At this inn on the banks of the Willamette River some rooms have an outdoor patio or balcony, some have river or pool views, and concierge rooms have access to a private lounge. The location is splendid, and current renovation should elevate the hotel's appearance to match its surroundings. The inn's restaurant is the popular

Sweetwaters. It also provides bicycles to help guests get out and about. **Pros:** river location, amenities, great restaurant. **Cons:** basic room decor. ⊠ *1000 Valley River Way, Eugene* ☎ *541/687–0123 or 800/543–8266* ⊕ *www.valleyriverinn.com* ⌐ *257 rooms* ⌂ *In-hotel: restaurant, bar, Wi-Fi, pool, gym, laundry service, parking* ⊟ *AE, D, DC, MC, V.*

NIGHTLIFE AND THE ARTS

Hult Center for the Performing Arts. This is the locus of Eugene's cultural life. Renowned for the quality of its acoustics, the center has two theaters that are home to Eugene's symphony and opera. ⊠ *1 Eugene Center, at 7th Ave. and Willamette St., Eugene* ☎ *541/682–5087* ⊕ *www. hultcenter.org.*

Conductor Helmuth Rilling leads the internationally known **Oregon Bach Festival** (☎ *541/682–5000 for tickets; 800/457–1486 for information* ⊕ *www.bachfest.uoregon.edu*) every summer. Concerts, chamber music, and social events—held mainly in Eugene at the Hult Center and the University of Oregon School of Music but also in Corvallis and Florence—are part of this 19-day event.

SHOPPING

Tourists coming to the Willamette Valley, especially to Eugene, can't escape without experiencing the **5th Street Public Market** in downtown Eugene. There are plenty of small crafts shops, and the food mall offers many cuisines, including vegetarian, pizza, and seafood.

Valley River Center (⊠ *Delta Hwy. and Valley River Dr., Eugene* ☎ *541/ 683–5511*) is the largest shopping center between Portland and San Francisco. There are five department stores, including Meier & Frank and JCPenney, plus 130 specialty shops and a food court.

SPORTS AND THE OUTDOORS

RECREATIONAL AREAS

Skinner Butte Park. Rising from the south bank of the Willamette River, this park provides the best views of any of the city's parks; it also has the greatest historic cachet, since it was here that Eugene Skinner staked the claim that put Eugene on the map. Children can scale a replica of Skinner Butte, uncover fossils, and cool off under a rain circle. Skinner Butte Loop leads to the top of Skinner Butte, from which Spencer Butte, 4 mi to the south, can be seen. The two main trails to the top of Skinner Butte traverse a sometimes difficult terrain through a mixed-conifer forest. ⊠ *2nd Ave. and High St., Eugene* ☎ *541/682–5521* ⊕ *www.eugene-or. gov/parks* ⊠ *Free* ☉ *Daily 10 AM–midnight.*

Splash! Lively Park Swim Center. This indoor water park has wave surfing and a waterslide. There are family, lap, and kids' pools; as well as a spa, concessions, playground, a park, and picnic shelters. ⊠ *6100 Thurston Rd., Springfield* ☎ *541/747–9283* ⊕ *www.willamalane.org* ⊠ *$6.25* ☉ *Mon., Wed., Sun. 1–7:30, Tues. and Thur. 1–5, Fri. and Sat. 1–9.*

OFF THE BEATEN PATH

Waldo Lake. Nestled in old-growth forest, Waldo Lake is famed as a remarkably clean and pristine body of water. The lake is accessible only after a short hike, so bring comfortable shoes. ⊠ *From Eugene, take Hwy. 58 to Oakridge and continue toward Willamette Pass; follow signs north to Waldo Lake.*

<table>
<tr><td>BIKING AND
JOGGING</td><td>The **River Bank Bike Path,** originating in Alton Baker Park on the Willamette's north bank, is a level and leisurely introduction to Eugene's topography. It's one of 120 mi of trails in the area. **Prefontaine Trail,** used by area runners, travels through level fields and forests for 1½ mi.</td></tr>
<tr><td>SKIING</td><td>**Willamette Pass** (⊠ *Hwy. 58, 69 mi southeast of Eugene* ☎ *541/345–7669 or 800/444–5030*), 6,666 feet high in the Cascade Range, packs an annual average snowfall of 300 inches atop 29 runs. The vertical drop is 1,563 feet. Four triple chairs and one double chair service the downhill ski areas, and 13 mi of Nordic trails lace the pass. Facilities here include a ski shop; day care; a bar and restaurant; and Nordic and downhill rentals, repairs, and instruction.</td></tr>
</table>

MCKENZIE BRIDGE

58 mi east of Eugene on Hwy. 126.

On the beautiful McKenzie River, lakes, waterfalls, and covered bridges surround the town of McKenzie Bridge and wilderness trails in the Cascades. Fishing, skiing, backpacking, and rafting are among the most popular activities in the area.

GETTING HERE

McKenzie Bridge is about an hour from Eugene, on Highway 126. It is just 38 mi from Hoodoo Ski Area, but its proximity can be deceiving if the snow is heavy. Bend also is close at 64 mi to the east.

VISITOR INFORMATION

Lane County Convention and Visitors Association (⊠ *754 Olive St., Eugene* ☎ *541/343–6335 or 800/547–5445* ⊕ *www.visitlanecounty.org*).

EXPLORING

McKenzie River Highway. Highway 126, as it heads east from Eugene, is known as the McKenzie River Highway. Following the curves of the river, it passes grazing lands, fruit and nut orchards, and the small riverside hamlets of the McKenzie Valley. From the highway you can glimpse the bouncing, bubbling, blue-green McKenzie River, one of Oregon's top fishing, boating, and white-water rafting spots, against a backdrop of densely forested mountains, splashing waterfalls, and jet-black lava beds. The small town of McKenzie Bridge marks the end of the McKenzie River Highway and the beginning of the 26-mi McKenzie River National Recreation Trail, which heads north through the Willamette National Forest along portions of the Old Santiam Wagon Road.

OFF THE
BEATEN
PATH

McKenzie Pass. Just beyond McKenzie Bridge, Highway 242 begins a steep, 22-mi eastward climb to McKenzie Pass in the Cascade Range. The scenic highway, which passes through the Mt. Washington Wilderness Area and continues to the town of Sisters (⇨ *Central Oregon*), is generally closed October–June because of heavy snow. Novice motorists take note, this is not a drive for the timid: it's a challenging exercise in negotiating tight curves at quickly fluctuating, often slow speeds—the skid marks on virtually every turn attest to hasty braking—so take it slow, and don't be intimidated by cars on your tail itching to take the turns more quickly.

WHERE TO EAT AND STAY

¢ ✕ **Takoda's Restaurant.** This restaurant has a full breakfast menu, burgers,
AMERICAN great soups, a salad bar, pizza, and daily specials. In addition, a video
🎮 game room keeps kids happy. ⊠ *91806 Mill Creek Rd, Milepost 47.5
McKenzie Hwy., Blue River* ☎ *541/822–1153* ▭ *AE, MC, V* ⊘ *Daily 8–8.*

$ 🏨 **Belknap Hot Springs Resort.** As the name implies, this resort is all about
getting into hot water—willingly. On the site of mineral springs 54 miles
(87 km) east of Eugene, Belknap Hot Springs is adjacent to two hot pools
and acres of lush gardens. Stay in the beautiful lodge or campground on
the McKenzie River. The Belknap Grill serves burgers and sandwiches.
Pros: hot springs, wooded location. **Cons:** 14-day cancellation policy,
two-night minimum on weekends. ⊠ *59296 Belknap Springs Rd., McK-
enzie Bridge* ☎ *541/822–3512* ⊕ *www.belknaphotsprings.com* ⇥ *19
rooms, 7 cabins, 39 RV sites, 13 tent sites* ▭ *D, MC, V* ⏹ *BP.*

$$ 🏨 **Eagle Rock Lodge.** This historic B&B on the McKenzie River is luxu-
rious and cozy for a lodge located in the woods. Rooms have wood,
quilts, and antiques, providing a romantic, relaxing atmosphere. The
lodge specializes in weddings, retreats, and just great living. Guided fish-
ing and rafting trips can be arranged. Their bodacious breakfasts include
homemade pastries, fruits and vegetables, sausage patties, vegetable
frittata, and roasted potatoes. Don't forget to pour on the house-made
roasted pepper sauce. **Pros:** great location, comfortable atmosphere.
Cons: a distance from non-outdoor activities. ⊠ *49198 McKenzie Hwy.,
Vida* ☎ *541/822–3630 or 888/773–4333* ⊕ *www.eaglerocklodge.com*
⇥ 8 rooms ⚒ *In-room: refrigerator (some)* ▭ *MC, V* ⏹ *BP.*

$$ 🏨 **Holiday Farm Resort.** Originally built in 1910, the Holiday Farm served
for many years as a stagecoach stop, and later a favorite stopover for
President Herbert Hoover. Its 13 cottages are on or near the McKenzie
River banks and can accommodate between 2 and 14 occupants. The
Holiday Farm Restaurant is just a short walk from most cabins. A great
feature of the property is the walking trails leading to the McKenzie
River and to nearby ponds for fishing or relaxing. Five of the cabins
are pet-friendly. There is a lounge and meeting room on the property.
Golf, fishing, and rafting are nearby. **Pros:** great place for relaxation
and outdoor activities. **Cons:** far from town. ⊠ *54455 McKenzie River
Dr., Blue River* ☎ *541/822–3725* ⊕ *www.holidayfarmresort.com* ⇥ *13
cottages* ⚒ *In-room: kitchens, Wi-Fi,* ▭ *AE, MC, V* ⏹ *BP, MAP, FAP.*

SPORTS AND THE OUTDOORS

Cougar Dam and Lake. Four miles outside of McKenzie Bridge is the highest embankment dam ever built by the Army Corps of Engineers—452
feet above the streambed. The resulting reservoir, on the South Fork
McKenzie River, covers 1,280 acres. The public recreation areas are
in the Willamette National Forest. A fish hatchery is in the vicinity.
You can visit the dam year-round, but the campgrounds are open only
from May to September. ⊠ *Forest Rd. 19 in Willamette National Forest* ☎ *541/822–3381* ✉ *Free* ⊘ *June–Sept., daily; most areas closed
rest of yr.*

Terwilliger Hot Springs (Cougar Hot Springs). An hour and 20 minutes east
of Eugene near Highway 126, take a short hike to a natural hot-springs
area. Hot-springs aficionados will find Terwilliger to be rustic, which

many regard as an advantage. The pools are in a forest of old-growth firs and cedars. No camping. ⊠ *5 mi east of Blue River McKenzie Bridge (Aufderheide Scenic Byway), McKenzie Bridge* ☎ *541/822–3799* ⊕ *www.hoodoo.com/Willamette_National_Forest/South_Fork_Area/ Terwilliger_Hot_Springs.htm* ⊠ *$5 day use only.*

Willamette National Forest. Stretching 110 miles along the western slopes of the Cascade Range, this forest boasts boundless recreation opportunities, including camping, hiking, boating, ATV riding, and winter sports. It extends from the Mt. Jefferson area east of Salem to the Calapooya Mountains northeast of Roseburg, encompassing 1,675,407 acres. ☎ *541/225-6300* ⊕ *www.fs.fed.us/r6/willamette/index.html.*

GOLF   Tokatee Golf Club. Ranked one of the best golf courses in Oregon by *Golf Digest,* this 18-hole beauty is near the McKenzie River with views of the Three Sisters Mountains, native ponds, and streams. Tokatee is a Chinook word meaning "a place of restful beauty." It offers a practice range, carts, lessons, rentals, a coffee shop and snack bar, and Wi-Fi. ⊠ *54947 McKenzie Highway, McKenzie Bridge* ☎ *541/822–3220 or 800/452–6376* ⊕ *www.tokatee.com* ⊠ *18 holes $42; 9 holes $24.*

WHITE-WATER   **High Country Expeditions.** Raft the white waters of the McKenzie River
RAFTING   on a guided full- or half-day tour. You'll bounce through rapids,
Fodor's Choice   admire old-growth forest, and watch osprey and blue herons fish-
★   ing. The outfit provides life jackets, splash gear, wet suits, booties (if
☾   requested), boating equipment, paddling instructions, river safety talk, a three-course riverside meal, and shuttle service back to your vehicle. ⊠ *Belknap Hot Springs Resort, 59296 Belknap Springs Rd., McKenzie Bridge* ☎ *541/822–8288 or 888/461–7238* ⌃ *reservations and deposit required* ⊕ *www.highcountryexpeditions.com* ⊠ *Full day $90.00, half day $60.00.*

The Columbia River Gorge and Mt. Hood

WORD OF MOUTH

"Next stop was Bridal Veil, which was really neat. The sound and power of these falls is amazing. This was a really good little hike, short, but with some good inclines that helped work off the cupcake from the previous night."

—aggiegirl

WELCOME TO THE COLUMBIA RIVER GORGE AND MT. HOOD

TOP REASONS TO GO

★ **Waterfall walkabout.** Hikers will discover dozens of gorgeous cascades along the Historic Columbia River Highway and its adjoining trail network, including 620-foot Multnomah Falls.

★ **Outdoor rec mecca.** From kiteboarding the gorge to mountain biking the slopes of Mt. Hood, this is a region tailor-made for adventure junkies. Get the gear and the beta from outfitters in Hood River and Government Camp.

★ **Historico-luxe.** Grand and gaudy landmarks like McMenamins Edgefield, Timberline Lodge, and the Columbia Gorge Hotel are guest favorites and entries on the National Register of Historic Places.

★ **Suds-tacular.** Western Oregon is the national seat of craft brewing, and the Gorge/Hood area has its share of inviting taprooms, from Stevenson's tiny Walking Man Brewing to Full Sail's upbeat national headquarters in Hood River.

1 Columbia River Gorge. The dams of the early twentieth century transformed the Columbia River from the raging torrent that vexed Lewis and Clark in 1805 to the breathtaking, but comparatively docile waterway that hosts kiteboarders and windsurfers today. Auto visitors have been scoping out the gorge's picturesque bluffs and waterfalls for quite a while now—the road between Troutdale and the Dalles, on which construction began in 1913, was the country's first planned scenic highway.

2 Mt Hood. Visible from 100 miles away, Mt. Hood (or "the Mountain," as Portlanders often call it) is the kind of rock that commands respect. It's holy ground for mountaineers, about 10,000 of whom make a summit bid each year. Sightseers are often shocked by the summer snows, but skiers rejoice, keeping the mountain's resorts busy year-round. Mingle with laid-back powderhounds and other outdoorsy types in the hospitality villas of Welches and Government Camp.

WASHINGTON

0   20 mi

0   20 km

Columbia River Gorge
National Scenic Area

Columbia River

Hood River

Mosier

Biggs Junction

84

Odell

The Dalles

Wasco

Dee

97

35

197

Moro

Mt. Hood

Deschutes River

Grass Valley

97

Badger Creek Wilderness

Government Camp

Kent

Maupin

218

26

197

218

216

Warm Springs Indian Reservation

Antelope

97

293

Warm Springs

Deschutes River

Lake Simtustus

Madras

Lake Billy Chinook

26

20

97

Ochoco National Forest

Prineville

26

Sisters

126

Redmond

20

97

GETTING ORIENTED

The mighty Columbia River flows west through the Cascade Range, past the Mount Hood Wilderness Area, to Astoria. It's is a natural border between Oregon and Washington to the north, and bridges link roads on both sides at Biggs Junction, the Dalles, Hood River, and Cascade Locks. The watery recreation corridor stretches from the Dalles in the east to the east Portland 'burbs. For most of that drive, snow-capped Mt. Hood looms to the southwest. Hood River drains the mountain's north side, emptying into the Columbia at its namesake town. Follow it upstream and you'll trade the warm, low-elevation climes of the gorge for the high country's tall pines and late-season snows. While it feels remote, the massive peak is just outside Portland. Look up from almost any neighborhood in town to see its white dome, just 60 miles east and accessible via U.S. 26 through Gresham.

5

THE COLUMBIA RIVER GORGE AND MT. HOOD PLANNER

When to Go

Winter weather in the Columbia Gorge and the Mt. Hood area is much more severe than in Portland and western Oregon. At times I–84 may be closed because of snow and ice. If you're planning a winter visit, be sure to carry plenty of warm clothes. High winds and single-digit temps are par for the course around 6,000 feet in January. Note that chains are a requirement for traveling over mountain passes.

Temperatures in the gorge are mild year-round, rarely dipping below 30 degrees in winter and hovering in the high 70s in mid-summer. As throughout Oregon, however, elevation is often a more significant factor than season, and an hour-long drive to Mt. Hood's Timberline Lodge can reduce those mid-summer temps by 20–30 degrees. Don't forget that the higher reaches of Mt. Hood retain snow as late as August.

In early fall, look for maple, tamarack, and aspen trees around the gorge, bursting with brilliant red and gold color. No matter the season, the basalt cliffs, the acres of lush forest, and that glorious expanse of water make the gorge worth visiting time and again.

About the Restaurants

A prominent locavore mentality pervades western Oregon generally, and low elevations around the gorge mean long growing seasons for dozens of local producers. Fresh foods grown, caught, and harvested in the Northwest dominate menus in gourmet restaurants around the gorge and Mt. Hood. Columbia River salmon is big, fruit orchards proliferate around Hood River, and the gorge nurtures a glut of excellent vineyards. Of course, beer culture is king across Oregon, and even the smallest towns around the region have their own lively brewpubs with casual American pub fare and tap after tap of craft ales. In keeping with the region's green and laid-back vibe, outdoor dining is big, Hood River's superb Stonehedge Gardens being the quintessential example.

About the Hotels

The hospitality industry is first-rate around the gorge and Mt. Hood, and the region's accommodations run the gamut from luxury hotels and sophisticated conference resorts to historic lodges, ski chalets, and cabin rentals. Cozy bed-and-breakfasts abound along the gorge, many of them historic structures overlooking the river. The slopes of Mt. Hood are spotted with smart ski resorts, and towns like Government Camp and Welches are long on rustic vacation rentals. The closer you are to Mt. Hood in any season, the earlier you'll want to reserve. With ski country working ever harder to attract summer patrons, Mt. Hood resorts like Timberline Lodge and Mt. Hood Skibowl offer some worthwhile seasonal specials.

WHAT IT COSTS IN U.S. DOLLARS					
	¢	$	$$	$$$	$$$$
Restaurants	under $10	$10–$16	$17–$23	$24–$30	over $30
Hotels	under $100	$100–$150	$151–$200	$201–$250	over $250

Restaurant prices are per person, for a main course at dinner. Hotel prices are for two people in a standard double room in high season, excluding tax.

Getting Here and Around

Air Travel. Portland International Airport (PDX) (☎ 877/739–4636 ⊕ www.portofportland.com) is the only nearby airport receiving commercial flights. Taxis out to Mt. Hood or the gorge are not particularly practical, but you can schedule a door-to-door shuttle with **Blue Star Transportation** (☎ 541/249–1837 ⊕ www.bluestarbus.com) or **Green Shuttle** (☎ 541/252–4422 ⊕ www.greentrans. com). Rates vary by destination, but a one-way trip to Hood River runs $80–$90. If you're heading to Hood, ski resorts like Mt. Hood Skibowl and Mt. Hood Meadows offer Portland shuttles in season.

Bus Travel. Greyhound (☎ 800/454–2487 ⊕ www. greyhound.com) provides service from Portland to Hood River and The Dalles. Portland's eco-friendly **Greasebus** (⊕ www.greasebus.com) runs seven days a week in winter between a Portland donut shop and Mt. Hood Meadows Ski Resort. On Thursdays, **Columbia Area Transit** (☎ 541/386–4202 ⊕ community.gorge.net/hrctd) runs a fixed-route bus between the Dalles and Portland via Hood River.

Car Travel. I–84 is the main east–west route into the Columbia River Gorge. U.S. 26, heading east from Portland and northwest from Prineville, is the main route into the Mt. Hood area. Portions of I–84 and U.S. 26 that pass through the mountains pose winter-travel difficulties, though the state plows these roadways regularly. The gorge is closed frequently during harsh winters due to ice and mud slides. Extreme winds can also make driving hazardous, and potentially result in highway closures.

The Historic Columbia River Highway (U.S. 30) from Troutdale to just east of Oneonta Gorge passes Crown Point State Park and Multnomah Falls. I–84/U.S. 30 continues on to the Dalles. Highway 35 heads south from the Dalles to the Mt. Hood area, intersecting with U.S. 26 at Government Camp. From Portland, the Columbia Gorge–Mt. Hood Scenic Loop is the easiest way to see the gorge and the mountain. Take I–84 east to Troutdale and follow U.S. 26 to Bennett Pass (near Timberline), where Highway 35 heads north to Hood River; then follow I–84 back to Portland. Or make the loop in reverse.

Major rental-car agencies are available in Gresham (3 miles west of Troutdale); Enterprise is also in Hood River and the Dalles.

Local Agencies **Apple City Rental Cars** (✉ 3250 Bonneville Rd., Hood River ☎ 541/386–5504).

Top Festivals

Columbia Gorge Bluegrass Festival. One of the premier bluegrass fests in the West takes place in Stevenson, Washington, every fourth weekend in July. **Mt. Hood Festival of the Forest.** Local bands and artists head to the woods the second full weekend in September for an earthy gathering on 580 acres of temperate rain forest in the shadow of Mt. Hood.

Tour Options

Americas Hub World Tours (☎ 800/673–3110 ⊕ www. americashubworldtours. com) offers waterfall and wine tours through the gorge. **Eco Tours of Oregon** (☎ 888/868–7733 ⊕ www. ecotours-of-oregon.com) combine trips to the waterfalls of the Historic Columbia River Highway with loops around Mt. Hood. **Explore the Gorge** (☎ 800/899–5676 ⊕ www.explorethegorge.com) designs customized van an0d bus tours of the gorge, Mt. Hood, and the Hood River Valley. **Martin's Gorge Tours** (☎ 888/290–8687 ⊕ www. martinsgorgetours.com) leads wine tours and waterfall hikes.

VISITOR INFORMATION

Columbia River Gorge Visitors Association (☎ 800/984–6743 ⊕ www.crgva.org). **Oregon Tourism Commission** (☎ 800/547–7842 ⊕ www. traveloregon.com).

Updated by
Brian Kevin

Volcanoes, lava flows, Ice Age floodwaters, and glaciers were Nature's tools of choice when carving a breathtaking 80-mi landscape now called the Columbia River Gorge. Proof of human civilization here reaches back 31,000 years, and excavations near the Dalles have uncovered evidence that salmon fishing is a 10,000-year-old tradition in these parts. In 1805 Lewis and Clark discovered the Columbia River to be the only waterway that led to the Pacific. Their first expedition was a treacherous route through wild, plunging rapids, but their successful navigation set a new exodus in motion.

Today the towns are laid-back recreation hamlets whose residents harbor a fierce pride in their shared natural resources. Sightseers, hikers, and skiers have long found contentment in this robust region, officially labeled a National Scenic Area in 1986. They're joined these days by epicures trolling the Columbia's banks in search of gourmet cuisine, artisan hop houses, and top-shelf vino. Highlights of the Columbia River Gorge include Multnomah Falls, Bonneville Dam, and the rich orchard land of Hood River. Sailboaters, windsurfers, and kiteboarders take advantage of the blustery gorge winds in the summer, their colorful sails decorating the waterway like windswept confetti.

To the south of Hood River are all the alpine attractions of the 11,245-foot-high Mt. Hood. With more than two million people living just up the road in Portland, you'd think this mountain playground would be overrun, but it's still easy to find solitude in the 67,000-acre wilderness surrounding the peak. Some of the world's best skiers take advantage of the powder on Hood, and they stick around in summertime for ski conditions that are as close to year-round as anyplace in the country.

COLUMBIA RIVER GORGE

When glacial floods carved out most of the Columbia River Gorge at the end of the last Ice Age, they left behind massive, looming cliffs where the river bisects the Cascade mountain range. The size of the canyon and the wildly varying elevations make this small stretch of Oregon as ecologically diverse as anyplace in the state. In a few days along the gorge you can mountain bike through dry canyons near the Dalles, hike through temperate rain forest in Oneonta Gorge, and take a woodland wildflower stroll just outside of Hood River. At night you'll be rewarded with historic lodging and good food in one of a half-dozen mellow river towns. The country's first National Scenic Area remains one of its most inviting ones.

TROUTDALE

16 mi east of Portland on I–84.

Troutdale is known for its great fishing spots, as well as antiques stores and the Columbia Gorge Premium Outlets. The city has a funky, walkable downtown, and it's the western terminus of the 22-mi-long **Historic Columbia River Highway,** U.S. 30 (also known as the Columbia River Scenic Highway and the Scenic Gorge Highway). In 1911, two years before work on the scenic road began, Troutdale became home to the Multnomah County Poor Farm, a massive Colonial Revival estate that housed Oregon's aged, indigent, and sick for most of the 20th century. After falling into disarray in the 1980s, the historic poor farm was reinvented in 1990 as the funky art resort McMenamins Edgefield, one of Troutdale's biggest draws today.

GETTING HERE

Troutdale is 16 mi east of downtown Portland on I–84, about a $40 cab ride from the airport. Reach Troutdale "the back way" by coming in from the east on U.S. 30, the Historic Columbia River Highway.

VISITOR INFORMATION

West Columbia Gorge Chamber of Commerce (✉ *226 W. Historic Columbia River Hwy., Troutdale* ☎ *503/669–7473* ⊕ *www.westcolumbiagorgechamber.com*).

WHERE TO EAT AND STAY

$$

NEW AMERICAN

✕ **Black Rabbit Restaurant & Bar.** Chef John Zenger's grilled rib-eye steak, old-fashioned roasted chicken, and Northwest cioppino are popular entrées at this McMenamins hotel restaurant. Vivid murals depicting the gorge's history enrich your view as you linger over dinner in a high-backed wooden booth. Enjoy an Edgefield wine or any one of five McMenamins brews (made on-site, approximately 50 yards away). Patio seating is available, with plenty of heaters to handle the unpredictable Oregon weather. Top off your meal with a homemade dessert and, wouldn't you know, a McMenamins home-roasted cup of coffee. ✉ *2126 S.W. Halsey St.* ☎ *503/492–3086* ⊕ *www.mcmenamins.com* ▭ *AE, D, MC, V.*

5

¢ ⬚ **McMenamins Edgefield.** As you explore the grounds of this Georgian
Fodor's Choice Revival manor, you'll feel like you've entered a twisted European vil-
★ lage, filled with activity and offbeat beauty. McMenamins Edgefield is
what the Four Seasons would be if it were operated by dreamers and
Deadheads—which essentially describes Northwest brewers and hospitality innovators par excellence Mike and Brian McMenamin. On
this former poor farm guests can wander through 74 acres of gardens,
murals, orchards, and vineyards with a drink in hand. Enjoy $3 movies
in the Power Station Theater, live music outdoors and in the winery, and
golf at one of two par-3 courses. There are three restaurants and nine
bars to choose from, with pool halls, distilleries, and tiny wine sheds
tucked away in unexpected places. Ruby's Spa offers an amplitude of
body treatments, and all guests have access to the outdoor soaking pool.
Edgefield is a western treasure, and even the most uptight vacationer
can't help but get swept up in Edgefield's mellow, bohemian vibe. Be
sure to make reservations ahead of time for the Black Rabbit restaurant and Ruby's Spa. **Pros:** plenty of choices for eating and drinking;
large variety of rooms and prices to choose from. **Cons:** crowds can
get large at this busy place. ⊠ *2126 S.W. Halsey St.* ☎ *503/669–8610
or 800/669–8610* ⊕ *www.mcmenamins.com* ⬎ *114 rooms, 20 with
private bath, 24 beds in men's/women's hostels* ⏧ *In-room: no phone,
no TV, Wi-Fi. In-hotel: 3 restaurants, bars, spa, parking (free)* ⊟ *AE,
D, DC, MC, V.*

SHOPPING

Columbia Gorge Premium Outlets. Forty-five outlet stores, including Eddie
Bauer and Guess, will keep you looking sharp for your trip through the
gorge. Oregon's lack of a sales tax is a big draw for out-of-towners.
⊠ *450 N.W. 257th Way* ☎ *503/669–8060* ⊕ *www.premiumoutlets.com/
columbiagorge* ☉ *Mon.–Sat. 10–8, Sun. 10–6.*

SPORTS AND THE OUTDOORS

RECREATIONAL **Rooster Rock State Park.** The most famous beach lining the Columbia
AREAS River is here, right below Crown Point. Three miles of sandy beaches,
panoramic cascades, and a large swimming area makes this a popular
spot. True naturists appreciate that one of Oregon's two designated
nude beaches is at the east end of Rooster Rock, and that it's not visible to conventional sunbathers. Rooster Rock is several miles east of
Troutdale, and it's accessible only via the interstate. ⊠ *I–84, 7 mi east
of Troutdale* ☎ *503/695–2261* ⊕ *www.oregonstateparks.org* ⬚ *Day
use $5 per vehicle* ☉ *Daily 7–dusk.*

FISHING Just east of town, the Sandy River is fed by Mt. Hood snowmelt, and
has a reputation as one of the state's best salmon and steelhead fisheries. **Jack's Snack N Tackle** can set you up with a license, bait, and tackle,
and they lead guided float trips throughout the year. ⊠ *1208 E. Historic
Columbia River Hwy.* ☎ *503/665–2257* ⊕ *www.jackssnackandtackle.
com* ⬚ *Half-day trips $100, full-day trips $175* ☉ *Feb.–mid-Oct., daily
8:30–5; mid-Oct.–Jan., Mon.–Sat. 7–5* ⊟ *MC, V.*

HISTORIC COLUMBIA RIVER HIGHWAY

U.S. 30, paralleling I–84 for 22 mi between Troutdale and interstate Exit 35

The oldest scenic highway in the U.S. is a construction marvel that integrates asphalt path with cliff, river, and forest landscapes. Paralleling the interstate to the south, U.S. 30 climbs to forested riverside bluffs, passes half a dozen waterfalls, and provides access to hiking trails leading to still more falls and scenic overlooks. Completed in 1922, the serpentine highway was the first paved road in the gorge built expressly for automotive sightseers. The route is peppered with state parks. Eight of them are day-use only, with camping only available at Ainsworth State Park. Near the Dalles, an additional 15 miles of U.S. 30 are designated as part of the scenic byway, but the 22-mile western segment is the real draw.

GETTING HERE

U.S. 30 heads out of downtown Troutdale going east, and the route can be accessed from I–84 along the way, via Exit 22 near Corbett, Exit 28 near Bridal Veil Falls, Exit 31 at Multnomah Falls, and Exit 35, where it rejoins the interstate.

VISITOR INFORMATION

West Columbia Gorge Chamber of Commerce (✉ *226 W. Historic Columbia River Hwy., Troutdale* ☎ *503/669–7473* ⊕ *www.westcolumbiagorgechamber. com*). **Multnomah Falls Visitor Center** (✉ *Exit 31 off I–84, 50000 Historic Columbia River Hwy., Bridal Veil* ☎ *503/695–2376* ⊕ *www.multnomahfallslodge. com* ☾ *Daily 9–5*).

EXPLORING

Fodor'sChoice ★ **Crown Point State Scenic Corridor.** A few miles east of Troutdale on U.S. 30 is a 730-foot-high bluff with an unparalleled 30-mi view down the Columbia River Gorge. **Vista House,** the two-tier octagonal structure on the side of the cliff, opened its doors to visitors in 1916; the rotunda has displays about the gorge and the highway. Vista House's architect Edgar Lazarus was the brother of Emma Lazarus, author of the poem displayed at the base of the Statue of Liberty. ✉ *10 mi east of Troutdale on U.S. 30* ☎ *503/695–2261 or 800/551–6949* ⊕ *www. oregonstateparks.org* ⌸ *Free* ☾ *Daily.*

Multnomah Falls. Multnomah Falls, a 620-foot-high double-decker torrent, the second-highest year-round waterfall in the nation, is by far the most spectacular of the cataracts east of Troutdale. The scenic highway leads down to a parking lot; from there a paved path winds to a bridge over the lower falls. A much steeper trail climbs to a viewing point overlooking the upper falls. It's quite a hike to the top, but worth it to avoid the crowds that swarm Multnomah in every season. ✉ *Exit 31 off I–84, or 15 mi east of Troutdale on U.S. 30, Bridal Veil* ☎ *503/695–2376* ⊕ *www.multnomahfallslodge.com.*

Oneonta Gorge. Following the old highway east from Multnomah Falls, you come to a narrow, mossy cleft with walls hundreds of feet high. Oneonta Gorge is most enjoyable in summer, when you can walk up the streambed through the cool green canyon, where hundreds of plant species—some found nowhere else—flourish under the perennially moist

conditions. At other times of the year, take the trail along the west side of the canyon. The clearly marked trailhead is 100 yards west of the gorge, on the south side of the road. The trail takes you to Oneonta Falls, about ½ mi up the stream, where it links with an extensive regional trail system exploring the region's bluffs and waterfalls. Bring boots or submersible sneakers—plus a strong pair of ankles—because the rocks are slippery. ⊠ *Exit 31 off I–84, 2 mi east of Multnomah Falls on U.S. 30* ☎ *503/308–1700* ⊕ *www.fs.fed.us/r6/columbia.*

WHERE TO EAT

$$ ✕**Multnomah Falls Lodge.** Vaulted ceilings, stone fireplaces, and exquisite
AMERICAN views of Multnomah Falls are complemented by wonderful service and an extensive menu at this restaurant, which is listed on the National Register of Historic Places. Consider the halibut fish-and-chips, the lemon- and herb-roasted wild salmon, or ancho chile and espresso-cured flatiron steak. Breakfast favorites include blueberry, buttermilk, or huckleberry pancakes. A particular pleaser for out-of-town guests, the champagne Sunday brunch is held 8–2. Try the brown sugar–glazed Salmon Multnomah. For a treat during warmer months, sit on the patio and get close to the falls without feeling a drop. ⊠ *Exit 31 off I–84, 50000 Historic Columbia River Hwy., Bridal Veil* ☎ *503/695–2376* ⊕ *www. multnomahfallslodge.com* ⊟ *AE, D, MC, V* ☉ *Daily 8* AM*–9* PM.

CASCADE LOCKS

7 mi east of Oneonta Gorge on Historic Columbia River Hwy. and I–84, 30 mi east of Troutdale on I–84.

In pioneer days, boats needing to pass the bedeviling rapids near the town of Whiskey Flats had to portage around them. The locks that gave the town its new name were completed in 1896, allowing waterborne passage for the first time. In 1938 they were submerged beneath the new Lake Bonneville when the Bonneville Lock and Dam became one of the most massive Corps of Engineers projects to come out of the New Deal. The town of Cascade Locks hung on to its name, though. A historic stern-wheeler still leads excursions from the town's port district, and the region's Native American tribes still practice traditional dip-net fishing near the current locks.

GETTING HERE

Reach Cascade Locks heading 45 mi east of Portland on I–84. If you're planning to come and go from Stevenson, Washington, carry cash for the $1 toll on the gorge-spanning Bridge of the Gods. The closest airport is Portland International, 40 mi west.

VISITOR INFORMATION

West Columbia Gorge Chamber of Commerce (⊠ *226 W. Historic Columbia River Hwy., Troutdale* ☎ *503/669–7473* ⊕ *www.westcolumbiagorgechamber.com*).

EXPLORING

☾ **Bonneville Dam.** This is the first federal dam to span the Columbia, and was dedicated by President Franklin D. Roosevelt in 1937. Its generators (visible from a balcony during self-guided powerhouse tours) have a capacity of more than a million kilowatts, enough to supply power

Dog Mountain Trail, Columbia River Gorge National Scenic Area

to more than 200,000 single-family homes. There is a modern visitor center on Bradford Island, complete with underwater windows where gaggles of kids watch migrating salmon and steelhead as they struggle up fish ladders. The best viewing times are between April and October. In recent years the dwindling runs of wild Columbia salmon have made the dam a subject of much environmental controversy. ⊠ *Bonneville Lock and Dam, U.S. Army Corps of Engineers, from I–84 take Exit 40, head northeast, and follow signs 1 mi to visitor center* ⊕ *www. nwp.usace.army.mil/op/b/home.asp* ☎ *541/374–8820* 🎫 *Free* ⊘ *Visitor center daily 9–5.*

Cascade Locks. This is the home port of the 600-passenger stern-wheeler *Columbia Gorge,* which churns upriver, then back again, on two-hour excursions through some of the Columbia River Gorge's most impressive scenery, mid-June to early October. The ship's captain will talk about the gorge's fascinating 40-million-year geology and about pioneering spirits and legends, as well as Lewis and Clark, who once triumphed over this very same river. Group bookings and private rentals are available. ⊠ *Cruises leave from Marine Park in Cascade Locks. Marine Park, 355 Wanapa St.* ☎ *541/224–3900 or 800/224–3901* ⊕ *www.portlandspirit.com* ⚓ *Reservations essential* 🎫 *Prices vary* ⊘ *May–Oct.* ⊟ *AE, D, DC, MC, V.*

WHERE TO EAT

$ ✕ **Pacific Crest Pub.** A woodsy tavern with cedar-shake walls, historical
AMERICAN photos, and a stone fireplace provides hearty servings of starters, salads, and main courses, including on-site-smoked salmon chowder and oven-roasted chicken accompanied by house-specialty, sinus-destroying

horseradish. If you like feta cheese with your pizzas, try the house favorite, the Greek "Pizza of the Gods." During warmer months, sit outside in the adjacent courtyard and take in mountain and river views while sipping one of a dozen or so featured microbrews, including Full Sail and Walking Man. ⊠ *500 Wanapa St.* ☎ *541/374–9310* ▭ *D, MC, V* ☉ *Closed Mon.*

SPORTS AND THE OUTDOORS

HIKING **Pacific Crest Trail.** Cascade Locks bustles with grubby thru-hikers refueling along the 2,650-mi Canada-to-Mexico Pacific Crest Trail. Check out a scenic and strenuous portion of it, heading south from the trailhead at Herman Creek Horse Camp, just east of town. The route heads up into the Cascades, showing off monster views of the gorge. Backpackers out for a longer trip will find idyllic campsites at Wahtum Lake, 14 mi south. ⊠ *1 mi east of Cascade Locks off N.W. Forest Ln.* ☎ *541/308–1700* ⊕ *www.pcta.org.*

STEVENSON, WASHINGTON

Across the river from Cascade Locks via the Bridge of the Gods and 1 mi east on Hwy. 14.

So it's not quite Oregon, but with the Bridge of the Gods toll bridge spanning the Columbia River above the Bonneville Dam, Stevenson acts as a sort of "twin city" to Cascade Locks. Tribal legends and the geologic record tell of the original Bridge of the Gods, a substantial landslide that occurred here sometime between AD 1000 and 1760, briefly linking the two sides of the gorge before the river swept away the debris. The landslide's steel namesake now leads to tiny Stevenson, where vacationers traverse the quiet Main Street, planning excursions to nearby Mt. Adams or Mt. St. Helens. Washington's Highway 14 runs through the middle of town, and since the cliffs on the Oregon side are more dramatic, driving this two-lane highway actually offers better views.

GETTING HERE

To get to Stevenson from the Oregon side of the gorge, cross the Columbia River at the Bridge of the Gods. Bring cash for the $1 toll. Stevenson proper is a mi east on Highway 14. The closest airport is Portland International, 43 mi west on the Oregon side of the river.

VISITOR INFORMATION

Skamania County Chamber of Commerce (⊠ *167 N.W. Second Ave., Stevenson, WA* ☎ *509/427–8911* ⊕ *www.skamania.org*).

EXPLORING

Bridge of the Gods. For a magnificent vista 135 feet above the Columbia, as well as a speedy route between Oregon and Washington, $1 will pay your way over the grandly named bridge. Here also, hikers cross from Oregon to reach the Washington segment of the **Pacific Crest Trail**, which picks up just west of the bridge. ⊕ *www.portofcascadelocks. org/bridge.htm.*

☾ **Columbia Gorge Interpretive Center.** A petroglyph whose eyes seem to look straight at you, "She Who Watches" or "Tsagaglalal" is the logo for this museum. Sitting among the dramatic basaltic cliffs on the north bank of the Columbia River Gorge, the museum explores the life of the gorge: its history, culture, architecture, legends, and much more. The younger crowd may enjoy the reenactment of the gorge's formation in the Creation Theatre. Or a 37-foot high fishwheel from the 19th century. Historians will appreciate studying the water route of the Lewis & Clark Expedition. There's also an eye-opening exhibit that examines current environmental impacts on the area. ⊠ *990 S.W. Rock Creek Dr., Stevenson, WA* ✛ *1 mi east of Bridge of the Gods on Hwy. 14* ☎ *509/427–8211 or 800/991–2338* ⊕ *www.columbiagorge. org* ⌦ *$7* ⊙ *Daily 10–5.*

NEED A BREAK? **Bahma Coffee Bar.** Funky and fun, '60s Haight-Ashbury meets Native American art, at *the* place in Stevenson for Wi-Fi (with purchase) and, of course, coffee. Or choose from grilled panini sandwiches, soups, fresh carrot juice, wine, sake, tea, and tasty homemade pastries. ⊠ *256 S.W. 2nd St., Hwy. 14* ☎ *509/427-8700* ⊕ *www.bahmacoffee.com* ⊙ *Daily 7:30-4* ⊟ *MC, V.*

WHERE TO EAT AND STAY

$$$
NEW AMERICAN
⨯ **The Cascade Room at Skamania Lodge**. Gaze at the perfect fusion of sky, river, and cliffscapes through the Cascade Room's expansive windows during an exquisite dining experience. Alder-plank potlatch salmon and oat-crusted trout stuffed with Northwest potatoes and herbs are signature dishes; also try the garlic sizzling shrimp and sautéed forest mushrooms. Melt-in-your-mouth chocolate soufflé and fresh mixed-berry cobbler are grand finales. Breakfast specialties include hazelnut pancakes and fresh berry crepes. A champagne brunch is offered on Sunday, and the seafood, salads, sushi, and pastas draw patrons from miles around. ⊠ *Skamania Lodge, 1131 S.W. Skamania Lodge Way* ☎ *509/427–7700* ⊟ *AE, D, DC, MC, V.*

$$$
AMERICAN
⨯ **Pacific Crest Dining Room**. After a rejuvenating spa treatment or hike, the fresh healthy cuisine is a special treat. You can dine in the low light of the muted main room (metal pine-tree light fixtures are custom made) or in the adjoining lounge, its 12-foot high glass wall overlooking the manicured courtyard and the forest beyond. The pastry chef works through the night, ensuring fresh-baked breads and pastries by sunrise. Healthy never tasted so good, with crisp salads, Pacific Northwest fish (amazing ahi tuna!), Cascades-area beef, and gourmet vegetarian fare. Late afternoons, the lounge serves goodies such as hazelnut-crusted Brie and Walking Man beer-battered halibut and chips. ⊠ *Bonneville Hot Springs Resort, 1252 E. Cascade Dr., North Bonneville, WA* ☎ *509/427–9711* ⊕ *www.bonnevilleresort.com* ⊟ *AE, D, MC, V.*

$$$
⛭ **Bonneville Hot Springs Resort and Spa**. Enter an architectural wonderland of wood, iron, rock, and water, water everywhere. Owner Pete Cam and his sons built the resort to share their love of these historic mineral springs with the public, especially those seeking physical renewal. The three-story lobby, with its suspended black iron trestle, Paul Bunyan-size river-rock fireplace, and floor-to-ceiling arched windows, is magnificent to behold. The unique redwood-paneled, 25-meter indoor lap pool is adjacent to an immaculate European spa, offering over 40 candlelit treatments (mineral baths, body wraps, massages).

Rooms are spacious, with upscale furnishings. **Pros:** glorious grounds, impressive architectural detail, attentive and knowledgeable spa staff; the Pacific Crest Trail passes directly through the property. **Cons:** must reserve spa appointments separately from room reservations; the dull, boxy exterior belies what's inside. ⊠ *1252 E. Cascade Dr., North Bonneville, WA* ☎ *509/427–7767 or 866/459–1678* ⊕ *www.bonnevilleresort.com* ⤳ *78 rooms* ⌂ *In-room: a/c, Wi-Fi. In-hotel: restaurant, bar, pool, spa, parking (free)* ▭ *AE, D, MC, V.*

$$ ⌂ **Skamania Lodge.** "Skamania," Chinook for "swift water," overlooks exactly that with its 175 acres sitting to the north of the Columbia River Gorge. So big you need a map to get around, the Lodge impresses with Montana slate tiling, Native American artwork, an immense word-burning fireplace, and a multitude of windows that take in the surrounding forests and the gorge. Think of a modern conference hotel spliced with a national park lodge. Outstanding recreational facilities include an 18-hole, par-70 golf course, 3 winding hiking trails, a large indoor pool, and even a sand volleyball court. The accommodating staff will pack you a box lunch if you're going out to explore for the day. **Pros:** addresses the active guest as well as the kids; U.S. Forest Service has a kiosk in the lobby; well suited to handle large events, conferences, weddings. **Cons:** costs can quickly multiply for a large family, can get crowded, sometimes there's a wait for table seating in the dining room. ⊠ *1131 S.W. Skamania Lodge Way* ☎ *509/427–7700 or 800/221–7117* ⊕ *www.skamania.com* ⤳ *254 rooms* ⌂ *In-room: a/c, Wi-Fi. In-hotel: restaurants, bars, golf course, tennis courts, pool, gym, spa, bicycles, Wi-Fi hotspot, parking (free), some pets allowed* ▭ *AE, D, DC, MC, V.*

NIGHTLIFE AND THE ARTS

Walking Man Brewing. Locals and tourists alike crowd this cozy brewery's sunshiny patio for creative pizzas and a dozen craft ales. After a couple of pints of the strong Homo Erectus IPA and Knuckle Dragger Pale ale, you may go a little ape. The house country-rock band plays every Sunday night. ⊠ *240 S.W. 1st St.* ☎ *509/427–5520* ⊕ *www.walkingmanbrewing.com* ☉ *Closed Mon.–Tues.* ▭ *MC, V.*

SPORTS AND THE OUTDOORS

RECRE-
ATIONAL AREA

Beacon Rock State Park. For several hundred years this 848-foot rock was a landmark for river travelers, including Native Americans, who recognized this point as the last rapids of the Columbia River. Lewis and Clark are thought to have been the first white men to see the volcanic remnant. Picnic atop old lava flows after hiking a 1-mi trail, steep but safe, which leads to tremendous views of the Columbia Gorge and the river. A round-trip hike takes 45–60 minutes. ⊠ *Off Hwy. 14, 7 mi west of Bridge of the Gods, North Bonneville, WA* ☎ *509/427–8265 or 360/902–8844* ⊕ *www.parks.wa.gov* ⊡ *Day use free.*

HOOD RIVER

17 mi east of Cascade Locks on I–84.

For years, the incessant easterly winds blowing through the town of Hood River were nothing more than a nuisance. Then somebody bolted a sail to a surfboard, waded into the fat part of the gorge, and a new recreational craze was born. A fortuitous combination of factors—mainly the reliable gale-force winds blowing against the current—has made Hood River the self-proclaimed windsurfing capital of the world. Especially in summer, this once-somnolent town swarms with colorful "boardheads" from as far away as Europe and Australia.

Hood River's rich pioneer past is reflected in its downtown historic district. The City of Hood River publishes a free self-guided walking tour (available through the city government office or the Hood River Chamber of Commerce) that will take you on a tour of more than 40 civic and commercial buildings dating from 1893 to the 1930s, some of which are listed in the National Register of Historic Places.

GETTING HERE

Reach Hood River by driving 60 mi east of Portland on I-84, or if you're coming from Mt. Hood, by heading north on Highway 35. The closest airport is in Portland.

VISITOR INFORMATION

Hood River County Chamber of Commerce (⊠ 405 Portway Ave. ☎ 541/386–2000 or 800/366–3530 ⊕ www.hoodriver.org).

EXPLORING

Western Antique Aeroplane and Automobile Museum. Housed at Hood River's tiny airport (general aviation only), the museum's meticulously restored, propeller-driven planes are all still in flying condition. The antique steam cars, Model Ts, and sleek Depression-era sedans are road-worthy, too. Periodic car shows and an annual fly-in draw thousands of history nerds and spectators. ⊠ 1600 Museum Rd., off Hwy. 281, 2½ mi south of town ☎ 541/308–1600 ⊕ www.waamuseum.org ⌨ $12 ⊙ Daily 9–5.

Fruit Loop. Either by car or bicycle, tour the quiet country highways of Hood River valley, whose vast orchards surround the river. You'll see apples, pears, cherries, and peaches fertilized by volcanic soil, pure glacier water, and a conducive harvesting climate. Along the 35 mi of farms are a host of outlets for delicious baked goods, wines, flowers, and nuts. Festive farm activities from April to November also give a taste of the agricultural life. While on the loop, consider stopping at the town of **Parkdale** to lunch, shop, and snap a photo of Mt. Hood's north face. ⊠ Rte. begins on Hwy. 35 ⊕ www.hoodriverfruitloop.com.

OFF THE BEATEN PATH

Lost Lake. One of the most-photographed sights in the Pacific Northwest, this lake's waters reflect towering Mt. Hood and the thick forests that line its shore. Cabins are available for overnight stays, and because no motorboats are allowed on Lost Lake, the area is blissfully quiet. ⊠ Lost Lake Rd., take Hood River Hwy. south to town of Dee ☎ 541/352–6002 ⌨ Day use $7.

Mt. Hood Railroad. An efficient and relaxing way to survey Mt. Hood and the Hood River, this passenger and freight line was established in 1906. Chug alongside the Hood River through vast fruit orchards before climbing up steep forested canyons, glimpsing Mt. Hood along the way. There are four trip options: a four-hour excursion (serves light concessions with two daily departures, morning and afternoon), dinner,

Vineyards in the Hood River Valley

brunch, and a themed murder-mystery dinner. Exceptional service is as impressive as the scenery. ⌧ *110 Railroad Ave.* ☎ *541/386–3556 or 800/872–4661* ⊕ *www.mthoodrr.com* ▤ *AE, D, V* ▱ *$25–$70* ◷ *Apr.–Dec.*

NEED A BREAK? A glass-walled microbrewery with a windswept deck overlooking the Columbia, the **Full Sail Tasting Room and Pub** (⌧ *506 Columbia St.* ☎ *541/386-2247*) is one of the great microbrew success stories in the West, having won major awards at the Great American Beer Festival and the World Beer Cup. Savory snack foods complement fresh ales. Free on-site brewery tours last about twenty-five minutes.

WINERY

Cathedral Ridge Winery. This six-acre vineyard was awarded Oregon Winery of the Year in 2007 by Wine Press Northwest, and in 2010 the same authority called it one of the region's best wine-country picnic spots. Popular varietals include Riesling, pinot gris, and syrah. The tasting room is open 11–5 daily. ⌧ *4200 Post Canyon Dr.* ☎ *800/516–8710* ⊕ *www.cathedralridgewinery.com* ▱ *Free* ◷ *Daily 11–5.*

WHERE TO EAT AND STAY

$ ✕ **Cornerstone Cuisine.** A tapas menu and a selection of small vegetable
NEW AMERICAN dishes make the Hood River Hotel restaurant a popular lunch stop. Try the sea-salted grilled asparagus or the wild mushrooms with garlic and thyme. Chef Mark Whitehead impresses with simple dishes and fresh ingredients, and the covered sidewalk patio lets you keep an eye

on comings and goings downtown. ⊠ *102 Oak St.* ☎ *541/386–1900* ⊕ *www.hoodriverhotel.com* ▭ *AE, D, MC, V.*

$$$
NEW AMERICAN
Fodor's Choice
★

✕ **Stonehedge Gardens.** It's not just the cuisine that's out of this world, Stonehedge is of another time and place, surrounding you with 7 acres of lush English gardens that gracefully frame its multitude of stone terraces and trickling fountains. There's a petanque court for quick pre-dinner activity, and music on Wednesday nights draws a full house of locals and visitors. Each of the four dining rooms in the restored 1898 home has a distinct personality, from cozy to verdant to elegant, but the tiered patio is where summer diners gather. Classics like steak Diane and filet mignon appeal to more traditional diners, while buffalo-style prawns and curry-shiitake mushroom soup show off the kitchen's creative side. Just when you think your meal is complete, along comes the Flaming Bread Pudding. This restaurant is a Columbia Gorge institution. ⊠ *3405 Cascade Ave.* ☎ *541/386–3940* ⊕ *www. stonehedgegardens.com* ▭ *AE, D, MC, V* ☽ *No lunch.*

$$$
▦ **Columbia Gorge Hotel.** One selling point of this grande dame of gorge hotels is the view of a 208-foot-high waterfall. Rooms with plenty of wood, brass, and antiques overlook the impeccably landscaped formal gardens. While watching the sun set on the Columbia River, dine in the hotel's restaurant; selections include quinoa-stuffed sweet onion or a worthy cioppino. **Pros:** historic structure built by Columbia Gorge Highway visionary Simon Benson; unbeatable gorge views. **Cons:** smallish rooms reflect their historic character. ⊠ *4000 Westcliff Dr.* ☎ *541/386–5566 or 800/345–1921* ⊕ *www.columbiagorgehotel.com* ⤸ *39 rooms* ♿ *In room: a/c, Wi-Fi. In-hotel: restaurant, bar* ▭ *AE, D, DC, MC, V.*

$
▦ **Hood River Hotel.** Another Hood River hospitality gem found on the National Register of Historic Places. The restored building has a grand, Old West façade with antiques-heavy interiors that feel more like a European inn. **Pros:** excellent downtown location, several available adventure packages, historic vibe. **Cons:** smallish rooms, no king-size beds. ⊠ *102 Oak St.* ☎ *541/386–1900* ⊕ *www.hoodriverhotel.com* ⤸ *41 rooms* ♿ *In-room: a/c, Wi-Fi, kitchen (some). In-hotel: restaurant, bar, some pets allowed.* ▭ *AE, D, DC, MC, V.*

$$
▦ **Lakecliff Bed & Breakfast.** Perched on a cliff overlooking the Columbia Gorge, this beautiful 1908 summer home has long been a favorite spot for weddings. Designed by architect A.E. Doyle (who also created the Multnomah Falls Lodge), this 3-acre magical land of ferns, fir trees, and water is a stunner. There's a deck at the back of the house, fireplaces and river views in three of the rooms, great artwork throughout, and top-notch service, including hot coffee right outside your door in the morning. "Large, spoiling breakfasts," says owner Allyson Pate, referring to her poached pears, blueberry pancakes, and butterscotch pecan rolls. For summer, make reservations as far ahead as possible. **Pros:** glorious views, friendly and accommodating hosts, convenient-to-town location with a remote feel. **Cons:** no king-size beds, Wi-Fi in living room only, and a bit spotty. ⊠ *3820 Westcliff Dr.* ☎ *541/386–7000* ⊕ *www.lakecliffbnb.com* ⤸ *4 rooms* ♿ *In-room: no phone, no TV, no a/c. In-hotel: Wi-Fi.* ▭ *MC, V.*

SPORTS AND THE OUTDOORS

KAYAKING **Columbia Gorge Kayak School.** Whether you want to practice your Eskimo roll in the safety of a pool, run the Klickitat River in an inflatable kayak, or take a mellow midnight paddle, the gorge's premier kayak guides can arrange the trip. Book online, by phone, or at the Kayak Shed downtown. ⊠ *6 Oak St.* ☎ *541/806–4190* ⊕ *www.gorgekayaker.com* ✉ *Lessons $40, flat-water and white-water trips $60–$220.*

WINDSURFING **Big Winds.** The retail hub for Hood River's windsurfing and kiteboarding culture also rents gear and provides windsurfing lessons for beginners. ⊠ *207 Front St.* ☎ *541/386–6086* ⊕ *www.bigwinds.com* ✉ *Lessons and clinics $65–$250* ▤ *AE, D, MC, V.*

THE DALLES

20 mi east of Hood River on I–84.

The Dalles lies on a crescent bend of the Columbia River where it narrows and once spilled over a series of rapids, creating a flagstone effect. French voyagers christened it *dalle,* or "flagstone." The Dalles is the seat of Wasco County and the trading hub of north–central Oregon. It gained fame early in the region's history as the town where the Oregon Trail branched, with some pioneers departing to travel over Mt. Hood on Barlow Road and the others continuing down the Columbia River. This may account for the small-town, Old West feeling that still permeates the area. Several historic Oregon moments as they relate to The Dalles' past are magnificently illustrated on eight murals painted by renowned Northwest artists, located downtown within short walking distance of one another.

GETTING HERE

The Dalles is best reached by car, 84 mi east of Portland or 126 mi west of Pendleton on I–84. The closest airport is Portland International.

VISITOR INFORMATION

The Dalles Area Chamber of Commerce (⊠ *404 W. 2nd St.* ☎ *541/296–2231* ⊕ *www.thedalleschamber.org*).

EXPLORING

☾ **Columbia Gorge Discovery Center–Wasco County Historical Museum.** Exhibits highlight the geological history of the Columbia Gorge, back 40 million years when volcanoes, landslides, and floods carved out the area. The museum focuses on 10,000 years of Native American life and exploration of the region by white settlers. ⊠ *5000 Discovery Dr.* ☎ *541/296–8600* ⊕ *www.gorgediscovery.org* ✉ *$8* ☉ *Daily 9–5.*

Dalles Lock and Dam. At this hydroelectric dam east of Bonneville Dam you can tour a visitor center with a surprisingly even-handed exhibit on differing views of Colombia River dams, with input from farmers, utility companies, environmentalists, and indigenous tribes. There's also a surreal live feed of salmon and sturgeon scaling the fish ladder. Call ahead for tours offered most weekends, photo ID required. ⊠ *Exit 87 (in summer) or Exit 88 other times off I–84, 2 mi east of The Dalles at Lake Celilo* ☎ *541/296–1181* ⊕ *www.nwp.usace.army.mil/op/d/ thedalles.asp* ✉ *Free* ☉ *Varied hrs throughout the year.*

Fort Dalles Museum. The 1856-vintage Fort Dalles Surgeon's Quarters is the site of the oldest history museum in Oregon. The museum's first visitors came through the doors in 1905. On display in authentic hand-hewn log buildings, originally part of a military base, are the personal effects of some of the region's settlers and a collection of early automobiles. The entrance fee gains you admission to the **Anderson Homestead** museum across the street, which also has pioneer artifacts. ⊠ *500 W. 15th St., at Garrison* ☎ *541/296–4547* ⊕ *www.fortdallesmuseum.org* ⊠ *$5* ☉ *Daily 10–4. Closed Nov.–Mar.*

WHERE TO EAT

$ ✕ **Baldwin Saloon.** The walls of this historic watering hole–turned-hip
AMERICAN restaurant are a weirdly authentic mix of landscape art and early American oil-painting erotica. The immense menu likewise runs the gamut from pastas to seafood to burgers. Stop in at lunch for a bowl of the popular bouillabaisse, and make weekend reservations for a dinner set to music from the saloon's 1894 mahogany Schubert piano. ⊠ *205 Court St.* ☎ *541/296–5666* ⊕ *www.baldwinsaloon.com* ☉ *Closed Sun.* ⊟ *AE, D, MC, V.*

$ ✕ **Petite Provence.** This popular downtown bistro/bakery/dessertery
CAFÉ serves eggs, crepes, and croissants for breakfast, hot and cold sandwiches and salads for lunch, and fresh-baked pastries and breads (you can take a loaf home). The sparkling display case tempts with a goodly selection of napoleons, éclairs, tarts, and mousses. ⊠ *408 E. 2nd St.* ☎ *541/506–0037* ⊕ *www.provence-portland.com* ⊟ *AE, MC, V.*

$ 🏨 **Celilo Inn.** The Celilo Inn benefits from a knockout concept: it's a
Fodor'sChoice prototypical motorlodge motel gone high-design, with exterior-entry
★ rooms and a '50s light-up sign that disguise the hotel's slick, boutique feel. The view doesn't hurt either, as Celilo sits on a high hill overlooking the Columbia, the Dalles Dam, and if you're in the right room, Mt. Hood. Flat-screen TVs, pillow-top mattresses, and smart decorating come standard, and the outdoor pool is mighty inviting during The Dalles' dry summers. **Pros:** sexy design, specializes in wine tours, bottles available on-site, complimentary espresso machine in lobby. **Cons:** not all rooms have views, those on the hotel's far end feel miles away from the front desk. ⊠ *3550 E. 2nd St.* ☎ *541/769–0001* ⊕ *www.celiloinn. com* ⤧ *46 rooms* ⚲ *In-room: Wi-Fi. In hotel: gym, pool.* ⊟ *AE, D, MC, V. Credit cards only.*

NIGHTLIFE AND THE ARTS

Rivertap Pub. Regional beers and wines are showcased at this hipster hangout with a feel like a friend's cool garage lair. Cocktails are also available, including the rare tap margarita, and the small menu appeals to a drinking crowd with nachos, hot wings, and fish tacos. Live music on Wednesday nights draws a crowd of slick young professionals. ⊠ *703 E. 2nd St.* ☎ *541/760–0059* ⊕ *www.rivertabpub.com* ☉ *Sun.–Thurs. 4–10, Sat.–Sun. noon–midnight* ⊟ *AE, D, MC, V.*

SPORTS AND THE OUTDOORS

RECREATIONAL AREAS

Celilo Park. Named for the falls that challenged spawning salmon here in the pre-dam days, this favorite spot for windsurfers also has swimming, sailboarding, and fishing. It's 7 mi east of The Dalles. ⊠ *Exit 99 off I–84* ☎ *541/296–1181* ⊡ *Free* ⊗ *Daily.*

Mayer State Park. Views from atop the park's Rowena Crest bluff are knockout, especially during the March and April wildflower season. Recreational activities include swimming, boating, fishing, and picnicking. ⊠ *Exit 77 off I–84* ☎ *800/551–6949* ⊕ *www.prd.state.or.us* ⊡ *Day use $5 per vehicle* ⊗ *Daily.*

MT. HOOD

The Multnomah tribe call Mt. Hood "Wy'East," named, according to popular legend, for a jealous lover who once sparred over a woman with his rival, Klickitat. When their fighting caught the Great Spirit's attention, Wy'East and Klickitat were transformed into two angry, smoke-bellowing mountains—one became Washington's Mt. Adams, the other became Mt. Hood. Wy'East has mellowed out a bit since then, but the mountain is still technically an active volcano, and it's had very minor, lava-free eruptive events as recently as the mid-1800s. Today Mt. Hood is better known for the challenge it poses to climbers, its deep winter snows, and a dozen glaciers and snowfields that make skiing possible almost year-round. Resort towns and colorful hospitality villages are arranged in a semi-circle around the mountain, full of ski bars and rental cabins that host hordes of fun-loving Portlanders each weekend. In every direction from the postcard-perfect peak the million-acre Mt. Hood National Forest spreads out like a big green blanket, and 300,000 acres of that are designated wilderness. Mule deer, black bears, elk, and the occasional cougar share the space with humans who come to hike, camp, and fish in the Pacific Northwest's quintessential wild ecosystem.

AROUND THE MOUNTAIN

About 60 mi east of Portland on I–84 and U.S. 26, 65 mi from the Dalles, west on I–84 and south on Hwy. 35 and U.S. 26.

Majestically towering 11,245 feet above sea level, Mt. Hood is what remains of the original north wall and rim of a volatile crater. Although the peak no longer spews ash or fire, active steam vents can be spotted high on the mountain. The mountain took its modern moniker in 1792, when a crew of the British Royal Navy, the first recorded Caucasians sailing up the Columbia River, spotted it and named it after a famed British naval officer by the name of—you guessed it—Hood.

Mt. Hood offers the only year-round skiing in the lower 48 states, with three major ski areas and some 30 lifts, as well as extensive areas for cross-country skiing and snowboarding. Many of the ski runs turn into mountain-bike trails in summer. The mountain is also popular with climbers and hikers. In fact, some hikes follow parts of the Oregon Trail, and signs of the pioneers' passing are still evident.

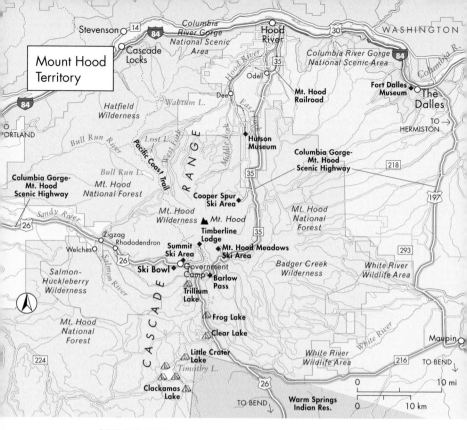

GETTING HERE

From Portland, U.S. 26 heads east into the heart of Mt. Hood National Forest, while Highway 35 runs south from Hood River along the mountain's east face. The roads meet 60 mi east of Portland, near Government Camp, forming an oblong loop with I–84 and the Historic Columbia Gorge Highway. The closest airport is Portland International, 53 mi northwest of Government Camp. Ski resorts like Mt. Hood Skibowl and Mt. Hood Meadows offer Portland shuttles in season—call for timetables and pick-up and drop-off sites.

VISITOR INFORMATION

Mt. Hood Area Chamber of Commerce (⊠ 24403 E. Welches Rd., Welches ☎ 503/622–3017 ⊕ www.mthood.org). **Mt. Hood National Forest Headquarters** (⊠ 16400 Champion Way, Sandy ☎ 503/668–1700 ⊕ www.fs.fed.us/r6/mthood).

WHERE TO EAT AND STAY

$$$$ ✕ **Cascade Dining Room.** If the wall of windows isn't coated with snow,
NEW AMERICAN you may get a good look at some of the neighboring peaks. Vaulted wooden beams and a wood-plank floor, handcrafted furniture, hand-woven drapes, and a lion-size stone fireplace set the scene. The atmosphere is historic, but new in 2010 is executive chef Jason Stoller Smith, a former wine-country Wunderkind whose resume includes

A snowboarder catches some air on Mt. Hood.

orchestrating a salmon bake at the White House. The dinner menu's local/organic emphasis embraces, for example, Oregon lamb with fig compote and rabbit pasta with root veggies, featuring hares raised at nearby Nicky Farms. The daily Farmers Market Brunch is itself worth the drive up to Timberline, highlighting different seasonal ingredients and purveyors each week, from Dungeness crab to local hazelnuts to Oregon cherries. Pick up a few culinary tips from the chef demonstrations. ✉ *Timberline Rd., Timberline* ☎ *503/272–3104* ⊕ *www. timberlinelodge.com* ⚅ *Reservations essential* ▭ *D, MC, V.*

$$$
🕐
Fodor's Choice
★

🏨 **Timberline Lodge**. The approach to Timberline Lodge builds excitement, an unforgettable 6-mi ascent that circles Mt. Hood. Now you see it, now you don't: The mountain teases you the whole way up, then quite unexpectedly, the Lodge materializes out of the mist and you momentarily forget about the snow-capped peak. It's no wonder that Stanley Kubrick used shots of the Lodge's exterior for the film *The Shining*. Built to complement the size and majesty of Mt. Hood, the massive structure was erected from timber and rock donated by the forests of the mountain itself. From 1936 to 1937 more than 500 men and women toiled, forging metal for furniture and fixtures, sculpting old telephone poles into beams and banisters, weaving, looming, sawing. But for once, the historical artifacts are not displayed behind a glass wall—they are the chairs you sit on, the doors you walk through, the floors you step on. You don't need to be a guest to appreciate Timberline. Check with the Forest Service desk in the front lobby for daily tours in summer. Enjoy the restaurants, snow sports, and hiking paths, or relax by the massive fireplace in the "headhouse," with its 96-foot stone chimney. Also, take in the marvelously detailed 22-minute film

Mt. Hood

(on the lower level) to learn about the building's genesis—it'll help you appreciate Timberline all the more. **Pros:** a thrill to stay on the mountain itself, great proximity to all snow activity, plush featherbeds, amazing architecture throughout, fun dining places. **Cons:** rooms are small, no a/c in summer, prepare yourself for carloads of tourists. ⊠ *Timberline* ☎ *503/231–5400 or 800/547–1406* ⊕ *www.timberlinelodge.com* ⇗ *70 rooms, 10 with shared baths* ⬠ *In-room: no a/c, no phone (some), no TV (some). In-hotel: restaurant, 2 bars, pool, gym, parking (free), Wi-Fi hotspot.* ⊟ *D, MC, V.*

SPORTS AND THE OUTDOORS

Mt. Hood National Forest. The highest mountain in Oregon and the fourth-highest peak in the Cascades, "the Mountain" is a focal point of the 1.1-million-acre park, an all-season playground attracting more than 7 million visitors annually. Starting twenty miles southeast of Portland, it extends south from the Columbia River Gorge for more than 60 mi and includes 189,200 acres of designated wilderness. These woods are perfect for hikers, horseback riders, mountain climbers, and cyclists. Within the forest are more than 80 campgrounds and 50 lakes stocked with brown, rainbow, cutthroat, brook, and steelhead trout. The Sandy, Salmon, and other rivers are known for their fishing, rafting, canoeing, and swimming. Both forest and mountain are crossed by an extensive trail system for hikers, cyclists, and horseback riders. The **Pacific Crest Trail,** which begins in British Columbia and ends in Mexico, crosses at the 4,157-foot-high Barlow Pass. As with most other mountain destinations within Oregon, weather can be temperamental, and snow and ice may affect driving conditions as early as October and as late as June. Bring tire chains and warm clothes as a precaution.

Since this forest is close to the Portland metro area, campgrounds and trails are potentially crowded over the summer months, especially on weekends. If you're planning to camp, get info and permits from the **Mt. Hood National Forest Headquarters.** The National Forest manages more than 80 campgrounds in the area, including a string of neighboring campgrounds that rest on the south side of Mt. Hood: Trillium Lake, Still Creek, Timothy Lake, Little Crater Lake, Clackamas Lake, Summit Lake, Clear Lake, and Frog Lake. Each varies in what it offers and in price. The mountain is overflowing with day-use areas, and passes can be obtained for $5–$7. There are also Mt. Hood National Forest maps with details about well-marked trails. From mid-November through April, all designated Winter Recreation Areas require a Sno*Park permit (✉ *Single day $7, three-day permit $ 10, season $20*), available from the Forest Service and many local resorts and sporting goods stores.

GOVERNMENT CAMP

45 mi from the Dalles, south on Hwy. 35 and west on U.S. 26, 54 mi east of Portland on I–84 and U.S. 26.

Government Camp is an alpine resort village with a bohemian vibe and a fair number of hotels and restaurants. A bonanza of ski and mountain-biking trails converge at "Govy," and it's a convenient drive to Welches, which also has restaurants and lodging. Several of Mt. Hood's five ski resorts are just outside of town, and the rest are a convenient drive away.

WHERE TO EAT AND STAY

¢ ✕ **Charlie's Mountain View.** Old and new ski swag plasters the walls, AMERICAN lift chairs function as furniture, and photos of famous (and locally famous) skiers and other memorabilia are as abundant as the menu selections. Open flame–grilled steaks and hamburgers are worthy here, and house specialties include creamy mushroom soup and chicken Caesar salad with dressing made from scratch. When they're in season, try the apple dumplings. Charlie's is a local institution for powderhounds, and the fun, divey bar in back stays busy with ski bums and other lively degenerates. Live music packs them in on Saturday nights from 9 to 1 AM. ✉ *88462 E. Government Camp Loop* ☎ *503/272-3333* ⊕ *www. charliesmountainview.com* ⊟ *AE, D, MC, V.*

¢ ✕ **Huckleberry Inn.** Whether it's 2 AM or 2 PM, Huckleberry Inn welcomes AMERICAN you 24 hours a day with soups, milk shakes, burgers, sandwiches, and omelets. Well-known treats are made with huckleberries, and include pie, pancakes, tea, jelly, and vinaigrette salad dressing. ✉ *88611 E. Government Camp Loop* ☎ *503/272-3325* ⊕ *www.huckleberry-inn. com* ⊟ *MC, V.*

$$ ▥ **Thunderhead Lodge.** Within walking distance of the Mt. Hood Ski Bowl (its night lights visible from your cabin), the condo units at the Lodge are great jumping-off sites for many activities in the area: hiking, mountain biking, fishing, white-water rafting, and in winter,

snowboarding, sledding, and cross-county and downhill skiing. Room sizes and capacities vary according to your needs, and there's a rec room with foosball, a pool table, wet bar, and fireplace. A special treat: no matter how cold, the outdoor pool is geothermally heated from underground. Note: this particular rental company, All Seasons Property Management, has many other properties as well, including pet-friendly facilities. Visit their Web site to find your ideal cabin. ⊠ *87577 E. Government Camp Loop* ☎ *503/622–1142* ⊕ *www.mthoodrent.com* ⤴ *10 units* ♿ *In-room: a/c, no phone, kitchen. In-hotel: pool, laundry facilities* ▭ *MC, V.*

SHOPPING

Govy General Store. Good thing this is a really nice grocery store, because it's the only one for miles around. Govy General stocks all the staples, plus a nice selection of gourmet treats like cheeses and chocolates. It's also a full-service liquor store and your one-stop shop for Mt. Hood sweatshirts, postcards, and other keepsake tchotchkes. Grab your Sno*Park permit here in winter. ⊠ *30521 E. Meldrum St.* ☎ *541/272–3107* ⊕ *www.govygeneralstore.com* ◷ *Daily 7* AM–8 PM ▭ *AE, D, MC, V.*

WELCHES AND ZIGZAG

14 mi west of Government Camp on U.S. 26, 40 mi east of Portland, I–84 to U.S. 26.

One of a string of small communities known as the Villages at Mt. Hood, Welches' claim to fame is that it was the site of Oregon's first golf course, built at the base of Mt. Hood in 1928. Another golf course is still going strong today, and summer vacationers hover around both towns for access to basic services like gas, groceries, and dining. Others come to pull a few trout out of the scenic Zigzag River or to access trails and streams in the adjacent Salmon-Huckleberry Wilderness.

GETTING HERE

Most of Welches is found just off U.S. 26, often called the Mt. Hood Corridor here, about 45 mi east of Portland. On weekdays the **Mountain Express** (☎ *541/668–3466* ⊕ *www.thevillagesatmthood.com/mel-bus*) bus line links the villages along the corridor, connecting in Sandy with a commuter line to Portland.

VISITOR INFORMATION

Mt. Hood Area Chamber of Commerce (⊠ *24403 E. Welches Rd., Welches* ☎ *503/622–3017* ⊕ *www.mthood.org*).

WHERE TO EAT AND STAY

$$
NEW AMERICAN

✕**Altitude.** The flagship restaurant at the Resort at the Mountain is a little schizophrenic, aiming for a sleek, modernist concept in a dining room that's filled with booths and bad hotel art. Don't let that stop you, though, as the kitchen steps it up with adventurous dishes like maple-fried quail and foie gras on a hazelnut waffle, plus you can still count on standards like grilled salmon and New York strip. There's an inexpensive kids' menu, and breakfast is also available. Ask to see the specialty cocktail menu in the small adjacent bar. ⊠ *68010 E. Fairway*

Ave., Welches ☎ *503/622–2214* ⊕ *www.altituderestaurant.com* ⊟ *AE, D, MC, V* ⊗ *No lunch.*

$$ ✕**The Rendezvous Grill & Tap Room.** "Serious food in a not-so-serious
AMERICAN place" is the slogan of this upscale roadhouse, a locals' favorite for
more than 15 years. For a landlocked joint, the 'Vous sure does a nice
job with seafood, turning out appetizing plates of trout almondine, Wil-
lapa Bay oysters, Dungeness crab, and more. In the adjacent tap room,
ask about the seasonal, house-infused vodkas. The bar's strong rhubarb
liqueur is good enough to drink by the glass. ⊠ *67149 E. Hwy. 26.,
Welches* ☎ *503/622–6837* ⊕ *www.rendezvousgrill.net* ⊟ *AE, D, MC, V.*

$ 🏠**The Cabins Creekside at Welches.** Affordability, accessibility to recre-
ational activities, and wonderful hosts make this a great lodging choice
in the Mt. Hood area. Comfortable, large studio units that accommo-
date from one to four people have knotty-pine vaulted ceilings and log
furnishings. As a bonus, full-size kitchens make cooking "at home" a
breeze. Surrounding woods offer privacy, and owners Bob and Mar-
garet Thurman have amassed an impressive collection of mid-century
and pioneer-era bric-a-brac that they display throughout the property.
Patios on each unit face the seasonal creek, and the cabins have lock-
storage units large enough to hold bikes, skis, or snowboards. ⊠ *25086
E. Welches Rd.* ☎ *503/622–4275* ⊕ *www.mthoodcabins.com* ⤴ *10 cab-
ins* ⌂ *In-room: a/c, kitchen, DVD, Wi-Fi. In-hotel: laundry facilities*
⊟ *AE, D, MC, V.*

$$$ 🏠**Mt. Hood Vacation Rentals.** Doggedly determined to ensure a great
time for the two and four-pawed vacationer alike, Mt. Hood Vacation
Rentals welcomes the family pet into the great majority of its homes/
cabins/condos. Yet the properties are still on the upscale side, with
fireplaces/woodburning stoves, hot tubs, river views, and full kitchens.
The management service has been accommodating Mt. Hood visitors
since 1991, carefully choosing properties that offer a true representation of a mountain home vacation spot with beauty as well as privacy.
For families and groups, most rentals can accommodate 8–10 guests.
Pros: knowledgeable, hospitable staff; gorgeous homes nestled throughout the Mt. Hood area, many secluded sites; family- and pet-friendly.
Cons: bring your own shampoo and hair dryer, two-night minimum.
⊠ *24403 E. Welches Rd.* ☎ *800/424–9168* ⊕ *www.mthoodrentals.com*
⌂ *In-room: a/c (some) kitchen, DVD, Internet, Wi-Fi (some). In-hotel:
laundry facilities, parking (free)* ⊟ *D, MC, V.*

$$ 🏠**The Resort at the Mountains.** Here in the highlands of Mt. Hood, the
Cascades are seemingly close enough for golfers to hit with a long
drive. You can croquet on the only court and lawn-bowling green in the
Northwest or choose from plenty of nearby outdoor activities such as
fly-fishing on the Salmon River, horseback riding, white-water rafting,
and all snow-related sports. Treatments at the serene new spa include
specialty massages for golfers and skiers. Accommodations run from
double rooms to two-bedroom condos, and each of the sharp, contem-
porary rooms has a deck or patio overlooking the forest, courtyard, or
fairway. Self-contained, the resort has its own golf shop (pros available
for lessons), tennis courts, pool/Jacuzzi, gym, restaurants, bars, etc.
Golf, skiing, and spa packages are available, as well as comprehensive

meeting and event facilities. **Pros:** every sport available, clean rooms, plenty of choices in size. **Cons:** there will be crowds, may not appeal if a guest isn't a fan of golf, the gorgeous grounds seem more designed for golf carts than pedestrians. ⊠ *68010 E. Fairway Ave.* ☎ *503/622–3101 or 800/669–7666* ⊕ *www.theresort.com* ⟿ *158 rooms* ⌂ *In-room: kitchen (some), Wi-Fi. In-hotel: 2 restaurants, bars, golf course, tennis courts, pool, gym, bicycles, laundry facilities, spa, Wi-Fi hotspot, some pets allowed (fee), parking (free)* ⊟ *AE, D, MC, V.*

SPORTS AND THE OUTDOORS

RECREATIONAL AREAS **Salmon–Huckleberry Wildernss.** Named for the two main food groups of both black bears and frequent Mt. Hood restaurant diners, this sizeable wilderness area just south of Welches occupies the eroded foothills of the "Old Cascades," ancient mountains made mellow by time, water, and wind. Not surprisingly, trailside huckleberry picking is big here in late August and September. Inquire at the Zigzag Ranger Station for regulations and recommended trails. ⊠ *Mt. Hood National Forest Zigzag Ranger Station, 70220 E. Hwy. 26.* ☎ *503/622–3191* ☉ *Daily 7:45–4:30.*

GOLF **The Courses.** The three nine-hole tracks at the Resort on the Mountain include the Pine Cone Nine, Oregon's oldest golf course, built on a rented hayfield in 1928. For families or more relaxed golfers, there's also an 18-hole putting course. Check the Web to review the club's dress code, or cover that tee with a collared shirt from the pro shop. ⊠ *68010 E. Fairway Ave.; follow signs south from U.S. 26 in Welches* ☎ *503/622–2216 or 800/669–7666* ⊕ *www.theresortcourses. com* ⊠ *Summer greens fees $81 weekday, $90 weekend for 27 holes; off-season rates vary month to month. Putting course $85 for adults, $5 for children.* ⊟ *AE, D, MC, V.*

FISHING **The Fly Fishing Shop.** This heritage shop full of self-proclaimed "fish-aholics" has been peddling flies and guiding trips for three decades. Drop in to ask about the huge variety of customizable float trips, clinics, and by-the-hour walking trips for seasonal steelhead and salmon. Great nearby rivers include the glacier-fed Sandy and its tributary the Zigzag, closed to steelhead and salmon, but rich in native cuthroat. ⊠ *67296 E. U.S. 26* ☎ *503/622–4607 or 800/266–3971* ⊕ *www.flyfishusa.com* ⊠ *Half-day wade-fishing trips $120; half-day trout and steelhead classes $150.* ⊟ *AE, D, MC, V.*

Central Oregon

WORD OF MOUTH

There is a nice hike/walk from the Old Mill District in Bend. When it starts out it feels like it will be an urban walk but soon you are in the woods and walking along the Deschutes. I am sure if you park in the Old Mill area, someone can point out the trail to you.

—sunbum1944

WELCOME TO CENTRAL OREGON

TOP REASONS TO GO

★ **Become one with nature.** Central Oregonians live on the flanks of the Cascade Range and are bracketed by rock formations, rivers, lakes, forests, ancient lava flows, and desert badlands. Bring your golf clubs, carabiners, snowboard, or camera, and explore deeper.

★ **Go on a Bend-er.** Downtown Bend is lively and walkable, with a variety of appealing restaurants, galleries, and stores. Within a few blocks you can buy a painting, eat jambalaya, sample brandies, feed geese, and hear live music.

★ **Kick back at Sunriver.** This family-oriented resort boasts bike paths, river trails, an airstrip, horse stables, tennis courts, a golf course, and several restaurants.

★ **Take down the craft brewing scene.** Nobody calls Bend "Munich on the Deschutes" yet, but it's home to eight breweries that make and pour distinctive, flavorful beers. Sisters and Redmond also have craft breweries.

1 West Central Oregon. The western portion of Central Oregon ranges from lush and green in the Cascades to dry and full of conifers down to the Deschutes River. It's the side with the ski areas, the high mountain lakes, most of the resorts, and the rushing waters. Conveniently, the region's largest town is Bend, and it straddles the forested west and the harshly beautiful east.

2 East Central Oregon. East of the Deschutes River this land is marked by rugged buttes, tough junipers, and bristly sagebrush. It's a place that still hugs the frontier, with weathered barns, painted desert hills, a caldera holding two popular lakes, and some world-class rock climbing.

Map Labels

97
Kent
Maupin
218
216
197
Simnasha
218
Warm Springs
Deschutes River
97
293
Antelope
218
Warm Springs
Ashwood
Lake
Simtustus
Hay
Creek
Madras
Lake
Billy
Chinook
Culver
26
2
EAST CENTRAL OREGON
97
Ochoco
National
Forest
Terrebonne
126
Redmond
Prineville
26
Lookout
Mtn.
20
97
Tumalo
Bend
20
Prineville
Reservoir
Ochoco
National
Forest
Sunriver
Newberry
National
Volcanic
Monument
Brothers
20
East Lake
Deschutes
National
Forest
31

GETTING ORIENTED

Oregonians talk periodically about breaking the state into two pieces along the Cascade range, but Central Oregon provides a natural meeting place between the urban west side and the rural east side. It nestles neatly below the Columbia River basin and is drained by the Deschutes River, which flows from south to north. Skiers and snowboarders flock to ski areas on the western edge, anglers head to the Deschutes, the Metolius, and the Cascade Lakes, and climbers, campers, rockhounds, and wanderers explore the arid landscapes on the east side. Bend, the largest town for more than 130 miles in any direction, sits roughly in the center of this region.

6

CENTRAL OREGON PLANNER

When to Go

Central Oregon is a popular destination year-round. Skiers and snowboarders come from mid-December through March, when the powder is deepest and driest. During this time, guests flock to the hotels and resorts along Century Drive, which leads from Bend to Mount Bachelor. In summer, when temperatures reach the upper 80s, travelers are more likely to spread throughout the region. But temperatures fall as the elevation rises, so take a jacket if you're heading out for an evening at the high lakes or Newberry Crater.

You'll pay a premium at the mountain resorts during ski season, and Sunriver and other family and golf resorts are busiest in summer. It's best to make reservations as far in advance as possible; six months in advance is not too early.

The **Sisters Rodeo** takes place in June, and Bend's **Pole, Pedal, Paddle**—a popular ski, bike, run, and kayak/canoe race—is in May. The **Sisters Folk Festival**, a celebration of American roots music, is in September. Bend celebrates the seasons with a **Fall Festival** in mid-September and **WinterFest** in February, featuring outdoor sports, ice carving, live music, beer, and wine.

About the Restaurants

The center of culinary ambition is in downtown Bend, where the industry remains strong after a brutal recession, but good-to-excellent restaurants also serve diners in Sisters, Redmond, Tumalo, Prineville, and the major resorts. Styles vary, but many hew to the Northwest preference for fresh foods grown, caught, and harvested in the region.

Central Oregon also has many down-home places and family-friendly brewpubs, and authentic Mexican restaurants have emerged to win faithful followings in Prineville, Redmond, Madras, and Bend.

About the Hotels

Central Oregon has lodging for every taste, from upscale resort lodges to an in-town brewpub village, eclectic bed-and-breakfasts, rustic Western inns, and a range of independent and chain hotels and motels. If you're drawn to the rivers, stay in a rustic fishing cabin along the Metolius near Camp Sherman. If you came for the powder, you'll want a ski/snowboard condo at Mount Bachelor Village. A range of choices lines Century Drive between Bend and the mountain. If you're soaking up the atmosphere, you might favor downtown Bend's newest option, a sophisticated boutique inn called the Oxford Hotel, or Old St. Francis, the Catholic school–turned-brewpub village.

WHAT IT COSTS IN U.S. DOLLARS					
	¢	$	$$	$$$	$$$$
Restaurants	under $10	$10–$16	$17–$23	$24–$30	over $30
Hotels		under $100	$100–$150	$151–$200	$201–$250	over $250

Restaurant prices are per person, for a main course at dinner. Hotel prices are for two people in a standard double room in high season, excluding tax.

Getting Here and Around

Air Travel. Visitors fly into **Roberts Field-Redmond Municipal Airport** (RDM) (☎ *541/548-0646*), about 10 miles north of downtown Bend. Rental cars are available for pickup at the airport from several national agencies. The **Redmond Airport Shuttle** (☎ *541/382-1687 or 888/664-8449* ⊕ *www.redmondairportshuttle.net*) provides transportation throughout the region (reservations requested); a ride from the airport to downtown Bend costs about $33. Taxis are available at curbside, or can be summoned from the call board inside the airport; a cab ride to Bend from the airport is about $40. Portland's airport is 160 miles northwest of Bend.

Bus Travel. Greyhound's (☎ *541/382-2151 or 800/231-2222* ⊕ *www.greyhound.com*) only service in Central Oregon is a shuttle from Salem to Bend. The **Central Oregon Breeze** (☎ *541/389-7469 or 800/847-0157* ⊕ *www.cobreeze.com*), a regional carrier, runs one bus a day each way between Portland and Bend, with stops in Redmond and Madras. It also serves Prineville by reservation. **Cascades East Transit** (☎ *541/385-8680 or 866/385-8680* ⊕ *www.cascadeseasttransit.com*) is Bend's intercity bus service, and connects Redmond, Prineville, and Sisters. Trips require a reservation.

Car Travel. U.S. 20 heads west from Idaho and east from the coastal town of Newport into central Oregon. U.S. 26 goes southeast from Portland to Prineville, where it heads northeast into the Ochoco National Forest. U.S. 97 heads north from California and south from Washington to Bend. Highway 126 travels east from Eugene to Prineville; it connects with U.S. 20 heading south (to Bend) at Sisters. Major roads throughout central Oregon are well maintained and open throughout the winter season, although it's always advisable to have tire chains in the car. Some roads are closed by snow during winter, including Oregon 242. Check the **Oregon Department of Transportation's TripCheck** (⊕ *www.tripcheck.com*) or call **ODOT** (☎ *800/977-ODOT*).

Tour Options

Cog Wild (☎ *541/385-7002 or 866/610-4822* ⊕ *www.cogwild.com*) runs bicycle tours for people of all skill levels and interests.

Gadabout Serene Adventures (☎ *541/593-6200* ⊕ *www.gadaboutadventures.com*) runs bus tours for seniors and people who want to cruise comfortably to Newberry Crater, Fort Rock, Smith Rocks, the Head of the Metolius, and other central Oregon sites.

Sun Country Tours (☎ *541/382-6277 or 800/770-2161* ⊕ *www.suncountrytours.com*) is a longtime provider of raft and tube trips on central Oregon's waterways. Trips range from half days to two days.

Wanderlust Tours (☎ *541/389-8359 or 800/962-2862* ⊕ *www.wanderlusttours.com*) offers popular and family-friendly half-day excursions in Bend, Sisters, and Sunriver. Options include kayaking, hiking, snowshoeing, caving, and volcano exploring.

Central Oregon Visitors Association (✉ *661 S.W. Powerhouse Dr., Suite 1301, Bend* ☎ *541/389-8799 or 800/800-8334* ⊕ *www.covisitors.com*).

6

Updated by
Mike Francis

After a day on the Sunriver bike paths, a first-time visitor from Germany shook her head. "This place is paradise," she declared. It's easy to see why she thought so. Central Oregon has snowfields so white they sharpen the edges of the mountains; canyons so deep and sudden as to induce vertigo; air so crisp that it fills the senses; water that ripples in mountain lakes so clear that boaters can see to the bottom, or rushes through turbulent rapids favored by rafters.

A region born of volcanic tumult is now a powerful lure for the adventurous, the beauty-seeking, and even the urbane—which, in Central Oregon, can all be found in the same person.

Bend has grown into a sophisticated city of 80,000-plus, a magnet for people retreating from larger, noisier urban centers. For most visitors it is the sunny face of central Oregon, a haven for hikers, athletes, and aesthetes, but with the charm and elegance of much larger cities.

From Bend it's easy to launch to the attractions that surround it. To the northwest, Camp Sherman is a stunning place to fish for rainbow trout or kokanee. The Smith Rocks formation to the north draws climbers and boulderers, and, to the south, Lava Lands and the Lava River Caves fascinate visitors more than 6,000 years after they were chiseled out of the earth. The Badlands Wilderness Study Area to the east draws hikers and horseback riders wanting to connect with the untamed landscape. Lake Billy Chinook to the north is a startling oasis, where summer visitors drift in houseboats beneath the high walls of the Deschutes River canyon. The Deschutes River itself carries rafters of all descriptions, from young families to solo adventurers.

The area's natural beauty has brought it a diverse cluster of resorts, whether situated on the shores of high mountain lakes or cradling golf courses of startling green. They dot the landscape from the dry terrain around Warm Springs to the high road to Mount Bachelor.

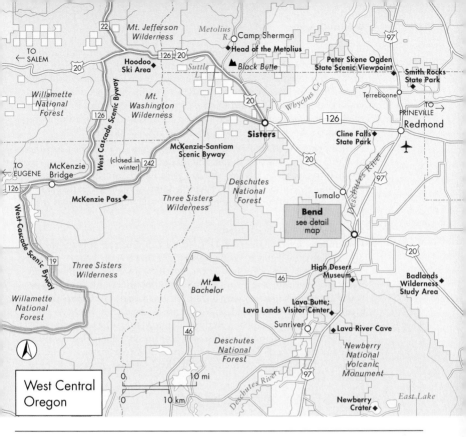

West Central
Oregon

WEST CENTRAL OREGON

Sunshine, crisp pines, pure air, rushing waters, world-class skiing and snowboarding at Mt. Bachelor, destination golf resorts, a touch of the frontier West at Sisters, an air of sophistication in Bend—the forested side of Central Oregon serves up many recreational flavors. The area draws young couples, seniors, families, athletes, and adventurers, all of whom arrive with a certain sense of purpose, but also with an appreciation for the natural world. Travelers will have no problem filling a week in central Oregon's western half with memorable activities, from rafting to enjoying a sensational meal.

BEND

160 mi from Portland, east and south on U.S. 26 and south on U.S. 97.

Bend, Oregon's largest city east of the Cascades, is emerging from a boom-and-bust cycle, one that caused it to go from being the state's fastest-growing city to the city with the nation's steepest fall in housing prices. As banks have worked through their inventories of foreclosed properties, the people of Bend have continued to enjoy the elements that attracted all the attention in the first place: an enviable climate, proximity to skiing, and a reputation as a playground and recreational escape. At times it seems that everybody in Bend is an athlete or a brewer, but it remains a tolerant, welcoming town, conscious of making a good first impression. Downtown Bend remains compact, vibrant, and walkable, and the Old Mill District draws shoppers from throughout the region. Chain stores and franchise restaurants have filled in along the approaches to town, especially along U.S. 20 and U.S. 97.

Neighboring Mt. Bachelor, though hardly a giant among the Cascades at 9,065 feet, is blessed by an advantage over its taller siblings—by virtue of its location, it's the first to get snowfall, and the last to see it go. Inland air collides with the Pacific's damp influence, creating skiing conditions immortalized in songs by local rock bands and raves from the ski press.

GETTING HERE AND AROUND

Portlanders arrive via car on U.S. 20 or U.S. 26, and folks from the mid-Willamette Valley cross the mountains on Oregon 126. Redmond Municipal Airport, 14 miles to the north, is an efficient hub for air travelers, who can rent a car or take a shuttle or cab into town. **Greyhound** also serves the area with a shuttle from Salem. The **Central Oregon Breeze**, a privately operated regional carrier, runs daily between Portland and Bend, with stops in Redmond and Madras. Bend is served by a citywide bus system called **Cascades East Transit,** which also connects to Redmond, Sisters, Prineville, Madras, and Warm Springs. To take a Cascades East bus between cities in Central Oregon, passengers must call to make a reservation.

If you're trying to head out of or into Bend on a major highway during the morning or 5 PM rush, especially on U.S. 97, you may hit congestion. Parking in downtown Bend is free for the first two hours, or park for free in the residential neighborhoods just west of downtown. In addition to the car-rental counters at the airport, Avis, Budget, Enterprise, and Hertz also have rental locations in Bend.

Contacts **Cascades East Transit** (☎ 541/385–8680 or 866/385–8680 ⊕ www. cascadeseasttransit.com). **Central Oregon Breeze** (☎ 541/389–7469 or 800/847–0157 ⊕ www.cobreeze.com). **Greyhound Bend** (✉ 1555 N.E. Forbes Rd. ☎ 541/382–2151).

VISITOR INFORMATION

Bend Chamber of Commerce (✉ 777 N.W. Wall St. ☎ 541/382–3221 ⊕ www. bendchamber.org). **Central Oregon Visitors Association** (✉ 661 S.W. Powerhouse Drive., Ste. 1301, Bend ☎ 541389–8799 or 800/800–8334 ⊕ www. visitcentraloregon.com).

EXPLORING

❶ **Des Chutes Historical Museum.** A striking 1914 building constructed from locally quarried volcanic tuff has Indian artifacts, historical photos of the region, and a pioneer schoolroom from 1915. It's operated by the Deschutes County Historical Society. Visit the 1915-era classroom and imagine yourself a student when Bend was young and largely untamed. ✉ 129 N.W. Idaho Ave. ☎ 541/389–1813 ⊕ www.deschuteshistory.org ☑ $5 ☉ Tues.–Sat. 10–4:30.

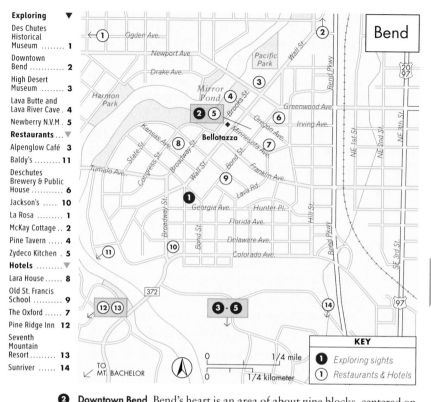

② **Downtown Bend.** Bend's heart is an area of about nine blocks, centered on
Wall and Bond streets. Here you'll find boutique shops, fine restaurants,
and lively nightlife establishments, as well as a few traditional pharma-
cies, taverns, and hardware stores keeping it real. At its western edge,
downtown Bend slopes down to **Drake Park and Mirror Pond.** Thirteen
acres of manicured greensward and trees line the edge of the Deschutes,
attracting flocks of Canada geese and strollers from downtown. Note
the marker at the edge of Mirror Pond, where, in 1928, Socialist Labor
Party presidential candidate Frank Johns finished his campaign speech,
then plunged into the water to rescue two boys that had fallen in from
a nearby bridge. He drowned in the attempt. ⊠ *Bounded on the west
by N.W. Brooks St. and Drake Park, N.W. Lava Rd on the east, N.W.
Franklin Ave. to the south, and N.W. Greenwood Ave. to the north.*
⊕ *www.downtownbend.org.*

Fodor's Choice
★

**NEED A
BREAK?**

A sleekly designed coffee shop with modernist blond-wood furnishings,
Bellatazza (⊠ *869 N.W. Wall St., #100* ☎ *541/318–0606* ⊟ *MC, V*) starts
with morning jolts and pastries in the heart of downtown Bend, and continues serving into the night. Wi-Fi is available with purchase.

❸ High Desert Museum. The West was truly wild, and this combo museum/
zoo proves it. Kids will love the up-close-and-personal encounters with
 gila monsters, snakes, porcupines, Ochoco the bobcat, and Snowshoe
the lynx. Actors in costume take part in the "Living History" series,
where you can chat with stagecoach drivers, boomtown widows, pioneers, and homesteaders. With 53,000 indoor square feet, a quarter-
mile trail, and an additional 32,000 square feet of outdoor exhibits and
live animal habitats, it's no wonder that the museum sells admission
tickets that cover a two-day visit. ⊠ *59800 S. Hwy. 97, 7 mi south
of downtown Bend* ☎ *541/382–4754* ⊕ *www.highdesertmuseum.org*
🖾 *$15* ☉ *Daily 9–5 May 1–Oct. 31, 10–4 other months.*

**EN
ROUTE** **Century Drive.** For 100 mi, this forest-highway loop beginning and ending in Bend meanders past dozens of high mountain lakes good for fishing, hiking, waterskiing, and camping in the summer months. (Much of
the road is closed by snow during the colder months.) To find it, take
Highway 46 for the first two-thirds of the trip, and then take U.S. 97
at LaPine to return to Bend.

❹ Lava Butte and Lava River Cave. On the north end of the Newberry
National Volcanic Monument, the Lava Butte area has several large
basalt lava flows as well as the 500-foot Lava Butte cinder cone—a
coal-black, symmetrical mound thrust from the depths 7,000 years ago.
The cone is now home to the recently expanded Lava Lands Visitor
Center, which features a variety of interpretive exhibits covering the
volcanic and early human history of the area. Lava River Cave is a
1-mi-long lava tube—a cave formed when molten lava drained from
the channel, leaving a crust as a roof—that takes about 90 minutes
to explore on your own. Lantern rental is $4. Enter by the tiny visi-
tor center. ⊠ *58201 S. Hwy. 97* ☎ *541/593–2421* ⊕ *www.fs.fed.us/r6/
centraloregon/newberrynvm/interest-lavabutte.shtml* 🖾 *$5 per vehicle*
☉ *May–Oct., daily 9–5.*

❺ Newberry National Volcanic Monument. The last time Newberry Volcano
blew its top was about 13 centuries ago. Paulina Peak, which is on an
unpaved road at the south end of the national monument, has the best
view into the crater and its two lakes, Paulina and East. Lava Butte and
Lava River Cave are at the north end of the monument near the visitor
center. You can also stay at rustic resorts on each lake. *58201 S. Hwy.
97* ☎ *541/593–2421* ⊕ *www.fs.fed.us/r6/centraloregon/newberrynvm/
index.shtml* 🖾 *$5 per vehicle* ☉ *Late Apr.–mid-Oct., daily 9–5; Labor
Day–Memorial Day, Wed.–Sun. 9–5.*

WHERE TO EAT

¢ ✕ **Alpenglow Café.** Locals will send you here for overstuffed breakfast
AMERICAN burritos, eggs Benedict, and buttermilk pancakes. The mandate for
freshness dictates that no can openers are permitted in the kitchen. The
good, strong coffee and fresh-squeezed orange juice are worthy com-
panions to any meal. Order breakfast until closing (2 PM) or pick from
tasty sandwiches and burgers. ⊠ *1133 N.W. Wall St, #100.* ☎ *541/383–
7676* ⊕ *www.alpenglowcafe.com* ▤ *MC, V* ☉ *No dinner.*

$ ✕ **Baldy's Barbeque.** With the arrival of Baldy's, Bend now has a top-
SOUTHERN notch, family-friendly barbecue joint with tender ribs, chicken, brisket,

Paulina and East lakes in Newberry National Volcanic Monument

pulled pork, and even catfish. The space is humble, but Baldy's isn't gunning for raves from *Architectural Digest*; it invests instead in serving up the tenderest, juiciest barbecue, seasoned with any of several house sauces. In warm weather, locals fill up the adjoining patio. ⊠ *235 S.W. Century Dr.* ☎ *541/385–7427* ⊕ *www.baldysbbq.com* ⊟ *MC, V.*

$ ✕**Deschutes Brewery & Public House.** Bendites are fiercely loyal to their
AMERICAN   city's original brewpub, established in 1988. Not only does the Brewery bake its own bread and pizza dough (adding in its own malt), it makes its sausages, sauces, mustards, dressings, soups, etc. House favorites include sweet-and-spicy mac and cheese and fish-and-chips. Though the always-popular Black Butte Porter is a Public House classic, Deschutes brews a diverse lineup of craft beers, including such seasonals as Jubelale (Christmastime) and Twilight Ale (summer). It is almost always hopping, and you may find yourself waiting to be seated, as there are no reservations. However, time flies as you admire the quasi-medieval murals of peasants downing ale, watch the four TVs broadcasting sports, or people-watch the boisterous crowd while you wait. ⊠ *1044 N.W. Bond St.* ☎ *541/382–9242* ⊕ *www.deschutesbrewery.com* ⊟ *AE, MC, V.*

$ ✕**Jackson's Corner.** This family-friendly community restaurant is housed
AMERICAN   in an unassuming two-story building tucked into a neighborhood outside downtown. The open, inviting space is a great place for casual gatherings, frequently with live music. The eclectic menu leans heavily on locally grown and organic dishes. It serves up cheesecake cups, mussels, pizza, fish, beef, and pork cutlets. ⊠ *845 N.W. Delaware Ave.* ☎ *541/647–2198* ⊟ *MC, V.*

$ | ✕ **La Rosa.** Come for the Red Cactus Margarita—stay for the food. Voted
MEXICAN | Best Mexican Restaurant in Bend time and again, La Rosa offers classic Mexican combination plates, as well as gourmet lobster-tail enchiladas, grilled prawns wrapped in apple-smoked bacon, and pork loin baked in banana leaves. There are plenty of vegetarian entrées offered as well. As one fan puts it, "La Rosa es la bomba!" Choose to dine indoors or on the heated patio. ⊠ *2763 N.W. Crossing Dr.* ☎ *541/647–1624* ⊕ *www. larosabend.com* ▭ *AE, MC, V.*

$ | ✕ **McKay Cottage.** This breakfast and lunch spot is housed in a 1916
AMERICAN | pioneer cottage that was home to a former state senator. Locals relax
Fodor'sChoice | throughout its cozy rooms and spill over on to the porch and patio
★ | below. The menu is long on comfort food, including fresh scones and sticky buns, and servers are friendly and attentive. On your way out, you can pick up baked goods and coffee drinks at the to-go bakery. ⊠ *62910 O.B. Riley Rd.* ☎ *541/383–2697* ⊕ *www.themckaycottage. com* ▭ *MC, V* ☻ *No dinner.*

$$ | ✕ **Pine Tavern.** This restaurant, named for the Ponderosa pine tree grow-
AMERICAN | ing through the back dining room, has been dishing up high-end meals in the heart of downtown Bend for more than 70 years. Its specialties are steaks and prime rib, especially Oregon Country Beef, which comes from hormone-free cattle raised on local ranches. Longtime regulars share the dining room with out-of-towners; in summertime, seek a spot on the patio, overlooking Mirror Pond and Drake Park. ⊠ *967 N.W. Brooks St.* ☎ *541/382–5581* ▭ *MC, V.*

$$ | ✕ **Zydeco Kitchen & Cocktails.** A local secret no longer. The menu is mostly
AMERICAN | American—fillet medallions, chicken, and pasta—although there are jambalaya and redfish dishes, as you'd expect. The owners emphasize the preparation of fresh, organic foods. The blended menu of Northwest specialties and Cajun influences has made Zydeco a popular spot. The bar is trendy, but welcoming. In warm weather, ask to sit on the patio. Bonus: Kids eat free on Sundays. ⊠ *919 N.W. Bond St.* ☎ *541/312– 2899* ⊕ *www.zydeckokitchen.com* ▭ *MC, V* ☻ *No lunch weekends.*

OFF THE BEATEN PATH | **Cowboy Dinner Tree Steakhouse.** Seventy miles south of Sunriver you'll find an authentic campfire cook, and he's firing up a genuine taste of the Old West. Oregonians will tell you that the 30-ounce steak or whole chicken over an open flame, plus all the fixings, is more than worth the trip. Serving the "true cowboy cut," the Dinner Tree ensures that leftovers will be enjoyed for days. Don't expect to plug in your laptop: there's no electricity, nor is alcohol served, nor credit cards accepted. If you journey from afar, lodging is available in the rustic buckaroo bunkhouse. Plates are $23.50 per adult, $10.25 for kids 7–13; kids 6 and under free. ⊠ *County Rd. 4–12/Forest Service Rd. 28, Silver Lake* ☎ *541/576–2426* ⊕ *www.cowboydinnertree.homestead.com* ☻ *June–Oct., Thurs.–Sun. 4* PM*–8:30; Nov.–May, Fri.–Sun. 4–8:30* PM.

WHERE TO STAY

$$$$ | ▣ **Lara House Lodge.** Fully refurbished in pure Craftsman style, this six-
Fodor'sChoice | suite B&B promises plenty of luxury. The kitchen gleams with modern
★ | appliances, and exposed dark-wood beams and wrought-iron appointments adorn the common rooms. An inviting fireplace is framed by artful tiles, and large-paned windows overlook Drake Park's Mirror

Pond. From the Bachelor Suite on the main floor with private entrance to the spacious Summit Suite at the top, each of the six rooms exudes high style and warmth. The gourmet breakfast, served on the front porch or in the sunroom or great dining room, may consist of a crustless salmon-rice torte, shortbread waffles, or herb-filled crepes. Try to arrive by 5 PM to enjoy the Northwest wine reception. **Pros:** clean lines and an uncluttered feel make a relaxing environment, park and town are a short walk away; wine and appetizer hour. **Cons:** no pets or kids. ⊠ *640 N.W. Congress St. NW* ☎ *541/388–4064 or 800/766–4064* ⊕ *www. larahouse.com* ↪ *6 rooms* ⌂ *In-room: a/c (central), no phone, refrigerator (some), Wi-Fi, DVD. In-hotel: parking (free) no guests younger than 18* ⊟ *D, MC, V* ℩◉℩ *BP.*

$ ⊓ **Old St. Francis School.** Not that you'd want to miss the rest of downtown Bend, but you could spend a charming weekend without leaving this delightful outpost of the McMenamin Brothers' regional hotel and brewpub empire. Old St. Francis is a restored 1936 Catholic schoolhouse converted to a destination village, with 19 classrooms that are now lodging rooms, a theater, and a pub. For a place that brews beer, bakes bread, shows movies, and exudes a laid-back charm, the property never lets you forget that it used to be a Catholic school. Enjoy the murals and the vintage photographs, and be sure to pick up the walking-tour primer, which explains why, for example, one mural depicts Catholic schoolkids releasing Monarch butterflies. Old St. Francis also rents nearby cottages that sleep 2 to 10 people. **Pros:** a self-contained destination village, yet only footsteps from downtown Bend and Drake Park. **Cons:** no pets; few modern appliances. ⊠ *700 N.W. Bond St.* ☎ *541/382–5174 or 877/661–4228* ⊕ *www.mcmenamins.com* ↪ *19 rooms* ⌂ *In-room: a/c, Wi-Fi. In-hotel: room service, 3 bars, pool, spa, parking (free)* ⊟ *AE, D, MC, V* ℩◉℩ *EP.*

$$ ⊓ **The Oxford Hotel.** A new and notable arrival in downtown Bend is this attractive boutique hotel, which features appealing views, a workout room, complimentary bikes, and loaner iPods. A step into the sleek, high-ceilinged lobby tells you you've found a new kind of accommodation in central Oregon, with comfortably elegant guest rooms and a confidently assured restaurant and lounge called 10 Below. Pets are welcome, and are even offered proportionately sized pet beds. **Pros:** stylish; generous amenities; attentive concierge. **Cons:** property is wedged into a half-block on the edge of downtown. ⊠ *10 N.W. Minnesota Ave.* ☎ *877/440–8436* ⊕ *www.oxfordhotelbend.com* ↪ *59 suites* ⌂ *In-room: a/c, safe, Wi-Fi., refrigerator, wet bar, kitchen (some), DVD players on request. In-hotel: restaurant, room service, bar, spa, loaner iPods, loaner bicycles, laundry facilities, Wi-Fi hotspot, parking (paid), some pets allowed* ⊟ *AE, D, MC, V.*

$$ ⊓ **Pine Ridge Inn.** This immaculate two-floor hotel is surrounded by ponderosa pines and junipers. The friendly staff goes out of its way to accommodate—if you can't make it to the 5 PM wine social, they'll be happy to bring a glass to your room upon request. All rooms have fireplaces, with either decks or patios. The suites have full sitting areas, seven with Jacuzzis. Hot breakfasts come with a choice of entrées, as well as the usual continental buffet spread of juices, pastries, and cereals.

The turndown service comes with a special homemade goodie on the pillow. **Pros:** clean spacious rooms; wine socials; nightlight embedded on the stairs in the suites. **Cons:** the river view is also the highway view; with 20 rooms, it has a less intimate feel than expected. ✉ *1200 S.W. Century Dr.* ☎ *541/389–6137 or 800/600–4095* ⊕ *www.pineridgeinn. com* ⤴ *20 rooms* ⚒ *In-room: a/c, kitchens (some), DVD, refrigerator, Wi-Fi. In-hotel: Wi-Fi hotspot, parking (free)* ═ *AE, D, MC, V* ⌑*BP.*

$$ ⌒ **Seventh Mountain Resort.** Proud of the fact that it's "the closest accommodation to Mt. Bachelor" (approximately 14 mi away), this resort has been a host to central Oregon's year-round outdoor activities since 1972. Lodging is distributed among 20 three-story buildings on the banks of the Deschutes River, with white-water rafting and fishing right outside. Among the recreational facilities there's a miniature golf course in a former roller rink, which converts to an ice-skating rink in winter. For younger guests, Camp Ranger Kids Camp has activities for ages 4 to 11. Accommodations include standard bedrooms with a queen-size bed, deluxe bedrooms with private deck, and studios with fireplaces and full kitchens, as well as private 2- and 3-bedroom homes. Consider Seasons Restaurant, the resort's latest upscale dining spot, specializing in Pacific Northwest cuisine. **Pros:** kid-friendly; varied accommodations, some moderately priced; setting is terrific. **Cons:** golf course is not on-site, but ½ mi away; some guests have complained that service is uneven. ✉ *18575 S.W. Century Dr., Deschutes National Forest* ☎ *541/382–8711 or 877/765–1501* ⊕ *www.seventhmountain.com* ⤴ *176 rooms* ⚒ *In-room: a/c, kitchen (most), refrigerator, DVD, Wi-Fi. In-hotel: 2 restaurants, bar, tennis and basketball courts, pools, gym, spa, water sports, bicycles, children's programs (ages 4–11), laundry facilities, Wi-Fi hotspot, parking (free)* ═ *AE, D, MC, V* ⌑*EP.*

$$$ ⌒ **Sunriver Resort.** Central Oregon's premier family playground continues to draw locals and faraway visitors for, in many cases, annual visits. They come because Sunriver encapsulates so many things that are distinctive about central Oregon, from the views of the central Cascades to the highly canoe- and raftable waters of the Deschutes River, which flows directly through the resort. An extensive system of paved bike-and-pedestrian paths connects all corners of the 3,300-acre resort. There are three golf courses, including the renowned Crosswater, 26 tennis courts, four swimming pools, and skiing at nearby Mt. Bachelor. If indoor fitness is more your style, check out Sage Springs Club. Lodging choices vary from vacation-house rentals to guest rooms in and around the lodge. Hundreds of houses on the property are available for rent through real-estate brokerages, separate from the hotel. For families, kids' programs are held at Fort Funnigan. Nature walks, raft trips, horseback excursions, bike tours, and night-sky observation sessions will keep everyone engaged. **Pros:** many activities; much pampering; dog-friendly. **Con:** when visitors throng the shops, restaurants, and bike paths, it can feel as if an entire city has relocated here. ✉ *17600 Center Dr., Sunriver* ☎ *800/801–8765* ⊕ *www.sunriver-resort. com* ⤴ *205 units* ⚒ *In-room: a/c, kitchen (some), refrigerator, Wi-Fi. In-hotel: 4 restaurants, room service, bars, golf courses, tennis courts, pools, gym, spa, bicycles, water sports, children's programs (ages 3–12),*

Fodor'sChoice
★

Sunriver Resort

Wi-Fi hotspot, laundry facilities, parking (free), pets allowed in some units (fee) ⊟ AE, D, DC, MC, V ⍾⊙⍾ EP.

NIGHTLIFE AND THE ARTS

The Astro Lounge. Bend's take on a space-age cocktail haven comes complete with matte black–and-chrome industrial furnishings, a loft-style layout, and 25 specialty martinis. There's an "Astrodiasiac" martini for two—'nuff said. The bar connects to a bistro sharing the out-of-this-world motif. ⊠ 147 N.W. Minnesota Ave. ☎ 541/388–0116 ⊕ www. astroloungebend.com.

Bendistillery. Oregon may be synonymous with craft-brewed ales and pinot noir, but Bendistillery expands the alcoholic range by handcrafting small batches of spirits flavored with local herbs. Bend sits in the middle of one of the world's great juniper forests, making the juniper-infused Cascade Mountain Gin a particular treat. This slick little tasting room stirs up bracing martinis and highballs incorporating Bendistillery's products, resulting in a perfect bar-crawl kickoff or classy, if sometimes noisy, nightcap. ⊠ 850 N.W. Brooks St. ☎ 541/318–0200 ⊕ www.bendistillery.com.

SHOPPING

Azila Nora. Carrying high-end Asian furniture and whimsical keepsakes from around the world, this store is a visual treat. It's also the only Oregon distributor of a highly-specialized line of handmade pottery from Zimbabwe called "Penzo." ⊠ 605 N.W. Newport Ave. ☎ 541/389–6552 ⊕ www.azilanora.com.

Cowgirl Cash. A funky Western outfitter also buys vintage boots and western apparel. You never know exactly what you'll find, but you can expect a fair share of leather, turquoise, silver, and, always, boots. It's a quirky and welcome addition to the downtown scene. ✉ *924 N.W. Brooks St.* ☎ *541/815–8996* ⊕ *www.cowgirlcashbend.com.*

Dudley's BookShop Café. Bend's leading independent bookseller has used books, Wi-Fi, and interesting people who take part in everything from knitting circles to Italian language classes. ✉ *135 N.W. Minnesota Ave.* ☎ *541/749–2010.*

Hot Box Betty. This fun, flashy shop sells high fashion for women and men, carrying DVF, Burning Torch, Frye Boots, and Isabelle Fiore bags. Visit the Hot Box if only to meet the delightful ladies running the store. ✉ *903 N.W. Wall St.* ☎ *541/288–1189* ⊕ *www.hotboxbetty.com.*

Old Mill District. Bend was once the site of one of the world's largest sawmill operations, a sprawling industrial complex along the banks of the Deschutes. In recent years the abandoned shells of the old factory buildings have been transformed into an attractive shopping center, a project honored with national environmental awards. Bend's national chain retailers can be found here, along with restaurants, the Central Oregon Visitors Association, a 16-screen multiplex movie house, and the Les Schwab Amphitheater. Don't miss the famous Old Mill District rockchucks, the groundhugging marmots who graze and hustle around the nearby rocks. ✉ *520 S.W. Powerhouse Dr.* ☎ *541/312–0131* ⊕ *www.theoldmill.com* ⊘ *Closed Sun.*

Patagonia by Pandora's Backpack. A friendly and attentive staff sells sleek modern outdoor gear and clothing at a Patagonia concept store that's still independently owned. ✉ *920 N.W. Bond St., Suite 101* ☎ *541/382–6694* ⊕ *www.pandorasbackpack.com.*

SPORTS AND THE OUTDOORS

RECREATIONAL AREAS
Deschutes National Forest. This 1.6-million-acre forest has 20 peaks higher than 7,000 feet, including three of Oregon's five highest mountains, more than 150 lakes, and 500 miles of streams. If you want to park your car at a trailhead, you'll need a Northwest Forest Pass. You'll also need day-use passes for boating and camping. ✉ *1001 S.W. Emkay Dr.* ☎ *541/383–5300* ⊕ *www.fs.fed.us/r6/centraloregon/* ✉ *Park pass required: day-use pass $5* ⊘ *Daily.*

BICYCLING
U.S. 97 north to the Crooked River Gorge and Smith Rock provides bikers with memorable scenery and a good workout. **Sunriver** has 26 mi of paved bike paths.

SKIING
Many Nordic trails—more than 165 mi of them—wind through the **Deschutes National Forest** (☎ *541/383–5300*). Call for information about conditions.

Mt. Bachelor is one of the best alpine resort areas in the U.S.—60 percent of the downhill runs are rated expert. One of 10 lifts takes skiers all the way to the mountain's 9,065-foot summit. The vertical drop is 3,265 feet; the longest of the 70 runs is 2 mi. Facilities and services include equipment rental and repair, a ski school, and ski shop, Nordic skiing, weekly races, and day care; you can enjoy restaurants, bars, and six lodges. Other activities include cross-country skiing, a tubing park, sled-dog rides, snowshoeing, and in summer, hiking and chair-lift rides. The 36 mi of trails at the **Mount Bachelor Nordic Center,** most of them near the base of the mountain, are intermediate.

> **DID YOU KNOW?**
>
> Sisters derived its name from a group of three Cascade peaks (Faith, Hope, and Charity) that rise to the southwest.

During the offseason, the lift to the **Pine Marten Lodge** provides stunning views. Visitors can play disc golf on a downhill course that starts near the lodge. At the base of the mountain, take dry-land dog sled rides with four-time Iditarod musher Rachael Scdoris. ✉ *Cascade Lakes Hwy.* ☎ *541/382–7888 or 800/829–2442* ⊕ *www.mtbachelor.com* ✆ *Lift tickets $59–$69 per day* ☉ *Nov.–May, daily 8–4, or as weather allows.*

SISTERS

18 mi northwest of Bend on U.S. 20.

If Sisters looks as if you've stumbled into the Old West, that's entirely by design. The town fathers—or perhaps we should say "sisters"—strictly enforce an 1800s-style architecture. Rustic cabins border a llama ranch on the edge of town. Western storefronts give way to galleries, a bakery occupies the former general store, and the town blacksmith's home now has a flower shop. Although its population remains under 2,000, Sisters increasingly attracts visitors as well as urban runaways who appreciate its tranquillity and charm. If you're driving over from the Willamette Valley, note how the weather seems to change to sunshine when you cross the Cascades at the Santiam Pass and begin descending toward the town.

Black Butte, a perfectly conical cinder cone, rises to the northwest. The Metolius River/Camp Sherman area to the west is a special find for fly-fishermen as well as springtime wildflower lovers.

GETTING HERE

Travelers from Portland and the west come to Sisters over the Santiam Pass on Oregon Highway 126. This is also the route for visitors who fly into Redmond Municipal Airport, rent a car, and drive 20 miles west. Those coming from Bend drive 20 miles northwest on U.S. 20. **Cascades East**, a regional bus carrier, runs routes between Sisters and Redmond by reservation.

Contacts Cascades East Transit (☎ *541/385–8680 or 866/385–8680* ⊕ *www. cascadeseasttransit.com*).

VISITOR INFORMATION

Sisters Chamber of Commerce (☎ *541/549–0251* ⊕ *www.sisterscountry.com*).

EXPLORING

Camp Sherman. Surrounded by groves of whispering yellow-bellied ponderosa pines, larch, fir, and cedars and miles of streamside forest trails, this small, peaceful resort community of 250 residents is part of a designated 86,000-acre conservation area. The area's beauty and natural resources are the big draw: the spring-fed Metolius River prominently glides through the community. In the early 1900s Sherman County wheat farmers escaped the dry summer heat by migrating here to fish and rest in the cool river environment. To help guide fellow farmers to the spot, devotees nailed a shoe-box top with the name CAMP SHERMAN to a tree at a fork in the road. Several original buildings still stand from the homesteader days, including some cabins, a schoolhouse, and a tiny chapel. The "action" is at the Camp Sherman Store, adjacent to the Post Office. ⊠ *25451 Forest Service Rd., 10 mi northwest of Sisters on U.S. 20, 5 mi north on Hwy. 14* ☎ *541/595–6711* ☾ *Mon.–Sat. 9-5, Sun. 9–4* ⊕ *www.metoliusriver.com.*

NEED A BREAK?

In a rustic-looking former general store, Sisters Bakery (⊠ *251 E. Cascade St.* ☎ *541/549–0361* ⊕ *www.sisters-bakery.com*) turns out high-quality pastries, coffee, and doughnuts. Sunday through Thursday the Oven Schedule starts with croissants and biscuits by 7 AM, dumplings and scones by 8, power cookies by 8:30, pies by 9, and breads by 10:30.

WHERE TO EAT

$$$
AMERICAN

✕ **The Boathouse.** From a simple marina tackle shop comes a woodsy boathouse, replete with pine, Mexican tiling, Native American art, and water as far as the eye can see. Dishes are ambitious and zesty variations on such core elements as salmon, halibut, tenderloin, and pheasant. Many fine Northwest and California wines are available by the bottle or glass. Lovely food and the management's genuine joie de vivre give the Boathouse its unique flavor. ⊠ *The Lodge at Suttle Lake, 13300 U.S. Hwy. 20* ☎ *541/595–2628* ⊕ *www.thelodgeatsuttlelake. com* ⊟ *AE, MC, V* ☾ *Closed Tues. and Wed.*

¢
AMERICAN

✕ **Depot Deli & Cafe.** A railroad theme prevails at this main-street deli. A miniature train circles above as the kitchen dishes out excellent, inexpensive sandwiches and burgers. Sit inside next to the rough-wood walls or out back on the deck. ⊠ *250 W. Cascade St.* ☎ *541/549–2572* ⊟ *MC, V.*

$$$$
FRENCH
Fodor's Choice
★

✕ **Jen's Garden.** This "garden" has grown to become the first world-class restaurant Sisters could claim in years. Jen's offers a three-course prix-fixe option as well as its traditional five-course meal. In keeping with the European custom of small servings, the courses are deliberately integrated so that the flavors complement each other. The menu changes every two weeks, with choices for each course; chantrelle-and-butternut-squash ravioli or New Zealand cockles/fennel/tomato/sausage broth, osso buco or berry-bread-pudding-stuffed roasted quail. If you prefer, you can always order à la carte. ⊠ *403 E. Hood Ave.* ☎ *541/549–2699* ⊕ *www.intimatecottagecuisine.com/* ⟐ *Reservations essential* ⊟ *MC, V* ☾ *No lunch.*

$$$
AMERICAN
Fodor's Choice
★

✕ **Kokanee Cafe.** The remarkable Kokanee draws diners from across the mountains to sample dishes at this homey hideaway on the banks of the Metolius. Crab cakes, rolled into smallish balls buried inside a crisscross of crisped vermicelli, are crunchy-succulent. Roast duck is enhanced by a sprinkling of organic chocolate bits; and wild salmon is just that when brushed with creamy potato and then heaped with calamari-corn salsa. As if brilliant appetizers, entrées, and a fine wine list weren't enough, enjoy hand-cranked ice cream daily. ⊠ *25545 S.W.*

The Lodge at Suttle Lake

Forest Service Rd., #1419, Camp Sherman ☎ *541/595–6420* ⊕ *www. kokaneecafe.com* ▭ *MC, V* ☉ *Closed Nov.–Apr. No lunch.*

WHERE TO STAY

$$ 🏨 **Five Pine Lodge.** This new property looks like a forest lodge, but it's conveniently located on the eastern fringe of downtown Sisters. The luxury Western-style resort features high-end furnishings hand-built by Amish craftsmen, lots of dark wood, and warm tile. The rooms and the campus behind the lodge exude Western, country charm. In front of the lodge, a brewpub, restaurant, spa, and movie theater share a parking area. **Pros:** top-quality craftsmanship; high-end fixtures, like the Kohler waterfall tubs. **Cons:** the lodge is only slightly set back from U.S. Highway 20, where traffic is sometimes quite heavy. ⊠ *1021 Desperado Trail* ☎ *541/549–5900 or 866/974–5900* ⊕ *www.fivepinelodge. com* 🛏 *8 rooms, 24 cabins* ⌂ *In-room: a/c, refrigerator, DVD, Wi-Fi. In-hotel: 2 restaurants, spa, gym, bicycles, pets allowed in some units (fee)* ▭ *AE, D, DC, MC, V.*

¢ 🏨 **The Lodge at Suttle Lake.** Built in the Grand Cascadian style, this

Fodor's Choice   10,000-square-foot lodge presides over the eastern side of Suttle Lake.
★   Supersized wooden architecture and whimsical charm characterize the main Great Room, which is often flooded with light beneath a sky-high ceiling. The 10 new lodge rooms are big on luxury, with fireplaces and glorious lake or forest views. The six exterior cabins vary in modern conveniences and size, and feature access to the high lake. For biking, hiking, boating, or just relaxing, beautiful Suttle Lake is well situated, inviting quiet contemplation. **Pros:** peaceful setting; accessibility to varied sports in all seasons; variation in room and price. **Cons:** no

a/c in summer. ⊠ *13300 U.S. Hwy. 20 (also known as Oregon Highway 126, 13 miles northwest of Sisters)* ☎ *541/595–2628* ⊕ *www.thelodgeatsuttlelake.com* ↪ *10 rooms, 14 cabins* ⎔ *In-room: no a/c, kitchen (some), refrigerator (some), DVD, Wi-Fi (some). In-hotel: restaurant, bar, spa, water sports, Wi-Fi, parking (free), pets allowed in some units (fee)* ⊟ *AE, MC, V* ⫟❘ *EP.*

$ ⊞ Metolius River Lodges. Homespun cottages give you cozy river views, fireplaces, and woodsy interiors complemented by top-notch hospitality. Pick from studiolike fourplex lodges or freestanding lodges with kitchen and bedrooms. Big picture windows bring in the pine scenery and blue sky reflecting off the water. Of the cabins, the Salmonfly is the most popular; its large front deck overhangs the current. Make reservations well in advance, especially for summer. **Pros:** within walking distance of the river and the Camp Sherman store. **Cons:** few amenities. ⊠ *12390 S.W. Forest Service Rd., #1419* ☎ *800/595–6290 or 541/595–6290* ⊕ *www.metoliusriverlodges.com* ↪ *13 cabins* ⎔ *In-room: no phone, refrigerator, kitchen (some), no TV. In hotel:* parking (free) ⊟ *MC, V* ⫟❘ *EP.*

$$$ ⊞ Metolius River Resort. Each of the 12 individually owned cabins at this
Fodor's Choice   resort has splendid views of the sparkling Metolius River, decks fur-
★   nished with Adirondack chairs, a full kitchen, and a fireplace—and are all in immaculate condition. Children are allowed, but management asks that they respect the resort's request to maintain a "peaceful and quiet area." And therein lies its beauty: the genuine get-away-from-it-all feel of a private residence nestled in ponderosa pines and aspen. Not to mention that one of the best fly-fishing rivers in the Cascades flows right outside your window and a gourmet restaurant is mere steps away. ⚠ **Make sure to drive in north from Hwy. 20—other routes are dangerous or ill-advised.** **Pros:** privacy; full view of the river; cabins that feel like home. **Cons:** no additional people (even visitors) allowed; no cell-phone service. ✛ *Off U.S. 20, northeast 10 mi from Sisters, turn north on Camp Sherman Rd, stay to left at fork (1419), and then right at only stop sign.* ⊠ *25551 S.W. Forest Service Rd. #1419, Camp Sherman* ☎ *800/818–7688* ⊕ *www.metoliusriverresort.com* ↪ *12 cabins* ⎔ *In-room: no a/c, kitchen, DVD (some), Wi-Fi. In-hotel: parking (free)* ⊟ *MC, V* ⫟❘ *EP.*

NIGHTLIFE AND THE ARTS

Three Creeks Brewing Co. The brewery has its own amber ale and IPA, but the seasonals are where it distinguishes itself. Look for the rye at Three Creeks. ⊠ *721 Desperado Ct.* ☎ *541/549–1963* ⊕ *www.threecreeksbrewing.com* ⊗ *Closed Sun.*

SHOPPING

Don Terra Artworks. A newcomer on the Sisters scene, this gallery represents local artists and craftspersons. You'll find stone sculptures, pottery, jewelry, glass, and paintings. ⊠ *222 W. Hood Ave.* ☎ *541/549–1299* ⊕ *www.donterra.com.*

High Desert Gallery. More than a dozen central Oregon artists are showcased here at "the art and soul of Central Oregon," a repository of affordable contemporary art that includes precious metal jewelry, clay jewelry, oil paintings, vases, and stained glass. ⊠ *281 W. Cascade Ave.* ☎ *541/549–6250 or 866/549–6250* ⊕ *www.highdesertgallery.info* ⊗ *Open by appointment in fall and winter.*

SPORTS AND THE OUTDOORS

RECREATIONAL AREAS

Metolius Recreation Area. On the eastern slope of the Cascades and within the 1.6-million-acre Deschutes National Forest, this bounty of recreational wilderness is drier and sunnier than the western side of the mountains, giving way to bountiful natural history, outdoor activities, and wildlife. Spectacular views of jagged, 10,000-foot snowcapped Cascade peaks—including Broken Top, the Three Sisters, and Mt. Jefferson, the second-highest peak in Oregon—sprawl high above the basin of an expansive evergreen valley carpeted by pine.

Five miles south of **Camp Sherman**, the dark and perfectly shaped cinder cone of **Black Butte** rises 6,400 feet. At its base the **Metolius River** springs forth. Witness the birth of this "instant" river by walking a paved ¼-mi path embedded in ponderosa forest, eventually reaching a viewpoint with the dramatic snow-covered peak of **Mt. Jefferson** on the horizon. At this point, water gurgles to the ground's surface and pours into a wide-trickling creek cascading over moss-covered rocks. Within feet it funnels outward, expanding its northerly flow; becomes a full-size river; and meanders east alongside grassy banks and a dense pine forest to join the Deschutes River 35 mi downstream. In 1988 the 4,600-acre corridor of the Metolius was designated a National Wild and Scenic River, and in 2009 the state legislature designated the entire Metolius Basin Oregon's first "Area of Critical State Concern." Within the area and along the river, there are ample resources for camping, hiking, biking, swimming, and boating. Enjoy fly-fishing for rainbow, brown, and bull trout in perhaps the best spot within the Cascades. ✉ *9 mi northwest of Sisters, off Hwy. 22* ⊕ *www.metoliusriver.com.*

FISHING

Fly-fishing the Metolius River attracts anglers who seek a challenge. A great fishing resource is the **Camp Sherman Store** (☎ *541/595–6711* ⊕ *www.campshermanstore.com*), which sells gear and provides information about where and how best to fish. For fishing guides, try **Fly and Field Outfitters** (☎ *541/389–7016* ⊕ *www.flyandfield.com*) out of Bend.

GOLF

Aspen Lakes. Golfers give high marks to this 18-hole bentgrass course designed by William Overdorf, which takes full advantage of the Sisters area's stunning vistas. ✉ *16900 Aspen Lakes Dr.* ☎ *541/549–4653* ⊕ *www.aspenlakes.com.*

Big Meadow at Black Butte. This 18-hole course wins praise for its stunning views and the stately stands of firs that girdle the fairways. ✉ *12930 Hawks Beard* ☎ *541/595–6211 or 866/901–2961* ⊕ *www. blackbutteranch.com.*

SKIING

On a 5,711-foot summit, **Hoodoo Ski Area** (✉ *U.S. 20, 20 mi west of Sisters* ☎ *541/822–3799* ⊕ *www.hoodoo.com*) has 806 acres of skiable terrain. With three quad lifts, one triple lift, one double lift, and 30 downhill runs, skiers of all levels will find suitable thrills. For tranquillity, upper and lower Nordic trails are surrounded by silence. At a 60,000-square-foot lodge at the mountain's base you can take in the view, grab bait, shop, or relax your weary feet. The ski area has kids' activities and child-care services available. Lift tickets range from $33 to $45 for adults, depending on time of day.

6

EAST CENTRAL OREGON

East of the Cascades, central Oregon changes to desert. The land is austere, covered mostly in sage and juniper, with a few hardy rivers and great extrusions of lava, which flowed or was blasted across the prehistoric landscape. In recent years resorts have emerged to draw west-side residents weary of the rain. They come over to bask in the sun and to soak up the feeling of the frontier, reinforced by ranches and resilient towns like Redmond and Prineville. They also come to fish and boat on the high lakes inside Newberry Crater and the man-made lakes near Culver and Prineville.

REDMOND

20 mi east of Sisters on Hwy. 126, 15 mi northeast of Bend on U.S. 97.

Redmond sits at the western end of Oregon's high desert, 4 mi from the Deschutes River and within minutes of several lakes. It is a place where desert ranches meet runways, as it serves as the regional hub for air travel. Its compact, historic downtown has been girdled—some would say strangled—by one-way highway couplets that slingshot travelers north to Hood River and south to Bend and Sunriver. It is the town nearest to Eagle Crest Resort and Smith Rock, a magnet for rock climbers. As with Deschutes County, Redmond has experienced some of the most rapid growth in the state during the past 10 years, largely owing to a dry and mild climate and year-round downhill and cross-country skiing, fishing, hiking, mountain biking, and rock hounding. Still, this is no gentrified resort town à la Bend, as a stroll through downtown will attest. A few blocks of vintage buildings remain, but north–south traffic hustles through the city core, with most residents in neighborhoods strung out to the west. Centennial Park, a small but attractive open space with fountains and an expansive lawn, opened downtown in the summer of 2010.

GETTING HERE

A couple of highways—U.S. 97 and Oregon 126—cross in Redmond. Highway 97 carries travelers north and south to Washington and California, and Highway 126 runs between Sisters in the west to Prineville in the east. Taxis and the **Redmond Airport Shuttle** ferry travelers to the Redmond Municipal Airport. Two bus lines, the **Central Oregon Breeze** and **Cascades East Transit**, serve Redmond. The Central Oregon Breeze links Bend, Redmond, Madras, and Portland, and Cascades East runs buses to and from Redmond and Madras, Prineville, and Bend on demand. Passengers should call to ensure a ride.

Contacts **Central Oregon Breeze** (☎ 541/389–7469 or 800/847–0157 ⊕ www.cobreeze.com). **Cascades East Transit** (☎ 541/385–8680 or 866/385–8680 ⊕ www.cascadeseasttransit.com). **Redmond Airport Shuttle** (☎ 541/382–1687 or 888/664–8449 ⊕ www.redmondairportshuttle.net).

VISITOR INFORMATION

Redmond Chamber of Commerce and Convention and Visitors Bureau (✉ 446 S.W. 7th St. ☎ 541/923–5191 ⊕ www.visitredmondoregon.com).

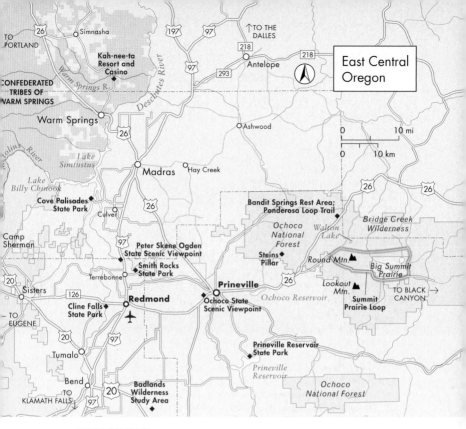

EXPLORING

Peter Skene Ogden Wayside. Even the most seasoned traveler may develop vertigo peering from the clifftop into a 300-foot-deep river canyon. It is a view that gives insight into why Oregon's high desert looks the way it does, with sheer drops and austere landscapes. You'll want to take pictures, but hang on to your camera. ⊠ *U.S. 97 N, 10 mi north of Redmond* ☎ *541/548–7501.*

Petersen's Rock Gardens. Rasmus Petersen, a Danish immigrant who died in 1952, created this 4-acre garden about halfway between Redmond and Bend. All of the petrified wood, agate, jasper, lava, and obsidian came from within an 85-mi radius of the garden, and was used to make miniature buildings and bridges, terraces, and towers. Among the structures are a micro–Statue of Liberty and five little castles up to 6 feet tall. The attraction includes a small museum and picnic tables. ⊠ *7930 S.W. 77th St.* ☎ *541/382–5574* ✉ *$4.50* ⊙ *Daily 9–5.*

WHERE TO EAT AND STAY

$$$ ✕ **The Brickhouse Steak and Seafood.** The most elegant dining experience in Redmond is at the Brickhouse, a white-tablecloth and brick-wall place that specializes in steaks and chops, but also offers attractive plates of seafood, especially shellfish. The lighting is muted, but bright enough to let you see what you're eating. You can get lost in the list of

Rock climbing in Smith Rock State Park

cocktails and wines from Oregon and around the world. ✉ *412 S.W. 6th St.* ☎ *541/526–1782* ⊕ *www.brickhouseredmond.com* 🖃 *MC, V* ☾ *Closed Sun. and Mon. No lunch.*

$$ ✕ **Terrebonne Depot.** Finally, a Smith Rock restaurant that matches the
AMERICAN view. The Terrebonne offers an array of reasonably priced, tasty dishes. The kitchen plays it straight down the middle, with nicely seasoned steaks, salmon, chicken, and pork chops. You can also get lunch baskets to take with you on the climb. Service is friendly, and the menu is a cut above what you'd expect in this off-the-beaten-track location. The view allows you to reflect on the climb you've just made—or will inspire you to embark on one. ✉ *400 N.W. Smith Rock Way* ☎ *541/548–5030* ⊕ *www.terrebonnedepot.com* 🖃 *MC, V* ☾ *Closed Tues.*

$$ 🏨 **Eagle Crest Resort.** Eagle Crest is 5 mi west of Redmond, above the
☾ canyon of the Deschutes River. In this high-desert area the grounds are covered with juniper and sagebrush, except for the lush golf course. Some rooms are vacation rentals, but others are clustered in a single building on the landscaped grounds, and some of the suites have gas fireplaces. The resort is on 1,700 acres. There are 10 mi of bike trails and a 2-mi hiking trail where you can fish in the river. **Pros:** a full-service resort; great for kids; pet-friendly. **Cons:** there can be crowds, kids, and pets. ✉ *1522 Cline Falls Hwy.* ☎ *800/682–4786* ⊕ *www. eagle-crest.com* ↪ *100 rooms, 45 suites, 75 town houses* ⟁ *In-room: a/c, kitchen (some), refrigerator, DVD, Wi-Fi. In-hotel: 4 restaurants, bar, golf courses, tennis courts, pools, gym, spa, bicycles, children's programs (ages 3–12), free parking, Wi-Fi hotspot, some pets allowed.* 🖃 *AE, DC, MC, V* ❙◯❙ *EP.*

SPORTS AND THE OUTDOORS

RECREATIONAL AREAS

Cline Falls State Park. Picnicking, fishing, and bicycling are popular at this nine-acre rest area commanding scenic views on the Deschutes River 5 mi west of Redmond. You'll feel free from civilization here. ⊠ *Hwy. 126, west of Redmond* ☎ *800/551–6949* ⊕ *www.oregonstateparks.org.*

ROCK CLIMBING

Fodor's Choice

★

Smith Rock State Park. Eight miles north of Redmond, this park is world famous for rock climbing, with hundreds of routes of all levels of difficulty. A network of trails serves both climbers and families dropping in for the scenery. In addition to the stunning rock formations, the Crooked River, which helped shape these features, loops through the park. You might spot golden eagles, prairie falcons, mule deer, river otters, and beavers. Due to the environmental sensitivity of the region, the animal leash law is strongly enforced. It can get quite hot in midsummer, so most prefer to climb in the spring and fall. ⊠ *Off U.S. 97, 9241 N.E. Crooked River Dr., Terrebonne* ☎ *541/548–7501 or 800/551–6949* ⊕ *www.oregonstateparks.org* ☞ *Day use $5 per vehicle.*

Smith Rock Climbing Guides (☎ *541/788–6225* ⊕ *www.smithrockclimbingguides.com*) is run by professionals with emergency medical training. They take visitors to the Smith Rock formation for climbs of all levels of difficulty and supply all equipment. Guided climbs can run a half-day or full day, and are priced according to the number of people in a group.

6

PRINEVILLE

17 miles east of Redmond on Hwy. 126.

Prineville is the oldest town in central Oregon, and the only incorporated city in Crook County. Tire entrepreneur Les Schwab founded his regional empire here, and it remains a key hub for the company. Recently, Facebook chose Prineville as the location for its new data center. Surrounded by verdant ranch lands and the purplish hills of the Ochoco National Forest, Prineville will likely interest you chiefly as a jumping-off point for some of the region's more secluded outdoor adventures. The area attracts thousands of anglers, boaters, sightseers, and rock hounds to its nearby streams, reservoirs, and mountains. Rimrocks nearly encircle Prineville, and geology nuts dig for free agates, limb casts, jasper, and thunder eggs. Downtown Prineville consists of a handful of small buildings along a quiet strip of Highway 26, dominated by the Crook County Courthouse, built in 1909. Shopping and dining opportunities are mostly on the basic side.

GETTING HERE

Travelers approaching Prineville from the west on Oregon 126 descend like a marble circling a funnel, dropping into a tidy grid of a town from a high desert plain. It's an unfailingly dramatic way to enter the seat of Crook County, dominated by the courthouse on Northeast Third Street, aka Highway 26, the main drag. Prineville is 20 miles east of Redmond Municipal Airport. If you're coming to Prineville from the airport, it's easiest to rent a car and drive. However, two bus lines, **Central Oregon Breeze** and **Cascades East** run routes by appointment.

CLOSE UP

Cove Palisades State Park

Fourteen mi west of Madras is **Cove Palisades State Park**, a mini–Grand Canyon of red-rock cliffs and gorges. On a clear day a column of snow-capped Cascades peaks lines the horizon during the drive from town. Lake Billy Chinook, a glittering oasis amid the rocks, snakes through the park.

High season here is summertime, when families camp on the lakeshore and houseboats drift unhurriedly from cliff to cleft. Nature lovers flock to the park in February for the annual eagle watch. The Crooked River Day Use Area is the most immediately accessible part of the park, a great place to cast a line into the water, launch a boat, or set a picnic. Nearby is the Cove Palisades Marina, where you can rent boats, clean fish, and buy sandwiches and boat supplies, including kids' water toys.

In addition to 10 mi of hiking trails, Cove Palisades has a driving loop around its craggy rim. Near the Ship Rock formation, you may see petroglyphs carved into a boulder by indigenous people who moved through the area centuries ago.

A full-service campground has 85 full hookups, 89 electrical sites with water, and 91 tent sites, houseboats, and cabins. ⊠ *Off U.S. 97, 15 mi S.W. of Madras, 7300 Jordan Rd., Culver* ☎ *541/546–3412 or 800/551–6949* ⊕ *www.oregonstateparks.org* 🖅 *Day use $5 per vehicle*

Contacts Central Oregon Breeze (☎ *541/389–7469 or 800/847–0157* ⊕ *www. cobreeze.com*). **Cascades East Transit** (☎ *541/385–8680 or 866/385–8680* ⊕ *www.cascadeseasttransit.com*).

VISITOR INFORMATION

Ochoco National Forest Headquarters and Prineville Ranger Station (⊠ *3160 N.E. 3rd St.* ☎ *541/416–6500* ⊕ *www.fs.fed.us/r6/centraloregon*). **Prineville-Crook County Chamber of Commerce and Visitor Center** (⊠ *102 N.W. 2nd St.* ☎ *541/447–6304* ⊕ *www.visitprineville.com*).

EXPLORING

Bowman Museum. A tough little stone building (it was a bank once, and banks aren't here needed to be tough) is the site of the museum of the Crook County Historical Society. The 1911 edifice is now on the National Register of Historic Places. Prominent are pioneer artifacts—agricultural implements, vintage mousetraps, firearms—that defined early Prineville. ⊠ *246 N. Main St.* ☎ *541/447–3715* ⊕ *www. bowmanmuseum.org* 🖅 *Free* ☉ *Memorial Day–Labor Day, weekdays 10–5, weekends 11–4; Labor Day–Dec. and Feb.–Memorial Day, Tues.–Fri. 10–5, Sat. 11–4. Closed Jan.*

SCENIC ROUTE

The 43-mi **Summit Prairie Loop** winds past Lookout Mountain, Round Mountain, Walton Lake, and Big Summit Prairie. The prairie abounds with trout-filled creeks and has one of the finest stands of ponderosa pines in the state; wild mustangs roam the area. The prairie can be glorious between late May and June, when wildflowers with evocative names like mule ears, wyethia, biscuit root, yellow bells, and desert shooting stars

burst into bloom. ✢ *Forest Service Rd. 22 east to Forest Service Rd. 30,*
which turns into Forest Service Rd. 3010, south, to Forest Service Rd. 42
heading west, which loops back to Forest Service Rd. 22 ☎ *541/416–6500.*

Ochoco Viewpoint. About ½ mi west of Prineville is a truly fantastic scenic overlook that commands a sweeping view of the city and the hills,
ridges, and buttes beyond. ✉ *½ mi west of Prineville on U.S. Hwy. 126.*

WHERE TO EAT AND STAY

$$ ✕ **Barney Prine's Steakhouse and Saloon.** Prineville has become home to
a startlingly appealing restaurant and saloon named after the town's
founder. It's a good place to get a filet mignon, pepper steak, T-bone,
or other good cuts. Chicken, lamb, fish, elk, and veal also are on the
menu. The waitstaff is cheerful and attentive, and the ambience is part
frontier Western, part contemporary. ✉ *380 N.E. Main St.* ☎ *541/447–*
3333 ⊕ *www.barneyprines.com* ▭ *MC, V* ✆ *Closed Mon. No lunch*
Sat.–Tues.

¢ ⌂ **Rustlers Inn.** From the old-style covered walkways to the large,
antiques-furnished rooms, this motel is Old West all the way. Each
room is decorated differently—if you call in advance, the managers
will attempt to match your room furnishings to your personality. The
Rustlers allows pets to stay for a one-time fee. **Pros:** Individually themed
rooms; friendly management. **Cons:** Little street appeal, no restaurant.
✉ *960 N.W. 3rd St. (U.S. 26)* ☎ *541/447–4185* ⊕ *www.rustlersinn.com*
⤳ *20 rooms* △ *In-room: a/c, kitchen (some), refrigerator, DVD, Wi-Fi.*
In-hotel: free parking, some pets allowed. ▭ *AE, D, DC, MC, V.*

SPORTS AND THE OUTDOORS

RECREATIONAL **Ochoco National Forest.** Twenty-five miles east of the flat, juniper-dotted
AREAS countryside around Prineville the landscape changes to forested ridges
covered with tall ponderosa pines and Douglas firs. Sheltered by the
diminutive Ochoco Mountains and with only about a foot of rain each
year, the national forest, established in 1906 by President Theodore
Roosevelt, manages to lay a blanket of green across the dry, high desert
of central Oregon. This arid landscape—marked by deep canyons, tow-
ering volcanic plugs, and sharp ridges—goes largely unnoticed except
for the annual influx of hunters during the fall. The Ochoco, part of the
old Blue Mountain Forest Reserve, is a great place for camping, hiking,
biking, and fishing in relative solitude. In its three wilderness areas—
Mill Creek, Bridge Creek, and Black Canyon—it's possible to see elk,
wild horses, eagles, and even cougars. ✉ *Ranger Station 3160 N.E. 3rd*
St., U.S. 26 ☎ *541/416–6500* ✆ *Ranger station weekdays 7:30–4:30.*

The Oregon Badlands Wilderness. This 30,000-acre swath of Oregon's
high desert was designated a national wilderness in 2009, following
the longtime advocacy of Oregonians enamored of its harshly beauti-
ful landscape riven by ancient lava flows and home to sage grouse,
pronghorn antelope, and elk. Motorized vehicles are prohibited, but
visitors can ride horses on designated trails and low-impact hikers are
welcome. Bring a camera to capture the ancient lava flows, jagged
rock formations, birds, and wildflowers. ✉ *3050 N.E. 3rd St., U.S. 26*
☎ *541/416–6700.*

6

Prineville Reservoir State Park. Mountain streams flow out of the Ochoco Mountains and join together to create the Crooked River, which is dammed near Prineville. Bowman Dam on the river forms the park. Recreational activities include boating, swimming, fishing, and hiking. The main campground has 22 full hookups, 23 electrical and 23 tent sites, and 3 cabins. Jasper Point Campground is open May 1– September 30 and has 30 electrical sites with water and a boat ramp. ✉ *19020 S.E. Parkland Dr.* ☎ *541/447–4363 or 800/452–5687* ⊕ *www. oregonstateparks.org* ⌦ *Campgrounds $22 May 1–Sept. 30.*

FISHING   It's a good idea to check the **Oregon Department of Fish and Wildlife**'s (⊕ *www.dfw.state.or.us/RR/index.asp*) weekly recreation report before you head out.

Ochoco Reservoir is stocked in the spring with fingerling trout, with hold-over rainbows available throughout the year. As the weather warms through the summer, bass, crappie and bluegill are the leading species. ✉ *7 miles east of Prineville on Highway 26* ☎ *541/447–1209* ⊕ *www. fs.fed.us/r6/centraloregon/recreation/fishing/lake-reservoir/ochoco.shtml.*

Some anglers return year after year to **Prineville Reservoir**, although temperatures can get uncomfortably hot and water levels relatively low by late summer. The reservoir is known for its bass, trout, and crappie, with fly fishing available on the Crooked River below Bowman Dam. ✉ *19020 S.E. Parkland Dr.* ☎ *541/447–4363 or 800/452–5687* ⊕ *www. oregonstateparks.org.*

HIKING   Pick up maps at the Ochoco/Prineville Ranger Station for trails through the 5,400-acre **Bridge Creek Wilderness** and the demanding Black Canyon Trail (24 mi round-trip) in the **Black Canyon Wilderness**. The 1½-mi **Ponderosa Loop Trail** follows an old logging road through ponderosa pines growing on hills. In early summer wildflowers take over the open meadows. The trailhead begins at Bandit Springs Rest Area, 29 mi east of Prineville on U.S. 26. A 2½-mi, one-way trail winds through old-growth forest and mountain meadows to **Steins Pillar,** a giant lava column with panoramic views; be prepared for a workout on the trail's poorly maintained second half, and allow at least three hours for the hike. To get to the trailhead, drive east 9 mi from Prineville on U.S. 26, head north (to the left) for 6½ mi on Mill Creek Road (also signed as Forest Service Road 33), and head east (to the right) on Forest Service Road 500.

SKIING   Two loops for cross-country skiers start at **Bandit Springs Rest Area,** 29 mi east of Prineville on U.S. 26. One loop is designed for beginners and the other for intermediate to advanced skiers. Both traverse the area near the Ochoco Divide and have great views. **Ochoco National Forest** headquarters has a handout on skiing trails, and can provide the required Sno-Park permits, which are also available from the **Department of Motor Vehicles** (✉ *Ochoco Plaza, 1595 E. 3rd St., Suite A-3, Prineville* ☎ *541/447–7855*).

Crater Lake National Park

WITH SOUTHERN OREGON

WORD OF MOUTH

"After arriving the evening before amidst fog and snow, we awoke to the incredible blue lake and fresh snow."
— photo by William A. McConnell, Fodors.com member

WELCOME TO CRATER LAKE NATIONAL PARK

TOP REASONS TO GO

★ **The lake:** Cruise inside the caldera basin and gaze into the extraordinary sapphire-blue water of the country's deepest lake.

★ **Native land:** Enjoy the rare luxury of interacting with totally unspoiled terrain.

★ **The night sky:** Billions of stars glisten in the pitch-black darkness of an unpolluted sky.

★ **Splendid hikes:** Accessible trails spool off the main roads and wind past colorful bursts of wildflowers and cascading waterfalls.

★ **Camping at its best:** Pitch a tent or pull up a motor home at Mazama Campground, a beautifully situated, guest-friendly, and well-maintained campground.

1 **Crater Lake.** The focal point of the park, this non-recreational, scenic destination is known for its deep blue hue.

2 **Wizard Island.** Visitors can take boat rides to this landmass protruding from the western section of Crater Lake; it's a great place for a hike or a picnic.

3 **Mazama Village.** This is your best bet for stocking up on snacks, beverages, and fuel in the park; it's about 5 mi from Rim Drive.

4 **Cleetwood Cove Trail.** The only safe, designated trail leading down to the lake's edge is on the rim's north side off Rim Drive.

GETTING ORIENTED

Crater Lake National Park covers 183,224 acres. In southern Oregon less than 100 mi from the California border, it's surrounded by several Cascade Range forests, including the Winema and Rogue River national forests. Of the nearby towns, Klamath Falls is closest, at 60 mi south of the park; Medford and Ashland, to the southwest, are approximately 80 mi and 90 mi from the lake, respectively. Bend is approximately 105 mi northeast (via seasonal Hwy. 138).

KEY
🏠 *Ranger Station*
△ *Campground*
🍽 *Picnic Area*
🍴 *Restaurant*
🏨 *Lodge*
🚶 *Trailhead*
🚻 *Restrooms*
⇥ *Scenic Viewpoint*
------ *Walking/Hiking Trails*

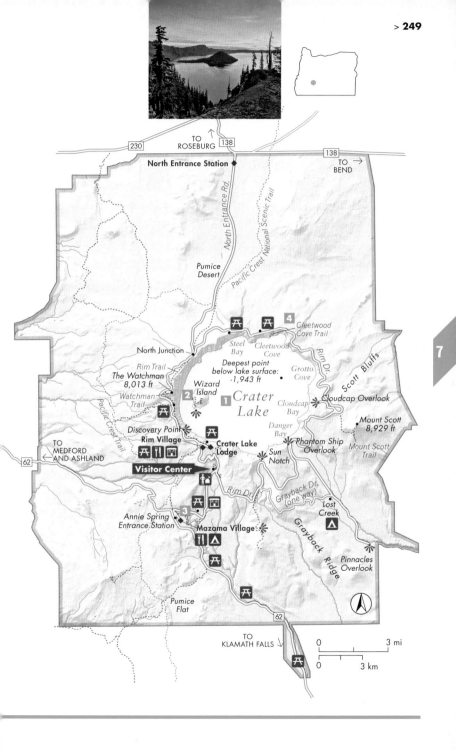

TO
ROSEBURG

TO
BEND

230 TO 138

138

North Entrance Station

North Entrance Rd.

Pacific Crest National Scenic Trail

Pumice
Desert

North Junction

4 Cleetwood
Cove Trail

Steel
Bay

Cleetwood
Cove

Rim Dr.

Scott Bluffs

Rim Trail
The Watchman
8,013 ft

Deepest point
below lake surface:
-1,943 ft

Grotto
Cove

Watchman
Trail

Wizard
Island

2

1 *Crater
Lake*

Cloudcap
Bay

Cloudcap Overlook

Discovery Point

Danger
Bay

Mount Scott
8,929 ft

Pacific Crest Trail

Rim Village

Crater Lake
Lodge

Phantom Ship
Overlook

Mount Scott
Trail

TO
MEDFORD
AND ASHLAND

62

Visitor Center

Sun
Notch

Rim Dr.

Grayback Dr.
(one way)

Lost
Creek

Annie Spring
Entrance Station

3

Grayback Ridge

Mazama Village

Pinnacles
Overlook

Pumice
Flat

62

TO
KLAMATH FALLS

0   3 mi

0   3 km

7

CRATER LAKE NATIONAL PARK PLANNER

When to Go

The park's high season is July and August. September and early October tend to draw smaller crowds. From October through most of May, most of the park closes due to heavy snowfall. The road is kept open just to the rim in winter, except during severe weather.

Getting Here and Around

Most of the park is only accessible from late June–early July through mid-October. The rest of the year, snow blocks all park roadways and entrances except Highway 62 and the access road to Rim Village from Mazama Village. Rim Drive is typically closed because of heavy snowfall from mid-October to mid-July, and you could encounter icy conditions any month of the year, particularly in early morning.

AVG. HIGH/LOW TEMPS.

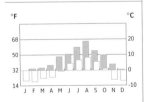

Flora and Fauna

Two primary types of fish swim beneath the surface of Crater Lake: kokanee salmon and rainbow trout. It's estimated that hundreds of thousands of kokanee inhabit the lake, but since boating and recreational access is so limited they elude many would-be sportsman. Kokanees average about 8 inches in length, but they can grow to nearly 18 inches. Rainbow trout are larger than the kokanee, but are less abundant in Crater Lake. Trout—including bull, Eastern brook, rainbow, and German brown—swim in the park's many streams and rivers; they usually remain elusive, because these waterways flow through inaccessibly steep canyons.

Remote canyons shelter the park's elk and deer populations, which can sometimes be seen at dusk and dawn feeding at forest's edge. Black bears and pine martens—cousins of the short-tailed weasel—also call Crater Lake home. Birds such as hairy woodpeckers, California gulls, red-tailed hawks, and great horned owls are more commonly seen in summer in forests below the lake.

Good Reads

■ *Crater Lake National Park: A Global Treasure,* by former park rangers Ann and Myron Sutton, celebrates the park's first 100 years with stunning photography, charts, and drawings.

■ Ron Warfield's *A Guide to Crater Lake National Park and The Mountain That Used to Be* gives a useful and lushly illustrated overview of Crater Lake's history and physical features.

■ The National Park Service uses Stephen Harris's *Fire Mountains of the West* in its ranger training; the detailed handbook covers Cascade Range geology.

■ *Wildflowers of the Olympics and Cascades,* by Charles Stewart, is an easy-to-use guide to the area's flora.

By Christine Vovakes

The pure, crystalline blue of Crater Lake astounds visitors at first sight. More than 5 mi wide and ringed by cliffs almost 2,000 feet high, the lake was created approximately 7,700 years ago, following Mt. Mazama's fiery explosion. Days after the eruption, the mountain collapsed on an underground chamber emptied of lava. Rain and snowmelt filled the caldera, creating a sapphire-blue lake so clear that sunlight penetrates to a depth of 400 feet (the lake's depth is 1,943 feet). Today it's both the clearest and deepest lake in the United States—and the seventh-deepest in the world.

PARK ESSENTIALS

ACCESSIBILITY

All the overlooks along Rim Drive are accessible to those with impaired mobility, as are Crater Lake Lodge, the facilities at Rim Village, and Steel Information Center. A half-dozen accessible campsites are available at Mazama Campground.

ADMISSION FEES AND PERMITS

Admission to the park is $10 per vehicle, good for seven days. Backcountry campers and hikers must obtain a free wilderness permit at Rim Visitor Center or Steel Information Center for all overnight trips.

ADMISSION HOURS

Crater Lake National Park is open 24 hours a day year-round; however, snow closes most park roadways October through May and sometimes into early July. Lodging and dining facilities usually are open from late May to mid-October. The park is located in the Pacific Time Zone.

ATMS/BANKS

There's an ATM at the Mazama Camper Store near the park's Annie Spring entrance station. Look for banks in nearby towns.

CELL-PHONE RECEPTION

Cell-phone reception is unreliable in the park, although Verizon carries a reliably good signal along most of the Rim Drive and around Crater Lake Lodge. You'll find public telephones at Steel Information Center, Rim Village, Crater Lake Lodge, and the Mazama Village complex.

PARK CONTACT INFORMATION

Crater Lake National Park ⬨ *P.O. Box 7, Crater Lake, OR 97604* ☏ *541/594–3000* ⊕ *www.nps.gov/crla.*

VISITOR CENTERS

Rim Visitor Center. In summer you can obtain park information here, take a ranger-led tour, or stop into the nearby Sinnott Memorial, with a small museum and a 900-foot view down to the lake's surface. In winter, snowshoe walks are offered on weekends and holidays. The Rim Village Gift Store and cafeteria are the only services open in winter. ⊠ *Rim Dr. on the south side of the lake, 7 mi north of Annie Spring entrance station* ☏ *541/594–3090* ⊕ *www.nps.gov/crla* ☉ *Late May–late Sept., daily 9:30–4:30.*

Steel Information Center. The information center is part of the park's headquarters; you'll find restrooms and a first-aid station here. There's also a small post office and a shop that sells books, maps, and postcards. In the auditorium, an ongoing 18-minute film, *The Mirror of Heaven,* describes Crater Lake's formation. ⊠ *Rim Dr., 4 mi north of Annie Spring entrance station* ☏ *541/594–3100* ⊕ *www.nps.gov/crla* ☉ *Early May–early Nov., daily 9–5; early Nov.–early May, daily 10–4.*

EXPLORING CRATER LAKE NATIONAL PARK

For most visitors, the star attractions of Crater Lake are the lake itself and the breathtakingly situated Crater Lake Lodge. Other park highlights include the natural, unspoiled beauty of the forest and the geological marvels that you can access along the 33-mi Rim Drive.

HISTORIC SITE

Fodor'sChoice
★
Crater Lake Lodge. First built in 1915, this classic log-and-stone structure still boasts the original lodgepole-pine pillars, beams, and stone fireplaces. The lobby, fondly referred to as the Great Hall, serves as a warm, welcoming gathering place, where you can play games, socialize with a cocktail, or gaze out of the many windows to view spectacular sunrises and sunsets by a crackling fire. ⊠ *Rim Village, just east of Rim Visitor Center.*

SCENIC DRIVE

Rim Drive. The 33-mi loop around the lake is the main scenic route, affording views of the lake and its cliffs from every conceivable angle. The drive alone takes up to two hours; frequent stops at overlooks and short hikes can easily stretch this to half a day. Be aware that Rim Drive is typically closed due to heavy snowfall from mid-October to mid-June, and icy conditions can be encountered any month of the year, particularly in early morning. ⊠ *Rim Dr. leads from Annie Spring entrance station to Rim Village, where the drive circles around the rim; it's about 7 mi from the entrance station to Rim Village. To get to Rim*

"The Great Hall" lobby and fireplace at Crater Lake Lodge

Dr. from the park's north entrance, access the north entrance road via either Hwy. 230 or Hwy. 138, and follow it for about 10 mi.

SCENIC STOPS

Cloudcap Overlook. The highest road-access overlook on the Crater Lake rim, Cloudcap has a westward view across the lake to Wizard Island and an eastward view of Mt. Scott, the volcanic cone that is the park's highest point, just 2 mi away. ⊠ *2 mi off Rim Dr., 13 mi northeast of Steel Information Center.*

Discovery Point. This overlook marks the spot at which prospectors first spied the lake in 1853. Wizard Island is just northeast, close to shore. ⊠ *Rim Dr., 1½ mi north of Rim Village.*

Mazama Village. In summer a campground, motor inn, amphitheater, gas station, post office, and small store are open here. ⊠ *Mazama Village Rd., off Hwy. 62, near Annie Spring entrance station* ☎ *541/594–2255 or 888/774–2728* ⊕ *www.nps.gov/crla* ☼ *June–Sept., daily 8–6.*

Phantom Ship Overlook. From this point you can get a close look at Phantom Ship, a rock formation that resembles a schooner with furled masts, and looks ghostly in fog. ⊠ *Rim Dr., 7 mi northeast of Steel Information Center.*

Pinnacles Overlook. Ascending from the banks of Sand and Wheeler creeks, unearthly spires of eroded ash resemble the peaks of fairy-tale castles. Once upon a time, the road continued east to a former entrance. A path now replaces the old road and follows the rim of Sand Creek (affording more views of pinnacles) to where the entrance arch still

CRATER LAKE IN ONE DAY

Begin at **Steel Information Center,** where interpretive displays and a short video introduce you to the story of the lake's formation and its unique characteristics. Then begin your circuit of the crater's rim by heading northeast on **Rim Drive,** allowing an hour to stop at overlooks—check out the Phantom Ship rock formation in the lake—before you reach the **Cleetwood Cove Trail** trailhead, the only safe and legal access to the lake. Hike down the trail to reach the dock, and hop aboard one of the **tour boats** for an almost-two-hour tour around the lake. If you have time, add on a trip to **Wizard Island** for a picnic lunch.

Back on Rim Drive, continue around the lake, stopping at the **Watchman Trail** for a short but steep hike to this peak above the rim, which affords not only a splendid view of the lake, but a broad vista of the surrounding southern Cascades. Wind up your visit at **Crater Lake Lodge**—allow time to wander the lobby of the 1915 structure perched on the rim. Dinner at the lodge restaurant, overlooking the lake and the Cascade sunset, caps the day.

stands. ⊠ *5 mi northeast of Steel Information Center, then 2 mi east on Pinnacles Spur Rd.*

Sun Notch. It's a moderate ¼-mi hike through wildflowers and dry meadow to this overlook, which has views of Crater Lake and Phantom Ship. Mind the cliff edges. ⊠ *Rim Dr., 4.4 mi east of Steel Information Center, east side of the lake.*

Wizard Island. To get here you've got to hike down Cleetwood Cove Trail (and back up upon your return) and board the tour boat for a 1¾-hour ride. Bring a picnic. If you're in top shape, take the very strenuous 2-mi hike to Wizard Summit that leads to a path around the 90-foot deep crater at the top. A more moderate hike is the 1.8-mi trek on a rocky trail along the shore of the island. ⊠ *Via Cleetwood Cove Trail to the Wizard Island dock* ☎ *541/594–2255 or 888/774–2728* ⊕ *www.craterlakelodges.com* ⊗ *Early July–mid-Sept., daily.*

WHERE TO EAT

There are a few casual eateries and convenience stores within the park. For fantastic upscale dining on the caldera's rim, head to the Crater Lake Lodge.

$
AMERICAN
⟳

✕**Annie Creek Restaurant.** It's family-style buffet dining here; pizza and pasta, along with ham and roast beef, are the main features. Breakfast, lunch, and dinner are served. The outdoor seating area is surrounded by towering pine trees. ⊠ *Mazama Village Rd., near Annie Spring entrance station* ☎ *541/594–2255 Ext. 4533* ▭ *AE, D, MC, V* ⊗ *Closed mid-Sept.–early June.*

$$$
AMERICAN
Fodor'sChoice
★

✕**Dining Room at Crater Lake Lodge.** Virtually the only place where you can dine well once you're in the park, the lodge emphasizes fresh, regional Northwest cuisine. The dining room is magnificent, with a large stone fireplace and views of Crater Lake's clear blue waters. Breakfast and lunch are enjoyable here, but the evening menu is the main attraction, with tempting delights such as tarragon-infused wild Alaskan salmon, roasted duck with citrus-chili glaze, filet mignon with a mushroom-merlot sauce, and roasted prime rib of bison. An extensive wine list tops off the gourmet experience. Book well ahead, as far as a week or two in advance for weekends. ⊠ *Crater Lake Lodge, Rim Village, east of Rim Visitor Center* ☎ *541/594–2255 Ext. 3217* ⚔ *Reservations essential* ⊟ *AE, D, MC, V* ☉ *Closed mid-Oct.–mid-May.*

PICNIC AREAS

Rim Drive. About a half-dozen picnic-area turnouts encircle the lake; all have good views, but they can get very windy. Most have pit toilets, and a few have fire grills, but none have running water. ⊠ *Rim Dr.*

Rim Village. This is the only park picnic area with running water. The tables are set behind the visitor center, and most have a view of the lake below. There are flush toilets inside the visitor center. ⊠ *Rim Dr. on the south side of the lake, 7 mi north of Annie Spring entrance station.*

Wizard Island. The park's best picnic spot is Wizard Island; pack a picnic lunch and book yourself on one of the early-morning boat-tour departures, reserving space on an afternoon return. There are no formal picnic areas and just pit toilets, but there are plenty of sunny, protected spots where you can have a quiet meal and appreciate the astounding scene that surrounds you. The island is accessible by boat tour only.

WHERE TO STAY

Crater Lake's summer season is relatively brief, and the park's main lodge is generally booked with guest reservations a year in advance. If you don't snag one, check availability as your trip approaches—cancellations are always possible. Outside the park are limited options in Prospect, and extensive choices in Klamath Falls, Roseburg, Medford, Ashland, and Bend.

Both tent campers and RV enthusiasts will enjoy the heavily wooded and well-equipped setting of Mazama Campground. Drinking water, showers, and laundry facilities help ensure that you don't have to rough it too much. Lost Creek Campground is much smaller, with minimal amenities and a more "rustic" Crater Lake experience.

$ ⛺ **The Cabins at Mazama Village.** In a wooded area 7 mi south of the lake, this complex is made up of several A-frame buildings. Most of the modest rooms have two queen beds and a private bath. These rooms fill up fast, so book early. A convenience store and gas station are nearby in the village. **Pros:** clean and well-kept facility. **Cons:** lots of traffic into adjacent campground, limited in-room amenities. ⊠ *Mazama Village, near Annie Spring entrance station* ☎ *541/594–2255 or 888/774–2728* ⊕ *www.craterlakelodges.com* ↩ *40 rooms* ♿ *In-room: no a/c, no phone, no TV. In-hotel: laundry facilities* ⊟ *AE, D, MC, V* ☉ *Closed mid-Oct.–late May.*

$$$ ⛺ **Crater Lake Lodge.** The period feel of this 1915 lodge on the caldera's rim is reflected in its lodgepole-pine columns, gleaming wood floors, and stone fireplaces in the common areas. With magnificent lake views,

rooms at this popular spot are often booked a year in advance. Plan ahead, as this is the only "in-park" place to stay by the lake. **Pros:** ideal location for watching sunrise and sunset reflected on the lake. **Cons:** difficult to reserve rooms. ⊠ *Rim Village, east of Rim Visitor Center, 1 Lodge Loop Rd., Crater Lake* ☎ *541/594–2255 or 888/774–2728* ⊕ *www.craterlakelodges.com* ⤴ *71 rooms* △ *In-room: no phone, no TV. In-hotel: restaurant* ═ *AE, D, MC, V* ⊘ *Closed mid-Oct.–late May.*

CAMPING   △ **Lost Creek Campground.** The small, remote sites here are available on a ¢ daily basis. In July and August arrive early to secure a spot. Lost Creek is for tent campers only; RVs must stay at Mazama. **Pros:** close to the fossil spires of Pinnacles Overlook. **Cons:** briefly open each summer; no reservations. ⊠ *3 mi south of Rim Rd. on Pinnacles Spur Rd. at Grayback Dr.* ☎ *541/594–3100* △ *16 tent sites* △ *Flush toilets, drinking water, fire grates* ⊘ *Closed early Oct.–mid-July.*

¢   △ **Mazama Campground.** Crater Lake National Park's major visitor accommodation, aside from the famed lodge on the rim, is set well below the lake caldera in the pine and fir forest of the Cascades. Not far from the main access road (Highway 62), it offers convenience more than outdoor serenity—although adjacent hiking trails lead away from the roadside bustle. About half the spaces are pull-throughs, some with electricity; no hookups are available. The best tent spots are on some of the outer loops above Annie Creek Canyon. **Pros:** close to the Annie Spring and Pacific Crest trails. **Cons:** because it's popular, it's a noisy, crowded place during the busiest summer weeks. ⊠ *Mazama Village, near Annie Spring entrance station* ☎ *541/594–2255 or 888/774–2728* ⊕ *www.craterlakelodges.com* △ *212 tent/RV sites* △ *Flush toilets, dump station, drinking water, guest laundry, showers, fire grates, public telephone* ═ *AE, D, MC, V* ⊘ *Mid-June–early Oct.*

OUTSIDE THE PARK

$$ ⛫ **Prospect Historic Hotel Bed and Breakfast.** Noted individuals such as Theodore Roosevelt, Zane Grey, Jack London, and William Jennings Bryan have stayed here (in rooms that now bear their names). Twenty-eight mi southwest of the park entrance on Highway 62, the main house has quaint, country-style guest accommodations. The historic Dinner House restaurant serves hearty pasta, chicken, and the signature prime rib special from May through October. Behind the main house are clean, economical, if rather basic motel units. **Pros:** three waterfalls within walking distance; beautiful, extensive grounds; motel units are very affordable. **Cons:** not much to do in tiny Prospect. ⊠ *391 Mill Creek Dr., Prospect* ☎ *541/560–3664 or 800/944–6490* ⊕ *www. prospecthotel.com* ⤴ *10 main house rooms, 14 motel rooms* △ *In-room: refrigerator (some), Wi-Fi. In-hotel: Wi-Fi hotspot, some pets allowed* ═ *D, DC, MC, V* ⛄ *BP.*

SPORTS AND THE OUTDOORS

FISHING

Fishing is allowed in the lake, but you may find the experience frustrating—in such a massive body of water, the problem is finding the fish. Try your luck near the Cleetwood Cove boat dock, or take poles on the boat tour and fish off Wizard Island. Rainbow trout and kokanee salmon lurk in Crater Lake's aquamarine depths, and some grow to enormous sizes. You don't need a state fishing license, but to protect the lake's pristine waters, use only artificial bait as opposed to live worms. Private boats are prohibited on the lake.

GUIDED TOURS

Boat Tours. The most extensively subscribed guided tours in Crater Lake are on the water, aboard launches that carry 49 passengers on a one-hour, 45-minute tour accompanied by a ranger. The boats circle the lake; two of the seven daily boats stop at Wizard Island, where you can get off and re-board a minimum of three hours later, or six hours later if you catch the morning boat. The first tour leaves the dock at 10 AM; the last departs at 3 PM. To get to the dock, you must hike down Cleetwood Cove Trail, a strenuous 1.1-mi walk that drops 700 feet; only those in excellent physical shape should attempt the hike. Bring adequate water with you. Purchase boat-tour tickets at the top of the trail. Restrooms are available at the top and bottom of the trail. ⊠ *Cleetwood Cove Trail, off Rim Dr., 10 mi north of Rim Village on the north side of the lake* ☎ *541/594–2255 or 888/774–2728* ⊕ *www.craterlakelodges.com* ⊠ *$28; $38 with island drop-off* ☾ *Early July–mid-Sept., daily.*

HIKING

EASY

Castle Crest Wildflower Trail. The 1.4-mi creek-side loop in the upper part of Munson Valley is one of the park's flatter and less demanding hikes. Wildflowers burst into full bloom here in July. ⊠ *Across the street from Steel Information Center parking lot, Rim Dr.*

Godfrey Glen Trail. This 1-mi loop trail is an easy stroll through an old-growth forest with canyon views. Its dirt path is accessible to wheelchairs with assistance. ⊠ *2.4 mi south of Steel Information Center.*

MODERATE

Annie Creek Canyon Trail. This somewhat strenuous 1.7-mi hike loops through a deep stream-cut canyon, providing views of the narrow cleft scarred by volcanic activity. This is a good spot to look for flowers and deer. ⊠ *Mazama Campground, Mazama Village Rd., near Annie Spring entrance station.*

Boundary Springs Trail. If you feel like sleuthing, take this moderate 5-mi round-trip hike to the headwaters of the Rogue River. The trail isn't always well marked, so a detailed trail guide is necessary. You'll see streams, forests, and wildflowers along the way before discovering Boundary Springs pouring out of the side of a low ridge. ⊠ *Pullout on Hwy. 230, near milepost 19, about 5 mi west of the junction with Hwy. 138.*

The Watchman Trail. This is the best short hike in the park. Though it's less than a mile each way, the trail climbs more than 400 feet—not counting the steps up to the actual lookout, which has great views of Wizard Island and the lake. ✉ *Watchman Overlook, 3.8 mi northwest of Rim Village on Rim Dr., west side of the lake.*

DIFFICULT

Cleetwood Cove Trail. This strenuous 2.2-mi round-trip hike descends 700 feet down nearly vertical cliffs along the lake to the boat dock. ✉ *Cleetwood Cove trailhead, Rim Dr., 11 mi north of Rim Village, north side of the lake.*

> **SERIOUS SAFETY**
>
> There is only one safe way to reach Crater Lake's edge: the Cleetwood Cove Trail from the north rim. The rest of the inner caldera is steep and composed of loose gravel, basalt, and pumice—extremely dangerous, in other words. That's why all hiking and climbing are strictly prohibited inside the rim, and rangers will issue citations for violations.

Fodor'sChoice ★ **Mt. Scott Trail.** This 5-mi round-trip trail takes you to the park's highest point—the top of Mt. Scott, Mt. Mazama's oldest volcanic cone, at 8,929 feet. It will take the average hiker 90 minutes to make the steep uphill trek—and nearly 60 minutes to get down. The trail starts at an elevation of about 7,450 feet, so the climb is not extreme, but does get steep in spots. Views of the lake and the broad Klamath Basin are spectacular. ✉ *14 mi east of Steel Information Center on Rim Dr., east side of the lake, across from the road to Cloudcap Overlook.*

Pacific Crest Trail. You can hike a portion of the Pacific Crest Trail, which extends from Mexico to Canada and winds through the park for 33 mi. For this prime backcountry experience, catch the trail off Highway 138 about a mile east of the north entrance road, where it heads toward the west rim of the lake and circles it for about 6 mi, then descends down Dutton Creek to the Mazama Village area. An online brochure offers further details. ✉ *Pacific Crest Trail parking lot, north access road off Hwy. 138, 2 mi east of the Hwy. 138–north entrance road junction* ⊕ *www.nps.gov/crla/planyourvisit/upload/2010 PCT.pdf.*

SOUTHERN OREGON

Updated by Andrew Collins

Southern Oregon begins where the verdant lowlands of the Willamette Valley give way to a complex collision of mountains, rivers, and ravines. The intricate geography of the "Land of Umpqua," as the area around Roseburg is somewhat romantically known, signals that this is territory distinct from neighboring regions to the north, east, and west.

Some locals refer to this sun-kissed, sometimes surprisingly hot landscape as the Mediterranean; others call it Oregon's banana belt. It's a climate built for slow-paced pursuits and a leisurely outlook on life, not to mention agriculture—the region's orchards, farms, and increasingly acclaimed vineyards have lately helped give southern Oregon cachet among food and wine aficionados. The restaurant scene has grown partly thanks to a pair of big cultural draws, Ashland's Oregon

Shakespeare Festival and Jacksonville's open-air, picnic-friendly Britt Festivals concert series.

Roseburg, Medford, and Klamath Falls are also all popular bases for visiting iconic Crater Lake National Park, which lies at the region's eastern edge, about an hour or two away by car.

PLANNING

GETTING HERE AND AROUND

Air Travel. Medford's **Rogue Valley International Airport (MFR)** (☎ *541/772–8068* ⊕ *www.co.jackson.or.us*) is the state's third-largest facility. Most national car-rental branches are at the airport, with rates starting at $25 a day. A few taxi and shuttle companies provide transportation from the airport to other towns in the area; these are used mostly by locals, as a car is the only practical way to explore this mostly rural part of Oregon. The one exception is Ashland, in which many attractions, restaurants, and accommodations are within walking distance. **Cascade Airport Shuttle** (☎ *541/488–1998*) offers door-to-door service from the airport to Ashland for about $30. Among taxi companies, Valley Cab (☎ *541/772–1818*) serves the Rogue Valley region, with fares costing $3 base per trip, plus $2.50 per mile thereafter.

Roseburg is a 75-mi drive from Oregon's second-largest airport, in Eugene (EUG). Ashland is about 300 mi south of the state's largest airport, in Portland; and 350 mi north of San Francisco. Although it's often cheaper to fly into these larger airports than it is to Medford, what you lose in gas costs, time, and inconvenience may outweigh the savings.

Car Travel. Unquestionably, your best way to explore the region is by car, although most of Ashland's key attractions, hotels, and dining are downtown and within walking distance of one another. Interstate 5 runs north–south the length of the Umpqua and Rogue River valleys, linking Roseburg, Grants Pass, Medford, and Ashland. Many regional attractions lie not too far east or west of Interstate 5. Jacksonville is a short drive due west from Medford. Highway 138 winds scenically along the Umpqua River east of Roseburg to the less-visited northern end of Crater Lake National Park. Highway 140 leads from Medford east to Klamath Falls, which you can reach from Bend via U.S. 97

ABOUT THE RESTAURANTS

Southern Oregon's dining scene varies greatly from region to region, with the more tourism-driven and upscale communities of Ashland and Jacksonville leading the way in terms of sophisticated farm-to-table restaurants, hip coffeehouses, and noteworthy bakeries and wine bars. Other larger towns in the valleys, including Roseburg, Grants Pass, and Medford, have grown in culinary stature and variety of late,

FAMILY PICKS

Boat Tour. Climb aboard for a close-up view of Crater Lake.

Annie Creek Restaurant. Feast on a picnic at this eatery's outdoor seating area.

Crater Lake Lodge. Tour this historic inn.

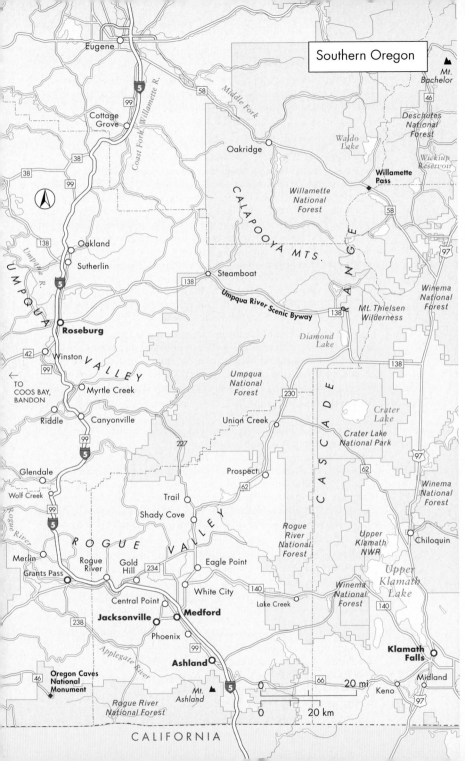

TOP REASONS TO GO

The other wine region. The underrated Umpqua and Rogue River wine regions offer picturesque pastoral views and numerous tasting rooms. The warmer climate and varied terrain makes southern Oregon conducive to many more varietals than the more famous Willamette Valley.

Oregon Shakespeare Festival. This acclaimed festival draws drama lovers to Ashland nine months a year, and presents a wide variety of theater at three distinctive venues.

Quaint towns. Southern Oregon's own throwback to the Old West, Jacksonville abounds with well-preserved buildings, good eateries and B&Bs. Ashland claims one of the prettiest downtowns in Oregon, with its hip cafés and urbane boutiques.

Wild wonders. Each fall more than 1 million waterfowl descend upon Klamath Basin National **Wildlife Refuge Complex.** The Rogue River is Oregon's white water–rafting capital.

while Klamath Falls and Cave Junction have few dining options of note. In the former communities you'll find chefs emphasizing Oregon-produced foods; Oregon wines, including many from the Rogue and Umqua valleys, also find their way onto many menus.

ABOUT THE HOTELS

Ashland has the region's greatest variety of distinctive lodgings, from the usual low- to mid-priced chain properties to plush B&Bs set in restored Arts and Crafts and Victorian houses. Nearby Jacksonville also has several fine, upscale inns. Beyond that, in nearly every town in southern Oregon you'll find two or three interesting B&Bs or small hotels, and in any of the communities along Interstate 5—including Roseburg, Grants Pass, and Medford—a wide variety of chain motels and hotels. Rooms in this part of the state book up earliest in summer, especially on weekends. If you're coming to Ashland or Jacksonville, try to book at least a week or two ahead. Elsewhere, you can usually find a room in a suitable chain property on less than a day's notice.

WHAT IT COSTS IN U.S. DOLLARS					
	¢	$	$$	$$$	$$$$
Restaurants	under $10	$10–$16	$17–$23	$24–$30	over $30
Hotels	under $100	$100–$150	$151–$200	$201–$250	over $250

Restaurant prices are per person, for a main course at dinner. Hotel prices are for two people in a standard double room in high season, excluding tax.

ROSEBURG

73 mi south of Eugene on Interstate 5.

Fishermen the world over hold the name Roseburg sacred. The timber town on the Umpqua River attracts anglers in search of a dozen popular fish species, including bass, brown and brook trout, and chinook, coho, and sockeye salmon. The native steelhead, which makes its run to the sea in the summer, is king of them all.

The north and south branches of the Umpqua River meet up just north of Roseburg. The roads that run parallel to this river provide spectacular views of the falls, and the North Umpqua route also provides access to trails, hot springs, and the Winchester fish ladder. White-water rafting is also popular here, although not to the degree that it is farther south in the Rogue Valley.

About 80 mi west of the northern gateway to Crater Lake National Park and in the Hundred Valleys of the Umpqua, Roseburg produces innovative, well-regarded wines. Wineries are sprouting up throughout the mild, gorgeous farm country around town, mostly within easy reach of Interstate 5.

GETTING HERE

Roseburg is the first large town you'll reach driving south from Eugene on Interstate 5. It's also a main access point into southern Oregon via Highway 138 if you're approaching from the east, either by way of Crater Lake or U.S. 97, which leads down from Bend. And from the Bandon–Coos Bay region of the Oregon Coast, windy but picturesque Highway 42 leads to just south of Roseburg. It's a 75-mi drive north to Eugene's airport, and a 95-mi drive south to Rogue Valley Airport in Medford. Attractions in the region are spread over a large area—a car is a must.

VISITOR INFORMATION

Roseburg Visitors & Convention Bureau (⊠ *410 S.E. Spruce St.* ☎ *541/672–9731 or 800/444–9584* ⊕ *www.visitroseburg.com*).

WINERY

Fodor's Choice **Abacela Vineyards and Winery.** The name derives from an archaic Spanish word meaning "to plant grapevines," and that's exactly what this winery's husband-wife team did not so very long ago. Abacela released its first wine in 1999, and has steadily established itself as one of the state's most acclaimed producers—arguably the best outside the Willamette Valley. Hot-blooded Spanish tempranillo is Abacela's pride and joy, though inky malbec and torrid sangiovese also highlight a repertoire heavy on Mediterranean varietals. ⊠ *12500 Lookingglass Rd.* ☎ *541/679–6642* ⊕ *www.abacela.com* ☉ *Open daily 11–3.*

EXPLORING

Douglas County Museum. One of the best county museums in the state surveys 8,000 years of human activity in the region. The fossil collection is worth a stop, as is the state's second-largest photo collection, numbering more than 24,000 images, some dating to the 1840s. ⊠ *123 Museum Dr.* ☎ *541/957–7007* ⊕ *www.co.douglas.or.us/museum* ✉ *$5* ☉ *Apr.–Sept., daily 10–5; Oct.–Mar., Mon.–Sat. 10–5*

☾ **Wildlife Safari.** Come face to face with some 550 free-roaming animals
Fodor's Choice at the 600-acre drive-through wildlife park. Inhabitants include alligators, bobcats, cougars, gibbons, lions, giraffes, grizzly bears, Tibetan yaks, cheetahs, Siberian tigers, and more than 70 additional species. There's also a petting zoo, a miniature train, and elephant rides. The

Wine production in southern Oregon

admission price includes two same-day drive-throughs. This nonprofit zoological park is a respected research facility with full accreditation from the American Zoo and Aquarium Assocation, with a mission to conserve and protect endangered species through education and breeding programs. ⊠ *1790 Safari Rd., Winston* ☎ *541/679–6761* ⊕ *www. wildlifesafari.net* ⊡ *$18* ⊗ *Apr.–Sept., daily 9–6; Oct.–Mar., daily 10–5.*

WHERE TO EAT AND STAY

$ ✕ **The Mark V.** This cheery corner bar and grill in downtown Roseburg
AMERICAN lends a bit of much-needed urbanity to this workaday downtown. Tall windows look onto the street from the plant-filled, warmly lighted dining room, where a friendly and easygoing staff serves both tapas-size and more substantial fare three meals a day. Try the blackened ahi tuna, clam chowder, and hefty steaks. ⊠ *563 S.E. Main St.* ☎ *541/229–6275* ⊟ *AE, D, MC, V.*

$$ ✕ **Tolly's.** Most folks head to this sweetly nostalgic restaurant in the
AMERICAN center of tiny and historic Oakland—18 mi north of Roseburg—for
Fodor's Choice inexpensive lunch (including exceptionally good burgers) or to enjoy
★ an old-fashioned soda or malt downstairs in the Victorian ice-cream parlor. On weekends, however, you can dine upstairs in the oak- and antiques-filled dining room on deftly prepared creative American cuisine. Try the wood-grilled salmon with a crimini-mustard sauce and herb polenta cake, or filet mignon sourced from Oregon's famed Carlton Farms ranch. There's also an excellent Sunday brunch. ⊠ *115 Locust St., Oakland* ☎ *541/459–3796* ⊕ *www.tollys-restaurant.com* ⊟ *AE, D, MC, V* ⊗ *No dinner Sun.–Thurs.*

$$$ ⛉ **The Steamboat Inn**. Every fall a Who's Who of the world's top fly-
Fodor's Choice   fishermen converges here, high in the Cascades above the emerald North
★   Umpqua River, in search of the 20-pound steelhead that haunt these
waters; guide services are available, as are equipment rentals and sales.
Others come simply to relax in the reading nooks or on the broad decks
of the riverside guest cabins nestled below soaring fir trees and sur-
rounded by verdant gardens. Lodging choices include riverside cabins,
forest bungalows (some sleep up to six), and riverside suites; the bunga-
lows and suites have kitchens. Make reservations well in advance, espe-
cially for a stay between July and October, the prime fishing months.
The exceptionally good restaurant, which offers occasional winemaker
and guest-chef dinners, caters primarily to guests, but also has a limited
number of tables available by reservation. It's also open for breakfast
and lunch to the general public. **Pros:** good option if en route to Cra-
ter Lake; access to some of the best fishing in the West; great escape.
Cons: extremely far from civilization. ✉ *42705 N. Umpqua Hwy., 38
mi east of Roseburg on Hwy. 138, near Steamboat Creek, Steamboat*
☎ *541/498–2230 or 800/840–8825* ⊕ *www.thesteamboatinn.com* 🛏 *8
cabins, 5 cottages, 2 suites, 5 houses* ⚄ *In-room: no a/c, some refrig-
erators, no TV, Wi-Fi. In-hotel: restaurant. some pets allowed (paid)*
🖃 *MC, V.*

SPORTS AND THE OUTDOORS

FISHING   You'll find some of the best river fishing in Oregon along the Umpqua,
with smallmouth bass, shad, steelhead, salmon (coho, chinook, and
sockeye), and sturgeon—the biggest reaching 10 feet in length—among
the most prized catches. In addition to the Steamboat Inn, several out-
fitters in the region provide full guide services, which typically include
all gear, boats, and expert leaders. There's good fishing in this region
year-round, with sturgeon and steelhead at their best during the colder
months, chinook and coho salmon thriving in the fall, and most other
species prolific in spring and summer.

The **Oregon Angler** (☎ *800/428–8585* ⊕ *www.theoregonangler.com*), run
by one of the state's most respected and knowledgeable guides, Todd
Hannah, specializes in jet-boat and drift-boat fishing excursions along
the famed "Umpqua Loop," an 18-mi span of river that's long been
lauded for exceptional fishing. Full-day trips start at $175 per person.

Set along a 10-mi span of the upper Umpqua River near Elkton (about
35 mi north of Roseburg), **Big K Guest Ranch** (☎ *800/390–2445* ⊕ *www.
big-k.com*) is a pastoral 2,500-acre guest ranch. The accommodations
are geared primarily to groups and corporate retreats, but the ranch
offers individual fishing packages starting at $350 per person, per day
(meals and lodging included), with three- and four-night deals available
at a better rate. Adventures include fly-fishing for smallmouth bass and
summer steelhead, as well as spin-casting and drift-boat fishing.

RAFTING   There's thrilling class-III and higher white-water rafting along the North
Umpqua River, with several outfitters providing trips ranging from a
few hours to a few days throughout the year.

Kayaking Rainey Falls on the Rogue River

Since 1987, **North Umpqua Outfitters** (☎ 888/454–9696 ⊕ *www.nuo-rafting.com*) has been a trusted provider of both half- and full-day rafting and kayaking trips along the frothy North Umpqua.

Oregon Ridge & River Excursions (☎ 888/454–9696, ⊕ *www.umpquarivers. com*) offers white-water rafting and kayaking throughout the Umpqua Basin. The company also has milder canoeing adventures on nearby lakes.

GRANTS PASS

70 mi south of Roseburg on I–5.

"It's the Climate!" So says a confident 1950s vintage neon sign presiding over Josephine County's downtown. Grants Pass bills itself as Oregon's white-water capital: the Rogue River, preserved by Congress in 1968 as a National Wild and Scenic River, runs right through town. Downtown Grants Pass is a National Historic District, a stately little enclave of 19th-century brick storefronts housing folksy businesses harking back to the 1950s. It's all that white water, however, that compels most visitors—and not a few moviemakers (*The River Wild* and *Rooster Cogburn* were both filmed here). If the river alone doesn't serve up enough natural drama, the sheer rock walls of nearby Hellgate Canyon rise 250 feet.

GETTING HERE

Grants Pass is easily reached from elsewhere in the region via Interstate 5, and it's also where U.S. 199 cuts southwest toward Oregon Caves National Monument and, eventually, the northernmost section of California's coast (as well as the northern sections of Redwood National

Park). Many visitors to the southern Oregon coastline backtrack inland up U.S. 199 to create a scenic loop drive, ultimately intersecting with Interstate 5 at Grants Pass. Medford's airport is a 30-mi drive away.

VISITOR INFORMATION

Grants Pass Visitors & Convention Bureau (⊠ *1995 N.W. Vine St.,* ☎ *541/476–5510* ⊕ *www.visitgrantspass.org*).

WINERY

Fodor'sChoice **Troon Vineyards.** Few winemakers in southern Oregon have generated ★ more buzz than Troon, whose swank tasting room and winery is patterned after a French country villa. Troon produces relatively small yields of exceptional wines more typical of Sonoma than Oregon (zinfandel, cabernet sauvignon, and syrah are the heavy hitters), but they've lately started planting less typical U.S. varietals, such as primitivo, rousanne, and sangiovese. The winery is 14 mi southeast of downtown Grants Pass, in the northern edge of the Applegate Valley. ⊠ *1475 Kubli Rd.* ☎ *541/846–9900* ⊕ *www.troonvineyard.com.* ⊗ *Jan., weekends 11–5; Feb.–late May and Oct.–Dec., daily 11–5; late May–Sept., daily 11–6.*

WHERE TO EAT AND STAY

$ ✕ **Blondie's Bistro.** Sophisticated but affordable Blondie's serves globally
ECLECTIC inspired food and cocktails in a dapper downtown space with high ceilings and hardwood floors—the lone aesthetic drawback is the sometimes boisterous acoustics. The kitchen, however, prepares first-rate food, including an especially good list of starters, from Portuguese-style steamed clams with herbed sausage to a substantial Mediterranean antipasto platter. Cedar plank–grilled wild coho salmon and the innovative Kung Pao chicken spaghetti rank among the better main courses. Live bands perform some nights. ⊠ *226 S.W. G St.* ☎ *541/479–0420* ⊕ *www. blondiesbistro.com* ⊟ *AE, D, DC, MC, V.*

$ ✕ **Taprock Northwest Grill.** This cavernous family-friendly restaurant
AMERICAN designed to resemble a Cascade mountain lodge lies on the southern edge of downtown, its dining room lined with tall windows overlooking the Rogue River. Expect hearty, reasonably priced fare that uses primarily regional ingredients, including such popular starters as panfried oysters and smoked chicken salad with candied Oregon hazelnuts. Burgers, sandwiches, and heftier main dishes like meatloaf and chicken potpie round out the menu. ⊠ *971 S.E. 6th St.* ☎ *541/955–5998* ⊟ *AE, D, DC, MC, V.*

$ ⌂ **Lodge at Riverside.** The pool and many of the rooms of this airy, contemporary downtown hotel overlook the Rogue River as it passes through the southern end of downtown Grants Pass. The setting is far enough from the bustle for peace and quiet, but still an easy walk to several good restaurants. All but a few rooms have private balconies or patios, and all are furnished with stylish country house–inspired armoires, plush beds, and oil paintings; suites have river-rock fireplaces and Jacuzzi tubs. A complimentary evening wine reception and continental breakfast are served in the log cabin–style lobby, beneath its soaring cathedral ceiling, or on the shaded patio. **Pros:** central location, beautiful modern furnishings, set directly on the Rogue River. **Cons:**

among the highest rates in town, no restaurant on-site. ✉ *955 S.E. 7th St.* ☎ *541/955–0600 or 877/955–0600* ⊕ *www.thelodgeatriverside.com* ⟋ *29 rooms, 4 suites* ♿ *In-room: a/c, Wi-Fi. In-hotel: pool* ⊟ *AE, D, MC, V* ⏐⊚⏐ *CP.*

$$$ ⛨ **Weasku Inn.** Although posh in a country-chic sort of way, the ram-

Fodor's Choice bling Weasku Inn fits in perfectly with its piney surroundings—the ram-

★ bling timber-frame home overlooking the Rogue River was built as a vacation retreat in 1924, and has hosted the likes of Walt Disney, Clark Gable, and Carol Lombard. In 1998 the owners added 11 handsomely outfitted cabins and restored an original A-frame bungalow to create the boutique resort that today ranks among the most luxurious accommodations between Ashland and Eugene. Pacific Northwest–inspired art, handmade furnishings, and fabrics fill the accommodations, which range from smaller doubles in the main lodge to romantic Jacuzzi suites with deep tubs and separate slate-wall walk-in showers. Many units have private decks with rocking chairs overlooking the river. A complimentary wine reception is offered each night. **Pros:** set directly on the Rogue River, impeccably decorated, fireplaces in many rooms. **Cons:** it's a 10-minute drive east of downtown; among the highest rates in the region. ✉ *5560 Rogue River Hwy.* ☎ *541/471–8000 or 800/493–2758* ⊕ *www.weaskuinn.com* ⟋ *5 rooms, 12 cabins* ♿ *In-room: a/c, Wi-Fi* ⊟ *AE, D, MC, V* ⏐⊚⏐ *CP.*

SPORTS AND THE OUTDOORS

RECREATIONAL AREAS **Rogue River and Siskiyou National Forests–Grants Pass.** In the Klamath Mountains and the Coast Range of southwestern Oregon, the 1.8-million-acre forest contains the 35-mi-long Wild and Scenic section of the Rogue River, which races through the Wild Rogue Wilderness Area, and the Illinois and Chetco Wild and Scenic rivers, which run through the 180,000-acre Kalmiopsis Wilderness Area. Activities include white-water rafting, camping, and hiking, but many hiking areas require trail-park passes—check the Web site for details. ✉ *Off U.S. 199* ☎ *541/858–2200* ⊕ *www.fs.fed.us/r6/rogue-siskiyou.*

Fodor's Choice **Valley of the Rogue State Park.** A 1¼-mi hiking trail follows the bank

★ of the Rogue, the river made famous by novelist and fisherman Zane Grey. A campground along 3 mi of shoreline has 88 full hookups ($24), 59 electrical ($24), 21 tent sites ($19), and 6 yurts ($36). There are picnic tables, walking trails, playgrounds, and restrooms. The park is 12 mi east of downtown Grants Pass. *3792 N. River Rd., Gold Hill* ☎ *541/582–1118 or 800/551–6949* ⊕ *www.oregonstateparks.org* ⏲ *Daily.*

RAFTING More than a dozen outfitters guide white-water rafting trips along the

Fodor's Choice Rogue River in and around Grants Pass. In fact, this stretch of class-

★ III rapids ranks among the best in the West. The rafting season lasts from about July through September, and the stretch of river running south from Grants Pass, with some 80 frothy rapids, is exciting but not treacherous, making it ideal for novices, families, and others looking simply to give this enthralling activity a try.

Orange Torpedo Trips (☎ *541/479–5061 or 866/479–5061* ⊕ *www. orangetorpedo.com*) is one of the most reliable operators on the Rogue

River, offering half-day to several-day trips, as well as relaxed dinner-and-wine float trips along a calmer stretch of river.

If you're up for an adventure that combines rafting with overnight accommodations, consider booking a trip with **Rogue River Raft Trips** (☎ 800/826–1963 ⊕ *www.rogueriverraft.com*). The rafting trips run along a 44-mi stretch of the Rogue River and last for four days and three nights, with options for both lodge and camping stays along the way.

MEDFORD

30 mi southeast of Grants Pass on I–5.

Medford is the professional, retail, trade, and service center for eight counties in southern Oregon and northern California. As such, it offers more professional and cultural venues than might be expected for a city of its size. The workaday downtown shows signs of gentrification and rejuvenation in recent years, and in the outskirts you'll find several major shopping centers and the famed fruit and gourmet-food mail-order company Harry & David.

Lodging tends to be cheaper in Medford than in nearby (and easily accessible) Ashland or Jacksonville, although fairly bland chain properties dominate the hotel landscape. But it's 71 mi southwest of Crater Lake and 80 mi northeast of the Oregon Caves, making it an affordable and convenient base for visiting either park.

GETTING HERE

Medford is in the heart of the Rogue Valley on I–5, and is home to the state's third-largest airport, Rogue Valley International. **Valley Cab** (☎ 541/772–1818) serves the Rogue Valley region, with fares costing $3 base per trip, plus $2.50 per mile thereafter. Most attractions in Medford lie outside the downtown area, however, so a cab isn't an especially practical or cost-effective way to explore. Your best option is renting a car.

Medford is the main regional Greyhound hub.

VISITOR INFORMATION

Medford Visitors & Convention Bureau (✉ *101 E. 8th St.* ☎ *541/779–4847 or 800/469–6307* ⊕ *www.visitmedford.org*).

WINERY

EdenVale Winery. Four mi southwest of downtown Medford amid a bucolic patch of fruit orchards, this winery and tasting room, called the Rogue Valley Wine Center, adjoins a rather grand 19th-century white-clapboard farmhouse surrounded by flower beds and vegetable gardens. Inside the tasting room you can sample and buy not only EdenVale's noted reds and late-harvest whites but also other respected labels from vineyards throughout the region. ✉ *2310 Voorhies Rd.* ☎ *541/512–2955* ⊕ *www.edenvalewines.com* ☉ *June–Aug., Mon.–Sat. 10–6, Sun. noon–4; Sept.–May, Mon.–Sat. 11–5, Sun. noon–4*

EXPLORING

Butte Creek Mill. This 1872 water-powered grist mill, which is 12 mi north of Medford, is listed in the National Historic Register and still produces whole-grain food products, which you can buy at the country store here. There's also a modest display of antiques. ✉ *402 Royal Ave. N, Eagle Point* ☎ *541/826–3531* ⊕ *www.buttecreekmill.com* ⌂ *Free* ☉ *Mon.–Sat. 9–5, Sun. 11–5.*

Crater Rock Museum. Jackson County's natural history and collections of the Roxy Ann Gem and Mineral Society are on display at this quirky museum in Central Point (6 mi northwest of Medford). Fossils, petrified wood, fluorescent rocks, and precious minerals from throughout Oregon and elsewhere in the West are included, plus works of glass by renowned artist Dale Chihuly. ✉ *2002 Scenic Ave., Central Point* ☎ *541/664–6081* ⌂ *$4* ☉ *Tues.–Sat. 10–4.*

WHERE TO EAT AND STAY

$$

AMERICAN

✕ **Porters Dining at the Depot.** Set in an opulent 1910 train station, Porters is a favorite spot for special-occasion meals or even just relaxed dinners on a wisteria-shaded patio. The menu features aged-beef steaks, pork tenderloin, rack of lamb, pastas, and fresh seafood. Leave room for the decadent desserts, including a rich bread pudding drizzled with Jack Daniels crème anglaise. The bar is a popular spot for drinks or, during the early- and late-evening happy hours, less expensive fare, such as prime-rib sandwiches and chicken satay with peanut-garlic sauce. ✉ *147 N. Front St.* ☎ *541/857–1910* ⊕ *www.porterstrainstation.com* ⌐ *AE, D, MC, V* ☉ *No lunch.*

$$

ELECTIC

Fodor's Choice

★

✕ **38 Central.** Set inside a handsomely restored 1910 downtown building, this casual yet smartly furnished bistro specializes in comfort-driven fare with notably urbane flourishes. The classic fish-and-chips, for instance, are prepared with fresh local lingcod and battered in a champagne sauce, while "grown up" mac-and-cheese comes with artisan cheddar and Parmesan cheeses and hardwood-smoked bacon. An oft-changing roster of starters, soups, salads, and sides (try haricots verts with shallots) are ideal for sharing. ✉ *38 N. Central Ave.* ☎ *541/776–0038* ⊕ *www.38oncentral.com* ⌐ *AE, D, MC, V* ☉ *No lunch Sat. No dinner Sun.*

$

⌂ **Under the Greenwood Tree.** Regulars at this B&B between Medford and Jacksonville find themselves hard-pressed to decide what they like most: the luxurious and romantic rooms, the stunning 10-acre farm, or the hearty three-course country-style breakfasts. Gigantic old oaks hung with hammocks shade the inn, an 1860s farmhouse exuding genteel charm. There's a manicured 2-acre lawn and a creaky three-story barn for exploring; an outbuilding holds the buckboard wagon that brought the property's original homesteaders westward on the Oregon Trail. The interior is decorated in Renaissance splendor, and all rooms have private baths. Afternoon tea is served. **Pros:** stunning setting amid farm fields and overlooking the Cascades, breakfast will fill you up well into the late afternoon. **Cons:** a few miles southwest of downtown (but en route to Jacksonville); old-fashioned rooms won't appeal to modernists or minimalists. ✉ *3045 Bellinger La.* ☎ *541/776–0000* ⊕ *www.*

greenwoodtree.com ☞ *4 rooms* ⚭ *In-room: a/c, no TV, Wi-Fi. In-hotel: bicycles.* ⊟ *AE, D, MC, V.*

SHOPPING

Famous for their holiday gift baskets, **Harry & David** (⊠ *1314 Center Dr.* ☎ *541/864–2278 or 877/322–8000* ⊕ *www.harryanddavid.com*) is based in Medford and offers hour-long tours of its huge facility on weekdays from 9:15 AM through 1:45 PM. The tours cost $5 per person, but the fee is refunded if you spend a minimum of $35 in the mammoth Harry & David store, great for snagging picnic supplies to carry with you on any winery tour.

Fodor's Choice
★
Just a few miles up the road from Medford in the small and otherwise drab little town of Central Point, you'll find one of the nation's most respected cheesemakers, **Rogue River Creamery** (⊠ *311 N. Front St.* ☎ *541/664–1537 or 866/396–4704* ⊕ www.roguecreamery.com), which was started in 1935 by Italian immigrants. Current owners Cary Bryant and David Gremmels bought the company in 2002, and promptly won one of the highest honors for cheesemaking, the London World Cheese Award. You can purchase any of the company's stellar cheeses here, from Smokey Blue to a lavender-infused cheddar, and you can watch the production through a window on most days. There's a wine-tasting room that carries vintages by a few local vineyards; the best nearby place to enjoy a picnic is the small neighborhood park a few blocks north at Laurel and North 6th streets.

Fodor's Choice
★
Next door to Rogue River Creamery, the artisan chocolatier **Lillie Belle Farms** (⊠ *211 N. Front St.* ☎ *541/664–2815* ⊕ *www.lilliebellefarms. com*) handcrafts outstanding chocolates using local, often organic ingredients. A favorite treat is the Smokey Blue Cheese ganache made with Rogue River blue, but don't overlook the dark-chocolate–marionberry bonbons (made with organic marionberries grown on-site) or the delectable hazelnut chews. Most unusual, however, is the chocolate-covered bacon. Yes, you read that correctly—the bacon is coated in chipotle and brown sugar, hand-dipped in chocolate, and sprinkled with sea salt.

SPORTS AND THE OUTDOORS

RECREATIONAL AREAS
Rogue River and Siskiyou National Forests–Medford. Covering 1.8 million acres, this immense tract of wilderness woodland has fishing, swimming, hiking, and skiing. Motorized vehicles and equipment—even bicycles—are prohibited in the 113,000-acre Sky Lakes Wilderness, south of Crater Lake National Park. Its highest point is the 9,495-foot Mt. McLoughlin. Access to most of the forest is free, but there are fees at some trailheads—check the Web site for details. ⊠ *I–5 to Exit 39, Hwy. 62 to Hwy. 140* ☎ *541/858–2200* ⊕ *www.fs.fed.us/r6/ rogue-siskiyou.*

OFF THE BEATEN PATH
Rogue River Views. Nature lovers who want to see the Rogue River at its loveliest can take a side trip to the Avenue of the Boulders, Mill Creek Falls, and Barr Creek Falls, off Highway 62, near Prospect. Here the wild waters of the upper Rogue foam past volcanic boulders and the dense greenery of the Rogue River National Forest.

You'll find an impressive array of kids' games and recreation at **Rogue Valley Fun Center**, just off Exit 33 of Interstate 5 (about 5 mi north of Medford). Miniature golf, batting cages, a golf driving range, bumper boats, and go-karts are among the offerings, and there's also a video arcade and game room. ⊠ *1A Peninger Rd., Central Point* ☎ *541/664– 4263* ⊕ *www.rvfamilyfuncenter.com.*

FISHING With close access to some of the best freshwater fishing venues in the Northwest, Medford has several companies that lead tours and provide gear. **Carson's Guide Service** (☎ *541/261–3279* ⊕ *carsonsguideservice. com*), based 22 mi north of Medford along Highway 62 (going toward Crater Lake), provides expert instruction and knowledge of many of the area's rivers, including the Rogue, Umpqua, Coquille, and Chetco, as well as several lakes. Steelhead, salmon, shad, and smallmouth bass are the most common catches.

GOLF There are a number of public golf courses in Medford and in nearby surrounding towns. By far the most challenging and best-designed in the area is **Eagle Point Golf Club** (⊠ *100 Eagle Point Dr., Eagle Point* ☎ *541/826–8225* ⊕ *eaglepointgolf.com; 7,099 yds; par 72; greens fees $32–$50*), which is 10 mi northeast of Medford and was designed by legendary golf-course architect Robert Trent Jones Jr.

HIKING One of the best venues for hiking in the Rogue Valley, **Table Rock** (⊠ *Off Fodor's* Choice *Table Rock Rd., Central Point* ☎ *541/618–2200* ⊕ www.blm.gov) com-
★ prises a pair of monolithic rock formations that rise some 700 to 800 feet above the valley floor about 10 mi north of Medford and just a couple of miles north of TouVelle State Park. Operated by a partnership between the Bureau of Land Management and the Nature Conservancy, the Table Rock formations afford panoramic valley views from their summits. You reach Lower Table Rock by way of a moderately challenging 1.75-mi trail, and Upper Table Rock via a shorter (1.25-mi) and less steep route. The trailheads to these formations are a couple of miles apart—just follow the road signs from Table Rock Road, north of TouVelle State Park (reached from Exit 33 of Interstate 5).

RAFTING Medford is close to a number of the region's great white-water rafting rivers, including the famed Rogue River. Both overnight and day trips are offered by several outfitters.

A popular outfitter for guided white-water rafting trips as well as fishing adventures (for salmon and steelhead) throughout the area, Medford's **Rogue Klamath River Adventures** (☎ *541/779–3708 or 800/231–0769,* ⊕ *www.rogueklamath.com*) also offers boating excursions on inflatable kayaks. The company visits a great variety of waterways, from gentle but scenic Class I rivers to wild and exciting Class V rapids.

JACKSONVILLE

5 mi west of Medford on Hwy. 238.

This perfectly preserved town founded in the frenzy of the 1851 gold rush has served as the backdrop for several Western flicks. It's easy to see why. Jacksonville is one of only eight towns corralled into the National Register of Historic Places lock, stock, and barrel. These days, living-history exhibits offering a glimpse of pioneer life and the world-renowned Britt Festivals of classical, jazz, and pop music are the draw, rather than gold. Trails winding up from the town's center lead to the festival amphitheater, mid-19th-century gardens, exotic madrona groves, and an intriguing pioneer cemetery.

GETTING HERE

Most visitors to Jacksonville come by way of Medford, 5 mi east, on Highway 238—it's a scenic drive over hilly farmland and past vineyards. Alternatively, you can reach the town coming the other way on Highway 238, driving southeast from Grants Pass. This similarly beautiful drive through the Applegate Valley takes about 45 minutes. **Valley Cab** (☎ 541/772–1818) serves the Rogue Valley region, with fares costing $3 base per trip, plus $2.50 per mile thereafter. A cab ride from Medford's airport to Jacksonville costs about $20, and downtown Jacksonville can easily be explored on foot. However, if you plan on visiting any of the region's wineries and parks, you're better off renting a car.

VISITOR INFORMATION

Jacksonville Chamber of Commerce & Visitor Center (✉ 185 N. Oregon St. ☎ 541/899–8118 ⊕ www.jacksonvilleoregon.org).

WINERY

Valley View Vineyard. Perched on a bench in the scenic Applegate Valley, you can sample acclaimed chardonnay, viogner, pinot gris, merlot, and cabernet sauvignon while soaking up some of the best views in southern Oregon. The valley's especially sunny, warm climate produces highly acclaimed vintages. Founded in the 1850s by pioneer Peter Britt, the vineyard was reestablished in 1972. A restored pole barn houses the winery and tasting room. ✉ *1000 Upper Applegate Rd., Ruch, 10 mi southwest of Jacksonville* ☎ *541/899–8468 or 800/781–9463* ⊕ *www.valleyviewwinery.com* ☉ *Daily 11–5.*

EXPLORING

Fodor's Choice ★

Jacksonville Cemetery. A trip up the winding road—or, better yet, a hike via the old cart-track marked "Catholic access"—leads to the resting place of the clans (the Britts, the Beekmans, and the Orths) that built Jacksonville. You'll also get a fascinating, if sometimes unattractive, view of the social dynamics of the Old West: older graves (the cemetery is still in use) are strictly segregated, Irish Catholics from Jews from Protestants. A somber granite plinth marks the pauper's field, where those who found themselves on the losing end of gold-rush economics entered eternity anonymously. The cemetery closes at sundown. ✉ *Oregon St.; follow direction signs from downtown.*

Jacksonville Museum. Set inside the old Jackson County Courthouse, this repository of regional memorabilia has intriguing gold rush–era artifacts. The "Jacksonville! Boomtown to Home Town" exhibit lays out the area's history. Inside the 1920 Jackson County Jail, the Children's Museum has hands-on exhibits of pioneer life and a collection of antique toys, and is open by appointment. A special display highlights local resident Pinto Colvig, the original Bozo the Clown, who co-composed "Who's Afraid of the Big Bad Wolf" and was the voice of a Munchkin, Goofy, both Sleepy and Grumpy, and many other animated film characters. ⊠ *206 N. 5th St.* ☎ *541/899–8123* ⊕ *www.sohs.org* ⟹ *$5 for both museums* ☉ *Wed.–Sun. 10–4.*

WHERE TO EAT AND STAY

$
SOUTHERN

✕**Back Porch BBQ.** For an excellent, mid-priced alternative to Jacksonville's several upscale eateries, head to this roadhouse-style clapboard building six blocks northeast of the town's historic main drag. Authentic central Texas–style barbecue is served here: char-grilled red-hot sausage, slow-cooked pork ribs, chicken-fried steak, and ½-pound burgers, plus a few dishes to remind you that you're in Oregon, including wild local salmon baked with Cajun spices. ⊠ *605 N. 5th St.* ☎ *541/899–8821* ⊕ *www.backporchbbqinc.com* ⊟ *D, MC, V.*

$$
ECLECTIC
Fodor'sChoice
★

✕**Gogi's.** Many visitors overlook this small, low-key restaurant just down the hill from Britt Gardens—it's a favorite of foodies and locals, and word seems to be spreading about the artful presentation and innovative style of chef-owner Gabriel Murphy's sophisticated international cuisine. The menu changes regularly, but has featured a tower of roasted beets and chevre topped with toasted walnuts and a balsamic-truffle reduction, followed by grilled pan-smoked pork chop atop a sweet-potato pancake with haricots verts and an orange-zest compound butter. The wine list is small but discerning. If you're in town on a Sunday, do not miss the super brunch. ⊠ *235 W. Main St.* ☎ *541/899–8699* ⊕ *www.gogis.net* ⬦ *Reservations essential* ⊟ *MC, V* ☉ *Closed Mon.– Tues. No lunch Wed.–Sat.*

$$

🍴**Jacksonville Inn.** The spotless period antiques and the host of well-chosen amenities at this 1861-vintage inn evoke what the Wild West might have been had Martha Stewart been in charge. In addition to the main building, the inn includes four larger and more luxurious cottages with fireplaces and saunas. One of the eight rooms in the main inn is named in honor of ubiquitous Jacksonville founding father Peter Britt, while another, the Blanchet Room, honors one of the area's earliest Catholic priests. All have meticulous pioneer-period furnishings. Some rooms and cottages have whirlpool tubs and double steam showers. Complimentary full breakfast is served in the elegant restaurant, which also serves lunch and dinner both to guests and nonguests. The Jacksonville Mercantile gourmet store and wine shop are on the ground floor. **Pros:** in heart of downtown historic district, one of the town's most historically significant buildings, very good restaurant on-site. **Cons:** rather old-fashioned decor for some tastes. ⊠ *175 E. California St.* ☎ *541/899–1900 or 800/321–9344* ⊕ *www.jacksonvilleinn.com* 🛏 *8 rooms, 4 cottages* ⚒ *In-room: a/c, refrigerator, Wi-Fi. In-hotel: restaurant* ⊟ *D, MC, V* ⊚⎮*BP.*

$$
Fodor'sChoice
★

🍴**TouVelle House B&B.** This six-room inn set inside a grand 1916 Craftsman-style home a few blocks north of Jacksonville's tiny commercial strip manages that tricky balance between exquisite and comfy. Museum-quality Arts and Crafts antiques fill the rooms, which include a common library, great room, and sunroom. Innkeepers Gary Renninger Balfour and Tim Balfour have filled the inn with welcoming touches, from CD players and down comforters in the understatedly elegant rooms to a DVD/TV with movie library, refrigerator, and guest computer in the common areas. During the warmer months you can slip

7

into the pool or sauna for a bit of relaxation. **Pros:** situated on a gentle bluff surrounded by beautiful gardens, downtown dining is a 5-minute walk away, knowledgeable and friendly hosts. **Cons:** no TVs or phones in rooms. ✉ *435 N. Oregon St.* ☎ *541/899–8938 or 800/846–8422* ⊕ *www.touvellehouse.com* ➷ *6 rooms* ⚲ *In-room: a/c, Wi-Fi. In-hotel: pool* ⊟ *D, MC, V* ❘◎❘ *BP.*

SHOPPING

Jacksonville's historic downtown has several engaging galleries, boutiques, and gift shops. It's best just to stroll along California Street and its cross streets to get a sense of the retail scene. Drop by the **Jacksonville Company** (✉ *115 W. California St.* ☎ *541/899–8912 or 888/271–1047* ⊕ *www.jacksonvillecompany.com*) to browse the stylish selection of handbags, footwear, and women's apparel. MOTO Denim, Nicole Shoes, and Bernardo Footwear are among the top brands carried here. The **Jacksonville Barn Co.** (✉ *150 S. Oregon St.* ☎ *541/702–0307* ⊕ *www.jacksonvillebarnco.com*) specializes in both antiques and contemporary home decor, from Victorian pieces that have come from many nearby estates to modern garden accessories and country-house furnishings. The racks of **Jacksonville Mercantile** (✉ *120 E. California St.* ☎ *541/899–1047* ⊕ *www.jacksonvillebarnco.com*) abound with gourmet sauces, oils, vinegars, jams, and tapenades. Watch for Chukar chocolate-covered cherries from Seattle's Pike Place Market, and the shop's own private-label merlot-wine jelly.

ASHLAND

20 mi southeast of Jacksonville and 14 mi southeast of Medford on I–5.

As you walk Ashland's twisting hillside streets, it seems like every house is a restored Victorian operating as an upscale B&B, though that's not quite all there is to this town: the Oregon Shakespeare Festival attracts thousands of theater lovers to the Rogue Valley every year, from mid-February to early November (though tourists don't start showing up en masse until June). That influx means that Ashland is more geared toward the arts, more eccentric, and more expensive than its size might suggest. The mix of well-heeled theater tourists, bohemian students from Southern Oregon University, and dramatic show folk imbues the town with some one-of-a-kind cultural frissons. The stage isn't the only show in town—skiing at Mt. Ashland and the town's reputation as a secluded getaway and growing culinary destination keep things hopping year-round.

GETTING HERE

Ashland is the first town you'll reach on Interstate 5 if driving north from California, and it's the southernmost community in this region. You can also get here from Klamath Falls by driving west on winding but dramatic Highway 66. **Cascade Airport Shuttle** (☎ *541/488–1998*) offers door-to-door service from the airport to Ashland for about $30. A car isn't necessary to explore downtown and to get among many of the inns and restaurants, but it is helpful if you're planning to venture farther afield or visit more than one town, which most visitors do.

Ashland's Main Street

VISITOR INFORMATION

Ashland Chamber of Commerce and Visitors Information Center (✉ *110 E. Main St.* ☎ *541/482–3486* ⊕ *www.ashlandchamber.com*).

WINERY

Weisinger's Winery. Although downtown Ashland has wine bars and tasting rooms, the only major winery of note here is Weisinger's, which set up shop in 1988 and is set a few miles south of town on a hilltop with broad views of the surrounding mountains. Specialties here include a semillon-chardonnay blend, a well-respected viogner, and a rich Bordeaux blend called Petite Pompadour. ✉ *3150 Siskiyou Blvd.* ☎ *541/488–5989 or 800/551–WINE* ⊕ *www.weisingers.com* ⊗ *May–Sept., daily 11–5; Oct.–Apr., Wed.–Sun. 11–5.*

EXPLORING

Fodor's Choice ★

Lithia Park. The Elizabethan Theatre overlooks this park, a 93-acre jewel that is Ashland's physical and psychological anchor. The park is named for the town's mineral springs, which supply a water fountain by the band shell as well as a fountain on the town plaza—be warned that the slightly bubbly water has a strong and rather disagreeable taste. Whether thronged with colorful hippie folk and picnickers on a summer evening or buzzing with joggers and dog walkers in the morning, Lithia is a well-used, well-loved, and well-tended spot. On summer weekend mornings the park plays host to a '60s-ish artisans' market. Each June the Oregon Shakespeare Festival opens its outdoor season by hosting the Feast of Will in the park, with music, dancing, bagpipes, and food. Tickets (about $12) are available through the festival box office (☎ *541/482–4331*).

Schneider Museum of Art. At the edge of the Southern Oregon University campus, this museum includes a light-filled gallery devoted to special exhibits by Oregon, West Coast, and international artists. The permanent collection has grown considerably over the years, and includes pre-Columbian ceramics and works by such notables as Alexander Calder, George Inness, and David Alfaro Siqueiros. Hallways and galleries throughout the rest of the 66,000-square-foot complex display many works by students and faculty. ⊠ *1250 Siskiyou Blvd.* ☎ *541/552–6245* ⊕ *www.sou.edu/sma* ⊗ *Mon.–Sat. 10–4* ⊠ *$5.*

WORD OF MOUTH

"In Ashland, there are a number of good restaurants including a micro-brewery and wine bars, and some nice shops as well as a pleasant walk along the stream that runs through the town center. Weekends include an outdoor market of high quality arts and crafts within a few steps of the theater area."   —saige

NEED A BREAK?

Zoey's Cafe (⊠ *199 E. Main St.* ☎ *541/482–4794*) scores high marks for its creative, house-made ice cream in such enticing flavors as mountain blackberry and Rogue Valley pear. The fair-trade, organic beans used in the espresso drinks at **Noble Coffee Roasting** (⊠ *281 4th St.* ☎ *541/488–3288*) are among the best in town.

WHERE TO EAT

$$$
ECLECTIC
Fodor's Choice
★

✕ **Amuse.** This locally celebrated restaurant features Northwest-driven French cuisine, infused with seasonal, organic meat and produce. Chef-owners Erik Brown and Jamie North prepare a daily-changing menu. You might sample wood-grilled white prawns with romesco sauce and fingerling potatoes, or truffle-roasted game hen with green beans and tarragon jus. Try your best to save room for the warm crepes filled with ricotta, honey, and local strawberries. ⊠ *15 N. 1st St.* ☎ *541/488–9000* ⊕ *www.amuserestaurant.com* ⌕ *Reservations essential* ═ *AE, D, MC, V* ⊗ *Closed Mon. and Tues. No lunch.*

$$
FRENCH

✕ **Chateaulin.** One of southern Oregon's most romantic restaurants is in an ivy-covered storefront a block from the Oregon Shakespeare Festival exhibit center, where it dispenses French food, local wine (there's a wine shop attached), and friendly, impeccable service with equal facility. This might be Ashland's most iconic restaurant, the fixed point in a hopping dining scene, where Shakespeare pilgrims return religiously year after year. The menu changes often, but mainstays include the pan-roasted rack of lamb rubbed with cocoa nibs and served with cream corn, a black-trumpet mushroom sauce, and braised spinach, accompanied by a bottle of Oregon pinot noir. But you have to begin with the escargots baked with garlic butter, parsley, and pernod. ⊠ *50 E. Main St.* ☎ *541/482–2264* ⊕ *www.chateaulin.com* ⌕ *Reservations essential* ═ *AE, D, MC, V* ⊗ *Closed Mon. Nov.–May. No lunch.*

$$$
AMERICAN

✕ **Larks.** In this restaurant off the lobby of the historic Ashland Springs Hotel, owners Doug and Becky Neuman are putting their "farm to table" philosophy into practice. Larks pairs the freshest foods from local farms with great wines, artisan-chocolate desserts, and drinks in a relaxing and soothing atmosphere. Modern interpretations of comfort food are the order of the day, with servings such as homemade meatloaf with mushroom gravy, Anniebelle's fried chicken, and maple-glazed pork chops with organic-apple compote and rosemary-roasted sweet potatoes. Dessert offerings include Dagoba chocolate sundaes, s'mores, and cheesecake of the day. The Sunday brunch is one of the best in town. ⊠ *212 E. Main St.* ☎ *541/488–5558* ⊕ *www.larksrestaurant.com* ⊟ *AE, D, MC, V.*

$ ✕**Morning Glory.** Breakfast reaches new heights at this distinctive café across the street from Southern Oregon University. In a blue Crafts-man-style bungalow, the café has eclectic furnishings and an attractive patio space bounded by arbors. The extraordinarily good food empha-sizes breakfast fare—omelets filled with crab, artichokes, Parmesan, and smoked-garlic cream; Tandoori tofu scrambles with cherry-cranberry chutney; lemon-poppy waffles with seasonal berries; and cranberry-hazel-nut French toast with lemon butter. No reservations; first-come, first-served. ⊠ *1149 Siskiyou Blvd.* ☎ *541/488–8636* ⊟ *MC, V* ⊗ *No dinner.*

AMERICAN

Fodor'sChoice

★

WHERE TO STAY

The Oregon Shakespeare Festival has stimulated one of the most exten-sive networks of B&Bs in the country—more than 50 in all. High season for Ashland-area bed-and-breakfasts is between June and October. The **Ashland B&B Network** (☎ *800/944–0329* ⊕ *www.abbnet.com*) provides referrals to roughly 25 of the town's top inns.

$$ 🛏 **Ashland Creek Inn.** Every one of the 10 plush suites in this converted mill has a geographic theme—the Normandy is outfitted with rustic country French prints and furniture, while Moroccan, Danish, and New Mexican motifs are among the designs in other units. Each sit-ting room–bedroom combo has its own entrance, either a full kitchen or kitchenette, and a deck just inches from burbling Ashland Creek. Privacy, space, high-concept elegance, and dynamite breakfast served in an understated central dining room make this well-run place an alterna-tive to up-close-and-personal traditional B&Bs. Downtown shopping, Lithia Park, and the theaters are within an easy walk. **Pros:** exception-ally good breakfasts, peaceful but central location, enormous suites. **Cons:** among the higher rates in the region, limited common areas. ⊠ *70 Water St.* ☎ *541/482–3315* ⊕ *www.ashlandcreekinn.com* ⇱ *10 suites* 🛆 *In-room: a/c, some kitchens, Wi-Fi. In-hotel: some pets allowed (paid)* ⊟ *MC, V* ❚◯❙ *BP.*

$$ 🛏 **Ashland Springs Hotel.** Ashland's stately landmark hotel is a totally restored version of an original 1925 landmark hotel that towers seven stories over the center of downtown. The 70 rooms soothe with a pre-ponderance of gentle fall colors and have work desks and flat-screen TVs. The unconventional decor—French-inspired botanical-print quilts and lampshades with leaf designs—makes for fascinating conversation in itself. The hotel offers theater, sports, and romance packages. A full range of soothing treatments is available at the hotel's adjacent Water-stone Spa. **Pros:** rich with history, upper floors have dazzling moun-tain views, the excellent Larks restaurant (see above) is on-site. **Cons:** Central location translates to some street noise and bustle, rooms are on the small side. ⊠ *212 E. Main St.* ☎ *541/488–1700 or 888/795–4545* ⊕ *www.ashlandspringshotel.com* ⇱ *70 rooms* 🛆 *In-room: a/c,*

7

refrigerator, Wi-Fi. In-hotel: restaurant, room service, bar, spa. ⊟ *AE, D, DC, MC, V* ⏆*CP.*

$$ ⏆**Chanticleer Inn.** This courtly, 1920 Craftsman-style B&B is one of the most picturesque structures in this hilly and historic residential neighborhood just a few blocks south of the Shakespeare theaters and Main Street restaurants. Owners Ellen Campbell and Howie Wilcox have given the rooms a tasteful, contemporary flair with muted, nature-inspired colors and Arts and Crafts furnishings and patterns. You can relax in a fragrant butterfly garden, and in-room massage can be arranged by appointment. Breakfast here is a treat, served communally (although owners are happy to set up a small table in the garden in good weather, if you'd prefer some morning privacy while you dine) and consisting of two courses—almond-pear clafouti and shiitake-sherry frittatas are among the specialties. **Pros:** rooms all have expansive views of the Cascade Mountains, owners use only eco-friendly products. **Cons:** it's intimate and homey, so fans of larger and more anonymous lodgings may prefer a bigger inn or hotel. ⊠ *120 Gresham St.* ☏ *541/482–1919 or 800/898–1950* ⊕ *www.ashland-bed-breakfast.com* ⤴*6 rooms* ⏆ *In-room: a/c, DVD, Wi-Fi. In-hotel: Some pets allowed (paid)* ⊟ *MC, V* ⏆*BP.*

Fodor's Choice
★

$$ ⏆**The Winchester Inn.** This posh yet unpretentious inn is often booked well in advance, so plan ahead. Not only are the meals smashing, the location is smack-dab in the center of Ashland's hopping theater scene. The 11 rooms and 8 suites have character and restful charm—some have fireplaces, refrigerators, and wet bars, and private exterior entrances. Some rooms have a fireplace and refrigerator, with Wi-Fi throughout. Its restaurant relies upon locally grown produce, fresh fish and meats, including liberal use of herbs from its own garden. The breakfasts are works of art (and available to nonguests as well). **Pros:** the adjacent wine bar and restaurant serve very good international fare. **Cons:** among the more expensive lodgings in town. ⊠ *35 S. 2nd St.* ☏ *541/488–1113 or 800/972–4991* ⊕ *www.winchesterinn.com* ⤴*11 rooms, 8 suites* ⏆ *In-room: a/c, some refrigerators, some TVs, Wi-Fi. In-hotel: restaurant, bar* ⏆*BP* ⊟ *AE, D, MC, V.*

NIGHTLIFE AND THE ARTS

With its presence of college students, theater types, and increasing numbers of tourists (many of them fans of local wine), Ashland has developed quite a festive nightlife scene. Much of the activity takes place at bars inside some of downtown's more reputable restaurants, such as Black Sheep and Creekside Pizza.

A good bet for local beers is **Standing Stone Brewing Company** (⊠ *101 Oak St.* ☏ *541/482–2448* ⊕ *www.standingstonebrewing.com*), which has live jazz on the patio and pours some excellent microbrews, including Milk & Honey Ale and Oatmeal Stout. The Nuevo Latino restaurant **Tabu** (⊠ *76 N. Pioneer St.* ☏ *541/482–3900* ⊕ *www.taburestaurant. com*) keeps busy with revelers into the later hours. Live comedy, reggae, salsa, and other entertainment takes place most Thursday through Saturday nights.

Fodor's Choice
★

From mid-February to early November, more than 100,000 Bard-loving fans descend on Ashland for the **Oregon Shakespeare Festival** (✉ *15 S. Pioneer St.* ☎ *541/482–4331* ⊕ *www.osfashland.org*), presented in three theaters. Its accomplished repertory company mounts some of the finest Shakespearean productions you're likely to see on this side of Stratford-upon-Avon—plus works by Ibsen, Williams, and contemporary playwrights. Between June and October plays are staged in the 1,200-seat Elizabethan Theatre, an atmospheric re-creation of the Fortune Theatre in London; the 600-seat Angus Bowmer Theatre, a state-of-the-art facility typically used for five different productions in a single season; and the 350-seat New Theater, which mostly hosts productions of new or experimental work. The festival generally operates close to capacity, so it's important to book ahead.

SHOPPING

Downtown Ashland abounds with galleries and one-of-a-kind shops. A few miles' drive south of town you'll find **Dagoba Organic Chocolate** (✉ *1105 Benson St.* ☎ *866/608–6944* ⊕ *www.dagobachocolate.com*), the retail outlet of the company that produces those small, handsomely packed, super-fine chocolate bars sold in fancy-food shops and groceries throughout the country. Although acquired by the Hershey Company in 2006, Dagoba was founded in Ashland, and its operation remains here, where a small retail shop sells its goods.

SPORTS AND THE OUTDOORS

OUTFITTERS The **Adventure Center** (✉ *40 N. Main St., Ashland* ☎ *541/488–2819 or 800/444–2819* ⊕ *www.raftingtours.com*) books outdoor expeditions in the Ashland region, including white-water rafting, fishing, and bike excursions.

RAFTING **Noah's River Adventures** (☎ *800/858–2811* ⊕ *www.noahsrafting.com*) is one of the most respected outfitters for white-water rafting and wilderness fishing trips in the region—the company can lead single- or multiple-day adventures along the mighty Rogue River as well as just across the border, in northern California, on the Salmon and Scott rivers.

SKIING **Mt. Ashland Ski Area**. This winter-sports playground in the Siskiyou Mountains is halfway between San Francisco and Portland. The ski runs get more than 300 inches of snow each year. There are 23 trails, virtually all of them intermediate and advanced, in addition to chute skiing in a glacial cirque called the Bowl. Two triple and two double chairlifts accommodate a vertical drop of 1,150 feet; the longest of the runs is 1 mi. Facilities include rentals, repairs, instruction, a ski shop, a restaurant, and a bar. Anytime of year the drive up the twisting road to the ski area is incredibly scenic, affording views of 14,162-foot Mt. Shasta, some 90 mi south in California. ✉ *Mt. Ashland Access Rd., 18 mi southwest of downtown Ashland; follow signs 9 mi from I–5 Exit 6* ☎ *541/482–2897* ⊕ *www.mtashland.com* ▨ *Lift ticket $39* ☉ *Nov.–Apr., daily 9–4.*

7

KLAMATH FALLS

65 mi east of Ashland via Hwy. 66, 75 mi east of Medford via Hwy. 140.

Often overlooked by visitors to the region, the greater Klamath Falls area is one of the most beautiful parts of Oregon. The small if not especially engaging city of Klamath Falls stands at an elevation of 4,100 feet, on the southern shore of Upper Klamath Lake. The highest elevation in Klamath County is the peak of Mt. Scott, at 8,926 feet. There are more than 82 lakes and streams in Klamath County, including Upper Klamath Lake, which covers 133 square mi.

The Klamath Basin, with its six national wildlife refuges, hosts the largest wintering concentration of bald eagles in the contiguous United States and the largest concentration of migratory waterfowl on the continent. Each February nature enthusiasts from around the world flock here for the Bald Eagle Conference, the nation's oldest birding festival.

The Nature Conservancy has called the basin a western Everglades, because it is the largest wetland area west of the Mississippi. But humans have significantly damaged the ecosystem through farming and development. More than 25% of vertebrate species in the area are now endangered or threatened. Only 35 years ago about 6 million birds used the area every year, today that number is down to 2 to 3 million. Environmental organizations are working to reverse some of the damage.

GETTING HERE

Klamath Falls lies along U.S. 97, one of the Northwest's main north–south routes—it's a prime stop between Bend, 140 mi north, and Weed, California, about 70 mi south. You can also get here from the Rogue Valley, either by way of Highway 66 from Ashland or Highway 140 from Medford, which is home to the nearest airport (about a 90-min drive).

VISITOR INFORMATION

Klamath County Chamber of Commerce (✉ *205 Riverside Dr.* ☎ *541/884–5193* ⊕ *www.klamath.org*).

EXPLORING

Klamath County Museum. The anthropology, history, geology, and wildlife of the Klamath Basin are explained at this extensive museum set inside the city's historic Armory building, with special attention given to the hardships faced by early white settlers. ✉ *1451 Main St.* ☎ *541/883–4208* ⊕ *www.co.klamath.or.us/museum* 🎟 *$5* ⊘ *Tues.–Sat. 9–5.*

Fodor's Choice **Klamath Basin National Wildlife Refuge Complex.** As many as 1,000 bald
   ★ eagles make Klamath Basin their rest stop, amounting to the largest wintering concentration of these birds in the contiguous United States. Located along the Pacific Flyway bird migration route, the vast acres of freshwater wetlands in the refuge complex—which comprises several different units, some in Oregon and some in California—serve as a stopover for nearly 1 million waterfowl in the fall. Any time of year is bird-watching season; more than 400 species of birds have been spotted in the Klamath Basin. It's best to begin your explorations at the refuge headquarters and visitor center, which are 24 mi south of Klamath Falls and 2 mi south of the California-Oregon border, in Tulelake. Here you

Klamath Basin National Wildlife Refuge

can pick up maps and get advice on other sections of the reserve, including Klamath Marsh, Upper Klamath, and Bear Valley, which are all on the Oregon side. For a leisurely ramble by car, take the tour routes in the Lower Klamath and Tule Lake refuges. ✉ *4009 Hill Rd. (for refuge headquarters and visitor center), 24 mi south of Klamath Falls via U.S. 97 or Hwy. 39, Tulelake, CA* ☎ *530/667–2231* ⊕ *www.fws.gov/ klamathbasinrefuges* ☉ *Weekdays 8–4:30, weekends 9–4.*

WHERE TO EAT AND STAY

$$
AMERICAN

✕ **Basin Martini Bar**. Although the name of this swell-elegant storefront spot in the heart of the downtown historic district suggests an option for evening cocktails, Basin Martini Bar is best known for its reliably tasty dinner fare—New York strip steaks, burgers topped with Crater Lake blue cheese, and bacon-wrapped scallops are among the highlights. There's seating in a handful of comfy booths or at stools along the modern bar. The creative drinks are notable, too—consider the lemon-basil martini. ✉ *632 Main St.* ☎ *541/884–6264* ▭ *AE, D, DC, MC, V* ☉ *No lunch*.

$$
FRENCH

✕ **Mr. B.'s Steakhouse**. The dark-wood dining room in this 1920s house suggests more formal pleasures, but maintains a relaxed mood. A talented French chef prepares tried-and-true classics like chicken Cordon Bleu, chateaubriand, shrimp scampi, veal dishes, and the house specialty, rack of lamb with rosemary and Dijon mustard. Fresh strawberry shortcake often appears on the menu, and there's a good wine list. It's in the unappealing but convenient strip of motels and fast-food restaurants about 2 mi southeast of downtown. ✉ *3927 S. 6th St.* ☎ *541/883–8719*

⊕ *www.mrbssteaks.com* ▭ *AE, D, DC, MC, V* ⊙ *Closed Sun.–Mon. No lunch.*

$ ⛳**Running Y Ranch Resort.** Golfers rave about the Arnold Palmer–
🄲   designed course here, which winds its way through a juniper-and-pon-
Fodor's Choice   derosa–shaded canyon overlooking Upper Klamath Lake. The resort
★   consists of a main lodge and several town-house complexes, with hiking, biking, spa services, ATV rentals, outdoor ice skating, swimming,
horseback riding, sailing, fishing, and wildlife watching the prime activities. A concierge can help arrange a variety of excursions. Rooms in the
lodge are spacious and modern; the two- to five-bedroom town houses
and custom homes have numerous amenities (kitchens, decks, grills,
outdoor hot tubs) and vary greatly in price according to size, with two-
bedroom town houses starting at $230 per night in summer. The prop-
erty has three restaurants, including an upscale steak house and lounge
with bar food. **Pros:** the myriad activities are great for families and outdoorsy types, rates in lodge are quite reasonable. **Cons:** it's a 15-minute
drive to town; those seeking an intimate hideaway won't find it here.
✉ *5500 Running Y Rd., 5 mi north of Klamath Falls* ☎ *541/850–5500
or 877/866–1266* ⊕ *www.runningy.com* ⇨ *82 rooms, 37 town houses*
⟳ *In-room: a/c, refrigerator, Internet. In-hotel: restaurants, bar, golf
course, tennis courts, pools, gym, spa, water sports, bicycles, laundry
service* ▭ *AE, D, DC, MC, V.*

$ ⛳**Thompson's B&B.** Set in a contemporary residential neighborhood on
a bluff high above Upper Lake Klamath, this low-keyed and reasonably
priced B&B has four rooms with simple, modern furnishings. A full
breakfast is served in the great room, with soaring windows overlooking
the lake. Guests can come and go through a separate exterior entrance,
which leads through a common room with a microwave and fridge
stocked with drinks. Just down the hill, Moore Park has a marina, tennis courts, fishing, and hiking. **Pros:** great lake views from two rooms,
relaxed alternative to downtown's uninteresting motel strip. **Cons:** cash
only, a 10-minute drive from downtown; homey personality may not
suit everybody. ✉ *1420 Wild Plum Court* ☎ *541/882–7938* ⊕ *www.
thompsonsbandb.com* ⇨ *4 rooms* ⟳ *In-room: a/c, Wi-Fi* ▭ *No credit
cards* ⧆ *BP.*

SPORTS AND THE OUTDOORS

OUTFITTERS   For advice, gear, clothing, books, and maps for hiking, birding, mountaineering, canoeing, camping, and fishing throughout the area, visit
The Ledge Outdoor Store (✉ *369 S. 6th St.* ☎ *541/882–5586* ⊕ *www.
theledgeoutdoorstore.com*) in downtown Klamath Falls. This well-
stocked store carries all kinds of equipment, and also offers guided
fly-fishing trips.

RECREATIONAL   **Winema National Forest.** Twelve miles north of Klamath Falls, the forest
AREAS   covers 2.3 million acres on the eastern slopes of the Cascades. It borders
Crater Lake National Park. Hiking, camping, fishing, and boating are
popular. In winter snowmobiling and cross-country skiing are available. ✉ *U.S. 97* ☎ *541/883–6714* ⊕ *www.fs.fed.us/r6/frewin* ⊙ *Daily;
campgrounds and picnic areas Memorial Day–Labor Day.*

BOATING For a chance to enjoy the beauty of Klamath Lake while also observing the region's abundant birdlife, consider a trip led by **Birding & Boating** (☎ 541/885–5450 ⊕ *www.birdingandboating.com*), which offers guided sailing tours of the lake with expert guidance on spotting wildlife. Fishing trips are also offered, and you can also rent canoes or kayaks and paddle around the lake on your own.

FISHING **Roe Outfitters Flyway Shop** (✉ *9349 U.S. 97 S* ☎ *541/884–3825* ⊕ *www.roeoutfitters.com*) leads fishing and hunting trips on nearby lakes and rivers. Also offered are guided canoe and white-water rafting excursions.

GOLF The outstanding Arnold Palmer–designed 18-hole course at **Running Y Ranch** (✉ *5115 Running Y Rd., 5 mi north of Klamath Falls* ☎ *541/850–5500 or 888/850–0275* ⊕ *wwww.runningy.com* ▭ *$50–$99 (discount for hotel guests* 6,581 yds. Par 72) delights golfers of all abilities. Ponderosa pines line the relatively short, undulating course, which is heavy on doglegs and has a number of holes in which water comes into play. There's also an 18-hole putting course that's ideal for honing your short game, and fun for families.

CAVE JUNCTION

30 mi southwest of Grants Pass via U.S. 199, 60 mi west of Jacksonville via Hwy. 238 and U.S. 199.

One of the least populated and most pristine parts of southern Oregon, the town of Cave Junction and the surrounding Illinois Valley attract outdoors enthusiasts of all kinds for hiking, backpacking, camping, fishing, and hunting. Expect rugged terrain and the chance to view some of the tallest Douglas fir trees in the state. Other than those passing through en route from Grants Pass to the northern California coast via U.S. 199, most visitors come here to visit the Oregon Caves National Monument, one of the world's only marble caves (formed by erosion from acidic rainwater). Sleepy Cave Junction makes an engaging little base camp, its main drag lined with a handful of quirky shops, short-order restaurants, and gas stations.

GETTING HERE

Cave Junction lies along U.S. 199, the main road leading from Grants Pass. You can also reach Cave Junction by heading west from Jacksonville on Hwy. 238 to U.S. 199. From Cave Junction, head east on Highway 46 to reach Oregon Caves National Monument. Cave Junction is a about a 75-minute drive southwest of Medford's regional airport. Alternatively, the small airport (served by United Airlines) in Crescent City, California, is the same distance.

VISITOR INFORMATION

Illinois Valley Chamber of Commerce (✉ *201 Caves Hwy., Cave Junction* ☎ *541/592–3326 or 541/592–4076* ⊕ *www.cavejunction.com*).

WINERY

Bridgeview Vineyard and Winery. The producers of the increasingly well-distributed and reasonably priced Blue Moon wines (known especially for Riesling, chardonnay, pinot gris, and merlot), as well as more premium vintages such as Black Beauty Syrah and a very nice reserve pinot noir, established the winery in 1986, and—despite considerable skepticism from observers—have gone on to tremendous success. ✉ *4210 Holland Loop Rd.* ☎ *541/592–4688 or 877/273–4843* 🌐 *www.bridgeviewwine.com* ⏲ *Daily 11–5.*

EXPLORING

Oregon Caves National Monument. The "Marble Halls of Oregon," high in the verdant Siskiyou Mountains, have enchanted visitors since 1874. Huge stalagmites and stalactites, the Ghost Room, Paradise Lost, and the River Styx are part of a ½-mi subterranean tour that lasts about 90 minutes. The tour includes more than 200 stairs, and is not recommended for anyone who experiences difficulty walking or has respiratory or coronary problems. The temperature inside the cave is 44°F (7°C) year-round. Be sure to wear warm clothing and comfortable closed-toe walking shoes. Children over six must be at least 42 inches tall and pass a safety and ability test, because they cannot be carried. ✉ *Hwy. 46, 20 mi southeast of Cave Junction* ☎ *541/592–2100* 🌐 *www.nps.gov/orca* 🎫 *$8.50* ⏲ *Tours: late Mar.–late Nov., hours vary.*

WHERE TO STAY

$ **Oregon Caves Chateau.** If you're looking for a quiet retreat in an unusual place, consider this six-story wood-frame lodge on the grounds of the national monument. Virtually unchanged since it was built in 1934, it has a rustic authenticity and steep gabled roofs. Rooms, all with their original furnishings, have canyon or waterfall views—the bare walls, old-fashioned radiators, and simple bedding are part of the charm. The dining room serves decent regional fare, using local wines, produce, and even buffalo from a nearby ranch. **Pros:** steps from national monument, historic and funky personality, wonderfully tranquil setting. **Cons:** no-frills rooms, no Internet or phones; location well out of the way if you aren't visiting the caves. ✉ *20000 Caves Hwy.* ☎ *541/592–3400 or 877/245–9022* 🌐 *www.oregoncaveschateau.com* *23 rooms* *In-room: no phone, no a/c, no TV. In-hotel: restaurant* 💳 *MC, V* ⏲ *Closed mid-Oct.–mid May.*

$$ **Out 'n' About.** You sleep among the leaves in the tree houses of this extraordinary resort—the highest is 37 feet from the ground. One has an antique claw-foot bath; another has separate kids' quarters connected to the main room by a swinging bridge. Other units have stained-glass windows, sleeping lofts, and other quirky features. There is also an earthbound cabin with a view of the old-growth forest. The least expensive units don't have bathrooms—guests use the common facilities, which also include a game area, fire pit, and common kitchen. **Pros:** kids love the Swiss Family Robinson atmosphere; it truly feels at one with the surrounding old-growth forest; amazingly quiet and peaceful. **Cons:** accommodations are extremely rustic, some units don't have bathrooms, 2-night minimum during week and 3-night minimum weekends during spring–fall. ✉ *300 Page Creek Rd.* ☎ *541/592–2208* 🌐 *www.treehouses.com* *15 tree houses, 1 cabin* *In-room: no phone, kitchen (some), no TV, Wi-Fi (some). In-hotel: laundry facilities* 💳 *MC, V* 🍽 *BP in spring–fall, CP winter.*

Eastern Oregon

WORD OF MOUTH

Joseph is a cute artsy town that has bronze foundries that you can tour. There is also the Wallowa Lake Tramway that takes you up above the lake. The views and hikes up above are beautiful. This area is where many of the scenes from the movie *Homeward Bound* were filmed.

—BarbAnn

WELCOME TO EASTERN OREGON

TOP REASONS TO GO

★ **Wallowa wonder.** The usually snowcapped peaks of the Wallowa Range ornament one of the West's most overlooked alpine playgrounds, with Wallowa Lake resting at its base.

★ **Time travel.** See architecture from Oregon's mining-era heyday in Baker City's authentically restored downtown, where a short walking tour takes you past more than 100 historic buildings.

★ **For the birds.** Visit countless feathered friends at the ruggedly idyllic Malheur National Wildlife Refuge.

★ **Let 'er buck.** Pendleton's famous rodeo attracts 50,000 people every September, but the cowboy mystique sticks around all year.

★ **Canyon country.** Oregon doesn't get more remote than along the wild and scenic Owyhee River or among the fascinating formations at Leslie Gulch. Only serious adventurers need apply.

1 East Gorge. The high plains around Umatilla and Pendleton are the heart of Oregon's ranching and agricultural communities. "Let 'er Buck!" is the rallying cry at the hugely popular Pendleton Round-Up rodeo, a phrase that sets the tone for the whole region's rootin', tootin' vibe.

2 Northeast Oregon. The superlative Wallowa and Blue mountains dominate this corner of the state. The peaks that once presented formidable obstacles to Oregon Trail pioneers now attract bands of hikers, mountain bikers, and other adventure types. In former frontier towns like Joseph and Baker City, old-school ranchers and cowboys mingle with a swelling population of artists, craftsmen, and foodies.

3 Southeast Oregon. The sprawling, scrubby ranchlands of Oregon's high desert country have a beauty all their own, and give way when you least expect it to majestic river canyons and stunning vistas. Food and lodging can be scarce out here, but outdoor enthusiasts will be rewarded with great campsites, serene hot springs, and small-town hospitality.

GETTING ORIENTED

At its eastern end, Oregon begins in a high, sage-scented desert plateau that covers nearly two-thirds of the state's 96,000 square miles. To the north, the border with Washington follows the Columbia River, then stretches eastward across the Colombia River Plateau to meet the Snake River, itself forming much of the state's eastern border with Idaho. East-central Oregon is carved out by the forks and tributaries of the John Day River, the country's third-largest undammed waterway. Its south–north course to the Columbia marks an invisible line extending southward, separating eastern Oregon from central Oregon's high plateaus and Cascades foothills. To the south, the Nevada border is an invisible line slicing through a high, desolate country sometimes known as the Oregon outback.

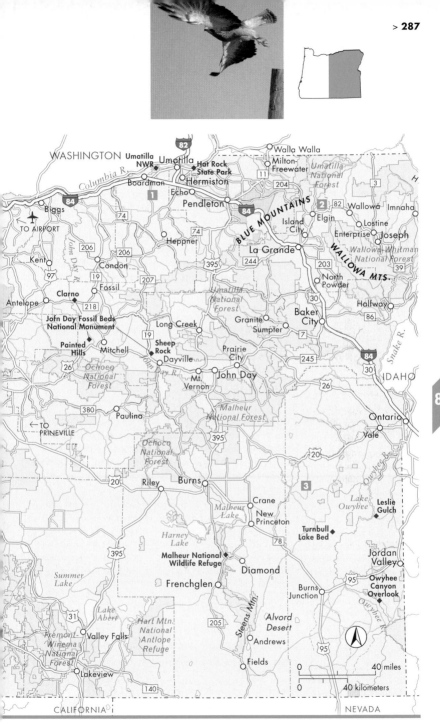

WASHINGTON

Columbia R.

I-82

Umatilla NWR

Umatilla

Hat Rock State Park

Walla Walla

Milton-Freewater

Umatilla National Forest

11

204

3

I-84

Biggs

TO AIRPORT

Boardman

Echo

Hermiston

Pendleton

I-84

BLUE MOUNTAINS

2

82

Wallowa

Imnaha

Elgin

Island City

Lostine

H

74

74

Heppner

395

La Grande

244

Enterprise

Joseph

Wallowa-Whitman National Forest

WALLOWA MTS.

39

Kent

206

206

Condon

19

207

North Powder

203

97

Fossil

Umatilla National Forest

30

Clarno

218

Antelope

John Day Fossil Beds National Monument

Long Creek

Granite

Sumpter

Baker City

Halfway

86

Painted Hills

Mitchell

19

Sheep Rock

Dayville

Prairie City

7

245

I-84

30

IDAHO

Snake R.

26

Mt. Vernon

John Day

Ochoco National Forest

380

Paulina

Malheur National Forest

26

Ontario

8

TO PRINEVILLE

Ochoco National Forest

395

Vale

Owyhee R.

20

Riley

Burns

3

Crane

Lake Owyhee

Leslie Gulch

Malheur Lake

New Princeton

Turnbull Lake Bed

Jordan Valley

Summer Lake

Harney Lake

78

395

Malheur National Wildlife Refuge

Diamond

Burns Junction

Owyhee Canyon Overlook

Owyhee R.

95

Frenchglen

31

Lake Abert

Hart Mtn. National Antelope Refuge

205

Steens Mtn.

Alvord Desert

95

Fremont-Winema National Forest

Valley Falls

Andrews

0   40 miles

Lakeview

Fields

0   40 kilometers

140

CALIFORNIA

NEVADA

EASTERN OREGON PLANNER

When to Go

Though skiers and snowboarders flock to the Blues and the Wallowas in winter, summer is eastern Oregon's primary travel season. It comes late in the state's northeast corner, where snow can remain on the mountains until July, and May flurries aren't uncommon at lower elevations. July and August are the best months for wildflowers in the high northeast, and they're also the only months when many remote-but-scenic Forest Service roads are guaranteed to be open. For visitors in the southeast, though, midsummer is often uncomfortably hot and dry, and avian action along the Pacific Flyway tends to peak around April and September.

Summer temps in northeast Oregon generally level out in the 80s around July and August. In mid-winter, 20-degree days are the norm. The deserts of southeastern Oregon are a bit warmer. Midsummer sees highs in the upper 90s, while January and February can remain in the 40s in the low country. Bear in mind: Elevation varies greatly in eastern Oregon, and this can render seasonal averages pretty meaningless. It's not uncommon to gain or lose several thousand feet during the course of an hour's drive, and for much of the year this can mean the difference between flip-flops and snow boots.

About the Restaurants

Gourmet cuisine and chef-driven restaurants are rare on the eastern Oregon range, but it's not hard to find a tasty, authentic meal if you know where to look. Restaurants around the Wallowas, in particular, have a burgeoning local/organic ethos—locally grown produce abounds, farmers' markets are a big draw, and the rural county even has its own Slow Food chapter.

Elsewhere in the high desert, an entrenched ranching culture means big eating: farm-boy breakfasts and steak house after spur-jangling steak house. Generations of braceros have left their mark on the region's culinary scene as well, and excellent taquerias can be found in even the dustiest ranch towns. Pack a lunch if you're touring the southeasternmost corner of the state—towns are few and far between.

About the Hotels

Chain hotels are easy to find along the gorge and in bigger towns like Baker City and Burns, but elsewhere small motels and B&Bs are more typical. Properties described as "rustic" or "historic" aren't kidding around—a lot of the region's lodging hasn't seen a renovation since the Eisenhower administration.

Triple-digit rates are an anomaly in eastern Oregon, and you'd have to work pretty hard to spend more than $150 on a night's lodging. In summer, book early in no-stoplight towns like Diamond and Frenchglen, where the handful of available rooms fill up fast. Much of eastern Oregon shuts down in the off-season, so don't count on winter lodging without calling first.

WHAT IT COSTS IN U.S. DOLLARS					
	¢	$	$$	$$$	$$$$
Restaurants	under $10	$10–$16	$17–$23	$24–$30	over $30
Hotels		under $100	$100–$150	$151–$200	$201–$250	over $250

Restaurant prices are per person, for a main course at dinner. Hotel prices are for two people in a standard double room in high season, excluding tax.

Getting Here and Around

Air Travel. Eastern Oregon Regional Airport at Pendleton (☎ 541/276–7754) receives daily flights from Portland and Seattle on SeaPort Airlines. Hertz Rental Car or **Elite Taxis** (☎ 541/276–8294) can get you into the city. Across the Washington border, **Tri-Cities Airport** (☎ 509/547–6352) is just 30 miles from Umatilla. Rental cars are available from most national agencies. Depending on where you're headed, check flights into Boise, ID (an hour from the Eastern Oregon border), Spokane, WA (three hours from the northern border), and Elko, NV (three hours from the southern border).

Bus Travel. Many of the cities in eastern Oregon can be reached by **Greyhound** (☎ 800/231–2222 ⊕ www.greyhound.com) or by a smaller, regional bus line, but bear in mind that once you get there public transportation is usually not available, and not all cities have car-rental outlets. Also, most area bus routes operate only once or twice a day, and some don't run on weekends.

The major Greyhound route travels along I–84, passing through Pendleton, La Grande, Baker City, and Ontario. A bus operated by **Porter Stage Lines** (☎ 541/269–7183) runs daily from Ontario to Coos Bay on the coast, with stops at Burns, Vale, Bend, Eugene, and elsewhere. A shuttle bus called the **People Mover** (☎ 541/575–2370) runs round-trip on Mondays, Wednesdays, and Fridays between John Day and Bend, where it connects with the **Central Oregon Breeze** bus line to Portland.

Car Travel. The vast majority of travelers in eastern Oregon get around by car. I–84 runs east along the Columbia River and dips down to Pendleton, La Grande, Baker City, and Ontario. U.S. 26 heads east from Prineville through the Ochoco National Forest, passing the three units of the John Day Fossil Beds. U.S. 20 travels southeast from Bend in central Oregon to Burns. U.S. 20 and U.S. 26 both head west into Oregon from Idaho.

In all these areas, equip yourself with chains for winter driving. Four-wheel drive is beneficial, if not essential, on a lot of eastern Oregon's designated Scenic Byways. Plan ahead for gas, since service stations can be few and far between. They often close early in small towns, and because drivers in Oregon can't legally pump their own gas, you'll be out of luck until morning.

Rental cars are available from Hertz at the Pendleton airport, and Sunray Auto in Ontario.

Local Agencies Sunray Auto Rentals (☎ 541/881–1383).

Top Festivals

Bronze, Blues & Brews. The title of Joseph's mid-August outdoor suds fest pretty much says it all. (⊕ www.bronzebluesbrews.com).
Pendleton Round-Up. This mid-September cowboy throwdown is the biggest one around. Saddle up for country music, flea markets, and plenty of bronc-ridin'. (⊕ www.pendletonroundup.com).

Tour Options

Hells Canyon Adventures (☎ 800/422–358 ⊕ www.hellscanyonadventures.com) leads full- and half-day jet-boat tours of the country's deepest gorge. **Jenkins Historical Tours** (☎ 888/493–2420 ⊕ www.roundbarn.net) are chatty, full-day van tours to the Steens Mountain and the Malheur National Wildlife Refuge areas.

VISITOR INFORMATION

Eastern Oregon Visitors Association (☎ 800/332–1843 ⊕ www.eova.com).

8

Updated by
Brian Kevin

Travel east from the Dalles, Bend, or any of the foothill communities blossoming in the shade of the Cascades, and you'll find a very different side of Oregon. The air is drier, clearer, often pungent with the smell of juniper. The vast landscape of sharply folded hills, wheat fields, and mountains shimmering in the distance evokes the mythic Old West. There is a lonely grandeur in eastern Oregon, a plain-spoken, independent spirit that can startle, surprise, and enthrall.

Much of eastern Oregon consists of national forest and wilderness, and the population runs the gamut from spur-janglin' cowboys to back-to-the-landers and urban expats. This is a world of ranches and rodeos, pickup trucks and country-western music. For the outdoor-adventure crowd, it's one of the West's last comparatively undiscovered playgrounds.

Some of the most important moments in Oregon's history took place in the towns of northeastern Oregon. The Oregon Trail passed through this corner of the state, winding through the Grande Ronde Valley between the Wallowa and Blue mountain ranges. The discovery of gold in the region in the 1860s sparked a second invasion of settlers, eventually leading to the displacement of the Native American Nez Perce and Paiute tribes. Pendleton, La Grande, and Baker City were all beneficiaries of the gold fever that swept through the area. Yet signs of even earlier times have survived, from the John Day Fossil Beds, with fragments of saber-toothed tigers, giant pigs, and three-toed horses, to Native American writings and artifacts hidden within canyon walls in Malheur County's Leslie Gulch.

Recreation and tourism are gaining a foothold in eastern Oregon today, but the region still sees only a fraction of the visitors that drop in on Mt. Hood or the coast each year. For off-the-beaten-path types, eastern Oregon's mountains and high desert country are as breathtaking as any landscape in the West, and you'd be pretty hard-pressed to get farther from the noise and distractions of city life.

EAST GORGE

Heading east along the interstate through the beige flats and monoculture croplands between Umatilla and Pendleton, you could be forgiven for supposing that the most interesting part of Oregon was behind you. But just off the beaten path in the East Gorge country are seasonal wetlands chock-full of avian wildlife, roadside relics of the Old West, and dusty frontier towns undergoing commercial rebirths. Parks like Hat Rock State Park offer boaters and anglers access to the vast Columbia River Gorge, one of the country's most impressive waterways. A few dozen miles away in Pendleton, one of the world's largest and oldest rodeos anchors a town with an unexpectedly hip dining and shopping scene. Look south and east to where the river plateau gives way to the forested foothills of the Blue Mountains—mule deer and bighorn sheep dot those hills in spots like the McKay Creek National Wildlife Refuge and Umatilla National Forest.

UMATILLA

180 mi east of Portland on I–84 and Hwy. 730; 40 mi northwest of Pendleton.

Umatilla is at the confluence of the Umatilla and Columbia rivers. It was founded in the mid-1800s as a trade and shipping center during the gold rush, and today is a center for fishing activities. Just east of Umatilla, Hat Rock State Park contains the unusual geological formation from which it gets its name. Farther upstream, McNary Dam generates extensive hydroelectric power and impounds a lake that extends from Umatilla to Richland, Washington, some 70 mi away. Umatilla is primarily a crossroads, but visitors crossing the Columbia here will appreciate the recreation opportunities along the massive river's banks.

GETTING HERE

Find Umatilla where I–82 crosses the Colombia River Gorge at the Washington-Oregon border. Commercial flights land at the Tri-Cities Airport in Pasco, Washington, 30 mi north on I–82, or in Pendleton's Eastern Oregon Regional Airport. From Portland, drive 165 mi east on I–84, then take a scenic, 15-mile shortcut along the gorge on Highway 730. It's a 40-mile trip from Pendleton, heading west on I–84, then cutting through Hermiston on Highway 395.

VISITOR INFORMATION

Umatilla Chamber of Commerce (✉ *100 Cline Ave.* ☎ *541/922–4825* ⊕ *www. umatillachamber.com*).

WHERE TO EAT AND STAY

$ ✕ **Desert River Inn Restaurant**. "Homemade clam chowder every day" AMERICAN is the claim of this casual and family-friendly spot serving breakfast, ☻ lunch, and dinner. Prime rib is a favorite at night. With large booths and pastel walls, the room's atmosphere is family-restaurant generic, but a meal here is a satisfying addition to a day of exploring. ✉ *705 Willamette Ave.* ☎ *541/922–1000 or 877/922–1500* ▭ *AE, D, MC, V.*

8

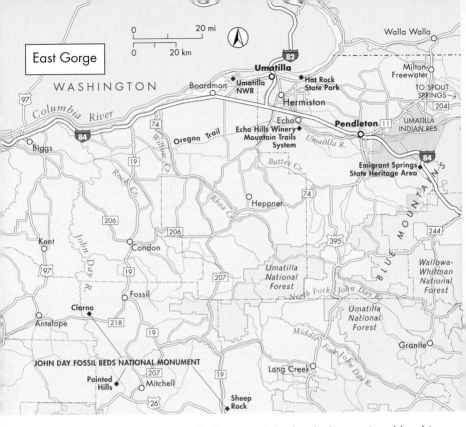

¢ 🖼 **Desert River Inn**. The largest and, by far, the best-equipped hotel in Umatilla, the Desert River Inn acts as the centerpiece of the town, with its restaurant, golf course, and banquet rooms making it more than just a place to spend the night. The rooms are large and comfortable, and there is a host of extras available, including Pasco & Hermiston airport pickup on request. **Pros:** some rooms have kitchenettes; horseshoe pits get a lot of action in the summer. **Cons:** not within walking distance into downtown. ⊠ *705 Willamette Ave.* ☎ *541/922–1000 or 877/922–1500* ⊕ *www.desertriverinn.com* ⤺ *66 rooms* ⌂ *In-room: kitchen (some), refrigerator, Wi-Fi, a/c. In-hotel: restaurant, room service, bar, golf course, pool, gym, pets allowed (fee)* ═ *AE, D, MC, V* ⑩ *CP.*

SPORTS AND THE OUTDOORS

RECREATIONAL AREAS

Hat Rock State Park. On the south shore of Lake Wallula, a 70-foot basalt rock is the first major landmark that Lewis and Clark passed on their expedition down the Columbia. In his notations, William Clark called it "Hat Rock," and the name stuck. Standing tall amid rolling sagebrush hills, it overlooks Lake Wallula, a popular spot for jet skiing, swimming, boating, and fishing for rainbow trout, walleye, and sturgeon. In addition to water sports, the park provides scenic picnic spots and expansive views of the stark, desertlike landscape. But because it abuts an upscale lakeside housing development that's visible from some portions of the park, it might be a challenge to pretend you're back in the days of Lewis and Clark. ✉ *U.S. 730, 9 mi. east of Umatilla, 82375 C St., Hermiston* ☎ *800/551–6949* ⊕ *www.oregonstateparks. org* 🖅 *Free* ☉ *Dawn–dusk year-round.*

Umatilla National Wildlife Refuge. The 23,555-acre refuge includes marsh, woodland, and wetland habitats that make it vital to migrating waterfowl and bald eagles, in addition to myriad species of resident wildlife. Although there are numerous routes to access portions of the refuge, the best and easiest way to view wildlife in ponds and wetlands is to drive along the McCormick Auto Tour Route, accessible from Paterson Ferry Road, off Route 730, 9 mi west of Umatilla. ✉ *Stretches from Boardman, 20 mi west of Umatilla, to Irrigon, 9 mi west of Umatilla, north of I–84 along Columbia River* ☎ *509/546–8300* ⊕ *www.fws.gov/ Umatilla* 🖅 *Free* ☉ *Daily dawn–dusk on designated roadways only.*

PENDLETON

210 mi east of Portland, 130 mi east of The Dalles on I–84.

At the foot of the Blue Mountains amid waving wheat fields and cattle ranches, Pendleton is a quintessential western town with a rip-snorting history. It was originally acquired in a swap for a couple of horses, and the town's history of wild behavior was evident from the first city ordinance, which outlawed public drunkenness, fights, and shooting off one's guns within the city limits. But Pendleton is also the land of the Umatilla Tribe—the herds of wild horses that once thundered across this rolling landscape were at the center of the area's early Native American culture. Later Pendleton became an important pioneer junction and home to a sizable Chinese community. Today's cityscape still carries the vestiges of yesteryear, with many of its century-old homes still standing, from simple farmhouses to stately Queen Annes.

Given its raucous past teeming with cattle rustlers, saloons, and bordellos, the largest city in eastern Oregon (population 17,500) looks unusually sedate. But all that changes in September when the **Pendleton Round-Up** *(⇨ Sports & the Outdoors)* draws thousands.

GETTING HERE

Pendleton has the region's only airport, the Eastern Oregon Regional Airport, which has incoming and outgoing flights daily on SeaPort Air to Portland and Seattle. Pendleton is located right on I–84 and is serviced by Greyhound.

VISITOR INFORMATION

Pendleton Chamber of Commerce (✉ *501 S. Main St.* ☎ *541/246–7411 or 800/547–9811* ⊕ *www.pendletonchamber.com).*

EXPLORING

Fodor's Choice ★ **Pendleton Underground Tours.** This 90-minute tour transports you below ground and back through Pendleton's history of gambling, girls, and gold. Originating in 1989, the Underground Tours depict town life from more than a century ago (when 32 saloons and 18 brothels were operating in full swing) to the 1953 closure of the "Cozy Rooms," the best-known bordello in town. The Underground Tour

8

eventually resurfaces, climbing the "31 Steps to Heaven" to those Cozy Rooms, where madam Stella Darby reigned. The secret gambling lairs, opium dens, and bathhouses that lie directly below the pavement will give you a whole new perspective of the streets of Pendleton. ⊠ *37 S.W. Emigrant Ave.* ☏ *541/276–0730 or 800/226–6398* ⊕ *www. pendletonundergroundtours.com* ☏ *$15* ⊘ *year-round, reservations necessary.*

Pendleton Woolen Mills. Perhaps Pendleton's main source of name-recognition in the country today comes from this mill, home of the trademark wool plaid shirts and colorful woolen Indian blankets. If you want to know more about the weaving process, the company gives 20-minute tours 4 times daily. The mill's retail store stocks blankets and clothing; there are good bargains on factory seconds. ⊠ *1307 S.E. Court Pl.* ☏ *541/276–6911 or 800/568–3156* ⊕ *www.pendleton-usa. com* ⊘ *Mon.–Sat. 8–6, Sun. 9–5; tours weekdays at 9, 11, 1:30, and 3.*

NEED A BREAK? A popular laid-back spot across from the Underground Tours, the **Cookie Tree** (⊠ **39 S.W. Emigrant Ave.** ☏ **541/278–0343**) is good for a quick breakfast, sandwich, pastry, or fresh bread.

WHERE TO EAT AND STAY

¢ AMERICAN ✕ **The Prodigal Son.** This is one of the newest brewpub entries in eastern Oregon's ambitious bid to catch up with the rest of this ale-obsessed state. A cavernous former car dealership (think Model Ts) houses this oh-so-hip hangout, complete with leather couches, tabletop Pac-Man, and a mini-library. The strong, malty house porter is a hit with young locals, and the menu sticks to tasty pub-food classics: fish-and-chips, Reubens, and scotch eggs. ⊠ *230 S.E. Court Ave.* ☏ *541/276–6090* ⊕ *www.prodigalsonbrewery.com* ▭ *MC, V.*

$$$ NEW AMERICAN ✕ **Raphael's.** Is it a restaurant—or a millionaire's seven-gabled home? It's both! The 1904 Raley House was sold and converted in 1991 to its current gastronomic glory, where art deco meets Native American cultural sensibilities. Husband/co-owner/chef Rob Hoffman is crazy for huckleberries—you might find them integrated in the Indian salmon, the pastas, chicken, or wild game (elk, pheasant, buffalo), as well as the crème brûlée. If you'd rather drink your berries, consider Raphael's signature huckleberry martinis and daiquiris. When chef Rob's not using huckleberries, he might mingle apples in his smoked prime rib, or apricots in a pork loin sauce. In sunnier months, consider dining alfresco in the garden out back. ⊠ *233 S.E. 4th St.* ☏ *541/276–8500 or 888/944–2433* ⊕ *www.raphaelsrestaurant.com* ▭ *AE, D, DC, MC, V* ⊘ *Closed Sun. and Mon. No lunch.*

¢ Fodor'sChoice ★ ▭ **Working Girls Hotel.** From boardinghouse to bordello to hotel, the refurbished 1890s edifice advertises it's "Old West Comfort" with a large vertical sign hanging from the top of the building. A redheaded lass looks down from the top of the sign, as if wanting to call to potential customers passing by. Exposed brick walls and 18-foot ceilings run throughout, but the individual Victorian antiques that decorate the rooms give them all their own personalities. Owned and operated by the Underground Tours, the inn has a full kitchen and dining room available to guests, and with no lobby or front office, you'll feel

Pendleton Underground Tours

more like you're renting a historic downtown apartment than booking a hotel room. **Pros:** centrally located in downtown Pendleton, fun decor, great prices. **Cons:** bathrooms in the hall instead of the room, no on-site reception. ✉ *17 S.W. Emigrant Ave.* ☎ *541/276–0730 or 800/226–6398* 🌐 *www.pendletonundergroundtours.com* *4 rooms with 2 shared baths, 1 suite* *In-room: a/c, no phone, no TV (some), no kids under 14* *MC, V.*

SPORTS AND THE OUTDOORS

RECREATIONAL AREAS

Emigrant Springs State Heritage Area. Near the summit of the Blue Mountains, this park in an old-growth forest is the site of a popular pioneer stopover along the Oregon Trail. The park has picnic areas, hiking trails, historical information, and gathering spaces for special events. At the campground, in addition to 18 full hookups and 32 tent sites, there are seven rustic cabins, including two totem cabins. ✉ *Off I–84 at Exit 234, 65068, Old Oregon Trail, Meacham* ☎ *541/983–2277 or 800/551–6949* 🌐 *www.oregonstateparks.org* *Day use free* *Year-round.*

Umatilla National Forest. Three rugged, secluded wilderness areas attract backpackers to this 1.4-million-acre forest: the Wenaha-Tucannon, the North Fork Umatilla, and the North Fork John Day. "Umatilla" is derived from a word in the indigenous Shahaptian language meaning "water rippling over sand," and the forest has its share of fishable rivers and streams as well. Home to the Blue Mountain Scenic Byway and 22 campgrounds, the diverse forestland is found both east and south of Pendleton, and extends south almost as far as John Day, where it borders the Malheur National Forest. To the east it is bordered by the Wallowa-Whitman National Forest. Major thoroughfares through the forest include I-84, U.S. 395, and Routes 204 and 244. ✉ *Forest Headquarters: 2517 S.W. Hailey Ave.* ☎ *541/278-3716* ⊕ *www.fs.fed. us/r6/uma* ✍ *Northwest Forest Pass required at some trailheads, $5/ day or $30 annual.*

RODEO **Pendleton Round-Up.** More than 50,000 people roll into town during the ㋡ second full week in September for one of the oldest and most prominent rodeos in the United States. With its famous slogan of "Let 'Er Buck," the Round-Up features eight days of parades, races, beauty contests, and children's rodeos, culminating in four days of rodeo events. Vendors line the length of Court Avenue and Main Street, selling beadwork and curios, while country bands twang in the background. ✉ *Rodeo grounds: 1205 S.W. Court Ave., at S.W. 12th St.* ✉ *Office, open year-round: 1114 S.W. Court Ave.* ☎ *541/276-2553 or 800/457-6336* ⊕ *www.pendletonroundup.com.*

SKIING **Spout Springs.** This ski resort in the Umatilla National Forest has an elevation of 4,950 feet at the base, 5,550 feet at the top, and a vertical drop of 550 feet. There are 11 runs and 21 km of Nordic trails, as well as a terrain park and large freestyle tubing hill. ✉ *Summit of Hwy. 204 at Tollgate, Milepost 22; 79327 Highway 204, Weston* ☎ *541/566-0320* ⊕ *www.spoutspringsskiresort.com* ✍ *$30 adult.*

SHOPPING

Bella Buck Leather Co. Though it shares space with a traditional tackle shop, this boutique puts a New West, punk-a-billy spin on frilly leather goods. Think skulls and mudflaps, ladies. ✉ *224 S.E. Court Ave.* ☎ *541/410-4023.*

Hamley & Co. Western Store & Custom Saddlery. On-site craftspeople at this Western superstore fashion hand-tooled saddles considered among the best in the world. You'll also find authentic cowboy/cowgirl gear and quality leather products, plus gifts and art. Bonus: in 2007 Hamley's opened a huge steak house on-site for lunch, dinner, and drinks. ✉ *30 S.E. Court Ave.* ☎ *541/278-1100 or 877/342-6539* ⊕ *www.hamley.com.*

NORTHEAST OREGON

No part of eastern Oregon repudiates the region's reputation for flat and barren landscapes quite like its lush and mountainous northeast corner. Simply put, the Wallowa Mountains are among the most underrated outdoor-rec hot spots in the Rockies, with 565 square miles of backpacker-friendly wilderness, abundant wildlife, and proximity to Hells Canyon, North America's deepest gorge. The nearby Blue Mountains are no slouches either, home to some of the state's best alpine and Nordic skiing. Towns like Baker City, Joseph, and La Grande have transitioned more thoroughly than much of the region from pastoral and extractive economies to hospitality and recreation, making them eastern Oregon's de facto capitals of art, food, and culture. Each city has a vibrant downtown and a chillbilly vibe, and you'll find locals swapping

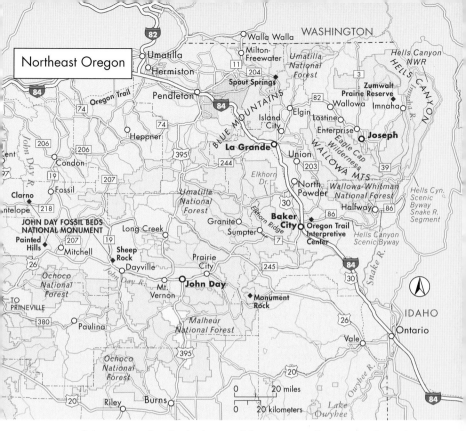

fish stories and trail tales in one of the area's excellent brewpubs. Baker City in particular has maintained its mining-era integrity—the restored Geiser Grand Hotel is a must-visit, especially for history buffs.

LA GRANDE

56 mi southeast of Pendleton on I–84 at Hwy. 82.

La Grande started life in the late 1800s as a farming community. It grew slowly while most towns along the Blue Mountains were booming or busting in the violent throes of gold-fueled stampedes. When the railroad companies were deciding where to lay their tracks through the valley, a clever local farmer donated 150 acres to ensure that the Iron Horse would run through La Grande. With steam power fueling a new boom, the town quickly outgrew its neighbors, took the title of county seat from fading Union City (Union City claims it "was robbed"), and with its current population of 12 thousand sits at the urban center of the Grand Ronde Valley. Though you can appreciate it for its own charms, La Grande is a convenient stop if you're heading to the nearby Wallowa Mountains.

GETTING HERE

La Grande sits at the intersection of I–84 and Highway 82, the primary route through the Wallowa Valley to Joseph and Enterprise. Cars and buses will get you into town from Portland, 260 mi west, and Boise, Idaho, 170 mi east. The closest airport is Eastern Oregon Regional, 50 mi northeast in Pendleton. The **Wallowa Link Bus** (☎ *541/963–2877* ⊕ *www.neotransit.org*) runs twice a week between La Grande and Joseph, stopping in Enterprise. The **Baker Bow** shuttle bus (☎ *541/963– 2877* ⊕ *www.neotransit.org*) runs Monday–Friday to Baker City and Haines. **Greyhound** also makes stops here.

VISITOR INFORMATION

La Grande Visitor Center (✉ *102 Elm St.* ☎ *541/963–8588 or 800/848–9969* ⊕ *www.visitlagrande.com*).

EXPLORING

Union's National Historic District. Fourteen miles southeast of La Grande is a Victorian-era town that's working to restore many of its historic buildings. In addition to the picturesque buildings lining Union's Main Street, the main attractions are the **Union Hotel** (✉ *326 N. Main St.* ☎ *541/562–6135* ⊕ *www.theunionhotel.com* ⇨ *Where to Stay and Eat*), a beautifully restored hotel with a restaurant and parlor, and the **Union County Museum** (✉ *331 S. Main St.* ☎ *541/562–6003* 🗐 *$4* ⊗ *mid-May–mid-Oct., Mon.–Sat. 10–4, or by appointment*), which has a fascinating exhibit on the Ku Klux Klan in Oregon, among other things.

NEED A BREAK?

If you want to remain an anonymous tourist, don't visit **Joe and Sugar's** (✉ *1119 Adams Ave.* ☎ *541/975–5282*). You can't avoid being chatted up by the funny, friendly, and helpful owner of this sweet-smelling café and coffee shop.

WHERE TO EAT AND STAY

$$$
NEW AMERICAN

✕**Foley Station.** This local favorite has an antique pressed-tin ceiling, an open kitchen, exposed-brick walls, and high-backed, rich wood-paneled booths. The snazzy bar has multiple happy hours, namely "Martinis & Munchies In The Lounge" 3–5 and 8–closing. The seasonal menu wanders from inexpensive burgers to high-end lobsters and steaks, incorporating Northwest ingredients as well as a pronounced Southwestern flair, and hush puppies with jalapeño jelly keep company with Vietnamese spring rolls. There's a full bar, with wines, microbrews, and a decent selection of after-dinner ports. Brunch starts at 9 AM on Sundays, and it's worth coming early for creative Benedicts (think pork loin and ahi tuna). ✉ *1114 Adams Ave.* ☎ *541/963–7473* ⊕ *www.foleystation. com* 🗖 *D, MC, V.*

$$$
AMERICAN

✕**Ten Depot St.** In a stylish historic brick building that has a VFW upstairs, Ten Depot St. has everything from burgers to nicely prepared steak and seafood dishes. With dark wood throughout accented by plum tablecloths and teal plates and napkins, it's an elegant place to dine. Start off your evening with a drink at the adjoining bar. ✉ *10 Depot St.* ☎ *541/963–8766* ⊕ *www.tendepotstreet.com* 🗖 *AE, MC, V* ⊗ *Closed Sun. No lunch.*

Wallowa Mountains

ç 🏨 **The Historic Union Hotel**. Cast-iron Victorian lampposts frame the entrance to this three-story, redbrick building, its white trim standing out against the red like icing on a cake. The Union Hotel, about 14 mi south of La Grande, offers 16 elegant, individually themed rooms. The forest-green Northwest Room has a kitchenette and a jetted tub for two; the Davis Bros.' Room comes with a wood-paneled shower with double showerheads; and for large parties up to 6, the Huffman Suite has a full kitchen. Per owners Dave and Rob, the best part of the hotel is "the guests." **Pros:** great prices, visual/historic treat, owners go out of their way to accommodate, RV spots. **Cons:** no TV, phones, Internet; front view of a trailer park doesn't impress. ✉ *326 N. Main St., Union* ☎ *541/562–6135* ⊕ *www.theunionhotel.com* ⤳ *16 rooms; RV accommodations, 8 spaces, for $25/night* ♨ *In-room: no phone, no TV, a/c. In-hotel: restaurant, parking (free), some pets allowed (fee), kids under 9 discouraged* ▭ *D, MC, V.*

SHOPPING

Sunflower Books, Etc. This unassuming yellow bungalow has been a cozy indie bookstore and coffeeshop for more than two decades. Find cookbooks in the kitchen and coffee-table books in the living room, then grab some shade-grown joe in the dining room before sitting down to use the free Wi-Fi. ✉ *1114 Washington Ave.* ☎ *541/963–5242* ⊕ *www. sunflowerbookstore.com.*

SPORTS AND THE OUTDOORS

RECREATIONAL AREAS **Eagle Cap Wilderness.** At more than 350,000 acres, this is the largest wilderness in Oregon, encompassing most of the Wallowa range with 534 mi of trails for hard-core backpackers and horseback riders. Most of the popular trailheads are along Eagle Cap's northern edge, accessible from Enterprise or Joseph, but you also can find several trailheads 20 to 30 mi southeast of La Grande along Route 203. (Some areas of the wilderness are accessible year-round, while the high-elevation areas are accessible only for a few months in summer.) To park at many trailheads you must purchase a Northwest Forest Pass for $5 per day, or $30 per year. To hike into the wilderness, you also need to get a free permit that will alert rangers of your plans. ⊠ *East of La Grande, via Hwy. 82 and Hwy. 203. Wallowa Mountains Visitor Center: 115 Tejaka Ln., off Hwy. 82, Enterprise* ☎ *541/426–4978* ⊕ *www.fs.fed.us/r6/w-w.*

Fodor'sChoice **Wallowa Mountains.** Forming a rugged U-shape fortress between Hells
★ Canyon on the Idaho border and the Blue Mountains, the Wallowas are sometimes called the American Alps or Little Switzerland. The granite peaks in this range are between 5,000 and 9,000 feet in height. Dotted with crystalline alpine lakes and meadows, rushing rivers, and thickly forested valleys that fall between the mountain ridges, the Wallowas have a grandeur that can take your breath away. Bighorn sheep, elk, deer, and mountain goats populate the area. Nearly all the trails in the Wallowa Mountains are at least partially contained within the Eagle Cap Wilderness. The offices and visitor center for the mountains are in Enterprise, but La Grande makes a good base for exploring both sides of the range. ⊠ *Wallowa Mountains Visitor Center: 115 Tejaka Ln., off Hwy. 82, Enterprise* ☎ *541/426–4978* ⊕ *www.fs.fed.us/r6/w-w.*

JOSEPH

80 mi east of La Grande on Hwy. 82.

The area around Wallowa Lake was the traditional home of the Nez Perce Indians—the town of Joseph is named for Chief Joseph, their famous leader. The peaks of the Wallowa Mountains, snow-covered until July, tower 5,000 feet above the regional tourist hubs of the town. Joseph itself isn't much more than a nice Main Street speckled with shops and cafés. Follow Main Street a mile out of town, though, to reach the gorgeous Wallowa Lake, where you'll find a whole separate hospitality village of rental cabins, outfitters, go-karts, and ice-cream stands. The busy area on the south end of the lake is also the site of two of the most popular access points for the mountains, the Wallowa Lake trailhead and the Wallowa Lake Tramway.

GETTING HERE

Highway 82 ends at Joseph, which is reachable primarily by car (or private plane at the town's postage-stamp airport). The **Wallowa Link Bus** (☎ *541/963–2877* ⊕ *www.neotransit.org*) runs twice weekly to and from La Grande, with a stop in Enterprise.

Main Street bisects tiny Joseph, then bends around Wallowa Lake to reach the tourism village on the south shore. In the summer a **shuttle bus** runs throughout the day between Joseph, Enterprise, and the south end of the lake (☎ *541/426–3840*).

Teepees overlooking Joseph Canyon

VISITOR INFORMATION

Joseph Chamber of Commerce (✉ *Kiosk at Main St. & Joseph Ave.* ☎ *541/432–1015* ⊕ *www.josephoregon.com*).

EXPLORING

Wallowa Lake Tramway. The steepest tram in North America rises 3,700 feet in 15 minutes, rushing you up to the top of 8,150-foot Mt. Howard. Vistas of mountain peaks, forest, and Wallowa Lake far below will dazzle you, both on the way up and at the summit. Early and late in the season, two and a half miles of cross-country skiing trails await at the top, and the interpretive trails are open for hiking during the snowless months of midsummer. Enjoy casual lunch with great views at the Summit Grill and Alpine Patio before making your return trip back down to earth. ✉ *59919 Wallowa Lake Hwy.* ☎ *541/432–5331* ⊕ *www.wallowalaketramway.com* 💲 *$24* ⊙ *May–Sept., daily 10–4; Oct. 11–3. Tram runs sporadically in winter.*

SCENIC ROUTE

Wallowa Mountain Loop. This is a relatively easy way to take in the natural splendor of the Eagle Cap Wilderness and reach Baker City without backtracking to La Grande. The 3-hour trip from Joseph to Baker City, designated the Hells Canyon Scenic Byway, winds through the national forest and part of Hells Canyon Recreation Area, passing over forested mountains, creeks, and rivers. Before you travel the loop, check with the Forest Service about road conditions; the route can be impassable when snowed over. ✉ *From Joseph, take Hwy. 350 east for 8 mi, turn south onto*

Forest Service Rd. 39, and continue until it meets Hwy. 86, which winds past town of Halfway to Baker City ⊕ www.fs.fed.us/r6/w-w/recreation/ byway/byway-hc.shtml.

WHERE TO EAT AND STAY

¢ ✕ **Terminal Gravity Brew Pub**. Beer connoisseurs from across the state,

AMERICAN and just about all the locals, rave about the India Pale Ale at this tiny

Fodor'sChoice microbrewery in a canary-yellow house six miles north of Joseph in

★ Enterprise. Aspens wave on a front yard dotted with picnic tables, and kids and dogs lounge on the wooden front porch. Between the indoor customers strumming guitars and outdoor customers playing volleyball, it can't just be about the hops at this friendly local hangout. The menu is short and simple, with creative sandwiches and burgers. There's a rotating selection of house-brewed beers on tap, complete with seasonals. The suds stack up favorably against the gazillion beers brewed over in Portland, but it's the vibe that really sells this place. ⊠ *803 S.E. School St., Enterprise* ☎ *541/426–3000* ⊕ *www.terminalgravitybrewing.com* ▭ *MC, V* ⊗ *Closed Sun.–Tues. No lunch.*

$ ✕ **Vali's Alpine Restaurant**. This Wallowa Lake institution serves a rotat-

EASTERN ing, single-entrée menu of classic Hungarian dishes like cabbage rolls

EUROPEAN and goulash. Drop in before 11 AM weekends for the out-of-this-world homemade donuts. ⊠ *59811 Wallowa Lake Hwy.* ☎ *541/432–5691* ⊕ *www.valisrestaurant.com* ⌂ *Reservations required* ▭ *No credit cards* ⊗ *Closed Labor Day–March. No lunch.*

$$ ⊞ **Wallowa Lake Lodge**. At this friendly 1920s lodge, handmade replicas of the structure's original furniture fill a large common area with a massive fireplace. The lodge's rooms are simple yet appealing; the grandest have balconies facing the lake. The cabins, some with fireplaces and lake views, are small, old-fashioned havens of knotty pine. The on-site restaurant serves standard American fare for breakfast, lunch, and dinner. **Pros:** affordable; visual/historical treat; owners go out of their way to accommodate. **Cons:** no TV, phones, Internet. ⊠ *60060 Wallowa Lake Hwy., Wallowa Lake* ☎ *541/432–9821* ⊕ *www.wallowalake.com* ⤵ *22 rooms, 8 cabins* ⌂ *In-room: no phone, no TV, Wi-Fi. In-hotel: restaurant, bar* ▭ *D, MC, V* ⊗ *Closed mid-Sept.–Memorial Day.*

SPORTS AND THE OUTDOORS

RECREATIONAL **Wallowa Lake**. A few miles south of Joseph proper on Highway 351 (or

AREAS the Wallowa Lake Highway), sparkling, blue-green Wallowa Lake is the highest body of water in eastern Oregon (elevation 5,000 feet). Boating and fishing are popular, and the lake supports a whole vacation village on its southern end, complete with cabins, restaurants, and mini-golf. ⊠ *Wallowa Lake Hwy.*

Wallowa Lake State Park. On the south shore of Wallowa Lake is a campground surrounded on three sides by 9,000-foot-tall snowcapped mountains. If you'd rather lose elevation than gain it, Hells Canyon is just 30 miles east. The park campground has 121 full hookups, 89 tent sites, a 2-story cabin (sleeps 8), and 2 yurts. Popular activities include fishing and powerboating on the adjacent Wallowa Lake, plus hiking on wilderness trails, horseback riding, and canoeing. Nearby are bumper boats, miniature golf, and the tramway to the top of Mt.

Howard. ⊠ *Off Hwy. 82, 6 mi south of Joseph, 72214 Marina La.*
☎ *541/432–4185 or 800/551–6949* ⊕ *www.oregonstateparks.org* ⊠ *$5
per vehicle* ☉ *Daily.*

RAFTING AND **Winding Waters River Expeditions.** Experienced river guides lead white-water
BOATING rafting and kayaking trips on the Snake River and the nearby Grande
Ronde River. ☎ *877/426–7238* ⊕ *www.windingwatersrafting.com.*

Wallowa Lake Marina Inc. From May to mid-September, rent paddleboats,
motorboats, rowboats, and canoes by the hour or by the day. ⊠ *Wallowa
Lake, south end* ☎ *541/432–9115* ⊕ *www.wallowalakemarina.com.*

HELLS CANYON

Fodor's Choice *30 mi northeast of Joseph on Route 350.*
★ This remote place along the Snake River is the deepest river-carved
gorge in North America (7,900 feet), with many rare and endangered
animal species. There are three different routes from which to view
and experience the canyon, though only one is accessible year-round.

Most travelers take a scenic peek from the overlook on the 45-mi **Wallowa Mountain Loop,** which follows Route 39 (part of the Hells Canyon
National Scenic Byway) from just east of Halfway on Route 86 to just
east of Joseph on Route 350. At the junction of Route 39 and Forest
Road 3965, take the 6-mi round-trip spur to the 5,400-foot-high rim
at Hells Canyon Overlook. This is the easiest way to get a glimpse of
the canyon, but be aware that Route 39 is open only during summer
and early fall. During the late fall, winter, and spring the best way to
experience Hells Canyon is to follow a slightly more out-of-the-way
route along the **Snake River Segment** of the Wallowa Mountain Loop.
Following Snake River Road north from Oxbow, the 60-mi round-trip
route winds along the edge of Hells Canyon Reservoir on the Idaho
side, crossing the Snake River at Hells Canyon Dam on the Oregon-Idaho
border. In some places the canyon is 10 mi wide. There's a visitor center near the dam, and hiking trails continue on into the Hells Canyon
Wilderness and National Recreation Area. Be sure you have a full tank
before starting out, since there are no gas stations anywhere along the
route. If you're starting from Joseph, you also have the option of heading to the **Hat Point Overlook.** From Joseph, take Route 350 northeast to
Imnaha, a tiny town along the Imnaha River. From there, Forest Road
4240 leads southeast to Route 315, which in turn heads northeast up
a steep gravel road to the overlook. This route is also open only during
the summer. Carry plenty of water.

GETTING HERE

Many seasonal Forest Service roads access Hells Canyon from Imnaha
east of Joseph and the Wallowa Mountain Loop. Four-wheel drive may
be necessary; check with rangers at the Wallowa Mountains Visitor
Center. Most float trips originate from the Hells Canyon Creek site
below the Hells Canyon Dam.

VISITOR INFORMATION

Wallowa Mountains Visitor Center (⊠ *115 Tejaka Ln., off Hwy. 82, Enterprise*
☎ *541/426–4978* ⊕ *www.fs.fed.us/r6/w-w*)

8

SPORTS AND THE OUTDOORS

RECREATIONAL AREAS

Hells Canyon National Recreation Area. This is the site of one of the largest elk herds in the United States, plus 422 other species, including bald eagles, bighorn sheep, mule deer, white-tailed deer, black bears, bobcats, cougars, beavers, otters, and rattlesnakes. The peregrine falcon has also been reintroduced here. Part of the area was designated as Hells Canyon Wilderness, in parts of Oregon and Idaho, with the establishment of the Hells Canyon National Recreation Area in 1975. Additional acres were added as part of the Oregon Wilderness Act of 1984, and the recreation area currently extends across more than 650,000 wild and rugged acres. Nine hundred miles of trails wind through the wilderness area, closed to all mechanized travel. If you want to visit the wilderness it must be on foot, mountain bike, or horseback. Three of its rivers, the Snake, Imnaha, and Rapid have all been designated as Wild and Scenic. Environmental groups have proposed the creation of Hells Canyon National Park to better manage the area's critical habitat. A wildlife-viewing guide is available from the Idaho Department of Fish and Game. ⊠ *115 Tejaka Ln., off Hwy. 82, Enterprise* ☎ *541/426–4978 or 541/426–5546* ⊕ *www.fs.fed.us/hellscanyon.*

Wild and Scenic Snake River Corridor. Sixty-seven miles of river are federally designated as part of the National Wild and Scenic Rivers system. Extending ¼ mi back from the high-water mark on each shore, the corridor is available for managed public use. Since the corridor itself is not designated as "wilderness," and wilderness area regulations do not therefore apply, there are developed campsites and man-made structures, and some motorized equipment is allowed. In season, both powerboaters and rafters must make reservations and obtain permits for access to the river corridor. ☎ *509/758–0616 general information; 509/758–1957 noncommercial float reservations; 509/758–0270 powerboat reservations* ⊘ *Daily Memorial Day–early Sept.*

BAKER CITY

44 mi south of La Grande on U.S. 30 off I–84.

During the 1860s gold rush, Baker City was the hub. The Big Apple, or rather, the Big Nugget. Many smaller towns dried up after the gold rush, but Baker City transformed itself into the seat of the regional logging and ranching industries that are still around today. Remnants of its turn-of-the-century opulence, when it was the largest city between Salt Lake and Portland, are still visible in the many restored Victorian houses and downtown storefronts.

Baker City may not have that much gold left in its surrounding hills— but what hills they are. The Wallowas and Eagle Cap, the Elkhorn Ridge of the Blue Mountains, the Umatilla National Forest, the Wallowa-Whitman, Hells Canyon, Monument Rock—the panorama almost completes a full circle. Outdoor enthusiasts flock here for the climbing, fishing, hunting, waterskiing, canoeing, hiking, cycling, and skiing. Baker City's gold rush has been supplanted by the "green rush."

GETTING HERE

Baker City is easily accessed by I–84, 305 mi east of Portland and 127 mi west of Boise, Idaho. The city is the hub for several smaller highways as well, including scenic Highway 7 through the Blue Mountains to John Day. The **Baker Bow** (☎ *541/963–2877* ⊕ *www.neotransit.org*) shuttle bus runs Monday–Friday to La Grande and nearby Haines, and the **Baker City Trolley** services the city Monday–Saturday (☎ *541/963–2877* ⊕ *www.neotransit.org*). **Greyhound** also makes stops here. The closest airport is Eastern Oregon Regional, 95 mi northeast in Pendleton.

VISITOR INFORMATION

Baker County Chamber of Commerce and Visitors Bureau (✉ *490 Campbell St.* ☎ *541/523–5855* ⊕ *www.visitbaker.com*).

EXPLORING

Baker Heritage Museum. Located in a stately brick building that once housed the community's swimming pool, Baker's history center has one of the most impressive rock collections in the West. Assembled over a lifetime by a local amateur geologist, the Cavin-Warfel Collection includes thunder eggs, glowing phosphorescent rocks, and a 950-pound hunk of quartz. Other exhibits highlight pioneering, ranching, mining, and antique furniture. The museum also operates the nearby **Adler House Museum** (✉ *2305 Main St.* ☐ *$6* ⊙ *Memorial Day–Labor Day*), an 1889 Italianate house that was once home to an eccentric publishing magnate and philanthropist. ✉ *2480 Grove St., at Campbell St.* ☎ *541/523–9308* ☐ *$6* ⊙ *Mid-Mar.–Oct., daily 9–4.*

SCENIC
ROUTE

Elkhorn Drive. This scenic 106-mi loop winds from Baker City through the Elkhorn Range of the Blue Mountains. Only white-bark pine can survive on the range's sharp ridges and peaks, which top 8,000 feet; spruce, larch, Douglas fir, and ponderosa pine thrive on the lower slopes. The route is well marked; start on Highway 7 west of Baker City, turn onto County Road 24 toward Sumpter, pass Granite on Forest Service Road 73, and then return to Baker City along U.S. 30.

8

National Historic Oregon Trail Interpretive Center. Head 5 mi east of Baker City to this sprawling facility perched on a high hillside for a superb exploration of pioneer life in the mid-1800s. From 1841 to 1861 about 300,000 people made the 2,000-mi journey from western Missouri to the Columbia River and the Oregon coast, looking for agricultural land in the West. A simulated section of the Oregon Trail will give you a feel for camp life and the settlers' impact on Native Americans; an indoor theater presents movies and plays. A 4-mi round-trip trail winds from the center to the actual ruts left by the wagons. ✉ *22267 Oregon Hwy. 86* ☎ *541/523–1843* ⊕ *www.blm.gov/or/oregontrail* ☐ *$8* ⊙ *Apr.–Oct., daily 9–6; Nov.–Mar., daily 9–4.*

NEED A
BREAK?

No historic Main Street would be complete without its soda fountain, and **Charley's Ice Cream Parlor** fits the bill, serving all manner of treats, frozen and otherwise. ✉ *2101 Main St.* ☎ *541/524–9307* ▭ *AE, D, DC, MC, V* ⊙ *Closed Sun.*

Historic Baker City mural in downtown Baker City

WHERE TO EAT AND STAY

$
AMERICAN

✕ **Barley Brown's.** It's the "Cheers" of Baker City–and everyone knows owner Tyler's name. A perennial winner at American beer festivals, their "Shredder's Wheat" American Wheat Ale recently beat out international contenders for a gold at the World Beer Cup. You can watch the process behind glass windows as they brew some eight different beers (e.g., "Hot Blonde" jalapeño ale, "Tank Slapper" India pale ale). Barley Brown's also makes tasty grub, from burgers and quesadillas to spicy pastas and the occasional alligator. Tyler is committed to using local produce (the hand-cut fries are Baker County potatoes) and hormone-free beef. ⊠ *2190 Main St.* ☎ *541/523–4266* ▭ *AE, MC, V* ☺ *Closed Sun. No lunch.*

$
NEW AMERICAN

✕ **Earth & Vine Art & Wine Gallery.** A chic little café on the ground-floor corner of one of Baker's numerous historic buildings, Earth & Vine sticks to sandwiches, flatbread pizza, fondue, and other simple treats. Regional varieties occupy much of the short wine list, but owner Mary Ellen Stevenson keeps many more bottles in the cellar than she prints on the menu, so ask for a recommendation. Local art, live music, and periodic sushi nights pack in the Baker City creative class. ⊠ *2001 Washington Ave.* ☎ *541/523–1687* ▭ *AE, D, V, MC.*

¢

☖ **Bridge Street Inn.** Right off Main Street, the Bridge Street Inn is one of the least-expensive motels in town. With rooms that are clean and reliable, it is an excellent option if you're looking for a bargain. All rooms have microwaves and refrigerators, new sinks, and double-pane windows. A substantial continental breakfast is included, and owner Thoy occasionally serves up free dinners in the lobby as well. **Pros:** inexpensive; well-insulated; comp breakfast. **Cons:** with 41 ground-floor units, neighbors may be noisy. ⊠ *134 Bridge St.* ☎ *541/523–6571 or 800/932–9220* ⊕ *www.bridgestreetinn.net* ↩ *41 rooms* ♿ *In-room: Wi-Fi, kitchen (some). In-hotel: parking (free), laundry facilities, some pets allowed* ⊟ *MC, V* ❏ *CP.*

$ ⊡ **Geiser Grand Hotel**. She sits like the dowager duchess of Main Street, her cupola clock tower still cutting a sharp figure against a wide Baker City sky. It's the Geiser Grand, built in 1889, the Italianate Renaissance Revival that was once known as the finest hotel between Portland and Salt Lake City—and arguably still is. Reopened in 1998 after an $8 million restoration, the rooms still have those 14-foot ceilings, old-fashioned transoms above the door, and 10-foot-tall windows. But of all the fascinating features, it's the custom-built stained-glass ceiling in hues of green, blue, purple, and red that takes center stage. The fact that it was created from photographs and an oldtimer's memory makes it even more astounding. No gym on-site, but guests have complimentary access to one across the street, plus nearby tennis courts. **Pros:** great downtown location; fascinating history; if possible, take the Saturday afternoon hotel tour. **Cons:** rooms, while well appointed, have a distinct femininity; Wi-Fi spotty in some rooms. ⊠ *1996 Main St.* ☎ *541/523–1889 or 888/434–7374* ⊕ *www.geisergrand.com* ↩ *30 rooms* ♿ *In-room: Wi-Fi, DVD. In-hotel: restaurant, bar, parking (free), some pets allowed* ⊟ *AE, D, MC, V.*

Fodor's Choice
★

SPORTS AND THE OUTDOORS

SKIING **Anthony Lakes Ski Area**. Find some of the state's best powder at this hill
♺ in the Wallowa-Whitman National Forest, along with a vertical drop of 900 feet and a top elevation of 8,000 feet. There are 21 trails, one triple chairlift, and a 30-km cross-country network. Snowboards are permitted. ⊠ *47500 Anthony Lake Hwy., North Powder* ☎ *541/856–3277* ⊕ *www.anthonylakes.com* 🎟 *Lift tickets $39* ⊙ *Nov.–Apr., Thurs.– Sun. 9–4.*

JOHN DAY

80 mi west of Baker City on U.S. 26.

More than $26 million in gold was mined in the John Day area. The town was founded shortly after gold was discovered there in 1862. Yet John Day is better known to contemporaries for the plentiful outdoor recreation it offers and for the nearby John Day Fossil Beds. The town is also a central location for trips to the Malheur National Wildlife Refuge and the towns of Burns, Frenchglen, and Diamond to the south.

As you drive west through the dry, shimmering heat of the John Day Valley on U.S. 26, it may be hard to imagine this area as a humid subtropical forest filled with lumbering 50-ton brontosauruses and 50-foot-long crocodiles. But so it was, and the eroded hills and sharp, barren-looking ridges contain the richest concentration of prehistoric plant and animal fossils in the world.

Two miles south of John Day, **Canyon City** is a small town that feels like it hasn't changed much since the Old West days. Memorabilia from the gold rush is on display at the town's small museum, **Grant County**

Historical Museum (✉ *101 S. Canyon City Blvd. Canyon City* ☎ *541/575–0362* ⊕ *wwwgchistoricalmuseum.com*), along with Native American artifacts and antique musical instruments. Drop in at the neighboring pioneer jail, which the locals pilfered years ago from a nearby crumbling ghost town.

GETTING HERE

You can get to John Day on the thrice-weekly **People Mover** (☎ *541/575–2370*) bus from Bend, but you really need a car to explore the nearby forests and fossil beds. The town is a scenic, 80-mi drive from Baker City on Highways 7 and 26. To the west, it's 152 mi to Bend and the closest commercial airport, primarily on U.S. 26.

JOHN DAY FOSSIL BEDS NATIONAL MONUMENT

40 mi from John Day, west 38 mi on U.S. 26 and north 2 mi on Hwy. 19.

Ⓒ Fodor's Choice ★ The geological formations that compose this peculiar monument cover hundreds of square miles and preserve a diverse record of plant and animal life spanning more than 40 million years of the Age of Mammals. The national monument itself is divided into three "units": Sheep Rock, Painted Hills, and Clarno—each of which looks vastly different and tells a different part of the story of Oregon's history. Each unit has picnic areas, restrooms, visitor information, and hiking trails. The main visitor center is in the Sheep Rock Unit, 40 mi northwest of John Day; Painted Hills and Clarno are about 70 and 115 mi northwest of John Day, respectively. If you only have time for one unit of the park, make it Painted Hills, where the namesake psychedelic mounds most vividly expose the region's unique geology.

GETTING HERE

Reach the Sheep Rock Unit of the John Day Fossil Beds Monument driving 38 mi west of John Day on U.S. 26, then 2 mi north on Highway 19. The Painted Hills unit is an additional 35 mi west on U.S. 26. To reach the Clarno unit, follow Highway 19 north from the Sheep Rock Unit, 60 mi northwest to Fossil. From Fossil, drive west on Highway 218 for 20 mi to the entrance. Be prepared to stop for frequent roadside interpretive exhibits between the three units. The fossil beds are between Eastern Oregon Regional Airport, 144 mi northeast in Pendleton, and Roberts Field-Redmond Municipal Airport, 104 mi west in Redmond.

VISITOR INFORMATION

Thomas Condon Paleontology Center (✉ *Hwy. 19, 2 mi north of U.S. 26, Kimberly* ☎ *541/987–2333* ⊕ *www.nps.gov/joda*).

EXPLORING

Clarno. The 48-million-year-old fossil beds in this small section have yielded the oldest remains in the John Day Fossil Beds National Monument. The drive to the beds traverses forests of ponderosa pines and sparsely populated valleys along the John Day River before traveling through a landscape filled with spires and outcroppings that attest to the region's volcanic past. A short trail that runs between the two parking lots contains fossilized evidence of an ancient subtropical forest.

John Day Fossil Beds

Another trail climbs ½ mi from the second parking lot to the base of the Palisades, a series of abrupt, irregular cliffs created by ancient volcanic mud flows. ⊠ *Off Hwy. 218, 20 mi west of Fossil* ☏ *541/763–2203* ⊕ *www.nps.gov/joda* ⊙ *Daily, during daylight hrs.*

Painted Hills. The fossils at Painted Hills, a unit of the John Day Fossil Beds National Monument, date back about 33 million years, and reveal a climate that has become noticeably drier than that of Sheep Rock's era. The eroded buff-color hills reveal striking red and green striations created by minerals in the clay. Come at dusk or just after it rains, when the colors are most vivid. If traveling in spring, the desert wildflowers are most intense between late April and early May. Take the steep, ¾-mi **Carroll Rim Trail** for a commanding view of the hills or sneak a peek from the parking lot at the trailhead, about 2 mi beyond the picnic area. A few Forest Service roads lead north toward the Spring Basin Wilderness and the town of Antelope, but these are appropriate only for high-clearance vehicles and only when dry. ⊠ *Off U.S. 26, 9 mi west of Mitchell* ☏ *541/462–3961* ⊕ *www.nps.gov/joda* ⊙ *Daily, during daylight hrs.*

Sheep Rock. The **Thomas Condon Paleontology Center** at Sheep Rock serves as the primary visitor center, with a museum dedicated to the fossil beds, fossils on display, in-depth informational panels, handouts, and an orientation movie. Two miles north of the visitor center on Highway 19 is the impressive **Blue Basin**, a badlands canyon with sinuous blue-green spires. Winding through this basin is the ½-mi **Island in Time Trail,** where trailside exhibits explain the area's 28-million-year-old fossils. The 3-mi Blue Basin Overlook Trail loops around the rim of the canyon, yielding some splendid views. Blue Basin is a hike with a high effort-to-reward ratio, and in summer rangers lead interpretive jaunts Friday–Sunday at 10 AM. ⊠ *32651 Hwy. 19, Kimberly* ☎ *541/987–2333* ⊕ *www.nps.gov/joda* ☉ *Daily, during daylight hrs.*

WHERE TO STAY

¢ ☷ **Fish House Inn and RV Park**. One of the only places to stay near the Sheep Rock fossil beds is 9 mi east, in the small town of Dayville. The piscatory touches at this lovely inn include fishing gear, nets, and framed prints of fish. The main house, built in 1908, has three bedrooms upstairs that share an outdoor deck and a separate entrance, and behind it is a cottage with a large bedroom and suite. The downstairs is available as a full suite with 3 bedrooms, 1 bath, kitchen, dining room, and living room. With a general store, a bar, and a gas station, Dayville can fill most of your traveling needs and has the only services in the area. **Pros:** great prices, fun atmosphere; ground floor of main house is great for a group traveling together. **Cons:** no food service other than the small Mercantile. ⊠ *110 Franklin St., Dayville* ☎ *541/987–2124 or 888/286–3474* ⊕ *www.fishhouseinn.com* ⤳ *5 rooms, 2 with shared bath, 1 suite* ␣ *In-room: no phone, refrigerator. In-hotel: some pets allowed* ⊟ *AE, D, MC, V.*

SOUTHEAST OREGON

"Oregon's Outback" is indeed a high and lonesome setting of sagebrush desert, one-horse towns, and acre after acre of grazing cattle. And while the region may be light-years away from cosmopolitan, southeast Oregon has historically been one of the West's more demographically diverse regions. The area's indigenous Paiute and Shoshone residents came to share the land with white pioneer families, Basque herders, Mexican bracero cowboys, Chinese mine workers, and a number of other groups who've helped to shape Oregon's high desert culturally. The impressively spare scenery, meanwhile, has been a constant. While the sagebrush horizon can be beautiful in its constancy, visitors need only to brave some of the region's gravel backroads to discover a collection of diverse and singular landscapes. Places like the blistering white Alvord Desert, the dramatic Owyhee Canyon, and the sculptural rock formations of Leslie Gulch can go toe-to-toe with any national park for straight-up natural beauty, but they host a comparative sliver of visitors each year.

BURNS

76 mi south of the town of John Day on U.S. 395.

Named after poet Robert Burns, this town was the unofficial capital of the 19th-century cattle empires that staked claims to these southeastern Oregon high-plateau grasslands. Today Burns is a working-class town of 3,000 residents, surrounded by the 10,185 square mi of sagebrush, rimrock, and grassy plains that compose Harney County, the ninth-largest county in the United States. As the only place in the county with basic tourist amenities, Burns serves as a convenient stopover for many

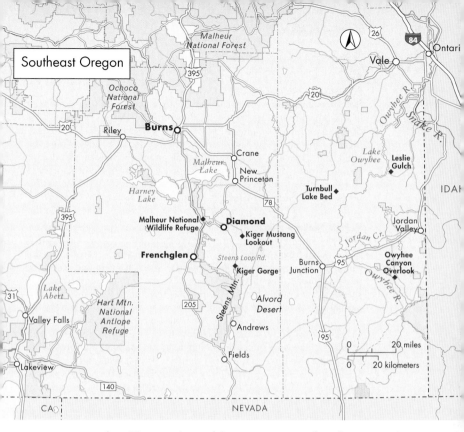

travelers. However, its usefulness as a source of modern convenience goes hand in hand with the sense that, unlike many of the region's smaller outposts, its Old West flavor has largely been lost. Rather than a final destination, think of Burns as a jumping-off point for exploring the poetry of the Malheur National Wildlife Refuge, Steens Mountain, and the Alvord Desert. Outdoor recreation at this gateway to Steens Mountain includes fishing, backpacking, camping, boating, and hiking.

GETTING HERE

Bend and the nearest commercial airport are 130 mi west of Burns on U.S. 20. From John Day to the north, it's a 70-mi drive through the sagebrush scrub along U.S. 395. **Porter Stage Lines** (☎ *541/269–7183*) runs a daily bus east to Ontario and west to the coast via Bend and Eugene.

VISITOR INFORMATION

Harney County Chamber of Commerce (✉ *484 N. Broadway, Burns* ☎ *541/573–2636* ⊕ *www.harneycounty.com*).

WHERE TO EAT

¢ ✕ **Bella Java & Bistro.** This simple, but elegant café is in a historic store-
CAFÉ front downtown, with high ceilings and an eclectic decor. Pastries, simple sandwiches, and delicious, house-made soups anchor the small menu. Locals are in and out all day for their espresso fix, and there's

local beer and wine behind the counter too. ⊠ *314A N. Broadway* 🕾 *541/573–3077* ▭ *MC, V* 🕙 *Mon.–Fri. 7:30–3, Sat. 9–3. No dinner.*

SPORTS AND THE OUTDOORS

RECREATIONAL AREAS

Malheur National Forest. You can cut through this 1.4-million-acre forest in the Blue Mountains as you drive from John Day to Burns on U.S. 395. It has alpine lakes, meadows, creeks, and grasslands. Black bears, bighorn sheep, elk, and wolverines inhabit dense stands of pine, fir, and cedar. Near Burns the trees dwindle in number and the landscape changes from mountainous forest to open areas covered with sagebrush and dotted with junipers. ⊠ *Between U.S. 26 and U.S. 20, accessible via U.S. 395 Emigrant Creek Ranger District Office: 265 Hwy. 20 S., Hines* 🕾 *541/573–4300* ⊕ *www.fs.fed.us/r6/malheur* 🖻 *Free* 🕙 *Daily.*

Malheur National Wildlife Refuge. This unusual desert environment covers 187,000 acres. The squat, snow-covered summit of Steens Mountain is the only landmark in this area of alkali playas, buttes, scrubby meadows, and, most surprising of all, marshy lakes. It's arid and scorching hot in summer, but in the spring and early summer more than 320 species of migrating birds descend on the refuge's wetlands for their annual nesting and mating rituals. Following an ancient migratory flyway, they've been coming here for nearly a million years. The 30-mi Central Patrol Road, which runs through the heart of the refuge, is your best bet for viewing birds. But first stop at the **Malheur National Wildlife Refuge Headquarters,** where you can pick up leaflets and a free map. The staff will tell you where you're most likely to see the refuge's winged inhabitants. The refuge is a short way from local petroglyphs (ask at the headquarters); a remarkable pioneer structure called the **Round Barn** (head east from the headquarters on Narrows–Princeton Road for 9 mi; road turns to gravel and then runs into Diamond Highway, a paved road that leads south 12 mi to the barn); and **Diamond Craters,** a series of volcanic domes, craters, and lava tubes (continue south from the barn 6 mi on Diamond Highway). Just outside the refuge is a rare sagebrush lek, the spring mating grounds where clusters of gray-brown sage grouse conduct morning strutting routines with fanned-out feathers. Visit at sunrise between mid-March and mid-June to see this peculiar display (8 mi west on Foster Flat Road, ask at the headquarters for more info). You'll need a car to get around Malheur National Wildlife Refuge, although the adventurous might enjoy exploring by bike or on foot. ⊠ *3691 Sodhouse La., Princeton* 🕾 *541/493–2612* ⊕ *www.fws. gov/malheur* 🖻 *Free* 🕙 *Park daily dawn–dusk; headquarters daily 8–4.*

DIAMOND

54 mi from Burns, south on Hwy. 205 and east on Diamond–Grand Camp Rd.

Though it's tucked into a verdant little valley just east of Malheur National Wildlife Refuge, Diamond has an average year-round population of something like seven people. You could probably do your own census as you take in the undisturbed cluster of a few houses and the hotel in the midst of this wildlife-rich, wide-open country. During its heyday at the turn of the 20th century, Diamond had a population of about 50, including the McCoy family ranchers, who continue to run the town's hotel today.

GETTING HERE

Diamond Lane turns off Highway 205 about 42 mi south of Burns, heading east through the Malheur National Wildlife Refuge for 12 mi. The last few miles are unpaved, but manageable for any passenger car. You can also catch up with Diamond Lane heading south from the refuge's Diamond Craters area. Eastern Oregon Regional Airport in Pendleton is the closest airport.

EXPLORING

Kiger Mustang Lookout. Not far from town is this wild horse viewing area run by the Bureau of Land Management. With their dun-color coats, zebra stripes on knees and hocks, and hooked ear tips, the Kiger mustangs are perhaps one of the purest herds of wild Spanish mustangs in the world today. Once thought to be the descendants of Barb horses brought by the Spanish to North America in the 16th century, the Kiger horses remain the most sought-after for adoption throughout the country. The viewing area is accessible to high-clearance vehicles only, and is passable only in dry weather. ⊠ *11 mi from Happy Valley Rd.* ☎ *541/573–4400* ⌧ *Free* ☉ *May–Oct., dawn–dusk.*

WHERE TO EAT AND STAY

¢ ✕ **Frazier's.** Owned by the Hotel Diamond, Frazier's is a small pub-style restaurant in a renovated stone icehouse, the oldest building in Diamond and maybe the coolest little bar in southeastern Oregon. Burgers, steaks, salads, and sandwiches are served for lunch. Aside from the dinners served in the hotel, this is the only place in town to buy a meal. And as the Bureau of Land Management firefighters can tell you, it's also the only place for many miles to play a game of pool. The unmarked restaurant is found around the back of the Hotel Diamond, and often looks like it might not be open, but head on in for friendly service in what feels like a subterranean speakeasy. ⊠ *Hotel Diamond, 49130 Main St.* ☎ *541/493–1898* ▭ *MC, V* ☉ *No dinner.*

AMERICAN

¢ ⌂ **Hotel Diamond.** In the early 1900s the Hotel Diamond served the local population of ranchers, Basque sheepherders, and cowhands. Now it caters to the birders, naturalists, and high desert lovers who flock to the Malheur refuge. The air-conditioned rooms are clean, comfortable, and pleasantly furnished with an eclectic mix of furniture, including wicker chairs, old wooden desks, and four-poster beds. From the comfortable screen porch guests can look out on the hotel's towering, narrow Lombardy poplars, often planted as de facto fences in ranch country. Family-style meals are served both to hotel guests and to the general public at 6:30 PM, by reservation only. A complimentary breakfast is served in the lounge. The hotel, owned and operated by a fifth-generation ranch family, is also the only place in town to buy gas or groceries. **Pros:** affordable, idyllic location, friendly owners. **Cons:** isolated, no Internet. ⊠ *49130 Main St., 10 mi east of Hwy. 205* ☎ *541/493–1898* ⊕ *www.central-oregon.com/hoteldiamond* ⤴ *8 rooms: 5 upstairs with 2 shared baths; 3 suites downstairs, each with private bath* ⧖ *In-room: no phone, no TV, a/c. In-hotel: restaurant, bar* ▭ *MC, V* ⧘ *CP* ☉ *Closed Nov.–March.*

Fodor'sChoice
★

FRENCHGLEN

61 mi south of Burns on Hwy. 205.

Frenchglen, the tiny town near the base of Steens Mountain, has no more than a handful of residents, and in the off-season offers no basic services to travelers. In other words: eat first. The only lodging in town, the historic Frenchglen Hotel, is a true classic of Oregon hostelry. In the spring and summer Frenchglen's main street is crowded with birders on break from exploring the adjacent Malheur refuge. The popular Steens Mountain Loop begins and ends here, and the town makes a nice setting-off point for adventures in the remote Alvord Desert.

GETTING HERE

Frenchglen is 60 mi south of Burns on Highway 205. It's an isolated, one-street town with minimal services, and the only gas station keeps sporadic hours. Fill up in Burns before heading down. Eastern Oregon Regional Airport in Pendleton is the closest airport.

VISITOR INFORMATION

Harney County Chamber of Commerce (⊠ *484 N. Broadway, Burns* 🕾 *541/573–2636* ⊕ *www.harneycounty.com*).

WHERE TO STAY

¢ 🖫 **Frenchglen Hotel.** A historic example of the 1895–1930 architecture called "American Foursquare," the 1920 Frenchglen Hotel is a simple white wooden house with a porch—Americana at its renovated best. State-owned, managed by John Ross, the hotel serves up a family-style dinner (reservations essential) to guests and the public at the long wooden tables in the combination lobby-dining room. Breakfast and lunch are also served, and meals sometimes incorporate produce grown in the cute garden out back. The small bedrooms, upstairs off a single hallway, share two bathrooms; five modern units with queen beds and private baths are in the back. Though still a part of the Frenchglen Hotel, the newer addition is called "Drover's Inn." **Pros:** historic "round barn" is on-site, close to Steens Mountain and Malheur Refuge; stay overnight in an authentic 1920s, rural American home. **Cons:** shared bathrooms; no phones or TV. ⊠ *39184 Hwy. 205* 🕾 *541/493–2825* ⤸ *8 rooms* ⚐ *In-room: no phone, no TV. In-hotel: restaurant, some pets allowed* ⊟ *D, MC, V* ⊙ *Closed Nov.–mid-Mar.*

SHOPPING

Frenchglen Mercantile. Frenchglen's only store has a small display of historic ranch items like old branding tools and turn-of-the-20th-century toiletries. Cold drinks, film, sunscreen, good coffee, snacks, and canned goods are also for sale. The store is only open in the summer, and the dates may change each year. It's also the only place in town for gas, and the owner has a sign on the door with a number to call if the store's closed—it's a $40 minimum charge, though, so fill up in Burns if you can. ⊠ *Hwy. 205* 🕾 *541/493–2738.*

SPORTS AND THE OUTDOORS

HIKING **Steens Mountain.** Amid the flat landscape of southeastern Oregon, the mountain is hard to miss, although the sight of its 9,700-foot summit is more remarkable from the east. There, its sheer face rises from the flat basin of the desolate Alvord Desert, which stretches into Idaho and Nevada. On the western side, Steens Mountain slopes gently upward over a distance of about 20 mi and is less astonishing. Steens is not your average mountain—it's a huge fault block created when the ancient lava that covered this area fractured. Except for groves of aspen, juniper, and a few mountain mahogany, Steens is almost entirely devoid of trees and resembles alpine tundra. But starting in June the wildflower displays are nothing short of breathtaking, as are the views: on Steens you'll encounter some of the grandest scenery in the West.

The mountain is a great spot for hiking over untrammeled and unpopulated ground, but you can also see it by car (preferably one with four-wheel drive) on the rough but passable 52-mi **Steens Loop Road,** open mid-July–October. You need to take reasonable precautions; storms can whip up out of the blue, creating hazardous conditions. On the drive up you might spot golden eagles, bighorn sheep, and deer. The view out over **Kiger Gorge,** on the southeastern rim of the mountain, includes a dramatic U-shape path carved out by a glacier. A few miles farther along the loop road, the equally stunning **East Rim viewpoint** is more than 5,000 feet above the valley floor. The view on a clear day takes in the Alvord Desert. ✉ *Northern entrance to Steens Loop Rd. leaves Hwy. 205 at south end of Frenchglen and returns to Hwy. 205 about 9 mi south of Frenchglen.*

OFF THE BEATEN PATH

Alvord Desert. With the eastern face of Steens Mountain in the background, the Alvord Desert conjures up Western movie scenes of parched cowboys riding through the desert—though today you're more likely to see wind sailors scooting across these hard-packed alkali flats (the "playa") and glider pilots using the basin as a runway. But once they go home, this desert is deserted. Snowmelt from Steens Mountain can turn it into a shallow lake until as late as mid-July. The mostly gravel Fields–Denio Road runs alongside the playa, accessing a number of rutted tracks maintained by the Bureau of Land Management. At the south end of the road, **Fields Station** (✉ *22276 Fields Dr.* ☎ *541/495–2275* ⊕ *www.fieldsoregon.com*) pretty much *is* the town of Fields, an all-in-one post office, general store, motel, and café. The old-fashioned milk shakes at this desert outpost are themselves worth the drive, made with old-school fountain syrups and served in enormous, 24-oz plastic cups. If the milk shakes aren't enough to justify a desert trip, then come for the **Alvord Hot Springs** (✉ *Off Fields–Denio Rd., 23 mi north of Fields* 💲 *Free*). Though the land is privately owned, the public is welcome to use the two concrete pools taking on superheated water from the nearby springs. From this roadside, ramshackle soaking station, the view of Steens Mountain is superb. Be warned, though, Alvord is a nudity-friendly spring. ✉ *From Frenchglen take Hwy. 205 south for about 33 mi until road ends at T-junction near town of Fields; go left (north) to Alvord Desert and Alvord Hot Springs.*

8

FURTHER OFF THE PATH

Leslie Gulch. The canyon country of the 280-mile Owyhee River extends through parts of Nevada, Idaho, and southeast Oregon, a sparsely populated area of deep gorges that cut through the high Owyhee Plateau. The gnarly spires of rock at Leslie Gulch are made from volcanic-ash tuff, rhyolitic leftovers from ancient eruptions, sculpted by erosion into towers and pinnacles. Much of Leslie Gulch is designated as Wilderness Study Area, and the canyon cliffs are home to a resident herd of bighorn sheep, along with coyotes, bobcats, mule deer, and the occasional elk. The 15-mi drive along Leslie Gulch Road descends from the Owyhee uplands into the river canyon, showing off dozens of spectacular formations along the way. At the end of the road are a boat launch and a free, 12-site primitive campground. You can only go a couple of miles up the side canyon of Juniper Gulch before it's too narrow to travel, but bring a camera along for a short hike past bizarre, pockmarked citadels. Keep your eyes peeled for rattlesnakes, too. ⊠ *Off U.S. 95, 19 mi north of Jordan Valley* ☎ *541/473–3144* ⊕ *www.blm.gov/or* ☑ *Free* ⊗ *March–mid-Nov.*

Seattle

WORD OF MOUTH

"Our daytime activities were: Coffee Walk with Seattle by Foot. That was fairly pleasant but if I had wanted to spend a few dollars more I probably would have liked a gourmet tour better. We took the watertaxi to West Seattle and rented bikes. That was a great day. We stopped by the Klondike Gold Rush museum one morning—FREE—that was well worth the hour or so spent there."

—suec1

WELCOME TO SEATTLE

TOP REASONS TO GO

★ **The World of SAM.**
The fantastic Seattle Art Museum (SAM) features modern and Native American art; Olympic Sculpture Park, in Belltown, showcases works by Calder and Serra amidst green space; and On Capitol Hill the Seattle Asian Art Museum, inside Volunteer Park, houses a fascinating collection.

★ **Discovery Park.** Densely forested trails spill out onto beaches with jaw-dropping vistas of Puget Sound at the city's best green space.

★ **Seattle Center.** There's something for everyone here: Pacific Science Center and Children's Museum; Experience Music Project/ Science Fiction Museum; a brand-new Seattle Center Skatepark; and the SIFF Film Center. You can catch opera or ballet at McCaw Hall and theater performances at Intiman Theatre.

★ **Local Farmers' Markets.** Start at glorious Pike Place Market. Then visit smaller markets in the University District, West Seattle, Columbia City, and along historic Ballard Avenue, and Broadway on Capitol Hill.

1 Downtown. The only part of Seattle with skyscrapers, along with most of the city's hotels and most popular tourist spots.

2 Seattle Center, South Lake Union, and Queen Anne. Queen Anne, north of Belltown, rises up from Denny Way to the Lake Washington Ship Canal. At the bottom are the Space Needle, the Seattle Center, and the Experience Music Project museum. South Lake Union—a neighborhood in transition—has the REI superstore, lakefront, and some eateries and hotels.

3 Pioneer Square. Seattle's oldest neighborhood has lovely redbrick and sandstone buildings, plus numerous galleries and antiques shops.

4 International District. The I.D. is a fun place to shop and eat. The stunning Wing Luke Asian Museum and Uwajimaya shopping center anchor the neighborhood.

5 Capitol Hill. The Hill has two faces: young and sassy and elegant and upscale. It has fantastic restaurants and nightlife.

6 Fremont. A mix of pricey boutiques and fantastic restaurants; up the hill, residential Phinney Ridge includes the Woodland Park Zoo.

7 Ballard. Ballard's main attraction is the Hiram M. Chittenden Locks. This historically Scandinavian neighborhood is beloved for its eateries, trendy shops, and farmers market.

8 Wallingford. At the ship canal is the wonderful Gas Works Park. The booming commercial strip along N. 45th Street has a

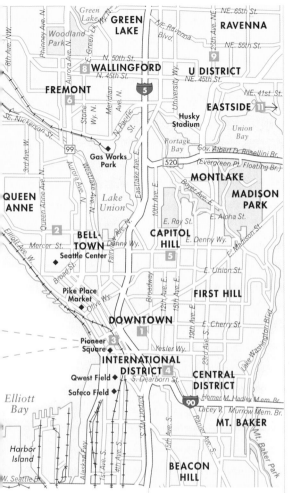

GETTING ORIENTED

Hemmed in by mountains, hills, and multiple bodies of water, Seattle is anything but a linear, grid-lined city. The city can be baffling to navigate, especially if you delve into its residential neighborhoods. Water makes the best landmark. Both Elliott Bay and Lake Union are pretty hard to miss. When you are trying to get your bearings Downtown, Elliott Bay is a much more reliable landmark than the Space Needle. Remember that I–5 bisects the city (north–south). The major routes connecting the southern part of the city to the northern part are I–5, Aurora Avenue/ Hwy. 99, 15th Avenue NW (Ballard Bridge), and Westlake (Fremont Bridge) and Eastlake avenues. Streets in the Seattle area generally travel east to west, whereas avenues travel north to south.

few excellent restaurants. Directly north is Green Lake, whose park has a paved path that circles the lake.

9 The "U District." The University's vast campus is truly lovely, and the surrounding neighborhood can be both gritty and charming. Loads of ethnic restaurants and a large student population keep things lively.

10 West Seattle. West Seattle's California Avenue has some lovely shops and restaurants. Gorgeous Alki Beach offers views of the Seattle skyline.

11 Eastside. East of Lake Washington, the Eastside suburbs are home to Microsoft. Bellevue is the most citylike, with its own skyline, an art museum, and high-end shops and restaurants.

SEATTLE PLANNER

Airport Ease

Your can take Sound Transit's **Central Link Light Rail** (⊕ www.soundtransit.org) from Sea-Tac to Downtown. The train runs every 10 to 15 minutes from 5 AM to 1 AM weekdays and Saturday, and every 15 minutes from 6 AM to midnight on Sunday. The Downtown terminus is Westlake Station, which is convenient to many hotels. The Sound Transit Central Link fare is $2.50 one-way. (⇨ For more airport transfer options, see Travel Smart Pacific Northwest.)

Visitor Information

Contact the **Seattle Visitors Bureau and Convention Center** (⊕ www.visitseattle. org ☎ 206/461–5800) for help with everything from sightseeing to booking spa services. You can also follow their Twitter feed (⊕ twitter. com/seattlemaven). The main visitor information center is Downtown, at the Washington State Convention and Trade Center on 8th Avenue and Pike Street; it has a full-service concierge desk open daily 9 to 5 (in summer; weekdays only in winter). There's also an info booth at Pike Place Market.

Getting Around

By Biking and Walking: Bicycling is popular but still somewhat of a cult endeavor, thanks to a shortage of safe bike routes and some daunting hills. Check out ⊕ www. ridethecity.com/seattle. Walking is fun, though distances and rain can sometimes get in the way. Several neighborhoods—from Pioneer Square to Downtown, or from Belltown to Queen Anne, for example—are close enough to each other that even hills and moisture can't stop walkers.

By Bus: The bus system will get you anywhere you need to go, although some routes require a time commitment and several transfers. Within the downtown core, however, the bus is efficient—and, most of the time it won't cost you a dime, thanks to the Ride-Free Area. The Trip Planner (⊕ trip-planner.kingcounty.gov) is a useful resource. (Fare: $2.25)

By Light Rail: Sound Transit's Central Link Light Rail (⊕ www.soundtransit.org)—the first link of which was completed in 2009—will eventually accomplish what the buses can't: an efficient way to go north–south in this vertically oriented city. (Fare: $2.50)

By Monorail: Built for the 1962 World's Fair, the monorail (⊕ www.seattlemonorail.com) is the shortest transportation system in the city. It runs from Westlake Center (on 5th and Pine) to Seattle Center. But this is great for visitors who plan to spend a day at the Space Needle and the Seattle Center's museums. (Fare: $2.00)

By Seattle Streetcar: The second-shortest system in the city (⊕ www.seattlestreetcar.org) was built to connect Downtown to South Lake Union (directly east of Seattle Center). It runs from Westlake and Olive to the southern shore of Lake Union. (Fare: $2.25)

By Taxi: Seattle's taxi fleet is small, but you can sometimes hail a cab, especially Downtown. Most of the time you must call for one. Except on Friday and Saturday nights, you rarely have to wait more than a few minutes. Cabs can be pricey but useful, especially late at night when buses run infrequently. Two major cab companies are **Yellow Cab** (☎ 206/622–6500) and **Farwest** (☎ 206/622–1717).

Plan Ahead

Hotel reservations. If you're arriving during high season or around major festivals and events, book as far in advance as possible. This extends past city limits—accommodations go fast (including campsites) on the San Juan Islands and the Olympic Peninsula. Waterfront or water-view hotels, like the Edgewater and the Inn at the Market, see their best rooms booked six months in advance.

Restaurant reservations. Seattle's latest (and certainly not greatest) dining trend is the two-hour wait at places that don't take reservations. It never hurts to ask if you can reserve, and you should definitely lock down your table at splurge restaurants. If you have a large party, a reservation is even more important and may be easier to come by.

Tickets. Nearly any act that makes it to Key Arena is going to sell out the show. National touring acts at smaller rock clubs like Neumos, Showbox, Triple Door, and the Croco-dile also play to full houses. Tickets for the most buzzed-about movies at the Seattle International Film Festival should be purchased as soon as they go on sale. Visits to the Bloedel Reserve on Bainbridge Island are by appoint-ment only, and booking well in advance on summer week-ends is advised. Tickets for major-league sports—such as Sounders and Mariners games—should be booked online in advance.

Car rentals. Though the parking lot that is Interstate 5 (I–5) may suggest otherwise, quite a few Seattleites don't own cars. On summer weekends you'll be competing not only with the thousands of other visitors in town but also with residents making an exodus toward the mountains. If you find a good rate, book it immediately, especially at the few downtown rental offices. (Remember: you'll find better rates—and no airport tax—if you book in town.)

Train tickets. Amtrak tickets to Portland and Vancouver, B.C., sell out on summer weekends, and last-minute fares can be quite expensive.

Ferries. Whale-watching/ferry ride vacation packages like those offered by the *Victoria Clipper* can be booked in advance. The Washington State Ferries rarely accepts reservations (only on international sailings to Sidney, B.C., for example), so be sure to plan island travel thoughtfully: leave enough time in your schedule to arrive at the piers early—and to wait for the next ferry if you're last in line.

When to Go

Seattle is most enjoyable May through October. July through September is mostly dry, with warm days reaching into the mid-70s and 80s, with cooler nights. Although the weather can be dodgy, spring and fall are also excellent times to visit, as lodging and tour costs are usually much lower (and the crowds much smaller). In winter the weather can be dreary, but temperatures rarely dip below the low 40s; days are short, as well, because of Seattle's far-north location.

Festivals

■TIP→ The Seattle Conven-tion and Visitors Bureau has a full calendar of events at ⊕ www.visitse-attle.org/cultural. Foodies will want to hit up **Taste of Washington** (spring; ⊕ *www. tastewashington.org*) and **Bite of Seattle** (July; ⊕ *www. biteofseattle.com*). The **Seat-tle International Film Fes-tival** presents more than 200 features (May–June; ⊕ *www. siff.net*). **Bumbershoot** (Sep-tember; ⊕ *www.bumbershoot. org*) is SIFF's musical equiva-lent, and includes dance and theater performances. The **Seattle Pride Festival** (June; ⊕ www.seattlepride.org) has the Northwest's biggest gay, lesbian, and transgender pride parade. **Seafair** (July– August; ⊕ *www.seafair.com*) is the biggest summer festival; hydroplane races are just one major event.

9

Updated by
Carissa Blue-
stone, Nick
Horton, Heidi
Johansen, &
Cedar Burnett

Seattle isn't just a city—it's a feat of environmental engineering. When the Denny party arrived on its shores, "Seattle" was a series of densely forested valleys covered by Douglas fir, Western hemlock, and red cedar; ridges that were far steeper than its current leg-burning hills surrounded it.

Present-day SoDo (the stadium district south of Downtown) was nothing but mudflats. Pioneer Square was actually an island of sorts, where Duwamish tribespeople crossed to the mainland over sandbars.

Once Seattle started to grow, its residents literally changed the city's geography. Massive Denny Hill once occupied the Belltown neighborhood—it simply had to go. The multi-stage "regrade" started in 1899 and was completed 32 years later. Dirt from the project helped fill in the tidelands, creating new land that supports what is now the entire waterfront district. The Denny Hill Regrade was just one of dozens of projects; other equally ambitious earth-moving missions created the city you see today. One of the largest was the digging of the canal that links Lake Washington to Puget Sound, which required, in addition to the carving of the canal itself, the construction of large fixed bridges with drawbridges. Today, construction of a new light rail line plus a replacement of the viaduct are examples of how the city is once again moving a lot of earth around.

It's hard to think of Seattle as anything but natural, though. After all, the city owes much of its appeal to its natural features—the myriad hills that did survive settlement offer views of mountain ranges and water, water, water. Outside of Downtown and other smaller commercial cores, Seattle's neighborhoods fan out in tangles of tree-lined streets. Massive parks like Discovery, Magnuson, and Washington Park Arboretum make Seattle one of the greenest and most livable cities in the nation. From the peaks of the Olympics or Cascades to an artistically landscaped garden in front of a classic Northwest bungalow, nature is in full effect every time you turn your head.

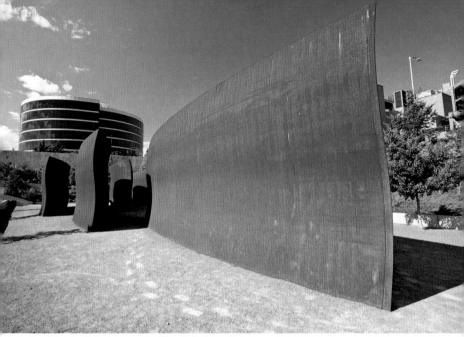

A steel sculpture by Richard Serra at the Olympic Sculpture Park

EXPLORING

Each of Seattle's neighborhoods is distinctive in personality, and taking a stroll, browsing a bookstore, or enjoying a cup of coffee can feel different in every one. It's the adventure of exploring these vibrant neighborhoods that will really introduce you to the character of Seattle.

DOWNTOWN AND BELLTOWN

Downtown Seattle may not be the soul of the city, but it's certainly the heart. There's big-city skyline, as well as plenty of marvelous things to see and do in the Downtown area: the city's premier art museum, the eye-popping Rem Koolhaus–designed Central Library, lively Pike Place Market, and a major shopping corridor along 5th Avenue and down Pine Street. And, of course, there's the water: Elliott Bay beckons from every crested hill.

WHAT TO SEE

Belltown is Downtown's younger sibling, just north of Virginia Street (up to Denny Way) and stretching from Elliott Bay to 6th Avenue. Not too long ago, Belltown was home to some of the most unwanted real estate in the city; the only scenesters around were starving artists. Today Belltown is increasingly hip, with luxury condos, trendy restaurants, swanky bars, and an ever-increasing number of boutiques. (Most of the action happens between 1st and 4th avenues and between Bell and Virginia streets.) You can still find plenty of evidence of its edgy past—including a gallery exhibiting urban street art, a punk-rock vinyl shop, and a major indie rock music venue that was a cornerstone

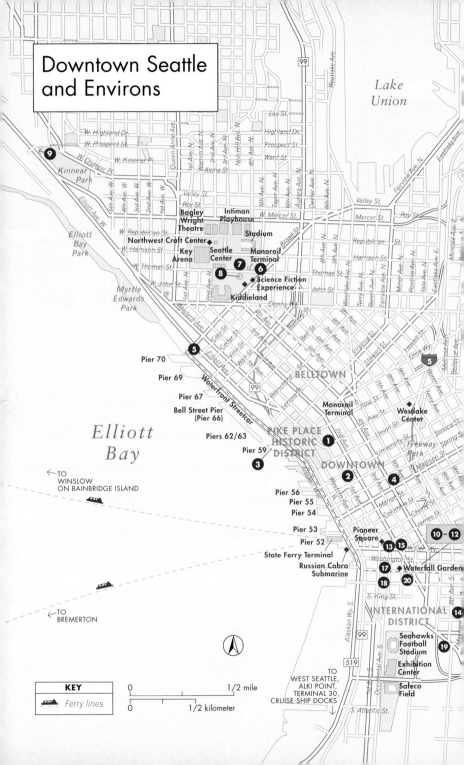

Downtown Seattle and Environs

9

Kinnear Park

Elliott Bay Park

Myrtle Edwards Park

Elliott Bay W.

W. Highland Dr.
W. Prospect St.
W. Kinnear Pl.
Aloha St.

Valley St.
Roy St.

Bagley Wright Theatre

Intiman Playhouse

Northwest Craft Center

Stadium

Key Arena

Seattle Center

7

8

Monorail Terminal

6

Science Fiction Experience

Kiddieland

W. Republican St.
W. Harrison St.
W. Thomas St.
W. John St.
W. Mercer St.
Republican St.
Harrison St.
Thomas St.
John St.
Denny Wy.

Lake Union

Lee St.
Highland Dr.
Prospect St.
Ward St.

Valley St.
Mercer St.
Roy St.

Elliott Bay

5

Pier 70
Pier 69
Pier 67
Bell Street Pier (Pier 66)
Piers 62/63
Pier 59 **3**

Waterfront Streetcar

BELLTOWN

Monorail Terminal

5

Westlake Center

PIKE PLACE HISTORIC DISTRICT

1

DOWNTOWN

2

4

Clay St.
Cedar St.
Vine St.
Wall St.
Battery St.
Bell St.
Blanchard St.
Lenora St.
Virginia St.
Stewart St.
Olive Wy.
Pine St.
Pike St.
Union St.
University St.
Seneca St.
Spring St.
Madison St.
Marion St.
Columbia St.

Freeway Park

Pier 56
Pier 55
Pier 54
Pier 53
Pier 52

State Ferry Terminal

Russian Cobra Submarine

Pioneer Square

13 **15**

10 – 12

17

Waterfall Garden

18

20

← TO WINSLOW ON BAINBRIDGE ISLAND

← TO BREMERTON

Elliott Bay

Columbia St.
Cherry St.
James St.
Jefferson St.
Terrace St.
Washington St.
S. Main St.
S. Jackson St.
S. King St.

INTERNATIONAL DISTRICT

14

Seahawks Football Stadium

Exhibition Center

Safeco Field

19

S. Atlantic St.

TO WEST SEATTLE, ALKI POINT, TERMINAL 30, CRUISE SHIP DOCKS

KEY

Ferry lines

0 ——— 1/2 mile
0 ——— 1/2 kilometer

of the grunge scene—but today Belltown is almost unrecognizable to long-term residents.

Fodor's Choice
★

Olympic Sculpture Park. This 9-acre open-air park is the spectacular outdoor branch of the Seattle Art Museum. Since opening in 2007, the Sculpture Park has become a favorite destination for picnics, strolls, and quiet contemplation. Nestled between Belltown and Elliott Bay, this gently sloping green space is planted with native shrubs and plants and crisscrossed with walking paths. On sunny days the park flaunts an astounding panorama of the Olympic Mountains, but even the grayest afternoon casts a favorable light on the site's sculptures. The grounds are home to works by such artists as Richard Serra, Roy McMakin, Louise Bourgeois, Mark di Suvero, and Alexander Calder, whose bright-red steel "Eagle" sculpture is a local favorite—indeed, you may even see a real bald eagle passing by overhead. The PACCAR Pavilion has a gift shop, café, and more information about the park. ⌂ *2901 Western Ave., between Broad and Bay Sts., Belltown* ☎ *206/654–3100* ⊕ *www.seattleartmuseum.org/visit/osp* ⊒ *Free* ⊘ *Park open daily sunrise–sunset. PACCAR Pavilion open May–Labor Day, Tues.–Sun. 10–5; Sept.–Apr., Tues.–Sun. 10–4.*

⌾ **Pike Place Market.** ⇨ *For an in-depth description of the Market, see the highlighted feature in this chapter.* Pike Place Market, one of the nation's largest and oldest public markets, plays host to happy, hungry crowds all year round, but summer is when things really start to heat up. Strap on some walking shoes and enjoy its many corridors: shops and stalls provide a pleasant sensory overload—stroll among the colorful flower, produce, and fish displays, plus bustling shops and lunch counters. Specialty-food items, tea, honey, jams, comic books, beads, and cookware—you'll find it all here. ⌂ *Pike Pl. at Pike St., west of 1st Ave., Downtown* ☎ *206/682–7453* ⊕ *www.pikeplacemarket.org* ⊘ *Stall hrs vary: 1st-level shops Mon.–Sat. 10–6, Sun. 11–5; underground shops daily 11–5.*

▌ A GOOD COMBO

If you plan to spend the morning exploring Pike Place Market or the Seattle Art Museum, but still have energy for a walk, head north into the Belltown neighborhood, grab lunch to go at Macrina Bakery, and stroll down to the Olympic Sculpture Park: Views, works of art, and chairs aplenty await.

⌾
Fodor's Choice
★

Seattle Aquarium. The city's renovated aquarium is more popular than ever. Among its most engaging residents are the sea otters—kids, especially, seem able to spend hours watching the delightful antics of these creatures and their river cousins. In the Puget Sound Great Hall, "Window on Washington Waters," a slice of Neah Bay life is presented in a 20-foot-tall tank holding 120,000 gallons of water. The aquarium's darkened rooms and large, lighted tanks brilliantly display Pacific Northwest marine life. The "Life on the Edge" tide pools re-create Washington's rocky coast and sandy beaches. Huge glass windows provide underwater views of seals and sea otters; go up top to watch them play in their pools. Kids love the Discovery Lab, where they can touch starfish, sea urchins, and sponges, then examine baby barnacles and jellyfish. Nearby, cylindrical tanks hold a fascinating octopus.

The stunning Seattle Central Library

■**TIP→** Spend a few minutes in front of the octopus tank even if you don't detect any movement. Your patience will be rewarded if you get to see this amazing creature shimmy up the side of the tank. If you're visiting in fall or winter, dress warmly—the Marine Mammal area is on the waterfront, and catches all of those chilly Puget Sound breezes. The café serves Ivar's chowder and kid-friendly food like burgers and chicken fingers; a balcony has views of Elliott Bay. ⊠ *1483 Alaskan Way, at Pier 59, Downtown* ☎ *206/386–4300* ⊕ *www.seattleaquarium.org* 🖂 *$17* ⊘ *Daily 9:30–6 (last entry at 5).*

Fodor's Choice
★

Seattle Art Museum. Long the pride of the city's art scene, SAM is now better than ever after a massive expansion that connects the iconic old building on University Street (where sculptor Jonathan Borofsky's several-stories-high *Hammering Man* still pounds away) to a sleek, light-filled high-rise adjacent space, on 1st Avenue and Union Street. Wander two floors of free public space. The first floor includes the museum's fantastic shop, a café that focuses on local ingredients, and drop-in workshops where the whole family can get creative. The second floor features free exhibitions, including awesome large-scale installations. ⊠ *1300 1st Ave., Downtown* ☎ *206/654–3100* ⊕ *www.seattleartmuseum.org* 🖂 *$15, free 1st Thurs. of month* ⊘ *Wed. and weekends 10–5, Thurs. and Fri. 10–9, 1st Thurs. until midnight.*

Fodor's Choice
★

Seattle Central Library. The hub of Seattle's 25-branch library system, the Central Library, is a stunning jewel of a building that stands out against the concrete jungle of Downtown. The bold construction brings to mind a futuristic, multifaceted gemstone covered in steel webbing—perched right on 4th Avenue. Designed by renowned Dutch architect

Rem Koolhaas and Joshua Ramus, this 11-story structure houses 1.45 million books—plus more than 400 computers with Internet access, an auditorium, a "mixing chamber" floor of information desks, an area with materials in foreign languages, and a café. The building's floor plan is anything but simple; standing outside the beveled glass-and-metal facade of the building, you can see the library's floors zigzagging upward. Tours focusing on the building's architecture are offered several times a week on a first-come, first-served basis; call for a current schedule. The reading room on the 10th floor has unbeatable views of the city and the water, and the building has Wi-Fi throughout. Readings and free film screenings happen on a regular basis; check the Web site for more information. ⊠ *1000 4th Ave., Downtown* ☎ *206/386–4636* ⊕ *www.spl.org* ⊗ *Mon.–Thurs. 10–8, Fri. and Sat. 10–6, Sun. noon–6.*

SEATTLE CENTER, SOUTH LAKE UNION, AND QUEEN ANNE

Seattle Center is the home to Seattle's version of the Eiffel Tower—the Space Needle—and is anchored by Frank Gehry's wild Experience Music Project building. Almost all visitors make their way here at least once, whether to visit the museums or catch a show at one of the many performing arts venues. The neighborhoods that bookend Seattle Center couldn't be more different: Queen Anne is all residential elegance (especially on top of the hill), while South Lake Union, once completely industrial, is becoming Seattle's next hot neighborhood.

WHAT TO SEE

ⓒ **The Children's Museum.** This colorful, spacious museum is located just off the Center House's food court, in the heart of Seattle Center. Enter through a Northwest wilderness setting, with winding trails, hollow logs, and a waterfall. From there, you can explore a global village where rooms with kid-friendly props show everyday life in Ghana, the Philippines, and Japan. The "Go Figure!" exhibit allows children to step inside the pages of their favorite storybooks. Cog City is a giant game of pipes, pulleys, and balls; and kids can also test their talent in a mock recording studio. There's a small play area for toddlers and lots of crafts to help kids learn more about the exhibits. ⊠ *305 Harrison St., Seattle Center* ☎ *206/441–1768* ⊕ *www.thechildrensmuseum.org* ⊠ *$7.50* ⊗ *Weekdays 10–5, weekends 10–6.*

ⓒ **Experience Music Project/Science Fiction Museum.** Seattle's most controversial architectural statement is the 140,000-square-foot complex designed by architect Frank Gehry, who drew inspiration from electric guitars to achieve the building's curvy metallic design. (Some say, however, that it looks more like robot open-heart surgery than a musical instrument.) Regardless, the building stands out among the city's cookie-cutter high-rises, and therefore it's a fitting backdrop for rock memorabilia from the likes of Bob Dylan and the grunge-scene heavies. The Science Fiction Museum (SFM) has its own wing and tackles the major themes of the genre in a way that's both smart and fun. ⊠ *325 5th Ave. N, between Broad and Thomas Sts., Seattle Center* ☎ *206/770–2700* ⊕ *www.empsfm.org* ⊠ *$15* ⊗ *Sept.–May, daily 10–5; rest of yr, daily 10–8.*

Space Needle. Almost 50 years old, Seattle's most iconic building is as quirky and beloved as ever. The distinctive, towering structure of the 605-foot-high Space Needle is visible throughout much of Seattle—but the view from the inside out is even better. A less-than-one-minute ride up to the observation deck yields 360-degree vistas of Downtown Seattle, the Olympic Mountains, Elliott Bay, Queen Anne Hill, Lake Union, and the Cascade Range. The Needle was built just in time for the World's Fair in 1962, but has since been refurbished with educational kiosks, interactive trivia game stations for kids, and the glass-enclosed SpaceBase store and Pavilion spiraling around the base of the tower. The top-floor SkyCity restaurant is better known for its revolving floor than its cuisine, but the menu has improved markedly in the last few years. ■ TIP➡ Don't bother doing the trip to the top of the Needle on rainy days—the view just isn't the same. If you can't decide whether you want the daytime or nighttime view, for $17 you can buy a ticket that allows you to visit twice in one day. ⊠ *5th Ave. and Broad St., Seattle Center* ☎ *206/905–2100* ⊕ *www.spaceneedle.com* ⊠ *$16* ☉ *Mon.–Thurs. 10 AM–9:30 PM, Fri.–Sat. 9:30 AM–10:30 PM, Sun. 9 AM–9:30 PM.*

OFF THE
BEATEN
PATH

Fodor's Choice
★

Discovery Park. Discovery Park is Seattle's largest park, and it has an amazing variety of terrain: shaded, secluded forest trails lead to meadows, saltwater beaches, sand dunes, a lighthouse, and views that include Puget Sound, the Cascades, and the Olympics. There are 2.8 mi of trails through this urban wilderness, but the North Beach Trail, which takes you along the shore to the lighthouse, is a must-see. Head to the South Bluff Trail to get a view of Mt. Rainier. The park has several entrances—if you want to stop at the visitor center to pick up a trail map before exploring, use the main entrance at Government Way. The North Parking Lot is much closer to the North Beach Trail and to Ballard and Fremont, if you're coming from that direction. ■ TIP➡ Note that the park is easily reached from Ballard and Fremont. It's easier to combine a park day with an exploration of those neighborhoods than with a busy Downtown itinerary. ⊠ *3801 W. Government Way, Magnolia ✛ From Downtown, take Elliot Ave. W (which turns into 15th Ave. W), and get off at the Emerson St. exit and turn left onto W. Emerson. Make a right onto Gilman Ave. W (which eventually becomes W. Government Way). As you enter the park, the road becomes Washington Ave.; turn left on Utah Ave.* ☎ *206/386–4236* ⊕ *www.cityofseattle.net/parks* ⊠ *Free* ☉ *Park daily 6 AM–11 PM, visitor center Tues.–Sun. 8:30–5.*

9

PIONEER SQUARE

The Pioneer Square district, directly south of Downtown, is Seattle's oldest neighborhood. It attracts visitors for its elegantly renovated (or in some cases replica) turn-of-the-20th-century redbrick buildings and its art galleries. It's undeniably the center of Seattle's arts scene—there are more galleries in this small neighborhood than we have room to list, and they make up the majority of its sights.

Continued on page 336

PIKE PLACE MARKET
Nine Acres of History & Quirky Charm

With more than a century of history tucked into every corner and plenty of local personality, the Market is one spot you can't miss. Office workers hustle past cruise-ship crowds to take a seat at lunch counters that serve anything from pizza to piroshkies to German sausage. Local chefs plan the evening's menu over stacks of fresh, colorful produce. At night, couples stroll in to canoodle by candlelight in tucked-away bars and restaurants. Sure, some residents may bemoan the hordes of visitors, and many Seattleites spend their dollars at a growing number of neighborhood farmers' markets. But the Market is still one of Seattle's best-loved attractions.

The Pike Place Market dates from 1907. In response to anger over rising food prices, the city issued permits for farmers to sell produce from wagons parked at Pike Place. The impromptu public market grew steadily, and in 1921 Frank Goodwin, a hotel owner who had been quietly buying up real estate around Pike Place for a decade, proposed to build a permanent space.

More than 250 businesses, including 70 eateries. Breathtaking views of Elliott Bay. A pedestrian-friendly central shopping arcade that buzzes to life each day beginning at 6:30 AM. Strumming street musicians. Cobblestones, flying fish, and the very first Starbucks. Pike Place Market—the oldest continuously operated public market in the United States and a beloved Seattle icon—covers all the bases.

The Market's vitality ebbed after World War II, with the exodus to the suburbs and the rise of large supermarkets. Both it and the surrounding neighborhoods began to deteriorate. But a group of dedicated residents, led by the late architect Victor Steinbrueck, rallied and voted the Market a Historical Asset in the early 1970s. Years of subsequent restoration turned the Market into what you see today.

Pike Place Market is many buildings built around a central arcade (which is distinguished by its huge red neon sign).

Shops and restaurants fill buildings on Pike Place and Western Avenue. In the main arcade, dozens of booths sell fresh produce, cheese, spices, coffee, crafts, and seafood—which can be packed in dry ice for flights home. Farmers sell high-quality produce that helps to set Seattle's rigorous dining standards. The shopkeepers who rent store spaces sell art, curios, clothing, beads, and more. Most shops cater to tourists, but there are gems to be found.

EXPLORING THE MARKET

TOP EATS

❶ THE PINK DOOR. This adored (and adorable) Italian eatery is tucked into Post Alley. Whimsical decor, very good Italian food (such as the scrumptious *linguine alla vongole*), and weekend cabaret and burlesque make this gem a must-visit.

❷ LE PANIER. It's a self-proclaimed "Very French Bakery" and another Seattle favorite. The pastries are the main draw, but sandwiches on fresh baguettes and stuffed croissants offer more substantial snacks.

❸ PIROSHKY PIROSHKY. Authentic piroshky come in both standard varieties (beef and cheese) and Seattle-influenced ones (smoked salmon with cream cheese). There are plenty of sweet piroshky, too, if you need a sugar fix.

❹ CAMPAGNE. This French favorite and its charming attached café have you covered, whether you want a quick Croque Madame for lunch, a leisurely and delicious weekend brunch, or a white-tablecloth dinner.

❺ BEECHER'S. Artisanal cheeses—and mac-n-cheese to go—make this a spot Seattle-ites will brave the crowds for.

❻ THREE GIRLS BAKERY. This tiny bakery turns out piles of pastries and sandwiches on their fresh-baked bread (the baked salmon is a favorite).

❼ MATT'S IN THE MARKET. Matt's is the best restaurant in the Market, and one of the best in the city. Lunch is casual (try the catfish po'boy), and dinner is elegant, with fresh fish and local produce showcased on the small menu. Reservations are essential.

❽ DAILY DOZEN DONUTS. Mini-donuts are made fresh before your eyes and are a great snack to pick up before you venture into the labyrinth.

❾ MARKET GRILL. This no-frills counter serves up the market's best fish sandwiches and a great clam chowder.

❿ CHUKAR CHERRIES. Look for handmade confections featuring—but not restricted to—local cherries dipped in all sorts of sweet, rich coatings.

TOP SHOPS

⓫ MARKET SPICE TEA. For a tin of the Market's signature tea, Market Spice Blend, which is infused with cinnamon and clove oils, seek out Market Spice shop on the south side of the main arcade.

⓬ PIKE & WESTERN WINE SHOP. The Tasting Room in Post Alley may be a lovely place to sample Washington wines, but Pike and Western is the place where serious oenophiles flock.

⓭ THE TASTING ROOM. With one of the top wine selections in town, the Tasting Room offers Washington wines for the casual collector and the experienced connoisseur. Stop by the bar for

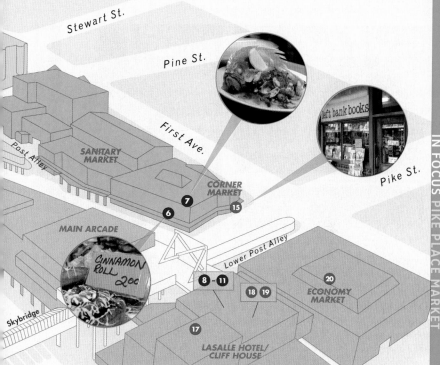

Stewart St.

Pine St.

First Ave.

Post Alley

Pike St.

SANITARY MARKET

CORNER MARKET

7

6

15

MAIN ARCADE

Lower Post Alley

8 - 11

18 19

20

ECONOMY MARKET

17

Skybridge

LASALLE HOTEL/ CLIFF HOUSE

9

large or small pours before you buy.

⑭ **WORLD SPICE.** Glass jars are filled with spices and teas from around the world here: Buy by the ounce or grab a pre-packaged gift set as a souvenir.

⑮ **LEFT BANK BOOKS.** A collective in operation since 1973, this tiny bookshop specializes in political and history titles and alternative literature.

⑯ **THE ORIGINAL STAR-BUCKS.** At 1912 Pike Place, you'll find the tiny store that opened in 1971 and started an empire. The shop is defi-

nitely more quaint and old-timey than its sleek younger siblings, and it features the original, uncensored (read: bare-breasted) version of the mermaid logo.

⑰ **THE SPANISH TABLE.** Though not technically in the Market, this amazing specialty store is nearby. It's the Spanish equivalent of DeLaurenti's, and carries hard-to-find cured meats and cheeses plus a nice stock of sweets and clay cookware like cazuelas.

⑱ **TENZING MOMO.** Your obligatory New Age stop, Tenzing sells high-quality essential oils, natural herbs, teas, tarot cards, incense, soaps, and much more.

⑲ **PAPPARDELLE'S PASTA.** There's no type of pasta you could dream up that isn't already in a bin at Pappardelle's.

⑳ **DELAURENTI'S.** This amazing Italian grocery has everything from fancy olive oil to digestifs and wine to meats and fine cheeses.

TOP EXPERIENCES

Pike Place Flowers

Pike Place Fish Co.

Market buskers

FISHMONGERS. There are four spots to visit if you want to see some serious fish: Pike Place Fish Co. (where the fish-throwers are—look for the awestruck crowds); City Fish (the place for fresh crab); Pure Food Fish Market (selling since 1911); and Jack's Fish Spot.

FLOWER STALLS. Flower growers, many of them Hmong immigrants, dot the main arcade. The gorgeous, seasonal bouquets are among the market's biggest draws.

PILES OF PRODUCE. The bounty of the agricultural valleys just outside Seattle is endless. In summer, seek out sweet peaches and Rainier cherries. In fall, look for cider made from Yakima Valley apples. There are dozens of produce vendors, but Sosio's and Manzo Brothers have been around the longest.

BUSKERS. The market has more than 240 street entertainers in any given year; the parade of Pacific Northwest hippie quirkitude is entertainment in itself.

POST ALLEY. There are some great finds in the alley that runs the length of the Market, paralleling First Avenue, from the highbrow (The Tasting Room) to the very lowbrow (the Gum Wall, a wall speckled with discarded gum supposedly left by people waiting in line at the Market Theater).

GHOSTS. If you listen to local lore, Pike Place Market may be the most haunted spot in Seattle. The epicenter seems to be 1921 First Avenue, where Butterworths & Sons Undertakers handled most of Seattle's dead in the early 1900s. You might see visitors sliding flowers into the building's old mail slot.

***SLEEPLESS IN SEATTLE* STOP.** Though it's been more than a decade since Rob Reiner and Tom Hanks discussed dating mores at the bar of The Athenian Inn, tourists still snap pictures of the corner they occupied. Look for the bright red plaque declaring: TOM HANKS SAT HERE.

A DAY AT THE MARKET

6:30 AM Delivery vans and trucks start to fill the narrow streets surrounding Pike Place Market. Vendors with permanent stalls arrive to stack produce, arrange flowers, and shovel ice into bins for displaying salmon, crab, octopus, and other delicacies.

7:30 AM Breakfast is served! ■TIP→ For freshly made pastries head to Three Girls and Le Panier.

9 AM Craftspeople vying for day stalls sign in and are assigned spots based on seniority.

10 AM Craftspeople set up Down Under —the levels below the main arcade—as the main arcade officially opens. The Heritage Center on Western Avenue opens. Market tours ($10) start at the information booth. ■TIP→ Make reservations for market tours at least a day in advance; call ☎ 206/774-5249.

11 AM The Market madness begins. In summer, midday crowds make it nearly impossible to walk through the street-level arcades. ■TIP→ Head Down Under where things are often a bit quieter.

12 PM–2 PM Lunch counters at places like the Athenian Inn and the Market Grill fill up.

Pike Place Market

5 PM Down Under shops close and the cobblestones are hosed down. (The Market closes at 6 PM Mon.–Sat. and 5 PM on Sun.)

7 PM–2 AM Patrons fill the tables at the Alibi Room, Zig Zag Café, the Pink Door, Matt's at the Market, and Maximilien's.

IN FOCUS PIKE PLACE MARKET

9

RACHEL THE PIG

Rachel, the 550-lb bronze pig that greets marketgoers at the main entrance on Pike and 1st Avenue, is a popular photo stop. But she's also a giant piggy bank that contributes up to $9,000 per year to the Market Foundation. Rachel was sculpted by Georgia Gerber, of Whidbey Island, and was named for the 750-pound pig that won the 1985 Island County Fair.

PARKING

There are numerous garages in the area, including one affiliated with the market itself (the Public Market Parking Garage at 1531 Western Ave.), at which you can get validated parking from many merchants; some restaurants offer free parking at this garage after 5 PM. You'll also find several pay lots farther south on Western Ave. and north on 1st Ave. Street parking is next to impossible to find midday. From Downtown hotels, the Market is easy to reach on foot or on city buses in the "Ride Free Zone."

WHAT TO SEE

Bill Speidel's Underground Tour. Present-day Pioneer Square is actually one story higher than it used to be. After the Great Seattle Fire of 1889, Seattle's planners regraded the neighborhood's streets one level higher. The result: there is now an intricate and expansive array of subterranean passageways and basements beneath Pioneer Square, and Bill Speidel's Underground Tour is the only way to explore them. Speidel was an irreverent historian, PR man, and former *Seattle Times* reporter who took it upon himself to preserve historic Seattle, and this tour is packed with his sardonic wit and playful humor. It's very informative, too—if you're interested in the general history of the city or anecdotes about the city's early politicians and residents, you'll appreciate it that much more. Kids will probably be bored, as there's not much to see at the specific sites, which are used more as launching points for the stories. ■TIP➔ **Comfortable shoes, a love for quirky historical anecdotes, and an appreciation of bad puns are musts.** Several tours are offered daily, and schedules change month to month: call or visit the Web site for a full list of tour times. ✉ *608 1st Ave., Pioneer Square* ☏ *206/682–4646* ⊕ *www.undergroundtour.com* ⊟ *$15* ⊙ *Tours daily; call for schedules.*

GALLERY WALKS

It's fun to simply walk around Pioneer Square and pop into galleries. South Jackson Street to Yesler between Western and 4th Avenue South is a good area. Visit ⊕ *www.artguidenw.com.*

Smith Tower. New York tycoon Lyman Cornelius Smith had big plans for Seattle in 1909—in the form of blueprints for a 14-story building. Turns out his son, Burns Lyman Smith, had even bigger plans, for a 21-story structure with an additional 21-story tower, topped by a pyramid-shaped Gothic cap. The building opened on July 4, 1914, and was the tallest office building outside New York City and the fourth-tallest building in the world. (It remained the tallest building west of the Mississippi for nearly 50 years.) The Smith Tower Observation Deck on the 35th floor is an open-air wrap-around deck providing panoramic views of the surrounding historic neighborhood, the city skyline, and the mountains on clear days. ✉ *506 2nd Ave. S, Pioneer Square* ☏ *206/622–4004* ⊕ *www.smithtower.com/Observation.html* ⊟ *$7.50* ⊙ *May–Sept., daily 10–sunset; Apr. and Oct., daily 10–5; Nov.–Mar., weekends only 10–4.*

OFF THE BEATEN PATH

Qwest Field. Located directly south of Pioneer Square, Qwest Field hosts two professional teams, the Seattle Seahawks (football) and the Seattle Sounders FC (soccer). The open-air stadium has 67,000 seats; sightlines are excellent, thanks to a cantilevered design and the close placement of lower sections—some seats are only 40 feet from the end zones. Tours start at the pro shop (be sure to arrive at least 30 minutes prior to purchase tickets) and last an hour and a half. ✉ *800 Occidental Ave. S, SoDo* ☏ *206/381–7555* ⊕ *www.qwestfield.com* ⊟ *$7* ⊙ *Sept.–May, Fri. and Sat. at 12:30 and 2:30; June–Aug., daily at 12:30 and 2:30.*

OFF THE BEATEN PATH

Safeco Field. This 47,000-seat, grass-turf, open-air baseball stadium with a retractable roof is the home of the Seattle Mariners. If you want to see the stadium in all its glory, take the one-hour tour, which brings you onto the field, into the dugouts, back to the press and locker rooms,

The Pioneer Square skyline is dominated by historic Smith Tower.

and up to the posh box seats. Wear comfortable shoes. Tours depart from the Team Store on 1st Avenue, and you purchase your tickets here, too. Afterward, head across the street to the Pyramid Alehouse for a brew. ⊠ *1st Ave. S, SoDo* ☎ *206/622–4487* ⊕ *www.mariners.mlb. com* ⊠ *$7* ☉ *Apr.–Oct. nongame-day tours at 10:30, 12:30, and 2:30, game-day tours at 10:30 and 12:30; Nov.–Mar. tours Tues.–Sun. at 12:30 and 2:30.*

Occidental Park. This picturesque cobblestone "park" and the ivy-covered wall on its western boundary show up in a lot of brochures. It's the geographical heart of the historic neighborhood—too bad its current layout is not that historic at all. Though it once was the site of the Savoy Hotel, the park actually spent a lot of time as a parking lot before the restoration of the neighborhood started in the late 1960s and early '70s. It can be lovely on sunny days, and there's a small outdoor café in seasonable weather. Note, however, that this square is a spot where homeless people congregate; depending on how intense the panhandling activity is, it may be more of a stroll-through than a sit-down-and-linger affair. The square is best avoided at night. ⊠ *Occidental Ave. S and S. Main St., Pioneer Square.*

GALLERIES

★ **Foster/White Gallery.** One of the Seattle art scene's heaviest hitters, Foster/White has digs as impressive as the works it shows: a century-old building with high ceilings and 7,000 square feet of exhibition space. Works by internationally acclaimed glass artist Dale Chihuly, and paintings, sculpture, and drawings by Northwest masters Kenneth Callahan, Mark Tobey, and George Tsutakawa are on permanent display. ⊠ *220*

A striking show at Greg Kucera Gallery

3rd Ave. S, Pioneer Square ☎ *206/622–2833* ⊕ *www.fosterwhite.com* ⌨ *Free* ⊗ *Tues.–Sat. 10–6.*

Fodor's Choice **G. Gibson Gallery.** Vintage and contemporary photography is on exhibit ★ in this elegant corner space, including shows by the likes of Michael Kenna as well as retrospectives of the works of Walker Evans and Berenice Abbott. The savvy gallery owner also shows contemporary paintings, sculpture, and mixed-media pieces. This is another institution of the Seattle art scene, and the gallery's taste is always impeccable. ⊠ *300 S. Washington St., Pioneer Square* ☎ *206/587–4033* ⊕ *www. ggibsongallery.com* ⌨ *Free* ⊗ *Tues.–Sat. 11–5.*

Fodor's Choice **Greg Kucera Gallery.** One of the most important destinations on the ★ First Thursday gallery walk, this gorgeous space is a top venue for national and regional artists. Be sure to check out the outdoor sculpture deck on the second level. If you have time for only one gallery visit, this is the place to go. You'll see big names that you might recognize along with newer artists, and the thematic group shows are consistently well thought out and well presented. ⊠ *212 3rd Ave. S, Pioneer Square* ☎ *206/624–0770* ⊕ *www.gregkucera.com* ⌨ *Free* ⊗ *Tues.–Sat. 10:30–5:30.*

James Harris. One of Seattle's oldest and most respected galleries, Harris is known for creating small shows that selectively and impeccably survey both local and international work. This strength is well showcased in the gallery's multiple tiny exhibition rooms, which provide intimacy and connectivity to tightly curated group shows, for example Alexander Kroll with Jason Hirata, or solo shows such as Margot Quan Knight, who is a regular. ✉ *312 2nd Ave. S, Pioneer Square* ☎ *206/903–6220* ⊕ *www.jamesharrisgallery.org* 🖼 *Free* ☉ *Tues.–Sat. 11–5.*

★ **Stonington Gallery.** You'll see plenty of cheesy tribal art knockoffs in tourist-trap shops, but this elegant gallery will give you a real look at the best contemporary work of Northwest Coast and Alaska tribal members (and artists from these regions working in the native style). Three floors exhibit wood carvings, paintings, sculpture, and mixed-media pieces. ✉ *119 S. Jackson St., Pioneer Square* ☎ *206/405–4040* ⊕ *www.stoningtongallery.com* 🖼 *Free* ☉ *Weekdays 10–6, Sat. 10–5:30, Sun. noon–5.*

INTERNATIONAL DISTRICT

Bright welcome banners, 12-foot fiberglass dragons clinging to lamp posts, and a traditional Chinese gate confirm you're in the International District. The I.D., as it's locally known, is synonymous with delectable dining—it has many cheap Chinese restaurants (this is the neighborhood for barbecued duck), but the best eateries reflect its Pan-Asian spirit: Vietnamese, Japanese, Malay, Cambodian. With the endlessly fun Uwajimaya shopping center, the gorgeously redesigned Wing Luke Asian Museum, and two up-and-coming galleries, you now have something to do in between bites.

WHAT TO SEE

★ **Lawrimore Project/Ohge Ltd.** The talk of the contemporary art scene, Lawrimore represents some of the hottest visual artists around, including large-scale installation provocateurs SuttonBeresCuller and Lead Pencil Studio. Lawrimore's former manager Alex Ohge opened his own gallery in the same building. Though much smaller in scope and size, Ohge Ltd. has already had some impressive shows, including a solo show of Nicholas Nyland's paintings and ceramics. ✉ *831 Airport Way S, International District* ☎ *206/501–1231 Lawrimore; 206/261–2315 Ohge* ⊕ *www.lawrimoreproject.com; www.ohgeltd.com* 🖼 *Free* ☉ *Lawrimore: Tues.–Sat. 10–5:30. Ohge: Fri. and Sat. 11–6.*

A GOOD COMBO

For a great day of walking and exploring, start your day with breakfast at Pike Place Market, then bus, cab, or stroll down 1st Avenue to Pioneer Square (you'll pass SAM en route—another option!). After visiting some art galleries (which generally open between 10:30 and noon) and stopping at any of the neighborhood's coffee shops, walk southeast to the International District for some retail therapy at Uwajimaya and a visit to the Wing Luke Asian Museum. Then cab it back to your hotel.

Fodor's Choice ★ **Uwajimaya.** This huge, fascinating Japanese supermarket is a feast for the senses. A 30-foot-long red Chinese dragon stretches above colorful mounds of fresh produce and aisles of delicious packaged goods—including spicy peas, sweet crackers, gummy candies, nut mixes, rice snacks, and colorful sweets—from countries throughout Asia. A busy food court serves sushi, Japanese bento-box meals, Chinese stir-fry combos, Korean barbecue, Hawaiian dishes, Vietnamese spring rolls, and an assortment of teas and tapioca drinks. This is the best place to pick up all sorts of snacks; dessert lovers won't know which way to turn first. The housewares section is well stocked with dishes, cookware, appliances, textiles, and gifts. There's also a card section, a Hello Kitty corner, and Yuriko's cosmetics, where you can find Shiseido products that are usually available only in Japan. Last but not least, there's a small branch of the famous Kinokuniya bookstore chain, selling paper goods, pens, stickers, gift items, and many Asian-language books. The large parking lot is free for one hour with a minimum $5 purchase (which will be no problem) or two hours with a minimum $10 purchase—don't forget to have your ticket validated by the cashiers. ✉ *600 5th Ave. S, International District* ☏ *206/624–6248* ⊕ *www.uwajimaya. com* ⊘ *Mon.–Sat. 7 AM–10 PM, Sun. 9–9.*

Fodor's Choice
★
Wing Luke Asian Museum. Named for the Northwest's first Asian-American elected official, this gorgeous museum is in a renovated 1910 hotel and commercial building that once was the first home for many new immigrants. The museum surveys the history and cultures of people from Asia and the Pacific islands who settled in the Pacific Northwest. It provides a sophisticated and often somber look at how immigrants and their descendants have transformed (and been transformed by) American culture. The evolution of the museum has been driven by community participation—the museum's library has an oral history lab, and many of the rotating exhibits are focused around stories from longtime residents and their descendants. ✉ *719 S. King St., International District* ☏ *206/623–5124* ⊕ *www.wingluke.org* ✉ *$12.95, free 1st Thurs. and 3rd Sat. of month* ⊘ *Tues.–Sun. 10–5.*

OFF THE
BEATEN
PATH
Seward Park (✉ *5895 Lake Washington Blvd. S, Columbia City–Seward Park*), 20 minutes south of Downtown, is a relatively undiscovered gem. The 300-acre park includes trails through old-growth forest, mountain views, and a small swimming beach complete with a swimming raft. Though you feel very far away from the city here, the park sits on the shores of Lake Washington. There are restrooms, picnic tables, and lifeguards on duty in summer. A large paved path circles the edge of the park, along Lake Washington, making for a lovely stroll.

CAPITOL HILL

With its mix of theaters and churches, quiet parks and nightclubs, stately homes and student apartments, Capitol Hill still deserves its reputation as Seattle's most eclectic neighborhood. Old brick buildings, modern apartment high-rises, colorfully painted two-story homes, and old-school mansions all occupy the same area. There are plenty of cute, quirky shops to browse and quite a few fantastic coffee shops.

WHAT TO SEE
Volunteer Park and the Seattle Asian Art Museum. High above the mansions of North Capitol Hill sits 45-acre Volunteer Park, a grassy expanse perfect for picnicking, sunbathing, reading, and strolling. You can tell this is one of the city's older parks by the size of the trees and the rhododendrons, many of which were planted more than a hundred years ago. The Olmsted Brothers, the premier landscape architects of the day, helped with the final design in 1904; the park has changed surprisingly

little since then. The manicured look of the park is a sharp contrast to the wilds of Discovery Park, but the design suits the needs of the densely populated neighborhood well—after all, Capitol Hill residents need someplace to set up Ultimate Frisbee games. In the center of the park is the **Seattle Asian Art Museum (SAAM, a branch of the Seattle Art Museum)**, housed in a 1933 art moderne–style edifice. It fits surprisingly well with the stark plaza stretching from the front door to the edge of a bluff, and with the lush plants of Volunteer Park. The museum's collections include thousands of paintings, sculptures, pottery, and textiles from China, Japan, India, Korea, and several Southeast Asian countries.

⊠ *Park entrance: 14th Ave. E at Prospect St., Capitol Hill* ⊕ *www. seattleartmuseum.org* ☎ *Museum 206/654–3100, conservatory 206/ 684–4743* ☎ *Park free; museum $7, free 1st Thurs. (all day) and 2nd Thurs. (5–9)* ☉ *Park daily sunrise–sunset; museum Wed.–Sun. 10–5, Thurs. until 9; conservatory Tues.–Sun. 10–4.*

OFF THE
BEATEN
PATH ☺
Fodor'sChoice
★

Washington Park Arboretum. As far as Seattle's green spaces go, this 230-acre arboretum is arguably the most beautiful. On calm weekdays the place feels really secluded; though there are trails, you feel like you're freer to roam here than at Discovery Park. The seasons are always on full display: in warm winters, flowering cherries and plums bloom in its protected valleys as early as late February, while the flowering shrubs in Rhododendron Glen and Azalea Way are in full bloom March through June. In autumn, trees and shrubs glow in hues of crimson, pumpkin, and lemon; in winter, plantings chosen specially for their stark and colorful branches dominate the landscape. From March through October, visit the peaceful **Japanese Garden**, a compressed world of mountains, forests, rivers, lakes, and tablelands. The pond, lined with blooming water irises in spring, has turtles and brightly colored koi. An authentic Japanese teahouse is reserved for tea ceremonies and instruction on the art of serving tea. The Graham Visitors Center at the park's north end has descriptions of the arboretum's flora and fauna (which include 130 endangered plants), as well as brochures, a garden gift shop, and walking-tour maps. ⊠ *2300 Arboretum Dr. E, Capitol Hill* ☎ *206/543– 8800 arboretum, 206/684–4725 Japanese garden* ⊕ *depts.washington. edu/uwbg/index.php* ☎ *Free, Japanese garden $5* ☉ *Park open daily 7* AM*–sunset, visitor center daily 10–4. Japanese garden May–Aug., daily 10–8, hrs vary seasonally, call to confirm.*

9

FREMONT AND PHINNEY RIDGE

If you ever wondered where the center of the universe is, look no further—the self-styled "Republic of Fremont" was declared just this by its residents in the 1960s. This pretty neighborhood isn't as eccentric as it used to be, but it's a great side trip when you're done sightseeing and want to do some shopping or strolling along the canal or sample artisan goodies (the neighborhood has both a chocolate factory and a craft brewery). Phinney Ridge, above Fremont, is almost entirely residential, though it shares the booming commercial street of Greenwood Avenue North with its neighbor to the north, Greenwood. Although not as strollable as similar districts in Fremont or Ballard, Greenwood Avenue has a lot of boutiques, coffee shops, and restaurants that range from go-to diner food to pricey Pacific Northwest.

WHAT TO SEE

⏲ **Theo Chocolate.** If it weren't for a small sign on the sidewalk pointing the way, you'd never know that Fremont has its own chocolate factory. Theo has helped to boost the Northwest's growing artisan chocolate scene, and has already taken the city by storm, thanks to high-quality chocolate creations. Theo uses only organic, Fair Trade cocoa beans, usually in high percentages—yielding darker, less sweet, and more complex flavors than some of their competitors. You'll see Theo chocolate bars for sale in many local businesses, from coffee shops to grocery stores. Stop by the factory to buy exquisite "confection" truffles—made daily in small batches—with unusual flavors like basil-ganache, lemon, fig-fennel, and burnt sugar. The super-friendly staff is known to be generous with samples. ■TIP→ **You can go behind the scenes as well: informative, yummy tours are offered daily; reservations aren't always necessary, but it's a good idea to call and make sure there's a spot, particularly on weekends.** ☒ *3400 Phinney Ave. N, Fremont* ☎ *206/632–5100* ⊕ *www.theochocolate.com* ☒ *Tour $6* ☉ *Store daily 10–6. Tours Mon.–Thurs. at 2 and 4, Fri. at 10, noon, 2, and 4, weekends at 10, 10:30, noon, 2, and 4.*

⏲ **Woodland Park Zoo.** Many of the 300 species of animals in this 92-acre botanical garden roam freely in habitat areas. A jaguar exhibit is the center of the Tropical Rain Forest area, where rare cats, frogs, and birds evoke South American jungles. The Humboldt penguin exhibit is environmentally sound—it uses geothermal heating and cooling to mimic the climes of the penguins native home, the coastal areas of Peru. With authentic thatch-roof buildings, the African Village has a replica schoolroom overlooking animals roaming the savanna; the Asian Elephant Forest Trail takes you through a Thai village; and the Northern Trail winds past rocky habitats where brown bears, wolves, mountain goats, and otters scramble and play. The terrain is mostly flat, making it easy for wheelchairs and strollers (which can be rented) to negotiate. The zoo has parking for $5; it's a small price to pay to avoid the headache of searching for a space on the street. ☒ *5500 Phinney Ave. N, Phinney Ridge* ☎ *206/684–4800* ⊕ *www.zoo.org* ☒ *Oct.–Apr. $11, May–Sept. $16.50* ☉ *Oct.–Apr., daily 9:30–4; May–Sept., daily 9:30–6.*

WORD OF MOUTH

"Right in the city, Volunteer Park on Capitol Hill is nice, even in winter. There's a plant conservatory, the [Seattle Asian Art Museum], plus a great view out over the city. [There are] great shops and restaurants nearby, along 15th Avenue East or on Broadway."   —suze

BALLARD

Ballard is Seattle's sweetheart. Locals of all stripes can't help but hold some affection for this neighborhood, even as it gets farther away from its humble beginnings. Ballard doesn't have many sights outside of the

Hiram M. Chittenden Locks; you'll spend more time strolling, shopping, and hanging out than crossing attractions off your list. It's got a great little nightlife, shopping, and restaurant scene on Ballard Avenue.

WHAT TO SEE

Golden Gardens Park. The waters of Puget Sound may be bone-chilling cold, but that doesn't stop folks from jumping in to cool off. Besides brave swimmers, who congregate on the small strip of sand between the parking lot and the canteen, this Ballard-area park is packed with sunbathers in summer. In other seasons, beachcombers explore during low tide, and groups gather around bonfires to socialize and watch the glorious Seattle sunsets. The park has drinking water, grills, picnic tables, phones, and restrooms. It also has two wetlands, a short loop trail, and unbelievable views of the Olympic Mountains. From Downtown, take Elliott Avenue N, which becomes 15th Avenue W, and cross the Ballard Bridge. Turn left to head west on Market Street and follow signs to the Ballard Locks; continue about another mile to the park. Note that even though the park has two dedicated parking lots, these quickly fill up on weekends, so be prepared to circle. ⌧ *8498 Seaview Pl. NW (near N.W. 85th St.), Ballard* ☎ *206/684–4075* ⌧ *Free* ☉ *Daily 6 AM–11:30 PM.*

ⓒ
Fodor's Choice
★
Hiram M. Chittenden Locks ("Ballard Locks"). The locks are an important passage in the 8-mi Lake Washington Ship Canal that connects Puget Sound to freshwater Lake Washington and Lake Union—and, on a sunny day this is a great place to visit. In addition to boat traffic, the Locks see an estimated half-million salmon and trout make the journey from saltwater to fresh each summer, with the help of a fish ladder. ⌧ *3015 N.W. 54th St., Ballard* ✥ *From Fremont, head north on Leary Way NW, west on N.W. Market St., and south on 54th St.* ☎ *206/783–7059* ⌧ *Free* ☉ *Locks daily 7 AM–9 PM; visitor center Thurs.–Mon. 10–4; call for tour information and reservations.*

OFF THE BEATEN PATH
ⓒ
Fodor's Choice
★
Gas Works Park. The park gets its name from the hulking remains of an old 1907 gas plant, which, far from being an eyesore, actually lends quirky character to the otherwise open, hilly, 20-acre park. Get a great view of Downtown Seattle while seaplanes rise up from the far shore of the lake; the best vantage point is from the zodiac sculpture at the top of the hill. The sand-bottom playground has monkey bars, wooden platforms, and a spinning metal merry-go-round. Crowds throng to picnic and enjoy outdoor summer concerts, movies, and the July 4th fireworks display over Lake Union. ■ TIP→ This lovely park can easily be reached from Fremont Center, via the waterfront Burke-Gilman Trail—remember to stay in the clearly designated pedestrian lane, as you'll be sharing the trail with many other walkers, joggers, and speed-demon bicyclists. ⌧ *2101 N. Northlake Way, at Meridian Ave. N (the north end of Lake Union) Wallingford* ☉ *Daily 4 AM–11:30 PM.*

9

UNIVERSITY DISTRICT

The U-District, as everyone calls it, is the neighborhood surrounding the University of Washington (UW or "U-Dub" to locals). The campus is extraordinarily beautiful (especially in springtime, when the cherry blossoms are flowering), and the Henry Art Gallery, on its western edge, is one of the city's best small museums. Beyond that, the appeal of the neighborhood lies in its variety of cheap, delicious ethnic eateries, its proximity to the waters of Portage and Union Bays and Lake Washington, and its youthful energy.

WHAT TO SEE

Fodor'sChoice
★
Henry Art Gallery. The Henry is perhaps the best reason to take a side trip to the U-District. The large gallery consistently presents sophisticated and thought-provoking work. Notable recent examples: large-scale installations by environmental artist Maya Lin, photography by Kiki Smith, and a comprehensive survey of the multimedia works of William Kentridge. Exhibits pull from many different genres and include mixed media, photography, 19th- and 20th-century paintings, and textiles from the permanent collection. Its permanent installation, *Light Reign,* is a "Skyspace" from artist James Turrell—an elliptical chamber that allows visitors to view the sky (more than a few people have used this as a meditation spot); at night the chamber is illuminated by thousands of LED lights. ⊠ *University of Washington campus, 15th Ave. NE and N.E. 41st St., University District* ☎ *206/543–2280* ⊕ *www.henryart. org* ☜ *$10* ☉ *Thurs. and Fri. 11–9, weekends 11–4.*

WEST SEATTLE

Cross the bridge to West Seattle and it's another world altogether. Jutting out into Elliott Bay and Puget Sound, separated from the city by the Duwamish waterway, this out-of-the-way neighborhood covers most of the city's western peninsula—and, indeed, it has an identity of its own. In summer throngs of people hang out at Alki Beach—Seattle's taste of California—while others head for the trails and playgrounds of Lincoln Park to the west.

WHAT TO SEE

Fodor'sChoice
★
Alki Point and Beach. In summer, West Seattle's Alki Beach is as close to California as Seattle gets—and some hardy residents even swim in the cold, salty waters of Puget Sound here (water temperature ranges from 46 to 56 degrees F). This 2½-mi stretch of sand has views of the Seattle skyline and the Olympic Mountains, and the beachfront promenade is especially popular with skaters, joggers, and cyclists. Year-round, Seattleites come to build sand castles, beachcomb, and fly kites; in winter, storm-watchers come to see the crashing waves. Facilities include drinking water, grills, picnic tables, phones, and restrooms; restaurants line the street across from the beach. ■TIP→ To get here from Downtown, take either I-5 south or Highway 99 south to the West Seattle Bridge (keep an eye out, as this exit is easy to miss) and exit onto Harbor Avenue SW, turning right at the stoplight. Alki Point is the place where David Denny, John Low, and Lee Terry arrived in September 1851, ready to found a

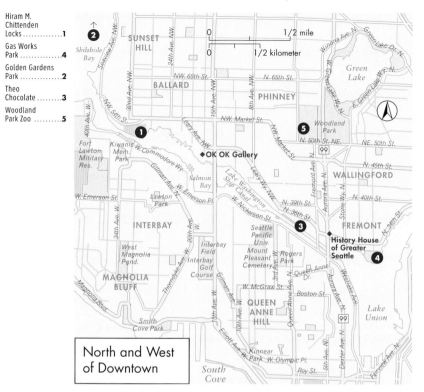

**North and West
of Downtown**

city. One of 195 Lady Liberty replicas found around the country lives near the 2700 block of Alki Avenue SW; it was erected by Boy Scouts in 1952 as part of their national "Strengthening the Arm of Liberty" campaign. The so-called Miss Liberty (or Little Liberty) is a popular meeting point for beachfront picnics and dates.

**OFF THE
BEATEN
PATH**

Museum of Flight. Boeing, the world's largest builder of aircraft, was founded in Seattle in 1916. So it's not surprising that this facility at Boeing Field, south of the International District, is one of the city's best museums. It's especially fun for kids, who can climb in many of the aircraft and pretend to fly, make flight-related crafts, or attend special programs. The Red Barn, Boeing's original airplane factory, houses an exhibit on the history of flight. The Great Gallery, a dramatic structure designed by Ibsen Nelson, contains more than 20 vintage airplanes. The Personal Courage Wing showcases World War I and World War II fighter planes. ■TIP→ **West Seattle is a good jumping-off point for a side trip to the Museum of Flight, which is farther south, close to Sea-Tac airport.** Take the West Seattle Bridge back toward I–5, and then head south on I–5. At Exit 158, merge right onto S. Boeing Access Road. Turn right at the first stoplight (E. Marginal Way S); the museum is on the right after ½ mi. ⊠ *9404 E. Marginal Way S, Tukwila* ✛ *Take I–5 south to Exit 158, turn right on Marginal Way S* ☎ *206/764–5720*

⊕ *www.museumofflight.org* ⊠ *$15* ⊗ *Daily 10–5, 1st Thurs. of every month until 9* PM.

THE EASTSIDE

The suburbs east of Lake Washington can easily supplement any Seattle itinerary. The center of East King County is Bellevue, a fast-growing city with its own downtown core, high-end shopping, and a notable dining scene. Kirkland, north of Bellevue, has a few shops and restaurants (including fabulous Café Juanita) plus lakefront promenades. Redmond and Issaquah, to the northeast and southeast respectively, are gateways to greenery. Woodinville, north of Redmond, is the ambassador for Washington State's wine industry, with many wineries and tasting rooms.

WHAT TO SEE

Bellevue Botanical Gardens. This beautiful, 36-acre public area in the middle of Wilburton Hill Park is encircled by spectacular perennial borders, brilliant rhododendron displays, and patches of alpine and rock gardens. ■ TIP→ **Docents lead tours of the gardens Saturdays and Sundays (April through October), beginning at the visitor center at 2** PM. The Yao Japanese garden is beautiful in fall, when the leaves change color. One of the most interesting features of the park is the Waterwise Garden, which was planted with greenery that needs little water in summer to demonstrate that not all great gardens require wasteful daily drenchings with a hose or sprinkler system. When you're tired of manicured gardens, take the Lost Meadow Trail, which winds through a heavily forested area, to see nature's disorganized beauty. The gardens are a short drive from Bellevue's core. ⊠ *12001 Main St., Bellevue* ☎ *425/452–2750* ⊕ *www. bellevuebotanical.org* ⊠ *Free* ⊗ *Gardens daily dawn–dusk, visitor center daily 9–4.*

⟲ **Marymoor Park.** This 640-acre park has the famous Marymoor Velo-
★ drome—the Pacific Northwest's sole cycling arena—a 45-foot-high climbing rock, game fields, tennis courts, a model airplane launching area, off-leash dog space, and the Pea Patch community garden. You can row on Lake Sammamish, fish off a pier, or head straight to the picnic grounds or to the Willowmoor Farm, an estate in the park. It has a Dutch-style windmill and the historic Clise Mansion, which contains the Marymoor Museum of Eastside History. Marymoor has some of the best bird-watching in this largely urban area. It's possible to spot some 24 resident species, including great blue herons, belted kingfishers, buffleheads, short-eared and barn owls, and red-tailed hawks. Occasionally, bald eagles soar past the lakefront. The Sammamish River, which flows through the western section of the park, is an important salmon spawning stream. King County Parks naturalists periodically give guided wildlife tours. With all these attractions, it's no wonder the park has more than 1 million visitors annually.

Ambitious hikers can follow the Burke-Gilman/Sammamish River Trail to access the park on foot. ⊠ *6046 W. Lake Sammamish Pkwy. NE, Redmond* ⊹ *Take Rte. 520 east to the West Lake Sammamish Pkwy. exit. Turn right (southbound) on W. Lake Sammamish Pkwy. NE. Turn left at the traffic light* ⊕ *www.metrokc.gov/parks/marymoor* ⊘ *Daily 8 AM–dusk.*

WHERE TO EAT

The number after the ⊕ *symbol indicates the property's coordinate on the map grid.*

Thanks to inventive chefs, first-rate local produce, adventurous diners, and a bold entrepreneurial spirit, Seattle has become one of the culinary capitals of the nation. Fearless young chefs have stepped in and raised the bar. Nowadays, fresh and often foraged produce, local seafood, and imaginative techniques make the quality of local cuisine even higher.

The city is particularly strong on New American, French, and Asian cuisines. Chefs continuously fine-tune what can best be called Pacific Northwest cuisine, which features fresh, local ingredients, including anything from nettles and mushrooms foraged in nearby forests; colorful berries, apples, and cherries grown by Washington State farmers; and outstanding seafood from the cold northern waters of the Pacific Ocean, including wild salmon, halibut, oysters, Dungeness crab, and geoduck. Seattle boasts quite a few outstanding bakeries, too, whose breads and desserts you'll see touted on many menus.

WHAT IT COSTS AT DINNER				
¢	$	$$	$$$	$$$$
under $8	$8–$16	$17–$24	$25–$32	over $32

Price per person for a median main course or equivalent combination of smaller dishes. Note: if a restaurant offers only prix-fixe (set-price) meals, it has been given the price category that reflects the full prix-fixe price.

DOWNTOWN AND BELLTOWN

$$$
NEW AMERICAN
Fodor's Choice
★

✕ **Boat Street Café & Kitchen.** Two rooms decorated in a French bistro–meets–Nantucket decor have a scattering of casual tables with fresh flowers and candles. Tables often fill up with couples at night, but the lunchtime scene runs the gamut from Downtown office workers to tourists. Food is understated, fresh, and divine: start with raw oysters and a crisp glass of white wine. Next up, sautéed Medjool dates sprinkled with *fleur de sel* and olive oil, a radish salad with pine nuts, or a plate of the famous housemade pickles. Entrées, too, take advantage of whatever is in season, so expect anything from Oregon hanger steak with olive tapenade to spring-onion flan and Alaskan halibut with cauliflower. Though it's housed in the ground floor of an odd office building (just north of the Olympic Sculpture Park), Boat Street positively blooms in the quirky space, and the food and dining experience are memorable and uniquely Seattle. Save room for desserts: wild blackberry clafouti, honey ice cream, and vanilla-bean *pot de crème* are just a few toothsome examples. Monday through Sunday, brunch and lunch are served from 10:30 to 2:30. ⊠ *3131 Western Ave., Belltown*

9

☎ *206/632–4602* ⊕ *www.boatstreetcafe.com* ▭ *D, MC, V* ⊙ *No dinner Sun.–Mon.* ⊹ *C3.*

$$$
FRENCH
Fodor'sChoice
★

✕ **Café Campagne/Campagne.** The white walls, picture windows, pressed linens, fresh flowers, and candles at charming French restaurant Campagne—which overlooks Pike Place Market and Elliott Bay—evoke Provence. So does the robust French country fare, with starters such as grilled housemade merguez sausage, pork rillettes, and potato gnocchi with braised artichokes and black-truffle butter. Main plates include pork short ribs with onion, raisin, and tomato compote; steamed mussels with expertly prepared *pommes frites*; and Oregon beef rib eye with parsley-crusted marrow bones. ■ TIP➔ Campagne is open only for dinner, but downstairs, the equally charming (some would say even more lovely and authentic) Café Campagne serves breakfast, lunch, and dinner daily. The café is an exceptional place for a satisfying weekend brunch before hitting Pike Place Market on foot. Try the impeccable quiche du jour with green salad; poached eggs with pearl onions, bacon, and champignons; or brioche French toast—plus a big bowl of *café au lait.* ⊠ *Inn at the Market, 86 Pine St., Downtown* ☎ *206/728–2800* ⊕ *www. campagnerestaurant.com* ▭ *AE, DC, MC, V* ⊹ *D4.*

$$$
MEDITERRANEAN
Fodor'sChoice
★

✕ **Lola.** Tom Douglas dishes out his signature Northwest style, spiked with Greek and Mediterranean touches here—another huge success for the local celebrity chef, if not his best. Try a glorious tagine of goat meat with mustard and rosemary; grape leaf–wrapped trout; lamb burgers with chickpea fries; and scrumptious spreads including hummus, tzatziki, and *harissa* (a red-pepper concoction). Booths are usually full at this bustling, dimly lighted restaurant, which anchors the Hotel Ändra. The fabulous weekend brunches are inventive: try Tom's Big Breakfast—octopus, mustard greens, cumin-spiced yogurt, bacon, and an egg. If you still have room, there are made-to-order doughnuts, too. ⊠ *2000 4th Ave., Belltown* ☎ *206/441–1430* ⊕ *www.tomdouglas.com* ▭ *D, MC, V* ⊹ *E4.*

¢–$
BAKERY

✕ **Macrina Bakery.** One of Seattle's favorite bakeries is also popular for breakfast and brunch. With its perfectly executed breads and pastries—from Nutella brioche and ginger cookies to almond croissants and dark-chocolate sugar-dusted brownies—it has become a true Belltown institution, even if this small spot is usually too frenzied to invite the hours of idleness that other coffee shops may inspire. ■ TIP➔ Macrina is an excellent place to take a delicious break on your way to or from the Olympic Sculpture Park. You can also wait for a table and have a larger breakfast or lunch—sandwiches, quiches, and salads are all yummy and fresh. ⊠ *2408 1st Ave., Belltown* ☎ *206/448–4032* ⊕ *www.macrinabakery. com* ⊹ *D4.*

$$$$
PACIFIC
NORTHWEST
Fodor'sChoice
★

✕ **Matt's in the Market.** Your first dinner at Matt's is like a first date you hope will never end. One of the most beloved of Pike Place Market's restaurants, Matt's is now owned by Dan Bugge, who continues to value intimate dining, fresh ingredients, and superb service. An expansion nearly doubled the number of seats, all the better to enjoy old favorites—and some new dishes, as well. Perch at the bar for pints and a delicious pulled pork or hot grilled-tuna sandwich or cup of gumbo, or be seated at a table—complete with vases filled with flowers from

Matt's in the Market

the market—for a seasonal menu that synthesizes the best picks from the restaurant's produce vendors and an excellent wine list. At dinner, starters might include such delectable items as Manila clams steamed in beer with herbs and chilies; entrées always include at least one catch of the day—such as whole fish in saffron broth or Alaskan halibut with pea vines—as well as such delectable entrées as seafood stew, beef short ribs, or braised lamb shank with ancho chili. Locals and visitors alike keep this low-key but special spot humming. ⊠ *94 Pike St., Suite 32, Downtown* ☎ *206/467–7909* ⊕ *www.mattsinthemarket.com* ⊼ *Reservations essential* ⊟ *MC, V* ⊗ *Closed Sun.* ✛ *E4.*

9

\$\$
SEAFOOD
✕ **McCormick's Fish House & Bar.** Evening happy hours (Monday to Friday 3:30–6 and 9:30–11:30) at this restaurant are popular with the after-work crowd; prices are very reasonable (there's a \$2 bar menu), and the rotating selection is satisfying—burgers, spring rolls, taquitos, oysters, and more. The dining room specializes in typical steak and seafood fare. The raw bar has a huge selection of oysters; in summer you can enjoy the bounty in the open-air dining area out front. The food and good times are good enough here that even some chain-hating Seattleites don't mind patronizing the place. Don't expect much in the way of atmosphere; come for the fresh fish. ⊠ *722 4th Ave., Downtown* ☎ *206/682–3900* ⊕ *www.mccormickandschmicks.com* ⊟ *AE, D, DC, MC, V* ⊗ *No lunch weekends* ✛ *E5.*

\$\$\$
JAPANESE
Fodor's Choice
★
✕ **Shiro's Sushi Restaurant.** Shiro Kashiba is the most famous sushi chef in Seattle; he's been in town for more than 40 years, and he still sometimes takes time to helm the sushi bar at his popular restaurant. ◾ TIP→ **If you get a seat at the sushi bar, in front of Shiro, don't be shy—this is one place where ordering omakase (chef's choice) is a must.** Willfully unconcerned

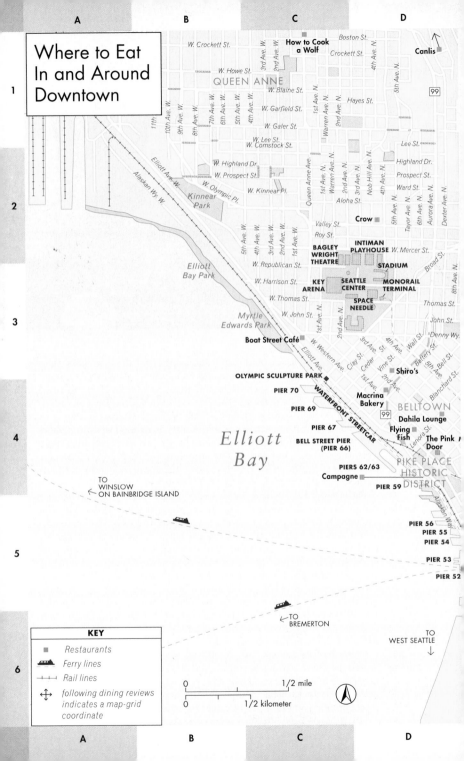

Where to Eat In and Around Downtown

KEY

- ■ *Restaurants*
- 🚋 *Ferry lines*
- ┼┼┼ *Rail lines*
- ✛ *following dining reviews indicates a map-grid coordinate*

QUEEN ANNE

How to Cook a Wolf

Canlis

W. Crockett St.
Boston St.
Crockett St.
W. Howe St.
W. Blaine St.
W. Garfield St.
Hayes St.
W. Galer St.
W. Lee St.
Lee St.
W. Comstock St.
W. Highland Dr.
Highland Dr.
W. Prospect St.
Prospect St.
W. Olympic Pl.
Ward St.
W. Kinnear Pl.
Aloha St.
Kinnear Park

Valley St.
Crow
Roy St.

INTIMAN PLAYHOUSE
BAGLEY WRIGHT THEATRE
W. Mercer St.
STADIUM
W. Republican St.
MONORAIL TERMINAL
KEY ARENA
SEATTLE CENTER
W. Harrison St.
SPACE NEEDLE
W. Thomas St.
Thomas St.
W. John St.
John St.

Myrtle Edwards Park
Denny Wy.
Boat Street Café
Shiro's
OLYMPIC SCULPTURE PARK
Macrina Bakery
BELLTOWN
PIER 70
Dahila Lounge
PIER 69
Flying Fish
The Pink Door
PIER 67
BELL STREET PIER (PIER 66)
PIKE PLACE HISTORIC DISTRICT
PIERS 62/63
Campagne
PIER 59

Elliott Bay

TO WINSLOW ON BAINBRIDGE ISLAND

PIER 56
PIER 55
PIER 54
PIER 53
PIER 52

TO BREMERTON

TO WEST SEATTLE

Elliott Ave. W.
Alaskan Wy. W.
11th
10th Ave. W.
9th Ave. W.
8th Ave. W.
7th Ave. W.
6th Ave. W.
5th Ave. W.
4th Ave. W.
3rd Ave. W.
2nd Ave. W.
1st Ave. W.
Queen Anne Ave. N.
Warren Ave. N.
2nd Ave. N.
3rd Ave. N.
Nob Hill Ave. N.
Taylor Ave. N.
6th Ave. N.
Aurora Ave. N.
Dexter Ave. N.
5th Ave. N.
8th Ave. N.
Broad St.
3rd Ave.
4th Ave.
Vine St.
Cedar St.
Clay St.
Wall St.
Battery St.
Bell St.
5th Ave.
Blanchard St.
Lenora St.
Elliott Ave.
W. Western Ave.
1st Ave.
2nd Ave.
Alaskan Wy.

WATERFRONT STREETCAR

99

Elliott Bay Park

0   1/2 mile
0   1/2 kilometer

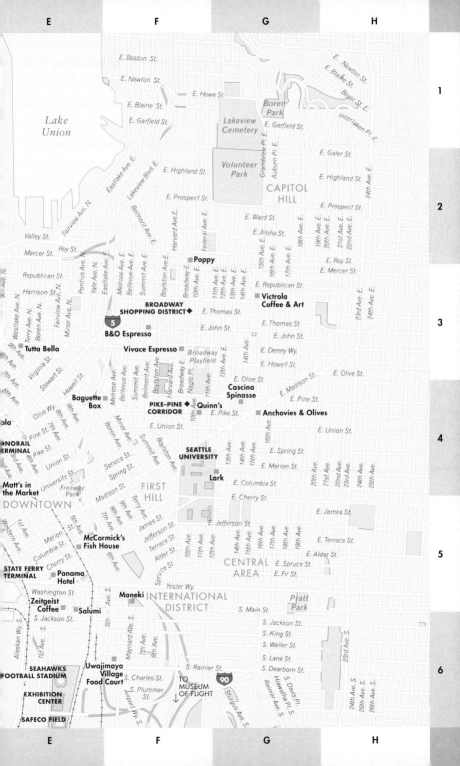

with atmosphere, this simple spot is a real curiosity amid Belltown's chic establishments, though it does seem to be charging Belltown prices for simpler pleasures like teriyaki and tempura dinners. Be forewarned that the place has a reputation for spotty table service. ✉ *2401 2nd Ave., Belltown* ☎ *206/443–9844* ⊕ *www.shiros.com* ▭ *AE, MC, V* ☺ *No lunch* ✛ *D3.*

SOUTH LAKE UNION, AND QUEEN ANNE

$$$$
PACIFIC
NORTHWEST

✕ **Canlis.** Canlis has been setting the standard for opulent dining in Seattle since the 1950s. And although there are no longer kimono-clad waitresses, the food and the views overlooking Lake Union are still remarkable. Executive chef Jason Franey (formerly of Manhattan's acclaimed Eleven Madison Park) has retained the restaurant's signature insistence on the finest cuts of meat and the freshest produce. To start, try fresh braised veal cheek with lemon confit, fresh carrot soup, foie-gras terrine, or a Dungeness crab cake with Granny Smith apple. The famous Canlis Salad boasts romaine, bacon, Romano cheese, and mint, in a dressing of fresh lemon, olive oil, and coddled egg—always a crowd-pleaser. But the entrées are the stars here: king salmon with lentils, Muscovy duck with hedgehog mushrooms, and Wagyu tenderloin served atop shallots and potatoes. ■ TIP➔ **The only way to wash this divine food down is with a bottle from one of the finest—if not the finest—wine cellars in town.** A banana-spiked *mille-feuille* or a "chocolate covered chocolate" molten creation should send you on your way happily. Canlis never fails to feel like a special-occasion splurge—make reservations well in advance, and request a table with a view. ✉ *2576 Aurora Ave. N, Queen Anne* ☎ *206/283–3313* ⊕ *www.canlis.com* ⏣ *Reservations essential*; *jacket required* ▭ *AE, DC, MC, V* ☺ *Closed Sun. No lunch* ✛ *D1.*

$$
NEW AMERICAN

✕ **Crow.** Inhabiting a converted warehouse space complete with artfully exposed ductwork, a modern comfort-food menu, and a list of shareable small plates, Crow feels very of-the-moment in Seattle. But this bistro has proved it has staying power and has become a Queen Anne institution. The food is the main component of locals' loyalty; share some appetizers and then move on to the pan-roasted chicken wrapped in prosciutto, portobello mushroom risotto, or the wonderful house lasagna with Italian sausage. Satisfy your sweet tooth with lavender crème brûlée. Service is good, even on busy nights. ✉ *823 5th Ave. N, Queen Anne* ☎ *206/283–8800* ⊕ *www.eatatcrow.com* ▭ *MC, V* ☺ *No lunch* ✛ *D2.*

$$$–$$$$
SEAFOOD

✕ **Flying Fish.** Chef-owner Christine Keff got the idea for Flying Fish on a trip to Thailand; she was impressed by the simplicity and quality of the seafood dishes grilled up in beachside restaurants. Even after almost 15 years, Flying Fish has stayed true to its inspiration: the fish is some of the freshest you'll find in Seattle, every ingredient is organic, and the dishes, while inventive, never get too busy. The menu changes daily, but you'll often find seafood and shellfish prepared with Thai curries and seasonings, and you'll always have the option of the delicious no-nonsense fried chicken. This joint is always jumping; dinner reservations are strongly recommended. ⊠ *300 Westlake Ave. N, South Lake Union* ☎ *206/728–8595* ⊕ *www.flyingfishrestaurant.com* ▭ *AE, DC, MC, V* ⊙ *No lunch weekends* ♦ *D4.*

$$–$$$ ✕ **How to Cook a Wolf.** This sleek eatery—complete with curving-wood
ITALIAN ceiling and loads of trendy young couples perched at its tables—"pays homage to MFK Fisher and her philosophy of taking simple ingredients and transforming them into culinary splendor." Fresh, artisanal ingredients are the major draws, with starters such as cured-meat platters, roasted almonds, pork terrine, chicken-liver mousse, and arugula salad, and tasty main dishes focused on handmade pastas—the *casarecce* features bacon, onion, and black pepper. Fresh skate with brown butter and capers or quail with saffron aioli are examples of the rustic-chic Italian-inspired dishes chef Ethan Stowell has perfected in his various eateries around town. This restaurant is worth the trip even if you're far from Queen Anne. ⊠ *2208 Queen Anne Ave. N, Queen Anne* ☎ *206/838–8090* ⊕ *www.howtocookawolf.com* ▭ *MC, V* ♦ *C1.*

¢ ✕ **Vivace Espresso.** A cozy and large outpost of this famed Capitol Hill
COFFEEHOUSE roaster, the Vivace coffee shrine in South Lake Union is housed right across from the REI megastore and amidst a growing number of hip boutiques and design shops. Grab a seat, order an expertly prepared espresso beverage, and munch on a small variety of snacks—this is a perfect stop after an exhausting jaunt through REI before you head to the next adventure. ⊠ *227 Yale Ave. N, South Lake Union* ☎ *206/388–5164* ⊕ *www.espressovivace.com* ▭ *AE, MC, V* ♦ *F3.*

PIONEER SQUARE

$ ✕ **Salumi.** The chef-owner Armandino Batali (father of famed New
ITALIAN York chef Mario Batali) makes superior cured meats for this miniature
Fodor's Choice lunch spot run by his daughter, who serves up hearty, unforgettable
★ sandwiches filled with all sorts of goodies. Order a salami, bresaola, porchetta, meatball, oxtail, sausage, or lamb prosciutto sandwich with onions, peppers, cheese, and olive oil. Most people do opt for takeout, though; be prepared for a long line, which most likely will be stretching well beyond the front door. ■ TIP➡ Note that Salumi is open only Tuesday–Friday from 11 AM to 4 PM. ⊠ *309 3rd Ave. S, Pioneer Square* ☎ *206/621–8772* ⊕ *www.salumicuredmeats.com* ▭ *AE, D, DC, MC, V* ⊙ *Closed Sat.–Mon.* ♦ *E5.*

¢–$ ✕ **Zeitgeist Coffee.** Not only is Zeitgeist one of the best coffee shops in
COFFEEHOUSE the southern part of the city, it is also a colorful local favorite. Even Seattleites who don't haunt Pioneer Square will happily hunt for parking to spend a few hours here. Housed in one of Pioneer Square's great brick buildings, with high ceilings and a few artfully exposed ducts and pipes, Zeitgeist has a simple, classy look that's the perfect backdrop for the frequent art shows held here. You'll feel smarter just sitting in here while you watch the parade of gallery-goers, locals, tourists, and Pioneer Square characters pass through. Plus, the sandwiches and pastries rival the fantastic espresso beverages. ⊠ *171 S. Jackson St., Pioneer Square* ☎ *206/583–0497* ⊕ *www.zeitgeistcoffee.com* ♦ *E5.*

9

INTERNATIONAL DISTRICT

$ ✕ **Maneki.** The oldest Japanese restaurant in Seattle, Maneki is no longer

JAPANESE   a hidden gem that caters to in-the-know locals and chefs from other Japanese restaurants in the area, but the food isn't any less authentic. Though the restaurant serves decent sushi, its better known for its home-style Japanese, which can be ordered as small plates—often enjoyed with copious amounts of sake. Try the miso black cod collar, a rice bowl with your choice of meat and greens, and any of the delicious daily fish specials. Rice-paper lamps and screens add a little bit of Old Japan to the otherwise uninspiring space. Larger parties can reserve a tatami room. Maneki is a mob scene on weekends—so don't even think about coming here without a reservation. ✉ *304 6th Ave. S, International District* ☎ *206/622–2631* ⊕ *www.manekirestaurant.com* ▭ *V* ☺ *Closed Mon. No lunch* ✛ *F5.*

¢   ✕ **Panama Hotel Tea and Coffee Shop.** On the ground floor of the historic

TEAHOUSE   Panama Hotel is a serene teahouse with tons of personality and a subtle Asian flair that reflects its former life as a Japanese bathhouse. The space is lovely, with exposed-brick walls, shiny, hardwood floors, and black-and-white photos of Old Seattle (many of them relating to the history of the city's Japanese immigrants). Kick back with an individual pot of tea—there are dozens of varieties—or an espresso. This is a good place to bring a book, as it's usually calm and quiet. ✉ *607 S. Main St., International District* ☎ *206/515–4000* ⊕ *www.panamahotelseattle. com/teahouse.htm* ▭ *No credit cards* ✛ *E5.*

$ ✕ **Uwajimaya Village Food Court.** Not only an outstanding grocery and

ASIAN   gift shop, Uwajimaya also has a hoppin' food court offering a quick tour of Asian cuisines at lunch-counter prices. For Japanese or Chinese, the deli offers sushi, teriyaki, and barbecued duck. For Vietnamese food, try the fresh spring rolls, served with hot chili sauce, at Saigon Bistro. Shilla has Korean grilled beef and *kimchi* stew, and there are Filipino *lumpia* (spring rolls) to be found at Inay's Kitchen. Finish your meal with some cream puffs at Beard Papa's or simply stroll the aisles in Uwajimaya to find fun snacks like rice candy, gummy delicacies, and mochi ice cream. ✉ *600 5th Ave. S, International District* ☎ *206/624–6248* ▭ *MC, V* ✛ *F6.*

CAPITOL HILL

$$$ ✕ **Anchovies & Olives.** A sleek, sophisticated space serves an equally posh

SEAFOOD   clientele. An utterly exposed, simple kitchen set-up anchors this spot

Fodor's Choice   in the ground floor of a residential high-rise at the eastern end of the

★   Pike–Pine Corridor. The food at this Ethan Stowell eatery is downright tantalizing, and the young line chefs and waitstaff are charming. Modern bent-wood wall coverings, artful lighting, a well-edited Italian wine list, and a lively small bar create the backdrop for some of the best, and most elegant, seafood dishes in the city, including mackerel with cauliflower and radicchio; skate wing with asparagus and saffron leeks; clams with pine nuts and hot pepper; and octopus with corona beans and fennel. Seafood is lovingly prepared and never overdone: the inherent texture and flavor of each fresh piece of fish is respected,

Anchovies & Olives

and the Mediterranean-inspired garnishes, sauces, and accompaniments that go with them are nothing if not graceful. A small *crudo* selection and salads such as golden beets with almonds and endive will get the meal started. Plates are smaller and are easily shared. A tiny selection of desserts is equally sublime. Reservations are highly recommended. ⊠ *1550 15th Ave., at Pine St., Capitol Hill* ☎ *206/838–8080* ⊕ *www. anchoviesandolives.com* ▭ *AE, MC, V* ✢ *G4.*

¢–$ **✕ B&O Espresso.** A cute, cozy neighborhood favorite that looks like a funky, shabby-chic version of a Victorian tearoom, B&O was one of Seattle's earliest purveyors of the latte, and the drinks are still going strong. The on-site bakery turns out memorable desserts and cakes—including devil's food, carrot, cheese, and lemon-chiffon varieties. The place is always packed for weekend brunch. B&O is much less of a hipster scene than many of the Hill's other coffeehouses. ⊠ *204 Belmont Ave. E, Capitol Hill* ☎ *206/322–5028* ⊕ *www.b-oespresso.com* ▭ *AE, MC, V* ✢ *F3.*

COFFEEHOUSE

$ **✕ Baguette Box.** A short walk up the hill from Downtown, perched on the western edge of Capitol Hill, this relaxed lunch (or early-dinner) spot serves Vietnamese-inspired sandwiches on crusty baguettes. You can eat at one of the simple tables here or take your meal to go. ■ TIP➔ **This is one of our favorite casual lunch options on Capitol Hill, especially if you're making your way to the Hill on foot after a morning Downtown. Simply start walking up Pine Street—Baguette Box will be on the right-hand side after you cross over I–5.** Standout sandwiches include roasted leg of lamb with cucumber yogurt; habit-forming crispy drunken chicken with tangy sauce; braised Berkshire pork belly; and grilled Asian eggplant with feta cheese and tomato. Truffle fries are also

DELI

fantastic. Its big-sister restaurant, Monsoon, is also divine. ⊠ *1203 Pine St., Capitol Hill* ☎ *206/332–0220* ⊕ *www.baguettebox.com* ⊗ *Closes at 8* PM ▭ *AE, MC, V* ✛ *F4.*

$$$
ITALIAN
Fodor's Choice
★

✕ **Cascina Spinasse.** A postage stamp–size eatery with cream-colored lace curtains and true Italian soul has bar seating and communal tables. Squeeze in, and come hungry, because chef Jason Stratton knows how to make pasta. It's made fresh daily and comes with such sauces and fillings as lamb or rabbit ragù, roasted carrot and goat cheese, or duck confit. Brussels sprouts and kale are vivified with pine nuts and aged balsamic; the melt-in-your-mouth gnocchi nearly float off the plate. *Secondi* options can range from braised pork belly with cabbage to stewed venison served over polenta. The dessert selections are lovely; two favorites are *panna cotta* with cardoon flower honey and delectable *gianduja* semifreddo. With the friendly service and dynamite grappa, amaro, and wine selection, you likely won't mind paying the price, even if it is loud and small. It's a night on the town to remember, and a perfect way to experience Capitol Hill's flourishing restaurant scene. ⊠ *1531 14th Ave., Capitol Hill* ☎ *206/251–7673* ⊕ *www.spinasse.com* ▭ *AE, MC, V* ⊗ *No lunch* ✛ *G4.*

$$$–$$$$
NEW AMERICAN
Fodor's Choice
★

✕ **Lark.** Just off the Pike–Pine Corridor in a converted garage with exposed beams and gauzy curtain dividers, Lark was one of the first restaurants to kick-start the small-plate trend in Seattle. And small plates often don't feel like enough, as the food is so mouth-wateringly delicious—the idea is to order several and enjoy to your heart's content. You can always order more, and the expert servers can help you choose from an impressive wine list, and will happily offer up their opinions of the long menu, which is divided into cheese; vegetables and grains; charcuterie; fish; meat; and, of course, dessert. Seasonally inspired dishes include chicken-liver parfait with grilled ramps; pork rillettes with bright radishes; carpaccio of yellowtail with preserved lemons; veal sweetbreads with black truffle; and poached organic egg with chorizo. For dessert, try the Theo-chocolate madeleines (lots of them!), which come wrapped in a white napkin with a small pot of dipping chocolate. ■ TIP ➜ **Reservations are recommended; if you do have to wait for a table, hop next door to Licorous (which also serves an abbreviated menu) for a distinctly cool libation.** ⊠ *926 12th Ave., Capitol Hill* ☎ *206/323–5275* ⊕ *www.larkseattle.com* ▭ *MC, V AE* ✛ *G4.*

$$$$
NEW AMERICAN
Fodor's Choice
★

✕ **Poppy.** Jerry Traunfeld's bright, airy restaurant on the northern end of Broadway is a feast for the senses. Deep-red walls, high-design lighting fixtures, friendly staff, and a happening bar area welcome you to this hip eatery with floor-to-ceiling windows. Start with one of the many interesting cocktails and eggplant fries with sea salt and honey; then you can peruse the interesting menu, which offers thali (and cleverly named "smalli")—inspired by an Indian meal of the same name in which a selection of different dishes is served in small compartments on a large platter. The inspired New American cuisine is completely dependent on seasonal bounty—you'll enjoy anything from stinging-nettle soup; braised Wagyu beef cheek with ginger; rhubarb pickles; onion-poppy naan; and roasted halibut with saffron leeks. Gimmicky, some say— we disagree. Somehow each small-portioned delight is better than the last, and your senses will be pulled happily in a variety of Asian- and Northwest-inspired directions. ■TIP➔ **Fantastic vegetarian and standard thali-style menus change regularly to reflect whatever is in season.** It's a fun way to dine—make reservations, and come hungry and ready to be delighted. ✉ *622 Broadway E, Capitol Hill* ☎ *206/324–1108* ⊕ *www. poppyseattle.com* ▭ *AE, MC, V* ☉ *No lunch* ✢ *F2.*

$–$$
GASTROPUB
Fodor's Choice
★
✕ **Quinn's.** Capitol Hill's coolest gastropub has friendly bartenders, an *amazing* selection of beers from all over the world on tap (with the West Coast and Belgium heavily represented), an extensive list of whiskies, and an edgy menu of quite good food, which you can enjoy at the long bar or at a table on either of the two floors of the industrial-chic space. Spicy fried peanuts, baby lettuces in sherry vinaigrette, and country-style rabbit pâté are good ways to start—then you can choose from Painted Hills beef tartare with pumpernickel crisps, a delicious beef burger with cheddar and bacon, perfect marrow bones with baguette and citrus jam, or a cheese and mostarda plate. The folks here take their libations seriously, so feel free to chat up the bartenders about their favorite whisky or brew. ✉ *1001 E. Pike St., Capitol Hill* ☎ *206/325–7711* ⊕ *www.quinnspubseattle.com* ▭ *AE, MC, V* ☉ *No lunch* ✢ *F4.*

¢
COFFEEHOUSE
Victrola Coffee. Victrola is probably the most loved of Capitol Hill's many coffeehouses, and it's easy to see why: The space is lovely—its walls feature constantly changing artwork from local painters and photographers—and the coffee, pastries, and sandwiches (especially the "Duke Ellington" version, with fresh basil, cheese, and turkey) are fantastic, the baristas are skillful, and everyone, from soccer moms to indie rockers, is made to feel like this neighborhood spot exists just for them. Unfortunately, it can be hard to score a table here, especially if you have a big group. If 15th Avenue E is too far off the beaten path for you, there's a branch at 310 East Pike Street (☎ *206/462–6259*), between Melrose and Bellevue. ✉ *411 15th Ave. E, Capitol Hill* ☎ *206/429–6269* ⊕ *www.victrolacoffee.com* ▭ *AE, MC, V* ✢ *G3.*

¢
COFFEEHOUSE
Vivace Espresso Bar at Brix. Vivace is considered by many (including us) to be the home of Seattle's finest espresso. A long, curving bar and a colorful mural add some character to a space that might otherwise feel ho-hum in Vivace's new home on the ground floor of the upscale Brix condo complex on Broadway (it was relocated out of its old digs due to construction of the future light rail station farther south on Broadway). The place has great energy—lively and bustling, where Hill residents tippity-tap on laptops and students hold study groups—but it's not necessarily a good spot for a quiet read. Pastries are a bit lackluster, but the espresso beverages more than make up for it. There's another branch right across the way from REI in South Lake Union, at 227 Yale Avenue North (☎ *206/388–5164*). ■TIP➔ **We're not the only ones who consider this the best espresso on Capitol Hill; if the weekend line is too long, there's also a Vivace sidewalk stand south of here at Broadway and Harrison Street** (☎ *206/324–8861*). ✉ *532 Broadway Ave. E, Capitol Hill* ☎ *206/860–2722* ⊕ *www.espressovivace.com* ▭ *AE, MC, V* ✢ *F3.*

9

BALLARD

$ ✕ **La Carta de Oaxaca.** True to its name, this low-key, bustling Ballard
MEXICAN   favorite serves traditional Mexican cooking with Oaxacan accents. The
Fodor's Choice   *mole negro* is a must, served with chicken or pork; another standout is
★   the *albondigas* (a spicy vegetable soup with meatballs). Halibut tacos
are served on fresh tortillas—and you can choose your spice at the
salsa bar. The menu is mostly small plates, which works out to your
advantage because you won't have to choose just one savory dish. The
small, casual space has an open kitchen enclosed by a stainless-steel
bar, the walls are covered in gorgeous black-and-white photos, and the
light-wood tables and black chairs and banquettes look more Scandinavian than Mexican. The place gets very crowded on weekends and
stays busy until late, though if you have a small party you usually
don't have to wait too long for a table. ⊠ *5431 Ballard Ave. NW, Ballard* ☎ *206/782–8722* ⊕ *www.lacartadeoaxaca.com* ⊟ *AE, DC, MC,
V* ☽ *No lunch Sun. and Mon.*

$$$ ✕ **Ray's Boathouse.** The view of Shilshole Bay might be the big draw
SEAFOOD   here, but the seafood is also fresh and well prepared. Perennial favorites
include broiled salmon, Kasu sake–marinated cod, Dungeness crab, and
regional oysters on the half shell. Ray's has a split personality: there's a
fancy dining room downstairs (reservations essential) and a casual café
and bar upstairs (reservations not accepted). In warm weather you can
sit on the deck outside the café and watch fishing boats, tugs, and plea-
sure craft floating past. Be forewarned that during happy hour (or early-
bird special time) in high season, the café's service can suffer greatly
because of the crowds. ■ TIP➔ **Sure, it's touristy, but snagging a spot on
the sun-drenched balcony here after an afternoon spent exploring the Bal-
lard Locks is quintessential Seattle summertime fun.** ⊠ *6049 Seaview Ave.
NW, Ballard* ☎ *206/789–3770* ⊕ *www.rays.com* ⊟ *AE, DC, MC, V.*

WALLINGFORD AND GREEN LAKE

$$$$ ✕ **Art of the Table.** You'll be in good hands here: the chef is absolutely
NEW AMERICAN   obsessive about finding the perfect ingredients for his utterly inspired
meals. The Supper Club (Thursday to Saturday) offers up a commu-
nal-dining experience with a prix-fixe menu highlighting local farmers'
markets finds. Dinner is served at 7:30, and reservations are essential.
"Happy Mondays" sees small plates, no reservations, and a more laid-
back and affordable atmosphere. Fresh local organic ingredients are
guaranteed. Small, pricey, but utterly unforgettable, Art of the Table is a
constantly changing tour de force. Sitting at a communal table while lis-
tening to the chef speak about each course is de rigeur; you'll enjoy any-
thing from braised ox tail, caramelized Brussels sprouts with pistachios,
and rockfish ceviche, to manila clams with cauliflower over pasta, hali-
but with asparagus and flavorful broth, and rhubarb soup with crème
fraiche. The wine pairings are elegant and worth the splurge. ⊠ *1054 N.
39th St., Wallingford* ☎ *206/282–0942* ⊕ *www.artofthetable.net* ⊟ *AE,
MC, V* ☽ *No lunch; no dinner Sun. or Tues.–Wed.*

DINING WITH KIDS

Seattle is just as serious about its food as it is about ensuring that no visiting parent leaves town without knowing why. Here are some picks you and your kids will enjoy.

Anthony's Pier 66, Downtown. Children are welcome at the fish bar (where they mix a mean Shirley Temple) and in the more formal dining room. Kids love to watch the tugboats and ferries in the busy harbor.

Café Flora, Capitol Hill. Local families love this vegetarian spot a short drive from the top of Capitol Hill—brunches are particularly fun.

Etta's, Downtown. Tom Douglas named this restaurant, one of many he owns, after his daughter. The jovial staff will make you feel right at home with your own kiddos.

The Hi-Life, Ballard. Ballard families love this casual restaurant in a converted firehouse. The menu is large; basics like great burgers are well represented, but fancier fusion dishes keep parents happy, too. The waitstaff is also very friendly.

Kidd Valley. Burgers, fries, shakes, and more in an indestructible fast-food restaurant that has branches in Queen Anne (on Queen Anne Avenue), Green Lake, and the University District.

Red Mill, Phinney Ridge. Some say the burgers here are the best in town, and this location is only a short walk north from the Woodland Park Zoo.

Tutta Bella, South Lake Union and Wallingford. Though Neapolitan pizza is a bit different from the classic slice, kids don't seem to mind. You won't be the only one with kids in tow if you're here on a weekend afternoon or early evening.

$$
KOREAN-FRENCH
Fodor's Choice
★

✕ **Joule.** Set in an adorable Wallingford storefront with graphic decor and an open kitchen, Joule is a true feast for your senses. Happy, casual Wallingford diners fill this bright space to feast on Chefs Rachel Yang and Seif Chirchi's exciting take on French-Korean fusion. The menu is divided into playful sections, including *Simmered* (such as spicy beef soup); *Tossed* (Japanese greens with Asian pear, Rogue blue cheese, and walnut agrodolce); *Crisped* (including Kimchi and trotter dumplings or braised cucumber, Chinese sausage, and shiitake); and *Sparked* (incredible whole branzino with salted shrimp fricasse; Kasu-brined pork chop; and Bison hanger steak with preserved garlic). The best approach is to order family-style so that you can try several dishes. You may not have room, but desserts are equally fascinating, such as a "Joule" box with tapioca pearls and ruby grapefruit brûlée. ✉ *1913 N. 45th St., Wallingford* ☎ *206/632–1913* ⊕ *www.joulerestaurant.com* ▭ *AE, DC, MC, V* ⊗ *No lunch; closed Mon.*

$$$
SUSHI

✕ **Kisaku.** One of the most outstanding sushi restaurants in Seattle is quietly nestled in Green Lake—and the diners come flocking. Fresh sushi is served up happily, along with signature rolls—such as the Green Lake variety, with salmon, flying-fish eggs, asparagus, avocado, and marinated seaweed, or the Wallingford, with yellowtail, green onion, cucumber, radish, sprouts, and flying-fish eggs. Definitely spring for the *omakase* (chef's menu), which can mean anything from fatty tuna,

9

shrimp, octopus, and albacore to salmon, yellowtail, hammer jack, and unagi. Straightforward decor and ambience mean that you can concentrate even more on the delicious food in front of you. Regulars swear by the agedashi tofu. Non-sushi entrées are also on offer, including terikayi and a tempura dinner with prawns. ⊠ *2101 N. 55th St., Green Lake* ☎ *206/545–9050* ⊕ *www.kisaku.com* ▤ *AE, MC, V.*

UNIVERSITY DISTRICT

$ × **Agua Verde Café and Paddle Club.** Baja California Mexican cuisine and
MEXICAN   a laid-back vibe define this casual spot that is done up in bright, beachy colors and has a lively deck come summertime. Regulars swear by the fresh fish tacos, black-bean cakes, and *mangodillas* (quesadillas with mango and poblano chilies). Be sure to pay a visit to the salsa bar. We like to wash it all down with a salt-rimmed margarita. ■TIP➔ In the warmer months, you can rent kayaks at Agua Verde and paddle around Portage Bay; Agua Verde is perched waterside on a street surrounded by quirky boat-repair shops. ⊠ *1303 N.E. Boat St., University District* ☎ *206/545–8570* ⊕ *www.aguaverde.com* ▤ *MC, V* ☉ *Closed Sun.*

$ × **Thai Tom.** This might be the cheapest Thai restaurant in town, but
THAI   rock-bottom prices aren't the only reason this place is always packed—the food is delicious, authentic, and spicy (two stars is usually pretty hot). But be forewarned: this is a hole-in-the-wall if there ever was one. Nevertheless, students and foodies pack in for garlic chicken, spicy curries, Thai coconut soup with shrimp, and rich, flavorful pad Thai. Tables can be hard to come by during the dinner rush, but there's usually space at the counter that lines the open kitchen. ⊠ *4543 University Ave., University District* ☎ *206/548–9548* ▤ *MC, V* ☉ *Closed Sun. No lunch Sat.*

WEST SEATTLE

$ × **Bakery Nouveau.** Widely considered one of the best bakeries in the
BAKERY   city, Bakery Nouveau has perfected many things, including cakes, croissants, and tarts. The chocolate cake, in particular, makes us swoon, though twice-baked almond croissants aren't too shabby either—so good, in fact, that you'll be thinking of France while you're on California Avenue. Sandwiches, quiches, and pizzas are also on offer if you need something deliciously substantial before a lemon meringue tart, banana mousse, or chocolate éclair. Artisan breads and good coffee make locals even happier. ⊠ *4737 California Ave. SW, West Seattle* ☎ *206/923–0534* ⊕ *www.bakerynouveau.com* ▤ *MC, V.*

$$$ × **Spring Hill.** West Seattle's most exciting culinary beacon, Spring Hill
NEW AMERICAN   takes quality and freshness seriously. A quietly hip vibe pervades this
Fodor'sChoice   large eatery on California Avenue, with polished wood floors, sim-
★   ple seating, a huge bar surrounding an open kitchen, and gently mod wooden wall treatments. Diners of all stripes relish the Pacific Northwest bounty, which is the star here, with raw oysters served atop a bundle of fresh seaweed; Dungeness crab with melted butter; house-made tagliatelle with crispy pork shoulder and fried parsley; Painted Hills hanger steak with beef-fat fries; Manila clams with razor-clam

Spring Hill

sausage and herbed mayo; and fresh halibut prepared to perfection and accompanied by smoked clam crumbs, corn grits chowder, and pea tendrils. Chef Mark Fuller creates dish after dish that combines expert execution of favorites, the finest ingredients, and subdued yet innovative flourishes. Weekend brunches are hoppin' and also more than worth the trek. This is a Seattle meal to be relished. ✉ *4437 California Ave. SW, West Seattle* ☎ *206/935–1075* ⊕ *www.springhillnorthwest.com* ▭ *AE, MC, V* ☻ *No dinner Sun.*

THE EASTSIDE

$$$
ITALIAN
Fodor's Choice
★

✕ **Café Juanita.** There are so many ways for a pricey "destination restaurant" to go overboard, making itself nothing more than a special-occasion spectacle, but Café Juanita manages to get everything just right. This Kirkland space is refined without being too design-y or too posh, and the food—much of which has a northern Italian influence—is also perfectly balanced: you won't find needlessly flashy fusion cooking or heavy sauces that obliterate subtle flavors. Chef Holly Smith (who won the "Best Chef Northwest" award from James Beard in 2008, among many other accolades) is a seasoned and elegant pro. One bite of the tender saddle of Oregon lamb with baby artichokes, fava beans, and lemon emulsion and you'll be sold. The daily fish specials are also worth the plunge, especially when the menu's featuring whole fish. Desserts are positively blissful, such as vanilla-bean panna cotta with honey and bittersweet chocolate torta with cherry-vinegar sauce and mint gelato. To top it all off, the restaurant has an *excellent* wine list. ✉ *9702 N.E.*

120th Pl., Eastside ☎ *425/823–1505* ⊕ *www.cafejuanita.com* ☰ *MC, V* ⊗ *Closed Mon. No lunch.*

$$$$ ✕ **The Herbfarm.** You may want to fast before dining at the Herbfarm.
PACIFIC   You'll get no fewer than nine courses here. "Dinner" takes at least
NORTHWEST   four hours and includes five fine Northwest wines, so you may also
want to arrange for transportation to and from the Woodinville-area
restaurant. Before you tuck in, you'll be treated to a delightful tour of
the herb garden. The dining room itself is in a century-old farmhouse
and is reminiscent of a country estate. The set menus change weekly;
if you have dietary restrictions, it's essential to call ahead. With all
products coming from the farm, or other local growers and suppliers,
you can always expect fresh seafood and shellfish, artisanal cheeses,
and luscious seasonal fruits. Book a room at elegant Willows Lodge to
make a true getaway of it (sometimes the hotel runs specials if you have
reservations here, so do call ahead). ⊠ *14590 N.E. 145th St., Eastside*
☎ *425/485–5300* ⊕ *www.theherbfarm.com* ⌂ *Reservations essential*
☰ *AE, MC, V* ⊗ *No lunch.*

WHERE TO STAY

The number after the ⊹ *symbol indicates the property's coordinate
on the map grid.*

Much like its culture, food, and fashion, Seattle's lodging offers something for everyone. There are grand, awe-inspiring vintage hotels; sleek,
elegant, modern properties; green hotels with yoga studios and enough
bamboo for an army of pandas; and wee B&Bs with sweet bedspreads
and home-cooked breakfasts. Travelers who appreciate the anonymity
of high-rise chains can comfortably stay here, while guests who want
to feel like family can find the perfect boutique inn in which to lay
their heads.

WHAT IT COSTS FOR TWO PEOPLE				
¢	$	$$	$$$	$$$$
under $100	$100–$180	$181–$265	$266–$350	over $350

Prices reflect the rack rate of a standard double room for two people in high season, excluding the 12% (for hotels with fewer than 60 rooms) or 15.6% (for hotels
with more than 60 rooms) city and state taxes. Check online for off-season rates
and special deals or discounts.

DOWNTOWN AND BELLTOWN

$–$$ 🏨 **Ace Hotel.** The Ace is a dream come true for both penny-pinching hip-
Fodor's Choice   sters and creative folks who appreciate unique minimalist decor. Almost
★   everything is white—even the wood floors and brick walls have been
painted over—making organic elements like driftwood lamps and ran-
domly placed tree stumps pop in this gallery-like space. Rooms continue
the theme, with such touches as army-surplus blankets, industrial metal
sinks, and street art, breaking up any notion of austerity. The cheapest

WHERE SHOULD I STAY?

	Neighborhood Vibe	Pros	Cons
Downtown and Belltown	Downtown is central, with the hottest hotels with water views. If you're a fan of galleries and bars, stay in Belltown.	A day in Downtown and Belltown can take you from the Seattle Art Museum to Pike Place Market.	Parking can be pricey and hard to come by. This is not your spot if you want quiet, relaxing respite.
Seattle Center, South Lake Union, and Queen Anne	Queen Anne boasts great water views and easy access to Downtown. South Lake Union can feel industrial.	Seattle Center's many festivals (such as Bumbershoot) means you'll have a ringside seat.	If you're mostly focused on seeing the key Downtown sights or have limited mobility, parking can be difficult.
Capitol Hill	One of Seattle's oldest and quirkiest neighborhoods, Capitol Hill has cozy accommodations.	A great place to stay if you want to mingle with creative locals in great bookstores and cafés.	If you're uncomfortable with the pierced, tattooed, or GLBT set, look elsewhere.
Fremont	From the Woodland Park Zoo to the Locks, funky Fremont is an excellent jumping-off point.	This quintessential Seattle 'hood is a short trek from Downtown and has restaurants and shops.	The only lodgings to be found here are B&Bs—book ahead.
Green Lake	Laid-back and wonderfully situated near the Woodland Park Zoo and Gas Works Park.	Outdoorsy types will love the proximity to Green Lake, a great place to stroll or jog.	You won't find anything trendy here, and, after a few days, you'll have seen everything.
University District	It offers everything you'd expect from a college area—from bookstores to ethnic food.	If you're renting a car, this area offers centrality with a lower price tag.	Decidedly college vibe. Not much in the way of sightseeing.
West Seattle	In summer, West Seattle can feel a lot like Southern California: It's a fun place to stay.	Alki Beach and Lincoln Park are fun, plus great restaurants and shopping on California Avenue.	You'll need a car to stay in this very removed 'hood. The only way in or out is over a bridge.
The Eastside	Proximity to high-end malls, Woodinville wineries, and Microsoft.	Woodinville is wine HQ; Kirkland offers cute boutiques; and Bellevue is a shopping mecca.	If you're here to experience Seattle, stick to the city. Traffic is a total nightmare.

9

rooms share bathrooms, which are clean and have enormous showers. Suites are larger, and have full private bathrooms hidden behind cool rotating walls. A small dining room hosts a continental breakfast and has a vending machine with unusual items like Japanese snacks and hangover cures. The Ace attracts guests of all ages (and levels of cool), but understand that this is a very specific experience and aesthetic: if you're not soothed (or stimulated) by the stripped-down quality of the rooms or not amused by finding a copy of the *Kama Sutra* where the Bible would be, you may want to stay elsewhere. **Pros:** ultratrendy spot with some the most affordable rates in town; cool art selection in rooms; good place to meet other travelers; free Wi-Fi. **Cons:** most rooms have shared bathrooms; not good for people who want pampering; neighborhood rife with panhandlers; lots of stairs to walk up

Fairmont Hotels & Resorts

Four Seasons Hotel

to get to lobby. ⊠ *2423 1st Ave., Belltown* ☎ *206/448–4721* ⊕ *www. acehotel.com* ⤳ *14 standard rooms, 14 deluxe rooms* ⚄ *In-room: no a/c (some), refrigerator (some), Wi-Fi. In-hotel: laundry facilities, Wi-Fi hotspot, parking (paid), some pets allowed* ⊟ *AE, D, DC, MC, V* ✛ *C3.*

$$$–$$$$ **Alexis Hotel.** Aesthetes and modern romantics will adore the Alexis Hotel, which occupies two historic buildings near the waterfront. Using slate gray, soft blue, taupe, and white against exposed brick, walls of windows, and nouveau-baroque touches, the Alexis has updated its look while maintaining a classic feel—the palette may be modern, but the ornate leather chairs and wood-burning fireplaces recall a different era. The Alexis has always had a focus on art (including a rotating collection of artwork selected by a Seattle Art Museum curator in the corridor between wings), and that tradition continues in the rooms as well—all have unique works of art. The property has 10 different types of specialty rooms in addition to themed suites. The Alexis Suite is hard to ignore: it's a full-blown two-bedroom apartment with two baths, a skylight, and exposed-brick walls. Downstairs, the Library bistro is one of the city's favorite lunchtime hideaways and bars. **Pros:** beautifully refurbished rooms; in-room spa services; specialty suites aren't prohibitively expensive. **Cons:** small lobby; not entirely soundproofed; some rooms can be a bit dark. ⊠ *1007 1st Ave., Downtown* ☎ *206/624–4844 or 888/850–1155* ⊕ *www.alexishotel.com* ⤳ *88 rooms, 33 suites* ⚄ *In-room: refrigerator, safe, Wi-Fi. In-hotel: restaurant, room service, bar, gym, spa, laundry service, Wi-Fi hotspot, parking (paid), some pets allowed* ⊟ *AE, D, DC, MC, V* ✛ *D4.*

$$–$$$ **Doubletree Arctic Club Hotel.** Close to the stadiums and in the heart
Fodor'sChoice of the financial district, this early-1900s landmark hotel was lovingly
★ restored from its gentlemen's club roots in 2006 to become a classy luxury hotel. From the Alaskan marble–sheathed foyer and the antique walrus heads on the third floor, to the Northern Lights Dome room with its leaded-glass ceiling and rococo touches, the Arctic Club pays homage to a different era of Gold Rush opulence. Guest rooms are done in earthy neutrals, with buttery leather chairs and dark-wood crown molding. Fun touches like trunks for bedside tables and walrus bottle openers continue the Arctic Club theme. Choose from rooms with whirlpools or deluxe showers; some standard rooms (and all the suites) also have sofa beds for those traveling with children; a few rooms have outdoor terraces. Enjoy cocktails in their Polar Bar or sit for serious noshing at the Northwest-influenced, urban-casual JUNO restaurant. **Pros:** cool, unique property; great staff; right on the bus line. **Cons:** fitness center is small; not in the absolute heart of Downtown; rooms are a bit dark. ⊠ *700 3rd Ave., Downtown* ☎ *206/340–0340* ⊕ *www. doubletree1.hilton.com* ⤳ *120 rooms* ⚄ *In-room: a/c, safe, refrigerator (some), DVD, Wi-Fi. In-hotel: restaurant, room service, 2 bars, gym, laundry service, Internet terminal, Wi-Fi hotspot, parking (paid), some pets allowed* ⊟ *AE, D, DC, MC, V* ✛ *E5.*

$$$$ **Edgewater.** Perched over Elliott Bay—with the waves lapping right underneath it—the Edgewater affords spectacular west-facing views of ferries and sailboats, seals and seabirds, and the distant Olympic Mountains. The whole hotel has a rustic-chic, elegant hunting-lodge

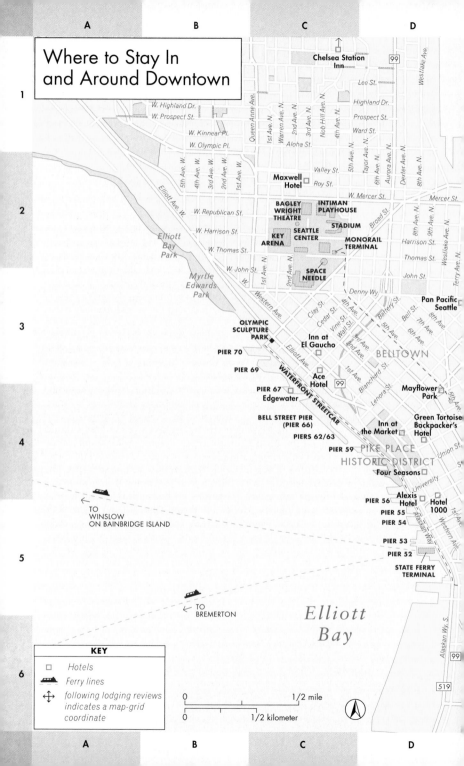

Where to Stay In and Around Downtown

KEY

☐ Hotels
🚋 Ferry lines
✢ following lodging reviews indicates a map-grid coordinate

A B C D

1 2 3 4 5 6

Chelsea Station Inn

99

Lee St.

W. Highland Dr.
W. Prospect St.
W. Kinnear Pl.
W. Olympic Pl.

Highland Dr.
Prospect St.
Ward St.

Queen Anne Ave. N.

1st Ave. N.
Warren Ave. N.
2nd Ave. N.
3rd Ave. N.
Nob Hill Ave. N.
4th Ave. N.

5th Ave. N.
Tayor Ave. N.
6th Ave. N.
Aurora Ave. N.
Dexter Ave. N.
8th Ave. N.

Aloha St.

5th Ave. W.
4th Ave. W.
3rd Ave. W.
2nd Ave. W.
1st Ave. W.

Valley St.

Maxwell Hotel ☐

Roy St.

W. Republican St.

W. Harrison St.

W. Thomas St.

W. John St.

1st Ave. W.
2nd Ave.

Western Ave.

BAGLEY WRIGHT THEATRE

KEY ARENA

SEATTLE CENTER

INTIMAN PLAYHOUSE

STADIUM

MONORAIL TERMINAL

SPACE NEEDLE

W. Mercer St.

Broad St.

Mercer St.

8th Ave. N.
9th Ave. N.
Westlake Ave. N.

Harrison St.
Thomas St.
John St.
Terry Ave. N.

Denny Wy.

Clay St.
Cedar St.
Vine St.
Wall St.

Battery St.
Bell St.

4th Ave.
5th Ave.
6th Ave.
7th Ave.
8th Ave.

Pan Pacific Seattle ☐

Elliott Bay Park

Myrtle Edwards Park

OLYMPIC SCULPTURE PARK ◆

PIER 70

PIER 69

Elliott Ave.

99

1st Ave.
2nd Ave.
3rd Ave.

Inn at El Gaucho ☐

BELLTOWN

Ace Hotel ☐

PIER 67
Edgewater ☐

Blanchard St.

Lenora St.

Mayflower Park ☐

5th Ave.

BELL STREET PIER (PIER 66)

PIERS 62/63

Inn at the Market ☐

Green Tortoise Backpacker's Hotel ☐

Union St.

PIER 59

PIKE PLACE HISTORIC DISTRICT

Four Seasons ☐

University

S

Alexis Hotel ☐

Hotel 1000 ☐

PIER 56

PIER 55

PIER 54

Alaskan Way.

1st Ave.
Western Ave.

PIER 53

PIER 52

STATE FERRY TERMINAL

← TO WINSLOW ON BAINBRIDGE ISLAND

← TO BREMERTON

Elliott Bay

Alaskan Wy. S.

99

519

0 ——— 1/2 mile
0 ——— 1/2 kilometer

look, with plaid rugs and fabrics and peeled-log furnishings. Many rooms have gas fireplaces. All that being said, the hotel has fallen short on service and guest satisfaction of late, and guests looking for luxury should probably head to the Four Seasons or Hotel 1000. There is a significant price jump here between the waterfront rooms and the waterfront premium rooms—unless you want a little more space, save your money. City-view rooms are very expensive, and probably not worth it unless you love the hotel's aesthetic or want to stay where the Beatles once slept in 1964. ■TIP➜ If you just want a taste of the hotel, stop into the elegant Six Seven restaurant for indoor-outdoor seating with a bay vista. **Pros:** amazing views; great upscale seafood restaurant; great public lounge area. **Cons:** overpriced for what you get; standard rooms are small; readers complain of poor service and thin walls. ⊠ *Pier 67, 2411 Alaskan Way, Pier 67, Belltown* ☎ *206/728–7000 or 800/624– 0670* ⊕ *www.edgewaterhotel.com* ⇨ *213 rooms, 10 suites* ♨ *In-room: Wi-Fi. In-hotel: restaurant, room service, bar, gym, laundry service, Wi-Fi hotspot, parking (fee), some pets allowed* ▭ *AE, D, DC, MC, V* ℣◯❙ *EP* ✢ *C4.*

$$$$ **The Fairmont Olympic Hotel.** Grand and stately, the Fairmont Olym-
♨ pic transports travelers to another time. With marble floors, brocade
Fodor'sChoice chairs, silk wallpaper, Corinthian columns, massive chandeliers, and
★ sweeping staircases worthy of Rhett Butler, this old-world hotel per-
sonifies class and elegance. It's no wonder that so many Seattleites get married in this Renaissance Revival hotel—it's as close to a princess palace as most of us will ever get to experience. Guest rooms are lovely and light, with French Country touches like pale yellow wallpaper and traditional floral patterns. The suites are a popular option for parents with kids—sofa beds are separated from the bedroom, and rollaway beds are available. The well-heeled leisure or business traveler will find everything he or she needs here: elegant dining and afternoon tea at the Georgian; an extensive fitness center with an indoor pool; a full-service business center; in-room massage; and a shopping arcade. Kids are even catered to, with child-size furniture and bathrobes, though wild tots might draw glances. **Pros:** elegant and spacious lobby; great location; excellent service; fabulous on-site dining. **Cons:** rooms are a bit small for the price; may be a little too old-school for trendy travelers. ⊠ *411 University St., Downtown* ☎ *206/621–1700 or 800/441–1414* ⊕ *www. fairmont.com/seattle* ⇨ *232 rooms, 218 suites* ♨ *In-room: safe, DVD (some), Wi-Fi. In-hotel: 2 restaurants, room service, bar, pool, gym, children's programs, laundry service, Wi-Fi hotspot, parking (fee), some pets allowed* ▭ *AE, D, DC, MC, V* ✢ *E4.*

$$$$ **Four Seasons Hotel Seattle.** The newest hotel jewel (or mega-diamond)
♨ in downtown Seattle gazes out over Elliott Bay. Just south of the Pike
Fodor'sChoice Place Market and steps from Benaroya Hall and the Seattle Art Museum,
★ the hotel is polished and elegant, with Eastern accents and plush fur-
nishings set against a definite modern-Northwest backdrop, in which materials, such as stone and fine hardwoods, take center stage, as seen in the sleek reception area. An extensive day spa and an infinity-pool terrace will help you relax after a day of exploring. Floor-to-ceiling windows in the guest rooms are unforgettable; lovely linens, comfortable

living spaces, and sleek marble bathrooms with deep soaking tubs, luxurious rain showers, and TVs embedded in the mirrors are added bonuses. The vibe here isn't pretentious, but it's certainly not laid-back either. Guests seem to know that they are in for a real treat. ■TIP➔ ART Restaurant and Lounge, headed up by Kerry Sear, offers up fabulous cocktails and good Northwest cuisine, with stunning views. A trip to the bar is a must if you're in the area for creative Northwest-inspired martinis and a tapas menu; happy hour is 5 to 7 Sunday through Thursday. **Pros:** amazing views; wonderful aesthetics; large rooms with luxurious bathrooms; lovely spa. **Cons:** Four Seasons regulars might not click with this modern take on the brand; some guests say service kinks need to be ironed out. ⊠ *99 Union St., Downtown* ☎ *206/749–7000* ⊕ *www. fourseasons.com* ⮡ *134 rooms, 13 suites* ⌂ *In-room: safe, refrigerator (some), DVD, Wi-Fi. In-hotel: restaurant, room service, bar, pool, gym, spa, children's programs, laundry service, parking (paid), some pets allowed* ☰ *AE, D, DC, MC, V* ✛ *D4.*

¢ 🏨 **Green Tortoise Backpacker's Hotel.** A Seattle institution, the Green Tortoise is still considered by many budget travelers to be the best deal in town. Even if you don't own a backpack and the word "hostel" gives you the heebie-jeebies, the impressive cleanliness here makes the Tortoise a viable option for all sorts of travelers who don't mind sacrificing a little comfort and privacy. Young (and young at heart) travelers might feel the most at home here, but anyone looking for a bargain is more than welcome. All rooms here share bathrooms, which are spacious, clean, and nicely tiled. Each bunk bed has its own locker, light, privacy curtains, four-plug outlet, and fan. The rate includes a fairly extensive breakfast buffet, and dinner Sunday, Tuesday, and Thursday nights. **Pros:** cheapest lodging in town; great place to make instant friends from around the globe; across the street from Pike Place Market. **Cons:** most guests are in their early twenties (and act like it); no frills rooms with shared bathrooms. ⊠ *105½ Pike St., Downtown* ☎ *206/340–1222* ⊕ *www.greentortoise.net* ⮡ *30 rooms without private bath* ⌂ *In-room: no phone, no TV, Wi-Fi. In-hotel: laundry facilities, Wi-Fi hotspot* ☰ *MC, V* ⧖|*BP* ✛ *D4.*

$$$ 🏨 **Hotel 1000.** Chic and cosmopolitan, Hotel 1000 is luxe and decidedly art-forward and modern—the centerpiece of the small lobby is a dramatically lighted glass staircase and original artwork by Pacific Northwest artist J.P. Canlis. Studio 1000, the small sitting room off the lobby, pairs an elegant fire pit with mid-century modern swiveling leather chairs. The designers wanted the hotel to have a distinctly Pacific Northwest feel, and they've succeeded without being campy. The whole hotel is done in dark woods and deep earth tones with an occasional blue accent. Rooms are full of surprising touches, including large tubs that fill from the ceiling. Hotel 1000 is without a doubt the most high-tech hotel in the city: Your phone will do everything from check the weather and airline schedules to give you restaurant suggestions; MP3 players and iPod docking stations are standard amenities. If you ever get tired of fiddling with the gadgets in your room, there's a state-of-the-art virtual golf club. **Pros:** lots of high-tech perks; guests feel pampered; hotel is hip without being alienating. **Cons:** rooms can be dark; rooms without

Fodor's Choice
★

9

views look out on a cement wall; restaurant can be overpriced. ✉ *1000 1st Ave., Downtown* ☎ *206/957–1000* ⊕ *www.hotel1000seattle.com* ⤵ *101 rooms, 19 suites* ⬳ *In-room: safe, refrigerator, DVD, Wi-Fi. In-hotel: restaurant, room service, bar, gym, spa, laundry service, Wi-Fi hotspot, parking (paid), some pets allowed* ▭ *AE, MC, V* ✛ *D4.*

$$–$$$
Fodor's Choice
★

🖼 **Hyatt at Olive 8.** In a city that's known for environmental responsibility, being the greenest hotel in Seattle is no small feat, but the Hyatt at Olive 8 has achieved the honor by becoming the first LEED-certified hotel in the city, and environmentally friendly has rarely been this chic. The hotel manages to be modern and minimalist without being austere, with a warm blue-and-brown palette, tasteful metal accents, and dark- and light-wood interplay. Maybe it's the floor-to-ceiling windows flooding the place with light or the extensive Elaia Spa, but the guests seem remarkably relaxed here. Middle-aged globe-trotters with sensible Euro shoes mix seamlessly with Tokyo hipsters and businessmen in the coffee and wine bar with (gasp) reasonable prices. Visitors also enjoy the on-site restaurant's extensive list of local wines and beer while seated around a reclaimed tree-turned-table that was downed by the '07 windstorm. Standard rooms are well appointed with fun enviro touches like dual-flush toilets, fresh-air vents, and low-flow showerheads. Allergy and asthma sufferers will also be happy with the complete absence of smells in the hotel—low VOC paint, wool carpeting, and natural materials were used throughout. From the green roof to the serene indoor pool and huge fitness center with yoga studio, this Hyatt proves that what's good for the planet can also be luxurious. **Pros:** central location; superb amenities; environmental responsibility; wonderful spa. **Cons:** standard rooms have showers only; fee for Wi-Fi use. ✉ *1635 8th Ave., Downtown* ☎ *206/695–1234* ⊕ *www.olive8.hyatt.com* ⤵ *333 rooms, 13 suites* ⬳ *In-room: safe, refrigerator, Wi-Fi. In-hotel: restaurant, room service, bar, pool, gym, spa, laundry service, Internet terminal, Wi-Fi hotspot, parking (paid; discounts for hybrid vehicles)* ▭ *AE, D, DC, MC, V* ✛ *E3.*

$–$$
Fodor's Choice
★

🖼 **Inn at El Gaucho.** Old Hollywood Rat Pack enthusiasts will want to move right in to this dark, swank, and sophisticated, retro-style inn. Upstairs from Belltown's beloved El Gaucho steak house and the Big Picture—a fabulous movie theater with a full bar—the Inn is hip and luxurious. Seventeen ultrachic suites have pale yellow walls, chocolate-color wood, workstations cleverly concealed in closets, and buttery leather furniture. They're filled with such goodies as featherbeds, Egyptian linens, Reidel stemware, fresh flowers from Pike Place Market, and large-screen plasma TVs. The sleek bathrooms have rain-style showers as well as L'Occitane and Philip B bath products. Rooms face Puget Sound, the city, or the hotel's atrium; atrium rooms are quieter than those that face the street. Additional perks include room service from El Gaucho and in-room massages and spa services from the Hyatt's spa team. ■ TIP➜ **One major drawback: the flight of stairs you'll have to climb to get to the Inn—there's no passenger elevator because it's a historic property.** **Pros:** beautiful rooms with upscale amenities; free long-distance calls from rooms; some great views; lovely location; warm, helpful staff. **Cons:** set of steep stairs with no elevator; some rooms only have showers; you have to go off-site for some amenities (such as a fitness center). ✉ *2505 1st Ave., Belltown* ☎ *206/728–1133 or 866/354–2824* ⊕ *inn.elgaucho.com* ↝ *17 suites* ♿ *In-room: Wi-Fi. In-hotel: restaurant, room service, bar, Wi-Fi hotspot, parking (paid)* ▭ *AE, MC, V* ✛ *C3.*

$$–$$$$
Fodor's Choice
★
🏨 **Inn at the Market.** From its heart-stopping views and comfortable rooms to its fabulous location and amazing fifth-floor deck perched above Puget Sound, the Inn at the Market is a place you'll want to visit again and again. The inn is well known locally and abroad for friendly, helpful service and excellent room service from French charmer Café Campagne and Northwest gastropub Bacco. Foodies, romantics, and nearly everyone in between will love the inn's prime location just off Pike Place Market, as well as the simple, sophisticated guest rooms with Tempur-Pedic beds, Northwest art, and bright, spacious bathrooms. Rooms are differentiated by the types of views they offer. You certainly won't be disappointed with the Partial Water View rooms—some have small sitting areas arranged in front of the windows. The four Deluxe Water View rooms—with glorious sundecks—are really spectacular, though. Even if you have to settle for a City Side room (a good deal even in high season), you can enjoy uninterrupted water views from the fifth-floor garden deck. **Pros:** outstanding views from most rooms and roof deck; steps from Pike Place Market; small and serene; complimentary town-car service for Downtown locations. **Cons:** little common space; not much in the way of amenities; a full renovation should take place in early 2011, so some rooms may be unavailable. ✉ *86 Pine St., Downtown* ☎ *206/443–3600 or 800/446–4484* ⊕ *www.innatthemarket.com* ↝ *63 rooms, 7 suites* ♿ *In-room: safe, refrigerator, Wi-Fi. In-hotel: 3 restaurants, room service, laundry service, Wi-Fi hotspot, parking (paid)* ▭ *AE, D, DC, MC, V* ✛ *D4.*

$–$$
🏨 **Mayflower Park Hotel.** Classic and comfortable, the Mayflower Park is unabashedly old school. Situated in a historic building, the hotel is decked out with sturdy antiques, Asian accents, brass fixtures, and florals. The standard rooms are on the small side, but all rooms have nice bathrooms with large mirrors and pedestal sinks. The main draw, however, is the location. The Mayflower Park is a quick walk from Pike Place Market and wonderfully central to Downtown shopping and Belltown sites. Despite its centrality, the hotel is so sturdily constructed that it's much quieter than many modern Downtown hotels. The Mayflower also boasts a star restaurant, Andaluca, as well as Oliver's, a well-known martini bar, which even locals flock to for its authentic cocktails. **Pros:** central Downtown location; access to spa next door; direct connection to the airport via light rail; excellent service. **Cons:** rooms are small; no pool. ✉ *405 Olive Way, Downtown* ☎ *206/623–8700 or 800/426–5100* ⊕ *www.mayflowerpark.com* ↝ *161 rooms, 29 suites* ♿ *In-room: safe, refrigerator, Wi-Fi. In-hotel: restaurant, room service, bar, gym, laundry service, Wi-Fi hotspot, parking (paid)* ▭ *AE, D, DC, MC, V* ✛ *D4.*

$$$–$$$$
🏨 **W Seattle.** The W Seattle is like an aging hipster—it once set the bar for Seattle's trendy hotels and, although its cool has been recently eclipsed by newer properties like Hotel 1000, it still thinks it can reel in the stylish with minimal effort. That said, it's a decent choice for a

9

Inn at the Market

Pan Pacific Hotel Seattle

Hotel 1000

boutique hotel with hip and reliable luxury. Custom-designed board games encourage lingering around the lobby fireplace on deep couches, and the hotel's bar is popular with guests and locals alike. A renovation to the fitness center will please exercise buffs. Decorated in black, brown, and French blue, guest rooms would almost be austere if they didn't have the occasional geometric print to lighten things up a bit. The beds are exceptionally comfortable, with pillow-top mattresses and 100% goose-down pillows and comforters (allergy sufferers may request hypoallergenic pillows). **Pros:** lively bar and restaurant; comfortable beds. **Cons:** unattractive (if central) location; self-consciously trendy; some folks complain about snotty staff members and poor concierge service. ⊠ *1112 4th Ave., Downtown* ☎ *206/264–6000 or 877/946–8357* ⊕ *www.whotels.com/seattle* ⇆ *415 rooms, 9 suites* ⚹ *In-room: safe, refrigerator, DVD, Wi-Fi. In-hotel: restaurant, room service, bar, gym, laundry service, Wi-Fi hotspot, parking (fee), some pets allowed* ▭ *AE, D, DC, MC, V* ✢ *E4.*

SOUTH LAKE UNION, AND QUEEN ANNE

$$–$$$
☼
Fodor's Choice
★

🏨 **Pan Pacific Hotel Seattle.** Views of the Space Needle and Lake Union are among the many perks at this stunning hotel. The lobby features a dramatic staircase, a fireplace, and plush brown-leather couches. The color palette blends blond and light woods, tan marble, cinnamon accents—and the result is that the hotel feels full of light even during the gray Seattle winter. In the rooms large soaking tubs are shielded by elegant sliding shoji doors, and Hypnos beds and ergonomic Herman Miller chairs at the desks ensure further comfort. The curving shape of the hotel causes rooms to be interestingly asymmetrical, and allows for fabulous views from many rooms. ■TIP→ **The South Lake Union Streetcar has a dedicated stop out front that will whisk travelers right into the heart of Downtown.** The Pan Pacific is part of a luxury condo development that includes a large fitness center (open to hotel guests), a spa, a courtyard of high-end specialty shops, a FedEx Office, a Starbucks, and an enormous Whole Foods with a fabulous outdoor dining area. Guests love the on-site restaurant and raw bar, and the delicious Tutta Bella pizzeria next door. **Pros:** warm, helpful staff; feels more luxurious than it costs; away from the tourist throngs. **Cons:** long walk to downtown sights if you don't take the streetcar; not many free amenities; shoji doors are pretty but cut down on bathroom privacy in smaller standard rooms. ⊠ *2125 Terry Ave., South Lake Union* ☎ *206/264–8111* ⊕ *seattle.panpacific. com* ⇆ *160 rooms, 1 suite* ⚹ *In-room: safe, refrigerator, DVD (some), Wi-Fi. In-hotel: restaurant, room service, bar, gym, laundry service, Wi-Fi hotspot, parking (fee)* ▭ *AE, DC, MC, V* ⊚*EP* ✢ *D3.*

$$$
🏨 **Maxwell Hotel.** Lower Queen Anne's newest hotel sits conveniently across from Seattle Center. This is *the* hotel for those visitors planning on frequenting Marion Oliver McCaw Hall for opera or performances by the Pacific Northwest Ballet company or for those going to Teatro Zinzanni, whose huge, colorful tent is just steps from the hotel's front door. Whimsical-but-functional decor is accented with art inspired by the performing arts. In the lively, open lobby area, take note of the tiled pineapple on the floor—this fruit is a theme here. Also at check-in are

9

mini-cupcakes (pineapple-flavored, of course), a small latte counter, and a glittering bead-and-glass chandelier. Rooms have graphic bed-spreads, colorful argyle-print chairs, outlines of chandeliers painted on the walls, and lovely (if small) bathrooms with black-marble counters. Among the amazing room amenities are iPod docking station alarm clocks and Keurig coffee machines; and a microwave with a complimentary bag of popcorn upon arrival. **Pros:** jazzy rooms are clean and comfortable; some rooms have great views of the Space Needle; loads of free amenities. **Cons:** most rooms do not have bathtubs (showers only); hotel is on a busy street; pool and gym are tiny; neighborhood is a bit shabby. ⊠ *300 Roy St., Queen Anne* ☏ *206/286–0629 or 877/298–9728* ⊕ *www.themaxwellhotel.com* ⤢ *139 rooms* ⌂ *In-room: safe, refrigerator, DVD, Internet, Wi-Fi. In-hotel: pool, gym, bicycles, laundry facilities, laundry service, Wi-Fi hotspot, parking (free), some pets allowed* ⊟ *AE, D, DC, MC, V* ✛ *C2.*

CAPITOL HILL

¢–$ **11th Avenue Inn Bed & Breakfast.** The closest B&B to Downtown, the

Fodor'sChoice 11th Avenue Inn offers all the charm of a classic bed-and-breakfast with

★ the convenience of being near the action. Exquisitely styled with antique beds, Oriental rugs, and a grand dining-room table draped in a lace-edged tablecloth, the Inn positively oozes vintage charm. The owner has impeccable taste, and even the small den that holds two public computers and stacks of travel guides, brochures, and laminated menus from the best local restaurants is thoughtfully arranged and appointed. Modest-size guest rooms are on two floors. The second floor has five rooms; the Citrine is our favorite for its regal antique headboard, but the Opal is a very close second because of the amount of light it gets. A full breakfast is served in the elegant dining room, which is the show-piece of the house. Don't worry about using the wrong fork, though—despite its formal appearance, the inn is a warm and laid-back place. **Pros:** unpretentious take on classic B&B; friendly staff. **Cons:** no a/c; although most guests are courteous, sound does carry in old houses. ⊠ *121 11th Ave. E, Capitol Hill* ☏ *206/720–7161 or 800/720–7161* ⊕ *www.11thavenueinn.com* ⤢ *8 rooms, 6 with bath* ⌂ *In-room: no phones, Wi-Fi. In-hotel: Wi-Fi hotspot, parking (paid), no kids under 12* ⊟ *AE, D, MC, V* ❧⊙ *BP* ✛ *F3.*

¢–$ **Gaslight Inn.** It's easy to imagine the splendor of this 1906 house when it was a single-family residence—the Gaslight retains much of the original charm, while offering contemporary and artistic touches not typically seen in B&Bs. Rooms here range from a crow's nest with peeled-log furniture and Navajo-print fabrics to a more traditional suite with Arts and Crafts–style furnishings, a fireplace, cloisonné vases, and stained-glass windows. The large common areas evoke a gentlemen's club, with deer mounts overlooking oak wainscoting, Oriental carpets, and leather chairs. There's room to move around in here, including a lovely backyard and a deck with fabulous views. The Gaslight also has something no other B&B can claim: a seasonal heated pool, nicely positioned in a private oasis of a backyard. **Pros:** great art collection; house and rooms are more spacious than at other B&Bs; heated pool. **Cons:**

breakfast is unimpressive; some readers find staff standoffish. ⊠ *1727 15th Ave., Capitol Hill* ☎ *206/325–3654* ⊕ *www.gaslight-inn.com* ⤶ *5 rooms with private bath; 3 rooms with shared bath* ⅏ *In-room: no a/c (some), refrigerator (some), Wi-Fi. In-hotel: pool, Wi-Fi hotspot, no kids under 16* ⊟ *AE, MC, V* ⚭⃒ *CP* ✛ *G3.*

$–$$ 🔲 **Salisbury House Bed & Breakfast.** If you like to start your mornings with
Fodor's Choice the *New York Times* and a full vegetarian breakfast with mouthwater-
★ ing choices like rhubarb coffee cake and fresh, fruit-laden huckleberry
pancakes, look no further. Built in 1904, this large Craftsman sits on a
wide, tree-lined street a few blocks south of Volunteer Park. The spacious rooms contain an eclectic collection of furniture. The decor isn't
eye-popping, but travelers who prefer a simpler, country-charm look
will appreciate the B&B's restraint. The basement suite has a private
entrance and phone line, a king-size bed, fireplace, and whirlpool bath.
The Blue Room is the best of the rest, for its private deck overlooking the garden. One of the common areas is a sun porch with wicker
furniture, where tea awaits guests each afternoon. A guest computer in
the library is available to all, and free Wi-Fi throughout is a plus. The
B&B is situated near the park and laid-back 15th Avenue, which is lined
with several great restaurants, bars, and coffee shops. A bus around
the corner will take you straight to Downtown. Allergy sufferers take
note: the owner has two cats. **Pros:** close to Volunteer Park; friendly
innkeeper can help you plan your stay; porches to relax on. **Cons:** a
bit far from Pike-Pine Corridor; some street noise. ⊠ *750 16th Ave. E,
Capitol Hill* ☎ *206/328–8682* ⊕ *www.salisburyhouse.com* ⤶ *4 rooms,
1 suite* ⅏ *In-room: no a/c (some), no TV (some), Wi-Fi. In-hotel: Wi-Fi
hotspot, no kids under 12* ⊟ *AE, MC, V* ⚭⃒ *BP* ✛ *G2.*

FREMONT

$$ 🔲 **Chelsea Station Inn Bed & Breakfast.** Situated on the south end of the
Fodor's Choice Woodland Park Zoo, on the edge of Fremont and Phinney Ridge, this
★ 1920s brick colonial B&B was reopened in 2009 and offers a conve-
nient jumping-off point for all the north end has to offer. Four beauti-
fully styled, 900-square-foot suites feature distressed hardwood floors
with colorful rugs, fireplaces, sleeper sofas, contemporary furnishings,
and a soft, modern palette. Guests enjoy breakfast delivered to their pri-
vate dining rooms and granite-counter kitchenettes stocked with local
treats. Master bathrooms are large and sumptuous, with double walk-in
rain showers and marble countertops, and each suite also boasts a sepa-
rate powder room—a fabulous benefit for couples or families. There are
several outdoor spaces for lounging, including a flower-filled patio and
outdoor fire pit and hot tub areas. This is a truly luxurious property,
suitable even for those who usually shy away from the B&B experience.
It's far from Downtown, but the nearby bus line takes travelers directly
to the core. **Pros:** great, unobtrusive host; 1½ bathrooms per suite;
sweet location. **Cons:** far from Downtown; no TVs; no elevator. ⊠ *4915
Linden Ave. N, Fremont* ☎ *206/547–6077* ⊕ *www.chelseastationinn.
com* ⤶ *4 suites* ⅏ *In-room: no phone, no a/c, kitchen, refrigerator, no
TV, Internet, Wi-Fi. In-hotel: laundry facilities, Wi-Fi hotspot, parking
(free)* ⊟ *MC, V* ⚭⃒ *BP* ✛ *C1.*

9

GREEN LAKE

$–$$

Fodor'sChoice

★

🔲 **Greenlake Guest House.** Outdoorsy types, visitors who want to stay in a low-key residential area, and anyone who wants to feel pampered and refreshed will enjoy this charming B&B. The house is directly across the street from the eastern shore of beautiful Green Lake; it's a short walk from several restaurants and the devilishly good Chocolati. The romantic Parkview Suite is the pièce de résistance, with a full view of the park, and pale green walls that play off the green of the leaves just outside the windows. All rooms have private baths with jetted tubs (except the Ballard room), fluffy robes, and heated tile floors. A public computer with Internet is available in the living room; a communal minibar in the hall has sodas, water, fresh fruit, cookies, and other snacks; and bookshelves in the upstairs hallway have an extensive DVD collection of Oscar-winning movies. To keep things interesting, the full breakfast alternates between made-to-order savory (a spinach-and-feta omelet, for example) and sweet (such as Brie-and-apple French toast). **Pros:** views of and quick access to Green Lake; thoughtful amenities; can accommodate kids over 4 years old. **Cons:** 5 mi from Downtown; on a busy street. ✉ *7630 E. Green Lake Dr. N, Green Lake* ☎ *206/729–8700 or 866/355–8700* ⊕ *www.greenlakeguesthouse.com* 🔖 *4 rooms* ⌂ *In-room: no phone, DVD, Wi-Fi. In-hotel: Internet terminal, Wi-Fi hotspot, no kids under 4* ▭ *DC, MC, V* ⎺⊙⎺ *BP* ✣ *F1.*

NIGHTLIFE

Seattle's amazing musical legacy is well known, but there's more to nightlife scene than live music. In fact, these days there are far more swanky bars and inventive pubs than music venues in the city. Seattle is, bluntly put, a great place to drink. You can sip overly ambitious and ridiculously named specialty cocktails in trendy lounges, get a lesson from an enthusiastic sommelier in a wine bar or restaurant, or swill cheap beer on the patio of a dive bar. Though some places have very specific demographics, most Seattle bars are egalitarian affairs, drawing loyal regulars of all ages.

The music scene is still kicking—there's something going on every night of the week in nearly every genre of music.

Every neighborhood has a little bit of everything, save for dance clubs, which are in short supply and mostly concentrated in Pioneer Square and Belltown. The number of bars in each neighborhood increases greatly if you take into account all of the great restaurants that also have thriving bar scenes—in some cases the line between restaurant and nightspot is quite blurred.

DOWNTOWN AND BELLTOWN

BARS AND LOUNGES

Alibi Room (✉ *85 Pike St., in Post Alley, Downtown* ☎ *206/623–3180* ⊕ *www.seattlealibi.com*), a wood-paneled bar in exquisitely hard-to-find Post Alley at Pike Place Market, is where well-dressed locals sip double martinis while taking in views of Elliott Bay or studying the scripts, handbills, and movie posters that line the walls. The lower level is more crowded and casual. It's an ever-cool yet low-key, intimate place. Stop by for a drink or a meal, or stay to listen and dance to live music. Happy hour from 3 to 6 is quiet and a good respite from the Market.

Black Bottle (⊠ 2600 1st Ave., Belltown ☎ 206/441–1500 ⊕ www. blackbottleseattle.com) is quite sleek and sexy, making the northern reaches of Belltown look good. The interior of this gastropub/wine bar is simple but very sleek, with black chairs and tables and shiny wood floors. It gets crowded with a chill but often dressed-up clientele on nights and weekends. A small selection of beers on tap and a solid wine list (with Washington, Oregon, California, and beyond well represented) will help you wash down the pub snacks, including wild boar ribs, grilled octopus, butter-bean salad, and seven-spice shrimp.

★ **Oliver's** (⊠ 405 Olive Way, Downtown ☎ 206/382–6995), in the Mayflower Park Hotel, is famous for its martinis. In fact, having a cocktail here is like having afternoon tea in some parts of the world. Wing chairs, low tables, and lots of natural light make it easy to relax after a hectic day. The likes of Frank Sinatra or Billie Holiday may be playing in the background; expect an unfussy crowd of regulars, hotel guests, and mature Manhattan-sippers who appreciate old-school elegance.

Purple Café and Wine Bar (⊠ 1225 4th Ave., Downtown ☎ 206/829–2280 ⊕ www.thepurplecafe.com) is certainly the biggest wine bar in the city and possibly its most dramatic—despite the cavernous quality of the space and floor-to-ceiling windows, all eyes are immediately drawn to the 20-foot tower ringed by a spiral staircase that holds thousands of bottles. There are full lunch and dinner menus (American and Pacific Northwest fare), as well as tasting menus. Try the popular lobster mac and cheese or a yummy baked Brie. Though Purple is surprisingly unpretentious for a place in the financial district of Downtown, it's sophisticated enough that you'll want to dress up a bit.

★ **Spur Gastropub** (⊠ 113 Blanchard St., Belltown ☎ 206/728–6706 ⊕ www.spurseattle.com) is a favorite among foodies. The inventive small plates and carefully curated drink menu (Spur is owned by the same folks who run Tavern Law on Capitol Hill), and stylish "pioneer-lite" space also make this a very popular nightspot. Sip a bourbon-infused cocktail and munch on stellar crostini with salmon, veal sweetbreads, or baby artichokes. Spur can be a bit spendy, so it may make sense to save your visit for happy hour (Sunday to Thursday 5–7) or for a late-night snack (it serves a special pairing menu from 11 to 1:30).

★ **Vessel** (⊠ 1312 5th Ave., Downtown ☎ 206/652–5222 ⊕ www.vessel-seattle.com) is the place to go Downtown for intricate and inventive cocktails. The specialty drinks are outstanding here, and you're bound to find a few concoctions that you won't find anywhere else. Service can be a bit slow on crowded weekends, but just spend the time people-watching in the attractive, supermodern bi-level space. The staircase leading to the mezzanine is backlighted in the type of unnatural yellow hue you'd expect to find in a cocktail with 10 ingredients—it's a surprisingly nice touch. This is a sophisticated place (leave the sport sandals at home) that knows it doesn't have to trade on pretension—it's all about the drinks, such as the Frick, with bourbon, Cinzano Rosso, peach bitters, and dried fig, or the Blueberry Flip, with brandy, crème de mûre, egg, and bitters.

Fodor's Choice ★ **Zig Zag Café** (✉ *1501 Western Ave., Downtown* ☎ *206/625–1146* ⊕ *zigzagseattle.com*) gives Oliver's at the Mayflower Hotel a run for its money when it comes to pouring perfect martinis—plus, it's much more eclectic and laid-back here. A mixed crowd of mostly locals hunts out this unique spot at Pike Place Market's Hillclimb (a nearly hidden stairwell leading down to the piers). Several memorable cocktails include the Don't Give Up the Ship (gin, Dubonnet, Grand Marnier, and Fernet Branca), the One-Legged Duck (rye whiskey, Dubonnet, Mandarine Napoleon, and Fernet Branca), and Satan's Soulpatch (bourbon, sweet and dry vermouth, Grand Marnier, orange, and orange bitters). A very simple, ho-hum food menu includes cheese and meat plates, bruschetta, soup, salad, olives, and nuts. A small patio is the place to be on a summery happy-hour evening. Zig Zag is friendly; retro without being obnoxiously ironic; and very Seattle—with the occasional live music show, to boot.

LIVE MUSIC

Fodor's Choice ★ **The Crocodile** (✉ *2200 2nd Ave., Belltown* ☎ *206/441–7416* ⊕ *www. thecrocodile.com*) is one of the few places that can call itself "the heart and soul of Seattle" without raising many eyebrows. Indeed, it is— and has been since 1991—the heart and soul of Seattle's music scene. Nirvana, Pearl Jam, Mudhoney, and REM have all taken the stage here. Seattleites mourned the abrupt closing of this Belltown club in 2007, and rejoiced even harder when it reopened, fully renovated with much improved sightlines, in 2009. Nightly shows are complemented by cheap beer on tap and pizza right next door at Via Tribunali. All hail the Croc!

Dimitriou's Jazz Alley (✉ *2033 6th Ave., Downtown* ☎ *206/441–9729* ⊕ *www.jazzalley.com*) is where Seattleites dress up to see nationally known jazz artists. The cabaret-style theater, where intimate tables for two surround the stage, runs shows nightly. Those with reservations for cocktails or dinner, served during the first set, receive priority seating.

Showbox (✉ *1426 1st Ave., Downtown* ☎ *206/628–3151* ⊕ *www. showboxonline.com*), near Pike Place Market, presents locally and nationally acclaimed artists. This is a great place to see some pretty big-name acts—the acoustics are decent, the venue's small enough that you don't feel like you're miles away from the performers, and the bar areas flanking the main floor provide some relief if you don't want to join the crush in front of the stage. In 2007, Showbox opened another venue, **Showbox SoDo** (✉ *1700 1st Ave. S, SoDo*) not far from the stadiums in SoDo (south of Downtown). The converted warehouse is larger than the original venue and features big national acts from Nas to The Hives.

The Crocodile

PIONEER SQUARE

BARS AND LOUNGES

Collins Pub (✉ *526 2nd Ave., Pioneer Square* ☎ *206/623–1016* ⊕ *www. thecollinspub.com*) is the best beer bar in Pioneer Square. It has 22 rotating taps of Northwest (including Boundary Bay, Chuckanut, and Anacortes, among others) and California beers and a long list of bottles from the region. Its full menu of upscale pub grub features local and seasonal ingredients—try smoked pork tenderloin or seared duck breast with your pint.

For an introduction to, or an advanced course on, sake, visit **Sake Nomi** (✉ *76 S. Washington St., Pioneer Square* ☎ *206/467–7253* ⊕ *www. sakenomi.us*), a shop and tasting bar open until 10 PM Tuesday through Saturday and from noon to 6 on Sunday. Don't be shy—have a seat, try a few of the rotating samples, and ask a lot of questions. Sake can be served up in a variety of temperatures, and it's fun to sample the sake-sipping tradition.

CAPITOL HILL

BARS AND LOUNGES

Capitol Club (✉ *414 E. Pine St., Capitol Hill* ☎ *206/325–2149* ⊕ *www. thecapitolclub.net*) is a sumptuous Moroccan-theme escape where you can sprawl upon tasseled floor cushions and dine on Mediterranean treats. Despite this being one of the neighborhood's see-and-be-seen spots, good attitudes prevail, and the waitresses are always affable and efficient, even during busy weekend nights.

Fodor's Choice   **Licorous** (✉ *928 12th Ave., Capitol Hill* ☎ *206/325–6947* ⊕ *www.*
★ *licorous.com*) is Lark restaurant's attractive next-door bar, complete
with a striking molded-tin ceiling, well-poured cocktails, and a dynamite whisky list (be sure to ask about it). This has provided something
that the Hill was once missing: a hip, well-designed space that attracts
an eclectic clientele, from young couples to larger groups and local
regulars—one where everyone can feel like a grown-up and enjoy a
low-key evening sipping tasty specialty cocktails and munching tasty
small dishes from an abbreviated Lark menu.

★ **Linda's Tavern** (✉ *707 E. Pine St., Capitol Hill* ☎ *206/325–1220*) is one
of the Hill's iconic dives—and not just because it was allegedly the last
place Kurt Cobain was seen alive. The interior has a vaguely Western
theme, but the patrons are pure Capitol Hill indie-rockers and hipsters.
The bartenders are friendly, the burgers are good (brunch is even better), and the always-packed patio is one of the liveliest places to grab
a happy-hour drink.

Fodor's Choice   **Quinn's** (✉ *1001 E. Pike St., Capitol Hill* ☎ *206/325–7711* ⊕ *www.*
★ *quinnspubseattle.com*) is our favorite go-to place for a dynamite beer
at a laid-back but very cool bar. A friendly, knowledgeable staff tends
the bar and the tables at the gastropub serving yummy food (especially
the burgers) and even better beers. It can be very busy on weekends,
but if you arrive in early evening on a weekday, you can sidle up to the
bar, order some nibbles, and chat up the bartender about the numerous
(rotating) brews on tap, including Belgian favorites, local IPAs, Russian
River winners, and more.

★ **Smith** (✉ *332 15th Ave. E, Capitol Hill* ☎ *206/709–1099* ⊕ *www.*
smithpub.com), a bit outside the Pike–Pine heart, on 15th Avenue East,
is a large, dark space with portraits of ex-presidents and taxidermied
birds all over the walls, plus a mixture of booth seating and large communal tables. Filled to brimming with tattooed hipsters on weekends,
this is actually a super-friendly and inviting space, with a very solid
menu of food (including a top-notch burger and sweet-potato fries)
and a full bar. Beer selection is small but good, and the cocktail list is
decent. It's great people-watching and very Capitol Hill.

BREWPUB

★ **Elysian Brewing Company** (✉ *1221 E. Pike St., Capitol Hill* ☎ *206/860–*
1920 ⊕ *www.elysianbrewing.com*) is a Capitol Hill mainstay with worn
booths and tables scattered across a bi-level warehouse space and decent
food (burgers, fish tacos, sandwiches, salads). The standouts here are
the beers, which are a good representation of the thriving brewing scene
in the Northwest. Seasonal brews are sometimes outstanding, with IPAs,
lagers, and ales showcasing hops, spices, and even pumpkin flourishes.
Always on tap are the hop-heavy Immortal IPA, the rich Perseus Porter,
and the crisp Elysian Fields Pale Ale. This is a favorite of Seattleites and
Capitol Hill residents and a good alternative to the hipster haunts and
swanky lounges in the area. There's another branch in Wallingford near
Green Lake on North 55th and Meridien, but it's a bit off the beaten
path unless you're staying in that area.

Elysian Brewing Company

GAY AND LESBIAN SPOTS

The Elite (✉ *1520 E. Olive Way, Capitol Hill* ☎ *206/860–0999* ⊕ *www. theeliteseattle.com*), technically the oldest gay bar on the Hill, has settled in well at its new location (it used to be on Broadway Avenue East). This laid-back pub and sports bar has a pool table, darts, and four TVs showing local sports.

Neighbours (✉ *1509 Broadway, Capitol Hill* ☎ *206/324–5358* ⊕ *www. neighboursnightclub.com*) is an institution thanks in part to its drag shows, great theme DJ nights, and relaxed atmosphere (everyone, including the straightest of the straights, seems to feel welcome here). It's no longer the center of the gay and lesbian scene, but the place is still usually packed Thursday through Saturday.

★ The original and short-lived **Pony** (✉ *1221 Madison St., Capitol Hill* ⊕ *www.ponyseattle.com*), which got bulldozed along with the rest of the 500 block of Pine Street, was notorious for wild fun. The newer, permanent incarnation is just a bit more polished and has an amazing patio, and retains some of the former space's decorating touches (vintage nude photos). There's a small dance floor and a mix of gays, lesbians, and hipsters.

Wildrose (✉ *1021 E. Pike St., Capitol Hill* ☎ *206/324–9210* ⊕ *www. thewildrosebar.com*) is Seattle's only dedicated lesbian bar, so expect a mob nearly every night. The crowd at weeknight karaoke is fun and good-natured, cheering for pretty much anyone. Weekends are raucous, so grab a window table early and settle in for perpetual ladies' night.

LIVE MUSIC

★ **Neumo's** (✉ *925 E. Pike St., Capitol Hill* ☎ *206/709–9467* ⊕ *www. neumos.com*) was one of the grunge era's iconic clubs (when it was Moe's), and it has managed to reclaim its status as a staple of the Seattle rock scene, despite being closed for a six-year stretch. And it is a great rock venue: acoustics are excellent and the roster of cutting-edge indie rock bands is the best in the city. Some lament that it's one of the most uncomfortable places in town to see a show (sightlines throughout the club can be terrible). It's also stuffy and hot during sold-out shows.

FREMONT AND PHINNEY RIDGE

BARS AND LOUNGES

★ **Brouwer's** (✉ *400 N. 35th St., Fremont* ☎ *206/267–2437* ⊕ *www. brouwerscafe.com*) is a Belgian-beer lover's heaven—even if it looks more like a trendy Gothic dungeon than a place with white clouds and harp-bearing angels. A converted warehouse provides an ample venue for a top selection of suds provided by the owners of Seattle's best specialty-beer shop, Bottleworks. There are plenty of German and American beers on offer, too, as well as English, Czech, and Polish selections. A menu of sandwiches, frites, and Belgian specialties helps to lay a pre-imbibing foundation (remember that Belgian beers have a higher alcohol content). Before settling on a seat downstairs, check out the balcony and the cozy parlor room.

BREWPUBS

Hales Ales Brewery and Pub (✉ *4301 Leary Way NW, Fremont* ☎ *206/706– 1544* ⊕ *www.halesbrewery.com*) is one of the city's oldest craft breweries (1983). Hales produces unique English-style ales, cask-conditioned ales and nitrogen-conditioned cream ales, plus a popular Mongoose IPA. The pub serves a full menu, and has a great view of the fermenting room. Order a taster's "flight" if you want to taste everything.

★ **Naked City Taphouse** (✉ *8564 Greenwood Ave. N, Phinney Ridge* ☎ *206/838–6299* ⊕ *www.nakedcitybrewing.com*) has its own small brewery, so expect to see a few of its ales and stouts. The rest of the 24 taps are dedicated to their peers, including a few you won't find everywhere, like Lazy Boy, Roslyn, and Snipes. Pub grub is simple but local and organic.

LIVE MUSIC

ToST (✉ *513 N. 36th St., Fremont* ☎ *206/547–0240* ⊕ *www.tostlounge. com*), pronounced "toast," is a swank-looking but super-laid-back martini bar that just happens to have great live music many nights. This is a good place to catch a smokin' jazz, funk, or jazz-funk act, but the club also presents everything from spoken word to alt-country. Thursday nights host the popular improv soul-and-funk show Marmalade.

BALLARD

BARS AND LOUNGES

Balmar (✉ *5449 Ballard Ave. NW, Ballard* ☎ *206/297–0500* ⊕ *www.balmar.com*) is one of Ballard's largest and most attractive bars—exposed-brick walls, hardwood floors, comfy cocoa-color couches and ottomans. The two-story space has areas to dine (serving a small-plates menu), drink, and shoot pool. It can be a bit of a fratty meat market on Saturday (it's definitely more New Ballard than Old Ballard), but other than that it's usually pretty mellow, and there's room enough to accommodate all the groups of friends and co-workers who enjoy having a slightly more upscale alternative to Ballard's neighborhood joints.

★ Japanese restaurant **Moshi Moshi** (✉ *5324 Ballard Ave., Ballard* ☎ *206/971–7424* ⊕ *www.moshiseattle.com*) has a tree with lighted faux-cherry blossoms branching out over the bar, and the inventive cocktails are expertly poured beneath it. Unlike at most Japanese restaurants, the cocktail menu steers clear of sake-tinis—there are one or two sake concoctions, but you're more likely to find whiskey, gin, brandy, or even tequila put to good use, as in the Bella Donna (gin, black muscat, vermouth blanc, and lavender bitters) or the Sweet Savage (whiskey, Aperol, maple syrup, and grapefruit). There always seems to be a happy hour or nightly special at the bar, including the evening-long happy hour on Sunday.

★ The **People's Pub** (✉ *5429 Ballard Ave. NW, Ballard* ☎ *206/783–6521*) is a Ballard institution and a great representative of what locals love about this unpretentious neighborhood. The pub (a dining room and a separate bar in the back) isn't much to look at—just a lot of wood paneling, simple wood tables and chairs, and some unfortunate floral upholstery—but it has a great selection of German beers and draws a true cross section of the neighborhood's denizens from hipsters to old-school fishermen.

Portalis (✉ *5205 Ballard Ave. NW, Ballard* ☎ *206/783–2007* ⊕ *www.portaliswines.com*) attracts serious oenophiles who gather around communal tables and at the long bar to sample wines from around the world in this cozy, brick-lined bar. It's a full-service retail shop as well, so you can pick up a few bottles to take home. Though it's a bit stuffy for Ballard, it's a nice alternative to the frenetic scene on the upper part of Ballard Avenue.

Fodor's Choice ★ If you manage to score a table at **Sambar** (✉ *425 NW Market St., Ballard* ☎ *206/781–4883*), a teeny-tiny bar attached to French restaurant Le Gourmand, you probably won't leave for hours—there's nothing else like it in Seattle. Though it claims to have French flair, the only thing that cries corner café is its small size. The interior is modern in a way that would look pretentious and stark if translated into a bigger space. Excellent cocktails are mixed with panache and made with premium liquors—just try to walk a straight line out the door when you're done. A small menu offers delicious bites from Le Gourmand, from fresh salads to guilty pleasures like the *croque monsieur* and rich desserts. The crowd is mixed and different every night. A small patio adds some additional and highly coveted seating in summer.

9

LIVE MUSIC

Tractor Tavern (✉ *5213 Ballard Ave. NW, Ballard* ☎ *206/789–3599* ⊕ *www.tractortavern.com*) is Seattle's top spot to catch local and national acts that specialize in roots music and alternative country. The large, dimly lighted hall has all the right touches—wagon-wheel fixtures, exposed-brick walls, and a cheery staff. The sound system is outstanding.

SHOPPING

Shopping in Seattle is something best done gradually. Don't expect to find it all in one or two days worth of blitz shopping tours. Downtown is the only area that allows for easy daylong shopping excursions. Within a few blocks along 4th and 5th avenues, you'll find the standard chains (The Gap, Urban Outfitters, H&M, Anthropologie, Sephora, Old Navy), along with Nike's flagship store, and a few more glamorous high-end stores, some featuring well-known designers like Betsey Johnson. Downtown is also where you'll find department stores like Nordstrom, Macy's, and Barneys New York. Belltown and Pioneer Square are also easy areas to patrol—most stores of note are within a few blocks.

To find many of the stores that are truly special to Seattle—such as boutiques featuring handmade frocks from local designers, independent record stores run by encyclopedic-minded music geeks, cozy used-book shops that smell of paper and worn wood shelves—you'll have to branch out to Capitol Hill, Queen Anne, and northern neighborhoods like Ballard. Shopping these areas will give you a better feel for the character of the city and its quirky inhabitants, all while you score that new dress or nab gifts for your friends.

DOWNTOWN

Best shopping: 4th, 5th, and 6th avenues between Pine and Spring streets, and 1st Avenue between Virginia and Madison streets.

BOOKS AND PRINTED MATERIAL

Fodor's Choice
★
Peter Miller Architectural & Design Books and Supplies. Aesthetes and architects regularly haunt this floor-to-ceiling-stocked shop for all things design. Rare international architecture, art, and design books mingle with high-end products from Alessi and Iittala, while sleek notebooks, bags, portfolios, and drawing tools round out the collection. This is a great shop for quirky, unforgettable gifts, like a Black Dot sketchbook, and Arne Jacobsen wall clock, or an aerodynamic umbrella. ✉ *1930 1st Ave., Downtown* ☎ *206/441–4114* ⊕ *www.petermiller.com.*

CHOCOLATE

Fodor's Choice
★
Fran's Chocolates. A Seattle institution, Fran's Chocolates (helmed by Fran Bigelow) has been making quality chocolates for decades. Their world-famous salted caramels are transcendent, as are delectable truffles, which are spiked with oolong tea, single-malt whisky, or raspberry, among other flavors. This shop is housed in the Four Seasons on

TOP SPOTS TO SHOP

Shopping becomes decidedly less fun when it involves driving around and circling for parking. You're better off limiting your all-day shopping tours to one of several key areas than planning to do a citywide search for a particular item. The following areas have the greatest concentration of shops and the greatest variety.

5th and 6th Avenues, Downtown. Depending on where you're staying, you may not need to drive to this area, but if you do, the parking garage at Pacific Place mall (at 600 Pine) always seems to have a space somewhere (it also has valet parking). Tackling either Pacific Place or the four blocks of 5th and 6th avenues between Olive Way and University Street will keep you very busy for a day.

1st Avenue, Belltown. From Wall Street to Pine Street you'll find clothing boutiques, shoe stores, and some sleek home and architectural design stores. 1st Avenue and Pike brings you to the Pike Place Market. There are numerous pay parking lots on both 1st and 2nd avenues.

Pioneer Square. Walk or bus here if you can. Art galleries are the main draw, along with some home decor and rug shops. If you do drive, many pay lots in the neighborhood participate in the "Parking Around the Square" program, which works with local businesses to offer shoppers validated parking; the Web site (⊕ www.pioneersquare.org) lists the lots and stores that offer it.

Pike–Pine Corridor, Capitol Hill. The best shopping in the Hill is on Pike and Pine streets between Melrose Avenue and 10th Avenue E. Most of the stores are on Pike Street; Pine's best offerings are clustered on the western end of the avenue between Melrose and Summit. There are pay lots on Pike Street (near Broadway) and one on Summit by E. Olive Way (next to the Starbucks).

Fremont and Ballard. Start in Fremont's small retail center, which is mostly along 36th Street. You may be able to snag street parking. After you've exhausted Fremont's shops, it's an easy drive over to Ballard. Ballard Avenue and NW Market Street are chockablock with great boutiques. Finding parking in Ballard can be tricky on weekends.

1st Avenue—how very elegant, indeed! ⊠ *1325 1st Ave., Downtown* ☎ *206/682–0168* ⊕ *www.franschocolates.com.*

CLOTHING

Alhambra. Sophisticated, casual, and devastatingly feminine, this pricey boutique delivers quality, European-style looks for women of all ages. Pop into the Moorish-inspired shop for a party dress, elegant jewelry, or separates, and be sure to check out their house line, designed by the owners. ⊠ *101 Pine St., Downtown* ☎ *206/621–9571* ⊕ *www. alhambrastyle.com.*

★ **Mario's of Seattle.** Known for fabulous service and designer labels, this high-end boutique treats every client like a superstar. Men shop the ground floor for Armani, Etro, and Zegna; women ascend the ornate staircase for Prada, Emilio Pucci, and Lanvin. A freestanding Hugo

Boss boutique sells the sharpest tuxedos in town. ⊠ *1513 6th Ave., Downtown* ☎ *206/223–1461* ⊕ *www.marios.com.*

DEPARTMENT STORES

Fodor'sChoice
★

Nordstrom. Seattle's own retail giant sells quality clothing, accessories, cosmetics, jewelry, and lots of shoes—in keeping with its roots in footwear—including many hard-to-find sizes. Browse the various floors for anything from trendy jeans to lingerie to goods for the home. A sky bridge on the store's fourth floor will take you to Pacific Place Shopping Center. Deservedly renowned for its impeccable customer service, the busy Downtown flagship has a concierge desk and valet parking. ■ TIP→ The Nordstrom Rack store at 1st Avenue and Spring Street, close to Pike Place Market, has great deals on marked-down items. ⊠ *500 Pine St., Downtown* ☎ *206/628–2111* ⊕ *www.nordstrom.com.*

GIFTS AND HOME DECOR

☺
Fodor'sChoice
★

Schmancy. Weird and wonderful, this toy store is more surreal art funhouse than FAO Schwarz. Pick up a crocheted zombie (with a cute little bow), a felted Ishmael's whale, your very own Hugh Hefner figurine—or how about a pork-chop pillow? With collectibles from cult favorites Plush You!, Kidrobot, and Lovemongers, kids of all ages will flip over this quirky shop. Warning: Sense of humor required. ⊠ *1932 2nd Ave., Downtown* ☎ *206/728–8008* ⊕ *www.schmancytoys.com.*

★ **Sur La Table.** Need a brass-plated medieval French duck press? You've come to the right place. Culinary artists and foodies have flocked to this popular Pike Place Market destination since 1972. Sur La Table's flagship shop is packed to the rafters with many thousands of kitchen items, including an exclusive line of copper cookware, endless shelves of baking equipment, tabletop accessories, cookbooks, and a formidable display of knives. ⊠ *84 Pine St., Downtown* ☎ *206/448–2244* ⊕ *www. surlatable.com.*

MALL

★ **Pacific Place Shopping Center.** Shopping, dining, and an excellent movie multiplex are wrapped around a four-story, light-filled atrium, making this a cheerful destination even on a stormy day. The mostly high-end shops include Tiffany & Co., MaxMara, Coach, and True Religion, though there's also L'Occitane, Brookstone, Victoria's Secret, Ann Taylor, and J.Crew. A third-floor sky bridge provides a rainproof route to neighboring Nordstrom. One of the best things about the mall is its parking garage, which is surprisingly affordable, given its location, and has valet parking for just a few bucks more. ⊠ *600 Pine St., Downtown* ☎ *206/405–2655* ⊕ *www.pacificplaceseattle.com.*

OUTDOOR CLOTHING AND EQUIPMENT

The North Face. This 1st Avenue location is one of the original stores by the California outfitter, and it doesn't take a rocket scientist to figure out why: You've probably heard about Seattle's often-dreary weather. If you showed up with an optimistic suitcase full of shorts and shirts, stop here for your requisite raincoat—an authentic souvenir if ever there was one. ⊠ *1023 1st Ave., Downtown* ☎ *206/622–4111* ⊕ *www. thenorthface.com.*

WINE AND SPECIALTY FOODS

Fodor's Choice **DeLaurenti Specialty Food and Wine.** Attention foodies: clear out your hotel
★ mini-bars and make room for delectable treats from DeLaurenti. And, if you're planning any picnics, swing by here first. Imported meats and cheeses crowd the deli cases, and packaged delicacies pack the aisles. Stock up on hard-to-find items like truffle-infused olive oil or excellent Italian vintages from the wine shop upstairs. Spring travelers will also want to stop by DeLaurenti's Pike Place nosh nirvana, called Cheesefest, in May. ⊠ *1435 1st Ave., Downtown* ☎ *206/622–0141* ⊕ *www.delaurenti.com.*

★ **Pike and Western Wine Shop.** The folks at Pike and Western have spent the last 35 years carving out the shop's reputation as one of the best wine shops in the city. With well over 1,000 wines personally selected from the Pacific Northwest and around the world—and expert advice from friendly salespeople to guide your choice—this shop offers taste-driven picks in a welcoming environment. ⊠ *1934 Pike Pl., Downtown* ☎ *206/441–1307* ⊕ *www.pikeandwestern.com.*

BELLTOWN

Best shopping: Along 1st Avenue between Cedar and Virginia streets.

CLOTHING

Karan Dannenberg Clothier. A favorite of Seattle executives and sophisticates, this boutique stocks classy, modern clothing for women, but doesn't bow to useless trends. The staff is very knowledgeable, and offers wardrobe consulting for their customers—they'll even make house calls to critique your closets in a What Not to Wear–style evaluation. Shop here for perfect jeans, business attire, or glamorous formal wear. ⊠ *2232 1st Ave., Belltown* ☎ *206/441–3442.*

MUSIC

Singles Going Steady. If punk rock is more to you than anarchy symbols sewn on Target sweatshirts, you must stop at Singles Going Steady. Punk and its myriad subgenres on CD and vinyl are specialties, though they also stock rockabilly, indie rock, and hip-hop. It's a nice foil to the city's indie-rock-dominated record shops and a good reminder that Belltown is still more eclectic than its rising rents may indicate. ⊠ *2219 2nd Ave., Belltown* ☎ *206/441–7396* ⊕ *www.singlesgoingsteady.com.*

OUTDOOR CLOTHING

Patagonia. If the person next to you on the bus isn't wearing North Face, he or she is probably clad in Patagonia. This popular and durable brand excels at functional outdoor wear—made with earth-friendly materials such as hemp and organic cotton—as well as technical clothing hip enough for mountaineers or urban hikers. The line of whimsically patterned fleece wear for children is particularly charming. Outdoor-chic trends of late have translated into seriously rising costs for a jacket here. ⊠ *2100 1st Ave., Belltown* ☎ *206/622–9700* ⊕ *www.patagonia.com.*

9

The REI superstore in South Lake Union

SOUTH LAKE UNION

OUTDOOR CLOTHING AND EQUIPMENT

Fodor'sChoice ★ **REI.** Recreational Equipment, Inc. (REI) is Seattle's sports-equipment mega-mecca. The enormous flagship store in South Lake Union has an incredible selection of outdoor gear—from polar-fleece jackets and wool socks to down vests, hiking boots, raingear, and much more—as well as its own 65-foot climbing wall. The staff is extremely knowledgeable; there always seems to be enough help on hand, even when the store is busy. You can test things out on the mountain-bike test trail or in the simulated rain booth. REI also rents gear such as tents, sleeping bags, skis, snowshoes, and backpacks. ⊠ *222 Yale Ave. N, South Lake Union* ☎ *206/223–1944* ⊕ *www.rei.com.*

QUEEN ANNE

Best shopping: Along Queen Anne Avenue N between W. Harrison and Roy streets, and between W. Galer and McGraw streets.

BOOKS AND MUSIC

★ **Easy Street Records.** Hip and huge, this lively independent music store at the base of Queen Anne Hill has a well-earned reputation for its inventory of new releases, imports, used CDs, and rare finds. With in-store performances a few times a month, you may just be treated to live music while you shop. ⊠ *20 Mercer St., Queen Anne* ☎ *206/691–3279* ⊕ *www.easystreetonline.com.*

★ **Queen Anne Books.** One of the most beloved neighborhood bookstores in Seattle, Queen Anne Books is well known for their friendly,

knowledgeable staff and extensive book selection. Pop in for their children's storytelling sessions on the third Sunday of every month, or
browse at night and catch one of the many author events. After you
grab your new books, slip into El Diablo, the incredibly cute coffee shop
adjacent to the bookstore. ✉ *1811 Queen Anne Ave. N, Queen Anne*
☎ *206/283–5624* ⊕ *www.queenannebooks.com.*

CLOTHING

Peridot Boutique. Strapless animal-print pocket dresses, retro gingham
tops, and ruffly skirts abound in this contemporary women's boutique
in lower Queen Anne. The prices are reasonable, the accessories are
abundant, and local designers are represented as well. ✉ *523 1st Ave. W,
Queen Anne* ☎ *206/284–3313* ⊕ *www.peridotboutique.blogspot.com.*

WINE AND SPECIALTY FOODS

★ **McCarthy & Schiering Wine Merchants.** One of the best wine shops in the city,
this attitude-free store offers an amazing selection of wines from around
the world in a range of prices. Check out their local specialty wines to
experience the true flavor of the Northwest. ✉ *2401B Queen Anne Ave.
N, Queen Anne* ☎ *206/282–8500* ⊕ *www.mccarthyandschiering.com.*

Teacup. Tea aficionados should not miss this aromatic shop on the top
of Queen Anne. In a city full of coffee drinkers, Teacup boldly salutes
the overlooked leaf with more than 150 varieties of tea sold loose by the
pound. The excellent selection includes seasonal favorites and delicious
blends like Provence Vanilla Rooibos and Elliott Bay Sunset. There are
a few tables if you want to sample some tea in-house. ✉ *2128 Queen
Anne Ave. N, Queen Anne* ☎ *206/283–5931* ⊕ *www.seattleteacup.com.*

PIONEER SQUARE

*Best shopping: 1st Avenue S between Yesler Way and S. Jackson Street,
and Occidental Avenue S between S. Main and Jackson streets.*

ANTIQUES AND COLLECTIBLES

★ **Kagedo Japanese Art and Antiques.** Museum-quality works from the early
20th century and Japanese art in a variety of mediums are on display
in this influential gallery. Among the treasures are intricately carved
okimono sculptures, stone garden ornaments, and studio basketry. The
gallery itself is worth a look—it's beautifully laid out, and includes a
small rock garden and rice-paper screens that cover the storefront's
picture windows. ✉ *520 1st Ave. S, Pioneer Square* ☎ *206/467–9077*
⊕ *www.kagedo.com.*

ART AND GIFTS

Agate Designs. Amateur geologists, curious kids, and anyone fascinated
by fossils and gems should make a trip to Agate Designs, where there's
no shortage of eye-popping items on display. Between the 500 million-
year-old fossils and the 250-pound amethyst geodes, this store is almost
like a museum (but a lot more fun). ✉ *120 1st Ave. S, Pioneer Square*
☎ *206/621–3063* ⊕ *www.agatedesigns.com.*

★ **Glass House Studio.** Seattle's oldest glassblowing studio and gallery lets
you watch fearless artisans at work in the "hot shop." Some of the best
glass artists in the country work out of this shop, and many of their

impressive studio pieces are for sale, along with around 40 other Northwest artists represented by the shop. ⊠ *311 Occidental Ave. S, Pioneer Square* ☎ *206/682–9939* ⊕ *www.glasshouse-studio.com.*

BOOKS AND TOYS

☺
★ **Magic Mouse Toys.** Since 1977, Magic Mouse has been supplying families with games, toys, puzzles, tricks, candy, figurines, and more in their two-story, 7,000-square-foot shop in the heart of Pioneer Square. They claim that a professional child runs the store—and it shows. The staff is friendly and fun, and the shop will surely put a smile on your face. ⊠ *603 1st Ave., Pioneer Square* ☎ *206/682-8097* ⊕ *www. magicmousetoys.net.*

CLOTHING

★ **Filson.** Seattle's flagship Filson store is a shrine to meticulously well-made outdoor wear for men and women. The hunting lodge–like decor of the space, paired with interesting memorabilia and pricey, made-on-site clothing, makes the drive south of Pioneer Square worth it (we recommend catching a cab, not hoofing it). The attention to detail paid to the plaid vests, oil-treated rain slickers, and fishing outfits is borderline fetishistic. ⊠ *1555 4th Ave. S, Pioneer Square* ☎ *206/622–3147* ⊕ *www.filson.com.*

Synapse 206. A near-seizure-inducing jumble of every imaginable fabric and color, Synapse 206 throws arty, innovative, and often audacious designs from local and international designers under one roof. Prices are actually reasonable, and whether or not you walk out with something, you'll have fun poking around in here. ⊠ *206 1st Ave. S, Pioneer Square* ☎ *206/447-7731* ⊕ *www.synapse206.com.*

CAPITOL HILL

Best shopping: E. Pike and E. Pine streets between Bellevue Avenue and Madison Avenue E, E. Olive Way between Bellevue Avenue E and Broadway E, and Broadway E between E. Denny Way and E. Roy Street.

BOOKS AND MUSIC

Fodor's Choice
★ **Elliott Bay Book Company.** After 36 years anchoring the Pioneer Square shopping district, Elliott Bay moved to new (but delightfully vintage) digs on Capitol Hill in 2010. Purist bibliophiles take heart: the new location is eerily like the old, as great pains were taken to move each and every massive cedar bookshelf onto the worn Douglas fir floors at the new space. With an expanded bargain-books section, underground parking, lovely skylights, and a new café run by restaurateur Tamara Murphy, some might argue the store is even better. Elliott Bay hosts hundreds of author events every year, so nearly every day is an exciting one to visit the store, and the staff is as knowledgeable and clever as ever. As you enter, check out the great selection of Pacific Northwest history books and fiction titles by local authors, complete with handwritten recommendation cards from staff members. Probably the only downside to the move is that the store will no longer carry used books—a small

sacrifice to pay to keep the literary heart of the city. ✉ *1521 10th Ave., Capitol Hill* ☎ *206/624–6600* ⊕ *www.elliottbaybook.com.*

Sonic Boom Records Like the mothership store in Ballard, Sonic Boom on Capitol Hill is one of the best music shops around. It carries a little bit of everything, but the emphasis is definitely on indie releases. Handwritten recommendation cards from the staff help you find local artists and the best new releases from independent Northwest labels. Discover new bands in the handy listening stations and check out the small but fantastic collection of books, gifts, and other rockin' paraphernalia. ✉ *1525 Melrose Ave., Capitol Hill* ☎ *206/568–2666* ⊕ *www. sonicboomrecords.com.*

Wall of Sound. If you're looking for Top 40 hits, this is not your record shop. If, however, you're on the hunt for Japanese avant-rock on LP, anti-war spoken word, spiritual reggae with Afro-jazz undertones, or old screen-printed show posters, you've found the place. Obscure, experimental, adventurous, and good? Wall of Sound probably has it. ✉ *315 E. Pine St., Capitol Hill* ☎ *206/441–9880* ⊕ *www.wosound.com.*

CLOTHING

★ **Le Frock.** It may look like just another overcrowded consignment shop, but Le Frock is Seattle's classiest vintage and consignment store. Among the racks, you'll find classic steals for men and women from Burberry, Fendi, Dior, Missoni, and the like, while contemporary looks from Prada, Gucci, and Chanel round out the collection. ✉ *317 E. Pine St., Capitol Hill* ☎ *206/623–5339* ⊕ *www.lefrockonline.com.*

★ **Red Light Clothing Exchange.** Nostalgia rules in this cavernous space filled with well-organized, good-quality vintage clothing. Fantasy outfits from decades past are arranged by era or by genre. There's plenty of denim, leather, and disco threads alongside cowboy boots and eveningwear. There's a smaller branch in the University District. ✉ *312 Broadway E, Capitol Hill* ☎ *206/329–2200* ⊕ *www.redlightvintage.com.*

FOOTWEAR

Edie's Shoes. Super-comfy, effortlessly cool shoes can be found at this small but carefully planned shop. Plop down on the big purple couch and try on trendy but sensible footwear by Camper, Onitsuka Tiger, Biviel, Tretorn, and Tsubo. You won't find any outrageous designs or one-of-a-kind items here, but it does have a great selection of favored brands in perhaps a few more styles than you'd find at Nordstrom. ✉ *319 E. Pine St., Capitol Hill* ☎ *206/839–1111* ⊕ *www.ediesshoes.com.*

GIFTS AND HOME DECOR

★ **Area 51.** Wander through this 10,000-square-foot temple of design and gape at the mix of retro-inspired new items and vintage, mid-century finds. Anything might materialize in this industrial space, from Eames replicas to clever coffee mugs, but it will all look like it's straight out of a handbook of the design trends from the middle of the last century. ✉ *401 E. Pine St., Capitol Hill* ☎ *206/568–4782* ⊕ *www.area51seattle.com.*

★ **NuBe Green.** An emphasis on recycled goods and sustainability is the mission of this well-presented store anchoring a corner of the Oddfellows Building. All items are sourced and made in the United States, including

9

linens, candles, glass art, and even dog beds made from old jeans. Our favorite items are by local **Alchemy Goods** (⊕ *www.alchemygoods. com*), which recycles bicycle tubes, reclaimed vinyl mesh, and seatbelts into distinctively cool wallets and messenger bags. ⊠ *912 E. Pine St., Capitol Hill* ☎ *206/402–4515* ⊕ *www.nubegreen.com.*

FREMONT

CHOCOLATE

Fodor'sChoice **Theo Chocolate.** Seattleites love their chocolate nearly as much as their
★ coffee (and preferably at the same time, thank you). This Fremont factory/storefront is one-stop fun, with factory tours on offer every day. Learn about the history of cacao, then stock up on free-trade organic tasty chocolate nibbles, such as spicy chile, cherry and almond, or coconut curry chocolate bars. ⊠ *3400 Phinney Ave. N, Fremont* ☎ *206/632–5100* ⊕ *www.theochocolate.com.*

CLOTHING

★ **Les Amis.** The most elegant boutique in Fremont, Les Amis is like a pop-up from a little girl's storybook set in a French country cottage. The over-35 set will breathe a sigh of relief when they see that the racks are not just filled with low-rise jeans: sophisticated dresses, gorgeous hand-knits, and the makings of great work outfits, much of it from Europe and Japan, fill the racks here. Younger fashionistas come here, too, for unique summer skirts and ultrasoft T-shirts. Everyone seems to love the whimsical lingerie collection. Les Amis carries some top designers such as Dosa, Rozae Nichols, and Nanette Lepore; accordingly, this is the most expensive store in Fremont. ⊠ *3420 Evanston Ave. N, Fremont* ☎ *206/632–2877* ⊕ *www.lesamis-inc.com.*

BALLARD

Best shopping: Ballard Avenue between 22nd Avenue NW and 20th Avenue NW; Northwest Market Street between 20th and 24th avenues.

BOOKS AND MUSIC

☾ **Secret Garden Bookshop.** Named after the Francis Hodgson Burnett classic, Secret Garden Books has been delighting readers for 34 years in their cozy shop in downtown Ballard. A favorite of teachers, librarians, and parents, the store stocks a wide array of imaginative literature and thoughtful nonfiction for all ages; their children's section is particularly notable. ⊠ *2214 N.W. Market St., Ballard* ☎ *206/789–5006* ⊕ *www. secretgardenbooks.com.*

CLOTHING AND ACCESSORIES

☾ **Clover.** Easily the cutest children's store in town, the always-charming
★ Clover carries wonderful handcrafted wooden toys, European figurines, works by local artists, and a variety of swoon-worthy, perfectly crafted little clothes. Even shoppers without children will be smitten—it's hard to resist their vintage French Tintin posters, knit-wool cow dolls, and classic Smurf figurines. ⊠ *5335 Ballard Ave. NW, Ballard* ☎ *206/782–0715* ⊕ *www.clovertoys.com.*

★ **Velouria.** The ultimate antidote to the mass-produced, unimaginative clothes choking much of the chains these days can be found at Velouria, where independent West Coast designers rule, and much on offer is one-of-a-kind. Step into this exquisitely feminine shop to find hand-made, '70s-inspired jumpsuits; romantic, demure eyelet dresses; and clever screen-printed tees. Superb bags, delicate jewelry, and fun cards and gifts are also on display. It's worth a look, just to check out all the wearable art. ✉ *2205 N.W. Market St., Ballard* ☎ *206/788–0330* ⊕ *shopvelouria.tripod.com.*

GIFTS AND HOME ACCESSORIES

Fodor's Choice **La Tienda.** Every item in La Tienda's showroom of handmade art from
★ around the world was lovingly selected by the owners, who pride themselves on procuring art directly from craftspeople for a fair price. You'll find delicate Chinese puppets, figurines from Peru, and Indonesian Buddha sculptures, but many American-made items are also included in the collection. This store has been a favorite shopping destination since 1962. ✉ *2050 N.W. Market St., Ballard* ☎ *206/297–3605* ⊕ *www. latienda-folkart.com.*

THE EASTSIDE

Best shopping: Bellevue Square and The Shops at the Bravern.

CENTERS AND MALLS

☺ **The Bellevue Collection (Bellevue Square, Bellevue Place, and Lincoln Center).**
★ In this impressive trifecta of shopping centers you'll find just about any chain store you've heard of (and some that you haven't). Bellevue Square alone has more than 200 stores, including Nordstrom, Macy's, Pottery Barn, Crate & Barrel, Aveda, Banana Republic, Coach, 7 For All Mankind, Build-a-Bear, and Helly Hansen. The Square's wide walkways and benches, many children's clothing stores, first-floor play area, and third-floor children's museum make this a great place for kids, too. You can park for free in the attached garage. Take the sky bridge to Lincoln Center, to catch a flick at their 16-screen cinema, organize your life at The Container Store, or sample an assortment of other retail and several popular chain restaurants. Bellevue Place, across from Lincoln Center, hosts a variety of retail along with the ever-popular Daniel's Broiler, STIR Martini & Wine Bar, and pickup-central Joey Bar. ✉ *Bellevue Way, Bellevue* ☎ *425/454–8096* ⊕ *www.bellevuesquare.com.*

The Shops at the Bravern. If you have some serious cash to burn, the sleek, upscale Bravern might be the Eastside spot for you. With über-high-end shops like Neiman Marcus, Hermès, Brooks Brothers, Jimmy Choo, Salvatore Ferragamo, and Louis Vuitton, it's tempting to empty your wallet—but save room for a spa treatment at the Elizabeth Arden Red Door Spa or a meal at Northwest favorite Wild Ginger. Valet and complimentary parking (with validation) are available. ✉ *11111 N.E. 8th St., Bellevue* ☎ *425/456–8780* ⊕ *www.thebravern.com.*

9

SPORTS AND ACTIVITIES

The question in Seattle isn't "Do you exercise?" Rather, it's "How do you exercise?" Athleticism is a regular part of most people's lives here, whether it's an afternoon jog, a sunrise rowing session, a lunch-hour bike ride, or an evening game of Frisbee.

To the west of the city is Puget Sound, where sailors, kayakers, and anglers practice their sports. Lake Union and Lake Washington also provide residents with plenty of boating, kayaking, fishing, and swimming opportunities. Spectator sports are also appreciated here. To see how excited Seattle citizens can get about crew racing, stop by the Montlake Cut on the official opening day of the unofficial boating season. The University of Washington (UW) has been a rowing powerhouse since the 1930s, and tickets to Husky football games have been hot items for years. Attendance at Mariners games is at an all-time high, and the Seattle Sounders—a Major League Soccer (MLS) franchise—may be the best-loved team in town.

PARKS INFORMATION

King County Parks and Recreation (☎ *206/296–4232 for information and reservations* ⊕ *www.metrokc.gov/parks*) manages many of the parks outside city limits. To find out whether an in-town park baseball diamond or tennis court is available, contact the **Seattle Parks and Recreation Department** (☎ *206/684–4075* ⊕ *www.seattle.gov/parks*), which is responsible for most of the parks, piers, beaches, playgrounds, and courts within city limits. The department issues permits for events, arranges reservations for facilities, and staffs visitor centers and naturalist programs. The state manages several parks and campgrounds in greater Seattle. For more information contact **Washington State Parks** (☎ *360/902–8844 for general information, 888/226–7688 for campsite reservations* ⊕ *www.parks.wa.gov/parkpage.asp*).

BASEBALL

The **Seattle Mariners** play in the West Division of the American League, and their home is **Safeco Field** (✉ *1st Ave. S and Atlantic St., SoDo* ☎ *206/346–4000* ⊕ *seattle.mariners.mlb.com*), a retractable-roof stadium where there really isn't a bad seat in the house. One local sports columnist referred to the $656 million venue—which finished $100 million over budget—as "the guilty pleasure." You can purchase tickets through Ticketmaster or StubHub; online or by phone from Safeco Field (to be picked up at the Will Call); in person at Safeco's box office (no surcharges), which is open daily 10–6; or from the Mariners team store at 4th Avenue and Stewart Street in Downtown. The cheap seats cost $9; better seats cost $38–$98, and the best seats will cost you up to $300.

BICYCLING

Biking is probably Seattle's most practiced sport. Thousands of Seattleites bike to work, and even more ride recreationally, especially on weekends. In the past, Seattle hasn't been a particularly bike-friendly

Bicyclists ride along Lake Washington in the Seattle-to-Portland (STP) event.

city. But in 2007 city government adopted a sweeping Bicycle Master Plan, calling for 118 new miles of bike lanes, 19 mi of bike paths, and countless route signs and lane markings throughout the city by 2017. The plan can't erase the hills, though—Queen Anne Hill and Phinney Ridge should only be attempted by sadists. Fortunately, all city buses have easy-to-use bike racks (on the front of the buses, below the windshield) and drivers are used to waiting for cyclists to load and unload their bikes. If you're not comfortable biking in urban traffic—and there is a lot of urban traffic to contend with here—you can do a combination bus-and-bike tour of the city or stick to the car-free Burke-Gilman Trail.

Seattle drivers are fairly used to sharing the road with cyclists. With the exception of the occasional road-rager or clueless cell-phone talker, drivers usually leave a generous amount of room when passing; however, there are biking fatalities every year, so be alert and cautious, especially when approaching blind intersections, of which Seattle has many. You must wear a helmet at all times (it's the law) and be sure to lock up your bike—though there are probably more car break-ins, bikes do get stolen, even in quiet residential neighborhoods.

The Seattle Parks Department sponsors Bicycle Sundays on various weekends from May through September. On these Sundays, a 4-mi stretch of Lake Washington Boulevard—from Mt. Baker Beach to Seward Park—is closed to motor vehicles. Many riders continue around the 2-mi loop at Seward Park and back to Mt. Baker Beach to complete a 10-mi, car-free ride. Check with the **Seattle Parks and Recreation Department** (☎ 206/684–4075 ⊕ *www.seattle.gov/parks/bicyclesunday*) for a complete schedule.

The trail that circles **Green Lake** is popular with cyclists, though runners and walkers can impede fast travel. The city-maintained **Burke-Gilman Trail**, a slightly less congested path, follows an abandoned railroad line 14 mi roughly following Seattle's waterfront from Ballard to Kenmore, at the north end of Lake Washington. (From there, serious cyclists can continue on the Sammamish River Trail to Marymoor Park in Redmond; in all, the trail spans 42 mi between Seattle and Issaquah.) **Discovery Park** is a very tranquil place to tool around in. **Myrtle Edwards Park**, north of Pier 70, has a two-lane waterfront path for bicycling and running. The **islands of the Puget Sound** are also easily explored by bike (there are rental places by the ferry terminals), though be forewarned that Bainbridge, Whidbey, and the San Juans all have some tough hills.

King County has more than 100 mi of paved and nearly 70 mi of unpaved routes including the Sammamish River, Interurban, Green River, Cedar River, Snoqualmie Valley, and Soos Creek trails. For more information contact the **King County Parks and Recreation** office (☏ *206/296–8687*).

RENTALS

BikeStation. This Pioneer Square bike storage facility also offers perhaps the cheapest rentals in town. Though the selection is not terribly large, you can procure a regular, mountain, or electric bike for a mere $3 per hour ($15 per day). ⊠ *311 3rd Ave. S, Pioneer Square* ☏ *206/332–9795* ⊕ *www.bikestation.org/seattle.*

Montlake Bicycle Shop (⊠ *2223 24th Ave. E, Montlake* ☏ *206/329–7333* ⊕ *www.montlakebike.com*), just one mile south of the University of Washington and within easy riding distance of the Burke-Gilman Trail, rents mountain bikes, road bikes, basic cruisers, and even tandems. Prices range from $25 to $85 for the day, with discounts for longer rentals. If you find yourself on the Eastside, rent a bike from their sister store, **Kirkland Bicycle Shop** (⊠ *208 Kirkland Ave., Kirkland* ☏ *425/828–3800* ⊕ *www.kirklandbikes.com*).

BOATING AND KAYAKING

The **Seafair Hydroplane Races** (☏ *206/728–0123* ⊕ *www.seafair.com*) are a highlight of Seattle's rowdy Seafair festivities, which occur from mid-July through the first Sunday in August. Races are held on Lake Washington near Seward Park. Tickets cost $25–$40. In summer, weekly sailing regattas take place on Lakes Union and Washington. Contact the **Seattle Yacht Club** (☏ *206/325–1000* ⊕ *www.seattleyachtclub.org*) for schedules.

★   **Alki Kayak Tours.** For a variety of day-long guided kayak outings—from a Seattle Sunset Sea Kayak Tour to an Alki Point Lighthouse Tour—led by experienced, fun staff, try this great outfitter in West Seattle. In addition to kayaks, you can also rent skates, fishing boats, and longboards here. Custom sea-kayaking adventures can be set up, so dream big! Note that to rent a kayak without a guide, you must be an experienced kayaker; otherwise, sign up for a guided tour, which is memorable and fascinating. ⊠ *1660 Harbor Ave. SW, West Seattle* ☏ *206/953–0237* ⊕ *www.kayakalki.com.*

Agua Verde Paddle Club and Café

Fodor's Choice **Agua Verde Paddle Club and Café.** Start out by renting a kayak and pad-
★ dling along either the Lake Union shoreline, with its hodgepodge of
funky-to-fabulous houseboats and dramatic Downtown vistas, or
Union Bay on Lake Washington, with its marshes and cattails. Afterward, take in the lakefront as you wash down some Mexican food
(halibut tacos, anyone?) with a margarita. Kayaks are available March
through October and are rented by the hour—$15 for singles, $18 for
doubles. It pays to paddle midweek: the third hour is free on weekdays.
✉ *1303 N.E. Boat St., University District* ☎ *206/545–8570* ⊕ *www.
aguaverde.com.*

★ **The Center for Wooden Boats.** Located on the southern shore of Lake
Union, Seattle's free maritime heritage museum is a bustling community hub. Thousands of Seattleites rent rowboats and small sailboats
here every year; the Center also offers workshops, demonstrations, and
classes. Rowboats are $20 an hour on weekdays and $25 an hour on
weekends. There's a $10 skills-check fee. Free half-hour guided sails and
steamboat rides are offered on Sunday from 2 to 4 (arrive an hour early
to reserve a spot). ✉ *1010 Valley St., Lake Union* ☎ *206/382–2628*
⊕ *www.cwb.org.*

Northwest Outdoor Center. This center on Lake Union's west side rents
one- or two-person kayaks (it also has a few triples) by the hour or day,
including equipment and basic or advanced instruction. The hourly
rate is $13 for a single and $18 for a double, with daily maximums of
$65 and $90, respectively. Third and fourth hours are free during the
week; a fourth hour is free on weekends. If you want to find your own
water, NWOC offers "to-go" kayaks; the rate for a single is $65 first

day, plus $35 each additional day. Doubles cost $90 the first day and $45 for each day thereafter. In summer, reserve at least three days ahead. NWOC also runs guided trips to the Nisqually Delta and Chuckanut Bay for $80 per person. Sunset tours to Golden Gardens Park ($55 per person) and moonlight tours of Portage Bay ($40 per person) are other options. Every May there are two overnight whale-watching trips to the San Juan Islands for $325 per person. ⊠ *2100 Westlake Ave. N, Lake Union* ☎ *206/281–9694* ⊕ *www.nwoc.com.*

Waterfront Activities Center. This center, located behind UW's Husky Stadium on Union Bay, rents three-person canoes and four-person rowboats for $8.50 an hour February through October. You can tour the Lake Washington shoreline or take the Montlake Cut portion of the ship canal and explore Lake Union. You can also row to nearby Foster Island and visit the Washington Park Arboretum. ⊠ *3854 Montlake Blvd. NE, University District* ☎ *206/543–9433.*

FOOTBALL

The **Seattle Seahawks** play in the $430 million, state-of-the-art **Qwest Field** (⊠ *800 Occidental Ave. S, SoDo* ☎ *425/203–8000* ⊕ *www. seahawks.com*). Single-game tickets go on sale in late July or early August, and all home games sell out quickly. Tickets are expensive, with the cheapest seats, in the 300 section (where you actually get a really good view of the field), starting at $42. Note that traffic and parking are both nightmares on game days; try to take public transportation—or walk the 1 mi from Downtown—if possible.

GOLF

★ **Gold Mountain Golf Complex.** Gold Mountain has two 18-hole courses, but most people make the trek to Bremerton to play the Olympic Course, a beautiful and challenging par 72 that is widely considered the best public course in Washington. The older, less-sculpted Cascade Course is also popular; it's better suited to those new to the game. There are four putting greens, a driving range, and a striking new clubhouse with views of the Belfair Valley. Prime-time greens fees are $27–$36 for the Cascade and $38–$49 for the Olympic. Carts are $32. You can drive all the way to Bremerton via I–5, or you can take the car ferry to Bremerton from Pier 52. The trip will take roughly an hour and a half no matter which way you do it, but the ferry ride (60 minutes) might be a more pleasant way to spend a large part of the journey. Note, however, that the earliest departure time for the ferry is 6 AM, so this option won't work for very early tee times. ⊠ *7263 W. Belfair Valley Rd., Bremerton* ☎ *206/415–5432* ⊕ *www.goldmt.com.*

Golf Club at Newcastle. Probably the best option on the Eastside, this golf complex, which includes a pair of courses and an 18-hole putting green, has views, views, and more views. From the hilly greens you'll see Seattle, the Olympic Mountains, and Lake Washington. The 7,000-yard, par-72 Coal Creek course is the more challenging of the two, though the China Creek course has its challenges and more sections of undisturbed natural areas. This is the Seattle area's most expensive golf club—greens fees for Coal Creek range from $125 to $160 depending on the season; fees for China Creek range from $80 to $110. Newcastle is about 35 minutes from Downtown—if you don't hit traffic. ✉ *15500 Six Penny La., Newcastle* ☎ *425/793–5566* ⊕ *www.newcastlegolf.com.*

★ **Harbour Pointe Golf Club.** Harbour Pointe is about 35 minutes north of Seattle in the town of Mukilteo. Its challenging 18-hole championship layout—with 6,800 yards of hilly terrain and wonderful Puget Sound views—is one of Washington's best. Greens fees range from $20 for twilight play to $49 for prime time on weekends. Carts cost $14 per person. There's also a driving range where you can get 65 balls for $5. Reserve your tee time online, up to 21 days in advance. Inquire about early-bird, twilight, off-season, and junior discounts. ✉ *11817 Harbour Pointe Blvd., Mukilteo* ☎ *425/355–6060* ⊕ *www.harbourpointegolf.com.*

Jefferson Park. This golf complex—where the PGA Tour pro Fred Couples grew up golfing— has views of the city skyline *and* Mt. Rainier. The par-27, 9-hole course has a lighted driving range with heated stalls that's open from dusk until midnight. And the 18-hole, par-72 main course is one of the city's best. Greens fees are $35 on weekends and $30 on weekdays for the 18-hole course; you can play the 9-hole course for $8.50 daily. Carts are $26 and $17, and $2 buys you a bucket of 30 balls at the driving range. You can book tee times online up to 10 days in advance or by phone up to 7 days in advance. ✉ *4101 Beacon Ave. S, Beacon Hill* ☎ *206/762–4513* ⊕ *www.seattlegolf.com.*

HIKING

■ TIP → Within Seattle city limits, the best nature trails can be found in Discovery Park, Lincoln Park, Seward Park, and at the Washington Park Arboretum.

9

★ **Larrabee State Park.** A favorite spot of the hippies and college students who call Bellingham home, Larrabee has two lakes, a coastline with tidal pools, and 15 mi of hiking trails. The Interurban Trail, which parallels an old railway line, is perfect for leisurely strolls or trail running. Head up Chuckanut Mountain to reach the lakes and to get great views of the San Juan Islands. ⊹ *Take I–5 North to Exit 231. Turn right onto Chuckanut Dr. and follow that road to the park entrance.*

Mt. Si. A good place to cut your teeth before setting out on more ambitious hikes—or a good place to just witness the local hiking and trail-running communities in all their weird and wonderful splendor—Mt. Si offers a challenging hike with views of a valley (slightly marred by the suburbs) and the Olympic Mountains in the distance. The main trail to Haystack Basin is 8 mi round-trip that climbs some 4,000 vertical feet, but there are several obvious places to rest or turn around if you'd like to keep the hike to 3 or 4 mi. Note that solitude is in short supply here—this is an extremely popular trail, thanks to its proximity to Seattle. ⊹ *Take I–90 East to Exit 31 (toward North Bend). Turn onto North Bend Way and then make a left onto Mt. Si Rd. and follow that road to the trailhead parking lot.*

Fodor's Choice   **Snow Lake.** Washington State's most popular wilderness trail may be
★   crowded at times, but the scenery and convenience of this hike make it
a classic. The 8-mile round-trip entails a relatively modest 1,300-foot
elevation gain; the views of the Alpine Lakes Wilderness are well worth
the sweat. The glimmering waters of Snow Lake await hikers at the
trail's end; summer visitors will find abundant wildflowers, huckleberries, and wild birds. ⊹ *Take I–90 East to Exit 52 (toward Snoqualmie
Pass West). Turn left (north), cross under the freeway, and continue on
to the trailhead, located in parking lot at the Alpental Ski Area.*

WALKING TOURS

With an abundance of lush city parks—with anything from meandering
paths through old-growth forests to beachside pathways—there's no
shortage of great places to walk in Seattle. Some of our favorite in-city
walking paths include those at **Seward Park, Green Lake, Alki Point,** and
Discovery Park. And, of course, the **Burke-Gilman Trail** meanders through
the city, passing many beautiful parks and bodies of water.

Bill Speidel's Underground Tour (✉ *608 1st Ave., Pioneer Square* ☎ *206/
682–4646* ⊕ *www.undergroundtour.com*) leads guests on fascinating
underground tours in the Pioneer Square area. Hear stories of Seattle's
pioneering past as you wander subterranean passageways that once
were the main roads of old Seattle.

Market Ghost Tours (✉ *1410 Post Alley, Downtown* ☎ *206/322–1218*
⊕ *www.seattleghost.com*) offers weekend tours around the Pike Place
Market, weaving in local ghost stories, eerie history, and fun facts about
the market and its haunted places.

Savor Seattle Food Tours (✉ *1st Ave. and Pike St., Downtown* ☎ *888/987–
2867* ⊕ *www.savorseattletours.com*) serves up two- to three-hour culinary walking tours around town, including a Chocolate Indulgence tour
(yum); a Gourmet Seattle tour (which includes stops at fine restaurants
to meet chefs, and tasty meals with wine and beer pairings); and a Pike
Place Market walking tour led by a local guide.

Seattle Environs

WITH WASHINGTON'S NORTH COAST

WORD OF MOUTH

"Tacoma has some really nice areas and the Silver Cloud is in one of them, along the waterfront. Point Defiance Pk is wonderful, as is the St Historical Society Museum, the Tacoma Art Museum and Glass Museum. The three museums are within walking distance of each other and there are nice restaurants and shops nearby."

—Orcas

WELCOME TO SEATTLE ENVIRONS

TOP REASONS TO GO

★ **Take Flight:** See a Boeing in mid-construction or see a World War II chopper up close at Everett's Paine Field.

★ **Tiptoe Through the Tulips:** Bike past undulating fields of tulips and other spring blooms in La Conner and Mt. Vernon.

★ **Hang in Glass Houses:** Check out Dale Chihuly's biomorphic sculptures at Tacoma's International Museum of Glass.

★ **Go Navy:** The Bremerton waterfront includes the *U.S. Turner Joy*, the Naval Museum, and other maritime attractions.

★ **Paddle Around Puget Sound:** Rent a kayak to explore the charming seaside communities of Poulsbo or Gig Harbor.

1 I–5 Corridor North of Seattle. North of Seattle are two important port towns. Edmonds has more of a seaside vibe, with waterfront parks and promenades, and a ferry terminal serving the islands of Puget Sound. Everett, on the other hand, is devoted to flight, with a Boeing factory tour and a collection of vintage airplanes being the main attractions. A short side trip off the highway leads you to Snohomish, a base of operations for the trails and slopes of Stevens Pass.

2 I–5 Corridor South of Seattle. Immortalized in song by Neko Case as the "dusty old jewel in the South Puget Sound," Tacoma is shining a bit more brightly these days with a walkable waterfront that includes several impressive museums. Farther south is the capital city Olympia, which is the perfect mix of quirky and stately. Short jaunts off the highway include attending a county fair in Puyallup, and winding down a day of hiking or biking near Snoqualmie Pass with a snack in the cute town of Snoqualmie.

3 Kitsap Peninsula. Crawling around Bremerton's collection of naval vessels is a favorite family activity. The smaller, less industrial port towns provide beach parks plus glimpses of the region's Scandinavian and logging pasts—a nice snapshot of coastal Washington life should you not be able to make it out to the Olympic Peninsula.

4 The North Coast and Skagit Valley. The sleepy college town of Bellingham is about as close as this area comes to bustle. Although not as tranquil as the central part of the state, the area is about roads less traveled: the farm roads that connect La Conner and Mt. Vernon and the bike and hiking paths that wind through state parks.

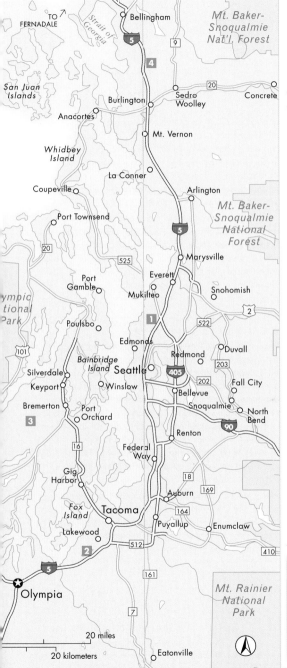

GETTING ORIENTED

Most of the major towns are along—or not far off from—the I–5 corridor, stretching from the capital city of Olympia, 60 mi south of Seattle, up to Bellingham, 90 mi north of Seattle and the last city of size before the Canadian border. Although I–5 jogs inland a bit through the Seattle suburbs, six of the cities along the route are ports. There's even more waterfront out on the Kitsap Peninsula, which is sandwiched between this corridor and the Olympic Peninsula. Two other outlying areas include the western edge of the Skagit Valley, an important agricultural area, and Snoqualmie, an unofficial cut-off point in the minds of locals—once you get past this and North Bend you're definitely out of the Seattle metropolitan area.

10

SEATTLE ENVIRONS PLANNER

Traveling from Seattle

Tacoma, Bremerton, and Everett are good choices for day trips. Tacoma is only 30–40 minutes by car or train from Seattle; Bremerton and Everett are also easy to reach in under an hour, plus their major attractions (exhibits on naval and flight history, respectively) are of the type that don't require overnights. Just don't get stuck driving the I–5 corridor during weekday rush hours or on Sunday nights in summer—the chaotic and heavy traffic will sour any outing.

Snohomish and Snoqualmie aren't far from Seattle, but are better as pit stops in longer itineraries that take in the natural areas surrounding Highway 2 and I–90, respectively.

Olympia is far enough from Seattle—technically it's only about 60 mi, but you almost always hit traffic, so expect a solid 1.5 hours in the car—that it's often better as a pit stop on the way to the southern part of the Olympic Peninsula (Ocean Shores or Moclips, for example). You can pick up Highway 101 on the outskirts of the city. Olympia can also be part of an itinerary to Mt. Rainier National Park or Mt. St. Helens National Monument. It's also a good leg-stretch between Seattle and Portland.

About the Restaurants

Tacoma and Olympia both have growing dining scenes, with everything from coffee shops to $$$$ splurge restaurants with water views. After those cities, Gig Harbor has the best scene—not terribly big, but with an across-the-board quality not found in Bellingham's more numerous restaurants. Bellingham, does however, have good brewpubs, as do Olympia and Snoqualmie.

On the road, refueling takes place at country-style cafés, farm stands, and kitschy or specialty shops like the '50s-style sweets shops of Port Gamble and Snoqualmie or the Norwegian bakeries of Poulsbo. None of these is in short supply, and many eateries, however small, pride themselves on using local ingredients.

About the Hotels

Many of the towns listed are easy day trips from Seattle, so staying in the city is always an option. Tacoma, Olympia, and Bellingham have the widest variety of accommodations, with pricey hotels, midrange chains, and bed-and-breakfasts. Almost all but the smallest rural towns have midrange chain motels; towns lacking those, like Port Gamble, have at least one B&B. Roughing it is unlikely—even most B&Bs and motels at this point have basic amenities like Wi-Fi; on the other end of the spectrum, the only truly great resort among this collection of towns is the Salish Lodge in Snoqualmie.

Frankly, except for the Salish Lodge, the Hotel Murano in Tacoma, the Chrysalis Inn in Bellingham, and one or two of our favorite B&Bs, lodging choices in the region can be lackluster. Prices tend to be a bit inflated, with Seattle rates even when the amenities don't match up.

WHAT IT COSTS IN U.S. DOLLARS

	¢	$	$$	$$$	$$$$
Restaurants	under $10	$10–$17	$18–$24	$25–$30	over $30
Hotels		under $100	$100–$150	$151–$200	$201–$250	over $250

Restaurant prices are per person, for a main course at dinner. Hotel prices are for two people in a standard double room in high season, excluding tax.

Getting Here and Around

Air Travel. Seattle-Tacoma International Airport (Sea-Tac), 15 mi south of Seattle, is the hub for the Seattle environs. There are several regional airports, but the only one that sees much action is Bellingham's International Airport, because Bellingham is a hub between northwestern Washington and Canada and has a ferry terminal for cruises to British Columbia and beyond.

Contacts Bellingham International (✉ *1801 Roeder Ave., Bellingham* ☎ *360/676-2500* ⊕ *www.portofbellingham. com*). **Sea-Tac Airport** (✉ *17801 Pacific Hwy. S, [Hwy. 99]* ☎ *206/433-5388* ⊕ *www.seatac.org*).

Airport Transfers. Shuttle Express provides scheduled ride-share service hourly from Sea-Tac Airport to all towns listed in this chapter. Bremerton–Kitsap Airporter shuttles passengers from Sea-Tac to points in Tacoma, Bremerton, Port Orchard, and Gig Harbor ($13–$20, double for round-trip). The Capital Aeroporter connects Sea-Tac with Olympia ($30–$40 one-way). The Bellair Airporter makes 10 round-trips daily between Sea-Tac and Bellingham ($34 one-way, $60 round-trip), with stops in Arlington, Mount Vernon, La Conner, and Ferndale.

Contacts Bellair Airporter (☎ *866/235-5247* ⊕ *www. airporter.com*). **Bremerton–Kitsap Airporter** (☎ *360/876-1737* ⊕ *www.kitsapairporter.com*). **Capital Aeroporter** (☎ *360/754-7113 or 800/962-3579* ⊕ *www.capair. com*). **Shuttle Express** (☎ *425/981-7000* ⊕ *www. shuttleexpress.com*).

Boat and Ferry Travel. Washington State Ferries ply Puget Sound, including from Seattle to Bremerton and between Edmonds and Kingston on the Key Peninsula. You can get updated ferry information on the company's Web site.

Contact Washington State Ferries (☎ *206/464-6400; 888/808-7977; 800/843-3779 automated line in WA and BC* ⊕ *www.wsdot.wa.gov/ferries*).

Bus Travel. Greyhound Lines and Northwestern Trailways cover Washington and the Pacific Northwest. From Seattle, Greyhound connects to Tacoma (45 minutes, $8.75), Olympia (1 hour and 35 minutes, $14–$18), Everett (40 minutes, $11.25), Bellingham (2 hours, $17), and Mount Vernon (1 hour and 25 minutes, $13.25). Pierce County Transit provides bus service around Tacoma.

Contacts Greyhound Lines (☎ *800/231-2222* ⊕ *www. greyhound.com*). **Northwestern Trailways** (⊕ *www. northwesterntrailways.com*). **Pierce County Transit** (☎ *253/581-8000* ⊕ *www.piercetransit.org*).

Car Travel. Interstate 5 runs south from the Canadian border through Seattle, Tacoma, and Olympia to Oregon and California. Interstate 90 begins in Seattle and runs east through North Bend all the way to Idaho. Highway 2 meanders east, parallel to I-90, from Everett to Spokane. Highways 7 and 167 connect the Tacoma area with the Puyallup suburbs and towns around Mt. Rainier. U.S. 101 begins northwest of Olympia and traces the coast of the Olympic Peninsula.

Train Travel. Amtrak's Cascades line serves Seattle, Tacoma, Olympia, Edmonds, Everett, Mt. Vernon, and Bellingham. Sound Transit's Sounder trains (commuter rail) leave Everett between 5:45 AM and 7:20 AM, with stops in Mukilteo and Edmonds before reaching Seattle; trains from Seattle do the reverse trip between 4:05 PM and 5:35 PM. Sounders leave Tacoma between 4:55 AM and 8 AM, as well as at 4:25 and 5 PM with stops in Puyallup and the Seattle suburbs before arriving at the city. Southbound trains leave Seattle for Tacoma between 3:15 and 6:15 PM. Fares range from $3.50 to $4.75 one-way. All trips are weekdays only.

Contacts Amtrak (☎ *800/872-7245* ⊕ *www. amtrak.com*). **Sound Transit** (☎ *206/398-5000 or 888/889-6368* ⊕ *www. soundtransit.org*).

10

Updated
by Carissa
Bluestone

Day trips—or long-weekend escapes—fan out from Seattle in every direction. The San Juan Islands, the Olympic Peninsula, and the great swaths of midstate wilderness get the most photo ops, but there are plenty of adventures that don't require bumping along Forest Service roads.

Up and down I–5 you'll find most of the state's major cities: the ports of Tacoma, Olympia, and Bellingham may feel more like overgrown towns, but each has enough cultural and outdoorsy attractions to warrant an overnight.

Slightly farther afield you'll find smaller towns with some very specific draws: Poulsbo's proud Norwegian heritage, Puyallup's traditional state fair, Port Gamble's painstakingly preserved mill-town vibe, and Everett's enthusiasm for all things flight-related, whether crafted by Boeing or not.

With "environs" encompassing so many distinct geographical areas like the Kitsap Peninsula and the western fringe of the Skagit Valley, exploring the northwestern part of the state can bring you from industrial areas to tulip fields in one day. From naval warships to thundering falls, there's a lot to see within two hours of the city.

I–5 CORRIDOR NORTH OF SEATTLE

The towns north of the city are a mixed bag. Edmonds and Everett, both close to Seattle, are important commuter hubs. Edmonds has a major ferry terminal and the more sophisticated dining and shopping scenes. Everett has slightly more tourist appeal because of its connection to Boeing and the great airplane-related attractions its Paine Field supports. Snohomish isn't technically in the corridor—it's about 15 minutes from Everett off of Highway 2—but it's the last major town between I–5 and the Stevens Pass ski area and Highway 2 hiking corridor.

EDMONDS

45 mi northwest of Snoqualmie, 15 mi north of Seattle.

Charming Edmonds has a waterfront lined by more than a mile of boutiques and restaurants, seaside parks and attractions, and a string of broad, windswept beaches. Just beyond is the small but lively downtown area, where you can wander into chic cafés and wine shops, peruse attractive antiques stores and chic galleries, and browse the colorful Summer Market, which runs Saturday 9 to 3 from May to September. The Third Thursday Art Walk shows off the work of local artists, and a host of events and festivals takes place year-round. On the east side of Puget Sound, Edmonds is also the gateway to the Kitsap Peninsula, as ferries from here connect with Kingston.

GETTING HERE

From Seattle, take I–5 north to 104 west, which will deliver you to the ferry terminal. Sound Transit also connects Seattle to Edmonds via commuter rail; the station in Edmonds is very close to the ferry dock. Additionally, Amtrak and Greyhound connect Edmonds with Seattle and towns along the I–5 corridor.

Contacts **Sound Transit** ☎ *800/201–4900* ⊕ *www.soundtransit.org*).

VISITOR INFORMATION

Edmonds Chamber of Commerce (✉ *120 5th Ave. N, Edmonds* ☎ *425/776–6711* ⊕ *edmondswa.com*).

EXPLORING

The lower level of the **Edmonds Historical Museum** is the place to find out about local legends and traditions; temporary exhibits upstairs often have a patriotic theme. The museum's Summer Garden Market sells handmade and hand-grown items on Saturday from 9 to 2 from May through June. ✉ *118 5th Ave. N* ☎ *425/774–0900* ⊕ *www.historicedmonds.org* ☜ *$2* ⊙ *Wed.–Sun. 1–4.*

The **Edmonds Underwater Park** (✉ *Next to the Edmonds terminal of the Kingston ferry* ⊕ *www.ci.edmonds.wa.us/parks.stm*), perhaps the best-known dive site in Puget Sound besides the Narrows Bridge area, has 27 acres of sunken structures and developed dive trails. It's immediately north of the ferry landing at the foot of Main Street. Dive outfitters in town have lessons, equipment rentals, and underwater tours of the park. The adjacent Brackett's Landing Park has trails, picnic areas, and restrooms.

The **Olympic Beach** fishing pier attracts anglers all year. Today the park is dedicated to such Olympic athletes and champions as figure skater Roslyn Summers, and it's an excellent spot to watch the sun set behind Whidbey Island and the Olympic Mountains. ✉ *Railroad Ave. at Dayton St.* ☎ *No phone.*

WHERE TO EAT

$$–$$$ ✕ **Arnie's in Edmonds.** Sitting directly across from the sound, the dining
SEAFOOD   room has views of the water. The restaurant's specialty, seafood, means that the menu is constantly changing according to what's in season. One famous dish is Prawns Undecided, which consists of prawns prepared in

10

three different ways—stuffed with crab, roasted with garlic, and coated in a beer batter and fried. Sunday-morning brunches, which last until 2, draw local crowds. ✉ *300 Admiral Way* ☎ *425/771–5688* w*www.arniesrestaurant.com* ▭ *AE, MC, V.*

$–$$ ✕ **Girardi's Osteria Italiana.** Coming here is like walking into an elegant
ITALIAN yet comfortable Italian kitchen, where every space beneath the high, peaked ceiling glows with warm country colors and muted light. Small tables, set with gleaming glass and white linens, are set along polished-wood floors and tucked in near exposed-brick walls. The menu is an induction to the Italian dining experience, with such entrées as *anitra della casa* (pan-seared duck breast on herb polenta) and *vitello del capitano* (veal medallions in a Madeira wine sauce). Come Monday for half-price bottled wines, and look for seasonal wine-tasting dinners following specific regions of Italy. ✉ *504 5th Ave. S* ☎ *425/673–5278* w*girardis-osteria.com* ▭ *AE, D, MC, V* ☉ *No lunch Sun. and Mon.*

¢–$ ✕ **Olives Café & Wine Bar.** Northwest wines are the focus of this chic,
WINE BAR gallery-style spot. With the restaurant's selection of 40-plus local labels, you could come here to just sip and smile. However, if you delve into the menu, you'll find eclectic meals to complement every bouquet. Lunch specialties include excellent grilled panini and overstuffed sandwiches as well as rich soups and tangy salads. Dinners surge forward into perfectly shareable antipasti and tapas that draw gourmands from all over the region. A chef's menu appears on Friday and Saturday evenings, and box lunches are available daily. Note that on Monday and Tuesday wines are half-price. ✉ *107 5th Ave. N, Suite 103* ☎ *425/771–5757* ⊕ *www.olivescafewinebar.com* ▭ *AE, MC, V* ☉ *Closed Sun. and Mon.*

WHERE TO STAY

$–$$ ⌂ **Best Western Edmonds Harbor Inn.** In the midst of downtown Edmonds, this inn has as much country style as a chain hotel can offer. It's fairly luxurious, as far as Best Westerns go; comfortable rooms are updated in modern, easy-on-the-eyes beiges and earth tones and have new flat-screen TVs and DVD players, and pillowtop mattresses. Some rooms have fireplaces, kitchens, and oversize jetted bathtubs. **Pros:** proximity to the waterfront, and only 1½ blocks from the Kingston ferry terminal. **Cons:** no beach views. ✉ *130 W. Dayton St.,* ☎ *425/771–5021 or 800/441–8033* ⊕ *bestwesternwashington.com* ⇖ *91 rooms* ⌂ *In-room: a/c, kitchen (some), refrigerator (some), DVD, Wi-Fi. In-hotel: pool, gym, laundry facilities, laundry service, some pets allowed* ▭ *AE, D, MC, V* ⦿*CP.*

EVERETT

19 mi north of Edmonds.

Everett is the county seat of Snohomish County. Much of this industrial town sits high on a bluff above Port Gardner Bay and the Snohomish River. The waterfront was once lined by so many lumber, pulp, and shingle mills that Everett proudly called itself "the city of smokestacks." Downtown Everett has many elegant old commercial buildings dating from the period when John D. Rockefeller heavily invested in the fledging town, hoping to profit from the nearby Monte Cristo mines—which turned out to be a flop. Another scheme failed when James J. Hill made Everett the western terminus of the Great Northern Railroad, hoping to turn it into Puget Sound's most important port. Everett is best known for the Boeing Aircraft plant and for having the second-largest Puget Sound port (Seattle has the largest). The naval station here is home to the U.S.S. *Abraham Lincoln* aircraft carrier and a support flotilla of destroyers and frigates.

The pleasant waterfront suburb of Mukilteo, about 5 mi southeast of Everett, is the main departure point for ferries to Clinton, on Whidbey Island. The old lighthouse and waterfront park are fun to explore. An important Indian treaty was signed in 1855 at nearby Point Elliott.

Marysville, 6 mi north of Everett, was set up as a trading post in 1877. Pioneers exchanged goods with the Snohomish Indians, who once occupied southeastern Whidbey Island and the lower Snohomish Valley. Settlers drained and diked the lowlands, raised dairy cows, planted strawberry fields, cleared the forests, and in no time a thriving community was established. Marysville kept to itself for a century, until the I–5 freeway was built; today it's a thriving community and the home of the popular Tulalip (Too-*lay*-lip) Casino.

GETTING HERE

To reach Everett by car, take I–5 north to exit 192. Driving is the best option, as many of the city's sights are spread out and public transportation between them is limited. That said, Everett is connected to Seattle by Amtrak train and by Greyhound bus, as well as by Sound Transit's Sounder commuter rail.

Contact **Sound Transit** ☎ *800/201–4900* ⊕ *www.soundtransit.org).*

VISITOR INFORMATION

Everett Area Chamber of Commerce (✉ *2000 Hewitt Avenue, Ste. 205 Everett* ☎ *425/257–3222* ⊕ *www.everettchamber.com).*

EXPLORING

The Flying Heritage Collection. Housed within a 51,000-square-foot airport hangar, this spectacular gathering of unique vintage aircraft belongs to local tycoon Paul Allen, who began collecting and restoring rare planes in 1988. The selections run the full length of 20th-century military history, including pieces from World War I, World War II, and other international battles. A favorite plane is the P-51D Mustang from the Second World War. Most tours are self-guided, though group tours are possible; exhibits help to explain the collection. In summer, try to time your visit for one of the Free Fly Days, when pilots are on-site to fly some of the craft as part of monthly maintenance. ✉ *Paine Field, 3407 109th St. SW* ☎ *206/342–3404* ⊕ *www.flyingheritage.com* ⌨ *$16* ☉ *Memorial Day–Labor Day, daily 10–5; Labor Day–Memorial Day, Tues.–Sun. 10–5.*

★ **Future of Flight Aviation Center & Boeing Tour** showcases the Boeing Everett line (747, 767, 777, and 787). The 62-acre site holds one of the world's largest buildings, second only to Canada's West Edmonton Mall—and so big that it often creates its own weather system inside. You can see planes in various stages of production on a 90-minute tour. Note that

10

Boeing Everett Facility

there are no bathroom breaks on the tour, and no purses, cameras, videos, or children under 50 inches tall are permitted. The tour includes a lot of walking and some stair-climbing, but the facility can accommodate people with mobility issues with advance arrangements. Reserving tour tickets a day in advance is recommended if you need a specific tour time, but same-day tickets are always available. The Future of Flight gallery includes cutaways of airplane fuselages, exhibits on the inner workings of navigation and hydraulic systems, and interactive exhibits that let you design your own commercial airliner. It also has a café. ⊠ *8415 Paine Field Blvd., at Hwy. 526 W, Mukilteo* ☎ *425/438–8100; 800/464–1476 reservations* ⊕ *www.futureofflight.org* ✉ *$15.50; gallery only $10* ☉ *Facility daily 8:30–5:30, tours hourly 9–3.*

Ⓒ The **Imagine Children's Museum** is on a pioneer homestead built in the 1800s. Interactive exhibits and crafts are part of the fun; wee ones will love the magic school bus as well. ⊠ *1502 Wall St.* ☎ *425/258–1006* ⊕ *www.imaginecm.org* ✉ *$7.50; Thurs. $3.75* ☉ *Tues.–Wed. 9–5, Thurs.–Sat. 10–5, Sun. 11–5.*

★ **Jetty Island** is a 2-mi-long, sand-fringed offshore haven full of wildlife
Ⓒ and outdoor opportunities. Seasonal programs include guided walks, bonfires, and midsummer Jetty Island Days festivities. A free ferry provides round-trip transport; group tours (book first) run daily at 10:45 and 3:30. ⊠ *W. Marine View Dr.* ☎ *425/257–8324* ⊕ *www.ci.everett. wa.us* ✉ *Free* ☉ *Ferry departures on the half-hour Mon.–Sat. 10–5:25, Sun. 11–5:25.*

The **Museum of Flight Restoration Center** is where vintage planes are restored by a volunteer staff who simply love bringing vintage aircraft back to life. You can wander among the mix of delicate and behemoth planes on a leisurely, self-guided tour at Paine Field. ☒ *2909 100th St. SW, Bldg. C-72* ☎ *425/745–5150* ⊕ *www.museumofflight.org* ✉ *$5* ☉ *June–Aug., Tues.–Sat. 9–5; Sept.–May, Tues.–Thurs. and Sat. 9–5.*

WHERE TO EAT

$–$$ ✕ **Alligator Soul.** The Louisiana cooking is straight from the bayou, and
SOUTHERN always receives rave reviews. It's a fun, noisy place where plates come piled high with thick smoked ribs, shrimp-packed gumbo, or fried green tomato salad. Spicy corn relish and hot barbecue sauce let you ratchet up the heat. Live music is on tap Friday and Saturday nights. ☒ *3121 Broadway Ave.* ☎ *425/259–6311* w*www.alligatorsoulrestaurant.com* ▭ *MC, V.*

$$–$$$ ✕ **Anthony's Homeport.** Tucked into chic Marina Village, this elegant
SEAFOOD waterfront restaurant has large windows opening to a panorama of Port Gardner Bay. In summer, sunsets appear to ooze into the water. The specials, which change daily, might include meaty Dungeness crab, wild Chinook salmon, and other sea creatures caught just offshore. Desserts are fabulous, especially those crafted from Washington's succulent berries and fruits. ☒ *1726 W. Marine View Dr.* ☎ *425/252–3333* w*www. anthonys.com* ▭ *AE, MC, V.*

¢ ✕ **The Sisters.** This funky breakfast and lunch café in Everett Public Mar-
AMERICAN ket is as popular now as it was a decade ago. Perhaps that's because the blueberry or pecan hotcakes, rich soups, and overflowing sandwiches are as good as ever. Eye-opening espresso drinks start the morning; homemade ice cream is a perfect end to the afternoon. Note that the café closes at 4 PM, but they shut down the grill at 3 PM. ☒ *2804 Grand St.* ☎ *425/252–0480* w*www.thesistersrestaurant.com* ▭ *MC, V* ☉ *Closed Sat. and Sun. No dinner.*

WHERE TO STAY

$ ⌂ **Gaylord House.** Down a lane lined by shady maples, this Craftsman
BED & BREAKFAST welcomes visitors to relax in the creaky rockers on its wide front porch. Themed guest rooms, filled with antiques and original art, include the Sunrise Mediterranean room; the nautical Commodore's Quarters; and the Victorian-style Lady Anne's Chamber. An exquisite breakfast is included, there's a bottomless cookie jar, and you can book ahead for equally exquisite high teas or dinners, when the table is set with fine china, sterling silver, and crystal. **Pros:** well-stocked library; piano concerts. **Cons:** not a lot of elbow room. ☒ *3301 Grand Ave.* ☎ *425/339– 9153 or 888/507–7177* 🖷 *425/303–9713* ⊕ *www.gaylordhouse.com* ⬎ *5 rooms* ⌂ *In-room: a/c, Wi-Fi. In-hotel: no kids under 12* ▭ *MC, V* ⦿*BP.*

$$ ⌂ **Inn at Port Gardner.** Stroll along the marina, and you'll encounter this grey, warehouse-style structure, which wraps around a cozy, modern hotel. Public spaces are done in summery colors and enhanced by modern art pieces, while the lobby is warmed by a fireplace. Rooms are contemporary, each with a DVD player and Wi-Fi; Marina View quarters add a water panorama from big glass windows or a French-door patio, and Harbor View suites have a kitchenette, fireplace, and soaking tub. All guests receive free gym passes to a nearby Gold's Gym and a bountiful breakfast basket. **Pros:** right on the waterfront close to area restaurants; nice patio and lobby. **Cons:** no pool; rooms are

10

nice, but look like standard chain hotel rooms. ⊠ *1700 W. Marine Dr.* ☎ *425/252–6779 or 888/252–6779* ⊕ *www.innatportgardner.com* ↪ *27 rooms, 6 suites* ♧ *In-room: a/c, DVD, kitchen (some) Wi-Fi. In-hotel: some pets allowed* ⊟ *AE, D, MC, V* ⊺❙ *CP.*

I-5 CORRIDOR SOUTH OF SEATTLE

A trip south down I–5 quickly yields two important port cities: Tacoma, and Olympia, the state capital. Although Olympia is more practiced in winning over visitors with its tidy legislative campus and laid-back charms, Tacoma is determined to follow suit with an ambitious if somewhat stalled revitalization plan. Both have the same good foundation to work with: beautiful waterfront locations with historic cores and lots of adjacent parkland.

Flanking the I–5 corridor are gateway towns to the state's natural areas: Snoqualmie and North Bend are tried-and-true pit stops for hikers, bikers, and skiers heading over Snoqualmie Pass. The town of Snoqualmie is itself day trip–worthy, with its stuck-in-time downtown full of vintage railway cars, and beautiful, easily accessed falls.

SNOQUALMIE

3 mi northwest of North Bend.

Spring and summer snowmelt turn the Snoqualmie (sno-*qual*-mie) River into a thundering torrent at **Snoqualmie Falls**, the sweeping cascades that provided the backdrop for the *Twin Peaks* opening montage. The water pours over a 268-foot rock ledge (100 feet higher than Niagara Falls) to a 65-foot-deep pool. These cascades, considered sacred by the Native Americans, are Snoqualmie's biggest attraction. A 2-acre park and observation platform afford views of the falls and the surrounding area. The 3-mi round-trip River Trail winds through trees and over open slopes to the base of the cascade.

GETTING HERE

To reach Snoqualmie from Seattle, take I–90 east to Exit 27. The old town area of Snoqualmie is very compact and walkable; reaching the falls and Salish Lodge requires another car trip.

EXPLORING

The vintage cars of the **Northwest Railway Museum** line a paved path along Railroad Avenue. Signs explain the origin of each engine, car, and caboose on display, and more history and memorabilia are on display inside the former waiting room of the stunning restored Snoqualmie depot. On weekends, a train made of cars built in the mid-1910s for the Spokane, Portland, and Seattle Railroad, travel between Snoqualmie Depot and North Bend. The 70-minute (round-trip) excursion passes through woods, past waterfalls, and around patchwork farmland. Crowds of families pack the winter Santa Train journeys and the mid-summer Railroad Days rides, when a helicopter drops balloons and prizes over the annual parade. ⊠ *Snoqualmie Depot: 38625 S.E. King St., at Hwy. 202* ☎ *425/888–3030* ⊕ *www.trainmuseum.org* ⊠ *Rides*

$12, depot free ⊗ *Rides Apr.–July and mid-Sept.–Oct., weekends at 12:01, 1:31, and 3:01; Aug.–mid-Sept., weekends 11:01, 12:31, 2:01, 3:31. Depot daily 10–5.*

WHERE TO EAT AND STAY

¢ ✕ **Chew Chew Cafe & Candy.** An Old West–style storefront leads to this combination candy store, gift shop, and soda fountain serving quick-cooked American burgers, hot dogs, and sandwiches. Homemade caramel corn, saltwater taffy, and nut brittles in pretty packages make great treats and souvenirs. The downtown Snoqualmie location attracts crowds during local railroad events. ⊠ *8102 Railroad Ave. SE* ☏ *425/888–0439 or 800/636–2263* w*chewchewcafeandcandy.com* ⊟ *AE, MC, V.*

AMERICAN

$ ✕ **Isadora's.** If the sight of all the candy at the Chew Chew makes your teeth hurt, you can go next door to this charming bookstore and have a quiet and kitsch-less snack at the small café. Weekend breakfasts include scrambles and French toast; daily lunch offerings are simple sandwiches and panini. Good espresso, tea, and chai are always available. ⊠ *8062 Railroad Ave. SE, Snoqualmie* ☏ *425/888–1345* ⊕ *www.isadorascafe. com* ⊟ *MC, V* ⊗ *No dinner.*

AMERICAN

$$$ ▥ **Salish Lodge.** The stunning, chalet-style lodge sits right over Sno-qualmie Falls. Eight rooms have gorgeous views of the cascades, while others have a river panorama. All the luxurious quarters have featherbeds, fireplaces, whirlpool baths, terry robes, and window seats or balconies. The world-famous spa offers relaxing and purifying treatments after a day of kayaking, golfing, or hiking. The elegant Dining Room restaurant serves such eclectic delicacies as wild Scottish partridge, herb-crusted John Dory fillet, and potato-wrapped elk loin; weekend brunches are elaborate. In the cozy and more casual Attic bistro, you can still sample fine Northwest wines and views of the falls beneath the eaves. Note that if you pay an extra $15 nightly resort fee, you'll have such privileges as valet service, 24-hour Wi-Fi, and unlimited access to the soaking pool, sauna, and fitness facilities. **Pros:** close to the falls; great food; great spa. **Cons:** extra charges for amenities that should be included in high prices; despite the view of the falls, the location's not that inspiring (in the sprawl part of town instead of the charming Old Town). ⊠ *6501 Railroad Ave. SE* ☏ *206/888–2556* ▤ *425/888–2420* ⊕ *www.salishlodge.com* ⤳ *81 rooms, 4 suites* ⌂ *In-room: a/c, refrigerator, Wi-Fi (some). In-hotel: 2 restaurants, room service, bar, gym, spa, laundry service* ⊟ *AE, D, DC, MC, V.*

Fodor's Choice
★

SPORTS AND THE OUTDOORS

☉ **The Summit at Snoqualmie,** 53 mi east of Seattle, combines the Alpental, Summit West, Summit East, and Summit Central ski areas along Snoqualmie Pass. Spread over nearly 2,000 acres at elevations of up to 5,400 feet, the facilities include 65 ski trails, 22 chairlifts, and two half-pipes. Those seeking tamer pursuits can head to the Summit Nordic Center, with groomed trails and a tubing area. Shops, restaurants, lodges, and ski schools are connected by shuttle vans; there's even child care. For a different take on the mountains, head up to the pass after dinner; this is the world's largest night-skiing area. Tickets, which let you ski and play at any of the above areas, start at $41–$51, depending

Fodor's Choice
★

10

The Summit at Snoqualmie

on the time of day. Ski and snowboard rental packages run $29–$35. Inner-tube rentals, including lighted rope tows, are $10. ⊠ *From Seattle, take I–90 east to Alpental Rd.* ☎ *425/434–7669; 425/236–1600 snow conditions* ⊕ *www.summitatsnoqualmie.com* ☽ *Oct.–Apr.*

NORTH BEND

40 mi northeast of Puyallap.

This truck stop gets its name from a bend in the Snoqualmie River, which here turns toward Canada. The gorgeous surrounding scenery is dominated by 4,420-foot Mt. Washington, 4,788-foot Mt. Tenerife, and 4,167-foot Mt. Si. Named for early settler Josiah "Si" Merrit, Mt. Si has a steep, four-hour trail that in summer provides views of the Cascade and Olympic peaks down to Puget Sound and Seattle. In winter, however, these mountains corner the rains: North Bend is one of the wettest places in western Washington, with an annual precipitation often exceeding 100 inches.

Scenes from the TV show *Twin Peaks*—notably the stunning opening waterfall sequence—were shot in North Bend, though most of the work was done in studios in Seattle. This is the last town on I–90 for gassing up before Snoqualmie Pass.

GETTING HERE

To reach North Bend from Seattle, take I–90 east to Exit 31. There's not much Old Town left in North Bend; navigating it requires a car.

EXPLORING

The **Snoqualmie Valley Historical Museum** focuses on life centuries ago, with Native American tools, crafts, and attire as well as pioneer artifacts. The timber industry is another focus. ⊠ *320 Bendego Blvd. S* ☎ *425/888–3200* ⊕ *www.snoqualmievalleymuseum.org* ✉ *$1* ⊙ *Apr.– Oct., Thurs.–Sun. 1–5; other times by appointment.*

WHERE TO EAT AND STAY

$ ⤫ **George's Bakery.** A reliable fueling stop on the way to Snoqualmie
BAKERY Pass, George's has shelves of fresh-made donuts, pastries, and breads; decent coffee; and a full deli menu of sandwiches, soups, quiches, and calzones. ⊠ *127 W. North Bend Way, North Bend* ☎ *425/888–0632* ⊟ *MC, V* ⊙ *No dinner. Closed Mon.*

$–$$ 🛏 **Roaring River Bed & Breakfast.** On 2½ acres above the Snoqualmie River, this secluded B&B has unbeatable mountain and wilderness views. Rooms with wainscoting and fireplaces have private entrances and decks. The Mountain View Room has a whirlpool tub; the Bear-Iris Room has a featherbed and a two-person Japanese soaking tub. Herb's Place is a hunting cabin with a kitchen and loft, and the Rock and Rose Room has its own sauna—behind a giant boulder. Homemade goodies are delivered to your room each morning. **Pros:** pretty location; rustic-chic and spacious Herb's Place hunting cabin is reasonably priced. **Cons:** rooms are a little cluttered and overdone. ⊠ *46715 S.E. 129th St.* ☎ *425/888–4834 or 877/627–4647* ⊕ *www.theroaringriver. com* ⇆ *4 rooms, 1 cabin* ⅙ *In-room: no phone, a/c, Wi-Fi. In-hotel: no kids under 12* ⊟ *AE, D, MC, V* ⋈ *BP.*

PUYALLUP

10 mi southeast of Tacoma.

Set before the towering forests and snowfields of Mt. Rainier is Puyallup (pyoo-*al*-lup), one of western Washington's oldest towns. The Puyallup Fair attracts all of western Washington to its carnival rides, performers, produce, and animals. The annual event is held at the fairgrounds on the northwest end of town each September. The Spring Fair and Daffodil Festival (known as "The Little Puyallup") is another beloved event that takes place each April. These special events are really the only reason to make a detour to Puyallup unless you need a leg-stretch or a bite to eat on your way elsewhere. The downtown area is pleasant enough and has a few boutiques and restaurants, but doesn't have enough charm to warrant a special visit.

10

GETTING HERE

To reach Puyallup, take I–5 south to 405 north and then 167 south. Alternatively, Sound Transit runs commuter trains from downtown Seattle to Puyallup. From the train station it's a 15-minute walk to the fairgrounds and shops of downtown.

Contact Sound Transit ☎ *800/201–4900* ⊕ *www.soundtransit.org).*

EXPLORING

The city's developing **Antique Shopping District**, has about a half-dozen cozy little stores clustered downtown. There are more vendors in the neighboring town of Sumner. Events and openings are guided by the Puyallup Antique District Association. ⊠ *101 S. Meridian* ☎ *253/845–4471* ⊕ *www.antiquedistrict.net.*

★ **Northwest Trek**, a spectacular wildlife park 35 mi south of Puyallup, is
☼ devoted to native creatures of the Pacific Northwest. Walking paths wind through natural surroundings—so natural that in 1998 a cougar entered the park and started snacking on the deer (it was finally trapped and relocated to the North Cascades). See beavers, otters, and wolverines; get close to wolves, foxes, coyotes; and observe several species of big cats and bears in wild environments. Admission includes a 55-minute tram ride through fields of wandering moose, elk, bison, and mountain goats. Note: Hours vary slightly by month, so check for specific times. ⊠ *11610 Trek Dr. E, Eatonville* ☎ *360/832–6117* ⊕ *www.nwtrek.org* ⌦ *$16* ⊙ *July–Labor Day, daily 9:30–6; Labor Day–early-Oct. and mid-Mar.–June, Mon.–Thurs. 9–4, Fri.–Sun. 9–5. Closed weekdays Oct.–mid-Mar.*

★ The **Pioneer Farm Museum and Ohop Indian Village**, 23 mi south of Puyal-
☼ lup, provides a look at pioneer and Native American life. Kids can learn how to hunt and fish in a realistic Indian village, grind grain, milk a cow, churn butter, and do other old-fashioned chores. A trading post shows the commodities of earlier eras. One-hour pioneer farm tours take place 11:15 to 4; Ohop Indian Village tours are at 1 and 2:30 from Memorial Day to Labor Day. ⊠ *Hwy. 7 off Ohop Valley Rd.* ☎ *360/832–6300* ⊕ *www.pioneerfarmmuseum.org* ⌦ *Farm $7.50, village $7, combined tour $13.50* ⊙ *Memorial Day–Labor Day, Fri.–Sun. 11:15–4; Sept.– mid-Nov., weekends 11–4.*

Puyallup's Outdoor Gallery (☎ *253/840–6015* ⊕ *www.artsdowntown. org*), presented by the Arts Downtown program, shows off dozens of rotating sculptures around the city via self-guided tours. Monthly Art Walks, held on first Saturdays, provide a look into all the new local galleries, and the semi-annual Art and Wine Walks bring Puget Sound residents southeast to explore the top creative projects of this offbeat community.

The **Ezra Meeker Mansion**, a grand, beige-colored Italianate palace built in 1891, was a fitting place for the richest man in the Northwest. Meeker, known locally as the "Hop King" for his beer empire, sank much of his profits into such elegant touches as inlaid fireplaces, ceiling murals, and stained-glass windows. Listed on the National Register of Historic Sites, the home is completely furnished in the style of its heyday. Seasonal events include the historic Meeker Days in June, the autumn Cider Squeeze, and Christmas at the Mansion each December. ⊠ *312 Spring St.* ☎ *253/848–1770* ⊕ *www.meekermansion.org* ⌦ *$4* ⊙ *Mar.–mid-Dec., Wed.–Sun. 12–4.*

WHERE TO EAT

¢–$ ✕ **Powerhouse Brewery and Restaurant**. The interior of what was once a
AMERICAN railroad powerhouse is adorned with glass insulators and high-voltage
signs. A dozen brews are served—six brewed on the premises and six
from a sister brewery. The pub fare includes salads, pizzas, burgers,
sandwiches, and pastas. ⊠ *504 E. Main Ave.* ☎ *253/845–1370* w*www.
powerhousebrewpub.com* ⊟ MC, V.

TACOMA

25 mi southeast of Gig Harbor, 34 mi southwest of Seattle.

The stories of Tacoma's renaissance are somewhat overstated. Development in select sections of the waterfront continues, and the galleries,
bars, and restaurants that have popped up around Union Station have
made a few blocks of Downtown seem vibrant and livable after decades
of decline. But there are far too many beautiful old buildings downtown
that are vacant or boarded up, and (at least before the housing market
collapsed) most developers seem interested only in building pricey condos far outside the historic core. Downtown can be a ghost town on
summer weekends—it'll take more than a glass museum before Tacoma
can claim to have any scene rivaling that of Seattle's.

Tacoma's got character, however, and it does have plenty to fill a day
or two. The museums, the waterfront promenade, and the attractive
old neighborhoods and suburbs make for a very pleasant side trip.
The waterfront stretches west from the busy port, past the city and
Puget Sound islands to the cliff-lined Tacoma Narrows. Renovated
19th-century homes, pretty beaches, and parks pocket the outskirts,
and a young population gives the city a spirited character. The Tacoma
Dome, that wooden, blue-and-gray half-sphere stadium visible along
I–5, hosts international expos, sporting events, and famous entertainers in its 28,000-seat arena. The city's convenient setting provides easy
access to Seattle to the north; Mt. Rainier to the southeast; Olympia to
the south; and the Kitsap and Olympic peninsulas to the west.

Tacoma was the first Puget Sound port connected by train to the East,
and its economy was once based on the railroad. Old photos show
tall-masted windjammers loading at the City Waterway, whose storage sheds were promoted by local boosters as the "longest warehouse
under one continuous roof in the world." The city's shipping industry
certainly weathered the tests of time, as Tacoma is the largest container
port in the Northwest.

GETTING HERE

Tacoma is close enough to Seattle that many people commute in both
directions. It's a straight shot down I–5 to Exit 133 toward the city
center. Tacoma is served by Greyhound and Amtrak, with connections
north to Seattle and beyond, as well as south to Olympia. Tacoma is
also served by Sound Transit's commuter rail, though trains are limited
to rush hours.

If you're not planning to go too far out of the downtown core—just
seeing the museums and the waterfront—you won't need a car to get

10

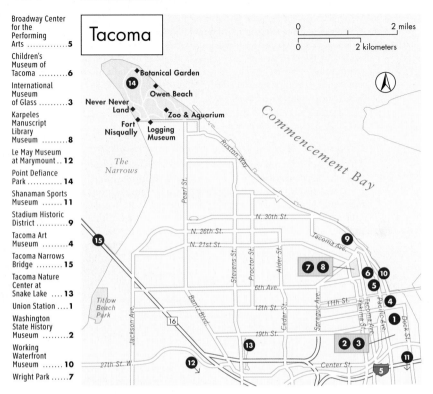

around, as Amtrak and Greyhound let you off at Union Station, which is within walking distance of the city's main museums and a handful of restaurants.

Contact Sound Transit (☎ 206/398–5000 or 888/889–6368 ⊕ www. soundtransit.org).

VISITOR INFORMATION

Tacoma Regional Convention & Visitors Bureau (✉ 1001 Pacific Ave., Suite 400, Tacoma ☎ 253/627–2836 or 800/272–2662 ⊕ www.tpctourism.org).

EXPLORING

TOP ATTRACTIONS

❸   **International Museum of Glass.** The showpiece of this spectacular, 2-acre

Fodor'sChoice   combination of delicate and creative exhibits is the 500-foot-long Chi-

★   huly Bridge of Glass, a tunnel of glorious color and light that stretches above I–705. Cross it to reach the building grounds, which sit above the bay and next to a shallow reflecting pool dotted with large modern-art sculptures. Inside, you can wander with the crowds through the quiet, light-filled galleries, take a seat in the theater-like Hot Shop to watch glass-blowing artists, or try your own hand at arts and crafts in the studio. You'll also find a souvenir shop and café. ✉ *1801 E. Dock*

Chihuly Bridge of Glass, Tacoma

St. ☎ *253/284–4750* ⊕ *www.museumofglass.org* 🎫 *$12* ⊘ *Mon.–Sat. 10–5, Sun. noon–5.*

⑭ **Point Defiance Park**. Jutting into Commencement Bay, this hilly, 698-acre
★ park surrounds Five Mile Drive with lush picnicking fields and patches
⊛ of forest. Hiking trails, bike paths, and numerous gardens draw crowds
year-round, particularly during summer festivals such as the Taste of
Tacoma, in June. The park begins at the north end of Pearl Street as you
drive toward the Point Defiance Ferry Terminal, where vehicles depart
for Vashon Island just across the Sound. A one-way road branches off
the ferry lane, past a lake and picnic area, a rose garden, and a Japanese
garden, finally winding down to the beach.

10

One of the Northwest's finest collections of regional and international
species is the winding and hilly **Point Defiance Zoo and Aquarium.**
Tigers, elephants, tapirs, and gibbons inhabit the Southeast Asian area,
where paw-print trails lead between lookouts so even the smallest tots
can spot animals. The aquarium is also fun to explore, with its glass-
walled, floor-to-ceiling shark tank; seahorse room; touch-tank marine
area; and open-topped, two-level Pacific Northwest reef display. Other
areas house such cold-weather creatures as beluga whales, wolves, polar
bears, and penguins. Thirty-minute animal shows, run two to four times
daily, let five different creatures show off their skills. The fantastic playground area has friendly farm animals running between the slides, and
seasonal special events include a Halloween trick-or-treat night and the
famous nightly Zoolights holiday displays around Christmas. ✉ *Point
Defiance Park: 5400 N. Pearl St.* ☎ *253/305–1000* ⊕ *www.pdza.org*
🎫 *Park free, zoo $13.50* ⊘ *Park daily dawn–dusk; zoo Oct.–Apr., daily*

A GOOD TOUR

Begin your tour early at **Union Station ❶**, with its sapphire-blue chandelier and other colorful glass pieces created by world-famous artist (and homeboy) Dale Chihuly. Linked by a courtyard to the station is the state-of-the-art **Washington State History Museum ❷**, connected to the **International Museum of Glass ❸** by the beautiful Chihuly Bridge of Glass. Have lunch downtown, then head north on Pacific Avenue to the **Tacoma Art Museum ❹**, where you'll see more Chihuly works amid the paintings and sculptures. Go west on 11th Street to Broadway, then walk north past the **Broadway Center for the Performing Arts ❺** and the compact **Children's Museum of Tacoma ❻**. At 9th Street begins **Antique Row**, a collection of shops. From here, continue north on Broadway and turn left on South 3rd Street until the intersection with G Street, which marks the entrance to **Wright Park ❼**. Stroll through the gardens and conservatory, then head across the street to the **Karpeles Manuscript Library Museum ❽**. Return to Broadway and walk north to North Third Street, where you can wander through the

Stadium Historic District ❾ neighborhood. If you have time, swing over to the **Working Waterfront Museum ❿** to learn more about the city's maritime history; explore the **Shanaman Sports Museum ⓫** and its collection of regional athletic memorabilia; or head across town to the **Le May Museum at Marymount ⓬** to view part of the world's largest collection of private cars.

You'll need a car to reach the **Tacoma Nature Center ⓭**, a cabin in the woods where kids can see local wildlife. From this point, aim for the sweeping afternoon views of Puget Sound and the Tacoma Narrows from **Point Defiance Park ⓮**, which includes the Point Defiance Zoo and Aquarium. Along Five Mile Drive, take a gander at the twin **Tacoma Narrows Bridge ⓯** spanning the deep chasm over the water; it's the only way to reach the Kitsap Peninsula from here. Follow Five Mile Drive back to the ferry landing, then drive southeast down the Ruston Way waterfront to end your tour at the restaurants and nightspots along Commencement Bay.

9:30–4; May and Sept., daily 9:30–5; Jun., daily 9:30–6; July and Aug., daily 8:30–6

On Five Mile Drive, the **Rhododendron Species Botanical Garden** is a 22-acre expanse of more than 10,000 plants—some 2,000 varieties of 450 species—which bloom in succession. It's one of the finest rhododendron collections in the world. ⊠ *2525 S. 336th St.* ☎ *253/927–6960* ⊕ *www.rhodygarden.org* ⊠ *$5* ⊗ *Mar.–Sept., Fri.–Wed. 10–4; Oct.–Feb., Sat.–Wed. 11–4.* A half-mile past the gardens is **Owen Beach,** a driftwood-strewn stretch of pebbly sand near the ferry dock and a wonderful place for beachcombing and sailboat-watching. Kayak rentals and concessions are available in summer. Continue around the looping drive, which offers occasional views of the narrows. Cruise slowly to take in the scenes—and watch out for joggers and bikers. Near the drive's end, the 15-acre **Camp Six Logging Museum** (☎ *253/752–0047*) has restored bunkhouses, hand tools, and other equipment illustrating the history of steam logging from 1880 to 1950. From here you can take a short ride through the woods on a steam train. The fare is $4.50, and the train runs every half hour on weekends between noon and 4. The museum is free, and open Wednesday to Sunday 10 to 4. West of the Camp Six Logging Museum is **Ft. Nisqually** (☎ 253/591–5339 ⊕ www.fortnisqually. org), a restored Hudson's Bay Trading Post. A British outpost on the Nisqually Delta in the 1830s, it was moved to Point Defiance in 1935. The compound houses a trading post, granary, blacksmith's shop, bakery, and officers' quarters. Docents dress in 1850s attire and demonstrate pioneer skills like weaving and loading a rifle. Queen Victoria's birthday in August is a big event, and eerie candlelight tours run throughout October. It's open September–April, Wednesday–Sunday 11–4; May, Wednesday–Sunday 11–5; and June–August, daily 11–5. Admission is $6. **Never Never Land,** a children's fantasy world of sculptured storybook characters, is across the parking lot from Ft. Nisqually.

⓯ **The Tacoma-Narrows Bridge**. A mile-wide waterway is the boundary between the Tacoma hills and the rugged bluffs of the Kitsap Peninsula. From the twin bridges that span it, the view plunges hundreds of feet down to roiling green waters, which are often busy with barge traffic or obscured by fog. The original bridge, "Galloping Gertie," famously twisted itself to death and broke in half during a storm in 1940. Today its mint-green replacement and a sister bridge opened in 2007 top the world's largest man-made reef, and is a popular dive site. Note: The $3.25 toll is for eastbound cars only; westbound it's free from Tacoma into Gig Harbor. ⊠ *Part of Hwy. 16.*

❼ **Wright Park**. The chief attraction at this 28-acre park, which is on the National Register of Historic Places, is the glass-dome **W. W. Seymour Botanical Conservatory** (⊠ 316 S. G St. ☎ 253/591–5330 ⊕ www. metroparkstacoma.org), a Victorian-style greenhouse (one of only three such structures on the West Coast) with exotic flora. ⊠ *Between 6th and Division Sts., Yakima and Tacoma Aves.* ☎ 253/591–5331 🎫 *Free* ☉ *Park daily dawn–dusk, conservatory Tues.–Sun. 10–4:30.*

WORTH NOTING

❺ **Broadway Center for the Performing Arts**. Cultural activity in Tacoma centers on this complex of performance spaces. The famous theater architect B. Marcus Pritica designed the **Pantages** (⊠ 901 Broadway ☎ 253/591–5894 ⊕ www.broadwaycenter.org), a 1918 Greco-Roman–influenced music hall with classical figures, ornate columns, arches, and reliefs. W. C. Fields, Mae West, Charlie Chaplin, Bob Hope, and Stan Laurel all performed here. The Tacoma Symphony and BalleTacoma perform at the Pantages, which also presents touring shows. Adjacent to the Pantages, the contemporary **Theatre on the Square** (⊠ *Broadway between 10th and 11th Sts.* ☎ 253/591–5894) is the home of the Tacoma Actors Guild, one of Washington's largest professional theater companies. In its early days, the **Rialto Theater** (⊠ 301 S. 9th St. ☎ 253/591–5894) presented vaudeville performances and silent films. The Tacoma Youth Symphony now performs in the 1918 structure.

10

6 **Children's Museum of Tacoma.** Fun activities for little ones take place in spacious exhibits. The Learning Lounge has touchable, movable pieces; Becka's Clubhouse has hands-on art; and New Digs goes from simple gardening to cooking. Older kids have fun on the climbing wall and at the cultural displays. Families get in free on the first Friday of the month. ⊠ *936 Broadway Ave.* ☎ *253/627–6031* ⊕ *www. childrensmuseumoftacoma.org* ⊠ *$6* ⊙ *Mon.–Sat. 10–5, Sun. noon–5.*

8 **Karpeles Manuscript Library Museum.** Housed in the former American Legion hall and across from Wright Park, the museum showcases rare and unpublished letters and documents by notables who have shaped history. Themes of temporary exhibits have included the War of 1812 and Einstein's theory of relativity. ⊠ *407 S. G St.* ☎ *253/383–2575* ⊕ *www.rain.org/~karpeles* ⊠ *Free* ⊙ *Tues.–Fri. 10–4.*

12 **The Le May Museum at Marymount.** Harold Le May was the ultimate collector of vintage cars; his collection is in the *Guinness Book of World Records* as the largest privately owned collection in the world. Highlights include a LaSalle, a Pierce-Arrow, a Packard, and a Tucker, along with fire engines, antique buses, and old-fashioned trucks. About 400 of the top models are on display; a new building, which is under construction at this writing, will house the full 4,000-vehicle collection. ⊠ *423 152nd St. E* ☎ *253/779–8490 or 877/902–8490* ⊕ *www.lemaymuseum. org* ⊠ *$15* ⊙ *May–Sept., Tues.–Sat. 9–5, Sun. 12–5; Oct.–Apr., Fri. and Sat. 9–5, Sun. 12–5. Tours on the hour; last tour at 3.*

11 **Shanaman Sports Museum.** Housed on the lower level of the atmospheric wooden Tacoma Dome, the museum highlights the accomplishments of local athletes. All sports are represented, from baseball, basketball, football, soccer, and tennis to gymnastics and volleyball. You must either hold a Tacoma Dome event ticket or make a tour by appointment. ⊠ *2727 E. D St.* ☎ *253/627–5857* ⊕ *www.tacomasportsmuseum.com* ⊠ *Free* ⊙ *Open during events or by appointment.*

9 **Stadium Historic District.** Several of the Victorian homes in this charming neighborhood, high on a hill overlooking Commencement Bay, have been converted to bed-and-breakfast inns. Stadium High School at 111 North E Street is in an elaborate château-style structure built in 1891 as a luxury hotel for the Northern Pacific Railroad. The building was converted into a high school after a 1906 fire.

4 **Tacoma Art Museum.** Adorned in glass and steel, this Antoine Predock masterpiece wraps around a beautiful garden. Inside, you'll find paintings, ceramics, sculptures, and other creations dating from the 18th century to the present. Look for the many glass sculptures by Dale Chihuly—especially the magnificent, flame-color *Mille Fiori* (Thousand Flowers) glass garden. ⊠ *1701 Pacific Ave.* ☎ *253/272–4258* ⊕ *www. tacomaartmuseum.org* ⊠ *$9, free on 3rd Thurs. of month* ⊙ *Wed.–Sun. 10–5, until 8 PM every 3rd Thurs. of month.*

13 **Tacoma Nature Center at Snake Lake.** Fifty-four acres of marshland, evergreen forest, and shallow lake break up the urban sprawl of west Tacoma and shelter 25 species of mammals and more than 100 species of birds. The lake has nesting pairs of wood ducks, rare elsewhere in western Washington, and the interpretive center is a fun place for kids to look at small creatures, take walks and nature quizzes, and dress up in animal costumes. ✉ *1919 S. Tyler St.* ☎ *253/591–6439* ⊕ *www. metroparkstacoma.org* ✍ *Free* ☉ *Center Tues.–Fri. 8–5, Sat. 10–4; trails daily dawn–dusk.*

❶ Union Station. This heirloom dates from 1911, when Tacoma was the western terminus of the Northern Pacific Railroad. Built by Reed and Stem, architects of New York City's Grand Central Terminal, the copper-domed, beaux arts–style depot shows the influence of the Roman Pantheon and Italian baroque style. The station houses federal district courts, but its rotunda contains a gorgeous exhibit of glass sculptures by Dale Chihuly. Hint: Since it's a highly guarded government facility, be prepared to walk through a metal detector and show photo ID. ✉ *1717 Pacific Ave.* ☎ *253/572–9310* ✍ *Free* ☉ *Weekdays 8–5.*

❷ Washington State History Museum. Adjacent to Union Station, and with the same opulent architecture, Washington's official history museum presents interactive exhibits and multimedia installations about the exploration and settlement of the state. Some rooms are filled with Native American, Eskimo, and pioneer artifacts, while others display logging and railroad relics. The upstairs gallery has rotating exhibits, and summer programs are staged in the outdoor amphitheater. ✉ *1911 Pacific Ave.* ☎ *253/272–3500* ⊕ *www.wshs.org* ✍ *$8* ☉ *Tues–Sun. 10–5, every 3rd Thurs. 10–8.*

❿ Working Waterfront Maritime Museum. With its beautiful setting right along the Thea Foss waterfront, the turn-of-the-20th-century, wharf-style structure is easily reached along a walk by the bay. Inside the enormous timber building, displays trace the history of Tacoma's brisk shipping business. Extensive exhibits cover boat-making, importing and exporting, and the development of the waterfront. Photos and relics round out the exhibits, and children's activities are staged monthly. ✉ *705 Dock St.* ☎ *253/272–2750* ⊕ *www.fosswaterwayseaport.org* ✍ *$6* ☉ *Wed.–Fri. 10–5, weekends 12–5.*

WHERE TO EAT

$–$$ ✕ **Engine House No. 9.** The 1907 brick building once housed the horse-
AMERICAN drawn fire-engine brigade, and today the structure is on the National Register of Historic Places. It's now a pub-style restaurant that's filled with firehouse memorabilia. The hearty, offbeat, Americanized ethnic fare (Thai chicken, soft tacos, pizza, and pasta) have made it a hit. The adjacent brewery, which serves microbrews and regional wines, is packed on weekends. ✉ *611 N. Pine St.* ☎ *253/272–3435* w*www. ehouse9.com* ☰ *AE, MC, V.*

$$ ✕ **Indochine.** The elegant, pan-Asian conglomeration of sounds, scents,
ASIAN and sights takes place in a sleekly modern, yet darkly cozy space. Black-leather seats, curving banquettes, and steely metal accents set off plush red curtains and pavilion tables. The taste-dazzling array of Thai, Chinese, Indian, and Japanese cuisines includes curries, stir-fries, soups, and seafood. Standouts include coconut and galangal chicken soup, and the Oceans Five seafood and cilantro, served over vegetables. ✉ *1924 Pacific Ave.* ☎ *253/272–8200* w*indochinedowntown.com* ☰ *MC, V* ☉ *Closed Sun.* ✉ *31254 Pacific Hwy. S, Federal Way* ☎ *253/946–3992.*

10

$$ ✕**Lobster Shop.** Built on stilts above the Dash Point tide flats, this former
SEAFOOD grocery store and beachside soda fountain is now an elite, two-story sea-
food spot with panoramic bay views. Start with a house martini (always
a double) or a taste of Washington wine, and perhaps coconut–maca-
damia nut prawns or lobster bisque. Move on to crab cakes, potato-
crusted lingcod, or pasta with wild-mushroom cream sauce. Finish with
white-chocolate banana-bread pudding—or the Ghirardelli's chocolate
brownie tower. Twilight meals, served before 5:30, provide a mix of
courses at a reduced price. ✉ *6912 Soundview Dr. NE, off Dash Point
Rd.* ☎ *253/927–1513* ✉ *4013 Ruston Way* ☎ *253/759–2165* w*www.
lobstershop.com* ⊟ *AE, DC, MC, V* ⊗ *No lunch.*

¢–$ ✕**Steamers.** A backdrop of deep-blue Narrows bay and the saltwater-
SEAFOOD soaked timber ruins of the old Tacoma ferry terminal surround this
popular little shack, where fresh-caught seafood is served up in a clap-
board, dockside-tavern environment. Specials are jotted in chalk in the
entry; the bar-style ordering area often has a line out the door; and
the close-set tables are usually jam-packed from noon until closing.
Portions lean toward the miniscule, but everything is simple, straight-
forward, and down-home Northwest, from the creamy clam chow-
der and hot beer-battered fish to the grilled salmon. ✉ *8802 6th Ave.*
☎ *253/565–4532* w*www.steamersseafoodcafe.com* ⌂ *Reservations not
accepted* ⊟ *MC, V.*

WHERE TO STAY

$–$$ ⌂**Chinaberry Hill.** Original fixtures and stained-glass windows are
among the grace notes in this 1889 Queen Anne–style B&B in the Sta-
dium Historic District. Suites have shining wood floors, antique feather
beds dressed in fine-quality linens, and ornate desks; three have a hot
tub. The two-story Catchpenny Cottage carriage house, which sleeps
six, has a claw-foot tub and memorabilia from its horse-and-buggy
days. A guest kitchen stocks complimentary drinks, cookies, and popcorn. **Pros:** wraparound porch with vast bay views. **Cons:** creaks and
quirks of a century-old mansion. ✉ *302 Tacoma Ave. N* ☎ *253/272–
1282* ✉ *253/272–1335* ⊕ *www.chinaberryhill.com* ⤳ *4 suites, 1 cottage*
⌂ *In-room: a/c, Wi-Fi* ⊟ *AE, D, MC, V* ⊠*BP.*

$–$$ ⌂**Courtyard by Marriott.** Although set in the late-19th-century Wad-
dell Building, this Marriott has spacious, modern rooms outfitted in
bright Northwest colors with lots of 21st-century touches, and you'll
find an upscale restaurant and wine bar. Many fitness and business
facilities and its proximity to the Tacoma Convention & Trade Center
(across the street) make this a favorite of business travelers. **Pros:** reliable chain hotel; close to convention center and museums; spa. **Cons:**
rooms get street noise; overpriced compared to amenities at Hotel
Murano. ✉ *1515 Commerce St.* ☎ *253/591–9100 or 800/321–2211*
✉ *253/591–9101* ⊕ *www.courtyard.com* ⤳ *148 rooms, 12 suites* ⌂ *In-
room: a/c, refrigerator, Internet, Wi-Fi. In-hotel: room service, spa, gym,
laundry services, Wi-Fi hotspot* ⊟ *AE, D, DC, MC, V* ⊠*CP.*

$ ⌂**DeVoe Mansion Bed and Breakfast.** On 1½ beautiful acres, this 1911
colonial-style mansion fronted with tall white columns is a national and
state historic site. Rooms, which are named after suffragettes, have such
antiques as an oak sleigh bed with claw feet. **Pros:** old-fashioned fun;

lavish breakfasts. **Cons:** streetside locale; away from main attractions. ✉ *208 E. 133rd St.* ☎ *253/539–3991 or 888/539–3991* 🖷 *253/539–8539* ⊕ *www.devoemansion.com* ⇨ *4 rooms* ♿ *In-room: a/c. In-hotel: no kids under 12* ▭ *AE, D, MC, V* ⦁◎⦁ *BP.*

$–$$ 🏠 **Green Cape Cod Bed & Breakfast.** Built in 1929, this house stands in a residential neighborhood only blocks from the historic Proctor shopping district. Three rooms with frilly linens and beautiful antiques provide the full scale of pampering with down comforters, soft robes, and bedside Almond Roca candy, a Northwest specialty. Guests receive passes to the downtown YMCA. **Pros:** cozy, frilly rooms. **Cons:** must drive to all Tacoma attractions. ✉ *2711 N. Warner St.* ☎ *253/752–1977 or 888/752–1977* 🖷 *253/756–9886* ⊕ *www.greencapecod.com* ⇨ *3 rooms* ♿ *In-room: no phone, a/c, Internet. In-hotel: laundry service, no kids under 10* ▭ *AE, MC, V* ⦁◎⦁ *BP.*

$$–$$$ 🏠 **Hotel Murano.** Named for the Italian island where some of the world's best glass is created, this big hotel with an intimate ambience centers around exhibits by world-famous glass artists. Bold colors and sleek metals infuse public spaces with style and energy, and each floor exhibits a different glass artist's pieces. Rooms are done in black and white with fiery accents; each has high-thread-count linens, iPod docks, and a flat-screen TV. The stark, chrome-and-glass restaurant sits spectacularly above glass creations in the hotel atrium. **Pros:** boutique feel; luxury amenities; top-flight service; convenient location. **Cons:** no pool; lots of breakables. ✉ *1320 Broadway Plaza* ☎ *253/238–8000 or 888/862–3255* ⊕ *www.hotelmuranotacoma.com* ⇨ *319 rooms, 10 suites* ♿ *In-room: a/c, Wi-Fi. In-hotel: restaurant, bar, spa* ▭ *AE, D, DC, MC, V.*

$$–$$$ 🏠 **Silver Cloud Inn.** Tacoma's only waterfront hotel juts right out into the bay along picturesque Ruston Way and the historic Old Town area. Views are of the forested surroundings and the boardwalk marina area stretching along either side. Rooms are elegant, extra-comfortable, and functional, each with a microwave, refrigerator, high-speed Internet connection, and glossy bay vistas. Suites feel like rooms in a posh mansion, with plush carpets, overstuffed chairs, fireplaces, and corner hot tubs that hang out over the water. On Tuesday evening the hotel hosts free wine-and-cheese receptions. **Pros:** waterside locale; Ruston Way walking paths and restaurants. **Cons:** summer traffic; compact rooms. ✉ *2317 N. Ruston Way* ☎ *253/272–1300 or 866/820–8448* 🖷 *253/274–9176* ⊕ *www.silvercloud.com* ⇨ *90 rooms* ♿ *In-room: a/c, refrigerator, Internet, Wi-Fi. In-hotel: room service, gym, laundry facilities, laundry service* ▭ *AE, D, MC, V* ⦁◎⦁ *CP.*

$$$$ 🏠 **Thornewood Castle Inn and Gardens Bed & Breakfast.** Spread over four lush acres along beautiful American Lake, this 27,000-square-foot, Gothic Tudor–style mansion built in 1908 has hosted two American presidents: William Howard Taft and Theodore Roosevelt. Among the exquisite details inside are medieval stained-glass windows, gleaming wood floors, large mirrors, antiques, fireplaces, and hot tubs. From the lakeside patio and sunken garden you can meditate on the spectacular sunsets. The inn is 12 mi south of Tacoma. **Pros:** castlelike ambience; lively events. **Cons:** very expensive; in a sort of no-man's-land between Tacoma and Fort Lewis. ✉ *8601 N. Thorne La. SW, Lakewood* ☎ *253/589–9052* 🖷 *253/584–4497* ⊕ *www.thornewoodcastle.com* ⇨ *2*

10

rooms, 5 suites, 1 apartment ♨ In-room: a/c, refrigerator, Wi-Fi. In-hotel: beachfront, no kids under 12 ⊟ AE, D, MC, V ⧉ BP.

NIGHTLIFE

BARS &
LOUNGES

1022 South. You can't claim to have a sophisticated nightlife scene until someone in a vest is mixing artisan cocktails, and 1022 South is Tacoma's answer to this Seattle nightlife trend. Drinks are made with strange infusions (nettles, yerba mate), housemade liqueurs and colas, premium liquors with hipster cachet (Portland's Aviation gin, for example). ⊠ 1022 South J St., Tacoma ☎ 253/627–8588 ⊕ www.1022south.com.

Six Olives (⊠ 2708 6th Ave. ☎ 253/272–5574 ⊕ www.sixoliveslounge. com) has a selection of innovative martini drinks Wednesday through Saturday, including the famous Eve at the Apple. Live jazz plays Friday and Saturday.

Dark, intimate **Shenanigans** (⊠ 3017 Ruston Way ☎ 253/752–8811), with gorgeous waterfront views, has a chic bar, excellent Northwest cuisine, and a line of sleek, cozy window booths.

Jazzbones (⊠ 2803 6th Ave. ☎ 253/396–9169 ⊕ www.jazzbones.com) is a classy no-cover, no-smoking, no-fuss, just-great-music joint on the Sixth Avenue strip, with live jazz on stage every night.

The **Swiss** (⊠ 1904 S. Jefferson Ave. ☎ 253/572–2821) has microbrews on tap, pool tables, and bands on stage Thursday through Saturday ($10 cover). Monday brings free admission for live blues night, and there's karaoke on Wednesday. The place is best early in the evening before the bands start playing—not only is the music not usually that good, but the pub morphs from a laid-back gem of a place to loud and obnoxious pretty quickly.

SHOPPING

Antique Row (⊠ Broadway Ave. at St. Helen's St., between 7th and 9th Sts.) contains upscale antiques stores and boutiques selling collectibles and 1950s paraphernalia. A farmers' market is held here every Thursday in summer. The **Proctor District** (⌂ Box 7291, Tacoma 98407 ☎ 253/370–1748 ⊕ www.proctorbusinessdistrict.com) is a gathering of upscale boutiques, restaurants, and specialty shops. The **Tacoma Mall** (⊠ 4502 S. Steele, off Tacoma Mall Blvd. and I–5 98409 ☎ 253/475–4565 ⊕ www.tacoma-mall.com) area, 1½ mi south of the Tacoma Dome, is a massive indoor-outdoor complex of department stores, specialty shops, and restaurants.

SPORTS AND THE OUTDOORS

AMUSEMENT
PARKS
☾

Wild Waves/ Enchanted Village, the only amusement park near Seattle, has a few moderately sized roller coasters and other rides. From Thanksgiving through New Year's the park shimmers with a nightly drive-through holiday light show. The **Wild Waves** section is the Northwest's largest water park, with giant slides, a 24,000-square-foot wave pool, and Splash Central, for younger children. Tickets get you into all pools and rides. Note: It's expensive and cash only, plus no outside food or drinks are allowed—but there's parking on the side streets, and discount coupons are available at local grocery and drug stores. The park is generally open Sunday–Thursday 10–7 and Friday and Saturday 10–8, but closing times vary wildly over the short season. ✉ *36201 Enchanted Pkwy. S* ☎ *253/925–8000* ⊕ *www.wildwaves.com* 💌 *Wild Waves: $40* 🕐 *June–Labor Day, call for hrs.*

HORSE RACING **Emerald Downs** is a Thoroughbred horse-racing stadium, with music, festivals, and picnics staged on summer weekends. Races are run every half hour Thursday–Monday, and free tours (which also include free track admission) take place Thursday at 10 and Saturday at 10:30. ✉ *2300 Emerald Downs Dr., Auburn* ☎ *253/288–7000 or 888/931–8400* ⊕ *www.emeralddowns.com* 💌 *$7* 🕐 *Mid-Apr.–mid-Sept., Wed.–Fri. 6 PM first post; weekends 2 PM first post.*

SCUBA DIVING **Tacoma Lighthouse Diving Center** (✉ *2502 Pacific Ave.* ☎ *253/627–7617*) is a full-service dive operation with lessons, equipment, and regional trips. **Tacoma Underwater Sports** (✉ *9606 40th Ave. SW, Lakewood* ☎ *253/588–6634*), the area's largest scuba center, sells and rents gear, plans trips, and has branches and repair facilities throughout Puget Sound. Open weekdays 10 to 7, weekends 9 to 5.

OLYMPIA

33 mi southwest of Puyallup.

Olympia has been the capital of Washington since 1853, the beginning of city and state. It is small for the capital city of a major state, but that makes it all the more pleasant to visit. The old and charming downtown area is compact and easy on the feet, stretching between Capitol Lake and the gathering of austere government buildings to the south, the shipping and yacht docks around glistening Budd Inlet to the west, the colorful market area capping the north end of town, and I–5 running along the eastern edge. There are little unexpected surprises all through town, from pretty little half-block parks and blossoming miniature gardens to clutches of Thai and Vietnamese restaurants and antiques shops. The imposing state capitol, finished in 1928, is set above the south end of town like a fortress, framed by a skirt of granite steps. The monumental 287-foot-high dome is the fourth-largest masonry dome in the world (only St. Peter's in Rome, St. Paul's in London, and the national Capitol in the other Washington are larger).

10

GETTING HERE

To reach Olympia from Seattle, take I–5 south to exit 105. Both Greyhound and Amtrak serve Olympia. Taking the bus, though less comfortable, is actually more convenient, as the bus station is centrally located and the sights clustered around downtown and the Capitol Campus are easily reached by foot. The train station is actually in Lacey, which is about 8 mi east of downtown Olympia. Intercity Transit buses (the #64) run between the train station and downtown roughly every hour. The fare is $2.50 one-way, and the trip takes a little over a half hour.

Contact **Intercity Transit** ☎ *360/786–1881* ⊕ *www.intercitytransit.com*).

EXPLORING

The **Capitol Campus** grounds, sprawling around the buildings perched above the Capitol Lake bluffs, contain memorials, monuments, rose gardens, and Japanese cherry trees. The 1939 conservatory is open year-round on weekdays from 8 to 3 and also on weekends in summer. Directly behind the legislative building, the modern state library has exhibits devoted to Washington's history. Free 45-minute campus tours from the visitor center take you around the area. If you want to see state government in action, the legislature is in session for 30 or 60 days from the second Monday in January, depending on whether it's an even- or odd-numbered year. ✉ *Capitol Way between 10th and 14th Aves.* ☎ *360/902–8880 group tour information* ⊕ *www.ga.wa.gov/visitor/ tour.htm* ✆ *Free* ☾ *Campus tours daily on the hr, 10–3 weekdays and 11–3 weekends.*

The Hands On Children's Museum is a fun little corner spot just a block north of the Capitol Campus where children can touch, build, and play with all sorts of crafts and exhibits. Fifty-plus interactive stations include an art studio and a special gallery for kids four and under. During the city's First Friday art walks the museum is open late and stages special programs and events. At this writing, a brand-new home for the museum is being constructed on Marine Drive by East Bay. It is scheduled to open in Fall 2011; check the Web site for updates on the project. ✉ *106 11th Ave. SW* ☎ *360/956–0818* ⊕ *www.hocm.org* ✆ *$7.95 ages 2 and over, $4.95 ages 12–23 months; half-price 3–5 on school weekdays; free 5–9 on first Fri. of the month* ☾ *Mon.–Sat. 10–5, Sun. noon–5.*

The **Olympia Farmers' Market** is a neat, clean, and well-run expanse of covered fruit, vegetable, pastry, and craft stalls at the north end of town. Much of the produce is organic, and you'll find all sorts of oddities such as ostrich eggs, button magnets, and glass sculptures. With a dozen tiny ethnic eateries tucked in between the vendors, it's also a terrific place to grab a bite and then walk over to the waterfront area. ✉ *700 N. Capitol Way* ☎ *360/352–9096* ⊕ *www.olympiafarmersmarket.com* ✆ *Free* ☾ *Apr.–Oct., Thurs.–Sun. 10–3; Nov. and Dec., weekends 10–3.*

The Olympic Flight Museum, housed in a hangar at the Olympic Regional Airport south of town, brings to life an ever-changing collection of vintage aircraft. Important pieces include a colorful P-51D Mustang, a sleek BAC-167 Strikemaster, and a serious-looking AH-1S Cobra helicopter. On the annual schedule are winter lectures, weekly tours, monthly flights, and the Gathering of Warbirds event each June. The shop sells a model of just about everything you see on-site. ✉ *7637 A Old Hwy. 99 SE* ☎ *360/705–3925* ⊕ *www.olympicflightmuseum.com* ✆ *$7* ☾ *May–Sept., daily 11–5; Oct.–Dec., Tues.–Sun. 11–5; Jan.–Apr., Wed.–Sun. 11–5.*

Percival Landing Waterfront Park, framing nearly an acre of landscaped desert gardens and bird-watching areas, stretches along a 1½-mi board-walk through a beachy section of the Ellis Cove coastline. To the south are yachts bobbing in the water at the wooden docks and the waterfront Anthony's restaurant; to the north are the shipyards and cargo cranes; and to the east is the market. In the center is an open space with an outdoor stage for summer shows, music, and festivals. You can see it all from three stories up by climbing the winding steps of the timber viewing tower, where open benches invite visitors to relax and enjoy the city views. At this writing, Percival Landing is at the start of a multi-phase restoration and expansion project. Sections of the boardwalk from Thurston Avenue north are closed through August 2011. Check the Web site for updates on accessibility. ⊠ *4th Ave. to Thurston Ave.* ☎ *360/753–8380* ⊕ *olympiawa.gov/community/parks/percival-landing.aspx* 🖃 *Free* ☉ *Daily dawn–dusk.*

Priest Point Park is a beautiful section of protected shoreline and wetlands. Thick swaths of forest and glistening bay views are the main attractions, with picnic areas and playgrounds filling in the open spaces. The 3-mi **Ellis Cove Trail,** with interpretive stations, bridges, and nature settings, runs right through the Priest Point Park area and around the Olympia coast. ⊠ *East Bay Dr.* ☎ *360/753–8380* ⊕ *olympiawa.gov/community/parks/parks-and-trails/priest-point-park.aspx.*

⟲ **Wolf Haven International** is an 80-acre sanctuary dedicated to wolf conservation. Guided tours of the wolf sanctuary are given every hour on the hour and run about 50 minutes, during which docents explain the recovery programs and visitors can view the wolves. You must join a tour. In summer the facility hosts a so-called Howl-In (reservations essential), with tours, storytelling, arts and crafts, and howling contests. Note that it's worth taking a look at the Web site before visiting—the sanctuary has a few rules regarding conduct and photography (certain zoom lenses can only be used on special photography tours). Most importantly, parents should know that although the sanctuary can be a wonderful place for kids, it does not provide as much stimulation as a typical zoo and may bore kids with short attention spans. ⊠ *3111 Offut Lake Rd. SE, Tenino* ⊕ *From Olympia, take I–5 south to Exit 99 and follow signs east for 7 mi* ☎ *800/448–9653* ⊕ *www.wolfhaven.org* 🖃 *Daily tours $9, Howl-Ins $17 in advance, $19 at gate* ☉ *Apr.–Sept., Mon., Wed.–Sat. 10–3, Sun. noon–3; Oct.–Jan., Mar. Sat. 10–3, Sun. noon–3. Closed Feb.*

The **Yashiro Japanese Garden,** a symbol of the sister-city relationship of Olympia and Yashiro, Japan, opened in 1989. Within it are a waterfall, a bamboo grove, a koi pond, and stone lanterns. ⊠ *1010 Plum St.* ☎ *No phone* 🖃 *Free* ☉ *Daily dawn–dusk.*

WHERE TO EAT

$$–$$$
AMERICAN

✕ **Falls Terrace.** An elegant, multilevel restaurant in front of the Olympia Brewery, Falls Terrace offers unobstructed views of Tumwater Falls. Steaks, burgers, and seafood are as fancy as the food gets. There is dining on the deck, but you have to be over 21. Inside is the place to be for a weekend brunch. ⊠ *106 S. Deschutes Way* ☎ *360/943–7830* w*www.fallsterrace.com* ▭ *AE, D, DC, MC, V.*

$–$$
MEDITERRANEAN

✕ **Mercato.** Tucked into a glitzy, glass-front office building on a sunny corner across from the Farmers' Market, the aptly named restaurant brings an Italian countryside ambience to this relaxed neighborhood. Tables line up against sponge-painted gold walls decorated with a series of Patés Baroni posters, with tiny stained-glass lamps lighting the scene. Specialties include the *piadina* sandwiches, slices of warmed flatbread slathered with such cold fillings as smoked duck on spinach vinaigrette. ⊠ *111 Market St. NE* ☎ *360/528–3663* ▭ *AE, D, MC, V.*

10

¢–$ ✗**Batdorf & Bronson's Dancing Goat Espresso Bar.** Here is a local roaster
CAFÉ   that can stand up to the best of Seattle's coffeehouses. Two spacious
and sleek shops, one across from the Farmers' Market and one in the
heart of downtown, pair the best beans with just-baked pastries and
tasty sandwiches. The tasting room at 200 Market Street is in the roastery. Free tours of the roastery are given the second Wednesday of each
month at 11; otherwise, you can sample about a half-dozen of Batdorf's
favorite blends in the tasting room Wednesday–Sunday from 9–4. ✉ *111
Market St. NE* ☎ *360/528–5555* ⊕ *www.dancinggoats.com* ▤ *AE, MC,
V* ☽ *No dinner.* ✉ *513 S. Capitol Way* ☎ *360/786–6717* ☽ *No dinner.*
✉ *200 Market St.* ☎ *360/753–4057* ☽ *Closed Mon. and Tues.*

WHERE TO STAY

$–$$ 🛏 **Phoenix Inn Suites.** This polished accommodation is nestled right up
to Budd Inlet and just a couple of blocks from the Farmers' Market.
The lobby is filled with gray-blue and lavender hues, crystal chandeliers,
and gilt-framed paintings, and rooms follow suit with plush fabrics in
deep charcoals, golds, and beiges. Splashy bonuses include corner jetted
tubs, chaise lounges, and jump-right-to-it service. Extra touches include
complimentary bottled water, coffee, and tea, free weekday newspa-
pers, and fresh-baked cookies served every evening. **Pros:** big place for
a small capital; lots of amenities; indoor pool open 24 hours. **Cons:**
pedestrian hotel appearance. ✉ *415 Capitol Way N* ☎ *360/570–0555 or
877/570–0555* 📠 *360/570–1200* ⊕ *www.phoenixinnsuites.com* 🛏 *102
suites* ⚿ *In-room: a/c, refrigerator, Internet, Wi-Fi. In-hotel: restaurant,
pool, gym, spa, laundry facilities* ▤ *AE, D, DC, MC, V* ⦿ *CP.*

$$ 🛏 **Swantown Inn.** Antiques and lace ornament every room of this stylish,
peak-roofed Victorian inn, built as a mansion in 1893 and then used as
a boardinghouse. Resting high above fragrant gardens and landscaped
lawns, the rooms have views of the capitol and the inn's breezy gazebo.
The Astoria Suite has a four-poster bed and a two-person hot tub; the
smaller Columbia Room has a claw-foot tub. **Pros:** 19th-century feel,
but modern and business-friendly. **Cons:** breakfast isn't outstanding;
a bit pricey for Olympia ✉ *1431 11th Ave. SE* ☎ *360/753–9123 or
877/753–9123* ⊕ *www.swantowninn.com* 🛏 *3 rooms, 1 suite* ⚿ *In-
room: no phone, a/c, no TV, Internet, Wi-Fi. In-hotel: no kids under
9* ▤ *MC, V* ⦿ *BP.*

KITSAP PENINSULA

Branching off the southeastern edge of the Olympic Peninsula, the Kit-
sap Peninsula has Puget Sound on one side and the Hood Canal on the
other. Though it doesn't possess the great wild beauty of the Olympic
Peninsula, it does have several charming waterfront towns with beach
parks, kayaking, and sailing opportunities, as well as a serene setting.
Bremerton is the most developed (and least attractive) city on the pen-
insula, but it's home to a navy base, and its waterfront has many naval
museums and retired ships to crawl around on. Gig Harbor's marinas,
on the other hand, are full of pretty sailboats—it's the town that has
the most to offer in terms of tourist amenities. Outside of these main
cities, Poulsbo and Port Gamble get the most attention. The former is a

Gig Harbor

pilgrimage point for anyone interested in tracing the Norwegian influence in the Pacific Northwest, and the latter is a twee little town made up mostly of historic buildings.

GIG HARBOR

23 mi south of Bremerton.

One of the most picturesque and accessible waterfront cities on Puget Sound, Gig Harbor has a neat, circular bay dotted with sailboats and fronted by hills of evergreens and million-dollar homes. Expect spectacular views all along the town's winding 2-mi bayside walkway, which is intermittently lined by boat docks, kitschy shops, cozy cafés, and broad expanses of open water.

The bay was a storm refuge for the 1841 survey team of Captain Charles Wilkes, who named the area after his small gig (boat). A decade later Croatian and Scandinavian immigrants put their fishing, lumber, and boat-building skills to profitable use, and the town still has strong seafaring traditions. By the 1880s, steamboats carried passengers and goods between the harbor and Tacoma, and auto ferries plied the narrows between the cities by 1917.

The town winds around the waterfront, centering at the intersection of Harborview Drive and Pioneer Way, where shops, art galleries, and restaurants often attract more foot traffic than vehicles. From here, Harborview makes a long, gentle curve around the bay toward the renovated Finholm Market building, which has shops, docks, a restaurant, kayak rentals, and more views. A Gig Harbor Historical Society self-guided walk brochure covers 49 sights (see if you can spot the 16 metal salmon sculptures, designed by local artists, placed in front of sights around town).

GETTING HERE

From Seattle, the fastest way (if there's no traffic) to Gig Harbor is to take I–5 south all the way through Tacoma and take Exit 132 to Highway 16 toward Bremerton. A slightly longer approach—in minutes, not miles—is to take the ferry from the West Seattle terminal to the Southworth landing on the Kitsap Peninsula and take 160 west to 16 east, which will take you into Gig Harbor. Taking the ferry from Seattle to Bremerton would also work—you'd take Highway 3 south to 16 east.

Contact **Washington State Ferries** (🕾 *888/808–7977* ⊕ *www.wsdot.wa.gov*).

VISITOR INFORMATION

Gig Harbor Chamber of Commerce (✉ *3302 Harborview Dr., Gig Harbor* 🕾 *253/851–6865* ⊕ *www.gigharborchamber.com*).

EXPLORING

Surrounding Gig Harbor, pine forests and open woods alternate with rolling pastures; it's enjoyable scenery (even on rainy days) during the 10-minute drive to **Fox Island**. Crossing the Fox Island Bridge over Echo Bay, you'll see stunning views of the Olympic Mountains to the right and the Tanglewood Lighthouse against a backdrop of Mt. Rainier to the left. **Tanglewood Island,** the small drop of forest on which the Tanglewood lighthouse sits, was once an Indian burial ground known as Grav Island. At low tide the boat ramp and boulder-strewn beach next to the bridge are scattered with stranded saltwater creatures.

The **Fox Island Historical Museum** displays island pioneer memorabilia in an authentic log cabin. Pioneer-days children's activities, such as Maypole dances, memory boxes, and old-fashioned Valentine crafts, are scheduled the first Saturday of every month, and the local farmer's market runs summer Wednesdays. ✉ *1017 9th Ave.* 🕾 *253/549–2461* ⊕ *www.foxislandmuseum.org* ▨ *$1* ⊙ *Wed. and weekends 1–4.*

The **Gig Harbor Museum** has an excellent collection of exhibits describing the city's maritime history, as well as photo archives, video programs, and a research library focusing on the area's pioneer and Native American ancestors. The facilities include a one-room, early-20th-century schoolhouse and a 65-foot, 1950s purse seiner, a type of fishing vessel from the community's famous seafaring fleets. News clippings and videos about "Galloping Gertie," the original bridge, are particularly eerie. The staff also stages major historic activities for the area, including a four-hour history cruise each summer ($60) and twice-yearly Harbor Heritage kayak outings from the city docks to locales around Puget Sound ($25 per person). At this writing, the museum is in the process of moving into its new facility on Harborview Drive. Call for updates, as it's only open sporadically, and hours and admission may change once the museum is fully operational. ✉ *4121 Harborview Dr.* 🕾 *253/858–6722* ⊕ *www.gigharbormuseum.org* ▨ *$2* ⊙ *Call for hrs.*

Kopachuk State Park, a 10-minute drive from Gig Harbor, is a wonderful beachcombing area at low tide. Indian tribes once fished and clammed here, and you can still see people trolling the shallow waters or digging deep for razor clams in season. Children and dogs alike delight in discovering huge Dungeness crabs, sea stars, and sand dollars. Picnic tables and walking trails are interspersed throughout the steep, forested hills, and the campground is always full in summer. ⊠ *11101 56th St. NW* ☎ *253/265–3606* ⊜ *Free* ☉ *Daily 6* AM–*10* PM.

WHERE TO EAT

$$$
CONTEMPORARY

✕ **Brix 25.** Simple seafood dishes and classic European fare are beautifully presented in this cozy, glass-fronted setting at the base of Harborview Drive and the Gig Harbor bay. Lunches run the gourmet gamut from spring rolls, salads, sandwiches, soups, and chowders to full-blown grilled steaks and fish. Dinners are formal affairs that focus on seafood and light meats accompanied by fresh local greens. Tempting desserts include an array of sugary cakes, sorbets, and cobblers, and there's a fine wine to match every course. Seasonal events include chef-hosted, multicourse dinners. ⊠ *7707 Pioneer Way* ☎ *253/858–6626* ⊕ *www.harborbrix.com* ⊟ *AE, D, MC, V* ☉ *No lunch.*

¢–$
MEXICAN

✕ **El Pueblito.** The mariachi music, cilantro and chili pepper scents from the kitchen, and a waitstaff that chats in Spanish are reminiscent of a compact cantina south of the border. Huge portions of better-than-average Mexican dishes and frothy margaritas are served amid much gaiety. The adjacent bar is a lively late-night hangout on weekends. ⊠ *3226 Harborview Dr.* ☎ *253/858–9077* ⊟ *AE, D, MC, V.*

$$–$$$
CONTEMPORARY

✕ **Green Turtle.** The unassuming exterior belies a dining room surrounded by a mural of an azure underwater world, one that includes a huge sea turtle. Wraparound windows show off the bayside setting, as does the front deck. Eclectic Northwest cuisine is beautifully presented in such dishes as halibut cheeks and filet mignon. It's difficult to leave without succumbing to crêpes suzette topped with vanilla ice cream and warm orange liqueur. ⊠ *2905 Harborview Dr.* ☎ *206/851–3167* w*www. thegreenturtle.com* ⊟ *AE, MC, V* ☉ *Closed Mon. No lunch weekends.*

WHERE TO STAY

$–$$

🏨 **Inn at Gig Harbor.** The city's largest hotel has a multicolor exterior that makes it seem more like a mansion than a member of the Heritage chain. Many rooms have Mt. Rainier views, and suites have a fireplace or jetted tub. The Heritage restaurant serves classic American fare with Northwest flair. Browse through the little shop, which is jam-packed with good-quality regional crafts and treats. The inn is a major base for business travelers driving into Seattle, Tacoma, and Bremerton. **Pros:** lodge-style ambience; professional staff. **Cons:** no pool; pricey for dated, unimpressive rooms. ⊠ *3211 56th St. NW* ☎ *253/858–1111 or 800/795–9980* ⊟ *253/851–5402* ⊕ *www.innatgigharbor.com* ⊅ *52 rooms, 12 suites* ⏃ *In-room: a/c, refrigerator (some), Internet, Wi-Fi. In-hotel: restaurant, room service, gym, laundry service, pets allowed* ⊟ *AE, D, DC, MC, V* ⎐⎜ *CP.*

$

🏨 **Maritime Inn.** On a hill across from Jersich Park and the docks, this boutique hotel combines class and comfort with water views. Individually decorated and themed rooms include the Captain's Room, the Canterwood Golf Room, and the Victorian Room. All have fireplaces, and several have decks. Cottages along the back of the hill

10

afford privacy and quiet; streetside rooms are noisy but have excellent views. **Pros:** right on the waterfront. **Cons:** front rooms absorb traffic noise. ⊠ *3112 Harborview Dr.* ☎ *253/858–1818* ⊕ *www.maritimeinn. com* ⇥ *15 rooms* ⅏ *In-room: a/c, Internet, pets not allowed* ⊟ *AE, D, DC, MC, V.*

SPORTS AND THE OUTDOORS

SAILING AND   **Arabella's Landing** (⊠ *Harborview Dr. at Dororitch La., just past the*
BOATING   *Bayview Dock* ☎ *253/851–1793* ⊕ *www.arabellaslanding.com*) provides moorage for those coming by boat into Gig Harbor. **Gig Harbor Rent-a-Boat** (⊠ *8829 N. Harborview Dr.* ☎ *253/858–7341* ⊕ *www. gigharborrentaboat.com*) has powerboats, kayaks, pedal boats, and a 22-foot sailboat for rent.

BREMERTON

18 mi west of Seattle by ferry, 68 mi southwest of Seattle by road, 25 mi south of Port Gamble by road.

Nearly surrounded by water, and with one of the largest Navy bases on the West Coast, Bremerton's attractions center on the waterfront, with its gardens, fountains, and ferry docks dwarfed by massive warships. Frankly, away from the waterfront, and especially in the area around the ferry terminal, Bremerton looks a bit depressed in some parts. The western Charlestown neighborhood seems to have the most going on, with a few art galleries and restaurants, but if you're not a fan of naval history and machinery, you probably won't find much here of interest.

GETTING HERE

From Seattle, Washington State Ferries make regular departures to Bremerton's ferry terminal. The crossing takes about an hour. The many navy sights are close to the terminal, but Bremerton isn't a very walkable place, so having a car is helpful. If you don't want to take the ferry, you can take the long way around by car, heading south through Tacoma on I–5, then swinging west across the Tacoma-Narrows Bridge onto the Kitsap Peninsula and heading west on Highway 16 until it merges with Highway 3 and heads into Bremerton. This trip takes about an hour and 40 minutes, and it's a pretty mind-numbing drive until you get across the Tacoma-Narrows Bridge.

Bremerton Area Chamber of Commerce (⊠ *301 Pacific Ave., Bremerton* ☎ *360/479–3579* ⊕ *www.bremertonchamber.org*).

EXPLORING

The waterfront expanse of the **Bremerton Marina**, lining the glistening blue bay between the warships and ferry docks, is the place to walk, bicycle, picnic, run through fountains in summer, and watch a mass of sailboats and military craft pass through the calm waters. It's an especially good place for spotting the host of birds and marine life around the docks. ⊠ *Off Washington Ave.*

The small **Kitsap County Historical Society Museum** has pioneer artifacts, nautical items, and a collection of old photographs. The staff plans such special children's events as costume dress-up sessions and treasure hunts for the first Friday of the month, when the museum is open late in conjunction with the town's monthly Art Walk. ✉ *280 4th St.* ☎ *360/479–6226* ⊕ *www.kitsaphistory.org* 🖃 *$2* ☉ *Tues.–Sat. 10–4, Sun. 12–4, 1st Fri. of month 10–8.*

☽ The **Naval Undersea Museum**, a 15-minute drive north of Bremerton, is fronted by a can't-miss sight: the 88-ton *Trieste II* submarine, which dove to the deepest spot in the ocean (the Marianas Trench) in 1960. In the main building are torpedoes, diving equipment, model submarines, and mines. ✉ *1 Garnett Way, Keyport* ☎ *360/396–4148* ⊕ *www.history. navy.mil* 🖃 *Free* ☉ *June–Sept., daily 10–4; closed Tues. Oct.–May.*

The **Puget Sound Navy Museum** right on the waterfront and near the ferry terminal, brings American naval history to life through war photos, ship models, historic displays, and American and Japanese war artifacts. ✉ *251 1st St. 98337* ☎ *360/479–7447* ⊕ *www.history.navy.mil* 🖃 *Free* ☉ *Mon.–Sat. 10–4, Sun. 1–4. Closed Tues. Oct.–Apr.*

☽ The **USS *Turner Joy*** Navy destroyer, along the marina near the ferry docks, is open for self-guided tours. Walk through the narrow passages to view the cafeteria, medical office, barbershop, prison cell, cramped bunk rooms, and captain's quarters. ✉ *300 Washington Beach Ave.* ☎ *360/792–2457* ⊕ *ussturnerjoy.org* 🖃 *$10* ☉ *Apr–Oct., daily 10–5; Nov.–Apr., Fri–Sun. 10–4.*

WHERE TO EAT

$$
CONTEMPORARY

✕ **Boat Shed**. At this deliberately rustic waterfront restaurant diners share a casual, seaside camaraderie as they slurp up clam chowder, steamed clams, and mussels. Sailors, who enjoy free boat moorage, arrive early for the famed Sunday brunch. ✉ *101 Shore Dr.* ☎ *360/377– 2600* 🖃 *AE, MC, V.*

WHERE TO STAY

¢
Flagship Inn. Although it's a budget spot, rooms here have private balconies overlooking Oyster Bay and the Olympic Mountains. It's close to everything, rooms have a microwave, refrigerator, and VCR, and there's even a free video library for rainy evenings. Free tea, coffee, fruit, and cookies are available all day. **Pros:** the price is right; nice views. **Cons:** place could use an update—some furnishings are worn. ✉ *4320 Kitsap Way* ☎ *360/479–6566 or 800/447–9396* 🖨 *360/479– 6745* ⊕ *www.flagship-inn.com* 🛏 *29 rooms* ♿ *In-room: a/c, kitchen, refrigerator, Internet, Wi-Fi. In-hotel: pool, some pets allowed* 🖃 *AE, D, DC, MC, V* ⑩ *CP.*

$
Hampton Inn & Suites Bremerton. Its splashy waterfront location—right in the center of the city marina, adjacent to the Bremerton Harborside Conference Center and just a block from the ferry terminal—makes this large, modern hotel a good choice. Disregard the gray, boxy exterior; inside it's plush furnishings, upgraded technology, and pure comfort all the way. There's free coffee and tea, weekday newspapers, a daily hot breakfast (with eggs, sausages, French toast, and more), and grab-and-go bag breakfasts at the desk. **Pros:** reliable chain hotel; good location. **Cons:** not much personality ✉ *150 Washington Ave.* ☎ *360/405–0200 or 800/426–7866* 🖨 *360/405–0618* ⊕ *www.hamptoninn.com* 🛏 *105 rooms, 21 suites* ♿ *In-room: a/c, Internet* 🖃 *AE, D, DC, MC, V* ⑩ *CP.*

10

$-$$ 🛏 **Illahee Manor Bed and Breakfast.** Six acres of woods, orchards, and gardens surround this 1920s bayfront manor with its own beach. Some rooms have fireplaces and balconies; those in the turret have wrap-around windows looking out onto grounds roamed by llamas and miniature deer. The Beach House has floor-to-ceiling windows, and the 1918 Cottage has rustic charm. The light- and plant-filled conservatory is a fine place to enjoy breakfast. **Pros:** Lovely grounds and private beach; Penthouse Suite with fireplace and whirlpool bath. **Cons:** decor in some suites is a bit frilly. ⊠ *6680 Illahee Rd. NE* ☎ *360/698–7555 or 800/693–6680* ⊕ *www.illaheemanorbnb.com* ⇄ *5 rooms, 2 cabins* ⚘ *In-room: no a/c, refrigerator. In-hotel: spa, beachfront* ⊟ *AE, D, MC, V* ⫶⃝❙ *BP.*

$-$$ 🛏 **Oyster Bay Inn.** This hotel sits at the lower curve of Oyster Bay, just outside of Bremerton but seemingly on an isle of its own. Panoramic views of the water are the highlight of the comfortable rooms, and you can see the bay up close on a stroll through the surrounding gardens and woods. The elegant restaurant is a lively spot to feast on seafood, steaks, and fancy pastas. Afterward head to the adjacent lounge, which has a piano bar. **Pros:** locale quiet but convenient. **Cons:** motel-style exterior. ⊠ *4412 Kitsap Way* ☎ *360/377–5510 or 800/393–3862* ⇄ *69 rooms, 4 suites, 3 apartments, 1 chalet* ⚘ *In-room: a/c, kitchen (some), refrigerator. In-hotel: restaurant, bar, gym, some pets allowed* ⊟ *AE, D, DC, MC, V* ⫶⃝❙ *CP.*

THE NORTH COAST AND SKAGIT VALLEY

Most people blow through places like La Conner, Mt. Vernon, or Bellingham on their way west to the San Juans, east to the Cascades, or north to the Canadian border. But between Everett and Canada are some lovely miles of coastline, some impressive parkland, and charming farm towns—all of which are fairly easy to access from I–5. Collectively, the towns that anchor the northwestern edge of the state are seriously underappreciated: La Conner is a pleasantly laid-back farming community, and Mt. Vernon is a riverfront town with some great festivals. Between the two towns are the best of the Skagit Valley flower farms, which do draw big crowds in spring when the tulips bloom. Bellingham is a college town that's a fun and quirky mix of hippie and yuppie, and nearby Ferndale has some interesting historic sights to supplement the natural wonders. Any one of these towns makes a good stopover on other itineraries.

LA CONNER

14 mi southeast of Anacortes, 68 mi north of Seattle.

Morris Graves, Kenneth Callahan, Guy Anderson, Mark Tobey, and other painters set up shop in La Conner in the 1940s, and the village on the Swinomish Channel (Slough) has been a haven for artists ever since. In recent years the community has become increasingly popular as a weekend escape for Seattle residents, because it can be reached after a short drive but seems far away.

Tulip fields, Mt. Vernon

La Conner has several historic buildings near the waterfront or a short walk up the hill—use the stairs leading up the bluff, or go around and walk up one of the sloping streets—as well as several good shops and restaurants. In summer the village becomes congested with people and cars, and parking can be hard to find. The flat land around La Conner makes for easy bicycling along levees and through the tulip fields. You'll see plenty of fields and farms, and a major attraction in fall and summer are farm stands selling local produce.

GETTING HERE

The center of La Conner is roughly 12 mi off of I–5 (from Seattle, take Exit 221 for Hwy. 534). The town is very close to both Anacortes and the northern tip of Whidbey Island, and therefore it makes sense to pass through here on the way to one or the other. A car is by far your best bet, as the only other option is to take the Airporter Shuttle from Sea-Tac or downtown Seattle; it makes one stop in La Conner on its way to the Anacortes ferry terminal (though it stops on Highway 20, about 5 mi from town).

In summer bike rentals ($15 for two hours; $35 per day) are available at the Port of Skagit Marina in La Conner from Tulip Country Bike Tours. The outfitter, which offers a guided tour of the farms of La Conner, operates out of Mt. Vernon the rest of the year.

Contact **Tulip Country Bike Tours** ☎ *360/424–7461* ⊕ *www.countrycycling.com).*

EXPLORING

The **Museum of Northwest Art** presents the works of regional creative minds past and present. Soaring spaces, circular exhibit rooms, a glass gallery, and a broad spiral staircase add to the free-form feeling of the displays. The small shop sells examples of what you see in the exhibits. ✉ *121 S. 1st St.* ☎ *360/466–4446* ⊕ *www.museumofnwart.org* ⬙ *$5* ⊗ *Sun. and Mon. 12–5, Tues.–Sat. 10–5.*

The hilltop **Skagit County Historical Museum** surveys domestic life in early Skagit County and Northwest Coastal Indian history. ✉ *501 4th St.* ☎ *360/466–3365* ⊕ *skagitcounty.net* ⬙ *$4* ⊗ *Tues.–Sun. 11–5.*

WHERE TO EAT

¢–$

CAFÉ

Fodor's Choice

★

✕ **Calico Cupboard.** A local favorite, this chain of storefront bakeries turn out some of the best pastries in Skagit County (there are branches in Anacortes and Mt. Vernon, too). Lunches focus on fresh, gourmet salads, soups, and burgers; you can also order big "breakfast for lunch" combos. No seats? Buy picnic goodies at the take-out counter. ✉ *720 S. 1st St.* ☎ *360/466–4451* w*www.calicocupboardcafe.com* ▭ *MC, V* ⊗ *No dinner.*

$$–$$$

CONTEMPORARY

✕ **Kerstin's.** The intimate dining room overlooks the channel. The menu, which changes seasonally, includes portobello mushrooms roasted in pesto, pan-braised fresh king salmon, pork tenderloin, rib-eye steak with Indonesian spices, halibut, and lamb shank with port wine sauce. The oysters baked in garlic-cilantro butter and finished with Parmesan are particularly popular. ✉ *505 S. 1st St.* ☎ *360/466–9111* w*www. kerstinsrestaurant.com* ▭ *AE, DC, MC, V* ⊗ *Closed Sun. No lunch Tues. and Wed.*

WHERE TO STAY

$–$$

☖ **La Conner Country Inn.** The multistory waterfront hotel is split into two sections: a large country inn and an understated lodge overlooking the narrow Swinomish Channel. Rooms, done in subdued gray tones with wooden trim, have a gas fireplace, flat-screen TV, DVD player, and a private balcony or patio. Twelve inn rooms have whirlpool baths. The lodge hosts weekend wine receptions and movie gatherings, and massage services are available in the privacy of your room. Nell Thorn's is a pub-style restaurant that serves hearty Northwest fare, organic seasonings, and fine wines. **Pros:** big stone fireplace; rustic charm wrapped around sleek modern amenities; two family suites. **Cons:** rooms are an odd mix of country coziness and chain hotel. ✉ *207 S. 2nd St.* ☎ *360/466–3101* ⊕ *www.laconnerlodging.com* ⬦ *28 rooms, 17 suites* ⬙ *In-room: a/c, DVD, Wi-Fi. In-hotel: Wi-Fi hotspot* ▭ *AE, D, DC, MC, V.*

$–$$

☖ **Wild Iris.** The garden-laced exterior is a sprawling model of a Victorian-style inn, and the elegantly decorated interior begins with a river-rock fireplace. Spacious rooms have soft, colorful fabrics and polished wood accents; suites have CD players, robes, fireplaces, whirlpool spa tubs, and private decks or balconies. Breakfast is served in the large, restaurant-style dining room. **Pros:** beautiful and tastefully decorated rooms; great amenities (good linens, DVD library, CD players). **Cons:** some rooms are small; layouts are a little odd, with whirlpool tubs plunked awkwardly close to the beds and fireplaces. ✉ *121 Maple Ave.*

☎ *360/466–1400 or 800/477–1400* ⊕ *www.wildiris.com* ⌐ *4 rooms, 12 suites* ⚒ *In-room: no a/c, DVD, Wi-Fi. In-hotel: Wi-Fi hotspot, no kids under 8* ▭ *AE, MC, V* ⦿ *BP.*

MOUNT VERNON

11 mi northeast of La Conner.

This attractive riverfront town is the county seat of Skagit County and was founded in 1871. After a giant logjam on the lower Skagit was cleared, steamers began churning up the river, and Mount Vernon soon became the major commercial center of the Skagit Valley, a position it has never relinquished. The city is surrounded by dairy pastures, vegetable fields, and bulb farms, and is famous for its annual Tulip Festival in April, when thousands of people visit to admire the floral exuberance. Rising above downtown and the river, 972-foot-high Little Mountain is a city park with a view. It used to be an island until the mudflats were filled in by Skagit River silt. Glacial striations in rocks near the top of the mountain, dating from the last continental glaciation (10,000–20,000 years ago), were made when the mountain (and all of the Puget Sound region) was covered by some 3,500 feet of ice.

GETTING HERE AND AROUND

The best way to reach Mt. Vernon is by car, taking I–5 north to any of several exits right in town. In Mt. Vernon I–5 connects with Highway 536, which then merges with Highway 20 toward Anacortes.

Amtrak's *Cascades* train stops in Mt. Vernon on its way north from Seattle to Vancouver, B.C.; this route also connects Mt. Vernon with Bellingham and Everett. Greyhound buses also serve Mt. Vernon from Seattle.

Skagit Transit provides limited bus service connecting Mt. Vernon with Bellingham and Everett. This is primarily a service for residents and commuters, so most of the stops are at places like schools, supermarkets, and park and rides, but it may be helpful if you, say, want to come into town for the day from Bellingham to take part in a bike tour of the tulip farms.

10

Tulip Country Bike Tours arranges spring trips through the tulip fields, starting at $65 per person. In summer, tours take in other Skagit Valley sights like berry farms and Padilla Bay.

Contacts Amtrak ☎ 800/872–7245 ⊕ www.amtrak.com). **Skagit Transit** ☎ 877/584–7528 ⊕ www.skagittransit.org). **Tulip Country Bike Tours** ☎ 360/424–7461 ⊕ www.countrycycling.com).

EXPLORING

Adjoining the small waterfront community of the same name, **Bay View State Park** has a campground in the woods and picnic tables on the low grassy bluff above the bay. Canoers and kayakers take note: Padilla Bay runs almost dry at low tide, when water is restricted to a few creek-like tidal channels. ⊠ *10905 Bay View–Edison Rd.* ☎ *360/757–0227* ⊕ *www.parks.wa.gov* ⛱ *$5 day use, $17–$23 camping* ☉ *Daily 8 AM–dusk.*

Atop Little Mountain at the southeastern edge of town, 480-acre **Little Mountain Park** has great views of the Skagit Valley (especially in March and April, when the daffodils and tulips are in full bloom), the San Juan Islands, and the distant Olympic Mountains. ⊠ *Blackburn Rd. W* ☎ *360/336–6213* ✆ *Free* ☉ *Daily dawn–dusk.*

At **Padilla Bay National Estuarine Reserve,** the Breazeale Interpretive Center has great birding: there are black brant geese, raptors, peregrine falcons, and bald eagles. Trails lead into the woods and to a rocky beach, with more good bird-watching opportunities. The 2¼-mi Padilla Bay Trail starts at the south end of Bayview; look for signs directing you to the parking area, which is away from the water off the east side of the road. ⊠ *10441 Bay View–Edison Rd.* ☎ *360/428–1558* ⊕ *www.padillabay. gov* ✆ *Free* ☉ *Wed.–Sun. 10–5.*

★ **Roozengaarde,** a 1,200-acre estate established by the Roozen family and Washington Bulb Company in 1985, is the world's largest family-owned tulip-, daffodil-, and iris-growing business. Fifteen acres of greenhouses are filled with multicolored blossoms, and more than 200,000 bulbs are planted in the show gardens each fall. The Skagit Valley Tulip Festival, held in April, is the main event, when the flowers pop up in neat, brilliant rows across the flat land, attracting thousands of sightseers. The garden and store are open year-round, and the staff and Web site are full of helpful advice for both novice and experienced gardeners. ⊠ *1587 Beaver Marsh Rd., Mt. Vernon* ☎ *360/424–8531 or 866/488–5477* ⊕ *www.tulips.com* ✆ *Free* ☉ *Mon.–Sat. 9–6, Sun. 11–4.*

WHERE TO EAT

$$$
ITALIAN
★
✕ **Il Grainaio.** Tucked deep into the town's historic Old Grainery, amid displays of century-old farming equipment, is this cozy and rustic Italian restaurant. Dark-wood floors, small tables, and lanternlike lighting give it the authentic ambience of a local trattoria. The waitstaff is quick and knowledgeable, turning out enormous pasta bowls, seafood salads, and pan-fried eggplant or salmon with flair. Excellent wines garnish the tables, and desserts are simple and rich. Slip in early on weekends, when dinners bustle with groups. ⊠ *100 E. Montgomery St.* ☎ *360/419–0674* w ▤ *AE, MC, V* ☉ *No lunch weekends.*

¢–$
AMERICAN
✕ **Rexville Grocery.** From Ben & Jerry's to Pocky sticks to local microbrews, Rexville is one well-stocked country store, with a great mix of everyday and gourmet snacks and drinks. There's a small café with a patio encircled by trees, vines, and blooming thistle. On weekends, you can sit down for a breakfast (served until noon) of scrambles or pancakes; the rest of the week, stop in for a sandwich or salad. You could put together quite a good picnic basket here. The store closes at 7 PM. ⊠ *19271 Best Rd., Mt. Vernon* ☎ *360/466–5522* ⊕ *www. rexvillegrocery.com* ▤ *MC, V* ☉ *No dinner.*

BELLINGHAM

29 mi northeast of Mount Vernon.

The fishing port and college community of Bellingham is transforming itself from a grungy blue-collar area to the arts, retirement, and pleasure-boating capital of Washington's northwest corner. Downtown has cafés, specialty shops, and galleries, and the waterfront, once dominated by lumber mills and shipyards, is slowly being converted into a string of parks with connecting trails. College students and professors from Western Washington University make up a sizable part of the town's population and contribute to its laid-back intellectual climate. The lushly green bayfront, creeks meandering through town, and Lakes Whatcom and Padden attract wildlife like deer, raccoons, river otters, beavers, ducks, geese, herons, bald eagles, and the occasional cougar.

GETTING HERE AND AROUND

From Seattle, Bellingham is nearly a straight shot on I–5 north (Exit 254 will get you into the center of town).

Amtrak's Cascades train stops in Bellingham on its way to Vancouver, B.C. It connects Bellingham with Mt. Vernon and Everett. Greyhound buses also serve Bellingham from Seattle, as does the Airporter Shuttle from Sea-Tac and downtown Seattle.

Biking is popular in and around Bellingham, which has a series of designated bike paths and park trails. The city of Bellingham has a good high-res bike-route map that can be downloaded from its Web site. The Whatcom Transportation Authority has more maps showing both bike and bus routes in Bellingham and the surrounding areas.

The Coast Millennium Trail will eventually connect Skagit and Whatcom counties to British Columbia. At this writing, 15 mi of the 50-mi trail were open to bikes and walkers. The Whatcom Council of Governments has a page discussing the trail plus a downloadable map of the completed segments.

Fairhaven Bike & Ski rents road bikes, full-suspension bikes, and standard mountain bikes starting at $55 per day.

Contacts Amtrak ☎ 360/733–4433 ⊕ www.amtrak.com). **City of Bellingham Bike Routes** ⊕ www.cob.org/services/transportation/biking.aspx).**Fairhaven Bike & Ski** ☎ 800/872–7245 ⊕ fairhavenbike.com). **Whatcom Council of Governments (Coast Millennium Trail info)** ⊕ www.wcog.org/Completed-Projects/Coast-Millennium-Trail/420.aspx). **Whatcom Transportation Authority** ⊕ www.ridewta.com).

EXPLORING

The **Bellingham Cruise Terminal** (✉ 355 Harris Ave. ☎ 360/676–2500), a massive brick building surrounded by gardens, dispatches daily ferries to the San Juan Islands, Victoria, and Alaska. There's terrific wildlife-watching right off the docks and adjacent shoreline, where sea lions, otters, and gray whales frolic out in the water as great blue herons, cormorants, and harlequin ducks bob on the surface.**Fairhaven Marine Park,** a long, sandy beach at the foot of Harris Street a few blocks south, is the place to launch sea kayaks. A rough trail runs south from the park along the railroad tracks to shingle beaches and rocky headlands, where you'll find clams, summer blackberries, and splendid views of Lummi Island.

The only public access in Bellingham to 14-mi-long Lake Whatcom is at its north end, in **Bloedel Donovan Park.** Locals swim in the sheltered waters of a cove, but you might find the water too cold. If so, spend some time trying to spot beavers, river otters, ducks, great blue herons, and yellow pond lilies at Scudder Pond, which is another 100 feet west (reached by trail from a parking area at Northshore and Alabama). ✉ *2214 Electric Ave.* ☎ *360/778–7000* 🖻 *Parking $3* ⊘ *Daily dawn–dusk.*

★ Highway 11, also known as **Chuckanut Drive,** was once the only highway heading south from Bellingham. The drive begins in Fairhaven, reaches the flat farmlands of the Samish Valley near the village of Bow, and joins up with I–5 at Burlington, in Skagit County; the full loop can be made in a couple of hours. For a dozen miles this 23-mi road winds along the cliffs above beautiful Chuckanut and Samish bays. It twists its way past the sheer sandstone face of Chuckanut Mountain and crosses creeks with waterfalls. Turnouts are framed by gnarled madrona trees and pines and offer great views of the San Juan Islands. Bald eagles cruise along the cliffs or hang out on top of tall firs. Drive carefully: the cliffs are so steep in places that rock slides are common; note that the road washes out once or twice each winter.

Fairhaven, the historic district just shy of 3 mi south of Bellingham and at the beginning of Chuckanut Drive (Highway 11), was an independent city until 1903, and still retains its distinct identity as an intellectual and artistic center. The beautifully restored 1890s redbrick buildings of the Old Fairhaven District, especially on Harris Avenue between 10th and 12th streets, house restaurants, galleries, and specialty boutiques.

Larrabee State Park, south of Chuckanut Bay along the Whatcom–Skagit county line, is one of the state's most scenic and popular parks. It straddles a rocky shore that has quiet, sandy coves and runs high up along the slopes of Chuckanut Mountain. Even though the mountain has been logged repeatedly, some of it is still wilderness. Miles of trails lead through ferny fir and maple forests to hidden lakes, caves, and cliff-top lookouts from which you can see all the way to the San Juan Islands. At the shore there's a sheltered boat launch; you can go crabbing here or watch the birds—and the occasional harbor seal—that perch on the offshore rocks. The area west of Chuckanut Drive has picnic tables as well as tent and RV sites with hookups, which are open all year. ✉ *245 Chuckanut Dr.* ☎ *360/676–2093* 🖻 *$5; tent campsites $21, RV sites $28* ⊘ *Daily 8 AM–dusk.*

☾ The **Maritime Heritage Park,** down a flight of stairs behind the Whatcom Museum, pays tribute to Bellingham's fishing industry. Self-guided Marine Heritage Center tours take you through a salmon's life cycle, winding past hatcheries, aquarium tanks, and fish ladders. A boardwalk route from Holly Street leads to the ponds and a waterfall, where Bellingham was founded in 1852. Note that salmon runs occur annually around September and October. ✉ *500 W. Holly St.* 🖻 *Free* ⊘ *Daily dawn–dusk.*

☾ A good place to fish, lounge, picnic, or walk is the **Squalicum Harbor Marina,** which holds more than 1,900 commercial and pleasure boats. Pete Zuanich Park, at the end of the spit, has a telescope for close-up views of the water and a marine-life center with touch tanks. ✉ *Roeder Ave. and Coho Way* ☎ *360/676–2542.*

The three-building **Whatcom Museum** has as its centerpiece the Light-catcher, a LEED-certified building with an 180-foot-long translucent wall. Bellingham's 1892 former city hall, a redbrick structure that was converted into a museum in 1940, is closed at this writing for renovations. Collections on display at the Lightcatcher Building include works by contemporary Northwest artists, Victorian clothing, toys, games, clocks, and history exhibits. The third building is a photo archive, generally open by appointment only. ⊠ *Lightcatcher Building, 250 Flora St.* ☎ *360/676–6981* ⊕ *www.whatcommuseum.org* ⤳ *$10* ☉ *Tues.–Sun. noon–5.*

WHERE TO EAT

$$–$$$
SEAFOOD
✕ **Big Fat Fish Company.** Have a fish craving? Head to this spacious, brew-pub-style restaurant for everything from panfried trout to cedar-planked salmon and sea bass Wellington. A lot of other fishy items round out the menu: king crab legs, scallops in truffle butter, and rich seafood cioppino. The sushi is spot-on, too; novices can try the sample platter. Aquaphobia? Dig into a rib eye with wild mushrooms, or the Big Fat Kobe Burger. Service is casual and fun, although weekends often bring long waits. ⊠ *1304 12th St.* ☎ *360/733–2284* ⊕ *www.bigfatfishco.com* ▤ *AE, D, MC, V.*

$$
AMERICAN
✕ **Chuckanut Manor.** The old-fashioned, glassed-in dining room and bar overlook the mouth of the Samish River, Samish Bay, and the mudflats, where great blue herons hang out. It's a popular spot for sunset- and bird-watching: bird feeders outside the bar's picture windows attract finches, chickadees, red-winged blackbirds, and other songbirds. Occasionally bald eagles can be seen gliding past. Besides the view, folks come here for traditional American fare with an emphasis on steak and fresh seafood. ⊠ *3056 Chuckanut Dr., Bow* ☎ *360/766–6191* w ▤ *AE, DC, MC, V* ☉ *Closed Mon.*

$$–$$$
PACIFIC NORTHWEST
✕ **Nimbus.** Downtown Fairhaven's upscale star is this small, posh spot rising 14 stories above the boutique neighborhood. Seasonal menus enhance fresh Washington produce, with delicacies including an apple-cider pork belly and caramelized sea scallops combination, and homemade melted leek ravioli. If you can't decide, go for the exquisite five-course tasting menu. After-hours tidbits, served until midnight, offer truffle fries, wild mushroom cannoli, and heirloom tomato soup. Service for all meals is professionally crisp, yet still relaxed and amiable. ⊠ *118 N. Commercial St., 14th fl.* ☎ *360/676–1307* w *www. nimbusrestaurant.com* ▤ *AE, MC, V* ☉ *No lunch.*

$$$
★
SEAFOOD
✕ **Oyster Bar.** Above the shore on a steep, wooded bluff, this intimate restaurant in the village of Bow is regionally famous for what is probably the best marine view from any Washington restaurant. People come here to dine and watch the sun set over the islands to the west or to watch the full moon reflect off the waters of Samish Bay. The menu changes regularly, so it's hard to predict what you might find, but the oyster bar, seafood dishes, wild game, and pastas never disappoint—and there are fine wines to complement every dish. ⊠ *2578 Chuckanut Dr., Bow* ☎ *360/766–6185* w *www.theoysterbaronchuckanutdrive.com* ▤ *AE, MC, V.*

10

WHERE TO STAY

$$$ ⊞ **Chrysalis Inn and Spa at the Pier.** The facade, which rises above the waterfront, is gray and stark, but in the lobby warm wood predominates. On sunny days you can see far across Bellingham Bay; on cloudy days, you can stare into the blaze of the big main fireplace. Rooms also have fireplaces, as well as double baths, window seats, and such amenities as coffeemakers, irons, hair dryers, and CD players. Artwork enlivens the walls of the modern Fino Wine Bar ($–$$$), and picture windows frame the bay. You can sample European and Pacific Northwest wines at the long back bar or dine on Mediterranean-inspired fare at white linen–clad tables. **Pros:** utterly relaxing; great water views from most rooms; attractive ultramodern decor. **Cons:** adjacent railway. ⊠ *804 10th St.* ☎ *360/756–1005 or 888/808–0005* ⊕ *www.thechrysalisinn.com* ⇨ *34 rooms, 9 suites* ⌂ *In-room: a/c, refrigerator, DVD, Internet, Wi-Fi. In-hotel: restaurant, bar, spa, Internet terminal, Wi-Fi hotspot* ⊟ *AE, D, DC, MC, V* ⫧⧄ *CP.*

$$–$$$ ⊞ **Hotel Bellwether.** Bellingham's original waterfront hotel overlooks ★ the entrance to bustling Squalicum Harbor. Its luxuriously appointed rooms are augmented by a lighthouse suite ensconced in its own tower. Rooms have gas fireplaces and private balconies for lounging and dining. The pleasant Harborside Bistro and comfortable bar have grand views across Bellingham Bay to Lummi Island. There's also an adjacent spa and boutique shopping area. **Pros:** beautiful bay views; large private dock; European feel. **Cons:** hub for groups; small pets in public areas; a bit pricey for Bellingham. ⊠ *1 Bellwether Way, Squalicum Harbor Marina* ☎ *360/392–3100 or 877/411–1200* 🖷 *360/392–3101* ⊕ *www.hotelbellwether.com* ⇨ *50 rooms, 15 suites, 1 lighthouse suite* ⌂ *In-room: a/c, DVD, Wi-Fi. In-hotel: restaurant, bar, gym, bicycles, Wi-Fi hotspot* ⊟ *AE, D, DC, MC, V.*

NIGHTLIFE AND THE ARTS

Boundary Bay Brewery & Bistro (⊠ *1107 Railroad Ave.* ☎ *360/647–5593* ⊕ *www.bbaybrewery.com*) turns out well-regarded microbrews; it also happens to serve some of Bellingham's best food, and displays eclectic local art. **Mt. Baker Theatre** (⊠ *104 N. Commercial St.* ☎ *360/734–6080* ⊕ *www.mountbakertheatre.com*), a restored vaudeville-era theater, has a 110-foot-tall Moorish tower and a lobby fashioned after a Spanish galleon. Home to the Whatcom Symphony Orchestra, it's also a venue for movies and headline performers. The mellowest place in Bellingham for a beer is the **Up and Up** (⊠ *1234 N. State St.* ☎ *360/733–9739*).

SPORTS AND THE OUTDOORS

WHALE-
WATCHING
Island Mariner Cruises (⊠ *5 Squalicum Harbor Loop* ☎ *360/734–8866* ⊕ *www.orcawatch.com*) conducts whale-watching and nature cruises to the Queen Charlotte Islands and Alaska, and sunset cruises around Bellingham Bay. **Victoria/San Juan Cruises** (⊠ *355 Harris Ave., inside Bellingham Cruise Terminal* ☎ *360/738–8099 or 800/443–4552* ⊕ *www.whales.com*) sails to Victoria, British Columbia, and the San Juan Islands on daylong or overnight trips. Under the right conditions, the views of whales and sunsets cannot be beat.

The Puget Sound and San Juan Islands

WORD OF MOUTH

"Our favorite is Whidbey Island, it's closer than the San Juans, you can drive onto the island at the north end and ferry back to the mainland, or Olympic Peninsula at the other. You won't find the resorts of the San Juans, but other than the Navy town of Oak Harbor it's a low key place with decent restaurants, historic spots and great views of Puget Sound."

—boom_boom

WELCOME TO THE PUGET SOUND AND SAN JUAN ISLANDS

TOP REASONS TO GO

★ **Bainbridge Island:** Take a peaceful stroll among trumpeter swans through the gardens of the Bloedel Reserve.

★ **Whidbey Island:** Gaze at the sparkling Strait of San Juan de Fuca from atop a windswept bluff at Ebey's Landing.

★ **Friday Harbor:** Spot whales and other sea life from a tour boat or sea kayak.

★ **Orcas Island:** Work out the kayaking kinks with a massage at the lovely seaside Rosario Spa & Resort.

★ **Lopez Island:** Rent a bike and cycle the scenic, sloping country roads.

1 The Puget Sound Islands. Seattleites never tire of day trips to Bainbridge, Whidbey, and Vashon islands, all reached via scenic trips on state ferries. Each island has its own pleasures: Bainbridge has swaths of coastal parkland and a winery. Whidbey has dramatic coastal trails dotted with historic forts and cute towns selling ice cream and antiques. Vashon has a distinct lack of attractions—beyond picnicking and biking, that is.

2 The San Juan Islands. With one of the islands named after the iconic orca, a trip to the San Juans is all about connecting with the sea. The excursion requires a bit more travel, planning, and expense, but that doesn't prevent tourists and Seattleites alike, who flock here to spot migrating whales. The most popular activities—boating and kayaking tours and seaplane rides—all include whale-watching, but each island has its share of parks, bluffs, and coastline to explore.

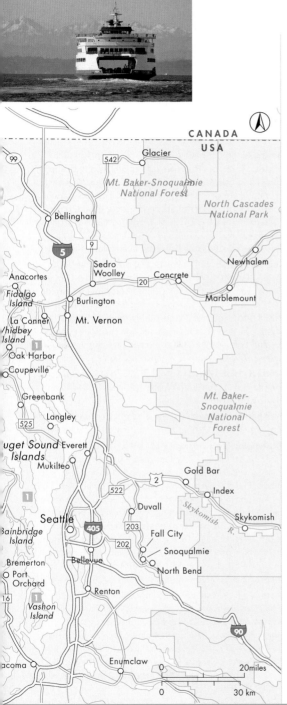

CANADA
USA

GETTING ORIENTED

The Puget Sound islands are at Seattle's doorstep, nestled between the mainland and the Olympic Peninsula. Both Bainbridge (directly west of Downtown) and Vashon (slightly more south of the city near the airport) are easily reached by ferry trips that take less than an hour. Whidbey is the northernmost island, and the largest, with several small towns and a naval base. It's the only island that can't be reached directly from Seattle, but it's also the only one easily reached by car through the town of Anacortes. The San Juan Islands are north of Whidbey, part of the same archipelago as the Gulf Islands of British Columbia—the San Juans are actually closer to Victoria, BC, than they are to Seattle. The closest Washington cities to them are Anacortes and Bellingham, about an hour and a half north of Seattle.

THE PUGET SOUND AND SAN JUAN ISLANDS PLANNER

When to Go

The Puget Sound region has a mild, maritime climate. Winter temperatures average in the low 40s, while summer temps average in the mid 70s. July and August are by far the most popular months to visit any of the islands. The San Juans, which are almost solely tourism destinations, get crowded during this time, with resorts, boating tours, and ferries filled to capacity. The Puget Sound islands are residential (Bainbridge and Vashon, in particular, are home to many Seattle commuters) and therefore tourism blends in more with daily activity. Still, expect to see bigger crowds on ferries and at restaurants and attractions. To beat the crowds and avoid the worst of the wet weather, visit in late spring or early fall—September and early October can be fair and stunningly gorgeous, as can May and early June (before schools let out for the summer). Hotel rates are generally lower everywhere during these shoulder seasons—and even lower once the winter drizzle starts—but be sure to check the calendar for major Seattle festivals that might drive up prices in the city, which is where you're likely to stay at least one night during your trip.

Getting Here and Around

Air Travel. Port of Friday Harbor is the main San Juan Islands airport, but there are also small airports on Lopez, Shaw, and Orcas islands. Seaplanes land on the waterfront at Friday Harbor and Roche Harbor on San Juan Island, Rosario Resort and West Sound on Orcas Island, and Fisherman Bay on Lopez Island. San Juan Islands flights are linked with mainland airports at Anacortes, Bellingham, Port Angeles, and Seattle-Tacoma International Airport. **Kenmore Air** (☎ 425/486–1257 or 866/435–9524 ⊕ www.kenmoreair.com) has regular flights from Seattle to Orcas, San Juan, and Lopez islands. **Northwest Seaplanes** (☎ 800/690–0086 ⊕ www.nwseaplanes.com) has service from Renton, south of Seattle, to San Juan, Orcas, and Lopez. The small propeller planes and seaplanes of Island Air and San Juan Airlines hop among the San Juans. All airlines have charter and sightseeing flights.

Contacts Island Air (☎ 360/378–2376 ⊕ www.sanjuanislandair.com). **San Juan Airlines** (☎ 800/874–4434 ⊕ www.sanjuanairlines.com).

Boat and Ferry Travel. *For more information on boat and ferry travel, see "Getting Here" in individual islands below.* **Washington State Ferries** (☎ 206/464–6400, 888/808–7977, 800/843–3779 automated line in WA and BC ⊕ www.wsdot.wa.gov/ferries) depart from two Seattle terminals (Pier 52 in downtown and Fauntleroy in West Seattle) for trips to Bainbridge and Vashon islands, respectively. Ferries from Mukilteo, about 45 minutes north of Seattle, sail to the southern tip of Whidbey Island. Anacortes, about 76 mi north of Seattle with a bridge connecting to the northern end of Whidbey, is a departure point for ferries to the San Juan Islands. That same ferry service also connects the San Juans to one another.

There is a ferry terminal in Bellingham, too, but it mostly serves private ferries and whale-watching cruises. **Victoria San Juan Cruises** (✉ Bellingham Cruise Terminal, 355 Harris Ave., No. 104, Bellingham ☎ 360/738–8099 or 888/443–4552 ⊕ www.whales.com), for example, has daily scheduled service in season to Orcas Island and Friday Harbor, as well as to Lopez Island and a few other smaller islands.

Getting Here and Around

Car Travel. Island roads have one or two lanes, and all carry two-way traffic. Slow down and hug the shoulder when passing another car on a one-lane road. Expect rough patches, potholes, fallen branches, wildlife, bicyclists, and other hazards—plus the distractions of sweeping water views. Be on the lookout for deer and rabbits. Carry food and water, since you may want to stop frequently to explore.

There are few car-rental agencies on the islands. **Angie's Cab Courier** (☎ *360/468–2227*) is the only office on Lopez. **M&W Rental Cars** (☎ *360/376–5266 Orcas, 360/376–5266 San Juan* ⊕ *www.sanjuanauto.com*) is the only agency on Orcas; they also have an office on San Juan. **Susie's Mopeds** (☎ *360/376–5244 or 800/532–0087* ⊕ *www.susiesmopeds.com*) rents cars and mopeds on San Juan. Summer rates for rentals run $50–$70 per day.

The Puget Sound Islands: You can reach Whidbey Island by heading north from Seattle or south from the Canadian border on I–5, west on Highway 20 onto Fidalgo Island, and south across Deception Pass Bridge. Interstate 5 is the main north–south route through western Whatcom and Skagit counties. From Tacoma or Bremerton, Bainbridge can be reached by car via Routes 16 W, 3 N, and 305 S, which crosses the Agate Pass Bridge.

San Juan Islands: To reach the San Juan Islands from Seattle, drive north on I–5 to Exit 230. From here, head west on Rte. 20 and follow signs to the ferry terminal in Anacortes. You may have to wait in long lines to take your car on the ferry. You can avoid the lines by leaving your car on the mainland and arranging for pickup service at the island ferry terminal. Most B&B owners provide this service with prior arrangement.

Travel Tips

The Washington State Ferries system can become overloaded during peak travel times, leading to lengthy waits at certain terminals, particularly for San Juan visitors bringing their vehicles aboard. Some of the ferries max out at 140 cars; some are even smaller, and on weekends arriving an hour before the ferry departure may not be enough time. It's rarely a problem to get a walk-on spot, although arriving a bit early to ensure you get a ticket is a good strategy, especially if you're traveling to the San Juans (the ferries to the Puget Sound Islands don't get quite as crowded). Expect to be delayed if you're headed toward the islands on Friday evening or Saturday morning. Backups are also likely when returning to the mainland on Sunday evening. Wait times vary depending on the route and terminal; contact **Washington State Ferries** for schedules, ferry terminal, and route information.

If traffic and ferry lines really aren't your thing, consider hopping aboard a seaplane for the quick flight from Seattle to the San Juan islands. **Kenmore Air** offers several departures from Seattle every day. Sure, the airfare isn't cheap—around $89–$130 each way—but the scenic, hour-long flight is an experience in itself. And the travel time saved is worth a pretty penny.

THE PUGET SOUND AND SAN JUAN ISLANDS PLANNER

Island Activities

Art enthusiasts will find excellent galleries and studios on Bainbridge and Whidbey islands. **Antiques shops** abound on these isles as well. And the islands of the Sound are becoming increasingly foodie-friendly, with bistros and cafés sprouting in sync with local organic farms. Vashon, in particular, has become known as a destination for lovers of locally sourced cuisine.

Beach walking is a favorite activity on Whidbey, which offers some of the region's most gorgeous strips of sand. Double Bluff and Ebey's Landing, in particular, are can't-miss destinations.

Cycling is particularly popular on the San Juan Islands, where there are multiday, island-hopping bicycle tours. Lopez and San Juan are delightfully bucolic (and relatively flat), while Orcas offers scenery as beautiful as its roads are hilly. During the summer, the San Juans are also a can't-miss **sea-kayaking** destination; outfitters offer paddles as brief as two hours or as long as a week. **Whale-watching**, whether from a charter boat, sea kayak, or ferry, is breathtaking, and the waters of the San Juans provide ample opportunities to view the majestic animals as they make their migrations.

About the Restaurants

The islands of Puget Sound offer top-notch restaurants serving local foods—including locally grown produce, seafood, and even island-raised beef. At the head of the pack is Vashon Island. There, small growers like Sea Breeze farm pride themselves on being "beyond organic," and island restaurants serve products from local farms. It doesn't get much more pastoral than this. Bainbridge, Whidbey, and the San Juans also have myriad small farms and restaurants serving local foods, and culinary agritourism—the recreational act of visiting local farmers, growers, and chefs at their places of business—is on the rise.

About the Hotels

For visits to the Puget Sound islands, most people stay in Seattle. This is particularly true for Bainbridge and Vashon islands, which don't have much to offer in terms of accommodations. Bainbridge has a few basic hotels close to the ferry terminal, but frankly, your money's better spent in Seattle. Whidbey, on the other hand, does have a few classic inns and B&Bs in the historic towns of Langley and Coupeville (as well as some nondescript chain hotels in the military town of Oak Harbor).

With the exception of Lopez Island, accommodations in the San Juans can be quite plush. Rosario Spa & Resort on Orcas Island is a favorite spot for special-occasion splurges. B&Bs and resorts are the best and most numerous properties in the San Juans, and although they can be pricey (you won't find a room for under $130), they have all the perks including on-site outfitters and tour operators.

WHAT IT COSTS IN U.S. DOLLARS					
	¢	$	$$	$$$	$$$$
Restaurants	under $10	$10–$17	$18–$24	$25–$30	over $30
Hotels		under $100	$100–$150	$151–$250	$251–$350	over $350

Restaurant prices are per person, for a main course at dinner. Hotel prices are for two people in a standard double room in high season, excluding tax.

Updated by
Carissa Blue-
stone & Holly
S. Smith

The coastal waters of the Pacific Northwest, between mainland Washington and Vancouver Island, contain hundreds of islands, some little more than sandbars, others rising 3,000 feet. Among these, the San Juans are considered by many to be the loveliest, but the islands of Puget Sound—particularly Bainbridge, Vashon, and Whidbey—are the easiest and most popular day trips for Seattle visitors.

About 80 mi northwest of Seattle, the San Juan Islands are a romantic's Valhalla. The rolling pastures, rocky shorelines, and thickly forested ridges of these isles are simply breathtaking, and their quaint villages draw art lovers, foodies, and burned out-city folk alike. Serene, well-appointed inns cater to visitors, and creative chefs operate small restaurants. Each of the San Juans maintains a distinct character, though all share in the archipelago's blessings of serene farmlands, unspoiled coves, blue-green or gray tidal waters, and radiant light. Offshore, seals haul out on sandbanks and orcas patrol the deep channels. Since the late 1990s, gray whales have begun to summer here, instead of heading north to their arctic breeding grounds; an occasional minke or humpback whale can also be seen frolicking in the kelp.

The Puget Sound islands offer spectacular scenery (starting with the ferry ride from Seattle) and a way of life even more laid-back than in the city itself—plus, they're easy to get to and easy to get around on. Bainbridge and Whidbey both have swaths of overdevelopment—Bainbridge is actually an island city of about 26,000—but their coastlines are still lovely and have miles of protected areas with inlets and bays and forest walks. Both islands still have farmland, though Bainbridge's is shrinking fast. You won't feel like you've gotten too far away from Seattle on either island, but their mix of outdoorsy fun and good restaurants are exactly why they're so popular. Vashon has more successfully held on to its agricultural roots despite an influx of Seattle commuters—it has the most greenery and least traffic of the three islands, plus plenty of beach parks with abundant bird and sea life.

THE PUGET SOUND ISLANDS

Whidbey Island has the most spectacular natural attractions, but it requires the biggest time commitment to get to (it's 30 mi northwest of Seattle). Bainbridge is the most developed island—it's something of a moneyed bedroom community—with a few decent restaurants and even a small winery supplementing its natural attractions. Vashon is the slowest and most pastoral of the islands—if you don't like leisurely strolls and bike rides, you might get bored there quickly. Bainbridge and Whidbey get tons of visitors in summer. Though you'll usually be able to snag a walk-on spot on the ferry, spaces for cars can fill up, so arrive early. You'll want a car on Whidbey (you can actually drive there, too). A car is handy on Bainbridge as well, especially if you want to tour the entire island. There's limited public transportation, which makes getting to some places, like the Bloedel Reserve, difficult. You can also tour Bainbridge on bicycle, just beware that there are some pretty intense hills. Vashon is best enjoyed on bicycle.

BAINBRIDGE ISLAND

35 mins west of Seattle by ferry.

Of the three main islands in Puget Sound, Bainbridge has by far the largest population of Seattle commuters. Certain parts of the island are dense enough to have rush-hour traffic problems, while other areas retain a semi-rural, small-town vibe. Longtime residents work hard to keep parks and protected areas out of the hands of condominium builders, and despite the increasing number of stressed-out commuters, the island still has resident artists, craftspeople, and old-timers who can't be bothered to venture into the big city. Though not as dramatic as Whidbey or as idyllic as Vashon, Bainbridge always makes for a pleasant day trip.

The ferry drops you off in the village of Winslow. Along its compact main street, Winslow Way, it's easy to while away an afternoon among the antiques shops, art galleries, bookstores, and cafés. There are two bike-rental shops in Winslow, too, if you plan on touring the island on two wheels. Getting out of town on a bike can be a bit nerve-wracking, as the traffic to and from the ferry terminal is thick, and there aren't a lot of dedicated bike lanes, but you'll soon be on quieter country roads. Be sure to ask for maps at the rental shop, and if you want to avoid the worst of the island's hills, ask the staff to go over your options with you before you set out.

GETTING HERE AND AROUND

Unless you're coming from Tacoma or points farther south, or from the Peninsula, the only way to get to Bainbridge is via the ferry from Pier 52 downtown. Round-trip fares start at $6.90 per person; $14.85 for car and driver. Crossing time is 35 minutes. If you confine your visit to the village of Winslow, as many visitors do, then you won't need anything other than a sturdy pair of walking shoes. Out on the island, besides driving or biking, the only way to get around is on buses provided by Kitsap Transit. Fares are only $2 one-way, but note that since routed buses are for commuters, they may not drop you off quite at the door-step of the park or attraction you're headed to. Be sure to study the route map carefully or call Kitsap at least a day in advance of your trip to inquire about their Dial-A-Ride services.

Contacts Kitsap Transit ☏ 800/422–2877 ⊕ www.kitsaptransit.com).

VISITOR INFORMATION

The **Chamber of Commerce** (☏ 866/805–3700 www.bainbridgechamber.com) operates a visitor's kiosk close to the ferry terminal, as well as a visitor's center at 395 Winslow Way E.

EXPLORING

Twice a year, the island's artists and craftspeople are in the spotlight with the **Bainbridge Island Studio Tour.** Participants put their best pieces on display for these three-day events, and you can buy everything from watercolors to furniture directly from the artists. Even if you can't make the official studio tours—held in mid-August and again in late November—check out the Web site, which has maps and information on studios and shops throughout the island, as well as links to artists' Web sites. Many of the shops have regular hours, and you can easily put together your own tour. ⊕ *www.bistudiotour.com*

Bainbridge Island Vineyards and Winery has 8 acres of grapes that pro-duce small batches of pinot noir, pinot gris, and Siegerrebe; it's the only winery in the Seattle area that grows all of its own grapes. Fruit wines are made from the seasonal offerings of neighboring farms. It's open for tastings Friday–Sunday 11–5. Tours are offered on Sunday at 2. If you first grab lunch provisions, you can picnic on the pretty grounds. ✉ *8989 Day Rd. E* ☏ *206/842–9463* ⊕ *www.bainbridgevineyards.com* ☻ *Closed Jan.–Mar.*

Fodor's Choice ★ The 150-acre **Bloedel Reserve** has fine Japanese gardens, a bird refuge, a moss garden, and other gardens planted with island flora. A French Renaissance–style mansion, the estate's showpiece, is surrounded by 2 mi of trails and ponds dotted with trumpeter swans. In 2009, the reserve was nominated as Garden of the Year by *Gardens Illustrated* magazine; it was one of only five gardens worldwide to receive the nomination. Dazzling rhododendrons and azaleas bloom in spring, and Japanese maples colorfully signal autumn's arrival. Picnicking is not permitted, and you'll want to leave the pooch behind—pets are not allowed on the property, even if they stay in the car. ✉ *7571 N.E. Dolphin Dr., 6 mi west of Winslow, via Hwy. 305* ☏ *206/842–7631* ⊕ *www.bloedelreserve.org* ✆ *$12* ☻ *Jun.–Aug., Wed.–Sat. 10–7, Sun. 10–4; Sept.–May, Wed.–Sun. 10–4.*

On the southwest side of the island is the lovely and tranquil 137-acre **Fort Ward State Park.** There are 2 mi of hiking trails through forest, a long stretch of sun-drenched beach, and even a spot for scuba diving. Along with views of the water and the Olympic Mountains, you might be lucky and get a crack view of Mt. Rainier—or of the massive sea lions that frequent the near-shore waters. A loop trail through the park is suitable for all ability levels, and will take you past vestiges of the park's previous life as a military installation. There are picnic tables

Bloedel Reserve, Bainbridge Island

in the park, but no other services are available. ✛ *Take Hwy. 305 out of Winslow; turn west on High School Rd. and follow signs to park* ☏ *206/842–3931* ⊕ *www.parks.wa.gov* ⊙ *Daily 8 AM–dusk.*

WHERE TO EAT

Many of the island's most reliable options are in Winslow—or close to it. You'll also find a major supermarket on the main stretch if you want to pick up some provisions for a picnic, though you can also easily do that in Seattle before you get on the ferry.

¢

BAKERY

✗ **Blackbird Bakery.** A great place to grab a cup of coffee and a snack before exploring the island, Blackbird serves up rich pastries and cakes along with quiche, soups, and a good selection of teas and espresso drinks. Though there is some nice window seating that allows you to watch the human parade on Winslow Way, the place gets very crowded, especially when the ferries come in, so you might want to take your order to go. ✉ *210 Winslow Way E, Winslow* ☏ *206/780–1322* ▭ *No credit cards* ⊙ *No dinner.*

$$$

BISTRO

✗ **Café Nola.** Café Nola is the best option for something a little fancier than pub grub or picnic fare. The bistro setting is pleasant, with pale yellow walls, white tablecloths, and jazz music, and there's a small patio area for alfresco dining. The food is basically American and European comfort cooking with a few modern twists. The lunch menu offers sandwiches, such as an open-faced Dungeness crab melt on foccacia; heartier mains include grilled Alaskan salmon or prawn puttanesca. At dinner, classics like Niman Ranch pork shank and pan-seared scallops steal the show. The restaurant is within walking distance of the main ferry terminal. ⊠ *101 Winslow Way E, Winslow* ☎ *206/842–3822* ⊕ *www. cafenola.com* ⊟ *AE, MC, V.*

¢–$ ✕**Harbor Public House.** An 1881 estate home overlooking Eagle Har-
SEAFOOD   bor was renovated to create this casual restaurant at Winslow's public
marina. Local seafood—including steamed mussels and clams—pub
burgers, and grilled flatiron steak sandwiches are typical fare, and there
are 12 beers on tap. This is where the kayaking and pleasure-boating
crowds come to dine in a relaxed, waterfront setting. When the sun
shines, the harbor-front deck is the place to be, and things get raucous
during Tuesday-night open-mike sessions. ⊠ *231 Parfitt Way SW, Win-
slow* ☎ *206/842–0969* ⊕ *www.harbourpub.com* ⊟ *AE, DC, MC, V.*

VASHON ISLAND

20–35 mins by ferry from West Seattle.

Vashon is the most peaceful and rural of the islands easily reached
from the city, home to fruit growers, rat-race dropouts, and Seattle
commuters.

Biking, strolling, picnicking, and kayaking are the main activities here.
A tour of the 13-mi-long island will take you down country lanes and
past orchards and lavender farms. There are several artists' studios
and galleries on the island, as well as a small commercial district in
the center of the island, where a farmers' market is a highlight every
Saturday from May to October. The popular Strawberry Festival takes
place every July.

GETTING HERE

Washington State Ferries leave from Fauntleroy in West Seattle for the
20-minute ride to Vashon Island. The ferry docks at the northern tip of
the island. Round-trip fares are $4.45 per person or $19 for a car and
driver. There's limited bus service on the island, but the best way to get
around is by car or by bicycle.

VISITOR INFORMATION

Vashon-Maury Island Chamber of Commerce (⊠ *17205 Vashon Hwy. SW*
☎ *206/463–6217* ⊕ www.vashonchamber.com) is open Tuesday–Thursday 9–4.

The site w*www.vashonmap.com* is also a good source of information.

EXPLORING

Vashon has many parks and protected areas. **Jensen Point** has trails, a
swimming beach, and boat and kayak rentals. ⊕ *From the ferry ter-
minal, take Vashon Highway SW to S.W. Burton Drive and turn left.
Turn left on 97 Avenue SW and follow it around as it becomes S.W.
Harbor Drive.*

You can stroll along the beach at **Point Robinson Park,** which is very pic-
turesque thanks to **Point Robinson Lighthouse.** Free tours of the light-
house are given from noon to 4 on Sunday from mid-May through the
summer; call to arrange tours at other times. ☎ *206/463–9602* w*www.
vashonparkdistrict.org.*

Vashon Allied Arts Center is the best representative of the island's diverse
arts community, presenting monthly exhibits that span all mediums.

The gift shop sells smaller items like jewelry. ⊠ *19704 Vashon Hwy.* ☎ *206/463–5131* ☉ *Weekdays 10–5, Sat. noon–5.*

WHERE TO EAT

$–$$

AMERICAN

✕ **Hardware Store.** The restaurant's unusual name comes from its former incarnation as a mom-and-pop hardware shop—it occupies the oldest commercial building on Vashon, and certainly looks like a relic from the outside. Inside, you'll find a charming restaurant that's a cross between a bistro and an upscale diner. Breakfast highlights include rustic French toast and housemade granola. On the lunch menu you'll find simple sandwiches, salads, and burgers; dinner includes hearty old standbys like buttermilk fried chicken, pasta, meat loaf, and grilled salmon. A decent wine list focuses on Northwest and Californian wines. ⊠ *17601 Vashon Hwy. SW* ☎ *206/463–1800* ⊕ *www.thsrestaurant.com* ▤ *AE, MC, V.*

$$–$$$

NEW AMERICAN

✕ **La Boucherie.** As the retail and restaurant side of the "beyond organic" Sea Breeze Farm, this outpost of ultralocal cuisine serves meats, poultry, and produce grown on or very close to the property. As a result, the menu is highly seasonal, but it always highlights Vashon's growers and farmers. You can order à la carte, but the prix-fixe menu is the way to go. Recent highlights included handmade tagliatelle pasta with Brussels sprouts, bacon, and pine nuts; a grilled lamb chop with celeriac remoulade and lentils; and a grilled Merguez sausage with fingerling mashed potatoes and a fried farm egg. Reservations are essential, and the restaurant serves lunch and dinner on Friday and Saturday only. ⊠ *17635 100th Ave. SW* ☎ *206/567–4628* ⊕ *www.seabreezefarm.net* ▤ *MC, V.*

WHIDBEY ISLAND

20 mins by ferry from Mukilteo (5 mi south of Everett) across Possession Sound to Clinton.

Whidbey is a blend of low pastoral hills, evergreen and oak forests, meadows of wildflowers (including some endemic species), sandy beaches, and dramatic bluffs with a few pockets of unfortunate suburban sprawl. It's a great place for a scenic drive, for viewing sunsets over the water, for taking ridge hikes that give you uninterrupted views of the Strait of Juan de Fuca, and for boating or kayaking along the protected shorelines of Saratoga Passage, Holmes Harbor, Penn Cove, and Skagit Bay.

The best beaches are on the west side, where wooded and wildflower-bedecked bluffs drop steeply to sand or surf—which can cover the beaches at high tide and can be unexpectedly rough on this exposed shore. Both beaches and bluffs have great views of the shipping lanes and the Olympic Mountains. Maxwelton Beach, with its sand, driftwood, and amazing sunsets, is popular with the locals. Possession Point includes a park and a beach, but it's best known for its popular boat launch. West of Coupeville, Ft. Ebey State Park has a sandy spread and an incredible bluff trail; West Beach is a stormy patch north of the fort with mounds of driftwood.

GETTING HERE

You can reach Whidbey Island by heading north from Seattle on I–5, west on Route 20 onto Fidalgo Island, and south across Deception Pass Bridge. The Deception Pass Bridge links Whidbey to Fidalgo Island. From the bridge it's just a short drive to Anacortes, Fidalgo's main town and the terminus for ferries to the San Juan Islands. It's easier—and more pleasant—to take the 20-minute ferry trip from Mukilteo (30 mi northwest of Seattle) to Clinton, on Whidbey's south end. It's a great way to watch gulls, terns, sailboats, and the occasional orca, gray whale, or bald eagle—not to mention the surrounding scenery, which takes in Camano Island and the North Cascades. Be sure to look at a map before choosing your point of entry; the ferry ride may not make sense if your main destination is Deception Pass State Park. Buses on Whidbey Island, provided by Island Transit, are free. Routes are fairly comprehensive, but keep in mind that Whidbey is big—it takes at least 35 minutes just to drive from the southern ferry terminal to the midway point at Coupeville—and if your itinerary is far-reaching, a car is your best bet.

Contact Island Transit (☎ 800/240–8747 ⊕ www.islandtransit.org).

VISITOR INFORMATION

Central Whidbey Chamber of Commerce (✉ 107 S. Main St., Coupeville ☎ 360/678–5434 ⊕ www.centralwhidbeychamber.com).

Langley/South Whidbey Chamber of Commerce (✉ 208 Anthes St., Langley ☎ 360/221–6765 ⊕ www.southwhidbeychamber.com).

LANGLEY

7 mi north of Clinton.

The historic village of Langley is above a 50-foot-high bluff overlooking Saratoga Passage, which separates Whidbey from Camano Island. A grassy terrace just above the beach is a great place for viewing birds on the water or in the air. On a clear day you can see Mt. Baker in the distance. Upscale boutiques selling art, glass, jewelry, books, and clothing line 1st and 2nd streets in the heart of town.

WHERE TO EAT AND STAY

$$–$$$
BISTRO
✕ **Prima Bistro.** Langley's most popular gathering spot occupies a second-story space on First Street, right above the Star Store Grocery. French cuisine is the headliner here; classic bistro dishes like steak frites, salade nicoise, and confit of duck leg are favorites. But Northwest food—and local, seasonal ingredients—are also present; Penn Cove mussels and oysters are popular. And the wine list is by far the best in town. The bistro's outdoor deck offers views of Saratoga Passage, Camano Island, and beyond, and ample heat lamps ensure that guests enjoy the beauty of Whidbey summer's night. ✉ 201½ 1st St. ☎ 360/221–4060 ⊕ www.primabistro.com ⊟ MC, V.

$$$–$$$$
Fodor's Choice
★
▦ **Inn at Langley.** Langley's most elegant inn, the concrete-and-wood Frank Lloyd Wright–inspired structure perches on a bluff above the beach, just steps from the center of town. Elegant, Asian-style guest rooms, all with fireplaces and balconies, have dramatic marine and mountain views. In-room highlights include open Jacuzzi tubs (all with

views of Saratoga Passage) and flat-panel televisions. The Inn's restaurant ($$$$; reservations essential), with its double-sided river-rock fireplace and full-view kitchen, is set above a pretty herb garden. In summer it serves sumptuous six-course dinners on Thursday, Friday, and Saturday at 7 and on Sunday at 6. During the off-season—October through May—dinner is served Friday–Sunday. **Pros:** island luxury; lovely views; amazing restaurant. **Cons:** some rooms can be on the small side; decor is starting to feel slightly dated. ⊠ *400 1st St.* ☎ *360/221–3033* ⊕ *www. innatlangley.com* ⤳ *28 rooms* ⚭ *In-room: a/c. In-hotel: restaurant, spa* ⊟ *AE, MC, V* ⦿ *CP.*

$–$$ 🛏 **Saratoga Inn.** At the edge of Langley, this cedar-shake, Nantucket-style accommodation is a short walk from the town's shops and restaurants, and it overlooks the waters of Saratoga Passage and the stunning North Cascades. Wood-shingle siding, gabled roofs, and wraparound porches lend the inn a neatly blended Euro–Northwest ambience. This theme extends to the interior, with wood floors and fireplaces. The carriage house, which has a deck as well as a bedroom with a king-size bed, a bathroom with a claw-foot tub, and a sitting area with a sleep sofa, offers more privacy. Included in the price are breakfast and a daily wine reception with hors d'oeuvres. **Pros:** breathtaking views; cozy interiors. **Cons:** a bit rustic; some small bathrooms. ⊠ *201 Cascade Ave.* ☎ *360/221–5801 or 800/698–2910* ⊕ *www.saratogainnwhidbeyisland. com* ⤳ *15 rooms, 1 carriage house* ⚭ *In-room: no a/c* ⊟ *AE, D, MC, V* ⦿ *BP.*

SHOPPING

At **Brackenwood Gallery** (⊠ *302 1st St.* ☎ *360/221–2978*) you can see pieces by Georgia Gerber, a famed island sculptor whose bronze pieces are regionally famous, and Bruce Morrow, whose Western-themed paintings and prints are popular. The gallery is closed on Tuesday.

Moonraker Books (⊠ *209 1st St.* ☎ *360/221–6962*) has been Langley's independent bookshop since 1972, and it stocks a wonderful array of fiction, nonfiction, cookbooks, and more. **Museo** (⊠ *215 1st St.* ☎ *360/221–7737* ⊕ *www.museo.cc*), a gallery and gift shop, carries contemporary art by recognized and emerging artists, including glass artists, of which there are many on Whidbey. **The Wayward Son** (⊠ *107-B 1st St.* ☎ *360/221–3911*) features the creations of local jeweler Sandrajean Wainwright, whose rings, bracelets, and pendants incorporate gemstones of all styles.

GREENBANK

14 mi northwest of Langely.

EXPLORING

★   About halfway up Whidbey Island is the hamlet of Greenbank, home to the 125-acre **Greenbank Farm**, a loganberry farm encircled by views of the Olympic and Cascade ranges. You can't miss the huge, chestnut-color, two-story barn with the wine vat out front, the centerpiece to this picturesque property. Volunteers harvest the loganberries—which are a cross between blackberries and raspberries—and turn them into rich jams and loganberry wine–filled chocolates. Greenbank's dessert wines can be sampled daily in the tasting room. The adjacent Whidbey Pies Café creates gourmet sandwiches, soups, and pies, all of which disappear quickly as visitors head for the scattered picnic tables, twisting meadow trails, and shimmering pond. Besides wildlife, be on the lookout for the herd of fluffy alpacas raised on-site by the Whidbey Island Alpacas company. The 1904 barn, which once housed a winery, is now a community center for farmers' markets, concerts, flea markets, and other events, including the famous Loganberry Festival each July. ⊠ *765 Wonn Rd.* ☎ *360/678–7700* ⊕ *www.greenbankfarm.com* ⌨ *Free* ☉ *Daily 10–5.*

The 53-acre **Meerkerk Rhododendron Gardens** contain 1,500 native and hybrid species of rhododendrons and more than 100,000 spring bulbs on 10 acres of display gardens with numerous walking trails and ponds. The flowers are in full bloom in April and May. Summer flowers and fall color provide interest later in the year. The 43 remaining acres are kept wild as a nature preserve. ⊠ *Hwy. 525 and Resort Rd.* ☎ *360/678–1912* ⊕ *www.meerkerkgardens.org* ⌨ *$8 (summer admission $5)* ☉ *Mar. 15–Sept. 15, daily 9–dusk; Sept. 16–Mar. 14, Weds.–Sun. 9–4.*

WHERE TO STAY

★
$$$

🏠 **Guest House Cottages.** Surrounded by 25 acres, each of these six private cabins, resembling cedar-sided barns with towering stone chimneys, comes with a feather bed, a Jacuzzi, country antiques, a kitchen, and a fireplace. The Cabin and the Tennessee and Kentucky cottages are built like classic log cabins; the colonial-style Farm Guest House has stained-glass windows and a private deck; the log cabin–style lodge has comfortable Northwest-style furnishings set around a river-rock fireplace. Rates include a continental breakfast on the first two days of your stay, and winter brings three-nights-for-the-price-of-two midweek specials. **Pros:** lots of privacy and amenities; good location between Langley and Coupeville. **Cons:** strict cancellation policy; basic breakfast foods are provided but you have to make your own. ⊠ *24371 State Route 525 E, Christianson Rd.* ☎ *360/678–3115 or 800/997–3115* ⊕ *www. guesthouselogcottages.com* ⌁ *6 cabins* ⌂ *In-room: no phone, a/c, kitchen, DVD. In-hotel: pool, gym, no kids* ═ *MC, V.*

COUPEVILLE

On the south shore of Penn Cove, 12 mi north of Greenbank.

Restored Victorian houses grace many of the streets in quiet Coupeville, Washington's second-oldest city. It also has one of the largest national historic districts in the state, and has been used for filming movies depicting 19th-century New England villages. Stores above the waterfront have maintained their old-fashioned character. Captain Thomas Coupe founded the town in 1852. His house was built the following year, and other houses and commercial buildings were built in the late 1800s. Even though Coupeville is the Island County seat, the town has a laid-back, almost 19th-century air.

EXPLORING

☾
Fodor'sChoice
★

Ebey's Landing National Historic Reserve encompasses a sand-and-cobble beach, bluffs with dramatic views down the Strait of Juan de Fuca, two state parks, and several privately held pioneer farms homesteaded in the early 1850s. The reserve, the first and largest of its kind, holds nearly 100 nationally registered historic structures, most of them from

This Historic Ferry House is part of Ebey's Landing National Historic Reserve on Whidbey Island.

the 19th century. Miles of trails lead along the beach and through the woods. Cedar Gulch, south of the main entrance to Ft. Ebey, has a lovely picnic area in a wooded ravine above the beach.

Ft. Casey State Park, on a bluff overlooking the Strait of Juan de Fuca and the Port Townsend ferry landing, was one of three forts built after 1890 to protect the entrance to Admiralty Inlet. Look for the concrete gun emplacement and a couple of 8-inch "disappearing" guns. The Admiralty Head Lighthouse Interpretive Center is north of the gunnery emplacements. There are also grassy picnic sites, rocky fishing spots, and a boat launch. ⊠ *2 mi west of Rte. 20* ☎ *360/678–4519* ⊕ *www. parks.wa.gov* ✉ *Free* ☽ *Daily sunrise–sunset.* In late May **Ft. Ebey State Park** blazes with native rhododendrons. West of Coupeville on Point Partridge, it has 645 acres of beaches, campsites in the woods, trails to the headlands, World War II gun emplacements, wildflower meadows, spectacular views down the Strait of Juan de Fuca, and a boggy pond. ⊠ *3 mi west of Rte. 20* ☎ *360/678–4636* ⊕ *www.parks.wa.gov* ✉ *Free* ☽ *Daily sunrise–sunset.*

☙ The **Island County Historical Museum** has exhibits on Whidbey's fishing, timber, and agricultural industries, and conducts tours and walks. The square-timber **Alexander Blockhouse** outside dates from 1855. Note the squared logs and dovetail joints of the corners—no overlapping log ends. This construction technique was favored by many western Washington pioneers. Several old-time canoes are exhibited in an open, roofed shelter. ⊠ *908 N.W. Alexander St.* ☎ *360/678–3310* ✉ *$3* ☽ *May–Sept., Mon.–Sat. 10–5, Sun. 11–5; Oct.–Apr., Mon.–Sat. 10–4, Sun. 11–4.*

WHERE TO EAT AND STAY

$–$$
AMERICAN

✕ **Christopher's on Whidbey.** A warm and casual place, Christopher's is in a house one block from the waterfront. The menu features many Whidbey favorites, including local oysters and mussels, and such flavorful fare as raspberry barbecued salmon, bacon-wrapped pork tenderloin with mushrooms, Penn Cove seafood stew, and linguine with a smoked-salmon cream sauce. The wine list is extensive. ⊠ *103 N.W. Coveland* ☎ *360/678–5480* ⊟ *AE, MC, V* ☹ *No dinner Sun.*

$$–$$$
Fodor's Choice
★
NEW AMERICAN

✕ **The Oystercatcher.** A dining destination for foodies from across the Northwest, the Oystercatcher is renowned for its local cuisine. The menu is crowded with Whidbey Island produce, seafood, meats, and cheeses, and is heavily influenced by fresh, in-season ingredients. Owners Joe and Jamie Martin have crafted an intimate, romantic dining space in the heart of town, and the restaurant's wine list is stellar. ⊠ *901 Grace St. NW* ☎ *360/678–0683* ⊕ *www.oystercatcherwhidbey. com* ⊟ *MC, V* ☹ *Closed Mon.–Wed. No lunch. Brunch offered Sun.*

$–$$

⌨ **Captain Whidbey Inn.** Almost a century old, this venerable madrone lodge on a wooded promontory offers a special kind of hospitality and charm now rarely found. Gleaming fir-paneled rooms and suites, which have pedestal sinks but share bathrooms, are furnished with antiques and modern amenities; quarters on the north side have views of Penn Cove. More luxurious Lagoon Rooms, in a separate cedar motel, over-look a quiet, marshy expanse. A cluster of small, one-bedroom cabins have stone fireplaces, private baths, and share a hot tub. The on-site Ship of Fools restaurant and tavern are popular with locals. **Pros:** private cabins with hot tubs; rustic yet comfortable. **Cons:** poor sound-proofing in the main inn; overpriced for rooms that share bathrooms. ⊠ *2072 Captain Whidbey Inn Rd., off Madrona Way* ☎ *360/678–4097 or 800/366–4097* ⊕ *www.captainwhidbey.com* ⇲ *23 rooms, 2 suites, 4 cabins* ⌂ *In-room: no phone (some), a/c (some), no TV. In-hotel: restaurant, bar* ⊟ *D, MC, V.*

$

⌨ **Compass Rose Bed and Breakfast.** Inside this stately 1890 Queen Anne Victorian a veritable museum of art, artifacts, and antiques awaits you. The proprietor's naval career carried him and his wife to all corners of the globe, from which they have collected the inn's unique adornments. The innkeepers' friendliness—and the location in the heart of Ebey's Landing National Historical Preserve—will make your stay all the more enjoyable and interesting. **Pros:** wonderful hosts; great breakfast; full of interesting antiques and collectibles. **Cons:** only two rooms, so it gets booked up fast. ⊠ *508 S. Main St.* ☎ *360/678–5318* ☎ *800/237–3881* ⊕ *www.compassrosebandb.com* ⇲ *2 rooms* ⌂ *In-room: no phone, no a/c, no TV* ⊟ *No credit cards* ⍟ *BP.*

OAK HARBOR
10 mi north of Coupeville.

Oak Harbor itself is the least attractive and least interesting part of Whidbey—it mainly exists to serve the Whidbey Island Naval Air Station, and therefore has none of the historic or pastoral charm of the rest of the island. It is, however, the largest town on the island and the one closest to Deception Pass State Park. In town, the marina, at the east side of the bay, has a picnic area with views of Saratoga Passage and the entrance of Penn Cove.

★ **Deception Pass State Park** has 19 mi of rocky shore and beaches, three freshwater lakes, and more than 38 mi of forest and meadow trails. Located 9 mi north of Oak Harbor, the park occupies the northernmost point of Whidbey Island and the southernmost tip of Fidalgo Island, on both sides of the Deception Pass Bridge. Park on Canoe Island and walk across the bridge for views of two dramatic saltwater gorges, whose tidal whirlpools have been known to swallow large logs. ⊠ *Rte. 20, 9 mi north of Oak Harbor* ☎ *360/675–2417* ⊕ *www.parks.wa.gov* ⊠ *Park free, campsite fees vary* ☉ *Apr.–Sept., daily 6:30 AM–dusk; Oct.–Mar., daily 8 AM–dusk.*

FIDALGO ISLAND

15 mi north of Oak Harbor.

The Deception Pass Bridge links Whidbey to Fidalgo, an island that hardly feels like one. (And it barely is: Fidalgo is separated from the mainland by the narrow waterways of Deception Pass to the south and the Swinomish Channel to the east.) Anacortes, Fidalgo's main town, has some well-preserved brick buildings along the waterfront, several well-maintained old commercial edifices downtown, and many beautiful older homes off the main drag. Still, it's little more than a waypoint for travelers heading to and from the San Juan Islands.

GETTING HERE

To reach Fidalgo, take the same route you would to reach the northern end of Whidbey Island: north from Seattle on I–5, west on Route 20 onto the island.

VISITOR INFORMATION

Anacortes Chamber of Commerce (⊠ *819 Commercial Ave., Suite G, Anacortes* ☎ *360/293–7911* ⊕ *www.anacortes.org*)

EXPLORING

The frequently changing exhibits at the **Anacortes History Museum** focus on the cultural heritage of Fidalgo and nearby Guemes Island. ⊠ *1305 8th St., Anacortes* ☎ *360/293–1915* ⊕ *museum.cityofanacortes.org* ⊠ *Free; donations accepted* ☉ *Mon.–Tues. and Thurs.–Sat. 10–4.*

West of Anacortes, near the ferry landing, **Washington Park** has dense forests, sunny meadows, trails, and a boat launch. A narrow loop road winds through woods to overlooks with views of islands and saltwater. You can picnic or camp under tall trees near the shore. There are six campsites with hookups ($22) and 27 tent sites ($16); restrooms and laundry facilities are at the park's exit. Only Anacortes residents are allowed to reserve campsites—first-come, first-served otherwise. ⊠ *12th St. and Oakes Ave.* ☎ *360/293–1927* ⊠ *Free* ☉ *Daily sunrise–sunset.*

WHERE TO EAT

$$ ✕ **Randy's Pier 61.** The dining room's nautical theme is in keeping with
SEAFOOD the waterfront setting. From here you can see across the channel to Guemes Island and the San Juans; don't be surprised if a sea lion looks

up from the tide rips or if a bald eagle cruises by. Specialties include seafood gumbo, crab cakes, salmon Wellington, crab-stuffed prawns, and a beautifully flavored (and expertly cooked) apples-and-almond salmon. While Randy's is far from haute cuisine, the staff is professional and friendly, and the food is consistently yummy. ⊠ *209 T Ave., Anacortes* ☎ *360/293–5108* w ▭ *AE, D, MC, V.*

SHOPPING

Compass Wines (⊠ *1405 Commercial Ave., Anacortes* ☎ *360/293–6500* ⊕ *www.compasswines.com*) may be the state's premier wine shop, with lots of hard-to-find vintages from small wineries whose annual releases sell out quickly. The focus here is on Washington wines, but the store carries an impressive selection of Californian and European vintages as well. Besides wines, Compass purveys artisan cheeses, provisions yachts and charter boats, and assembles delectable lunch baskets. If you're headed in for a tasting, be sure to wear a coat—the entire store is kept at cellar temperature.

THE SAN JUAN ISLANDS

In the course of a soggy, gray Northwest winter, Seattleites often dream of an escape, and the vision that fills their minds is usually of the San Juans. There are 176 named islands in the San Juan archipelago. Sixty are populated (though most have only a house or two), and 10 are state marine parks, some of which are accessible only to kayakers navigating the Cascadia Marine Trail.

The San Juan Islands have valleys and mountains where eagles soar, and forests and leafy glens where the tiny island deer browse. Even a species of prickly pear cactus (*Opuntia fragilis*) grows here. Beaches can be of sand or shingle, but all are scenic and invite beachcombers and kayakers to explore them. The islands are visited by ducks and swans, herons and hawks, otters and whales. The main draw of the islands is the great outdoors, but there's plenty to do once you've seen the whales or hiked. Each island, even tiny Lopez, has at least one commercial center, where you'll find shops, restaurants, and history museums. Not surprisingly, many artists take inspiration from the dramatic surroundings, and each island has a collection of galleries; Friday Harbor even has an impressive sculpture park and art museum. Lavender and alpaca farms, spas and yoga studios, whale museums and lighthouse tours—the San Juans have a little bit of everything.

Ferries stop at the four largest islands: Lopez, Shaw, Orcas, and San Juan. Others, many privately owned, can be reached by commuter ferries from Bellingham and Port Townsend. Seaplanes owned by local airlines regularly splash down near the public waterfronts and resort bays around San Juan, Orcas, and Lopez, while charters touch down in private waters away from the crowds.

■TIP→ **Orcas, Lopez, and San Juan islands are extremely popular in high season; securing hotel reservations in advance is essential. Car lines for the ferries during this time can experience very long delays because of limited capacity. If you're traveling light, consider walking or biking on. Lot**

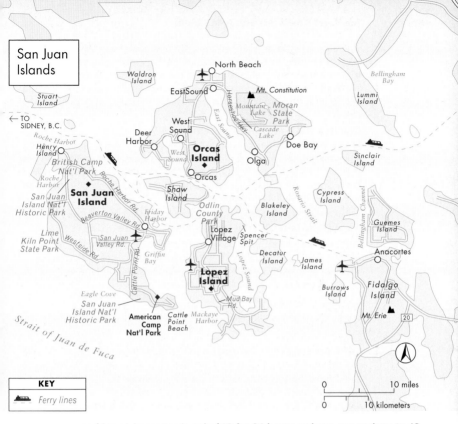

San Juan
Islands

Waldron
Island

North Beach

EastSound

Mt. Constitution

Bellingham
Bay

Stuart
Island

Lummi
Island

← TO
SIDNEY, B.C.

Roche Harbor

Henry
Island

British Camp
Nat'l Park

Roche
Harbor

San Juan
Island Nat'l
Historic Park

Deer
Harbor

West
Sound

West
Sound

Orcas
Island

Olga

Doe Bay

Sinclair
Island

Mountain
Lake

Moran
State
Park

Cascade
Lake

East Sound

Horseshoe Hwy

Orcas

Shaw
Island

Cypress
Island

Blakeley
Island

San Juan
Island

Friday
Harbor

Odlin
County
Park

Lopez
Village

Spencer
Spit

Rosario Strait

Guemes
Island

Anacortes

Beaverton Valley Rd.

San Juan
Valley Rd.

Lime
Kiln Point
State Park

Westside Rd.

Griffin
Bay

Lopez
Island

Decatur
Island

James
Island

Lopez Sound

Bellingham Channel

Eagle Cove

San Juan
Island Nat'l
Historic Park

Cattle Point Rd.

American
Camp
Nat'l Park

Cattle
Point
Beach

Mackaye
Harbor

Mud Bay
Rd.

Burrows
Island

Fidalgo
Island

Mt. Erie

20

Strait of Juan de Fuca

KEY

Ferry lines

0   10 miles

0   10 kilometers

parking at Anacortes is only $10 for 24 hours and you can park up to 48
or 72 hours. Ferry lines are also far more common than in the winter
months; contact Washington State Ferries (☎ 888/808–7977 ⊕ *www.
wsdot.wa.gov/ferries*) before you travel.

LOPEZ ISLAND

45 min by ferry from Anacortes.

Known affectionately as "Slow-pez," the island closest to the mainland is a broad, bay-encircled bit of terrain amid sparkling blue seas, a
place where cabinlike homes are tucked into the woods, and boats are
moored in lonely coves. Of the three San Juan islands with facilities
to accommodate overnight visitors, Lopez has the smallest population
(approximately 2,200), and with its old orchards, weathered barns,
and rolling green pastures, it's the most rustic and least crowded during high season. Gently sloping roads cut wide curves through golden
farmlands and trace the edges of pebbly beaches, while peaceful trails
wind through thick patches of forest. Sweeping country views make
Lopez a favorite year-round biking locale, and except for the long hill
up from the ferry docks, most roads and designated bike paths are easy
enough for novices to negotiate.

The only settlement is Lopez Village, really just a cluster of cafés and boutique shops, as well as a summer market and outdoor theater, visitor information center, and grocery store. Other attractions—such as seasonal berry-picking farms, small wineries, kitschy galleries, intimate restaurants, and isolated bed-and-breakfasts—are scattered around the island.

GETTING HERE AND AROUND

Lopez Island is reached via Washington State Ferries from Anacortes. The crossing takes about 45 minutes. Round-trip fares are $13.45 per person, $36.80 for a car and driver. You can also fly directly to Lopez from Seattle on a seaplane or Cessna. One-way fares range from $89 to $149. The flight takes one hour.

Once on the island, the way to get around is either by car or by bicycle. There are bike-rental facilities by the ferry terminal.

Contacts Island Air (☎ 360/378–2376 ⊕ www.sanjuan-islandair.com).**Kenmore Air** ☎ 425/486–1257 or 866/435–9524 ⊕ www.kenmoreair.com). **Northwest Seaplanes** (☎ 800/690–0086 ⊕ www.nwseaplanes.com).**San Juan Airlines** (☎ 800/874–4434 ⊕ www.sanjuanairlines.com).

VISITOR INFORMATION

Lopez Island Chamber of Commerce (☎ 360/468–4664 ⊕ www.lopezisland.com).

EXPLORING

The **Lopez Island Historical Museum** has artifacts from the region's Native American tribes and early settlers, including some impressive ship and small-boat models and maps of local landmarks. ✉ *28 Washburn Pl., Lopez Village* ☎ *360/468–2049* ⊕ *www.lopezmuseum.org* ✉ *Donations accepted* ☉ *May–Sept., Wed.–Sun. noon–4, year-round by appointment.*

Lopez Island Vineyard is spread over 6 acres about 1 mi north of Lopez Village. The winery produces estate-grown white wines including Madeleine Angevine and Siegerrebe, as well as dessert wines, such as those made from raspberries, blackberries, and other local fruits. Red wines—including Malbec and cabernet sauvignon—are also made here, albeit with grapes grown in the warmer climates of eastern Washington. ✉ *724 Fisherman Bay Rd., north of Cross Rd.* ☎ *360/468–3644* ⊕ *www.lopezislandvineyards.com* ✉ *Free* ☉ *July and Aug., Wed.–Sat. noon–5; May, June, and Sept., Fri. noon–5; Apr. and Oct., Sat. noon–5.*

★ A quiet forest trail along beautiful **Shark Reef** leads to an isolated headland jutting out above the bay. The sounds of raucous barks and squeals mean you're nearly there, and eventually you may see throngs of seals and seagulls on the rocky islets across from the point. Bring binoculars to spot bald eagles in the trees as you walk, and to view sea otters frolicking in the waves near the shore. The trail starts at the Shark Reef Road parking lot south of Lopez Village, and it's a 15-minute walk to the headland. ✛ *Off Shark Reef Rd., 2 mi south of Lopez Island Airport* ✉ *Free* ☉ *Daily dawn–dusk.*

Spencer Spit State Park is on former Native American clamming, crabbing, and fishing grounds. The spit is a stop along the Cascadia Marine Trail for kayakers, and it's a good place for summer camping. Hike or bike-in sites are $14, and car camping sites are $24; there are a few

Continued on page 472

WHALE-WATCHING
IN THE PACIFIC NORTHWEST

The thrill of seeing whales in the wild is, for many, one of the most enduring memories of a trip to the Pacific Northwest. In this part of the world, you'll generally spot two species—gray whales and killer "orca" whales.

About 20,000 grays migrate up the West Coast in spring and back down again in early winter (a smaller group of gray whales live off the Oregon coast all summer). From late spring through early autumn about 80 orcas inhabit Washington's Puget Sound and BC's Georgia Strait. Although far fewer in number, the orcas live in pods and travel in predictable patterns; therefore chances are high that you will see a pod on any given trip. Some operators claim sighting rates of 90 percent; others offer guaranteed sightings, meaning that you can repeat the tour free of charge until you spot a whale.

COMMON PACIFIC NORTHWEST SPECIES

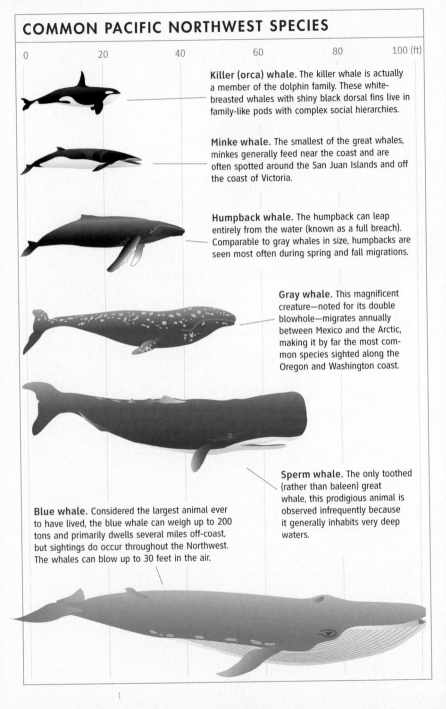

0   20   40   60   80   100 (ft)

Killer (orca) whale. The killer whale is actually a member of the dolphin family. These white-breasted whales with shiny black dorsal fins live in family-like pods with complex social hierarchies.

Minke whale. The smallest of the great whales, minkes generally feed near the coast and are often spotted around the San Juan Islands and off the coast of Victoria.

Humpback whale. The humpback can leap entirely from the water (known as a full breach). Comparable to gray whales in size, humpbacks are seen most often during spring and fall migrations.

Gray whale. This magnificent creature—noted for its double blowhole—migrates annually between Mexico and the Arctic, making it by far the most common species sighted along the Oregon and Washington coast.

Sperm whale. The only toothed (rather than baleen) great whale, this prodigious animal is observed infrequently because it generally inhabits very deep waters.

Blue whale. Considered the largest animal ever to have lived, the blue whale can weigh up to 200 tons and primarily dwells several miles off-coast, but sightings do occur throughout the Northwest. The whales can blow up to 30 feet in the air.

(

TAKING A TOUR

Spotting an orca in the Haro Strait between British Columbia and Washington

CHOOSING YOUR BOAT

The type of boat you choose does not affect how close you can get to the whales. For the safety of whales and humans, government regulations require boats to stay at least 100 meters (328 feet) from the pods, though closer encounters are possible if whales approach a boat when its engine is off.

Motor Launches. These cruisers carry from 30 to more than 80 passengers. They are comfortable, with washrooms, protection from the elements, and even snack-and-drink concessions. They can be either glass-enclosed or open-air.

Zodiacs. Open inflatable boats, Zodiacs carry about 12 passengers. They are smaller and more agile than cruisers and offer both an exciting ride bouncing over the waves and an eye-level view of the whales. Passengers are supplied with warm, waterproof survival suits. **Note: Zodiac tours are not recommended for people with back or neck problems, pregnant women, or small children.**

Most companies have naturalists on board as guides, as well as hydrophones that, if you get close enough, allow you to listen to the whales singing and vocalizing. Although the focus is on whales, you also have a good chance of spotting marine birds, Dall's porpoises, dolphins, seals, and sea lions, as well as other marine life. And, naturally, there's the scenery of forested islands, distant mountains, and craggy coastline.

MOTION SICKNESS

Seasickness isn't usually a problem in the sheltered waters of Puget Sound and the Georgia Strait, but seas can get choppy off the Washington and Oregon coasts. If you're not a good sailor, it's wise to wear a seasickness band or take anti-nausea medication. Ginger candy often works, too.

THE OREGON AND WASHINGTON COAST

A full breach in open waters is a thrilling sight

WHEN TO GO

Mid-December through mid-January is the best time for viewing the southbound migration, with April through mid-June the peak period for the northbound return (when whales swim closer to shore). Throughout summer, several hundred gray whales remain in Oregon waters, often feeding within close view of land. Mornings are often the best time for viewing, as it's more commonly overcast at this time, which means less glare and calmer seas. Try to watch for vapor or water expelled from whales' spouts on the horizon.

WHAT IT COSTS

Trips are generally 2 hours and prices for adults range from $25 to $35.

RECOMMENDED OUTFITTERS

Depoe Bay, with its sheltered, deepwater harbor, is Oregon's whale-watching capital, and here you'll find several outfitters.

Dockside Charters (☎ 800/733–8915, ⊕ www. docksidedepoebay.com) and **Tradewind Charters** (☎ 800/445–8730, ⊕ www. tradewindscharters.com) have excellent reputations. Offering a twist on the theme, **Tillamook Air Tours** (☎ 503/842–1942, ⊕ www. tillamookairtours.com) offers gray-whale flightseeing tours along the coast in restored 1942 Stinson Reliant V-77 aircraft.

Along the Washington coast, several of the fishing-charter companies in Westport offer seasonal whale-watching cruises, including **Deep Sea Charters** (☎ 800/562–0151, ⊕ www.deepseacharters.

biz) and **Ocean Charters** (☎ 800/562–0105, ⊕ www. oceanchartersinc.com).

BEST VIEWING FROM SHORE

Washington: On Long Beach Peninsula, the North Head Lighthouse at the mouth of the Columbia River, makes an excellent perch for whale sightings. Westport, farther up the coast at the mouth of Grays Harbor, is another great spot.

Oregon Coast: You can spot gray whales all summer long and especially during the spring migration—excellent locales include Neahkanie Mountain Overlook near Manzanita, Cape Lookout State Park, the Whale Watching Center in Depoe Bay, Cape Perpetua Interpretive Center in Yachats, and Cape Blanco Lighthouse near Port Orford.

PUGET SOUND AND GEORGIA STRAIT

Killer whales in the Puget Sound

WHEN TO GO

Prime time for viewing the three pods of orcas that inhabit this region's waterways is April through September. Less commonly, you may see minke, gray, and humpback whales around the same time.

WHAT IT COSTS

Trips in the San Juan waters are from 3 to 6 hrs and prices range from $59 to $99 per adult. Trips in Canada are generally 4 to 6 hrs and prices range from $115 to $175 per adult.

RECOMMENDED OUTFITTERS

Many tours depart from Friday Harbor on San Juan Island, among them **Salish Sea Charters** (☎ 877/560–5711, ⊕ www. salishsea. com), **San Juan Excursions** (☎ 800/809–4253, ⊕ www. watchwhales.com), and **Western Prince Cruises** (☎ 800/757–6722, ⊕ www.

orcawhalewatch.com). **Victoria/San Juan Cruises** (☎ 800/443–4552, ⊕ www. whales.com) offers both day- and overnight whale-watching cruises between Bellingham and Victoria.

One rather fortuitous approach to whale-watching is simply to ride one of the **Washington State Ferries** (☎ 888/808–7977, ⊕ www. wsdot.wa.gov/ferries) out of Anacortes through the San Juans. During the summer killer-whale season, naturalists work on the ferries and talk about the whales and other wildlife.

In Canada, **Wild Whales Vancouver** (☎ 604/699–2011, ⊕ www.whalesvancouver.com) departs from Granville Island on both glass-domed and open-air vessels. **Vancouver Whale Watch** (☎ 604/274–9565, ⊕ www.vancouverwhale-

watch.com) is another first-rate company.

Victoria has an even greater number of whale-watching outfitters. **Great Pacific Adventures** (☎ 877/733–6722, ⊕ www.greatpacificadventures.com), **Ocean Explorations** (☎ 888/442–6722, ⊕ www.oceanexplorations. com), **Springtide Whale Tours** (☎ 800/470–3474, ⊕ www.springtidecharters. com) and **Prince of Whales** (☎ 888/383–4884, ⊕ www. princeofwhales.com) use boats equipped with hydrophones. The latter also offer trips on a 74-passenger cruiser.

BEST VIEWING FROM SHORE

A prime spot for viewing orcas is Lime Kiln State Park, on the west side of San Juan Island. On the Canadian side, you can sometimes see whales right off Oak Bay in Victoria.

group sites for $40. It's also one of the few Washington beaches where cars are permitted. ✛ *2 mi northeast of Lopez Village via Port Stanley Rd.* ☎ *360/468–2251* 🎫 *Free* ⊗ *Mar.–Oct., daily 8–dusk.*

WHERE TO EAT AND STAY

$$–$$$ ✕ **Bay Café.** Boats dock right outside this pretty waterside mansion at
AMERICAN   the entrance to Fisherman Bay. In winter, sunlight streams into the window-framed dining room; in summer you can relax on the wraparound porch before a gorgeous sunset panorama. The menu is highlighted by Lopez Island beef and seafood tapas—such as basil prawns with saffron rice and sea scallops with sun-dried tomatoes. Homemade sorbet and a fine crème caramel are among the desserts. Weekend breakfasts draw huge crowds. ⊠ *9 Old Post Rd., Lopez Village* ☎ *360/468–3700* ⊕ *www.bay-cafe.com* 🖃 *AE, DC, MC, V* ⊗ *Closed Mon.–Wed. Oct.–May. No lunch.*

¢–$ ✕ **Holly B's Bakery.** Tucked into a small, cabinlike strip of businesses
★   set back from the water, this cozy, wood-paneled dining room is the
BAKERY   highlight of daytime dining in the village. Fresh pastries and big homemade breakfasts are the draws. Sunny summer mornings bring diners out onto the patio, where kids play and parents relax. ⊠ *Lopez Plaza* ☎ *360/468–2133* ⊕ *www.hollybsbakery.com* 🖃 *No credit cards* ⊗ *Closed Dec.–Mar. No dinner.*

$–$$ 🛏 **Edenwild.** This large Victorian-style farmhouse, surrounded by gardens and framed by Fisherman Bay, looks as if it's at least a century old, but it actually dates from 1988. Large rooms, each painted or papered in different pastel shades, are furnished with simple antiques; some have claw-foot tubs and brick fireplaces. The sunny dining room is a cheery breakfast spot. In summer you can sip tea on the wraparound ground-floor veranda or relax with a book on the garden patio. **Pros:** bicycles provided; nice breakfast buffet using local produce. **Cons:** few in-room amenities (no TVs, Wi-Fi, etc). ⊠ *132 Lopez Rd., Lopez Village* ☎ *360/468–3238 or 800/606–0662* ⊕ *www.edenwildinn.com* 🛏 *6 rooms, 2 suites* ⚲ *In-room: a/c, no TV. In-hotel: no kids under 12* 🖃 *MC, V* ⊗❙*BP.*

$$ 🛏 **Mackaye Harbor Inn.** This former sea captain's house, built in 1904, rises two stories above the beach at the southern end of the island. Rooms have golden-oak and brass details and wicker furniture; three have views of MacKaye Harbor. Breakfast includes Scandinavian specialties like Finnish pancakes; tea, coffee, and chocolates are served in the evening. Rooms are simple, with colorful coverlets. The Harbor Suite has a private bath, deck, and fireplace. Kayaks are available for rent, and mountain bikes are complimentary. **Pros:** fantastic water views; bikes and kayaks available; attentive hosts. **Cons:** on the far end of the island; several miles from the ferry terminal and airport. ⊠ *949 MacKaye Harbor Rd., Lopez Village* ☎ *360/468–2253 or 888/314–6140* ⊕ *www.mackayeharborinn.com* 🛏 *4 rooms, 2 with bath; 1 suite* ⚲ *In-room: no phone, a/c, no TV. In-hotel: beachfront, bicycles* 🖃 *MC, V* ⊗❙*BP.*

SPORTS AND THE OUTDOORS

BICYCLING   Mountain-bike rental rates start at around $7 an hour and $30 a day. Reservations are recommended, particularly in summer.

Cascadia Kayak & Bike (✉ *Lopez Village* ☎ *360/468–3008* ⊕ *www.cascadiakayakandbike.com*) makes deliveries to the ferry docks or to your hotel, for an extra $10, has a full repair shop, and organizes bike tours. **Lopez Bicycle Works** (✉ *2847 Fisherman Bay Rd.* ☎ *360/468–2847* ⊕ *www.lopezbicycleworks.com*), at the marina 4 mi from the ferry, can bring bicycles to your door or the ferry. In addition to cruisers and mountain bikes, Lopez Bicycle Works rents tandem ($20 per hour/$70 per day) and recumbent ($45 per hour/$60 per day) bikes.

SEA KAYAKING **Cascadia Kayak & Bike** (✉ *Lopez Village* ☎ *360/468–3008* ⊕ *www.cascadiakayakandbike.com*) rents kayaks for half days ($45) or full days ($55) and organizes half-day ($69), full-day ($99), or multiday ($300–$400) guided tours. Hour-long private lessons are available, too, if you need a little coaching before going out on your own.

Elakah! Expeditions (☎ *360/734–7270 or 800/434–7270* ⊕ *www.elakah.com*), a family-run sea-kayaking company, leads kayaking clinics on Lopez and two- to five-day trips ($225 to $495) around the San Juans. Specialty trips, such as tours for women only, are also organized. **Lopez Kayaks** (☎ *360/468–2847* ⊕ *www.lopezkayaks.com*), open May to October at Fisherman Bay, has a huge selection of kayaks, both plastic and fiberglass touring models. Rentals start at $15 an hour or $40 per day, and the company can deliver kayaks to any point on the island for an additional $10 fee.

SHOPPING

The **Chimera Gallery** (✉ *Village Rd.* ☎ *360/468–3265*), a local artists' cooperative, exhibits and sells crafts, jewelry, and fine art. **Islehaven Books** (✉ *Village Rd.* ☎ *360/468–2132*) is stocked with publications on San Juan Islands history and activities, as well as books about the Pacific Northwest. There's also a good selection of mysteries, literary novels, children's books, and craft kits, plus greeting cards, art prints, and maps. Many of the items sold here are the works of local writers, artists, and photographers.

ORCAS ISLAND

75 mins by ferry from Anacortes.

Orcas Island, the largest of the San Juans, is blessed with wide, pastoral valleys and scenic ridges that rise high above the neighboring waters. (At 2,409 feet, Orcas's Mt. Constitution is the highest peak in the San Juans.) Spanish explorers set foot here in 1791, and the island is actually named for their ship—not for the black-and-white whales that frolic in the surrounding waters. The island was also the home of Native American tribes, whose history is reflected in such places as Pole Pass, where the Lummi people used kelp and cedar-bark nets to catch ducks, and Massacre Bay, where in 1858 a tribe from southeast Alaska attacked a Lummi fishing village.

Today farmers, fishermen, artists, retirees, and summer-home owners make up the population of about 4,500. Houses are spaced far apart, and the island's few towns typically have just one major road running through them. Resorts dotting the island's edges are evidence of the thriving local tourism industry. The beauty of this island is beyond compare; Orcas is a favorite place for weekend getaways from the Seattle area any time of the year, as well as one of the state's top settings for summer weddings.

GETTING HERE AND AROUND

Orcas Island is reached via Washington State Ferries from Anacortes to Orcas Village in the Westsound area of the island. The crossing takes about 1 hour 10 minutes. Round-trip fares are $13.45 per person, $44.15 for a car and driver. You can also fly directly to Orcas from Seattle by seaplane or Cessna. One-way fares range from $89 to $149. The flight takes one hour. Planes land at Deer Harbor, Eastsound, Westsound, and at the Rosario Spa & Resort.

Once on the island the best way to get around is either by car or by bicycle. Most resorts offer transfers from the ferry terminal. A public shuttle bus operates from the terminal in July and August, stopping at each major town and Moran State Park. Fares are $6 one-way or $12 for a day pass.

Contacts Orcas Island Shuttle Bus ☎ *360/376–7433* ⊕ *www. orcasislandshuttle.com).*

Island Air (☎ *360/378–2376* ⊕ *www.sanjuan-islandair.com).* **Kenmore Air** ☎ *425/486–1257 or 866/435–9524* ⊕ *www.kenmoreair.com).* **Northwest Seaplanes** (☎ *800/690–0086* ⊕ *www.nwseaplanes.com).* **San Juan Airlines** (☎ *800/874–4434* ⊕ *www.sanjuanairlines.com).*

VISITOR INFORMATION

Orcas Island Chamber of Commerce (☎ *360/376–2273* ⊕ *www. orcasislandchamber.com).*

EXPLORING

Eastsound, the main town, lies at the head of the East Sound channel, which nearly divides the island in two. Small shops here sell jewelry, pottery, and crafts by local artisans. Along Prune Alley is a handful of stores and restaurants.

↻   The **Funhouse** is a huge, nonprofit activity center and museum for families. Interactive exhibits on age, hearing, kinetics, and video production, among other subjects, are all educational. Kids can explore an arts-and-crafts yurt, a climbing wall, a library, Internet stations, and a big metal "Jupiter" tree fort. Sports activities include indoor pitching cages and games, as well as an outdoor playground. Kids and adults can also take classes on music, theater, digital film, and poetry. There are free programs for preteens and teenagers on Friday and Saturday nights from 6 to 11 (hint to Mom and Dad, who might want to enjoy dinner alone on this romantic island). ✉ *30 Pea Patch La., Eastsound* ☎ *360/376-7177* ⊕ *www.thefunhouse.org* 🎫 *$7* ☽ *Sept.–June, weekdays 3–5:30; July and Aug., Wed.–Sat. 11–5.*

★   **Moran State Park** comprises 5,000 acres of hilly, old-growth forests dotted with sparkling lakes, in the middle of which rises Mt. Constitution. A drive to the summit affords exhilarating views of the islands, the Cascades, the Olympics, and Vancouver Island. You can explore the terrain along 14 hiking trails and choose from among 151 campsites if

Rosario Point at Rosario Resort, on Orcas Island in the San Juans

you'd like to stay longer (reservations are available May–Sept., or first-come, first-served at other times). ✛ *Star Rte. 22; head northeast from Eastsound on Horseshoe Hwy. and follow signs* ⬧ *Box 22, Eastsound 98245* ☎ *360/902–8844, 888/226–7688 for reservations* ⊕ *www.parks. wa.gov* ✉ *Camping $21–$28* ☉ *Daily dawn–dusk.*

WHERE TO EAT

$$
PACIFIC
NORTHWEST
Fodor'sChoice
★

✕ **The Inn at Ship Bay.** This boutique inn is just 1 mi from Eastsound, and the on-site restaurant may be the best dining experience on the island. Tucked into a renovated 1869 farmhouse, the dining room and bar offer a menu that's heavy on local, seasonal ingredients. Island greens, fruits, and seafood are served alongside a regionally focused wine list, and the results are spectacular. An example: during early summer, troll-caught king salmon is accompanied by local spring greens and a bing cherry/sweet herb dressing. Even the bread is memorable; the restaurant serves housemade sourdough from a starter that's more than 100 years old. ✉ *326 Olga Rd., Orcas Island* ☎ *877/276–7296* ⊕ *www.innatshipbay. com* ⊟ *AE, MC, V* ☉ *Closed Sun.–Mon. Oct.–May. No lunch.*

WHERE TO STAY

$$ ⬚ **Deer Harbor Inn.** This lodge has eight wood-paneled rooms, each with a balcony and peeled-log furniture. Four cottages—including one with three bedrooms—and the Harborview Suite have whirlpool tubs and propane fireplaces; two houses have kitchens and laundry facilities. The century-old apple orchard is lovely, making it a favorite spot for weddings. **Pros:** cute spa cabin for solo or couples' massage; cottages are good for longer stays. **Cons:** decor is a bit outdated; cottages are the best accommodations, but they're expensive and some require a

two-night minimum stay. ✛ *5½ mi southwest of West Sound via Deer Harbor Rd.* ☎ *360/376–4110* ⊕ *www.deerharborinn.com* ⌁ *8 rooms, 1 suite, 4 cottages, 2 houses* ⌂ *In-room: no phone, a/c, kitchen (some), no TV (some), Wi-Fi. In-hotel: restaurant, laundry facilities, Wi-Fi hotspot* ⊟ *AE, MC, V* ⓄⅠ *CP.*

$–$$ ▦ **Kingfish Inn.** Located on the quiet, lesser-visited shore of West Sound, the quaint little Kingfish boasts water views from three of its four rooms. (The West Sound marina is a stone's throw away.) Each room is equipped with a king or queen bed, private bath, and all the serenity a guest could ever want. The Club Suite, with a king and two single beds, is ideal for families. **Pros:** decor is less frilly or dated than most B&Bs; good café. **Cons:** small bathrooms; location isn't as secluded or special as some properties (expect some traffic noise). ✛ *7 mi southwest of Eastsound via Crow Valley Rd.* ☎ *360/376–4440* ⊕ *www.kingfishinn. com* ⌁ *3 rooms, 1 suite.* ⌂ *In-room: a/c. In-hotel: restaurant* ⊟ *MC, V.*

$$–$$$ ▦ **Rosario Spa & Resort.** Shipbuilding magnate Robert Moran built this Arts and Crafts–style mansion on Cascade Bay in 1906. It's now on the National Register of Historic Places and worth a visit even if you're not staying here. The house has retained its original Mission-style furniture and numerous antiques; its centerpiece, an Aeolian organ with 1,972 pipes, is used for year-round concerts in the music room. All 17 rooms are in a nearby waterfront building; all have views. You can hike, whale-watch, and kayak nearby or stay in for a day of pampering in the on-site spa. From your room you can watch seaplanes splash down in the bay and fishing and sailboat charters come into the marina. **Pros:** gorgeous location; historic mansion to explore; great spa. **Cons:** the guest rooms are the least special part of this property; often busy with weddings and special events; service has been uneven as the resort has transitioned to new ownership and undergone renovations. ⊠ *1400 Rosario Rd., Eastsound* ☎ *360/376–2222 or 800/562–8820* ⊕ *www.rosarioresort. com* ⌁ *17 rooms* ⌂ *In-room: a/c, Wi-Fi. In-hotel: 2 restaurants, bar, pools, gym, spa, Internet terminal* ⊟ *AE, DC, MC, V.*

$$–$$$ ▦ **Turtleback Farm Inn.** Eighty acres of meadow, forest, and farmland in the shadow of Turtleback Mountain surround this forest-green inn. Rooms are divided between the carefully restored late-19th-century green-clapboard farmhouse and the newer cedar Orchard House. All are well lighted and have hardwood floors, wood trim, and colorful curtains and quilts, some of which are made from the fleece of resident sheep. The inn is a favorite place for local weddings. Breakfast is in the dining room or on the deck overlooking Crow Valley, one of the island's most beautiful nooks. **Pros:** lovely grounds to stroll through; good location reasonably close to marina, ferries, and Moran State Park. **Cons:** Orchard House gets some traffic noise; two-night minimum stay often required. ⊠ *1981 Crow Valley Rd., Eastsound* ☎ *360/376–3914 or 800/376–4914* ⊕ *www.turtlebackinn.com* ⌁ *11 rooms* ⌂ *In-room: no phone, a/c, Wi-Fi, no TV* ⊟ *MC, V* ⓄⅠ *BP.*

SHOPPING

Crow Valley Pottery (⊠ *2274 Orcas Rd., Eastsound* ☎ *360/376–4260 or 877/512–8184* ⊕ *www.crowvalley.com*) carries ceramics, metalworks, blown glass, and sculptures. **Darvill's Bookstore** (⊠ *Eastsound*

☎ *360/376–2135*) specializes in literary fiction, nautical literature, local guidebooks, and more. **Orcas Island Artworks** (⊠ *Main St., Olga* ☎ *360/376–4408* ⊕ *www.orcasisland.com/artworks*) displays pottery, sculpture, jewelry, art glass, paintings, and quilts by resident artists.

SPORTS AND THE OUTDOORS

BICYCLES AND MOPEDS Mountain bikes rent for about $30 per day or $100 per week. Tandem, recumbent, and electric bikes rent for about $50 per day. Mopeds rent for $20 to $30 per hour or $60 to $70 per day.

Dolphin Bay Bicycles (⊠ *Orcas Village* ☎ *360/376–4157 or 360/376–6734* ⊕ *www.rockisland.com/~dolphin*), at the ferry landing, rents road, mountain, and BMX bikes for children and adults. **Orcas Moped Rentals** (⊠ *Orcas Village* ☎ *360/376–5266* ⊕ *www.orcasmopeds.com*), at the ferry landing, rents mopeds and bicycles. **Wildlife Cycles** (⊠ *Eastsound* ☎ *360/376–4708* ⊕ *www.wildlifecycles.com*) rents bikes and can recommend routes all over the island.

BOATING AND SAILING **Deer Harbor Charters** (⊠ *Deer Harbor* ☎ *360/376–5989 or 800/544–5758* ⊕ *www.deerharborcharters.com*), an eco-conscious outfitter (they were the first in the San Juans to use biodiesel), has several small sailboats making half-day cruises around the San Juans for marine-wildlife viewing. Rates are $69 to $75 per person. Outboards and skiffs are also available, as is fishing gear. **Orcas Boat Rentals** (⊠ *Deer Harbor* ☎ *360/376–7616* ⊕ *www.orcasboats.com*) has sailboats, outboards, and skiffs for full- and half-day trips. **West Beach Resort** (⊹ *3 mi west of Eastsound* ☎ *360/376–2240 or 800/937–8224* ⊕ *www.westbeachresort.com*) rents motorized boats, kayaks and canoes, and fishing gear.

SCUBA DIVING **West Beach Resort** (⊠ *West Beach* ☎ *360/376–2240 or 877/937–8224*) is a popular dive spot where you can fill your own tanks.

SEA KAYAKING All equipment is usually included in a rental package or tour. One-hour trips cost around $30; three-hour tours, about $50; day tours, $95–$120; and multiday tours, about $125 per day.

Crescent Beach Kayaks (⊠ *Eastsound* ☎ *360/376–2464* ⊕ *crescentbeachkayaks.com*) caters to families with free instruction and kayak rentals. **Orcas Outdoors Sea Kayak Tours** (⊠ *Orcas Village* ☎ *360/376–2222* ⊕ *www.orcasoutdoors.com*) has one-, two-, and three-hour journeys, as well as day trips, overnight tours, and rentals. **Shearwater Adventures** (⊠ *Eastsound* ☎ *360/376–4699* ⊕ *www.shearwaterkayaks.com*) holds kayaking classes and runs three-hour, day, and overnight tours from Rosario, Deer Harbor, West Beach, and Doe Bay resorts.

WHALE-WATCHING Cruises, which run about four hours, are scheduled daily in summer and once or twice weekly at other times. The cost is around $72 per person, and boats hold 20 to 40 people. Wear warm clothing and bring a snack.

Deer Harbor Charters (☎ *360/376–5989 or 800/544–5758* ⊕ *www.deerharborcharters.com*) has whale-watching cruises around the island straits. **Eclipse Charters** (☎ *360/376–6566* ⊕ *www.orcasislandwhales.com*) searches around Orcas Island for whale pods and other wildlife.

SAN JUAN ISLAND

45 mins by ferry from Orcas Island, 75 mins by ferry from Anacortes.

San Juan is the cultural and commercial hub of the archipelago that shares its name. Friday Harbor, the county seat, is larger and more vibrant than any of the towns on Orcas or Lopez, yet San Juan still has miles of rural roads, uncrowded beaches, and rolling woodlands. It's easy to get here, too, making San Juan the preferred destination for travelers who have time to visit only one island.

Lummi Indians were the first settlers on San Juan, with encampments along the north end of the island. North-end beaches were especially busy during the annual salmon migration, when hundreds of tribal members would gather along the shoreline to fish, cook, and exchange news. Many of the Lummi tribe were killed by smallpox and other imported diseases in the 18th and 19th centuries. Smallpox Bay was where tribal members plunged into the icy water to cool the fevers that came with the disease.

The 18th century brought explorers from England and Spain, but the island remained sparsely populated until the mid-1800s. From the 1880s Friday Harbor and its newspaper were controlled by lime-company owner and Republican bigwig John S. McMillin, who virtually ran San Juan Island as a personal fiefdom from 1886 until his death in 1936. The town's main street, rising from the harbor and ferry landing up the slopes of a modest hill, hasn't changed much in the past few decades, though the cafés and shops are snazzier now than they were in the 1960s and '70s.

GETTING HERE AND AROUND

San Juan is the most convenient Pacific Northwest island to visit, since you can take the ferry here and explore the entire island by public transportation or bicycle.

BY AIR You can fly directly to San Juan's Friday Harbor or Roche Harbor from Seattle on a seaplane or Cessna. One-way fares range from $89 to $149. The flight takes 30 minutes to one hour depending on the craft.

Contacts Island Air (☎ 360/378–2376 ⊕ www.sanjuan-islandair.com). **Kenmore Air** ☎ 425/486–1257 or 866/435–9524 ⊕ www.kenmoreair.com). **Northwest Seaplanes** (☎ 800/690–0086 ⊕ www.nwseaplanes.com). **San Juan Airlines** (☎ 800/874–4434 ⊕ www.sanjuanairlines.com).

BY BUS On San Juan Island, San Juan Transit & Tours operates shuttle buses from mid-May to mid-September. Hop on at Friday Harbor, the main town, to get to all the island's significant points and parks, including the San Juan Vineyards, Pelindaba Lavender Farm, Lime Kiln Point State Park, and Snug Harbor and Roche Harbor resorts. Note that only a few of the scheduled buses stop at all of these sights; some only stop at the vineyard, IMA Sculpture Park at Westcott Bay, and Roche Harbor, so be sure to check the schedule before you plan your day. Tickets are $5 one-way, or $15 for a day pass.

Contact San Juan Transit & Tours (☎ 360/378–8887 ⊕ sanjuantransit.com).

San Juan Island's Friday Harbor can be reached via Washington State Ferries from Anacortes. The crossing takes about an hour. Round-trip fares are $13.45 per person, $52.55 for a car and driver.

Clipper Navigation operates the passenger-only *Victoria Clipper* jet catamaran service between Pier 69 in Seattle and Friday Harbor. Boats leave daily in season (end of May through September) at 7:45 AM; reservations are strongly recommended. The journey costs $42.50 one way, $80 round-trip (kids under 11 are $21.25 one-way).

Victoria/San Juan Cruises sends *Island Commuter* ferries from the Bellingham Cruise Terminal in Bellingham to Friday Harbor via Orcas Island from May through September. Regular fares are $48 one way and $58 round-trip. There's a whale-watching-only option ($49) from Friday Harbor, or a combination cruise from Bellingham that includes the whale-watching trip ($89).

Contacts Clipper Navigation (☎ *250/382–8100 in Victoria, 206/448–5000 in Seattle, 800/888–2535 in the U.S.* ⊕ *www.clippervacations.com/ferry*). **Victoria/ San Juan Cruises** (☎ *360/738–8099 or 800/443–4552* ⊕ *www.islandcommuter. com*).

VISITOR INFORMATION
San Juan Islands Visitors Bureau (✉ *Box 98, Friday Harbor 98250* ☎ *360/468–3701 or 888/468–3701* ⊕ *www.visitsanjuans.com*).

EXPLORING

★ ☯ The **IMA Sculpture Park at Westcott Bay** is essentially a 19-acre open-air art gallery within the spectacular Westcott Bay Reserve. You can stroll along winding trails to view more than 100 sculptures spread amid freshwater and saltwater wetlands, open woods, blossoming fields, and rugged terrain. The park is also a haven for birds; more than 120 species nest and breed here. Art workshops and events are scheduled throughout the year in the tented area. ✉ *Westcott Dr. off Roche Harbor Rd.* ☎ *360/370–5050* ⊕ *www.sjima.org* 🎫 *Free* ☉ *Daily dawn–dusk.*

To watch whales cavorting in Haro Strait, head to **Lime Kiln Point State Park,** on San Juan's western side just 6 mi from Friday Harbor. A rocky coastal trail leads to lookout points and a little white 1914 lighthouse. The best period for sighting whales is from the end of April through August, but a resident pod of orcas regularly cruises past the point. This park is also a beautiful spot to soak in a summer sunset, with expansive views of Vancouver Island and beyond. ✉ *1567 Westside Rd.* ☎ *360/378–2044* ⊕ *www.parks.wa.gov* 🎫 *Free* ☉ *Daily 8 AM–dusk; lighthouse tours May–Sept. at 3 and 5.*

At **Pelindaba Lavender Farm,** a spectacular 20-acre valley is smothered with endless rows of fragrant purple-and-gold lavender blossoms. The oils are distilled for use in therapeutic, botanical, and household products, all created on-site. If you can't make it to the farm, stop at the outlet in the Friday Harbor Center on First Street, where you can buy their products and sample delicious lavender-infused baked goods and beverages. ✉ *33 Hawthorn La., Friday Harbor* ☎ *360/378–4248* ⊕ *www.pelindaba.com* 🎫 *Free* ☉ *May–Sept., daily 9:30–5:30; Closed Nov.–Apr.*

It's hard to believe that fashionable **Roche Harbor** at the northern end of San Juan Island was once the most important producer of builder's lime on the West Coast. In 1882 John S. McMillin gained control of the lime company and expanded production. But even in its heyday as a limestone quarrying village, Roche Harbor was known for abundant flowers and welcoming accommodations. McMillin transformed a bunkhouse into private lodgings for his invited guests, who included such notables as Teddy Roosevelt. The guesthouse is now the Hotel de Haro, which displays period photographs and artifacts in its lobby. The staff has maps of the old quarry, kilns, and the Mausoleum, an eerie Greek-inspired memorial to McMillin.

McMillin's heirs operated the quarries and plant until 1956, when they sold the company to the Tarte family. Although the old lime kilns still stand below the bluff, the company town has become a posh resort. Locals say it took two years for the limestone dust to wash off the trees around the harbor. McMillin's former home is now a restaurant, and workers' cottages have been transformed into comfortable visitors' lodgings. With its rose gardens, cobblestone waterfront, and well-manicured lawns, Roche Harbor retains the flavor of its days as a hangout for McMillin's powerful friends—especially since the sheltered harbor is very popular with well-to-do pleasure boaters.

★ ☾ **San Juan Island National Historic Park** commemorates the Pig War, in which the United States and Great Britain nearly went to war over their respective claims on the San Juan Islands. The dispute began in 1859 when an American settler killed a British soldier's pig, and escalated until roughly 500 American soldiers and 2,200 British soldiers with five warships were poised for battle. Fortunately, no blood was spilled, and the disagreement was finally settled in 1872 in the Americans' favor, with Kaiser Wilhelm I of Germany as arbitrator.

The park comprises two separate areas on opposite sides of the island. English Camp, in a sheltered cove of Garrison Bay on the northern end, includes a blockhouse, a commissary, and barracks. A popular (though steep) hike is to the top of Young Hill, from which you can get a great view of northwest side of the island. American Camp, on the southern end, has a visitor center and the remains of fortifications; it stretches along driftwood-strewn beaches. Many of the American Camp's walking trails are through prairie; in the evening, dozens of rabbits emerge from their warrens to nibble in the fields. Great views greet you from the top of the Mt. Finlayson Trail—if you're lucky, you might be able to see Mt. Baker and Mt. Rainier along with the Olympics. From June to August you can take guided hikes and see reenactments of 1860s-era military life. ✉ *American Camp, 6 mi southeast of Friday Harbor; English Camp, 9 mi northwest of Friday Harbor; park headquarters, 125 Spring St., Friday Harbor* ☎ *360/378–2240* ⊕ *www.nps.gov/sajh* ☞ *Free* ☉ *American Camp visitor center, June–Sept., daily 8:30–5; Oct.–May, Wed.–Sun. 8:30–4:30. English Camp visitor center, June–Sept., daily 9–5.*

☾ A stairwell painted with a life-size underwater mural leads you to the **Whale Museum.** Models of whales and whale skeletons, recordings of

A solitary boat in San Juan Island's Friday Harbor

whale sounds, and videos of whales are the attractions. Head around to the back of the first-floor shop to view maps of the latest orca pod trackings in the area. ⊠ *62 1st St. N, Friday Harbor* ☎ *360/378–4710* ⊕ *www.whale-museum.org* ▧ *$6* ⊗ *Daily 9–6.*

WHERE TO EAT AND STAY

$$–$$$
ECLECTIC

✕ **Backdoor Kitchen.** This local favorite has finally become known beyond San Juan County. As the name might indicate, it's a bit hard to find: The restaurant is tucked in an elegant courtyard a few blocks uphill from the water. The excellent service here complements the star dishes, which include fresh mahimahi baked in tomato-saffron broth, and a Vietnamese-style seared duck breast. Local greens and produce are used often, and the Northwest-heavy wine list cements the Backdoor's status as a regional gem. ⊠ *400B A St., Friday Harbor* ☎ *360/378–9540* ⊕ *backdoorkitchen.com* ▭ *AE, MC, V* ⊗ Closed Tues.

$$$–$$$$
PACIFIC
NORTHWEST
Fodor's Choice
★

✕ **Duck Soup Inn.** Blossoming vines thread over the cedar-shingled walls of this restaurant. Inside, island-inspired paintings and a flagstone fireplace are the background for creative meals served at comfortable booths. Everything is made from scratch daily, from the sourdough bruschetta to the ice cream. You might start with shrimp- and cheese-stuffed hot chilis, served with a lime-mango sauce and cilantro; or perhaps house-smoked Jones Family Farm oysters from Lopez Island. For a second course, you might have grilled Alaskan sea scallops or a juniper-rubbed filet mignon. Vegetarian options and child portions are available. An excellent selection of Northwest, Californian, and European wines is also on hand. ⊠ *50 Duck Soup La.* ☎ *360/378–4878* ⊕ *www.*

ducksoupinn.com ⊟ *MC, V* ⊗ *Closed Nov.–Mar.; Mon.–Thurs. Oct., Apr., and May; Mon. and Tues. in June; Mon. July–Sept. No lunch.*

¢–$ ╳**The Market Chef.** Only 50 yards from the ferry holding area, this café
CAFE makes some unbelievable sandwiches (try the roast-beef-and-rocket version, which is served on a house-baked roll with spicy chili aioli). The soups and deli items—including a decadent macaroni and cheese—are also top-notch. Beer, wine, juices, and espresso are served as well. There may be no better place to wait for your ferry to depart. ⊠ *225 A St., Friday Harbor* ☎ *360/378–4546* ⊟ *MC, V* ⊗ Open daily 10–4.

$$–$$$ ▦**Kirk House Bed and Breakfast.** Steel magnate Peter Kirk had this Crafts-
★ man bungalow built as a summer home in 1907. Rooms are all differ-ently decorated: the Garden Room has a botanical motif, the sunny Trellis Room is done in soft shades of yellow and green, and the Arbor Room has French doors leading out to the garden. You may take break-fast in the parlor—or have it in bed, served on antique Limoges china. Bountiful wicker-basket picnics, with all the trimmings, can be prepared for a day's excursion—but you might not need one after the full break-fast provided each morning. There is a two-night minimum stay in high season. **Pros:** gorgeous house full of lovely details liked stained-glass windows; within walking distance of town. **Cons:** some noise from nearby airport; some rooms are small and cluttered. ⊠ *595 Park St., Friday Harbor* ☎ *360/378–3757 or 800/639–2762* ⊕ *www.kirkhouse. net* ⤳ *4 rooms* ♨ *In-room: no phone, no a/c, DVD, Wi-Fi. In-hotel: no kids under 10* ⊟ *MC, V* ⓘ◎ⓘ *BP.*

$–$$ ▦**Roche Harbor Resort.** First a log trading post built in 1845, and later an 1880s lime-industry complex, including hotel, homes, and offices, this sprawling resort is still centered around the lime deposits that made John S. McMillin his fortune in the late 19th century. Rooms are filled with notable antiques, like the claw-foot tub where actor John Wayne used to soak. Luxury suites in the separate McMillin House have fire-places, heated bathroom floors, and panoramic water views from a private veranda. The beachside Company Town Cottages, once the homes of lime-company employees, have rustic exteriors but modern interiors. Elsewhere are contemporary condos with fireplaces; some have lofts and water views. Walking trails thread through the resplen-dent gardens and the old lime quarries. **Pros:** lots of different options for families and groups; very convenient for boaters docking at the marina; beautiful grounds. **Cons:** condos are nothing special and far from the resort; a bit isolated from the rest of the island if you don't have a car. ⊠ *248 Reuben Memorial Dr., 10 mi northwest of Friday Harbor off Roche Harbor Rd., Roche Harbor* ☎ *360/378–2155 or 800/451–8910* ⊕ *www.rocheharbor.com* ⤳ *16 rooms without bath, 18 suites, 9 cot-tages, 20 condos* ♨ *In-room: a/c, kitchen (some), refrigerator (some), DVD (some), no TV (some). In-hotel: 3 restaurants, tennis court, pool, spa* ⊟ *AE, MC, V.*

SHOPPING

Friday Harbor is the main shopping area, with dozens of shops sell-ing a variety of art, crafts, and clothing created by residents, as well as a bounty of island-grown produce. From May to September, the **San Juan Island Farmers' Market** (⊠ *2nd St., Friday Harbor* ☎ *360/378–5240*

⊕ *www.sjifarmersmarket.com*) fills a parking lot two blocks northwest of town on Saturday from 10 to 1.

Waterworks Gallery (✉ *315 Spring St., Friday Harbor* ☎ *360/378–3060* ⊕ *www.waterworksgallery.com*) represents eclectic, contemporary artists.

The **San Juan Vineyards** (✉ *3136 Roche Harbor Rd.* ☎ *360/378–9463* ⊕ *www.sanjuanvineyards.com*), 3 mi north of Friday Harbor, has a winery, tasting room, and gift shop, and organizes such special events as May barrel tastings, "Bottling Day" in July, volunteer grape harvesting in October, and winter wine classes and tastings.

SPORTS AND THE OUTDOORS

BEACHES **American Camp** (✛ *6 mi southeast of Friday Harbor* ☎ *360/468–3663*), part of San Juan Island National Historical Park, has 6 mi of public beach on the southern end of the island. **San Juan County Park** (✉ *380 Westside Rd., Friday Harbor* ☎ *360/378–2992*) has a wide gravel beachfront where orcas often frolic in summer, plus grassy lawns with picnic tables and a small campground.

BICYCLES AND MOPEDS You can rent standard, mountain, and BMX bikes for $30 per day or $100 per week. Tandem, recumbent, and electric bikes rent for about $50 per day. You can rent mopeds for $20 to $30 per hour or $60 to $70 per day. Make sure to reserve bikes and mopeds a few days ahead in summer.

Island Bicycles (✉ *380 Argyle Ave., Friday Harbor* ☎ *360/378–4941* ⊕ *www.islandbicycles.com*) is a full-service shop that rents bikes. **Susie's Mopeds** (✉ *125 Nichols, Friday Harbor* ☎ *360/376–5244 or 800/532–0087* ⊕ *www.susiesmopeds.com*) rents mopeds and bicycles. There is another location in Roche Harbor near the airport.

BOATING AND SAILING At public docks, high-season moorage rates are 75¢–$1.75 per foot (of vessel) per night.

Port of Friday Harbor (☎ *360/378–2688* ⊕ *www.portfridayharbor.org*) provides marina services including guest moorage, vessel assistance and repair, bareboat and skippered charters, overnight accommodations, and wildlife and whale-watching cruises. **Roche Harbor Marina** (☎ *360/378–2155* ⊕ *www.rocheharbor.com*) has a fuel dock, pool, grocery, and other guest services. **Snug Harbor Resort Marina** (☎ *360/378–4762* ⊕ *www.snugresort.com*) provides marina services and van service to and from Friday Harbor, including ferry and airport shuttle service, and rents small powerboats.

CHARTERS Charter sailboat cruises start at about $225 per day and run up to $400 per day for deluxe vessels. Charter powerboat trips start at about $150 per day. Extra costs for overnight cruises may include skipper fees ($150–$175), meals ($10–$15 per person daily), preboarding fees ($50–$100), and so on.

Cap' n Howard's Sailing Charters (☎ *360/378–3958 or 360/317–8421* ⊕ *www.capnhoward.com*) hires out full-size vessels for sailing excursions around the islands. **Charters Northwest** (☎ *800/426–2313* ⊕ *www. abcyachtcharters.com*) offers three-day and weeklong full-service sailboat and powerboat charters. **Harmony Charters** (☎ *360/468–3310*

⊕ *www.interisland.net/countess*) conducts daylong and multiday sailboat charters throughout the San Juan Islands and the Pacific Northwest.

SEA KAYAKING Many experienced kayakers bring their own vessels to the San Juans. But if you're a beginner or didn't bring your own kayak, you'll find many places to rent in Friday Harbor, as well as outfitters providing classes and tours. Be sure to make reservations in summer. One-hour trips start at $30, three-hour tours run about $50, day tours cost $90–$125, and overnight tours cost $100–$125 per day with meals. Equipment is always included in the cost.

A Leisure Kayak Rentals (☎ *360/378–5992 or 800/836–8224*) will shuttle you from the ferry to the start of your kayaking class; hourly, daily, and overnight tours are also scheduled. **Crystal Seas Kayaking** (☎ *360/378–4223 or 877/732–7877/625–7245* ⊕ *www.crystalseas.com*) has many trip options, including sunset tours and multisport tours that might include biking and camping. **Discovery Sea Kayaks** (☎ *360/378–2559 or 866/461–2559* ⊕ *www.discoveryseakayak.com*) offers both sea-kayaking adventures, including sunset trips and multiday excursions, and whale-watching tours. **San Juan Kayak Expeditions** (☎ *360/378–4436* ⊕ *www.sanjuankayak.com*) runs kayaking and camping tours in two-person kayaks. **Sea Quest** (☎ *360/378–5767 or 888/589–4253* ⊕ *www.sea-quest-kayak.com*) conducts kayak eco-tours with guides who are trained naturalists, biologists, and environmental scientists.

WHALE-WATCHING *For more information about whale-watching see our special feature in this chapter.*

Whale-watching expeditions run three to four hours and cost around $50 per person. ■TIP→ For the best experience, look for tour companies with small boats that accommodate no more than 20 or 30 people; if booking on a larger vessel, inquire whether or not they always fill the boat to capacity or leave a little breathing room. Bring warm clothing even if it's a warm day.

Island Adventures (☎ *360/293–2428 or 800/465–4604* ⊕ *www.island-adventures.com*) has two tours per day from June through August that get you right up next to the orcas. **San Juan Excursions** (☎ *360/378–6636 or 800/809–4253* ⊕ *www.watchwhales.com*) offers daily whale-watching cruises. **Western Prince Cruises** (☎ *360/378–5315 or 800/757–6722* ⊕ *www.orcawhalewatch.com*) operates a four-hour narrated whale-watching tour.

Olympic National Park

WITH THE OLYMPIC PENINSULA AND LONG BEACH PENINSULA

WORD OF MOUTH

"There are several lodges in Olympic National Park. They are in gorgeous locations but the rooms themselves aren't great, but that's not why you stay there. You stay for the opportunity to be in the gorgeous location.If you're looking for something nicer, the area between Port Angeles and Sequim has some lovely b and bs. Colette's is my favorite but there are others."

—NWWanderer

WELCOME TO OLYMPIC NATIONAL PARK

TOP REASONS TO GO

★ **Exotic rain forest:** A rain forest in the Pacific Northwest? Indeed, Olympic National Park is one of a few places in the world with this unique temperate landscape.

★ **Beachcombing:** Miles of spectacular, rugged coastline dotted with tidal pools, sea stacks, and driftwood hem the edges of the Olympic Peninsula.

★ **Nature's hot tubs:** Take a relaxing dip in the wooded heart of the park at the Sol Duc Hot Springs, a series of geothermal mineral pools.

★ **Lofty vistas:** The Olympics have plenty of peaks you can climb—or just drive up to Hurricane Ridge for endless views over the ranges.

★ **A sense of history:** The first evidence of humans on the Olympic Peninsula dates back 12,000 years. Today, eight tribes still have traditional ties to lands in Olympic National Park, and there are ample opportunities for exploring Native American history in and around the region.

1 Coastal Olympic.
Here the Pacific smashes endlessly into the rugged coastline, carving out some of the park's most memorable scenes in the massive, rocky sea stacks and islets just offshore. Back from the water are beaches and tide pools full of starfish, crabs, and anemones.

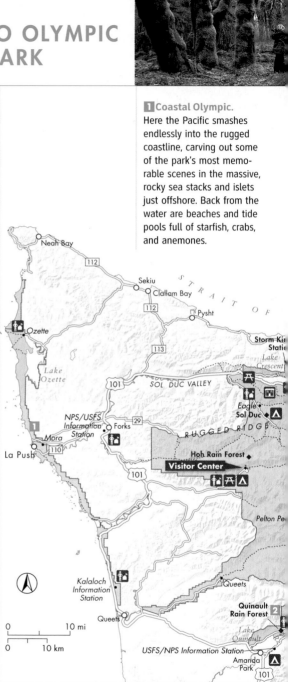

2 **The Rain Forest.** Centered on the Hoh, Queets, and Quinault river valleys, this is the region's most unique landscape. Fog-shrouded Douglas firs and Sitka spruces, some at more than 300 feet tall, huddle in this moist, pine-carpeted area, shading fern- and moss-draped cedars, maples, and alders.

3 **The Mountains.** Craggy gray peaks and snow-covered summits dominate the skyline. Low-level foliage and wildflower meadows make for excellent hiking in the plateaus. Even on the sunniest days, temperatures are brisk. Some roads are closed in winter months.

4 **Alpine Meadows.** In midsummer the swath of colors is like a Monet canvas spread over the landscape, and wildlife teems among the honeyed flowers. Trails are never prettier, and views are crisp and vast.

GETTING ORIENTED

The Olympic Peninsula's elegant snowcapped and forested landscape is edged on all sides by water: to the north, the Strait of Juan de Fuca separates the United States from Canada, a network of Puget Sound bays laces the east, the Chehalis River meanders along the southern end, and the massive gray Pacific Ocean guards the west side.

12

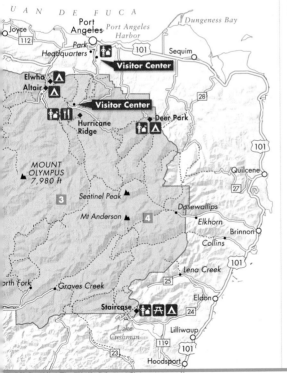

KEY	
👫	Ranger Station
⛺	Campground
🌲	Picnic Area
🍴	Restaurant
🏠	Lodge
🚶	Trailhead
🚻	Restrooms
⇘	Scenic Viewpoint
-----	Walking/Hiking Trails

OLYMPIC NATIONAL PARK PLANNER

When to Go

Summer, with its long stretches of sun-filled days, is prime touring time for Olympic National Park. **June through September are the peak months;** Hurricane Ridge, the Hoh Rain Forest, Lake Crescent, and Ruby Beach are bustling by 10 AM.

Late spring and early autumn are also good bets for clear weather; any time between April and October, and you'll have a good chance of fair skies. Between Thanksgiving and Easter, it's a toss-up as to which days will turn out fair; prepare for heavy clouds, rain showers, and chilly temperatures, then hope for the best.

Winter is a great time to visit if you enjoy isolation. Locals are usually the only hardy souls during this time, except for weekend skiers heading to the snowfields around Hurricane Ridge. Many visitor facilities have limited hours or are closed from October to April.

AVG. HIGH/LOW TEMPS.

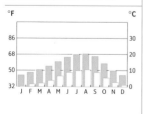

Flora and Fauna

Along the high mountain slopes hardy cedar, fir, and hemlock trees stand tough on the rugged land; the lower montane forests are filled with thickets of silver firs; and valleys stream with Douglas firs and western hemlock. The park's famous temperate rain forests are on the peninsula's western side, marked by broad western red cedars, towering red spruces, and ferns festooned with strands of mosses and patchwork lichens. This lower landscape is also home to some of the Northwest's largest trees: massive cedar and Sitka spruce near Lake Quinault can measure more than 700 inches around, and Douglas firs near the Queets and Hoh rivers are nearly as wide.

These landscapes are home to a variety of wildlife, including many large mammals and 15 creatures found nowhere else in the world. Hikers often come across Roosevelt's elk, black-tailed deer, mountain goats, beavers, raccoons, skunks, opossums, and foxes; Douglas squirrels and flying squirrels populate the heights of the forest. Less common are black bears (most prevalent from May through August); wolves, bobcats, and cougar are rarely seen. Birdlife includes bald eagles, red-tailed hawks, osprey, and great horned owls. Rivers and lakes are filled with freshwater fish, while beaches hold crabs, starfish, anemones, and other shelled creatures. Get out in a boat on the Pacific to spot seals, sea lions, and sea otters—and perhaps a pod of porpoises, orcas, or gray whales.

Beware of jellyfish around the shores—beached jellyfish can still sting. In the woods, check for ticks after every hike and after each shower. Biting nasties include black flies, horseflies, sand fleas, and the ever-present mosquitoes. Yellow-jacket nests populate tree hollows along many trails; signs throughout the Hoh Rain Forest warn hikers to move quickly through these sections. If one or two chase you, remain calm and keep walking; these are just "guards" making sure you're keeping away from the hive. Poison oak is common, so familiarize yourself with its appearance. Bug repellent, sunscreen, and long pants and sleeves will go a long way toward making your experience more comfortable.

12

Getting Here and Around

U.S. 101 essentially encircles the main section of Olympic National Park, and a number of roads lead from the highway into the park's mountains and toward its beaches. You can reach U.S. 101 via Interstate 5 at Olympia, via Route 12 at Aberdeen, or via Route 104 from the Washington State Ferries terminals at Bainbridge or Kingston. The ferries are the most direct route to the Olympic area from Seattle; contact **Washington State Ferries** (📞 888/808–7977, 800/843–3779, or 206/464–6400 ⊕ www.wsdot. wa.gov/ferries) for information. You can enter the park at a number of points, though access roads do not penetrate far, since the park is 95% wilderness. The best way to get around and to see many of the park's key sites is on foot.

Grays Harbor Transit (📞 360/532–2770 or 800/562–9730 ⊕ www.ghtransit.com) runs daily buses from Aberdeen, Hoquiam, and Forks to Amanda Park, on the west end of Lake Quinault. **West Jefferson Transit** (📞 360/385–4777 or 800/436–3950 ⊕ www.jeffersontransit.com) runs a Forks–Amanda Park route Monday through Saturday.

Good Reads

■ Robert L. Wood's *Olympic Mountain Trail Guide* is a great resource for both day hikers and those planning longer excursions.

■ Stephen Whitney's *A Field Guide to the Cascades and Olympics* is an excellent trailside reference, covering more than 500 plant and animal species found in the park.

■ The park's newspaper, the *Olympic Bugler*, is a seasonal guide for activities and opportunities in the park. You can pick it up at the visitor centers. A handy online catalog of books, maps, and passes for Northwest parks is available from **Discover Your Northwest** (📞 877/874–6775 ⊕ www. discovernw.org).

Festivals and Events

MAY Irrigation Festival. Highlights of this Sequim festival include an antique-car show, logging demonstrations, arts and crafts, dancing, and a parade. 📞 360/683–6197 ⊕ www.irrigationfestival.com.

JUNE–AUG. Centrum Summer Arts Festival. Fort Worden State Park, a 19th-century army base near Port Townsend, stages a summer-long lineup of concerts and workshops. 📞 360/385–3102 ⊕ www.centrum.org.

JUNE–SEPT Olympic Music Festival. A variety of classical concerts are performed in a renovated barn; picnic on the farm while you listen. 📞 360/732–4800 ⊕ www. olympicmusicfestival.org.

JULY Fourth of July. A salmon bake, a parade, a demolition derby, and arts and crafts exhibits mark Forks' celebration. 📞 360/374–2531 or 800/443–6757.

Lavender Festival. Mid-month, a street fair and farm tours celebrate Sequim's many fragrant lavender fields. 📞 360/681–3035 or 877/681–3035 ⊕ www. lavenderfestival.com.

SEPT Wooden Boat Festival. Hundreds of antique boats sail into Port Townsend. 📞 360/385–3628 ⊕ www. woodenboat.org.

Updated by
Shelley Arenas
& Holly S.
Smith

A spellbinding setting is tucked into the country's far-northwestern corner, within the heart-shaped Olympic Peninsula. Edged on all sides by water, the forested landscape is remote and pristine, and works its way around the sharpened ridges of the snow-capped Olympic Mountains.

Big lakes cut pockets of blue in the rugged blanket of pine forests, and hot springs gurgle up from the foothills. Along the coast the sights are even more enchanting: wave-sculpted boulders, tidal pools teeming with sealife, and tree-topped sea stacks.

PARK ESSENTIALS

ACCESSIBILITY
There are wheelchair-accessible facilities—including trails, campgrounds, and visitor centers—throughout the park; contact visitor centers for more information.

ADMISSION FEES AND PERMITS
Seven-day vehicle admission fee is $15; individuals on bike, foot, or motorcycle are $5; an annual pass is $30. An overnight wilderness permit, available at visitor centers and ranger stations, is $5 (covers registration of your party for up to 14 days), plus $2 per person per night. A frequent-hiker pass, which covers all wilderness use fees, is $30 per year. Fishing in freshwater streams and lakes within Olympic National Park does not require a Washington State fishing license; however, anglers must acquire a salmon-steelhead punch card when fishing for those species. Ocean fishing and harvesting shellfish and seaweed require licenses, which are available at sporting goods and outdoor supply stores.

ADMISSION HOURS
Six park entrances are open 24/7; gate kiosk hours (for buying passes) vary widely according to season and location, but most kiosks are staffed during daylight hours. Olympic National Park is located in the Pacific time zone.

ATMS/BANKS

If you'll need cash for kayak rentals, groceries, or souvenirs during your visit, stop in the nearby towns before entering the park—several gas stations near the park in Port Angeles and Forks have ATMs, and major banks and grocery chains with ATMs are found in these towns and in Sequim.

CELL-PHONE RECEPTION

Note that there is no cell-phone reception in wilderness areas. There are public telephones at the Olympic National Park Visitor Center, Hoh River Rain Forest Visitor Center, and the lodging properties within the park—Lake Crescent, Kalaloch, and Sol Duc Hot Springs. Fairholm General Store also has a phone.

PARK CONTACT INFORMATION

Olympic National Park. ⊠ *600 E. Park Ave., Port Angeles, WA* ☎ *360/565–3130* ⊕ *www.nps.gov/olym.*

VISITOR CENTERS

Forks Park and Forest Information Center. The office has park maps and brochures; they also provide permits and rent bear-proof containers. ⊠ *U.S. 101, Forks* ☎ *No phone* ⊕ *www.nps.gov/olym* ⊗ *June–Aug., daily 9–4; Sept.–May, Fri.–Sun. 10–4.*

Hoh Rain Forest Visitor Center. Pick up park maps and pamphlets, permits, and activities lists in this busy, woodsy chalet; there's also a shop and exhibits on natural history. Several short interpretive trails and longer wilderness treks start from here. ⊠ *Upper Hoh Rd., Forks* ☎ *360/374–6925* ⊕ *www.nps.gov/olym* ⊗ *Open daily in summer; Fri.–Sun. off-season (hours vary, call for info).*

Hurricane Ridge Visitor Center. The upper level of this visitor center has exhibits; the lower level has a gift shop and café (open seasonally) and open seating with nice views. Guided walks and programs start in late June, and you can also get details on the surrounding Winter Use Area ski and sledding slopes. Guided snowshoe walks are offered on winter weekends, too. ⊠ *Hurricane Ridge Rd., Port Angeles* ☎ *360/565–3131* ⊕ *www.nps.gov/olym* ⊗ *Hours vary by season; building is open daily when Hurricane Ridge Road is open.*

Olympic National Park Visitor Center. This modern, well-organized facility, staffed by park rangers, provides everything: maps, trail brochures, campground advice, listings of wildlife sightings, educational programs and exhibits, information on road and trail closures, and weather forecasts. ⊠ *3002 Mount Angeles Rd., Port Angeles* ☎ *360/565–3130* ⊕ *www.nps.gov/olym* ⊗ *May–Sept., daily 8–6; Oct.–Apr., daily 10–4.*

South Shore Quinault Ranger Station. This office next door to the Lake Quinault Lodge has maps, campground information, and program listings. ⊠ *353 S. Shore Lake Quinault Rd., Lake Quinault* ☎ *360/288–0232* ⊕ *www.fs.fed.us/r6/olympic* ⊗ *Daily weekdays 8–4:30, weekends 9–4.*

Wilderness Information Center (WIC). Located inside the Olympic National Park Visitor Center, this facility provides all the information you'll need for a trip in the park, including trail conditions, safety tips, and weather bulletins. The office also issues camping permits, takes campground

OLYMPIC IN ONE DAY

Start at the **Lake Quinault Lodge**, in the park's southwest corner. From here, drive a half hour into the Quinault Valley via **South Shore Road**. Tackle the forested **Graves Creek Trail**, then head up **North Shore Road** to the Quinault Rain Forest Interpretive Trail. Next, head back to Highway 101 and drive to **Ruby Beach**, where a shoreline walk presents a breathtaking scene of sea stacks and sparkling, pink-hued sands.

Forks, and its **Timber Museum**, are your next stop; have lunch here, then drive 20 minutes to the beach at **La Push**. Next, head to **Lake Crescent**, around the corner to the northeast, where you can rent a boat, take a swim, or enjoy a picnic next to the sparkling teal waters. Drive through **Port Angeles** to **Hurricane Ridge**; count on an hour's drive from bottom to top if there aren't too many visitors. At the ridge, explore the visitor center or hike the 3-mi loop to **Hurricane Hill**, where you can see over the entire park north to Vancouver Island and south past Mt. Olympus.

reservations, and rents bear-proof food canisters for a $3 donation. ⊠ *3002 Mount Angeles Rd., Port Angeles* ☎ *360/565–3100* ⊕ *www. nps.gov/olym* ☉ *Late June–Labor Day, Sun.–Thurs. 7:30–6, Fri. and Sat. 7:30–7.*

EXPLORING OLYMPIC NATIONAL PARK

Most of the park's attractions are found either off Highway 101 or down trails that require hikes of 15 minutes or longer. The west coast beaches are linked to the highway by downhill tracks; the number of cars parked alongside the road at the start of the paths indicate how crowded the beach will be.

HISTORIC SITE

Fodor's Choice ★ **Lake Ozette.** The third-largest glacial impoundment in Washington anchors the coastal strip of Olympic National Park at its north end. The small town of Ozette, home to a coastal tribe, is the trailhead for two of the park's better one-day hikes. Both 3-mi trails lead over boardwalks through swampy wetland and coastal old-growth forest to the ocean shore and uncrowded beaches. ⊠ *At the end of Hoko-Ozette Rd., 26 mi southwest of Hwy. 112 near Sekiu* ☎ *360/963–2725 Ozette Ranger Station.*

SCENIC DRIVE

Fodor's Choice ★ **Port Angeles Visitor Center to Hurricane Ridge.** The premier scenic drive in Olympic National Park is a steep ribbon of curves, which climbs from thickly forested foothills and subalpine meadows into the upper stretches of pine-swathed peaks. At the top, the visitor center at Hurricane Ridge has some truly spectacular views over the heart of the peninsula and across the Strait of Juan de Fuca. (Backpackers note wryly that you have to hike a long way in other parts of the park to get the kinds of views you can drive to here.) Hurricane Ridge also has an uncommonly fine display of wildflowers in spring and summer.

SCENIC STOPS

12

Fodor'sChoice
★

Hoh River Rain Forest. South of Forks, an 18-mi spur road links Highway 101 with this unique temperate rain forest, where spruce and hemlock trees soar to heights of more than 200 feet. Alders and big-leaf maples are so densely covered with mosses they look more like shaggy prehistoric animals than trees, and elk browse in shaded glens. Be prepared for precipitation: the region receives 140 inches or more each year. The visitor center is open daily July through September, and Friday through Sunday in other months. ⊠ *From U.S. 101, at about 20 mi north of Kalaloch, turn onto Upper Hoh Rd. 18 mi east to Hoh Rain Forest Visitor Center* ☎ *360/374–6925.*

Fodor'sChoice
★

Hurricane Ridge. The panoramic view from this 5,200-foot-high ridge encompasses the Olympic range, the Strait of Juan de Fuca, and Vancouver Island. Guided tours are given in summer along the many paved and unpaved trails, where wildflowers and wildlife such as deer and marmots flourish. ⊠ *Hurricane Ridge Rd., 17 mi south of Port Angeles* ☎ *360/565–3130 visitor center* ⊘ *Visitor center open daily; staffed daily mid-June–mid-Sept.; weekends in winter and spring.*

Kalaloch. With a lodge, a huge campground, miles of coastline, and easy access from the highway, this is another popular spot. Keen-eyed beachcombers may spot sea otters just offshore; they were reintroduced here in 1970. ⊠ *U.S. 101, 32 mi northwest of Lake Quinault* ☎ *360/962–2283 Kalaloch ranger station.*

Lake Crescent. Visitors see Lake Crescent as Highway 101 winds along its southern shore, giving way to gorgeous views of teal waters rippling in a basin formed by Tuscan-like hills. In the evening, low bands of clouds caught between the surrounding mountains often linger over its reflective surface. ⊠ *U.S. 101, 16 mi west of Port Angeles and 28 mi east of Forks* ☎ *360/928–3380 Storm King ranger station.*

Fodor'sChoice
★

Lake Quinault. This glimmering lake, 4½ mi long and 300 feet deep, is the first landmark you'll reach when driving the west-side loop of U.S. 101. The rain forest is thickest here, with moss-draped maples and alders, and towering spruce, fir, and hemlock. Enchanted Valley, high up near the Quinault River's source, is a deeply glaciated valley that's closer to the Hood Canal than to the Pacific Ocean. A scenic loop drive circles the lake and travels around a section of the Quinault River. ⊠ *U.S. 101, 38 mi north of Hoquiam* ☎ *360/288–2525 Quinault ranger station* ⊘ *Ranger station weekdays 8–4:30; weekends 9–4.*

Second and Third Beaches. During low tide the pools here brim with life, and you can walk out to some sea stacks. Gray whales play offshore during their annual spring migration, and most of the year the waves are great for surfing and kayaking (bring a wet suit). ⊠ *U.S. 101, 32 mi north of Lake Quinault* ☎ *360/374–5460 Mora ranger station.*

DID YOU KNOW?

Encompassing more than 70 miles of beachfront, Olympic is one of the few national parks of the West with an ocean beach (Redwood, Channel Islands, and some of the Alaskan parks are the others). This rare feature means that the park is home to many marine animals, including sea otters, whales, sea lions, and seals.

Sol Duc. Sol Duc Valley is one of those magical places where all the Northwest's virtues seem at hand: lush lowland forests, sparkling river scenes, salmon runs, and serene hiking trails. Here the popular Sol Duc Hot Springs area includes three attractive sulfuric pools ranging in temperature from 98°F to 104°F. ✉ *Sol Duc Rd. south of U.S. 101, 1 mi past the west end of Lake Crescent* ☎ *360/374–6925 Hoh Rain Forest visitor center.*

12

WHERE TO EAT

The major resorts are your best bets for dining in the park. Each has a main restaurant, café, and/or kiosk, as well as casually upscale dinner service, with regional seafood, meat, and produce complemented by a range of microbrews and good Washington and international wines. Reservations are either recommended or required.

Outside the park, The town of Port Angeles (⇨ *see below*) is the place to go for a truly spectacular meal. Dozens of small, easygoing eateries offering hearty American-style fare line the main thoroughfares in Forks and Sequim.

$$
AMERICAN
✕**Kalaloch Lodge.** A tranquil country setting and ocean views create the perfect backdrop for savoring local dinner specialties like cedar-planked salmon, fresh shellfish, wild mushrooms, and well-aged beef. Note that seating is every half hour after 5, and reservations are recommended. Hearty breakfasts and sandwich-style lunches are more casual. ✉ *157151 U.S. 101, Kalaloch* ☎ *866/525–2562* ▭ *AE, MC, V.*

$$–$$$
AMERICAN
✕**Lake Crescent Lodge.** Part of the original 1916 lodge, the fir-paneled dining room overlooks the lake; you also won't find a better spot for a view of the sunset. Entrées include crab cakes, grilled salmon, fish-and-chips, and classic American steaks. A good Northwest wine list complements the menu. Note that meals are only offered during set hours, but appetizers are served in the lounge—or out on the Sun Porch—from 2 to 10. ✉ *416 Lake Crescent Rd., Port Angeles* ☎ *360/928–3211* ▭ *AE, D, MC, V* ☉ *Closed Nov.–Apr.*

$$
AMERICAN
✕**The Springs Restaurant.** The main Sol Duc Hot Springs Resort restaurant is a rustic, fir-and-cedar-paneled dining room surrounded by trees. Big breakfasts are turned out daily 7:30 to 10; dinner is served daily between 5:30 and 9 (lunch and snacks are available 11 to 4 at the Poolside Deli or Espresso Hut). Evening choices include Northwest seafood and game highlighted by fresh-picked fruits and vegetables. ✉ *12076 Sol Duc Rd., at U.S. 101, Port Angeles* ☎ *360/327–3583* ▭ *AE, D, MC, V* ☉ *Closed mid-Oct.–mid-May.*

PICNIC AREAS
All Olympic National Park campgrounds have adjacent picnic areas with tables, some shelters, and restrooms, but no cooking facilities. The same is true for major visitor centers, such as Hoh Rain Forest. Drinking water is available at ranger stations, interpretive centers, and inside campgrounds.

East Beach Picnic Area. Set on a grassy meadow overlooking Lake Crescent, this popular swimming spot has six picnic tables and vault toilets. ✉ *At the far east end of Lake Crescent, off U.S. 101, 17 mi west of Port Angeles.*

La Poel Picnic Area. Tall firs lean over a tiny gravel beach at this small picnic area, which has five picnic tables and a splendid view of Pyramid Mountain across Lake Crescent. ⊠ *Off U.S. 101, 22 mi west of Port Angeles.*

Rialto Beach Picnic Area. Relatively secluded at the end of the road from Forks, this is one of the premier day-use areas in the park's Pacific coast segment. This site has 12 picnic tables, fire grills, and vault toilets. ⊠ *Rte. 110, 14 mi west of Forks.*

WHERE TO STAY

ABOUT THE HOTELS

Major park resorts run from good to terrific, with generally comfortable rooms, excellent facilities, and easy access to trails, beaches, and activity centers. Midsize accommodations, like Sol Duc Hot Springs Resort, are often shockingly rustic—but remember, you're here for the park, not for the rooms.

The towns around the park have motels, hotels, and resorts for every budget. For high-priced stays with lots of perks, base yourself in Port Angeles. Sequim has many attractive, friendly bed-and-breakfasts, plus lots of inexpensive chain hotels and motels. Forks is basically a motel town, with a few guesthouses around its fringes.

ABOUT THE CAMPGROUNDS

Note that only a few places take reservations; if you can't book in advance, you'll have to arrive early to get a place. Each site usually has a picnic table and grill or fire pit, and most campgrounds have water, toilets, and garbage containers; for hookups, showers, and laundry facilities, you'll have to head into the towns. Firewood is available from camp concessions, but if there's no store you can collect dead wood within 1 mi of your campsite. Dogs are allowed in campgrounds, but not on trails or in the backcountry. Trailers should be 21 feet long or less (15 feet or less at Queets Campground). There's a camping limit of two weeks.

If you have a backcountry pass, you can camp virtually anywhere throughout the park's forests and shores. Overnight wilderness permits are $5—plus $2 per person per night—and are available at visitor centers and ranger stations. Note that when you camp in the backcountry, you must choose a site at least ½ mi inside the park boundary.

$$–$$$ ⊡ **Kalaloch Lodge**. A two-story cedar building overlooking the Pacific, Kalaloch has cozy rooms with sea views. The surrounding log cabins have a fireplace or woodstove, knotty-pine furnishings, earth-tone fabrics, and kitchenettes; the main lodge houses rustic oceanview rooms and suites; and wood-paneled motel-style quarters are in the Seacrest Building. Guests have pool privileges at the Lake Quinault Resort; towels are provided. The restaurant's ($–$$) menu changes seasonally, but usually includes local oysters, crab, and salmon. **Pros:** ranger tours; clam digging; supreme storm watching in winter. **Cons:** some units are two blocks from main lodge; cabins can smell like pets. ⊠ *157151 U.S. 101, Forks* ☎ *360/962–2271 or 866/525–2562* ⊕ *www.visitkalaloch.*

com ✍ 9 lodge rooms, 2 lodge suites, 6 motel rooms, 3 motel suites, 44 cabins △ In-room: no phone, kitchen (some), refrigerator (some), no TV (some). In-hotel: restaurant, bar, some pets allowed ═ AE, D, MC, V.

$–$$ ▦ **Lake Crescent Lodge.** Deep in the forest at the foot of Mt. Storm King, this comfortable 1916 lodge has a wraparound veranda and picture windows that frame the lake's sapphire waters. Rooms in the rustic Roosevelt Cottage have polished wood floors, stone fireplaces, and lake views, while Tavern Cottage quarters resemble modern motel rooms. The historic lodge has second-floor rooms with shared baths. The lodge's fir-paneled dining room ($$–$$$) overlooks the lake, and the adjacent lounge is often crowded with campers. Seafood dishes like grilled salmon or steamed Quilcene oysters highlight the restaurant menu; reservations are required. **Pros:** gorgeous setting; free wireless access in the wilderness. **Cons:** no laundry; Roosevelt Cottages must be booked a year in advance. ✉ *416 Lake Crescent Rd., Port Angeles* ☎ *360/928–3211 or 866/574–2708* ⊕ *www.lakecrescentlodge.com* ✍ *30 motel rooms, 17 cabins, 5 lodge rooms with shared bath △ In-room: no phone, refrigerator (some), no TV, Wi-Fi. In-hotel: restaurant, bar, beachfront, water sports, some pets allowed ═ AE, D, MC, V* ⊘ *Closed Nov.–Apr.*

$$–$$$ ▦ **Lake Quinault Lodge.** On a lovely glacial lake in Olympic National Forest, this beautiful early-20th-century lodge complex is within walking distance of the lakeshore and hiking trails in the spectacular old-growth forest. A towering brick fireplace is the centerpiece of the great room, where antique wicker furnishings sit beneath ceiling beams painted with Native American designs. In the rooms, modern gadgets are traded in for old-fashioned comforts, such as claw-foot tubs, fireplaces, and walking sticks. The lively bar is a good place to unwind after a day outdoors, and the restaurant ($$–$$$) serves upscale seafood entrées like baked salmon with capers and onions. **Pros:** hosts summer campfires with s'mores; family-friendly ambience. **Cons:** kayaks and canoes rent out quickly in the summer. ✉ *South Shore Rd., P.O. Box 7, Quinault* ☎ *360/288–2900 or 800/562–6672* ⊕ *www.visitlakequinault.com* ✍ *91 rooms △ In-room: no phone, no a/c, no TV (some). In-hotel: restaurant, bar, pool, Wi-Fi hotspot, some pets allowed ═ AE, D, MC, V.*

$$ ▦ **Sol Duc Hot Springs Resort.** Deep in the brooding forest along the Sol Duc River, this remote 1910 resort is surrounded by 5,000-foot-tall mountains. The main draw is the pool area, which surrounds a gathering of soothing mineral baths, and has a freshwater swimming pool. Some forest cabins have kitchens, but all are spartan; however, after a day's hike, a dip, and dinner at the Springs Restaurant ($–$$), you'll hardly notice. The attractive fir-and-cedar-paneled dining room serves unpretentious meals during breakfast and dinner hours, drawing on top Northwest seafood and produce; the poolside deli is open for lunch. **Pros:** nearby trails; peaceful setting. **Cons:** very remote, no Wi-Fi, strong sulfur smell from hot springs. ✉ *12076 Sol Duc Rd.* ⌖ *P.O. Box 2169, Port Angeles 98362* ☎ *360/327–3583 or 866/476–5382* ⊕ *www. visitsolduc.com* ✍ *33 cabins, 17 RV sites △ In-room: no phone, no a/c, kitchen (some), no TV. In-hotel: restaurant, bar, pool, spa, some pets allowed ═ AE, D, MC, V* ⊘ *Closed Nov.–Mar.*

$ △ **Deer Park Campground.** At 5,400 feet, this is the park's only drive-to alpine campground. The part-gravel access road is steep and winding; RVs are prohibited. **Pros:** shaded sites; easy access by road. **Cons:** motor noises. ⊠ *Deer Park (Blue Mountain) Rd., 21 mi south of U.S. 101, Olympic National Park* 🕾 *No phone* ↪ *14 tent sites* ♿ *Pit toilets, drinking water, fire grates* ⊘ *Closed Oct.–Apr.*

$ △ **Elwha Campground.** The larger of the Elwha Valley's two campgrounds, this is one of Olympic's year-round facilities. Two campsite loops lie in an old-growth forest. **Pros:** spur-of-the-moment camping opportunity because it's not usually full; amphitheater nearby. **Cons:** no water in winter. ⊠ *Elwha River Rd., 7 mi south of U.S. 101, Olympic National Park* 🕾 *No phone* ↪ *40 tent/RV sites* ♿ *Flush toilets, drinking water (summer only), fire grates, public telephone, ranger station* 🖃 *MC, V.*

$ △ **Fairholme Campground.** One of just three lakeside campgrounds in the
Fodor's Choice   park, Fairholm is near the Lake Crescent Resort. There is an on-site
★   boat launch. **Pros:** gorgeous setting; well placed for lakeside explorations. **Cons:** very popular. ⊠ *U.S. 101, 28 mi west of Port Angeles, on the west end of Lake Crescent, Olympic National Park* 🕾 *No phone* ↪ *88 tent/RV sites* ♿ *Flush toilets, dump station, drinking water, fire grates, public telephone, swimming (lake)* ⊘ *Closed Nov.–Mar.*

$ △ **Heart O' the Hills Campground.** At the foot of Hurricane Ridge in a grove of tall firs, this popular year-round campground offers a regular slate of summer programs. **Pros:** lots of activities; closest campground to the ridge. **Cons:** only accessible on foot during off-season. ⊠ *Hurricane Ridge Rd., 4 mi south of the main park visitor center in Port Angeles, Olympic National Park* 🕾 *No phone* ↪ *105 tent/RV sites (tent-only in winter)* ♿ *Flush toilets, drinking water, fire grates, public telephone, ranger station.* 🖃 *MC, V.*

$ △ **Hoh Campground.** Crowds flock to this rain-forest site, near the Hoh Visitor Center under a canopy of moss-draped maples and towering spruce trees. **Pros:** kid-friendly day hikes; animal sightings. **Cons:** bears are sometimes spotted, especially during salmon season. ⊠ *Hoh River Rd., 17 mi east of U.S. 101, Olympic National Park* 🕾 *No phone* ↪ *88 tent/RV sites* ♿ *Flush toilets, dump station, drinking water, fire grates, public telephone, ranger station* 🖃 *MC, V.*

$–$$ △ **Kalaloch Campground.** Kalaloch is the biggest and most popular Olympic campground, and it's open all year. Its vantage of the Pacific is unmatched on the park's coastal stretch—although the campsites themselves are set back in the spruce fringe. **Pros:** bluff-top views, beach access. **Cons:** no reservations taken mid-September–mid-June. ⊠ *U.S. 101, ½ mi north of the Kalaloch Information Station, Olympic National Park* 🕾 *360/962–2271 group bookings* ↪ *170 tent/RV sites* ♿ *Flush toilets, dump station, drinking water, fire grates, public telephone, ranger station* 🖃 *MC, V.*

$$ △ **Lake Quinault Rain Forest Resort Village Campground.** Stretching along the south shore of Lake Quinault, this RV campground has many recreation facilities, including beaches, canoes, ball fields, and horseshoe pits. Cabins, suites, motel rooms, and an apartment are also available. **Pros:** Salmon House restaurant ($); on-site grocery and gift shop. **Cons:**

very busy in summer. ✉ *3½ mi east of U.S. 101, South Shore Rd., Lake Quinault* ☎ *360/288–2535 or 800/255–6936* ⊕ *www.rainforestresort. com* ⤳ *31 RV sites, 16 rooms, 10 cabins, 2 suites* ⚭ *Flush toilets, full hookups, drinking water, showers, grills, picnic tables, electricity, public telephone, general store* ⊟ *AE, D, MC, V* ⊗ *Open year-round, campground restaurants closed in winter.*

$ ⚠ **Mora Campground.** Along the Quillayute estuary, this campground doubles as a popular staging point for hikes northward along the coast's wilderness stretch. **Pros:** some sites have river views; quick drive to Rialto Beach. **Cons:** throngs of hikers in summer. ✉ *Rte. 110, 13 mi west of Forks, Olympic National Park* ☎ *No phone* ⤳ *94 tent/RV sites (1 walk-in)* ⚭ *Flush toilets, dump station, drinking water, fire grates, public telephone, ranger station.*

$ ⚠ **Ozette Campground.** Hikers heading to Cape Alava, a scenic promontory that is the westernmost point in the lower 48 states, use this lakeshore campground as a jumping-off point. There's a boat launch and a small beach. **Pros:** water activities; stunning panoramas. **Cons:** often closes in winter. ✉ *Hoko-Ozette Rd., 26 mi south of Hwy. 112, Olympic National Park* ☎ *No phone* ⤳ *15 tent/RV sites* ⚭ *Pit toilets, fire grates, ranger station* ⊟ *MC, V* ⊗ *Call ahead in winter.*

$ ⚠ **Sol Duc Campground.** Sol Duc resembles virtually all Olympic campgrounds save one distinguishing feature—the famed hot springs are a short walk away. **Pros:** easy access to pools; waterfalls close by, too. **Cons:** no water off-season (November through April). ✉ *Sol Duc Rd., 11 mi south of U.S. 101, Olympic National Park* ☎ *360/327–3534* ⤳ *82 tent/RV sites* ⚭ *Flush toilets, dump station, drinking water (spring–fall), fire grates, public telephone, ranger station, swimming (hot springs).*

$ ⚠ **Staircase Campground.** In deep woods away from the river, this campground is a popular jumping-off point for hikes into the Skokomish River Valley and the Olympic high country. **Pros:** some sites are next to the river; running water in summer. **Cons:** Staircase Road is closed to vehicles November to May. ✉ *Rte. 119, 16 mi northwest of U.S. 101, Olympic National Park* ☎ *No phone* ⤳ *50 tent/RV sites (tent-only in winter)* ⚭ *Flush toilets, drinking water, fire grates, public telephone, ranger station* ⊟ *MC, V.*

SPORTS AND THE OUTDOORS

BEACHCOMBING

Fodor'sChoice ★ The wild, shell-strewn Pacific coast teems with tide pools and clawed creatures. Crabs, sand dollars, anemones, starfish, and all sorts of shellfish are exposed at low tide, when flat beaches can stretch out for hundreds of yards. The most easily accessible sand-strolling spots are Rialto, Ruby, First, and Second beaches, near Mora and La Push, and Kalaloch Beach and Fourth Beach in the Kalaloch stretch.

The Wilderness Act and the park's code of ethics instruct visitors to leave all nonliving materials where they are for others to enjoy.

Ruby Beach, Olympic National Park

CLIMBING

At 7,980 feet, Mt. Olympus is the highest peak in the park and the most popular climb in the region. To attempt the summit, participants must register at the Glacier Meadows Ranger Station. Mt. Constance, the third-highest Olympic peak at 7,743 feet, has a well-traversed climbing route that requires technical experience; reservations are recommended for the Lake Constance stop, which is limited to 20 campers. Mt. Deception is another possibility, though tricky snows have caused fatalities and injuries in the last decade. Climbing season runs from late June through September. Note that crevasse skills and self-rescue experience are highly recommended. Climbers must register with park officials and purchase wilderness permits before setting out. The best resource for climbing advice is the Wilderness Information Center in Port Angeles.

OUTFITTERS AND EXPEDITIONS **Alpine Ascents** (✉ *121 Mercer St., Seattle* ☎ *206/378–1927* ⊕ *www.alpineascents.com*) leads tours of the Olympic ranges. **Mountain Madness** (✉ *3018 S.W. Charlestown St. Seattle* ☎ *206/937–8389 or 800/328–5925* ⊕ *www.mountainmadness.com*) offers adventure trips to summits around the Olympic Peninsula.

FISHING

Bodies of water throughout the park offer numerous fishing possibilities. Lake Crescent is home to cutthroat and rainbow trout, as well as petite kokanee salmon; Lake Cushman, Lake Quinault, and Ozette Lake have trout, salmon, and steelhead; and Lake Mills has three trout varieties. As for rivers, the Bogachiel and Queets have steelhead salmon in season. The glacier-fed Hoh River is home to chinook salmon April to November, and coho salmon from August through November; the Sol

12

Duc River offers all five species of salmon, plus cutthroat and steelhead trout. Rainbow trout are also found in the Dosewallips, Elwha, and Skykomish rivers. Other places to go after salmon and trout include the Duckabush, Quillayute, Quinault, and Salmon rivers. A Washington state punch card is required during salmon-spawning months; fishing regulations vary throughout the park. Licenses are available from sporting-goods and outdoor-supply stores.

OUTFITTERS AND EXPEDITIONS
Bob's Piscatorial Pursuits (☎ 866/347–4232 ⊕ *www.piscatorialpursuits. com*), based in Forks, offers year-round fishing trips around Olympic. **Blue Sky Outfitters** (⊠ *9674 50th Ave. SW, Seattle* ☎ *206/938–4030 or 800/228–7238* ⊕ *www.blueskyoutfitters.com*), in Seattle, organizes custom-tailored fishing trips. White-water rafting trips are another specialty. **Kalaloch Lodge** (⊠ *157151 U.S. 101, Forks* ☎ *360/962–2271 or 866/525–2562* ⊕ *www.visitkalaloch.com*) organizes guided fishing expeditions around the Olympic Peninsula.

HIKING

Know your tides, or you might be trapped by high water. Tide tables are available at all visitor centers and ranger stations. Remember that a wilderness permit is required for all overnight backcountry visits.

OUTFITTERS AND EXPEDITIONS
Peak 6 (⊠ *4883 Upper Hoh Rd., Forks* ☎ *360/374–5254*) runs guided hiking and camping trips. **Timberline Adventures** (☎ *800/417–2453* ⊕ *www.timbertours.com*) does weeklong excursions around the Olympic Peninsula.

EASY

⟳ **Hoh Valley Trail**. Leaving from the Hoh Visitor Center, this rain-forest jaunt takes you into the Hoh Valley, wending its way alongside the river, between moss-draped maple and alder trees, and past open meadows where elk roam in winter. ⊠ *Hoh Visitor Center, 18 mi east of U.S. 101.*

Fodor's Choice ★

⟳ **Hurricane Ridge Trail**. A 0.25-mi alpine loop, most of it wheelchair-accessible, leads through wildflower meadows overlooking numerous vistas of the interior Olympic peaks to the south and a panorama of the Strait of Juan de Fuca to the north. ⊠ *Hurricane Ridge Rd., 17 mi south of Port Angeles.*

MODERATE

Boulder Creek Trail. The 5-mi round-trip walk up Boulder Creek leads to a half-dozen hot-spring pools of varying temperatures; some are clothing-optional. ⊠ *End of the Elwha River Rd., 4 mi south of Altair Campground.*

⟳ **Cape Alva Trail**. Beginning at Ozette, this 3-mi trail leads from the forest to wave-tossed headlands. ⊠ *End of the Hoko-Ozette Rd., 26 mi south of Hwy. 112, west of Sekiu.*

Graves Creek Trail. This 6-mi-long, moderately strenuous trail climbs from lowland rain forest to alpine territory at Sundown Pass. Due to spring floods, a fjord halfway up is often impassable in May and June. ⊠ *End of S. Quinault Valley Rd., 23 mi east of U.S. 101.*

⟳ **Sol Duc Trail**. The 1.5-mi gravel path off Sol Duc Road winds through thick Douglas fir forests toward the thundering, three-chute Sol Duc Falls. Just 0.1 mi from the road, below a wooden platform over the

Fodor's Choice ★

Sol Duc River, you'll come across the 70-foot Salmon Cascades. In late summer and autumn, thousands of salmon negotiate 50 mi or more of treacherous waters to reach the cascades and the tamer pools near Sol Duc Hot Springs. The popular 6-mi **Lovers Lane Loop Trail** links the Sol Duc falls with the hot springs. You can continue up from the falls 5 mi to the **Appleton Pass Trail**, at 3,100 feet. From there you can hike on to the 8.5-mi mark, where views at the High Divide are from 5,050 feet. ⊠ *Sol Duc Rd., 11 mi south of U.S. 101.*

DIFFICULT

High Divide Trail. A 9-mi hike in the park's high country defines this trail, which includes some strenuous climbing on its last 4 mi before topping out at a small alpine lake. A return loop along High Divide wends its way an extra mile through alpine territory, with sensational views of Olympic peaks. This trail is only for dedicated, properly equipped hikers who are in good shape. ⊠ *End of Sol Duc River Rd., 13 mi south of U.S. 101.*

KAYAKING AND CANOEING

Lake Crescent, a serene expanse of teal-colored waters surrounded by deep-green pine forests, is one of the park's best boating areas. Note that the west end is for swimming only; no speedboats are allowed here.

Lake Quinault has boating access from a gravel ramp on the north shore. From U.S. 101, take a right on North Shore Road, another right on Hemlock Way, and a left on Lakeview Drive. There are plank ramps at Falls Creek and Willoughby campgrounds on South Shore Drive, 0.1 mi and 0.2 mi past the Quinault Ranger Station, respectively.

Lake Ozette, with just one access road, is a good place for overnight trips. Only experienced canoe and kayak handlers should travel far from the put-in, since fierce storms occasionally strike—even in summer.

OUTFITTERS AND EXPEDITIONS **Fairholm General Store** (⊠ *U.S. 101, Fairholm* ☎ *360/928–3020* ⊕ *www.fairholmstore.com*) rents kayaks on Lake Crescent for $9/hour, $25/half-day, $4/full day. It's at the lake's west end, 27 mi west of Port Angeles. **Lake Crescent Lodge** (⊠ *416 Lake Crescent Rd.* ☎ *360/928–3211* ⊕ *www.lakecrescentlodge.com*) rents rowboats for $8.50 per hour and $35 per day. **Log Cabin Resort** (⊠ *Piedmont Rd., off U.S. 101* ☎ *360/928–3325* ⊕ *www.logcabinresort.net*), 17 mi west of Port Angeles, has boat rentals for $10 to $30. The dock provides easy access to Lake Crescent's northeast section. **Rain Forest Paddlers** (⊠ *4882 Upper Hoh Rd., Forks* ☎ *360/374–5254 or 866/457–8398* ⊕ *www.rainforestpaddlers.com*) takes kayakers down the Lizard Rock and Oxbow sections of the Hoh River.

RAFTING

Olympic has excellent rafting rivers, with Class II to Class V rapids. The Elwha River is a popular place to paddle, with some exciting turns. The Hoh is better for those who like a smooth, easy float.

OUTFITTERS AND EXPEDITIONS **Olympic Raft and Kayak** (☎ *360/452–1443 or 888/452–1443* ⊕ *www.raftandkayak.com*), based in Port Angeles, is the only rafting outfit allowed to venture into Olympic National Park.

DID YOU KNOW?

If you wander for just 1 mi on the Sol Duc Trail, you'll arrive at the breathtaking Sol Duc Falls.

WINTER SPORTS

Hurricane Ridge is the central spot for winter sports. Miles of downhill and Nordic ski tracks are open late December through March, and a ski lift, towropes, and ski school are open 10 to 4 weekends and holidays. Tubing areas for adults and children are open Friday through Sunday across from Hurricane Ridge Lodge.

OUTFITTERS AND EXPEDITIONS **Hurricane Ridge Visitor Center** (⊠ *Hurricane Ridge Rd., Port Angeles* ☎ *360/565–3131 information, 360/565–3136 tour reservations* ⊕ *www.nps.gov/olym*) rents ski equipment December through March; prices are $15 to $35. Free 90-minute snowshoe tours also depart from here every weekend from late December through March. Group bookings are at 10:30, with informal group tours at 2; sign-ups are at 1:30 and are first-come, first-served. A $5 per person donation is requested to cover trail and equipment maintenance. **Lost Mountain Lodge** (⊠ *303 Sunny View Dr., Sequim* ☎ *360/683–2431 or 888/683–2431* ⊕ *www. lostmountainlodge.com*), in Sequim, offers weekend Olympic Mountains snowshoe packages.

THE OLYMPIC PENINSULA

Wilderness covers much of the rugged Olympic Peninsula, the westernmost corner of the continental United States. Its heart of craggy mountains is safeguarded in Olympic National Park, 95% of which is designated wilderness land. The Olympic Coast National Marine Sanctuary shares the 65-mi stretch of ocean shore with the National Park and extends to Cape Flattery on the Makah Indian Reservation, the northwesternmost point in the lower 48 states. Several thousand acres more are protected in Olympic National Forest, five wilderness areas, and seven Indian reservations.

This is a landscape whose primeval ecosystem has remained in large part intact, and it's a land of almost incredible variety. The rain forest of the western river valleys soaks up 140 to 167 inches of precipitation per year, while the dry slopes of the northeastern peninsula, in the so-called "rain shadow" of the mountains, generally receive fewer than 16 inches. With some of the wettest and driest climates in the coastal Pacific Northwest, the peninsula supports a great diversity of plants and animals.

At its southwestern corner, the peninsula is defined by Grays Harbor, Washington's second-largest estuary and one of only eight natural harbors between Mexico and Canada. The harbor is named for discoverer and fur trader Robert Gray, who in 1792 became the first European-American to enter the harbor. Two long, forested sand spits separate and protect Grays Harbor from the fury of the Pacific Ocean. Although rugged terrain and a lack of roads make much of the Olympic Peninsula's interior accessible only to backpackers, the 300-mi-long outer loop of U.S. 101 provides fabulous views over ocean, rain forest, and mountains. Side roads provide excellent opportunities for exploring remote villages, beaches, and valleys. The following section describes a clockwise journey, primarily via U.S. 101, beginning and ending in Olympia.

GETTING HERE AND AROUND

AIR TRAVEL Port Angeles is the major northern gateway to the Olympic Peninsula, while Olympia is the major entry point in the south. Kenmore Air connects Port Angeles with Boeing Field, near Seattle, where passengers make the 15-minute trip to Sea-Tac Airport via a free shuttle bus. Fairchild International Airport, the largest on the Olympic Peninsula, is 6 mi southwest of Port Angeles off U.S. 101 (take Airport Rd. north from U.S. 101). Jefferson County Airport, a small charter-flight base, is 4 mi southwest of Port Townsend off Highway 19.

> ## TOP REASONS TO GO
>
> **1. Makah Cultural Center.** Exhibits at this impressive complex display authentic scenes of early life in the Northwest.
>
> **2. Ocean Shores.** The expansive beach community is a great seaside getaway.
>
> **3. Westport.** Head herefor explorations of coastal boating history.
>
> **4. Hurricane Ridge.** Drive to the top of this spectacular ridge for splendid summer hikes and winter snow sports.
>
> **5. Ruby Beach.** Make this a stop for heart-stopping vistas of rugged, ocean-carved rock formations.

12

Contacts Fairchild International Airport (✉ *1404 Fairchild International Airport Rd.* ☎ *360/457–1138*). **Jefferson County International Airport** (✉ *310 Airport Rd.* ☎ *360/385–0656*). **Kenmore Air** (☎ *866/435–9524* ⊕ *www.kenmoreair.com*). **San Juan Airlines** (☎ *425/277–1590 or 800/874–4434* ⊕ *www.sanjuanairlines.com*).

Airports and Transfers. Olympic Bus Lines, a Greyhound affiliate, transports passengers twice daily from Port Angeles and Sequim to Sea-Tac Airport ($49) and downtown Seattle ($39).

Contacts Olympic (☎ *360/417–0700 or 800/457–4492* ⊕ *www.olympicbuslines.com*).

BOAT AND FERRY TRAVEL Washington State Ferries charge $11.45 per vehicle from Port Townsend to Keystone; it's $2.65 each way if you walk on. From Port Angeles you can reach Victoria, British Columbia, on the *Victoria Express* passenger ferry, which makes the one-hour trip ($10) two to three times daily from mid-May to mid-October. Four times a week during summer, the boat continues on 2½ hours longer to Friday Harbor, on San Juan Island. Or, take your car on the M.V. *Coho*, operated by Black Ball Transport, which makes 1½-hour Port Angeles–Victoria crossings four times daily from mid-May through mid-October and twice daily the rest of the year (except when it's docked for maintenance, from mid-January through mid-March). Rates are $55 per car and driver, $15.50 per passenger, and $6.00 per bike; you can reserve ahead for an additional fee. The *Victoria Express* departs from the Landing Mall terminal, while the *Coho* departs from the ferry terminal at the foot of Laurel Street.

Contacts Black Ball Transport (☎ *360/457–4491 in Port Angeles, 250/386–2202 in Victoria* ⊕ *www.ferrytovictoria.com*). **Victoria Express** (☎ *360/452–8088* *in Port Angeles, 250/361–9144 in Victoria ⊕ www.victoriaexpress.com).* **Washington State Ferries** (⊠ *Colman Dock, Pier 52, Downtown, Seattle* ☎ *206/464–6400, 888/808–7977, 800/843–3779 automated line in WA and BC ⊕ www.wsdot.wa.gov/ferries).*

CAR TRAVEL   U.S. 101, the main thoroughfare around the Olympic Peninsula, is a two-lane, well-paved highway. Rural back roads are blacktop or gravel, and tend to have potholes and get washed out during rains. In winter, landslides and wet weather frequently close roads. Highway 112 heads west from U.S. 101 at Port Angeles to Neah Bay. Highway 113 winds north from U.S. 101 at Sappho to Highway 112. Highway 110 travels west from U.S. 101 at Forks to La Push. Highway 109 leads west from U.S. 101 at Hoquiam to Copalis Beach, Moclips, and Taholah. Highway 8 heads west from Olympia and connects with U.S. 12, which travels west to Aberdeen.

VISITOR INFORMATION

Contacts **North Olympic Peninsula Visitor and Convention Bureau** (⊠ *Port of Port Angeles, 338 W. 1st St., Suite 104, Port Angeles* ☎ *360/452–8552 or 800/942–4042 ⊕ www.olympicpeninsula.org).* **Northwest Interpretive Association** (⊠ *3002 Mt. Angeles Rd., Port Angeles* ☎ *360/565–3195 ⊕ www.nwpubliclands.com).* **Olympic National Forest** (⊠ *1835 Blacklake Blvd., Olympia* ☎ *360/956–2400).* **Olympic National Park** (⊠ *1835 Blacklake Blvd., Olympia* ☎ *360/956–4501).* **Washington Coast Chamber of Commerce** (⊠ *2272 Hwy. 109, Box 562, Ocean City* ☎ *360/289–4552 ⊕ www.washingtoncoastchamber.org).*

PORT TOWNSEND

99 mi north from Olympia.

A Victorian-era city with a restored waterfront historic district, Port Townsend is the most picturesque gateway to the Olympic Peninsula. You could easily spend a weekend exploring its art galleries, shops, and trendy restaurants.

Settled in 1851, and fondly dubbed the "City of Dreams," Port Townsend was laid out with two separate urban quarters: Watertown, on the waterfront, catered to sailors, while uptown, on the plateau above the bluffs, was where Watertown merchants and other permanent citizens lived and raised their families. Today the city has a strong community of writers, musicians, painters, and other artists, and the waterfront is where you'll find chic stores and seafood restaurants. Handsomely restored brick buildings from the 1888–90 railroad boom line the bay, and the crowd of impressive yachts beyond attest to the town's status as one of the state's premier sailing spots. At the east edge of town, the Point Hudson Maritime District is a beach-side educational area with historic walks, traditional wooden boatbuilding demonstrations, and historic exhibits.

GETTING HERE

From Seattle, Port Townsend is reached via the Washington State Ferries traveling from Edmonds (north of Seattle via I–5) to Kingston, then west via Hwy. 104 and north via Hwy. 19; roughly an 1 hour

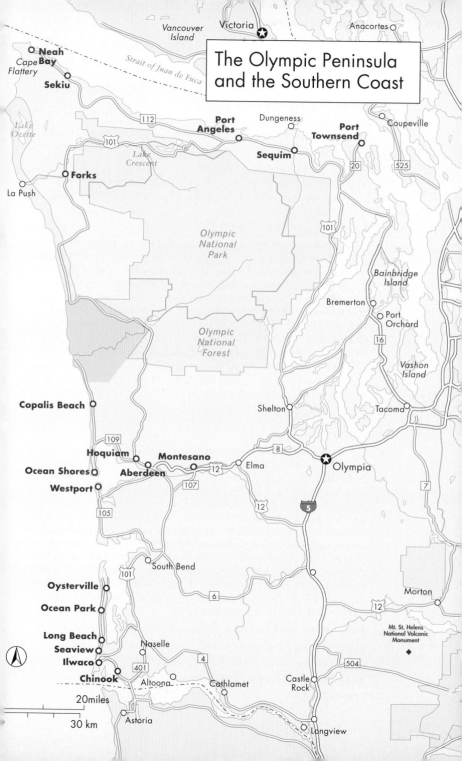

The Olympic Peninsula and the Southern Coast

Victoria

Anacortes

Vancouver Island

Strait of Juan de Fuca

Neah Bay

Cape Flattery

Sekiu

Lake Ozette

112

101

Lake Crescent

Port Angeles

Dungeness

Sequim

Port Townsend

Coupeville

20

525

Forks

La Push

Olympic National Park

101

Bainbridge Island

Bremerton

Port Orchard

16

Olympic National Forest

Vashon Island

Copalis Beach

Shelton

Tacoma

109

Hoquiam

Montesano

Elma

8

Olympia

Ocean Shores

Aberdeen

12

Westport

107

7

105

12

5

South Bend

Oysterville

101

Morton

Ocean Park

6

12

Long Beach

Naselle

Mt. St. Helens National Volcanic Monument

Seaview

Ilwaco

401

Chinook

Altoona

Cathlamet

504

Castle Rock

20 miles

30 km

Astoria

Langview

and 45-min trip (not including ferry waits). From Olympia and points south, there are two routes northbound: U.S. 101 and Hwy. 14. Both take about two hours.

Contact Washington State Ferries ☎ *888/808-7977, 800/843-3779, or 206/464-6400* ⊕ *www.wsdot.wa.gov/ferries*).

GUIDED TOURS

Guided Historical Tours (✉ *820 Tyler St., Port Townsend* ☎ *360/385-1967*) conducts two- to three-hour walking tours of Port Townsend for $10 to $20.

VISITOR INFORMATION

Port Townsend Chamber of Commerce and Visitor Information Center (✉ *440 12th St., Port Townsend* ☎ *360/385-7869 or 888/365-6978* ⊕ *www. ptchamber.org*).

EXPLORING

The **Fire Bell Tower,** set high along the bayside bluffs, is recognizable by its pyramid shape. Built in 1890, it was once the key alert center for local volunteer firemen, and a century later it's considered one of the state's most valuable historic buildings. Inside are firefighting equipment and regional artifacts from pioneer days, including a 19th-century horse-drawn hearse. You can reach the tower by climbing the stairs at Tyler Street. ✉ *Jefferson St.* ☎ *360/385-1003* 🖾 *$3* ⊗ *By appointment with Jefferson Co. Historical Society.*

The manicured grounds of 443-acre **Fort Worden State Park** include a row of restored Victorian officers' houses, a World War II balloon hangar, and a sandy beach that leads to the Point Wilson Lighthouse. The fort, which was built on Point Wilson in 1896, 17 years after the lighthouse, hosts art events, kayaking tours, camping, and outdoor activities. ✉ *200 Battery Way* ☎ *360/385-4730* ⊕ *www.parks.wa.gov* 🖾 *Free* ⊗ *Daily dawn–dusk.*

★ The **Northwest Maritime Center** opens the myriad traditions and trades of the Pacific Northwest's seafaring history to the public, specifically citing the importance of Port Townsend as one of only three Victorian-era seaports on the country's register of National Historic Sites. It's the core of the Point Hudson district and the center of operations for the Wooden Boat Foundation, which stages the annual Wooden Boat Festival early each September. The center has interactive exhibits, hands-on sailing and boatbuilding crafts, a wood shop, and a pilot house where you can test navigational tools. The boardwalk, pier, and sandy beach that front the buildings are laced with marine life, and are the perfect points to launch a kayak or watch sloops and schooners gliding along the coast. ✉ *431 Water St.* ☎ *360/379-2629* ⊕ *www.nwmaritime.org* 🖾 *Free* ⊗ *Weekdays 9–5, weekends 9–6.*

NEED A BREAK?

Stop at the Elevated Ice Cream Company (✉ *627 and 631 Water St.* ☎ *360/385-1156* ⊕ *www.elevatedicecream.com*) for coffee, pastries, candy, or a scoop of ice cream. The proprietors first served their homemade ice cream from an antique Victorian elevator cage in 1977. The shop is open daily 10–10.

The **Port Townsend Marine Science Center,** along the seafront at Fort Worden State Park, is divided into two sections. The actual Science Center, set at the end of a long pier and within a former World War II military storage facility, houses numerous aquarium displays, as well as touch tanks of starfish, crabs, and anemones. The separate, on-shore Natural History Exhibit Center is filled with displays following the region's geography and marine ecology. Beach walks, nature camps, cruises, and day camps run throughout the summer, and there's a Low Tide Festival each July. ⊠ *520 Battery Way* ☎ *360/385–5582 or 800/566–3932* ⊕ *www.ptmsc.org* ✉ *$3 each bldg., $5 combined ticket* ⊙ *Marine Science Center: Sept.–mid-June, weekends noon–4; mid-June–Sept., Wed.–Mon. noon–5; Natural History Exhibit Center: Sept.–mid-June, weekdays noon–5; mid-June–Sept., Wed.–Mon. 11–5.*

EN ROUTE Alongside the highway next to the bay sits **Discovery Bay Railroad Park,** marked by four brightly colored vintage rail cars. Grab a hot dog, burger, sugared ice-cream cone, or a half-pound of candy, then take it out to the water-view deck to relax before views of passing sailboats and kayaks. You'll find it—in fact, you can't miss it—a few miles before the Hood Canal Bridge on the way to Port Townsend. ⊠ *282023 U.S. 101, Port Townsend* ☎ *360/379–1903.*

WHERE TO EAT

$$
AMERICAN
✕**The Belmont.** The town's only remaining 1880s saloon is tucked into the line of brickfront buildings along the busy main street. Tall windows let in the light and afford broad harbor views, which make a perfect backdrop to the innovative seafood and Northwest dishes. Dig into scallops carbonara, or try crisp crostini with warmed Dungeness crab and artichoke dip. The second floor is a hotel with Victorian furnishings to match the history and architecture; three of the four rooms have lofts with second queen beds. ⊠ *925 Water St.* ☎ *360/385–3007* w*www.thebelmontpt.com* ⊟ *AE, D, DC, MC, V.*

$–$$
SEAFOOD
✕**Fins Coastal Cuisine.** Hike upstairs to the spacious Northwest-style dining room, set above the main street and timber-lined harbor, to sample fresh catch, from appetizers to full dinners of succulent, beautifully presented shellfish and grilled meats. Look for mains like Portuguese fisherman's stew, Tuscan-style boneless lamb loin with goat-cheese ravioli, and filet mignon and cold-water lobster on whipped potatoes with a red-wine glaze. In warm weather you can dine on the terrace, which overlooks the oncoming ferries. ⊠ *1019 Water St.* ☎ *360/379–3474* ⊕ *www.finscoastal.com* ⊟ *AE, D, MC, V.*

$$
CAFE
✕**Fountain Café.** This funky, art- and knickknack-filled café is a town favorite. Although it's known for sumptuous vegetarian dishes and delicate warm salads, you'll find tender steaks and other hearty choices on the rotating menu as well. Delicious seafood entrées appear nightly, along with a selection of Northwest beers and wines. ⊠ *920 Washington St.* ☎ *360/385–1364* ⊟ *MC, V.*

¢–$
CAFE
✕**Salal Café.** Informal and bright, the restaurant is especially beloved for its ample, all-day breakfasts. Try to get a table in the glassed-in solarium, where you can brunch in style facing a plant-filled courtyard. After 11:30, lunch items appear, mixing sandwiches and soups with fresh salads and vegetarian options. The town's top-rated Elevated Ice

Cream is the perfect dessert. Note that the restaurant closes at 2. ⊠ *634 Water St.* ☎ *360/385–6532* ▭ *MC, V* ⊘ *No dinner.*

$$
ITALIAN
✕ **T's Restaurant.** Italian cuisine is the focus of this rustic local favorite, which is decked out in white linen and fresh local flowers. The aroma of fresh-baked breads leads you into a comfortable dining room filled with fragrant seasonings of pungent garlic, sweet basil, crumbled oregano, and spicy tomato. Handsome wood furnishings and ochre walls provide the background for pasta and seafood, including pan-roasted wild sea scallops and ginger-and-scallion-crusted wild salmon. Vegetarian dishes are also offered, like rigatoni Gorgonzola, doused in rich garlic and cream sauce and dotted with basil. Fine wines and espresso round out the menu. ⊠ *2330 Washington St.* ☎ *360/385–0700* ⊕ *www. ts-restaurant.com* ▭ *AE, D, MC, V* ⊘ *Closed Tues.*

WHERE TO STAY

$
Fodor's Choice
★
☷ **Ann Starrett Mansion.** Gables, turrets, and gingerbread trim decorate this glorious 1889 mansion, a gift from a wealthy contractor to his young bride. You can climb the three-tiered hanging spiral staircase to a 70-foot-high cupola tower, where outdoor murals and red stained-glass windows catch the first light of each changing season. Each guest room is unique and beautifully decorated with American antiques. Two separate cottages have more modern furnishings and facilities and are more suitable for families. **Pros:** seasonal decorations; tours for nonguests. **Cons:** can bustle with nonstop activities during high seasons. ⊠ *744 Clay St.* ☎ *360/385–3205 or 800/321–0644* ⊕ *www.starrettmansion. com* ⇨ *8 rooms, 2 cottages* ⌂ *In-room: no phone, no a/c, kitchen (some), no TV (some). In-hotel: some pets allowed* ▭ *AE, MC, V.*

$–$$
☷ **Bishop Victorian Hotel.** Once an office building and warehouse, this brick-front inn abounds with elegant 19th-century living spaces and thoughtful service. One- and two-bedroom suites are adorned with lush fabrics, antique furnishings, and authentic brass and glass features, and each has a fireplace and pull-out couch. Some quarters even have a large bathtub, and most have spectacular garden, mountain, or water views. The in-house gallery exhibits the works of local artists, and the gorgeous backyard Victorian gardens and a gazebo are a favorite wedding site. A breakfast basket and passes to a nearby athletic club are included. **Pros:** the chance to meet area artists and celebrities. **Cons:** Amenities are very basic. ⊠ *714 Washington St.* ☎ *360/385–6122 or 800/824–4738* ⊕ *www.bishopvictorian.com* ⇨ *16 suites* ⌂ *In-room: no a/c, kitchen (some), refrigerator, DVD, Wi-Fi. In-hotel: some pets allowed* ▭ *AE, D, MC, V* ⓘ◍ *CP.*

$–$$
☷ **Manresa Castle.** An immense, imposing stone structure, this mansion was built in 1892 for Port Townsend businessman and mayor Charles Eisenbeis and his wife Kate. Later tenants included Jesuit priests, who named the castle after the town in Spain where their order was founded. A hotel since the late 1960s, the castle retains its Victorian character, although it's been renovated to offer modern amenities. Rooms have wood trim and furniture, patterned wallpaper, and lace curtains covering tall windows. The austere, period Castle Key Restaurant and Lounge ($–$$; closed Monday) serves Wienerschnitzel, cioppino, jambalaya, and several steak and seafood selections, plus a lavish Sunday

brunch. Make time for a round in the Edwardian-style cocktail lounge, set around the bar from San Francisco's old Savoy Hotel. **Pros:** staying in a real slice of history. **Cons:** somewhat of a spooky vibe. ⊠ *7th and Sheridan Sts.* ☎ *360/385–5750 or 800/732–1281* 📠 *360/385–5883* ⊕ *www.manresacastle.com* ⤴ *30 rooms, 9 suites* ⌂ *In-room: no a/c, Wi-Fi. In-hotel: restaurant, bar* ▭ *D, MC, V* ⎮⃝⃞ *CP.*

$–$$ ⊡ **Palace Hotel.** Built in 1889, this is one of the most famous buildings in town, a former bordello. Walk inside, and you're surrounded by cream walls, mint-color woodwork, and complete 19th-century grandeur. A half-level up, the mezzanine lounge has a balcony overlooking the entryway scene, and a circular mural decorating the soaring ceiling. Rooms, named for the ladies who used to work here, are light-filled and packed with elegant period furnishings like hand-carved dressers and big claw-foot baths. The Miss Ruby has graceful, arched windows and a kitchenette; Miss Rose has a whirlpool tub; and Miss Marie is a corner suite with a fireplace. **Pros:** fun and funky architectural layout. **Cons:** some shabbiness might detract from charm. ⊠ *1004 Water St.* ☎ *360/385–0773 or 800/962–0741* ⊕ *www.palacehotelpt.com* ⤴ *19 rooms, 17 with bath* ⌂ *In-room: no phone, no a/c, refrigerator, Wi-Fi. In-hotel: Internet terminal, some pets allowed* ▭ *AE, D, MC, V.*

¢–$ ⊡ **Port Townsend Inn.** Set midway along a bluff about a half-mile east of downtown, the two-story inn blends hotel-style elegance with small-town charm and tourist conveniences. Rooms are large and light-filled, lined with front and back windows to catch the constant ocean breeze, and done in cream and sea colors. This is also Port Townsend's only accommodation with an indoor pool and hot tub. There are bay views from most rooms, and it's a five-minute stroll to town and the ferry docks. **Pros:** pool; modern comforts. **Cons:** hot tub sometimes on the fritz; central location heightens traffic sounds. ⊠ *2020 Washington St.* ☎ *360/385–2211 or 800/216–4985* 📠 *360/385–7443* ⊕ *www.porttownsendinn.com* ⤴ *36 rooms* ⌂ *In-room: no a/c, kitchen (some), refrigerator, Wi-Fi. In-hotel: pool, some pets allowed* ▭ *AE, D, MC, V* ⎮⃝⃞ *CP.*

$–$$ ⊡ **Tides Inn.** The multistory, peak-roofed inn resembles a classic San Francisco mansion, and its setting next to the ferry docks makes it one of the town's most popular accommodations. A slim brown beach and blue bay front the property, which includes two separate sections; a wing of small, basic, budget rooms, and another wing with newer, more spacious rooms that have refrigerators and microwaves, jetted tubs, and private decks right over the water. Rooms are done in Victorian light Northwest hues with wood trimmings. Note to movie buffs: scenes from *An Officer and a Gentleman* were filmed here. **Pros:** beach locale; choice of rooms and prices. **Cons:** need to book far in advance for festivals and summer weekends. ⊠ *1807 Water St.* ☎ *360/385–0595 or 800/822–8696* ⊕ *www.tides-inn.com* ⤴ *22 rooms, 21 suites* ⌂ *In-room: kitchen (some), refrigerator (some), Wi-Fi. In-hotel: beachfront, laundry facilities* ▭ *AE, D, DC, MC, V* ⎮⃝⃞ *CP.*

NIGHTLIFE

Secluded **Sirens** (⊠ *832 Water St.* ☎ *360/379–0776* ⊕ *www.sirenspub. com*) overlooks the water from the third floor and books rock, blues, and jazz acts on weekends.

SHOPPING

Port Townsend is packed with art galleries, New Age-y book and gift shops, and pseudo-hippie clothing boutiques, especially along Water Street and its offshoots. The Fountain District, along Washington and Taylor streets a block west of the water, brims with charming clothing boutiques and craft shops. More stores are uptown on Lawrence Street near an enclave of Victorian houses.

William James Bookseller (⊠ *829 Water St.* ☎ *360/385–7313*) stocks used and out-of-print books in all fields, with an emphasis on nautical, regional history, and theology titles. For a little bit of everything—including arts, crafts, furnishings, bath items, books, and antiques—head to the **Perfect Season** (⊠ *918 Water St.* ☎ *360/385–9265*).

In the Fountain District, **All Things Lavender** (⊠ *230 Taylor St.* ☎ *360/379–2573*) brings a wealth of fragrant bath, bedroom, and food items in from Sequim's famous lavender farms. **Simply Charming** (⊠ *234 Taylor St.* ☎ *360/379–2977*) is filled with locally created home furnishings and decorations. Three-dozen dealers at the two-story **Port Townsend Antique Mall** (⊠ *802 Washington St.* ☎ *360/385–2590*) sell merchandise ranging from pricey Victorian collectors' items to cheap flea-market kitsch.

Sport Townsend (⊠ *1044 Water St.* ☎ *360/379–9711*) is stocked with high-quality outdoor gear, including backpacks, hiking boots, camping supplies, and boating and fishing equipment. Winter sports gear is also sold here, including downhill and cross-country ski accessories, cold-weather clothing, and snowshoes.

SPORTS AND THE OUTDOORS

BICYCLING   The nearest place to go biking is Fort Worden State Park, but you can range as far afield as Fort Flagler, the lower Dungeness trails (no bikes are allowed on the spit itself), or across the water to Whidbey Island.

P. T. Cyclery (⊠ *100 Tyler St.* ☎ *360/385–6470* ⊕ www.ptcyclery.com) rents mountain bikes and can advise you on where to start your journey.

BOAT CRUISE   **P. S. Express** (⊠ *431 Water St.* ☎ *360/385–5288* ⊕ *www.pugetsoundexpress. com*) has run summer speedboat connections between Port Townsend and Friday Harbor for more than 20 years. The round-trips cost $68.50 to $78.50, depending on season May through September; boats depart from Port Townsend at 9, arriving in Friday Harbor at noon; the return trip departs from Friday Harbor at 2:30 and arrives back in Port Townsend at 5. Four-hour guaranteed killer whale-watching trips from Friday Harbor depart at 10 and 2:30 and cost $85.

KAYAKING   **PT Outdoors** (⊠ *10178 Water St.* ☎ *360/379–3608 or 888/754–8598* ⊕ *www.ptoutdoors.com*) offers kayaking classes and guided trips. Waterfront tours are $60; three-hour tours to Bird Island are $80; specialty tours can also be arranged. Single kayaks rent for $25 per hour; double kayaks rent for $40 per hour.

SEQUIM

31 mi west of Port Townsend

Sequim (pronounced *skwim*), incorporated in 1913, is a pleasant farming and mill town between the northern foothills of the Olympic Mountains and the southeastern stretch of the Strait of Juan de Fuca. With neat, quiet blocks and lovely views, it's also a popular place to retire. A few miles to the north is the shallow and fertile Dungeness Valley. Though it has some of the lowest rainfall in western Washington, fragrant purple lavender flourishes in local fields.

GETTING HERE

Sequim is about 2 hours from Seattle, via the Edmonds–Kingston ferry and U.S. 101. It's served by Clallam Transit to local Olympic Peninsula towns, and Olympic Bus Lines to Silverdale, Seattle, and Sea-Tac airport.

Contacts Clallam Transit ☎ *360/452–4511 or 800/858–3747* ⊕ *www. clallamtransit.com.* **Olympic Bus Lines** ☎ *360/417–0700 or 800/457–4492* ⊕ *www.olympicbuslines.com.*

VISITOR INFORMATION

Sequim Chamber of Commerce (✉ *1192 E. Washington St., Sequim* ☎ *360/683–6197 or 800/737–8462* ⊕ *www.sequimchamber.com*).

EXPLORING

Fodor's Choice ★ **Dungeness Spit.** Curving 5½ mi into the Strait of Juan de Fuca, the longest natural sand spit in the United States is a wild, beautiful section of shoreline. More than 30,000 migratory waterfowl stop here each spring and fall, but you'll see plenty of birdlife any time of year. The entire spit is part of the **Dungeness National Wildlife Refuge.** At the end of the Dungeness Spit is the towering white **New Dungeness Lighthouse** (☎ *360/683–9166* ⊕ *www.newdungenesslighthouse.com*); tours are available, though access is limited to those who can hike or kayak out 5 mi to the end of the spit. An adjacent 64-site camping area, on the bluff above the Strait of Juan de Fuca, is open February through September. ✉ *Kitchen Rd., 3 mi north from U.S. 101, 4 mi west of Sequim* ☎ *360/457–8451 wildlife refuge; 360/683–5847 campground* ⊕ *www. fws.gov/washingtonmaritime/dungeness* 🖾 *$3 per family* ⊗ *Wildlife refuge daily sunrise–sunset.*

The 200-acre **Olympic Game Farm**—part zoo, part safari—is Sequim's biggest attraction after the Dungeness Spit. For years, the farm's exclusive client was Walt Disney Studios, and many of the bears here are former movie stars. On the drive-through tour, be prepared to see large animals like buffalo surround your car (and lick your windows). You'll view leopards, pumas, and small indigenous animals on the walk-through. Facilities also include an aquarium, a studio barn with movie sets, a snack kiosk, and a gift shop. You can drive through the park at any time of year; one-hour guided walking tours are offered June–September between 11 and 2 on weekdays, 10 and 4 on Saturday, and 10 and 3 on Sunday. ✉ *1423 Ward Rd.* ☎ *360/683–4295 or 800/778–4295* ⊕ *www.olygamefarm.com* 🖾 *Drive-through tour $11, mini tour*

12

The Dungeness National Wildlife Refuge

$5, combined tour $13 ⊙ *May–Sept., weekdays 9–5, weekends 9–6; Oct.–Apr., daily 9–3.*

You'll find lavender and other local produce in abundance at the Saturday **Open Aire Market** (⊠ *Cedar St., between Seal St. and 2nd Ave.* ☎ *360/460–2668* ⊕ *www.sequimopenairemarket.com*), a tented affair with lots of color and live music, open from 9 to 3 between mid-May and mid-October.

★ **Railroad Bridge Park,** set along a beautifully serene, 25-acre stretch of the Dungeness River, is centered on a lacy ironwork bridge that was once part of the coastal line between Port Angeles and Port Townsend. Today the park shelters a pristine river environment. The River Walk hike-and-bike path leads from the River Center educational facility, on the banks of the Dungeness, into the woods, and a horseback track links Runnion Road with the waterway. In summer, families picnic at the River Shed pavilion, students participate in science programs at the Dungeness River Audubon Society office, and locals come to watch performances at the River Stage amphitheater. Free guided bird walks run every Wednesday morning from 8:30 to 10:15. You'll find the park 2 mi west of town, and a five-minute drive from the coast. ⊠ *2151 Hendrickson Rd.* ☎ *360/681–4076* ⊕ *www.dungenessrivercenter.org* ⊡ *Free* ⊙ *Park, daily dawn–dusk. Audubon office Tues.–Sat. 10–4, Sun. noon–4.*

Sequim Bay State Park, an inlet 4 mi southwest of Sequim, is protected by a sand spit. The woodsy park has picnic tables, campsites, hiking trails, tennis courts, and a boat ramp. ⊠ *Off U.S. 101* ☎ *360/683–4235* ⊕ *www.parks.wa.gov* ⊡ *Free, camping $21–$28* ⊙ *Daily 8–sunset.*

12

WHERE TO EAT

$–$$
ECLECTIC

✕ **Alder Wood Bistro.** An inventive menu of local and organic dishes makes this one of the most popular restaurants in Sequim. Pizzas from the wood-fired oven include unique creations like the Nash's Spinach with lamb, sausage, goat cheese, and pickled onions; chicken pesto, and several that feature Mt. Townsend Creamery's cheeses. The menu's sustainably harvested seafood selections highlight whatever is in season, from black cod to salmon; they also get the wood-fire treatment. Even the basic meatloaf features local beef, along with buttermilk mashed potatoes and greens. For dessert, try the housemade apple pie or organic carrot cake. On warmer days, enjoy alfresco dining in the pretty garden courtyard. ⊠ *139 W. Alder St., Sequim* ☎ *360/683-4321* ⊕ *www.alderwoodbistro.com* ⊟ *AE, D, MC, V* ⊗ *Closed Sun. and Mon.; closed 2–5 PM between lunch and dinner. Reservations recommended.*

$–$$
CAFÉ

✕ **Cedarbrook Garden Cafe.** The greenhouse-enclosed restaurant overlooks Cedarbrook Lavender and Herb Farm. Many of the menu items feature lavender, including lavender cheesecake, crème brûlée, and lavender-flavored beverages. There are also carefully crafted soups, salads, burgers, fish-and-chips, and the special flower-pot brioche. ⊠ *1345 S. Sequim Ave.* ☎ *360/683–4541* w*www.cedarbrookgardencafe.com* ⊟ *D, MC, V* ⊗ *Closed Sun. and Mon. No dinner.*

$$–$$$
AMERICAN

✕ **Deckside Grill.** With tremendous views of John Wayne Marina and Sequim Bay, this family restaurant is a fun place to watch the ships placidly sail by. The casual menu includes coconut prawns, pasta, grilled chicken, and sandwiches. The kitchen also serves up excellent steak and lamb. ⊠ *2577 W. Sequim Bay Rd., Sequim* ☎ *360/683–7510* ⊟ *AE, D, MC, V* ⊗ *Closed Mon. and Tues.*

¢–$
AMERICAN

✕ **Oak Table Café.** Pancakes, waffles, and omelets are made using creative techniques at this breakfast and lunch restaurant. Eggs Nicole, for instance, is a medley of sautéed mushrooms, onions, spinach, and scrambled eggs served over an open-face croissant and covered with hollandaise sauce. You can get breakfast all day, or opt for the lunch menu, which includes burgers, salads, and sandwiches. ⊠ *292 W. Bell St.* ☎ *360/683–2179* ⊟ *AE, D, DC, MC, V* ⊗ *No dinner.*

$$
SEAFOOD
Fodor's Choice
★

✕ **Three Crabs.** An institution since 1958, this large crab shack on the beach, 5 mi north of Sequim, specializes in Dungeness's famed crustacean. Although the clawed creatures are served many ways here, these crabs are so fresh that it's best to simply have them with lemon and butter. ⊠ *11 Three Crabs Rd., Sequim* ☎ *360/683–4264* ⊕ *www.the3crabs.com* ⊟ *MC, V* ⊗ *Closed Mon. and Tues.*

WHERE TO STAY

$–$$
★

🏠 **Greywolf Inn Groveland.** On a 5-acre hilltop overlooking the town and bay, this country retreat among the trees is right on the Olympic Discovery Trail. A gazebo, Japanese-style hot tub, and warm front room encourage convivial gatherings. Berry bushes and occasionally elk dot the 5 acres of wild grounds. Room themes are inspired by diverse places and cultures like the south of France, the African savanna, and Bavaria. One room has a fireplace, another has a featherbed, and two have magnificent views. The glass-enclosed dining room and deck overlook a meadow. Cozy rooms are done in country style and filled with antiques;

there's also a rustic 19th-century bungalow. The pastoral setting is a favorite for weddings. **Pros:** pretty garden setting; inexpensive. **Cons:** decor too frilly for some. ✉ *395 Keeler Rd., Sequim* ☎ *360/683–5889 or 800/914–9653* ⊕ *www.greywolfinn.com* ⇆ *5 rooms* ☖ *In-room: no phone, a/c, Wi-Fi. In-hotel: restaurant, Wi-Fi, no kids under 16* ⊟ *AE, D, MC, V* ⎮○⎮ *BP.*

$–$$ ⊡ **Red Caboose Getaway.** Vintage metal railcars form the centerpiece of **Fodor's Choice** this bed-and-breakfast, where you get to sleep in a luxury train, each ★ decorated with a different famous theme. Track 1 is the Casey Jones, outfitted with the original conductor's desk and intercom; Track 2 holds the bright-red Orient Express, a cozy, wood-infused space with two-person whirlpool bath; Track 3 is the family-size Circus Caboose, with a boat-shape jetted tub and two extra bunks; Track 4 captures an Old West theme with desert decor and an antique claw-foot bathtub; Track 5 has a lavender theme and two-person whirlpool tub; and Track 6 honors the area's wine industry and accommodates four guests. The gleaming Silver Eagle restaurant, in an elegant 1937 Zephyr dining car, turns out hot, four-course breakfasts on china and crystal. **Pros:** unique decor; great breakfast. **Cons:** kids under 12 aren't allowed. ✉ *24 Old Coyote Way* ☎ *360/683–7350* ⊕ *www.redcaboosegetaway.com* ⇆ *6 suites* ☖ *In-room: a/c, refrigerator, DVD, Wi-Fi. In-hotel: no kids under 12* ⊟ *AE, D, MC, V.*

¢   ⊡ **Sequim Bay Lodge.** This sprawling, modern hotel on 17 acres is as resort-style as you'll get for the area. Rooms are done in pastel florals and set above woodland views, and most of the suites have a fireplace or balcony. The 7 Cedars Casino is nearby. **Pros:** good value; suites are convenient for families; varied room styles. **Cons:** decor is somewhat dated. ✉ *268522 U.S. 101* ☎ *360/683–0691 or 800/622–0691* 🖷 *360/683–3748* ⊕ *www.sequimbaylodge.com* ⇆ *54 rooms* ☖ *In-room: a/c, refrigerator, Wi-Fi. In-hotel: pool, some pets allowed* ⊟ *AE, D, MC, V* ⎮○⎮ *CP.*

NIGHTLIFE

The Jamestown S'Klallam tribe's enormous **7 Cedars Casino** (✉ *270756 U.S. 101* ☎ *360/683–7777* ⊕ *www.7cedarsresort.com*) has blackjack, roulette, and slots. One end of the casino is devoted to bingo. The tribe also runs an excellent art gallery and gift shop across the highway near the information kiosk, which is accessed via an underpass footpath.

PORT ANGELES

17 mi west of Sequim on U.S. 101.

Sprawling along the hills above the deep-blue Strait of San Juan de Fuca, Port Angeles is the crux of the Olympic Peninsula's air, sea, and land links. The town is capped off at the water's edge by a gathering of glittering hotels, restaurants, shops, and attractions, all set around the modern marina and the bone-white swath of Hollywood Beach. With a population of about 19,000, the town is the largest on the Olympic Peninsula and a major gateway to Olympic National Park. Summer foot traffic is shoulder-to-shoulder downtown with hopefuls rushing to ferries, vacationers strolling the waterfront, and locals relaxing at outdoor cafés.

It didn't start out this way, though, as the seasonal crowds have only been a phenomenon since the 1950s. The area was first settled by the Hoh, Makah, Quileute, Quinault, and S'Klallam tribes, and others had little reason to visit until a Greek pilot named Apostolos Valerianus—aka Juan de Fuca—sailed into the strait in 1610. In 1791 Spanish explorer Juan Francisco de Eliza followed him and named the Puerto de Nuestra Señora de Los Angeles, or Port of Our Lady of the Angels. George Vancouver shortened the name to Port Angeles in 1792, and the site was settled by pioneers in 1856. In the century that followed Port Angeles became a timber-mill town, a military base, and a key regional fishing port.

GETTING HERE

Port Angeles is about 2 hours from Seattle via the Edmonds–Kingston ferry and Highway 104; it's about 20 mi west of Sequim. It's served by Clallam Transit to local Olympic Peninsula towns, and Olympic Bus Lines to Silverdale, Seattle, and Sea-Tac airport. Kenmore Air runs flights between Port Angeles and Boeing Field, near Seattle.

Contacts Clallam Transit ☎ *360/452–4511 or 800/858–3747* ⊕ *www. clallamtransit.com.* **Olympic Bus Lines** ☎ *360/417–0700 or 800/457–4492* ⊕ *www.olympicbuslines.com.* **Kenmore Air** *866/435-9524* ⊕ *www.kenmoreair.com.*

GUIDED TOURS

Diamond Back Guide Service (✉ *140 Dolan Ave., Port Angeles* ☎ *360/452–9966*) leads fishing trips and scenic boat excursions around the peninsula. **Olympic Raft & Kayak** (✉ *123 Lake Aldwell Rd., Port Angeles* ☎ *360/452–1443* ⊕ *www.raftandkayak.com*) conducts white-water and scenic float trips on the Hoh and Elwha rivers. **Sound Dive Center** has scuba certification classes, dive equipment, and tours around the region.

VISITOR INFORMATION

Port Angeles Chamber of Commerce (✉ *121 E. Railroad Ave.* ☎ *360/452–2363* ⊕ *www.portangeles.org*).

EXPLORING

☺ **Ediz Hook,** at the western end of Port Angeles, is a long natural sand spit that protects the harbor from big waves and storms. The Hook is a fine place to take a walk along the water and watch shore- and seabirds, and to spot the occasional seal, orca, or gray whale. From downtown, take Front Street west and follow it as it meanders past the shuttered lumber mill.

The **Fiero Marine Life Center,** at the corner of the marina and Hollywood Beach, is brightly painted with an array of life-size ocean murals. Meander along the boardwalk overlooking the bay, then step inside to see just what's down in those waters. A variety of touch and display tanks along the walls house octopus, scallops, rockfish, and anemones, and volunteers are on hand to answer questions. ✉ *Port Angeles City Pier, Railroad St. at Lincoln St.* ☎ *360/417–6254* ⊕ *www.feiromarinelifecenter. org* 🏷 *Summer $3; free off-season* ⊗ *Memorial Day–Labor Day, daily 10–5; otherwise weekends noon–4.*

The small, sophisticated **Port Angeles Fine Arts Center** is inside the former home of the late artist and publisher Esther Barrows Webster, one of Port Angeles's most energetic and cultured citizens. Outdoor sculpture and trees surround the center, which has panoramas of the city and harbor. Exhibitions emphasize the works in various mediums of emerging and well-established Pacific Northwest artists. ☒ *1203 W. Lauridsen Blvd.* ☎ *360/417–4590* ⊕ *www.pafac.org* ⊠ *Free* ☉ *Indoor exhibits Mar.–Oct., Wed.–Sun. 11–5; Nov.–Feb., Wed.–Sun. 11–4. Outdoor exhibits daily dawn–dusk.*

WHERE TO EAT

$$
STEAK

✕ **The Bushwhacker.** More than three decades of excellent surf-and-turf keep the locals coming back to this Northwest-style restaurant just east of the city. It's a big, friendly place where families gather to dig into huge cuts of meat or seafood dishes. Other tasty fare includes jam-packed seafood fettucine, and stout bread-bowl Guinness stew topped with garlic mashed potatoes. A salad and soup bar comes with every meal—but save room for decadent desserts like triple berry cobbler with ice cream. ☒ *1527 E. 1st St.* ☎ *360/457–4113* ⊕ *www.bushwhackerpa. com* ☐ *AE, MC, V* ☉ *No lunch Sat.*

$$$–$$$$
FRENCH
Fodor's Choice
★

✕ **C'est Si Bon.** Far more Euro-savvy than is typical on the Olympic Peninsula, this first-rate restaurant stands out for its decor as well as for its food. The fanciful dining room is done up in bold red hues, with crisp white linens, huge oil paintings, and glittering chandeliers; the spacious solarium takes an equally formal approach. The changing menu highlights homemade onion soup, Cornish hen, Dungeness crab soufflé, and filet mignon. The wine list is superb, with French, Australian, and Northwest choices to pair with everything. ☒ *23 Cedar Park Rd., Port Angeles* ☎ *360/452–8888* ⊕ *www.cestsibon-frenchcuisine.com* ☐ *AE, DC, MC, V* ☉ *Closed Mon. No lunch.*

$–$$
SEAFOOD

✕ **Crab House.** This waterfront restaurant, linked to the Red Lion Inn in front of the Port Angeles Pier, is one of the region's most famous spots for fresh local seafood. Crab is the specialty, of course, and it shows up in a tasty variety of dishes, including crab hash, crab bisque, crab cakes, and crab-stuffed fish specials. Windows surrounding the elegant dining room let you view the serene gray waters where much of what's on the menu is caught daily. ☒ *221 N. Lincoln St.* ☎ *360/457–0424* ⊕ *www. redlion.com* ☐ *AE, D, DC, MC, V.*

$$–$$$
CONTEMPORARY
★

✕ **Dupuis Restaurant.** Flower-filled gardens surround this little log cabin, painted a cheery yellow and blue and trimmed with bright flower boxes. One of the dining rooms was a tavern in the 1920s, and today close-set tables in the elegant main dining room are lit by small chandeliers. Grilled local fish, steamed crabs and oysters, seafood sautés, and a selection of continental choices, like cheese-topped French onion soup, round out the menu. It's a dress-up dinner spot that's a highlight of a trip to the region. Hint: The owner will open the restaurant during lunch and off days for groups of 10 or more. ☒ *256861 U.S. 101* ☎ *360/457–8033* w*www.dupuisrestaurant.com* ☐ *AE, D, MC, V* ☉ *Closed Tues. in winter. No lunch.*

Colette's Bed & Breakfast

WHERE TO STAY

$$$

Fodor's Choice
★

Colette's Bed & Breakfast. A contemporary mansion curving around 10 acres of gorgeous waterfront property, this B&B offers more space, service, and luxury than any other property in the area. Leather sofas and chairs and a river-rock fireplace make the front room a lovely spot to watch the water through expansive 20-foot windows. The suites, which have such names as Iris, Azalea, and Cedar, also overlook the water and have fireplaces, balconies, CD and DVD players, and two-person hot tubs. A specially made outdoor fireplace means you can enjoy the deck even in winter. Multicourse breakfasts include espresso-based drinks and fresh fruit. **Pros:** water views to Victoria, BC; discreet personal service. **Cons:** does not cater to families. ⊠ *339 Finn Hall Rd., 10 mi east of town, Port Angeles* ☎ *360/457–9197 or 877/457–9777* ⊕ *www.colettes.com* ↩ *5 suites* ⚂ *In-room: a/c, refrigerator (some), DVD, Wi-Fi. In-hotel: laundry facilities, no kids under 18* ⊟ *MC, V* ⏀ *BP.*

$–$$

Five Sea Suns Bed & Breakfast. The clever name of this cozy 1926 inn refers to its rooms, each elegantly appointed in the theme of a time of year: the four seasons plus an Indian summer. If you stay in Lente (spring), you can enjoy a breezy balcony. Na Zomer (Indian summer) is in a separate carriage house. The B&B overlooks the mountains and the bay, which you can view from the pond-side pergola and award-winning gardens. In the morning, coffee is served in a silver tea set in your room. **Pros:** garden setting is steps from town; the owner's home-baked chocolate-chip cookies. **Cons:** on a busy street. ⊠ *1006 S. Lincoln St.* ☎ *360/452–8248 or 800/708–0777* ⊕ *www.seasuns.com* ↩ *5 rooms*

♿ *In-room: no phone, no a/c, refrigerator (some), DVD (some), no TV (some), Wi-Fi. In hotel: no kids under 12* ☰ *AE, D, MC, V* ¶Ol *BP.*

$$ ⌕ **Sea Cliff Gardens Bed & Breakfast.** A gingerbread-style porch fronts Fodor'sChoice this waterfront Victorian home on three acres of landscaped grounds. ★ Exquisitely appointed guest rooms include Victoria's Repose, which has a finely carved half-tester English oak bed and a balcony with a private two-person hot tub. All rooms have fireplaces, CD players and DVDs, plus panoramic water views through floor-to-ceiling windows. Three suites have indoor whirlpool tubs, and one has a private outdoor hot tub. Antiques are artfully arranged throughout the living and dining rooms, which have expansive views of the strait. **Pros:** gorgeous flower gardens have been featured in national commercials; very romantic setting; new owners are adding their touches. **Cons:** a bit off the beaten path. ✉ *397 Monterra Dr.* ☎ *360/452–2322 or 800/880–1332* ⊕ *www. seacliffgardens.com* ⛵ *5 suites* ♿ *In-room: a/c, DVD, Wi-Fi. In-hotel: bicycles, no kids under 12* ☰ *AE, D, MC, V* ¶Ol *BP.*

SEKIU

28 mi northwest of Forks.

The village of Sekiu (pronounced *see*-kyu) rests on the peninsula's northern shore, a rocky and roiling stretch of coastline inhabited for centuries by the Makah (ma-*kah*), Ozette, and S'Klallum tribes. White settlers moved to Sekiu after a salmon cannery opened near the fishing grounds in 1870. Logging became the mainstay of the local economy in the early 1900s. Both industries shut down when resources became overexploited, and now Sekiu is a scenic vacation town known for excellent fishing and scuba diving. As the twisted two-lane road rises and dips along the rugged edge of the land, the forest often yields to a panorama of surf-thrashing, boulder-strewn beaches, with distant views of mountainous Vancouver Island. Autumn attracts fishing pros to the Sekiu River for cutthroat trout and steelhead, and the town jetty is a base for sports divers.

GETTING HERE

Seiku is about an hour and 15 min from Port Angeles, via U.S. 101 west to Hwy. 113 then north.

GUIDED TOURS

Curley's Resort & Dive Center (✉ *291 Front St., Sekiu* ☎ *360/963–2281 or 800/542–9680* ⊕ *www.curleysresort.com*) is a regional scuba shop.

VISITOR INFORMATION

Clallam Bay/Sekiu Chamber of Commerce (⌖ *Box 355, Clallam Bay 98326* ☎ *360/963–2339* ⊕ *www.sekiu.com*).

EXPLORING

On the former site of an Indian fishing village, the 33-acre **Clallam Bay Spit** brings beachcombers, fishers, and divers. The 4-acre Pillar Point Fishing Camp to the east has campsites and a boat ramp. Dress warmly: Pysht Bay takes its name from a S'Klallam term meaning "where the wind blows from all directions." ✉ *Off Hwy. 112 at Clallum Bay and Pysht Bay.*

WHERE TO EAT AND STAY

$ ✕**Breakwater Restaurant.** This restaurant above the Strait of San Juan
SEAFOOD de Fuca claims to be the most northwesterly dining establishment in
the continental United States. Look for seafood, of course, served by
a friendly and accommodating staff. Chicken dishes, burgers, steaks,
and breakfasts fill out the menu. While you wait for your food, enjoy
the collection of "Messy Palette" locally painted works hung along the
walls. ☒ *15582 Hwy. 112, Clallam Bay* ☎ *360/963–2428* ▭ *MC, V.*

¢–$ 🛏 **Winter Summer Inn.** The late-1800s home is the community's oldest,
and its walls are appropriately adorned with American antiques and
works by local artists. The master suite has a full kitchen and private
deck, and the Quilt Room has a whirlpool tub. You can see panoramas
of the Clallam River and Strait of Juan de Fuca from all around the inn.
Pros: central to upper Olympic Peninsula sights; stunning water views.
Cons: two rooms have private half-bath but share the shower. ☒ *16651
Hwy. 112, Clallam Bay* ☎ *360/963–2264* ⊕ *www.wintersummerinn.
com* 🛏 *3 rooms, 1 suite* ⚐ *In-room: no phone, no a/c, kitchen (some),
DVD, no TV (some), Wi-Fi. In-hotel: no kids under 12* ▭ *AE, D, MC,
V* ⦿ *BP.*

NEAH BAY

15 mi northwest of Sekiu.

One of the oldest villages in Washington, Neah (pronounced *nee*-ah)
Bay is surrounded by the Makah Indian Reservation at the northwestern tip of the Olympic Peninsula. Today it's still a quiet, seldom-visited
seaside settlement of one-story homes, espresso stands, and bait shops
stretched along about a mile of gravelly coastal road, which parallels
the glistening, boat-filled bay. Stroll along the docks to watch boot-clad
fishermen and shaggy canines motoring out on warped and barnacled
vessels, and peer into the oil-stained water for views of anemones, shellfish, and sea lions. The rocky bulkhead rises behind the marina; look
beyond that to view sunsets and Cape Flattery, the northwesternmost
point in the contiguous United States.

Explorer James Cook named the cape in 1778 when his ship missed the
fog-smothered Strait of Juan de Fuca and landed here instead. In 1792
Spanish mariners established a short-lived fort here, which was the first
European settlement in what is now Washington State. The local Makah
tribe is more closely related to the Nootka of Vancouver Island, just
across the water, than to any Washington tribe. Like their ancestors,
they embark on whale hunts by canoe, although fleets of kayaks skim-
ming through the calm bay are all you're likely to see during your visit.

GETTING HERE
Neah Bay is quite remote, accessed only by Highway 112 west of Sekiu
(about a 30-min drive).

EXPLORING

☺ The outstanding **Makah Cultural and Research Center** displays thousands
Fodor's Choice of Makah art pieces and artifacts, many eons old. Done in low lights
★ and rich timbers, the space is divided into an easy route of intriguing exhibits. The centerpiece is a full-size cedar longhouse, complete

Makah Indian Art

with hand-woven baskets, fur skins, cattail wool, grass mats on the bed planks, and a background of tribal music. Another section houses full-size whaling and seal-hunting canoes and weapons. Other areas show games, clothing, crafts, and relics from the ancient Ozette Village mudslide. The small shop stocks a collection of locally made art pieces, books, and crafts; plan to spend some time looking around. This is an impresssive a museum as you'd find in any major city, and should be a stop on any itinerary in the region. ⊠ *1880 Bayview Ave.* ☎ *360/645–2711* ⊕ *www.makah.com* ✉ *$5* ⊗ *Daily 10–5.*

At the **Makah National Fish Hatchery** you can view Chinook salmon as they make their way over fish ladders to the hatchery's spawning area. Spawning months are October and November, and the salmon are released in late April. Smaller numbers of coho and chum salmon and steelhead trout also populate the hatchery. From Neah Bay, follow signs south for 7 mi. ⊠ *897 Hatchery Rd.* ☎ *360/645–2521* ✉ *Free* ⊗ *Daily 7:30–4.*

WHERE TO STAY

$$ 🏨 **King Fisher Inn.** The three-story, sky-gray chalet above the Strait of Juan de Fuca is decked out in Northwest style, trimmed with timber and a fringe of colorful flowers. Each room comes with fluffy robes, and a breakfast buffet is included. One unique focus of the inn is quilting, and you can view many local creations in the gallery; quilting classes and workshops run autumn through winter. Note that a two-night minimum stay is required on weekends. **Pros:** chairlift service up to rooms; full meal plan for groups. **Cons:** scrapbooking and meeting groups can disrupt serene atmosphere. ⊠ *1562 Hwy. 112* ☎ *360/645–2150* *or 888/622–8216 ⊕ www.kingfisherenterprises.com ↩ 4 rooms ⚏ In-room: no phone, no a/c, DVD, Wi-Fi. In-hotel: laundry facilities, no kids under 12 ⊟ MC, V ⏀ BP.*

FORKS

99 mi north of Copalis Beach.

The former logging town of Forks is named for two nearby river junctions: the Bogachiel and Calawah rivers merge west of town, and a few miles farther they are joined by the Soleduck to form the Quileute River, which empties into the Pacific at the Native American village of La Push. Forks is a small, quiet gateway town for Olympic National Park's Hoh River valley unit. The surrounding countryside is exceptionally green, with an annual precipitation of more than 100 inches. As the setting for the popular Twilight movie series, the town has become a popular destination for fans in recent years.

GETTING HERE

From the Seattle area, Forks is about 3 1/2 hours via the Edmonds–Kingston ferry and U.S. 101 west; it's about an hour past Port Angeles. Coming from the south, U.S. 101 north from Aberdeen to Forks takes about 2 hours. Clallam Transit runs from Forks to Port Angeles and other north peninsula towns. West Jefferson Transit provides service between Forks and Lake Quinault, including a stop at Kalaloch.

GUIDED TOURS

Extreme Adventures (⌂ *Box 1991, Forks* ☎ *360/374–8747*) runs two-hour and overnight float trips on the Hoh River. **Peak Six Tours** (⊠ *4883 Upper Hoh Rd., Forks* ☎ *360/374–5254*) provides gear and information for hiking, biking, camping, climbing, and sightseeing on the Olympic Peninsula. Guided hikes cost about $50 per day.

VISITOR INFORMATION

Forks Chamber of Commerce (⊠ *1411 S. Forks Ave., Forks* ☎ *360/374–2531 or 800/443–6757* ⊕ *www.forkswa.com*).

EXPLORING

The **Big Cedar,** thought to be the world's largest cedar tree, stands 178 feet tall and is 19 feet 5 inches in diameter. Area loggers left it standing when they realized just how enormous it really was. The tree is off Nolan Creek Road. From U.S. 101, turn right onto Highway N1000 for 1.3 mi, then turn right onto N1100 for 2.4 mi. Turn right again onto N1112 for 0.4 mi, and then turn right once more for 0.1 mi.

WHERE TO EAT

$–$$

CAFE

✕**Forks Coffee Shop.** This modest restaurant on the highway in downtown Forks serves terrific, home-style, classic American fare. From 5 AM onward you can dig into giant pancakes and Sol Duc scrambles (eggs, sausage, hash browns, and veggies tumbled together). At lunch there's a choice of soups, salads, and hot and cold sandwiches, which the waitstaff will bag for pickup if you're on the run. Dinner specials come with free trips to the salad bar and include entrées like baby back ribs and grilled Hood Canal oysters. Top off the meal with a home-baked treat, like a slice of flaky-crust pie made with locally grown marionberries, blueberries, strawberries, cherries, or apples. ✉ *241 Forks Ave.* ☎ *360/374–6769* ⊕ *www.forkscoffeeshop.com* 🖃 *D, DC, MC, V.*

¢–$ ✕ **Plaza Jalisco.** On the outside you can tell it was once a gas station, but
MEXICAN head past the painted Mexican bandit statue and suddenly you're in a colorful world south of the border. Desert colors, ceramic bells, hand-painted masks, and hand-knit blankets decorate the small, airy dining room, where locals gather to down heaping plates of rice, beans, and meat-filled burritos. Frothy and potent margaritas are the big draw on weekends. This is a top budget stop, where the home-cooked flavors and low prices keep both your stomach and your wallet full. ✉ *90 N. Forks Ave.* ☎ *360/374–3108* 🖃 *MC, V.*

$–$$ ✕ **Smoke House Restaurant.** Rough-panel walls give a rustic appeal to the
STEAK dining room of this two-story Forks favorite. Successful surf-and-turf specials remain unchanged since the place opened as a smokehouse in 1975. Smoked salmon is a top-seller, but the steaks and prime rib are also delicious. Burgers, fries, and milk shakes will please the kids. ✉ *193161 U.S. 101* ☎ *360/374–6258* 🖃 *D, MC, V.*

WHERE TO STAY

$ 🏨 **Manitou Lodge.** If seclusion is what you seek, turn off your cell phone (they're useless here) and visit this cedar lodge in the rain forest, which bills itself as the westernmost B&B in the continental United States. The cathedral-size main room has a towering stone fireplace, a tall bookcase, and multiple couches. Five lodge rooms of varying sizes and two suites in the adjacent cottage have cedar paneling, handmade quilts, driftwood headboards, and oak furnishings; the large Sacagawea room even has a fireplace. Two small, rustic cabins are available from May through October. Snacks and coffee are served in the Great Room. **Pros:** guests are welcomed with cookies in their rooms; some lodgings are family-friendly. **Cons:** no TV or phones, though there is Wi-Fi. ✉ *813 Kilmer Rd.* ☎ *360/374–6295* 🖷 *360/374–7495* ⊕ *www.manitoulodge.com* ⤳ *5 rooms, 2 suites, 2 cabins, 2 tents* △ *In-room: no phone, no a/c, no TV, Wi-Fi. In-hotel: no kids under 5 (except in cottage), some pets allowed* 🖃 *AE, MC, V* ⓘ◯ⓘ *BP.*

$ 🏨 **Miller Tree Inn Bed and Breakfast.** Built as a farmhouse in 1916, this pale yellow B&B is still bordered on two sides by pastures. Numerous windows make the rooms bright, cheerful places to relax amid antiques, knickknacks, and quilts. Premier rooms have king-size beds, gas fireplaces, and whirlpool tubs for two. A separate apartment has a private entrance and kitchenette. One parlor has a library and piano, the other has games. In summer, lemonade and cookies are served on the lawn or the wide front porch. From October through April, nearby rivers offer prime salmon and steelhead fishing. **Pros:** nice location; good breakfast. **Cons:** some guests have complained about cleanliness and functionality of rooms. ✉ *654 E. Division St.* ☎ *360/374–6806 or 800/943–6563* ⊕ *www.millertreeinn.com* ⤳ *6 rooms, 1 apartment* △ *In-room: no phone, no a/c, kitchen (some), DVD (some), no TV (some), Wi-Fi. In-hotel: some pets allowed* 🖃 *AE, D, MC, V* ⓘ◯ⓘ *BP.*

COPALIS BEACH

12

3 mi north of Ocean Shores.

A Native American village for several thousand years, this small coastal town at the mouth of the Copalis (pronounced coh-*pah*-liss) River was settled by European-Americans in the 1890s. The beach here is known locally for its innumerable razor clams, which can be gathered by the thousands each summer, and for its watchtowers, built between 1870 and 1903 to spot and stalk sea otters—the animals are now protected by Washington state law. The first oil well in the state was dug here in 1901, but it proved to be unproductive. However, some geologists still claim that the continental shelf off the Olympic Peninsula holds major oil reserves.

GETTING HERE

Copalis Beach is about 30 mi from Aberdeen, via Highway 109. Bus service is provided by Grays Harbor Transit.

Contact **Grays Harbor Transit** ☎ *360/532–2770 or 800/562–9730* ⊕ *www. ghtransit.com.*

EXPLORING

You can hike or ride horses at **Griffiths-Priday Ocean State Park,** a 364-acre marine park stretching more than a mile along both the Pacific Ocean and the Copalis River. A boardwalk crosses low dunes to the broad, flat beach. The Copalis Spit section of the park is a designated wildlife refuge for thousands of snowy plover and other bird life. There is no camping at this park. ⊠ *3119 Hwy. 109* ☎ *360/902–8844* ☑ *Free* ☉ *Daily dawn–dusk.*

Pacific Beach State Park, between Copalis Beach and the town of Moclips, is a lovely spot for walking, surf-perch fishing, and razor-clam digging. There's also excellent fishing for sea-run cutthroat trout in the Moclips River—but be careful not to trespass onto Indian land, as the Quinault Reservation starts north of the river. The park has developed tent and RV sites, as well as a few primitive beachfront campsites. ⊠ *Hwy. 109 S, 5 mi north of Copalis Beach* ☎ *360/289–3553* ☑ *Camping $14–$28* ☉ *Daily dawn–dusk.*

WHERE TO EAT AND STAY

¢–$
AMERICAN

✕ **Green Lantern Tavern.** The Copalis River flows beside this rustic, cedar shake–covered local favorite, in business since the 1930s. Huge picture windows show off ocean views, and the flowery outdoor beer garden attracts beachgoers in summer. Breakfasts, BLTs, grilled cheese, and fish are on the menu, and there are specials every night, including New York steak on Tuesdays, served with a baked potato and garlic bread. The tavern has shuffleboard and a 10-foot-long clam-digging shovel in the corner adds some local flavor. You must be 21 to enter. ⊠ *3119 Hwy. 109* ☎ *360/289–2297* ▭ *No credit cards.*

¢–$

🏨 **Sandpiper Beach Resort.** This resort is on a secluded beach 3 mi south of Moclips. The clean, contemporary studios and one-, two-, and three-bedroom suites each have a fireplace except one, a kitchen, exposed wood ceilings, and sliding glass doors leading to a porch overlooking the ocean. Little extras include heated towel bars, and

Seabrook Cottage Rentals

there's housekeeping service every third day. No restaurant is on-site, but you're within walking distance of local cafés. **Pros:** great place for seclusion and getting close to nature in spacious lodgings. **Cons:** not for technology-dependent folks. ✉ *4159 Hwy. 109, Pacific Beach* ☎ *360/276–4580 or 800/567–4737* ⊕ *www.sandpiper-resort.com* ⤸ *31 units* ⚲ *In-room: no phone, no a/c, kitchen, no TV. In-hotel: beachfront, laundry facilities, Wi-Fi hotspot, some pets allowed* ▭ *MC, V.*

$$–$$$$
Fodor's Choice
★
☾

🍴 **Seabrook Cottage Rentals.** Seabrook is a charming new beach town that is being strategically planned and developed. At this writing, it has just over 150 homes, and more than half of those are available as rentals, ranging from small cottages that are perfect for a couple's getaway to large homes (some with separate carriage houses) big enough for multiple families to share. Most of the homes are set around the walkable village, which has its own café, small market, and pottery studio and eventually will have other retail services. (When complete, there will be nearly 500 homes at Seabrook). The Cape Cod–style homes are individually owned and decorated; some have private hot tubs and all have access to beachy style cruiser bikes for exploring the small town and its parks, recreation (including bocce ball and shuffle board), shops, common areas, and the natural environment. Nearly all of the current homes are on the east side of the highway; visitors take a private trail and stairs to get to the beach. Oceanfront homes are just beginning to be developed. **Pros:** community's recreational amenities and beach are within walking distance; homes are all new with full amenities. **Cons:** as a developing town, there is ongoing construction. ✉ *4275 State Route 109, Pacific Beach* ☎ *360/276–0265 or 877/779–9990* ⊕ *www. seabrookcottagerentals.com* ⤸ *76 cottages* ⚲ *In-room: a/c (some),* *kitchen, DVD (some), Wi-Fi (some). In-hotel: restaurant, bicycles, laundry facilities, Wi-Fi hotspot, some pets allowed* ⊟ *AE, D, MC, V.*

EN ROUTE

Ruby Beach, named for the rosy fragments of garnet that color its sands, is one of the peninsula's most beautiful stretches of coastline. A short trail leads to the wave-beaten sands, where sea stacks, caves, tidal pools, and bony driftwood make it a favorite place for beachcombers, artists, and photographers. It's 15 mi south of Forks, off U.S. 101.

12

OCEAN SHORES

18 mi west of Hoquiam, 4 mi northwest of Westport.

Ocean Shores, a long stretch of resorts, restaurants, shops, and attractions, sits on the northern spit that encloses Grays Harbor. The whole area was planned by housing developers in the 1960s, and with its broad, flat white beach, shallow surf, and sunset panoramas, it's been a favorite seaside getaway since. Come summer, dune buggies and go-karts buzz up and down the sand road, weaving around clusters of horses trotting tourists over the dunes. Colorful kites flap overhead, dogs romp in the waves, and tide pools are filled with huge orange Dungeness crabs, live sand dollars, and delicate snails, to the delight of small children. It's no tropical haven, however, as summer can bring chilly breezes, and the water never warms up much for swimming—hence jackets are mandatory even in July. A fog of sea mist often blows in during the late afternoon, and in winter massive thunderstorms billow onto land directly before the line of coastal hotels. An indoor pool and in-room fireplace are coveted amenities year-round in this cool climate, and well worth the added expense.

GETTING HERE

Ocean Shores is the closest developed ocean-beach town to Seattle; it's about a 2 1/2-hour drive via I–5 south to Olympia then west via U.S. 101 and north via Highway 109. The traffic through Aberdeen and Hoquiam can slow to a crawl on busy summer weekends; try especially to avoid heading back east on Sunday or holiday afternoons. Grays Harbor Transit serves the community locally.

Contact Grays Harbor Transit ☎ *360/532–2770 or 800/562–9730* ⊕ *www.ghtransit.com.*

VISITOR INFORMATION

Ocean Shores Information Center (⊠ *873 Point Brown Ave. NW, Ste. 1, Ocean Shores* ☎ *360/289–2451 or 800/762–3224* ⊕ *www.oceanshores.org).*

EXPLORING

The **Ocean Shores Interpretive Center,** a great stormy-day educational spot for families, highlights the seaside environment, local history, and Native American traditions. Displays include dried local wildflowers, a rock identification table, Native American basketry, and a model of the Quinault River's Chow Chow Bridge. Reproduction seabirds, whale bones, and a vast shell collection let you examine the shoreline wildlife up close. ⊠ *1033 Catala Ave. SE* ☎ *360/289–4617* ⊕ *www.*

oceanshoresinterpretivecenter.com 🖃 *Free* 🕙 *April–Sept., daily 11–4; Oct.–Mar., weekends 11–4.*

WHERE TO EAT

$$ ✕ **Alec's by the Sea.** Some of the region's best seafood is served at this
AMERICAN elegant restaurant conveniently set between town and beach. The best dishes are made with creatures caught locally, such as razor clams and Willapa Bay oysters. For a light meal, try the garlic bread served with bouillabaisse, or one of the salads. Steaks and burgers are also on the menu. ⊠ *131 E. Chance a la Mer Blvd.* ☎ *360/289–4026* ▭ *AE, D, MC, V.*

$–$$ ✕ **Mike's Seafood.** Wander through the small, roadside seafood shop to
SEAFOOD see what's cooking before you sit down in the adjacent restaurant. Every-
★ thing served is fresh-caught, and salmon is smoked on the premises. Italian specialties round out the menu—one of the best ways to sample it all is in the tomato-based cioppino. ⊠ *830 Point Brown Ave. NE* ☎ *360/289–0532* w*www.oceanshoresseafood.com* ▭ *AE, D, MC, V.*

WHERE TO STAY

$–$$ 🏨 **Quinault Beach Resort & Casino.** A half mile of dunes and wild beach grasses separates this enormous resort from the crowds. Shades of green, gray, and gold appear throughout the rooms, which all have 10-foot ceilings, gas fireplaces, and twin bathroom sinks. Enormous suites have sea vistas, corner jetted tubs, and plasma TVs. The full-ser-vice spa has private sauna and Jacuzzi rooms and an ocean-view patio. Surrounded by 200 acres of protected wetlands, there's plenty of room to swim, hike, and watch for wildlife. **Pros:** grand rooms for low rates; upscale setting. **Cons:** gambling crowds can be rowdy. ⊠ *78 Hwy. 115* ☎ *360/289–5001 or 888/461–2214* ⊕ *www.quinaultbeachresort.com* ᨏ *150 rooms, 9 suites* ⌂ *In-room: a/c, refrigerator, DVD (some), Wi-Fi. In-hotel: 5 restaurants, room service, bar, pool, gym, spa, beachfront, laundry service* ▭ *AE, D, DC, MC, V.*

$$ 🏨 **Shilo Inn.** Framed by a Pacific Ocean seascape to the west and a dune-covered state park to the south, this all-suites hotel welcomes guests resort-style. The lower floor opens into an expanse of elegant lounging areas, each dotted with hand-carved models of international sailing vessels and life-size marble sea creatures—and it's all backed by a 3,000-gallon aquarium that looks into the pool. Large, modern accommodations are like apartments, each with a living area, fireplace, and a balcony overlooking the beach. A five-minute walk takes you to the surf, local shops, and outdoor activities. The restaurant and lounge serves a mix of American fare and fine Northwest cuisine. **Pros:** great location; attractive lobby; lots of amenities. **Cons:** lots of tourists, fami-lies, and groups make hallways noisy late and early; rates spike during summer and special events. ⊠ *707 Ocean Shores Blvd.* ☎ *360/289–4600 or 800/222–2244* 🖷 *360/289–0355* ⊕ *www.shiloinns.com* ᨏ *113 suites* ⌂ *In-room: a/c, refrigerator, Wi-Fi. In-hotel: restaurant, bar, pool, gym, beachfront, laundry facilities, Wi-Fi hotspot, some pets allowed* ▭ *AE, D, DC, MC, V.*

HOQUIAM

10 mi west of Aberdeen.

Hoquiam (pronounced *hoh*-quee-ahm) is a historic lumber town near Aberdeen and the mouth of the Hoquiam River. Both river and town were named with the Chehalis word meaning "hungry for wood." The town was settled in the mid–19th century, around the same time as Aberdeen, and is now a major Grays Harbor port for cargo and fishing vessels. Its industries include canneries and manufacturers of wood products and machine tools.

GETTING HERE

Hoquiam is about an hour from Olympia via U.S. 101. Grays Harbor Transit serves Hoquiam and neighboring towns.

Contact Grays Harbor Transit (☎ *360/532–2770 or 800/562–9730* ⊕ *www. ghtransit.com*).

VISITOR INFORMATION

Grays Harbor Chamber of Commerce (⊠ *506 Duffy St., Aberdeen* ☎ *800/321– 1924* ⊕ *www.graysharbor.org*).

EXPLORING

In fall and spring, **Grays Harbor National Wildlife Refuge** is a perfect place to observe the multitude of migrating shorebirds that visit the area. Keep your binoculars handy as you stroll along the 1,800-foot-long boardwalk, and make sure to stop at the visitor center's shop and bookstore. To get here from Hoquiam, drive west on Highway 109 to Pawlson Road, then turn left and continue to Airport Way, where you make a right toward the refuge. ⊠ *Airport Way* ☎ *360/753–9467* ⊕ *www. fws.gov/graysharbor* ⊠ *$3 (admits 4 adults)* ⊙ *Park: daily dawn–dusk; visitor center: Wed.–Sun. 9–4.*

The Polson Museum, in a 26-room mansion built in 1924, is filled with artifacts and mementos relating to Grays Harbor's past. You can walk through the remodeled dining room, kitchen, and living room, where an exhibit traces the history of tall ships in the Pacific Northwest. Upstairs is the logging exhibit, with a replica Little Hoquiam Railroad; a period-costume room; and the Polson children's room and dollhouse. Outside you can wander the riverside grounds, which have exotic trees and a rose garden. ⊠ *1611 Riverside Ave.* ☎ *360/533–5862* ⊕ *www. polsonmuseum.org* ⊠ *$4* ⊙ *Jan.–Aug., Wed.–Sat. 11–4, Sun. noon–4.*

WHERE TO STAY

$–$$ **Hoquiam's Castle Bed & Breakfast.** A registered National Historic Site, this imposing, 10,000-square-foot Victorian mansion was built in 1887 by lumber baron Robert Lytle. Three floors are filled with exquisite antique and reproduction furnishings, including crystal chandeliers, Tiffany-style lamps, stained-glass windows, and canopy beds. The charming bedrooms overlook the town and harbor. Nonguests can take a 45-minute tour, scheduled by appointment, for $5; guests receive a free guided walk-through. ⊠ *515 Chenault Ave.* ☎ *360/533–2005* ⊕ *www. hoquiamscastle.com* ↘ *4 rooms* ⚘ *In-room: no phone, no a/c. In-hotel: no kids under 12* ▤ *AE, D, MC, V* ⦿| *CP.*

ABERDEEN

6 mi west of Montesano.

The pretty town of Aberdeen, on Grays Harbor at the mouth of the Chehalis River, was settled in 1867 by farmers. Some of the earliest residents were Scottish immigrants who named it after their own city set along a harbor at the mouth of a river. Growth and prosperity came to the town after Scotsman George R. Hume started a salmon cannery here in 1878 and the town's first sawmill was built in 1884. Soon tall ships crowded the narrow harbor to load lumber, and waterfront bars were busy with sailors and lumberjacks.

Early homesteaders found the cleared forest land too soggy to support anything except cranberries, which still thrive in the bogs. Other farmers turned to cultivating oysters in the shallow harbor bays. In 1903 most of Aberdeen's buildings, made of wood and surrounded by streets of sawdust, burned down during a dry spell. These were replaced with stone and brick buildings, many of which still stand in the downtown area.

Aberdeen is known for its lovely harbor, spread glittering and gray along the west edge of town, where the bay bobs with sailboats and speed cruisers. Vast swaths of lumberyards are broken up by towering cranes, which transport the massive timbers onto immense metal barges. Forested hills serve as a backdrop to town, promising a picturesque entry into the Olympic Peninsula to the north. The town is also dotted with the classic, century-old mansions built by shipping and timber barons of the 20th century, and the "Aberdeen Walking Tour" brochure ($4) provides a self-guided look at more than four dozen of the largest and most beautiful homes. The contemporary Walk of Fame tour follows the local highlights from some of the town's best-known former residents, including Bill Boeing and Kurt Cobain.

GETTING HERE

Aberdeen is 4 miles east of Hoquiam and is also served by Grays Harbor Transit.

Contact Grays Harbor Transit ☎ *360/532–2770 or 800/562–9730* ⊕ *www.ghtransit.com.*

EXPLORING

For a general look at the lay of Aberdeen, take the 1½-mi-long, paved **Morrison Riverfront Park Walk** to the 40-foot-wide Compass Rose mosaic, inlaid at the confluence of the Wishkah and Chehalis rivers.

Tall, billowing white sails in the harbor mark the presence of the ***Lady Washington,*** a replica of the 1750s coastal freighter from Boston, which in 1792, under the command of famous explorer Captain Robert Gray, was the first American vessel to reach the northwest American coast. The replica was famously converted into the multimasted HMS *Interceptor* sloop for the 2002 Disney movie *Pirates of the Caribbean.* Its main base is the Grays Harbor Historic Seaport, but you'll find the vessel at local coastal towns throughout the region, where it's open for self-guided tours.Three-hour cruises include the hands-on "Adventure Sail" and a mock "Battle Sail" war between two vessels, and if you're

12

at least 18 you can volunteer as a deckhand for multiday trips. The free **Seaport Learning Center,** a 214-acre site spread across the harbor and surrounding wetlands, runs tours on two historic longboats, and schedules monthly boatbuilding, rope-climbing, and marine-trade programs for families and students. ⊠ *712 Hagara St.* ☎ *360/532–8611 or 800/200–5239* ⊕ *www.ladywashington.org* ✉ *Tours by donation, sailings $55–$60* ⊙ *Tours weekdays 4–5, Sat. 10–1, sailings weekends 2–5.*

WHERE TO EAT AND STAY

$

AMERICAN

✕**Billy's.** This bar and grill used to be the most popular saloon and brothel in town, and the restaurant has a collection of prints recalling those bawdy days. Even the establishment's name was taken from the saloon's notorious original owner, Billy Ghol. It's said his ghost haunts the premises. Standard fare includes burgers and salads, but you can go exotic with grilled yak. ⊠ *322 E. Heron St.* ☎ *360/533–7144* ⊟ *AE, DC, MC, V.*

$–$$

AMERICAN

✕**Bridges.** This café takes its name not from its location between the Wishkah and Chehalis river spans but from owner Sonny Bridges, who's been running local restaurants for more than 30 years. This classy, pastel-hue place has excellent seafood and huge steaks. ⊠ *112 N. G St.* ☎ *360/532–6563* ⊟ *AE, D, DC, MC, V* ⊙ *No lunch Sun.*

$–$$

🛏**A Harbor View Inn.** You can see the harbor from every room in this 1905 Victorian mansion. Hand-stenciled walls surround the elegant parlors, where two fireplaces warm the air on cool autumn evenings. Three of the rooms have fireplaces and all have king-size beds. Sunrooms bring in the light to help a variety of plants flourish. Take the ballroom staircase to the old-fashioned rooms, where handmade quilts cover the antique beds. ⊠ *111 W. 11th St.* ☎ *360/533–7996 or 877/533–7996* ⊕ *www.aharborview.com* ⌨ *5 rooms, 1 suite* ⌂ *In-room: no phone, no a/c, refrigerator (some), DVD. In-hotel: Internet terminal, Wi-Fi hotspot, no kids under 8* ⊟ *AE, D, MC, V* ⑩ *BP.*

WESTPORT

15 mi southwest of Aberdeen.

Westport is a bayfront fishing village on the southern spit that helps protect the entrance to Grays Harbor from the fury of the Pacific Ocean. Numerous charter companies based here offer salmon, lingcod, rockfish, and albacore fishing trips, as well as whale-watching tours. If you're not taking a cruise, you can stand on Westport's beach to look for gray whales migrating southward in November and December, toward their breeding grounds in Baja California, and northward in April and May, toward their feeding grounds in the Bering Sea. The serene beach is perfect for walking, surfing, or kite-flying—although it's too dangerous for swimming and too cold for sunbathing. In winter it's one of the best spots on the coast to watch oncoming storms.

GETTING HERE

Westport is about 30 min southwest of Aberdeen via Highway 105. Grays Harbor Transit serves the town.

Contact Grays Harbor Transit ☎ *360/532–2770 or 800/562–9730* ⊕ *www.ghtransit.com.*

VISITOR INFORMATION

Westport-Grayland Chamber of Commerce (✉ *2985 S. Montesano, Westport* ☎ *360/268–9422 or 800/345–6223* ⊕ *www.westportgrayland-chamber.org*).

EXPLORING

Westport's **Harbor Walkway** is a 2-mi-long paved promenade that winds along the sandy beach. ✉ *Ocean Ave. between Grays Harbor Lighthouse and West Haven State Park.*

☼ **Westport Aquarium** has exhibits of local marine life, including a wolf eel, an octopus, and a dog shark. Touch tanks let you feel shells, starfish, anemones, and other sea creatures. You can even hand-feed two live seals. ✉ *321 Harbor St.* ☎ *360/268–0471* ☒ *$5* ☉ *Thurs.–Mon, 10–4, and by appointment.*

In a former Coast Guard station, the **Westport Maritime Museum** displays historic photos, equipment, clothing, and other relics from the life-saving service and such local industries as fishing, logging, and cranberry farming. Among the exhibits is a collection of sea-mammal bones, and the 17-foot-tall Destruction Island Lens, a lighthouse beacon that was built in 1888 and weighs almost 6 tons. The octagonal **Grays Harbor Lighthouse,** a 107-foot structure built in 1898, is the tallest on the Washington coast. It stands near the museum and adjacent to Westport Light State Park, a day-use area with picnic tables and a beach. A tour of the lighthouse base is included with museum admission; if you want to climb to the top, it's $4. ✉ *2201 Westhaven Dr.* ☎ *360/268–0078* ⊕ *www.westportwa.com/museum* ☒ *$5 museum, lighthouse base free* ☉ *Apr.–Sept., daily 10–4; Oct.–Mar., Fri.–Mon. noon–4; lighthouse closed Dec. and Jan.*

WHERE TO STAY

$ 🍽 **Chateau Westport Motel.** This big motel sits near the dunes and is perfect for families who want a base near the beach. Rooms are large and have contemporary furniture; some have fireplaces and kitchenettes with microwaves. **Pros:** Guests 21 and older receive a voucher for free wine and cheese tasting at local winery. **Cons:** Parking lot can be noisy. ✉ *710 Hancock* ☎ *360/268–9101 or 800/255–9101* ⊕ *www. chateauwestport.com* ⚲ *104 rooms* ⚹ *In-room: no a/c, kitchen (some), Wi-Fi. In-hotel: pool, beachfront, laundry facilities, Internet terminal, some pets allowed* ☰ *AE, D, DC, MC, V* 🍽 *CP.*

LONG BEACH PENINSULA

Town of Ilwaco is 169 mi southwest of Seattle, 106 mi northwest of Portland, Oregon.

Long Beach Peninsula stretches north from Cape Disappointment, protecting Willapa Bay from the ocean. The peninsula has vast stretches of sand dunes, friendly beach towns, dank cranberry bogs, and forests and meadows. Willapa Bay was once known as Shoalwater Bay because it runs almost dry at low tide. It's a prime oyster habitat, producing more of the creatures than any other estuary in the country.

12

The 28-mi-long, uninterrupted stretch of sand that runs along the peninsula's ocean shore is a great place to beachcomb. Don't even think about swimming here, however. Though surfers in wet suits brave the waves in some areas, the water is too cold and the surf too rough for most people; hypothermia, shifting sands underfoot, and tremendous undertows account for several drownings each year.

The peninsula is a great place to hike, bike, and bird-watch. Lakes and marshes attract migrating birds, among them trumpeter swans. Long Island, in southeastern Willapa Bay, has a stand of old-growth red cedar trees, home to spotted owls, marbled murrelets (a western seabird), elks, and black bears. The island is accessible only by private boat (the boat ramp is on the bay's eastern shore).

GETTING HERE

The Long Beach peninsula is a little more than 3 hours from Seattle via I–5 south to Olympia and then southwest via U.S. 101. From Portland, the drive takes about 2.25 hours via I–5 north to Kelso then west via Highway 30. Pacific Transit busses serve the towns of Aberdeen, Bay Center, Chinook, Ilwaco, Long Beach, Nahcottta, Naselle, Ocean Park, Oysterville, South Bend, Surfside, Raymond, and Astoria, Oregon.

Contact **Pacific Transit** ☎ 360/642–9418 ⊕ www.pacifictransit.org).

CHINOOK

172 mi southwest of Seattle, 99 mi northwest of Portland, OR.

The pleasant Columbia River fishing village of Chinook (*shi*-nook) takes its name from the tribe that once controlled the river from its mouth to Celilo Falls. The same group encountered Lewis and Clark during their stay on the Pacific coast. Chinook is a great base from which to explore the lower Columbia River by boat.

☺ ★ **Ft. Columbia State Park and Interpretive Center** blends so well into a rocky knob above the river that it's all but invisible from land or water (U.S. 101 passes underneath, via tunnel). The 1902 bastions offer great views of the river's mouth and of the river flowing past the foot of the cliff. In spring the slopes are fragrant with wildflowers. The interpretive center has displays on barracks life and Chinook Indian culture. Two historic buildings on the property are available for vacation rental. ⊠ *U.S. 101, 2 mi east of Chinook* ☎ *360/642–3078 or 888/226–7688* ⊕ *www.parks.wa.gov* ▧ *Free* ☉ *Park: daily, dawn to dusk. Center: Memorial Day–Sept., Wed.–Sun. 10–5 (subject to change, depending on volunteer staffing).*

ILWACO

13 mi west of Chinook.

Ilwaco (ill-*wah*-co) has been a fishing port for thousands of years, first as a Native American village and later as an American settlement. A 3-mi scenic loop winds past Ft. Canby State Park to North Head Lighthouse and through the town. The colorful harbor is a great place for watching gulls and boats. Lewis and Clark camped here before moving their winter base to the Oregon coast at Ft. Clatsop.

WHAT TO SEE

The dioramas and miniatures of Long Beach towns at the **Columbia Pacific Heritage Museum** illustrate the history of southwestern Washington. Displays cover Native Americans; the influx of traders, missionaries, and pioneers; and the contemporary workers of the fishing, agriculture, and forest industries. The original Ilwaco Freight Depot and a Pullman car from the Clamshell Railroad highlight rail history. ⊠ *115 S.E. Lake St., off U.S. 101* ☎ *360/642–3446* ⊕ *columbiapacificheritagemuseum.org* ⊠ *$5; free on Thurs.* ⊙ *Tues.–Sat. 10–4, Sun. noon–4; closed New Year's, Thanksgiving, Christmas.*

Cape Disappointment was named in 1788 by Captain John Meares, an English fur trader who had been unable to find the Northwest Passage. This rocky cape and treacherous sandbar—the so-called graveyard of the Pacific—has been the scourge of sailors since the 1800s. More than 250 ships have sunk after running aground on its ever-shifting sands. A ½-mi-long path from the Lewis & Clark Interpretive Center in Cape Disappointment State Park leads to the Cape Disappointment Lighthouse. Built in 1856, it's the oldest lighthouse on the West Coast still in use.

The **U.S. Coast Guard Station Cape Disappointment** (☎ *360/642–2382*) is the Northwest Coast's largest search-and-rescue station. The rough conditions of the Columbia River provide plenty of lessons for the students of the on-site National Motor Life Boat School. The only institution of its kind, the school teaches elite rescue crews from around the world advanced skills in navigation, mechanics, firefighting, and lifesaving. The observation platform on the north jetty in Cape Disappointment State Park is a good place to watch the motor lifeboats.

☾ Fodor'sChoice ★ The 1,700-acre **Cape Disappointment State Park (formerly Ft. Canby)** was an active military installation until 1957. Emplacements for the guns that once guarded the Columbia's mouth remain, some of them hidden by dense vegetation. Trails lead to stunning beaches. Be on the lookout for eagles on the cliffs. All of the park's 240 campsites have stoves and tables; some have water, sewer, and electric hookups. The park also has three lightkeepers' residences (houses) available for rent, as well as 14 yurts and three cabins.

Exhibits at the park's **Lewis & Clark Interpretive Center** tell the tale of the duo's 8,000-mi round-trip expedition. Displays include artwork, journal entries, and other items that elaborate on the Corps of Discovery, which left Wood River, Illinois, in 1804; arrived at Cape Disappointment in 1805; and got back to Illinois in 1806. ⊠ *Robert Gray Dr., 2½ mi southwest of Ilwaco off U.S. 101* ☎ *360/642–3029 or 360/642–3078* ⊕ *www.parks.wa.gov* ⊠ *Interpretive center $5, park admission free, campsites $21–$28* ⊙ *Park: daily dawn–dusk. Interpretive center: daily 10–5.*

★ **North Head Lighthouse** was built in 1899 to help skippers sailing from the north who couldn't see the Cape Disappointment Lighthouse. Stand

Cape Disappointment State Park

high on a bluff above the pounding surf here, amid the windswept trees, for superb views of the Long Beach Peninsula. Lodging is available in the Lighthouse Keepers' Residence. ⊠ *From Cape Disappointment follow Spur 100 Rd. for 2 mi* ☏ *360/642–3029* ⊕ *www.parks.wa.gov* ☏ *$2.50* ⊗ *Hrs vary; call for updated info.*

WHERE TO EAT AND STAY

$-$$ ✕ **Imperial Schooner.** This is the place to go for fish-and-chips; they also
SEAFOOD offer fried shrimp and six varieties of local Willapa Bay oysters, including chicken-fried and Angels and Devils on Horseback (wrapped in bacon). Thursday is oyster day, with varying specials. ⊠ *133 Howerton Way SE* ☏ *360/642–8667* ▭ *MC, V.*

$$-$$$ ▦ **China Beach Retreat.** Between the port of Ilwaco and Ft. Canby State Park, this secluded B&B is surrounded by wetlands and has wonderful views of Baker's Bay and the mouth of the Columbia River. Each of the three rooms has antiques and original art. The Audobon Cottage opened in late 2006, and offers a secluded, romantic experience in nature, with a river-view outdoor soaking tub for two. Decorated with stained glass, rare woods, and period antiques, the cottage also has a flat-screen TV, microwave, small refrigerator, and wireless Internet. **Pros:** secluded, back-to-nature setting; new cottage is very nice. **Cons:** rooms need updating according to some guests; no a/c; breakfast is not on-site but at nearby sister property, Shelburne Inn. ⊠ *222 Robert Gray Dr.* ☏ *360/642–5660* ⊕ *www.chinabeachretreat.com* ⇨ *3 rooms, 1 cottage* ⌂ *In-room: no a/c, no TV, Wi-Fi (some). In-hotel: no kids under 16* ▭ *AE, D, MC, V* ⓞ*BP.*

OUTDOOR ACTIVITIES

FISHING AND WHALE-WATCHING

Gray whales pass the Long Beach Peninsula twice a year: December to February, on their migration from the Arctic to their winter breeding grounds in Californian and Mexican waters, and March to May, on the return trip north. The view from the **North Head Lighthouse** is spectacular. ■TIP➜ **The best time for sightings is in the morning, when the water is calm and overcast conditions reduce the glare.** Look on the horizon for a whale blow—the vapor, water, or condensation that spouts into the air when the whale exhales. If you spot one blow, you're likely to see others: whales often make several shorter, shallow dives before a longer dive that can last as long as 10 minutes.

The fish that swim in the waters near Ilwaco include salmon, rock cod, lingcod, flounder, perch, sea bass, and sturgeon. Charters generally cost from $100 to $200 per person. Free tide charts are available from the **Port of Ilwaco** (☎ *360/642–3143* ⊕ *www.portofilwaco.com*); check the Web site for information about fishing season dates.

SEAVIEW

3 mi north of Ilwaco.

Seaview, an unincorporated town, has 750 year-round residents and several homes that date from the 1800s. The Shelburne Inn, built in 1896, is on the National Register of Historic Places. In 1892 U.S. Senator Henry Winslow Corbett built what's now the Sou'wester Lodge.

WHERE TO EAT AND STAY

$$

CONTEMPORARY

Fodor's Choice

★

✕ **42nd Street Cafe.** Chef Jake Burden's fare is inspired, original, and reasonably priced. Make a meal of small plates like fried green tomatoes or Willapa Bay steamer clams Provençal. Dinner entrées—such as cranberry barbecue glazed baby back ribs with polenta, pan-fried oysters or clams, and eight-hour pot roast—come with house-baked bread, marionberry conserve, and seasonal local vegetables. Most come in two sizes, small and full. Chocolate lovers should save room for the rich chocolate rum truffle cheesecake for dessert, or go for the lighter mini mint chocolate sorbet. The excellent wine list has Pacific Northwest labels. ⊠ *Hwy. 103 and 42nd Pl.* ☎ *360/642–2323* ⊕ *www.42ndstreetcafe. com* ⊟ *AE, MC, V.*

$–$$

Fodor's Choice

★

 Shelburne Inn. A white picket fence surrounds rose and other gardens as well as an 1896 Victorian that's home to Washington's oldest continuously run hotel. Fresh flowers, antiques, fine-art prints, and original works adorn guest rooms, a few of which have decks or balconies. The Shelburne Restaurant and Pub ($–$$$) has a dark wooden interior and a contemporary American menu dominated by seafood dishes. Homemade pastries and specialty desserts feature fresh local ingredients. The cozy Pub serves lighter fare. **Pros:** excellent breakfast; historic appeal as state's oldest hotel; attentive service. **Cons:** like many B&Bs, there are no in-room phones or TVs; some rooms are rather small. ⊠ *Hwy. 103 and N. 45th St.* ☎ *Inn: 360/642–2442; restaurant: 800/466-1896 or 360/642–4150* 🖷 *360/642–8904* ⊕ *www.theshelburneinn.com* ⟿ *13 rooms, 2 suites* ⊲ *In-room: no phone, no a/c, no TV, Wi-Fi. In-hotel: restaurant, bar, Wi-Fi hotspot, some pets allowed* ⊟ *AE, D, MC, V* ❙◎❙ *BP.*

LONG BEACH

½ mi north of Seaview.

Long Beach bears a striking resemblance to Brooklyn's Coney Island in the 1950s. Along its main drag, which stretches southwest from 10th Street to Bolstadt Street, you'll find everything from cotton candy and hot dogs to go-carts and bumper cars.

WHAT TO SEE

At the **Cranberry Museum,** learn about the 100-plus-year history of cranberries in this area, take a self-guided walking tour through the bogs, try some cranberry tea, and buy cranberry products to take home. ⊠ *2907 Pioneer Rd.* ☎ *360/642–5553* ⊕ *www.cranberrymuseum.com* ☞ *Free* ⊙ *Apr.–mid-Dec., daily 10–5.*

⟳ Created to memorialize Lewis and Clark's explorations here in 1805–
★ 06, the 8-mi **Discovery Trail** traces the explorers' moccasin steps from Ilwaco to north Long Beach. ☎ *800/451–2542* ☎ *360/642–3900* ⊕ *www.funbeach.com.*

⟳ The ½-mi-long **Long Beach Boardwalk** runs through the dunes parallel
★ to the beach, and is a great place for strolling, bird-watching, or just sitting and listening to the wind and the roar of the surf. It's ¼ mi west of downtown.

⟳ If you've got kids in your group, or simply an appreciation of oddities, be sure to visit the quirky **Marsh's Free Museum.** Best known for "Jake the Alligator Man," Marsh's is filled with plenty of other curiousities, like real shrunken heads, skeletons, and an eight-legged lamb. ⊠ *400 S. Pacific* ☎ *360/642–2188* ⊕ *www.marshsfreemuseum.com* ☞ *Free* ⊙ *Daily 9–6, later in summer.*

Each August Long Beach hosts the Washington State International Kite Festival; the community is also home to the Northwest Stunt Kite Championships, a competition held each June. At the **World Kite Museum and Hall of Fame,** the only U.S. museum focused solely on kites and kiting, you can view an array of kites and learn about kite making and history. ⊠ *303 Sid Snyder Dr. SW* ☎ *360/642–4020* ⊕ *www.worldkitemuseum. com* ☞ *$5* ⊙ *May–Sept., daily 11–5; Oct.–Apr., closed Wed. and Thurs.*

WHERE TO EAT AND STAY

$$ ✕ **Doogers.** Locals will urge you to eat here—listen to them. The place
SEAFOOD serves seafood from 11 AM to 9 PM in winter, and until 10 on summer weekends. The ample portions come with potatoes, shrimp-topped salad, and garlic toast. Clam chowder and fish-and-chips are popular lunch choices. ⊠ *900 Pacific Hwy. S* ☎ *360/642–4224* ▭ *AE, D, MC, V.*

¢–$ ⌂ **Anchorage Cottages.** Most of the cottages have fireplaces, free fire-
⟳ wood, and unobstructed views of the dunes. There's a private ¼-mile path to the ocean. Kitchens are stocked with cooking and dining essentials, but don't forget to do your dishes—there's a $25 fee if you don't. The sports court, volleyball, and play area make this a great place to bring kids. **Pros:** pretty gardens and courtyard; affordable. **Cons:** not very private; town is a mile away. ⊠ *2209 Boulevard N* ☎ *800/646–2351* ⊕ *www.theanchoragecottages.com* ↰ *10 cottages* △ *In-room: no a/c, kitchen, DVD, Wi-Fi. In-hotel: some pets allowed* ▭ *AE, D, MC, V.*

$$ ⊡ **Boreas Bed and Breakfast.** A private path leads from this vintage 1920s beach house, on the Lewis and Clark Trail, through the dunes to the shore. Antiques are scattered throughout the B&B, and there's a good selection of books. Rooms have balconies or decks and ocean views. Innkeepers and chefs Susie Goldsmith and Bill Verner prepare extravagant three-course breakfasts. The inn also provides full concierge service. **Pros:** great breakfast; helpful innkeepers. **Cons:** no bathtubs in two rooms; not for families. ⊠ *607 N. Ocean Beach Blvd.* ☎ *360/642–8069 or 888/642–8069* ⊕ *www.boreasinn.com* ↩ *5 suites, 3 with shower only* ⌂ *In-room: no phone, no a/c, no TV, Wi-Fi. In-hotel: no kids under 16* ⊟ *AE, D, MC, V* ⏀ *BP.*

$$ ⊡ **Breakers Motel and Condominiums.** Each of the contemporary one- and ⟳ two-bedroom condominiums has a private balcony or patio. Many also have fireplaces and exceptional views of the dunes and the surf. Some units have kitchenettes. There's lots to do on-site, including volleyball, a sports court, a playground, and a private walk to the beach. **Pros:** very family-friendly, with lots of activities. **Cons:** units are individually owned, so decor and quality differs. ⊠ *26th St. and Hwy. 103* ☎ *360/642–4414 or 800/219–9833* 🖶 *360/642–8772* ⊕ *www. breakerslongbeach.com* ↩ *144 rooms* ⌂ *In-room: no a/c, kitchen (some), refrigerator, DVD, Wi-Fi. In-hotel: pool, laundry facilities, some pets allowed* ⊟ *AE, D, DC, MC, V.*

¢ ⊡ **Our Place at the Beach.** Located a couple blocks from the main highway, the setting for this older motel is both quiet and convenient. The beach, restaurants, and shops are a five-minute walk from this establishment. New owners have recently upgraded the rooms, and all have refrigerators and microwaves. Room styles vary from basic, budget accommodations with a queen bed to family suites that sleep 8 and have kitchens. Two home-like cabins have two bedrooms, kitchen, and fireplace. The fitness center has two hot tubs and a sauna. ⊠ *1309 S. Ocean Beach Blvd.* ☎ *360/642–3793 or 800/538–5107* 🖶 *360/642– 3896* ⊕ *www.ourplacelongbeach.weebly.com* ↩ *26 rooms* ⌂ *In-room: no a/c, DVD (some), kitchen (some), refrigerator, Wi-Fi. In-hotel: gym, some pets allowed* ⊟ *AE, D, MC, V* ⏀ *CP.*

SHOPPING

⟳ **Long Beach Kites** (⊠ *115 Pacific Ave. S* ☎ *360/642–2202*) stocks box, ★ dragon, and many other kites. **Rainy Day Gallery** (⊠ *600 S. Pacific Hwy.* ☎ *360/484–3681*) is a funky little shop stuffed with antiques, collectibles, art, and unique apparel.

SPORTS AND THE OUTDOORS

Back Country Horse Rides (⊠ *10th St. next to Edgewater Inn* ☎ *360/642– 2576*) offers one-hour horseback rides for $15 and two-hour rides for $30. **Our Wonderful World (O.W.W.) Inc.** (⊠ *1st Place Shopping Center, 106 Sid Snyder Dr. SW* ☎ *360/642–4260*) rents bikes for $7 per hour. The **Peninsula Golf Course** (⊠ *9604 Pacific Hwy.* ☎ *360/642–2828*) consists of two 9-hole, par-33 courses on Long Beach's northern edge. Greens fees are $11 for 9 holes and $19 for 18 holes.

North Cascades National Park

WITH NORTH CENTRAL WASHINGTON

WORD OF MOUTH

"We were very glad we decided to go to North Cascades, it is such an amazingly beautiful place. We stopped at Cascadian and had the raspberry ice cream on the way in and a pint of blueberries on the way out of the park. Both were delicious."

—regalada

WELCOME TO
NORTH CASCADES NATIONAL PARK

TOP REASONS TO GO

★ **Pure wilderness:** Nearly 400 mi of mountain and meadow trails immerse hikers in pristine natural panoramas, with sure sightings of bald eagles, deer, elk, and other wildlife.

★ **Majestic glaciers:** The North Cascades are home to 318 moving ice masses, more than half of the glaciers in the United States.

★ **Splendid flora:** A bright palette of flowers blankets the hillsides in midsummer, while October paints the landscape in vibrant autumn hues.

★ **Thrilling boat rides:** Lake Chelan, Lake Ross, and the Stehekin River are the starting points for kayaking, white-water rafting, and ferry trips.

★ **19th-century history:** Delve into the state's farming, lumber, and logging pasts in clapboard towns and homesteads around the park.

1 **North Unit.** The park's creek-cut northern wilderness, centered on snowy Mount Challenger, stretches north from Highway 20 over the Picket Range toward the Canadian border. It's an endless landscape of pine-topped peaks and ridges.

2 **South Unit.** Hike the South Unit's lake-filled mountain foothills in summer to take in vistas of blue skies and flower-filled meadows. Waterfalls and wildlife are abundant here.

3 **Ross Lake National Recreation Area.** Drawing a thick line from British Columbia all the way down to the North Cascades Scenic Highway, placid Ross Lake is edged with pretty bays that draw swimmers and boaters.

4 **Lake Chelan National Recreation Area.** Ferries steam between small waterfront towns along this pristine waterway, while kayakers and hikers follow quiet trails along its edges. This is one of the Northwest's most popular summer escapes, with nature-bound activities and rustic accommodations.

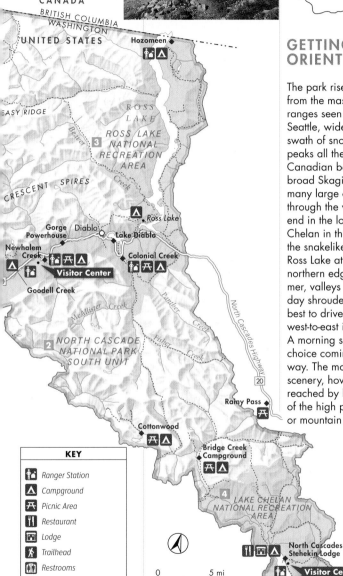

CANADA
BRITISH COLUMBIA
WASHINGTON
UNITED STATES

Hozomeen

EASY RIDGE

ROSS LAKE

ROSS LAKE
NATIONAL
RECREATION
AREA

3

CRESCENT SPIRES

Beaver Creek

Ross Lake

Gorge Diablo
Powerhouse
Lake Diablo
Newhalem Creek
Colonial Creek
Visitor Center
Goodell Creek

McAllister Creek

Panther Creek

Fisher Creek

North Cascades Highway

20

**NORTH CASCADE
NATIONAL PARK
SOUTH UNIT**

2

Rainy Pass

Cottonwood

Bridge Creek
Campground

**LAKE CHELAN
NATIONAL RECREATION
AREA**

4

North Cascades
Stehekin Lodge
Visitor Center
Stehekin

Lake
Chelan

KEY

👫	Ranger Station
⛺	Campground
🎪	Picnic Area
🍴	Restaurant
🏨	Lodge
🚶	Trailhead
🚻	Restrooms
⚜	Scenic Viewpoint
-----	Walking/Hiking Trails

0   5 mi
0   5 km

GETTING ORIENTED

13

The park rises upward from the massive Cascade ranges seen northeast of Seattle, widening in a swath of snow-covered peaks all the way to the Canadian border. The broad Skagit River and many large creeks cut through the valleys; most end in the long arm of Lake Chelan in the south or in the snakelike expanse of Ross Lake at the park's northern edge. Even in summer, valleys can start the day shrouded in fog; it's best to drive the highway west-to-east in afternoon. A morning start is a good choice coming the other way. The most sensational scenery, however, is reached by hiking to one of the high park passes or mountain lookouts.

NORTH CASCADES NATIONAL PARK PLANNER

When to Go

The spectacular, craggy peaks of the North Cascades—often likened to the Alps—are breathtaking in any season. **Summer is peak season,** especially along the alpine stretches of Route 20; weekends and holidays can be crowded. Summer is short and glorious in the high country, extending from snowmelt (late May to July, depending on the elevation and the amount of snow) to early September.

The North Cascades Highway is a popular autumn drive in September and October, when the changing leaves put on a colorful show. The lowland forest areas, such as the complex around Newhalem, can be visited almost any time of year. These can be wonderfully quiet in early spring or late autumn on mild, rainy days. Snow closes the North Cascades Highway from November through mid-April.

Note that a day trip isn't nearly enough to make a thorough exploration of the park: roads are narrow and closed from October to June, many sights are off the beaten path, and the scenery is so spectacular that, once you're in it, you won't want to hurry through anyway.

Getting Here

Highway 20, the North Cascades Highway, splits the park's north and south sections. The gravel Cascade River Road, which runs southeast from Marblemount, peels off Highway 20; Sibley Creek/Hidden Lake Road (USFS 1540) turns off Cascade River Road to the Cascade Pass trailhead. Thornton Creek Road is another rough four-wheel-drive track. For the Ross Lake area in the north, the unpaved Hozomeen Road (Silver–Skagit Road) provides access between Hope, British Columbia; Silver Lake; and Skagit Valley provincial parks. From Stehekin, the Stehekin Valley Road continues to High Bridge, Car Wash Falls, Bridge Creek, and Cottonwood campgrounds—although seasonal floods may cause washouts.

About the Restaurants and Hotels

There are no restaurants in North Cascades National Park, just a lakeside café at the Environmental Learning Center. The only other places to eat are in Stehekin. (*See Chelan, below.*) Towns within a few hours of the park on either side all have a few small eateries, and some lodgings have small dining rooms.

Accommodations in North Cascades National Park are rustic and comfortable. Options range from plush Stehekin lodges (*see Chelan, below*) and homey cabin rentals to spartan Learning Center bunks and campgrounds. Expect to pay roughly $50 to $200 per night, depending on the rental size and the season. Book at least three months in advance, or even a year for popular accommodations in summer. Outside the park are numerous resorts, motels, bed-and-breakfasts, and even overnight boat rentals in Chelan, Glacier, Marblemount, Sedro-Woolley, Twisp, and Winthrop.

WHAT IT COSTS

	¢	$	$$	$$$	$$$$
Restaurants	under $10	$11–$20	$21–$30	$31–$40	over $40
Hotels	under $100	$100–$150	$151–$200	$201–$250	over $250

Restaurant prices are per person, for a main course at dinner. Hotel prices are for two people in a standard double room in high season, excluding tax.

Updated by
Holly S. Smith
& Shelley
Arenas

Countless snow-clad mountain spires dwarf narrow glacial valleys in this 505,000-acre expanse of the North Cascades, which actually encompasses three diverse natural areas.

North Cascades National Park is the core of the region, flanked by Lake Chelan National Recreation Area to the south and Ross Lake National Recreation Area to the north; all are part of the Stephen T. Mather Wilderness Area. This is an utterly spectacular gathering of snowy peaks, glacial meadows, plunging canyons, and cold, deep-blue lakes. Traditionally the lands of several American Indian tribes, it's fitting that it's still completely wild—and wildlife filled.

PARK ESSENTIALS

ACCESSIBILITY

All visitor centers along North Cascades Highway are accessible by wheelchair. Accessible hikes include Sterling Munro, Skagit River Loop, and Newhalem Creek Rockshelter, three short trails into lowland old-growth forest, all at mile 120 along Route 20 near Newhalem.

ADMISSION FEES AND PERMITS

A Northwest Forest Pass, required for use of various park and forest facilities and trails, is $5 per vehicle for one calendar day or $30 for one year. A free wilderness permit is required for all overnight stays in the backcountry; these permits are limited and are available in person only, no more than 24 hours before your stay (no advance reservations). Dock permits for boat-in campgrounds are also $5 per day. Passes and permits are sold at visitor centers and ranger stations around the park area.

ADMISSION HOURS

The park never closes, but access is limited by snow in winter. Route 20 (North Cascades Highway), the major access to the park, is partially closed from around mid-November to mid-April (dates vary).

ATMS/BANKS

There are no ATMs in the park. Marblemount, Winthrop, and Chelan have banks with 24-hour ATMs.

CELL-PHONE RECEPTION

Cell-phone reception in the park is not reliable. Public telephones are found at the North Cascades Visitor Center and Skagit Information Center in Newhalem; and at the Golden West Visitor Center and Stehekin Landing Resort in Stehekin.

PARK CONTACT INFORMATION

North Cascades National Park. ⊠ *810 Rte. 20, Sedro-Woolley, WA* ☏ *360/856–5700 or 360/854–7200* ⊕ *www.nps.gov/noca.*

VISITOR CENTERS

Chelan Ranger Station. The base for the Chelan National Recreation Area and Wenatchee National Forest has an information desk and a shop selling regional maps and books. ⊠ *Edge of Lake Chelan, Chelan* ☏ *509/682–2549* ⊗ *Weekdays 7:45–4:30.*

Glacier Public Service Center. This office doubles as a headquarters for the Mt. Baker–Snoqualmie National Forest; it has maps, a book and souvenir shop, and a permits desk. The center is also right on the way to some of the park's main trailheads. ⊠ *Mt. Baker Hwy., east of Glacier* ☏ *360/599–2714* ⊗ *Memorial Day–Sept., daily 8–4:30; off-season schedule varies; open weekends and some Thursdays and Fridays. Closed mid-Mar.–mid-Apr.*

Golden West Visitor Center. Rangers here offer guidance on hiking, camping, and other activities, as well as audiovisual and children's programs and bike tours. There's also an arts and crafts gallery. Maps and concise displays explain the layered ecology of the valley, which encompasses in its length virtually every ecosystem in the Northwest. Note that access is by floatplane, ferry, or trail only. ⊠ *Stehekin Valley Rd., ¼ mi north of Stehekin Landing, Stehekin* ☏ *360/854–7365 Ext. 14* ⊗ *Memorial Day–Sept., daily 8:30–5; limited hours off-season.*

North Cascades National Park Headquarters Information Station. This is the park's major administrative center, and the place to pick up passes, permits, and information about current conditions. ⊠ *810 Rte. 20, Sedro-Woolley* ☏ *360/856–5700 Ext. 515* ⊗ *Memorial Day–mid-Oct., daily 8–4:30; mid-Oct.–Memorial Day, weekdays 8–4:30.*

North Cascades Visitor Center. The main visitor facility for the park complex has extensive displays on the surrounding landscape. Learn about the history and value of old-growth trees, the many creatures that depend on the rain-forest ecology, and the effects of human activity on the ecosystem. Park rangers frequently conduct programs; check bulletin boards for schedules. ⊠ *Milepost 120, N. Cascades Hwy., Newhalem* ☏ *206/386–4495 Ext. 11* ⊗ *May–June, daily 9–6; July–Labor Day., daily 9–7; Labor Day–Oct., daily 9–6.*

Wilderness Information Center. The main stop to secure backcountry and climbing permits for North Cascades National Park and the Lake Chelan and Ross Lake recreational areas, this office has maps, a bookshop, and nature exhibits. If you arrive after hours, there's a self-register permit stop outside. ⊠ *Ranger Station Rd., off milepost 105.9, N. Cascades Hwy., Marblemount* ☏ *360/854–7245* ⊗ *May–June, Sun.–Thurs. 8–4:30, Fri. and Sat. 7 AM–6 PM; July–Aug., Sun.–Thurs. 7 AM–6 PM, Fri. and Sat. 7 AM–8 PM.*

EXPLORING NORTH CASCADES NATIONAL PARK

HISTORIC SITE

Buckner Homestead. Founded in 1912, this restored pioneer farm includes an apple orchard, farmhouse, barn, and many ranch buildings. One-hour ranger-guided tours of the property are offered weekends from July 4 through mid-September at 2:15; otherwise, you can pick up a self-guided tour booklet from the drop box. ⊠ *Stehekin Valley Rd., 3½ mi from Stehekin Landing, Stehekin* ☎ *360/854–7365 option 14.*

SCENIC DRIVE

Fodor's Choice ★ **North Cascades Highway.** Also known as Highway 20, this classic scenic route first winds through the green pastures and woods of the upper Skagit Valley, the mountains looming in the distance. Beyond Concrete, a former cement-manufacturing town, the highway climbs into the mountains, passes the Ross and Diablo dams, and traverses Ross Lake National Recreation Area. Here several pullouts offer great views of the lake and the surrounding snowcapped peaks. From June to September the meadows are covered with wildflowers, and from late September through October the mountain slopes flame with fall foliage. The pinnacle point of this stretch is 5,477-foot-high Washington Pass: look east, to where the road descends quickly into a series of hairpin curves between Early Winters Creek and the Methow Valley. Remember, this section of the highway is closed from roughly November to April, depending on snowfall. From the Methow Valley, Highway 153 takes the scenic route along the Methow River's apple, nectarine, and peach orchards to Pateros, on the Columbia River; from here you can continue east to Grand Coulee or south to Lake Chelan.

SCENIC STOP

Gorge Powerhouse/Ladder Creek Falls and Rock Gardens. A powerhouse is a powerhouse, but the rock gardens overlooking Ladder Creek Falls, 7 mi west of Diablo, are beautiful and inspiring. ⊠ *Rte. 20, 2 mi east of North Cascades Visitor Center, Newhalem* ☎ *206/684–3030* 🖃 *Free* ☉ *May–Sept., daily, dawn to dusk.*

WHERE TO EAT AND STAY

ABOUT THE RESTAURANTS

There are no formal restaurants in North Cascades National Park, just a lakeside café at the North Cascades Environmental Learning Center. The only other place to eat out is in Stehekin, at the Stehekin Valley Ranch dining room or the Stehekin Pastry Company; both serve simple, hearty, country-style meals and sweets. *(See Where to Eat in Chelan below.)* Towns within a few hours of the park on either side all have a few small eateries, and some lodgings have small dining rooms. Don't

NORTH CASCADES IN ONE DAY

The **North Cascades Highway,** with its breathtaking mountain and meadow scenery, is one of the most memorable drives in the United States. Although many travelers first head northeast from Seattle into the park and make this their grand finale, if you start out from Winthrop, at the south end of the route, traffic is lighter and there's less morning fog. Either way, the main highlight is **Washington Pass,** the road's highest point, where an overlook affords a sensational panorama of snow-covered peaks.

Rainy Pass, where the road heading north drops into the west-slope valleys, is another good vantage point. Old-growth forest begins to appear, and after about an hour you reach **Gorge Creek Falls Overlook** with its 242-foot cascade. Continue west to Newhalem and stop for lunch, then take a half-hour stroll along the **Trail of the Cedars.** Later, stop at the **North Cascades Visitor Center** and take another short hike. It's an hour drive down the Skagit Valley to Sedro-Woolley, where bald eagles are often seen along the river in winter.

expect fancy decor or gourmet frills—just friendly service and generally delicious homemade stews, roasts, grilled fare, soups, salads, and baked goods.

PICNIC AREAS   Developed picnic areas at Rainy Pass (Route 20, 38 mi east of the park visitor center) and Washington Pass (Route 20, 42 mi east of the visitor center) each have a half-dozen picnic tables, drinking water, and pit toilets. The vistas of surrounding peaks are sensational at these two overlooks. More picnic facilities are located near the visitor center in Newhalem and at Colonial Creek Campground 10 mi east of the visitor center on Highway 20.

ABOUT THE HOTELS

Accommodations in North Cascades National Park are rustic, cozy, and comfortable. Options range from plush Stehekin lodges *(see Where to Stay in Chelan, below)* and homey cabin rentals to spartan Learning Center bunks and campgrounds. Expect to pay roughly $50 to $200 per night, depending on the rental size and the season. Book at least three months in advance, or even a year for popular accommodations in summer. Outside the park are numerous resorts, motels, bed-and-breakfasts, and even overnight boat rentals in Chelan, Concrete, Glacier, Marblemount, Sedro-Woolley, Twisp, and Winthrop.

¢–$ **Skagit River Resort.** The Clark Family runs this rambling resort at the western entrance to the North Cascades. Many of the country cabins with kitchens have a gas or log fireplace; you also can stay in one of the charming second-floor bed-and-breakfast rooms, motel rooms in a triplex, RVs with kitchens, or campsites along the Skagit River. You can book adventure tours, rent DVD and VCR players, enjoy the spacious picnic grounds, play volleyball, badminton, and horseshoes; and try "bunny-hole golf" on a course dug by local rabbits. The Eatery—a quaint, country-style restaurant and museum fronted by a huge sawmill mural—serves homemade cinnamon rolls and chicken-fried steak.

Savory pies are made by Tootsie Clark, whose grandmother arrived here in 1888 by Indian canoe and later named Marblemount. **Pros:** convenient location; great food; online coupons add discounts. **Cons:** a lot of rabbit droppings. ⊠ *58468 Clark Cabin Rd. (milepost 103.5 on North Cascades Hwy.), Rockport* ☎ *360/873–2250 or 800/273–2606* ⊕ *www.northcascades.com* ↝ *37 cabins, 3 motel rooms, 4 B&B rooms, 5 trailers, 30 RV sites, 15 tent sites* ⭣ *In-room: no a/c, kitchen (some), refrigerator, no TV (some), no phone, Wi-Fi. In-hotel: restaurant, bicycles, laundry facilities* ▭ *AE, D, MC, V.*

13

ABOUT THE CAMPGROUNDS

Tent campers can choose between forest sites, riverside spots, lake grounds, or meadow spreads encircled by mountains. Here camping is as easy or challenging as you want to make it; some campgrounds are a short walk from ranger stations, while others are miles from the highway. Note that many campsites, particularly those around Stehekin (*see Where to Stay in Chelan, below*), are completely remote and without road access anywhere, so you have to walk, boat, ride a horse, or take a floatplane to reach them. Most don't accept reservations, and spots fill up quickly May through September. If there's no ranger on-site, you can often sign in yourself—and always check in at a ranger station before you set out overnight. Note that some areas are occasionally closed due to flooding, forest fires, or other factors. Outside the park, each town has several managed camping spots, which can be at formal campgrounds or in the side yard of a motel.

$ ⚠ **Ross Lake National Recreation Area.** The National Park Service maintains three upper Skagit Valley campgrounds near Newhalem. All have fire grates and picnic tables. Colonial Creek and Newhalem Creek have RV sites as well as tent sites, flush toilets, and drinking water, but are only open late May through early October. Goodell Creek is open year-round, with 21 sites for tents and small RVs; there's drinking water (summer only) but only pit toilets. All sites are on a first-come, first-served basis, except campsites in Loop C of Newhalem Creek campground can be reserved in advance through **Recreation.gov** (☎ *877/444-6777* ⊕ *www.recreation.gov*). **Pros:** set amid forest. **Cons:** two are seasonal only. ☎ *360/856–5700 Ext. 515* ▭ *No credit cards.*

SPORTS AND THE OUTDOORS

BICYCLING

Mountain bikes are permitted on all highways, unpaved back roads, and a few designated tracks around the park; however, you can't take a bike on any footpaths. Ranger stations have details on the best places to ride in each season, as well as notes on spots that are closed due to weather, mud, or other environmental factors. It's $24 round-trip to bring a bike on the Lake Chelan ferry.

OUTFITTER You can rent mountain bikes at a self-serve rack in front of the Courtney Log Office in Stehekin for $4 per hour, $20 a day through **Discovery Bikes** (⊕ *www.stehekindiscoverybikes.com*); helmets are provided.

BOATING

The boundaries of North Cascades National Park touch two long and sinewy expanses: Lake Chelan in the far south, and Ross Lake, which runs toward the Canadian border. Boat ramps, some with speed- and sailboat, paddleboat, kayak, and canoe rentals, are situated all around Lake Chelan, and passenger ferries cross between towns and campgrounds. Hozomeen, accessible via a 39-mi dirt road from Canada, is the boating base for Ross Lake; the site has a large boat ramp, and a boat taxi makes drops at campgrounds all around the shoreline. Diablo Lake, in the center of the park, also has a ramp at Colonial Creek. Gorge Lake has a public ramp near the town of Diablo.

HIKING

⚠ **Black bears are often sighted along trails in the summer; DO NOT approach them!** Back away carefully, and report sightings to a park ranger. Cougars, which are shy of humans and well aware of their presence, are rarely sighted in this region. Still, keep kids close and don't let them run ahead too far or lag behind on a trail. If you do spot a cougar, pick up children, have the whole group stand close together, and make yourself look as large as possible.

EASY

☺ **Happy Creek Forest Walk.** Old-growth forests are the focus of this kid-friendly boardwalk route, which loops just 0.3 mi through the trees right off the North Cascades Highway. Interpretive signs provide details about flora along the way. ⊠ *Trailhead at Milepost 135, Hwy. 20.*

Rainy Pass. An easy and accessible 1-mi paved trail leads to Rainy Lake, a waterfall, and a glacier-view platform. ⊠ *Trailhead off Hwy. 20, 38 mi east of visitor center at Newhalem.*

River Loop. Take this flat and easy, 1.8-mi, wheelchair-accessible trail down through stands of huge, old-growth firs and cedars toward the Skagit River. ⊠ *Trailhead at northeast corner of North Cascades Visitor Center.*

Sterling Munro Trail. Starting from the North Cascades Headquarters and Information Station, this popular introductory stroll follows a boardwalk path to a lookout above the forested Picket Range peaks. ⊠ *Trailhead just outside the northwest corner of the North Cascades Visitor Center.*

"To Know a Tree" Nature Trail. Plaques identify the large trees and plants along this mostly flat, 0.5-mi gravel trail around the Newhalem Creek Campground and along the river. ⊠ *Trailhead at Newhalem Creek Campground, Milepost 120, Hwy. 20 (also accessible via Sterling Munro Trail).*

Fodor'sChoice **Trail of the Cedars.** Only 0.5-mi long, this trail winds its way through
★ one of the finest surviving stands of old-growth western red cedar in Washington. Some of the trees on the path are more than 1,000 years old. ⊠ *Trailhead near North Cascades Visitor Center.*

Stehekin River Valley

MODERATE

Fodor'sChoice ★ **Cascade Pass.** The draws of this extremely popular 3.7-mi, four-hour
trail are stunning panoramas from the great mountain divide. Dozens
of peaks line the horizon as you make your way up the fairly flat,
hairpin-turn track, the scene fronted by a blanket of alpine wildflowers from July to mid-August. Arrive before noon if you want a parking
spot at the trailhead. ⊠ *Trailhead at end of Cascade River Rd., 14 mi
from Marblemount.*

Diablo Lake Trail. Explore nearly 4 mi of waterside terrain on this moderate route, which is accessed from the Sourdough Creek parking lot. An
excellent alternative for parties with small hikers is to take the Seattle
City Light Ferry one way. ⊠ *Trailhead at Milepost 135, Hwy. 20.*

DIFFICULT

Thornton Lakes Trail. A 5-mi climb into an alpine basin with two pretty
lakes, this steep and strenuous hike takes about five to six hours round-
trip. ⊠ *Trailhead off Hwy. 20, 3 mi west of Newhalem.*

HORSEBACK RIDING

Many hiking trails and backwoods paths are also popular horseback-
riding routes, particularly around the park's southern fringes.

OUTFITTERS
AND
EXPEDITIONS
Cascade Corrals (⊕ *www.cascadecorrals.com* ✉ *$50* ۞ *June–mid-Sept.,
daily at 8:15 and 2:15*), a subsidiary of Stehekin Outfitters, organizes
2½-hour horseback trips to Coon Lake. English- and western-style rid-
ing lessons are also available. Reservations are taken at the Courtney
Log Office at Stehekin Landing.

KAYAKING

The park's tangles of waterways offer access to remote areas inaccessible by road or trail; here are some of the most pristine and secluded mountain scenes on the continent. Bring your own kayak and you can launch from any boat ramp or beach; otherwise, companies in several nearby towns and Seattle suburbs offer kayak and canoe rentals, portage, and tours. The upper basin of Lake Chelan (at the park's southern end) and Ross Lake (at the top edge of the park) are two well-known kayaking expanses, but there are dozens of smaller lakes and creeks between. The Stehekin River also provides many kayaking possibilities.

OUTFITTERS AND EXPEDITIONS

Based in the mountain-sports center of Mazama, **Outward Bound U.S.A.** (☎ 866/467–7651 ⊕ *www.outwardbound.com*) stages canoe expeditions on Ross Lake. **Ross Lake Resort** (☎ 206/386–4437) rents kayaks and offers portage service for exploring Ross Lake; a water-taxi service is also available. Book a two-hour kayak trip along the lake's upper estuary and western shoreline with **Stehekin Adventure Company** (⌂ *P.O. Box 36, Stehekin 98852* ☎ *509/682–4677 or 800/536–0745* ⊕ *www. stehekinoutfitters.com* ✉ *Tour $35* ☉ *Tours June–Sept., daily at 10.*

RAFTING

June through August is the park's white-water season, and rafting trips run through the lower section of the Stehekin River. Along the way, take in views of cottonwood and pine forests, glimpses of Yawning Glacier on Magic Mountain, and placid vistas of Lake Chelan.

OUTFITTERS AND EXPEDITIONS

Downstream River Runners (☎ *206/910–7102* ⊕ *www.riverpeople.com*) covers rafting throughout the Northwest. White-water tours are available on the Skykomish and other area rivers April through September with **Orion River Expeditions** (☎ *509/548–1401 or 800/553–7466* ⊕ *www. orionexp.com*). Guided trips on the Class III Stehekin River leave from **Stehekin Valley Ranch** (☎ *509/682–4677 or 800/536–0745* ⊕ *www. stehekinvalleyranch.com* ✉ *$50* ☉ *June–Sept.*).Exciting half- and full-day rafting excursions with **Wildwater River Tours** (☎ *253/939–3337 or 800/522–9453* ⊕ *www.wildwater-river.com*) include transportation and a picnic.

WINTER SPORTS

Mt. Baker, just off the park's far northwest corner, is one of the Northwest's premier skiing, snowboarding, and snowshoeing regions—the area set a U.S. record for most snow in a single season during the winter of 1998–99 (1,140 inches). The Mt. Baker Highway (Route 542) cuts through the slopes toward several major ski sites; main access is 17 mi east of the town of Glacier, and the season runs roughly from November to April. Salmon Ridge, 46 mi east of Bellingham at Exit 255, has groomed trails and parking.

Stehekin is another base for winter sports. The Stehekin Valley alone has 20 mi of trails; some of the most popular are around Buckner Orchard, Coon Lake, and the Courtney Ranch (Cascade Corrals).

Mt. Baker. Off the park's northwest corner, this is the closest winter-sports area, with facilities for downhill and Nordic skiing, snowboarding, and other recreational ventures. The main base is the town of Glacier, 17 mi west of the slopes. Equipment, lodgings, restaurants, and tourist services are on-site. ✉ *Mt. Baker Hwy. 542, 62 mi east of Bellingham* ☎ *360/734–6771; 360/671–0211 for snow reports* ⊕ *www. mtbaker.us* ✉ *All-day lift ticket weekends and holidays $41, weekdays $34* ⊙ *Nov.–Apr.*

NORTH CENTRAL WASHINGTON

Although the Cascade Range in general is of volcanic origin, the North Cascades have only two prominent volcanic peaks, both more than 10,000 feet tall. Glacier Peak is almost hidden amid tall nonvolcanic mountains, but Mt. Baker, to the north, stands west of the main range and can be seen from far out to sea. This is the ultimate hiking and backpacking country, but it also has good fishing, quiet streams and lakes for boating, and shady trails for taking refreshing strolls.

Some parts of this region can be challenging to reach by car. The North Cascades Highway closes for winter on the west just east of Diablo at milepost 134 and on the east at milepost 171, 14 miles west of Mazama. The Stehekin area at the north end of Lake Chelan can

> ## TOP REASONS TO GO
>
> 13
>
> 1. To hike the stunning glacial peaks and vibrantly-colored valleys of the North Cascades.
>
> 2. To shop, eat, and enjoy seasonal festivals in the Bavarian-style mountain village of Leavenworth.
>
> 3. To get away from it all in remote Stehekin at the north end of Lake Chelan.
>
> 4. To explore the Western-themed town of Winthrop and and nearby Sun Mountain Lodge.
>
> 5. To partake in white-water rafting, horseback riding, fishing, camping, hiking, and mountain biking.

be accessed only by boat, plane, or on foot, but this seclusion certainly adds to the back-to-the-nature experience.

The town of Glacier in the far north is close to Mt. Baker, where there's skiing in winter and hiking and biking in summer. The former logging town of Sedro-Woolley, called the "Gateway to the Cascades," has a fun steam-train ride through the forest in summer. Marblemount, another former logging town, is a good base for exploring North Cascades National Park. On the other side of the mountains, the Western-theme town of Winthrop has shops, restaurants, basic and luxury lodgings, and a brewery that features live music by the river on summer weekends. Farther south, Chelan is a popular beach resort town and provides access via ferry or floatplane to Stehekin. The larger town of Wenatchee has an airport and Amtrak station. Bavarian-style Leavenworth can be reached via Amtrak, and there are plenty of shopping, dining, and lodging options right in town if you travel without a car. Otherwise, it's an easy two-hour drive from the Seattle area, which makes the town a favorite getaway from western Washington.

Hiking in North Cascades National Park

GLACIER

41 mi northeast of Ferndale.

The canyon village of Glacier, just outside the Mt. Baker–Snoqualmie National Forest boundary, has a few shops, cafés, and lodgings. Highway 542 winds east from Glacier into the forest through an increasingly steep-walled canyon. It passes 170-foot-high Nooksack Falls, about 5 mi east of Glacier, and travels up the north fork of the Nooksack River and the slopes of Mt. Baker to a ski area, which is bright with huckleberry patches and wildflowers in summer.

GETTING HERE

Glacier is about 2 hours and 15 minutes from Seattle. Take I–5 north to Exit 230 at Burlington; go east 6 mi on Highway 20 then north via Highway 9, then northeast via Highway 542.

EXPLORING

Mt. Baker–Snoqualmie National Forest is a vast area including much of the mountain and forest land around North Cascades National Park. The region has many trails, but because the snowline is quite low in Washington State, the upper ridges and mountains are covered by snow much of the year. This makes for a short hiking, climbing, and mountain-biking season, usually from mid-July to mid-September or October—but winter brings skiing and snowmobiling. The wildflower season is also short but spectacular; expect fall color by late August and early September. The 10,778-foot-high, snow-covered volcanic dome of **Mt. Baker** is visible from much of Whatcom County and from as far north as Vancouver and as far south as Seattle. ✉ *2934 Wetmore*

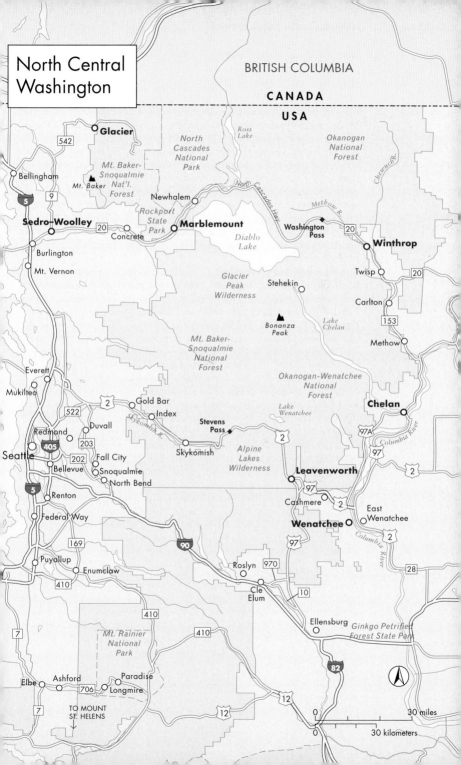

Rd., Everett ☎ *360/783–6000 or 800/627–0062* ⊕ *www.fs.fed.us/r6/ mbs* ◲ *$5* ⊙ *Daily 24 hrs.*

$–$$ ⬚ **The Inn at Mt. Baker.** Nestled into the upper Cascades, this stately country home offers airy spaces with vaulted ceilings—and sweeping mountain panoramas from every angle. Each bedroom, named for an area river, gold mine, or peak, has down-soft beds, a rocking chair, and big views. Guests relax in the reading room, TV lounge, or on the patio, and there's a hot tub and an on-call massage therapist. Big breakfasts in the sunny dining room feature upside-down peach pancakes, potato pancakes, and homemade granola. **Pros:** easy to find; European-style luxuries; recreation packages can be arranged. **Cons:** simple room decor can seem sparse. ✉ *Hwy. 542, Milepost 28* ☎ *360/599–1776 or 877/567–5526* ⊕ *www.theinnatmtbaker.com* ➳ *5 rooms* △ *In-room: a/c (some), no phone, DVD, Wi-Fi. In-hotel: no kids under 14* ▭ *AE, D, MC, V* ⦿*| BP.*

¢ ⬚ **Kale House Bed & Breakfast.** The charming home gleams with polished wood and large windows, which look out to knobby apple trees and a weeping willow. The pastel main-floor bedroom has a private bath, while the bright, two-room second-floor suite has a unique cupboard sleeping nook. Public spaces include the cozy dining room, the comfortable fireplace lounge, and a gift shop and gallery. **Pros:** small and inviting. **Cons:** no services or amenities. ✉ *201 Kale St, Everson* ☎ *360/966–7027* ⊕ *www.kalehouse.net* ➳ *2 rooms* △ *In-room: no phone, no a/c, no TV, Wi-Fi. In-hotel: Wi-Fi hotspot* ▭ *MC, V* ⦿*| BP.*

$ ⬚ **The Logs at Canyon Creek.** This comfortable back-country resort, set on a creek and surrounded by forest, is a haven for deer, eagles, and other wildlife. Rustic two-bedroom cabins have a full kitchen, plus a living room with a rock fireplace—your wood is even provided. A cedar chalet vacation home has three bedrooms and comes fully equipped with such amenities as hot tub, pool table, DVD player, and dishwasher. The property is open year-round, but rates plummet September through June, when you can stay two nights and get a third night free Sunday through Thursday. **Pros:** your home in the woods; great ski access. **Cons:** a long drive from civilization. ✉ *7577 Canyon View Dr. Glacier* ☎ *360/599–2711* ⊕ *www.thelogs.com* ➳ *5 cabins, 1 vacation home* △ *In-room: no phone (some), no a/c, kitchen, DVD (some), no TV (some). In-hotel: laundry facilities (some)* ▭ *No credit cards.*

At the **Mt. Baker Ski Area** you can snowboard and ski downhill or cross-country from roughly November to the end of April. The area set a world snowfall record in winter 1998–99. Ski and snowboard equipment is available to rent. ✉ *Hwy. 542, Mt. Baker* ☎ *360/734–6771, 360/671–0211 snow reports* ⊕ *www.mtbakerskiarea.com* ▱ *Lift ticket weekdays $33.90, weekends and holidays $41.32.*

SEDRO-WOOLLEY

42 mi southwest of Glacier, 9 mi northeast of Mount Vernon.

On its way east from I–5, Highway 20 skirts Burlington and Sedro-Woolley, the latter a former mill and logging town now considered "The Gateway to the Cascades." Fronted by a huge black steam engine, the settlement has a bit of an old downtown and a smattering of Tar Heel culture, as it was settled by pioneer loggers and farmers from North Carolina. It also has an institute that arranges trips into the North Cascades National Park and a nearby park headquarters.

GETTING HERE

Sedro-Woolley is about 1 hr 20 min from Seattle via I–5 north to Burlington (Exit 230), then 5 mi east via Highway 20.

VISITOR INFORMATION

Sedro-Woolley Chamber of Commerce (⊠ *714-B Metcalf St., Sedro-Woolley* ☎ *360/855–1841 or 888/225–8365* ⊕ *www.sedro-woolley.com*).

EXPLORING

Lake Whatcom Railway. The steam-powered train makes short jaunts through the woods 11 mi north of Sedro-Woolley. Excursions run all summer and during special events, such as the December Christmas train rides with Santa. During peak weekends, tours depart around 9:30, noon, and 2:30, and children pay half-price. Note that the schedule changes seasonally. ⊠ *Hwy. 9, Wickersham* ☎ *360/595–2218* 🎫 *$18* ☉ *Call for hrs.*

WHERE TO STAY

$ 📺 **Three Rivers Inn.** This pleasant two-story motel is a handy place to stay on the way to or from North Cascades National Park. Each room has either a deck or balcony and some overlook the manicured lawn and seasonal pool and hot tub. Continental breakfast is served in the lobby; there's also an Alfy's Pizza restaurant adjacent. **Pros:** rooms are well-equipped with microwaves and refrigerators. **Cons:** no elevator, past guests have complained about cleanliness and noise. ⊠ *210 Ball St., Sedro-Woolley* ☎ *360/855–2626* ⊕ *www.thethreeriversinn.com* 📞 *40 rooms* ♿ *In-room: a/c, refrigerator, Wi-Fi. In-hotel: restaurant, bar, pool, Wi-Fi hotspot, some pets allowed* ▭ *D, MC, V.* ☞ *CP*

MARBLEMOUNT

40 mi east of Sedro-Woolley.

Like Sedro-Woolley, Marblemount is a former logging town now depending on outdoor recreation for its fortunes. Anglers, campers, hikers, bird-watchers, and hunters come and go from the town's collection of motels, cafés, and stores, while day-trippers head in for sips at the area's small wineries. It's also a good base for exploring North Cascades National Park.

GETTING HERE

Marblemount is about two hours northeast of Seattle. It can be reached via I–5 north to Burlington then east past Sedro-Woolley on Highway 20. An alternate route is to take the exit from I–5 to Arlington/

Darrington and proceed on Highway 530 until it reaches Highway 20, then continue east.

WHERE TO EAT

$$ ✕ **Buffalo Run Restaurant.** Buffalo, venison, elk, and ostrich are the spe-
AMERICAN cialties at this little place next to the Marblemount post office. Veg-
etarians need not worry, though—there are a few non-meat options.
The atmosphere is completely casual, with buffalo heads and Old
West memorabilia lining the dining room walls. Outside, the patio
adds warm-weather seating and garden views; it's a good spot to kick
back with a glass of wine. The adjacent inn, run by the same man-
agement, is an inexpensive overnight option. ✉ *60084 Hwy. 20, Mar-
blemount* ☎ *360/873–2461* ⊕ *www.buffaloruninn.com* ▤ *AE, D, MC,
V* ⊗ *Closed Wed. and Nov.–Dec. and Mar.; closed Mon–Fri. Jan.–Feb.,
Apr. and May.*

$ ✕ **Marblemount Diner.** Standard diner fare is featured at this family-
AMERICAN owned restaurant, including burgers, fish-and-chips, soup, and grilled-
chicken sandwiches. An emphasis on local ingredients is evident and
service is friendly. The weekend breakfast buffet is a hearty way to fill
up before a day of hiking in the mountains. ✉ *60147 Hwy. 20, Mar-
blemount* ☎ *360/873–4503* ▤ *MC, V.* ⊗ *Closed Tue. and Wed. Limited
hours off-season; call ahead.*

WINTHROP

87 mi east of Marblemount, 128 mi east of Sedro-Woolley.

Before the cowboys came, the Methow Valley was a favorite gather-
ing place for Indian tribes, who dug the plentiful and nutritious bulbs
and hunted deer while their horses fattened on the tall native grasses.
For wayward pioneers who came later, the cool, glacier-fed streams
provided welcome relief on hot summer days, and the rich fields were
a starting point for vast crops and orchards. The 1800s saw the bur-
geoning riverside settlement of Winthrop grow into a cattle-ranching
town, whose residents inspired some of Owen Wister's colorful char-
acters in his novel *The Virginian*. Today Winthrop, in the center of the
Methow Valley, still retains its Wild West character throughout the
business district, where many of the original, turn-of-the-20th-century
buildings still stand.

Getting to town through the Washington countryside is a picturesque
drive, with endless vistas of golden meadows, neatly sown crop fields,
and rustic old barn frames. In winter the land is a crisp blanket of glit-
tering frost; in summer little fruit-and-vegetable stands pop up along the
back roads. Massive tangles of blackberry bushes produce kumquat-size
fruit you can eat right off the vines, and the pungent aroma of apples
pervades the breezes in autumn. Flat roads, small towns, incredible
views, and plenty of camp spots make this the perfect weekend wander-
ing territory by bike, car, or motorcycle.

GETTING HERE

When the North Cascades Highway is open, Winthrop can be reached
via that scenic route; it takes about 3 hrs, 45 min from Seattle. The rest
of the year, it will take about an extra hour via Stevens Pass (Hwy. 2)

or Snoqualmie Pass (I–90 then Hwy. 970 to Hwy. 2) to Wenatchee then north via Highways 97, 153, and 20. From Spokane, Winthrop is about 3½ hrs west via Highway 2, then Highways 174, 17, 97, 153, and 20.

VISITOR INFORMATION

Winthrop Chamber of Commerce (⌧ *202 Hwy. 20, Winthrop* ☎ *509/996–2125 or 888/463–8469* ⊕ *www.winthropwashington.com*).

WHERE TO EAT

$$$–$$$$

ECLECTIC

✕**Dining Room at Sun Mountain Lodge.** Cozy tables are surrounded by a woodsy decor in this spacious restaurant, where you can enjoy the mountain scenery while you dine. Farm-fresh produce, Washington beef, and locally caught fish highlight the excellent menu, which includes such delicacies as rich forest-mushroom strudel; melt-in-your-mouth glazed pork chops with apple-sage compote and roasted fingerling potatoes; and wild antelope fillet with huckleberry sauce, served with spaetzle and local vegetables. Desserts range from individually baked apple pies to a luscious huckleberry chocolate hazelnut torte. The 5,500-bottle wine cellar is one of the best in the region. ⌧ *Sun Mountain Lodge, Patterson Lake Rd., Winthrop* ☎ *509/996–2211* ⊕ *www.sunmountainlodge.com/ dining* ▭ *AE, DC, MC, V.*

$–$$

SOUTHERN

✕**Heenan's Burnt Finger Bar-B-Q & Steak House.** You can't get more authentic than a barbecue joint that serves slow-smoked sauce-slathered ribs and chicken right out of an old Conestoga wagon. Sidled up to the Methow River, the corral-style restaurant provides sweeping views of the water, the valley, and the farmlands beyond. Creamy coleslaw, crisp corn on the cob, and an assortment of salads and chilies round out the menu. Diners can relax inside the cozy dining rooms or outside by the grill, where evenings bring campfires and guitar-strumming cowboys on weekends. *716 Hwy. 20 S, Winthrop* ☎ *509/996–8221* ▭ *D, MC, V* ⊘ *Closed Wed. Oct.–Memorial Day; no lunch Mon., Tues., Thurs., and Fri.*

¢–$

AMERICAN

✕**Old Schoolhouse Brewery.** Casey and Laura Ruud purchased the old Winthrop Brewery in 2008. Son Blaze, with a degree in physics and background in chemistry and math, is the head brewer; he's already won a gold medal from the North American Brewers Association for the Hooligan Stout. The long, one-room pub sits between the town's main street and the river; live music plays on the outdoor stage by the Chewuch River on summer weekend nights. While you're waiting for big burgers, fish-and-chips, or a healthy wrap, sip your Ruud Awakening IPA or Epiphany Pale. Save room for a mini chocolate Bundt cake for dessert, great with local organic, fair-trade coffee from Backcountry Coffee Roasters. ⌧ *155 Riverside Ave.* ☎ *360/996–3183* w*www. oldschoolhousebrewery.com* ⊘ *Closed Tues.* ▭ *D, MC, V.*

$–$$

AMERICAN

✕**Twisp River Pub.** Buffalo wings, nachos, and an array of homemade soups are tasty partners for the brewery's crisp house beers and regional wines. Choose from burgers, fish-and-chips, wraps, and meaty sandwiches at lunch; dinners include steak, salmon, pastas, and pad thai. Brunch is served Sunday. Kids can get a Shirley Temple or Roy Rogers drink, along with fairly standard kids' menu fare. There's live music every weekend and jazz in the beer garden each Wednesday evening in summer. The shop sells quality T-shirts, beer glasses, and coffee mugs,

13

as well as pub gift cards. Free Wi-Fi throughout the building is a bonus. ✉ *201 Hwy. 20, Twisp* ☎ *509/997–6822 or 888/220–3360* ⊕ *www. methowbrewing.com* ⊟ *AE, D, DC, MC, V* ⊙ *Closed Mon. and Tues.*

WHERE TO STAY

$$–$$$ ☷ **Freestone Inn.** At the heart of a 120-acre farm amid more than 2 mil-
Fodor's Choice   lion acres of forest, this rustic resort embraces luxury in a pioneer-style
★   setting. One side of the massive log-cabin main building holds simple,
☺   spacious guest rooms, each done in Northwest colors and enhanced
with a gas fireplace, soaking tub, mini-refrigerator, and balcony or deck;
two suites also have jetted tubs and separate living areas. On the other
side of the inn there are five new, spacious condos with full kitchens,
flat-screen TVs in living rooms and bedrooms, and very private decks
with Adirondack chairs. A hot tub by the inn overlooks Freestone Lake,
and all the rooms and condos have lake views too. Several spacious
lodges stand lakeside, and wood-paneled cabins snuggle up to Early
Winters Creek; some have stone fireplaces, others have wrought-iron
fireplaces and decks over the water. The inn houses a library, a Great
Room with a three-story fireplace, and a restaurant serving Northwest
cuisine (**$–$$**). Jack's Hut Adventure Center organizes everything from
hot-air balloon trips and mountaineering expeditions to sleigh rides and
children's activities. Note that this is also one of the Northwest's top
heli-skiing bases. **Pros:** beautiful setting; myriad activities; very family-friendly; **Cons:** a bit off the beaten path. ✉ *31 Early Winters Dr.,
Mazama* ☎ *509/996–3906 or 800/639–3809* 🖶 *509/996–3907* ⊕ *www.
freestoneinn.com* ⤴ *12 rooms, 15 cabins, 5 condos, 4 lodges* ☺ *In-
room: a/c (some), kitchen (some), refrigerator, DVD (some), Wi-Fi.
In-hotel: restaurant, pool, bicycles, laundry facilities (some), some pets
allowed* ⊟ *AE, D, MC, V.*

¢–$ ☷ **Methow Valley Inn.** Guest rooms in this lovely 1912 home are appointed
with antiques and quilt-covered iron beds. A large stone fireplace fronts
the Great Room; there's also a cozy library and light-filled sunroom.
Fresh flowers and organic fruits come from the surrounding gardens,
and seasonal events are hosted in the adjacent courtyard. **Pros:** gorgeous
gardens in summer; lovely holiday decorations in winter; family-style
friendliness. **Cons:** there isn't much to do in Twisp. ✉ *234 2nd Ave.,
Twisp* ☎ *509/997–2253* ⊕ *www.methowvalleyinn.com* ⤴ *8 rooms, 5
with private bath* ☺ *In-room: no phone, no TV, Wi-Fi. In-hotel: Wi-Fi
hotspot, no kids under 12* ⊟ *AE, MC, V* ⧆ *BP.*

$$$–$$$$ ☷ **Sun Mountain Lodge.** A hilltop location gives guests panoramic views
Fodor's Choice   of the Cascade Mountains and Methow Valley; experiencing the spec-
★   tacular setting is a prime reason to visit. In the main lodge the rooms
☺   are basic hotel-style, but almost all have mountain views; the few that
have valley views are the only ones with TVs at the resort. The best
rooms are in the Mt. Gardner and Mt. Robinson buildings, where
accommodations mirror the lodge-style elegance of the main building;
all have a fireplace, CD player, and a private patio or balcony. In the
Mt. Robinson rooms, doors open above the jetted tubs allowing a full
outdoor view, and mirrors are strategically placed to further enhance
the views. Throughout the property, furniture and decor are by local
artisans. Spacious cabins are off-site, 1½ mi below on the Patterson

Sun Mountain Lodge

lakefront, and have full kitchens and fireplaces. There are 100 mi of hiking, horseback-riding, and skiing trails nearby; afterward, you can indulge your sore muscles at the spa or in the hot tubs, open year-round. Two pools, playgrounds, boat and bike rentals, fishing at Patterson Lake, outdoor games, an indoor game room, and numerous special activities make this an all-seasons destination. The Cowboy Dinner (or breakfast) is fun for all ages; guests can ride to the outdoor barbecue dinner on a horse or be transported by a horse-drawn wagon. The Dining Room (⇨ *Where to Eat above*), with snowy mountain views from every table, serves Northwest fare and has an impressive wine cellar. **Pros:** year-round outdoor activities; views are incredible; friendly and helpful staff. **Cons:** no TVs and limited cell-phone service; somewhat isolated; pricey but ask about specials. ⊠ *Patterson Lake Rd., Winthrop* ☎ *509/996–2211 or 800/572–0493* ⊕ *www.sunmountainlodge. com* ⊷ *96 rooms, 16 cabins* ⬥ *In-room: a/c, kitchen (some), refrigerator (some), no TV, Wi-Fi. In-hotel: restaurant, room service, bar, tennis court, pools, gym, spa, water sports, bicycles, children's programs (ages 5–12), Wi-Fi hotspot* ⊟ *AE, DC, MC, V.*

CHELAN

61 mi south of Winthrop.

Long before the first American settlers arrived at the long, narrow lake, Chelan (sha-*lan*) was the site of a Chelan Indian winter village. The Indians would range far and wide on their horses in spring and summer, following the newly sprouting grass from the river bottoms into the mountains; in winter they converged in permanent villages to feast, perform sacred rituals, and wait out the cold weather and snow. During the winter of 1879–80, Chelan served briefly as an army post, but the troops were soon transferred to Fort Spokane. American settlers arrived in the 1880s.

Today Chelan serves as the favorite beach resort of western Washingtonians. In summer Lake Chelan is one of the hottest places in Washington, with temperatures often soaring above 100°F. The mountains surrounding the 55-mi-long fjordlike lake rise from a height of about 4,000 feet near Chelan to 8,000 and 9,000 feet near the town of Stehekin, at the head of the lake. There is no road circling the lake, so the only way to see the whole thing is by boat or floatplane. Several resorts line the lake's eastern (and warmer) shore. Its northwestern end, at Stehekin, just penetrates North Cascades National Park. South of the lake, 9,511-foot Bonanza Peak is the tallest nonvolcanic peak in Washington.

GETTING HERE

From Seattle it takes about 3 hrs 15 min to reach Chelan by either Highway 2 (Stevens Pass) or I–90 (Snoqualmie Pass) then north via Highway 97. From Spokane it's about 3 hrs via Highways 2 and 17.

VISITOR INFORMATION

Purple Point Information Center. Rangers here offer guidance on hiking and camping and information about the national parks and recreation areas. This is a good place to pick up permits and passes. Maps and concise displays explain the complicated ecology of the valley, which encompasses in its length virtually every ecosystem in the Northwest. Hours vary in spring and fall. ⊠ *Stehekin Valley Rd., ¼ mi north of Stehekin Landing, Stehekin* ☎ *360/856–5700 option 14* ☼ *Mid-Mar.– mid-Oct., daily 8:30–5.*

EXPLORING

Fodor's Choice
★

Lake Chelan. This sinewy, 55-mi-long fjord—Washington's deepest lake— works its way northwest between the towns of Chelan, at its south end, and Stehekin, at the far northwest edge. The scenery is unparalleled, the flat blue water encircled by plunging gorges, with a vista of snow-slathered mountains beyond. No roads access the lake except for Chelan, so a floatplane or boat is needed to see the whole thing. Resorts dot the warmer eastern shores. ⊠ *Alt. 97, Chelan* ☎ *360/856–5700 Ext. 340 option 14* ⊕ *www.nps.gov/lach.*

Lake Chelan Boat Co. Working boats for this company haul supplies, mail, cars, and construction materials across Lake Chelan to Stehekin, but travelers are welcome aboard as well. The *Lady of the Lake II* makes journeys from May to October, departing from Chelan at 8:30 and returning at 6. Tickets are $39 round-trip, half price for ages two to 11. The *Lady Express,* a speedy catamaran, runs between Stehekin, Holden Village, the national park, and Lake Chelan from June to October, departing daily at 8:30 and returning at 2:45; tickets are $59 round-trip. Its schedule varies in the off-season. The vessels also can drop off and pick up at lakeshore trailheads. ⊠ *1418 Woodin Ave., Chelan* ☎ *509/682–4584 or 888/682–4584* ⊕ *www.ladyofthelake.com* ✉ *$39– $59* ☼ *Schedule varies by season and boat; check Web site.*

Lake Chelan State Park, right on the lake and 9 mi west of Chelan on the opposite (less crowded) shore, is a favorite hangout for folks from the cool west side of the Cascades who want to soak up some sun. There are docks, a boat ramp, RV sites with full hookups, and lots of campsites for those who prefer a less "citified" approach to camping. ⊠ *U.S. 97A, west to South Shore Dr. or Navarre Coulee Rd.* ☎ *800/452–5687* ⊕ *www.parks.wa.gov* ⌦ *Camping $21–$28* ⊙ *Memorial Day–Labor Day, daily 6:30* AM*–10* PM*; Labor Day–Memorial Day, 8–5.*

Fodor's Choice ★ **Stehekin.** One of the most beautiful and secluded valleys in the Pacific Northwest, Stehekin was homesteaded by hardy souls in the late 19th century. It's actually not a town, but rather a small community set at the northwest end of Lake Chelan, and it's accessible only by boat, floatplane, or trail. Year-round residents—who have intermittent outside communications, boat-delivered supplies, and just two-dozen cars between them—enjoy a wilderness lifestyle. Even during the peak summer season only around 200 visitors make the trek here.

Directly north of Lake Chelan State Park, **Twenty-Five Mile Creek State Park** also abuts the lake's eastern shore. It has many of the same facilities as the park in Chelan, as well as a swimming pool. Because it's the more remote of the two, it's often less crowded. ⊠ *South Shore Dr.* ☎ *509/687–3610 or 800/452–5687* ⊕ *www.parks.wa.gov* ⊙ *Apr.–Sept., daily dawn–dusk.*

WHERE TO EAT

¢
CAFÉ
✕ **Stehekin Pastry Company.** As you enter this lawn-framed timber chalet, you're immersed in the tantalizing aromas of a European bakery. Glassed-in display cases are filled with trays of homemade baked goods, and the pungent espresso is eye-opening. Sit down at a window-side table and dig into an over-filled sandwich or rich bowl of soup—and don't forget dessert: we're guessing you'll never taste a better slice of pie, made with fruit fresh-picked from local orchards. Although it's outside of town, the shop is conveniently en route to Rainbow Falls and adjacent to the Norwegian Fjord Horses stables, which also makes it a popular summertime ice-cream stop for sightseers. ⊠ *Stehekin Valley Rd., about 2 mi from Stehekin Landing, on the way to Rainbow Falls, Stehekin* ☎ *509/682–4677* w*www.stehekinpastry.com* ⊟ *No credit cards* ⊙ *Closed mid-Oct.–mid-May.*

$–$$
AMERICAN
✕ **Stehekin Valley Ranch.** Meals in the rustic log ranch house, served at long, polished log tables, include buffet dinners of steak, ribs, hamburgers, salad, beans, and dessert. Note that breakfast is served 7 to 9, lunch is noon to 1, and dinner is 5:30 to 7; show up later, and the kitchen's closed. Transportation from Stehekin Landing is included for day visitors. ⊠ *Stehekin Valley Rd., 9 mi north of Stehekin Landing, Stehekin* ☎ *509/682–4677 or 800/536–0745* w*www.stehekinvalleyranch.com* ⊟ *No credit cards* ⊙ *Closed Oct.–mid-June.*

WHERE TO STAY

$$
▢ **Campbell's Resort.** Open for more than a century, this sand-color apartment-style resort sits on landscaped grounds alongside Lake Chelan. Every room has a balcony or patio with lake views and at least a microwave and refrigerator; some have kitchens and fireplaces.

Campbell's Bistro ($–$$) serves Northwest fare and wines in a comfortable atmosphere; the second-floor Pub and Veranda, with views over the lake, dishes out simpler meals. The parklike, family-friendly setting includes pristine beaches, picnic areas, barbecues, and lots of room to romp. **Pros:** lots of activity, but also tranquil spaces; rates are very low in the off-season. **Cons:** busy high season. ⊠ *104 W. Woodin Ave., Chelan* ☎ *509/682–2561 or 800/553–8225* ⎙ *509/682–2177* ⊕ *www. campbellsresort.com* ⟿ *170 rooms* ⇘ *In-room: a/c, kitchen (some), refrigerator, Wi-Fi. In-hotel: 2 restaurants, bar, pools, gym, spa, children's programs (ages 4–15), laundry facilities* ⊟ *AE, MC, V.*

$–$$ ⊡ **Stehekin Landing Resort.** Large log cabins welcome you with crackling fires and Lake Chelan views. Standard rooms are in the Alpine House, which has a shared lounge and a lakeside deck; larger rooms in the Swiss Mont building each have a private deck overlooking the water. Kitchen units are also available, and the fully equipped four-bedroom Lake House comes with a fireplace, hot tub, and laundry facilities. American fare is served in the restaurant, which is open all day in high season (lunch only October through April). For deep discounts, check out the lodge's seasonal packages, which combine accommodations, round-trip boat fare across Lake Chelan, a bus tour, parking, and sports equipment (like snowshoes). **Pros:** right on the water; boat slips. **Cons:** as in all of Stehekin, modern-day technology is largely absent here. ⊠ *About 5 mi south of Stehekin Landing on Lake Chelan* ☎ *509/682–4494* ⊕ *www. stehekinlanding.com* ⟿ *27 rooms, 1 house* ⇘ *In-room: no phone, no a/c, kitchen (some), no TV. In-hotel: restaurant, laundry facilities, Wi-Fi hotspot* ⊟ *MC, V.*

$$ ⊡ **Stehekin Valley Ranch.** Nestled along pretty meadows at the edge of pine forest, this classic ranch is a center for hikers and horseback riders. Barnlike ranch cabins have cedar paneling, tile floors, and a private bath; canvas-roof tent cabins have bunk beds, kerosene lamps, and shared facilities; and two kitchen cabins have modern equipment. Enormous breakfasts and meaty dinner buffets are turned out family-style at picnic tables in the rustic wood restaurant (dinners for nonguests by reservation only; $–$$). Rates for ranch and tent cabins include accommodations, linens, meals, and transport from Stehekin Landing. Credit cards are accepted only by phone. **Pros:** many activities; free vehicle use with kitchen cabins. **Cons:** no bathrooms in tent cabins. ⊠ *Stehekin Valley Rd., 9 mi north of Stehekin Landing, Stehekin* ☎ *509/682–4677 or 800/536–0745* ⊕ *www.stehekinvalleyranch.com* ⟿ *14 cabins* ⇘ *In-room: no phone, no a/c, kitchen (some), no TV. In-hotel: restaurant, bicycles, some pets allowed* ⊟ *MC, V* ☉ *Closed Oct.–mid-June* �‖ *FAP.*

CAMPING ⚠ **Lake Chelan National Recreation Area.** Many backcountry camping
 ¢ areas are accessible via park shuttles or boat. All require a free backcountry permit; 12 boat-in sites also require a $5 per day dock fee. Everything you bring must be hung on bear wires, so rethink those big coolers. **Purple Point,** the most popular campground due to its quick access to Stehekin Landing, has seven tent sites, bear boxes, and nearby road access. Reservations are not accepted, but group requests must be made in writing. **Pros:** beautiful location; easy water access. **Cons:** crowded in July and August. ⊠ *Stehekin Landing, NPS, P.O. Box 7,*

Stehekin, WA ☎ *360/856–5700 Ext. 360 option 14* ⇝ *7 tent sites* ⚿ *Pit toilets, drinking water, bear boxes.* ⊘ *Closed mid-October–mid-March* ⊟ *No credit cards.*

SPORTS AND THE OUTDOORS

On a scenic half-day raft trip you can traverse the lower section of the Stehekin River, which winds through cottonwood and pine forest, from Yawning Glacier on the slopes of Magic Mountain southeast to Lake Chelan. From June through September, guided trips on Class III waters leave from the **Stehekin Valley Ranch** (⊠ *Stehekin Valley Rd., 3½ mi from Stehekin Landing, Stehekin* ☎ *509/682–4677 or 800/536–0745*). Trip prices are $35–$75.

Mountain bikers also make their way into this rugged terrain, and **Stehekin Landing Resort** (☎ *509/682–4494* ⊕ *www.stehekin.com*) rents bikes for $5 per hour or $40 per day, and organizes seasonal trips.

WENATCHEE

39 mi southwest of Chelan.

Wenatchee (we-*nat*-chee), the county seat of Chelan County, is an attractive city in a shallow valley at the confluence of the Wenatchee and Columbia rivers. Surrounded by orchards, Wenatchee is known as the "Apple Capital of Washington." Downtown has many old commercial buildings as well as apple-packing houses where visitors can buy locally grown apples by the case (at about half the price charged in supermarkets). The paved Apple Valley Recreation Loop Trail runs on both sides of the Columbia River. It crosses the river on bridges at the northern and southern ends of town and connects several riverfront parks. The Wenatchee section is lighted until midnight.

The town was built on an ancient Wenatchi Indian village, which may have been occupied as long as 11,000 years ago, as recent archaeological finds of Clovis hunter artifacts suggest. (The Clovis hunters, also known as Paleo-Indians, were members of the oldest tribes known to have inhabited North America.)

GETTING HERE

Horizon Air serves Wenatchee's Pangborn Memorial Airport. Amtrak's *Empire Builder,* which runs from Chicago to Seattle, stops in Wenatchee; Greyhound Bus Lines serves the town too. From Seattle it's about a 2½ hr drive to Wenatchee via Highway 2 or I-90 and Highway 97; from Spokane it takes about 3 hrs via Highway 2 or I-90.

Contacts Amtrak (☎ *800/872–7245* ⊕ *www.amtrak.com*). **Greyhound Bus Lines.** ☎ *509/662–2183* ⊕ *www.greyhound.com*). **Pangborn Memorial Airport** ☎ *509/884–2494* ⊕ *www.pangbornairport.com*).

VISITOR INFORMATION

Wenatchee Chamber of Commerce (⊠ *300 S. Columbia St., Wenatchee* ☎ *509/662–2116 or 800/572–7753* ⊕ *www.wenatcheevalley.org*).

EXPLORING

The **Wenatchee Valley Museum & Cultural Center** has displays of local Indian and pioneer artifacts, as well as Northwest artist exhibits. ⊠ *127 S. Mission St.* ☎ *509/888–6240* ⊕ *www.wvmcc.org* ⊠ *$5* ☉ *Tues.–Sat. 10–4.*

Ohme Gardens provides a lush green oasis, high atop bluffs near the confluence of the Columbia and Wenatchee rivers, where you can commune with a blend of native rocks, ferns, mosses, waterfalls, rock gardens, and conifers. ⊠ *North of Wenatchee near U.S. 2 at U.S. 97A, 3327 Ohme Rd.* ☎ *509/662–5785* ⊕ *www.ohmegardens.com* ⊠ *$7* ☉ *Memorial Day–Labor Day, daily 9–7; mid-April–Memorial Day and Labor Day–mid-Oct, daily 9–6, closed mid-Oct.–mid-April.*

Rocky Reach Dam has a museum and visitor center as well as picnic tables and elaborately landscaped grounds. The Gallery of the Columbia has the pilothouse of the late-19th-century Columbia River steamer *Bridgeport*, replicas of Indian dwellings, and Indian, loggers', and railroad workers' tools. The Gallery of Electricity has exhibits explaining why dams are good for you. ⊠ *U.S. 97A N, about 10 mi north of Wenatchee* ☎ *509/663–7522 or 509/663–8121* ⊠ *Free* ☉ *Park, daily dawn–dusk. Museum, daily 8:30–5. Visitor center, daily 8:30–5:30.*

Okanogan-Wenatchee National Forest, a pine forest, covers 2.2 million acres, from the eastern slopes of the Cascades to the crest of the Wenatchee Mountains and north to Lake Chelan. Camping, hiking, boating, fishing, hunting, and picnicking are popular activities. ⊠ *215 Melody La., Wenatchee* ☎ *509/664–9200* ⊕ *www.fs.fed.us/r6/ wenatchee* ⊠ *$5 daily parking pass, or $30 Northwest Forest Pass* ☉ *Daily 24 hrs.*

WHERE TO EAT AND STAY

$$
ECLECTIC
✕ **Shakti's.** Fine dining in a classy yet comfortable atmosphere is the vibe at Shakti's, making it popular for dates and special occasions. Entrée prices are very reasonable considering the large serving sizes. The eclectic menu has several pasta dishes, including a spicy-hot chicken puttanesca and a seafood linguini; steaks, fish, crab, and lamb also are featured. The small, two-level restaurant and bar has twinkling white lights that add to the romantic ambience. There's also patio dining in the charming garden, open during the warmer months. ⊠ *218 N. Mission* ☎ *509/662–3321* ⊕ *www.shaktisfinedining.com* ⊟ *AE, D, MC, V.*

$$
AMERICAN
✕ **The Windmill.** The comfortable old roadhouse, gamely topped by a windmill, opened in 1937. Here it's all about home-style food, particularly steak: famous entrées include whiskey pepper steak (pepper-coated New York strip sautéed, flamed with whiskey, and finished with mushrooms in a rich demi-glace) and the marinated tenderloin chunks. Seafood isn't overlooked, though; try the charbroiled salmon coated with apple brandy barbecue sauce. Save room for fresh-baked pies and regional wines. ⊠ *1501 N. Wenatchee Ave.* ☎ *509/665–9529* w*www. thewindmillrestaurant.com* ⊟ *AE, DC, MC, V* ☉ *No lunch.*

$$
☖ **Coast Wenatchee Center Hotel.** A skywalk links this hotel to a convention center. Although it tends to attract business travelers, the Coast Wenatchee has enough facilities and amenities to appeal to vacationing families. Rooms are tidy and comfortable, and suites have a kitchenette.

The ninth-floor restaurant serves a blend of American and European fare from breakfast until late. You can walk from the hotel to the riverfront park and downtown. **Pros:** convenient access to local sights and activities. **Cons:** standard hotel atmosphere. ⊠ *201 N. Wenatchee Ave.,* ☏ *509/662–1234* or *800/716–6199* ⊕ *www.coasthotels.com* ↪ *147 rooms, 5 suites* ⟁ *In-room: a/c, refrigerator, Wi-Fi. In-hotel: restaurant, bar, pool, laundry service, some pets allowed* ⊟ *AE, D, DC, MC, V.*

$ ⌂ **Warm Springs Inn Bed & Breakfast.** Roses planted along the driveway lead you to this 1917 mansion amid 10 acres of gardens and trees. The rooms, some of which look out onto the Wenatchee River, are filled with a tasteful selection of art and antiques. The Chandelier Suite is the largest, bedecked with the glittering namesake fixture and complete with a private bath and attached twin bedroom. The Garden Room, done in pastel yellows and blues, has a four-poster bed and a shower. The River Room and the Autumn Leaf Room, both on the lower level, have private entrances along a riverside deck. **Pros:** charming, quiet setting. **Cons:** wedding bookings fill rooms far in advance. ⊠ *1611 Love La.* ☏ *509/662–8365* or *800/543–3645* ☏ *509/663–5997* ⊕ *www. warmspringsinn.com* ↪ *6 rooms* ⟁ *In-room: no phone, a/c, refrigerator (some), DVD (some), Wi-Fi. In-hotel: no kids under 10* ⊟ *AE, D, MC, V* ⏺ *BP.*

SKIING

Four lifts, 33 downhill runs, powder snow, and some 30 mi of marked cross-country trails make **Mission Ridge Ski Area** one of Washington's most popular ski areas. There's a 2,100-foot vertical drop, and the snowmaker scatters whiteness from the top to bottom slopes during the season. Snowboarding is allowed. Lift tickets cost $50–$54 per day, but look for deals like the Bomber Card, which gives you discounted tickets and direct lift access for $65. (Note: The pass takes its name from the Bomber Bowl, a ski run where a B-52 bomber crashed on the slopes during World War II.) ⊠ *7500 Mission Ridge Rd.* ☏ *509/663–6543, 800/374–1693 snow conditions* ⊕ *www.missionridge.com* ⊙ *mid-Nov.– Apr., Thurs.–Mon. 9–4 (daily during school breaks).*

EN ROUTE Surrounded by snow-capped mountain peaks, Cashmere is one of Washington's oldest towns, founded by Oblate missionaries back in 1853, when the Wenatchi and their vast herds of horses still roamed free over the bunch grasslands of the region. Some of the great Wenatchi leaders are buried in the mission cemetery. Today Cashmere is the apple, apricot, and pear capital of the Wenatchee Valley. **Aplets and Cotlets/Liberty Orchards Co., Inc.** was founded by two Armenian brothers who escaped the massacres of Armenians by Turks early in the 20th century, settled in this peaceful valley, and became orchardists. When a marketing crisis hit the orchards in the 1920s, the brothers remembered dried-fruit confections from their homeland, re-created them, and named them aplets (made from apples) and cotlets (made from apricots). Sales took off almost immediately, and today Aplets and Cotlets are known as the combination that made Cashmere famous. Free samples are offered during the 15-minute tour of the plant. ⊠ *117 Mission St.* ☏ *509/782–2191* ⊕ *www.libertyorchards.com* ⊡ *Free* ⊙ *Daily 8:30–5:30, tours every 20 min. with some exceptions for breaks.*

LEAVENWORTH

22 mi northwest of Wenatchee, 118 mi northeast of Seattle.

Leavenworth a favorite weekend getaway for Seattle folks, and it's easy to see why: the charming (if occasionally *too* cute) Bavarian-style village, home to good restaurants and attractive lodgings, is a hub for some of the Northwest's best skiing, hiking, rock climbing, rafting, canoeing, and snowshoeing.

A railroad and mining center for many years, Leavenworth fell on hard times around the 1960s, and civic leaders, looking for ways to capitalize on the town's setting in the heart of the Central Cascade Range, convinced shopkeepers and other businesspeople to maintain a gingerbread-Bavarian architectural style in their buildings. Today, even the Safeway supermarket and the Chevron gas station carry out the theme. Restaurants prepare Bavarian-influenced dishes, candy shops sell Swiss-style chocolates, and stores and boutiques stock music boxes, dollhouses, and other Bavarian items.

GETTING HERE

From Seattle, Leavenworth can be reached by either of Washington's most-developed mountain passes—Stevens (Hwy. 2) or Snoqualmie (I–90 then a short jog up Hwy. 97/Blewett Pass); either takes about 2½ hrs. From Spokane, traveling west via Highway 2 takes about 3½ hrs. Amtrak's *Empire Builder* now makes daily trips from Spokane and Seattle to Leavenworth, and Greyhound Bus Lines also serves the town.

Contacts **Amtrak** (☎ *800/872-7245* ⊕ *www.amtrak.com*). **Greyhound Bus Lines** (☎ *509/548-9601* ⊕ *www.greyhound.com*).

EXPLORING

Icicle Junction is an amusement arcade in the wilderness replete with miniature golf, a rock wall, a movie theater, and other activities. ⊠ *565 Hwy. 2, at Icicle Rd.* ☎ *509/548-2400 or 800/558-2438* ⊕ *www. iciclejunction.com* ☉ *School year, Mon.–Thurs. 3–8, Fri. 3–10, Sat. 10–10, Sun. 10–8. Summer, daily 10–10.*

Settled into the 19th-century, barn-style Big Haus, the **Leavenworth Upper Valley Museum** (⊠ *347 Division St.* ☎ *509/548–0728*) invokes pioneer days in the Cascades. The riverside grounds were once Arabian stallion–grazing terrain, and Audubon programs take advantage of plentiful bird sightings. Exhibits highlight the lives and times of the Field family, local Native American tribes, and other prominent residents of Leavenworth and the Upper Wenatchee Valley. The gallery is open 11 to 5 Thursday through Sunday and holiday Mondays; admission is by donation.

The **Nutcracker Museum** (⊠ *735 Front St.* ☎ *509/548–4573 or 800/892–3989* ⊕ *www.nutcrackermuseum.com*), which contains more than 5,000 kinds of antique and modern nutcrackers, is housed in the Nussknacker House, a shop selling nutcrackers and other knickknacks. The store is open daily 10 to 6, the museum 2 to 5 daily May through October, and weekends November through April. Admission is $2.50.

Holiday season in Leavenworth

WHERE TO EAT

$$
AUSTRIAN

✕ **Andreas Keller German Restaurant.** Merry "oompah" music bubbles out from marching accordion players at this fun-focused dining hub, where the theme is "Germany without the Passport." Laughing crowds lap up strong, cold brews and feast on a selection of brat-, knack-, weiss-, and mettwursts, Polish sausage, and Wienerschnitzel, all nestled into heaping sides of sauerkraut, tangy German potato salad, and thick, dark rye bread. Get a taste of it all with the sampler plate—and save room for the knockout apple strudel. Note that service can be slow at times, so just sit back and enjoy the ambience. ✉ *829 Front St.* ☎ *509/548–6000* w*ww.andreaskellerrestaurant.com* ▭ *AE, D, MC, V.*

$$–$$$
CAFÉ
★

✕ **Cafe Mozart.** This café looks like the upstairs apartments of a central European town house: it captures the essence of Gemütlichkeit (coziness) in the way the small dining rooms are decorated and the curtains are cut, as well as with the authentic aromas that drift from the kitchen. The food is superb, with ingredients blending together beautifully. Menu highlights include slow-roasted duck with pear and raspberry confiture, pork medallions accompanied by flavorful red cabbage, and chicken breast topped with Black Forest ham and melted Gouda cheese. A pianist plays during weekend dinners. ✉ *829 Front St.* ☎ *509/548–0600* w*ww.cafemozartrestaurant.com* ▭ *AE, D, MC, V.*

$–$$
AMERICAN

✕ **Baren Haus.** The cuisine at this spacious, noisy, and often crowded beer hall–style room may not be haute, or even particularly interesting, but the generous servings and low prices will appeal to those traveling on a budget. Fill up on generous servings of basic American fare, like burgers and fries, sandwiches, salads, pizza, and pasta. ✉ *208 9th St.* ☎ *509/548–4535* ⊕ *www.barenhaus.com* ▭ *MC, V.*

¢ ✕ **Home Fires Bakery.** This homey bakery with a German wood-fired oven
BAKERY turns out delicious breads, muffins, cinnamon rolls, and other baked
goods. On a sunny day you can sit outside at a picnic table and enjoy
the scenery while sipping coffee and munching on goodies. ⊠ *11007
Hwy. 2.* ☎ *509/548–7362* w*www.homefiresbakery.com* ▭ *D, MC, V*
☻ *Closed Mon. and Tues. No dinner.*

$ ✕ **South.** A nice change from all the Bavarian food in town, South fea-
LATIN tures an innovative menu of Latin-inspired dishes, including sweet-
potato and roasted poblano chili enchiladas, Yucatan chicken rojo, and
Oaxacan black mole with chicken or pork. It's not all Latin, though.
Although there's no Wienerschnitzel on the menu, they do have German sausage, burgers, steaks, and a popular pulled pork sandwich
at lunch. The children's menu includes tacos, quesadillas, and even
prawns, and oranges can be substituted for chips. More than two dozen
kinds of tequila and a margarita infused with basil are among the drink
choices. ⊠ *913 Front St.* ☎ *509/888–4328* ⊕ *www.southleavenworth.
com* ▭ *AE, D, MC, V.*

WHERE TO STAY

$$ ⊡ **Abendblume Pension.** The carved-wood walls and ceilings of this
Austrian-style country chalet give it an authentic alpine appearance.
The B&B, ¾ mi from downtown, overlooks the Leavenworth Val-
ley. Wonderful views of the mountains and valley are afforded from
each room's private balcony. Rooms are individually decorated and all
have fireplaces. **Pros:** very romantic; Bavarian breakfast is authentic
and ample. **Cons:** fills up quickly during festivals. ⊠ *12570 Ranger
Rd.* ☎ *509/548–4059 or 800/669–7634* ⊕ *www.abendblume.com* ⤸ *7
rooms* ⚴ *In-room: no phone, a/c, DVD, Wi-Fi. In-hotel: no kids under
12* ▭ *AE, D, MC, V* ⎺⎺⎺ *BP.*

$$–$$$ ⊡ **Icicle Village Resort.** This nearly five-acre property has an array of
☻ unique amenities, including its own movie theater, soda fountain, mini-
golf, two outdoor pools (one covered and open year-round), two hot
tubs, a day spa, sport court, and game arcade. The Best Western Icicle
Inn's hotel rooms have been recently upgraded with flat screen TVs and
new decor. All have refrigerators, microwaves, and coffeemakers; some
also have fireplaces, whirlpool tubs, and an extra sleeping area for fami-
lies. The Aspen Suites are newer condominiums in separate buildings
on the property. Great for longer stays, families, and groups, they have
1 to 3 bedrooms, fully-equipped kitchens, washer/dryer, access to all of
the resort facilities, and a separate shared barbecue area and workout
room. A full hot breakfast buffet at J.J. Hills Restaurant is included
for guests staying at both the Inn and the condominiums. A free shut-
tle bus to downtown Leavenworth runs daily except Sunday. **Pros:**
Lots of on-site activities, very kid-friendly. **Cons:** 10-minute walk to
town. ⊠ *505 Hwy. 2 Leavenworth* ☎ *800/961–0162 or 509/888–2776*
⊕ *www.iciclevillage.com* ⤸ *92 rooms, 27 condominiums* ⚴ *In-room:
a/c, kitchen (some), refrigerator, DVD, Wi-Fi. In-hotel: 2 restaurants,
bar, room service, mini-golf course, 2 pools, gym, spa, laundry facilities,
Internet terminal, some pets allowed.* ▭ *AE, D, DC.* ⎺⎺⎺ *BP.*

$$ ⊡ **Mountain Home Lodge.** This contemporary mountain inn, built of
sturdy cedar and redwood, sits on a 20-acre alpine meadow with

breathtaking Cascade Mountains views. Peeled-pine and vine-maple furniture fill the rooms, which also contain handmade quilts, binoculars, robes, and port wine; self-contained cabins are also available. Forty miles of trails thread through the property, and sports options range from hiking and skiing to tennis and horseshoes. Winter rates include all meals, plus Sno-Cat transportation from the parking lot below. **Pros:** pristine luxury; high-quality sports and activities. **Cons:** tough winter transport; some rooms on the small side. ⊠ *8201 Mountain Home Rd., 3 mi south of Leavenworth* ☎ *509/548–7077 or 800/414–2378* 🖷 *509/548–5008* ⊕ *www.mthome.com* ⇆ *10 rooms, 2 cabins* ♿ *In-room: no phone, a/c, refrigerator (some), no TV (some), DVD (some), Wi-Fi. In-hotel: tennis court, pool, spa, Wi-Fi hotspot, no kids under 16* ☰ *D, MC, V* ⊧Ⓞ▯ *BP.*

$–$$ ⌘ **Pension Anna.** Rooms at this family-run Austrian-style pension in the heart of the village are decorated with sturdy alpine imported furniture and fresh flowers; the beds have cozy comforters. Each suite has a fireplace and a Jacuzzi tub. A solid European breakfast of coffee, fruit, cereal, meats and cheeses, and coffeecake is served in a room decorated in traditional European style, with crisp linens, pine decor, dark-green curtains, and a cuckoo clock. **Pros:** German breakfast is unique; very European feel; nice location. **Cons:** No elevator, some guests have complained about noisy plumbing. ⊠ *926 Commercial St.* ☎ *509/548–6273 or 800/509–2662* ⊕ *www.pensionanna.com* ⇆ *13 rooms, 4 suites* ♿ *In-room: a/c, refrigerator (some), Wi-Fi* ☰ *AE, D, MC, V* ⊧Ⓞ▯ *BP.*

$$–$$$
Fodor's Choice
★
⌘ **Run of the River.** This intimate, relaxed mountain inn stands on the banks of the Icicle River near Leavenworth, placing the rustic rooms with timber furnishings close to nature. All rooms have private outside entrances and decks with views of the Pinnacles (a dramatic rock formation), an aspen grove, meadows (where deer browse), or Icicle and Tumwater canyons. Ravenwood Lodge is a spacious, chalet-style luxury retreat complete with a full kitchen, river-rock fireplace, loft bedroom, and its own outdoor hot tub. Cushy bathrobes, a fireplace, a two-person jetted tub, a DVD player, a refrigerator, and an old-fashioned typewriter are in every room. Guests have free access to mountain bikes to explore the country roads. **Pros:** close to town; abundant healthy breakfasts; lots of outdoor activities. **Cons:** popular longtime owners recently sold the inn, but new owners are adding their own touches. ⊠ *9308 E. Leavenworth Rd.* ☎ *509/548–7171 or 800/288–6491* 🖷 *509/548–7547* ⊕ *www.runoftheriver.com* ⇆ *6 rooms, 1 lodge* ♿ *In-room: a/c, kitchen (some), refrigerator, DVD, Wi-Fi. In-hotel: bicycles, Wi-Fi hotspot, no kids under 18* ☰ *D, MC, V* ⊧Ⓞ▯ *BP.*

SPORTS AND THE OUTDOORS

FISHING Trout are plentiful in many streams and lakes around Lake Wenatchee. **Leavenworth Ranger Station** (☎ *509/782–1413*) issues permits for the Enchantment Lakes and Alpine Lake Wilderness area.

GOLF **Leavenworth Golf Club** (⊠ *9101 Icicle Rd.* ☎ *509/548–7267*) has an 18-hole, par-71 course. The greens fees are $20, plus $20 for an optional cart.

13

HIKING   The Leavenworth Ranger District has more than 320 mi of scenic trails, among them Hatchery Creek, Icicle Ridge, the Enchantments, Tumwater Canyon, Fourth of July Creek, Snow Lake, Stuart Lake, and Chatter Creek. Both of the following sell the Northwest Forest Pass ($5 day pass; $30 annual pass), which is required year-round for parking at trailheads and for camping in the upper Chiwawa Valley. The **Lake Wenatchee Ranger Station** (⊠ *22976 Hwy. 207* ☎ *509/763–3101*) provides updates on trails and fire closures. Contact the **Leavenworth Ranger District** (⊠ *600 Sherburne St.* ☎ *509/782–1413*) for information on area hikes.

HORSEBACK RIDING   Rent horses by the hour, or take daylong rides (including lunch) or overnight pack trips ($26–$60) at **Eagle Creek Ranch** (⊠ *7951 Eagle Creek Rd.* ☎ *509/548–7798* ⊕ *www.eaglecreek.ws*). **Icicle Outfitters & Guides** (⊠ *7373 Icicle Rd.* ☎ *800/497–3912* ⊕ *www.icicleoutfitters.com*) has 2- to 4-mi trail rides ($25–$50 per person) and daylong rides ($150). **Mountain Springs Lodge** (⊠ *19115 Chiwawa Loop Rd.* ☎ *509/763–2713 or 800/858–2276* ⊕ *www.mtsprings.com*) offers horseback rides from 40 minutes to all day ($25–$145) long, as well as daytime sleigh rides ($19), moonlight dinner sleigh rides ($65), and snowmobile tours one to five hours long ($55–$130).

SKIING   More than 20 mi of cross-country ski trails lace the Leavenworth area. In winter enjoy a Nordic ski jump, snowboarding, tubing, and really great downhill and cross-country skiing at **Leavenworth Ski Hill** (⊠ *Ski Hill Dr.* ☎ *509/548–5477* ⊕ *www.skileavenworth.com*). In summer, enjoy the wildflowers or view the Leavenworth Summer Theatre's production of *The Sound of Music*. The ski hill is 1 mi north of downtown Leavenworth. The Play All Day Pass is $22; there's also a Nordic Day Pass ($15), an Alpine Day Pass ($15), and a Tubing Pass ($15).

Stevens Pass (⊠ *Summit Stevens Pass, U.S. 2, Skykomish* ☎ *360/973–2441 or 360/634–1645* ⊕ *www.stevenspass.com*) has snowboarding and cross-country skiing as well as 37 major downhill runs and slopes for skiers of every level. Lift tickets cost $60.

WHITE-WATER RAFTING   Rafting is popular from March to July; the prime high-country runoff occurs in May and June. The Wenatchee River, which runs through Leavenworth, is considered one of the best white-water rivers in the state—a Class III on the International Canoeing Association scale.

Alpine Adventures (☎ *206/323–1220 or 800/723–8386* ⊕ *www.alpine-adventures.com*) conducts challenging white-water and relaxing river floats through spectacular scenery. An all-day Wenatchee River drift costs $79 (lunch included); a half-day drift is $64 (no lunch). The Methow River drift is $79. **Blue Sky Outfitters** (☎ *509/682–8026* ⊕ *www.blueskyoutfitters.com*) makes half- and full-day rafting trips on the Methow and Wenatchee rivers.

Osprey Rafting Co. (⊠ *Icicle Rd.* ☎ *509/548–6800 or 800/743–6269* ⊕ *www.ospreyrafting.com*) offers 4½-hour trips on the Wenatchee River for $74, which includes wet suits and booties, transportation, and lunch; a $56, two-hour trip includes gear and transportation but no lunch.

Mount Rainier
National Park

WORD OF MOUTH

"I took this photo at Paradise on Mt. Rainier. It is the nearest thing to Switzerland this side of the Atlantic!"

—photo by chinana, Fodors.com member

WELCOME TO
MOUNT RAINIER NATIONAL PARK

TOP REASONS
TO GO

★ **The mountain:** Some say Mt. Rainier is the most magical mountain in America. At 14,411 feet, it is a popular peak for climbing, with more than 10,000 attempts per year—half of which are successful.

★ **The glaciers:** About 35 square mi of glaciers and snowfields encircle Mt. Rainier, including Carbon Glacier and Emmons Glacier, the largest glaciers by volume and area, respectively, in the continental United States.

★ **The wildflowers:** More than 100 species of wildflowers bloom in the high meadows of the national park; the display dazzles from midsummer until the snow flies.

★ **Fabulous hiking:** More than 240 mi of maintained trails provide access to old-growth forest, river valleys, lakes, subalpine meadows, and rugged ridges.

★ **Unencumbered wilderness:** Under the provisions of the 1964 Wilderness Act and the National Wilderness Preservation System, 97% of the park is preserved as wilderness.

1 Longmire. Inside the Nisqually Gate, explore the Longmire historic district's museum and visitor center, ruins of the park's first hotel, or the nature loop. Nearby, delicate footbridges span the thundering Christine and Narada falls.

2 Paradise. The park's most popular destination is famous for wildflowers in summer and skiing in winter. Skyline Trail is one of many hiking routes that crisscross the base of the mountain; the larger of the two park lodges is also here.

3 Ohanapecosh. Closest to the southeast entrance and the town of Packwood, the old-growth trees of the Grove of Patriarchs are a must-see. Another short trail around nearby Tipsoo Lake has great views.

4 Sunrise and White River. This side of the park is easy to visit in summer if you enter from the east side, but it's a long drive from the southwest entrance. Sunrise is the highest stretch of road in the park and a great place to take in the alpenglow—reddish light on the peak of the mountain near sunrise and sunset. Mt. Rainier's premier mountain-biking area, White River, is also the gateway to more than a dozen hiking trails.

5 Carbon River and Mowich Lake. Near the Carbon River Entrance Station is a swath of temperate forest, but to really get away from it all, follow the windy gravel roads to remote Mowich Lake.

GETTING ORIENTED

The jagged white crown of Mount Rainier is the showpiece of the Cascades and the focal point of this 337-square-mi national park. The most popular destination in the park, Paradise, is in the park's southern region, and Ohanapecosh, the Grove of Patriarchs, and Tipsoo Lake are in the southeastern corner. Mount Rainier National Park's eastern and northern areas are dominated by wilderness. The snowy folds of the Cascade mountain range stretch out from this Washington park; Seattle is roughly 50 mi north, and the volcanic ruins of Mt. St. Helens 100 mi south.

14

SOUDOUGH MOUNTAINS

Huckleberry Creek

SUNRISE RIDGE

410

White River

Mather Memorial Parkway

Pacific Crest Trail

Sunrise
Visitor Center

White River Entrance

White River

AT ISLAND MOUNTAIN

GOVERNORS RIDGE

410

410

Tipsoo Lake

123

Wonderland Trail

COWLITZ DIVIDE

0   2 mi

0   2 km

3

Grove of the Patriarchs

Stevens Canyon Entrance

Visitor Center

123

MOUNT RAINIER NATIONAL PARK PLANNER

When to Go

Rainier is the Puget Sound's weather vane: if you can see it, the weather is going to be fine. Visitors are most likely to see the summit in July, August, and September. Crowds are heaviest in summer, too, meaning that the parking lots at Paradise and Sunrise often fill before noon, campsites are reserved months in advance, and other lodgings are reserved as much as a year ahead.

True to its name, Paradise is often sunny during periods when the lowlands are under a cloud layer. The rest of the year, Rainier's summit gathers clouds whenever a Pacific storm approaches; once the peak vanishes from view it's time to haul out rain gear. The rare periods of clear winter weather bring residents up to Paradise for cross-country skiing.

AVG. HIGH/LOW TEMPS.

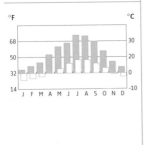

Flora and Fauna

Wildflower season in the meadows at and above timberline is mid-July through August. Large mammals like deer, elk, black bears, and cougars tend to occupy the less accessible wilderness areas of the park and thus elude the average visitor; smaller animals, such as squirrels and marmots are easier to spot. The best times to see wildlife are at dawn and dusk at the forest's edge. Fawns are born to the park's does in May, and the bugling of bull elk on the high ridges can be heard in late September and October, especially on the park's eastern side.

Getting Here and Around

The Nisqually entrance is on Highway 706, 14 mi east of Route 7; the Ohanapecosh entrance is on Route 123, 5 mi north of U.S. 12; and the White River entrance is on Route 410, 3 mi north of the Chinook and Cayuse passes. These highways become mountain roads as they reach Rainier, winding up and down many steep slopes, so cautious driving is essential: use a lower gear, especially on downhill sections, and take care not to overheat brakes by constant use. These roads are subject to storms any time of year, and are repaired in the summer from winter damage and washouts. Expect to encounter roadwork delays.

The side roads going into the park's western slope are all narrower, unpaved, and subject to frequent flooding and washouts. All are closed by snow in winter except Highway 706 to Paradise and Carbon River Road, though the latter is washed out beyond the park boundary due to the major 2006 flood. (Route 410 on the northeast side is open to the Crystal Mountain access road entrance.)

Park roads have a maximum speed of 35 MPH in most places, and you have to watch for pedestrians, cyclists, and wildlife. Parking can be very difficult to find during the peak summer season, especially at Paradise, Sunrise, the Grove of Patriarchs, and at the trailheads between Longmire and Paradise; it's best to arrive early in the day if you plan to visit these sites. A free shuttle runs from Ashford to Paradise on weekends and from Paradise to Longmire Friday through Sunday, from mid-June through Labor Day.

Updated by
Holly S. Smith
& Shelley
Arenas

14

Like a mysterious, white-clad woman, often veiled in clouds even when the surrounding forests and fields are bathed in sunlight, Mt. Rainier is the centerpiece of its namesake park. The impressive volcanic peak stands at an elevation of 14,411 feet, making it the fifth-highest peak in the lower 48 states. More than 2 million visitors a year enjoy spectacular views of the mountain and return home with a lifelong memory of its image.

The mountain holds the largest glacial system in the contiguous United States, with more than two-dozen major glaciers. On the lower slopes you find silent forests made up of cathedral-like groves of Douglas fir, western hemlock, and western red cedar, some more than 1,000 years old. Water and lush greenery are everywhere in the park, and dozens of thundering waterfalls, accessible from the road or by a short hike, fill the air with mist.

PARK ESSENTIALS

ACCESSIBILITY

The only trail in the park that is fully accessible to those with impaired mobility is Kautz Creek Trail, a short boardwalk that leads to a splendid view of the mountain. The entrance to the Trail of the Shadows at Longmire is flat and also somewhat accessible but not paved. At Paradise there is a new ramp that allows access to the meadows and some of the paved trails. Campgrounds at Cougar Rock, Ohanapecosh, and White River have several accessible sites. All main visitor centers, as well as National Park Inn at Longmire, are accessible.

ADMISSION FEES AND PERMITS

The entrance fee of $15 per vehicle and $5 for those on foot, motorcycle, or bicycle, is good for seven days. Annual passes are $30. Climbing permits are $30 per person per climb or glacier trek. Wilderness camping permits must be obtained for all backcountry trips, and advance reservations are highly recommended.

ADMISSION HOURS

Mount Rainier National Park is open 24/7 year-round, but with limited access in winter. Gates at Nisqually (Longmire) are staffed year-round during the day; facilities at Paradise and Ohanapecosh are open daily from late May to mid-October; and Sunrise is open daily July to early October. During off-hours you can buy passes at the gates from machines that accept credit and debit cards. Winter access to the park is limited to the Nisqually entrance, and the Jackson Memorial Visitor Center at Paradise is open on weekends and holidays in winter.

ATMS/BANKS

There are no ATMs in the park. ATMs are available at stores, gas stations, and bank branches in Ashford, Packwood, and Eatonville.

CELL-PHONE RECEPTION

Cell-phone reception is unreliable throughout much of the park, although access is clear at Paradise, Sunrise, and Crystal Mountain. Public telephones are at all park visitor centers, at the National Park Inn at Longmire, and at Paradise Inn at Paradise.

PARK CONTACT INFORMATION

Mount Rainier National Park ⊠ *Tahoma Woods, Star Rte., Ashford, WA* ☎ *360/569–2211* ⊕ *www.nps.gov/mora.*

TOURS

Fodor's Choice ★ **Gray Line Bus Tours.** Join one-day or overnight sightseeing tours from Seattle to Mount Rainier National Park. ⊠ *4500 W. Marginal Way SW, Seattle* ☎ *206/626–5200 or 800/824–8897* ⊕ *www.graylineofseattle.com.*

VISITOR CENTERS

Jackson Memorial Visitor Center. High on the mountain's southern flank, this center houses exhibits on geology, mountaineering, glaciology, and alpine ecology. Multimedia programs are staged in the theater; there's also a snack bar and gift shop. This is the park's most popular visitor destination, and it can be quite crowded in summer. ⊠ *Hwy. 706 E, 19 mi. east of the Nisqually park entrance* ☎ *360/569–6036* ☉ *May–June and early-Sept.–mid-Oct., daily 10–6; July–mid-Aug., daily 9–7; mid-Aug.–Labor Day, daily 10–7; Nov.–Apr., weekends and holidays 10–5.*

★ **Longmire Museum and Visitor Center.** Glass cases inside this museum preserve plants and animals from the park—including a stuffed cougar—and historical photographs and geographical displays provide a worthwhile overview of the park's history. The visitor center area has some perfunctory exhibits on the surrounding forest and its inhabitants, as well as pamphlets and information about park activities. ⊠ *Hwy. 706, 17 mi east of Ashford* ☎ *360/569–2211 Ext. 3314* ☒ *Free* ☉ *July–early Sept., daily 9–6; Sept.–June, daily 9–5.*

Ohanapecosh Visitor Center. Learn about the region's dense old-growth forests through interpretive displays and videos at this visitor center; a couple miles away at the Grove of the Patriarchs, roving rangers are available to answer questions in person. ⊠ *Rte. 123, 11 mi north of Packwood* ☎ *360/569–6046* ☉ *Late May–Oct., daily 9–7.*

Sunrise Visitor Center. Exhibits at this center explain the region's sparser alpine and subalpine ecology. A network of nearby loop trails leads you

MOUNT RAINIER IN ONE DAY

The best way to get a complete overview of Mount Rainier in a day is to enter via Nisqually and begin your tour by browsing in **Longmire Museum**. When you're done, get to know the environment in and around Longmire Meadow and the overgrown ruins of Longmire Springs Hotel on the ½-mi **Trail of the Shadows** nature loop.

From Longmire, Highway 706 East climbs northeast into the mountains toward Paradise. Take a moment to explore gorgeous **Christine Falls**, just north of the road 1½ mi past Cougar Rock Campground, and **Narada Falls**, 3 mi farther on; both are spanned by graceful stone footbridges. Fantastic mountain views, alpine meadows crosshatched with

nature trails, a welcoming lodge and restaurant, and the excellent **Jackson Memorial Visitor Center** combine to make lofty Paradise the primary goal of most park visitors. One outstanding (but challenging) way to explore the high country is to hike the 5-mi round-trip **Skyline Trail** to Panorama Point, which rewards you with stunning 360-degree views.

Continue eastward on Highway 706 East for 21 mi and leave your car to explore the incomparable, thousand-year-old **Grove of the Patriarchs**. Afterward, turn your car north toward White River and **Sunrise Visitor Center**, where you can watch the alpenglow fade from Mt. Rainier's domed summit.

14

through alpine meadows and forest to overlooks that have broad views of the Cascades and Rainier. ⊠ *Sunrise Rd., 15 mi from the White River park entrance* ☎ *360/663–2425* ☉ *Early July–early Sept, daily 10–6.*

EXPLORING MOUNT RAINIER

HISTORIC SITE

National Park Inn. Even if you don't plan to stay overnight, you can stop by year-round to admire the architecture of this 1917 inn, which is on the National Register of Historic Places. While you're here, relax in front of the fireplace in the lounge, stop at the gift shop, or dine at the restaurant. ⊠ *Longmire Visitor Complex, Hwy. 706, 10 mi east of Nisqually entrance, Longmire* ☎ *360/569–2411.*

SCENIC DRIVES

Chinook Pass Road. Route 410 (the highway to Yakima) follows the eastern edge of the park to Chinook Pass, where it climbs the steep, 5,432-foot pass via a series of switchbacks. At its top, take in broad views of Rainier and the east slope of the Cascades.

Mowich Lake Road. In the northwest corner of the park, this 24-mi gravel mountain road begins in Wilkeson and heads up the Rainier foothills to Mowich Lake, traversing beautiful mountain meadows along the way. Mowich Lake is a pleasant spot for a picnic, though remote and with no facilities except restrooms.

Paradise Road. This 9-mi stretch of Highway 706 winds its way up the mountain's southwest flank from Longmire to Paradise, taking you from lowland forest to the ever-expanding vistas of the mountain above. Visit on a weekday if possible, especially in peak summer months, when the road is packed with cars. The route is open year-round.

Fodors Choice ★ **Sunrise Road.** This popular (read: crowded) scenic road carves its way 11 mi up Sunrise Ridge from the White River Valley on the northeast side of the park. As you top the ridge there are sweeping views of the surrounding lowlands. The road is open late June to October.

SCENIC STOPS

Christine Falls. These two-tiered falls were named in honor of Christine Louise Van Trump, who climbed to the 10,000-foot level on Mt. Rainier in 1889 at the age of nine, despite having a crippling nervous-system disorder. ⊠ *Next to Hwy. 706, about 2½ mi east of Cougar Rock Campground.*

Fodors Choice ★ **Grove of the Patriarchs.** Protected from the periodic fires that swept through the surrounding areas, this small island of 1,000-year-old trees is one of Mount Rainier National Park's most memorable features. A 1½-mi loop trail heads through the old-growth forest of Douglas fir, cedar, and hemlock. ⊠ *Rte. 123, west of the Stevens Canyon entrance.*

Fodors Choice ★ **Narada Falls.** A steep but short trail leads to the viewing area for these spectacular 168-foot falls, which expand to a width of 75 feet during peak flow times. ⊠ *Along Hwy. 706, 1 mi west of the turnoff for Paradise, 6 mi east of Cougar Rock Campground.*

☺ **Tipsoo Lake.** The short, pleasant trail that circles the lake here—ideal for families—provides breathtaking views. Enjoy the subalpine wildflower meadows during the summer months; in early fall there is an abundant supply of huckleberries. ⊠ *Off Cayuse Pass east on Hwy. 410.*

WHERE TO EAT

ABOUT THE RESTAURANTS

There are a limited number of restaurants inside the park, and a few worth checking out lie beyond its borders. Mount Rainier's picnic areas are justly famous, especially in summer, when wildflowers fill the meadows—resist the urge to feed the yellow pine chipmunks darting about.

WHAT IT COSTS				
¢	$	$$	$$$	$$$$
Restaurants	under $8	$8–$12	$13–$20	$21–$30	over $30

$–$$
ECLECTIC
 National Park Inn. Photos of Mt. Rainier taken by some of the Northwest's top photographers adorn the walls of this inn's large dining room, a bonus on the many days the mountain refuses to show itself. Meals, served family-style, are simple but tasty: orange-pecan chicken, pot roast, and sautéed trout. For breakfast, don't miss the Camp Muir

Mount Rainier, Looking North

Little Tahoma Peak 11,138 ft

Disappointment Cleaver

Ingraham Glacier

Paradise Glaciers

Anvil Rock 9,584 ft

CATHEDRAL ROCKS

McClure Rock 7,385 ft

Muir Snowfield

Camp Muir 10,188 ft

Columbia Crest 14,411 ft

Gibraltar Rock 12,660 ft

Panorama Point 6,800 ft

Nisqually Glacier

Skyline Trail

Alta Vista

Paradise

The Castle

Louise Lake

Unicorn Peak 6,917 ft

KEY
— Paved Roads
--- Hiking Trails
⋯ Climbing Routes

Point Success 14,153 ft

Wilson Glacier

Liberty Cap 14,122 ft

SUNSET AMPHITHEATER

Henry M. Jackson Memorial Visitor Center

Pinnacle Peak 6,562 ft

Reflection Lakes

St. Andrews Rock 10,992 ft

SUCCESS CLEAVER

Van Trump Glaciers

WAPOWETY CLEAVER

Success Glacier

Kautz Glacier

CUSHMAN CREST

Plummer Peak 6,370 ft

TATOOSH RANGE

Lane Peak 6,012 ft

VAN TRUMP PARK

Tahoma Glacier

PUYALLUP CLEAVER

GLACIER ISLAND

South Tahoma Glacier

Pyramid Glaciers

DIVIDE

PYRAMID PARK

Mildred Point

Wahpenayo Peak 6,231 ft

Chutla Peak

Tokaloo Rock 7,684 ft

Pyramid Peak 6,937 ft

Eagle Peak 5,958 ft

EMERALD RIDGE

Iron Mountain 6,283 ft

PYRAMID RIDGE

Cougar Rock

Rampart Ridge Trail

RAMPART RIDGE

THE RAMPARTS

Creek

Longmire

MOUNT RAINIER

French toast. ⊠ *Hwy. 706, Long-mire* ☎ *360/569–2411* ⊕ *www.mtrainierguestservices.com* ⊟ *AE, D, MC, V.*

¢ ✕ **Paradise Camp Deli.** Tasty deli
AMERICAN fare, including pizza, sandwiches,
ⓒ soups, salads, and hot entrées are
served daily from May through
early October and on weekends
and holidays during the rest of the
year. ⊠ *Jackson Memorial Visitors
Center* ☎ *360/569–2211* ⊕ *www.mtrainierguestservices.com* ⊟ *No
credit cards* ⊙ *Closed weekdays
early Oct.–Apr.*

$–$$ ✕ **Paradise Inn.** Where else can you
CONTINENTAL get a decent Sunday brunch in a historic heavy-timbered lodge halfway
up a mountain? Tall, many-paned windows provide terrific views of
Rainier, and the warm glow of native wood permeates the large dining
room. The lunch menu is simple and healthy—grilled salmon, salads,
and the like. For dinner, there's nothing like a hearty plate of the inn's
signature bourbon buffalo meat loaf. ⊠ *Hwy. 706, Paradise* ☎ *360/569–
2413* ⊕ *www.mtrainierguestservices.com* ⌦ *Reservations not accepted*
⊟ *AE, D, MC, V* ⊙ *Closed early Oct.–late May.*

¢ ✕ **Sunshine Lodge Food Service.** A cafeteria and grill here serve inexpen-
AMERICAN sive hamburgers, chili, hot dogs, and snacks from early July to early
ⓒ September. ⊠ *Sunrise Rd., 15 mi from the White River park entrance*
☎ *360/663–2425* ⊕ *www.mtrainierguestservices.com* ⊟ *No credit cards*
⊙ *Closed early Sept.–early July.*

PICNIC AREAS Park picnic areas are open July through September only.

Paradise Picnic Area. This site has great views on clear days. After picnicking at Paradise, you can take a hike to one of the many waterfalls
in the area—Sluiskin, Myrtle, or Narada, to name a few. ⊠ *Hwy. 706,
11 mi east of Longmire.*

Sunrise Picnic Area. Set in an alpine meadow that's filled with wildflowers in July and August, this picnic area provides expansive views of the
mountain and surrounding ranges in good weather. ⊠ *Sunrise Rd., 11
mi west of the White River entrance.*

WHERE TO STAY

ABOUT THE HOTELS

The Mount Rainier area is remarkably bereft of quality lodging. Rainier's two national park lodges, at Longmire and Paradise, are attractive and well maintained. They exude considerable history and charm,
especially Paradise Inn, but unless you've made summer reservations a
year in advance, getting a room can be a challenge. Dozens of motels
and cabin complexes are near the park entrances, but the vast majority
are overpriced and no-frills. With just a few exceptions, you're better
off camping.

Paradise Inn at Mt. Rainier National Park

ABOUT THE CAMPGROUNDS

Three drive-in campgrounds are in the park—Cougar Rock, Ohana-pecosh, and White River—with almost 500 sites for tents and RVs. None have hot water or RV hookups. For backcountry camping, you must obtain a free wilderness permit at one of the visitor centers. Primitive sites are spaced at 7- to 8-mi intervals along the Wonderland Trail and on other trails. A copy of *Wilderness Trip Planner: A Hiker's Guide to the Wilderness of Mount Rainier National Park*, available from any of the park's visitor centers or through the superintendent's office, is an invaluable guide if you're planning backcountry stays. Reservations for specific wilderness campsites are available from April 1 to September 30 for $20; for details, call the Wilderness Information Center at ☎ 360/569–4453.

WHAT IT COSTS					
	¢	$	$$	$$$	$$$$
Hotels	under $70	$70–$100	$101–$150	$151–$200	over $200
Camping	under $10	$10–$17	$18–$35	$36–$50	over $50

$ 🏨 **National Park Inn.** A large stone fireplace sits prominently in the common room of this country inn, the only one of the park's two inns that's open year-round. Rustic details such as wrought-iron lamps and antique bentwood headboards adorn the rooms. Simple American fare is served in the restaurant (⇨ *Where to Eat, above*). **Pros:** classic national park ambience; only lodging inside park open in winter and spring. **Cons:** jam-packed in summer; must book far in advance; some rooms have shared bath. ⊠ *Longmire Visitor Complex, Hwy. 706, 10 mi east of Nisqually entrance, Longmire* ☎ *360/569–2275* ⊕ *www. mtrainierguestservices.com* ⇨ *25 rooms, 18 with bath* ⌂ *In-room: no phone, no a/c, no TV. In-hotel: restaurant* ⊟ *AE, D, MC, V.*

$–$$ 🚩 **Paradise Inn.** With its hand-carved Alaskan cedar logs, burnished
Fodor's Choice parquet floors, stone fireplaces, Indian rugs, and glorious mountain
★   views, this 1917 inn is a classic example of a national park lodge. German architect Hans Fraehnke designed the decorative woodwork. In addition to the full-service dining room (⇨ *Where to Eat, above*), there's a café for lighter fare. **Pros:** central to trails; pristine vistas; nature-inspired details. **Cons:** noisy in high season; some shared bathrooms. ⊠ *Hwy. 706, Paradise* ☎ *c/o Mount Rainier Guest Services, P.O. Box 108, Star Rte., Ashford 98304* ☎ *360/569–2275* ⊕ *www. mtrainierguestservices.com* ⇨ *121 rooms* ⌂ *In-room: no phone, no TV. In-hotel: 2 restaurants* ⊟ *AE, D, MC, V* ⊙ *Closed early Oct.–late May.*

CAMPING   ⚠ **Cougar Rock Campground.** A heavily wooded campground with an
¢   amphitheater, Cougar Rock is one of the first to fill up. Five group sites are available. Reservations are accepted by calling the toll-free number. **Pros:** ranger programs; located near Paradise. **Cons:** often crowded. ⊠ *2½ mi north of Longmire* ☎ *360/569–2211 or 800/365–2267* ⇨ *173 tent/RV sites* ⌂ *Flush toilets, dump station, drinking water, fire grates, ranger station* ⊟ *AE, D, MC, V* ⊙ *Closed mid-Oct.–Apr.*

¢   ⚠ **Mowich Lake Campground.** This is Rainier's only lakeside campground. At 4,959 feet, it's also peaceful and secluded. Note that the campground is accessible only by 5 mi of convoluted gravel roads, which are subject to weather damage and potential closure at any time. **Pros:** Mowich Lake setting; isolated. **Cons:** long drive on unpaved roads. ⊠ *Mowich Lake Rd., 6 mi east of the park boundary* ☎ *360/569–2211* ⇨ *10 tent sites, 3 group sites* ⌂ *Pit toilets, running water (non-potable), picnic tables, ranger station* ⌂ *Reservations not accepted* ⊙ *Closed Nov.–mid July.*

¢   ⚠ **Ohanapecosh Campground.** This lush, green campground in the park's southeast corner has a visitor center, amphitheater, and self-guided trail. It's often one of the first campgrounds to open. Reservations are accepted by calling the toll-free number listed. **Pros:** great for families; open in early summer. **Cons:** popularity means busy facilities. ⊠ *Ohanapecosh Visitor Center, Hwy. 123, 1½ mi north of park boundary* ☎ *360/569–6046 or or 800/365–2267* ⇨ *188 tent/RV sites* ⌂ *Flush toilets, dump station, drinking water, fire grates, ranger station* ⊟ *AE, D, MC, V* ⊙ *Closed mid-Oct.–late May.*

¢   ⚠ **White River Campground.** At an elevation of 4,400 feet, White River is one of the park's highest and least-wooded campgrounds. Here you can enjoy campfire programs, self-guided trails, and partial views of Mt. Rainier's summit. Sites are first-come, first-served. **Pros:** breathtaking scenery. **Cons:** more exposure to the elements. ⊠ *5 mi west of White River entrance* ☎ *360/569–6030* ⇨ *112 sites* ⌂ *Flush toilets, drinking water, fire grates, ranger station* ⊟ *AE, D, MC, V* ⌂ *Reservations not accepted* ⊙ *Closed late-Sept.–early June.*

SPORTS AND THE OUTDOORS

BIRD-WATCHING

Be alert for kestrels, red-tailed hawks, and, occasionally, golden eagles on snags in the lowland forests. Also present at Rainier, but rarely seen, are great horned owls, spotted owls, and screech owls. Iridescent rufous hummingbirds flit from blossom to blossom in the drowsy summer lowlands, and sprightly water ouzels flutter in the many forest creeks. Raucous Steller's jays and gray jays scold passersby from trees, often darting boldly down to steal morsels from unguarded picnic tables. At higher elevations, look for the pure-white plumage of the white-tailed ptarmigan as it hunts for seeds and insects in winter. Waxwings, vireos, nuthatches, sapsuckers, warblers, flycatchers, larks, thrushes, siskins, tanagers, and finches are common throughout the park.

HIKING

Fodor's Choice
★
Although the mountain can seem remarkably benign on calm summer days, hiking Rainier is not a city-park stroll. Dozens of hikers and trekkers annually lose their way and must be rescued—and lives are lost on the mountain each year. Weather that approaches cyclonic levels can appear quite suddenly, any month of the year. With the possible exception of the short loop hikes listed here, all visitors venturing far from vehicle access points should carry day packs with warm clothing, food, and other emergency supplies.

⇨ *Multisport Outfitters box, below, for hiking outfitters and expeditions.*

EASY

Grove of the Patriarchs. A 1½-mi loop trail heads through the old-growth forest of Douglas fir, cedar, and hemlock. ⊠ *Rte. 123, west of the Stevens Canyon entrance.*

Nisqually Vista Trail. Equally popular in summer and winter, this trail is a 1¼-mi round-trip through subalpine meadows to an overlook point for Nisqually Glacier. The gradually sloping path is a favorite venue for cross-country skiers in winter; in summer, listen for the shrill alarm calls of the area's marmots. ⊠ *Trailhead at lower Paradise parking lot.*

Sourdough Ridge Trail. The mile-long loop of this self-guided trail takes you through the delicate subalpine meadows near the Sunrise Visitor Center. A gradual climb to the ridgetop yields magnificent views of Mt. Rainier and the more distant volcanic cones of Mts. Baker, Adams, Glacier, and Hood. ⊠ *Access trail at Sunrise Visitor Center, Sunrise Rd., 15 mi from the White River park entrance.*

Trail of the Shadows. This ½-mi walk is notable for its glimpses of meadowland ecology, its colorful soda springs (don't drink the water), James Longmire's old homestead cabin, and the foundation of the old Longmire Springs Hotel, which was destroyed by fire around 1900. ⊠ *Trailhead at Hwy. 706, across from Longmire Museum, 7 mi east of Nisqually entrance.*

MODERATE

Fodor's Choice
★
Skyline Trail. This 5-mi loop, one of the highest trails in the park, beckons day-trippers with a vista of alpine ridges and, in summer, meadows filled with brilliant flowers and birds. At 6,800 feet, Panorama Point,

the spine of the Cascade Range, spreads away to the east, and Nisqually Glacier tumbles downslope. ⊠ *Jackson Memorial Visitor Center.*

Van Trump Park Trail. You gain an exhilarating 2,200 feet on this route while hiking through a vast expanse of meadow with views of the southern Puget Sound. The 5-mi track provides good footing, and the average hiker can make it up in three to four hours. ⊠ *Hwy. 706 at Christine Falls, 4.4 mi east of Longmire.*

DIFFICULT

Fodor's Choice ★ **Wonderland Trail.** All other Mt. Rainier hikes pale in comparison to this stunning 93-mi trek, which completely encircles the mountain. The trail passes through all the major life zones of the park, from the old-growth forests of the lowlands to the alpine meadows and goat-haunted glaciers of the highlands—pick up a mountain-goat sighting card from a ranger station or visitor center if you want to help in the park's effort to learn more about these elusive animals. Wonderland is a rugged trail; elevation gains and losses totaling 3,500 feet are common in a day's hike, which averages 8 mi. Most hikers start out from Longmire or Sunrise and take 10–14 days to cover the 93-mi route. Snow lingers on the high passes well into June (sometimes July); count on rain any time of the year. Campsites are wilderness areas with pit toilets and water that must be purified before drinking. Only hardy, well-equipped, and experienced wilderness trekkers should attempt this trip, but those who do will be amply rewarded. Wilderness permits are required, and reservations are strongly recommended. ⚠ **Parts of the Wonderland Trail can be severely damaged due to floods. Check with a visitor center for the trail's current status.** For a summer-day hike, it's easiest to explore from Longmire, where a broad, easy section of track climbs through open, wildflower-filled slopes toward a vast panorama of ice-covered ridges. ⊠ *Longmire Visitor Center, Hwy. 706, 17 mi east of Ashford; Sunrise Visitor Center, Sunrise Rd., 15 mi west of the White River park entrance.*

MOUNTAIN CLIMBING

Fodor's Choice ★ Climbing Mt. Rainier is not for amateurs; each year, climbers die on the mountain, and many climbers become lost and must be rescued. Near-catastrophic weather can appear quite suddenly, any month of the year. If you're experienced in technical, high-elevation snow, rock, and ice-field adventuring, Mt. Rainier can be a memorable adventure. Climbers can fill out a climbing card at the Paradise, White River, or Carbon River ranger stations and lead their own groups of two or more. Climbers must register with a ranger before leaving and check out upon return. A $30 annual climbing fee applies to anyone venturing above 10,000 feet or onto one of Rainier's glaciers. During peak season it is recommended that you make a climbing reservation ($20 per group) in advance; reservations are taken by fax beginning in April on a first-come, first-served basis (find the reservation form at ⊕ *www.nps. gov/mora/planyourvisit/climbing.htm*). For climbing outfitters, ⇨ *Multisport Outfitters box*

MULTISPORT OUTFITTERS

Alpine Ascents International.
The Seattle-based company shuttles climbers directly from the city. The 3-day climb includes a high camp on the last night, which makes for a shorter climb to the summit the final day. There's a 2:1 guide ratio on the summit day for added safety. ✉ 109 W. Mercer St., Seattle☎ 206/378-1927 ⊕ www.alpineascents.com 🖃 $1325 for 3-day summit climb package (includes transportation to and from Seattle).

International Mountain Guides.
Guided climbs of Mt. Rainier for all ability levels from beginners to experts are offered; the ratio of one guide per two beginner climbers helps to ensure a greater chance of success. IMG also offers mountaineering workshops, glacier skills seminars, and winter climbing programs. ✉ 31111 Hwy 706 E, Ashford ☎ 360/569-2609 ⊕ www.mountainguides.com 🖃 $1225 for 3.5-day summit climb package.

Rainier Mountaineering Inc.
Reserve a private hiking guide through this highly regarded outfitter, or take part in its one-day mountaineering classes (mid-May through September), where participants are evaluated on their fitness for the climb and must be able to withstand a 16-mi round-trip hike with a 9,000-foot gain in elevation. The company also arranges private cross-country skiing and snowshoeing guides. ✉ 30027 Hwy. 706 E, Ashford ☎ 888/892-5462 or 360/569-2227 ⊕ www.rmiguides.com 🖃 $926 for three-day summit climb package.

Whittaker Mountaineering
(✉ 30027 Hwy. 706 E, Ashford ☎ 800/238-5756 or 360/569-2142 ⊕ www.whittakermountaineering. com). You can rent hiking and climbing gear, skis, snowshoes, snowboards, and other outdoor equipment at this all-purpose Rainier Base Camp outfitter, which also arranges for private cross-country skiing and hiking guides.

SKIING AND SNOWSHOEING

Mt. Rainier is a major Nordic ski center for cross-country and telemark skiing. Although trails are not groomed, those around Paradise are extremely popular. If you want to ski with fewer people, try the trails in and around the Ohanapecosh–Stevens Canyon area, which are just as beautiful and, because of their more easterly exposure, slightly less subject to the rains that can douse the Longmire side, even in the dead of winter. You should never ski on the plowed main roads, especially in the Paradise area—the snowplow operator can't see you. No rentals are available on the eastern side of the park.

Deep snows make Mt. Rainier a snowshoeing pleasure. The Paradise area, with its network of trails, is the best choice. The park's east-side roads, Routes 123 and 410, are unplowed, and provide other good snowshoeing venues, although you must share the main parts of the road with snowmobilers.

Paradise Area. You can cross-country ski or, in the Snowplay Area north of the upper parking lot at Paradise, sled using inner tubes and soft platters from December to April. Check with rangers for any restrictions. In summer, many trails around this side of the mountain are accessible from Paradise. During winter, the easy, 3½-mile Nordic ski route begins at the Paradise parking lot, and follows Paradise Valley/Stevens Canyon Road to Reflection Lakes. Equipment rentals are available at Whittaker Mountaineering in Ashford, or at the National Park Inn's General Store in Longmire. ⊠ *Accessible from Nisqually entrance at park's southwest corner and (summer only) from Stevens Canyon entrance at park's southeast corner* ☎ *360/569–2211* ⊕ *www.nps.gov/mora* ۞ *May–mid-Oct., daily, sunrise–sunset; mid-Oct.–Apr., weekends sunrise–sunset.*

OUTFITTERS AND EXPEDITIONS
Adjacent to the National Park Inn, **Rainier Ski Touring Center** (⊠ *Hwy. 706, 10 mi east of Nisqually entrance, Longmire* ☎ *360/569–2411, 360/569–2271*) rents cross-country ski equipment and provides lessons from mid-December through Easter, depending on snow conditions. Park rangers lead **Snowshoe Walks** (⊠ *Hwy. 706 E, 19 mi. east of the Nisqually park entrance* ☎ *360/569–2211 Ext. 2328* ⊠ *Free; suggested donation* ۞ *Late Dec.–Apr., weekends and holidays*) that start at Jackson Memorial Visitor Center at Paradise and cover 1¼ mi in about two hours. Check park publications for exact dates.

⇨ *For additional outfitters, see Multisport Outfitters box.*

MT. RAINIER ENVIRONS

The Cascade Mountains south of Snoqualmie Pass are more heavily eroded than those to the north and generally not as high. But a few peaks do top 7,000 feet, and two volcanic peaks are taller than any of the state's northern mountains. Mt. Adams is more than 12,000 feet high, and Mt. Rainier rises to more than 14,000 feet. The third of the southern peaks, Mt. St. Helens, blew its top in 1980, and is now little more than 8,000 feet tall.

Ashford sits astride an ancient trail across the Cascades used by the Yakama Indians to trade with the coastal tribes of western Washington. The town began as a logging railway terminal; today, it's the main gateway to Mount Rainier—and the only year-round access point to the park—with lodges, restaurants, grocery stores, and gift shops. Surrounded by Cascade peaks, Packwood is a pretty mountain village on U.S. 12, below White Pass. Between Mt. Rainier and Mt. St. Helens, it's a perfect jumping-off point for exploring local wilderness areas. The small town of Mossyrock is located between the large lakes of Riffe and Mayfield, which are popular for fishing, camping, and boating. Centralia (and its twin city Chehalis, the county seat) is right off I–5 and steeped in history—from its historic downtown district to numerous antiques stores. There's an outlet mall that spans two sides of the Interstate, and good options for dining and inexpensive lodging. Longview, a few miles west of I–5 past Kelso, has an interesting layout with curving streets and a city park that encircles one-third of the downtown. A 1,200-foot-long bridge over the Columbia River connects Longview to Oregon.

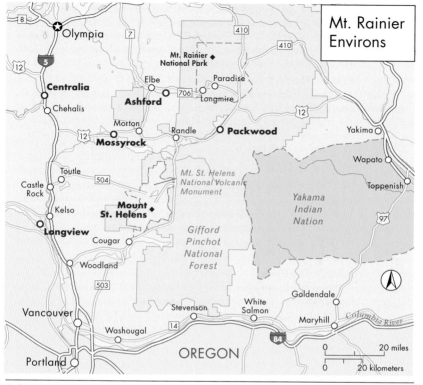

Mt. Rainier
Environs

14

ASHFORD

Adjacent to Nisqually (Longmire) entrance to Mount Rainier National
Park.

Ashford sits astride an ancient trans-Cascades trail used by the Yakama
Indians to trade with the people of western Washington. The town
began as a logging railway terminal; today the village provides access
to the Nisqually (Longmire) entrance to Mount Rainier National Park,
and caters to 2 million annual visitors with lodges, restaurants, groceries, and gift shops along Highway 706.

GETTING HERE

Ashford is about 85 miles from Seattle via I–5 southbound to Highway
7, then southeast to Highway 706. An alternate route is via I–5 southbound to Highway 167, then continuing south to Highway 161 through
Eatonville to Highway 7, then east to Highway 706. From the Portland
area, its about 130 miles via I–5 northbound, then east on Highway 12
to Morton and north via Highway 7 to Highway 706.

EXPLORING

Fodor'sChoice   **Mount Rainier Scenic Railroad.** Beginning at Elbe, 11 mi west of Ashford,
★   the train takes you southeast through lush forests and across scenic
☺   bridges, covering 14 mi of incomparable beauty. Seasonal theme trips,

such as the Great Pumpkin Express and the Santa Express, are popular and often sell out. ✉ *54124 Mountain Hwy E., Elbe* ☎ *360/569–2588 or 888/783–2611* ⊕ *www.mrsr.com* ✉ *$20–$23* ⊙ *Memorial Day–Sept. Thurs.–Sun. at 10:00 AM and 1:30 PM; lunch or dinner on select Sat. and Sun. at 3:30; Dec., weekends, call for hrs.*

WHERE TO EAT

$–$$
AMERICAN
Fodor's Choice
★

✕ **Alexander's Country Inn & Restaurant.** This classic, woodsy Northwest country inn built in 1912 serves the best food in the area. Ceiling fans and wooden booths lining the walls make it look like a country kitchen. Try the steak or trout—freshly caught from the pond on the grounds. The homemade bread is fantastic, and the blackberry pie is a must for dessert. Box lunches for adventurers are available upon request. ✉ *37515 Hwy. 706, Ashford* ☎ *360/569–2323 or 800/654–7615* ⊕ *www.alexanderscountryinn.com* ▤ *D, MC, V* ⊙ *Closed Nov.–Apr.*

¢
AMERICAN
☺

✕ **Scaleburgers.** Once a 1939 logging-truck weigh station, the building is now a popular restaurant serving homemade hamburgers, fries, and milk shakes. Eat outside on tables overlooking the hills and scenic railroad. The restaurant is 11 mi west of Ashford. ✉ *54109 Mountain Hwy. E, Elbe* ☎ *360/569–2247* ▤ *No credit cards.*

WHERE TO STAY

$

⛺ **Alexander's Country Inn.** Serving guests since 1912, Alexander's offers premier lodging just a mile from Mt. Rainier. Antiques and fine linens lend the main building romance; there are also two adjacent guesthouses. Rates include a hearty breakfast and evening wine. The cozy restaurant (⇨ *Where to Eat, above;* closed to off-site guests in winter) is the best place in town for lunch or dinner. Stroll out back to view verdant gardens, or take a dip in a hot tub set over the trout pond. **Pros:** luxury extras; on-site day spa. **Cons:** lots of breakables means it's not the best place for children. ✉ *37515 Hwy. 706 E, 4 mi east of Ashford, Ashford* ☎ *360/569–2323 or 800/654–7615* ⊕ *www.alexanderscountryinn. com* ⇱ *12 rooms, 2 3-bedroom houses* ⚭ *In-room: no phone, no a/c, no TV. In-hotel: restaurant, spa, Wi-Fi hotspot* ▤ *D, MC, V* ¶⦿¶ *BP.*

¢

⛺ **Nisqually Lodge.** Crackling flames from the massive stone fireplace lend warmth and cheer to the great room of this hotel, a few miles west of Mount Rainier National Park. The decor is standard for a motel, but two king rooms have a balcony and microwave. **Pros:** spacious rooms; central to mountain activities and just miles from park. **Cons:** no frills. ✉ *31609 Hwy. 706 E, Ashford* ☎ *360/569–8804 or 888/674–3554* ⊕ *www.escapetothemountains.com* ⇱ *24 rooms* ⚭ *In-hotel: laundry facilities, Wi-Fi hotspot* ▤ *AE, D, DC, MC, V* ¶⦿¶ *CP.*

$

⛺ **Wellspring.** In the woodlands outside Ashford, the nontraditional accommodations here include tastefully designed log cabins, tent cabins, a tree house, and a room in a greenhouse. The Tatoosh lodge, with space for 14, has a huge stone fireplace. Each space is individually decorated: for example, a queen-size feather bed is suspended by ropes beneath a skylight in the Nest Room. This forest-inspired collection of units, the only property of its kind in the area, is the creation of a massage therapist; a variety of spalike amenities are available. **Pros:** unique lodging option; some rooms good for groups or kids; relaxing spa influence. **Cons:** limited amenities. ✉ *54922 Kernehan Rd. E.,*

Mt. Rainier was named after British admiral Peter Rainier in the late 18th century.

Ashford ☎ *360/569–2514* ⊕ *www.wellspringspa.com* ➥ *2 rooms, 1 lodge, 6 cabins, 3 tent cabins, 1 tree house, 1 cottage* ⚲ *In-room: no phone, no a/c, kitchen (some), refrigerator, no TV (some). In-hotel: spa* ▭ *MC, V* ⎰❍⎱*EP, CP.*

¢   **Whittaker's Bunkhouse.** This 1912 motel once housed loggers and mill workers. In those days it was referred to as "the place to stop on the way to the top." In the early 1990s famed climber Lou Whittaker bought and renovated the facility. Today it's a comfortable hostelry, with inexpensive bunk spaces (available May–September) as well as large private rooms and a cottage. The hot tub is a welcome amenity after a day of recreation. **Pros:** inexpensive; convenient; historical draw for mountain buffs. **Cons:** no frills in most rooms except Wi-Fi; some shared bathrooms. ✉ *30205 Hwy. 706 E, Ashford* ☎ *360/569–2439* ⊕ *www.whittakersbunkhouse.com* ➥ *20 private rooms, bunk room has 12 beds, 1 cottage* ⚲ *In-room: refrigerator (some), DVD (some), no TV (some), Wi-Fi. In-hotel: restaurant, Wi-Fi hotspot* ▭ *MC, V.*

PACKWOOD

25 mi southeast of Ashford via Skate Creek Rd. (closed in winter).

Packwood is a pretty mountain village on U.S. 12, below White Pass. It's a great base for exploring wilderness areas because it's between Mt. Rainier and Mt. St. Helens.

GETTING HERE

Packwood is about 140 miles from Portland via I–5 northbound to Exit 68, then 64 miles east via Highway 12 (also called the White Pass Scenic Byway). From Seattle (about 120 miles away), take I–5 south to

MT. ST. HELENS

One of the most prominent peaks in the Northwest's rugged Cascade Range, Mount St. Helens National Volcanic Monument affords visitors an up-close look at the site of the most destructive volcanic blast in U.S. history.

Just 55 mi northeast of Portland, and 155 mi southeast of Seattle, this once soaring, conical summit stood at 9,665 feet above sea level. Then, on May 18, 1980, a massive eruption launched a 36,000-foot plume of steam and ash into the air and sent nearly 4 million cubic yards of debris through the Toutle and Cowlitz river valleys. The devastating eruption leveled a 230-square-mi area, claiming 57 lives and more than 250 homes. The mountain now stands at 8,365 feet, and a horseshoe-shape crater—most visible from the north—now forms the scarred summit. A modern highway carries travelers to within about 5 mi of the summit, and the surrounding region offers thrilling opportunities for climbing, hiking, and learning about volcanology.

BEST TIME TO GO

It's best to visit from mid-May through late October, as the last section of Spirit Lake Highway, Johnston Ridge Observatory, and many of the park's forest roads are closed the rest of the year. The other visitor centers along the lower sections of the highway are open year-round, but overcast skies typically obscure the mountain's summit in winter.

WORD OF MOUTH

"The Visitor Centers were excellent—far from the usual NPS centers that make one feel like they are on a 5th grade field trip. I remember standing outside in awe at the power of the volcano."

—gail

PARK HIGHLIGHTS

Ape Cave. The longest continuous lava tube in the continental U.S., Ape Cave is one of the park's outstanding attractions. Two routes traverse the tube. The lower route is an easy hour-long hike; the upper route is challenging (expect uneven ground and some scrambles) and takes about three hours. Be sure to bring your own light source and warm clothing—temperatures in the cave don't rise above the mid-40s. In high season ranger-led walks are sometimes available; inquire at the **Apes' Headquarters** (☎ *360/449–7800*), which is off Forest Service road 8303, 3 mi north of the junction of Forest Roads 83 and 90.

Johnston Ridge Observatory. The visitor center closest to the summit, Johnston Ridge is named for scientist David Johnston, who was killed by the mountain's immense lateral blast. Open only from mid-May through October, **Johnston Ridge Observatory Visitor Center** (*end of Hwy. 504* ☎ *360/274–2140* ⊕ *www.fs.fed.us./gpnf/mshnvm*) stands at the end of the park's Spirit Lake Highway, and contains exhibits on the mountain's geology and instruments measuring volcanic activity and seismic activity. Several short trails afford spectacular views of the summit.

Spirit Lake Highway Officially known as Highway 504, this twisting, turning paved road rises some 4,000 feet from the town of Castle Rock (just off I–5, Exit 49) to within about 5 mi of the Mt. St. Helens summit. Along this road are several visitor centers that interpret the region's geology and geography, and several turnouts afford views of the destruction wrought upon the Toutle and Cowlitz river valleys. Don't miss the **Mount St. Helens Visitor Center** (*Hwy. 504, 5 mi east of I–5,* ☎ *360/274–0962* ⊕ *www.parks.wa.gov/interp/mountsthelens*) at Seaquest State Park, which shows chilling video footage of the eruption, contains superb exhibits on the region's geologic beginnings, and houses a scale model of the mountain that you can actually climb into.

STAY THE NIGHT

Mt. St. Helens is in a remote area, and the nearest town, Castle Rock, has little in the way of lodging options. You'll find plenty of chain motels in Kelso and Longview, about 10 to 15 mi south. In Woodland, 30 mi south of Castle Rock but right on Highway 503, the gateway for approaching great Mt. St. Helens hiking from the south, the charming **Lewis River B&B** (*2339 Lewis River Rd., Woodland,* ☎ *360/225–8630* ⊕ *www. lewisriverbedandbreakfast. com*) is a terrific lodging option. The five rooms have upscale, contemporary furnishings, and most overlook the scenic Lewis River. For a memorable meal midway up Spirit Lake Highway, drop by **19 Mile House** (*9440 Spirit Lake Hwy., Kid Valley,* ☎ *360/274–8779*), a rustic roadhouse with a veranda overlooking the North Fork Toutle River—burgers are a specialty—and be sure to save room for the fresh-fruit cobblers.

14

Highway 167 near Renton, then south via Highway 161 through Eatonville and southeast on Highway 7 through Morton, then east on Highway 12. Packwood is also served by Lewis Mountain Highway Transit.

Contact **Lewis Mountain Highway Transit** ☎ 360/496–5405.

VISITOR INFORMATION
Destination Packwood Association ☎ *360/494–2223 or 800/963–7898* ⊕ *www.destinationpackwood.com.*

EXPLORING

Goat Rocks Wilderness. The crags in Gifford Pinchot National Forest, south of Mt. Rainier, are aptly named: you often see mountain goats here, especially when you hike into the backcountry; Goat Lake is a particularly good spot for viewing the elusive creatures. See the goats without backpacking by taking Forest Road 2140 south from Highway 12 near Packwood to Stonewall Ridge. Ask for exact directions in Packwood, or ask a national forest ranger. The goats will be on Stonewall Ridge looming up ahead of you. ⊠ *Gifford Pinchot National Forest, 10600 N.E. 51st St. Circle, Vancouver* ⊕ *Wilderness entrance points along U.S. 12, 2–10 mi east of White Pass* ☎ *360/891–5000* ⊕ *www.fs.fed.us/gpnf/recreation/wilderness* ✉ *Free* ☉ *Call for weather conditions.*

WHERE TO STAY

¢ 🏨 **Cowlitz River Lodge.** You can't beat the location of this comfortable two-story family motel: it's just off the highway in Packwood, the gateway to Mount Rainier National Park *and* the Mount St. Helens National Volcanic Monument. A lodgelike construction and a large stone fireplace in the great room add some character—a good thing, since guest rooms have standard motel furniture and bedding. **Pros:** convenient location; helpful manager. **Cons:** no pool; no restaurant; rooms are basic motel style. ⊠ *13069 U.S. 12* ☎ *360/494–4444 or 888/305–2185* 🖷 *360/494–2075* ⊕ *www.escapetothemountains.com* ➲ *31 rooms* ⚬ *In-room: a/c, refrigerator, Wi-Fi. In-hotel: laundry facilities, Wi-Fi hotspot, some pets allowed* ⊟ *AE, D, MC, V* ⏇ *CP.*

¢ 🏨 **Mountain View Lodge.** Just east of the town of Packwood, this conve-
☾ nient, quiet motel is 40 mi from both Mt. Rainier and Mt. St. Helens, and 17 mi from White Pass Ski Resort. Rooms have pine paneling, and some have log furniture, microwaves, and refrigerators. Family suites have fireplaces and sleep six. There's also a year-round hot tub and picnic area. **Pros:** roomy accommodations (some with kitchens); close to ski resort; friendly and helpful owners. **Cons:** no restaurant on-site. ⊠ *13163 U.S. Hwy. 12* ☎ *360/494–5555 or 877/277–7192* ⊕ *www. mtvlodge.com* ➲ *22 rooms* ⚬ *In-room: a/c, kitchen (some), refrigerator (some). In-hotel: Wi-Fi hotspot* ⊟ *AE, D, MC, V.*

MOSSYROCK

45 miles west of Packwood.

Mossyrock is a charming small town nestled between two large lakes—Riffe and Mayfield—that were created by dams in the 1960s. The area is a haven for camping, fishing, and boating; two lakefront parks are owned and operated by Tacoma Power (which generates power from the dams and stocks the lakes with fish). At Mayfield Lake there are also a state park and a privately owned marina and resort.

GETTING HERE

Mossyrock is reached from Portland or Seattle via I–5's Exit 68, then 21 mi east via Highway 12 (also called the White Pass Scenic Byway). An alternate route from Seattle that is more scenic and travels closer to Mt. Rainier is Highway 167 and Highway 161 through Eatonville, then Highway 7 to Morton and west on Highway 12. Coming from the southwest (Nisqually) entrance to Mt. Rainier, take Highway 706 West to Highway 7 South, then follow the same route via Morton to Mossyrock. Mossyrock is also served by Lewis Mountain Highway Transit.

Contact Lewis Mountain Highway Transit (☎ 360/496–5405).

EXPLORING

Just outside of town, fields of tulips and other flowers grown at the **DeGoede Bulb Farm** provide a colorful backdrop along Highway 12. Stroll through the manicured show gardens year-round. ⊠ *409 Mossyrock Rd.* W ☎ *360/983–9000* 🖙 *Free* ☉ *Closed most Sun. except Apr.–June and Nov.–Dec; also closed Mon. in Jan.*

Ike Kinswa State Park is on the north side of Mayfield Lake, about 4 mi from Mossyrock. Many of the forested campsites provide a nice sense of seclusion, and some lake-view spots are situated for prime sunset views. Five cabins have electricity and bunk beds, but no bathrooms. There's year-round camping, two boat ramps, hiking trails, and fish (including the challenging tiger muskie, stocked from a nearby hatchery). The park is named after a Cowlitz Indian; the Cowlitz tribe lived in this area and their burial grounds are nearby. ⊠ *873 Harmony Rd.* ☎ *360/983–3402* ⊕ *www.parks.wa.gov* 🖙 *Camping $21–$28; Cabins $55–$65* ☉ *Summer, daily 6:30–dusk; winter, daily 8:30–dusk.*

Mayfield Lake Park has a handy boat launch right off Highway 12, 4 mi west of Mossyrock. Camping spots are especially scenic, with lake views, forest settings, and even lakefront spots. Fish for trout, bass, and coho salmon. ⊠ *180 Beach Rd.* ☎ *360/985–2364 or 888/502–8690* 🖙 *Parking $5 (summer weekends and holidays); camping $15–$27* ☉ *Mid-Apr.–mid-Oct.*

Fish, camp, and boat at **Mossyrock Park,** on Riffe Lake, just a few miles east of town. The lake is stocked with cutthroat, rainbow and brown trout, coho salmon, steelhead, and bass. ⊠ *202 Ajlune Rd.* ☎ *360/983–3900 or 888/502–8690* 🖙 *Parking $5 (summer weekends and holidays); camping $27–$29* ☉ *Closed Dec. 20–Jan 1.*

WHERE TO STAY

$–$$ ⬚ **Adytum Retreat.** Opened in 2010, this bed-and-breakfast is all about luxury in nature. Set on a hill on nearly 16 acres of forested property, the castle-like home, with its stone front, towers, and 75 windows, faces Mayfield Lake and the valleys below. The Star of the North Suite on the third floor has 2 bedrooms, whirlpool tub, gas fireplace, private entrance from outside, and a balcony where guests can see the sun rise and set. On the main floor, the smaller First Light Suite for two has a eucalyptus steam sauna and its own private garden patio. On the lowest level, the Orion Suite includes a kitchenette, living room with 50-inch plasma TV and DVD player, FAR infrared sauna, gas fireplace, and private courtyard. All suites have access to the Retreat's serene outdoor amenities, including a saltwater hot tub, firepit, walking trails, koi pond, fountains, and gardens. Indoors, common areas include the third floor Cloud Nine Library and the Tower Room, where organic breakfast is served; there's a baby grand piano and some of the owners' extensive art collection on display there too. **Pros:** Amazing views, beautiful grounds, unique amenities. **Cons:** a bit of a drive to restaurants and shopping. ⊠ *186 Skyview Drive, Mossyrock* ☎ *360/983-8008* ⊕ *www.adytumsanctuary.com* ⌁ *3 suites* ♿ *In-room: a/c (some), no phone, refrigerator, DVD (some), no TV (some), Wi-Fi. In-hotel: Wi-Fi hotspot, some pets allowed, no kids under 21* ⊟ *D, MC, V* ¶⊙¶*BP.*

CENTRALIA

Centralia is 35 mi northwest of Mossyrock.

Centralia (sen-*trail*-ya) was founded by George Washington, a freed slave from Virginia, who faced serious discrimination in several states and territories before settling here in 1852. The town has a well-maintained historic business district. In a park just off I–5 stand the Borst Blockhouse (built during the 1855–56 Indian Wars) and the elegant Borst farmhouse. Centralia is an antiques-hunter's paradise, with 350 dealers in 11 malls. It's also known for its 17 murals depicting the region's history. Pick up a brochure about the murals at the Centralia Train Depot. Six miles to the south is the sister city of Chehalis (sha-*hay*-liss), where there's a historical museum and the Chehalis–Centralia Steam Train.

GETTING HERE

Centralia is almost halfway between Seattle (85 mi north) and Portland (92 mi south) via I–5. Greyhound Bus Lines and Amtrak both serve the town. Local options include Twin Transit for getting around Centralia and neighboring Chehalis, Rural Public Transit with daily stops in towns along the I–5 corridor between Longview and Tumwater, and Lewis Mountain Highway Transit, which travels several times a day between Centralia and the towns of eastern Lewis County, including Mossyrock, Morton, and Packwood.

Contacts Amtrak (☎ 360/736–8653 ⊕ *www.amtrakcascades.com*). **Greyhound Bus Lines** (☎ 360/736–9811 ⊕ *www.greyhound.com*). **Lewis Mountain Highway Transit** (☎ 360/496–5405). **Rural Public Transit** (☎ 360/425–3430 or 800/383–2101). **Twin Transit** (☎ 360/330–2072).

EXPLORING

☪ Through scenic landscapes and over covered bridges, the authentic engines of the **Chehalis–Centralia Steam Train** will carry you on rails originally laid for logging. The line runs through farmland and rolling hills, and crosses several wooden bridges. The 12-mi round-trip ride (departing at 1 and 3 on Saturday) costs $11; the 18-mi ride (departing at 5 PM on Saturday) is $14. Call for dinner train and special-event schedules and pricing. ⊠ *1945 S. Market Blvd., Chehalis* ☎ *360/748–9593* ⊕ *www.steamtrainride.com* ☉ *Memorial Day–Labor Day, weekends.*

Constructed during the Indian Wars, **Ft. Borst** was later used for grain storage. Standing within a 100-acre park, the Borst Home is a Greek Revival mansion, built in 1857. ⊠ *Borst Park, 2500 Bryden Ave. W* ☎ *360/330–7688* 🎫 *$2* ☉ *Thanksgiving–Christmas and Memorial Day–Labor Day, weekends 1–4.*

The small **Lewis County Historical Museum** has regional pioneer memorabilia, some Chehalis Indian art, and a collection of children's dolls and toys. ⊠ *599 N.W. Front Way, Chehalis* ☎ *360/748–0831* ⊕ *www.lewiscountymuseum.org* 🎫 *$4* ☉ *Tues.–Sat. 10–5, also Sun. 1–5 in summer.*

14

☪ The wooded, 125-acre **Rainbow Falls State Park** is en route to the coast. Along the way are several shallow waterfalls cascading down shelves of rock. The park, which opened in 1935, has towering old-growth forest and 3,400 feet of freshwater shoreline along the Chehalis River. ⊠ *Hwy. 6, 17 mi west of Chehalis* ☎ *360/291–3767 or 888/226–7688* ⊕ *www.parks.wa.gov* 🎫 *$21–$27 camping fee* ☉ *Daily dawn–dusk.*

WHERE TO EAT AND STAY

$–$$ ✕ **Mary McCrank's Dinner House.** It's an elegant yet cozy farmhouse restaurant that opened in 1928 as the Dutch Mill Inn and was acquired by namesake Mary McCrank in 1935. There are armchairs in the waiting parlor and fireplaces in some of the dining rooms. The chicken-and-dumplings Sunday night special is sublime; so are the dessert pies and homemade ice cream. ⊠ *2923 Jackson Hwy., Chehalis* ☎ *360/748–3662* *wwww.marymccranks.com* ▭ *D, MC, V* ☉ *Closed Mon.*

AMERICAN

¢ 🛏 **McMenamins Olympic Club Hotel & Theater.** When it opened in 1908, the Olympic Club was an exclusive gentlemen's resort. It's now owned by the Portland, Oregon, microbrewery moguls the McMenamin brothers, and it houses a restaurant, a bar, and a pool hall. The Tiffany chandeliers, the card room, and various signs (one reading WOMEN'S PATRONAGE NOT SOLICITED hangs above the entrance) remain almost as they were when the club first opened. The restaurant ($) serves up burgers, sandwiches, pastas, steak, fish, and signature chicken wings. McMenamins is part of a northwest chain of hotels and pubs in historic settings; the company not only brews its own beer but also bottles its own wine, distills its own spirits, and has its own line of coffee as well. The hotel has 27 European-style rooms with bathrooms down the hall. Some rooms have bunk beds, others are queen and king rooms. Hotel guests receive free movie passes to the house theater. **Pros:** restored historic facility complete with its own theater; inexpensive rates and restaurant. **Cons:** rooms are comfortable but nearby train tracks may prove too noisy for light sleepers; shared bathrooms; small rooms. ⊠ *112 N. Tower Ave.,* ☎ *360/736–5164 or 866/736–5164* ⊕ *www.mcmenamins. com* ⟐ *In-room: no phone, no a/c, no TV, Wi-Fi. In-hotel: restaurant, Wi-Fi* ▭ *AE, D, DC, MC, V.*

LONGVIEW

46 mi south of Centralia.

Longview, which was founded on the site of an 1805 Lewis and Clark encampment, is the largest planned community in the United States after Washington, D.C., but it's so well put together that it looks anything but planned. For one thing, the city isn't laid out on the familiar grid system, but has a roundabout where the civic center is located, surrounded by curving streets that are crossed by diagonal roads (which creates a somewhat out-of-kilter grid). To top it off, there's Lake Sacajawea, a former oxbow of the Cowlitz, that's part of a city park that encircles about one-third of downtown. Downtown itself is cut off from the Columbia River by a rather grungy industrial district and port. A 1,200-foot-long, 195-foot-high bridge, built in 1950, crosses to the Oregon side of the river.

GETTING HERE

Longview is right off of I–5, about 50 mi north of Portland. It's served by both Amtrak (in neighboring Kelso) and Greyhound Bus Lines. Community Urban Bus System provides in-city transit in Longview and Kelso. Rural Public Transit offers daily stops in towns along the I–5 corridor between Longview and Tumwater.

Contacts Amtrak (☎ 360/578–1870 ⊕ www.amtrakcascades.com). **Community Urban Bus System** (☎ *360/442–5663* ⊕ www.cubs-bus.com). **Greyhound Bus Lines** (☎ 360/423–7380 ⊕ www.greyhound.com). **Lewis Mountain Highway Transit** (☎ 360/496–5405). **Rural Public Transit** (☎ 360/425–3430 or-800/383–2101).

EXPLORING

☺ **Nutty Narrows** isn't a traditional bridge: it's only for squirrels, and serves as a safe passage for the animals across Olympia Way, between the Public Library and Civic Center. ⊠ *Olympia Way.*

WHERE TO EAT AND STAY

$–$$
AMERICAN

✕ **Henri's Carousel and Beachway Bar** This large but comfortable restaurant is the local businessmen's lunch hangout, but dinner is also popular for such hearty fare as good seafood bisque, rack of lamb, and steaks. New owners have added a sports bar with activities every night, including live music on weekends to appeal to a younger crowd. ⊠ *4545 Ocean Beach Hwy.* ☎ *360/425–7970* w*www.beachwaybar.com* ⊟ *AE, D, DC, MC, V.*

¢

⊞ **Quality Inn & Suites.** The lobby's many antiques make this quiet hotel, 3 mi from the highway, homey. Rooms have microwaves and have been recently updated by new owners. There are standard rooms, minisuites, and a full Jacuzzi suite. **Pros:** great value; ample breakfast buffet selection; good service. **Cons:** no pool; nothing much within walking distance. ⊠ *723 7th Ave.* ☎ *360/414–1000* ⊕ *www.choicehotels.com* ⇗ *50 rooms* ⚷ *In-room: a/c, refrigerator, Wi-Fi. In-hotel: pool, some pets allowed* ⊟ *AE, D, DC, MC, V* ⊙❘ *CP.*

Yakima River Valley

WORD OF MOUTH

"In addition to the vineyard areas of Oregon . . . there are also some excellent wine-producing areas in east/central Washington (around the Yakima Valley) and some in the Columbia River basin and near the Columbia Gorge. The Yakima areas would be drier than Seattle/Portland—and might be worth investigating."

—Gardyloo

WELCOME TO YAKIMA RIVER VALLEY

TOP REASONS TO GO

★ **To Stay at a Spectacular Mountain Lodge.** The Lodge at Suncadia is one of Washington's premier resorts. Golfers, cross-country skiers, hikers, and families will enjoy this terrific lodge in the beautiful Cascade Mountains.

★ **For Washington History.** Yakima Valley Museum is one of the finest museums in the state, with plenty of history of the real West.

★ **For a Classic Diner.** Diners in wine country? There are two terrific ones here. The Red Horse Diner in Ellensburg is more than a hamburger joint, it's a restaurant and museum all in one, built around a mid-1900s Mobil gas station. And Miner's Drive-In, a Yakima icon, serves great old-fashioned hamburgers, fries, and shakes in a truly vintage setting.

★ **And Perhaps for a Bit of Wine.** There are more than 70 wineries in this region, and nearly all of them are excellent. Washington wines' reputation extends globally, and Yakima Valley may be the state's finest wine region.

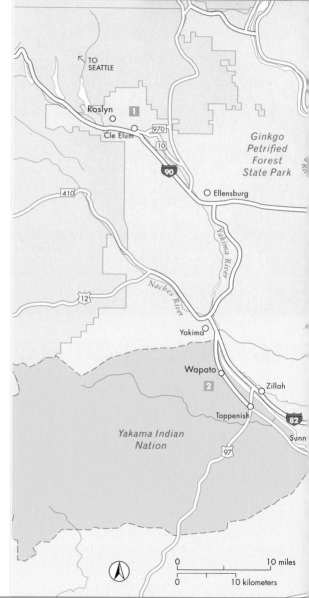

TO SEATTLE

Roslyn

Cle Elum

Ginkgo Petrified Forest State Park

Ellensburg

Yakima River

Naches River

Yakima

Wapato

Zillah

Toppenish

Yakama Indian Nation

Sunn

| 0 | 10 miles |
| 0 | 10 kilometers |

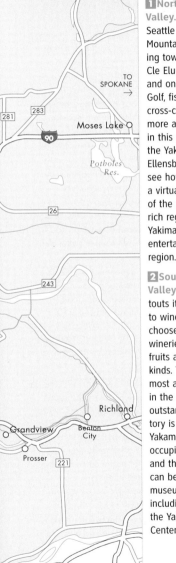

1 Northern Yakima River Valley. Just 80 mi from Seattle over the Cascade Mountains, the historic mining towns of Roslyn and Cle Elum offer quaint shops and one very plush resort. Golf, fishing, hiking, biking, cross-country skiing, and more are readily available in this region. As you follow the Yakima River down past Ellensburg to Yakima, you'll see how irrigation turns a virtual desert into one of the most agriculturally rich regions in the nation. Yakima is the shopping and entertainment hub of the region.

2 Southern Yakima River Valley. From Yakima, which touts itself as the gateway to wine country, visitors can choose from more than 70 wineries, as well as fresh fruits and vegetables of all kinds. The area is one of the most agriculturally diverse in the country, with some outstanding restaurants. History is rich here as well. The Yakama Indian Reservation occupies much of the land, and the history of its people can be seen in several museums around the region, including the museum at the Yakama Nation Cultural Center in Toppenish.

GETTING ORIENTED

The Yakima River valley encompasses a region of south central Washington that starts just east of Snoqualmie Pass in the Kittitas Valley. It includes the forested eastern slopes and the foothills of the Central Cascades, from Chinook and White Pass all the way down through the Yakima Valley near Benton City. Two interstates meet in Ellensburg. I–90 links Seattle to Cle Elum and Ellensburg before heading east toward Spokane. I–82 branches south off I–90 just east of Ellensburg, and runs through the Yakima Valley to the so-called Tri-Cities (Richland, Pasco, and Kennewick). U.S. 97 is the primary link from Ellensburg north (Wenatchee, Canada's Okanagan Valley) and from Yakima south toward central Oregon.

15

YAKIMA RIVER VALLEY PLANNER

When to Go

Much of the area is considered high desert, with annual rainfall of just 7 inches a year. But in winter, in the higher elevations, it is quite common to have snow on the ground from November until March. This is a decidedly four-season region, with wet, cool, windy springs, beautiful warm summer days, and gorgeous falls with colors to match those of any Northeastern state. Best time to visit is April through October, unless, of course, you're looking to ski, snowboard, or snowmobile.

The main wine-tasting season begins in late April and runs to the end of the fall harvest in November. Winery hours vary in winter, when you should call ahead before visiting. The Yakima Valley Winery Association (⊕ www.wineyakimavalley. org) publishes a map-brochure that lists wineries with tasting-room hours. Most are owned and managed by unpretentious enthusiasts, and their cellar masters are often on hand to answer questions.

Getting Here and Around

Air Travel. Although major airlines serve the region's two airports, most people fly into Seattle or Portland, Oregon, and drive to the area.

Horizon Air (☎ 800/547-9308 ⊕ www.horizonair.com) has two nonstops daily between Sea-Tac and Yakima, a 45-minute flight. Tri-Cities Airport has a similar schedule from Seattle, a 60-minute trip, with additional nonstop connections to Denver, Portland, and Salt Lake City. Both Yakima and the Tri-Cities are served by Horizon. The Tri-Cities are also served by Delta and United.

Airline Contacts Delta (☎ 800/221-1212 ⊕ www.delta. com). **United** (☎ 800/241-6522 ⊕ www.ual.com).

Airports. Yakima International Airport (✉ 2300 W. Washington Ave. ☎ 509/575-6150) is 4 mi southeast of downtown Yakima. **Tri-Cities Regional Airport** (✉ 3601 N. 20th Ave., Pasco ☎ 509/547-6352) is more convenient to Grandview, Prosser, and Benton City.

Transfers. Taxis and public transit are available at both airports. The **Airporter Shuttle** (☎ 866/235-5247) offers shuttle services from Sea-Tac airport (between Seattle and Tacoma) and Seattle Amtrak to Yakima ($43.50 in either direction), with stops in downtown Seattle, Cle Elum ($32.50), and Ellensburg ($37.50). In Yakima, **Yakima City Transit** (☎ 509/575-6175) can provide transportation to hotels.

Airport Transportation. Diamond Cab (☎ 509/453-3113).

Car Travel. The Yakima Valley Highway is a reliable, off-the-beaten-track alternative to I–82 for wine-country visits; but it can be slow, especially through towns, or if farm machinery is on the road. Because of unmarked turns and other potential hazards, it's wise to stick to the freeway after dark. Gas stations in towns, and at major freeway intersections, are typically open well after dark.

Major car rental companies in Yakima include **Avis** (☎ 800/831-2847), Budget (☎ 509/248-6767), **Enterprise** (☎ 888/305-8051), and **Hertz** (☎ 509/452-9965). Hertz and Budget are available at Yakima International Airport.

About the Restaurants

South central Washington has a fair share of Mexican food, from taco wagons to fine Mexican restaurants. National fast-food chains, local eateries, and Chicago-style steak houses can be found scattered throughout the region, or sometimes right along-side one another. As a huge agricultural area, the Yakima Valley supplies many of its local restaurants with fresh fruits and vegetables. Yakima Valley wines are a staple at virtually all of the fine-dining establishments. Pacific Northwest seafood (particularly salmon) is another staple of the region.

About the Hotels

Two major freeways, I–90 and I–82, pass through the cities of Ellensburg and Yakima where you'll find the highest concentration of lodgings. A few independent motels are available, but the majority are independently operated under familiar chain names. At the far northeastern end of the region sits Suncadia Resort, offering possibly the finest accommodations in the area. Several bed-and-breakfasts are also available, particularly in the lower Yakima Valley, near the plethora of wineries in the area. Times when it's best to call ahead for vacancy include the third week in April, for Spring Barrel Tasting, and from Memorial Day through Labor Day.

WHAT IT COSTS IN U.S. DOLLARS

	¢	$	$$	$$$	$$$$
Restaurants	under $10	$10–$17	$18–$24	$25–$30	over $30
Hotels	under $100	$100–$150	$151–$200	$201–$250	over $250

Restaurant prices are per person, for a main course at dinner. Hotel prices are for two people in a standard double room in high season, excluding tax.

Tour Options

Lifelong residents run Yakima Valley Tours' custom agricultural, historical, wine-tasting, and adventure-sports tours. Accent! Tours has informative trips to area wineries. Bus companies such as A & A Motorcoach, and limo services, including Moonlit Ride, conduct charter tours of the Yakima area.

Contacts A & A Motorcoach (✉ 2410 S. 26th Ave., Yakima ☎ 509/575–3676 ⊕ www. aamotorcoach.com). **Accent! Tours** (✉ 1017 So. 48th Ave. Suite C., Yakima ☎ 509/575–3949 or 800/735–0428 ⊕ www.accenttours.com). **Moonlit Ride Limousine** (✉ 3908 River Rd., Yakima ☎ 509/575–6846 ⊕ www. moonlitride.com). **Yakima Valley Tours** (✉ 551 N. Holt Rd., Mabton ☎ 509/985–8628 or 509/840–4777 ⊕ www. yakimavalleytours.com).

VISITOR INFORMATION

Yakima Valley Visitor Information Center (✉ 101 Fair Ave., Exit 34 off I–82 ☎ 509/573–3388 or 800/221–0751 ⊕ www. visityakima.com). **Wine Yakima Valley Association** (☎ 800/258–7270 ⊕ www. wineyakimavalley.org).

15

YAKIMA RIVER VALLEY WINERIES

Farmers first plowed the Yakima Valley more than 150 years ago, but there's still sagebrush on the driest and rockiest slopes. Now, though, long rows of grapevines snake along the high edge between the irrigated fields on the valley floor and the steppe grasslands of the hills where the screams of eagles and the cries of curlews resound.

(Above and opposite page top) Hyatt Vineyards (Opposite page bottom) Rows of grapevines are a common sight in the Yakima River Valley

The Yakima Valley produces excellent reds, among them cabernet sauvignon, cabernet franc, merlot, nebbiolo, sangiovese, and syrah. Whites also do well here: chardonnay, muscat, sauvignon blanc, sémillon, viognier, and, in cooler vineyards, gewürztraminer, chenin blanc, and Riesling.

Support for local wineries took a long time to build when the apple growers reigned supreme, but after a quarter-century of serious wine-making, the valley is finally beginning to recognize the significance of its new industry.

APPLES AND GRAPES

Yakima Valley is at an agricultural crossroads. Apples are on their way out; grapes are in. Among the mistakes of the pioneering grape growers of the 1960s and 70s was overplanting Riesling and chenin blanc, which proved hard to market. They compensated by grafting over their vines to more desirable varieties or by replanting. Today Yakima Valley chardonnay, cabernet sauvignon, merlot, sangiovese, and syrah are ranked among the world's best.

YAKIMA'S BEST WINERIES

Stop at the Yakima Valley Visitor Information Center (Exit 34 off I–82) to pick up a wine-tour brochure and map of more than 30 wineries. Most are within a few miles of the freeway and there are directional signs. Nearly all of Yakima's wineries are worth a visit, but here are three of our favorites.

ZILLAH

Hyatt Vineyards. Hyatt Vineyards is big in a physical as well as an enological sense, comprising 97 acres of estate vineyards. Established in 1985, the winery, owned by Leland and Linda Hyatt, has always been well respected locally for its merlot and cabernet sauvignon, but lately those wines have been attracting national attention. The late-harvest Riesling here is also worth tasting. The winery has spacious grounds for picnicking. On clear days spectacular views of the Yakima Valley, Mt. Adams, and the Cascade Mountains can be had. ✉ *2020 Gilbert Rd., off Bonair Rd.* ☎ *509/829–6333* ⊕ *www.hyattvineyards.com*

SUNNYSIDE

Tucker Cellars. The Tucker family came to the Yakima Valley as sharecroppers during the Great Depression. They became successful farmers and were among the first to grow vinifera grapes on a commercial scale. Dean and Rose

15

Tucker founded the winery in 1981; both it and the estate vineyards are family operations involving their four children. Tucker plantings include Riesling, pinot noir, gewürztraminer, chenin blanc, chardonnay, and Muscat canelli. Attached to the Tucker Cellars tasting room is the family's produce stand, which sells, in season, some of the Yakima Valley's best fruits and vegetables. There's a picnic area. ✉ *70 Ray Rd.* ☎ *509/837–8701* ⊕ *www.tuckercellars.net*

PROSSER

Kestrel Vintners. Kestrel has established itself as one of the Yakima Valley's premium wineries. Although visiting the winery, in the Port of Benton's Prosser Wine and Food Park, doesn't necessarily rank as a great sensory pleasure, tasting the wines does. Kestrel makes mainly reds (cabernet sauvignon, merlot, syrah), as well as some white (chardonnay, viognier), from grapes—some of them estate-grown—that are deliberately stressed to increase the intensity of their flavors. The tasting room sells cheeses and deli items to go with the wines. ✉ *2890 Lee Rd., in Prosser Wine and Food Park* ☎ *509/786–2675* ⊕ *www.kestrelwines.com*

–John Doerper

Updated by
Rob Phillips

The Yakima River binds a region of great contrasts. Snow-capped volcanic peaks and and evergreen-covered hills overlook a natural shrub steppe turned green by irrigation. Famed throughout the world for its apples and cherries, its wine and hops, this fertile landscape is also the ancestral home of the Yakama people from whom it takes its name.

The river flows southeasterly from its source in the Cascade Mountains near Snoqualmie Pass. Between the college town of Ellensburg, at the heart of the Kittitas Valley, and Yakima, the region's largest city, the river cuts steep canyons through serried, sagebrush-covered ridges before merging with the Naches River. Then it breaks through Union Gap to enter its fecund namesake, the broad Yakima Valley. Some 200 mi from its birthplace, the river makes one final bend around vineyard-rich Red Mountain before joining the mighty Columbia River at the Tri-Cities.

Mount Rainier stands west of the Cascade crest but is often more readily seen east of the mountains, where the air is clear and clouds are few. South of Rainier is the broad-shouldered Mt. Adams, the sacred mountain of the Yakama people. The 12,276-foot-tall mountain marks the western boundary of their reservation, second-largest in the Pacific Northwest. Here, today as they have for centuries, wild horses run free through the Yakama Nation and can be seen feeding along Highway 97 south of Toppenish. Deer and elk roam the evergreen forests, eagles and ospreys soar overhead.

Orchards and vineyards dominate Yakima Valley's agricultural landscape. Cattle and sheep ranching initially drove the economy; apples and other produce came with the first irrigation schemes in the 1890s. The annual asparagus harvest begins in April, followed by spring cherries; apricots and peaches ripen in early to mid-summer. Exported throughout the world for the brewing of beer, hops are ready by late August; travelers may see the bushy vines spiraling up fields of twine. The apple harvest runs from late summer through October.

The valley's real fame, however, rests on its wines, which have a growing reputation as among the best in the world. Concord grapes were first planted here in the 1960s, and they still take up large tracts of land. But *vinifera* grapes, the noble grapes of Europe, now dominate the local wine industry. Merlot and white burgundies boosted the region, and syrah is often regarded as the grape of the future. There are fine cabernets, grenaches, Rieslings, chardonnays, gewürztraminers, sémillons, sauvignon blancs, chenin blancs, and muscats, as well as such lesser known varietals as sangioveses, nebbiolos, and lembergers.

NORTHERN YAKIMA RIVER VALLEY

In the upper Kittitas Valley, tucked between the Cascade Mountains to the west and the rugged, snowcapped Sawtooth Mountains to the east, visitors will find the newest in championship golf courses, resort amenities, and fine dining. Plentiful shops, restaurants, museums, and outdoor activities make this one of the most diverse regions of the state. The old-time coal mining towns of Roslyn and Cle Elum are being discovered by more and more travelers seeking good food, fun, and relaxation. The college town of Ellensburg, home of the annual Ellensburg Rodeo on Labor Day, offers a variety of entertainment, restaurants, and hotels. Through it all runs the Yakima River, the lifeblood of this agricultural region, and one of Washington's best trout-fishing streams.

The city of Yakima is the region's hub, offering tons of shopping and, thanks to a newly refurbished downtown core district, many new restaurants, wineries, and nightlife options. Thousands of acres of orchards, producing cherries, apricots, peaches, pears, plums, nectarines and apples, surround the city. In spring and summer, outdoor enthusiasts flock here to hike, bike, canoe, raft, swim, and fish. Snow lovers delight in the multitude of cross-country skiing, snowshoing, and snowmobiling options, along with downhill skiing at White Pass.

CLE ELUM

86 mi southeast of Seattle.

A former railroad, coal, and logging town, Cle Elum (pronounced "klee *ell*-um") now caters to travelers stopping for a breath of air before or after tackling Snoqualmie Pass. It's also home to the ever-growing Suncadia Resort, possibly Washington's finest destination resort.

GETTING HERE

Cle-Elum is hard to miss; it's just off I–90. Exit 80 will get you to SunCadia Resort. Exit 84 will put you at the west end of Cle Elum, placing you in the business district if you're approaching from Seattle and points west. Exit 85 will deliver you into the eastern boundaries of Cle Elum, but will also put you directly in the business district. Most of the amenities are found within the city limits of Cle Elum and Roslyn.

VISITOR INFORMATION

Cle Elum/Roslyn Chamber of Commerce (✉ *401 W. 1st St., Cle Elum* ☎ *509/674–5958* ⊕ *www.cleelumroslyn.org*).

EXPLORING

The Cle Elum Bakery. A local institution, this establishment has been doing business from the very same spot since 1906. Delectable treats from fresh-baked donuts and pastries to a fabulous sticky bun–cinnamon roll are available daily. ⊠ *501 E. 1st St.* ☎ *509/674–2233*

Owens Meats. Across from the Cle Elum bakery is this marvelous smoke-house; established in 1889, it's been run by the Owens family since 1937. No processed jerky and meats here—just the freshest smoked and dried meats around, including beef jerky that is addictive. ⊠ *502 E. 1st St.* ☎ *509/674–2530.*

Roslyn. A former coal-mining town just 3 mi northwest of Cle Elum, Roslyn gained notoriety as the stand-in for the fictional Alaskan village of Cicely on the 1990s TV show *Northern Exposure.* A map locating sites associated with filming is available from the city offices at First Street and Pennsylvania Avenue. Roslyn is also notable for its 28 ethnic cemeteries. Established by communities of miners in the late 19th and early 20th centuries, they are clustered on a hillside west of town.

WHERE TO EAT

$$
ITALIAN
✕ **Lentine's Italian Restaurant.** A quaint café style motif with a huge wine rack dominating one wall, provides diners a comfortable setting in which to enjoy some excellent Italian food. Italian classics are available nightly, along with specialties such as Gorgonzola-stuffed tenderloin with a port demi-sauce. Lentine's has one of the best private wine cellars in the region. ⊠ *212 W. Railroad St., Cle Elum* ☎ *509/674–9609* ⊕ *www.eat-at-lentines.com* ⌂ *Reservations recommended* ▭ *MC, V* ⊘ *No lunch. Closed Mon. and Tues.*

$–$$
STEAK
✕ **MaMa Vallone's Steak House and Inn.** Set in a building constructed in 1906, the upscale but rustic Western look makes the perfect decor for this cozy and informal restaurant that once was a boarding house for unmarried miners. Guests dine at antique tables, and the works of several local artists hang on the walls. Pasta dishes such as the tomato-based *fagioli* (soup with vegetables and beans) and *bagna calda* (a bath of olive oil, garlic, anchovies, and butter for dredging vegetables and meat) attract diners from as far away as Seattle. ⊠ *302 W. 1st St.* ☎ *509/674–5174* ▭ *AE, DC, MC, V* ⊘ *No lunch.*

$
AMERICAN
✕ **Sunset Café and Loose Wolf Lounge.** Since 1936 this restaurant has been serving breakfast delectables such as Texas-sized cinnamon rolls made on-site and comfort food such as homemade ravioli. Italian dishes share the menu with traditional American favorites such as hamburgers and fried chicken at this Western-themed establishment. ⊠ *318 E. 1st St.* ☎ *509/674–2241* ▭ *AE, D, DC, MC, V.*

WHERE TO STAY

¢
⛱ **Cascade Mountain Inn.** Decor is simple at this well-kept two-story motel east of downtown. The large rooms provide home-away-from-home comfort with many amenities, including in-room refrigerators and microwaves. Kitchenette and Jacuzzi rooms are also available. **Pros:** Clean, affordable rooms. **Cons:** No-frills, no pool. ⊠ *906 E. 1st St.* ☎ *509/674–2380 or 888/674–3975* w*www.cascadeinncleelum.com*

Lodge at Suncadia

↪ *43 rooms* ⚲ *In-room: refrigerator.* In-hotel: *some pets allowed* ═ *AE, D, DC, MC, V* ⍩ *CP.*

ȼ–$ 🏠 **Iron Horse Inn Bed and Breakfast.** What was once a boardinghouse for rail workers (1909–74) is now a comfortable country inn owned by the daughter and son-in-law of a one-time lodger. Rooms are named for former crewmen, and are full of railroad memorabilia. Four adjacent cabooses have been transformed into guest quarters complete with microwaves and refrigerators. **Pros:** unique lodging experience; on the National Registry of Historic Places. **Cons:** some sharing of bathrooms. ✉ *526 Marie Ave., South Cle Elum* ☏ *509/674–5939, 800/228–9246 in WA and OR* ⊕ *www.ironhorseinnbb.com* ↪ *12 rooms, 9 with private bath* ⚲ *In-room: no phone, refrigerator (some), no TV (some)* ═ *MC, V* ⍩ *BP.*

$$$ 🏠 **The Lodge at Suncadia.** Situated in the middle of one of the region's premier golf courses (Prospector), this great stone-and-wood lodge blends
Fodor's Choice beautifully with its mountain and forest surroundings. More than 250
⟳ rooms, most with gas fireplaces, are beautifully elegant while maintaining a rustic, homespun appeal. The Glade Spring Spa blends seamlessly with the lush, outdoor gardens, and feels like a forest oasis. It offers a full menu of treatments, massages, and facials. Other amenities include indoor and outdoor pools, hot tub, sauna, a huge exercise room, an amphitheatre that doubles as an outdoor skating rink in the winter, hiking and biking trails, and more. Portals restaurant serves fresh Pacific Northwest fare. **Pros:** intimate mountain-retreat environment; golfing, fly-fishing, cross-country skiing, and hiking just minutes away. **Cons:** costs can quickly add up for a family visit. ✉ *3320 Suncadia Trail, Cle Elum* ☏ *509/649–6405 or 866/904–6300* ⊕ *www.suncadia.com* ↪ *253*

rooms, ♿ In-room: refrigerator, Internet, Wi-Fi. In-hotel: restaurant,
pool, gym, spa, some pets allowed ▭ AE, MC, V.

ELLENSBURG

24 mi southeast of Cle Elum.

This university town is one of the state's friendliest and most easygoing places. "Modern" Ellensburg had its origin in a July 4 fire that
engulfed the original city in 1889. Almost overnight, Victorian brick
buildings rose from the ashes; many still stand, though their functions
have changed. Stroll downtown to discover art galleries, comfortable
cafés, secondhand-book and -record stores, an old-fashioned hardware
store, and one antiques shop after another.

Central Washington's single biggest event is the Ellensburg Rodeo, held
Labor Day weekend. On the national circuit since the 1920s, the rodeo
has a year-round headquarters on Main Street where you can buy tickets
and souvenirs. You can also get a bird's-eye view of the rodeo grounds
from Reed Park, in the 500 block of North Alder Street.

GETTING HERE
Ellensburg is adjacent to I–90, with two exits that will take you right
to gas, fast food, and lodging. Follow Main Street north and it will put
you into the heart of downtown and Central Washington University.

VISITOR INFORMATION
Ellensburg Chamber of Commerce (✉ 609 N. Main St. ☎ 509/925–3183 or
888/925–2204 ⊕ www.ellensburg-chamber.com).

EXPLORING

Central Washington University. The nearly 11,000 students here enjoy a
pleasant, tree-shaded campus marked by tasteful redbrick architecture.
Its 8th Avenue side has several handsome buildings dating from its
founding in 1891 as the State Normal School. Near the center of campus is a serene Japanese garden.

Rotating exhibits at the **Sarah Spurgeon Art Gallery** (✉ Nicholson Blvd.
☎ 509/963–2665 ⬚ Free ⊙ Sept.–June, weekdays 8:30–4:30, weekends
noon–3), in Randall Hall, feature the work of regional and national artists as well as students and faculty. ✉ 400 E. 8th Ave. ☎ 509/963–1111
⊕ www.cwu.edu ⬚ Free ⊙ Tours weekdays 10–2.

Clymer Museum of Art. Half the museum houses the largest collection
of works by painter John Clymer (1907–89). The Ellensburg native
was one of the most widely published illustrators of the American
West, focusing his oils and watercolors on wildlife and traditional lifestyles. The other half features other well-known and aspiring Western and wildlife artists. ✉ 416 N. Pearl St. ☎ 509/962–6416 ⊕ www.
clymermuseum.com ⬚ Free ⊙ Weekdays 10–5, weekends noon–4.

○ **Dick and Jane's Spot.** Nestled in suburbia is the area's most peculiar
attraction. The home of artists Dick Elliott and Jane Orleman is a
continuously growing whimsical sculpture: a collage of 20,000 bottle
caps, 1,500 bicycle reflectors, and other bits. Their masterpiece stands
on private property near downtown, but it's still possible to see the

recycled creation from several angles; sign the guestbook mounted on the surrounding fence. ✉ *101 N. Pearl St.* ☎ *509/925–3224* ⊕ *www. reflectorart.com.*

Gallery One. In the 1889 Stewart Building you'll find a community art center with rotating shows by regional artists, a fine gift shop, and art classes. ✉ *408 N. Pearl St.* ☎ *509/925–2670* ▭ *Free* ⊙ *Tues.–Sat. 11–5.*

Ginkgo and Wanapum State Parks. Separated by I-90, 28 mi east of Ellensburg on the Columbia River, are two state parks. Ginkgo Petrified Forest State Park preserves a fossil forest of ginkgos and other trees. A 3-mi-long trail leads from the interpretive center. Wanapum State Park, 3 mi south, has camping and river access for boaters. ✉ *I-90 east to Exit 136, Vantage* ☎ *509/856–2700* ⊕ *www.parks.wa.gov* ▭ *Free; parking $5, camping $17* ⊙ *Apr.–Sept., daily 6:30 AM–dusk; Oct.–Mar., daily 8 AM–dusk.*

Olmstead Place State Park. This park and 217-acre working farm encompasses the grounds of an original pioneer farm built in 1875. A 1-mi interpretive trail links eight buildings, including a barn and schoolhouse. ✉ *N. Ferguson Rd., ½ mi south of Kittitas Hwy., 4 mi east of Ellensburg* ☎ *509/925–1943* ⊕ *www.parks.wa.gov* ▭ *Free, parking $5* ⊙ *Apr.–Oct., 6:30 AM–dusk; Nov.–Mar., 8 AM–dusk.*

Wanapum Dam Visitor Center. Indian and pioneer artifacts are exhibited here as well as displays on modern hydroelectric power. ✉ *Hwy. 243 S* ☎ *509/932–3571 Ext. 2571* ▭ *Free* ⊙ *Weekdays 8:30–4:30, weekends 9–5.*

WHERE TO EAT

¢ ✕ **The Palace Cafe.** This café has been serving good food to hungry travelers and locals since 1892. They offer a solid menu with standard varieties of steaks, burgers, chicken, and pasta in a Western setting. Their specialty is a prawn strawberry salad, and they have a chicken linguini that is excellent. ✉ *323 Main St., Ellensburg* ☎ *509/925–2327* ⊕ *www. thepalacecafe.net* ▭ *MC, V.*

AMERICAN

¢ ✕ **Red Horse Diner.** Step back in time to a 1930s-era service station. Now, however, the service at this refurbished Mobil station includes specialty sandwiches, shakes, and more. While you wait for your burger and fries, check out the hundreds of old metal signs and advertisements that enhance the vintage appeal of this classic burger joint. ✉ *1518 W. University Way* ☎ *509/925–1956* ⊕ *www.redhorsediner.com* ▭ *MC, V.*

AMERICAN
Fodor's Choice

$ ✕ **Valley Cafe.** Meals at this vintage art deco eatery consist of Mediterranean bistro-style salads, pastas, and other plates. Featured dinner entrées include rack of lamb, seared ahi tuna, and chicken marsala. An impressive wine list offers dozens of Yakima Valley options. Owner Greg Beach also owns the wine shop next door. ✉ *105 W. 3rd Ave.* ☎ *509/925–3050* ▭ *AE, D, DC, MC, V.*

CONTEMPORARY
★

¢–$ ✕ **Yellow Church Café.** Built in 1923 as a Lutheran church, this house of culinary worship now offers seating in the nave or choir loft. Soups, salads, sandwiches, pastas, and home-baked goods are served, as well as dinner specials. Breakfast is popular on weekends. ✉ *111 S. Pearl St.* ☎ *509/933–2233* ⊕ *www.yellowchurchcafe.com* ▭ *AE, MC, V.*

AMERICAN

15

WHERE TO STAY

$ ☷ **Best Western Lincoln Inn and Suites.** A spacious hostelry one block off Ellensburg's main north–south arterial, the Lincoln Inn offers travelers plenty of elbow room, minimal noise, and lots of amenities and services. Guests can use the outdoor picnic and barbecue area. All rooms have separate sitting areas with desks. **Pros:** Very nice motel close to the freeway. Caters to business travelers **Cons:** If you are looking for a less expensive place for a one night's stay, this may be a bit much. ⊠ *211 W. Umptanum Rd.,* ☎ *509/925–4244 or 866/925–4288* 🖷 *509/925– 4211* ⊕ *www.bestwestern.com* ⬥ *55 rooms* ♨ *In-room: kitchen (some), refrigerator, Internet, Wi-Fi. In hotel: pool, fitness center, hot tub, business center, Wi-Fi, free parking* ⊟ *AE, D, DC, MC, V* ⋈ *CP.*

¢–$ ☷ **Inn at Goose Creek.** Each room of this modern house—sparse from the outside, elegant within—has its own theme. The Homespun Room contains an assortment of black Shaker-style furniture, plain walls, and (like all the rooms) a handmade rug. The Timber Creek Lodge Room appeals to fishing enthusiasts. **Pros:** close to freeway and amenities; rooms have the feel of a B&B. **Cons:** although the rooms are very quiet, lots of car traffic. ⊠ *1720 Canyon Rd.* ☎ *509/962–8030 or 800/533–0822* ⊕ *www.innatgoosecreek.com* ⬥ *10 rooms* ♨ *In-room: refrigerator, Jacuzzi tubs, Wi-Fi. In hotel: Wi-Fi, free parking* ⊟ *AE, MC, V* ⋈ *CP.*

YAKIMA

38 mi south of Ellensburg.

The gateway to Washington wine country is sunny Yakima (pronounced *yak*-imah), home to about 80,000 people within the city limits and another 25,000 in the surrounding area. Spread along the west bank of the Yakima River just south of its confluence with the Naches River, Yakima is a bustling community with lovely parklands and a downtown in the midst of revitalization. Downtown street improvements with period lighting, trees, and planters have created a fresh new "old" feel that is inviting to residents and visitors alike.

Yakima was settled in the late 1850s as a ranching center where Ahtanum Creek joins the Yakima River, on the site of earlier Yakama tribal villages at present-day Union Gap. When the Northern Pacific Railroad established its terminal 4 mi north in 1884, most of the town picked up and moved to what was then called "North Yakima."

Yakima's Mission-style Northern Pacific Depot (1912) is the highlight of its historic North Front Street. Other old buildings face the depot; behind it, colorful Track 29 Mall is in old rail cars. Four blocks east is the ornate Capitol Theatre, built in 1920. The former vaudeville and silent-movie hall is now a performing arts center. Opposite is Millennium Plaza, a public art installation that celebrates the importance of water to the Yakima Valley. Residents and visitors alike enjoy year-round natural beauty in the heart of Yakima, thanks to the city's ongoing restoration and preservation of the Yakima Greenway. The nature area and trails stretch from Selah Gap to Union Gap, and west along the Naches River. The greenway includes more than 10 mi of paved

Yakima Valley Museum

pathway that connects parks, trails, and adjacent protected natural areas.

GETTING HERE

Yakima can be reached via air and road. The Yakima International Airport offers commercial flights to and from Seattle daily, and also welcomes private flights from all over. Interstate 82 from Ellensburg to the Tri-Cities and beyond, runs right through the city limits. Highways 12 and 410, known as White and Chinook Pass, pass on either side of Mount Rainier and connect with I–82 at Yakima, as does Highway 97, which brings travelers from Oregon and points south.

Yakima is the only city in the region with a public transportation system. **Yakima City Transit** (☎ *509/575–6175* ⊕ *www.ci.yakima.wa.us/services/transit*) buses operate weekdays 6 AM to 6:45 PM and Saturday from 8:45 to 6:45 at half-hour intervals on nine routes. The one-way fare is 75 cents.

VISITOR INFORMATION

Yakima Valley Visitors and Convention Bureau (✉ *10 N. 8th St., Yakima* ☎ *509/576-6385* ⊕ *www.visityakima.com*).

EXPLORING

McAllister Museum of Aviation. The history of aviation in Central Washington unfolds at the site of this pioneering flight school at Yakima International Airport. The museum, which includes Charlie McAllister's original pilot's license signed by Orville Wright, is open Thursday and Friday 10–4 and Saturday 9–4. Donations are accepted. ✉ *2008 S. 16th Ave.* ☎ *509/457–4933* ⊕ *www.mcallistermuseum.org.*

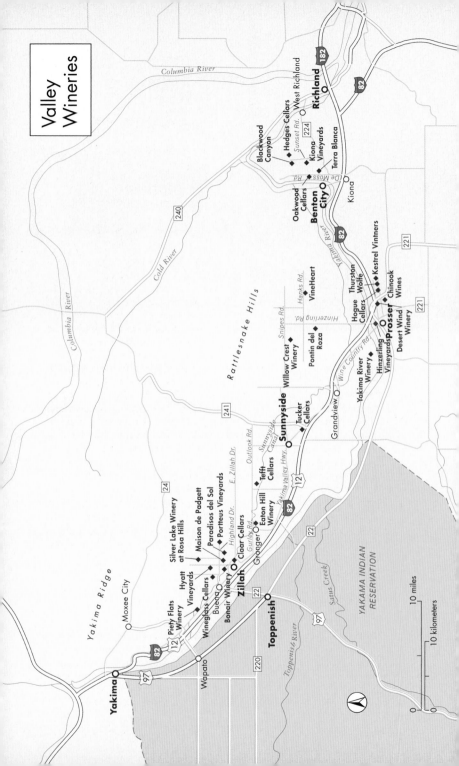

Valley Wineries

Columbia River

182

West Richland

Richland

82

Hedges Cellars

Blackwood Canyon

Sunset Rd.

224

Kiona Vineyards

Terra Blanca

De Moss Rd.

Oakwood Cellars

Benton City

Kiona

Yakima River

82

Kestrel Vintners

221

Thurston Wolfe

VineHeart

Chinook Wines

Hanks Rd.

Hogue Cellars

Prosser

221

Hinzerling

Hinzerling Winery

Desert Wind Winery

Yakima River Winery

Wine Country Rd.

Snipes Rd.

Willow Crest Winery

Pontin del Roza

Rattlesnake Hills

Cold River

240

Columbia River

Yakima Vineyards

Grandview

241

Sunnyside

Tucker Cellars

Sunnyside Canal

Outlook Rd.

Tefft Cellars

12

82

E. Zillah Dr.

Eaton Hill Winery

Yakima Valley Hwy.

24

Maison de Padgett

Silver Lake Winery at Rosa Hills

Paradisos del Sol

Porteus Vineyards

Highland Dr.

Claar Cellars

Granger

Gurley Rd.

Hyatt Vineyards

Piety Flats Winery

Wineglass Cellars

Bonair Winery

Buena

Zillah

22

Toppenish

Yakima Ridge

Moxee City

82

12

97

Wapato

220

22

97

Satus Creek

Toppenish River

YAKAMA INDIAN RESERVATION

10 miles

10 kilometers

Yakima

82

97

Yakima Area Arboretum. Just off I–82, the Yakima Arboretum features hundreds of different plants, flowers, and trees. The park-like Arboretum also sits along side the Yakima River and the the 10-mi-long Yakima Greenway, a paved path that links a series of riverfront parks. A Japanese garden and a wetland trail are the arboretum's highlights. ✉ *1401 Arboretum Dr., off Nob Hill Blvd.* ☎ *509/248–7337* ⊕ *www. ahtrees.org* 🎫 *Free* ☉ *Daily dawn–dusk.*

★ ☺ **Yakima Valley Museum.** Constant exhibits here focus on Yakama native, pioneer, and 20th-century history, ranging from horse-drawn vehicles to a "neon garden" of street signs. Highlights include a fully operating 1930s soda fountain and a model of Yakima native and Supreme Court Justice William O. Douglas's Washington, D.C., office. Other visiting and rotation exhibits are also scheduled throughout the year. ✉ *2105 Tieton Dr.* ☎ *509/248–0747* ⊕ *www.yakimavalleymuseum.org* 🎫 *$5* ☉ *Mon.–Sat. 10–5, Sun. 11–5.*

WHERE TO EAT

$$–$$$
ITALIAN
✕ **Gasperetti's.** John Gasperetti's restaurant keeps an elegant low profile in a high-traffic area north of downtown. Moderately priced pasta dishes share the menu with a short list of special weekly dinners—meat or seafood entrées with organically grown local produce. The cellar has an excellent selection of wines, including Italian varietals. ✉ *1013 N. 1st St.* ☎ *509/248–0628* ▤ *AE, D, DC, MC, V* ☉ *Closed Sun. No lunch Sat.*

$$
CONTEMPORARY
✕ **Greystone Restaurant.** The 1899 Lund Building has come a long way since its days as a sheep-ranchers' hotel, saloon, and brothel. Beneath the pressed-tin ceiling and between the gray stone walls, the same creative steak-and-seafood menu is served in the dining room and bistro bar. Specialties include a scrumptious Muscovy duck breast with julienne of apples or short ribs braised in a Yakima Valley syrah and mushrooms. ✉ *5 N. Front St., at Yakima Ave.* ☎ *509/248–9801* ⊕ *www.greystonedining.com* ▤ *AE, MC, V* ☉ *Closed Sun. Open for lunch weekdays.*

¢
AMERICAN
★ ☺
✕ **Miner's Drive-In** This Yakima icon (actually located in Union Gap) is a must-visit for many travelers coming to or through Yakima. It's an authentic 1940s hamburger joint that has expanded from a traditional drive-in to a family sit-down diner. Plenty of great-tasting items on the menu from salads to fish-and-chips, but the real crowd pleaser is the giant "Big Miner"—an old-fashioned burger that knocks any chain burger out of the park. Add a huge basket of fries and a shake, and chances are you'll be full for most of your day. ✉ *2415 S. 1st St., Yakima* ☎ *509/457–8194* ▤ *MC, V.*

¢
AMERICAN
✕ **Museum Soda Fountain.** Soda jerks at the Yakima Valley Museum's café make shakes and sundaes plus soups, hot dogs, and other sandwiches while a period Wurlitzer spins 1930s big-band records. ✉ *2105 Tieton Dr.* ☎ *509/248–0747* 🖎 *Reservations not accepted* ▤ *MC, V* ☉ *Closed Mon. No dinner Sept.–mid-June.*

$
MEXICAN
★
✕ **Santiago's.** Elegant and charming, Jar and Deb Arcand's skylit establishment puts a new spin on Mexican dishes. For chili verde, chunks of pork loin are slow-cooked in jalapeño sauce; the Yakima apple-pork mole is prepared with chocolate and cinnamon. ✉ *111 E. Yakima Ave.*

☎ 509/453–1644 ⊕ *www.santiagos.org* ⚱ *Reservations accepted for 5 or more* ▭ *MC, V* ☺ *Closed Sun. No lunch Sat.*

$$$
CONTEMPORARY

✕ **Tony's Steakhouse & Lounge.** The newest steak house in the region features Kobe rib-eye steaks and other cuts. The specialty menu changes every three months, but standard-cut steaks including filet mignon, New York, and smoked American Kobe prime rib are the specialty here and are available at all times. Unique appetizers and recipes featuring Northwest salmon and other seafood are also featured. Beautiful stone work outside and more stone and hardwood accents inside create elegant dining areas. Tony's is also one of the most popular nightspots in the area for dining or just meeting friends for a glass of Yakima Valley wine. ⊠ *221 W. Yakima Ave., Yakima* ☎ *509/853–1010* ⊕ *www. tonysteakhouse.com* ▭ *AE, D, MC, V* ☺ *Closed Sun.*

WHERE TO STAY

$$
★

⌂ **Birchfield Manor.** The valley's most luxurious accommodation is on a plateau just east of Yakima surrounded by hop yards (the fields where most of the brewery hops in the United States are grown), corn, and cattle. The Old Manor House contains the restaurant and five upstairs rooms. Rooms in a newer cottage are more private and have such amenities as steam-sauna showers and gas fireplaces. Chef-owner Brad Masset oversees the continental-style restaurant ($$$–$$$$, no lunch; one seating Thursday and Friday, two seatings Saturday; reservations essential), often assisted by his father Will, a European-trained chef who established the inn in 1978, and his brother Greg, a local vintner. The limited prix-fixe menu changes seasonally. The wine cellar has an excellent selection of local and imported vintages. **Pros:** a unique experience for this region. **Cons:** a little difficult to find. ⊠ *2018 Birchfield Rd., just south of Hwy. 24* ☎ *509/452–1960 or 800/375–3420* ⊕ *www. birchfieldmanor.com* ⇗ *11 rooms* ⚏ *In-room: no phone (some), fireplaces (some), whirlpool tubs (some), Wi-Fi. In-hotel: restaurant, pool.* ▭ *AE, DC, MC, V* ❢⦾❢ *BP.*

$–$$

⌂ **Hilton Garden Inn.** Modern, spacious, and comfortable rooms make this hotel in the heart of downtown Yakima one of the city's finest upscale lodgings. With an atypical lobby that is more akin to a New York town house, it combines elegance and simplicity. A two-sided gas fireplace near the open-air restaurant, adjacent to the lobby, offers guests a comfy place to read a book or check e-mails. Close to boutiques, downtown wineries, restaurants, and the Capitol Theatre. Full-service restaurant allows guests to stay in if desired. **Pros:** one block from the convention center and within walking distance of dozens of shops. **Cons:** in the midst of the concrete jungle. ⊠ *402 E. Yakima Ave., Yakima* ☎ *509/454–1111* ⊕ *www.yakima.stayhgi.com* ⇗ *111 rooms, 3 suites* ⚏ *In-room: refrigerator, Internet, Wi-Fi. In-hotel: pool, business center, fitness center, valet parking, laundry service, Wi-Fi.* ▭ *AE, MC, V.*

¢–$

⌂ **North Park Lodge.** This 2009 luxury addition to the region offers 53 rooms, with grand suites also available. Rustic, outdoor designs and premium comfort, including overstuffed leather furniture and hand-made wood furniture in the lobby and breakfast nook, add to the appeal of this very inviting hotel. You're close to shopping, parks, and the

Yakima River in Selah here. **Pros:** quiet and affordable, with plenty of room for the family. **Cons:** eight miles from Yakima. ✉ *659 N. Wenas Rd., Selah* ☎ *509/698–6004* ⊕ *www.northparklodge.com* ⤳ *53 rooms* ♺ *In-room: refrigerator, Internet (some), Wi-Fi. In-hotel: pool, gym, spa, laundry facilities, Internet terminal, Wi-Fi hotspot, parking (free), some pets allowed* ▭ *AE, MC, V* ⦿ *BP.*

$ ▥ **Oxford Inn & Oxford Suites.** Overlooking the Yakima Greenway and the Yakima River, these adjacent properties give scant clue that they lie just off the freeway. All the suites, which are in a contemporary white-adobe building, have patios or river-view balconies. About half the rooms in the Oxford Inn, which is surrounded by evergreens, have balconies, too. **Pros:** the Yakima River and Greenway are right out the back door for fishing and hiking. **Cons:** Wal-Mart and car lots across the street. ✉ *1603 Terrace Heights Dr.* ☎ *509/457–4444, 800/521–3050 inn; 509/457–9000, 800/404–7848 suites* ▤ *509/453–7593* ⊕ *www. oxfordsuites.com* ⤳ *96 rooms, 107 suites* ♺ *In-room: kitchen (some), refrigerator. In hotel: fitness center, complementary breakfast, evening appetizers, Wi-Fi hotspot, free parking* ▭ *AE, D, DC, MC, V* ⦿ *CP.*

15

SPORTS AND THE OUTDOORS

Apple Tree Golf Course (✉ *8804 Occidental Rd.* ☎ *509/966–5877*) This beautiful course cut through the apple orchards of West Yakima is rated as one of the state's top 10. The signature hole on the 18-hole, par-72 course is Number 17, shaped like a giant apple surrounded by a lake. Greens fees run $45–$60.

White Pass Ski Area, a full-service ski area 50 mi west of Yakima toward Mt. Rainier, is the home mountain of former Olympic medalists Phil and Steve Mahre. Five lifts serve a vertical drop of 1,500 feet from the 6,000-foot summit. Here you'll find condominiums, a gas station, grocery store, and snack bar. Open woods are popular with cross-country skiers and summer hikers. ✉ *48935 U.S. 12* ☎ *509/672–3101* ⊕ *www. skiwhitepass.com.*

SHOPPING

Johnson Orchards (✉ *4906 Summitview Ave.* ☎ *509/966–7479*) has been growing and selling fruit—including cherries, peaches, apples, and pears—to the public since 1904.

Central Washington's largest shopping center, **Valley Mall** (✉ *2529 Main St., Union Gap* ☎ *509/453–8233*) has all kinds of specialty shops including two major department stores: Sears, and Macy's. Produce vendors gather in downtown Yakima every Sunday, June through October, for the **Yakima Farmers' Market**. At other times, roadside stands and farms welcome visitors.

SOUTHERN YAKIMA RIVER VALLEY

The lower Yakima Valley encompasses hundreds of thousands of acres both on and off the Yakama Indian Reservation and includes dozens of small towns. Agriculture is the name of the game in this part of the lower valley where everything from apples to zucchinis are grown. Throughout the summer visitors buy or pick all kinds of fresh vegetables and fruits in season. In early May the asparagus grows to cutting height, and soon after it is time for the cherries to be harvested. Basically, it is one harvest after the next, culminating with apples in late October. Growing conditions also make this area the hot spot for wine-grape growing, and where there are grapes, there are wineries. Some 70 different wineries now call the Yakima Valley home, with many of the best wines in the country coming from these vintners. The history of this region stretches back hundreds of years from the time of the native Yakama Indians and early white settlers. Much of this history can be seen in several museums around the region, including the museum at the Yakama Nation Cultural Center in Toppenish.

ZILLAH

15 miles southeast of Yakima.

The south-facing slopes above Zillah, a tiny town named after the daughter of a railroad manager, are covered with orchards and vineyards. Several wineries are in or near the community; more are near Granger, 6 mi southeast.

GETTING HERE

The outskirts of Zillah, which is growing to include many new businesses, sits right on I–82 southeast out of Yakima. Downtown Zillah is just up the hill a half-mile or so.

WINERIES

Bonair Winery. After years of amateur wine-making in California, the Puryear family began commercial wine production in their native Yakima Valley in 1985 under the Bonair Winery name. One of the older Yakima Valley wineries, Bonair offers a large tasting room that sits among the vineyards and a koi pond, which was voted one of Washington's best places to kiss. Bonair makes cabernets, cabernet francs, chardonnays, gewürztraminer port, merlots, Rieslings and more. ⊠ *500 S. Bonair Rd.* ☎ *509/829–6027* ⊕ *www.bonairwine.com* ☉ *Mar. 1–Oct. 31, daily 10–6; Nov.–Dec., daily 10–5; Jan.–Feb., weekends noon–5.*

Claar Cellars. Right off of I–82 at Exit 52, Claar Cellars has one of the highest visitor rates of any Yakima Valley winery. The family-owned estate produces a variety of wines including some ice wines, sangiovese, and rare varieties such as Corneauxcopia (a blended variety) and Fouled Anchor Port, which includes cherries, raisins, honey, and maple syrup. They also produce traditional merlots, cabernets, chardonnays, sauvignon blanc, and Rieslings. Their grapes come from vineyards in the White Bluffs region. ⊠ *1001 Vintage Valley Pkwy.* ☎ *509/829–6810* ⊕ *www.claarcellars.com* ☉ *Apr.–Nov., daily 10–6; Dec.–Mar., daily 11–5.*

Eaton Hill Winery. Inside the restored Rinehold Cannery building, the rustic Eaton Hill Winery produces cabernet, merlot, chardonnay, Riesling, sémillon, and various sweeter and fortified wines. ⊠ *530 Gurley Rd., off Yakima Valley Hwy., Granger* ☎ *509/854–2220* ☉ *Feb.–Nov., daily noon–5; closed Dec. and Jan.*

Horizon's Edge Winery. With a spectacular view of the Yakima Valley, Mt. Adams, and Mt. Rainier, it is easy to see where Horizon's Edge got its name. The winery makes sparkling wine, chardonnay, pinot noir, merlot, cabernet sauvignon, and muscat canelli. ⊠ *4530 E. Zillah Dr., east of Yakima Valley Hwy.* ☎ *509/829–6401* ⊕ *www.horizonsedgewinery. com* ⊙ *June–Nov., Thurs.–Mon. 11–5; Mar.–June, Fri.–Mon. 11–5.*

Hyatt Vineyards. This 97-acre estate vineyard and winery sits in the middle of the Rattlesnake appellation and specializes in chardonnay, merlot, syrah, and cabernet sauvignon. ⊠ *2020 Gilbert Rd., off Bonair Rd.* ☎ *509/829–6333* ⊕ *www.hyattvineyards.com* ⊙ *Apr.–Nov., daily 11–5; Dec.–Mar., daily 11–4:30.*

Maison de Padgett Winery. Owned and operated by a small family, Maison de Padgett produces specialized handcrafted wines in a beautiful winery highlighted by adjoining European-style gardens. Groups of 10 or more should call ahead. ⊠ *2231 Roza Dr., at Highland Dr.* ☎ *509/829–6794* ⊕ *www.maisondepadgettwinery.com* ⊙ *Mar.–Nov., Thurs.–Mon. 11–5; Dec.–Feb., by appointment.*

Paradisos del Sol. This is another family-owned winery, operated by veteran winemaker Paul Vandenberg. Specialties are gewürztraminer, Riesling, cabernet, and a lemberger-cabernet blend designed especially for pizza. ⊠ *3230 Highland Dr.* ☎ *509/829–9000* ⊕ *www.paradisosdelsol. com* ⊙ *Daily 11–6.*

Piety Flats Winery. Just off 1–82 (Exit 44), this former mercantile (circa 1911) and fruit stand is now a winery and tasting room. Offering syrah, merlot, Mercantile Red, Carmenere, Junkyard Red, Back Muscat, and more, the winery also offers a number of other Yakima Valley specialty foods and goods, which makes it still a mercantile of sorts. ✉ *2560 Donald–Wapato Rd.* ☎ *509/877–3115* ⊕ *www.pietyflatswinery.com* ☉ *Mar.–Nov., Mon.–Sat. 10–6, Sun. 10–5; Nov.–Dec., daily 10–5; Jan.–Feb., Sat.–Sun., noon–5.*

Portteus Vineyards. One of the early Yakima Valley wineries, established in 1981, Portteus is beloved by red-wine drinkers. Production is limited to cabernet sauvignon and franc, merlot, syrah, zinfandel, and port—as well as a robust chardonnay. Grapes are grown at 1,440-foot elevation on 47 acres above Zillah. ✉ *5201 Highland Dr.* ☎ *509/829–6970* ⊕ *www.portteus.com* ☉ *Daily 10–5.*

★ **Silver Lake at Roza Hills.** Bands serenade picnickers on summer weekends on what Silver Lake calls the "viniferanda" sitting above their historic winery. Large windows afford views of the cabernets, merlots, chardonnays, Rieslings, and other vintages in production. ✉ *1500 Vintage Rd., off Highland Dr.* ☎ *509/829–6235* ⊕ *www.silverlakewinery.com* ☉ *Apr.–Nov., daily 10–5; Dec.–Mar., Thurs.–Mon. 11–4.*

Tefft Cellars. Once an old Concord grape vineyard, the land at Tefft Cellars was replanted in the late 1980s with *vinifera*. Today it produces cabernet, merlot, syrah, sangiovese, pinot grigio, pinot meunier, late-harvest dessert wines, and champagne. The owners' original three-bedroom house, adjacent to the winery, is now the Outlook Inn with rooms for rent. ✉ *1320 Independence Rd. via Gurley Rd., Outlook* ☎ *509/837–7651* ⊕ *www.tefftcellars.com* ☉ *Feb.–Dec., daily 10–5; Jan., by appointment.*

Wineglass Cellars. This small winery got its name from an unusual collection of antique wine glasses. In the interest of quality and priority, the winery produces limited lots of merlot, cabernet sauvignon, zinfandel, sangiovese, chardonnay, and port. ✉ *206 N. Bonair Rd.* ☎ *509/829–3011* ⊕ *www.wineglasscellars.com* ☉ *Mid-Feb.–Nov., Thurs.–Sun. 10:30–5.*

WHERE TO EAT AND STAY

¢–$

MEXICAN

✕ **El Porton.** Authentic, yet inexpensive Mexican fare is what you get at El Porton. Savory seafood dishes such as *mariscos al mojo de ajo*—sautéed prawns with mushrooms and garlic—are favorites. Traditional offerings such as beef or chicken burritos and enchiladas served up in a variety of Mexican styles round out the menu. ✉ *905 Vintage Valley Pkwy., Exit 52 off I–82* ☎ *509/829–9100* ⚄ *Reservations not accepted* ▭ *MC, V.*

¢–$

▦ **Comfort Inn–Zillah.** Just a few steps from Claar Cellars off I–82, this clean and modern hotel is a favorite of winery visitors. Kids love the free cookies and milk served each evening. **Pros:** right on the freeway and the only motel within miles. **Cons:** potential freeway traffic noise. ✉ *911 Vintage Valley Pkwy.* ☎ *509/829–3399 or 800/501–5433* 🖷 *509/829–3428* ⊕ *www.comfortinnzillah.com* ⤳ *40 rooms* ♿ *In-room: refrigerator, Wi-Fi. In-hotel: pool, laundry facilities, some pets allowed* ▭ *AE, D, MC, V* ⦿ *CP.*

TOPPENISH

17 mi southeast of Yakima.

An intriguing small town with a rustic Old West sensibility, Toppenish—which lies within the Yakama Indian Reservation—blends history and culture, art and agriculture. You can't miss the 70 colorful murals that adorn the facades and exterior walls of businesses and homes: commissioned since 1989 by the Toppenish Mural Association, done in a variety of styles by regional artists, they commemorate the town's history and Western spirit. Tours in a horse-drawn covered wagon leave from the association's office on Toppenish Avenue.

GETTING HERE

Take Highway 97 out of Yakima, and the four-lane road will take you through Wapato and right to Toppenish. Or follow the signs from I–82 at Zillah. From Oregon and points south Highway 97 also brings you right to Toppenish over Satus Pass.

VISITOR INFORMATION

Toppenish Chamber of Commerce (⊠ *5A S. Toppenish Ave.* ☎ *509/865–3262 or 800/863–6375* ⊕ *www.toppenish.net*).

EXPLORING

★ **American Hop Museum.** The Yakima Valley grows 75% of the nation's hops and 25% of the world's. The industry's story is well told at this museum. Exhibits describe the history, growing process, and unique biology of the plant, a primary ingredient in beer. It's open Wednesday through Saturday 10–4 and Sunday 11–4 from early May until late September. Admission is $3. ⊠ *22 S. B St.* ☎ *509/865–4677* ⊕ *www. americanhopmuseum.com.*

Ft. Simcoe Historical State Park. The residential quarters of an 1856 army fort 30 mi west of Toppenish look like a Victorian summer retreat. Exhibits focus on relations between the Yakama people—in the heart of whose reservation the fort stands—and American settlers. ⊠ *5150 Ft. Simcoe Rd.* ☎ *509/874–2372* ⊕ *www.parks.wa.gov* 🏷 *Free* 🕐 *Apr.– Sept., daily 8–dusk; Oct.–Mar., weekends and holidays 8–dusk.*

★ **Yakama Nation Cultural Center.** This six-building complex has a fascinating museum of tribal history and culture, including costumes, basketry, beadwork, and reconstructions of traditional lodges. Tribal dances and other cultural events are often staged in the Heritage Theater; the complex also includes a gift shop, library, and restaurant. The center is open daily 8–5; admission is $5. ⊠ *Buster Dr. at U.S. 97* ☎ *509/865–2800* ⊕ *www.yakamamuseum.com.*

SUNNYSIDE

14 mi southeast of Zillah.

The largest community in the lower Yakima Valley and the hometown of astronaut Bonnie Dunbar, Sunnyside runs along the sunny southern slopes of the Rattlesnake Hills.

15

GETTING HERE

I–82 runs right past Sunnyside as it threads its way down through the Lower Yakima Valley. Three exits put you at either end, and in the middle of Sunnyside.

VISITOR INFORMATION

Sunnyside Chamber of Commerce (✉ *230 E. Edison* ☎ *509/837–5939 or 800/457–8089* ⊕ *www.sunnysidechamber.com*).

WINERY

Tucker Cellars. Established in 1981 by renowned Washington grape growers Dean and Rose Tucker, Tucker Cellars produces gewürztraminer, chenin blanc, Riesling, chardonnay, and pinot noir. It's next to a fruit and produce market just off the Yakima Valley Highway, about 4 mi east of Sunnyside. ✉ *70 Ray Rd.* ☎ *509/837–8701* ⊙ *10–5 year-round.*

EXPLORING

☺   **Darigold Dairy Fair.** South of I–82 and the city of Sunnyside, you'll find this large, automated cheesemaking factory. It allows self-guided tours. There's also an expansive gift shop, an ice-cream bar, and a deli. ✉ *400 Alexander Rd.* ☎ *509/837–4321* ⊙ *Mon.–Sat. 8–6, Sun. 10–6.*

WHERE TO EAT

$–$$
AMERICAN
★   ✕ **Dykstra House.** In a wine valley with few upscale restaurants, this 1914 Craftsman house in quiet Grandview (6 mi southeast of Sunnyside) has held its own for nearly two decades. Breads are made from hand-ground wheat grown locally. Lunch, which is quite a bit less expensive than dinner, features salads, sandwiches, and daily specials. Casual Friday night dinners are Italian; grand Saturday night dinners revolve around chicken, beef, or fish. Local beers and wines are served. ✉ *114 Birch Ave., Grandview* ☎ *509/882–2082* ⌣ *Reservations essential* ▭ *AE, D, DC, MC, V* ⊙ *Closed Sun. and Mon. No dinner Tues.–Thurs.*

¢–$
MEXICAN
✕ **El Conquistador.** The bright, lively colors and clean, modern-Mexican decor belie the aging facade of this quaint eatery. The menu ranges from burritos, fajitas, and enchiladas mole to shrimp sautéed with green peppers and onions and served with a tangy salsa. Egg dishes are also on the menu, as are some unique Mexican salads and soups. Hand-crafted clay masks on the walls add a festive flair. ✉ *612 E. Edison Ave.* ☎ *509/839–2880* ▭ *AE, D, DC, MC, V.*

$
AMERICAN
✕ **Snipes Mountain Microbrewery & Restaurant.** In an imposing log structure that resembles a hunting or ski lodge, the lower valley's oldest and largest brewpub is a grand restaurant with fare ranging from burgers and wood-fired pizzas to pasta dishes, fresh king salmon, prime rib, and rack of lamb. Head brewer Chris Miller makes handcrafted beers. ✉ *905 Yakima Valley Hwy.* ☎ *509/837–2739* ⊕ *www.snipesmountain. com* ▭ *AE, MC, V.*

WHERE TO STAY

¢–$
🛏 **Sunnyside Inn Bed & Breakfast.** Built in 1919 as a doctor's residence and office, this two-house inn, remodeled in 2007, is larger than the usual B&B. Eight rooms have whirlpool tubs; several have small sunrooms, and all have private entrances. Breakfast consists of breads, pastries, meats, and a griddle entrée. Families are welcome. **Pros:** in the heart of

Desert Wind Winery

wine country; offering a short drive to several different wineries. **Cons:** immediate surroundings are not the most appealing. ✉ *800–804 E. Edison Ave.* ☏ *509/839–5557 or 800/221–4195* ⊕ *www.sunnysideinn.com* ⇥ *12 rooms* ⚲ *In room: Refrigerators (some). In hotel: Wi-Fi* ▭ *AE, MC, V* ⦿| *BP.*

PROSSER

13 mi southeast of Sunnyside.

On the south bank of the Yakima River, Prosser feels like small-town America of the 1950s. The seat of Benton County since 1905, it has a 1926 courthouse and a charming museum in City Park. In 2005, Prosser's Horse Heaven Hills, on the Columbia River's north slope, became Washington's seventh federally recognized wine region.

GETTING HERE
On the lower end of the Yakima Valley, Prosser sits alongside I–82 as it works its way to Benton City and then on to the Tri-Cities (Richland/Kennewick/Pasco). Two exits put you at either end of town.

VISITOR INFORMATION
Prosser Chamber of Commerce (✉ *1230 Bennett Ave.* ☏ *509/786–3177 or 800/408–1517* ⊕ *www.prosserchamber.org*).

WINERIES
Chinook Wines. A small house winery, Chinook Wines is run by Kay Simon and Clay Mackey, vintners known for their dry wines, including merlot, chardonnay, sémillon and sauvignon blanc. ✉ *Wittkopf Loop*

at Wine Country Rd. ☎ *509/786–2725* ⊕ *www.chinookwines.com*
⊙ *May–Oct., weekends noon–5.*

★ **Desert Wind Winery.** With an expansive tasting room housed in an elegant Southwestern-style building featuring a vast patio overlooking the Yakima River, Desert Wind is one of the highlights of any wine tour in the Valley. Tasters will delight in sémillon, barbera, ruah, viognier, and various other unique wine selections. Just off I–82, the winery also includes Mojave by Picazo, a small lunch restaurant (open for lunch Thursday–Saturday), and a gift shop with Yakima Valley food products and gift items. Also available on the second floor are four luxury guest suites, $175–$300 per night depending on season and room size. ⊠ *2258 Wine Country Rd.* ☎ *800/437–2313* ⊕ *www.desertwindvineyard.com* ⊙ *May–Sept., daily 10–5, Oct.–Apr., daily 11–5.*

★ **Hinzerling Vineyards.** Billed as the valley's first winery, Hinzerling specializes in dessert and appetizer wines including port, sherry, and muscat. Vintner Mike Wallace is one of the state's wine pioneers: he planted his first Prosser-area vines in 1972, and established the small winery in 1976. ⊠ *1520 Sheridan Rd., at Wine Country Rd.* ☎ *509/786–2163* ⊕ *www.hinzerling.com* ⊙ *Apr.–Dec. 24, Mon.–Sat. 11–5, Sun. 11–3; Dec. 26–Mar., Mon.–Sat. 11–4.*

Hogue Cellars. Founded in 1982, Hogue has grown to be one of the largest wineries in the state and has earned multiple awards for its wines. The gift shop carries the winery's famous pickled beans and asparagus as well as cabernet sauvignon, merlot, chenin blanc, Rieslings, and fume blanc, among other wines. ⊠ *2800 Lee Rd., in Prosser Wine and Food Park* ☎ *509/786–4557* ⊕ *www.hoguecellars.com* ⊙ *Daily 10–5.*

Kestrel Vintners. Featuring one the oldest vineyards in the Valley, planted in 1973, Kestrel vintners focus on dark red wines including rich cabernets, merlots, and syrahs, among others ⊠ *2890 Lee Rd., in Prosser Wine and Food Park* ☎ *509/786–2675* ⊕ *www.kestrelwines.com* ⊙ *Daily 10–5.*

Pontin del Roza. Named for its owners, the Pontin family, and the grape-friendly slopes irrigated by the Roza Canal, Pontin del Roza produces Italian-style sangioveses and pinot grigios, as well as Rieslings, chenin blancs, chardonnays, sauvignon blancs, and cabernet sauvignons. ⊠ *35502 N. Hinzerling Rd., 3½ mi north of Prosser* ☎ *509/786–4449* ⊕ *www.pontindelroza.com* ⊙ *Daily 10–5.*

Thurston Wolfe. Established in 1987, Thurston Wolfe features Wade Wolfe's unusual blends of specialty wines, including a white pinot gris–viognier, for instance, and a red mix of zinfandel, syrah, lemberger, and turiga. One of their popular varieties is Sweet Rebecca, an orange muscat. ⊠ *2880 Lee Rd., in Prosser Wine and Food Park* ☎ *509/786–3313* ⊕ *www.thurstonwolfe.com* ⊙ *Apr.–early Dec., Thurs.–Sun. 11–5.*

VineHeart. This pleasant boutique winery offers a buttery Riesling, a raspberry-toned sémillon, a Lemberger, and a sangiovese, as well as zinfandel, cabernet sauvignon, and syrah. ⊠ *44209 N. McDonald Rd., 7 mi northeast of Prosser* ☎ *509/973–2993* ⊕ *www.vineheart.com* ⊙ *Thurs.–Mon. 10–5.*

Thurston Wolfe Winery

Willow Crest Winery. Founded by David Minick in 1995, Willow Crest is a small winery with a Tuscan-themed tasting room that pours its own award-winning syrah as well as cabernet franc and pinot gris. ⊠ *135701 Snipes Rd., 6 mi north of Prosser* ☎ *509/786–7999* ⊕ *www. willowcrestwinery.com* ⊙ *Apr.–Nov., daily 10–5.*

Yakima River Winery. Another of the pioneer wineries in the Valley, established by John and Louise Rauner in 1977, Yakima River specializes in barrel-aged reds and a memorable port, along with a new variety, petit verdot. ⊠ *143302 N. River Rd., 1½ mi south of Wine Country Rd.* ☎ *509/786–2805* ⊕ *www.yakimariverwinery.com* ⊙ *Daily 9–5.*

WHERE TO STAY

¢ 🛏 **Vintners Inn.** You'll think you have time-warped back to the turn of the 20th century when you arrive at this 1905 Queen Anne that has been remodeled into a farmhouse-style B&B. Located next to the Hinzerling Winery, it offers two cozy rooms that may remind you of the comfort of Grandma's. ⊠ *1520 Sheridan Ave.* ☎ *509/786–2163 or 800/727–6702* ⊕ *www.hinzerling.com* 🛏 *2 rooms* 🗲 *In-room: no phone, no TV. In-hotel: bar, some pets allowed, no kids under 18* ▤ *D, MC, V* ⦿⊺*BP.*

BENTON CITY

16 mi east of Prosser.

The Yakima River zigzags north, making a giant bend around Red Mountain and the West Richland district before pouring into the Columbia River. Benton City—which, with a mere 3,000 residents, is hardly a city—is on a bluff west of the river facing vineyard-cloaked Red Mountain. High-carbonate soil, a location in a unique high-pressure pocket, and geographical anomalies have led to this district's being given its own appellation. You can access the wineries from Highway 224.

GETTING HERE

You'll find Benton City just off of I–82 about halfway between Prosser and Richland. One exit takes off from the Interstate and funnels traffic into the little town and to Highway 224.

WINERIES

★ **Blackwood Canyon Vintners.** Winemaker Michael Taylor Moore freely admits he's pushing the edge, meticulously crafting wines by hand, in the traditional European style of yesteryear. He shuns modern filters, pumps, and even sulfites, and carefully avoids pesticides. Chardonnays, sémillons, merlots, cabernets, and late-harvest wines age *sur lies* (on their sediment) for as long as eight years before release. ⊠ *53258 N. Sunset Rd.* ☎ *509/588–7124* ⊕ *www.blackwoodwine.com* ◎ *Daily 10–6.*

★ **Hedges Cellars.** This spectacular hillside château winery dominates upper Red Mountain and produces robust red wines. The estate blends cabernet sauvignon, cabernet franc, merlot, syrah, and reserve blends are superb. ⊠ *53511 N. Sunset Rd.* ☎ *509/588–3155* ⊕ *www.hedgesfamilyestate.com* ◎ *Apr.–Dec., Fri.–Sun. noon–4.*

Kiona Vineyards Winery. John Williams planted the first grapes on Red Mountain in 1975, made his first wines in 1980, and produced the first commercial Kiona lemberger, a light German red, in the United States. Today Williams's newly constructed 10,000-square-foot tasting room features 180-degree views of Red Mountain and the Rattlesnake Hills. Kiona also produces premium Riesling, chenin blanc, chardonnay, cabernet sauvignon, merlot, syrah, sangiovese, and dessert wines. ⊠ *44612 Sunset Rd.* ☎ *509/588–6716* ⊕ *www.kionawine.com* ◎ *Daily noon–5.*

Oakwood Cellars. This tiny boutique winery overlooking the Yakima River from the west slope of Red Mountain produces Lemberger, merlot, cabernet sauvignon, Estate Blanc, and Riesling. ⊠ *40504 N. Demoss Rd.* ☎ *509/588–5332* ⊕ *www.oakwoodcellars.com* ◎ *Mar.–Nov., Fri.–Sun. noon–5.*

Terra Blanca. Named for the calcium carbonate in its soil, Terra Blanca means "white earth" in Latin, and from the unique soil grow wine grapes that produce such specialties as syrah, merlot, cabernet sauvignon, and chardonnay. ⊠ *34715 N. Demoss Rd.* ☎ *509/588–6082* ⊕ *www.terrablanca.com* ◎ *Daily 11–6.*

Eastern Washington

WORD OF MOUTH

"If you want dry weather stay east of the Cascades. Soap Lake is 75 miles southeast of Chelan and is reputed to be a source of healing waters by the local Native Americans. Moses Lake is the home of an alternate Space Shuttle Landing area. Spokane has some very interesting sights and great restuarants. "

—kelsojim

WELCOME TO EASTERN WASHINGTON

TOP REASONS TO GO

★ **Historic Lodgings.** Take a step back in time. Visit the historic hotels and inns in Spokane, Walla Walla, and Dayton, which have been updated with modern amenities and high-tech touches, yet retain the flavor of yesteryear.

★ **Natural Wonders.** Get off the beaten path to experience the unique waters of Soap Lake, see the cliffs and canyons along the Columbia River, and hike in national forests.

★ **Wineries.** Explore the many wineries in Walla Walla, Tri-Cities, and Spokane.

★ **Family Attractions.** Slip in a little education on your family vacation by visiting pioneer museums, then play at water parks and Spokane's sprawling Riverfront Park.

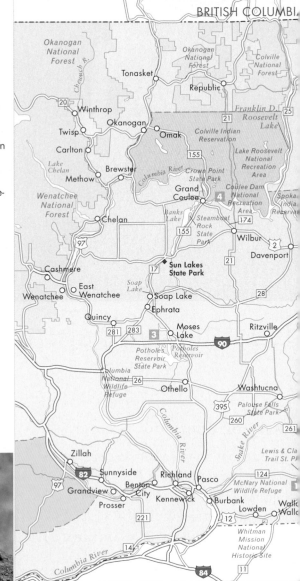

1 **Southeastern Washington.** In the wide-open areas of the Walla Walla and Columbia Valleys, hillsides are covered with rows of grapevines and wind turbines. Lodging, restaurants, museums, and wine-tasting opportunities can be found in Walla Walla and the Tri-Cities. Farther east are historic Dayton, the college town of Pullman, and Clarkston by the Snake River.

2 **Spokane.** The second-largest city in Washington is home to several historic lodgings and numerous restaurants; a fun kids' museum and interesting history museum; and two especially notable parks (Manito and Riverfront).

3 **Along Route 90.** Venture off the main route to discover the stunning Cave B Inn at Sagecliffe by the Columbia River, see pioneer history displays in Ephrata, and experience the healing waters of Soap Lake, before heading back on I–90 through Moses Lake.

4 **Northeastern Washington.** Travelers to this region will find the "Eighth Technological Wonder of the World"—the Grand Coulee Dam—which features a daily laser light show in summer. Further exploration brings you to the Colville and Okanogan national forests, and the small towns of Grand Coulee, Coulee City, Omak, and Colville (the latter two towns have city-quality dining at two noted restaurants).

GETTING ORIENTED

The main route through eastern Washington is I–90. As you leave the Cascade Mountains and its foothills behind, the terrain turns to desert and sagebrush, before crossing over the Columbia River and reaching the irrigated areas where fields of crops grow. In this area's barren, dry lands a new type of farming has emerged—wind farms with giant turbines that transform the landscape and provide electricity. The southeast part of the state offers a more verdant setting—rolling hills and fields where rain helps produce abundant crops of grains and wine grapes. The northeast part of the state is flanked by three mountain ranges (Selkirk, Okanogan, and Kettle River), which are considered foothills of the Rocky Mountains; this area is rich with lakes, rivers, cliffs, and meadows, and home to diverse wildlife.

16

EASTERN WASHINGTON PLANNER

When to Go

Eastern Washington has four distinct seasons, with generally very hot summers and sometimes very snowy winters. Recreational activities are geared to the specific season, with several downhill ski resorts open for skiing and snowboarding, and Nordic skiing available in the national forests, too. In summer, water activities on the lakes and rivers are popular, and there are many places to pursue hiking, backpacking, cycling, fishing, and hunting. Eastern Washington rarely feels crowded, though popular campgrounds may fill in summer. Lodging rates tend to be higher between Memorial Day and Labor Day, so visiting off-season can reduce costs. Spring and fall are both beautiful seasons to explore the region. In smaller towns certain attractions are open only from May through September, so call ahead to plan visits to sights. Also call well in advance to make reservations during college special-event weekends in Pullman and Walla Walla.

Getting Here and Around

Air Travel. Spokane International Airport is the main hub for air travel in eastern Washington. Smaller airports include Pullman, Tri-Cities, Walla Walla, and Lewiston, Idaho (across the border from Clarkston). Spokane International Airport is served by the airlines listed below, including Horizon, which also serves the smaller regional airports. Tri-Cities is served by Delta and United Express.

Contacts **Alaska Airlines** (📞 800/426–0333 ⊕ www. alaskair.com). **Delta** (📞 800/221–1212 ⊕ www.delta. com). **Frontier Airlines** (📞 800/432–1359 ⊕ www. frontierairlines.com). **Horizon** (📞 800/547–9308 ⊕ www. horizonair.com). **Lewiston-Nez Perce County Airport** (✉ 406 Burrell Ave., Lewiston 📞 208/746–7962 ⊕ www. lcairport.net). **Northwest** (📞 800/225–2525 ⊕ www. nwa.com). **Southwest** (📞 800/435–9792 ⊕ www. southwest.com). **Tri-Cities Airport** (✉ 3601 N. 20th, Pasco 📞 509/547–6352 ⊕ www.portofpasco.org). **United** (📞 800/241–6522 ⊕ www.united.com). **US Airways** (📞 800/428–4322 ⊕ www.usairways.com).

Car Travel. I–90 is the most direct route from Seattle to Spokane, over the Cascade Mountains (Snoqualmie Pass). U.S. 2 (Stevens Pass), an alternate route, begins north of Seattle near Everett, and passes through Wenatchee and Coulee City. South of I–90, U.S. 395 leads to the Tri-Cities from the east; the Tri-Cities can also be accessed via I–82 from the west. Past the Tri-Cities, continue on I–82 then U.S. 12 to reach Walla Walla. U.S. 195 traverses southeastern Washington to Pullman. Leave U.S. 195 at Colfax, heading southwest on Highway 26 and then 127, and finally U.S. 12 to Dayton and Walla Walla. Gas stations along the main highways cater to truckers, and some are open 24 hours.

For Travel in the region by Bus and Train, see Getting Here in the Spokane section below.

About the Restaurants

Nearly every small town in eastern Washington has at least one fast-food drive-through for a quick meal on the go, but choosing a slower pace will reward visitors with an authentic dining experience that often doesn't cost much more. Local diners and cafés are great spots for getting a hearty breakfast of traditional favorites like farm-fresh eggs or biscuits and gravy. Somewhat surprisingly, several of the small towns have outstanding dining options too; check out our restaurant reviews for Clarkston, Omak, Colville, and Dayton. At most restaurants there's an increasing emphasis on locally-grown, organic foods. With the region's many farms, it's easy to source produce, grains, poultry, meat, and dairy items, and some restaurants have their own gardens on-site for the freshest produce of all. Spokane has a good diversity of cuisines and some highly-acclaimed restaurants, but up-and-coming Walla Walla is becoming a mecca for foodies and wine lovers too.

About the Hotels

Family-owned motels and budget chains are prevalent in small towns like Colville, Omak, Grand Coulee, Moses Lake, and Pullman. More of these properties are updating their amenities to include modern touches such as flat-screen TVs; others can feel dated, but at least the prices are reasonable, except during special events when demand spikes create rate hikes. Several pleasant bed-and-breakfasts with friendly innkeepers are found in Spokane, Walla Walla, Dayton, and Uniontown (near Pullman), but with no more than six suites at each it's usually necessary to call ahead for a reservation. There are several historic hotels built in the early 1900s and restored in recent years that are definitely worth visiting in Spokane, Walla Walla, and Dayton. A stay at the Cave B Inn by the Columbia River—in one of its cliff houses, cavern rooms, or new yurts—is a recommended destination experience too.

WHAT IT COSTS IN U.S. DOLLARS					
	¢	$	$$	$$$	$$$$
Restaurants	under $10	$10–$17	$18–$24	$25–$30	over $30
Hotels		under $100	$100–$150	$151–$200	$251–$350	over $350

Restaurant prices are per person, for a main course at dinner. Hotel prices are for two people in a standard double room in high season, excluding tax.

Festivals and Events

April Spring Release Weekend, Walla Walla wineries

June Taste Washington!, Spokane

Vintage Walla Walla, Walla Walla wineries

July Grant County Wine Festival, Moses Lake

August Celebrate the Crush Wine Fest, Quincy

Peach Festival, Green Bluff (near Spokane)

September Balloon & Wine Festival, Quincy

Farmer Consumer Awareness Day, Quincy

Pig Out in the Park, Spokane

Apple & Harvest Festival, Green Bluff (near Spokane)

Sustainable September Festival, Spokane

Fiery Foods Festival, Pasco

Harvest Festival, West Richland

October Apple & Harvest Festival, Green Bluff (near Spokane)

November Tri-Cities Wine Festival, Kennewick

Fall Release Weekend, Walla Walla wineries

Spokane Cork & Keg Festival

December Holiday Barrel Tasting, Walla Walla wineries

Wine Country Holiday Open House, Red Mountain wineries, Tri-Cities

16

Updated by
Shelley Arenas

The Columbia Plateau was created by a series of lava flows that were later deeply cut by glacial floods. Because its soil is mostly made up of alluvial deposits and windblown silt (known to geologists as loess), it's very fertile. But little annual rainfall means that its vast central section—more than 30,000 square mi from the foothills of the Cascades and the northeastern mountains east to Idaho and south to Oregon—has no forests. In fact, except for a few scattered pine trees in the north, oaks in the southwest, and willows and cottonwoods along creeks and rivers, it has no trees.

This treeless expanse is part of an even larger steppe and desert region that runs north into Canada and south to California and the Sea of Cortez. There is water, however, carried from the mountains by the great Columbia and Snake rivers and their tributaries. Irrigation provides the region's cities with shrubs, trees, and flowers, and its fields bear a great variety of crops: asparagus, potatoes, apples, peaches, alfalfa, sweet corn, wheat, lentils, and much more. This bounty of agriculture makes the region prosperous, and provides funds for symphony halls and opera houses, theaters, art museums, and universities.

Southeast of the Columbia Plateau lies a region of rolling hills and fields. Farmers of the Palouse region and of the foothills of the Blue Mountains don't need to irrigate their fields, as rain here produces record crops of wheat, lentils, and peas. It's a blessed landscape, flowing green and golden under the sun in waves of loam. In the Walla Walla Valley the traditional crops of wheat and sweet onions remain, but more than 1,800 acres of grapes now supply more than 100 wineries that have opened in the past few decades. The region is not only fertile, it is historically significant as well. The Lewis and Clark expedition passed through the Palouse in 1805, and Walla Walla was one of the earliest settlements in the inland Northwest.

The northeastern mountains, from the Okanogan to the Pend Oreille Valley, consist of granite peaks, glaciated cliffs, grassy uplands, and sunlit forests. Few Washingtonians seem to know about this region's attractions, however. Even at the height of the summer its roads and trails are rarely crowded.

The hidden jewel of these mountains is the Sanpoil River valley, which is a miniature Yosemite Valley, with vertical rock walls rising 2,000–3,000 feet straight from the river, their height accentuated by the narrowness of the canyon. The valley has no amenities, and is still in the possession of its original owners, the Indians of the Colville Reservation, who have preserved its beauty. These wild highlands have few visitor facilities. Towns in the Okanogan Valley and the regional metropolis of Spokane, on the fringes of the region, offer more services.

SOUTHEASTERN WASHINGTON

The most populated area in this region is the Tri-Cities—Pasco, Kennewick, and Richland. Each town has its own character, but their proximity makes it easy to access an array of services and attractions like local wineries and pleasant riverfront parks. The town of Walla Walla has an historic downtown shopping district with innovative restaurant choices, wine-tasting rooms, elegant B&Bs, and the impressive Marcus Whitman Hotel. Just outside of town, wineries in bucolic country settings are as enjoyable for picnickers as for serious wine connoisseurs. If you continue east and north on quiet two-lane highways you'll discover Dayton, another historic small town; Pullman, home of Washington State University; and Clarkston, farther south by the roaring Snake River that serves as a boundary to its twin city, Lewiston, on the Idaho side.

16

RICHLAND

202 mi southeast of Seattle, 145 mi southwest of Spokane.

Richland is the northernmost of the three municipalities along the bank of the Columbia River known as the Tri-Cities (the others are Pasco and Kennewick). Founded in the 1880s, Richland was a pleasant farming village until 1942, when the federal government built a nuclear reactor on the nearby Hanford Nuclear Reservation. The Hanford site was instrumental in the building of the Tri-Cities, and still plays a major role in the area's economy. In recent years this has also become a major wine producing area. You can find more than 100 wineries within a 50-mi radius, many with tasting rooms.

GETTING HERE

The Tri-Cities have an airport in Pasco that is served by Delta and United Express. Taxis and rental cars are available there. Some hotels also offer an airport shuttle. Greyhound Bus Lines and Amtrak's *Empire Builder* both stop in Pasco. Ben Franklin Transit serves all three cities. By car, I–82 is the main east–west highway; from Ritzville or Spokane, take Highway 395 to reach the Tri-Cities; from Ellensburg and Yakima, take Highway 82 south and east.

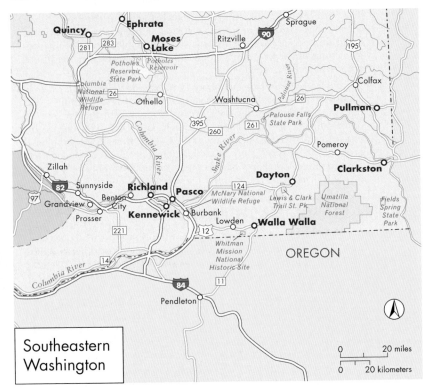

Ephrata
Quincy
Moses
Lake
281 283
Ritzville
90 Sprague
195
Potholes Potholes
Reservoir Reservoir
State Park
Columbia
National 26
Wildlife
Refuge
Othello
Washtucna
395
260 261
Palouse Falls
State Park
26 Colfax
Pullman
Pomeroy
Clarkston
Zillah
Sunnyside
82
97
Grandview
Prosser
Richland
Benton
City
Kennewick
221
Pasco
124
Dayton
McNary National
Wildlife Refuge
Burbank
Lowden
12
Walla Walla
Whitman
Mission
National
Historic Site
Lewis & Clark
Trail St. Pk.
Umatilla
National
Forest
Fields
Spring
State
Park
OREGON
14
Columbia River
84
11
Pendleton

Southeastern Washington

0   20 miles
0   20 kilometers

Contact Ben Franklin Transit ☎ 509/735–5100 ⊕ www.bft.org).

VISITOR INFORMATION
City of Richland (✉ 505 Swift Blvd., Richland ☎ 509/942–7390 ⊕ www.
ci.richland.wa.us). For winery information and maps, contact **Tri-Cities Visitor
and Convention Bureau** (☎ 800/254–5824 ⊕ www.visittri-cities.com).

WINERIES
Barnard Griffin Winery and Tasting Room. Owners Rob and Deborah Griffin offer a variety of fine wines, including excellent merlot and cabernet.
The art gallery adds class to the wine-tasting experience. ✉ *878 Tulip
La.* ☎ *509/627–0266* ⊕ *www.barnardgriffin.com* ⊘ *Daily 10–6.*

Bookwalter Winery. Next door to Barnard Griffin Winery, Bookwalter
produces red wines aged in French oak barrels and whites that are
100% stainless-steel fermented. The classic merlot is celebrated. Blends
are prevalent in both reds and whites. Live music plays Wednesday–Saturday evenings year-round. The lounge features a changing variety of
artisan cheeses, antipasto plates, other light fare, and desserts. ✉ *894
Tulip La.* ☎ *509/627–5000* ⊕ *www.bookwalterwines.com* ⊘ *Mar.–
Oct., Sun.–Tues. 11–8, Wed.–Sat. 11–11; Nov.–Feb., Sun. noon–6,
Mon.–Tues. noon–8, Wed.–Sat. 11–10.*

EXPLORING

CREHST Museum (*Columbia River Exhibition of History, Science, and Technology*). Displays show the area's development from prehistoric times to the nuclear age. There are educational exhibits, some of which are hands-on. The outdoor Boomers on Wheels exhibit depicts local trailer life in the 1940s, when the Hanford Construction Camp was the largest trailer camp in the world. A Lewis and Clark exhibit tells the story of the famous explorers and their expedition through the area more than 200 years ago. Another exhibit highlights fish species of the Columbia River. The area's geology is depicted in a mural and hands-on rock display. ⊠ *95 Lee Blvd.* ☎ *509/943–9000 or 877/789–9935* ⊕ *www.crehst.org* ➘ *$4* ☉ *Mon.–Sat. 10–5, Sun. noon–5.*

WHERE TO EAT

$$$ ✕ **Anthony's at Columbia Point.** For years the Anthony's chain has been
SEAFOOD known for fine waterfront dining in western Washington; since 2004 the Tri-Cities has had its own Anthony's on the Columbia River waterfront. Seafood is the specialty—even the appetizers are fish-focused, including pan-fried Willapa Bay oysters and fresh Puget Sound mussels. Dungeness crab (whole, in fettuccine, or in crab cakes), Columbia River sturgeon, char-grilled Alaskan halibut, Northwest cioppino, and several steaks are among the many entrée offerings. Anthony's weekday sunset four-course dinners are also popular. ⊠ *550 Columbia Point Dr.* ☎ *509/946–3474* ⊕ *www.anthonys.com* ▤ *AE, D, DC, MC, V.*

$ ✕ **Atomic Ale Brewpub and Eatery.** The staff is friendly at this small, casual
AMERICAN brewpub, which serves mainly house-brewed beers. The delicious pizzas are cooked in a wood-fired oven; sandwiches, salads, and soups (including potato, made with the in-house brew) are also fine. Local memorabilia is displayed throughout the restaurant, and the history of the Hanford nuclear plant is depicted in photos on the walls. ⊠ *1015 Lee Blvd.* ☎ *509/946–5465* ⊕ *www.atomicalebrewpub.com* ▤ *AE, D, MC, V.*

$$ ✕ **Katya's Bistro & Wine Bar.** A favorite of both locals and tourists, Katya's
CONTINENTAL has a devoted following who come to enjoy the skillful efforts of executive chef Josh Trunnell, a graduate of the Western Culinary Institute. Select from more than 200 regional wines to accompany such dishes as osso bucco, lamb chops, wild salmon, lasagna, and several steak and chicken choices. Ukrainian dishes include borscht and dumplings called *pelmini*. The menu changes to highlight local produce in season. Save $2 on wine by the glass during happy hour in the wine bar. ⊠ *430 George Washington Way* ☎ *509/946–7777* ⊕ *www.katyasbistro.com* ▤ *AE, D, MC, V* ☉ *No lunch, except groups by reservation. Closed Sun.*

WHERE TO STAY

$ 🏠 **Red Lion Hotel Richland Hanford House.** Richland's Red Lion overlooks the Columbia River and is near many major Hanford contractors and government facilities. The hotel borders a greenbelt riverfront park and has easy access to trails along the levee; ask for a room with a river view. Ripples Riverside Bar & Grill features steak, salmon, salads, pasta, and burgers, and an early-bird dinner special 5–6. Some rates include breakfast; the "Roaring Start" breakfast buffet is offered to all guests for $4.95. **Pros:** nice location; free airport shuttle; some rooms have views

16

of river. **Cons:** older hotel; some say the rooms need updating. ⊠ *802 George Washington Way* ☎ *509/946–7611* ⊕ *www.redlion.com* ⇌ *142 rooms, 7 suites* ⌂ *In-room: a/c, refrigerator, Wi-Fi. In-hotel: restaurant, room service, bar, pool, gym, laundry service, Internet terminal, some pets allowed* ▭ *AE, D, DC, MC, V.*

$

☺

⊞ **Shilo Inn Rivershore.** Bordering the Columbia River above the mouth of the Yakima, the Shilo Inn has easy access to riverside trails and parks. Rooms are simple in style yet well equipped with coffeemakers, microwaves, refrigerators, a fold-down ironing unit, and free unlimited local and long-distance calls. In O'Callahan's Restaurant and Lounge ($–$$), enjoy the river view from inside or out on the deck as you indulge in prime rib, halibut-and-chips, pastas, or salads. **Pros:** excellent value; convenient riverfront location walking distance to town and park. **Cons:** rooms by outdoor pool can be noisy; room keys are not electronic and they have the room number on them. ⊠ *50 Comstock St.* ☎ *509/946–4661* ⊕ *www.shiloinns.com* ⇌ *151 rooms, 13 suites* ⌂ *In-room: a/c, kitchen (some), refrigerator, Wi-Fi. In-hotel: restaurant, room service, bar, pool, gym, laundry facilities, laundry service, Internet terminal, some pets allowed* ▭ *AE, D, DC, MC, V* ⦿*BP.*

PASCO

10 mi east of Richland.

Tree-shaded Pasco, a college town and the Franklin County seat, is an oasis of green on the Columbia River near a site where the Lewis and Clark expedition made camp in 1805. The city began as a railroad switchyard and now has a busy container port. The neoclassical Franklin County Courthouse (1907) is worth a visit for its fine marble interior.

The Pasco Basin has first-rate vineyards and wineries and some of the state's most fertile land. You can purchase the regional bounty at the farmers' market, held downtown every Wednesday and Saturday morning during the growing season.

GETTING HERE
The Tri-Cities Airport is in Pasco; Delta and United Express operate there. Taxis and rental cars are both available and some hotels offer an airport shuttle. Ben Franklin Transit serves all three cities. By car, I–82 is the main east–west highway; from Ritzville or Spokane, take Highway 395 to reach the Tri-Cities; from Ellensburg and Yakima, take I–82 south and east.

Contact Ben Franklin Transit ☎ *509/735-5100* ⊕ *www.bft.org).*

VISITOR INFORMATION
City of Pasco ☎ *509/544-3080* ⊕ *www.pasco-wa.gov*

WINERIES
Gordon Brothers Family Vineyards. Just off Highway 182, Gordon Brothers produces some of the region's most acclaimed wines. Try the chardonnay, merlot, or cabernet sauvignon. All wine grapes are grown in their south-facing vineyard along the Snake River. ⊠ *671 Levey Rd.* ☎ *509/547–6331* ⊕ *www.gordonwines.com* ⊠ *Free* ☉ *Open by appointment.*

Preston Premium Wines. This is one of the Pasco Basin's oldest wineries. The tasting room has great views of surrounding fields, and visitors are welcome to picnic in the winery's park setting. ⊠ *502 E. Vineyard Dr.* ☎ *509/545–1990* ⊕ *www.prestonwines.com* ⊠ *Free* ☉ *Daily 10–5:30.*

EXPLORING

Franklin County Historical Museum. Here you'll find numerous items illustrating local history, including artifacts from Native American tribes. Revolving exhibits have featured the Lewis and Clark expedition, the railroad, and World War II. ⊠ *305 N. 4th Ave.* ☎ *509/547–3714* ⊕ *www.franklincountyhistoricalsociety.org* ⊠ *Donations accepted* ☉ *May–Oct., Tues.–Fri. noon–4, Sat. 9–noon.*

Sacajawea State Park. At the confluence of the Snake and Columbia rivers, this park occupies the site of Ainsworth, a railroad town that flourished from 1879 to 1884. It's named for the Shoshoni Indian woman who guided the Lewis and Clark expedition over the Rocky Mountains and down the Snake River. The 284-acre day-use park has an interpretive center and a large display of Native American tools. A beach, boat launch, picnic area, and children's playground round out the facilities; sand dunes, marshes, and ponds are great for watching wildlife. ⊠ *2503 Sacajawea Park Road* ⚓ *Off U.S. 12, 5 mi southeast of Pasco* ☎ *509/545–2361* ⊕ *www.parks.wa.gov* ⊠ *Free* ☉ *Apr.–Oct., 6:30 AM–dusk.*

WHERE TO EAT AND STAY

\$\$
AMERICAN
✕ **Bin 20 Steak and Seafood Restaurant.** Bin 20 opened as a wine bar, and still carries over 120 kinds of wine, most from Washington state. In 2007 it expanded beyond the wine focus to become a full-fledged steak and seafood restaurant. In 2010 Charles Reed, a veteran of 36 years with the American Culinary Federation Apprenticeship programs and winner of more than 45 awards, became executive chef. Signature dishes include the Bin 20 chop salad and blended meatloaf with forest mushroom demi-glace. On Friday and Saturday nights live smooth jazz accompanies the dinner hours. Happy hour runs 4 to 7 Monday through Thursday. ⊠ *2525 N. 20th St.* ☎ *509/544–3939* ⊕ *www.bin20. com* ⊟ *AE, D, MC, V* ☉ *No lunch.*

\$
🏨 **Red Lion Hotel Pasco.** This full-service hotel is the largest in the Tri-Cities and popular for conventions. The outdoor pool area is attractive and there is a spacious, open lobby. The rooms are in three separate wings of low-rise buildings; most rooms have either a patio or balcony. They are equipped with in-room coffeemakers, irons, and ironing boards, and microwaves. The hotel is four blocks from the airport. **Pros:** as at all other Red Lions, the Roaring Start breakfast buffet is available for \$4.95; there's also a Red Lion club for dogs. **Cons:** very large hotel, so some rooms can be a long walk from the lobby. ⊠ *2525 N. 20th St.* ☎ *509/547–0701* ⊕ *www.redlion.com* ⇆ *279 rooms, 10 suites* ⬩ *In-room: a/c, refrigerator, Wi-Fi. In-hotel: 3 restaurants, room service, bar, pool, gym, Internet terminal, some pets allowed* ⊟ *AE, D, DC, MC, V.*

16

KENNEWICK

3 mi southwest of Pasco, directly across the Columbia River.

In its 100-year history, Kennewick (*ken*-uh-wick) evolved from a railroad town to a farm-supply center and then to a bedroom community for Hanford workers and a food-processing capital for the Columbia Basin. The name Kennewick translates as "grassy place," and Native Americans had winter villages here long before Lewis and Clark passed through. Arrowheads and other artifacts aside, the 9,000-year-old skeleton of Kennewick Man has been studied by scientists at the University of Washington to determine whether its features are American Indian or, as some claim, Caucasian.

GETTING HERE

The Tri-Cities Airport is in nearby Pasco, served by Delta and United Express. Taxis and rental cars are available and some hotels offer an airport shuttle. Ben Franklin Transit serves all three cities. By car, I-82 is the main east–west highway; from Ritzville or Spokane, take Highway 395 to reach the Tri-Cities; from Ellensburg and Yakima, take I-82 south and east.

Contact **Ben Franklin Transit** ☎ *509/735–5100* ⊕ *www.bft.org).*

VISITOR INFORMATION

City of Kennewick ⊕ *www.ci.kennewick.wa.us*

WINERY

Badger Mountain Vineyard. A beautiful view of the valley and wine made without pesticides or preservatives is what you'll find here. Badger Mountain was the first wine-grape vineyard in Washington State to be certified organic. ⊠ *1106 N. Jurupa St.* ☎ *509/627–4986 or 800/643–9463* ⊕ *www.badgermtnvineyard.com* ⊟ *$5 tasting fee; applied to purchases of bottles* ⊗ *Daily 10–5.*

BREWERY

Ice Harbor Brewing Company. If you prefer a fine-crafted brew, this 7,000-square-foot brewery has a tasting room, gift shop, and a pub with an antique bar. ⊠ *206 N. Benton St.* ☎ *509/582–5340 or 888/701–2350* 🖷 *509/545–0571* ⊕ *www.iceharbor.com* ⊟ *Free* ⊗ *Mon.–Wed. 11–9, Thurs. 11–10, Fri. and Sat. 11–11, Sun. noon–7.*

EXPLORING

Columbia Park. One of Washington's great parks. Its 4½-mi-long, riverfront has boat ramps, a golf course, picnic areas, playgrounds (including an aquatic one), train ride, ropes course, and family fishing pond. In summer, hydroplane races are held here. ⊠ *Columbia Trail Dr., between U.S. 240 and the Columbia River* ☎ *509/585–4293.*

East Benton County Historical Museum. The entire entryway to the museum is made of petrified wood. Photographs, agricultural displays, petroglyphs, and a large collection of arrowheads interpret area history. Kennewick's oldest park, Keewaydin, is across the street. ⊠ *205 Keewaydin Dr.* ☎ *509/582–7704* ⊕ *www.ebchs.org* ⊟ *$4* ⊗ *Tues.–Sat. noon–4.*

Ice Harbor Lock and Dam. At 103 feet, the single-lift locks here are among the world's highest. It's about 12 mi southeast of Kennewick. ⊠ *2763*

Monument Dr., Burbank ☎ *509/547–7781* ✉ *Free* ◷ *Visitor center open Apr.–Sept., daily 9–5.*

McNary National Wildlife Refuge. More than 200 species of birds have been identified here, and many waterfowl make it their winter home. But its 15,000 acres of water and marsh, croplands, grasslands, trees, and shrubs are most enjoyable in spring and summer, when there is no hunting. A new Environmental Education Center opened in 2008 with some hands-on exhibits. A self-guided 2-mi trail winds through the marshes, and a cabinlike blind hidden in the reeds allows you to watch wildlife up close. Other recreation includes boating, fishing, hiking, and horseback-riding. ⊠ *64 Maple Rd., Burbank* ✦ *¼ mi east of U.S. 12, south of Snake River Bridge* ☎ *509/546–8300* ⊕ *www.fws.gov/ refuges* ✉ *Free, $10 hunting fee* ◷ *Daily during daylight hrs. Center is open some weekdays when staff or volunteers are available; call ahead.*

WHERE TO EAT AND STAY

$$–$$$ ✕ **The Cedars.** Right on the edge of the Columbia River, Cedars has
AMERICAN beautiful views and a 200-foot dock for boaters coming to dine. A deck is open seasonally, and it's popular as an after-work gathering place. The menu includes top-quality steaks, pasta, poultry, and wild salmon, and the extensive wine list features many local labels. Save room for the house-made mud pie. ⊠ *355 Clover Island Dr.* ☎ *509/582–2143* ⊕ *www.cedarsrest.com* ⊟ *AE, D, DC, MC, V* ◷ *No lunch.*

$ ⌂ **Red Lion Columbia Center.** Talk about convenience: it's next to a regional shopping mall and a block from the convention center. The recently renovated rooms have microwaves. The Red Lion chain's Roaring Start breakfast buffet in the morning costs $4.95 for guests and is the only time the restaurant is open. Food is available in the evenings in the lounge, which also has karaoke on Saturday and Sunday nights. **Pros:** handy location; good value. **Cons:** no full-service restaurant (many at the nearby mall); best for business guests. ⊠ *1101 N. Columbia Center Blvd.* ☎ *509/783–0611 or 800/733–5466* ⊕ *www.redlion.com* ⇆ *162 rooms, 9 suites* ♿ *In-room: a/c, refrigerator, Wi-Fi. In-hotel: bar, pool, gym, laundry service, Internet terminal, some pets allowed* ⊟ *AE, D, DC, MC, V.*

WALLA WALLA

52 mi southeast of Kennewick.

Walla Walla, founded in the 1850s on the site of a Nez Perce village, was Washington's first metropolis. As late as the 1880s its population was larger than that of Seattle. Walla Walla occupies a lush green valley below the rugged Blue Mountains. Its beautiful downtown boasts old residences, green parks, and the campus of Whitman College, Washington's oldest institution of higher learning.

A successful downtown restoration has earned Walla Walla high praise. The heart of downtown, at 2nd and Main streets, looks as pretty as it did 60 years ago, with beautifully maintained old buildings and newer structures designed to fit in. Walla Walla's Main Street is the winner of the "Great American Main Street Award" from the National Trust for

16

Historic Preservation. Residents and visitors come here to visit shops, wineries, cafés, and restaurants.

West of town, the green Walla Walla Valley—famous for asparagus, sweet onions, cherries, and wheat—has emerged as Washington's premier viticultural region. Tall grain elevators mark Lowden, a few miles west of Walla Walla, a wheat hamlet that now has several wineries.

GETTING HERE

Coming from points west, Walla Walla is reached via I–82 east of the Tri-Cities, then Highway 12, which is still a two-lane highway in places. From Spokane and the northeast, travel is all by two-lane highway, going south on Highway 195 to Colfax, then southwest via Highways 26 and 127 to Highway 12, then continuing south through Dayton and Waitsburg. Horizon Air runs two daily flights (one on Saturday) each way between Walla Walla and Seattle.

Contacts **Horizon Air** (☎ 800/547–9308 ⊕ www.horizonair.com). **Walla Walla Regional Airport** (✉ 45 Terminal Loop Rd., Walla Walla ☎ 509/525–3100 ⊕ www.wallawallaairport.com).

VISITOR INFORMATION

Walla Walla Valley Chamber of Commerce (✉ 29 E. Sumach St. ☎ 509/525–0850 or 877/998–4748 ⊕ www.wwvchamber.com).

WINERIES

Canoe Ridge Vineyards, owned by the Chalone Wine Group, produces merlot, cabernet, chardonnay, and other wines. The tasting room is in Walla Walla's historic Engine House. ✉ 1102 W. Cherry St. ☎ 509/527–0885 ⊕ www.canoeridgevineyard.com ⊙ Oct.–Apr., daily 11–4; May–Dec., daily 11–5.

★ **L'Ecole No. 41,** housed in the lower floors of a circa-1915 schoolhouse, produces outstanding sémillon and merlot, among other wines. The tasting room is in one of the old classrooms, and details like chalkboards and books add to the restored school's character. ✉ 41 Lowden School Rd., Lowden ☎ 509/525–0940 ⊕ www.lecole.com ⊙ Daily 10–5.

At **Seven Hills Winery**, owner Casey McClellan makes well-balanced merlot, cabernet sauvignon, and syrah. The winery is in Walla Walla's historic Whitehouse-Crawford building. ✉ 212 N. 3rd Ave. ☎ 509/529–7198 or 877/777–7870 ⊕ www.sevenhillswinery.com ⊙ Thurs.–Mon. 10–5, and by appointment.

The tasting room for one of Walla Walla's newest wineries, **Sinclair Estate Vineyards**, opened downtown in spring 2010. Owners Tim and Kathy Sinclair also own the new Vine and Roses Bed and Breakfast, and their love for French antiques and fine art is evident in the elegant tasting room, which even has a grand piano. Their first releases include a syrah and two blends. ✉ 109-B E. Main St. ☎ 509/876–8300 ⊕ www.sinclairestatevineyards.com ⊙ Thurs.–Sat. 11–5, Sun. 11–4.

About a mile east of L'Ecole N. 41 is **Three Rivers Winery**. Just off U.S. 12 and surrounded by vineyards, the winery is home to premium cabernet sauvignon, merlot, sangiovese, and syrah. It also has a nice

L'Ecole No. 41

tasting room, a gift shop, summer concerts, and a 3-hole golf course. ✉ *5641 W. U.S. Hwy. 12* ☎ *509/526–9463* ⊕ *www.threeriverswinery. com* ☉ *Daily 10–5.*

Waterbrook Winery. The tasting room, part of a facility on 75 acres, has an indoor-outdoor feel, with a spacious patio and outdoor fireplace, hillside views, and natural landscaping and ponds. Waterbrook is best known for chardonnay, sauvignon blanc, and viognier. ✉ *10518 W. U.S. Hwy. 12* ☎ *509/522–1262* ⊕ *www.waterbrook.com* ☉ *Sun.–Thurs., 10–6, Fri.–Sat, 10–8.*

★ Lovers of fine wines make pilgrimages to **Woodward Canyon Winery**, 12 mi west of Walla Walla, for the superb cabernet sauvignon, merlot, and chardonnay. The winery occasionally produces other varietals. ✉ *11920 W. U.S. 12, Lowden* ☎ *509/525–4129* ⊕ *www.woodwardcanyon.com* ☉ *Daily 10–5.*

EXPLORING

☉ **Ft. Walla Walla Museum**, a few miles west of Walla Walla, occupies 15 acres at Fort Walla Walla Park. A 17-building pioneer village depicts the region's life in the 1800s, and four halls house military, agricultural, and penitentiary exhibits. ✉ *755 Myra Rd., at Dalles Military Rd.,* ☎ *509/525–7703* ⊕ *www.fortwallawallamuseum.org* ✉ *$7* ☉ *Apr.– Oct., daily 10–5.*

Planted with native and exotic flowers and trees, **Pioneer Park** is a shady, turn-of-the-20th-century park with a fine aviary. It was originally landscaped by sons of Frederick Law Olmsted, who designed New York City's Central Park. ✉ *E. Alder St. and Division St.*

Large, tree-lined lawns surround the many beautiful 19th-century stone and brick structures of the **Whitman College** campus. The school began as a seminary in 1859 and became a college in 1883. ⊠ *345 Boyer Ave.* ☎ *509/527–5111.*

☼ **Whitman Mission National Historic Site,** 7 mi west of downtown Walla Walla, is a reconstruction of Waiilatpu Mission, a Presbyterian outpost established on Cayuse Indian lands in 1836. The park preserves the foundations of the mission buildings, a short segment of the Oregon Trail, and, on a nearby hill, the graveyard where the Native American victims of an 1847 measles epidemic and subsequent uprising are buried. ⊠ *328 Whitman Mission Rd.* ☎ *509/522–6360 or 509/529–2761* ⊕ *www.nps.gov/whmi* ⊡ *$3* ⊙ *Daily dawn–dusk (except New Year's Day, Thanksgiving, and Christmas); visitor center open 8–6 summer, 8–4:30 winter.*

WHERE TO EAT

$
CAFÉ
✕ **Olive Marketplace & Cafe.** Kick back and enjoy good food in a casual environment right downtown on Main Street. In 2010 the owners of nearby T. Maccarones restaurant opened this two-level café in the space that housed Merchants Ltd. Deli for more than 30 years. Between pouring its first cup of coffee when it opens at 6, and the last glass of wine from the wine bar before closing at 9 (10 on Friday and Saturday), the café serves a reasonably-priced and varied menu. Standards like spaghetti and meatballs and vegetarian pasta are offered at dinner, while the lunch menu includes several sandwiches, salads, and seasonal soups. Flatbread pizzas are available from 11 until closing; try the unique prosciutto and grape pizza, pancetta pizza with a farm egg, or sausage pizza with house-smoked chili sausage and pink lady apples. ⊠ *21 E. Main St.* ☎ *509/526–0200* ⊕ *www.tmaccarones.com/olive* ⊟ *AE, D, MC, V.*

$$
ITALIAN
Fodor'sChoice
★
✕ **T. Maccarones.** Italian food with a very contemporary flare is the draw at "T-Mac's," along with the neighborly feel of the small, two-level restaurant. It's the kind of place that quickly becomes a favorite for locals. Customers are often greeted personally by friendly owner Tom Maccarone, a native of Walla Walla who returned in 2005 after years in the Seattle area. Executive Chef Jacob Crenshaw, now a co-owner, came from the Marc Restaurant at the Marcus Whitman Hotel and Brasa in Seattle. He's responsible for the inventive menu that focuses on sustainable practices and fresh, local, and organic ingredients for dishes like summer-vegetable gnocchi and free-range chicken. The T-Mac and Cheese is rich and delicious; desserts are baked in-house. ⊠ *4 N. Colville* ☎ *509/522–4776* ⊕ *www.tmaccarones.com* ⊟ *AE, D, MC, V* ⊙ *No lunch.*

$$–$$$
AMERICAN
Fodor'sChoice
★
✕ **Whitehouse-Crawford Restaurant.** In a former wood mill, this restaurant has gained a reputation for quality and excellence over its decade of existence, thanks to chef Jamie Guerin. Local is the watchword here, where hamburgers are made with beef from the Thundering Hooves Farm in nearby Touchet, and more than a dozen nearby purveyors supply produce, cheese, meat, eggs, and coffee. Try the smoked trout and warm spinach salad, Wagyu beef tenderloin steak, or roasted Alaskan king salmon, and save room for the homemade ice cream, which you can take home by the pint. The extensive wine list features many Walla

T. Maccarones

Walla Valley winemakers. ⊠ *55 W. Cherry St.* ☎ *509/525–2222* ⊕ *www. whitehousecrawford.com* 🖃 *AE, MC, V* ⊘ *Closed Tues. No lunch.*

WHERE TO STAY

$$–$$$ 🖼 **Inn at Abeja**. Twenty-five acres of gardens and vineyards surround
Fodor's Choice a turn-of-the-20th-century farm with guest cottages and suites. Each
★ accommodation has board games, books and magazines, binoculars (to better enjoy the bucolic views), CD players, and satellite TV. Breakfast can be delivered to your room or served in the small barn. It's a short drive to both downtown Walla Walla and valley wineries. **Pros:** beautiful grounds; high-end; very spacious accommodations with kitchens; private tours of the winery on-site. **Cons:** The Inn is closed Tuesday and Wednesday and from mid-December to February. ⊠ *2014 Mill Creek Rd.* ☎ *509/522–1234* ⊕ *www.abeja.net/inn* 🛏 *4 cottages, 4 suites* ♿ *Inroom: a/c, kitchen (some), refrigerator, DVD, Wi-Fi. In-hotel: some pets allowed, no kids under 13* 🖃 *AE, MC, V* ⫦ *BP.*

$$ 🖼 **Marcus Whitman Hotel**. This 1928 hotel is *the* landmark in downtown
Fodor's Choice Walla Walla. Guest quarters in the historic tower building are spa-
★ cious two-room parlor suites and spa suites with king beds, flat-screen TVs in the bedroom and living room, refrigerators, and microwaves. Adorned with Renaissance-style Italian furnishings, these rooms are well worth the splurge. ■TIP➜ **Ask for a high floor to enjoy the best city and hillside views.** For business guests or those on a budget, the rooms in the West Wing are more standard hotel style. The Marc restaurant ($$–$$$) has fine dining and a wine list that has won several awards from the Washington Wine Commission. Chef Bear Ullman has led the restaurant since it opened; his seasonal menu focuses on local and

Vine and Roses Bed & Breakfast

organic foods and innovations like microgreens grown in-house and an on-site bakery. "Chef's Table" multicourse dinners (paired with wine) for eight are held several times a month right in the kitchen. You can sample local wines at the Vineyard Lounge. **Pros:** range of accommodations to choose from; central downtown location; full breakfast buffet and parking included. **Cons:** no pool; no bathtubs in historic rooms. ⊠ *6 W. Rose St.* ☎ *509/525–2200 or 866/826–9422* 🖷 *509/524–1747* 🌐 *www.marcuswhitmanhotel.com* 📌 *127 rooms, 16 suites* ⚒ *In-room: a/c, refrigerator (some), DVD (some), Internet, Wi-Fi. In-hotel: restaurant, bar, gym, some pets allowed* ▤ *AE, D, DC, MC, V* 🍽 *BP.*

$$–$$$

Fodor'sChoice
★

🏠 **Vine and Roses Bed & Breakfast.** Walla Walla's newest Bed & Breakfast is most certainly its finest. Located a block from Pioneer Park (⇨ *Exploring above*), the 1893 Victorian was extravagantly renovated by transplanted Seattleites Tim and Kathy Sinclair to create an in-town oasis of luxury and grace. Rooms are decorated with French antiques, yet boast an array of upscale amenities, including flat-screen TVs, gas fireplaces, deep soaking tubs (some with jets), and separate walk-in showers. Some have balconies, garden and creek views, or sunrooms. All are quiet and secluded, though the inn does have expansive common areas where guests can interact, including a Great Room, library, porch, and deck overlooking the gardens and creek. The owners are very gracious and knowledgeable about the area. They can recommend many fine restaurants in the area and help secure reservations. **Pros:** guests get free tastings at the Sinclairs' other business, Sinclair Estate Vineyards; the couple will also help arrange exclusive visits to other wineries. **Cons:** breakfast is the only meal prepared in the beautiful kitchen. ⊠ *516 S.*

Division St. ☎509/876–2113 ⊕www.vineandroses.com ➲5 rooms ☖In-room: a/c, Wi-Fi. In-hotel: no kids under 18 ⊟AE, D, MC, V.

DAYTON

31 mi northeast of Walla Walla.

The tree-shaded county seat of Columbia County is the kind of Currier & Ives place many people conjure up when they imagine the best qualities of rural America. This tidy town has 117 buildings listed on the National Register of Historic Places, including the state's oldest railroad depot and courthouse.

GETTING HERE

Dayton is northeast of Walla Walla via Highway 12. From the Spokane area, take Highway 195 to Colfax, then veer southwest via Highways 26 and 127 before reaching Highway 12 and continuing into the town.

EXPLORING

At Washington's oldest standing depot, the **Dayton Historical Depot Society** houses exhibits illustrating the history of Dayton and surrounding communities. ✉222 E. Commercial Ave. ☎509/382–2026 ⊕www. daytonhistoricdepot.org ➲$5 ☉May–Oct., Wed.–Sat. 10–5 (closed noon–1); Nov.–Apr., Wed.–Sat. 11–4.

16

OFF THE
BEATEN
PATH

Palouse Falls State Park. Just north of its confluence with the Snake River, the Palouse River gushes over a basalt cliff higher than Niagara Falls and drops 198 feet into a steep-walled basin. Those who are surefooted can hike to an overlook above the falls, which are at their fastest during spring runoff in March. Just downstream from the falls at the Marmes Rock Shelter, remains of the earliest-known inhabitants of North America, dating back 10,000 years, were discovered by archaeologists. The park has 10 primitive campsites. ✉U.S. 12, 50 mi north of Dayton ☎509/646–9218 or 888/226–7688 ➲Campsites $12 ☉Park daily summer 6:30 AM–dusk, winter 8 AM–dusk; campsites open year-round but no water Sept.–April.

WHERE TO EAT AND STAY

$$$

FRENCH

✗**Patit Creek Restaurant.** The chef turns out inspired beef, duck, and lamb dishes at this small café, which has been a favorite southeastern Washington eatery for more than 30 years. Portobello mushroom saltimbocca is favorite vegetarian option. Not only can the food be truly sublime, but the service is also excellent. The wine list is short, but has some rare Walla Walla Valley vintages. ✉725 E. Dayton Ave. ☎509/382–2625 ⊟AE, MC, V ☉Closed Sun.–Tues. No lunch Sat.

$–$$

AMERICAN

✗**Weinhard Café.** The past seems to echo through this restaurant, which is near the Weinhard Hotel and in what was once a pharmacy. Try a panini sandwich for lunch; for dinner, the New York strip steak with tarragon butter and potato-thyme gratin or the sesame-crusted tuna are good bets. The raspberry-rhubarb pie and coconut-lemon pie are dessert favorites. The menu changes frequently to highlight seasonal specialties. ✉258 E. Main St. ☎509/382–1681 ⊕www.weinhard-cafe.com ⊟MC, V ☉Closed Sun. and Mon.

$ ▦ **Weinhard Hotel**. Step back into the Old West at this hotel, which was built as a saloon and lodge in the late 1800s by the nephew of beer baron Henry Weinhard. Rooms have modern amenities but period antiques; fruit baskets and bouquets of flowers are thoughtful touches. An Internet coffeehouse provides free Wi-Fi to hotel guests and nonguests using their own laptop. Enjoy sparkling cider and live music at weekend evening socials; catch a breeze in the pleasant rooftop garden. **Pros:** weekend live music is fun; rooms reflect the history of the era but have modern features. **Cons:** some rooms face highway and can be noisy; some guests have complained about the continental breakfast. ⊠ *235 E. Main St.* ☎ *509/382–4032* ⊕ *www.weinhard.com* ⤵ *15 rooms* △ *In-room: a/c, Internet, Wi-Fi. In-hotel: Internet terminal, Wi-Fi hotspot, some pets allowed* ⊟ *MC, V* �◖◗ *CP.*

PULLMAN

33 mi northwest of Clarkston.

This funky, liberal town—home of Washington State University—is in the heart of the rather conservative Palouse agricultural district. The town's freewheeling style can perhaps be explained by the fact that most of the students come from elsewhere in Washington.

The Palouse River, whose upper course flows though the town, is an exception among Washington rivers: because of the high erosion rate of the light Palouse loess soils it usually runs muddy, almost like a gruel during floods (most Washington Rivers run clear, even after major storms). The 198-foot-high Palouse Falls farther downstream, near Washtucna, dramatically drop as a thin sheet of water into a steep box canyon.

GETTING HERE

Horizon Air flies into the local airport, where taxis and rental cars are available to get you to your destination. Most of the hotels have free airport shuttles, too. Pullman is reached via Highway 195, about 80 miles from Spokane.

Pullman-Moscow Regional Airport (⊠ *3200 Airport Complex N, Pullman* ☎ *509/338–3223* ⊕ *www.pullman-wa.gov/airport*).

VISITOR INFORMATION

Pullman Chamber of Commerce (⊠ *415 N. Grand Ave.* ☎ *509/334–3565 or 800/365–6948* ⊕ *www.pullmanchamber.com*).

EXPLORING

Kamiak Butte County Park has a 3,360-foot-tall butte that's part of a mountain chain that was here long before the lava flows of the Columbia basin erupted millions of years ago. Ten miles north of Pullman, the park has great views of the Palouse hills and Idaho's snow-capped peaks to the east, as well as nine primitive campsites, a picnic area, and a 1-mi trail to the top of the butte. ⊠ *Hwy. 272 to Rd. 5100 to Rd. 6710, Palouse* ☎ *509/397–6238* ▱ *Free* ☉ *Daily 7–dusk.*

Washington State University

Opened in 1892 as the state's agriculture school, **Washington State University** today sprawls almost all the way to the Idaho state line. To park on campus, pick up a parking pass in the Security Building on Wilson Road. On weekdays between 9:30 and 4:30, you can pop into **Ferdinand's** (⊠ *S. Ferdinand La.* ☎ *509/335–2141*), a soda fountain–cheese shop in the food-science building, to buy Aged Cougar Gold, a cheddar-type cheese in a can. The small **Museum of Art** (⊠ *WSU Fine Arts Center, Wilson Rd. and Stadium Way* ☎ *509/335–1910*) has lectures, as well as exhibitions that might include turned-wood art, Native American art, or landscaping displays. It's open Monday–Wednesday, Friday and Saturday 10–4, Thursday 10–7 during the regular school year (call for summer hours); admission is free. The **Charles R. Conner Museum of Zoology** (⊠ *Science Hall* ☎ *509/335–3515*) has the finest collection of stuffed birds and mammals and preserved invertebrates in the Pacific Northwest. It's open daily 8–5, and there's no admission fee. ⊠ *1 S.E. Stadium Way* ☎ *509/335–4636* ⊕ *www.wsu.edu* ✉ *Free* ◷ *Daily.*

Fodor's Choice ★

WHERE TO EAT AND STAY

¢ ✕ **Basilio's Italian Café**. In the heart of downtown, Basilio's serves up such classics as pasta, lasagna, and chicken parmigiana in addition to an assortment of sandwiches and pizzas. Gaze at scenic downtown from the sidewalk seating area. ⊠ *337 E. Main St.* ☎ *509/334–7663* ⊕ *www. basilios.net* ▭ *MC, V.*

ITALIAN

¢ ✕ **Sella's Calzone and Pastas**. Made daily from scratch, the calzones are always fresh at this cozy storefront. The most popular is the Coug (pepperoni, mushrooms, and black olives), followed by Gourmet (artichoke hearts, sundried olives, pesto sauce, and mozzarella). Pizzas,

PIZZA

sandwiches, pastas, and salads are also served. ✉ *1115 E. Main St.* ☎ *509/334–1895* ▭ *MC, V.*

¢–$ ⌨ **Churchyard Inn.** Registered as a national and state historic site, this 1905 Flemish-style inn, 15 mi southeast of Pullman in Uniontown, was once a parish house for the adjacent church, and then a convent, before becoming a B&B in 1995. Kids are sometimes allowed; ask in advance. And book well in advance during WSU games/events. Afternoon tea parties can be scheduled by advance reservation for groups up to 14 on Friday–Sunday afternoons. A common social room has games,TV, and a piano. **Pros:** welcoming and helpful innkeeper; interesting history; quiet and scenic. **Cons:** no a/c or TVs in rooms. ✉ *206 St. Boniface St., Uniontown* ☎ *509/229–3200 or 800/227–2804* ⊕ *www.churchyardinn. com* ⇆ *6 rooms* ♿ *In-room: no a/c, no TV, Wi-Fi. In-hotel: laundry facilities, Wi-Fi.* ▭ *AE, D, MC, V* ⍑ *BP.*

SPOKANE

75 mi north of Pullman, 282 mi east of Seattle.

Washington's second-largest city, Spokane (spo-*can*, not spo-*cane*) takes its name from the Spokan tribe of Salish Indians. It translates as "Children of the Sun," a fitting name for this sunny city. It's also a city of flowers and trees, public gardens, parks, and museums. Known as the "Capital of the Inland Empire," Spokane is the cultural and financial center of the inland Northwest.

Spokane began as a Native American village at a roaring waterfall where each autumn salmon ascended in great numbers. American settlers built a sawmill at the falls in 1873. Several railroads arrived after 1881, and Spokane soon became the transportation hub of eastern Washington. In 1885 Spokane built the first hydroelectric plant west of the Mississippi. Downtown boomed after the fire of 1889, as the city grew rich from mining ventures in Washington, Idaho, and Montana, and from shipping the wheat grown on the Palouse hills.

Until they were cleared away for the 1974 World's Fair, bridges and railroad trestles hid Spokane's magnificent falls from view. Today they form the heart of downtown's Riverfront Park, and the city rises from the falls in a series of broad terraces to the valley's rim. Urban parks are among Spokane's assets. The dry, hot summers here make it easy to plan golf, fishing, and hiking excursions; long, snowy winters provide nearly six months to enjoy skiing, snowboarding, and sledding.

GETTING HERE AND AROUND

Airport Transfers. Many hotels offer a free airport shuttle service. Spokane Transit runs about hourly, 6–6 daily, and costs $1. Wheatland Express has shuttle service between the Spokane Airport and Pullman and Moscow, Idaho. Reservations are recommended; the cost is $39 one-way. Yellow Cab serves the Spokane area. Metered fares run about $2.50 a mile. A taxi ride from the Spokane airport to downtown costs about $20.

Contacts Spokane International Airport (✉ *9000 W. Airport Dr., Spokane* ☎ *509/455–6455* ⊕ *www.spokaneairports.net*). **Spokane Transit Authority**

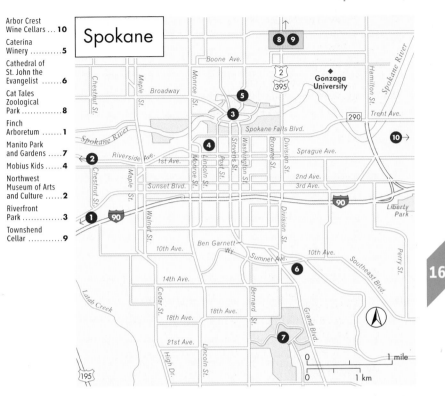

(☎ 509/456–7277). **Wheatland Express** (☎ 509/334–2200 or 800/334–2207).
Yellow Cab (☎ 509/624–4321).

Bus Travel. Greyhound Lines runs daily to Spokane from Seattle (5–6½
hours) and Portland (8–13 hours). The line serves Ephrata, Moses Lake,
Okanogan, Omak, Pasco, Pullman, Quincy, Ritzville, and Walla Walla.
Spokane has an extensive local bus system. The fare is $1.50; exact
change or a token is required. Pick up schedules, maps, and tokens at
the bus depot or the Plaza, the major downtown transfer point.

Contact Greyhound Lines (⊠ 221 W. 1st Ave., in Amtrak station ☎ 509/624–
5251 ⊕ www.greyhound.com). **The Plaza** (⊠ 701 W. Riverside Ave. ☎ 509/456–
7277 ⊕ www.spokanetransit.com).

Car Travel. Spokane can be reached by I–90 from the east or west. U.S.
395 runs north from Spokane to Colville and the Canadian border.
Downtown Spokane is laid out along a true grid: streets run north–
south, avenues east–west; many are one-way. Spokane's heaviest traffic
is on I–90 between Spokane and Spokane Valley on weekday evenings.
Metered parking is available on city streets; there are also several downtown lots.

Train Travel. Amtrak's *Empire Builder* runs daily between Spokane
and Seattle and between Spokane and Portland, stopping at points in

between (including Ephrata and Pasco). Reservations are recommended. Round-trip fares vary depending on season; $160 is an average fare between Seattle and Spokane.

Contact Amtrak (☎ *800/872–7245* ⊕ *www.amtrak.com*).

VISITOR INFORMATION

Spokane Area Visitors Information (✉ *201 W. Main St.* ☎ *509/747–3230 or 888/776–5263* ⊕ *www.visitspokane.com*).

EXPLORING

TOP ATTRACTIONS

❻ Cathedral of St. John the Evangelist. An architectural masterpiece, the church was constructed with sandstone from Tacoma and Boise and limestone from Indiana. It's considered one of America's most important and beautiful Gothic cathedrals. The cathedral's renowned 49-bell carillon has attracted international guest musicians. ✉ *127 E. 12th Ave.* ☎ *509/838–4277* ⊕ *www.stjohns-cathedral.org* ☞ *Free* ☉ *Tours Wed., Fri., Sat. 11–2.*

❼ Manito Park and Gardens. A pleasant place to stroll in summer, this 90-acre park has a formal Renaissance-style garden, conservatory, Japanese garden, duck pond, and rose and perennial gardens. Snowy winters find its hills full of sledders and its frozen pond packed with skaters. ✉ *S. Grand Blvd. between 17th and 25th Aves.* ☎ *509/363–5422* ☞ *Free* ☉ *Daily; summer 4 AM–11 PM, winter 5 AM–10 PM; Japanese garden daily Apr.–Oct., 8 AM to ½ hr before dusk.*

 Fodor's Choice ★

❹ Mobius Kids. Spokane's 16,000-square-foot children's museum is on the first floor of River Park Square and has seven interactive galleries for hands-on learning. Exhibits include a Safety Town with a fire truck and medical area, an art studio, a science exhibit called Geotopica, and a Filipino village with home, market, and boat. A Mobius Science Center is currently being developed as well, with 2011 projected as the opening date. ✉ *808 W. Main St.* ☎ *509/624–5437* ⊕ *www.mobiusspokane.org* ☞ *$5.75* ☉ *Mon.–Sat. 10–5, Sun. 11–5.*

❷ Northwest Museum of Arts and Culture. What is affectionately referred to as the MAC is in an impressive six-level glass-and-wood structure. The museum has an audiovisual display and artifacts that trace Spokane's history as well as a fine Native American collection that includes baskets and beadwork of the Plateau Indians. The MAC also hosts several traveling exhibits each year. Wander the adjacent Victorian, the Campbell House, to admire the interior or view mining-era exhibits; guided tours are available by reservation only. ✉ *2316 W. 1st Ave.* ☎ *509/456–3931* ⊕ *www.northwestmuseum.org* ☞ *$7* ☉ *Wed.–Sat. 10–6, 1st Fri. until 8.*

❸ Riverfront Park. The 100-acre park is what remains of Spokane's Expo '74. Sprawling across several islands in the Spokane River, near the falls, the park was developed from old railroad yards. One of the modernist buildings houses an IMAX theater. The opera house occupies the former Washington State pavilion. The outdoor Ice Palace is open mid-October through March. The stone clock tower of the former Great Northern

A GOOD TOUR

Numbers correspond to points of interest on the Spokane map.

Begin your tour of Spokane west of downtown at the ❶**Finch Arboretum** on Woodland Boulevard off Sunset Boulevard. From the arboretum, head east on Sunset Boulevard, left on Chestnut Street, and left on First Avenue to get to the ❷**Northwest Museum of Arts and Culture**. Riverside Avenue, a block north of First Avenue, leads east to ❸**Riverfront Park**. From here you can see Spokane Falls. If you have kids in tow, make a stop before or after the park at ❹**Mobius Kids**, the children's museum in River Park Square shopping center. Across from Riverfront Park, check out the ❺**Caterina Winery**. About 1 mi south of downtown off Grand Boulevard is the ❻**Cathedral of St. John the Evangelist**, and the pleasant ❼**Manito Park and Gardens** are about six blocks south of here.

If you have time to venture out of the city, head north on Division Street, which becomes U.S. 2 (Newport Highway) to ❽**Cat Tales Zoological Park**, about 13 mi from downtown. From here a 2-mi drive east will take you to ❾**Townshend Cellar**, where you can sample Columbia Valley and huckleberry wines (open Fri.–Sun., noon–6). Drive through the countryside another 10 mi south to reach ❿**Arbor Crest Wine Cellars** and its pleasant views of the Spokane River. From here, head north to I–90 for the 6-mi drive back to downtown.

TIMING

You could easily drive the in-city route in an hour. Plan to spend a half day at Riverfront Park and two hours at the Northwest Museum of Arts and Culture, with at least a half hour to an hour for stops at the other sights. For the destinations outside of the city, figure on driving about 1½ hours round-trip from downtown and making half-hour stops at each site.

16

Railroad Station, built in 1902, stands in sharp architectural contrast to the Expo '74 building. A children's train chugs around the park in summer, and a 1909 carousel, hand-carved by master builder Charles I. D. Looff, is a local landmark. Another icon here is the giant red slide shaped like a Radio Flyer wagon. ⊠ *507 N. Howard St.* ☎ *509/625–6600 or 800/336–7275* ⊕ *www.spokaneriverfrontpark.com* ⊠ *Park: free. Fees for some attractions. Summer and winter day passes for seasonal activities: $13–$16* ☉ *Park, daily 4 AM–midnight. Attraction hrs vary.*

WORTH NOTING

❿ **Arbor Crest Wine Cellars.** The eclectic mansion of Royal Riblet, the inventor of a square-wheel tractor and the poles that hold up ski lifts, was built in 1924. Sample complimentary Arbor Crest wines, enjoy the striking view of the Spokane River below, or meander through the impeccably kept grounds (the house isn't open to tours). Enjoy Sunday evening concerts (5:30 PM–sunset) for $5 from June through September. Local musicians perform Thursday evenings in summer too; no cover charge. ⊠ *4705 N. Fruithill Rd.* ☎ *509/927–9463* ⊕ *www.arborcrest. com* ⊠ *$5 tasting fee* ☉ *Daily noon–5; extended hrs in summer.*

Riverfront Park

⑤ Caterina Winery. Featuring wines that have won both national and international awards, this is also one of Washington's few downtown wineries. It's now also home to Lone Canary Winery. It's in the Broadview Building, formerly home to Carnation Dairy, across the river from Riverfront Park. In 2010 Don Townshend of Townshend Cellars bought the winery. Enjoy live music and wine specials during citywide First Friday events. ⊠ *905 N. Washington St.* ☎ *509/328–5069* ⊕ *www.caterinawinery.com* ⊗ *Wed.–Sun. noon–6.*

⑧ Cat Tales Zoological Park. Among the large cats living at this zoo are lions, tigers, ligers (a combination of lion and tiger), leopards, pumas, and lynxes. Guided tours give background on the animals. There's also a petting zoo. ⊠ *N. 17020 Newport Hwy., 12 mi north of I–90, Mead* ☎ *509/238–4126* ⊕ *www.cattales.org* ⊠ *$8* ⊗ *May–Sept., Tues.–Sun. 10–6; Oct.–Apr., Tues.–Sun. 10–4.*

① Finch Arboretum. This mile-long green patch along Garden Springs Creek has an extensive botanical garden with more than 2,000 labeled trees, shrubs, and flowers. Follow the walking tour on well-manicured paths along the creek, or follow your whim—depending on the season—through flowering rhododendrons, hibiscus, magnolias, dogwoods, hydrangeas, and more. ⊠ *3404 W. Woodland Blvd., off Sunset Blvd.* ☎ *509/624–4832* ⊠ *Free* ⊗ *Daily dawn–dusk.*

⑨ Townshend Cellar. A drive to the Green Bluff countryside about 13 mi northeast of downtown leads wine lovers to this small winery and its tasting room. Open since 1998, it's won awards for its cabernet sauvignon, and also makes merlot, chardonnay, syrah, port, gewürztraminer, and chenin blanc. Berries from nearby Idaho are used in huckleberry port, blush, and sparkling wine. ✉ *16112 N. Greenbluff Rd., via N. Division and U.S. 2 N, Colbert* ☎ *509/238–1400* ⊕ *www.townshendcellar.com* 🏷 *Free* ☉ *Open Fri.–Sun. noon–6 and by appointment.*

EN ROUTE

About 20 mi west of Spokane, the tree-shaded Cheney campus of **Eastern Washington University** (✉ *526 5th St., Cheney* ☎ *509/359–6200* ⊕ *www.ewu.edu*) has six original buildings on the National Register of Historic Places, but most of the 300-acre campus consists of post–World War II concrete-and-glass structures. **The Gallery of Art** (☎ *509/359–2494*) has changing exhibits of works by local and nationally known artists throughout the school year. It's open weekdays 9–5; admission is free.

WHERE TO EAT

$–$$
CONTINENTAL

✕ **Catacombs.** Catacombs wins accolades for its unique setting and menu. The underground restaurant is in the former boiler room of the Montvale Hotel. Modeling his creation on pubs and underground restaurants he's visited on his travels, owner Rob Brewster has incorporated stone walls, iron chandeliers, lots of brick, and wall tapestries. Try a thin-crust pizza or one of the European specialties, such as Hungarian goulash. For dessert, pretend you're camping and toast s'mores at your table. ✉ *10 S. Monroe St.* ☎ *509/838–4610* ⊕ *www.catacombspub.com* 🍽 *AE, D, MC, V* ☉ *No lunch.*

$$–$$$
SEAFOOD

✕ **Clinkerdagger.** In a former flour mill with great views of the Spokane River, Clink's has been a Spokane institution since 1974. The seafood, steaks, and prime rib are excellent; the mac and cheese and Kobe meat loaf are both popular at lunch. Happy hour runs daily 4–6 and also 9–close on Fridays and Saturdays. ✉ *621 W. Mallon Ave.* ☎ *509/328–5965* ⊕ *www.clinkerdagger.com* 🍽 *AE, D, DC, MC, V* ☉ *No lunch Sun.*

¢–$
AMERICAN

✕ **Elk Public House.** This eatery in the relaxed Browne's Addition neighborhood, west of downtown, serves pub food such as lamb sandwiches, pastas, salads, and many vegetarian dishes, together with 18 microbrews, most from the Northwest. A copper bar stands along one wall, in front of a mirror, giving the interior a saloonlike appearance. ✉ *1931 W. Pacific Ave.* ☎ *509/363–1973* ⊕ *www.wedonthaveone.com* 🍽 *Reservations not accepted* 🍽 *MC, V.*

¢–$
AMERICAN

✕ **Frank's Diner.** Right off the Maple Street Bridge, this is the state's oldest railroad-car restaurant. Built as an observation car in 1906, it has original light fixtures, stained-glass windows, and mahogany details. Breakfast is the specialty here, and portions are large; for dinner there's such comfort food as turkey with mashed potatoes. Everything is made from scratch. The North Spokane branch, which opened in 2005, is housed in a luxury Pullman car built in 1913. ✉ *1516 W. 2nd Ave.* ☎ *509/747–8798* ✉ *10929 N. Newport Hwy.* ☎ *509/465–2464* ⊕ *www.franksdiners.com* 🍽 *AE, MC, V.*

$–$$
ECLECTIC
Fodor'sChoice
★

✕ **Latah Bistro.** Tucked into a strip mall in south Spokane near Qualchan Golf Course, Dave and Heather Dupree's neighborhood restaurant serves a diverse menu that changes frequently and includes pasta, duck, pork, beef, shrimp, and ahi tuna. Pizzas, including the eclectic coconut-curry-chicken pizza, are baked in a wood-burning oven. Try

16

the Idaho rainbow trout with hazelnut-sage pesto, crimini mushrooms, and roasted potatoes. Save room for dessert. You'll want to try the pumpkin-bread pudding or the "bucket of love" (flourless mini-chocolate cakes dusted with spices). On Monday, bottles of wine are half off; Thursday martinis are $5. Enjoy live music on Wednesday. ⊠ *4241 S. Cheney–Spokane Rd.* ☎ *509/838–8338* ⊕ *www.latahbistro.com* ⊟ *AE, D, MC, V.*

$$–$$$
ECLECTIC
Fodor's Choice
★
✕ **Luna**. You'll find inventive approaches to classics here, including pork, chicken, salmon, and lamb. The menu highlights fresh ingredients grown in the restaurant's garden and changes seasonally. Sunday brunch has such treats as scrambled-egg salad with field greens and smoked bacon and French toast with apple butter. Luna is especially known for its extensive wine list, with more than 900 vintages, and has a wine bar as well. The rose terrace and courtyard are open in summer. ⊠ *5620 S. Perry St.* ☎ *509/448–2383* ⊕ *www.lunaspokane.com* ⊟ *AE, D, MC, V.*

$$–$$$
SEAFOOD
✕ **Milford's Fish House**. This brick and terra-cotta tile structure was built in 1925, and the terrazzo floor and tin ceiling are relics of that era. The interior's exposed brick walls and wood details, lit by candles, create a romantic environment in which to enjoy the wide array of seafood dishes and steaks. Everything is fresh here, and it is hard to predict what the menu will include, but you might find such offerings as tuna, cod, salmon, snapper, mahimahi, clams, and prawns. Pan-fried oysters are a house specialty. ⊠ *719 N. Monroe St.* ☎ *509/326–7251* ⊕ *www. milfordsfishhouse.com* ⊟ *AE, D, MC, V* ۞ *No lunch.*

$$$–$$$$
ECLECTIC
✕ **Mizuna Restaurant**. Fresh flowers and redbrick walls lend both color and charm to this downtown eatery. Local produce is the inspiration for such scrumptious vegetarian fare as white cheddar–and-apple salad and fried latkes with leeks and dill apple-pear chutney. Natural Brandt Ranch steak is served with gremolata, crimini quinoa, charred peppers, and seasonal vegetables. Ask about weekly specials, too. The wine bar highlights Northwest wines. The patio is open for outdoor dining May through September. ⊠ *214 N. Howard St.* ☎ *509/747–2004* ⊕ *www. mizuna.com* ⊟ *AE, D, MC, V* ۞ *No lunch Sun.*

$$–$$$
GREEK
✕ **Niko's Greek Restaurant and Wine Bar**. Sunlight streaming through the large storefront windows renders the dining room bright and cheerful. Lamb is the specialty here, served in a variety of ways, including curried, grilled with rosemary, and grilled on skewers in a marinade of lemon, garlic, and white wine. There are several vegetarian dishes, including spanakopita and roasted red-pepper orzo. Niko's boasts the largest wine list in the inland Northwest—more than 1,200 choices. ⊠ *725 W. Riverside Ave.* ☎ *509/624–7444* ⊕ *www.nikosspokane.com* ⊟ *AE, D, MC, V* ۞ *No lunch except on Fri.*

¢–$
AMERICAN
✕ **Post Street Ale House**. Adjacent to Hotel Lusso, the Post Street Ale House is a casual eatery with an affordable menu. There's standard pub fare like fish-and-chips, burgers, and sausage dogs, and several kinds of pasta and salads, too. Seared halibut tacos with pineapple salsa, served with a cup of black-bean soup, are a great value. About 20 beers are on tap, and Guinness-braised short ribs also pay homage to the ale. ⊠ *1 N. Post St* ☎ *509/789–6900* ⊕ *www.hotellusso.com/dining/alehouse* ⊟ *AE, D, MC, V*

S–SS
ITALIAN
✕ **Rock City Grill**. This upbeat restaurant, which is close to Riverfront Park, has excellent pastas and gourmet wood-fired pizzas, including their most popular, the Thai, with marinated chicken and prawns. Expect some kidding around from the outgoing staff, who will make sure your soft drinks and lemonades never go empty. Save room for such desserts as tiramisu and the Italian favorite, spumoni ice cream. If you love Thai peanut sauce, take some home; it's available by the bottle. ⊠ 808 W. Main St. ☎ 509/455–4400 ⊕ www.rockcitygrill.com ▤ AE, MC, V.

$$$
FRENCH
✕ **Sante Restaurant and Charcuterie**. Spectacular French cuisine that isn't too rich and saucy is the focus here. Local and organic ingredients are creatively presented in such items as goat cheese–and-leek-stuffed crepes. The cold fromage plate brings to mind an outdoor picnic, with three cheeses, salami (from the on-site charcuterie), local fruit, and a baguette. For a heartier meal, try the Kobe rib-eye steak, free-range chicken, or pepper-encrusted tofu. The restaurant is small, and service can sometimes be slow; ask for a window seat to people-watch, and remember that the European approach to eating is all about savoring. If there's a wait to be seated, consider browsing in Auntie's Bookstore right next door. Brunch is offered daily. ⊠ 404 W. Main ☎ 509/315–4693 ⊕ www.santespokane.com ▤ AE, D, MC, V.

¢–S
AMERICAN
✕ **Steelhead Bar & Grill**. This casual pub-style eatery is popular for its convenient downtown location and affordable prices. Housed in one of Spokane's many older brick buildings, the interior design has an urban contemporary vibe, with lots of burnished-metal artwork by local artists. About a dozen beers are on tap, but this is a place the whole family can enjoy; there's a decent kids' menu with the usual favorites. Sandwiches and burgers make this a handy place for lunch; kebabs, steak, and halibut-and-chips are heartier fare for dinner, and steelhead is definitely on the menu too. ⊠ 218 N. Howard ☎ 509/747–1303 ⊕ www. steelheadbarandgrille.com ⧄ Reservations not accepted on Fri. and Sat. nights ▤ AE, D, MC, V.

16

WHERE TO STAY

¢–S
▦ **Angelica's Bed and Breakfast**. On a tree-lined residential street, this 1907 brick mansion is a paradigm of Victorian elegance, with polished-wood floors, lace curtains, beautiful antique furniture, and period lighting. Each individually appointed room has its own charm: Jessica, for example, has a tile fireplace and view of the trees. **Pros:** bountiful breakfast; pleasant and helpful innkeeper. **Cons:** previous on-site culinary services no longer available, but restaurants are nearby. ⊠ 1321 W. 9th Ave. ☎ 509/324–8428 ⊕ www.angelicasbedandbreakfast.com ⧄ 4 rooms ⧄ In-room: no phone, a/c, no TV (some), Wi-Fi. In-hotel: Wi-Fi hotspot ▤ MC, V ⦿ BP.

$$–$$$
Fodor's Choice
★
▦ **The Davenport Hotel & Tower**. Elegant rooms in the main hotel have hand-carved mahogany furniture and fine Irish linens, as well as high-speed Internet access and flat-screen TVs. Though the sleeping areas are not huge, the marble bathrooms, with big soaking tubs and separate showers, are spacious and inviting. You can dine in the restaurant or in the Peacock Lounge, which serves light fare. On the lobby level are an

espresso bar, candy and flower shops, and an art gallery. Helpful concierges were recently equipped with iPads as a new way to help guests get the most from their stay. The 21-floor Tower building across the street, more than doubles the number of rooms, making the Davenport the fourth-largest hotel in Washington. The contemporary-style rooms have 32-inch flat-screen LCD TVs and marble showers and vanities, but no bathtubs. The Safari Grill restaurant in the new Tower serves breakfast, lunch, dinner, and a late-night menu, and often has great specials. **Pros:** main hotel's historical restoration is a marvel to see; abundant resort-like amenities; experienced service. **Cons:** no coffeemakers or minibars in rooms; no bathtubs in Tower rooms. ⊠ *10 S. Post St.* ☎ *509/455–8888 or 800/899–1482* 🖷 *509/624–4455* ⊕ *www.davenporthotel.com* ⟿ *563 rooms, 48 suites* ⚬ *In-room: a/c, safe, Internet, Wi-Fi. In-hotel: 3 restaurants, room service, bars, pools, gym, spa, laundry service, parking (paid), some pets allowed* ⊟ *AE, D, DC, MC, V.*

$ 🏨 **Hotel Lusso.** This classy boutique hotel features Italian marble tile ornamenting the floor, archways, and fountains of its elegant lobby. Guest rooms are appointed with European furnishings and many modern amenities, including flat-screen TVs. In 2009 the hotel was purchased by the owners of the Davenport Hotel, who have been busy upgrading and improving it. **Pros:** small and intimate; luxurious rooms. **Cons:** no pool or similar amenities, though a day pass to the Davenport across the street can be purchased; no coffeemaker or minibar. ⊠ *N. 1 Post St.* ☎ *509/747–9750* 🖷 *509/747–9751* ⊕ *www.hotellusso.com* ⟿ *36 rooms, 12 suites* ⚬ *In-room: a/c, safe, Wi-Fi. In-hotel: gym, laundry service, parking (paid)* ⊟ *AE, D, DC, MC, V.*

¢–$ 🏨 **Marianna Stolz House.** Across from Gonzaga University on a tree-lined street, this B&B is an American foursquare home built in 1908. Listed on Spokane's historical register, it's decorated with leaded-glass china cabinets, Renaissance Revival armchairs, and original dark-fir woodwork. **Pros:** convenient location; rich history. **Cons:** shared bathroom for some rooms. ⊠ *427 E. Indiana Ave.* ☎ *509/483–4316 or 800/978–6578* ⊕ *www.mariannastoltzhouse.com* ⟿ *4 rooms, 2 with bath* ⚬ *In-room: no phone, a/c, Wi-Fi. In-hotel: Internet terminal, Wi-Fi hotspot* ⊟ *AE, D, MC, V* ⊖*BP.*

$$ 🏨 **Montvale Hotel.** Housed in one of Spokane's recently-restored historic buildings, this intimate boutique hotel has spacious rooms with comfortable beds, classy retro decor, and flat-screen TVs. Bathrooms are spacious too, some with two-headed showers. (A few of the standard queens don't have tubs, so if that's important to you, ask about that when reserving.) The second-floor lobby is a welcoming place to read a book or admire the glass atrium and art deco steel canopy. **Pros:** helpful and pleasant service; good value. **Cons:** noise from trucks, trains, and nearby nightlife can be distracting; very small hotel, so no recreational amenities. ⊠ *105 First Ave.* ☎ *509/747–1919 or 866/668–8253* ⊕ *www. montvalehotel.com* ⟿ *36 rooms* ⚬ *In-room: a/c, Internet, Wi-Fi. In-hotel: restaurant, bar, Wi-Fi hotspot, parking (paid)* ⊟ *AE, D, MC, V* ⊖*CP.*

$–$$ 🖫 **Red Lion Hotel at the Park.** This hotel is adjacent to Riverfront Park
☺   and just a two-block walk from the downtown shopping district. All
floors in the main building open onto an atrium lobby; more guest
rooms are in two newer wings. Bathrooms feature granite counters
and multi-spray shower heads, and rooms have been upgraded with
flat-screen TVs. In summer, cool off in the swimming lagoon's waterfalls and waterslide. An indoor pool and hot tub are open year-round.
Pros: Pool area is popular with families; location is great; good service. **Cons:** Very large hotel; some say it needs updating and have had
issues with cleanliness. ⊠ *303 W. North River Dr.* ☎ *509/326–8000 or
800/733–5466* 🖶 *509/325–7329* ⊕ *www.redlion.com* ⇥ *400 rooms, 25
suites* ⌂ *In-room: a/c, refrigerator (some), Wi-Fi. In-hotel: 3 restaurants,
room service, bar, 2 pools, gym, laundry service, parking (paid), some
pets allowed* ⊟ *AE, D, DC,MC, V.*

$–$$ 🖫 **Red Lion River Inn.** East of Riverfront Park in the heart of downtown,
☺   this hotel overlooks the Spokane River. The property strives for a resort-
like atmosphere, with tennis, volleyball, and basketball courts, horseshoes, a Jacuzzi, and two outdoor pools. In summer, enjoy views of the
river from the patio while eating at Ripples Riverside Grill restaurant.
Pros: pleasant setting; lots to do on-site. **Cons:** no elevator; some say it
feels dated. ⊠ *N. 700 Division St.* ☎ *509/326–5577 or 800/733–5466*
⊕ *www.redlion.com* ⇥ *245 rooms, 2 suites* ⌂ *In-room: a/c, Wi-Fi. In-
hotel: restaurant, room service, bar, tennis courts, pools, gym, laundry
facilities, laundry service, parking (free), some pets allowed* ⊟ *AE, D,
DC, MC, V.*

16

NIGHTLIFE AND THE ARTS

NIGHTLIFE

At the **Blue Spark** (⊠ *15 S. Howard St.* ☎ *509/838–5787*) the '80s are
still trendy, as evidenced by the music and decor. It's known for great
service, great drinks, and a party atmosphere. Check out Monday open-
mike night, Tuesday trivia, and live music on the weekends.

Downstairs at **Dempsey's Brass Rail** (⊠ *909 W. 1st St.* ☎ *509/747–5362*)
is Spokane's most popular gay bar and restaurant; upstairs it's a dance
club popular with the local college crowd, both gay and straight. There's
a cover on weekends after 9 and dancing until 2 AM, a daily happy hour,
and karaoke Monday and Wednesday nights.

Named Spokane's best new nightspot in 2010 by a local magazine, **Gib-
liano Brothers** (⊠ *718 W. Riverside Ave.* ☎ *509/315–8765*) has brought
dueling pianos to town. Every Thursday through Saturday three pianists
duke it out on the ivories, playing both popular and offbeat tunes—
and, of course, they take requests. Monday is open mike night. There's
karaoke on Tuesday, and on Wednesday solo pianists are scheduled.

The **MarQuee Lounge** (⊠ *522 W. Riverside Ave.* ☎ *509/838–3332*) is
Spokane's most happening dance club, where the young and stylish
go to see and be seen. Calling itself a "London" style bar, it features a
two-story wall of liquor and VIP sections encased in glass.

THE ARTS

Interplayers Ensemble (✉ *174 S. Howard St.* ☎ *509/455–7529*) is a professional theater company whose season runs September–May. The 200-seat **Spokane Civic Theatre** (✉ *1020 N. Howard St.* ☎ *509/325–2507 or 800/446–9576*) presents musicals and dramas on two stages August–June.

The Knitting Factory Concert House (✉ *919 W. Sprague* ☎ *509/244–3279* ⊕ *sp.knittingfactory.com*) hosts national acts ranging from the Deftones to Hanson to the Reverend Horton Heat in its 1,500-seat venue.

The **Spokane Symphony** (✉ *818 W. Riverside Ave.* ☎ *509/624–1200*) plays classical and pops concerts from September to May in the newly restored historic Martin Woldson Theater at The Fox, presents special events such as the *Nutcracker* at the INB Performing Arts Center, gives free outdoor concerts at city parks in summer, and performs chamber music in the elegant Davenport Hotel.

A THEATER IS REBORN

Built in 1931, the Fox Theater was an impressive art deco–style venue where generations of Spokanites made memories. In 2000, after years of neglect, it was slated for the wrecking ball when civic- and culture-minded citizens came to the rescue. The Spokane Symphony Orchestra purchased it and began raising funds from public and private sources to restore it and make it the orchestra's permanent home. In November 2007 the Fox reopened with 1,600 seats and a new name—Martin Woldson Theater at The Fox—in honor of the inaugural donor's father.

SHOPPING

When the **Flour Mill** (✉ *621 W. Mallon Ave.*) was built in 1895, it was a huge technical innovation. Today it's home to shops, restaurants, and offices. The mill sits virtually atop the falls, north of the river.

Upscale **River Park Square** (✉ *808 W. Main St.* ⊕ *www.riverparksquare. com*) has Nordstrom, Talbots, Williams-Sonoma, Restoration Hardware, Pottery Barn, and other national retailers—more than 30 stores in all. Several restaurants are here or nearby, and there's a 20-screen movie theater.

The two-story **Spokane Valley Mall** (✉ *14700 E. Indiana Ave.* ⊕ *www. spokanevalleymall.com*), about 12 mi east of downtown in Spokane Valley, is anchored by Macy's, Sears Roebuck, and JCPenney. It also has a movie theater and many restaurants.

SPORTS AND THE OUTDOORS

GOLF

Hangman Valley (✉ *2210 E. Hangman Valley Rd.* ☎ *509/448–1212*), an 18-hole, par-72 course, has greens fees of $26 weekdays, $28 weekends. **Indian Canyon** (✉ *4304 W. West Dr.* ☎ *509/747–5353*), an 18-hole course on the slope of a basalt canyon, has great views of North Spokane and Mt. Spokane. The greens fees are $27 weekdays, $29 weekends. At **Liberty Lake** (✉ *24403 E. Sprague Ave., Liberty Lake* ☎ *509/255–6233*), a $4.5-million course renovation was completed in 2010, giving it a whole new look. It's near MeadowWood, so avid golfers can visit both and play 36 holes. The greens fees are $26 weekdays, $28 weekends. **MeadowWood** (⊠ *24501 E. Valleyway Ave., Liberty Lake* ☎ *509/255–9539*) is Spokane's newest golf course. A Scottish-style course, it has been ranked in Washington's top 10. Greens fees are $27 weekdays, $29 weekends.

HIKING

The hills around Spokane are laced with trails, almost all of which connect with 37-mi-long **Centennial Trail**, which winds along the Spokane River. Beginning in Nine Mile Falls, northwest of Spokane, the well-marked trail ends in Idaho. Maps are available at the visitor center at 201 West Main Street. Northwest of downtown at **Riverside State Park**, a paved trail leads through a 17-million-year-old fossil forest in Deep Creek Canyon. From there it's easy to get to the western end of the Centennial Trail by crossing the suspension bridge at the day-use parking lot; trails heading both left and right will lead to the Centennial.

SKIING

49° North (⊠ *U.S. 395, Chewelah* ☎ *509/935–6649 or 866/376–4949* ⊕ *www.ski49n.com*), an hour north of Spokane in the Colville National Forest, is a 1,200-acre family-oriented resort. Lift tickets cost $42–$48; snowboards and ski package rentals are about $35. **Mt. Spokane** (⊠ *29500 N. Mt. Spokane Park Dr., Mead* ☎ *509/238–2220* ⊕ *www.mtspokane.com*), 28 mi northeast of downtown Spokane, is a modest downhill resort with a 2,000-foot drop and 10 mi of groomed cross-country ski trails. Snowshoeing and tubing are also options. There's night skiing Wednesday–Saturday. Lift tickets cost $36–$42. A state Sno-Park permit, available at the resort, is required.

ALONG ROUTE 90

If you travel along the Interstate at 70+ mph, it might seem that this area is mainly a lot of crop fields and a single town with a big lake. But slow the pace a bit and get off the beaten path to discover family-friendly activities in Moses Lake, including a lively water park and lakefront park for swimming on hot summer days. North in the town of Ephrata, local history is depicted in a pioneer village. Soap Lake is a body of water like no other, with bubbly, mineral-rich water that has been purported to have healing effects for more than a century. Closer to the Columbia River just west of Quincy, the award-winning Gorge Amphitheatre hosts concerts through the summer. Adjacent to the Gorge is the not-to-be-missed Cave B Inn at Sagecliffe, which has luxurious accommodations, fabulous river and canyon views, an estate winery, pool, spa, fine dining, and recently added upscale yurts.

MOSES LAKE

105 mi west of Spokane.

The natural lake from which this sprawling town takes its name seems to be an anomaly in the dry landscape of east-central Washington. But ever since the Columbia Basin Project took shape, there's been water everywhere. Approaching Moses Lake from the west on I–90, you'll pass lushly green irrigated fields; to the east lie vast stretches of wheat. The lakes of this region have more shorebirds than Washington's ocean beaches. Potholes Reservoir is an artificial lake that supports as much wildlife as does the Columbia Wildlife Refuge. The Winchester Wasteway, west of Moses Lake, is a great place to paddle a kayak or canoe and watch birds as you glide along the reedy banks. The airfield north of town was once a major Air Force base, and now serves as a training facility for airline pilots.

GETTING HERE

Moses Lake straddles I–90, it's about 100 mi from Spokane and 175 mi from Seattle. To the north, Highway 17 connects Moses Lake to Ephrata and points north, including Soap Lake and Coulee City.

VISITOR INFORMATION

Moses Lake Area Chamber of Commerce (⊠ *324 S. Pioneer Way, Moses Lake* ☎ *509/765–7888 or 800/992–6234* ⊕ *www.moseslake.com*).

EXPLORING

Columbia National Wildlife Refuge attracts a great number of birds: hawks, falcons, golden eagles, ducks, sandhill cranes, herons, American avocets, black-necked stilts, and yellow-headed and red-winged blackbirds. The refuge is also home to beavers, muskrats, badgers, and coyotes. It's 8 mi northwest of the town of Othello, about 20 mi southeast of Moses Lake. ⊠ *Refuge headquarters at 735 E. Main St., Othello* ☎ *509/546–8300* ⊕ *www.fws.gov/columbia* ⊠ *Free* ☉ *Daily 5–dusk; office open Mon.–Thurs. 7–4:30, Fri. 7–3:30.*

Claw-shaped, 38-foot-deep, 18-mi-long **Moses Lake** is filled by Crab Creek—which originates in the hills west of Spokane—with three side branches known as Parker Horn, Lewis Horn, and Pelican Horn. The city sprawls over the peninsulas formed by these "horns," and can therefore be a bit difficult to get around. This is the state's second-largest lake. ⊠ *Hwy. 17, off I–90.*

Fossils collected all over North America, including prehistoric land and marine animals, are exhibited at the **Moses Lake Museum and Art Center**. One gallery also has visual-arts displays. ⊠ *228 W. 3rd Ave.* ☎ *509/766–9395* ⊠ *Free* ☉ *Tues.–Sat. 11–5.*

Potholes State Park is 20 mi southwest of Moses Lake on the west side of O'Sullivan Dam. Camping and boating, as well as fishing for trout, perch, and walleye, are popular diversions. ⊠ *6762 Hwy. 262 E, Othello* ☎ *360/902–8844 or 888/226–7688* ⊕ *www.parks.wa.gov* ⊠ *$21–$28 for camping* ☉ *Summer, daily 6:30–dusk; winter, daily 8–dusk.*

★ Cool off from the hot central Washington sunshine at the **Surf 'n Slide**
☺ **Water Park**. In addition to the Olympic-sized pool, there are two 200-foot waterslides, a tube slide, a "baby octopus" slide, and diving boards. ⊠ *McCosh Park, 4th and Cedar* ☎ *509/766–9246* ⊠ *$9* ☉ *Mid-June–Aug., Mon.–Thurs. 11–6:30, Fri. and Sat. 11–7; Memorial Day–mid-June and Sept. 1–Labor Day, weekdays 4–8, weekends 11–7.*

WHERE TO EAT

$$
AMERICAN
✕ **Michael's on the Lake.** In the late afternoon golden rays of sunset wash over the dining room and deck at this lakeside restaurant. Indulge in prime rib or Parmesan-crusted halibut over linguini, or go for the lighter soups and sandwiches. There's breakfast on weekends and happy-hour specials daily 4–6 and 9–close. ⊠ *910 W. Broadway Ave.* ☎ *509/765–1611* ⊕ *www.michaelsonthelake.com* ⊟ *AE, D, MC, V.*

$$
STEAK
✕ **Porter House Steakhouse.** New owners took over one of Moses Lake's oldest restaurants in late 2009 with the goal of making it a favorite family and group gathering place. Candlelight sets a subdued tone in the dining room, and the fireplace provides further warmth and ambience. As the name implies, steaks are the main event here; complementing the beef entrées are a variety of chicken, seafood, and pasta dishes. Check out the hearty Sunday brunch and house-made desserts, including Texas sheet cake and Sherry Berry pie. ⊠ *217 N. Elder St.* ☎ *509/766–0308* ⊕ *www.porterhousesteakhouse.net* ⊟ *AE, D, MC, V.*

WHERE TO STAY

$–$$
🏨 **Comfort Suites.** New to the area, this hotel shines with modern style and conveniences, including granite counters in the bathroom, and flat-screen TVs. Clean, spacious, and comfortable rooms are considered suites because there's a sitting area separate from the beds, though not a wall. All rooms have microwaves and refrigerators. Five extended-stay suites include kitchens; there are also three Jacuzzi suites. **Pros:** clean and modern; nice pool; friendly service. **Cons:** no restaurant; prices very steep during some events. ⊠ *1700 E. Kittleson Road* ☎ *509/765–3731 or 827/424–6423* ⊕ www.comfortsuites.com 🛏 *60 rooms, 8 suites* ⚒ *In-room: a/c, refrigerator, Wi-Fi. In-hotel: pool, gym, laundry facilities, laundry service, Internet terminal, Wi-Fi hotspot, some pets allowed* ⊟ *AE, D, DC, MC, V* ❑ *CP.*

SHOPPING

Vendors come to the **Columbia Basin Farmers' Market** each Saturday in summer and early fall to sell fresh produce and handmade arts and crafts. ⊠ *Civic Center Park, 5th and Balsam Sts.* ☎ *509/765–7888* ⊙ *Mid-June–mid-Oct., Wed. 3–7, Sat. 7:30–1.*

QUINCY

34 mi northwest of Moses Lake.

On the fences along I-90 to George and north on Highway 281 to Quincy, crop identification signs highlight what the Quincy Valley is known for: agriculture. From Thanksgiving to New Year's Eve, these same fields are filled with Christmas motion-light displays, powered by electricity from farmers' irrigation lines—a delightful sight for highway travelers in the dark winter nights. Agriculture hasn't always been king in this area. Though the rich soils attracted many settlers after the railroad made the region accessible in the early 1900s, several serious droughts proved that Mother Nature could not be relied on to water the crops consistently. In the mid-1930s the federal government began to assist with irrigation plans, and by the early 1950s the first systems were in place.

Today the area has 200,000 irrigable acres growing corn, alfalfa, wheat, potatoes, seed, apples, and more. An annual Farmer Consumer Awareness Day is held the second Saturday of September, with farm tours, entertainment, food, arts and crafts, and plenty of fresh produce. Tourism is also growing here, with visitors from across the state and beyond coming to summer concerts at the Gorge Amphitheatre, touring wineries between Quincy and Wenatchee, and hiking and climbing near the Columbia River.

GETTING HERE

Quincy is 11 mi north of I-90's Exit 149, via Highway 281. It's about 2 hrs 45 min. from Seattle and 2 hrs 30 min from Spokane.

EXPLORING

Gorge Amphitheatre. The Gorge is a 20,000-seat amphitheater that has won accolades as best outdoor concert venue due to its fine acoustics and stunning vistas of the Columbia River—a setting compared to the Grand Canyon's. Set in one of the sunniest parts of the state, the concert season runs from May to September. Concertgoers often overnight at the adjacent campground or at motels and hotels in Quincy, Moses Lake, and Ellensburg. ⊠ *754 Silica Rd. NW, George* ☎ *206/628–0888 tickets* ⊕ *www.livenation.com/gorge-amphitheatre-tickets-george/venue/122913*

WHERE TO EAT AND STAY

¢

CAFÉ

☺

⤫**The Grainery.** Quincy farmers David and Harriet Weber opened their café in 2010 to feature their own farm products, including the grains used for breads and pastries baked in-house. Mornings, the locals stop in for espresso and giant cinnamon rolls to start their day. Lunch is served from 11 to 2; the café stays open until 5 on weekdays and 3 on Saturdays. Menu items change to reflect what's in season, such as the strawberry summer salad. Some Friday nights live music plays in the spacious, brightly decorated, country-cozy setting. ⊠ *101 E St. SE,* ☎ *509/797–7240* ▭ *D, MC,V* ☺ *Closed Sun. No dinner.*

$$$

Fodor's Choice

★

🏨 **Cave B Inn at Sagecliffe.** Washington's first destination winery resort is built on (and into) ancient basalt cliffs 900 feet above the Columbia River. The 15 cliff houses, cavern (with 12 rooms), and inn (with three rooms, restaurant, meeting rooms, and spacious lobby) all were designed to blend into the natural environment. The buildings' exterior walls are made of precast concrete embedded with rocks taken from the land. The inn's restaurant, Tendrils ($$–$$$), highlights local produce and Northwest beef and seafood, complemented by the wines produced on-site. Guests can tour the Cave B Estate Winery to taste and learn about the wine-making process. A pleasant spa offers an array of treatments. River views are stunning from the outdoor pool, which is open seasonally and adds a family-friendly aspect to the upscale Inn. Bikes are available to rent, and energetic guests can hike down to the river and past waterfalls. Dogs are welcome at Cave B, and the Inn's own dog Cuvée is friendly and welcoming to guests. In summer 2010 Chiwana Village, a cluster of 25 luxury yurts, opened. With views of

Cave B Inn at Sagecliffe

either the river or vineyards, they provide a close-to-the-land experience and lower-cost option to enjoy all the amenities of the resort. The yurt village is open May through October. **Pros:** fantastic place to stargaze at night; quiet and secluded; gorgeous accommodations. **Cons:** very expensive during Gorge Amphitheatre events; no local meal options besides on-site restaurant. ⊠ *344 Silica Rd. NW,* ☎ *509/785–2283 or 888/785–2283* 🖨 *509/785–3670* ⊕ *www.sagecliffe.com/Inn.htm* ⚄ *In-room: a/c, refrigerator, DVD, Internet, Wi-Fi. In-hotel: restaurant, room service, pool, gym, spa, bicycles, some pets allowed* ⊟ *AE, MC, V.*

EPHRATA

18 mi northeast of Quincy.

Ephrata (e-*fray*-tuh), a pleasant small farm town and the Grant County seat, is in the exact center of Washington. It was settled quite early because its abundant natural springs made it an oasis in the dry steppe country of the Columbia Basin. Native Americans visited the springs, as did cattle drovers after American ranchers stocked the open range. Ephrata began to grow after the Great Northern Railroad established a terminal here in 1892. Cattlemen took advantage of the railroad to round up and ship out thousands of wild horses that roamed the range. The last great roundup was held in 1906, when the remaining 2,400 horses of a herd that once numbered some 25,000 were corralled and shipped off.

GETTING HERE

Ephrata is about 20 miles north of Moses Lake via Highway 17. Continuing north on the highway leads to the town of Soap Lake, then past state parks, up to Coulee City

VISITOR INFORMATION

Ephrata Chamber of Commerce (⊠ *1 Basin St. SW,* ☎ *509/754–4656* ⊕ *www. ephratawachamber.com*).

EXPLORING

Built in the 1920s, the redbrick **Grant County Courthouse** has a facade framed by white columns and a majestic set of stairs. Although it may seem antique from the exterior, the building has a unique and progressive feature: it's heated by thermal springs. ⊠ *35 C St. NW* ☎ *509/754–2011* ⊙ *Weekdays 8–5.*

🖑 The **Grant County Historical Museum and Village** consists of more than 30 pioneer-era buildings brought here from other parts of Grant County. They include a blacksmith forge, saloon, barber shop, and printing office. ⊠ *742 Basin St. N.* ☎ *509/754–3334* ⊠ *$3.50* ⊙ *May–Sept., Mon.–Tues. and Thurs.–Sat. 10–5, Sun. 1–4.*

Soap Lake, 6 mi north of Ephrata, has water high in dissolved carbonates, sulfates, and chlorides. Even though the lake has long been famous for its mineral waters and therapeutic mud baths, the eponymous small town has never quite succeeded as a resort—perhaps because the miraculous waters have been heavily diluted by irrigation waters. But agriculture is much more profitable anyway, and many other beautiful recreation areas are nearby.

WHERE TO STAY

¢ 🏨 **Inn at Soap Lake.** Built in 1905 as a stable and blacksmith shop, this beachside structure was converted to an inn in 1915. Each room contains a soaking tub in which to enjoy Soap Lake's natural mineral water. Floral patterns dominate most rooms, which are appointed with contemporary furnishings and modern amenities. Most rooms have a wet bar with microwave, refrigerator, coffeemaker, and supply of dishes and cutlery. Some cottages are fully equipped with their own kitchens, grills, and decks for a comfortable vacation experience for families. **Pros:** beautifully landscaped gardens; private beach has lounge chairs; cozy lobby. **Cons:** no pool; registration desk is not staffed, but management is on-site. ⊠ *226 Main Ave. E, Soap Lake* ☎ *509/246–1132 or 800/557–8514* ⊕ *www.innsoaplake.com* ⇥ *20 rooms, 8 cottages* ☖ *In-room: a/c, kitchen (some), refrigerator, DVD (some), Wi-Fi. In-hotel: gym, beachfront, Wi-Fi hotspot* ⊟ *AE, D, MC, V.*

¢ 🏨 **Notaras Lodge.** The spacious rooms at this four-building lodge on
🖑 the shore of Soap Lake are individually decorated; all have a rustic log-style construction. Bathtubs offer a choice of mineral water piped in from the lake or regular water. All the spacious rooms have both a refrigerator and microwave; several have whirlpool baths, and some have a washer/dryer. **Pros:** room decor is very unusual and fun; helpful staff; interesting grounds **Cons:** not all rooms have lake views. ⊠ *13 Canna St.* ☎ *509/246–0462* ⎙ *509/246–1054* ⊕ *www.notaraslodge.com*

com 15 *rooms* In-room: *a/c, refrigerator, Wi-Fi. In-hotel: room service, beachfront, some pets allowed* D, MC, V.

NORTHEASTERN WASHINGTON

A technological marvel, the Grand Coulee Dam took nearly a decade to build in the 1930s. Its fascinating history is on display at the year-round visitors center, where tours are also available. The dam created a 150-mile long lake; several campgrounds surround it and recreational activities abound. Farther north, the Colville and Okanogan national forests are comprised of three mountain ranges that are foothills of the Rockies. These wild areas teem with wildlife and natural beauty, yet remain pristine and uncrowded. The small towns of Omak and Colville provide basic services for travelers and a couple of outstanding restaurants.

COULEE DAM NATIONAL RECREATION AREA

60 mi northeast of Ephrata, 239 mi northeast of Seattle, 87 mi northwest of Spokane.

16

Grand Coulee Dam is the one of the world's largest concrete structures. At almost a mile long, it justly deserves the moniker "Eighth Technological Wonder of the World." Beginning in 1932, 9,000 men excavated 45 million cubic yards of rock and soil and dammed the Grand Coulee, a gorge created by the Columbia River, with 12 million cubic yards of concrete—enough to build a sidewalk the length of the equator. By the time the dam was completed in 1941, 77 men had perished and 11 towns were submerged under the newly formed Roosevelt Lake. The waters backed up behind the dam turned eastern Washington's arid soil into fertile farming land, but not without consequence: salmon-fishing stations that were a source of food and spiritual identity for Native Americans were destroyed. Half the dam was built on the Colville Indian Reservation on the north shore of the Columbia; the Colville tribes later received restitution in excess of $75 million from the U.S. government.

In 1946 most of Roosevelt Lake and the grassy and pine woodland hills surrounding it were designated the Coulee Dam National Recreation Area. Crown Point Vista, about 5 mi west of Grand Coulee on Highway 174, may have the best vantage for photographs of the dam, Roosevelt Lake, Rufus Woods Lake (below the dam), and the town of Coulee Dam.

After nightfall from Memorial Day through September the dam is transformed into an unlikely entertainment complex by an extravagant, free laser-light show. With 300-foot eagles flying across the white water that flows over the dam, the show is spectacular, if hokey. The audio portion is broadcast on 90.1 FM. Show up early to get a good seat. The show starts at 10 PM Memorial Day–July, 9:30 PM in August, and 8:30 PM in September.

GETTING HERE

From Ephrata, take Highway 17 north to reach Grand Coulee. From the Spokane area, U.S. 2 and Highway 174 are the most direct route.

VISITOR INFORMATION

Grand Coulee Dam Area Chamber of Commerce (✉ *306 Midway Ave., Grand Coulee* ☎ *800/268–5332 or 509/633–3074* ⊕ *www.grandcouleedam.org*).

EXPLORING

Highway 155 passes through the **Colville Indian Reservation**, one of the largest reservations in Washington, with about 7,700 enrolled members of the Colville Confederated Tribes. This was the final home for Chief Joseph and the Nez Perce, who fought a series of fierce battles with the U.S. Army in the 1870s after the U.S. government enforced a treaty that many present-day historians agree was fraudulent. Chief Joseph lived on the Colville reservation until his death in 1904. There's a memorial to him off Highway 155 east of the town of Nespelem, 17 mi north of the dam; four blocks away (two east and two north) is his grave. You can drive through the reservation's undeveloped landscape, and except for a few highway signs you'll feel like you've time-traveled to pioneer days.

☾ The **Coulee Dam National Recreation Area Visitors Arrival Center** has colorful displays about the dam, a 13-minute film on the site's geology and the dam's construction, and information about the laser-light show. The U.S. Bureau of Reclamation, which oversees operation and maintenance of the dam, conducts tours year-round, weather and maintenance schedules permitting. You can also pick up a self-guided historical walking tour that will take you from the visitors center through the old part of town, across the bridge, and into the old engineers' town. ✉ *Hwy. 155 north of Grand Coulee* ☎ *509/633–9265* ⊕ *www.grandcouleedam. org* ✉ *Free* ☉ *Late May–July, daily 8:30 AM–11 PM; Aug., daily 8:30 AM–10:30 PM; Sept., daily 8:30 AM–9:30 PM; Oct. and Nov. and Feb.– late May, 9–5.*

The **Lake Roosevelt National Recreation Area** contains the 150-mi-long lake created by the Columbia River when it was backed up by Grand Coulee Dam. Several Native American villages, historic sites, and towns lie beneath the waters. ✉ *1008 Crest Dr., headquarters address* ☎ *509/633–9441* ⊕ *www.nps.gov/laro* ✉ *Free day use; camping $10 May–Sept., $5 Oct.–Apr.* ☉ *Daily dawn–dusk.*

At **Steamboat Rock State Park** a 2,200-foot-high flat-topped lava butte rises 1,000 feet above Banks Lake, the 31-mi-long irrigation reservoir filled with water from Lake Roosevelt by giant pumps and siphons. Water is distributed from the south end of the lake throughout the Columbia Basin. The state park has campsites, a small store, and swimming area. In summer it's popular with boaters and anglers, and in winter there's Nordic skiing. ✉ *Hwy. 155, 16 mi north of Coulee City* ☎ *360/902–8844 or 888/226–7688* ⊕ *www.parks.wa.gov* ✉ *Camping $21–$28* ☉ *Daily 6:30–dusk.*

Sun Lakes State Park is a high point in the coulee. Campgrounds, picnic areas, and a state-run golf course attract visitors year-round; in summer the lakes bristle with boaters. From the bluffs on U.S. 2, west of the dam, you can get a great view over this enormous canyon. To the

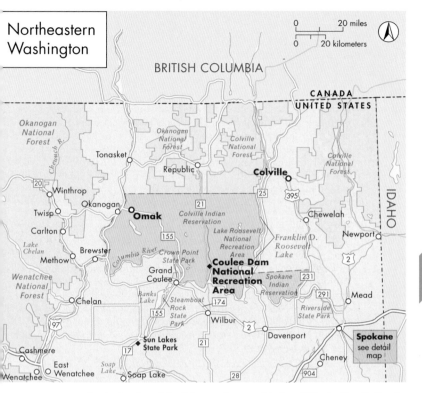

Northeastern
Washington

BRITISH COLUMBIA

CANADA
UNITED STATES

north, the banks of the lake are hemmed in by cliffs. At Dry Falls, the upstream erosion of the canyon caused by the floods stops. Below Dry Falls, steep, barren cliffs—some 1,000 feet tall—rise from green meadows, marshes, and blue lakes bordered by trees. Most of the water is irrigation water seeping through the porous rock, but the effect is no less spectacular. Eagles and ravens soar along the cliffs, while songbirds, ducks, and geese hang out in the bottomlands.

South of the Sun Lakes, the landscape turns even wilder. The coulee narrows and the cliffs often look like they are on fire, an illusion created by the bold patterns of orange and yellow lichens. The waters of the lakes change, too. The deep blue waters of the small lakes below Dry Falls are replaced by lapis lazuli in the Sun Lakes and turn milky farther south. Presentations at the park's interpretive center at Dry Falls survey the area's geology, and an excellent film describes the great floods. ⊠ *From Grand Coulee Dam take Hwy. 155 south, U.S. 2 east, and Hwy. 17 south* ☎ *360/902–8844 or 888/226–7688* ⊕ *www.parks. wa.gov* ⌨ *$21–$28 camping* ⊙ *Daily 6:30–dusk.*

WHERE TO EAT AND STAY

¢ ✕ **Flo's Cafe**. One mile south of the dam, this diner dishes up heaps
AMERICAN of local color along with loggers' food: biscuits and gravy, corned-beef hash, hamburgers, chicken-fried steak, and chef's salads. Flo's is

open for breakfast but closes at 1. ⊠ *316 Spokane Way, Grand Coulee* ☎ *509/633–3216* ▤ *D, MC, V* ◷ *No dinner.*

$ ✕ **Melody Restaurant**. This casual, family-friendly spot with excellent
AMERICAN views of Grand Coulee Dam prepares sandwiches, steaks, seafood,
☾ and pasta, and is open for breakfast. ⊠ *512 River Dr., Coulee Dam*
☎ *509/633–1151* ▤ *AE, D, MC, V.*

$ ⊡ **Columbia River Inn**. The well-appointed rooms all have private decks
at this inn across the street from Grand Coulee Dam, with easy access
to hiking trails and fishing. The sauna and hot tub are useful amenities after a day of active recreation. **Pros:** rooms have microwaves
and refrigerators; pretty location. **Cons:** basic rooms on the small side;
some visitors have complained about noise. ⊠ *10 Lincoln St., Coulee
Dam* ☎ *509/633–2100 or 800/633–6421* 🖨 *509/633–2633* ⊕ *www.
columbiariverinn.com* ⤴*35 rooms* ⌂ *In-room: a/c, kitchen (some),
refrigerator, Internet, Wi-Fi. In-hotel: pool, gym, laundry facilities*
▤ *AE, D, MC, V.*

¢ ⊡ **Coulee House Motel**. This motel with "the best dam view in town"
(someone had to say it) has modern rooms decorated in earth tones.
The gift shop is open daily and stocked with souvenirs. **Pros:** rooms
have microwaves and refrigerators; good location. **Cons:** room view of
dam is from small balcony; some visitors have complained about lack
of cleanliness. ⊠ *110 Roosevelt Ave., Coulee Dam* ☎ *509/633–1101
or 800/715–7767* 🖨 *509/633–1416* ⊕ *www.couleehouse.com* ⤴*61
rooms* ⌂ *In-room: a/c, safe (some), kitchen (some), refrigerator, DVD
(some), Internet, Wi-Fi. In-hotel: pool, gym, laundry facilities, some
pets allowed* ▤ *AE, D, DC, MC, V.*

OMAK

52 mi northwest of Grand Coulee Dam.

Omak is a small mill and orchard town in the beautifully rustic Okanogan Valley of north-central Washington. Lake Omak to the southeast,
on the Colville Reservation, is part of an ancient channel of the Columbia River, which ran north prior to the last Ice Age before turning south
at Omak in what is now the lower Okanogan Valley.

For years Omak has been criticized by animal lovers for its mid-August
Omak Stampede and Suicide Race. During the annual event, wild horses
race down a steep bluff and across the Okanogan River. Some horses
have been killed and riders seriously injured. Many of the riders are
from the Colville Reservation, and elders defend the race as part of
Indian culture. Despite the detractors, more spectators attend the event
each year.

GETTING HERE
Omak can be reached from the west via Highway 20 from the Methow
Valley area. From Ephrata, head north via Highway 17, then Highway
97. From Grand Coulee Dam, take WA 155N.

EXPLORING
☾ At the **Okanogan County Historical Museum** you'll find displays of Okanogan pioneer life and a replica of an Old West town. Outside are Okanogan's oldest building, a 19th-century log cabin, and antique farm

equipment. ⊠ *1410 2nd Ave. N* ☎ *509/422–4272* 🖃 *$2* ⊙ *Memorial Day weekend–Labor Day, daily 10–4; otherwise by appointment.*

The **Okanogan National Forest** is a region of open woods, meadows, and pastoral river valleys in the Okanogan highlands. There's lots of wildlife: deer, black bears, coyotes, badgers, bobcats, cougars, grouse, hawks, and golden eagles. Campgrounds are scattered throughout the region. There are 11 snow parks with groomed trails for snowmobilers, and open areas for cross-country skiing. Ski areas are at Loup Loup Pass (Nordic and alpine) and Sitzmark (alpine only). ⊠ *1240 2nd Ave. S (office)* ☎ *509/826–3275* ⊕ *www.fs.fed.us/r6/oka* 🖃 *Free* ⊙ *Office: weekdays 7:45–4:30.*

WHERE TO EAT AND STAY

$–$$
ECLECTIC
Fodor'sChoice
★

✕ **Breadline Cafe.** For nearly 30 years, Breadline has been a top destination for dinner and live music in the Okanogan Valley. A varied menu highlights local organic produce, locally-raised natural Angus beef, crepes, and seafood. You'll find Cajun dishes such as jambalaya, as well as an around-the-world assortment of cuisines, including Italian and Greek. Enjoy the breakfast buffet on Saturdays. Enjoy half-price appetizers at Thursday-night wine tastings. ⊠ *102 S. Ash St.* ☎ *509/826–5836* ⊕ *www.breadlinecafe.com* ▭ *AE, D, DC, MC, V* ⊙ *Closed Sun. and Mon.*

¢

🛏 **Omak Inn.** Just off U.S. 97, this motel is close to restaurants and shopping. A small patio and expansive lawn behind the pool allow for relaxing in the summer heat or walking the dog. All rooms are "mini-suites," with a separate sitting area. **Pros:** most rooms have microwaves and refrigerators; reasonable rates. **Cons:** room decor is basic; some complaints about customer service. ⊠ *912 Koala Dr.* ☎ *509/826–3822 or 800/204–4800* 🖶 *509/826–2980* ⊕ *www.omakinnwa.com* ⤴ *66 rooms* ⚮ *In-room: a/c, refrigerator (some), Internet (some), Wi-Fi (some). In-hotel: pool, gym, laundry facilities, some pets allowed* ▭ *AE, D, MC, V* ⋔⃝*| CP.*

16

COLVILLE

115 mi east of Omak.

This small town, the seat of Stevens County, sits in a valley surrounded by lakes, forests, and mountains. The town has many well-maintained old houses and a pleasant, well-to-do atmosphere. Colville became regionally famous in 1983 when Mike Hale opened Hale's Microbrewery—which later moved to the Seattle area.

GETTING HERE
Colville is a direct drive north of Spokane via Highway 395.

VISITOR INFORMATION
Colville Chamber of Commerce (⊠ *121 E. Astor Ave.* ☎ *509/684–5973* ⊕ *www.colville.com*).

EXPLORING
Colville National Forest is a vast region encompassing mountains, forests, and meadows in the state's northeast corner. Here the desert area ends, and three mountain ranges (Selkirks, Kettle River, and

Okanogan)—considered foothills of the Rocky Mountains—traverse the region from north to south. It's a beautiful, wild area, where only the river bottoms are dotted with widely spaced settlements and where the mountains (whose average height is about 4,500 feet) are largely pristine. The streams abound with trout, and the forests with deer and black bears. This is perfect backpacking country, with many trails to remote mountain lakes. ⊠ *765 S. Main St.* ☎ *509/684–7000* ⊕ *www. fs.fed.us/r6/colville* ⊒ *Free* ☉ *Daily dawn–dusk.*

At the **Keller Heritage Center** you can see a farmstead, lookout tower, trappers' cabins, blacksmith shop, sawmill, and museum. ⊠ *700 N. Wynne St.* ☎ *509/684–5968* ⊕ *www.stevenscountyhistoricalsociety.org* ⊒ *$5* ☉ *May–Sept., daily 1–4; Oct.–April, by appointment.*

WHERE TO EAT AND STAY

$–$$
AMERICAN
Fodor's Choice
★

✕ **Lovitt Restaurant.** As it's located in a 1908 farmhouse, it's no surprise that the emphasis here is on farm-fresh ingredients. While "eat local" has become a trendy concept in recent years, owners Norman and Kristen Six are sincerely committed to utilizing products from local farms and vendors. Their original Lovitt Restaurant in Chicago won numerous accolades, and their talents have been well received in the inland Northwest since their move back in 2005 to where Norman grew up. The menu changes frequently depending on what's in season, but you can expect to find at least one vegetarian dish, as well as steak and burgers made from grass-fed beef. Chocolate bonbons are a favorite dessert item. In summer, enjoy outside dining with views of the bucolic Colville Valley. ⊠ *149 Hwy. 395 S* ☎ *509/684–5444* ⊕ *www.lovittrestaurant. com* ⊟ *AE, MC, V* ☉ *Closed Mon. and Tues. Closed Sun. Oct.–April. No lunch.*

¢

⊞ **Benny's Colville Inn.** This is a comfortable family motel nestled in a pristine valley between the Kettle River and Selkirk mountain ranges. Larger king suites have both hot tubs and fireplaces. There's no gym on-site, but guests get a pass to use a nearby fitness center for free. Restaurant is adjacent. **Pros:** family-owned; friendly staff; very affordable. **Cons:** some have complained that beds are hard and rooms are small. ⊠ *915 S. Main St.* ☎ *509/684–2517 or 800/680–2517* ⊟ *509/684–2546* ⊕ *www.colvilleinn.com* ⊅ *100 rooms, 5 suites* ☖ *In-room: a/c, refrigerator (some), Wi-Fi. In-hotel: pool, laundry service, some pets allowed* ⊟ *AE, D, MC, V* ⧖ *CP.*

Vancouver and Victoria

WORD OF MOUTH

"If you loved the Museum of Anthropology in Vancouver, I hope you also got to see the Royal BC Museum in Victoria as well. That latter is also such a gem for artifacts of Pacific Coast First Nations!"
—Daniel_Williams

WELCOME TO VANCOUVER AND VICTORIA

TOP REASONS TO GO

★ **Stanley Park:** The views, the activities, and the natural wilderness beauty here are quintessential Vancouver.

★ **Granville Island:** Ride the mini-ferry across False Creek to the Granville Island Public Market, where you can shop for delicious lunch fixings; eat outside when the weather's fine.

★ **Museum of Anthropology:** The phenomenal collection of First Nations art and cultural artifacts, and the incredible backdrop, make this a must-see.

★ **The Journey here:** Yup, getting here is one of the best things about Victoria. Whether by ferry meandering past the Gulf or San Juan islands, by floatplane (try to travel at least one leg this way), or on a whale-watching boat, just getting to Victoria from the mainland is a memorable experience.

★ **Butchart Gardens:** A million and a half visitors can't be wrong—these lavish gardens north of town truly live up to the hype.

1 Vancouver. Many people say that Vancouver is the most gorgeous city in North America, and situated as it is, between mountains and water, it's hard to disagree. The Vancouver area actually covers a lot of ground, but the central core—Downtown, Gastown, Yaletown, Chinatown, Stanley Park, and Granville Island—is fairly compact. An excellent public transportation system makes getting around a snap. When in doubt, remember that the mountains are north.

2 Victoria. British Columbia's capital city, Victoria, is a lovely, walkable city with waterfront paths, lovely gardens, fascinating museums, and splendid 19th-century architecture. In some senses remote, it's roughly midway between Vancouver and Seattle and about three hours by car and ferry from either city.

Powell River

East Cove

Strait of Georgia

Parksville

Nanaimo

VANCOUVER ISLAND

Lake Cowichan

| 0 | | 15 miles |
| 0 | | 15 kilometers |

Pacific Rim National Park

Port Renfrew

Juan de Fuca Strait

British Columbia

GETTING ORIENTED

The city of Victoria is on Vancouver Island (not Victoria Island). The city of Vancouver is on the British Columbia mainland, not on Vancouver Island, or on Victoria Island (which isn't in British Columbia but rather way up north, spanning parts of Nunavut and the Northwest Territories). For the most part, Vancouver central sits on a peninsula, which makes it compact and easy to explore on foot, especially since most streets are laid out on a grid system. To get your bearings, use the mountains as your "true north" and you can't go too far wrong. All the avenues, which are numbered, have east and west designations; the higher the number, the farther away from the inlet you are. At the southern tip of Vancouver Island, forming the western point of a triangle with Seattle and Vancouver, Victoria dips slightly below the 49th parallel. That puts it farther south than most of Canada, giving it the mildest climate in the country, with virtually no snow and less than half the rain of Vancouver.

17

VANCOUVER PLANNER

Making the Most of Your Time

If you don't have much time in Vancouver, you'll probably still want to spend at least a half day in Stanley Park: start out early for a walk, bike, or trolley ride through the park to see the Vancouver Aquarium Marine Science Centre, enjoy the views from Prospect Point, and stroll the seawall. If you leave the park at English Bay, you can have lunch on Denman or Robson Street, and meander past the trendy shops between Jervis and Burrard streets. Or, exit the park at Coal Harbour and follow the Seawall Walk to Canada Place, stopping for lunch at a harbor-front restaurant. A couple of hours at the Granville Island Public Market are also a must.

Walking the downtown core is a great way to get to know the city. Start at Canada Place and head east to Gastown and Chinatown; that's a good half day. Then head north to Yaletown and travel back via Robson Street, by which time you'll have earned yourself a glass of British Columbia wine at one of Vancouver's excellent restaurants.

If you're traveling with children, make sure to check out Science World, Grouse Mountain, and the Capilano Suspension Bridge or Lynn Canyon.

Getting Here and Around

Central Vancouver is extremely walkable, and TransLink, Metro Vancouver's public transport system—a mix of bus, ferry, and the SkyTrain (a fully automated rail system)—is easy and efficient to use. Transfer tickets enable you to travel from one system to the other. The hop-on-hop-off Vancouver Trolley buses circle the city in a continuous loop, and are a great way to see the sights.

Contacts SkyTrain (☎ 604/953–3333 ⊕ www.translink.bc.ca). **Translink** (⊕ www.translink.bc.ca). **Vancouver Trolley** (☎ 888/451–5581 ⊕ www.vancouvertrolley.com).

Air Travel. There are direct flights from most major U.S. and international cities to Vancouver International Airport (YVR), with connecting services to Victoria.

Car Travel. Interstate highway I–5 heads straight up the U.S. coast into Vancouver. However you travel, carry a passport. Without one, even U.S. citizens might not be allowed home. That includes minors. Check out full details in the Travel Smart chapter.

Ferry Travel. Twelve-passenger ferry boats bypass busy bridges and are a key reason why you don't need a car in Vancouver. Aquabus Ferries and False Creek Ferries are private commercial enterprises that provide passenger services between key locales on either side of False Creek. Tickets average C$5 depending on the route; day passes are C$14. Aquabus Ferries connections include Science World, Plaza of Nations, Granville Island, Stamp's Landing, Spyglass Place, Yaletown, and the Hornby Street dock. False Creek Ferries provides service between the Aquatic Centre on Beach Avenue, Granville Island, Science World, Stamp's Landing, and Vanier Park. False Creek and Aquabus ferries are not part of the TransLink system.

Contacts Aquabus Ferries (☎ 604/689–5858 ⊕ www.theaquabus.com). **False Creek Ferries** (☎ 604/684–7781 ⊕ www.granvilleislandferries.bc.ca). **SeaBus** (☎ 604/953–3333 ⊕ www.translink.bc.ca).

Taxi Travel. It can be hard to hail a cab in Vancouver. Unless you're near a hotel or find a taxi rank (designated curbside parking areas), you'll have better luck calling a taxi service. Try Black Top or Yellow Cab.

Taxi Companies Black Top Cabs (☎ 604/681–2181). **Yellow Cab** (☎ 604/681–1111).

About the Restaurants

Vancouver has hundreds of restaurants, but if you're looking for a uniquely Vancouver experience, remember that Pacific Northwest seafood is always a good choice, and many restaurants emphasize fresh seasonal produce, Canadian cheeses, and locally raised meats. Vancouver also has some of the best Asian food in North America. Dining is informal. Neat casual dress is appropriate everywhere; nice jeans are fine, though you might want something dressier than sneakers in the evening. A 15% tip is expected. A 12% Harmonized Sales Tax (HST) is levied on restaurant bills.

About the Hotels

Accommodations in Vancouver range from luxurious waterfront hotels to neighborhood B&Bs, chain hotels (both luxury and budget), basic European-style pensions, and backpackers' hostels. There are also many top-quality choices that epitomize countryside—within a 30-minute drive of the downtown core. Although the city is quite compact, each area has its distinct character and accommodation options. All our recommendations are within easy reach of transit that will take you to the major attractions, though if you choose to stay outside of the downtown core, a car will still be the easiest way to tour neighborhoods on the West Side or North Shore.

The trend toward self-catered apartment suites really struck gold in Vancouver with the 2010 Winter Olympics. The site ⊕ www.makeyourselfathome.com (☎ 604/874–7817) provides a terrific range of private homes and suites available for short-term rentals; this site is especially good for last-minute bookings.

WHAT IT COSTS IN CANADIAN DOLLARS

	¢	$	$$	$$$	$$$$
RESTAURANT	under C$8	C$8–C$12	C$13–C$20	C$21–C$30	over C$30
HOTEL	under C$75	C$75–C$125	C$126–C$175	C$176–C$250	over C$250

Restaurant prices are for an average main course or equivalent combination of smaller dishes, at dinner. Hotel prices are for a standard double room in high season, excluding 2% room tax and 12% HST.

Rainy-Day Activities

While most Vancouverites don't let a little drizzle stop them, heavier rains might inspire you to seek indoor activities. Obvious options include museums—the Museum of Anthropology at UBC is a worthwhile trek. If you're downtown, the Vancouver Art Gallery is good for an hour or two, as is the Vancouver Aquarium and Science World. Less obvious choices are the Bill Reid Gallery, the Dr. Sun Yat-Sen Classical Chinese Garden (it has covered walkways), or Granville Island Market (it's inside; you just have to get there, but then you can spend hours browsing the goods and having lunch). Lonsdale Quay is another colorful indoor market on the North Shore, and getting there, via the SeaBus, is half the fun.

17

Tours

A company called **Edible British Columbia** provides guided tours of Granville Island, with the market as its focus. They also have culinary tours around Vancouver's Chinatown. ☎ 604/662–3606 ⊕ www.edible-britishcolumbia.com.

VICTORIA PLANNER

Making the Most of Your Time

You can see most of the sights in downtown Victoria's compact core in a day, although there's enough to see at the main museums to easily fill two days. Many key sights, including the Royal BC Museum and the Parliament Buildings, are open on some summer evenings as well. You can save time by prebooking tea at the Empress Hotel and buying tickets to the Royal British Columbia Museum online.

You should also save at least half a day or a full evening to visit the Butchart Gardens. The busiest but most entertaining time is during the Saturday-evening fireworks shows. If you have a car, you can make a day of it visiting the nearby town of Sidney and some of the Saanich Peninsula wineries.

An extra day allows for some time on the water, either on a whale-watching trip—it's fairly easy to spot orcas in the area during summer—or on a Harbour Ferries tour, with stops for a microbrew at Spinnakers' Brewpub or fish-and-chips at Fisherman's Wharf. You can also explore the shoreline on foot, following all, or part, of the 7-mi (11-km) waterfront walkway.

Getting Here and Around

It's easy to visit Victoria without a car. Most sights, restaurants, and hotels are in the compact walkable core, with bikes, ferries, horse-drawn carriages, double-decker buses, step-on tour buses, taxis, and pedicabs on hand to fill the gaps. Bike paths lace downtown and run along much of Victoria's waterfront, and long-haul car-free paths run to the ferry terminals as far west as Sooke. Most buses and ferries carry bikes.

Air Travel. Victoria International Airport (YYJ) is 25 km (15 mi) north of downtown Victoria. The flight from Vancouver to Victoria takes about 25 minutes. The Airporter bus service drops off passengers at most major hotels. There is floatplane service to Victoria's Inner Harbour with West Coast Air and Harbour Air. Kenmore Air has daily floatplane service from May–September from Seattle to Victoria's Inner Harbour.

Contacts and Local Airlines **Airporter** (☎ 250/386–2525 or 877/386–2525 ⊕ www.victoriaairporter.com). **Harbour Air** (☎ 604/274–1277 or 800/665–0212 ⊕ www.harbour-air.com). **Kenmore Air** (☎ 425/486–1257 or 866/435–9524 ⊕ www.kenmoreair.com). **West Coast Air** (☎ 604/606–6888 or 800/347–2222 ⊕ www.westcoastair.com).

Ferry Travel. Victoria Harbour Ferries serve the Inner Harbour; stops include the Fairmont Empress, Chinatown, Point Ellice House, the Delta Victoria Ocean Pointe Resort, and Fisherman's Wharf. Fares start at C$4; multiple-trip and two-day passes are available. Boats make the rounds every 15 to 20 minutes, daily, March–October. The 45-minute harbor tours cost $20, and Gorge cruises cost $25. At 10:45 AM on summer Sundays the little ferries perform a water ballet set to classical music in the Inner Harbour.

Victoria Harbour Ferries (☎ 250/708–0201 ⊕ www.victoriaharbourferry.com).

Taxi Travel. In Victoria, call Bluebird, Victoria Taxi, or Yellow Cabs. Salt Spring and Pender also have cab companies.

Contacts **Bluebird Taxi** (☎ 250/382–2222). **Pender Island Cab Company** (☎ 250/629–2222). **Salt Spring Silver Shadow Taxi** (☎ 250/537–3030). **Victoria Taxi** (☎ 250/383–7111). **Yellow Cabs** (☎ 250/381–2222).

About the Restaurants

Wild salmon, locally made cheeses, Pacific oysters, organic vegetables, local microbrews, and even wines from the island's farm-gate wineries (The B.C. government allows really small wineries to sell their wines "at the farm gate") are tastes to watch for. Vegetarians and vegans are well catered for in this health-conscious town, and seafood choices go well beyond traditional fish-and-chips. You may notice an Ocean Wise symbol on a growing number of menus: this indicates that the restaurant is committed to serving only sustainably harvested fish and seafood.

Some of the city's best casual (and not-so-casual) fare is served in pubs—particularly in brewpubs; most have an all-ages restaurant as well as an adults-only bar area.

Afternoon tea is a Victoria tradition, as is good coffee in any number of funky local caffeine purveyors around town.

About the Hotels

Victoria has a vast range of accommodation, with what seems like whole neighborhoods dedicated to hotels. Options range from city resorts and full-service business hotels to mid-priced tour-group haunts, family-friendly motels, and backpacker hostels, but the city is especially known for its lavish B&Bs in beautifully restored Victorian and Edwardian mansions.

WHAT IT COSTS IN CANADIAN DOLLARS

	¢	$	$$	$$$	$$$$
Restaurants	under C$8	C$8–C$12	C$13–C$20	C$21–C$30	over C$30
Hotels	under C$75	C$75–C$125	C$126–C$175	C$176–C$250	over C$250

Restaurant prices are for a main course at dinner, not including 12% HST. Hotel prices are for two people in a standard double room in high season, excluding 2% rooms tax, service charge, and 12% HST.

When to Go

Victoria has the warmest, mildest climate in Canada: snow is rare and flowers bloom in February. Summers are mild, too, rarely topping 75°F. If you're here for dining, shopping, and museums, winter is a perfectly nice time for a visit: it's gray and wet, and some minor attractions are closed, but hotel deals abound. If your focus is the outdoors—biking, hiking, gardens, and whale-watching—you need to come with everyone else, between May and October. That's when the streets come to life with crafts stalls, street entertainers, blooming gardens, and the inevitable tour buses. It's fun and busy, but Victoria never gets unbearably crowded.

17

Best Fests

Victoria's top festivals take place in summer, when you're apt to encounter the best weather. For 10 nights in late June, international musicians perform during JazzFest International. Victoria's Inner Harbour becomes an outdoor concert venue in early August for Symphony Splash, when the Victoria Symphony plays a free concert from a barge moored in the middle of the harbor. August and September is the time for the Victoria Fringe Theatre Festival, during which you can feast from a vast menu of offbeat, original, and intriguing performances around town.

Updated by Chris McBeath and Carolyn B. Heller

Consistently ranked as one of the world's most livable cities, Vancouver lures visitors with its abundance of natural beauty, multicultural vitality, and cosmopolitan flair. Victoria, the capital of a province whose license plates brazenly label it "The Best Place on Earth," is a walkable, livable seaside town of fragrant gardens, waterfront paths, engaging museums, and beautifully restored 19th-century architecture.

The mountains and seascape make Vancouver an outdoor playground for hiking, skiing, kayaking, cycling, and sailing—and so much more—while the cuisine and arts scenes are equally diverse, reflecting the makeup of Vancouver's ethnic (predominantly Asian) mosaic. Yet despite all this vibrancy, the city still exudes an easy West Coast style that can make New York or London feel, in comparison, edgy and claustrophobic to some.

Victoria was the first European settlement on Vancouver Island, and in 1868 it became the capital of British Columbia. In summer the Inner Harbour—Victoria's social and cultural center—buzzes with visiting yachts, horse-and-carriage rides, street entertainers, and excursion boats heading out to visit pods of friendly local whales. Yes, it might be a bit touristy, but Victoria's good looks, gracious pace, and manageable size are instantly beguiling, especially if you stand back to admire the mountains and ocean beyond.

VANCOUVER

More than 8 million visitors each year come to Canada's third-largest metropolitan area, and thousands more are expected now that it has strutted its stuff on the Olympic world stage. Because of its peninsula location, traffic flow is a contentious issue. Thankfully, Vancouver is wonderfully walkable, especially in the downtown core. The North Shore is a scoot across the harbor, and the rapid-transit system to Richmond and the airport means that staying in the more affordable 'burbs doesn't have to be synonymous with sacrificing convenience. The mild climate, exquisite natural scenery, and relaxed outdoor lifestyle keep attracting residents, and the number of visitors is increasing for the same reasons. People often get their first glimpse of Vancouver when catching an Alaskan cruise, and many return at some point to spend more time here.

EXPLORING

The city's downtown core includes the main business district between Robson Street and the Burrard Inlet harbor front; the West End that edges up against English Bay; Stanley Park; trendy Yaletown; and Gastown and Chinatown, which are the oldest parts of the city. Main Street, which runs north-south, is roughly the dividing line between the east and west sides. The entire downtown district sits on a peninsula bordered by English Bay and the Pacific Ocean to the west; by False Creek to the south; and by Burrard Inlet, the city's working port, to the north, where the North Shore Mountains loom.

Elsewhere in the city you'll find other places of interest: the North Shore is across Burrard Inlet (Whistler is a two-hour drive from here); Granville Island is south of downtown across False Creek; the West Side comprises several neighborhoods across from English Bay in the West End. Richmond, where the airport is, is to the south; the suburbs of Burnaby and the Fraser Valley are to the east.

17

DOWNTOWN AND THE WEST END

Vancouver's compact downtown juxtaposes historic architecture with gleaming brand-new buildings. Sightseeing venues include museums, galleries, and top-notch shopping, most notably along Robson Street, and in and around couture-savvy Sinclair Centre. The harbor front, with the convention center expansion, has a fabulous water's-edge path all the way to Stanley Park, epitomizing what Vancouver is all about.

Fodor's Choice ★ **The Bill Reid Gallery of Northwest Coast Art.** Named after one of B.C.'s pre-eminent artists, Bill Reid (1920–98), this aboriginal art gallery is as much a legacy of Reid's works as it is a showcase of current artists. Displays include wood carvings, jewelry, prints, and sculpture. The gallery may be small, but its expansive offerings often include artist talks and noon-hour presentations. Bill Reid is best known for his bronze statue *The Spirit of Haida Gwaii, The Jade Canoe*—measuring 12 ft x 20 ft; the original is an iconic meeting place at the Vancouver International Airport and its image is on the back of the Canadian $20 bill. ⊠ *639 Hornby St., Downtown* 🕾 *604/682–3455* ⊕ *www.billreidgallery. ca.* 🖾 *C$10* ⊗ *Wed.–Sun. 11–5.*

Canada Place. Extending four city blocks north into Burrard Inlet, this complex (once a cargo pier) mimics the style and size of a luxury ocean liner, with exterior esplanades. The Teflon-coated fiberglass roof, shaped like five sails (the material was invented by NASA and once used in astronaut space suits), has become a Vancouver skyline landmark. Home to Vancouver's main cruise-ship terminal, Canada Place can accommodate up to four luxury liners at once. It's also home to the luxurious **Pan Pacific Hotel** and the east building of the **Vancouver**

Convention Centre (☎ 604/647–7390). Outdoor promenades, which wind all the way to Stanley Park, present spectacular vantage points to view Burrard Inlet and the North Shore Mountains; plaques posted at intervals offer historical information about the city and its waterfront. ✉ *999 Canada Place Way, Downtown* ☎ *604/775–7200* ⊕ *www.canadaplace.ca.*

Robson Street. Vancouver's busiest shopping street is lined with see-and-be-seen sidewalk cafés, chain stores, and high-end boutiques. The street, which links downtown to the West End, is particularly lively between Jervis and Burrard streets, and stays that way into the evening with buskers and entertainers.

OFF THE BEATEN PATH

Roedde House Museum. Two blocks south of Robson Street, on Barclay, is the Roedde (pronounced *roh*-dee) House Museum, an 1893 house in the Queen Anne Revival style, set among Victorian-style gardens. Tours of the restored, antiques-furnished interior take about an hour. On Sunday, tours are followed by tea and cookies. The gardens (free) can be visited anytime. ✉ *1415 Barclay St., between Broughton and Nicola, West End* ☎ *604/684–7040* ⊕ *www.roeddehouse.org* 🎫 *C$5; Sun. C$6, including tea* ⊘ *Tues.–Sat. 10–5, Sun. 2–4.*

Vancouver Art Gallery. Painter Emily Carr's haunting evocations of the British Columbian hinterland are among the attractions at western Canada's largest art gallery. Carr (1871–1945), a grocer's daughter from Victoria, fell in love with the wilderness around her and shocked middle-class Victorian society by running off to paint it. Her work accentuates the mysticism and the danger of B.C.'s wilderness, and records the diminishing presence of native cultures during that era (there's something of a renaissance now). The gallery, which also hosts touring historical and contemporary exhibitions, is housed in a 1911 courthouse that Canadian architect Arthur Erickson redesigned in the early 1980s as part of the Robson Square redevelopment. Stone lions guard the steps to the parklike Georgia Street side; the main entrance is accessed from Robson Square at Hornby Street. ✉ *750 Hornby St., Downtown* ☎ *604/662–4719* ⊕ *www.vanartgallery.bc.ca* 🎫 *C$22.50; higher for some exhibits; by donation Tues. 5–9* ⊘ *Daily 10–5, Tues. 10–9.*

GASTOWN AND CHINATOWN

Gastown and Chinatown are favorite destinations for visitors and residents alike. Gastown is fast becoming überhip as boutiques, ad agencies, and restaurants take over refurbished brick warehouses. Chinatown's array of produce stalls and curious alleyways make it look as if they're resisting gentrification, but inside many of the historic buildings are getting a new lease on life.

Dr. Sun Yat-Sen Classical Chinese Garden. The first authentic Ming Dynasty–style garden outside China, this small garden was built in 1986 by 52 artisans from Suzhou, China. It incorporates design elements and traditional materials from several of Suzhou's centuries-old private gardens. No power tools, screws, or nails were used in the construction. Guided tours (45 minutes long), included in the ticket price, are conducted on the hour between mid-June and the end of August (call ahead for off-season tour times); they are valuable for understanding the philosophy and symbolism that are central to the garden's design. A concert series, including classical, Asian, world, jazz, and sacred music, plays on Friday evenings in July, August, and early September. The free public park next door is also designed as a traditional Chinese garden. ■TIP➜ Covered walkways make this a good rainy-day choice. ✉ *578 Carrall St., Chinatown* ☎ *604/662–3207* ⊕ *www.vancouverchinesegarden. com* ✉ *C$14* ☉ *May–mid-June and Sept., daily 10–6; mid-June–Aug., daily 9:30–7; Oct., daily 10–4:30; Nov.–Apr., Tues.–Sun. 10–4:30.*

Steam Clock. An underground steam system, which also heats many local buildings, supplies the world's first steam clock—possibly Vancouver's most-photographed attraction. On the quarter hour a steam whistle rings out the Westminster chimes, and on the hour a huge cloud of steam spews from the apparatus. The ingenious design, based on an 1875 mechanism, was built in 1977 by Ray Saunders of Landmark Clocks (at 123 Cambie Street) to commemorate the community effort that saved Gastown from demolition. ✉ *Water St., Gastown.*

YALETOWN AND FALSE CREEK

In 1985–86 the provincial government cleaned up a derelict industrial site on the north shore of False Creek, built a world's fair, and invited everyone; 20 million people showed up at Expo '86. Now the site of the fair has become one of the largest urban-redevelopment projects in North America, as well as the site for the Winter Olympics Athlete's Village.

Tucked into the forest of green-glass condo towers is the old warehouse district of Yaletown. It's one of the city's most fashionable neighborhoods, and the Victorian-brick loading docks have become terraces for cappuccino bars.

Science World. In a gigantic shiny dome built over the Omnimax theater, this hands-on science center encourages children to participate in interactive exhibits and demonstrations. Exhibits change throughout the year, so there's always something new to see. It's an easy walk (and mini-ferry ride) from Yaletown; there's a SkyTrain station on its doorstep, and there's plenty of parking. ✉ *1455 Quebec St., False Creek* ☎ *604/443–7443 or 604/443–7440* ⊕ *www.scienceworld.ca* ✉ *Science World C$21, Science World and Omnimax theater C$26.50* ☉ *July–Labor Day, daily 10–6; Sept.–June, weekdays 10–5, weekends 10–6.*

STANLEY PARK

Fodor's Choice
★

A 1,000-acre wilderness park, only blocks from the downtown section of a major city, is a rare treasure. Stanley Park is, perhaps, the single most prized possession of Vancouverites, who make use of it fervently to cycle, walk, jog, Rollerblade, play cricket and tennis, and enjoy outdoor art shows and theater performances alongside attractions such as the renowned aquarium.

For information about guided nature walks in the park, contact the **Lost Lagoon Nature House** (☎ *604/257–8544* ⊕ *www.stanleyparkecology.ca*) on the south shore of Lost Lagoon, at the foot of Alberni Street. They operate May to September on Sunday afternoons; call for times.

17

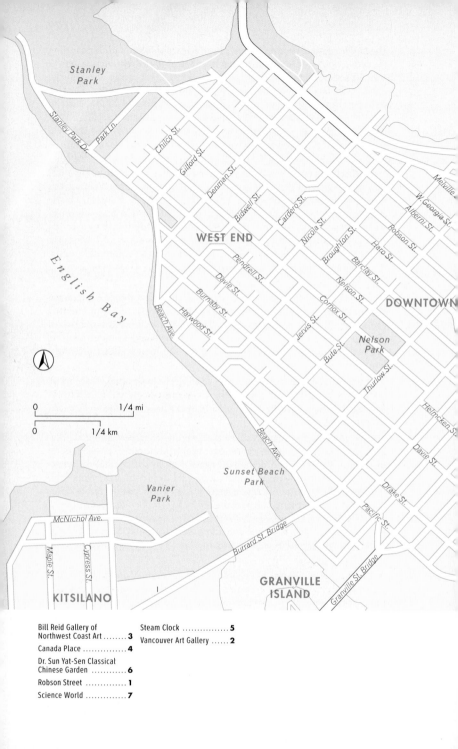

Stanley
Park

Stanley Park Dr.

Park Ln.

Chilco St.

Gilford St.

Denman St.

Bidwell St.

Cardero St.

WEST END

Nicola St.

Broughton St.

Barclay St.

Haro St.

Robson St.

Melville

W. Georgia St.

Alberni St.

English Bay

Pendrell St.

Davie St.

Burnaby St.

Harwood St.

Beach Ave.

Nelson St.

Comox St.

Jervis St.

Bute St.

DOWNTOWN

Nelson
Park

Thurlow St.

Helmcken St.

0   1/4 mi

0   1/4 km

Beach Ave.

Davie St.

Sunset Beach
Park

Vanier
Park

McNichol Ave.

Drake St.

Pacific St.

Maple St.

Cypress St.

Burrard St. Bridge

KITSILANO

GRANVILLE
ISLAND

Granville St. Bridge

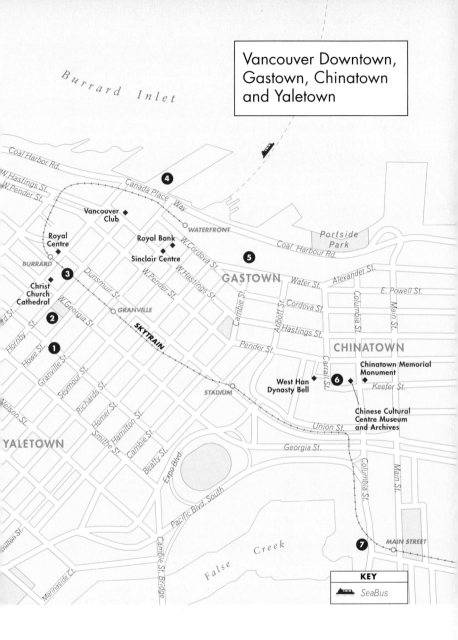

Vancouver Downtown, Gastown, Chinatown and Yaletown

Burrard Inlet

Coal Harbor Rd.

W.Hastings St.
W.Pender St.

Canada Place Way

❹

WATERFRONT

Vancouver Club

Royal Bank

W.Cordova St.

Coal Harbour Rd.

Portside Park

Royal Centre

Sinclair Centre

W.Hastings St.

❺

GASTOWN

Water St.

Alexander St.

BURRARD

W.Pender St.

Cambie St.

Cordova St.

Columbia St.

Main St.

E. Powell St.

❸

Dunsmuir St.

Abbott St.

Christ Church Cathedral

W.Georgia St.

GRANVILLE

Hastings St.

CHINATOWN

❷

SKYTRAIN

Pender St.

Carrall St.

Chinatown Memorial Monument

Hornby St.

Howe St.

❶

West Han Dynasty Bell

❻

Keefer St.

Granville St.

Seymour St.

STADIUM

Chinese Cultural Centre Museum and Archives

Nelson St.

Richards St.

Homer St.

Hamilton St.

Union St.

YALETOWN

Smithe St.

Cambie St.

Beatty St.

Georgia St.

Columbia St.

Main St.

Expo Blvd.

Pacific Blvd. South

Creek

amilton St.

Cambie St. Bridge

False

Marinaside Ct.

❼

MAIN STREET

KEY

SeaBus

Prospect Point. At 211 feet, Prospect Point is the highest point in the park and provides striking views of the Lions Gate Bridge (watch for cruise ships passing below), the North Shore, and Burrard Inlet. There's also a year-round souvenir shop, a snack bar with terrific ice cream, and a restaurant (May–September only). From the seawall, you can see where cormorants build their seaweed nests along the cliff ledges.

Seawall. The seawall path, a 9-km (5½-mi) paved shoreline route popular with walkers, cyclists, and in-line skaters, is one of several car-free zones within the park. If you have the time (about a half day) and the energy, strolling the entire seawall is an exhilarating experience. It extends an additional mile east past the marinas, cafés, and waterfront condominiums of Coal Harbour to Canada Place downtown, so you could start your walk or ride from there. From the south side of the park, the seawall continues for another 28 km (17 mi) along Vancouver's waterfront, to the University of British Columbia, allowing for a pleasant, if ambitious, day's bike ride. Along the seawall, cyclists must wear helmets and stay on their side of the path. Within Stanley Park, cyclists must ride in a counterclockwise direction.

The seawall can get crowded on summer weekends, but inside the park is a 28-km (17-mi) network of peaceful walking and cycling paths through old- and second-growth forest. The wheelchair-accessible Beaver Lake Interpretive Trail is a good choice if you're interested in park ecology. Take a map—they're available at the park-information booth and many of the concession stands—and don't go into the woods alone or after dusk.

☺ **Vancouver Aquarium Marine Science Centre.** Massive pools with windows below water level let you come face to face with beluga whales, sea otters, sea lions, dolphins, and harbor seals at this research and educational facility. In the Amazon rain-forest gallery you can walk through a jungle populated with piranhas, caimans, and tropical birds, and in summer you'll be surrounded by hundreds of free-flying butterflies. Other displays, many with hands-on features for kids, show the underwater life of coastal British Columbia and the Canadian Arctic. A Tropic Zone is home to exotic freshwater and saltwater life, including clown fish, moray eels, and black-tip reef sharks. Beluga whale, sea lion, and dolphin shows, as well as dive shows (where divers swim with aquatic life, including sharks) are held daily. Make sure to check out the 4-D film experience; it's a multisensory show that puts mist, smell, and wind into the 3-D equation. For an extra fee, you can help the trainers feed and train otters, belugas, and sea lions. There's also a café and a gift shop. Be prepared for lines on weekends and school holidays. ■TIP➔ The quietest time to visit is before 11 AM or after 3 PM. ⊠ *845 Avison Way, Stanley Park* ☎ *604/659–3474* ⊕ *www.vanaqua.org* ✍ *C$27* ⊙ *July–Labor Day, daily 9:30–7; Labor Day–June, daily 9:30–5.*

GRANVILLE ISLAND

The creative redevelopment of this former industrial wasteland vies with Stanley Park as the city's top attraction. An active cement works remains at its heart, and is oddly complemented with a thriving diversity

Robson Square, in front of the Vancouver Art Gallery, is a downtown focal point; there's a skating rink here in winter.

of artists' studios, performing arts spaces, an indoor farmers' market, specialty shops, and a jammed-to-the-gunnels marina.

If your schedule is tight, you can tour Granville Island in two to three hours. If you like to shop, you could spend a full day.

Fodor's Choice ★ **Granville Island Public Market.** Because no chain stores are allowed in this 50,000-square-foot building, each shop here is unique. Dozens of stalls sell locally grown produce direct from the farm; others sell crafts, chocolates, cheese, fish, meat, flowers, and exotic foods. On Thursdays in summer, market gardeners sell fruit and vegetables from trucks outside. At the north end of the market you can pick up a snack, lunch, or coffee at one of the many food stalls. The Market Courtyard, on the waterside, is a good place to catch street entertainers—be prepared to get roped into the action, if only to check the padlocks of an escape artist's gear. Weekends can get madly busy. ⊠ *1689 Johnston St., Granville Island* ☎ *604/666–5784* ⊕ *www.granvilleisland.com* ☉ *Daily 9–7.*

Kids' Market. A converted factory warehouse sets the stage for a slice of kids' heaven on Granville Island. The Kids' Market has an indoor play area and two floors of small shops that sell all kinds of toys, magic gear, books, and other fun stuff. ⊠ *1496 Cartwright St., Granville Island* ☎ *604/689–8447* ⊕ *www.kidsmarket.ca* ☉ *Daily 10–6.*

Net Loft. This blue-and-red building—a former loft where fishermen used to dry their nets—includes a bookstore, a café, and a collection of high-quality boutiques selling imported and locally made crafts, exotic fabrics, handmade paper, and First Nations art. ⊠ *1666 Johnston St., Granville Island* ☎ *No phone* ☉ *Daily 10–7.*

Part of the attraction of the Museum of Anthropology are the exhibits outside the museum, on the cliffs overlooking the water.

THE WEST SIDE AND KITSILANO

Once a hippie haven, Kitsilano has gone upmarket. Character homes and specialty shopping now make up some of the country's most expensive few square miles of real estate. The West Side has the city's best gardens and natural sights; "Kits," however, is really where all the action is.

Museum of Anthropology. Part of the University of British Columbia, the MOA has one of the world's leading collections of Northwest Coast First Nations art. The Great Hall displays dramatic cedar poles, bentwood boxes, and canoes adorned with traditional Northwest Coast–painted designs. On clear days the gallery's 50-foot-tall windows reveal a striking backdrop of mountains and sea. Another highlight is the work of the late Bill Reid, one of Canada's most respected Haida artists. In *The Raven and the First Men* (1980), carved in yellow cedar, he tells a Haida story of creation. Reid's gold-and-silver jewelry work is also on display, as are exquisite carvings of gold, silver, and argillite (a black shale found on Haida Gwaii, also known as the Queen Charlotte Islands) by other First Nations artists. The museum's visible storage-section displays, in drawers and cases, contain thousands of examples of tools, textiles, masks, and other artifacts from around the world. Behind the museum are two Haida houses, set on the cliff over the water. Free guided tours—given three times daily in summer (call to confirm times)—are immensely informative. Arthur Erickson designed the cliff-top structure that houses the MOA, which also has a book and fine-art shop and a café. To reach the museum by transit, take any UBC-bound bus to the university loop; from there, it's a 10-minute walk, or a quick ride on the C20 shuttle bus, to the museum. ■ TIP→ Pay parking is available in the Rose Garden parking lot, across Marine Drive from the museum. ⊠ *University of British Columbia, 6393 N.W. Marine Dr., Point Grey* ☏ *604/822–5087* ⊕ *www.moa.ubc.ca* ⊡ *C$14, Tues. 5–9 C$7* ☉ *Late May–mid-Oct., Tues. 10–9, Wed.–Mon. 10–5; Mid-Oct.– late May, Tues. 11–9, Wed.–Sun. 11–5.*

☽ **Queen Elizabeth Park.** At the highest point in the city, showcasing 360-degree views of downtown, this 52-hectare (130-acre) park has lavish sunken gardens (in a former stone quarry), a rose garden, and an abundance of grassy picnicking spots. Other park facilities include 18 tennis courts, pitch and putt (an 18-hole putting green), and a restaurant. On summer evenings there's free outdoor dancing on the Plaza— everything from Scottish country dance to salsa, for all ages and levels. In the **Bloedel Floral Conservatory** you can see tropical and desert plants and 100 species of free-flying tropical birds in a glass geodesic dome—the perfect place to be on a rainy day. To reach the park by public transportation, take a Cambie Bus 15 from the corner of Robson and Burrard streets downtown to 33rd Avenue; it should take about 20 minutes. Hop on board the SkyTrain for an even faster trip, although the stop requires a six-block walk. ■ TIP➔ **Park activities make for a great family excursion, as well as being a gardener's delight.** ⊠ *Cambie St. and 33rd Ave., Cambie* ☏ *604/257–8584* ⊕ *www.vancouver.ca/parks/* ⊡ *Conservatory C$5* ☉ *Apr.–Sept., weekdays 9–8, weekends 10–9; Oct.–Mar., daily 10–5.*

NORTH SHORE

The North Shore and its star attractions—the Capilano Suspension Bridge, Grouse Mountain, Lonsdale Quay, and, farther east, the lovely hamlet of Deep Cove—are just a short trip from downtown Vancouver.

☽ **Capilano Suspension Bridge.** At Vancouver's oldest tourist attraction (the

Fodor's Choice ★ original bridge was built in 1889) you can get a taste of rain-forest scenery and test your mettle on the swaying, 450-foot cedar-plank suspension bridge that hangs 230 feet above the rushing Capilano River. Across the bridge is the Treetops Adventure, where you can walk along 650 feet of cable bridges suspended among the trees; there's also a scenic pathway along the canyon's edge, appropriately called Cliff Hanger Walk. Without crossing the bridge, you can enjoy the site's viewing decks, nature trails, totem park, and carving center (where you can watch First Nations carvers at work), as well as history and forestry exhibits, a massive gift shop in the original 1911 teahouse, and a restaurant. May through October, guides in 19th-century costumes conduct free tours on themes related to history, nature, or ecology, while fiddle bands, First Nations dancers, and other entertainers keep things lively. ■ TIP➔ **Catch the attraction's free shuttle service from Canada Place; it also stops along Burrard and Robson streets.** ⊠ *3735 Capilano Rd., North Vancouver* ☏ *604/985–7474* ⊕ *www.capbridge.com* ⊡ *C$30.95, plus C$5 for parking* ☉ *May–Labor Day, daily 8:30–8; Nov.–Mar., daily 9–5; Sept., Oct., and Apr.–mid-May call for hrs.*

☽ **Grouse Mountain.** North America's largest aerial tramway, the **Skyride** is a great way to take in the city, sea, and mountain vistas (be sure to pick a clear day or evening). The Skyride makes the 2-km (1-mi) climb

17

to the peak of Grouse Mountain every 15 minutes. Once at the top you can watch a half-hour video presentation at the Theatre in the Sky (it's included with your Skyride ticket). Other free mountaintop activities include, in summer, lumberjack shows, chairlift rides, walking tours, hiking, falconry demonstrations, and a chance to visit the grizzly bears and gray wolves in the mountain's wildlife refuge. For an extra fee you can also try zip-lining and tandem paragliding, or take a helicopter tour. In winter you can ski, snowshoe, snowboard, ice-skate on a mountain-top pond, or take Sno-Cat-drawn sleigh rides. A stone-and-cedar lodge is home to a café, a pub-style bistro, and a high-end restaurant, all with expansive city views. ■TIP→ **The Grouse Grind—a hiking trail up the face of the mountain—is one of the best workouts on the North Shore. Depending on your fitness level, allow about 90 minutes to complete it. Then you can take the Skyride down.** (⇨ *See the Vancouver Outdoors chapter for more info.*) ✉ *6400 Nancy Greene Way, North Vancouver* ☎ *604/980–9311* ⊕ *www.grousemountain.com* ⌦ *Skyride and most activities C$39.95* ☉ *Daily 9* AM–10 PM.

WHERE TO EAT

From inventive downtown bistros to waterfront seafood palaces, to Asian restaurants that rival those in Asia, Vancouver has a diverse array of gastronomical options. Many cutting-edge establishments are defining and perfecting Modern Canadian fare, which incorporates Pacific Northwest seafood—notably salmon and halibut—and locally grown produce, often accompanied by British Columbia wines.

British Columbia's wine industry is enjoying great popularity, and many restaurants feature wines from the province's 100-plus wineries. Most B.C. wines come from the Okanagan Valley in the province's interior, but Vancouver Island is another main wine-producing area. Merlot, pinot noir, pinot gris, and chardonnay are among the major varieties; also look for ice wine, a dessert wine made from grapes that are picked while they are frozen on the vines.

DOWNTOWN VANCOUVER

Use the coordinate (✛ B2) at the end of each listing to locate a site on the corresponding map.

$$$–$$$$
SEAFOOD
Fodor's Choice
★

✕ **Blue Water Cafe.** Executive chef Frank Pabst features both popular and lesser-known local seafood (including frequently overlooked varieties like mackerel or herring) at this fashionable restaurant. You might start with B.C. sardines stuffed with pine-nut *gremolata*, a pairing of Dungeness crab and flying squid, or a selection of raw oysters. Main dishes are seafood-centric, too—perhaps white sturgeon grilled with wheat berries, capers, and peppery greens, or a Japanese-style seafood stew. Ask the staff to recommend wine pairings from the B.C.-focused list. You can dine in the warmly lit interior or outside on the former loading dock that's now a lovely terrace. ■TIP→ **The sushi chef turns out both classic and new creations—they're pricey, but rank among the city's best.** ✉ *1095 Hamilton St., Yaletown* ☎ *604/688–8078* ⊕ *www.bluewatercafe.net* ▭ *AE, DC, MC, V* ☉ *No lunch* ✛ *E5.*

$$$
MODERN
CANADIAN

✕ **Boneta.** Some of the city's most innovative dishes—and drinks—grace the tables of this Gastown restaurant, named after co-owner Mark Brand's mother. The exposed-brick walls and high ceilings make the room feel like a downtown loft, as do the almost-too-cool-for-school cocktails, including the Tharseo (lemon-thyme-infused gin, sherry, apple juice, honey, and citrus) and the B.K. (gin, Campari, chamomile syrup, and grapefruit). Vancouver is buzzing about such creations as smoked bison carpaccio served with arugula salad and a quail egg; squid-ink farfalle pasta topped with sablefish, calamari, and a briny puttanesca sauce; and grilled tuna with lobster mushrooms and eggplant caviar—dishes that would make any foodie mother proud. And mama wouldn't say no to the Valrhona chocolate "bar" paired with honey-and-chili ice cream. ⊠ *1 W. Cordova St., Gastown* ☎ *604/684–1844* ⊕ *www.boneta. ca* ▭ *AE, MC, V* ⊗ *Closed Sun. No lunch* ✛ *G3.*

$$$$
SEAFOOD
Fodor's Choice
★

✕ **C Restaurant.** Save your pennies, fish fans—dishes such as crispy trout served with oven-dried tomato and braised fennel, spice-rubbed tuna grilled ultrarare, or lingcod paired with smoked-ham-hock broth have established this spot as Vancouver's most innovative seafood restaurant. Start with shucked oysters from the raw bar or perhaps the seared scallops wrapped in octopus "bacon," and finish with an assortment of handmade chocolate truffles and petits fours. The elaborate six- or 14-course tasting menus with optional wine pairings highlight regional seafood. Both the ultramodern interior and the waterside patio overlook False Creek, but dine before dark to enjoy the view. ⊠ *2–1600 Howe St., Downtown* ☎ *604/681–1164* ⊕ *www.crestaurant.com* ▭ *AE, DC, MC, V* ⊗ *No lunch weekends or Nov.–Feb.* ✛ *C5.*

$$$–$$$$
SEAFOOD

✕ **The Fish House in Stanley Park.** This 1930s former sports pavilion with two verandas and a fireplace is surrounded by gardens, tucked between Stanley Park's tennis courts and putting green. Chef Karen Barnaby's food, including fresh oysters, grilled ahi tuna steak with a green-peppercorn sauce, and corn-husk-wrapped salmon with a maple glaze, is flavorful and unpretentious. Check the fresh sheet for the current day's catch. Traditional English afternoon tea is served between 2 and 4 daily. ⊠ *8901 Stanley Park Dr., Stanley Park* ☎ *604/681–7275 or 877/681–7275* ⊕ *www.fishhousestanleypark.com* ▭ *AE, DC, MC, V* ✛ *A1.*

$–$$
JAPANESE

✕ **Hapa Izakaya.** *Izakayas* are Japanese pubs that serve tapas-style small plates designed for sharing, and they've sprouted up all over Vancouver. This sleek izakaya has three locations, all popular with twenty- and thirtysomethings. Choose from the daily "fresh sheet," or sample other tasty tidbits, such as the mackerel (cooked table-side—with a blowtorch), udon noodles coated with briny cod roe, or the *ishi-yaki*, a Korean-style stone bowl filled with rice, pork, and vegetables. Sake or Japanese beer are the drinks of choice. If you're dining alone, sit at the counter facing the open kitchen to watch the action. The Robson branch is located city center; the Kitsilano branch is one block from Kits Beach, while the newest location is in Yaletown. ⊠ *1479 Robson St., West End* ☎ *604/689–4272* ⊕ *www.hapaizakaya.com* ▭ *AE, MC, V* ⊗ *No lunch* ⊠ *1516 Yew St., Kitsilano* ☎ *604/738–4272* ▭ *AE, MC, V* ⊗ *No lunch* ⊠ *1193 Hamilton St., Yaletown* ☎ *604/681–4272* ▭ *AE, MC, V* ⊗ *No lunch Sat.–Sun.* ✛ *C2.*

17

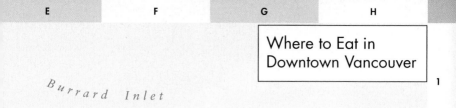

E   **F**   **G**   **H**

Burrard Inlet

Coal Harbor Rd.

l. Hastings St.

W. Pender St.

Thurlow St.

CANADA PLACE

Canada Place Way

Waterfront

SINCLAIR CENTRE

Ⓜ Waterfront

W. Cordova St.

◆ **WATERFRONT STATION**

Coal Harbour Rd.

Portside Park

GASTOWN

Water St.

Alexander St.

E. Powell St.

Burrard

Ⓜ Burrard

W. Hastings St.

W. Pender St.

Richards St.

Homer St.

Hamilton St.

Cambie St.

Cordova St.

Abbott St.

Salt Tasting Room

■ **Boneta**

Hastings St.

Carrall St.

Columbia St.

Main St.

Gore Ave.

Burrard St.

Hornby St.

Howe St.

Granville St.

Seymour St.

Ⓜ Granville

Dunsmuir St.

W. Georgia St.

Robson St.

Smithe St.

Vancouver City Centre Ⓜ

Pender St.

CHINATOWN

Keefer St.

Stadium

Union St.

YALETOWN

Cambie St.

Beatty St.

Georgia St.

Columbia St.

Main St.

■ **Blue Water Cafe**

Hamilton St.

Expo Blvd.

Pacific Blvd. South

Ⓜ **Yaletown-Roundhouse**

Creek

■ **Rodney's Oyster House**

Marinaside Ct.

Cambie St. Bridge

False Creek

Main Street

Ⓞ

Olympic Village Ⓜ

KEY

■ *Restaurants*

Ⓜ *CanadaLine stations*

Ⓞ *SkyTrain stations*

✛ *following dining reviews indicates a map-grid coordinate*

1   **2**   **3**   **4**   **5**   **6**

Izakaya are Japanese small plates, similar to Spanish tapas.

$$$–$$$$
FRENCH

✗ **Le Crocodile.** Chefs prepare classic Alsatian-inspired food (such as the signature onion tart) at this long-established downtown restaurant. Despite the white-tablecloth sophistication, the golden yellow walls, café curtains, and burgundy banquettes keep things cozy. Favorite dishes include lobster with beurre blanc, veal medallions with morel sauce, and sautéed Dover sole. Many lunch options, including a black-truffle omelet and a mixed grill of halibut, prawns, and wild salmon, are moderately priced. ⊠ 100–909 Burrard St., Downtown ☎ 604/669–4298 ⊕ www.lecrocodilerestaurant.com ⊟ AE, DC, MC, V ✆ Closed Sun. No lunch Sat. ✛ D3.

$$$–$$$$
MODERN
CANADIAN

✗ **Market by Jean-Georges.** Vancouver was all abuzz when celebrity chef Jean-Georges Vongerichten opened this contemporary dining room in the Shangri-La Hotel. While the globetrotting chef is rarely on-site, his signature Asian influences abound, as in the rice cracker–crusted tuna with a citrus-Sriracha (chili sauce) emulsion or the soy-glazed short ribs. These global flavors frequently garnish local ingredients; you might find Pacific halibut in a lemon-garlic broth or B.C.-raised venison sauced with cabrales (blue cheese) foam. If you don't fancy a full meal, you can dine lightly (and less expensively) on stylish salads or creative appetizers. Either way, you'll want to dress up a bit to match the sleek space. ⊠ 1115 Alberni St., Downtown ☎ 604/695–1115 ⊕ www.shangri-la. com ⊟ AE, DC, MC, V ✛ D2.

$$$–$$$$
MODERN
CANADIAN

✗ **Raincity Grill.** One of the best places to try British Columbian food and wine is this lovely candlelit bistro overlooking English Bay. The menu changes regularly and relies almost completely on local and regional products, from salmon and shellfish to game and fresh organic vegetables. Vegetarian selections are always available, and the exclusively

Pacific Northwest and Californian wine list has at least 40 choices by the glass. One popular alternative is the 100 Mile Tasting Menu—all ingredients in this multicourse dinner are sourced from within 100 mi of the restaurant. Another prix-fixe option, the early dinner (C$30), is a steal; it's served from 5 to 6 PM. Reservations are required for these prix-fixe dinners. ⊠ *1193 Denman St., West End* ☎ *604/685–7337* ⊕ *www. raincitygrill.com* ▭ *AE, DC, MC, V* ✢ *B2.*

$$
SEAFOOD
✕**Rodney's Oyster House.** This fishing-shack look-alike in Yaletown has one of the widest selections of oysters in town (up to 18 varieties), from locally harvested to exotic Japanese *kumamotos.* You can pick your oysters individually—they're laid out on ice behind the bar—or try the clams, scallops, mussels, and other mollusks from the steamer kettles. Oyster lovers can also relax over martinis and appetizers in the attached Mermaid Room lounge. ⊠ *1228 Hamilton St., Yaletown* ☎ *604/609–0080* ⊕ *www.rodneysoysterhouse.com* ▭ *AE, DC, MC, V* ☺ *No lunch Sun.* ✢ *E5.*

$–$$
ECLECTIC
✕**Salt Tasting Room.** If your idea of a perfect lunch or light supper revolves around fine cured meats, artisanal cheeses, and a glass of wine from a wide-ranging list, find your way to this sleek spare space in a decidedly unsleek Gastown lane. The restaurant has no kitchen and simply assembles its first-quality provisions, perhaps meaty *bunderfleisch* (cured beef), smoked pork chops, or B.C.-made Camembert, with accompanying condiments, into artfully composed grazers' delights— more like an upscale picnic than a full meal. There's no sign out front, so look for the salt-shaker flag in Blood Alley, which is off Abbott Street, half a block south of Water Street. ⊠ *45 Blood Alley, Gastown* ☎ *604/633–1912* ⊕ *www.salttastingroom.com* ▭ *AE, MC, V* ✢ *G3.*

GREATER VANCOUVER

$$$$
MODERN
CANADIAN
✕**Bishop's.** Before "local" and "seasonal" were all the rage, this highly regarded room was serving West Coast cuisine with an emphasis on organic regional produce. The menu changes regularly, but highlights have included such starters as marinated Pacific sardines paired with Barlotti beans, bacon, and tomatoes, and mains like Qualicum Bay scallops with potato confit, slow-roasted pork with rosemary gravy, and locally raised beef tenderloin. All are expertly presented and impeccably served with suggestions from Bishop's extensive local wine list. The split-level room displays elaborate flower arrangements and selections from owner John Bishop's art collection. ⊠ *2183 W. 4th Ave., Kitsilano* ☎ *604/738–2025* ⊕ *www.bishopsonline.com* ▭ *AE, DC, MC, V* ☺ *Closed 1st wk in Jan. No lunch.*

$$–$$$
CHINESE
✕**Kirin Seafood Restaurant.** Take in cityscapes and mountain views from this spacious room opposite City Hall, where the focus is on Cantonese-style seafood, including whole fish, crab, and lobster fresh from the tanks. They do an excellent job with vegetables, too; ask for whatever's fresh that day. Dim sum is served daily. There's another location in suburban Richmond. Both branches are an easy ride on the Canada Line from downtown. ⊠ *555 W. 12th Ave., 2nd fl., City Sq. Shopping Centre, Fairview* ☎ *604/879–8038* ▭ *MC, V* ⊠ *Three West Centre,*

17

2nd fl., 7900 Westminster Hwy., Richmond ☎ *604/303–8833* ⊕ *www. kirinrestaurants.com* ▭ *MC, V* ✛ *B4.*

$$
✕ Maenam. Chef Angus An has applied his creative sensibilities to a

THAI   moderately priced Thai menu that brings this Asian cuisine to a new level. While some dishes may sound familiar—green papaya salad, pad thai, curries—they're amped up with local ingredients, fresh herbs, and vibrant seasonings. Look for delicious innovations, too: perhaps crispy B.C. oysters, a chicken-and-clam salad, or "three flavor fish" that balances sweet, salty, and sour tastes. The bar sends out equally exotic cocktails, such as the Siam Sun Ray (vodka, lime, chili, ginger, coconut juice, and soda). The sleek Kitsilano dining room is stylish enough that you could dress up a bit, but you wouldn't be out of place in jeans. ⊠ *1938 W. 4th Ave., Kitsilano* ☎ *604/730–5579* ⊕ *www.maenam.ca* ▭ *AE, MC, V* ☽ *No lunch Sun.–Mon.*

$$$–$$$$ **✕ Tojo's.** Hidekazu Tojo is a sushi-making legend in Vancouver, with

JAPANESE   thousands of special preparations stored in his creative mind. In this strikingly modern, high-ceilinged space, complete with a separate sake lounge, the prime perch is at Tojo's sushi bar, a convivial ringside seat for watching the creation of edible art. The best way to experience Tojo's creativity is to reserve a spot at the sushi bar and order *omakase* (chef's choice); chef Tojo will keep offering you wildly more adventurous fare, both raw and cooked, until you cry uncle. Budget a minimum of C$70 per person (before drinks) for the omakase option; tabs topping C$120 per person are routine. ⊠ *1133 W. Broadway, Fairview* ☎ *604/872–8050* ⊕ *www.tojos.com* ⌲ *Reservations essential* ▭ *AE, DC, MC, V* ☽ *Closed Sun. No lunch.*

$$$ **✕ Vij's.** At Vancouver's most innovative Indian restaurant, genial propri-

INDIAN   etor Vikram Vij and his wife and business partner Meeru Dhalwala use

Fodor'sChoice   local ingredients to create exciting takes on South Asian cuisine. Dishes

★   such as lamb "popsicles" in a creamy fenugreek-scented curry, or B.C. spot prawns and halibut with black chickpeas, are far from traditional but are spiced beautifully. Mr. Vij circulates through the room, which is decorated with Indian antiques and whimsical elephant-pattern lanterns, greeting guests and suggesting dishes or cocktail pairings. Expect to cool your heels at the bar sipping chai or a cold beer while you wait for a table (lineups of more than an hour are common), but if you like creative Indian fare, it's worth it. ⊠ *1480 W. 11th Ave., South Granville* ☎ *604/736–6664* ⊕ *www.vijs.ca* ⌲ *Reservations not accepted* ▭ *AE, DC, MC, V* ☽ *No lunch.*

$$$$ **✕ West.** Contemporary regional cuisine is the theme at this chic res-

MODERN   taurant, one of the city's most innovative dining rooms. Among the

CANADIAN   kitchen's creations are octopus, quinoa, and black tobiko salad; smoked

Fodor'sChoice   sablefish with Tarbais beans and watermelon radishes; and sake-braised

★   pork cheeks served with plum puree, broccolini, and späetzle. There's an extensive selection of cheeses and decadent desserts that might include a mascarpone–espresso cake or a frozen lime parfait served on a coconut macaroon with fresh strawberries. If you can't decide, opt for one of the elaborate multicourse tasting menus (C$76–C$88). Marble floors, high ceilings, and warm caramel leather set into red walls make the space feel simultaneously energetic and cozy. ⊠ *2881 Granville St., South*

Chefs prepare regional Canadian cuisine at the popular restaurant West.

Granville ☎ *604/738–8938* ⊕ *www.westrestaurant.com* ⊟ *AE, DC, MC, V* ⊙ *No lunch Sun.*

WHERE TO STAY

Unless stated in the review, hotels are equipped with elevators, and all guest rooms have air-conditioning, TV, telephone, and private bathroom. Internet (meaning some form of high-speed dial-up) and wireless access are noted when available.

DOWNTOWN

Use the coordinate (✥ B2) at the end of each listing to locate a site on the corresponding map.

$$$$ ⊺ **Fairmont Hotel Vancouver.** The copper roof of this 1939 château-style hotel dominates Vancouver's skyline, and the hotel itself—one of the last railway-built hotels in Canada—is considered the city's gracious grande dame, redone to its original elegance. Guest rooms vary in size, but even the standard rooms have an aura of prestige, with high ceilings, lush draperies, and 19th-century-style mahogany furniture. Two friendly dogs are on hand for petting and walking, and the full-service spa here was Canada's first to cater to men, with big-screen TVs, Wi-Fi, and black-leather pedicure chairs; women are welcome, though. **Pros:** the male-oriented spa; great location for shopping; the architecture. **Cons:** diversity of "standard" room sizes can be irritating if you're expecting a room similar to the one you stayed in before. ⊠ *900 W. Georgia St., Downtown* ☎ *604/684–3131* ⊕ *www.fairmont. com/hotelvancouver* ⇲ *556 rooms, 37 suites* ⚲ *In-room: refrigerator*

(some), Internet. In-hotel: 2 restaurants, room service, bar, pool, gym, spa, laundry service, Wi-Fi, parking (paid), some pets allowed ▭ *AE, D, DC, MC, V* ✛ *E3.*

$$$$ 🏨 **Fairmont Waterfront.** This luxuriously modern 23-story hotel is across the street from the Convention and Exhibition Centre and the Canada Place cruise-ship terminal, but it's the floor-to-ceiling windows with ocean, park, and mountain views in most guest rooms that really make this hotel special. Adorned with blond-wood furniture and contemporary Canadian artwork, each room also has a window that opens. Elevator waits can be frustrating, so consider asking for a room on a lower floor, though you'll be sacrificing a view for this minor convenience. Next to the mountain-view pool is a rooftop herb garden—an aromatic retreat that includes a number of beehives. **Pros:** harbor views; proximity to cruise-ship terminal; the lovely terraced pool near the patio herb garden; fresh honey products. **Cons:** long elevator queues; the seemingly always-busy lobby lounge; the garden patio if you're at all bee phobic. ✉ *900 Canada Pl. Way, Downtown* ☎ *604/691–1991* ⊕ *www.fairmont.com/waterfront* ☞ *489 rooms, 29 suites* ☍ *In-room: safe (some), kitchen (some), refrigerator, Internet. In-hotel: restaurant, room service, bar, pool, gym, laundry service, Wi-Fi, parking (paid), some pets allowed* ▭ *AE, D, DC, MC, V* ✛ *F2.*

$–$$ 🏨 **The Kingston Hotel Bed & Breakfast.** Convenient to shopping and the entertainment district, the family-owned and family-operated Kingston is an old-style four-story elevator building (circa 1910), the type of establishment you'd expect to find in Europe. Small and immaculate, the spartan rooms are decorated in a contemporary style, with flower-pattern bedspreads and pastel colors. Some rooms have private bathrooms; others have a sink in the room and share a bath down the hall. North-facing rooms overlook a restaurant and bar–patio next door. That's not an issue in wet winter, but in summer the burble of bar talk below might disturb early-to-bed types. **Pros:** great location for the price; continental breakfast included. **Cons:** some shared bathrooms; limited amenities. ✉ *757 Richards St., Downtown* ☎ *604/684–9024 or 888/713–3304* ⊕ *www.kingstonhotelvancouver.com* ☞ *52 rooms, 13 with bath* ☍ *In-room: no TV (some), Wi-Fi. In-hotel: restaurant, bar, laundry facilities, Wi-Fi* ▭ *AE, MC, V* ⎊ *CP* ✛ *F3.*

$$$–$$$$ 🏨 **L'Hermitage Hotel.** Get beyond the marble floors, silk-velvet fabric
Fodor'sChoice   walls, and gold-cushion benches in the lobby, and you'll discover a
★   warm residential character to this mixed-use condo-boutique hotel. The studio, one-, and two-bedroom suites come with kitchenettes and in some cases fireplaces; faux-leather wall coverings convey an organic feel, and the oversized mirrors from Paris add just the right amount of bling. East-side rooms overlook a pool and garden patio. Breakfast is available in the elegant L'Orangerie guest-only lounge, which leads to a small library and free Internet terminals. Ideally located in the entertainment district, this is the choice for feeling chicly at home. The hotel has HD satellite. **Pros:** uptown hotel has refreshingly residential vibe; excellent concierge; weekly rates. **Cons:** lacks full-service restaurant (but near many great eateries). ✉ *788 Richards St., Downtown* ☎ *778/327–4100 or 888/855–1050* ⊕ *www.lhermitagevancouver.com*

40 rooms, 20 suites ⌂ In-room: safe, kitchen, refrigerator, Wi-Fi. In-hotel: room service, pool, gym, laundry service, Internet terminal, Wi-Fi, parking (paid) ☰ AE, D, DC, MC, V ✛ F4.

$$$$ 🏨 **Loden Hotel.** An ultrasophisticated boutique inn that has all manner of plug-and-play amenities, including in-room iPod stations and TVs with oversized LCD screens. Floor-to-ceiling windows fill the spacious guest rooms with natural light—and if you slide open the bathroom half wall you can enjoy the views from the soaker tub. The Voya restaurant has an Asian-infused French menu and a retro 1940s design with lots of mirrors and crystal chandeliers. The glitter continues on the outside, where the reflective glass covering the building creates the illusion that it's constructed entirely of mirrors. **Pros:** the lounge's intimacy lends it to discreet rendezvous; side-of-center location is a real find. **Cons:** limited spa services; dark lobby. ✉ *1177 Melville St., Downtown* ☎ *604/669–5060 or 877/225–6336* ⊕ *www.theloden.com* *70 rooms, 7 suites ⌂ In-room: safe, refrigerator, Wi-Fi. In-hotel: restaurant, room service, bar, gym, spa, laundry service, Wi-Fi, parking (paid), some pets allowed ☰ AE, D, DC, MC, V ✛ E2.*

$$$$ 🏨 **Shangri-la Hotel.** It's the tallest building in Vancouver—a 61-story tower of angled glass studded with gold squares that glint in the sunshine. Shangri-la relishes in over-the-top superlatives, and this is the upscale Asian brand's first hotel in North America. Soaring windows make spacious rooms feel even roomier, and a scheme of warm latte tones and dark-wood paneling captures a sleek contemporary Asian aesthetic. Such high-tech perks as bedside curtain controls and "do not disturb" doorbell indicators further establish the property's five-star credentials, as do the luxurious linens, cuddly robes, and bathroom LCD TVs. The Chi Spa provides wonderful Asian and European therapies. **Pros:** first-rate concierge service; stellar Chi Spa. **Cons:** public areas could be a shade more inviting; on the city's busiest thoroughfare (though still relatively peaceful). ✉ *1128 W. Georgia St., Downtown* ☎ *604/689–1120* ⊕ *www.shangri-la.com* *81 rooms, 38 suites ⌂ In-room: safe, refrigerator, DVD, Wi-Fi. In-hotel: restaurant, room service, bar, gym, spa, laundry service, Wi-Fi, parking (paid) ☰ AE, D, DC, MC, V ✛ D2.*

$$–$$$ 🏨 **The Victorian Hotel.** Budget hotels can be handsome, witness the gleaming hardwood floors, high ceilings, and chandeliers at this prettily restored 1898 European-style pension. This is one of Vancouver's best-value accommodations—guest rooms in the two connecting three-story buildings have down duvets, Oriental rugs atop hardwood floors, lush draperies, and period furniture; a few have bay windows or mountain views. Some of the private bathrooms are outfitted with marble tiles and granite countertops (though some have a shower and no tub). Even the shared baths are spotlessly clean and nicely appointed. With three queen beds, Room 15 is a good choice for families. **Pros:** great location for the price; helpful staff; clean; comfortable. **Cons:** location near the "rummy part of town" a few blocks east. It's relatively safe (honest), but common sense says you would probably take a cab to the door after midnight rather than walk. ✉ *514 Homer St., Downtown* ☎ *604/681–6369 or 877/681–6369* ⊕ *www.victorianhotel.ca* *39 rooms, 18 with*

17

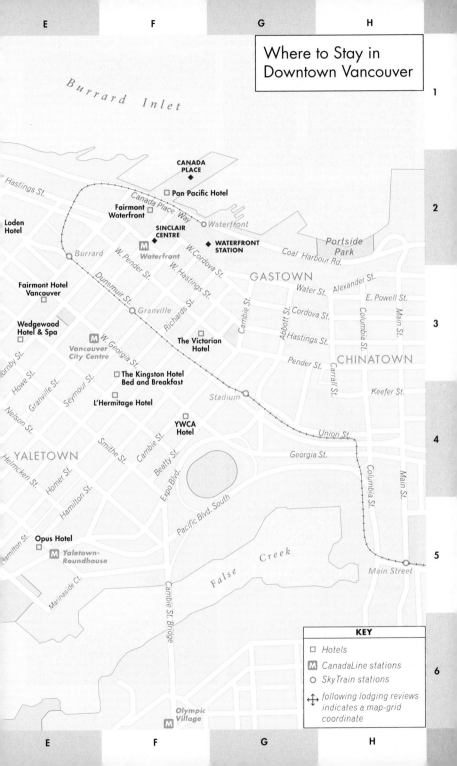

Where to Stay in Downtown Vancouver

Burrard Inlet

E **F** **G** **H**

1

2

3

4

5

6

CANADA PLACE ◆

□ Pan Pacific Hotel

Canada Place Way

Hastings St.

Fairmont Waterfront

Loden Hotel

SINCLAIR CENTRE ◆

W. Cordova St.

WATERFRONT STATION ◆

○ *Waterfront*

Ⓜ *Waterfront*

Burrard ○

W. Pender St.

W. Hastings St.

Coal Harbour Rd.

Portside Park

GASTOWN

Water St.

Alexander St.

Dunsmuir St.

Fairmont Hotel Vancouver □

Cambie St.

Abbott St.

Cordova St.

E. Powell St.

Granville ○

Richards St.

Hastings St.

Columbia St.

Main St.

Wedgewood Hotel & Spa □

Pender St.

Carrall St.

CHINATOWN

Ⓜ

Vancouver City Centre

W. Georgia St.

□ **The Victorian Hotel**

Keefer St.

Thornby St.

Howe St.

Granville St.

Seymour St.

□ **The Kingston Hotel Bed and Breakfast**

Stadium ○

L'Hermitage Hotel □

Nelson St.

YALETOWN

Smithe St.

Cambie St.

Beatty St.

□ **YWCA Hotel**

Union St.

Georgia St.

Columbia St.

Helmcken St.

Homer St.

Hamilton St.

Expo Blvd.

False Creek

Main St.

Hamilton St.

□ **Opus Hotel**

Ⓜ **Yaletown-Roundhouse**

Marinaside Ct.

Pacific Blvd. South

Main Street ○

Cambie St. Bridge

Olympic Village Ⓜ

KEY	
□	*Hotels*
Ⓜ	*CanadaLine stations*
○	*SkyTrain stations*
✛	*following lodging reviews indicates a map-grid coordinate*

L'Hermitage

Opus

Sylvia

Wedgewood Hotel & Spa

bath ⚌ In-room: Internet, refrigerator (some). In-hotel: laundry service, Wi-Fi, parking (paid) ▭ *MC, V* ⍾◎⍾ *CP* ✥ *E3.*

$$$$

Fodor's Choice

★

▦ **Wedgewood Hotel & Spa.** The small lavish Wedgewood is a member of the exclusive Relais & Châteaux Group, and is run by an owner who cares fervently about her guests. The lobby and guest rooms display a flair for old-world Italian luster with original artwork and antiques selected by the proprietor on her European travels. Guest rooms are capacious and each has a balcony. The four penthouse suites have fireplaces, luxury spa bathrooms, and private garden terraces. All the extra touches are here, too: afternoon ice delivery, dark-out drapes, robes, and a morning newspaper. The turndown service includes homemade cookies and bottled water. The sophisticated Bacchus restaurant and lounge ($$$–$$$$) is in the lobby; it's also a terrific stop for afternoon tea after shopping along Robson Street. The tiny but posh on-site spa is incredibly popular—book ahead for an appointment. **Pros:** personalized and attentive service; afternoon tea with finesse; great location close to top shops. **Cons:** small size means it books quickly. ✉ *845 Hornby St., Downtown* ☎ *604/689–7777 or 800/663–0666* ⊕ *www.wedgewoodhotel.com* ⤳ *41 rooms, 43 suites ⚌ In-room: safe, refrigerator, Wi-Fi. In-hotel: restaurant, room service, bar, gym, spa, laundry facilities, laundry service, Wi-Fi, parking (paid)* ▭ *AE, D, DC, MC, V* ✥ *E3.*

WEST END

$$–$$$

Fodor's Choice

★

▦ **Sylvia Hotel.** To stay at the Sylvia in June through August, you must book six months to a year ahead: this Virginia-creeper-covered 1912 building is popular because of its low rates and near-perfect location: about 25 feet from the beach on scenic English Bay, 200 feet from Stanley Park, and a 20-minute walk from Robson Street. The rooms and apartment-style suites vary from tiny to spacious. Many of the basic but comfortable rooms are large enough to sleep four, and all have windows that open. The restaurant and bar are popular, and its tenure on English Bay has made it a nostalgic haunt for Vancouverites. **Pros:** beachfront location; close to restaurants; a good place to mingle with the locals. **Cons:** older building; parking can be difficult if the lot is full; the 15-minute walk to the downtown core is slightly uphill. ✉ *1154 Gilford St., West End* ☎ *604/681–9321* ⊕ *www.sylviahotel.com* ⤳ *97 rooms, 22 suites ⚌ In-room: kitchen (some), Wi-Fi. In-hotel: restaurant, room service, bar, laundry service, Internet terminal, parking (paid), some pets allowed* ▭ *AE, DC, MC, V* ✥ *B2.*

YALETOWN

$$$$

Fodor's Choice

★

▦ **Opus Hotel.** The design team had a good time with this boutique hotel, creating fictitious characters and designing rooms for each. Billy's room is fun and offbeat, with pop art and lime-green accents. Dede's room has leopard skin, velveteen, and faux-fur accents, while Bob and Carol's place has softer edges and golden tones. Amenities are fun, too: look for mini-oxygen canisters in the bathrooms—a whiff'll clear your head if you have a hangover, and it'll stimulate blood flow for other pursuits. Most rooms have a full wall of windows, lots of natural light, and views of the city or the Japanese garden in the courtyard. Two rooms have private access to the garden; seventh-floor rooms have balconies. Other

17

perks include dog walking if you've brought Fido along, personal shopping, and free car service anywhere downtown. The Canada Line from the airport is steps away. **Pros:** the central Yaletown location, right by a rapid transit station; it's funky and hip; the lobby bar is a fashionable meeting spot. **Cons:** renovated heritage building has no views; surrounding neighborhood is mostly high-rises; trendy nightspots nearby can be noisy at night. ⊠ *322 Davie St., Yaletown* ☎ *604/642–6787 or 866/642–6787* ⊕ *www.opushotel.com* ⇆ *85 rooms, 11 suites* ♿ *Inroom: safe, refrigerator, DVD (some), Wi-Fi. In-hotel: restaurant, room service, bar, gym, bicycles, laundry service, Wi-Fi, parking (paid), some pets allowed* ⊟ *AE, DC, MC, V* ⊹ *E5.*

$–$$ 🖥 **YWCA Hotel.** A secure, modern high-rise in the heart of the entertainment district and steps from Yaletown, the YWCA has bright, comfortable rooms—a few big enough to sleep five. Some share a bath down the hall, some share a bath between two rooms, and others have private baths. TV lounges and shared kitchens are available for all guests, and rates include use of the YWCA adults-only pool and fitness facility, a 15-minute walk away at 535 Hornby Street. **Pros:** clean and friendly; access to high-quality fitness center; a terrific alternative to hostel accommodation. **Cons:** shared facilities. ⊠ *733 Beatty St., Downtown* ☎ *604/895–5830 or 800/663–1424* ⊕ *www.ywcahotel.com* ⇆ *155 rooms, 40 with bath* ♿ *In-room: refrigerator, no TV (some), Wi-Fi. In-hotel: laundry facilities, Internet terminal, Wi-Fi, parking (paid)* ⊟ *AE, MC, V* ⊹ *F4.*

NIGHTLIFE

Updated by
Crai S. Bower

There's plenty to choose from in just about every neighborhood: hipster Gastown has usurped Yaletown for the coolest cluster of late-night establishments, and is now the place to go for swanky clubs and trendy wine bars. The gay-friendly West End is all about bumpin' and grindin' in retro bars and clubs, while a posh crowd of glitterati flocks to Yaletown's brewpubs and stylish lounges. Meanwhile, Kitsilano (the Venice Beach of Vancouver) attracts a laid-back bunch who like to sip beer and frilly cocktails on cool bar patios with killer views, especially in the summer. And with its fair share of galleries, film festivals, cutting-edge theater, comedy, opera, and ballet, Vancouver (also known as Hollywood North) also has all manner of cultural stimuli that you might be looking for.

WHERE TO GET INFORMATION

For event information, pick up a copy of the free *Georgia Straight* (available at cafés and bookstores and street boxes around town) or look in the entertainment section of the *Vancouver Sun*: Thursday's paper has listings in the "Queue" section. Web-surf over to ⊕ *www. gayvan.com* and ⊕ *www.gayvancouver.net* for an insider's look at the gay-friendly scene.

WHERE TO GET TICKETS

Ticketmaster. Tickets for many venues can be booked by calling or visiting their Web site. ☎ *604/280–4444* ⊕ *www.ticketmaster.ca.*

Tickets Tonight sells half-price day-of-the-event tickets and full-price advance tickets to the theater, concerts, festivals, and other performing-arts events in Vancouver. Located at the Vancouver Tourist Info Centre. ✉ *200 Burrard St., Downtown* ☎ *604/684–2787* ⊕ *www.ticketstonight.ca.*

BARS AND LOUNGES

If you're headed to any of the more happening spots, dress to impress and prepare to wait in line, though doorman have been known to make magic happen for the right price.

Fodor'sChoice ★ **The Diamond.** At the top of a narrow staircase above Maple Tree Square, in one of the city's oldest buildings, the Diamond merges speakeasy simplicity with lounge cool. The large windows provide an ideal vantage point from which to observe the Square's impromptu street theater as you sip something special. And oh what cocktails; bartender and co-owner Josh Pape's passion for mixology flows over his room like a conductor before a symphony. You can choose between "boozy," "proper," or "delicate" options on the drinks menu. The Buck Buck Mule is a refreshing mix of gin, sherry, cucumber juice, cilantro, lime juice, and ginger beer; the Tequila Martinez features tequila, vermouth, Lillet, peach bitters, and an orange twist. ✉ *6 Powell St., Gastown* ☎ *604/408–2891.*

Fodor'sChoice ★ **Pourhouse.** Paying homage to the Klondike Gold Rush and Pioneer Square spirit, Pourhouse has quickly appeared on numerous local Top Ten lists. Gold Fashioned, Centennial, and Prospector take libation lovers on a historical tour of the city's highlights, while Pork and Beans, Welsh Rarebit, and Carpet Bag Steak show what a little imagination and fresh ingredients can do to transform tried-and-true dining options. ✉ *162 Water St., Gastown* ☎ *604/568--7022.*

BREWPUBS

Dockside Brewing Company. This popular local hangout has a seaside patio, casual Pacific Northwest restaurant, and house-brewed German-style beer. ✉ *Granville Island Hotel, 1253 Johnston St., Granville Island* ☎ *604/685–7070.*

Yaletown Brewing Company. Based in a renovated warehouse with a glassed-in brewery turning out several tasty beers, this always-crowded pub has a lively singles'-scene pub, a patio, and a restaurant. ✉ *1111 Mainland St., Yaletown* ☎ *604/681–2739.*

HOTEL BARS

Fodor'sChoice ★ **Market by Jean George, at Shangri-la.** Besides boasting the best rainy-season patio (it's covered and heated) in Vancouver, the Shangri La's bar and restaurant became the city's hottest spot the instant it opened in 2009. ✉ *1128 W. Georgia St., Downtown* ☎ *604/689–1120.*

Fodor'sChoice ★ **Opus Bar.** Local hipsters, international jet-setters, and film industry types sip martinis and lounge on Jacobsen egg chairs and Eames stools at this happening destination, which doubles as the hotel's lobby. It's small, but it's still one of the hippest cocktail destinations in the city. ✉ *350 Davie St., in the Opus Hotel, Yaletown* ☎ *604/642–0557.*

YEW Bar at the Four Seasons. Glass, natural woods, and granite reflect B.C.'s stunning natural environment, while the more than 150 wines

17

The Yale is one of Vancouver's top spots for live music.

by the glass and a perpetually changing cocktail list have established YEW among the city's top hotel bars. Happy hour attracts executives, and at other times you'll see Canucks fans or late nightcappers eager to stretch out on the low-rise banquettes or cozy up to the raw bar. ⊠ *791 W. Georgia St., Downtown* ☎ *604/689–9333.*

WINE BARS

Bin 942 Tapas Parlour. This cozy South Granville room dishes up Asian- and Latin-influenced small plates that pair well with the eclectic wine list. The sister restaurant, **Bin 941,** in raucous Davie Street, also has a small, albeit expertly selected, wine list, but the scene is more chaotic and definitely louder. ⊠ *1521 W. Broadway, Downtown* ☎ *604/734– 9421* ⊠ *941 Davie St., Downtown* ☎ *604/683–1246.*

★ **Salt Tasting Room.** This hip wine bar and charcuterie has communal tables, concrete floors, and a killer selection of local and international wines perfect for pairing with cured meats and artisanal cheeses. ⊠ *45 Blood Alley, Gastown* ☎ *604/633–1912.*

GAY NIGHTLIFE

The city's gay community is centered in two distinctive neighborhoods: the West End (⊕ *www.westendbia.com*), with its flashy bars and flam- boyant shops on Davie Street, and the thriving lesbian community of Commercial Drive (⊕ *www.thedrive.ca*), where authentic Italian cafés, Greek delis, and chill restaurants set the come-as-you-are vibe.

1181. This addition to the gayborhood is all about stylish interior design—plush sofas, glass coffee tables, wood-paneled ceiling—and fancy cocktails (think caipirinhas and mojitos). It gets particularly crowded on Saturdays, when a DJ spins behind the bar. ⊠ *1181 Davie St., West End* ☎ *604/687–3991.*

The Fountainhead Pub. You won't find anyone poring over Ayn Rand books at "The Head." Instead, this friendly local pub attracts gays, straights, and undecideds to their street-side patio, ideally placed for watching the parade of local boys strutting their stuff on Davie Street. ⊠ *1025 Davie St., West End* ☎ *604/687–2222.*

Lick. Vancouver's most popular lesbian dance bar sizzles as girls who like girls dance to kick-ass electronic, hip-hop, and drum-and-bass beats. A quiet chill-out area in front provides respite from the noise and heat. Two other dance clubs, **Honey** and **Lotus,** at the same site, are open to all. ⊠ *455 Abbott St., Gastown* ☎ *604/685–7777.*

MUSIC

JAZZ Vancouver is home to one of the most accessible jazz scenes in Canada, with clubs and restaurants hosting local and international talent. **Coastal Jazz and Blues Society** has a hotline that details upcoming concerts and clubs. The society also runs the **Vancouver International Jazz Festival,** which lights up venues around town every June. ☎ *604/872–5200* ⊕ *www.coastaljazz.ca.*

Cellar Restaurant and Jazz Club. The city's top jazz venue features a who's who of the Canadian jazz scene. ⊠ *3611 W. Broadway, Kitsilano* ☎ *604/738–1959.*

ROCK AND **Railway Club.** In the early evening this spot attracts film and media types
BLUES to its pub-style rooms; after 8 it becomes a venue for local bands. Technically it's a private social club, so patrons must sign in, but everyone of age is welcome. ⊠ *579 Dunsmuir St., Downtown* ☎ *604/681–1625.*

Yale. Live bands perform most nights at Vancouver's most established rhythm-and-blues bar. ⊠ *1300 Granville St., Downtown* ☎ *604/681–9253.*

THE ARTS

From performing arts to theater, classical music, dance, and a thriving gallery scene, there's much for an art lover to choose from in Vancouver.

CLASSICAL MUSIC

Vancouver Opera. The city's opera company stages four productions a year, from October through May, at the Queen Elizabeth Theatre. ☎ *604/682–2871.*

Vancouver Symphony Orchestra. The resident company at the **Orpheum Theatre** presents classical and popular music performances to a wide variety of audiences. ⊠ *884 Granville St., Downtown* ☎ *604/876–3434.*

DANCE

Scotiabank Dance Centre. The hub of contemporary dance in British Columbia, this striking building with an art deco facade has performances, studio showings, and other types of events by national and international artists. ⊠ *677 Davie St., Downtown* ☎ *604/606–6400.*

17

THEATER

Arts Club Theatre Company. This company operates two theaters. The **Arts Club Granville Island Stage** (⊠ *1585 Johnston St., Granville Island* ☎ *604/687–1644*) is an intimate venue and a good place to catch works by local playwrights. The **Stanley Industrial Alliance Stage** (⊠ *2750 Granville St., South Granville* ☎ *604/687–1644*) is a lavish former movie palace staging works by such perennial favorites as William Shakespeare and Noël Coward.

Queen Elizabeth Theatre. This is a major venue for ballet, opera, and similar large-scale events. ⊠ *600 Hamilton St., Downtown* ☎ *604/665–3050.*

Vancouver Playhouse. The leading venue in Vancouver for mainstream theater is in the same complex as the Queen Elizabeth Theatre. ⊠ *649 Cambie St., Downtown* ☎ *604/665–3050.*

SHOPPING

Updated by
Carolyn B.
Heller

Unlike many cities where suburban malls have taken over, Vancouver is full of individual boutiques and specialty shops. Ethnic markets, art galleries, gourmet-food shops, and high-fashion outlets abound, and both Asian and First Nations influences in crafts, home furnishings, and foods are quite prevalent.

Stretching from Burrard to Bute, **Robson Street** is the city's main fashion-shopping and people-watching artery. The Gap and Banana Republic have their flagship stores here, as do Canadian fashion outlets Club Monaco and Roots. Souvenir shops and cafés fill the gaps. One block north of Robson, **Alberni Street** is geared to the higher-income visitor, and is where you'll find duty-free shopping. At the stores in and around Alberni, and around Burrard, you'll find names such as Tiffany & Co., Louis Vuitton, Gucci, Coach, Hermés, and Betsey Johnson. Treasure hunters like the 300 block of **West Cordova Street** in **Gastown**, where off-beat shops sell curios, vintage clothing, and locally designed clothes. Bustling **Chinatown**—centered on Pender and Main streets—is full of Chinese bakeries, restaurants, herbalists, tea merchants, and import shops. Frequently described as Vancouver's SoHo, **Yaletown** on the north bank of False Creek is home to boutiques and restaurants—many in converted warehouses—that cater to a trendy, moneyed crowd. On the south side of False Creek, **Granville Island** has a lively food market and a wealth of galleries, crafts shops, and artisans' studios.

DEPARTMENT STORES AND SHOPPING CENTERS

The **Hudson's Bay Co.** A Canadian institution (even though it's now owned by Americans), The Bay was founded as part of the fur trade in the 17th century. A whole department sells the signature tri-color Bay blankets and other Canadiana. ⊠ *674 Granville St., at Georgia St., Downtown* ☎ *604/681–6211.*

Aberdeen Centre. First-rate Asian restaurants and cheap-and-cheerful food stalls, clothing stores stocking the latest Hong Kong styles, and Daiso—a Japanese bargain-hunters' paradise where most goods sell for just $2—make this swank mall a good introduction to Vancouver's Asian shopping experience. Take the Canada Line south to Aberdeen station, about 20 minutes from downtown. ⊠ *4151 Hazelbridge Way, Richmond* ☎ *604/270–1234.*

Metropolis at Metrotown. With 450 (give or take) stores—mostly North American chains—it's the province's largest shopping destination, easily reached via a 20-minute SkyTrain ride from downtown. Teens and serious shoppers alike flock to this sprawling mall; wear comfortable shoes. ⊠ *4800 Kingsway, Burnaby* ☎ *604/438–3610.*

SPECIALTY STORES

ART AND CRAFTS GALLERIES

DOWNTOWN — A number of notable galleries are on the downtown peninsula.

Fodor's Choice
★ — **Hill's Native Art.** This highly respected store has Vancouver's largest selection of First Nations art. If you think the main level is impressive, go upstairs where the collector-quality stuff is. ⊠ *165 Water St., Gastown* ☎ *604/685–4249.*

GALLERY ROW — Gallery Row along Granville Street is home to about a dozen high-end contemporary-art galleries. Most are clustered between 5th Avenue and Broadway, but the gallery district extends up to 15th Avenue.

Douglas Reynolds Gallery. In this collection of Northwest Coast First Nations art, particularly strong in woodwork and jewelry, some pieces date back to the 1800s, while others are strikingly contemporary. ⊠ *2335 Granville St., South Granville* ☎ *604/731–9292.*

Robert Held Art Glass. At Canada's largest "hot glass" studio, located two blocks west of Granville Street, you can watch glassblowers in action, then browse the one-of-a-kind vases, paperweights, bowls, ornaments, and perfume bottles. Held's glass pieces have been exhibited at the Canadian Museum of Civilization in Ottawa and at galleries across North America. ⊠ *2130 Pine St., between 5th and 6th Aves., South Granville* ☎ *604/737–0020.*

GRANVILLE
ISLAND — Granville Island is a must-do destination for crafts aficionados. Stroll Railspur Alley (off Old Bridge Street), which is lined with working artists' studios; the Net Loft building opposite the Public Market also has several galleries. The "Artists & Artisans of Granville Island" brochure (available at shops around the island or online at ⊕ *www. granvilleislandartists.com*) has a complete listing of galleries and studios.

CLOTHES

MEN'S AND
WOMEN'S
CLOTHING — West Coast casual is the predominant look in Vancouver, but if you're looking for "made in Vancouver" fashions, head for Gastown or Main Street, where young, up-and-coming labels are sold at stores committed to giving local designers a leg up.

Barefoot Contessa. These cute shops mix creative looks with '40s-style glamour. Look for frilly feminine clothing (the homemade camisoles are in hot demand), jewelry, and bags—some by local designers—as well as vintage linens and decorative accessories. ⊠ *3715 Main St., Main St./Mt. Pleasant* ☎ *604/879–1137* ⊠ *1928 Commercial Dr., East Side* ☎ *604/255–9035.*

Dream Apparel & Articles for People. Come here to find a variety of wares by local designers. The creative selections target the hip twentysomething crowd. Under the same ownership, **Little Dream** (⊠ *130–1666*

CLOSE UP

Vancouver's Top Spas

Vancouver's spa scene is as diverse as its multicultural makeup, and includes everything from exotic steam experiences to over-the-top indulgence. While many services give the nod to ancient wisdoms such as Ayurveda, you'll also find holistic spa and wellness destinations that incorporate elements of traditional Chinese medicine, Japanese Reiki, and New Age energy therapies, alongside medical aesthetics like Botox, microdermabrasion, and teeth whitening. For authentic spa experiences, here are our top choices:

Absolute Spa at the Century. ⊠ *1015 Burrard St., Downtown* ☎ *604/684–2772.*

Absolute Spa at Hotel Vancouver. ⊠ *900 W. Georgia St., Downtown* ☎ *604/684–2772.*

Miraj. ⊠ *1495 W. 6th Ave., South Granville* ☎ *604/733–5151.*

Spa Utopia. ⊠ *999 Canada Pl., at Pan Pacific Hotel, Downtown* ☎ *604/641–1351.*

Spruce Body Lab. ⊠ *1128 Richards St., Yaletown* ☎ *604/683–3220.*

Wedgewood Hotel Spa. ⊠ *2nd floor, 845 Hornby St., Downtown* ☎ *604/608–5340.*

Johnston St., Net Loft, Granville Island ☎ *604/683–6930*) is a smaller version of this fashion-forward shop. ⊠ *311 W. Cordova St., Gastown* ☎ *604/683–7326.*

Fodor'sChoice ★ **Holt Renfrew.** High on the city's ritzy scale, Holts is a swanky showcase for international high fashion and accessories for men and women. Think Prada, Dolce & Gabbana, and other designer labels. ⊠ *Pacific Centre, 737 Dunsmuir St., Downtown* ☎ *604/681–3121.*

Lululemon Athletica. This is a real Vancouver success story: everyone from power-yoga devotees to soccer moms covets the fashionable, well-constructed workout wear with the stylized "A" insignia. The stores also provide free drop-in yoga classes; call or check ⊕ *www.lululemon.com* for details. ⊠ *1148 Robson St., West End* ☎ *604/681–3118* ⊠ *2113 W. 4th Ave., Kitsilano* ☎ *604/732–6111* ⊠ *Metropolis at Metrotown, 4800 Kingsway, Burnaby* ☎ *604/430–4659.*

Roots. For outdoorsy clothes that double as souvenirs (many sport maple-leaf logos), check out these Canadian-made sweatshirts, leather jackets, and other comfy casuals. ⊠ *1001 Robson St., West End* ☎ *604/683–4305* ⊠ *2665 Granville St., South Granville* ☎ *604/629–1300* ⊠ *Metropolis at Metrotown, 4700 Kingsway, Burnaby* ☎ *604/435–5554.*

FOOD

FOOD MARKET
Fodor'sChoice ★ **Granville Island Public Market.** Locals and visitors alike crowd this indoor market that's part farm stand, part gourmet grocery, and part upscale food court. Stalls are packed with fresh produce, meats, just-caught fish, baked goods, and prepared foods from exotic cheeses and handmade fudge to frothy cappuccinos. If the sun is out, dine on your purchases out on the decks. At the **Salmon Shop** (☎ *604/669–3474*), you can pick up fresh or smoked salmon vacuum-packed and wrapped for travel. For

A selection of goodies from Les Amis du Fromage.

other local specialties (and great gifts for foodie friends), visit **Edible British Columbia** (☎ 604/662–3606), which sells jams, sauces, chocolates, and hundreds of other edible items from around the province. ✉ *1689 Johnston St., Granville Island* ☎ *604/666–5784.*

FOOD AND WINE SHOPS **Les Amis du Fromage.** If you love cheese, don't miss the mind-boggling array of selections from B.C., the rest of Canada, France, and elsewhere at this shop of delicacies. The extremely knowledgeable mother-and-daughter owners, Alice and Allison Spurrell, and their staff encourage you to taste before you buy. Yum. ✉ *1752 W. 2nd Ave., Kitsilano* ☎ *604/732–4218.* ✉ *843 E. Hastings St., East Side* ☎ *604/253–4218*

Taylorwood Wines. To learn more about British Columbia wines, or to pick up a bottle (or a few), visit the knowledgeable staff at this Yaletown store that stocks only wines produced within the province. Weekly tastings let you try before you buy; check the Web site ⊕ *www. taylorwoodwines.com* for a schedule. ✉ *1185 Mainland St., Yaletown* ☎ *604/408–9463.*

OUTDOOR EQUIPMENT

Outdoor-oriented Vancouver is a great place to pick up camping and hiking gear. There's a cluster of outdoor-equipment shops on West Broadway between Yukon and Manitoba streets, and there are several snowboard, skiing, and bicycle outlets on West 4th Avenue, just east of Burrard Street.

Mountain Equipment Co-op. The massive warehouse-style outlet is a local institution with a good selection of high-performance and midprice clothing and equipment for hiking, cycling, climbing, kayaking, traveling, and just hanging around outdoors. A onetime C$5 membership is required. ✉ *130 W. Broadway, Fairview* ☎ *604/872–7858.*

SHOES

John Fluevog. You might've seen these shops in New York and Los Angeles, but did you know the funky shoe shops were started by a Vancouverite? The Gastown location is worth a look for the store itself, with its striking glass facade and soaring ceilings. ✉ *837 Granville St., Downtown* ☎ *604/688–2828.* ✉ *65 Water St., Gastown* ☎ *604/688–6228.*

OUTDOOR ACTIVITIES AND ATTRACTIONS

Updated by Alison Appelbe

Exceptional for North American cities, the downtown peninsula is almost entirely encircled by a seawall along which you can walk, in-line skate, cycle, or otherwise propel yourself. Indeed, it's so popular that it qualifies as a, albeit unofficial, national treasure. There are places along the route where you can hire a bike, Rollerblades, canoe, or kayak, or simply go for a swim or play tennis. Top-rated skiing, snowboarding, mountain biking, fishing, diving, and golf are just minutes away.

BEACHES

Greater Vancouver is well endowed with beaches—from the pebbly coves of West Vancouver to a vast tableau of sand at Spanish Banks—but the waters are decidedly cool, even in summer, and, aside from the kids and the intrepid, the preferred activity is sunbathing. That said, the city provides several exceptional outdoor pools—right smack on the ocean. The most spectacular is Kitsilano Pool, where you can gander up at the North Shore Mountains while swimming lengths or lolling in the shallows. At the city's historic beach and round-the-clock social venue, English Bay, you can swim, rent a kayak—or simply stroll and people-watch. Cosmopolitan Vancouver is also known for its clothing-optional beaches.

All city beaches have lifeguards, washrooms, and concession stands, and most have paid parking. Liquor is prohibited in parks and on beaches. With a few exceptions, dogs are not permitted on beaches. For more information, check out the Vancouver Parks Web site (⊕ *vancouver.ca/ parks/rec/beaches*).

Fodor'sChoice
★

Kitsilano Beach. To the west of the south end of the Burrard Bridge, this is the city's busiest beach—in-line skaters, volleyball games, and sleek young people are ever-present. Facilities include a playground, a restaurant and concession stand, and tennis courts. **Kitsilano Pool** is also here: at 137 meters (445 feet), it's the longest pool in Canada, and one of the few heated saltwater pools in the world. ✉ *2305 Cornwall Ave., Kitsilano* ☎ *604/731–0011* ⊙ *Late May–mid-September.*

Stanley Park beaches. There are several beaches accessed from Stanley Park Drive in Stanley Park. **Second Beach** has a playground, a small sandy area, and a large heated pool with a slide. **Third Beach** has a larger stretch of sand, fairly warm water, and great sunset views. It's a popular evening picnic spot.

West End beaches. English Bay, the city's best-known beach, lies just to the east of the south entrance to Stanley Park, at the foot of Denman

Beaches might not be the first thing you think of in Vancouver, but in summer, Kits Beach is quite a hot spot.

Street. A waterslide, street performers, and artists keep things interesting all summer. Farther along Beach Drive, **Sunset Beach** is too close to the downtown core for clean safe swimming, but is a great spot for an evening stroll. You can catch a ferry to Granville Island here, or swim at the **Vancouver Aquatic Centre** (⊠ *1050 Beach Ave.* ☎ *604/665–3424*), a public indoor pool and fitness center.

CYCLING

While Vancouver is increasingly bike friendly, its major arteries and busier streets can be uncomfortable for all but the experienced cyclist. As a helpful gesture, the city introduced 26 interconnected bikeways, identified by green bicycle signs; although most routes share the road with cars, they're well chosen for safety. The city has also introduced protected bike lanes on the Burrard Bridge and on Dunsmuir Street. Many TransLink buses have bike racks, and bikes are welcome on the SeaBus and on the SkyTrain at off-peak times. Aquabus Ferries transport bikes and riders across False Creek. If cycling is a key component of your visit, check in with the Vancouver Cycling Coalition (⊕ *www.vacc.bc.ca*) for events and cycling-awareness information.

Lower Seymour Conservation Reserve. Nestled into the precipitous North Shore Mountains, this reserve has 25 km (15.5 mi) of challenging rainforest trails. The **Seymour Valley Trailway** is a 10-km (6-mi) paved pathway, suitable for cyclists, in-line skaters, baby strollers, and wheelchairs; it meanders over streams and through woods. Other trails, like Corkscrew and Salvation, are classified as advanced or even extreme. ⊠ *End of Lillooet Rd., North Vancouver* ☎ *604/432–6286*.

Fodor'sChoice
★

The most popular recreational route, much of it off-road, is the **Seaside route.** It runs about 32 km (20 mi) from the seawall in Coal Harbour, around Stanley Park and False Creek, through Kitsilano to Spanish Banks. For detailed route descriptions and a downloadable map, check out ⊕ *www.metrovancouver.ca*. Vancouver cycling routes connect with routes on the North Shore, in Richmond and Delta to the south, and in municipalities to the east. For sub-area and region-wide maps, go to the regional transportation authority, TransLink (⊕ *www.translink.bc.ca*) or the Metro Vancouver Web site (⊕ *www.metrovancouver.ca*). Cycling maps are also available from most bike shops and bike-rental outlets. Helmets are required by law and a sturdy lock is essential.

BIKE RENTALS   Most bike-rental outlets also rent Rollerblades and jogging strollers. Cycling helmets, a legal requirement in Vancouver, come with the rentals. Locks and maps are also normally supplied.

Bayshore Bicycles. If you're starting your bike ride near Stanley Park, try this friendly store. It has a range of bikes and Rollerblades as well as baby joggers and bike trailers. ⊠ *745 Denman St., West End* ☎ *604/688–2453* ⊕ *www.bayshorebikerentals.ca.*

Spokes Bicycle Rentals. Located at Denman and Georgia, near Stanley Park, Spokes has a wide selection of bikes, including kids' bikes, tandems, mountain bikes, and Rollerblades. ⊠ *1798 W. Georgia St., West End* ☎ *604/688–5141* ⊕ *www.spokesbicyclerentals.com.*

ECOTOURS AND WILDLIFE-VIEWING

Given a temperate climate and forest, mountain, and marine environments teeming with life, it's no surprise that wildlife-watching is an important pastime and growing business in and around Vancouver. Many people walk the ocean foreshores or park and mountain trails, binoculars or scopes in hand, looking for exceptional or rare birds. Others venture onto the water to see seals, sea lions, and whales—as well as the birds that inhabit the maritime world.

Sewell's Marina Horseshoe Bay. This longtime marina at the foot of Howe Sound runs two-hour ecotours of the surrounding marine and coastal mountain habitat from April through October. Sightings range from seals to soaring eagles. High-speed rigid inflatable hulls are used. ⊠ *6409 Bay St., Horseshoe Bay* ☎ *604/921–3474* ⊕ *www.sewellsmarina.com.*

Between mid-November and mid-February the world's largest concentration of bald eagles gathers to feed on salmon at **Brackendale Eagles' Park** (⊠ *Government Rd. off Hwy. 99, Brackendale*), about an hour north of Vancouver.

WHALE-
WATCHING   Between April and October pods of orca whales travel through the Strait of Georgia, near Vancouver. The area is also home to harbor seals, elephant seals, bald eagles, minke whales, porpoises, and a wealth of birdlife.

Lotus Land Tours. High-speed covered boats take you out to watch for whales and other wildlife in the Strait of Georgia. The five-hour cruise costs C$175 and includes pickup anywhere in Vancouver and an on-board lunch. ☎ *604/684–4922 or 800/528–3531* ⊕ *www. VancouverNatureAdventures.com.*

Prince of Whales. This established Victoria operator runs several different trips from the downtown waterfront (near Waterfront Station) across Georgia Strait to the Victoria area in season. ✉ *812 Wharf St., Victoria* ☎ *250/383–4884 or 888/383–4884* ⊕ *www.princeofwhales.com.*

Wild Whales Vancouver. Boats leave Granville Island in search of orca pods in Georgia Strait, traveling as far as Victoria. Rates are C$125 for a three- to seven-hour trip in either an open or glass-domed boat. Each boat leaves once daily, April through October, conditions permitting. ✉ *1806 Mast Tower Rd., Granville Island* ☎ *604/699–2011* ⊕ *www. whalesvancouver.ca.*

FISHING

You can fish for salmon all year in coastal British Columbia, weather and marine conditions permitting. Halibut, at 50 pounds and heavier, is the area's other trophy fish. Charters ply waters between the Capilano River mouth in Burrard Inlet and the outer Georgia Strait and Gulf Islands. Your fishing license can be purchased from the boat-rental or tour operator.

Bonnie Lee Charters. From moorings in the Granville Island Maritime Market, this company runs five-hour fishing trips into Burrard Inlet and Georgia Strait year-round. Guided outings start at C$395 for one person, less per person for groups. ✉ *1676 Duranleau St., Granville Island* ☎ *604/290–7447* ⊕ *www.bonnielee.com.*

Steveston Seabreeze Adventures. From docks in Steveston village in Richmond, just south of Vancouver, Seabreeze operates fishing charters as far west as the Gulf Islands, between mid-June and September. Its 12-passenger boats, with guides, cost C$1,400 on weekends, C$1,300 on weekdays. ✉ *12551 No. 1 Rd., Richmond* ☎ *604/272–7200* ⊕ *www. seabreezeadventures.ca.*

GOLF

Vancouver-area golf courses offer challenging golf with great scenery. Most are open year-round. For advance tee-time bookings at about 20 Vancouver area courses, or for a spur-of-the-moment game, call **Last Minute Golf** (☎ *604/878–1833 or 800/684–6344* ⊕ *www.lastminutegolfbc. com*). The company matches golfers and courses, sometimes at substantial greens-fee discounts.

Fodor's Choice ★ The Vancouver Park Board operates three public courses, all located on the city's south-facing slope. The most celebrated is the 18-hole, par-72, 6,700-yard **Fraserview Golf Course** (✉ *7800 Vivian Dr., South Vancouver* ☎ *604/257–6923, 604/280–1818 advance bookings*), where facilities include a driving range and a clubhouse. The greens fees are C$58–C$65. The other two, both 18 holes and with slightly lower greens fees, are **Langara Golf Course** (✉ *6706 Alberta St.* ☎ *604/713–1816*) and **McCleery Golf Course** (✉ *7188 Macdonald St.* ☎ *604/257–8191*).

HIKING

If you're heading into the mountains, hike with a companion, pack warm clothes (even in summer) and extra food and water, and leave word of your route and the time you expect to return. Remember that weather can change quickly in the mountains here. You can check for a weather forecast with **Environment Canada** (⊕ *weatheroffice.ec.gc.ca*).

Fodor'sChoice **Capilano River Regional Park.** This small but spectacular park is where
★ you'll find the Capilano River canyon, several old-growth fir trees approaching 61 meters (200 feet), a salmon hatchery open to the public, and the Cleveland Dam, as well as 26 km (16 mi) of hiking trails. It's at the end of Capilano Park Road, off Capilano Road, in North Vancouver. ☎ *604/224–5739.*

Grouse Mountain. Vancouver's most famous, or infamous, hiking route, the Grind, is a 2.9-km (1.8-mi) climb straight up 2,500 vertical feet to the top of Grouse Mountain. Thousands do it annually, but climbers are advised to be in "excellent physical condition"; it's not for children. The route is open daily, 6:30 AM to 7:30 PM, from spring through autumn (conditions permitting). Or you can take the Grouse Mountain Skyride (gondola) to the top; a round-trip ticket is C$39.95, one-way down is C$10. Eco-walks are led along the paths accessed from the Skyride, and there are additional hiking trails from this point, like the Goat Mountain Trail, which can take you even farther up. ✉ *6400 Nancy Greene Way, North Vancouver* ☎ *604/980–9311 Grouse Mountain, 604/432–6200 Metro Vancouver (formerly GVRD)* ⊕ *www.grousemountain.com.*

Fodor'sChoice **Stanley Park.** Stanley Park is well suited for moderate walking and easy
★ hiking. The most obvious and arguably most picturesque route is the 8.8-km (5.5-mi) seawall around its perimeter, but this 1,000-acre park also offers 27 km (16.7 mi) of interior trails through the coniferous forest, including a few small patches of original forest, or old growth. The interior paths are wide and well maintained; here you'll experience something of the true rain forest, and spot some of the birds and small mammals that inhabit it. An easy interior trail runs around Lost Lagoon, and a popular interior destination is Beaver Lake. You can download a trail map at the Park Board Web site. ⇨ *For more information, see the Stanley Park listing in Exploring above.* ☎ *604/257–8400.*

HOCKEY

The Canucks have sold out every game since 2004, though tickets can be purchased at legal resale outlets. Watching NHL hockey in a Canadian city is one of sport's greatest spectacles, so try and catch a game if possible. If you can't attend in person, head into any bar on game night, especially Saturdays ("Hockey Night" in Canada), as game nights light up the city's bars and restaurants.

The **Vancouver Canucks** play at **General Motors Place** (✉ *800 Griffiths Way, Downtown* ☎ *604/899–7400*).

JOGGING

Vancouverites jog at any time of day, in almost any weather, and dozens of well-trodden routes go through the leafy streets of the city's West Side; there is also the wider Greenways network of "calmed roads." The seawall around the downtown peninsula and False Creek, into Kitsilano, remains the most popular route, though the hilly byways of the North Shore are also popular with serious runners. Visiting runners staying downtown will be drawn to the 8.8-km (5.5-mi) route around Stanley Park, or the 4 km (2.5 mi) around Lost Lagoon.

The hike up Grouse Mountain is no easy feat, but the views from the top, and from Goat Mountain, slightly farther up, are breathtaking.

SKIING AND SNOWBOARDING

While Whistler Resort, a two-hour drive from Vancouver, is the top-ranked ski destination in the region, the North Shore Mountains hold three excellent ski and snowboard areas. All have rentals, lessons, night skiing, eateries, and a variety of runs suitable for all skill levels. The ski season generally runs from early December through early spring. While ski areas and trails are generally well marked, once you ski outside the boundaries you're entering rugged wilderness that can be distinctly unfriendly to humans. All mountain-goers are strongly advised to respect maps and signposts.

Grouse Mountain can be reached by TransLink buses. Cypress and Seymour each run shuttle buses from Lonsdale Quay and other North Shore stops.

Cypress Mountain. The most recent of three North Shore commercial ski destinations, Cypress is well equipped and was made even more so with the completion of freestyle skiing and snowboarding venues built for the 2010 Winter Olympics. Facilities include six quad or double chairs, 53 downhill runs, and a vertical drop of 1,750 feet. The mountain also has a snow-tubing area and snowshoe tours, as well as 19 km (10 mi) of cross-country trails. ⊠ *Cypress Bowl Rd., West Vancouver ⌖ Exit 8 off Hwy. 1 westbound* ☎ *604/419–7669* ⊕ *www.cypressmountain.com.*

Grouse Mountain. Reached by gondola (with an entrance fee) from the upper reaches of North Vancouver, much of the Grouse Mountain resort inhabits a slope overlooking the city. While views are fine on a clear day, at night (the area is known for its night skiing) they're spectacular. Facilities include four quad chairs, 26 skiing and snowboarding runs, and several all-level freestyle-terrain parks. The vertical drop is 1,210 feet. There's a choice of upscale and casual dining in a good-looking stone-and-timber lodge. ⊠ *6400 Nancy Greene Way, North Vancouver* ☎ *604/980–9311, 604/986–6262 snow report* ⊕ *www. grousemountain.com.*

Mount Seymour. Described as a full-service winter activity area, the Mount Seymour resort sprawls over 200 acres accessed from eastern North Vancouver. With three chairs for varying abilities; a beginner's rope tow, equipment rentals, and lessons; and toboggan and tubing runs, it's a popular destination for families. Snowboarding is particularly popular. The eateries aren't fancy. ⊠ *1700 Mt. Seymour Rd., North Vancouver* ☎ *604/986–2261, 604/718–7771 snow report* ⊕ *www. mountseymour.com.*

WATER SPORTS

BOATING AND SAILING
With an almost limitless number and variety of waterways, southwestern British Columbia is a boater's paradise. And much of this territory has easy access to marine and public services. One caution: this ocean territory is vast and complex; maritime maps are required. And one should always consult the Environment Canada marine forecasts (⊕ *www.weatheroffice.gc.ca*).

Blue Pacific Yacht Charters. This company rents motor- and sailboats for use between Vancouver Island and Seattle. ⊠ *1519 Foreshore Walk, Granville Island* ☎ *604/682–2161 or 800/237–2392* ⊕ *www. bluepacificcharters.ca.*

Cooper Boating charters sailboats and cabin cruisers, with or without instructing skippers. ⊠ *1815 Mast Tower Rd., Granville Island* ☎ *604/687–4110 or 888/999–6419* ⊕ *www.cooperboating.com.*

CANOE-ING AND KAYAKING
Kayaking—seagoing and river kayaking—has become something of a lifestyle in Vancouver. While many sea kayakers start out (or remain) in False Creek, others venture into the open ocean and up and down the Pacific Coast. You can white-water kayak or canoe down the Capilano River and several other North Vancouver rivers. And paddling in a traditional, seagoing aboriginal-built canoe is an increasingly popular way to experience the maritime landscape.

Deep Cove Canoe and Kayak Rentals. Ocean-kayak rentals, guided trips, and lessons for kids and adults are all available at their North Shore base, from May to mid-October. ⊠ *2156 Banbury Rd., North Vancouver* ☎ *604/929–2268* ⊕ *www.deepcovekayak.com.*

Ecomarine Ocean Kayak Centre. Lessons and rentals are offered year-round from Granville Island, and from early May to early September at Jericho Beach and English Bay. ⊠ *1668 Duranleau St., Granville Island* ☎ *604/689–7575 or 888/425–2925* ⊕ *www.ecomarine.com* ⊠ *English Bay* ⊠ *Jericho Beach.*

VICTORIA

Updated
by Sue
Kernaghan

Despite its role as the provincial capital, Victoria was largely bypassed, economically, by Vancouver throughout the 20th century. This, as it turns out, was all to the good, helping to preserve Victoria's historic downtown and keeping the city free of freeways. For much of the 20th century Victoria was marketed to tourists as "The Most British City in Canada," and it still has more than its share of Anglo-themed pubs, tea shops, and double-decker buses. These days, however, Victorians prefer to celebrate their combined indigenous, Asian, and European heritage, and the city's stunning wilderness backdrop. Locals do often venture out for afternoon tea, but they're just as likely to nosh on dim sum or tapas. Decades-old shops sell imported linens and tweeds, but newer upstarts offer local designs in hemp and organic cotton. And let's not forget that fabric favored by locals: Gore-Tex. The outdoors are ever present here. You can hike, bike, kayak, sail, or whale-watch straight from the city center, and forests, beaches, offshore islands, and wilderness parklands lie just minutes away.

EXPLORING

Exploring Victoria is easy. A walk around downtown, starting with the museums and architectural sights of the Inner Harbour, followed by a stroll up Government Street to the historic areas of Chinatown and Old Town, covers most of the key attractions, though seeing every little interesting thing along the way could easily take two days.

17

DOWNTOWN VICTORIA

Numbers in the margin correspond to the Downtown Victoria map.

4 **Chinatown.** Chinese immigrants built much of the Canadian Pacific Railway in the 19th century, and their influence still marks the region. Covering just two square blocks, Victoria's Chinatown, founded in 1858, is the oldest and most intact such district in Canada. If you enter from Government Street, you'll pass under the elaborate **Gate of Harmonious Interest,** made of Taiwanese ceramic tiles and decorative panels. Along Fisgard Street, merchants display paper lanterns and exotic produce. Mah-jongg, fan-tan, and dominoes were games of chance played on **Fan Tan Alley,** said to be the narrowest street in Canada. Once the gambling and opium center of Chinatown, it's now lined with offbeat shops, few of which sell authentic Chinese goods. Look for the alley on the south side of Fisgard Street between Nos. 545½ and 549½. ⊠ *Fisgard St., between Government and Store Sts., Chinatown.*

2 **Emily Carr House.** One of Canada's most celebrated artists and a respected writer, Emily Carr (1871–1945) was born and raised in this extremely proper, wooden Victorian house before she abandoned her middle-class life to live in, and paint, the wilds of British Columbia. Carr's own descriptions, from her autobiography *Book of Small,* were used to restore the house. Catch, if you can, one of the days when an actress playing Carr tells stories of her life. Artwork on display includes work by modern-day B.C. artists and reproductions of Carr's work. You'll need to visit the Art Gallery of Greater Victoria or the Vancouver

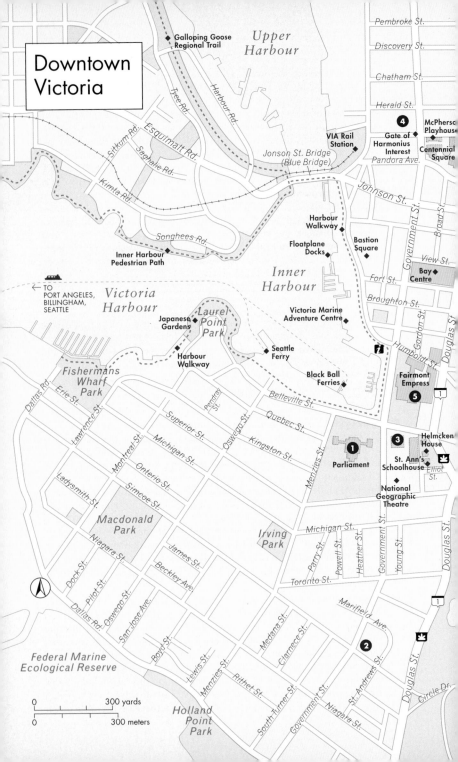

Downtown Victoria

Upper Harbour

Galloping Goose Regional Trail

Pembroke St.

Discovery St.

Chatham St.

Herald St.

VIA Rail Station

Jonson St. Bridge (Blue Bridge)

4 Gate of Harmonius Interest

McPherson Playhouse

Centennial Square

Pandora Ave.

Johnson St.

Harbour Walkway

Floatplane Docks

Bastion Square

Government St.

Broad St.

View St.

Bay Centre

Fort St.

Broughton St.

Inner Harbour

Victoria Marine Adventure Centre

Gordon St.

Humboldt St.

Douglas St.

Esquimalt Rd.

Tyee Rd.

Harbour Rd.

Sitkum Rd.

Saghalie Rd.

Kimta Rd.

Songhees Rd.

Inner Harbour Pedestrian Path

← TO PORT ANGELES, BILLINGHAM, SEATTLE

Victoria Harbour

Japanese Gardens

Laurel Point Park

Harbour Walkway

Seattle Ferry

Black Ball Ferries

Fairmont Empress

5

Fishermans Wharf Park

Dallas Rd.

Erie St.

Lawrence St.

Montreal St.

Michigan St.

Superior St.

Pendray St.

Oswego St.

Quebec St.

Kingston St.

Menzies St.

Betteville St.

Parliament

1

3

Helmcken House

St. Ann's Schoolhouse

Elliot St.

National Geographic Theatre

Ontario St.

Ladysmith St.

Simcoe St.

Macdonald Park

Niagara St.

James St.

Beckley Ave.

Irving Park

Michigan St.

Parry St.

Powell St.

Heather St.

Government St.

Young St.

Douglas St.

Toronto St.

Dock St.

Pilot St.

Dallas Rd.

Oswego St.

San Jose Ave.

Boyd St.

Marifield Ave.

2

St. Andrews St.

Douglas St.

Circle Dr.

Medana St.

Clarence St.

Lewis St.

Menzies St.

Rithet St.

South Turner St.

Government St.

Niagara St.

Federal Marine Ecological Reserve

0   300 yards
0   300 meters

Holland Point Park

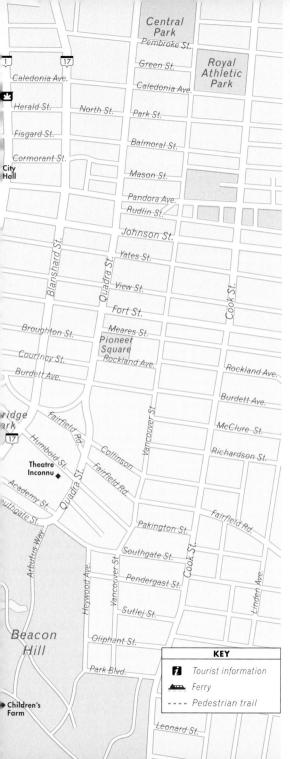

KEY

🄵 *Tourist information*

🚢 *Ferry*

---- *Pedestrian trail*

More than 3,300 lights outline Victoria's Parliament Buildings; like the Fairmont Empress hotel, the buildings have a prominent position in the Inner Harbor, and were designed by the same architect: Francis Rattenbury.

Art Gallery to see Carr originals. ⊠ *207 Government St., James Bay* ☏ *250/383–5843* ⊕ *www.emilycarr.com* 🎟 *C$6; C$10 for actress performances and other special events* ⊗ *May–Sept., Tues.–Sat. 11–4; Oct.–Apr. by arrangement or during special events.*

⑤ Fairmont Empress. Opened in 1908 by the Canadian Pacific Railway, the Empress is one of the grand château-style railroad hotels that grace many Canadian cities. Designed by Francis Rattenbury, who also designed the Parliament Buildings across the way, the Empress, with its solid Edwardian grandeur, has become a symbol of the city. The elements that made the hotel an attraction for travelers in the past—Old World architecture, ornate decor, and a commanding view of the Inner Harbour—are still here. Nonguests can stop by for afternoon tea (reservations are recommended; the dress code is smart casual), meet for a curry under the tiger skin in the Bengal Room, enjoy a treatment at the hotel's Willow Stream spa, browse the shops and galleries in the hotel's arcade, or sample the superb Pacific Northwest cuisine in the Empress Room restaurant. ⊠ *721 Government St., entrance at Belleville and Government, Downtown* ☏ *250/384–8111, 250/389–2727 tea reservations* ⊕ *www.fairmont.com/empress* 🎟 *Free, afternoon tea C$55.*

❶ Parliament Buildings. Officially the British Columbia Provincial Legislative Assembly Buildings, these massive stone structures are more popularly referred to as the Parliament Buildings. Designed by Francis Rattenbury (who also designed the Fairmont Empress Hotel) when he was just 25 years old, and completed in 1897, they dominate the Inner Harbour. Two statues flank the main entrance: one of Sir James Douglas (1803–77), who chose the site where Victoria was built, and the other of Sir Matthew Baille Begbie (1819–94), the man in charge of law and order during the Gold Rush era. Atop the central dome is a gilded statue of Captain George Vancouver (1757–98), the first European to sail around Vancouver Island. A statue of Queen Victoria (1819–1901) reigns over the front of the complex. More than 3,300 lights outline the buildings at night. When the legislature is in session, you can sit in the public gallery and watch British Columbia's democracy at work (custom has the opposing parties sitting 2½ sword lengths apart). Free, informative, 30- to 60-minute tours run every 20 to 30 minutes in summer and several times a day in the off-season (less frequently if school groups or private tours are coming through). Tours are obligatory on summer weekends (mid-May until Labor Day) and optional the rest of the time. ☒ *501 Belleville St., Downtown* ☎ *250/387–3046* ⊕ *www.leg. bc.ca* ☒ *Free* ⊙ *Mid-May–early Sept., Mon.–Thurs. 9–5, Fri.–Sun. 9–6; early Sept.–mid-May, weekdays 9–4.*

3 **Royal British Columbia Museum.** This excellent museum, one of Victoria's leading attractions, traces several thousand years of British Columbian history. Its First Peoples Gallery, home to a genuine Kwakwaka'wakw big house and a dramatically displayed collection of masks and other artifacts, is especially strong. The Environmental History Gallery traces B.C.'s natural heritage, from prehistory to modern-day climate change, in realistic dioramas. An Ocean Station exhibit gets kids involved in running a Jules Verne–style submarine. In the Modern History Gallery, a replica of Captain Vancouver's HMS *Discovery* creaks convincingly, and a re-created frontier town comes to life with cobbled streets, silent movies, and the rumble of an arriving train. Also on-site is the National Geographic Theater showing a variety of IMAX films on a six-story-tall screen.

Fodor'sChoice ★

17

Optional one-hour tours, included in the admission price, run roughly twice a day in summer and less frequently in winter. Most focus on a particular gallery, though the 90-minute Highlights Tour touches on all galleries. Special exhibits, usually held between April and October, often attract crowds (and higher admission prices). Skip ticket lines by booking online. ☒ *675 Belleville St., Downtown* ☎ *250/356– 7226 or 888/447–7977; theater show times: 877/480–4887* ⊕ *www. royalbcmuseum.bc.ca* ☒ *C$15, IMAX theater C$11, combination ticket C$24. Family rate (2 adults and 2 youths) C$39.50. Rates may be higher during special-exhibit periods* ⊙ *Museum: daily 10–5 (open until 10 PM most Fri. and Sat. early June–late Sept.). Theater: daily 10–8; call for show times.*

OAK BAY, ROCKLAND, AND FAIRFIELD

The winding shady streets of Victoria's older residential areas—roughly bordered by Cook Street, Fort Street, and the seaside—are lined with beautifully preserved Victorian and Edwardian homes. These include many stunning old mansions now operating as bed-and-breakfasts, and Victoria's most elaborate folly: Craigdarroch Castle. With mansions come gardens, and several of the city's best are found here. Clusters of high-end shops include the extraordinarily British Oak Bay Village, described as a place "behind the Tweed Curtain" for its adherence to Tudor facades and tea shops. Among the lavish waterfront homes are plenty of public parks and beaches offering views across Juan de Fuca Strait to the Olympic Mountains of Washington State.

GETTING AROUND

A car or a bike is handy, but not essential, for exploring this area. No wheels? Big Bus, Gray Line, and other tour companies offer Oak Bay and Marine Drive tours.

By public transit, take bus No. 11 or 14 from the corner of Fort and Douglas streets to Moss Street (for the Art Gallery of Greater Victoria), or to Joan Crescent (for Craigdarroch Castle). The walk, about a mile past the antiques shops of Fort Street, is also interesting. Another useful route is bus No. 7: from Johnson and Douglas streets, it travels to Abkhazi Garden and Oak Bay Village.

Abkhazi Garden. Called "the garden that love built," this once-private garden is as fascinating for its history as for its innovative design. Seeds for the 1-acre residential garden were planted, figuratively, in Paris in the 1920s, when Englishwoman Peggy Pemberton-Carter met exiled Georgian Prince Nicholas Abkhazi. Separate World War II internment camps (his in Germany, hers near Shanghai) interrupted their romance, but they reunited and married in Victoria in 1946. They spent the next 40 years together cultivating their garden. Rescued from developers and now operated by the Land Conservancy of British Columbia, the Zen-like 1-acre site is recognized as one of Canada's most significant gardens and a leading example of West Coast horticultural design, resplendent with native Garry Oak trees, Japanese maples, and mature rhododendrons. The tearoom, in the sitting parlor of the modest, modernist home, serves lunch and afternoon tea. Watch for evening concerts in the garden. ✉ *1964 Fairfield Rd., Fairfield* ☎ *250/598–8096* ⊕ *www.conservancy. bc.ca* ✎ *C$10* ⊙ *Mar.–Oct., daily 11–5 (last admission at 4).*

Craigdarroch Castle. This resplendent mansion complete with turrets and Gothic rooflines was built as the home of one of British Columbia's wealthiest men, coal baron Robert Dunsmuir, who died in 1889, just a few months before the castle's completion. Now a museum depicting life in the late 1800s, the castle's 39 rooms have ornate Victorian furnishings, stained-glass windows, carved woodwork, and a beautifully restored painted ceiling in the drawing room. A winding staircase climbs four floors to a tower overlooking Victoria. Castles run in the family: son James went on to build the even-more-lavish Hatley Castle just west of Victoria. Note that the castle is not wheelchair accessible and has no elevators. ✉ *1050 Joan Crescent, Rockland* ☎ *250/592–5323* ⊕ *www. thecastle.ca* ✎ *C$13.75* ⊙ *Mid-June–early Sept., daily 9–7; early Sept.– mid-June, daily 10–4:30.*

SIDNEY AND THE SAANICH PENINSULA
30 km (18 mi) north of Victoria on Hwy. 17.

Home to the B.C. and Washington State ferry terminals as well as the Victoria International Airport, the Saanich Peninsula, with its rolling green hills and small family farms, is the first part of Vancouver Island that most visitors see. Although it's tempting to head straight for downtown Victoria, 25 minutes to the south, there are many reasons to linger here, including the Butchart Gardens, one of the province's leading attractions. Sidney's parklike waterfront is home to an aquarium and marine ecology center, as well as cafés, restaurants, and a wheelchair-accessible waterfront path.

GETTING HERE AND AROUND

To reach the area by car from downtown Victoria, follow the signs for the ferries straight up Highway 17, or take the Scenic Marine Drive starting at Dallas Road and following the coast north. It joins Highway 17 at Elk Lake (but take a map—even locals get lost traveling this way). Victoria transit buses serve the area, though not frequently. Bus tours to the Butchart Gardens run several times a day, and many tours take in other sights in the area; several companies also offer winery tours. Gray Line West also runs a low-cost shuttle service to the Butchart Gardens and the Butterfly Gardens. Cyclists can take the Lochside Trail, which runs from Victoria to Sidney, detouring, perhaps, to some wineries along the way.

The Butchart Gardens. This stunning 55-acre garden and National Historic Site has been drawing visitors since it was planted in a limestone quarry in 1904. Seven hundred varieties of flowers grow in the site's Japanese, Italian, rose, and sunken gardens. Highlights include the view over the ivy-draped and flower-filled former quarry, the dramatic 21-meter-high (70-foot-high) Ross Fountain, and the formal and intricate Italian garden, complete with a gelato stand. From mid-June to mid-September the gardens are illuminated at night with hundreds of hidden lights. In July and August, kids' entertainers perform Sunday through Friday afternoons; jazz, blues, and classical musicians play at an outdoor stage each evening; and fireworks draw crowds every Saturday night. The wheelchair- and stroller-accessible site is also home to a seed-and-gift shop, a plant identification center, two restaurants (one offering traditional afternoon tea), and a coffee shop; you can even call ahead for a picnic basket on fireworks nights. To avoid crowds, try to come at opening time, in the late afternoon or evening (except Saturday evenings, which also draw many visitors), or between September and June, when the gardens are still stunning. The grounds are especially magical at Christmas, with themed lighting and an ice rink.

The gardens are about 20 minutes' drive north of downtown; parking is free and plentiful, but fills up on fireworks Saturdays. You can get here by city bus 75 from Douglas Street downtown, but service is slow and infrequent. The Butchart Gardens Express Shuttle, operated by Gray Line West, runs every 45 minutes between downtown Victoria and the Butchart Gardens in spring and summer; buses leave from the bus depot at 700 Douglas Street, behind the Fairmont Empress Hotel, daily between 9 AM and 5:45 PM. The C$43 round-trip fare includes admission to the gardens. ⊠ *800 Benvenuto Ave., Brentwood Bay* ☎ *250/652–5256 or 866/652–4422. Gray Line West: 800/667–0882* ⊕ *www.butchartgardens.com* ⧎ *Mid-June–late Sept. C$28, discounted*

17

Butchart Gardens

rates rest of yr ⊙ *Mid-June–Labor Day, daily 9 AM–10 PM; Sept.–mid-June, daily 9 AM–dusk; call for exact times.*

🐾 **Shaw Ocean Discovery Centre.** A simulated ride underwater in a deep-sea elevator is just the beginning of a visit to this fun and educational marine interpretive center on Sidney's waterfront. Devoted entirely to the aquatic life and conservation needs of the Salish Sea—the waters south and east of Vancouver Island—the center displays local sealife, including luminous jellyfish, bright purple starfish, wolf eels, rockfish, and octopi, while hands-on activities, touch tanks, and knowledgeable volunteers inspire learning. Kids love the high-tech effects, including a floor projection that ripples when stepped on, streaming video, and a pop-up tank you can poke your head into. ⊠ *9811 Seaport Pl., Sidney* ☎ *250/665–7511* ⊕ *www.oceandiscovery.ca* ☒ *$12* ⊙ *Daily 10–4:30.*

WHERE TO EAT

Victoria has a tremendous number of restaurants for such a small city, and the glorious pantry that is Vancouver Island—think wild salmon and Pacific oysters, locally made cheese, and organic fruits and veggies—keeps standards up. Restaurants in the region are generally casual. Smoking is banned in all public places, including restaurant patios, in Greater Victoria. Victorians tend to dine early—restaurants get busy at 6, and many kitchens close by 9. Pubs, lounges, and the few open-late places mentioned here are your best options for an after-hours nosh.

DOWNTOWN

Use the coordinate (⊕ B2) at the end of each listing to locate a site on the corresponding map.

$$$ ✕ **Aura.** One of Canada's top young chefs (Culinary Olympics star Brad
CANADIAN Horen) meets the city's best waterfront patio at this chic eatery on the
Fodor's Choice Inner Harbour's south shore. The seasonally changing fare is locally
★ sourced with Asian leanings: think wild local halibut and salmon; a
"surf-and-turf" done with a sukiyaki-braised short rib, smoked scal-
lops, and a maki roll; and a cellar full of hard-to-find Vancouver Island
farm-gate wines. Sleek lines, warm colors, and water-view windows
create a room that's both stylish and cozy. Live music plays Thurs-
day evenings. ⊠ *680 Montreal St., at the Inn at Laurel Point, James
Bay* ☎ *250/414–6739* ⊕ *www.aurarestaurant.ca* ⊟ *AE, D, DC, MC,
V* ⊕ *C4.*

$–$$ ✕ **Barb's Place.** Funky Barb's, a tin-roofed take-out shack, floats on the
SEAFOOD quay at Fisherman's Wharf, west of the Inner Harbour off St. Lawrence
Street. Halibut, salmon, oysters, mussels, crab, burgers, and chowder
are all prepared fresh. The picnic tables on the wharf provide a front-
row view of the brightly colored houseboats moored here, or you can
carry your food to the grassy park nearby. Ferries sail to Fisherman's
Wharf from the Inner Harbour. ⊠ *Fisherman's Wharf, St. Lawrence St.,
Downtown* ☎ *250/384–6515* ⊟ *AE, MC, V* ⊗ *Closed Nov.–Feb.* ⊕ *B5.*

$$–$$$ ✕ **Brasserie L'école.** French-country cooking shines at this informal Chi-
FRENCH natown bistro, and the historic room—once a schoolhouse for the Chi-
Fodor's Choice nese community—evokes a timeless brasserie, from the white linens and
★ patina-rich fir floors to the chalkboards above the slate bar listing the
day's oyster, mussel, and steak options. Sean Brennan, one of the city's
better-known chefs, works with local farmers and fishers to source the
best seasonal, local, and organic ingredients. The menu changes daily,
but lists such classic bistro fare as duck confit, braised lamb shank,
and trout with gnocchi. Be prepared for lines, though, as this 12-table
spot does not take reservations. ⊠ *1715 Government St., Downtown*
☎ *250/475–6260* ⊕ *www.lecole.ca* ⌕ *Reservations not accepted* ⊟ *AE,
MC, V* ⊗ *Closed Sun. and Mon. No lunch* ⊕ *F2.*

$$$ ✕ **Cafe Brio.** "Charming, comfortable, and hip with walls of art—all
CANADIAN backed by city's best chef and kitchen," is how one fodors.com user
Fodor's Choice describes this bustling Italian villa–style room. The frequently chang-
★ ing menu highlights regional, organic fare; favorites include roast veal
strip loin with crispy sweetbreads, butter-poached pheasant breast, local
sablefish, albacore tuna, Cowichan Bay duck breast, and house-made
charcuterie. Virtually everything, including the bread, pasta, and des-
serts, is made in-house—even the butter is hand churned. The 400-label
wine list has a top selection of B.C. choices. ⊠ *944 Fort St., Downtown*
☎ *250/383–0009 or 866/270–5461* ⊕ *www.cafe-brio.com* ⊟ *AE, MC,
V* ⊗ *No lunch* ⊕ *H4.*

$$$ ✕ **Camille's.** Working closely with independent farmers, the chef at this
CANADIAN long-established favorite concentrates on such locally sourced products
as lamb, duck, and seafood; quail, venison, and ostrich often make an
appearance, too. The menu is based on what's fresh, but might include
lemon, ginger, and rock-prawn bisque; halibut with sea scallops and

17

tiger prawns; or organic beef tenderloin. The five-course tasting menu, with optional wine matching, is popular. The wine cellar–like backdrop, on the lower floor of a historic building in Bastion Square, is candlelit and romantic, with exposed brick, local art, soft jazz and blues, and lots of intimate nooks and crannies. The wine list is well selected. ⊠ *45 Bastion Sq., Downtown* ☎ *250/381–3433* ⊕ *www.camillesrestaurant. com* ☰ *AE, MC, V* ⊗ *Closed Sun. and Mon. No lunch* ✛ *E3.*

$–$$
CANADIAN

✕ **Mo:Lé.** It's been called "fine dining for vegans," but this tiny brick-lined Chinatown café has plenty of wholesome, organic, local fare for meat eaters, too. At breakfast, large helpings of free-range eggs, locally made sausages, and organic, spelt griddle cakes fuel a post-party, pre-yoga crowd. At lunch, locals might pop in for an avocado, dulse (seaweed), and sprout sandwich, a yam wrap, or an organic beef burger. ⊠ *554 Pandora St., Downtown* ☎ *250/385–6653* ⊕ *www.molerestaurant.ca* ⌲ *Reservations not accepted* ☰ *MC, V* ⊗ *No dinner* ✛ *F2.*

$–$$
ASIAN

✕ **The Noodle Box.** Noodles, whether Indonesian style with peanut sauce, thick Japanese udon in teriyaki, or Thai-style chow mein, are piled straight from steaming woks in the open kitchen to bowls or cardboard take-out boxes at this local answer to fast food. Malaysian, Singapore, and Cambodian-style curries tempt those who like it hot. The brick, rose, and lime walls keep things modern and high-energy at the Douglas Street location near the Inner Harbour. The Fisgard Street outlet is a tiny hole-in-the-wall near Chinatown. ⊠ *818 Douglas St., Downtown* ☎ *250/384–1314* ⊕ *www.thenoodlebox.net* ⌲ *Reservations not accepted* ☰ *AE, MC, V* ✛ *F4* ⊠ *626 Fisgard St., Downtown* ☎ *250/360–1312* ⌲ *Reservations not accepted* ☰ *AE, MC, V* ✛ *F2.*

$–$$
SEAFOOD

✕ **Red Fish Blue Fish.** If you like your fish both yummy *and* ecologically friendly, look no further than this former shipping container on the pier at the foot of Broughton Street. From the soil-topped roof and biodegradable packaging to the sustainably harvested, local seafood, this waterfront take-out shop minimizes its ecological footprint. Portuguese buns are baked daily for the seafood sandwiches, fish tacos come in grilled tortilla cones, and even plain old fish-and-chips are taken up a notch with a choice of wild salmon, halibut, or cod in tempura batter with hand-cut, thick fries. Be prepared for queues on sunny days. ⊠ *1006 Wharf St., Downtown* ☎ *250/298–6877* ⊕ *www.redfish-bluefish.com* ⌲ *Reservations not accepted* ☰ *MC, V* ✛ *E4.*

$–$$
CANADIAN

✕ **Spinnakers Gastro Brewpub.** Victoria's longest menu of handcrafted beer is just one reason to trek over the Johnson Street Bridge or hop a Harbour Ferry to this Vic West waterfront pub. Canada's oldest licensed brewpub, Spinnakers relies almost exclusively on locally sourced ingredients for its top-notch casual fare. Opt for the pubby adults-only taproom, with its covered waterfront deck, double-sided fireplace, and wood-beam rooms; or dine in the all-ages waterfront restaurant. Either way you can enjoy such high-end pub grub as mussels steamed in ale, wild salmon fettuccine, or fish-and-chips with thick-cut fries. A take-away deli, bakery, and chocolatier is another place to try the house-made fare. ⊠ *308 Catherine St., Downtown* ☎ *250/386–2739 or 877/838–2739* ⊕ *www.spinnakers.com* ⌲ *Reservations not accepted in the Taproom* ☰ *AE, MC, V* ✛ *B2.*

WHERE TO STAY

Unless stated in the review, hotels are equipped with elevators, and all guest rooms have air-conditioning, TV, telephone, and private bathroom. Internet (meaning some form of high-speed dial-up) and wireless access are noted when available.

DOWNTOWN

Use the coordinate (✛ B2) at the end of each listing to locate a site on the corresponding map.

$$–$$$$
★

Beaconsfield Inn. This 1905 registered historic building four blocks from the Inner Harbour is one of Victoria's most faithfully restored Edwardian mansions. Though the rooms and suites all have antique furniture, high ceilings, and period details, each also has a unique look; several rooms have jetted tubs or fireplaces, and one room even includes an Edwardian, wooden canopied tub. Three-course breakfasts and tea and sherry in the conservatory or around the library fire complete the English country-manor experience. In-room spa services are a nice touch, too. **Pros:** luxurious; kid-free. **Cons:** kids not permitted; several blocks from shopping and dining. ⊠ *998 Humboldt St., Downtown* ☏ *250/384–4044 or 888/884–4044* ⊕ *www.beaconsfieldinn.com* ↪ *5 rooms, 4 suites* ⚘ *In-room: no a/c, Wi-Fi. In-hotel: Internet terminal, Wi-Fi, parking (free), no kids under 10* ▭ *AE, MC, V* ⦿| *BP* ✛ *H6.*

$$$$

Delta Victoria Ocean Pointe Resort and Spa. Across the Johnson Street Bridge from downtown Victoria, this waterfront property has all sorts of resort facilities, from tennis and squash courts to a popular spa, a 24-hour gym, and a waterfront walking path. Rooms, many with views of the Parliament Buildings across the water, are spacious and airy. Conferences do play a big role here, though kids are made welcome with check-in treats, discounted meals, and evening story time. The hotel's restaurant, Lure ($$$), offers fresh local seafood and expansive harbor views. **Pros:** water views; full range of facilities; free Internet; downtown shuttle and harbor ferry service. **Cons:** not central; gets busy with conferences and groups. ⊠ *45 Songhees Rd., Downtown* ☏ *250/360–2999 or 800/667–4677* ⊕ *www.deltahotels.com* ↪ *233 rooms, 6 suites* ⚘ *In-room: kitchen (some), refrigerator, Internet (some). In-hotel: restaurant, room service, bar, tennis courts, pool, gym, spa, laundry service, Wi-Fi, parking (paid), some pets allowed* ▭ *AE, D, DC, MC, V* ✛ *D3.*

$$$$

The Fairmont Empress. A hundred years old in 2008, this ivy-draped harborside château and city landmark has aged gracefully, with top-notch service and sympathetically restored Edwardian furnishings. The 176 different room configurations include standard and harbor-view rooms with 11-foot ceilings. State-of-the-art gym equipment and an indoor pool are welcome touches. If you stay on the Fairmont Gold floor, you will enjoy a private lounge, a continental breakfast, and evening snacks. The hotel is a tourist attraction, but a guests-only lobby separates hotel guests from the throng. **Pros:** central location; professional service; great spa and restaurant. **Cons:** small-to-average-size rooms and bathrooms; tourists in the public areas; pricey. ⊠ *721 Government St., Downtown* ☏ *250/384–8111 or 800/257–7544* ⊕ *www. fairmont.com/empress* ↪ *436 rooms, 41 suites* ⚘ *In-room: no a/c*

17

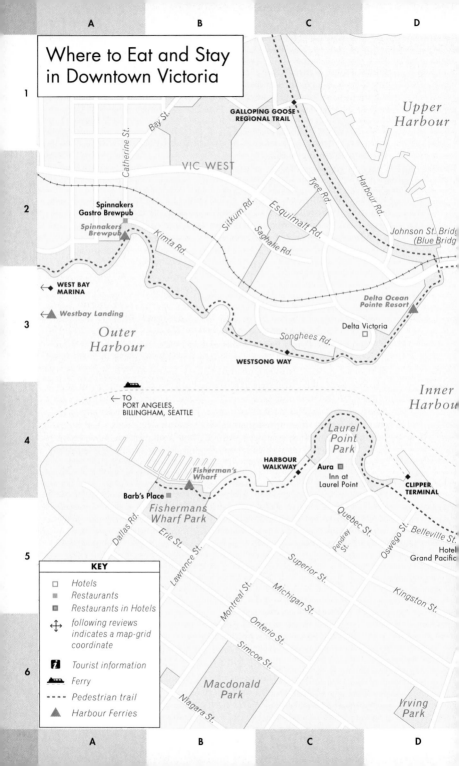

Where to Eat and Stay in Downtown Victoria

A **B** **C** **D**

1

GALLOPING GOOSE
REGIONAL TRAIL

Upper Harbour

Bay St.

Catherine St.

2

VIC WEST

Tyee Rd.

Harbour Rd.

Spinnakers Gastro Brewpub

Spinnakers Brewpub

Sitkum Rd.

Esquimalt Rd.

Saghalie Rd.

Kimta Rd.

Johnson St. Bridge
(Blue Bridge)

WEST BAY MARINA

3

Westbay Landing

Outer Harbour

Songhees Rd.

Delta Ocean Pointe Resort

Delta Victoria

WESTSONG WAY

Inner Harbour

← TO PORT ANGELES,
BILLINGHAM, SEATTLE

Laurel Point Park

4

HARBOUR WALKWAY

Aura

Inn at Laurel Point

CLIPPER TERMINAL

Fisherman's Wharf

Barb's Place

Fishermans Wharf Park

Quebec St.

Oswego St.

Belleville St.

Dallas Rd.

Erie St.

Pendray St.

Hotel Grand Pacific

5

Lawrence St.

Superior St.

Michigan St.

Kingston St.

KEY

☐ *Hotels*

◼ *Restaurants*

◼ *Restaurants in Hotels*

⊕ *following reviews indicates a map-grid coordinate*

🛈 *Tourist information*

⛴ *Ferry*

- - - *Pedestrian trail*

▲ *Harbour Ferries*

Montreal St.

Onterio St.

Simcoe St.

6

Macdonald Park

Niagara St.

Irving Park

A **B** **C** **D**

Inn at Laurel Point

Brentwood Bay Lodge & Spa

(some), refrigerator, Internet. In-hotel: 2 restaurants, room service, bar, pool, gym, spa, laundry service, Internet terminal, Wi-Fi, parking (paid), some pets allowed = *AE, D, DC, MC, V* ⊕ *E5.*

$$$–$$$$ **Hotel Grand Pacific.** The city's best health club (with yoga classes, squash courts, and state-of-the-art equipment) and a prime Inner Harbour location appeal to savvy business and leisure regulars, including Seattleites stepping off the ferry across the street. Feng shui design elements apply throughout, lending a calm energy to the gleaming marble lobby. Rooms are large and surprisingly quiet, with deep soaker tubs, floor-to-ceiling windows, and a muted decor. Upper-floor rooms have views of the harbor, the Parliament Buildings, or mountains, which you can admire from your private balcony. **Pros:** great health club; staffed business center; prime location; balconies and views. **Cons:** standard hotel decor; markup on local calls and Internet. ⊠ *463 Belleville St., Downtown* ☎ *250/386–0450 or 800/663–7550* ⊕ *www. hotelgrandpacific.com* ⇨ *258 rooms, 46 suites* ⌂ *In-room: safe, refrigerator, DVD (some), Internet. In-hotel: 3 restaurants, room service, bar, pool, gym, spa, laundry service, Internet terminal, Wi-Fi, parking (paid), some pets allowed* = *AE, D, MC, V* ⊕ *D5.*

$$$–$$$$

Fodor'sChoice
★

Inn at Laurel Point. Set on a peninsula on the Inner Harbour's quiet south shore, this Asian-inspired hotel affords harbor views from every room. A seaside Japanese garden, a resort's worth of facilities, and a museum-quality art collection make this freshly renovated, independent hotel a favorite among Victoria regulars. Rooms—especially in the Arthur Erickson–designed southern wing—are light and airy, with blond wood and Asian touches; all have balconies, and some suites have large harbor-view decks. In-room spa services, free local calls and Internet, and an indoor pool are among the pluses. The restaurant is one of the city's best. **Pros:** views; quiet, parklike setting. **Cons:** 10-minute walk to downtown. ⊠ *680 Montreal St., Downtown* ☎ *250/386–8721 or 800/663–7667* ⊕ *www.laurelpoint.com* ⇨ *135 rooms, 65 suites* ⌂ *In-room: safe, refrigerator, Internet, Wi-Fi (some). In-hotel: restaurant, room service, bar, pool, gym, laundry service, Internet terminal, Wi-Fi, parking (paid), some pets allowed* = *AE, D, DC, MC, V* ⊕ *C4.*

¢–$ **Ocean Island Backpackers Inn.** The backpacker grapevine is full of praise for this fun and friendly downtown hostel. Impeccably managed by a thought-of-everything owner, the historic warren of a building houses 60 private rooms (three of which have private baths), several four- to six-bed dorms, secured entry, bike and bag storage, group day trips, heaps of travel information, a shared kitchen, and, best of all, an evening snack and beer lounge hopping with planned events. You can even borrow a guitar for open-mike night. ■ **TIP→ Ask for a room away from the café if you want an early night.** Seniors and families mix well with the clean-cut young crowd, but ask, too, about the Ocean Island Suites ($), self-contained accommodations with kitchens in nearby James Bay. **Pros:** cheap, clean, and cheerful; loads of services; a great place to meet other travelers; $5 meals at the on-site café. **Cons:** shared bathrooms; private rooms are tiny; the few parking spaces go quickly. ⊠ *791 Pandora Ave., Downtown* ☎ *250/385–1785 or 888/888–4180* ⊕ *www. oceanisland.com* ⇨ *9 4- to 6-bed dorms, 60 private rooms* ⌂ *In-room:*

17

no a/c, no phone, refrigerator (some), no TV, Wi-Fi. In-hotel: restaurant, bar, laundry facilities, Internet terminal, parking (paid) ⊟ AE, MC, V ⊹ G3.

OAK BAY AND ROCKLAND

$$$ **Abbeymoore Manor Bed & Breakfast Inn.** This 1912 mansion has the wide verandas, dark wainscoting, and high ceilings of its era but the attitude is informal, from the helpful hosts to the free snacks and coffee on tap all day. Two modern, one-bedroom suites on the ground floor have kitchens, while five upper-level rooms charm with such period details as claw-foot tubs or four-poster king beds, and verandas or antique-tile fireplaces. The Penthouse Suite has a full kitchen and private entrance. Multicourse breakfasts are served family style or at tables for two in the sunroom or on the patio. In-room spa services include Thai massage. **Pros:** good value; friendly hosts; well staffed with excellent service. **Cons:** kids not permitted; a mile from the Inner Harbour; often booked in advance. ⊠ *1470 Rockland Ave., Rockland* ☎ *250/370–1470 or 888/801–1811* ⊕ *www.abbeymoore.com* ⟿ *5 rooms, 3 suites* ⏶ *In-room: no a/c, no phone (some), kitchen (some), DVD (some), no TV (some), Wi-Fi. In-hotel: Internet terminal, parking (free), no kids under 12* ⊟ *MC, V* ⏐◎⏐ *BP.*

$$$$ **Villa Marco Polo.** A classical European garden with a stone terrace, reflecting pool, and fountains is all part of the Tuscan-hideaway feel at this 1923 Italian Renaissance–style manor. Fireplaces, duvet-topped king beds, Persian carpets, and Italian art—along with pre-loaded iPods with docking stations—grace each of the four sumptuous rooms. The most romantic, though, are the Persia suite with its bed curtains and garden view, and the Zanzibar suite with its bay window and small balcony. The lavish four-course breakfast includes organic local produce; services at the on-site spa include Thai massage and mud-wraps. **Pros:** lots of comfy common areas; gracious hosts; full concierge services. **Cons:** a mile from downtown; no elevator. ⊠ *1524 Shasta Place, Rockland* ☎ *250/370–1524 or 877/601–1524* ⊕ *www.villamarcopolo. com* ⟿ *4 rooms* ⏶ *In-room: no a/c, Wi-Fi. In hotel: spa, laundry service, Internet terminal, Wi-Fi, parking (free), no kids under 12* ⊟ *AE, MC, V* ⏐◎⏐ *BP.*

SIDNEY AND THE SAANICH PENINSULA

$$$$ **Brentwood Bay Lodge & Spa.** Every room has a private ocean-view patio
Fodor's Choice or balcony at this adult-oriented boutique resort in a tiny seaside village.
★ Handmade furniture, fireplaces, king beds topped with crisp Italian linens and sensuous black bedspreads, and original local art decorate each of the clean-lined, earth-toned rooms. Slate-lined bathrooms have jetted tubs and multihead showers, and shuttered windows bring ocean views to the tub. Handy to the Butchart Gardens (a five-minute hop on the resort's water taxi) and to local wineries, Brentwood Bay is known for the wine-based treatments at its lavish spa. The ocean-view restaurant and casual marine pub serve locally raised organic fare. Marine eco-cruises, kayak tours, and a dive center are among the many distractions. **Pros:** magnificent setting; great food; free Wi-Fi and calls across North America. **Cons:** pricey; 30-minute drive from downtown. ⊠ *849 Verdier*

Ave., Brentwood Bay ☎ *250/544–2079 or 888/544–2079* ⊕ *www.brentwoodbaylodge.com* ⤳ *30 rooms, 3 suites* ⌂ *In-room: safe, refrigerator, DVD, Wi-Fi. In-hotel: 2 restaurants, room service, bar, pool, gym, spa, diving, water sports, laundry facilities, laundry service, Internet terminal, Wi-Fi, parking (free)* ▭ *AE, MC, V.*

$$–$$$$ 🛏 **The Sidney Pier Hotel & Spa.** Stylish and ecologically friendly, this glass-and-stone boutique hotel on Sidney's parklike waterfront has helped put Sidney on the hipster radar. Rooms, done in chic black, crisp white, and sea-toned neutrals, with tall windows, rain-forest showers, and flat-screen TVs, range from excellent value ($$) non-view rooms to apartment-size suites with private ocean-view balconies. Sustainable local seafood is the focus at Haro's ($$$), the ocean-view restaurant. The marine theme continues from seaweed treatments at the spa to seashore walks with a resident marine biologist, and a marine concierge who'll set up whale-watching, kayaking, scuba diving, and more. **Pros:** views, style, and eco-cred; close to ferries and airport. **Cons:** 30 minutes from downtown, no pool. ✉ *9805 Seaport Pl., Sidney* ☎ *250/655–9445 or 866/659–9445* ⊕ *www.sidneypier.com* ⤳ *46 rooms, 9 suites* ⌂ *In-room: safe, kitchen (some), refrigerator, DVD, Internet. In hotel: 2 restaurants, room service, bar, gym, spa, laundry facilities, laundry service, Wi-Fi, parking (paid), some pets allowed* ▭ *AE,DC, MC, V.*

NIGHTLIFE AND THE ARTS

17

For entertainment listings, pick up a free copy of **Monday Magazine** (it comes out every Thursday) or see the listings online at ⊕ *www.mondaymag.com.*

Tourism Victoria also has event listings, and you can buy tickets for many events at the **Visitor Information Centre** (✉ *812 Wharf St.* ☎ *250/953–2033 or 800/663–3883* ⊕ *www.tourismvictoria.com*).

NIGHTLIFE

Victoria's nightlife is low-key and casual, with many wonderful pubs, but a limited choice of nightclubs. Pubs offer a casual vibe for lunch, dinner, or an afternoon pint, often with a view and an excellent selection of beer. The pubs listed here all serve food, and many brew their own beer. Patrons must be 19 or older to enter a bar or pub in British Columbia, but many pubs have a separate restaurant section open to all ages. Several of Victoria's trendier restaurants double as lounges, offering cocktails and small plates well into the night. Dance clubs attract a young crowd, and most close by 2 AM. A dress code (no jeans or sneakers) may be enforced, but otherwise, attire is casual. Smoking is not allowed in Victoria's pubs, bars, and nightclubs—this applies both indoors and on the patio.

BARS AND LOUNGES **Bengal Lounge.** Deep leather sofas and a Bengal tiger skin help to re-create the days of the British Raj at this iconic lounge in the Fairmont Empress Hotel. Martinis and a curry buffet are the draws through the week. On Friday and Saturday nights a jazz combo takes the stage. ✉ *721 Government St., Downtown* ☎ *250/384–8111* ⊕ *www.fairmont.com/empress.*

Canoe Brewpub. One of Victoria's biggest and best pub patios overlooks the Gorge, the waterway just north of the Inner Harbour. Inside, the former power station has been stylishly redone, with high ceilings, exposed brick and beams, a wide range of in-house brews, top-notch bar snacks, and an all-ages restaurant. ⊠ *450 Swift St., Downtown* ☎ *250/361–1940* ⊕ *www.canoebrewpub.com.*

The Superior. Live nightly acoustic blues and jazz and a small-plates menu of local organic fare attract a hip grown-up crowd to this café and nightspot near Fisherman's Wharf. ⊠ *106 Superior St., James Bay* ☎ *250/380–9515* ⊕ *www.thesuperior.ca.*

Swans Brewpub. A stunning array of First Nations masks and other artworks hangs from the open rafters in this popular downtown brewpub, where jazz, blues, and swing bands play nightly. ⊠ *506 Pandora Ave., Downtown* ☎ *250/361–3310.*

DANCE CLUBS **Hermann's Jazz Club.** Dinner, dancing, and live jazz are on the menu at this venerable downtown restaurant and jazz club. ⊠ *753 View St., Downtown* ☎ *250/388–9166* ⊕ *www.hermannsjazz.com.*

Paparazzi Nightclub. Victoria's only gay club draws a mixed crowd with fun drag, karaoke, and club nights. ⊠ *642 Johnson St., Downtown* ☎ *250/388–0505* ⊕ *www.paparazzinightclub.com.*

THE ARTS

MUSIC **Summer in the Square.** Free jazz, classical, and folk concerts; cultural events; and more run all summer at Centennial Square, next to City Hall at Pandora and Douglas streets. Events start weekdays at noon. ☎ *250/361–0388* ⊕ *www.victoria.ca.*

Victoria Jazz Society. Watch for music events hosted by this group, which also organizes the annual JazzFest International in late June. ☎ *250/388–4423* ⊕ *www.jazzvictoria.ca.*

Victoria Symphony. The Royal Theatre and the University Centre Farquhar Auditorium are the venues for regular season concerts. Watch, too, for **Symphony Splash** on the first Sunday in August, when the Victoria Symphony plays a free concert from a barge in the Inner Harbour. *Symphony Information:* ☎ *250/385–6515* ⊕ *www.victoriasymphony. ca.* **Royal Theatre** ⊠ *805 Broughton St., Downtown* ☎ *250/386–6121 or 888/717–6121.* **University Centre Farquhar Auditorium** ⊠ *3800 Finnerty Rd., University of Victoria Campus* ☎ *250/721–8480.*

THEATER **McPherson Playhouse and the Royal Theatre.** These two historic downtown theaters work together to host touring theater, dance, and musical performances. **Royal Theatre** ⊠ *805 Broughton St., Downtown* **McPherson Playhouse** ⊠ *3 Centennial Sq., Downtown* ☎ *250/386–6121 or 888/717–6121* ⊕ *www.rmts.bc.ca.*

SHOPPING

Shopping in Victoria is easy: virtually everything is in the downtown area on or near Government Street stretching north from the Fairmont Empress hotel. Victoria stores specializing in English imports are plentiful, though Canadian-made goods are usually a better buy.

Fan Tan Alley, in Victoria's Chinatown, is said to be the narrowest street in Canada.

SHOPPING DISTRICTS AND MALLS

Chinatown. Exotic fruits and vegetables, toys, wicker fans, fabric slippers, and other Chinese imports fill the shops and the baskets set up in front of them along Fisgard Street. Fan Tan Alley, a narrow lane off Fisgard Street, has more nouveau-hippie goods, with an art gallery, a Nepalese import shop, and a record store tucked in among its tiny storefronts.

The Design District. Wharf and Store streets, between Johnson and Fisgard, contains a cluster of Victoria's home-decor shops. The two floors of import furnishings and lush fabrics at Chintz & Co. (*1720 Store St.*) are especially fun to browse through. ⊕ *www.victoriadesigndistrict.com*.

Fodor'sChoice
★
Lower Johnson Street. This row of candy-color Victorian shopfronts between Government and Store streets is Victoria's hub for independent fashion-designer boutiques. Storefronts—some closet size—are filled with local designers' wares, funky boutiques, and no fewer than three shops selling ecologically friendly clothes of hemp and organic cotton. ⊠ *Johnson St. between Government and Store Sts., Downtown.*

SPECIALTY STORES

Artina's. Canadian-made jewelry—all handmade, one-of-a-kind pieces—fills the display cases at this unique jewelry shop. ⊠ *1002 Government St., Downtown* ☎ *250/386–7000 or 877/386–7700.*

Munro's Books. This beautifully restored 1909 building houses one of Canada's prettiest bookstores. ⊠ *1108 Government St., Downtown* ☎ *250/382–2464.*

Silk Road Aromatherapy & Tea Company & Spa. For exotic teas (which you can sample at the tasting bar), aromatherapy remedies, and spa treatments (think green-tea facials), stop at this chic and multifaceted shop. ✉ *1624 Government St., Downtown* ☎ *250/704–2688.*

OUTDOOR ACTIVITIES AND ATTRACTIONS

BIKING

Victoria is a bike-friendly town, with more bicycle commuters than any other city in Canada. Bike racks on city buses, bike lanes on downtown streets, and tolerant drivers all help, as do the city's three long-distance cycling routes, which mix car-free paths and low-traffic scenic routes.

BC Ferries will transport bikes for a nominal fee (just C$2 from Vancouver). You can also rent bikes, bike trailers, and tandem bikes at several Victoria outlets for a few hours, a day, or a week. Helmets are required by law and are supplied with bike rentals.

BIKE ROUTES   **Galloping Goose Regional Trail.** Following an old rail bed, this 55-km (33-mi) route officially starts at the Johnson Street Bridge downtown. The multi-use trail runs across old rail trestles and through forests to the town of Sooke, finishing at the abandoned gold-mining town of Leechtown. ☎ *250/478–3344* ⊕ *www.crd.bc.ca/parks.*

The Lochside Regional Trail. This fairly level, mostly car-free, 29-km (18-mi) route follows an old rail bed past farmland, wineries, and beaches from the ferry terminals at Swartz Bay and Sidney to downtown Victoria. It joins the Seaside Touring route at Cordova Bay and meets the Galloping Goose Trail just north of downtown Victoria. ☎ *250/478–3344* ⊕ *www.crd.bc.ca/parks.*

The Seaside Touring Route. Starting at Government and Belleville on the Inner Harbour, this 11-km (7-mi) route, marked with bright yellow signs, leads past Fisherman's Wharf and along the Dallas Road waterfront to Beacon Hill Park. It then follows the seashore to Cordova Bay, where it connects with Victoria's other two long-distance routes: the Lochside and Galloping Goose regional trails.

BIKE RENTALS
AND TOURS   **Cycle BC Rentals.** You can rent bikes, kids' bikes, and bike trailers at Cycle BC's Humboldt Street outlet and (between May and October) at their Wharf Street location. ✉ *685 Humboldt St., Downtown* ☎ *250/380–2453* ✉ *950 Wharf St., Downtown* ☎ *250/385–2453 or 866/380–2453* ⊕ *www.cyclebc.ca.*

CycleTreks. Besides renting bikes, this company also runs bike tours of Victoria, the Gulf Islands, and various parts of Vancouver Island, including a Cowichan Valley vineyard tour. They can also give you a ride to the start of Galloping Goose Trail or to the Butchart Gardens so you can pedal back. ✉ *1000 Wharf St.* ☎ *250/386–2277 or 877/733–6722* ⊕ *www.cycletreks.com.*

GOLF

You can golf year-round in Victoria and southern Vancouver Island, and you almost have to, just to try all the courses. Victoria alone has several public golf courses, ranging from rolling sea-view fairways to challenging mountaintop sites. Southern Vancouver Island is home

VICTORIA'S TOP SPAS

Since health, nature, and relaxing seem to be the major preoccupations in Victoria, it's not surprising that the city has enjoyed a boom in spas. Aesthetics are important, but natural healing, ancient practices, and the use of such local products as wine and seaweed are more the focus here. Local specialties include vinotherapy (applying the antioxidant properties of wine grapes externally, rather than internally). Here are some local favorites.

The Aveda Institute. ⊠ 1402 Douglas St., Downtown ☎ 250/386–7993 ⊕ www.avedainstitutevictoria.ca.

Le Spa Sereine. ⊠ 1411 Government St., Downtown ☎ 250/388–4419 or 866/388–4419 ⊕ www.lespasereine.com.

The Spa at the Delta Victoria Ocean Pointe Resort. ⊠ 45 Songhees Rd., Downtown ☎ 250/360–5938 or 800/575–8882 ⊕ www.thespadeltavictoria.com.

Spa at the Grand. ⊠ 463 Belleville St., Grand Pacific HotelDowntown ☎ 250/380–7862 ⊕ www.hotelgrandpacific.com.

Willow Stream Spa at the Fairmont Empress Hotel. ⊠ 633 Humboldt St., Downtown ☎ 250/995–4650 or 866/854–7444 ⊕ www.willowstream.com.

to the Vancouver Island Golf Trail, where you'll find 12 championship courses along a 250-km (150-mi) corridor. Golf Vancouver Island (☎ 888/465–3239 ⊕ *www.golfvancouverisland.ca*) has details.

Bear Mountain Golf & Country Club. Built near the top of a 335-meter (1,100-foot) mountain about 20 minutes north of Victoria, this is widely regarded as the island's most exciting course. Designed by Jack Nicklaus and his son Steve, the Mountain Course has an extra 19th hole built on a cliff ledge with striking views across the city. A second Nicklaus-designed layout, called the Valley Course, is at a slightly lower elevation. ⊠ *1999 Country Club Way, off Millstream Rd. and Bear Mountain Pkwy., The West Shore* ☎ *250/744–2327 or 888/533–2327* ⊕ *www.bearmountain.ca.*

HIKING AND WALKING

Victoria is one of the most pedestrian-friendly cities in North America. Waterfront pathways make it possible to stroll virtually all around Victoria's waterfront. For some interesting self-guided walks around the city's historic areas, check out ⊕ *www.victoria.ca/tours* or pick up a free walking-tour map at the city's visitor information center. Though popular with cyclists, the area's long-distance paths are also great for long walks. For views and elevation, check out the trail networks in the area's many provincial and regional parks.

Juan de Fuca Marine Trail. This tough 47-km (30-mi) coastal hike begins at China Beach, near the village of Jordan River, about 48 km (29 mi) west of Victoria. There are three other trailheads, each with a parking lot, at Sombrio Beach, Parkinson Creek, and Botanical Beach (which is 5 km [3 mi] southeast of Port Renfrew), allowing hikers to tackle the trail in day-hike sections. ⊠ *Off Hwy. 14, between Jordan River*

17

(southeast end) and Port Renfrew (northwest end) ☎ *800/689–9025 camping reservations* ⊕ *www.env.gov.bc.ca/bcparks.*

Mount Douglas Regional Park. Trails through the forest to the 213-meter (758-foot) summit of Mt. Douglas reward hikers with a 360-degree view of Victoria, the Saanich Peninsula, and the mountains of Washington State. ✉ *Off Cedar Hill Rd., Saanich* ☎ *250/475–5522* ⊕ *www. saanich.ca.*

SCUBA DIVING

The waters off Vancouver Island have some of the best scuba diving in the world, with clear waters and rich marine life; visibility is best in winter. The Ogden Point Breakwater and Race Rocks Underwater Marine Park are popular spots close to town. In Brentwood Bay on the Saanich Peninsula are the Glass Sponge Gardens, a sea mountain covered with sponges that were thought to be extinct. Off Thetis Island, near Chemainus, in the Cowichan Valley, divers can explore a sunken 737 jetliner. Dive BC (⊕ *www.divebc.ca*) has details.

Ogden Point Dive Centre. Fills, rentals, guided dives, weekend charters, and a water-view café are all available at this PADI (Professional Association of Diving Instructors) dive center at the Ogden Point Breakwater near downtown Victoria. ✉ *199 Dallas Rd., Downtown* ☎ *250/380– 9119 or 888/701–1177* ⊕ *www.divevictoria.com.*

Rockfish Divers. This internationally accredited PADI dive outfitter, based at the Brentwood Bay Lodge & Spa on the Saanich Peninsula, offers charters, courses, and equipment rentals. ✉ *849 Verdier Ave., Brentwood Bay* ☎ *250/889–7282* ⊕ *www.brentwoodbaylodge.com.*

Travel Smart Pacific Northwest

WORD OF MOUTH

"For sightseeing downtown Seattle, you don't need a rental car—there is good public transportation and/or getting around on foot."

—suze

GETTING HERE AND AROUND

See also Pacific Northwest Planner in chapter 1.

▌ AIR TRAVEL

It takes about 5 hours to fly nonstop to Seattle or Portland from New York, 4 hours from Chicago, and 2½ hours from Los Angeles. Flights from New York to Vancouver take about 6 hours nonstop; from Chicago, 4½ hours nonstop; and from Los Angeles, 3 hours nonstop. Flying from Seattle to Portland takes just under an hour; flying from Portland to Vancouver takes an hour and 15 minutes.

Airlines and Airports **Airline and Airport Links.com** (⊕ *www.airlineandairportlinks.com*) has links to many of the world's airlines and airports.

Airline Security Issues **Transportation Security Administration** (⊕ *www.tsa.gov*) has answers for almost every question that might come up. Check here as well for the latest safety regulations. As threat levels ebb and flow, new regulations can pop up overnight. It's best to check the day before your flight for any recent additions to ensure that you aren't stuck throwing out any expensive products or scrambling to find the right identification.

AIRPORTS

The main gateways to the Pacific Northwest are Portland International Airport (PDX), Sea-Tac International Airport (SEA), and Vancouver International Airport (YVR).

Airport Information **Portland International Airport (PDX)** (✉ *N.E. Airport Way at I–205* ☎ *877/739–4636* ⊕ *www.flypdx. com*). **Sea-Tac International Airport (SEA)** (☎ *206/433–5388* ⊕ *www.portseattle.org/ seatac*). **Vancouver International Airport (YVR)** (☎ *604/207–7077* ⊕ *www.yvr.ca*).

▌TIP→ Long layovers don't have to be only about sitting around or shopping. These days they can be about burning off vacation calories. Check out ⊕ *www.airportgyms.com* for lists of health clubs that are in or near many U.S. and Canadian airports.

AIRLINE TICKETS

The least expensive airfares to the Pacific Northwest are often priced for round-trip travel and usually must be purchased in advance. Airlines generally allow you to change your return date for a fee; most low-fare tickets, however, are nonrefundable.

You can also save money on your car rental (a must for most Pacific Northwest itineraries) by booking a fly/drive package through your airline. Many airlines offer deals on rental cars if you book through them.

FLIGHTS

Many international carriers serve the Pacific Northwest, including Air France, British Airways, Cathay Pacific (Vancouver), Japan Airlines (Vancouver), KLM, Lufthansa, and Qantas. Vancouver has the most connections with international cities, but Seattle's a close second. U.S. carriers serving the area include Alaska Airlines, Continental, Delta, and United. American Airlines has frequent flights to Seattle and Vancouver. JetBlue has daily direct flights from New York's JFK airport and Los Angeles' Long Beach airport to both Seattle and Portland. Virgin America has daily direct flights to Seattle from San Francisco and Los Angeles (LAX). USAirways flies from Portland and Seattle to Las Vegas, Phoenix, Charlotte, and Philadelphia, and from Vancouver to Las Vegas and Phoenix. Frontier Airlines, Horizon Air, and United Express provide frequent service between cities in Washington, Oregon, Idaho, Montana, and California. Southwest Airlines has frequent service to Seattle and Portland from cities in California, Nevada, Idaho, and Utah, as well as some other parts of the country. The major regional carrier in western Canada is Air Canada (and its subsidiary,

Air Canada Jazz), which has flights from Seattle and Portland to Vancouver and Victoria, along with many direct flights between Vancouver and major U.S. cities outside the Northwest.

Airline Contacts **Air Canada/Air Canada Jazz** (☎ 888/247–2262 ⊕ www.aircanada. com or www.flyjazz.ca). **Alaska Airlines** (☎ 800/252–7522 ⊕ www.alaskaair.com). **American Airlines** (☎ 800/433–7300 ⊕ www. aa.com). **Continental Airlines** (☎ 800/523–3273 for U.S. and Mexico reservations, 800/231–0856 for international reservations ⊕ www.continental.com). **Delta Airlines** (☎ 800/221–1212 for U.S. reservations, 800/241–4141 for international reservations ⊕ www.delta.com). **Frontier** (☎ 800/432–1359 ⊕ www.frontierairlines.com). **Horizon Air** (☎ 800/547–9308 ⊕ www.alaskaair. com). **Japan Airlines** (☎ 800/525–3663 ⊕ www.jal.com). **jetBlue** (☎ 800/538–2583 ⊕ www.jetblue.com). **Southwest Airlines** (☎ 800/435–9792 ⊕ www.southwest.com). **United Airlines** (☎ 800/864–8331 for U.S. reservations, 800/538–2929 for international reservations ⊕ www.united.com). **US Airways** (☎ 800/428–4322 for U.S. and Canada reservations, 800/622–1015 for international reservations ⊕ www.usairways.com). **Virgin America** (☎ 877/359–8474 ⊕ www. virginamerica.com).

▌ BOAT AND FERRY TRAVEL

Ferries play an important part in the transportation network of the Pacific Northwest. Some are the sole connection to islands in Puget Sound and to small towns and islands along the west coast of British Columbia. Each day ferries transport thousands of commuters to and from work in the coastal cities. Always comfortable, convenient, and surrounded by spectacular views, ferries are also one of the best ways for you to get a feel for the region and its ties to the sea.

Generally, the best times for travel are 9–3 and after 7 PM on weekdays. In July and August you may have to wait hours to take a car aboard one of the popular ferries, such as those to the San Juan Islands. Walk-on space is always available; if possible, leave your car behind. Reservations aren't taken for domestic routes.

WASHINGTON AND OREGON

Washington State Ferries carries millions of passengers and vehicles each year on 11 routes between 20 points on Puget Sound, the San Juan Islands, and Sidney, British Columbia. Onboard services vary depending on the size of the ferry, but many ships have a cafeteria, vending machines, newspaper and tourist-information kiosks, arcade games, and restrooms with family facilities. There are discounted fares in off-peak months.

Black Ball Transport's MV *Coho* makes daily crossings year-round from Port Angeles, WA, to Victoria. The *Coho* can carry 800 passengers and 100 cars across the Strait of Juan de Fuca in 1½ hours. Clipper Vacations operates the passenger-only *Victoria Clipper* jet catamaran service between Seattle and Victoria year-round and between Seattle and the San Juan Islands May through September. ▌TIP→ Victoria Clipper fares are less expensive if booked at least one day in advance, children under 12 are free with select trips (be sure to ask about any promotions or deals), and there are also some great package deals available online.

Black Ball Transport (☎ 250/386–2202 in Victoria, 360/457–4491 in Port Angeles ⊕ www.cohoferry.com). **Clipper Vacations** (☎ 800/888–2535 in the U.S., 250/382–8100 in Victoria, 206/448–5000 in Seattle ⊕ www. clippervacations.com). **Puget Island Ferry** (☎ 360/795–3301 ⊕ www.co.wahkiakum. wa.us/depts/pw). **Washington State Ferries** (☎ 800/843–3779 automated line in WA and BC, 888/808–7977, 206/464–6400 ⊕ www. wsdot.wa.gov/ferries).

BRITISH COLUMBIA

British Columbia Ferries operates passenger and vehicle service between the mainland and Victoria and elsewhere. Most ferries take reservations.

Information British Columbia Ferries
(☎ 250/386–3431 in Victoria, 888/223–3779
⊕ www.bcferries.bc.ca).

SIGHTSEEING

Argosy cruising vessels make sightseeing, dinner, weekend brunch, and special-event cruises around Elliott Bay, Lake Union, Lake Washington, the Ballard Locks, and other Seattle waterways.

From Portland, the *Portland Spirit, Willamette Star,* and *Crystal Dolphin* make sightseeing and dinner cruises on the Willamette and Columbia Rivers. Departing from Cascade Locks, Oregon (45 minutes east of Portland), the sternwheeler *Columbia Gorge* cruises the Columbia Gorge and the Willamette River (December only).

Information Argosy Cruises (☎ 206/623–1445 or 800/642–7816 ⊕ www.argosycruises.com). **Portland Spirit River Cruises** (☎ 503/224–3900 or ⊕ www.portlandspirit.com).

▌ BUS TRAVEL

Greyhound services the whole Washington-Oregon region. Northwest Trailways services Washington and Idaho, with most service between Eastern Washington and Idaho. Experience Oregon in Eugene operates charter bus services and scheduled sightseeing tours that last from a few hours to several days. People Mover travels on Highway 26 between Bend and John Day. Greyhound serves most towns in British Columbia, and provides frequent service on popular runs. Quick Shuttle runs buses from Sea-Tac airport and downtown Seattle to various Vancouver spots and hotels.

Pacific Coach Lines runs multiple daily buses between Vancouver and Victoria, including a ferry ride across the Strait of Georgia. The company also has connections from Vancouver to Vancouver International Airport and the cruise ship terminal, and operates numerous package tours around British Columbia.

Greyhound's domestic and international Discovery Passes (www.discoverypass.com) allow unlimited bus travel in North America—including Canada and Mexico—for periods of 7 to 60 days.

Bus Information Experience Oregon
(☎ 541/342–2662 or 888/342–2662 ⊕ www.experienceoregon.com). **Greyhound Lines** (☎ 800/231–2222 in U.S. ⊕ www.greyhound.com ☎ 800/661–8747 in Canada ⊕ www.greyhound.ca). **Northwestern Trailways** (☎ 800/366–3830 ⊕ www.northwesterntrailways.com). **Pacific Coach Lines** (☎ 800/661–1725 in U.S., 604/662–7575 in Vancouver ⊕ www.pacificcoach.com). **People Mover** (☎ 541/575–2370). **Quick Shuttle** (☎ 800/665–2122 in U.S., 604/940–4428 in Vancouver ⊕ www.quickcoach.com).

SIGHTSEEING

Gray Line operates a few day trips from Portland, Seattle, and Vancouver, including tours out to Mt. Hood and Mt. Rainier, Vancouver, and Victoria, schedules a variety of popular bus tours and overnight packages around the Pacific Northwest.

Gray Line (☎ 503/684–3322, 888/684–3322 in Portland ⊕ www.grayline.com ☎ 206/624–5077, 800/426–7532 in Seattle ⊕ www.graylineseattle.com ☎ 800/667–0882 in Vancouver ☎ 250/388–6539, 800/663–8390 in Victoria ⊕ www.graylinewest.com).

▌ CAR TRAVEL

Driver's licenses from other countries are valid in the United States and Canada. International driving permits (IDPs)—available from the American and Canadian automobile associations and, in the United Kingdom, from the Automobile Association and Royal Automobile Club—are a good idea. Valid only in conjunction with your regular driver's license, these permits are universally recognized; having one may save you a problem with local authorities.

TRAVEL TIMES FROM SEATTLE BY CAR	
Portland	3–3½ hours
Vancouver	2½–3 hours
Victoria	2½–3 hrs drive to Vancouver; 1½ hrs ferry ride from Vancouver
Mt. Rainier National Park (Paradise or Longmire entrances)	2½ hours
North Cascades National Park	3–3½ hrs
Olympic National Park	2½ hrs to Port Angeles; 1 hr from Port Angeles to Hurricane Ridge
Mt. St. Helens	3–3½ hours
Spokane	4½–5 hours
Yakima Valley	2–2½ hours

TRAVEL TIMES FROM PORTLAND BY CAR	
Bend	3½–4 hours
Crater Lake National Park	4½–5 hours
Columbia River Gorge/ Mt. Hood	1½ hours
Willamette Valley	1½–2 hours

BORDER CROSSING

⇨ *See also Passports in Essentials below.*

You will need a valid passport to cross the border. In addition, drivers must carry owner registration and proof of insurance coverage, which is compulsory in Canada. The Canadian Non-Resident Inter-Provincial Motor Vehicle Liability Insurance Card, available from any U.S. insurance company, is accepted as evidence of financial responsibility in Canada. If you are driving a car that is not registered in your name, carry a letter from the owner that authorizes your use of the vehicle.

The main entry point into British Columbia from the United States by car is on I–5 at Blaine, Washington, 48 km (30 mi) south of Vancouver. Three highways enter British Columbia from the east: Highway 1, or the Trans-Canada Highway; Highway 3, or the Crowsnest Highway, which crosses southern British Columbia; and Highway 16, the Yellowhead Highway, which runs through northern British Columbia from the Rocky Mountains to Prince Rupert. From Alaska and the Yukon, take the Alaska Highway (from Fairbanks) or the Klondike Highway (from Skagway or Dawson City).

Border-crossing procedures are usually quick and simple. Every British Columbia border crossing is open 24 hours (except the one at Aldergrove, which is open from 8 AM to midnight). The I–5 border crossing at Blaine, Washington (also known as the Douglas, or Peace Arch, border crossing), is one of the busiest border crossings between the United States and Canada. Listen to local radio traffic reports for information about wait times.

CAR RENTAL

■TIP→ Make sure that a confirmed reservation guarantees you a car. Agencies sometimes overbook, particularly for busy weekends and holiday periods.

Unless you only visit Seattle, Portland, and Vancouver, you will need to rent a car for at least part of your trip. It's possible to get around the big cities by public transportation and taxis, but once you go outside city limits, your options are limited. National lines like Greyhound do provide service between major towns, and Amtrak has limited service between Washington and Oregon (allowing you to get from, say, Seattle to Portland, by train), but it is nearly impossible to get to and around the major recreation areas and national parks of each state without your own wheels. For example, there is no public transportation from Seattle to Mt. Rainier National Park.

Rates in Seattle begin at $29 a day ($146 per week) for an economy car. This does not include the 19.2% tax. The tax on rentals at Sea-Tac Airport, which includes an airport concession fee, is more than 30%, so try to rent from a downtown branch. Rates in Portland begin at $30 a day and $138 a week, not including the 17% tax. Rates in Vancouver begin at about C$32 a day or C$196 a week, usually including unlimited mileage. Note that summer rates in all cities can be absurd (up to $60 per day for a compact); book as far in advance as possible, and if you find a good deal, grab it.

Car rentals in British Columbia also incur a 15% sales tax, a C$1.50-per-day social services tax, and a vehicle licensing fee of C$1.18 per day. An additional 17% Concession Recovery Fee, charged by the airport authority for retail space in the terminal, is levied at airport locations.

All the major agencies are represented in the region. If you're planning to cross the U.S.–Canadian border with your rental car, discuss it with the agency to see what's involved.

In the Pacific Northwest you must be 21 to rent a car. Car seats are compulsory for children under four years *and* 40 pounds; older children are required to sit in booster seats until they are eight years old *and* 80 pounds. (In British Columbia, children up to 40 pounds or 18 kilos in weight must use a child seat.) In the United States nonresidents need a reservation voucher, passport, driver's license, and insurance for each driver.

ROAD CONDITIONS

Tire chains, studs, or snow tires are essential equipment for winter travel in mountain areas. If you're planning to drive into high elevations, be sure to check the weather forecast beforehand. Even the main-highway mountain passes can close because of snow conditions. In winter state and provincial highway departments operate snow advisory telephone lines that give pass conditions.

ROADSIDE EMERGENCIES

Contacts For **police, ambulance,** or **other emergencies** dial 911. **Oregon State Police** (☎ *503/378-3720 or 800/452-7888*).

▌ TRAIN TRAVEL

Amtrak, the U.S. passenger rail system, has daily service to the Pacific Northwest from the Midwest and California. The *Empire Builder* takes a northern route through Minnesota and Montana from Chicago to Spokane, from which separate legs continue to Seattle and Portland. The *Coast Starlight* begins in Los Angeles; makes stops throughout California, western Oregon, and Washington; and terminates in Seattle.

Amtrak's *Cascades* trains travel between Seattle and Vancouver and between Seattle, Portland, and Eugene. The trip from Seattle to Portland takes roughly 3½ hours and costs $28–$49 for a coach seat; this is a pleasant alternative to a mind-numbing drive down I–5. The trip from Seattle to Vancouver takes roughly 4 hours and costs $39–$59. The *Empire Builder* travels between Portland and Spokane (7 hours, $75), with part of the route running through the Columbia River gorge. From Portland to Eugene, it's a 3-hour trip; the cost is $23–$35.

▌TIP➔ Book Amtrak tickets at least a few days in advance, especially if you're traveling between Seattle and Portland on summer weekends.

VIA Rail has train service from Victoria along the coast of Vancouver Island. The line terminates at Courtenay (4½ hours from Victoria); the fare for this journey is $37.

Information **Amtrak** (☎ *800/872-7245* ⊕ *www.amtrak.com*). **VIA Rail Canada** (☎ *888/842-7245* ⊕ *www.viarail.ca*).

ESSENTIALS

■ ACCOMMODATIONS

The lodgings we list are the cream of the crop in each price category. We always list the facilities that are available, but we don't specify whether they cost extra; when pricing accommodations, always ask what's included and what costs extra. Properties are assigned price categories based on the range between their least and most expensive standard double rooms at high season (excluding holidays).

All prices are for a standard double room in high season, based on the European Plan (EP) and excluding tax and service charges. Seattle room tax: 15.6%. Elsewhere in WA: ranges from 10% to 16%. Portland room tax: 11.5%. Elsewhere in Oregon: ranges from 6 to 10%. Vancouver room tax: 12%. Elsewhere in BC: 8%. Most hotels and other lodgings require you to give your credit-card details before they will confirm your reservation. If you don't feel comfortable e-mailing this information, ask if you can fax it (some places even prefer faxes). However you book, get confirmation in writing and have a copy of it handy when you check in.

■TIP➜ Assume that hotels operate on the European Plan (EP, no meals) unless we specify that they use the Breakfast Plan (BP, with full breakfast), Continental Plan (CP, continental breakfast), Full American Plan (FAP, all meals), or Modified American Plan (MAP, breakfast and dinner), or are all-inclusive (AI, all meals and most activities).

BED AND BREAKFASTS

The Pacific Northwest is known for its vast range of bed-and-breakfast options, which are found everywhere from busy urban areas to casual country farms and coastal retreats. Many B&Bs here provide full gourmet breakfasts, and some have kitchens that guests can use. Other popular amenities to ask about are fireplaces, jetted bathtubs, outdoor hot tubs, and area activities.

The regional B&B organizations listed below can provide information on reputable establishments.

Reservation Services **American Bed & Breakfast Association** (⊕ *www.abba.com*). **BBCanada.com** (⊕ *www.bbcanada.com*). **British Columbia Bed & Breakfasts** (⊕ *www. bcbbonly.com*). **The Canadian Bed & Breakfast Guide** (☎ *877/213–0089 or 905/262– 4597* ⊕ *www.canadianbandbguide.ca*). **Oregon Bed & Breakfast Guild** (☎ *800/944–6196* ⊕ *www.obbg.org*). **Washington Bed & Breakfast Guild** (☎ *800/647–2918* ⊕ *www.wbbg. com*). **British Columbia Bed & Breakfast Innkeepers Guild** (⊕ *www.bcsbestbnbs.com*).

CAMPING

Oregon, Washington, and British Columbia have excellent government-run campgrounds. A few accept advance camping reservations, but most do not. National park campsites—even backcountry sites—fill up quickly and should be reserved in advance. Note that federal forests allow free camping almost anywhere along trails—a good failsafe if you're unable to secure last-minute arrangements at designated sites, and don't mind hauling your gear.

Privately operated campgrounds sometimes have extra amenities such as laundry rooms and swimming pools. For more information, contact the state or provincial tourism department. Campground Reservations **British Columbia Lodgings & Campground Association** (⊕ *www.camping.bc.ca*). **Discover Camping (British Columbia)** (☎ *800/689– 9025* ⊕ *www.discovercamping.ca*). **Oregon Parks and Recreation Dept.** (☎ *800/452– 5687 reservations* ⊕ *www.oregon.gov/oprd/ parks*). **Washington State Parks and Recreation Commission** (☎ *888/226–7688 reservations* ⊕ *www.parks.wa.gov*).

HOTELS

When booking a room, always call the hotel's local toll-free number (if one is available) rather than the central reservations number—you'll often get a better price. Deals can often be found at hotel Web sites. Always ask about special packages or corporate rates. Many properties offer special weekend rates, sometimes up to 50% off regular prices. However, these deals are usually not extended during peak summer months, when hotels are normally full. All hotels listed have private bath unless otherwise noted.

▌CUSTOMS AND DUTIES

You're always allowed to bring goods of a certain value back home without having to pay any duty or import tax. But there's a limit on the amount of tobacco and liquor you can bring back duty-free, and some countries have separate limits for perfumes; for exact figures, check with your customs department. The values of so-called "duty-free" goods are included in these amounts. When you shop abroad, save all your receipts, as customs inspectors may ask to see them as well as the items you purchased. If the total value of your goods is more than the duty-free limit, you'll have to pay a tax (most often a flat percentage) on the value of everything beyond that limit.

U.S. Information U.S. Customs and Border Protection (⊕ www.cbp.gov).

Information in Canada Canada Border Services Agency (☎ 204/983–3500 or 800/461–9999 ⊕ www.cbsa-asfc.gc.ca).

▌EATING OUT

Pacific Northwest cuisine highlights regional seafood and locally grown, organic produce, often prepared in styles that reflect an Asian influence (Seattle, Victoria, and Vancouver have large Asian populations) or incorporate European (often French or Italian) influences. *See our the Flavors of the Pacific Northwest feature at the beginning of this book.*

The restaurants we list are the cream of the crop in each price category.

MEALS AND MEALTIMES

Unless otherwise noted, the restaurants listed in this guide are open daily for lunch and dinner.

PAYING

Credit cards—Visa and MasterCard, in particular—are widely accepted in most restaurants, especially in Seattle, Portland, and Vancouver. Debit cards are widely accepted in coffeehouses, delis, and grocery stores.

WINES, BEER & SPIRITS

Both Oregon and Washington have thriving wineries—restaurants in Seattle take their wine lists very seriously. Most of Washington's wineries are east of the Cascades in the south-central part of the state, but you'll find a few close to Seattle as well. Oregon's wineries mostly lie in the valleys between the southern Cascades and the coast. The Washington State Wine Commission (⊕ *www.washingtonwine.org*) and the Oregon Wine Board (⊕ *www.oregonwine.org*) both maintain Web sites with facts, history, and information on local wineries. British Columbia winemaking has become increasingly prominent. The British Columbia Wine Institute's Web site (⊕ *www.winebc.com*) has facts and information on individual wineries.

Oregon has more than 60 microbreweries, and Washington has no shortage of excellent local microbrews. Both states have festivals and events celebrating their brews—Seattle's Fremont neighborhood has its own Oktoberfest. The Web site for the Washington Brewers Guild (⊕ *www. washingtonbeer.com*) has info on breweries in the state and events throughout the Pacific Northwest. The Oregon Brewers Guild (⊕ *www.oregonbeer.org*) also has links to breweries and information on events.

You must be 21 to buy alcohol in Washington and Oregon. The legal drinking age in British Columbia is 19.

▌ MONEY

Prices throughout this guide are given for adults. Substantially reduced fees are almost always available for children, students, and senior citizens.

CREDIT CARDS

Throughout this guide, the following abbreviations are used: **AE**, American Express; **D**, Discover; **DC**, Diners Club; **MC**, MasterCard; and **V**, Visa.

CURRENCY AND EXCHANGE

The units of currency in Canada are the Canadian dollar (C$) and the cent, in almost the same denominations as U.S. currency ($5, $10, $20, 1¢, 5¢, 10¢, 25¢, etc.). The C$1 and C$2 bill are no longer used; they have been replaced by C$1 and C$2 coins (known as a "loonie," because of the loon that appears on the coin, and a "toonie," respectively). Check with a bank or other financial institution for the current rate. A good way to be sure you're getting the best exchange rate is by using your credit card or ATM/debit card. The issuing bank will convert your bill at the current rate.

▌TIP➡ Even if a currency-exchange booth has a sign promising no commission, rest assured that there's some kind of huge, hidden fee. (Oh . . . that's right. The sign didn't say no *fee*.) And as for rates, you're almost always better off getting foreign currency at an ATM or exchanging money at a bank.

▌ PASSPORTS

All people traveling by air between the United States and Canada are required to present a passport to enter or reenter the United States. To enter Canada (or more precisely, to reenter the U.S. from Canada) by land or sea you need to present either a valid passport or a U.S. Passport Card—sort of a "passport lite" that is only valid for land or sea crossings from Canada, Mexico, Caribbean, or Bermuda, based on the latest Western Hemisphere Travel Initiative info.

For more information on border crossings see Car Travel above

U.S. passports are valid for 10 years. You must apply in person if you're getting a passport for the first time; if your previous passport was lost, stolen, or damaged; or if your previous passport has expired and was issued more than 15 years ago or when you were under 16. All children under 18 must appear in person to apply for or renew a passport. Both parents must accompany any child under 14 (or send a notarized statement with their permission) and provide proof of their relationship to the child.

The cost to apply for a new passport is $97 for adults, $82 for children under 16; renewals are $67. Allow at least six weeks, sometimes longer for processing, both for first-time passports and renewals. For an expediting fee of $60 you can reduce this time to about two weeks. If your trip is less than two weeks away, you can get a passport even more rapidly by going to a passport office with the necessary documentation. Private expediters can get things done in as little as 48 hours, but charge hefty fees for their services.

U.S. Passport Information U.S. Department of State (☎ 877/487–2778 ⊕ *www.travel.state. gov/passport*).

Canadian Passports Passport Office (✉ *To mail in applications: 70 Cremazie St., Gatineau, Québec* ☎ *819/994–3500 or 800/567–6868* ⊕ *www.ppt.gc.ca*).

U.S. Passport & Visa Expediters **American Passport Express** (☎ 800/455–5166 or 800/841–6778 ⊕ www.americanpassport.com). **Passport Express** (☎ 800/362–8196 ⊕ www. passportexpress.com). **Travel Document Systems** (☎ 800/874–5100 or 202/638–3800 ⊕ www.traveldocs.com). **Travel the World Visas** (☎ 866/886–8472 or 301/495–7700 ⊕ www.world-visa.com).

▌TAXES

Oregon has no sales tax, although many cities and counties levy a tax on lodging and services. Room taxes, for example, vary 6%–9½%. The state retail sales tax in Washington is 6.5%, but there are also local taxes that can raise the total tax to 11.5%, depending on the goods or service and the municipality; Seattle's retail sales tax is 8.9%. A Goods and Services Tax (GST) of 5% applies on virtually every transaction in Canada except for the purchase of basic groceries.

In 2010 British Columbia merged it's provincial sales tax with the GST; the Harmonized Sales Tax is 12% and it applies to most goods and services. You can get a GST refund on purchases taken out of the country and on short-term accommodations of less than one month, but not on food, drink, tobacco, car or motor-home rentals, or transportation; rebate forms, which must be submitted within a year of leaving Canada, may be obtained from certain retailers, duty-free shops, customs officials, or from the Canada Customs and Revenue Agency. Instant cash rebates up to a maximum of C$500 are provided by some duty-free shops when you leave Canada, and most provinces do not tax goods that are shipped directly by the vendor to the purchaser's home. Always save your original receipts from stores and hotels (not just credit-card receipts), and be sure the name and address of the establishment are shown on the receipt. Original receipts are not returned. For you to be eligible for a refund, your receipts must total at least C$200, and each individual receipt for goods must show a minimum purchase of C$50 before tax. Some agencies in Vancouver and Whistler offer on-the-spot cash GST refunds. Although they charge a commission of about 20%, some visitors may find it worth it for the convenience, especially as Canadian Government checks may be difficult to cash in some countries.

Information **Canada Customs and Revenue Agency** (✉ Visitor Rebate Program, Summerside Tax Centre, 275 Pope Rd., Suite 104, Summerside, PE ☎ 902/432–5608, 800/668–4748 in Canada ⊕ www.ccra-adrc.gc.ca).

▌VISITOR INFORMATION

British Columbia **Tourism Vancouver Island** (✉ 203–335 Wesley St., Nanaimo ☎ 250/754–3500 ⊕ www.tourismvictoria.com). **Tourism Victoria** (⊕ www.tourismvictoria.com). **Vancouver Tourist InfoCentre** (✉ Plaza Level, 200 Burrard St., Vancouver ☎ 604/683–2000 ⊕ www.tourismvancouver.com).

Oregon **Oregon Tourism Commission** (✉ Jantzen Beach State Welcome Center, 12348 N. Center Ave., Portland ☎ 503/289–7535 or 800/547–7842 ⊕ www.traveloregon. com). **Portland Oregon Visitors Association** (✉ 1000 S.W. Broadway, Suite 2300, Portland ☎ 503/275–9750 or 800/962–3700 ⊕ www. travelportland.com).

Washington **Seattle Convention and Visitor's Bureau** (✉ 520 Pike St., Suite 1300, Seattle ☎ 206/461–5840 or 206/461–5888 ⊕ www.visitseattle.org). **Washington State Tourism** (✉ 101 General Administration Bldg., Olympia ☎ 800/544–1800 ⊕ www. experiencewashington.com).

INDEX

PHOTO CREDITS

1, Konrad Wothe / age fotostock. 2-3, Jeanne Hatch/iStockphoto. 5, Liem Bahneman/Shutterstock. **Chapter 1: Experience the Pacific Northwest.** 8-9, Martin Bydalek Photography. 10, Rebecca Kennison/ wikipedia.org. 11 (left), Lijuan Guo/iStockphoto. 11 (right), Ashok Rodrigues/iStockphoto. 12, Steve Whiston/Burke Museum. 13 (left), Stacey Lynn Payne/iStockphoto. 13 (right), 2008 Washington Wine Commission. 16 (left), neelsky/Shutterstock. 16 (top right), moohaha/Flickr. 16 (bottom center), Elena Korenbaum/iStockphoto. 16 (bottom right), Neta Degany/iStockphoto. 17 (top left), Chuck Pefley / Alamy. 17 (bottom left), Thomas Barrat/Shutterstock. 17 (top center), MAY FOTO / age fotostock. 17 (bottom center), Pike Place Market PDA. 17 (right), fotofriends/Shutterstock. 18, Kirk Hirota. 19 (left), Victrola Coffee/Kent Colony. 19 (right), ABC.pics/Shutterstock. 20, Glenn R. McGloughlin/Shutterstock. 21, Andy Simonds. 22, Matt McGee/flickr. 23, Pacific Science Center. 24, Martin Bydalek Photography. 25 (left), Ben Tobin. 25 (right), Campbelll Gordon. 27 (left), Rachell Coe/Shutterstock. 27 (right), Geoffrey Smith. 28, fotofriends/Shutterstock. 30, Andrew Lachance. **Chapter 2: Portland.** 31, Brian A. Ridder/Flickr. 32, --b--/Flickr. 33 (left), David Owen/Flickr. 33 (right), Michael Hashizume/ Flickr. 37, Karen Massier/iStockphoto. 41 and 44, Greg Vaughn. . 47, Rigucci/Shutterstock. 53, Jeff Hobson. 57, Basil Childers. 70 (top), McMenamins Kennedy School. 70 (bottom left), Hotel deluxe. 70 (bottom right), Heathman Hotel. 81, EvanLovely/Flickr. 89, LWY/Flickr. 95, Jason Vandehey/Shutterstock. **Chapter 3: The Oregon Coast.** 101, Greg Vaughn. 102 (bottom), Jeramey Jannene/Flickr. 102 (center), Aimin Tang/iStockphoto. 102 (top), scaredy_kat/Flickr. 103 (top), Oksana Perkins/iStockphoto. 103 (bottom), CVA/Flickr. 106, Tom Wald/iStockphoto. 107 (bottom), John Norris/Flickr. 107 (top), Scott Catron/wikipedia.org. 108, Pacific Northwest USCG/Flickr. 114, Greg Vaughn. 119, OCVA/ Flickr. 127, Greg Vaughn. 130, Oregon Coast Aquarium. 137, Greg Vaughn. **Chapter 4: Willamette Valley and Wine Country.** 149, Greg Vaughn. 150 (bottom), Gathering Together Farms. 150 (top), Don Hankins/Flickr. 151, Doreen L. Wynja. 154, Craig Sherod. 158, Greg Vaughn. 160, Randy Kashka/ Flickr. 164-84, Greg Vaughn. **Chapter 5: The Columbia River Gorge and Mt. Hood.** 191, Laura Cebulski/iStockphoto. 192, Timberline Lodge. 193 (top), Robert Crum/iStockphoto. 193 (bottom), Christian Sawicki/iStockphoto. 196, Rigucci/Shutterstock. 200, zschnepf/Shutterstock. 202 and 207, Greg Vaughn. 213, Melissa & Bryan Ripka/Flickr. 214, William Blacke/iStockphoto. **Chapter 6: Central Oregon.** 219, Mike Houska. 220 (bottom), Black Butte Ranch. 220 (top), Robert O. Brown Photography/ iStockphoto. 221, JonDissed/flickr. 224, Sunriver Resort. 229, USGS photo by Lyn Topinka/wikimedia. 233, Sunriver Resort. 237, mccun934/flickr. 242, mariachily/flickr. **Chapter 7: Crater Lake National Park.** 247, William A. McConnell. 248 (bottom), Aimin Tang/iStockphoto. 248 (center), Steve Terrill. 248 (top), Ashok Rodrigues/iStockphoto. 249, Michael Rubin/iStockphoto. 251, Vivian Fung/Shutterstock. 253, Greg Vaughn. 263, Larry Turner. 265, nwrafting/flickr. 275 and 281, Greg Vaughn. **Chapter 8: Eastern Oregon.** 285, Fokket/flickr. 286 (top), Fokket/flickr. 286 (bottom), Jan Tik/flickr. 287, salvez/ flickr. 290, Jeffrey T. Kreulen/iStockphoto. 295, Pendleton Underground Tours. 299, araddon/flickr. 301, IDAK/Shutterstock. 306, Cacophony/wikimedia. 309, AmySelleck/flickr. **Chapter 9: Seattle.** 317, José Fuste Raga / age fotostock. 319, Stephen Finn/Shutterstock. 322, Gregory Olsen/iStockphoto. 323, Mariusz S. Jurgielewicz/Shutterstock. 327, jeffwilcox/Flickr. 330 (top), Mark B. Bauschke/Shutterstock. 330 (bottom), Charles Amundson/Shutterstock. 332 (top), The Tasting Room. 332 (bottom left), piroshky bakery. 332 (bottom right), Beecher's Handmade Cheese. 333 (left), Phillie Casablanca/Flickr. 333 (center), Nick Jurich of flashpd.com. 333 (right), eng1ne/Flickr. 334 (top left), Liem Bahneman/ Shutterstock. 334 (bottom left), Pike Place Market PDA. 334 (right), World Pictures/Phot / age fotostock. 335 (left), Stephen Power / Alamy. 335 (right), Rootology/wikipedia.org. 337, Chris Cheadle / age fotostock. 338, Laura Komada. 349, Nick Jurich of flashpd.com. 355 and 361, Geoffrey Smith. 364 (top), Fairmont Hotels & Resorts. 364 (bottom), Benjamin Benschneider. 372 (top), Mark Bauschke. 372 (bottom left), Pan Pacific Hotel Seattle. 372 (bottom right), Hotel 1000. 379, HeyRocker/Flickr. 381, Elysian Brewing Company. 388, Chris Howes/Wild Places Photography / Alamy. 395, ebis50/ Flickr. 397, Agua Verde Paddle Club. **Chapter 10: Seattle Environs.** 401, Michael Sedam / age fotostock. 402 (top), Northwest Trek Wildlife Park. 402 (bottom), Adrian Baras/Shutterstock. 403, Rodefeld/Flickr. 406, Mrs. Flinger/Flickr. 410, Rodefeld/Flickr. 414, John Carlson. 419, amanderson2/Flickr.

431, Richard Cummins / age fotostock. 437, Carlos Arguelles/Shutterstock. **Chapter 11: The Puget Sound and San Juan Islands.** 445, Christina T. Mallet / age fotostock. 446, GlennFleishman/Flickr. 447, tobiaseigen/Flickr. 449, stevevoght/Flickr. 451, yel02/Flickr. 454, LegalAdmin/Flickr. 457, Richard Cummins / age fotostock. 461, Joe Becker / age fotostock. 467, Stuart Westmorland/age fotostock. 469, Thomas Kitchin & Vict/age fotostock. 470, San Juan Safaris. 471, Sylvain Grandadam/age fotostock. 475, Hauke Dressler / age fotostock. 481, Bill Stevenson / age fotostock. **Chapter 12: Olympic National Park.** 485, Rita Bellanca. 486-89, Washington State Tourism. 490, Andrey Lukashenkov/ Shutterstock. 494, Lindsay Douglas/Shutterstock. 500, P Frischknecht / age fotostock. 503, Martin Rugner / age fotostock. 514, UnGePhoto SS/Shutterstock. 519, Keith Lazelle Nature Photography. 522, Konrad Wothe / age fotostock. 526, Seabrook Cottage Rentals. 535, Alan Majchrowicz / age fotostock. **Chapter 13: North Cascades National Park.** 539, Alan Kearney/age fotostock. 540, Washington State Tourism. 541, Iwona Erskine-Kellie/Flickr. 543, Alan Kearney/age fotostock. 549, brewbooks/ Flickr. 552, Kurt Werby / age fotostock. 559, Sun Mountain Lodge. 567, Natalia Bratslavsky/Shutterstock. **Chapter 14: Mount Rainier National Park.** 571, chinana, Fodors.com member. 573 (top and bottom), Washington State Tourism. 575, Pat Leahy/Flickr. 581, Lee Coursey/Flickr. 589, zschnepf/ Shutterstock. 590, neelsky/Shutterstock. 591 (bottom), Bill Perry/Shutterstock. 591 (top), Donald A. Swanson/Wikimedia Commons. **Chapter 15: Yakima River Valley.** 597, Bruce Block/iStockphoto. 598, Jackie Johnston. 599 (top), L'Ecole N 41. 599 (bottom), Desert Wind Winery. 601, Chinook Wines. 602 and 603 (top), Lincoln Potter. 603 (bottom), Karen Massier/iStockphoto. 604, Hogue Cellars. 607, Lodge at Suncadia. 611, David Lynx. 617, Lincoln Potter. 621, Lynn Howlett. 623, RSD Photography. **Chapter 16: Eastern Washington.** 625, Michael Sedam / age fotostock. 626 (bottom), fotofriends/Shutterstock. 626 (top), Mark Wagner/wikipedia.org. 630, James Hawley/Flickr. 639, Kirk Hirota. 641, Kim Miner. 642, Ted Wolfe Photography. 645, Andre Jenny / Alamy. 650, James Hawley/Flickr. 661, Cave B Inn at SageCliffe.**Chapter 17: Vancouver and Victoria.** 669, Barrett & MacKay / age fotostock. 670, Natalia Bratslavsky/Shutterstock. 671, Xuanlu Wang/Shutterstock. 675, Hannamariah/Shutterstock. 676, ABC.pics/Shutterstock. 683, Douglas Williams / age fotostock. 684, SuperStock / age fotostock. 690, Geoff604/Flickr. 693, West Restaurant. 698 (top left), L'Hermitage Hotel. 698 (bottom left), SqueakyMarmot/Flickr. 698 (top right), Opus Hotel. 698 (bottom right), Relais & Chateaux. 702, Mike McHolm. 707, sashafatcat/Flickr. 709, Chris Cheadle / age fotostock. 713, Rich Wheater / age fotostock. 718, North Light Images / age fotostock. 722, Xuanlu Wang/Shutterstock. 728, (top) Inn at Laurel Point. 728, (bottom) Brentwood Bay Lodge & Spa. 733, Chuck Pefley / Alamy.

NOTES

ABOUT OUR WRITERS

Shelley Arenas grew up in Spokane and has lived in the Seattle area all of her adult life. She has contributed to several Fodor's books, co-authored a guidebook to Seattle for families, and writes for regional publications, including *Seattle Woman* magazine.

Former Fodor's editor Carissa Bluestone has written about the Emerald City for Fodor's *Pacific Northwest*, TravelandLeisure.com, and Concierge.com; explored the future of sustainable tourism for Worldchanging.com; and updated several other Fodor's guides, including *Mexico, Seattle,* and *Alaska.*

Andrew Collins, former Fodor's editor and a Portland resident since 2007, has authored more than a dozen guidebooks and is the gay travel expert for *The New York Times* Web site, About.com.

England-born and Midwest-raised, Mike Francis has worked as a reporter, editor, and producer in Oregon for 27 years. He lives with his family in Portland, where he is an associate editor for *The Oregonian.* Mike updated the Central Oregon chapter.

A writer by vocation, troubadour by avocation, Matt Graham has performed and watched shows all over the City of Roses, making him a well-versed person to cover the Portland music scene.

Carolyn B. Heller is the author of the book Living Abroad in Canada, and has contributed to more than 25 Fodor's guides. Her travel and food articles have appeared in publications ranging from the Boston Globe and Los Angeles Times to FamilyFun, Real Weddings, and Perceptive Travel.

Heidi Johansen, a native Seattlelite, relished the opportunity to explore and write about the Emerald City, which lured her back from New York.

Vancouver-born freelance writer Sue Kernaghan has written about British Columbia for dozens of publications. She has contributed to several editions of Fodor's

Guide to Vancouver & British Columbia, as well as to Fodor's *Alaska, Great Canadian Vacations,* and *Healthy Escapes.*

Brian Kevin explored Mt. Hood, the Columbia River Gorge, and the high desert country of eastern Oregon from a home base in the Wallowa Mountains. He writes about travel and adventure for publications such as *Outside, Sierra,* and *Afar,* and he tweets about the same at twitter.com/brianMT.

Janna Mock-Lopez is enamored of the spirit, beauty, and vitality of Portland, and loved writing the city chapter. Janna is a publisher of two magazines: *Portland Family* and *Goodness,* of which more than 60,000 copies are distributed monthly in the greater metropolitan area.

A sixth-generation Oregonian, Deston S. Nokes spent his childhood traveling Latin America and the East Coast. Today he makes Portland his home, where he works as a travel journalist and business communications consultant.

Freelance writer Rob Phillips has lived in Central Washington for nearly 50 years. He has written for dozens of publications, mostly on outdoor subjects. His award-winning "Northwest Outdoors" column appears every Tuesday in the *Yakima Herald-Republic.*

Allecia Vermillion is a Portland native who loves dining out and drinking local. She is a freelance writer pleased to once again reside in the Pacific Northwest after stints in San Francisco and Chicago.

Christine Vovakes's travel articles and photographs have appeared in such publications as *The Washington Post, The Christian Science Monitor, The Sacramento Bee,* and the *San Francisco Chronicle.* For this book, Christine wrote our Crater Lake chapter.

After more than ten years living in Oregon, Crystal Wood still loves playing tour guide to friends and family. Crystal's vast knowledge of Portland made her the perfect person to update that chapter.